The Solicitor's Handbook
2022

Related titles from Law Society Publishing:

Anti-Money Laundering Toolkit (3rd edn)
Alison Matthews

Financial Crime
Rebecca Atkinson

Regulation and In-house Lawyers (2nd edn)
Tracey Calvert and Bronwen Still

Solicitors and Money Laundering (4th edn)
Peter Camp and Amy Bell

Solicitors and the Accounts Rules (4th edn)
Andrew Allen and Janet Taylor

Titles from Law Society Publishing can be ordered from all good bookshops or direct (telephone 0370 850 1422 or visit our online shop at www.lawsociety.org.uk/bookshop).

THE
SOLICITOR'S HANDBOOK
2022

By

**Gregory Treverton-Jones QC, Nigel West,
Susanna Heley and Robert Forman**

Contents

Foreword to the 2008 edition

The authors have asked me to write a short foreword to this book. I am delighted to do so because I entirely agree with the views expressed in the Preface. Although I quite understand that it may be necessary to use the Internet in order for practitioners to be fully up to date at any given moment, many people (and not only the very old like me) like to have a book which sets out the basic principles and which they can readily consult. *The Solicitor's Handbook* is precisely that. It concisely sets out the relevant position under a number of different headings and is very user friendly.

The authors express the hope that the book will prove to be a valuable resource for regulator and regulated alike and that it will contribute to good regulation by identifying and explaining areas of particular concern and risk, especially where practitioners have, in the past, made innocent mistakes which have nevertheless had serious consequences.

I know that hope springs eternal, but in this case I am confident that the authors' hopes will be fulfilled. I wish it well.

Sir Anthony Clarke

Master of the Rolls
Royal Courts of Justice
October 2007

Preface to the 2008 edition

For generations of solicitors *The Guide to the Professional Conduct of Solicitors* (first published in 1960 and always provided free of charge) was the source of all knowledge in relation to the rules that controlled the profession. If you could not find it in the Guide, or if the available published guidance still left you in a quandary, you could always 'ring Redditch' – the Law Society's ethics helpline. Looking it up in the Guide and seeking the Law Society's advice was a total solution. After all; how could you be criticised for following the Law Society's own advice?

The Guide is no more. The eighth edition, published in 1999, was the last. We have moved into the modern era; the paperless age. The Solicitors' Code of Conduct 2007 (which henceforth we will refer to as 'the Code') appears on the website of the Solicitors Regulation Authority (SRA); so do the Solicitors' Accounts Rules 1998, and the Financial Services Rules and other rules. Diligent searching on the Law Society website will reveal much in the way of published guidance, pronunciations and edicts. Information about how clients can complain about you, and what will happen when they do, can be found on the website of the Legal Complaints Service (LCS).

Only in the two thick volumes of the mighty *Cordery on Solicitors* will practitioners find in written form all the law and professional rules relating to solicitors.

But the paperless age and rapidly changing regulatory rules carry with them real dangers for practitioners who may find it difficult or impossible to discover what rules were in force when they did things which later become the subject of regulatory concern. This Handbook, which will be updated annually, seeks to remove those problems.

This Handbook brings together all the professional rules governing the conduct and regulation of solicitors in a manner that is convenient and inexpensive. We hope that we have added much more of value, by drawing upon our professional experience to explain how the rules and the regulatory machinery work in practice.

We have addressed our book to 'you' the practitioner: it has been written from the perspective of the practitioner, to whom it is intended to provide information and guidance. We have included material that we consider relevant and important to the practitioner but which is not included within the formal rules (for example, how money laundering, mortgage fraud and investment scams work), so that independently of the published guidance you can spot problems before they develop into loss to clients and others, damage to reputation, and regulatory interest.

We have included guidance on the workings of the Solicitors Disciplinary Tribunal, on the powers of intervention available to the SRA and the regime for the imposition of conditions on practising certificates.

And we have included a section on where you can obtain further specialist advice and help if all else fails.

It is unlikely that any practitioner currently feels that the profession is under-regulated; the weight of regulation, and dealings with the SRA, can be daunting. The Solicitors' Practice Rules 1936 (made by virtue of section 1 of the Solicitors Act 1933) comprised seven rules (in reality only four) and could be printed on one page.[1] The latest Code, if printed on A4, occupies 253 pages (and 190 pages of this book). We also live in a rapidly changing regulatory environment. The Code came into force on 1 July 2007: one month later it was amended for the first time. An updated version of the Accounts Rules to be incorporated into the Code by amendment is already in contemplation. We now have two regulators – the LCS, dealing with client complaints and redress for poor service, and the SRA, dealing with every-thing else. Under the previous system, if a complaint engaged both conduct and service issues it was a 'hybrid' and both aspects were dealt with together. Now, all consumer complaints and redress will be dealt with first by the LCS and if any conduct issues are considered to arise they will be referred to the SRA to be dealt with subsequently (although, if very serious concerns are raised and the interests of the public require it, more urgent action will no doubt be taken).

You can still 'ring Redditch' for advice on issues of professional conduct, but the official and published position of the SRA is that for the purpose of any investiga-tion or adjudication it is 'not bound' by any opinion or advice given by its own staff on the ethics helpline. In other words, you can follow the advice of the regulator, but – in theory at least – the regulator can nevertheless find you guilty of miscon-duct and impose sanctions. It is also not clear to what extent, if at all, information provided for the purposes of seeking such advice will be regarded as confidential, as opposed to being useful intelligence for regulatory purposes about the person making the enquiry.

The Legal Services Act 2007 maintains the division between conduct and service, hiving off consumer complaints and redress to the independent Office for Legal Complaints, which will succeed the LCS. The Act grants significant new powers to the SRA (which we have touched upon in Chapter 2) and sweeps away significant parts of the current statutory regime, for example in relation to conditions on prac-tising certificates. Where changes will occur, we explain what the future holds.

We hope that this book will prove to be a valuable resource for regulator and regu-lated alike, and that it will contribute to good regulation in identifying and explaining areas of particular concern and risk – especially where practitioners have in the past made innocent mistakes that have nevertheless had serious consequences.

We would welcome feedback from practitioners, and particularly any requests and recommendations for the inclusion of material in areas we have not covered in this first edition.

We are grateful to the following for their drafting and other suggestions: Euros Jones of James Saunders & Co., who conducted extensive research and provided considerable input for the money laundering chapter; Mike Calvert of the SRA and Che Odlum of the Law Society, who shared their practical experience of money laundering and investment fraud issues; Iain Miller of Bevan Brittan for his substan-tial contributions to the chapter on the Code; and Geoffrey Williams QC for reviewing and suggesting amendments to Chapter 14. Many other members of the SRA and SDT, notably Sue Elson and Liz Aldred, answered our queries constructively and with unfailing courtesy. All provided invaluable assistance, although the responsibility for any errors and omissions is ours alone. Others deserve particular thanks. Michael Hoyle was the inspiration for Andrew Hopper's original interest in solicitors' regulatory law and practice. When legal complications arose after we finished the writing, we received matchless assistance from Nick Gardner and David Mayhew at Herbert Smith, and valuable advice from Tony Grabiner at 1 Essex Court, and Sean Wilken and Ben Williams at 39 Essex Street. Finally, we are both deeply grateful to our respective wives, Ros and Tamsin, for their support and forbearance while their otherwise apparently sane husbands buried themselves in some of the more esoteric material contained in this book.

1   In brief – Rule 1: no touting; Rule 2: no charging under the published scale fees; Rule 3: no fee sharing; Rule 4: no association with ambulance chasers; Rule 5: provision for waivers; Rule 6: definitions; Rule 7: commencement.

Preface to the 2022 edition

In the two years since the publication of the 2019 edition in September of that year, life in the United Kingdom has been dominated by the country's withdrawal from the European Union, and the coronavirus pandemic. Each of these has had profound effects upon the solicitors' profession. Brexit has altered the rules of the country's international trade, and has rendered the species of registered European lawyer almost extinct, but has not affected the Human Rights Act or the European Convention on Human Rights: the protections provided by those instruments to those charged with disciplinary offences remain.

As for the pandemic, the effects are subtler but will be felt for years to come. By and large, the profession coped admirably with the enforced changes. Clients were served, and court hearings were able to proceed, due to the wonders of modern technology. Indeed the Solicitors Disciplinary Tribunal coped more easily than most with remote hearings, having already introduced its Caselines system before the pandemic struck. But that superficially positive picture may mask some deep issues. Many young and inexperienced members of the profession will have found it stressful to be cooped up in often small accommodation, having to try to work at home for weeks on end without face-to-face supervision, or the enjoyable social interaction which is part of office life. Those with small or not-so-small children will have faced the daunting challenge of trying to work and parent at the same time. Solicitors have had to get used to meeting clients remotely, and conducting matters through computer screens. Any non-compliant behaviour during the pandemic will be slowly revealed in the months and years to come.

The suite of rule changes made in 2019 have been bedding in. One of the most important changes was the lowering of the reporting 'bar' for solicitors. The result has been a significant increase in the number of reports made to the SRA. This must have increased the regulator's workload, and all of the authors of this edition have come across unacceptable and often gross delays in the conduct of SRA investigations which may result in part from the regulator's caseload.

In the courts, the most important judgment for some years was the Divisional Court decision in *Beckwith*, which is dealt with in some detail in **CHAPTER 19**. Although we believe the decision in that case to have been correct, some of the court's reasoning may prove to be controversial. The Supreme Court's decision in the *Harcus Sinclair* case in July 2021 has clarified the law as to solicitors' undertakings, although the court declined to extend the reach of the supervisory jurisdiction over solicitors to cover the entities in which solicitors work and it remains to be seen whether, as a result, undertakings will maintain their central role in commercial transactions in general and conveyancing in particular. In early 2022, the Supreme Court will revisit in the case of *Pharma Flynn*, the default position since *Baxendale-Walker* in 2006 that costs do not follow the event where a disciplinary prosecution fails, and that the regulator should not be ordered to pay the respondent's costs unless there is good reason (beyond the result of the case) to make such an order.

The amount of commentary in the present edition has grown somewhat since 2019. This is largely because the SRA has issued a great deal of guidance in the meantime, and we have sought to capture and summarise for our readers the most important examples of that guidance.

The law is stated as at 1 October 2021.

We are very grateful to Andrew Blatt of Messrs Murdochs for his contribution to CHAPTER 17 on interventions. As ever, we are indebted to those at Law Society Publishing who have worked on the book. Particular thanks are due to Laura Armentano, David Crosby, Suzanne Giles and Sarah Kent.

GT-J QC

Table of cases

Table of statutes

Paragraph references printed in **bold type** indicate where the enactment is set out in part or in full.

Table of statutory instruments

Paragraph references printed in **bold type** indicate where the enactment is set out in part or in full.

Table of European legislation and other international materials

Table of other enactments

Paragraph references printed in **bold** type indicate where the enactment is set out in part or in full.

PART I
Overview

CHAPTER I

The regulatory and disciplinary landscape

1.1

In the earliest times only the courts exercised disciplinary jurisdiction over solicitors, as officers of the court. When Mr Brounsall was struck off the roll of attorneys in 1778, having been convicted of stealing a guinea, for which he had been sentenced 'to be branded on the hand, and to be confined to the house of correction for nine months' the question was raised as to whether the striking off would amount to a second, and unlawful, penalty. Lord Mansfield announced that as this raised issues concerning the dignity of the profession, 'a solemn opinion should be given' and that the matter should be mentioned 'to all the judges'. On 27 June 1778, a Saturday, Lord Mansfield announced:

> 'We have consulted all the judges upon this case, and they are unanimously of opinion, that the defendant's having been burnt in the hand, is no objection to his being struck off the roll. And it is on this principle; that he is an unfit person to practise as an attorney.'[1]

The nineteenth century saw a move towards control of the profession by its own professional body. The Law Society was formed in 1823, as a successor to the Society of Gentleman Practisers, and incorporated by Royal Charter in 1831. By virtue of the Solicitors Act 1888, complaints of misconduct against solicitors were made to a Committee of the Incorporated Law Society, whose members were appointed by the Master of the Rolls. The Committee made findings which were embodied in a report to the court, but the court continued to exercise the disciplinary jurisdiction. No report from the Society's Committee was necessary however; the court could still act on its own motion.[2]

1   *Ex parte Brounsall* [1778] 2 Cowp 829.
2   Sections 12, 13 and 19 of the Solicitors Act 1888; and see *Re Weare* [1893] 2 QB 439, CA.

1.2

The Solicitors Act 1919 granted the powers of the court, to strike solicitors from the roll and to impose other penalties, to the Disciplinary Committee of the Law Society, but preserved the court's inherent jurisdiction. The Disciplinary Committee was not a committee of the Council of the Law Society, but a separate statutory body whose members continued to be appointed by the Master of the Rolls. The Disciplinary Committee was replaced by the Solicitors Disciplinary Tribunal (the Tribunal or SDT) in 1975, by the Solicitors Act (SA) 1974. The members continued (and still continue) to be appointed by the Master of the Rolls. Section 50 of SA 1974 preserves the court's parallel and inherent jurisdiction. The functions of the investigator and prosecutor have remained with the Law Society throughout, as they still do (although such powers are formally delegated to the Solicitors Regulation Authority Ltd (SRA), the Law Society's wholly owned subsidiary which operates independently of the Society).

1.3

In January 2007 the Law Society split into three organisations:

(1)   the Society itself, based in Chancery Lane, which remains the representative body for solicitors; their 'trade union' – though not in the fullest sense of that phrase; the Society represents solicitors as a membership organisation whether they are employers or employees. It also remains impossible, for example, for the Law Society to assist directly in the defence of any individual solicitor in dealings with the SRA;

(2)   the SRA, which since October 2012 is based in Birmingham, with a satellite City of London office, and which is the regulator; and

(3)   the now defunct Legal Complaints Service (LCS) which between 2007 and October 2010 dealt with client complaints.

The functions of the LCS were brought to an end in respect of all complaints made on and after 6 October 2010 and it ceased to exist. Consumer or client complaints were removed by the Legal Services Act (LSA) 2007 from the existing regulators altogether[1] and vested in the Office for Legal Complaints (which uses the title of Legal Ombudsman (LeO)). Part 6 of LSA 2007 established a comprehensive ombudsman scheme for the handling of complaints by consumers. For the Legal Ombudsman see **CHAPTER 14**.

The SRA is run by its own directors as a company limited by guarantee. As the statutory powers remain vested in the Council of the Law Society, under SA 1974 as amended, those powers are delegated by the Council to and through the SRA, to enable the SRA to operate independently of the Law Society.

1   Section 157 of LSA 2007.

1.4

Under LSA 2007, the Legal Services Board (LSB) is established to promote and maintain regulatory objectives relating to the provision of legal services, namely:

(1)   protecting and promoting public interest;

(2)   supporting the constitutional principle of the rule of law;

(3)   improving access to justice;

(4)   protecting and promoting the interests of consumers;

(5)   promoting competition in the provision of legal services;

(6)   encouraging an independent, strong, diverse and effective legal profession;

(7)   increasing public understanding of the citizen's legal rights and duties; and

(8)   promoting and maintaining adherence to professional principles.[1]

The professional principles are:

(1)   acting with independence and integrity;

(2)   maintaining proper standards of work;

(3)   acting in the best interests of clients;

(4)   complying with the duty to the court to act with independence in the interests of justice in relation to litigation and advocacy; and

(5)   keeping the affairs of clients confidential.[2]

The LSB regulates the regulators, delegating the primary role to approved regulators (including the Law Society/SRA) but maintaining oversight. A detailed consideration of the Board's powers is outside the parameters of this book.

1   Section 1(1) of LSA 2007.
2   Section 1(3).

1.5

Part 5 of LSA 2007 is concerned with alternative business structures (ABSs) – the licensing of bodies, not owned or controlled by lawyers, to provide legal services. The Council for Licensed Conveyancers (CLC) began licensing ABSs from 6 October 2011, providing legal services restricted to conveyancing and probate, and the SRA began taking applications in January 2012.

In order to ensure that the existing suite of rules was appropriate for the changed landscape that would exist when ABSs became licensed, the SRA undertook the mammoth task of amending it. The result was the SRA Handbook 2011, which brought together a new set of Principles and a new Code of Conduct, Accounts Rules, the various rules covering authorisation and practising requirements, client protection (insurance and compensation), discipline and costs recovery, and specialist services. The SRA Handbook was officially replaced by the SRA Standards and Regulations with effect from 25 November 2019. By that time, there had been 21 editions of the SRA Handbook with the 21st edition coming into force on 6 December 2018.

The SRA Standards and Regulations were introduced following extensive public consultations on new regulatory arrangements, which dealt with a new Code of Conduct in two parts (one for individuals and one for entities), new Accounts Rules and proposals for changes in regulation for individual solicitors. Several of the changes were very controversial, in particular the perceived risks of permitting solicitors to use the title of solicitor when working for unregulated organisations in specified circumstances. The long-term effect of the Standards and Regulations is yet to be fully determined and the true impact is likely to have been delayed somewhat by wider societal issues such as the COVID-19 pandemic and the enforced changes in working habits which have resulted.

Duties of approved regulators

1.6

Under section 28 of LSA 2007, approved regulators are under a statutory duty to act in a way that is compatible with the regulatory objectives (see **1.4**) and in a way most appropriate for the purpose of meeting those objectives. Those objectives require, of course, regulation in the public interest, but a strong and independent profession is in the view of Parliament an essential requirement in the public interest. It is therefore part of the function of the SRA to work towards improving access to justice, promoting competition in the provision of legal services, encouraging an independent, strong, diverse and effective legal profession, and increasing public understanding of the citizen's legal rights and duties, all of which involve support for the profession.

Approved regulators must also have regard to the principles under which regulatory activities should be transparent, accountable, proportionate, consistent and targeted only at cases in which action is needed.[1] It has not always been the case (so it has seemed to informed commentators and so it may have seemed to the profession following encounters with the SRA) that these principles have been rigorously applied in practice, although they are officially adopted as SRA policy.

In April 2014 the Better Regulation Delivery Office of the Department for Business, Innovation and Skills issued a 'Regulators' Code' (see **APPENDIX 13**), which sets out six principles each with accompanying detailed requirements. The general principles are:

(1)   Regulators should carry out their activities in a way that supports those they regulate to comply and grow.

(2)   Regulators should provide simple and straightforward ways to engage with those they regulate and hear their views.

(3)   Regulators should base their regulatory activities on risk.

(4)   Regulators should share information about compliance and risk.

(5)   Regulators should ensure clear information, guidance and advice is available to help those they regulate meet their responsibilities to comply.

(6)   Regulators should ensure that their approach to their regulatory activities is transparent.

The Regulators' Code is not fully applicable to the SRA but does apply to the LSB and is likely to be adopted in principle by the SRA or to be imposed on all the approved regulators by the LSB.

1   Section 28(3) of LSA 2007.

CHAPTER 2

The regulation and authorisation of business entities

Entity or firm-based regulation

2.1

The year 2009 saw the beginning of a series of substantial changes in the way that the profession is regulated. The Solicitors Regulation Authority (SRA) moved to firm-based regulation, although the first signs of this happening in practice did not emerge until the third quarter of 2010. The intention was that the focus of investigation and regulatory action would more frequently be the business within which solicitors practise, rather than individual practitioners. Explanations were to be sought from the firm, in relation to matters perceived to have gone wrong, and less from individual solicitors. The business entity became liable to rebukes, fines and controls on the way it is permitted to operate, although individual solicitors, or other managers or employees of the business, may also be targeted. In practice, through 21 editions of the SRA Handbook 2011, the emphasis remained for the most part on individual responsibility. The introduction of separate codes for firms and individuals in the 2019 regulatory arrangements acknowledged the need for clearer dividing lines. For a consideration of the practical consequences of this see **15.11**.

Secondly, the Legal Services Act (LSA) 2007 created an environment in which businesses that provide legal services may have a choice as to which of the available approved regulators is to regulate the firm. For example, the Council for Licensed Conveyancers (CLC) regulates those who supply conveyancing and probate services; the Institute of Chartered Accountants of England and Wales (ICAEW) regulates the supply of probate (at present). The regulatory arm of the Chartered Institute of Legal Executives, CILEx Regulation, authorises and regulates firms, and grants individual practising rights (litigation, advocacy, conveyancing, probate and immigration).

Following the rise of firm-based regulation and the approval of the Bar Standards Board (BSB) and CILEx Regulation alongside the CLC and ICAEW as licensing authorities (regulators able to license alternative business structures (ABSs) to provide legal services), the number of potential regulators is growing and solicitors may elect to work in a firm regulated by a regulator other than the SRA if the entity meets the authorisation requirements of the other regulator.

2.2

In consequence, individual solicitors may find themselves subject to two different regulatory regimes simultaneously. For example, the business by which they are employed may be an entity regulated by the BSB, CLC, CILEx Regulation or ICAEW, while the solicitors as individuals may be regulated by the SRA. LSA 2007 provides[1] that if a conflict arises between the regulations that apply to the entity and those that apply to an employee or manager of the entity, the regulations applying to the entity prevail. Thus, a solicitor who is a manager of or employed by a business regulated by

7

the CLC must comply with the rules of the CLC in relation to, for example, referral fees and deposit interest. However, the SRA Principles apply to a solicitor who is practising as such, whether or not the entity through which the individual practises is subject to the Principles.[2] The SRA Code of Conduct for Solicitors, RELs and RFLs 2019 (the 'Code for Individuals') will also apply to individuals irrespective of the entity through which they may practise, although the extent of the obligations varies when individuals are not providing services to the public as set out in that Code. Solicitors are also subject to the requirement to have a practising certificate issued by the SRA, even if employed by a legal services provider regulated by another regulator, or if they are managers of such a body, if the solicitor's involvement in the firm, or the work undertaken, depends on the individual being a solicitor, or the individual is employed or held out explicitly or implicitly as a solicitor.[3] A publication concerned with the regulation of solicitors can no longer focus exclusively on the rules promulgated by the SRA. Therefore, a brief consideration of the CLC rules is contained in **CHAPTER 13** and the CLC Code of Conduct is reproduced at **APPENDIX 12**.

One of the principal changes introduced by the 2019 regulatory arrangements is to permit solicitors, as individuals, to provide unregulated legal services through unregulated businesses. It was considered anomalous, for example, that the effect of the SRA Practice Framework Rules 2011 (see **2.25**) was that a solicitor may not work, using the title of solicitor, in an unregulated will-writing business.

The effect of this is that in-house solicitors are no longer restricted to acting for their employers only (with limited exceptions as formerly set out in rule 4 of the Practice Framework Rules). Solicitors may (for example) provide legal advice to anyone, not just to their employers, because legal advice is not a reserved legal activity. The restrictions on in-house solicitors providing reserved legal activities for persons other than their employer remain. If the employer wishes to provide reserved legal services to the general public, or a sector of the public, it will have to be regulated as an entity. This is a natural consequence of the general requirement that persons providing reserved legal activities must be authorised to do so.[4]

Solicitors may (using their title as solicitors) set up businesses which are unregulated to provide advice and any other legal service provided they are not undertaking reserved legal activities. They will be regulated as solicitors in terms of their personal conduct, but the business will not have to comply with the regulatory burdens of an SRA authorised firm. For example, there will be no compulsory insurance, no compliance officer for legal practice (COLP) or compliance officer for finance and administration (COFA), no Compensation Fund contributions. However, clients will have less protection and dealings may not be covered by legal professional privilege. Solicitors must make clear to clients the extent of the regulatory protections available to them under paragraph 8.11 of the Code for Individuals.[5]

Firms are able to hive off non-reserved legal services into such unregulated businesses, provided that clients are properly informed.[6]

---

1 Section 52(4) of LSA 2007.
2 SRA Principles – Introduction.
3 This is the natural consequence of sections 1 and 21 of the Solicitors Act (SA) 1974, although there are no longer any express provisions in SRA regulations explaining this.
4 Section 14 of LSA 2007.
5 See **CHAPTER 4**.
6 See paragraphs 8.10 and 8.11 of the Code for Individuals and paragraph 7.1(c) of the SRA Code of Conduct for Firms 2019 (the 'Code for Firms').

Authorisation

2.3

'Authorisation' is one of the three strands of regulation covered by the SRA regulations, the other two being supervision and enforcement.

Authorisation as an area of regulation covers the processes whereby individuals may be permitted to provide legal services, including the process of being admitted as a solicitor, and thus includes the SRA Authorisation of Firms Rules 2019, SRA Authorisation of Individuals Regulations 2019 (as amended), SRA Education, Training and Assessment Provider Regulations 2019 and the SRA Assessment of Character and Suitability Rules 2019 (the 'Suitability Rules') which, as well as being relevant to the enrolment of students and admission to the roll, is applicable in relation to the approval of non-lawyer managers of law firms (within legal disciplinary partnerships and ABSs), of COLPs and COFAs (see **CHAPTER 7**), and of non-lawyers who own a material interest in a law firm.

Authorisation also encompasses the procedures regulating firms and individuals in the manner in which they provide legal services, through the SRA Authorisation of Firms Rules 2019 and the SRA Authorisation of Individuals Regulations 2019 (as amended).

SRA Authorisation Rules

2.4

These rules are the core of the SRA's control mechanism for all forms of practice. They comprise the SRA Authorisation of Firms Rules 2019 and the SRA Authorisation of Individuals Regulations 2019. We will refer to the rules collectively as the 'Authorisation Rules' and individually as the 'Firm Rules' and the 'Individual Rules'.

The Firm Rules apply to ABSs ('licensable bodies' or 'licensed bodies' depending on the context) and to all other more traditional forms of practice ('legal services bodies' or 'recognised bodies'), including legal disciplinary partnerships. From 1 November 2015, sole practitioners (who had previously been regulated separately through 'sole practitioner recognition' are regulated in the same way as any other recognised body.

There are two key elements to the Firm Rules:

- the process of authorisation, including applications and conditions; and

- the approval process for managers, owners and compliance officers.

There are also provisions relating to the duration, suspension and revocation of authorisation; the effect of unforeseen breaches in relation to the requirements for authorisation; appeals and transitional arrangements.

'Authorisation' is used to describe the recognition process for recognised bodies, *and* the licensing process for ABSs. Once authorised a firm, including a sole practice, will not need to renew its authorisation (recognition or licence); it will continue in force until withdrawn or revoked, although there will be a requirement to make annual returns with specified information and to pay annual fees.

Applications

2.5

The SRA must make a decision on an application that has been duly made, using the correct form and accompanied by all the required information, within six months unless an extension notice is served, which may be done only once, so as to bring the maximum period for any decision to nine months.[1] This is plainly intended to provide for the most complex ABS authorisation applications which require extensive investigation. More routine applications are dealt with far faster. This is an area in which the SRA has improved very considerably and genuinely urgent applications, such as the grant of a new ABS licence to enable an existing ABS to acquire the shares in a failing business as a 'rescue', can be processed very quickly indeed.

The SRA may only grant an application for authorisation if the applicant satisfies, in terms of the business structure, the statutory requirements for a legal services body (non-ABS) or a licensable body (ABS). The body must have at least one practising address in England and Wales.[2]

The applicant will also have to: satisfy the requirements as to the appointment of compliance officers, and obtain the SRA's approval; demonstrate that all managers and owners of the business are approved as necessary, and not disqualified (for example, as a result of having been struck off); and comply with rule 9.4 of the Firm Rules as to supervision of regulated work by a lawyer of England and Wales who has practised as such for a minimum of three years.

The SRA will refuse an application even though these conditions are satisfied:

- if it is not satisfied that the applicant body's managers, interest holders or management and governance arrangements are suitable to operate or control a business providing regulated legal services;

- if it is not satisfied that, if the authorisation is granted, the applicant body will comply with the SRA's regulatory arrangements; or

- if for any other reason, the SRA considers that it would be against the public interest or otherwise incompatible with the regulatory objectives to grant authorisation.[3]

1   Rules 1.5 and 1.6 of the SRA Application, Notice, Review and Appeal Rules 2019.
2   Rule 1.3(b) of the Firm Rules.
3   Rule 2.2 of the Firm Rules.

Conditions

2.6

All authorisations will be subject to standard conditions (under rules 6–11 of the Firm Rules) as well as any specific conditions the SRA decides to impose (under rule 3). These conditions are designed to protect the public, ensure compliance with regulatory arrangements and promote the regulatory objectives.

The standard conditions impose duties as to regulatory compliance; as to making suitable arrangements to ensure compliance; as to the payment of periodical fees; as to any limits on the activities that may be carried out; as to the appointment of compliance officers; as to those permitted to have management responsibilities and control; and as to the provision of information by means of an annual return.[1]

1   Rules 6–11 of the Firm Rules.

2.7

The Firm Rules should be read in conjunction with the Code for Firms, which requires that all managers of a firm are jointly and severally responsible for compliance with that Code and that compliance officers must take all reasonable steps to ensure compliance with the SRA's regulatory arrangements (see **CHAPTER 5**).

Managers and COLPs should be particularly aware of the ongoing compliance requirements embodied in the Firm Rules.

Rule 5.3 specifies that an authorised body may only carry on a regulated activity if that is done through a person (a body or an individual) who is authorised to carry on that activity.

Rule 7.1 requires that every authorised body must pay to the SRA the prescribed periodical fees by the prescribed date. In the case of merger or demerger, an authorised body is required to provide notice to the SRA within 28 days if it wishes the change to be taken into account in the calculation of the fee (see rule 16.1).

Rule 9.1 requires that an authorised body must ensure that any manager or owner of the authorised body, or any manager of a body corporate which is a manager or owner of the authorised body, has been approved by the SRA. Solicitors with a current practising certificate and existing authorised bodies are deemed to be approved in the absence of any regulatory or disciplinary investigations or adverse findings by the SRA, the Solicitors Disciplinary Tribunal (the Tribunal or SDT), or other regulatory body.[1] No manager of a licensed body may be a person who is disqualified from being a manager.[2] An authorised body (or manager or employee of such a body) and a recognised body (or manager or employee) must not employ or remunerate a person without the written permission of the SRA if they are in certain categories, for example, struck off or suspended solicitors or persons subject to an order under section 43 of SA 1974. Nor may such a person be permitted to be a manager or owner of the body.

Rule 9.4 requires that an authorised body must have at least one manager or employee, or must procure the services of an individual who is a lawyer of England and Wales (and has practised as such for a minimum of three years) who supervises the work undertaken by the authorised body in so far as it is regulated by the SRA. This requirement replaces the requirement that a firm have an individual who is 'qualified to supervise'. The requirement should be read in conjunction with the supervision requirements of the Codes of Conduct (see **4.43** and **5.40**).

Rule 14.1 deals with the matters that must be addressed by, respectively, partnerships, recognised bodies and licensed bodies where the last remaining individual whose presence ensures that there is a valid partnership, or that a recognised body meets the requirements for a legal services body, or that a licensed body remains a licensable body, ceases to be able to fulfil that role, through imprisonment, illness, loss of mental capacity, abandonment or the imposition of regulatory conditions. In any such case the body must inform the SRA within seven days and must within 28 days ensure that the body regularises the position or (in the case of a recognised body or licensed body) ceases to practise.

1   Rule 13.2 of the Firm Rules.
2   Rule 10.1(d) of the Firm Rules.

Additional conditions and modifications

2.8

Under rule 3.1 of the Firm Rules the SRA may at any time impose further conditions.

> 3.1   The *SRA* may at any time, whether on grant of an application for authorisation or otherwise, impose such conditions on a body's authorisation (whether indefinite or for a specified period), where it considers it appropriate in the public interest to do so and in accordance with rules 3.2 and 3.3.
>
> 3.2   The *SRA* may impose conditions under rule 3.1 if it is satisfied that the *authorised body*, or a *manager, compliance officer, employee, owner,* or *interest holder* of the *authorised body*:
>
> (a)   is unsuitable to undertake certain activities or engage in certain business or practising arrangements;
>
> (b)   is putting or is likely to put at risk the interests of *clients*, third parties or the public;
>
> (c)   will not comply with the *SRA's regulatory arrangements*, or requires monitoring of compliance with the *SRA's regulatory arrangements*; or
>
> (d)   should take specified steps conducive to the *regulatory objectives*.
>
> 3.3   The conditions imposed by the *SRA* under rule 3.1 may:
>
> (a)   specify certain requirements that must be met or steps that must be taken;
>
> (b)   restrict the carrying on of particular activities or holding of particular roles; or
>
> (c)   prohibit the taking of specified steps without its approval.

A condition imposed under rule 3.1 takes effect from the date on which the condition is imposed unless otherwise specified by the SRA.

Under rule 12.1 the SRA may at any time extend, revoke or vary any terms or conditions on a body's authorisation, imposed in accordance with rule 3 or otherwise, either on the application of the body or on its own initiative.

Approval

2.9

As part of the authorisation process express approval is required by the SRA of an authorised body's managers, owners and compliance officers. Solicitors who hold a current practising certificate and existing authorised bodies will be deemed to be approved to be owners or managers of an authorised body, provided that there are no practising certificate conditions or conditions on the body's authorisation which would be inconsistent with approval, and provided that the SRA has been notified that the person or body should be a manager or owner, and has not withdrawn approval.[1]

It should be noted that the deeming provisions in relation to the appointment of compliance officers are not the same and in particular only apply to authorised bodies with a turnover of no more than £600,000.[2] The position of COLPs and COFAs is considered in more detail in **CHAPTER 7**.

1 Rules 13.3, 13.4 and 13.10 of the Firm Rules.
2 See rule 13.5.

SRA Assessment of Character and Suitability Rules 2019

2.10

Those who are not deemed to be approved for their roles must be expressly approved by the SRA which will apply its Suitability Rules. These are largely designed to exclude those who have been convicted of criminal offences of varying degrees of seriousness, and those with other serious lapses in their history.

Those with a conviction for an offence for which they received a custodial or suspended sentence; or which involved dishonesty, fraud, perjury and/or bribery; or which was of a violent or sexual nature; or which was associated with obstructing the course of justice; or which demonstrated behaviour showing signs of discrimination towards others; or which was associated with terrorism; those who have been convicted by a court of more than one criminal offence; those who have accepted a caution from the police for an offence involving dishonesty, violence or discrimination, or a sexual offence; and those included on the Violent and Sex Offender Register are all likely to be refused approval.

This test has been relaxed slightly from the requirements of the former Suitability Test, which was found to be too rigid in its approach.

An application may still fail, but has some prospect of success, if the applicant has received a local warning from the police; accepted a caution from the police for an offence not involving dishonesty; received a Penalty Notice for Disorder from the police; received a final warning or reprimand from the police (youths only); and/or received a referral order from the courts (youths only).

The onus is very firmly on individuals to provide to the SRA all material information regarding their character and suitability. Any failure to disclose any material information may be taken into consideration by the SRA when making a determination (rule 6.7). The express suggestion in the former Suitability Test that a failure to disclose will be treated as prima facie evidence of dishonesty has been removed, replaced with the more generic provision allowing the SRA greater flexibility. However, historically the SRA has regarded a failure to make full and proper disclosure of previous brushes with the criminal law as being almost as serious as the criminal offences themselves, and this is unlikely to change.

2.11

It is not only criminal convictions that are relevant. A raft of other issues may be taken into account, as set out in rule 4.1; however, there is no longer any automatic outcome associated with the listed factors. While it can reasonably be predicted that, in practice, there will still be no approval for those who have been responsible for behaviour which is dishonest or violent; or where there is evidence of discrimination towards others; or where the individual has misused his or her position to obtain pecuniary advantage; or abused a position of trust in relation to vulnerable people; or been responsible for other forms of behaviour which demonstrate that he or she could not be relied upon to comply with regulatory responsibilities, it is no longer an express requirement that there be exceptional circumstances. Instead, these are matters which must be assessed and taken into account as seems appropriate in any particular case.

Similarly, those who have committed or have been adjudged by an education establishment to have committed a deliberate assessment offence which amounts to plagiarism or cheating to gain an advantage, whether for the individual or others, will face extreme difficulty in securing approval.

Past financial failings are relevant. The SRA will take into account evidence that finances have not been managed properly and carefully; or evidence that the applicant has deliberately sought to avoid responsibility for his or her debts, particularly if there is evidence of dishonesty in relation to the management of finances.

2.12

A poor regulatory history is relevant. The SRA will take into account any serious disciplinary finding, sanction or action by a regulatory body and/or any court or other body hearing appeals in relation to disciplinary or regulatory findings; or any failure to disclose information to a regulatory body when required to do so; or the provision of false or misleading information or significant breach of the requirements of a regulatory body; or the refusal of registration by a regulatory body; or the failure to comply with the reasonable requests of a regulatory body.

The SRA will also take into account a disqualification as a charity trustee or a company director and any offences under the Companies Act 2006, as well as any case in which the applicant has been rebuked, reprimanded or received a warning about his or her conduct by a regulatory body.

2.13

All the above considerations apply to those seeking to be admitted as a solicitor and those seeking approval for any role covered by the Authorisation Rules: that is, any COLP, COFA, owner or manager.

The current approach to assessing character as set out in the Suitability Rules is (in keeping with the SRA's approach since 2019 generally) more streamlined. The abandonment of rigid requirements enables the test simply to list relevant factors without prescribing outcomes if those factors are present. Instead, the SRA lists aggravating and mitigating factors. Despite this attempt to relax the overly prescriptive requirements of the Suitability Test in force until 2019, little has changed in practice.

The SRA is obliged by LSA 2007 to consider the associates of those to be approved as owners of material interests in ABSs,[1] and has extended the same requirement to all covered by the Authorisation Rules. Applications for approval may be refused if the SRA has evidence reflecting on the honesty and integrity of a person the applicant is related to, affiliated with, or acts together with, where there is reason to believe that the person may have an influence over the way in which the applicant will exercise his, her or its authorised role.

1   Paragraph 6 of Schedule 13 to LSA 2007.

2.14

It is important to bear in mind that the onus is on applicants to satisfy the regulator. There is no entitlement to an appointment. The law and the relevant tests to be applied are considered in the context of appeals in relation to licensing matters; see **23.15.**

Withdrawal of approval

2.15

The SRA may withdraw approval where approval, including deemed approval, has been granted if it is not satisfied that the person is fit and proper to undertake the designated role.[1] Fitness and propriety are determined in accordance with the Suitability Rules.

Where withdrawal of approval relates to a director of a company, the SRA may set separate dates for that individual ceasing to be a director and disposing of his or her shares.[2]

1   Rule 13.9 of the Firm Rules.
2   Rule 13.12 of the Firm Rules.

Revocation and suspension of authorisation

2.16

The SRA may revoke or suspend a body's authorisation where, in the case of an authorised body (that is, any practice that the SRA has authorised, ABS or non-ABS):

- authorisation was granted as a result of error, misleading or inaccurate information, or fraud;

- the body is or becomes ineligible to be authorised in accordance with the criteria set out in the Firm Rules;

- the body has failed to provide any information reasonably requested by the SRA;

- the body has failed to pay any prescribed fee to the SRA;

- a relevant insolvency event has occurred in relation to the body;

- the body makes an application to the SRA for its authorisation to be revoked or suspended but the SRA may refuse the application if the applicant is subject to any proceedings, investigation or consideration of their conduct or practice by the SRA or the Tribunal;

- the SRA has decided to exercise its intervention powers;

- the body has failed to comply with any obligation under the SRA's regulatory arrangements;

- in the case of a licensed body (applicable to ABSs alone), the body fails to comply with the prohibition on appointing disqualified managers; or in the case of any authorised body, the body fails to comply with the prohibition on employing disqualified persons (struck off solicitors and the like) if the manager or employee concerned was disqualified as a result of breach of the duties imposed upon the manager or employee by sections 176 or 90 of LSA 2007 (the general duties imposed to comply with all regulatory arrangements for ABSs); or

- for any other reason it is in the public interest.

A 'relevant insolvency event' is defined as occurring when:

'(a) a resolution for a voluntary winding up of the body is passed without a declaration of solvency under section 89 of the Insolvency Act 1986;

(b) the body enters administration within the meaning of paragraph 1(2) (b) of Schedule B1 to that Act;

(c) an administrative receiver within the meaning of section 251 of that Act is appointed;

(d) a meeting of creditors is held in relation to the body under section 95 of that Act (creditors' meeting which has the effect of converting a members' voluntary winding up into a creditors' voluntary winding up);

(e) an order for the winding up of the body is made;

(f) all of the managers in a body which is unincorporated have been adjudicated bankrupt; or

(g) the body is an overseas company or a societas Europaea registered outside England, Wales, Scotland and Northern Ireland and the body is subject to an event in its country of incorporation analogous to an event as set out in paragraphs (a) to (f) above.'

The SRA may also revoke or suspend a body's authorisation where, in the case of a *licensed* body (applicable to ABSs alone), a non-authorised person holds an interest in the licensed body:

- as a result of the person taking a step in circumstances where that constitutes an offence under paragraph 24(1) of Schedule 13 to LSA 2007 (whether or not the person is charged with or convicted of an offence under that paragraph) – this is failing to give notice as to the proposed or actual acquisition of a material interest in an ABS;

- in breach of conditions imposed on the owners of material interests in the ABS; or

- the person's holding of which is subject to an objection by the licensing authority.

2.17

Before the SRA can revoke or suspend an authorisation it must first give the authorised body an opportunity to make representations to it on the issues that have led the SRA to consider this course, and it must also give at least 28 days' notice of its intention to make the decision to revoke or suspend.[1]

Guidance notes to rule 22 of the SRA Authorisation Rules 2011 emphasised that the SRA was unlikely to revoke or suspend authorisation if to do so would present any risk to clients, the public, the protection of public money or to any SRA investigation. This guidance has not been reissued but the approach would be consistent with the proper exercise of the SRA's duty and is likely to be maintained in practice.

1   Rule 4.5 of the Firm Rules.

Unforeseen temporary breach

2.18

Rule 14.1 of the Firm Rules provides for a variety of situations in which authorised bodies (ABSs and non-ABSs) could cease to be eligible to be authorised; for example, if an ABS no longer has a manager who is a qualified lawyer, or a recognised body no longer has one manager who is a solicitor. The body has seven days to notify the SRA of the event and must remedy the situation within 28 days or cease to carry on reserved legal activities and to hold itself out as an authorised body.

Partnership changes and temporary emergency authorisation

2.19

The express provisions of rule 24.2 of the Authorisation Rules 2011 have not survived the reform of the SRA's regulatory arrangements. The express provisions dealing with changes in the composition of an authorised body have been replaced by the generic and unhelpful rule 14.2 of the Firm Rules, which provides:

> 14.2 Subject to any *prescribed* application requirements, the *SRA* may:
>
> (a) transfer a body's authorisation to another body where the first body ceases to exist and the second body succeeds to the whole or substantially the whole of its business;
>
> (b) substitute a body's authorisation for another type of authorisation where it is satisfied that the body is materially carrying on the same practice, notwithstanding a change in its management or control; and

> (c)   permit any *person* previously approved as a *manager, owner,* or *compliance officer* of the body to continue to act in their designated role, notwithstanding the transfer or substitution.

While this omission is unlikely to trouble incorporated practices which have separate legal identities, it may require traditional partnerships to consider their position more carefully upon a change in the composition of the partnership – particularly if there is no partnership agreement in place.

Under the Authorisation Rules 2011, a change in composition of a partnership did not generally affect the firm's authorisation. However, if the change in composition resulted in there being no individual who was a partner after the change who was also a partner before the change, that was not a change in composition at all, but the cessation of one firm and the creation of another. The new firm could not adopt the authorisation of the old firm.[1]

It may be suggested that any change in composition which does not result in a complete loss of eligibility does not require an application to be made for authorisation of the changed entity – however, the position is unclear under the Firm Rules. Rule 4.2, for example, provides that authorisation ceases to have effect when a body ceases to exist, subject to the limited savings in rules 14 and 15, essentially permitting the SRA to continue authorisation by allowing firms a short period to rectify unforeseen problems through the temporary emergency recognition process.

It is implicit under rule 15.1 that a change in management or control of an authorised body can bring into being a new unauthorised body. That is one of the grounds upon which an application for temporary emergency recognition can be made. What is not clear is *when* a change in management and control *can* bring into being a new unauthorised entity and, in the absence of any express provision, it must be assumed that the general law will apply.

1   Rule 24.2(a) of the Authorisation Rules 2011 (now superseded).

Review and appeals

2.20

The SRA reserves to itself the right to review any decision made by a decision-maker. Historically, this power has been used in disciplinary investigations when adjudicators have made decisions which the SRA staff had not expected or did not agree with (see **20.15**). A review may be undertaken on the SRA's own initiative or on the application of the person affected by the decision.[1]

1   Rules 3.1(b) and 3.2 of the SRA Application, Notice, Review and Appeal Rules 2019.

2.21

The appeal provisions vary depending on whether the authorised body is or is not an ABS, because the licensing and appeal decisions for an ABS are dictated by LSA 2007.

An ABS may appeal to the Tribunal against a refusal of authorisation, a decision to impose a condition on an authorisation, a decision to revoke or suspend an authorisation, a refusal to approve a step which under a condition requires prior approval, a decision to modify, or to refuse to modify the conditions of an authorisation.[1]

An ABS or the person affected may appeal to the Tribunal against a refusal to approve a person as a manager or compliance officer, a decision to impose conditions on an approval or to withdraw approval, a decision to grant approval or conditional approval of the holding of a material interest in an ABS and a decision to withdraw approval of a manager, an owner or a compliance officer of an ABS.[2]

There are also ABS-specific provisions concerning financial penalties, disqualification and ownership issues, dealt with in **Chapters 25** and **26**.

1   Rule 5.1 of and Annex 2 to the SRA Application, Notice, Review and Appeal Rules 2019.
2   Ibid.

2.22

Traditional firms (legal services bodies/recognised bodies) do not have any right of appeal to the Tribunal, nor do individuals within them affected by authorisation or approval decisions. The statutory background to the process of approval of recognised bodies is the Administration of Justice Act (AJA) 1985 as amended by LSA 2007, and under Schedule 2 to that statute[1] appeal lies where relevant to the High Court.

A legal services body may appeal to the High Court against a refusal of authorisation, a decision to impose a condition on an authorisation, or a decision to revoke or suspend an authorisation.[2]

A legal services body or the person affected may appeal to the High Court against the withdrawal of approval for the roles of COLP, COFA, manager or owner of a recognised body.[3]

If the body is not an ABS, but a legal services body/recognised body, there is no external right of appeal at all, and only the prospect of an appeal to a different decision-maker in the SRA[4] in relation to decisions:

- to refuse to approve a person to be an owner of the body;[5]

- to refuse to approve a person as a compliance officer – COLP or COFA;

- to approve a manager, owner or compliance officer subject to conditions; or

- to modify or to refuse to modify terms and conditions of authorisation.

1   See **Appendix 19**.
2   Annex 3 to the SRA Application, Notice, Review and Appeal Rules 2019.
3   Annex 3 to the SRA Application, Notice, Review and Appeal Rules 2019.
4   Annex 1 to the SRA Application, Notice, Review and Appeal Rules 2019. This would not prevent an application for judicial review in appropriate cases.
5   If a non-authorised person has an interest in a regulated firm that is equivalent to 10 per cent or more the firm is licensable as an ABS and the interest holder must be expressly approved (see **25.1** and **25.3**). If a non-authorised person has an interest that is less than 10 per cent, the body does not qualify as an ABS but the SRA still has to be satisfied that the body's managers and interest holders are suitable, as a group, to operate or control a business providing regulated legal services; see rule 2.2(a) of the Firm Rules.

2.23

The SRA's decision to adopt the same authorisation principles for all practices regardless of the statutory background has therefore created serious anomalies. A decision, for example, to impose conditions on a manager or to refuse approval of a compliance officer where the individual's role is in an ABS may be subject to an internal review process but is also subject to external review by the Tribunal, potentially with costs consequences if the SRA got it wrong.

Exactly the same decisions, made under the same rules applying the same principles and the same procedures, but where the individual's role is within an authorised practice that is not an ABS, can only be appealed internally. If the SRA decision-maker on appeal endorses the decision of the SRA first instance decision-maker there is no further right of appeal, leaving only the unsatisfactory remedy of judicial review.

2.24

The time limit for internal review is 28 days from notification of the decision and reasons. The SRA specifies that unless otherwise provided in rules of the High Court or the Tribunal appeals to the court or Tribunal must be made within 28 days.[1] Appeals to the High Court are governed by Part 52 of the Civil Procedure Rules and should be entered in the Administrative Court within 21 days of the decision, or of receipt of the reasons for the decision if later.[2] The Tribunal has set the time for appeal as 28 days from receipt of the decision in all cases; see **23.6**.

1   Rule 5.1 of the SRA Application, Notice, Review and Appeal Rules 2019.
2   CPR rule 52.4; Part 52 Practice Direction 52D, paragraphs 3.3A and 27.1.

The SRA Authorisation of Individuals Regulations 2019

2.25

The Individual Rules deal with the requirements for seeking admission to the roll, the admission of qualified lawyers, the formalities of obtaining practising certificates and explain what authorisation entitles you to do.

The lists of the various ways in which solicitors, registered European lawyers (RELs), registered foreign lawyers (RFLs) and authorised bodies could practise when regulated by the SRA, which characterised the now defunct Practice Framework Rules 2011, have been abandoned.

Matters considered likely to be relevant in everyday practice are in part considered elsewhere in this book; for RELs and RFLs see **CHAPTER 12**; for in-house and overseas practice see **CHAPTER 10**.

Two particularly relevant and important issues are dealt with in these rules – the circumstances in which practising certificates are required and the rules permitting solicitors to act as a solicitor through an unregulated entity.

All solicitors require practising certificates (unless they are in the privileged group exempted by section 88 of SA 1974, such as those employed in central government) if:

- they provide reserved legal activities;[1]

- they act as a solicitor within the meaning of section 20 of SA 1974;

- the individual is held out explicitly or implicitly as a practising solicitor within the meaning of section 21 of SA 1974; or

- section 1A of SA 1974 applies.

Section 1A of SA 1974 states that a person who has been admitted as a solicitor and whose name is on the roll shall be taken to be acting as a solicitor (if this would not otherwise be so) if he or she is employed in connection with the provision of any legal services by any person who is qualified to act as a solicitor, by a partnership at least one member of which is qualified to act as a solicitor, by a recognised body, or by any other person or body who is authorised under LSA 2007 to provide reserved legal services.

Thus by section 1A any solicitor employed in what may be loosely termed private practice must always have a practising certificate. Solicitors employed by other bodies, for example, in industry or local government or by charities, will need to consider whether their employment depends on them being solicitors, whether they are employed on that basis, or whether they are held out as practising solicitors.[2]

1 Section 14 of LSA 2007.
2 See SRA guidance, 'When do I need a practising certificate?', issued 4 July 2019, updated 25 November 2019.

2.26

From 25 November 2019, it has been possible for the first time for solicitors to describe themselves as solicitors and to provide certain legal services to the public through an unregulated entity. This arrangement, when proposed in consultation, generated significant resistance from the Law Society and from the Legal Services Consumer Panel due to perceived consumer detriment and potential damage to the reputation of solicitors.

The SRA's approach to this issue has been that it is better for consumers to have some regulatory protection than none.

Solicitors who intend to call themselves a solicitor will need a practising certificate to comply with SA 1974, irrespective of the entity through which they may practise. All solicitors will be subject to the requirements of the Code for Individuals and should pay particular attention to the information requirements set out at paragraphs 8.10 and 8.11 of the Code.

Solicitors who intend to practise other than through an authorised body, including a recognised sole practice, may provide reserved legal activities in the extremely limited circumstances set out at regulation 10.2(b) of the Individual Rules, which provides:

(b) any *reserved legal activities* you carry on are provided through an *authorised body* or an *authorised non-SRA firm*, or in circumstances in which you:

　　(i) have practised as a *solicitor* or an *REL* for a minimum of three years since admission or registration;

　　(ii) are self-employed and practise in your own name, and not through a trading name or service company;

    (iii)   do not employ anyone in connection with the services that you provide;

    (iv)   are engaged directly by the *client* with your *fees* payable directly to you;

    (v)   have a practising address in the *UK*;

    (vi)   take out and maintain indemnity insurance that provides adequate and appropriate cover in respect of the services that you provide or have provided, whether or not they comprise *reserved legal activities*, taking into account any alternative arrangements you or your *clients* may make; and

    (vii)   do not hold *client money*, save that you may hold money which falls within the category of *client money* set out in rule 2.1(d) of the SRA Accounts Rules so long as:

        (A)   any money held for *disbursements* relates to costs or expenses incurred by you on behalf of your *client* and for which you are liable; and

        (B)   you have informed your *client* in advance of where and how the money will be held,

and you choose for your practice not to be authorised as a *recognised sole practice*.

It is not possible to provide reserved legal services through an unauthorised body. Such services can only be provided directly and in person and with the benefit of professional indemnity (PI) insurance.[1] Solicitors practising within the limits of regulation 10.2(b) will be described as independent solicitors.[2]

It is not permissible to provide regulated immigration services in this way as regulation 9.5 of the Individual Rules requires that such services be provided through an authorised body. Similar considerations apply to claims management services (regulation 9.8) and financial services (regulation 9.9).

Solicitors wishing to provide unreserved legal services to members of the public may do so through an unregulated entity. They may not provide reserved legal services, immigration services, claims management services or financial services unless the entity is duly regulated to enable the provision of such services. Solicitors practising in this way may not hold client money.[3]

---

1   This does not have to comply with the SRA minimum terms and conditions; however the SRA has published guidance on what information must be provided to clients. See 'Unregulated organisations giving information to clients', issued 23 July 2019, updated 25 November 2019, at www.sra.org.uk.

2   SRA guidance, 'Preparing to become a sole practitioner or an SRA-regulated freelance solicitor', issued 4 July 2019, updated 25 November 2019.

3   Regulation 9.1 of the Individual Rules, incorporating the restrictions in regulation 10.2(b) listed above.

PART 2
The SRA Principles and Codes

CHAPTER 3

Overview of the Principles and the Codes

Introduction

3.1

The rather modest regulatory impact of the 1936 Solicitors' Practice Rules has been mentioned in the Preface to the 2008 edition of this book. The Practice Rules changed very little in subsequent decades. A new rule was made in 1967, requiring that only solicitors with practising certificates should be listed on notepaper and the office nameplate. Rule 2 (which prohibited the sin of charging less than scale fees) was replaced in 1972 with a rule against acting for both parties in conveyancing transactions subject to specified exceptions. A comprehensive new set of Rules was made in 1987, which are recognisably the precursor to the Solicitors' Practice Rules 1990 (SPR 1990) and very little different from the 1990 Rules in their original form. The 1990 Rules were amended and supplemented extensively after they were implemented; not all the changes were readily accessible.

The Law Society embarked on the preparation of a new comprehensive set of rules in and before 2004, and the resulting Solicitors' Code of Conduct 2007 (2007 Code) came into force on 1 July 2007. The 2007 Code abandoned the historical approach of relatively narrow practice rules and wider but non-exclusive (official and published) guidance. Instead, it created a comprehensive regulatory framework for all aspects of a solicitor's conduct. The 2007 Code comprised 25 individual rules and was supplemented by guidance produced by the Solicitors Regulation Authority (SRA) which amplified and explained its provisions. The guidance was not mandatory and did not form part of the 2007 Code; however, the SRA added a note to the preamble to the 2007 Code with effect from 31 March 2009 to the effect that if solicitors did not follow the guidance they could be required to demonstrate (ie prove) how they nevertheless complied with the rules.

The 2007 Code's life was short. Because of its all-encompassing nature, the 2007 Code and the guidance associated with each rule had to be amended regularly, which caused problems for solicitors who found it difficult to pinpoint what rule or guidance was in force at a given time. This was accompanied by an approach to regulation by the SRA which appeared to concentrate on minutiae – for example, precisely what needed to be said to clients about referral arrangements, and when it had to be said, about which it was not difficult to make mistakes, even when solicitors were doing what they thought was entirely proper.

3.2

The passing of the Legal Services Act (LSA) 2007, the inevitable need to create a regulatory environment which would work for both traditional law firms and alternative business structures (ABSs) and strong guidance from the Legal Services Board (LSB), created the need to move to a different basis and style of regulation.

Principles-based regulation had been pioneered by the financial services profession, and was then introduced to the legal profession in October 2011 under the title 'outcomes-focused regulation' (OFR). Instead of professionals being bound, and often hamstrung, by a prescriptive set of rules, the onus shifted to the regulated individual or entity to deliver satisfactory outcomes for consumers based upon an overarching set of ethical principles. The regulated individual, the solicitor, is (or should be) trusted to think for him- or herself in order to achieve satisfactory outcomes for clients.

OFR was designed to move away, both in the form of rules and by the way in which they were policed, from the tick-box, strict liability, 'every breach is a breach' approach described above, which had seriously damaged the relationship between the profession and the regulator. The problem with that former approach was that it was too easy to hit the wrong target – the solicitor trying to get it right but making mistakes, as opposed to the one who does not care, or deliberately breaks the rules.

3.3

During the consultation process before the introduction of the SRA Code of Conduct 2011 (2011 Code), the SRA announced that:

> 'We know that the current rule book is too prescriptive. OFR will give firms the flexibility to do new and better things for consumers. It will lead to a more grown-up relationship between the SRA and the regulated community.'

and:

> 'The introduction of OFR will give a simplified rulebook and freedom to practise innovatively, which will be good for consumers and providers of legal services alike. OFR is risk-based regulation; firms will have to comply with broad principles rather than detailed rules. Firms will be able to comply with the principles in the ways which best suit their businesses. Formal rules will still apply in important areas including accounts and indemnity, where they are necessary. ...
>
> The SRA's enforcement of OFR will be effective, fair and proportionate. We will focus on the things which really matter to consumers; for example risks which may lead to a loss of their money, justice, or social or economic wellbeing.'[1]

That, as an announcement, was welcome as it stated an intention to turn the clock back to a time when the consequence of something going wrong – whether there was in fact any mischief or prejudice caused, as opposed to being a 'bare breach' – was an important if not determinative factor in how the regulator could be expected to treat the solicitor concerned.

Accordingly, we anticipated that we would see a refreshingly different approach to enforcement of the 2011 Code by the SRA. The experience of practitioners after October 2011 was mixed. Many found the relationship with their regulator easier than it had been in the past, but others reported that little had changed, with all the 'old' tendencies towards disproportionate reaction and judgement by hindsight.

There was also a tendency to move back towards a prescriptive approach to the rules. That can be demonstrated by the use of indicative behaviours in the 2011 Code. When the indicative behaviours were introduced in 2011, it was stated that they were not mandatory and were designed to specify the kind of behaviour which may establish compliance with, or contravention of, the Code. There was always a fear in the profession that they would gradually acquire the status of rules, despite an absolute disavowal that they had that force. By 2016 it was common for the SRA to send disciplinary letters to practitioners informing them that they had breached indicative behaviours.

1   'Freedom in practice: better outcomes for consumers. A passport to regulatory reform' issued by the SRA in April 2010.

3.4

In June 2016 the SRA announced a decision to change the profession's rules again. The new rules were submitted to the LSB for approval in August 2018. The announcements made at that time by the SRA were very similar to the announcements made before the introduction of the 2011 Code:

> 'In developing our new rules, we have sought to reduce unnecessary regulation – we have removed prescriptive drafting to produce requirements that:
>
> - are clearer and more accessible, with duplication removed
> - are easier to understand in terms of purpose and effect
> - are targeted at the issues that really matter
> - operate at a higher level, and so are less detailed and less prescriptive, providing flexibility to apply to changing circumstances ...'

and:

> 'We are removing restrictions we cannot justify and will allow more freedom for those we regulate to innovate and provide services to meet consumers' needs ...
>
> Our current Handbook is long and complex. We have therefore reviewed all our rules to create a shorter, sharper, clearer set of regulatory arrangements ...
>
> Many we regulate agree and consider that the current Handbook duplicates other legislative and regulatory obligations, is too prescriptive and needs changing too often ...
>
> [The new codes] allow more flexibility for individuals and firms to decide how best to comply with our rules than is provided under our current prescriptive rulebook.'[1]

Those rules, given the new description 'SRA Standards and Regulations', came into force on 25 November 2019 and included a revised set of SRA Principles and separate codes of conduct for firms and individuals.

1   'Application for the approval of regulatory arrangements', issued by the SRA in August 2018, paras 12–26.

3.5

There are no indicative behaviours in the SRA Standards and Regulations 2019, and the SRA said it was removing them because some had started to give them the status of rules. It announced that the new regulatory arrangements would instead be supported by new guidance to help those it regulates, that the guidance would not have the force of rules and would be there to help support solicitors in the judgements they make.[1]

At the time of writing this edition of *The Solicitor's Handbook*, the SRA has published more than 120 guidance notes and case studies relating to the SRA Standards and Regulations. It is difficult to reconcile the sheer volume of that guidance with the SRA's aim of creating a shorter and clearer set of regulatory arrangements, and it remains to be seen whether a departure from the guidance will in the future be relied on per se as evidence of a breach of the rules.

1   'Application for the approval of regulatory arrangements', issued by the SRA in August 2018, para 61.

3.6

In this Part of *The Solicitor's Handbook* we consider the 2019 Principles and Codes, and the guidance relating to them, which govern all acts and omissions occurring after the SRA Standards and Regulations came into force on 25 November 2019. The 2011 rules will continue to be relevant to disciplinary proceedings relating to acts and omissions that occurred before the introduction of the 2019 regulatory arrangements, and detailed commentary on the 2011 rules can be found in *The Solicitor's Handbook 2017*.

3.7

Taking an overview of the history, from 1936 when nearly all the 'rules' were unwritten but clearly understood, through successive Guides to Professional Conduct and changes in the Solicitors' Practice Rules (SPR), and the succession of Codes of Conduct from 2007 onwards, little has really changed, because the standards of behaviour required of solicitors have largely remained constant. There cannot be any solicitors who do not know that they have to behave honestly, or that they have to keep their clients' affairs confidential, or that they cannot ordinarily act where there is a conflict of interest. The moves from Rules to Codes, from rules to outcomes, and from outcomes to new regulatory arrangements have been costly, as firms need to ensure that their internal arrangements comply with each set of new rules, but have not, in our view, caused any changes in behaviour, nor would they be expected to.

Arguably, what needs to change is not a matter of drafting, though any simplification of the rule book is welcome, but an approach to enforcement which is reliably consistent and proportionate, and in accordance with the Regulators' Code (see **APPENDIX 13**).

The SRA Principles 2019

The seven Principles

3.8

The SRA Principles 2019 are relatively short and are set out in full, with the introduction, below:

'Introduction

The SRA Principles comprise the fundamental tenets of ethical behaviour that we expect all those that we regulate to uphold. This includes all individuals we authorise to provide legal services (solicitors, RELs and RFLs), as well as authorised firms and their managers and employees. For licensed bodies, these apply to those individuals, and the part of the body (where applicable), involved in delivering the services we regulate in accordance with the terms of your licence.

Should the Principles come into conflict, those which safeguard the wider public interest (such as the rule of law, and public confidence in a trustworthy solicitors' profession and a safe and effective market for regulated legal services) take precedence over an individual client's interests. You should, where relevant, inform your client of the circumstances in which your duty to the Court and other professional obligations will outweigh your duty to them.

The Principles and Codes are underpinned by our Enforcement Strategy, which explains in more detail our approach to taking regulatory action in the public interest.

This introduction does not form part of the SRA Principles.

The principles are as follows:

SRA Principles

You act:

1. in a way that upholds the constitutional principle of the rule of law, and the proper administration of justice.
2. in a way that upholds public trust and confidence in the solicitors' profession and in legal services provided by authorised persons.
3. with independence.
4. with honesty.
5. with integrity.
6. in a way that encourages equality, diversity and inclusion.
7. in the best interests of each client.'

3.9

The SRA Principles 2019 apply, as did their predecessors, to every person and body regulated by the SRA: solicitors of course, but also registered European lawyers (RELs),[1] registered foreign lawyers (RFLs), the business entity itself; partnerships, limited liability partnerships (LLPs), limited liability companies, recognised sole practitioners, legal disciplinary practices, and the managers and employees of those entities and licensed bodies. That is subject to one exception: regulated individuals who are practising overseas and are subject to the Overseas Principles must comply with those Overseas Principles rather than the SRA Principles 2019.[2] In the case of

CHAPTER 3
PRINCIPLES AND CODES
OVERVIEW

licensed bodies the Principles apply to the individuals and the part of the body (where applicable) involved in delivering the regulated service under the terms of the licence. Although this book is written principally for solicitors, the reach of regulation should not be overlooked.

1   On 1 January 2021 the Services of Lawyers and Lawyer's Practice (Revocation etc.) (EU Exit) Regulations 2020 (SI 2020/1342) ('the 2020 Regulations') revoked the rights of all European lawyers apart from Swiss lawyers to practise as RELs. The rights of Swiss lawyers to practise as RELs continue under transitional provisions in the 2020 Regulations. See **Chapter 12**.

2   See the SRA Overseas and Cross-border Practice Rules 2019 (the 'Overseas Rules' or 'OCB Rules') and **4.6**. The Overseas Principles are set out in rule 2.1 of the Overseas Rules.

3.10

The emphasis placed by the regulatory arrangements on different core duties has varied from time to time over the past 30 years. The Solicitors' Practice Rules 1987 identified five principles, which were the solicitor's independence and integrity, the client's freedom of choice, the best interests of the client, the good repute of the solicitor and the profession, and the solicitor's proper standard of work. SPR 1990 added, importantly, the solicitor's duty to the court. Rule 1 of the 2007 Code identified six core duties: justice and the rule of law; integrity; independence; the best interests of the client; the solicitor's good standard of service; and public confidence in the profession. Those six core duties were virtually identical to principles 1 to 6 of the ten principles in the SRA Principles 2011. Principles 7 to 10 of the SRA Principles 2011 added a further four principles: compliance with legal and regulatory obligations; sound management; encouraging equality of opportunity and respect for diversity; and protecting client money and assets.

In 2019 four of the SRA's 2011 Principles were entirely jettisoned, namely providing a proper standard of service (principle 5), complying with legal and regulatory obligations (principle 7), sound management (principle 8) and protecting client money and assets (principle 10). Those four principles are now found in the 2019 Codes.[1] A new principle was added in 2019: the requirement to act honestly. It was questionable whether that really needed to be expressly provided for, but other regulators do make such a requirement of those they regulate, and it may be that the SRA considered that it should fall into line.

1   See in particular paragraph 3.2 of the SRA Code of Conduct for Solicitors, RELs and RFLs 2019 (the 'Code for Individuals') (proper standard of service), paragraph 7.1 of the Code for Individuals (compliance with legal and regulatory obligations), paragraphs 2.4 and 2.5 of the SRA Code of Conduct for Firms 2019 (the 'Code for Firms') (sound management) and paragraph 4.2 of the Code for Individuals (protecting client money and assets).

Public and private life

3.11

Neither the introduction nor the Principles themselves expressly state that the Principles apply to activities conducted in a private as well as a business capacity. However, the introduction does state that the Principles are underpinned by the Enforcement Strategy, and the Enforcement Strategy contains the following statement on private life:

> 'Our key role is to act on wrongdoing which relates to an individual or a firm's legal practice. We will not get involved in complaints against a

solicitor which relate solely to, for example, their competence as a school governor or their involvement in a neighbour dispute. However, our Principles set out the core ethical values we require of all those we regulate and apply at all times and in all contexts – and apply both in and outside of practice (as the context permits).

We are concerned with the impact of conduct outside of legal practice including in the private lives of those we regulate if this touches on risk to the delivery of safe legal services in future. The closer any behaviour is to professional activities, or a reflection of how a solicitor might behave in a professional context, the more seriously we are likely to view it. For example, an allegation of financial impropriety against a solicitor when acting as a Member of Parliament, will raise a question as to their fitness to manage client funds. However, we will also be interested in matters that are so serious that they are capable of damaging public confidence, such as dishonest or discriminatory conduct in any context.

As stated above, the Principles apply outside of practice but only insofar as the context permits: So for example, the obligation to act in a client's best interests relates to their best legal interests in any matter in which you act for them; and would not extend to how you behave towards them in a personal or social matter.

In addition, whilst the Principles apply outside of practice to individuals who are not themselves authorised (such as employees or non-lawyers holding roles that are approved by us – such as managers of firms), we will take their role into consideration. Our interest in employees relates to their role as an employee and any behaviour that touches on their suitability as such, which will generally derive from their conduct in practise. When it comes to other role holders, we will also consider their wider fitness or suitability to be approved in that role; and, for example, to have management or control over a legal business. So conduct such as mishandling funds relating to a non-legal business or appointment, will potentially bring our regulation into play.'[1]

1   SRA Enforcement Strategy, 7 February 2019, updated 25 November 2019. The SRA has also published Guidance Notes which apply SRA Principles to private life; see **3.15–3.29**.

3.12

The principles which could apply to a solicitor's private life are principles 1 (rule of law), 2 (public trust and confidence), 4 (honesty), 5 (integrity) and 6 (equality, diversity and inclusion). The SRA routinely takes disciplinary proceedings against solicitors who have been convicted of criminal offences for conduct in their private lives, and the convictions almost invariably lead to findings by SRA Adjudicators and the Solicitors Disciplinary Tribunal (the Tribunal or SDT) that the solicitors have breached principle 2 (on the grounds that public trust and confidence in the solicitors' profession is damaged by criminal convictions). More serious offences can also result in findings that other principles such as principles 4 (honesty) and 5 (integrity) have been breached. Conduct in other areas of private life can, and does, lead to disciplinary proceedings. For example, offensive comments on a person's race or sexual orientation on social media platforms, or discrimination in separate businesses such as restaurants operated by solicitors, can lead to disciplinary proceedings and findings for breach of the principle 6 requirement to encourage equality, diversity and inclusion.

CHAPTER 3
PRINCIPLES AND CODES OVERVIEW

3.13

The extent to which the SRA should apply the Principles to conduct in private life was considered in 2020 in *Beckwith v SRA*. *Beckwith* involved a consensual sexual encounter outside the office between a partner in the firm and a junior employee. The SDT found that the partner had not abused his position of seniority but said that his conduct was 'inappropriate' and that he had breached the principles of integrity and maintaining public trust and confidence in the profession. The SDT order was quashed by the High Court, which decided that the circumstances in which a solicitor should be required to act with integrity or uphold public trust and confidence in the profession should be identified by reference to the contents of the SRA Handbook (and primarily the rules in the code of conduct) as the Handbook is the best guide to the occasions and contexts where solicitors should be held to the higher standards required from members of the profession.[1] The High Court also said that the decision in the case should not be treated as 'any form of permission to expand the scope of the obligation to act with integrity simply by making rules that extend ever further into personal life'.[2]

The decision in *Beckwith* highlights complex issues on the extent to which the SRA is entitled to regulate conduct in a solicitor's private life, but does not provide an easy answer which sits readily with former decisions on professional conduct. *Beckwith* concentrated on the professional standards arising from the rules made by the SRA under section 31 of the Solicitors Act (SA) 1974 which are set out in the Handbook, but professional standards are not simply based on the rules made under section 31. Professional standards also stem from a number of other sources such as the court's inherent jurisdiction, the common law, LSA 2007 and the LSB. Some of those sources place an emphasis on overarching principles rather than the rules, such as the LSB's emphasis on principles-based regulation and the common law principle in *Bolton*[3] that the most fundamental purpose of the Tribunal is to maintain the reputation of the profession as one in which every member of whatever standing may be trusted to the ends of the earth. It is therefore unclear after *Beckwith* whether professional standards should be determined by reference to overarching principles or specific rules.

There is as a result uncertainty on the extent to which the SRA Principles can regulate a solicitor's private life, and that uncertainty is reflected in the commentary on the Principles below.

For further commentary on *Beckwith* see **19.3–19.4** and **19.6**.

1 *Beckwith v SRA* [2020] EWHC 3231 (Admin). The High Court made it clear that it was considering the Handbook containing the 2011 Principles and Code of Conduct, but the decision applies equally to the 2019 regulatory arrangements.
2 *Beckwith v SRA* [2020] EWHC 3231 (Admin) at [39].
3 *Bolton v Law Society* [1994] 1 WLR 512, CA.

Professional misconduct and the Principles

3.14

In *SRA v Day*[1] the High Court held that a decision whether an alleged breach of a principle amounts to professional misconduct depends on an assessment of the seriousness of the breach; not all breaches are so serious that they amount to professional misconduct; see **19.2**.

1 [2018] EWHC 2726 (Admin) at [156] to [162]. See also **19.2**.

Principle 1 – the constitutional principle of the rule of law and the proper administration of justice

3.15

Somehow, along the way, the solicitor's duty to the court has become rephrased as a duty to 'uphold the administration of justice'. Upholding the administration of justice could be said to equate to a duty to the court, but could also be said to be wider than that. The duty to the court is one of the 'professional principles' set out in section 1(3)(d) of LSA 2007, and is reinforced by section 188 of LSA 2007, which states that a person who exercises a right of audience or conducts litigation has a duty to the court to act with independence in the interests of justice. It is also reinforced by section 2 of the Code for Individuals which sets out specific conduct obligations relating to proceedings before courts, tribunals and inquiries (see **4.16**).

Upholding 'the constitutional principle of the rule of law' may be more controversial, and possibly a mistake. Upholding the rule of law is not the same as upholding the law or complying with the law (as it occasionally seems to be suggested in proceedings before the Tribunal; see for example *SRA v Olujinmi*).[1] The rule of law is a constitutional principle (see section 1(1)(b) of LSA 2007) the basic concept of which is:

> 'that all persons and authorities within the state, whether public or private, should be bound by and entitled to the benefit of laws publicly made, taking effect (generally) in the future and publicly administered in the courts.'[2]

That is primarily an obligation of the state, not of individuals. However, principle 1 is interpreted by the SRA as a principle which imposes an obligation on every regulated person to comply with the law in their practice and their personal lives, and also on every regulated entity to comply with the law.

In many cases, the SDT also equates principle 1 with a failure to comply with the law. However, in *SRA v Main* the Tribunal decided after hearing detailed submissions on principle 1 that a solicitor's conviction for a failure to comply with the law did not mean that the solicitor had failed to uphold the rule of law.[3]

1   11442-2015, SDT.
2   Bingham, *The Rule of Law*, Penguin Books, 2010.
3   11698-2017, SDT. The case concerned the comparable principle in the SRA Principles 2011. In *Main*, the Tribunal found that the solicitor had breached principles 2 (integrity) and 6 (public confidence) and imposed a suspension. The SRA appealed the sentence, but did not appeal the Tribunal decision that the solicitor had not breached principle 1 – see *SRA v Main* [2018] EWHC 3666 (Admin).

Principle 2 – public trust and confidence

3.16

Principle 2 relates to preserving the reputation of, and public confidence in, the regulated legal profession.[1] A comparable core duty was set out in rule 1(d) of SPR 1990, rule 1.06 of the 2007 Code, and the 2011 Principles.

An SRA guidance note states that public trust and confidence in solicitors is at the heart of the legal system, and stresses that clients place their confidence in solicitors to protect their interests, money, other assets and personal information.[2]

The SRA applies the principle to standards of behaviour in a solicitor's private life, as well as behaviour within the context of professional practice. It has stated that it is required to act on any report of conduct outside practice that may damage public confidence or suggest that the solicitor might present a risk while in practice (such as a report of a lack of financial probity).[3] It has also stated the type of conduct outside practice which is likely to result in disciplinary action includes behaviour involving violence, sexual harassment or offensive social media posts and conduct resulting in criminal convictions.[4]

For case law on the extent to which principle 2 applies to private life see **3.13** and **CHAPTER 19**, and for the question whether an alleged breach amounts to professional misconduct see **3.14** and **19.2**.

1   See *SRA v Wingate* [2018] EWCA Civ 366 at [105], on the comparable provision in the 2011 Principles.
2   SRA guidance, 'Public trust and confidence' 25 November 2019.
3   'Application for the approval of regulatory arrangements', issued by the SRA in August 2018, para 94.
4   SRA guidance, 'Public trust and confidence' 25 November 2019.

Principle 3 – independence

3.17

The duty to act with independence is one of the professional principles enshrined in section 1(3) of LSA 2007. It is a core duty which was also included in rule 1(a) of SPR 1990, rule 1.03 of the 2007 Code, and the 2011 Principles. It encompasses obligations such as the duties to avoid conflicts of interest and to not take unfair advantage of a client.

Principle 4 – honesty

3.18

The SRA Principles 2011 included a duty to act with integrity but did not include a duty to act with honesty. In 2017 Mostyn J stated that the SRA Principles did not additionally include honesty because honesty and integrity were the same thing.[1] That decision was overruled by the Court of Appeal, which held that honesty and integrity are different concepts,[2] and the addition of a new principle of honesty reinforces the fact that the two principles are different. Integrity is a broader concept than honesty[3] and encompasses conduct such as sexual harassment and reckless misconduct, which can involve a lack of integrity even if the conduct is not dishonest.

In *Ivey* the Supreme Court said that the test for dishonesty is objective, although the mindset of the individual is highly relevant to the fact-finding process. Lord Hughes set out the test as follows:

> 'When dishonesty is in question the fact-finding tribunal must first ascertain (subjectively) the actual state of the individual's knowledge or belief as to the facts. The reasonableness or otherwise of his belief is a matter of evidence (often in practice determinative) going to whether he held the belief, but it is not an additional requirement that his belief must be reasonable; the question is whether it is genuinely held. When once his actual

state of mind as to knowledge or belief as to facts is established, the question whether his conduct was honest or dishonest is to be determined by the fact-finder by applying the (objective) standards of ordinary decent people. There is no requirement that the defendant must appreciate that what he has done is, by those standards, dishonest.'[4]

For further commentary on *Ivey* see **19.12**.

1   *Malins v SRA* [2017] EWHC 835 (Admin) at [30].
2   *SRA v Wingate* [2018] EWCA Civ 366 at [95].
3   Ibid.
4   *Ivey v Genting Casinos (UK) Ltd* [2017] UKSC 67 at [74]. For application of the *Ivey* test in Tribunal proceedings, see *Zivancevic v SRA* [2019] EWHC 1950 (Admin) at [19].

Principle 5 – integrity

3.19

The duty to act with integrity is one of the professional principles enshrined in section 1(3) of LSA 2007. It is a core duty which was also included in rule 1(a) of SPR 1990, rule 1.02 of the 2007 Code and the 2011 Principles.

In *Wingate*, Jackson LJ said:

'In professional codes of conduct, the term "integrity" is a useful shorthand to express the higher standards which society expects from professional persons and which the professions expect from their own members ... The underlying rationale is that the professions have a privileged and trusted role in society. In return they are required to live up to their own professional standards ...

Integrity connotes adherence to the ethical standards of one's own profession ...

The duty of integrity does not require professional people to be paragons of virtue. In every instance, professional integrity is linked to the manner in which that particular profession professes to serve the public ...'[1]

In *Newell-Austin* Morris J observed that the test for lack of integrity is objective but an individual's state of knowledge of, and intentions relating to, the underlying facts are relevant to determining whether they have acted without integrity.[2] It is submitted that this is plainly correct: a deliberate or reckless breach of rules or standards of professional conduct may demonstrate a lack of integrity, whereas an inadvertent or negligent breach may not.[3]

For case law on the extent to which principle 5 applies to private life see **3.13** and **CHAPTER 19**, and for the question whether an alleged breach amounts to professional misconduct see **3.14** and **19.2**.

1   *SRA v Wingate* [2018] EWCA Civ 366 at [97]–[102].
2   *Newell-Austin v SRA* [2017] EWHC 411 (Admin) at [48]–[50].
3   For examples of lack of integrity see the SRA's guidance, 'Acting with integrity', issued 23 July 2019, updated 25 November 2019 and the SRA's case study, 'Acting without integrity', issued 23 July 2019.

Principle 6 – equality, diversity and inclusion

3.20

The importance that the SRA attaches to equality, diversity and inclusion (EDI) is emphasised by the fact that it is treated as a core principle and not a standard.

Equality and diversity were first made the subject of regulatory requirements by the Solicitors' Anti-Discrimination Rules 2004. These were replaced by rule 6 of the 2007 Code, which simply imposed obligations not to discriminate in a way that would be unlawful, and to have a written policy.

Section 1(1)(f) of LSA 2007 introduced the regulatory objective of 'encouraging an independent, strong, diverse and effective legal profession'.

The language in the 2011 Code wholly changed. Principle 9 of the 2011 Code stated you must 'run your business or carry out your role in the business in a way that encourages equality of opportunity and respect for diversity'. That was supplemented by Chapter 2 of the 2011 Code, which concerned equality and diversity, and the introduction to Chapter 2 of the 2011 Code stated that it 'is about encouraging equality of opportunity and respect for diversity, and preventing unlawful discrimination'.

The emphasis on encouragement has been carried forward into the 2019 Principles and widened in scope: principle 6 states that you must act 'in a way that encourages equality, diversity and inclusion'.

The SRA has published a guidance note[1] on principle 6 which describes EDI in the following manner:

'1.   Equality is about making sure there is a level playing field and people are treated fairly.

2.   Diversity is about encouraging and valuing people with a broad range of different backgrounds, knowledge, skills, and experiences.

3.   Inclusion is about accepting people for who they are and encouraging everyone to participate and contribute.'

The word 'encourage' is probably to be treated as a regulatory obligation to approach issues of equality, diversity and inclusion in a positive frame of mind; to be alive to opportunities and, in a manner falling short of positive discrimination, seek to ensure that issues of EDI remain at the forefront when decisions are made. In short, principle 6 is about having the right attitude of mind.

1   SRA guidance, 'The SRA's approach to equality, diversity and inclusion', notes, issued 17 July 2019, updated 25 November 2019.

3.21

The regulatory emphasis on encouragement goes beyond the statutory requirements in the Equality Act (EqA) 2010 which prohibit direct and indirect discrimination, harassment and victimisation in relation to a protected characteristic (age, disability, gender reassignment, marriage and civil partnership, pregnancy and maternity, race, religion or belief, sex and sexual orientation).[1]

There are also provisions in EqA 2010 which contemplate positive action by employers, such as the duty to make reasonable adjustments for disabled persons,[2] and the ability of service providers to take positive action in recruitment and promotion.[3] However, those provisions do not impose a statutory obligation on businesses to encourage equality, diversity and inclusion.

1   Section 4 of EqA 2010.
2   Section 20 of EqA 2010.
3   Sections 158 and 159 of EqA 2010.

3.22

EqA 2010 imposes a public sector equality duty on public authorities, including the LSB and the SRA, in the exercise of their functions to have regard to the need to eliminate discrimination, harassment, victimisation and any other conduct that is prohibited by EqA 2010, advance equality of opportunity between persons who share a protected characteristic and those who do not, and foster good relations between those who share a protected characteristic and those who do not.

The LSB describes one of its equality objectives under the equality duty as follows:

'Through our regulatory oversight role, encourage and work with the approved regulators to promote equality and diversity, including developing a diverse workforce across the legal sector at all levels by:

●   Assessing regulators' implementation plans to gather and evaluate diversity data.

●   Reviewing and monitoring the progress made by regulators in delivering their implementation plans.

●   Continuing to engage with approved regulators and others on how best to enhance a more diverse workforce across the legal sector.'[1]

That equality duty overlaps with the LSB's regulatory objective under section 1 of LSA 2007 of encouraging an independent, strong, diverse and effective legal profession. In 2017 the LSB published guidance for regulators on encouraging a diverse workforce which stated that regulators were expected to have activities in place to deliver the following four outcomes:

'1)   The regulator continues to build a clear and thorough understanding of the diversity profile of its regulated community (beginning at entry), how this changes over time and where greater diversity in the workforce needs to be encouraged;

2)   The regulator uses data, evidence and intelligence about the diversity of the workforce to inform development of, and evaluate the effectiveness of, its regulatory arrangements, operational processes and other activities;

3)   The regulator collaborates with others to encourage a diverse workforce, including sharing good practice, data collection and other relevant activities;

4)   The regulator accounts to its stakeholders for its understanding, its achievements and plans to encourage a diverse workforce.'[2]

The SRA is under an obligation to meet the LSB's equality and diversity outcomes, and also to comply with its public sector equality duty and the regulatory objective of encouraging a diverse legal profession.

1   LSB, 'Diversity and inclusion', at https://legalservicesboard.org.uk/about-us/diversity-and-inclusion.
2   LSB, 'Guidance for legal services regulators on encouraging a diverse workforce', February 2017.

3.23

In the SRA's Risk Outlook for 2018/19, the SRA said that to improve diversity and inclusion, firms can:

- create a culture where people feel able to talk about diversity and staff feel included and valued;

- offer mentoring schemes, which can improve access to the profession and diversity at management levels;

- use the SRA's law firm diversity tool to benchmark their diversity, and encourage all staff to respond to all questions;

- carry out pay audits to identify any pay gaps between different groups of people;

- consider unconscious biases and help staff overcome these to make objective decisions about recruitment and selection;

- offer flexible working, such as home working, to help the work–life balance of all staff, particularly those with caring responsibilities;

- ask senior managers to lead by example, such as challenging any offensive behaviour in the workplace;

- support different routes to the profession, including apprentices, paralegals and legal executives, so talented people from all backgrounds can access the profession; and

- consider the wellbeing of staff and help staff manage stress levels.[1]

1   SRA Risk Outlook 2018/19, 'Diversity in the profession', issued by the SRA in July 2018.

3.24

In November 2019 the SRA updated its guidance note on EDI.[1] The guidance note states that, while legislation sets minimum legal obligations, a solicitor's regulatory obligations extend beyond strict compliance with the law. Those obligations extend to how solicitors run their firms and provide services, how they interact with people they work with, including employees and how they meet the diverse needs of clients and others. The obligations include:

- compliance with EqA 2010;

- not unfairly discriminating against others;

- providing reasonable adjustments to disabled clients and employees;

- taking positive steps for disabled employees and clients so that they have fair and equitable access to opportunities and can participate in services provided by the firm;

- encouraging diversity at all levels of the workforce;

- collecting, reporting and publishing data about the diversity of the workforce;

- treating people fairly and with dignity and respect; and

- having a complaints procedure in place to make sure complaints relating to discrimination, harassment and victimisation are dealt with.

The guidance note also states that it is good practice for firms to put in place appropriate policies for EDI which are proportionate to the size of the firm. The policies should include information on the firm's approach to recruitment, retention and progression and explain to clients the firm's approach to equality of opportunity and respect for diversity. Firms are encouraged to produce a policy statement which articulates support for EDI, and to monitor and analyse the diversity of staff and clients.

1   SRA guidance, 'The SRA's approach to equality, diversity and inclusion', issued 17 July 2019, updated 25 November 2019.

3.25

The SRA collects data from firms through data questionnaires which all firms are currently required to complete every two years, and the SRA states that it uses the data to 'inform our publications or engagement with people as part of our work to promote diversity in the profession' and to monitor the impact of the changes the SRA makes.[1]

The SRA periodically publishes reports on its EDI work in strategy reviews, risk outlook publications[2] and the diversity sections of its website. The reports summarise the work carried out by the SRA, identify areas of concern and set out the SRA's expectations of practitioners, which change over time as the profession responds to EDI issues and as new data is collected.

1   SRA, 'Reporting your firm data', 2 August 2021.
2   See for example, SRA Risk Outlook, 'Diversity in the profession', 23 November 2020.

3.26

The SRA intends that all regulated individuals and entities should play a role in implementing EDI policies and procedures by embedding appropriate values in the workplace and by challenging inappropriate behaviour and processes. The individual's responsibility for embedding these values will vary depending on the role in the organisation. The managers of the firm, the compliance officer for legal practice (COLP) and the firm have a wider responsibility than junior employees to ensure that appropriate policies and procedures are in place. The guidance note states that senior leaders in particular have a responsibility to encourage EDI and identify and remove barriers in recruitment, promotion and progression.[1]

Although it is plainly intended that principle 6 should supplement rather than merely restate the obligations of solicitors and firms under the general law, the extent to which the SRA expects firms and individuals to go beyond their statutory obligations is unclear.

1   SRA guidance, 'The SRA's approach to equality, diversity and inclusion', issued 17 July 2019, updated 25 November 2019.

3.27

Principle 6 applies to solicitors in their private and professional lives. A solicitor who, for example, carries on a separate business unrelated to legal activities, could face disciplinary proceedings if the separate business does not encourage equality, diversity and inclusion. Similarly, a solicitor who expresses personal views on social

CHAPTER 3
PRINCIPLES AND CODES
OVERVIEW

media platforms which are incompatible with the principles of equality, diversity and inclusion could breach principle 6.[1]

1   See the SRA's warning notice, 'Offensive communications', issued 24 August 2017, updated 25 November 2019.

3.28

The Law Society operates a Diversity and Inclusion Charter, and encourages firms to become signatories to the Charter. The signatories make a commitment to:

> 'Strive to achieve best practice in our recruitment, retention and career progression practices as employers.
>
> Support the development of good diversity practice by collecting and sharing examples of practical activities that contribute to progress with other signatories.
>
> Assign responsibility for meeting our charter commitments to a named, senior level individual.
>
> Work together to develop and adopt future protocols that support the practical implementation of the aims of this charter.
>
> Annually publish the diversity profile of our UK employees and details of our work on equality, diversity and inclusion.
>
> Publish a joint annual report on the basis of a monitoring exercise to measure the impact of this charter and its protocols. These reports will form the basis of regular dialogue with stakeholders, employees and clients.'

The Law Society makes available, free of charge to the firms which commit to the Charter, its Diversity and Inclusion Standards, best practice guidance, facilities for measuring the effectiveness of the firm's diversity and inclusion measures, access to research and reports and protocols on matters such as monitoring diversity and inclusion within the firm and flexible working.[1]

1   For further details visit www.lawsociety.org.uk/campaigns/Diversity-and-inclusion-charter.

Principle 7 – best interests of the client

3.29

The duty to act in the best interests of clients arises out of the solicitor's status as a fiduciary, and is one of the professional principles enshrined in section 1(3) of LSA 2007. It is a core duty which was also included in rule 1(c) of SPR 1990, rule 1.04 of the 2007 Code, and the 2011 Principles. It encompasses obligations such as the duty of confidentiality, the obligation to avoid conflicts of interest and the obligation not to take unfair advantage of a client.

The SRA Code of Conduct for Solicitors, RELs and RFLs

Introduction

4.1

There have been four different sets of conduct rules since the start of 2007.

Until 1 July 2007, solicitors were governed by the Solicitors' Practice Rules 1990 (SPR 1990) as amended from time to time, and wider non-codified provisions which might be described as the common law of conduct. The Law Society periodically issued *The Guide to the Professional Conduct of Solicitors*, free of charge to the profession. The final edition, the eighth, was published in 1999, and so was considerably out of date by July 2007, although attempts had been made to keep it current by postings on the Solicitors Regulation Authority (SRA) website under the style of the 'Guide Online'.

The Solicitors' Code of Conduct 2007 (2007 Code) came into force on 1 July 2007, but both the rules and the associated guidance were regularly amended thereafter.

The SRA Code of Conduct 2011 (2011 Code) came into force on 6 October 2011. The 2011 Code was also regularly amended and, by the time of the 2019 Codes, the 2011 Code had been amended 21 times.

The SRA Standards and Regulations came into force on 25 November 2019, and the 2011 Code was replaced with two codes of conduct: one for individuals (solicitors, registered European lawyers (RELs) and registered foreign lawyers (RFLs)), and one for regulated firms, including their managers, compliance officers and employees.

Aside from the separation into two codes, the main change affecting conduct rules was a change in approach. The drafting was designed to lead to shorter and less prescriptive codes which introduced 'more flexibility to require those to whom the Codes apply to use their own judgment when applying the Code to their practice and conduct'.[1]

There were also some changes to specific rules. New provisions were added to the SRA Code of Conduct for Solicitors, RELs and RFLs 2019 (the 'Code for Individuals') relating to litigation (paragraphs 2.4 and 2.5), continuing competence (paragraph 3.3), supervision (paragraph 3.5), keeping up to date with the law (paragraph 7.1), identification of clients (paragraphs 3.1 and 8.1) and alternative dispute resolution (ADR) in complaints handling (paragraph 8.4).

In addition there were some changes to take account of the two policy changes introduced by the 2019 regulatory arrangements relating to the manner in which solicitors could practise. Solicitors became able to provide unreserved legal services to the public while working in businesses not regulated by the Legal Services Act (LSA) 2007 and using their solicitor title. Individual solicitors working on their own became able to practise in some circumstances without applying for authorisation as a recognised sole practitioner. Those changes primarily affected the rules on authorisation, but they led to some new provisions in the Code for Individuals, such as the provision of information to clients in paragraph 8.10.

As at the date of this edition of *The Solicitor's Handbook* there have been no amendments to the 2019 Codes.

1   'Looking to the future – flexibility and public protection', issued by the SRA in June 2016, Annex 4, p 13.

4.2

The Codes are supplemented by a series of guidance notes, case studies and warning notices which are published on the SRA's website. As at the date of this edition of *The Solicitor's Handbook*, there are over 120 such documents relating to the 2019 regulatory arrangements, and a large number of them relate to the provisions of the Principles and the Codes.

4.3

In this chapter, we examine the Code for Individuals section by section, making practical suggestions as to how solicitors can best achieve compliance with the standards.

Solicitors will continue to be prosecuted for breaches of the 2011 Principles and Code, as some of the alleged misconduct brought before the Solicitors Disciplinary Tribunal (the Tribunal or SDT) occurs over a significant period of time. If a commentary on the 2011 Principles and Code is needed, it can found in *The Solicitor's Handbook 2017*.

4.4

The introduction to the Code for Individuals is as follows:

Introduction

The Code of Conduct describes the standards of professionalism that we, the SRA, and the public expect of individuals (solicitors, registered European lawyers and registered foreign lawyers) authorised by us to provide legal services.

They apply to conduct and behaviour relating to your practice, and comprise a framework for ethical and competent practice which applies irrespective of your role or the environment or organisation in which you work (subject to the Overseas Rules which apply to your practice overseas); although paragraphs 8.1 to 8.11 apply only when you are providing your services to the public or a section of the public.

You must exercise your judgement in applying these standards to the situations you are in and deciding on a course of action, bearing in mind your role and responsibilities, areas of practice, and the nature of your clients (which in an in house context will generally include your employer and may include other persons or groups within or outside your employer organisation).

You are personally accountable for compliance with this Code – and our other regulatory requirements that apply to you – and must always be prepared to justify your decisions and actions.

A serious failure to meet our standards or a serious breach of our regulatory requirements may result in our taking regulatory action against you. A failure or breach may be serious either in isolation or because it comprises a persistent or concerning pattern of behaviour. In addition to the regulatory requirements set by us in our Codes, Principles and our rules and regulations, we directly monitor and enforce the requirements relating to referral fees set out in section 56 of the Legal Aid, Sentencing and Punishment of Offenders Act (LASPO) 2012, and provisions relating to anti money laundering and counter terrorist financing, as set out in regulations made by the Treasury as in force from time to time [Link].

All these requirements are underpinned by our Enforcement Strategy. That strategy explains in more detail our views about the issues we consider to be serious, and our approach to taking regulatory action in the public interest.

4.5

The introduction to the Code for Individuals states that the code applies to 'conduct and behaviour relating to your practice'. That can be contrasted with the 2019 Principles, which are intended to apply to an individual's conduct in private life as well as in practice.

4.6

The Code for Individuals does not apply to solicitors and other regulated individuals who are practising overseas, unless the practice predominantly comprises the provision of legal services to clients within England and Wales, or in relation to assets located in England and Wales.[1] A solicitor who is practising overseas, and whose practice does not fall within that exception, must instead comply with the SRA Overseas and Cross-border Practice Rules 2019 (the 'Overseas Rules' or 'OCB Rules'). The SRA Glossary defines 'practising overseas' in relation to a solicitor to mean 'a practice … of a solicitor established outside England and Wales for the purpose of providing legal services in an overseas jurisdiction', and 'overseas' means outside England and Wales.

1   Rules 1.1(a) and 1.3 of the Overseas Rules.

Maintaining trust and acting fairly

4.7

1.1   You do not unfairly discriminate by allowing your personal views to affect your professional relationships and the way in which you provide your services.

1.2   You do not abuse your position by taking unfair advantage of *clients* or others.

1.3   You perform all *undertakings* given by you, and do so within an agreed timescale or if no timescale has been agreed then within a reasonable amount of time.

> 1.4   You do not mislead or attempt to mislead your *clients*, the *court* or others,
> either by your own acts or omissions or allowing or being complicit in the
> acts or omissions of others (including your *client*).

Discrimination

4.8

It is probably no coincidence that the first standards in the Code for Individuals and the SRA Code of Conduct for Firms 2019 (the 'Code for Firms') relate to discrimination. The SRA is committed to encouraging equality, diversity and inclusion and preventing discrimination.

The SRA intends that everyone should contribute to compliance with those requirements by embedding appropriate values in the workplace and by challenging inappropriate behaviour and processes. The responsibility falls on the individual as well as the firm.

Under the Equality Act (EqA) 2010, the protected characteristics are age, disability, gender reassignment, marriage and civil partnership, pregnancy and maternity, race, religion or belief, and sex or sexual orientation.[1]

Direct discrimination is defined in EqA 2010 as follows: 'A person (A) discriminates against another (B) if, because of a protected characteristic, A treats B less favourably than A treats or would treat others'. There are detailed statutory provisions in EqA 2010 which qualify or extend the statutory definition in differing ways for differing protected characteristics. For example, in relation to age, direct discrimination can be justified if it is a proportionate means of achieving a legitimate aim. Direct discrimination also covers a situation where someone is treated less favourably than another person because they are thought to have a protected characteristic or because they associate with someone who has a protected characteristic.[2]

Paragraph 1.1 goes hand in hand with principle 6 (you must act in a way that encourages equality, diversity and inclusion). See the commentary on principle 6 at **3.20–3.28**.

Paragraph 1.1 also prohibits indirect discrimination. For indirect discrimination see the commentary on paragraph 1.1 of the Code for Firms at **5.12**.

The use of the phrase 'unfairly discriminate' rather than 'unlawfully discriminate' in paragraph 1.1 could extend the standard to behaviour beyond the discrimination prohibited by EqA 2010.

1   Section 4 of EqA 2010.
2   See sections 13 to 18 of EqA 2010.

4.9

On 25 November 2019 the SRA published a warning notice on offensive communications after receiving a number of complaints relating to inappropriate communications in emails and on social media. The notice includes warnings that solicitors should not make derogatory, discriminatory or inappropriate comments about others by email or online, that solicitors should not endorse derogatory or discriminatory comments made by clients or others, or pass them on if it is unnecessary to do so, and that the conduct cannot be justified on the basis that a communication was intended to be humorous or was not intended to cause offence or was only sent to a colleague within the firm.[1]

1   SRA warning notice, 'Offensive communications', 24 August 2017, updated 25 November 2019.

Taking unfair advantage

4.10

Paragraph 1.2 reflects a long-standing rule of professional conduct that solicitors must not take unfair advantage of anyone.

The introduction to the Code for Individuals states that the standards apply to conduct and behaviour relating to the solicitor's practice. However, if a solicitor uses his or her status as a solicitor to gain an unfair advantage when acting in a personal capacity, there will be a breach of principle 2 (upholding public trust and confidence in the profession) and possibly also principle 5 (integrity) of the SRA Principles 2019.

Paragraph 1.2 could be breached if, for example, a solicitor communicates with a third party after becoming aware that the third party has instructed another solicitor; or takes advantage of an opposing party's lack of legal knowledge where they have not instructed a lawyer; or knowingly makes a demand in litigation for a remedy which is not legally recoverable, such as a demand for a debtor to pay the cost of a letter of claim when it cannot be said at that stage that the cost is legally recoverable.[1]

1   For an SRA report on circumstances in which litigation tactics could amount to a breach of paragraph 1.2 see SRA, 'Balancing duties in litigation', 27 November 2018.

4.11

The SRA has published a warning notice on non-disclosure agreements (NDAs) which states that it is improper to use an NDA to prevent a person from reporting an offence or misconduct to a law enforcement agency or regulatory authority, and warns solicitors against taking unfair advantage of an opposing party. The warning notice states that the obligation not to take unfair advantage is heightened if the opposing party is vulnerable or unrepresented. Examples of unfair advantage include imposing oppressive time limits on a vulnerable person to agree an NDA, preventing someone who has entered into an NDA from keeping a copy of the agreement and proposing a clause known to be unenforceable when dealing with an opposing party with limited access to legal advice.[1]

1   SRA warning notice, 'Use of non disclosure agreements (NDAs)', 12 March 2018, updated 12 November 2020. Particular care needs to be taken in sexual harassment cases where the victim is likely to be vulnerable. For a Court of Appeal decision enforcing an NDA see *ABC v Telegraph Media Group Limited* [2018] EWCA Civ 2329. See also **4.116**.

4.12

In *SRA v Andersons*[1] the High Court held that the comparable rule in the 2007 Code (which was rule 10 of the 2007 Code) would only be breached if a solicitor intended to take an unfair advantage. There was no breach if the unfair advantage was an unintended consequence. Lord Justice Treacy said:

'It seems to me that the wording of Rule 10 prohibiting the use of a solicitor's position to take advantage of another must involve an element of consciously taking unfair advantage. This gives a natural meaning to the words used. It is not in my judgment sufficient … for the solicitor to have taken deliberate action which in fact had the consequence of taking unfair advantage of the client. To look at the end result is not, in my judgment, enough. The phrase "you must not use your position to take unfair advantage" clearly imports a degree of purpose underlying the use of position … I am satisfied that Rule 10 properly construed requires a subjective element in the way I have indicated.'

1   [2013] EWHC 4021 (Admin) at [67] and [68]. Rule 10.01 of the 2007 Code was headed 'Not taking unfair advantage' and stated: 'You must not use your position to take unfair advantage of anyone either for your own benefit or for another person's benefit.'

Undertakings

4.13

Paragraph 1.3 is concerned with undertakings. An undertaking is defined in the SRA Glossary to mean:

'a statement, given orally or in writing, whether or not it includes the word "undertake" or "undertaking", to someone who reasonably places reliance on it, that you or a third party will do something or cause something to be done, or refrain from doing something.'

4.14

Not every undertaking given by a solicitor is a 'solicitor's undertaking', breach of which may be professional misconduct. In *Harcus Sinclair Ltd LLP v Your Lawyers Ltd*[1] two firms had agreed not to compete against each other when acting for groups of claimants in a piece of group litigation. The agreement contained the following clause:

'The Recipient further undertakes not to accept instructions for or to act on behalf of any other group of Claimants in the contemplated Group Action without the express permission of the Discloser.'

At [103] the Supreme Court observed that:

'The mere fact that the undertaking is given by a solicitor does not make it a solicitor's undertaking. The generally accepted test is that the undertaking must be given by the solicitor in his or her "capacity as a solicitor" – see, for example, *United Mining and Finance Corpn Ltd v Becher* at p 306 per Hamilton J; *Geoffrey Silver & Drake v Baines* at 402G per Lord Denning MR; the *Fox* case at 928 per Nicholls LJ; *United Bank of Kuwait v Hammoud* [1988] 1 WLR 1051 at 1063 per Staughton LJ. It is the fact that the undertaking is given professionally that engages the court's supervisory jurisdiction. The court is concerned with undertakings given by solicitors in their professional capacity rather than in some other capacity, such as their private capacity – see *Geoffrey Silver & Drake v Baines* at 403G per Widgery LJ.'

The Supreme Court provided further guidance at [112]:

> 'As further guidance, we consider that in many cases it will be helpful to consider the following two questions when determining whether an undertaking is given by solicitors in their "capacity as solicitors". The first concerns the subject matter of the undertaking and whether what the undertaking requires the solicitor to do (or not to do) is something which solicitors regularly carry out (or refrain from doing) as part of their ordinary professional practice. The second concerns the reason for the giving of the undertaking and the extent to which the cause or matter to which it relates involves the sort of work which solicitors regularly carry out as part of their ordinary professional practice. If both questions are answered affirmatively then the undertaking is likely to be a solicitor's undertaking.'

Adopting this test, the court ruled that the undertaking contained in the agreement was not a solicitor's undertaking, holding at [119] that 'in giving the undertaking Harcus Sinclair was acting in a business capacity rather than a professional capacity'.

1   [2021] UKSC 32.

Misleading others

4.15

If a solicitor deliberately misleads others (whether clients, third parties, or the court), or attempts to do so, he is at risk of being struck off for dishonesty. For commentary on paragraph 1.4 in relation to the courts see **4.22**.

Dispute resolution and proceedings before courts, tribunals and inquiries

4.16

2.1	You do not misuse or tamper with evidence or attempt to do so.
2.2	You do not seek to influence the substance of evidence, including generating false evidence or persuading witnesses to change their evidence.
2.3	You do not provide or offer to provide any benefit to witnesses dependent upon the nature of their evidence or the outcome of the case.
2.4	You only make assertions or put forward statements, representations or submissions to the *court* or others which are properly arguable.
2.5	You do not place yourself in contempt of *court*, and you comply with *court* orders which place obligations on you.
2.6	You do not waste the *court's* time.
2.7	You draw the *court's* attention to relevant cases and statutory provisions, or procedural irregularities of which you are aware, and which are likely to have a material effect on the outcome of the proceedings.

Section 2

4.17

There is nothing unusual in the requirements of section 2 and any practitioner familiar with the proper standards of behaviour of litigators and advocates need have no concern that section 2 presents any traps or creates obligations that have not hitherto been owed. Section 2 is supplemented by paragraph 1.4 (you do not mislead or attempt to mislead your clients, the court or others), which is contained in section 1 of the Code as its scope is not limited to the courts.

Paragraph 1.4 and section 2 are not an exhaustive list of the professional obligations relating to the court. Every solicitor is an officer of the court, and owes duties to the court under case law, statute and procedural rules. The professional obligation to comply with the duties owed to the court falls within the general obligation under paragraph 7.1 of the Code for Individuals to follow the law governing the way solicitors work. If a solicitor breaches any of the duties owed to a senior court it is open to the court either to admonish the solicitor under the court's inherent jurisdiction or to refer the matter to the SRA as professional misconduct.[1] Inferior courts are restricted to referring the matter to the SRA. In practice the matter would normally be referred to the SRA, as the inherent jurisdiction is rarely invoked.[2]

1   *Sathivel v Secretary of State for the Home Department* [2018] EWHC 913 (Admin) at [2].
2   See **Chapter 24**.

Balancing duties to the court and the client

4.18

LSA 2007 imposes statutory duties on litigators. Section 1(3) of LSA 2007 states that one of the five professional principles is that persons who exercise before any court a right of audience, or conduct litigation in relation to proceedings in any court, by virtue of being authorised persons should comply with their duty to the court to act with independence in the interests of justice. Sections 176(1) and 188(3) of LSA 2007 impose a duty on regulated persons to comply with their conduct rules relating to the exercise of a right of audience and the conduct of litigation. Any conflict between those statutory duties and other professional duties (such as the duty to act in the best interests of the client) is governed by section 188(3) of LSA 2007, which provides that the duties to act with independence in the interests of justice, and to comply with the relevant conduct rules, override any obligations which the person who is conducting the litigation or exercising a right of audience may have (otherwise than under the criminal law) if they are inconsistent with them.

4.19

A solicitor's role in the administration of justice means that duties to the client can be overridden by duties to the court. In the House of Lords in *Arthur JS Hall v Simons*[1] Lord Hoffmann said:

> 'Lawyers conducting litigation owe a divided loyalty. They have a duty to their clients, but they may not win by whatever means. They also owe a duty to the court and the administration of justice. They may not mislead the court or allow the judge to take what they know to be a bad point in

their favour. They must cite all relevant law, whether for or against their case. They may not make imputations of dishonesty unless they have been given the information to support them. They should not waste time on irrelevancies even if the client thinks that they are important. Sometimes the performance of these duties to the court may annoy the client. So, it was said, the possibility of a claim for negligence might inhibit the lawyer from acting in accordance with his overriding duty to the court. That would be prejudicial to the administration of justice.'

1   [2000] UKHL 38. For an example of a case where the duty to the court overrides the duty to the client even if the solicitor is not on the record see *Ip v SRA* [2018] EWHC 957 (Admin) at [118] (a case involving an immigration solicitor drafting grounds for a lay applicant to lodge personally for an unmeritorious application for judicial review).

4.20

The SRA has issued a number of publications over the past eight years on the need to strike the correct balance between duties owed to the court and the obligation to act in the client's best interests. For example, in March 2015 the SRA published a risk resource paper[1] which highlighted instances in which litigators unduly prioritise clients' interests by using the threat of litigation in unmeritorious cases to obtain settlement, mislead the court by knowingly or recklessly permitting false information to be given to the court and use the litigation process for purposes that are not directly connected to resolving a specific dispute. Cases in that third category include immigration cases in which last-minute applications are made for injunctions as a strategy to defeat removal proceedings.[2] On 6 September 2017 the SRA issued a warning notice on holiday sickness claims warning practitioners that clients' instructions on holiday sickness claims should be examined by retrieving and analysing the evidence, that cases should not be commenced or continued if there is a serious concern about the reliability of the evidence and that 'turning a blind eye' to unhelpful issues in a case could be treated as dishonesty.[3] On 27 November 2018 the SRA published a report on balancing duties in litigation which included warnings on taking unfair advantage of an unrepresented opponent by exploiting their lack of legal knowledge, 'excessive' litigation in which solicitors advance arguments which they do not consider to be properly arguable, and disregarding obligations to the court by attempting to persuade experts to alter reports to the benefit of the client.[4]

For improper use of litigation see also **22.32**.

1   'Walking the line: the balancing of duties in litigation', issued by the SRA in March 2015.
2   See *R (Hamid) v Secretary of State for the Home Department* [2012] EWHC 3070 (Admin) and *Sathivel v Secretary of State for the Home Department* [2018] EWHC 913 (Admin). See also *Ip v SRA* [2018] EWHC 957 (Admin) in which the High Court affirmed a Tribunal decision to strike off a solicitor for making judicial review applications in asylum cases which were totally without merit.
3   SRA warning notice, 'Holiday sickness claims', 6 September 2017, updated 25 November 2019.
4   SRA, 'Balancing duties in litigation', 27 November 2018.

4.21

The obligation in paragraph 2.4, that you only put forward statements, representations or submissions to the court which are properly arguable, is comparable to the former rule 11.01(3)(a) of the 2007 Code, which provided that a solicitor could not draft documents containing any allegation that he or she did not consider properly arguable.[1] Rule 11 was considered by the Court of Appeal in *Richard Buxton (Solicitors) v Mills-Owens*[2] in which it was held that solicitors could lawfully terminate their retainer when required by a client to advance an argument which they considered to be untenable.

1   Rule 11 of the 2007 Code replaced the Law Society's Code for Advocacy and the principles that were previously contained in Chapter 21 of *The Guide to the Professional Conduct of Solicitors* (8th edn), and imposed on all solicitors who conduct litigation some of the obligations that had previously been imposed only on advocates – including the provision in rule 11.01(3)(a) that a solicitor could not draft documents containing any allegation that he or she did not consider properly arguable. Rule 11 of the 2007 Code was replaced by indicative behaviour 5.7 of the 2011 Code, and indicative behaviour 5.7 of the 2011 Code was in turn replaced by paragraph 2.4 of the 2019 Code for Individuals.
2   [2008] EWHC 1831 (QB).

Misleading the court

4.22

Paragraph 1.4 of the Code for Individuals states: 'You do not mislead or attempt to mislead your clients, the court or others, either by your own acts or omissions or allowing or being complicit in the acts or omissions of others (including your client)'.

In *Brett v SRA*[1] Lord Thomas CJ said:

'... misleading the court is regarded by the court and must be regarded by any disciplinary tribunal as one of the most serious offences that an advocate or litigator can commit. It is not simply a breach of a rule of a game, but a fundamental affront to a rule designed to safeguard the fairness and justice of proceedings. Such conduct will normally attract an exemplary and deterrent sentence. That is in part because our system for the administration of justice relies so heavily upon the integrity of the profession and the full discharge of the profession's duties and in part because the privilege of conducting litigation or appearing in court is granted on terms that the rules are observed not merely in their letter but in their spirit. Indeed, the reputation of the system of the administration of justice in England and Wales and the standing of the profession depends particularly upon the discharge of the duties owed to the court.'

For misleading the court, see also **22.31**.

1   [2014] EWHC 2974 (Admin) at [111]. See also the comment of Carr J in *Shaw v SRA* [2017] EWHC 2076 (Admin) at [107] that misleading the court is 'a matter of the utmost gravity'.

4.23

In the context of criminal proceedings, the scope of an advocate's duty not to mislead the court was considered by the House of Lords in *Ali v Sydney Mitchell & Co*. Lord Diplock set out the law as follows:

'A barrister must not wilfully mislead the court as to the law nor may he actively mislead the court as to the facts; although, consistently with the rule that the prosecution must prove its case, he may passively stand by and watch the court being misled by reason of its failure to ascertain facts that are within the barrister's knowledge.'[1]

The permission to 'passively stand by' is preserved by the Bar Standards Board (BSB) Handbook. The duty not to mislead the court is expressed as follows:

'R C3.1 you must not knowingly or recklessly mislead or attempt to mislead the *court*;'

and the following guidance is provided on that duty:

'gC4: As to your duty not to mislead the court:

1. knowingly misleading the *court* includes being complicit in another person misleading the court;

2. knowingly misleading the *court* also includes inadvertently misleading the court if you later realise that you have misled the *court*, and you fail to correct the position;

3. recklessly means being indifferent to the truth, or not caring whether something is true or false; and

4. the duty continues to apply for the duration of the case.

gC12: For example, if your *client* tells you that they have previous *convictions* of which the prosecution is not aware, you may not disclose this without their consent. However, in a case where mandatory sentences apply, the non-disclosure of the previous *convictions* will result in the *court* failing to pass the sentence that is required by law. In that situation, you must advise your *client* that if consent is refused to your revealing the information you will have to cease to act. In situations where mandatory sentences do not apply, and your *client* does not agree to disclose the previous *convictions*, you can continue to represent your *client* but in doing so must not say anything that misleads the court. This will constrain what you can say in mitigation.'[2]

The paragraph 1.4 rule that a solicitor must not mislead the court by '*allowing or being complicit* in the acts or omissions of others' is wider than the BSB Handbook guidance that the advocate must not be *complicit* in another person misleading the court. The word 'allowing' suggests there may be a duty to correct prosecution errors relating to previous convictions.

The use of the word 'allow' was considered during the consultation period for the drafting of the 2011 Code. The first draft of the comparable rule stated: 'You do not knowingly allow another person to deceive or mislead … the court'. The draftsman changed the rule so that the rule (outcome 5.2) stated: 'you are not complicit in another person deceiving or misleading the court'.

The retention of the word 'complicit' in paragraph 1.4 is indicative of a lack of intention to change the legal position, but the use of the word 'allowing' leaves room for doubt, and raises the question whether the draftsman of the 2019 Codes has inadvertently created a standard which is inconsistent with the duty set out by the House of Lords.

1   *Saif Ali v Sydney Mitchell & Co* [1980] AC 198, HL per Lord Diplock at 220.
2   BSB Handbook, version 4.6, guidance gC4 and gC12.

Solicitor advocates

4.24

For solicitors who appear as advocates, it is worth repeating some of the contents of rule 11 of the 2007 Code, which were included in earlier editions of *The Solicitor's Handbook* but which have not found their way into the Code for Individuals, as there can be no doubt that they still hold good. Rule 11.05 provided that:

'If you are appearing as an advocate:

(a)   you must not say anything which is merely scandalous or intended only to insult a witness or any other person;

(b)   you must avoid naming in open court any third party whose character would thereby be called into question, unless it is necessary for the proper conduct of the case;

(c)   you must not call into question the character of a witness you have cross-examined unless the witness has had the opportunity to answer the allegations during cross-examination; and

(d)   you must not suggest that any person is guilty of a crime, fraud or misconduct unless such allegations:

   (i)   go to a matter in issue which is material to your client's case; and

   (ii)   appear to you to be supported by reasonable grounds.'

Rule 11.08 provided that:

'If you are acting in the defence or prosecution of an accused and you have in your possession a copy of an audio or video recording of a child witness which has been identified as having been prepared to be admitted in evidence at a criminal trial in accordance with the relevant provisions of the Criminal Justice Act 1991 or the Youth Justice and Criminal Evidence Act 1999, you must:

(a)   not make or permit any person to make a copy of the recording;

(b)   not release the recording to the accused;

(c)   not make or permit any disclosure of the recording or its contents to any person except when, in your opinion, it is necessary in the course of preparing the prosecution, defence or appeal against conviction and/or sentence;

(d)   ensure that the recording is always kept in a locked, secure container when not in use; and

(e)   return the recording when you are no longer instructed in the matter.'

The solicitor as potential witness

4.25

The rule relating to cases in which solicitors are potential witnesses has not been included in the Code for Individuals. The principle has caused difficulties in the past because it has not always seemed to be wholly logical. It was first expressed as guidance in successive editions of *The Guide to the Professional Conduct of Solicitors*, and appeared in the 1999 edition as principle 21.12. There the principle was:

'A solicitor must not accept instructions to act as advocate for a client if it is clear that he or she or a member of the firm will be called as a witness on behalf of the client, unless the evidence is purely formal.'

It will be noted that the focus is not only on advocacy, but on the sequence of events. The question was whether a solicitor could 'accept instructions to act' – in other words the mischief at which the principle is aimed is a situation in which it is *already* clear that the solicitor is or is likely to be a material witness. One can well see that if the solicitor had, for example, been a witness to a road accident and one of the drivers or passengers subsequently instructed that solicitor's firm, professional issues would be likely to arise.

The 2007 Code went further than the earlier principle 21.12. The guidance notes to rule 11.06 of the 2007 Code provided that it would be 'extremely rare' for it to be proper for a solicitor to act in litigation where that solicitor is also a witness.

That rule had far less logical application as it extended to situations in which the solicitor acts for the client perfectly properly, and then something arises as a result of the solicitor/client relationship which makes it appropriate or necessary for the solicitor to give supportive evidence. It is commonplace for solicitors to give evidence for their clients about matters arising in the course of the retainer, for example, on procedural matters and as to dealings with opposing solicitors in civil proceedings, and in criminal proceedings where, for instance, evidence may be needed to explain that the defendant exercised his right of silence on advice. The proposition that, in this situation, the solicitor would be obliged to cease to act would make little sense.

The rule 11.06 provisions were dropped from the 2011 Code. Indicative behaviour 5.6 of the 2011 Code provided that a solicitor should not appear as an advocate, or act in litigation, if it is clear that the solicitor, or anyone in the firm, will be called as a witness in the matter unless the solicitor is satisfied that it would not prejudice his independence as an advocate, or litigator, or the interests of clients or the interests of justice. That indicative behaviour moved away from rule 11.06 towards the former principle 21.12, by shifting the focus from the giving of evidence, per se, to whether giving evidence would offend any of the Principles requiring independence, the interests of the client and the interests of justice to be considered. No such concerns tend to arise in the everyday situations in which most solicitors find themselves giving evidence.

In our view the primary historical concern which lay behind the previous rules was the situation in which a solicitor who is a material witness to matters unrelated to the solicitor/client relationship is subsequently asked to act in the case.

Service and competence

4.26

3.1   You only act for *clients* on instructions from the *client*, or from someone properly authorised to provide instructions on their behalf. If you have reason to suspect that the instructions do not represent your *client's* wishes, you do not act unless you have satisfied yourself that they do. However, in circumstances where you have legal authority to act notwithstanding that it is not possible to obtain or ascertain the instructions of your *client*, then you are subject to the overriding obligation to protect your *client's* best interests.

3.2 You ensure that the service you provide to *clients* is competent and delivered in a timely manner.

3.3 You maintain your competence to carry out your role and keep your professional knowledge and skills up to date.

3.4 You consider and take account of your *client's* attributes, needs and circumstances.

3.5 Where you supervise or manage others providing legal services:

(a) you remain accountable for the work carried out through them; and

(b) you effectively supervise work being done for *clients*.

3.6 You ensure that the individuals you manage are competent to carry out their role, and keep their professional knowledge and skills, as well as understanding of their legal, ethical and regulatory obligations, up to date.

Paragraph 3.1: Client instructions

4.27

The SRA has stated that the paragraph 3.1 requirement relating to proper authorisation has been included in the Code for Individuals because of the increase in theft, fraud and cybercrime.[1]

---

1 'Looking to the future – flexibility and public protection', issued by the SRA in June 2016. See also 'Application for the approval of regulatory arrangements', issued by the SRA in August 2018, para 88.

4.28

When a solicitor is acting on the basis that instructions are to be provided directly by a client, the solicitor needs to ensure that the instructions are in fact being provided by the client, and not by a fraudster. That involves standard identification checks under the firm's anti-money laundering (AML) procedures, but solicitors also need to be aware of the particular risks in their area of work. In conveyancing, for example, there have been cases in which properties have been sold on the basis of instructions from fraudsters masquerading as the owner. A significant risk is email modification fraud, where a fraudster breaks into a client's email account and intercepts and falsifies emails between the client and the firm on conveyancing matters, in order to divert completion monies to the fraudster's bank account. Most of these frauds take place on Fridays just before a property completion, and a property lawyer receiving an email of that type shortly before completion would have good reason to suspect that the instructions do not represent the client's wishes, and that the completion monies should not be sent to the bank account without speaking to the client. The growing prevalence of cybercrime means that it is advisable for every solicitor to read the SRA's Risk Outlook, which is published on an annual basis and highlights risks of all types identified by the SRA, including cybercrime. Given the fast changing nature of cybercrime, it is also advisable to periodically check the SRA website for any additional warnings. For cybercrime, see also **5.43**.

4.29

Where instructions are provided by a third party, paragraph 3.1 imposes an obligation on the solicitor to ensure that the third party is properly authorised to provide the instructions. The Code for Individuals does not specify what steps should be taken, and that is a matter for the solicitor to decide in the circumstances of the case. For example, in the case of a manager below board level providing instructions on behalf of a corporate client, it may require written confirmation from the directors at board level that the manager has authority to provide the instructions. In the case of a relative providing instructions on behalf of an individual, it may require a direct discussion with the individual and written confirmation of the authorisation. In the case of joint clients, where the instructions are provided by one of the joint clients, it may again require written confirmation of the authorisation from the other joint client(s). The obligation continues throughout the retainer. If there is reason at any time to suspect that instructions do not represent the client's wishes, the solicitor must satisfy himself or herself that they do, and that is likely to involve the need to take instructions directly from the client.

4.30

When deciding whether to take instructions from a third party, the solicitor needs to consider whether the client is vulnerable, whether the client is giving informed consent, whether it is in the best interests of the client to take instructions from the third party and whether there are any conflicts of interest between the third party and the client. It may also be necessary to warn the client that the third party will be sharing confidential information, which carries with it an inherent risk of subsequent misuse of the confidential information. In litigation matters, the solicitor also needs to consider whether certain steps require the direct authorisation of the client such as certification of a statement of truth in a pleading and confirmation that proper disclosure of documents has been made.

4.31

The obligation to act in the best interests of the client means that the solicitor should consider whether significant steps require direct authorisation from the client despite a general authorisation relating to third party instructions (such as decisions in litigation to issue proceedings or settle claims), whether the client should be kept directly informed of events and whether the authorisation instructions need to be reviewed directly with the client during the course of the retainer.

4.32

If a solicitor acts without proper authority there is a risk of civil claims, such as negligence, by the underlying client, as well as disciplinary action. In court proceedings, the proceedings could be an abuse of process. There could be a risk of a wasted costs order and possibly also in extreme cases a finding of contempt of court.

4.33

In March 2016 the SRA published a warning notice on personal injury claims, which stated that the role of referral organisations in the sector meant that solicitors should be particularly cautious in ensuring that they are acting on valid instructions. It also warned that they are likely to have to take instructions from, or check them directly with, the client throughout the course of the case, particularly in relation to significant decisions such as whether to settle and, if so, for how much.[1]

CHAPTER 4
SRA CODE OF CONDUCT FOR
SOLICITORS, RELS AND RFLS

1   SRA warning notice, 'Risk factors in personal injury claims', issued 21 March 2016, updated
    December 2017 and 25 November 2019.

4.34

By paragraph 3.1, in circumstances where a solicitor has legal authority to act
notwithstanding that it is not possible to obtain or ascertain the instructions of the
client, the solicitor is subject to an overriding obligation to protect the client's best
interests. The solicitor therefore needs to be satisfied that it is in the best interests of
the client to agree to act on that basis. That could involve ensuring that the client
has been warned of the risks of permitting steps to be taken without specific instructions, so that authorisation is provided on the basis of informed consent. It could also
involve ensuring that there is no conflict between the client and any third party
providing instructions on the client's behalf.

Paragraph 3.2: The service provided to clients

4.35

Solicitors are generally free to decide whether or not to accept instructions, but
must refuse to act or cease to act when acting for the client would involve a breach of
the law or professional rules, or when the solicitor has insufficient resources or
competence.[1]

1   A decision not to act should not offend the Principle 6 obligations of equality, diversity and inclu-
    sion; see **3.20–3.28**.

4.36

The Code for Individuals does not contain detailed rules on the level of service to be
provided to clients. That is consistent with the SRA's overall approach in the 2019
Standards and Regulations of allowing flexibility for individuals and firms to decide
how best to comply with the rules of professional practice.[1]

1   See 'Application for approval of regulatory arrangements', issued by the SRA in August 2018, para
    26.

4.37

The SRA has stated that a high proportion of complaints regarding the standard of
service currently relate to client care, including delays and poor communication.[1]
Identified shortcomings in previous years relate to a failure to give clear, concise and
accessible information throughout the work about the cost (which should be
updated when the cost is likely to change), the legal work required, the progress of
the work, and complaints processes.[2]

The SRA has also stated that it receives more reports of poor service relating to
personal injury firms than other types of firm, and that is often because of training
and supervision issues.[3] It has published a warning notice on personal injury claims
referring to the need properly to train and supervise staff, and has also published a
guidance note on mis-sold PPI claims which refers to the need to ensure that the
staff dealing with the claims receive proper training and supervision. A common
theme in both notices is staff training and supervision in firms dealing with volume
claims.[4]

1   SRA Risk Outlook 2020/21, 'Standards of service'.
2   SRA Risk Outlook 2018/19, 'Standards of service'.
3   SRA Risk Outlook 2020/21, 'Standards of service'.
4   SRA warning notice, 'Risk factors in personal injury claims', 21 March 2016, updated 25 November 2019; SRA guidance, 'Dealing with claims for mis-sold payment protection insurance', 4 January 2012, updated 25 November 2019.

4.38

In general, matters of poor service are investigated or considered by the Legal Ombudsman (LeO) or the courts, rather than the SRA. Mere negligence is not professional misconduct. In *Preiss v GDC*, the Privy Council said that gross negligence can amount to professional misconduct but, for the opprobrium which attaches to a disciplinary offence, something more is required than the degree of negligence which gives rise to civil liability.[1] In *Re a Solicitor* (1972) Lord Denning said that negligence can amount to professional misconduct if it is inexcusable and such as to be regarded as deplorable by the profession.[2]

In February 2019 the SRA published a guidance note on competence and standard of service which confirmed that mere negligence will not be regarded as a disciplinary matter, but stated that the SRA would 'investigate competence or service issues where these are particularly grave or suggest multiple failures or repeat or persistent poor conduct'. Aggravating features include circumstances in which a firm or an individual knowingly or recklessly acts outside their competence or fails to take reasonable steps to update their knowledge and skills or fails to properly supervise work.[3]

1   *Preiss v GDC* [2001] UKPC 36 at [28].
2   *Re a Solicitor* [1972] 1 WLR 869, CA; see also **19.16–19.19**.
3   SRA topic guide, 'Competence and standard of service', 7 February 2019, updated 25 November 2019.

4.39

The question of whether solicitors can cease to act when it transpires they have insufficient resources or lack the competence to deal with a matter was considered by the Court of Appeal in *R v Ulcay*.[1] In a criminal trial the judge had refused an adjournment for the amount of time requested by defence counsel and solicitors who had been instructed in place of the original defence team at the end of the prosecution case. The new solicitors had withdrawn on the basis that the time allowed did not enable them to prepare their client's case to the necessary standard. It was held that they were wrong to do so and that the rule did not allow a solicitor to refuse to act or to cease to act where an order of the court creates difficulties and makes it harder for him to discharge his professional duties. Those difficulties arose because of the judge's ruling, and not as a result of the absence of appropriate resources or competence.

1   [2007] EWCA Crim 2379.

4.40

The common law position that solicitors must not cease acting for a client except for good cause and on reasonable notice was considered in *Richard Buxton (Solicitors) v Mills-Owens*[1] in a situation in which the client was persisting in a course that his solicitors and counsel considered unwise. He insisted on points being advanced and argued on his behalf that his lawyers considered to be wholly unarguable. They considered their position to be untenable, obtained supportive advice to this effect from the Law Society and ceased to act on reasonable notice. It was held at first instance that they were not entitled to do so (at [21]):

> 'if a client who is prepared to pay for a case to be advanced, and who wants the claim advanced on a particular basis, which does not involve impropriety on the part of the solicitor or counsel, then it is no answer for the solicitor to say that he believes it is bound to fail therefore he will not do it.'

In consequence, a claim for costs by the solicitor for the work done up to the date the retainer was terminated was disallowed on the basis that he was required to complete the retainer: to carry on the action to the end. This was (fortunately) reversed by the Court of Appeal[2] which held that the solicitors had good reason to terminate the retainer, and were entitled to be paid their costs to date. The Law Society intervened in the appeal in support of the firm. The court noted (at [32]) that rule 11.01(3) of the 2007 Code provided:[3]

> 'you must not construct facts supporting your client's case or draft any documents relating to any proceedings containing … any contention which you do not consider to be properly arguable.'

Dyson LJ (with whom Sir Mark Potter P and Maurice Kay LJ agreed) stated (at [41]):

> 'There is no comprehensive definition of what amounts to a good reason to terminate in the Solicitors' Practice Rules or the Code of Conduct (although examples are given in both documents), or in any of the authorities that have been cited to us. That is not surprising, since whether there is a good reason to terminate is a fact-sensitive question. I accept the submission of Mr Drabble [for the Law Society] that it is wrong to restrict the circumstances in which a solicitor can lawfully terminate his retainer to those in which he is instructed to do something improper.'

And at [43]:

> 'I am in no doubt that even before the point was spelt out in the 2007 Code, it would have been understood by all solicitors that, as officers of the court, they were under a professional duty (i) not to include in the court documents that they drafted any contention which they did not consider to be properly arguable and (ii) not to instruct counsel to advance contentions which they did not consider to be properly arguable. That duty was reinforced by CPR 1.3.'

1   [2008] EWHC 1831 (QB).
2   [2010] EWCA Civ 122.
3   See also indicative behaviour 5.7 of the 2011 Code.

Paragraph 3.3: Keeping knowledge and skills up to date

4.41

On 1 November 2016 the SRA replaced the continuing professional development (CPD) programme with continuing competence. Under continuing competence, every solicitor with a practising certificate should reflect on their practice to identify learning needs, plan how to address those needs, complete the planned activities, record the process and make an annual declaration when applying for renewal of their practising certificate that they have reflected on their practice and addressed any identified learning and development needs. The SRA's guidance note on competence and standards of service states that a failure to consider or address training needs will be treated as an aggravating feature in professional issues relating to standard of service.[1]

1   SRA topic guide, 'Competence and standard of service', 7 February 2019, updated 25 November 2019.

Paragraph 3.4: The client's attributes, needs and circumstances

4.42

The SRA places particular emphasis on the requirement to recognise the needs of vulnerable clients. The SRA Enforcement Strategy categorises vulnerable clients to include those facing barriers preventing access to legal services for cost or geographical reasons, those involved in sensitive family matters, those facing loss of personal liberty or deportation and those with health or learning disabilities. Vulnerability could be short term or permanent, and does not only result from the client's personal circumstances. It could result from the structure of the market or the nature of legal services and could mean that corporate clients are vulnerable in some circumstances. The Enforcement Strategy states that the SRA will consider a breach of the standards to be particularly serious where the client's vulnerability is relevant to the culpable behaviour.[1]

1   SRA Enforcement Strategy, issued 7 February 2019, updated 25 November 2019. In *Ip v SRA* [2018] EWHC 957 (Admin) at [181] the court stated that 'it should not be forgotten that [spurious and hopeless applications for judicial review in asylum cases] … cost the applicants, both financially and in engendering prolonged and unjustified expectations'.

Paragraphs 3.5 and 3.6: Supervision and management

4.43

Paragraphs 3.5 and 3.6 place responsibilities for supervision and training relating to matters that affect client work on all solicitors who supervise or manage others, regardless of their seniority within the firm. The responsibility does not simply fall on the managers or partners in a firm.

The standards apply to solicitors working in firms which are not regulated, as well as solicitors working in firms regulated by the SRA. In guidance for solicitors working in firms which are not regulated, the SRA has stated 'you will remain responsible for the work of those you supervise as far as we are concerned … the Legal Ombudsman may also accept a complaint where it is clear that this has been supervised by a solicitor'.[1]

1   SRA, 'Giving information to clients of businesses that are not authorised by a legal services regulator', issued in August 2018. See also 'SRA Standards and Regulations guidance for the not for profit sector', 23 July 2019, para 7.6.2. and SRA guidance, 'Unregulated organisations for employers of SRA regulated lawyers', 25 November 2019.

Client money and assets

4.44

> 4.1 You properly account to *clients* for any *financial benefit* you receive as a result of their instructions, except where they have agreed otherwise.
>
> 4.2 You safeguard money and *assets* entrusted to you by *clients* and others.
>
> 4.3 You do not personally hold *client money* save as permitted under regulation 10.2(b)(vii) of the Authorisation of Individuals Regulations, unless you work in an *authorised body*, or in an organisation of a kind *prescribed* under this rule on any terms that may be *prescribed* accordingly.

Commissions and financial benefits

4.45

The SRA Glossary states that 'financial benefit includes any commission, discount or rebate, but does not include your fees or interest earned on any client account'. The paragraph 4.1 requirement relating to financial benefits is comparable to the general law. Under the general law, a solicitor must not make a secret profit, or obtain any secret advantage, and must disclose to the client any interest in the transaction for which the solicitor is retained. The general law is satisfied if the fiduciary obtains the informed consent of the client at the outset of the retainer to retention of a financial benefit.[1]

A fiduciary is under no obligation in law to account for benefits which he is authorised to take under the terms of the agreement under which he acts as a fiduciary.[2]

Commissions and payments for introductions are a normal part of business life. Clients are generally, in our experience, unconcerned with the business arrangements solicitors make with third parties provided that they are transparent and cause no prejudice to the clients. The fact that solicitors may take a commission raises no eyebrows.

---

1 The 2007 Code, and its predecessors for many years, only imposed a professional duty to account in respect of commissions of £20 or more. The £20 *de minimis* exception no longer exists; a secret profit is a secret profit, whether of £20 or £20 million, and it is arguable as a matter of legal principle that the Law Society should never have created the *de minimis* exception in the first place.
2 The liability to account arises if there is no such authority: 'If the person in a fiduciary position does gain or receive any financial benefit arising out of the use of the property of the beneficiary he cannot keep it unless he can show such authority', *Brown v Inland Revenue Commissioners* [1965] AC 244, HL per Lord Reid at 256G.

4.46

Solicitors should be aware that financial benefits received from third parties in the course of personal injury work may be prohibited under section 56(2) of LASPO 2012, which provides that a regulated person is in breach of section 56 if, while providing legal services in the course of prescribed legal business, the regulated person arranges for a third party to provide services to the client and is paid or has been paid for making that arrangement. This is likely to be relevant, for example, where the solicitor arranges for the client to be examined by a medical practitioner who is on the books of a medical agency, and/or helps the client obtain after-the-event insurance, and/or helps to arrange car hire for the injured claimant following a road traffic accident. Such arrangements are caught by the referral fee ban, and outlawed if the solicitor is paid for the referral, or if there is any other consideration for the referral.[1]

1   See also paragraphs 5.1 and 5.2 of the Code for Individuals and **4.51**.

Client money and assets

4.47

The requirement in paragraph 4.2 to safeguard money and assets applies to third parties as well as clients.

Since 2017 the SRA has often asserted in disciplinary proceedings that there has been a breach of the obligation to protect client money when a shortfall arises on client account. The question whether there needs to be a degree of culpability and seriousness for a breach of the SRA Accounts Rules to translate into a breach of a professional code of conduct is often overlooked. Managers of a practice are strictly liable for shortfalls under the SRA Accounts Rules.[1] An extension of the SRA Accounts Rules principle of strict liability to a rule of strict liability in a code of conduct would be a departure from the principle that there has to be a degree of seriousness and a culpable act or omission to act for there to be a breach of a code setting out standards of professional behaviour.[2] Human error and shortfalls can arise in the best-run firms.

1   Rule 1.2 of the SRA Accounts Rules 2019.
2   See *SRA v Day* [2018] EWHC 2726 (Admin) at [156] to [158] and [215] to [228] and **19.2**.

4.48

Client money can only be held by solicitors working in authorised bodies unless one of the two exceptions in paragraph 4.3 applies. The 'authorised bodies' are recognised sole practices, recognised bodies (including traditional firms) and licensed bodies.[1]

The first exception relates to sole solicitors who practise on their own without being authorised as a recognised sole practice and who are entitled to carry out reserved legal activities.[2] They are entitled to hold client money on account of fees and unpaid disbursements provided that (a) the client is told in advance where the money will be held and (b) any money held for disbursements relates to expenses which the sole solicitor has incurred on the client's behalf and is personally liable to pay.[3] The money need not be held in a client account.[4] As the expenses have to be incurred before the money on account can be obtained, the sole solicitor is at risk of personal liability for the incurred expenses (such as counsel's and expert's fees) until the money is obtained on account.

The second exception relates to prescribed organisations. A prescribed organisation is a 'non-commercial body', which is defined by the SRA Glossary to be a body that falls within section 23(2) of LSA 2007.[5]

By section 23(2) of LSA 2007 three types of entity, not for profit bodies, community interest companies and trade unions, are entitled to carry out reserved legal activities without the need to be licensed as an alternative business structure (ABS) during a transitional period which comes to an end by order of the Lord Chancellor on the recommendation of the Legal Services Board (LSB). The LSB has announced that the transitional protection will remain in force for the foreseeable future and that it will only make the recommendation when satisfied that there is at least one licensing authority with appropriate arrangements in place to license the different bodies.[6]

Solicitors, RELs and RFLs working in a non-commercial body are permitted to hold client money subject to prescribed terms. The prescribed terms are based on the SRA Accounts Rules 2019 and include provisions that client money must be kept separate from money belonging to the lawyer or the prescribed organisation, and must be paid into a client account (unless the client agrees an alternative arrangement in writing, the money has been received from the Legal Aid Agency (LAA) for costs or the money is received as a trustee or holder of an office or appointment such as a Court of Protection Deputy and the payment into client account would conflict with the terms of the appointment). Client account reconciliations must be completed at least every five weeks, and the SRA is entitled to require the lawyer to obtain an accountant's report on reasonable notice if the SRA considers it is in the public interest to do so.[7]

1   See the SRA Glossary.
2   The conditions which sole solicitors need to meet to carry out reserved legal activities are set out in regulation 10.2(b) of the SRA Authorisation of Individuals Regulations 2019.
3   Regulation 10.2(b)(vii) of the SRA Authorisation of Individuals Regulations 2019.
4   Rule 2.2 of the SRA Accounts Rules 2019.
5   SRA statement, 'The prescribed organisations and terms under which solicitors, RELs and RFLs are allowed to hold client money in their own name', in force with effect from 25 November 2019.
6   LSB, 'Transitional protections from ABS licensing', https://legalservicesboard.org.uk/our-work/work-related-to-previous-years/transitional-protections-from-abs-licensing.
7   SRA statement, 'The prescribed organisations and terms under which solicitors, RELs and RFLs are allowed to hold client money in their own name', in force with effect from 25 November 2019.

4.49

See **5.43** for steps which can be taken by a firm to protect client money from cybercrime.

Business requirements

Referrals, introductions and separate businesses

4.50

> 5.1   In respect of any referral of a *client* by you to another *person*, or of any third party who introduces business to you or with whom you share your *fees*, you ensure that:
>
> (a)   *clients* are informed of any financial or other interest which you or your business or employer has in referring the *client to another person* or which an *introducer* has in referring the *client* to you;
>
> (b)   *clients* are informed of any fee sharing arrangement that is relevant to their matter;

(c)   the fee sharing agreement is in writing;

(d)   you do not receive payments relating to a referral or make payments to an *introducer* in respect of *clients* who are the subject of criminal proceedings; and

(e)   any *client* referred by an *introducer* has not been acquired in a way which would breach the *SRA's regulatory arrangements* if the *person* acquiring the *client* were regulated by the *SRA*.

5.2   Where it appears to the *SRA* that you have made or received a *referral fee*, the payment will be treated as a *referral fee* unless you show that the payment was not made as such.

5.3   You only:

(a)   refer, recommend or introduce a *client* to a *separate business*; or

(b)   divide, or allow to be divided, a *client's* matter between you and a *separate business*;

where the *client* has given informed consent to your doing so.

Referral fees: introduction

4.51

No subject has been more controversial for solicitors than the payment of referral fees by solicitors to introducers. The profession itself has been sharply divided over the issue. One part regards the whole idea of buying work, and thereby increasing the basic overhead cost of conducting a client's case, to be distasteful, and damaging in tending to increase costs. The other maintains that solicitors' practices are businesses, that the payment of commissions for the introduction of work is a common and inevitable feature of business life, and that a return to more restrictive practices would defy the marketplace, which never really works, and in any event it would probably be unlawful as being anti-competitive. From 2004 until the passing of LASPO 2012, this liberal attitude prevailed. However, LASPO 2012 turned the clock back and, with effect from 1 April 2013, the profession again had to come to terms with the fact that in personal injury cases, solicitors cannot pay referral fees.

In his *Review of Civil Litigation Costs: Final Report* (published in 2010), Lord Justice Jackson recommended the abolition of referral fees, alternatively their capping at £200. The Government issued a Green Paper late in 2010, and consultation upon it closed at the end of February 2011. The Green Paper did not make any recommendation as to the future of referral fees: the Government was apparently awaiting the Report of the LSB before making its decision. That Report emerged in May 2011 and concluded that the purely regulatory case for a general ban in the legal services market had not been made out. This was because sufficient evidence of consumer detriment, which would have been needed to merit a ban, had not been found.

During the summer of 2011, a number of politicians called publicly for the banning of referral fees. They had become concerned both by the so-called 'compensation culture' that had grown over the previous decade leading to some spurious or exaggerated claims, and by the aggressive, often unscrupulous, and on occasions fraudulent activities of those who sought, for commercial gain, to incite personal injury victims to make legal claims in respect of the injuries they had sustained. This political campaign proved to be very successful, and the necessary provisions were somewhat hastily inserted into the Bill that was making its way through Parliament.

4.52

Other than arrangements caught by sections 56 to 60 of LASPO 2012, there is no prohibition against the payment by solicitors of referral fees in the general law.

As for agreements between introducers and their clients entered into before the client is introduced to the solicitor, solicitors may need to consider the doctrine of unconscionable bargain. In *Strydom v Vendside Limited*,[1] an attempt was made to set aside an agreement with a claims handling company associated with the Union of Democratic Mineworkers. Blair J, on appeal from the county court judge's decision, summarised the law on unconscionable bargains as follows (at [36]):

> 'before the court will consider setting a contract aside as an unconscionable bargain, one party has to have been disadvantaged in some relevant way as regards the other party, that other party must have exploited that disadvantage in some morally culpable manner, and the resulting transaction must be overreaching and oppressive. No single one of these factors is sufficient – all three elements must be proved, otherwise the enforceability of contracts is undermined (see the reasoning in Goff & Jones, *The Law of Restitution*, 7th edition, para 12-006). Where all these requirements are met, the burden then passes to the other party to satisfy the court that the transaction was fair, just and reasonable (*Snell's Equity*, 31st edition, para 8-47).'

1   [2009] EWHC 2130 (QB).

The referral fee ban in personal injury cases: sections 56 to 60 of LASPO 2012

4.53

LASPO 2012[1] received Royal Assent on 1 May 2012, and sections 56 to 60, which contain the referral fee ban, came into force in April 2013. The SRA has published a guidance note on what the regulator regards as acceptable and unacceptable arrangements. This is particularly helpful in explaining the SRA's interpretation of the statute, what is prohibited and, constructively, what in the SRA's interpretation is not prohibited.[2]

1   LASPO 2012 currently only affects the relationship between introducers and law firms in relation to claims for personal injury or death.
2   SRA guidance, 'The prohibition of referral fees in LASPO 56 60', 25 March 2013, updated 25 November 2019.

4.54

The SRA has also issued a warning notice to practitioners who have arrangements with introducers in connection with personal injury work. The reason for issuing the warning notice is explained thus:

'We know that the ban on referral fees has raised difficult issues in relation to its application and interpretation. We are also aware that, because of the wording of LASPO, it is possible to have arrangements that involve the introduction or referral of personal injury work without being in breach of LASPO. We are concerned, however, that by setting up arrangements in a way that does not breach LASPO, some of those we regulate are failing to consider their wider duties to clients and others, and in doing so may breach the Standards and Regulations. Examples include:

- agreeing with an introducer to deduct money from clients' damages;

- inappropriate outsourcing of work to introducers;

- referrals to other service providers which are not in the best interests of clients;

- failure to properly advise clients about the costs and how their claim should be funded; and

- lack of transparency about the arrangement.'[1]

1   SRA warning notice, 'Referral fees, LASPO and the SRA principles', 11 October 2013, updated 25 November 2019. The warning notice is at **Appendix 8**.

Mechanism of the ban

4.55

By section 56(1) and (2), a regulated person is in breach of the section if he refers prescribed legal business to another and is paid for the referral; or if the regulated person pays or has paid for the referral of prescribed legal business. Regulated persons are defined in section 59, and in simple terms are persons regulated by the Financial Conduct Authority (FCA), the Ministry of Justice, the Law Society and the Bar Council, in other words barristers, solicitors, claims management companies and insurers. The definition of prescribed legal business is complex and requires consideration of section 56(4) and (6) of LASPO 2012, and section 12(3) of LSA 2007. To date, the ban has been restricted to legal services relating to claims for personal injury and death: other areas of legal work where referral fees are commonplace, such as conveyancing and non-personal injury claims, eg damage-only accidents, and claims arising out of allegedly mis-sold payment protection insurance, are untouched. However, the Lord Chancellor has power to make regulations to widen the definition of prescribed legal business.[1]

1   See section 56(4)(c) of LASPO 2012.

4.56

A referral is defined in section 56(5): there is a referral if a person (not the client) provides information to another person and it is information that a solicitor would need to make an offer to act for a client. Thus in the typical scenario of a claims management company and a solicitor, the introducer will pass on the details of the prospective client: the solicitor will then make contact with the client. Such a situation is clearly caught by the legislation if a payment is made. Where, however, the flow of information is in a different direction, eg where the introducer gives information about the solicitor to the prospective client, and the client is then left to contact the solicitor if he or she so chooses, this would not be a referral within the meaning of the Act.

The following extract from the guidance note published by the SRA confirms the correctness of this analysis:

> 'We consider that the communication of a client's name and contact details to or by a regulated person would amount to a referral, as this information would enable the recipient to make an offer to the client to provide relevant services.
>
> Example 1: An insurance company has an agreement with a firm of solicitors for the referral of clients. The insurance company is contacted by the claimant who notifies the insurer of a claim involving personal injury. The client's details are provided to the firm, who write to the claimant/client offering their services. The firm pays a fee for each email sent from the website.
>
> We would regard this as a referral because the insurer has passed to the firm information which will enable the firm to offer to act for the claimant.
>
> Example 2: A website offers to find a suitable firm of solicitors for members of the public. The potential client is required to input their postcode and the area of law in which they need help. They then receive an email providing contact details of a suitable firm in their area.
>
> We do not consider that this amounts to a referral within the terms of LASPO as the potential client's details are not being provided to the firm.'[1]

---

1   SRA guidance, 'The prohibition of referral fees in LASPO 56–60', 25 March 2013, updated 25 November 2019.

4.57

By section 56(8), payment includes any form of consideration (whether the benefit is received by the solicitor or a third party) but excludes the provision of reasonable hospitality.

Enforcing the ban

4.58

Parliament has thrown the responsibility for monitoring and enforcing the referral fee ban upon the regulators, who must ensure that they have appropriate arrangements in place and may make rules for this purpose.[1] LASPO 2012 can be enforced by the general requirement of paragraph 7.1 to follow the law and regulation governing the way you work and by the requirement of principle 1 to uphold the principle of the rule of law.[2] The introduction to the Code for Individuals states that the SRA monitors the ban:

> 'In addition to the regulatory requirements set by us in our Codes, Principles and our rules and regulations, we directly monitor and enforce the requirements relating to referral fees set out in section 56 of [LASPO 2012]'.

---

1   See section 57(1)–(3) of LASPO 2012.
2   But see **3.15** on principle 1.

4.59

LASPO 2012 provides that a breach of section 56 does not make the perpetrator guilty of a criminal offence, nor does it give rise to an action for breach of statutory duty.[1] A breach of section 56 does not make anything void or unenforceable, but a contract to make or pay for a referral or arrangement in breach of that section is unenforceable.[2]

1   See section 57(5) of LASPO 2012.
2   See section 57(6).

Anti-avoidance provisions

4.60

The pre-2004 ban was widely circumvented by solicitors. Instead of paying referral fees per se, solicitors paid 'administration fees' or 'marketing fees' for services allegedly provided of such description. As a result LASPO 2012 includes within it some important anti-avoidance provisions, in sections 57(2), (7) and (9).

4.61

Section 57(2) provides that a regulator may make rules for the purposes of ensuring that it has appropriate arrangements for monitoring and enforcing the referral fee ban. That is a statutory mechanism, created in deliberately vague terms (to cater for business ingenuity), to enable regulators to identify arrangements which on the surface do not offend section 56, but avoid the legislative intent.

Section 57(7) provides in substance from a solicitor's perspective that where a referral is made to a solicitor and it appears to the SRA that payment by the solicitor may be a referral fee, subsection (8) will apply. That subsection provides that rules under section 57(2) may provide for the payment to be treated as a referral fee unless the solicitor shows that the payment was made (a) as consideration for the provision of services, or (b) for another reason, and not as a referral fee. Paragraph 5.2 of the Code for Individuals contains a rule to that effect (and is the only rule made by the SRA under section 57(2) and (7) in the 2019 Codes).

Section 57(9) provides that a payment which would otherwise be regarded as consideration for the provision of services of any description may be treated as a referral fee if it exceeds the amount specified in relation to services of that description in regulations made by the Lord Chancellor. No regulations have been made.

The referral fee ban and ABSs

4.62

Although the creation of ABSs under LSA 2007 was unconnected with the new referral fee ban, on the face of it introducers and solicitors should be able to surmount the difficulties caused by the ban by joining forces in an ABS. As soon as solicitor and introducer are under the same legal roof as part of the same legal entity there can no longer be a 'referral', which requires information flowing from one legal person to another. In a publication headed 'Q&As on the ban of personal injury referral fees',[1] the SRA recognises this:

'Can I set up an ABS to avoid the ban?

Becoming an … ABS will not necessarily enable you to avoid the ban.

The ABS itself will be a regulated person for the purposes of LASPO and its referral arrangements will be subject to the ban and the standards set out in paragraphs 5.1 to 5.3 of the Code of Conduct for solicitors, RELs and RFLs … and paragraph 7.1 (b) of the Code of Conduct for Firms … If you merge your firm with another business to become an ABS, any referrals within the new business will not be caught. However, if the ABS is part of a group of companies, referrals within the group will be caught.'

1   SRA, 'Q&As on the ban of personal injury referral fees', 1 April 2013, updated 3 December 2019.

The referral fee ban and collective advertising by solicitors

4.63

There have been a number of successful schemes under which solicitors have pooled resources and created a third party organisation such as Injury Lawyers 4U, and National Accident Helpline, to carry out advertising and marketing on behalf of the firms, and then to refer claims generated by such activities to the solicitors on their panels. On the face of it, these collective schemes have the potential to be caught by the referral fee ban. However, where enforcement of the ban has been delegated by Parliament to the regulators, the view of the latter will be of decisive importance. The SRA's guidance note contains the following:

'Our view is that where there is a referral of a matter to or by a regulated person, or an arrangement for another person to provide services, a payment will be prohibited to the extent that it is being paid for the referral or arrangement. Where a payment is for the provision of other services of for another reason, the payment would not be in breach of LASPO.

This may cause difficulties where a third party refers clients to a firm of solicitors in addition to or in the course of providing other services such as marketing.

Example […]: a company carries out marketing for a group of firms. Enquiries are made to a call centre, details of potential clients are passed to member firms on a rota basis and each firm pays an equal share of the costs of advertising and operating the scheme. There has been a referral within the terms of LASPO because the details of potential clients have been passed to firms by the company carrying out the marketing. The firms involved will need to be satisfied that any payments they make to the marketing company are for the marketing and not for the referral of clients. If a payment is made for each "lead" or the payment varies according to the number of referrals made, this is likely to suggest that the payment is for the referrals rather than for the marketing. Even if there is no specific number of leads guaranteed the solicitor would need to be satisfied that the payment they are making is reasonable in view of the services being provided.

If it appears to us that a payment may have been made for a referral or for making an arrangement, we will treat that as a prohibited referral fee for the purposes of LASPO, unless the regulated person can show that the payment was made for services or for another reason and not as a referral fee. Where you advertise jointly and pay only for that service, you are unlikely to breach the provisions of LASPO – however, you will need to be satisfied that the arrangement does not contain a referral fee element.

Example [...]: A CMC advertises in local newspapers in its own name and has a panel of firms to which they refer cases. When a potential client contacts the CMC, the CMC takes brief details and asks a standard set of questions to ensure the claim is not time barred. The client is told that a solicitor will contact them within the next 24 hours. Firms pay a fixed fee in respect of each client referred. The CMC says that the payments are for advertising, operating the call centre and vetting potential claims.

A firm in this situation would need to show that the payments were genuinely for the services described. In this case the vetting would appear to be minimal and it is difficult to see how the payment for advertising could be genuine as it is being paid "per client" rather than reflecting the actual cost of advertising. It is therefore likely that the payment would include a referral fee element.

When determining whether referral fees are being paid, we will take into account all of the circumstances but the following factors may indicate a prohibited referral fee:

- payment for services appear to be excessive;

- an arrangement where receipt of referrals is conditional upon payment;

- payments that are made per referral or which are otherwise linked to the number of referrals;

- no evidence that a genuine service is being provided.

Where it appears to us that a referral fee may have been paid, the onus will be on the regulated person to demonstrate that the payment was not for the referral (see section 57(7) of LASPO). Firms should therefore fully investigate all relevant matters before making or receiving referrals of prescribed legal business.'[1]

1   SRA guidance, 'The prohibition of referral fees in LASPO 56–60', 25 March 2013, updated 25 November 2019.

The LASPO warning notice

4.64

A solicitor needs to consider very carefully any request by an introducer to deduct payments from a client's damages, or forward the client's damages to the introducer. The SRA's warning notice on LASPO states that a solicitor who deducts payments at the request of a claims management company (CMC) or forwards damages to a CMC is 'unlikely to be able to comply' with the Principles and Codes, as the payment is unlikely to ever be in the client's best interests and could compromise the solicitor's obligation of independence.[1]

Although there may be arguments that payments can in some circumstances be justified where for example a CMC is entitled to charge for a genuine service arising from a regulated activity, the SRA is likely to take enforcement action on the basis of the terms of the warning notice.[2]

1   SRA warning notice, 'Referral fees LASPO and SRA Principles', 11 October 2013, updated 25 November 2019.
2   It should be noted that Parliament has previously expressly sanctioned deductions from damages: the Damages-Based Agreements Regulations 2013 (SI 2013/609) provided for damages-based agreements (DBAs) with claims management companies.

4.65

The warning notice imposes the following obligation to ensure that arrangements between the referrer and the client are fair:

> 'You have a duty to ensure that contracts or other arrangements between your client and a referrer are fair. You must stop dealing with a referrer whose contractual terms or whose behaviours are contrary to your clients' interests or to the rule of law … For this reason, you should review your referral arrangements regularly.'[1]

It is difficult to see how a solicitor can always ensure that the contractual arrangements are fair. The warning notice does at least place the solicitor in a position where the solicitor should obtain a right to review the arrangements between the clients and the referrer, and regularly review them, and the solicitor should stop accepting referrals if the arrangements are known to be unfair. If a solicitor enters into or continues an arrangement with a referrer in order to generate fee income, in circumstances where the solicitor is aware that the referrer is entering into unfair agreements with the clients, he or she is at risk of allegations of lack of integrity as well as a breach of paragraph 5.1(e).[2]

1   SRA warning notice, 'Referral fees LASPO and SRA Principles', 11 October 2013, updated 25 November 2019.
2   See also **4.76–4.78** and **4.128**.

4.66

The warning notice also highlights SRA concerns on outsourcing work to the referrer, obtaining insurance products and medical reports which generate commissions for the firm or the referrer and failure to discuss funding options with clients. The full text of the warning notice is at **APPENDIX 8**.

Paragraph 5.1: Referral arrangements and fee sharing in the Code for Individuals

4.67

It should be stressed that the LASPO referral fee ban currently applies only to personal injury and fatal accident cases. In most other areas of practice[1] solicitors may pay referral fees to introducers, and the solicitor's conduct is governed by the Principles and the provisions of the Code for Individuals.

1   There is a prohibition against referral fees in criminal proceedings – see paragraph 5.1(d).

4.68

Paragraphs 5.1(a) and (b) centre upon transparency and financial arrangements. The section 1 standards are also relevant to referrals: the client must be treated fairly. Principles 3 (independence) and 7 (acting in the best interests of each client) should also be taken into account. In particular, the solicitor must ensure that an arrangement with an introducer, and the solicitor's interest in receiving referrals, does not compromise the duty to act with independence and in the client's best interests.

4.69

Although paragraph 5.1(a) and (b) require that clients are informed of any financial or other interest which an introducer has in referring the client to the solicitor, and of any fee sharing arrangement, the provision does not mandate when this has to be done. The nearest that the SRA has come to giving guidance on the timing was in a series of 'Q and As' on its website relating to the comparable provision in the 2011 Code (which was outcome 9.3). The answer to the question 'When do I have to give this information to clients?' was:

> 'The outcomes do not specify when the information should be provided. However, in order to achieve outcome 9.3, you will need to consider whether you need to give the information before the client has committed themselves to instructing your firm i.e. at the outset of the matter. The nature of the referral arrangement may affect the client's decision to instruct your firm.'

It would however be equally logical, and much easier in pragmatic terms, if solicitors used the medium of routine client care documents to provide this information, provided there is no detriment or prejudice to clients or potential clients if they were to decide to terminate the retainer in the light of the disclosure of a referral arrangement.

4.70

Paragraphs 5.1(a) and (b) do not state whether the information to be supplied to clients should be in writing. Principle 7 (acting in the best interests of clients) is likely to mean in most circumstances that the information should be clear and in writing, so that the client can make an informed decision.

4.71

Paragraph 5.1(c) states that 'in respect of any referral of a client by you to another person, or of any third party who introduces business to you or with whom you share your fees, you ensure that … the agreement is in writing'.

Read literally, that standard is difficult to understand. It is presumably not intended to cover referrals made between solicitors on a one-off basis to overcome a conflict of interest where there is no underlying agreement to pay a fee. It appears to require a written document for any agreement or arrangement for referrals, introductions or fee sharing.

4.72

Paragraph 5.1(d) outlaws referral fees in respect of clients who are the subject of criminal proceedings.

4.73

The 2007 Code imposed obligations on the solicitor to require the introducer to provide information to the client. In the absence of any specific rule to that effect in subsequent Codes, solicitors can safely abandon that obligation. The obligation was onerous and difficult to perform, and it was not missed.

4.74

By paragraph 5.1(e) solicitors must ensure that the introducers have not referred clients who have been acquired in a way which would breach the SRA's regulatory arrangements if the person acquiring the client were regulated by the SRA. The phrase 'SRA regulatory arrangements' has a very wide meaning. The SRA Glossary states it 'has the meaning given to it by section 21 of the LSA'. Section 21 of LSA 2007 defines 'regulatory arrangements' to include all authorisation arrangements, practice rules, conduct rules, qualification regulations and indemnification arrangements. The standard places a potentially onerous burden on solicitors, and it may be impossible to ensure that introducers have not breached such a wide-ranging requirement.

The comparable provisions in the 2011 Code were indicative behaviours which identified specific types of conduct. The 2011 Code included indicative behaviours which suggested that acting in the following ways would tend to show that solicitors had complied with the 2011 Code and Principles:

- only entering into arrangements with reputable third parties (indicative behaviour 9.1);

- in any case where a client has entered into, or is proposing to enter into, an arrangement with an introducer in connection with their matter which is not in their best interest, advising the client that this is the case (indicative behaviour 9.2); and

- being satisfied that any client referred by the introducer has not acquired the client as a result of marketing or other activities which if done by a person regulated by the SRA would be contrary to the Principles or any requirements of the Code (indicative behaviour 9.4).

The indicative behaviours also provided that acting in the following way would tend to show that the solicitor had not complied with the 2011 Code and Principles:

- accepting referrals where you have reason to believe that clients have been pressurised or misled into instructing you (indicative behaviour 9.12).

Adopting those indicative behaviours as guidelines, it can be said that, under paragraph 5.1(e), solicitors should not accept referrals from introducers if there has been marketing such as cold calling, or there is reason to believe that clients have been pressurised or misled into instructing the introducer, or the introducer is entering into unfair agreements with clients relating to, for example, payment of disproportionate fees.[1] However, the standard is wider than that, and in practice it may often be impossible to ensure that the introducer complies with all applicable regulatory arrangements.

Paragraph 5.1(e) does not exclude introducers subject to other regulatory regimes. Claims management companies are regulated by the FCA and are subject to their own suite of regulatory rules. By paragraph 5.1(e) a solicitor is required to ensure claims management companies do not offend the SRA regulations, despite that regulation by the FCA.[2]

1   See **4.76–4.78**.
2   Claims management services have been regulated by the FCA under the Financial Services and Markets Act (FSMA) 2000 since 1 April 2019. Before that date they were regulated by the Claims Management Regulation Unit of the Ministry of Justice under the Competition Act 2006.

4.75

The referral provisions in section 5 of the Code for Individuals apply to referrals between lawyers. Referral agreements need to be in writing. Any referral fees or fee sharing arrangements need to be disclosed to the client under paragraphs 5.1(a) and (b).

Pre-retainer arrangements between clients and introducers

4.76

The question of whether solicitors should advise their clients on pre-retainer arrangements between the client and an introducer, when those arrangements are not in the client's best interests, requires special mention.

Until recent years, it has not been suggested that solicitors are under any duty to advise their clients as to the wisdom or otherwise of contractual arrangements that they (the clients) may have made before instructing the solicitor. Indeed the imposition of such a duty in the general law is fraught with danger, and the courts have consistently pointed out the limits of a solicitor's retainer. In the words of Lord Jauncey in *Clark Boyce v Mouat*:[1]

> 'When a client in full command of his faculties and apparently aware of what he is doing seeks the assistance of a solicitor in the carrying out of a particular transaction, that solicitor is under no duty whether before or after accepting instructions to go beyond those instructions by proffering unsought advice on the wisdom of the transaction. To hold otherwise could impose intolerable burdens on solicitors.'

However, in some of the disciplinary prosecutions arising out of the miners' compensation cases, and later in disciplinary prosecutions arising out of the activities of an organisation known as Justice Direct, the Tribunal held that solicitors should have advised clients about agreements with introducers entered into before instruction of the solicitors, by which the client agreed to yield up a proportion of their compensation to the introducer.

1   [1994] 1 AC 428, PC at 437D.

4.77

The extent of the obligation is difficult to define. For instance, what is the solicitor to do where the client is introduced by an estate agent who charges significantly more than its competitors, with no apparent added value for the client? Is the solicitor to advise the new client that he or she is paying far too much to the estate agency which has introduced the client to the solicitor? In the judgment in the *Beresford* appeal[1] the Divisional Court discussed this issue at some length ([61]–[80] inclusive) but declined to decide it; observing that:

> 'It would for instance be a distraction to set about determining whether the Vendside agreements were indeed unenforceable in law. They were certainly questionable, as Beresfords knew or ought to have known. Vendside were not providing the services for which the fee was stated to be payable.'

The court appeared to take the view that there was an obligation to advise that the agreement was 'questionable' (at [75]). There remains uncertainty. In the *Beresford* case itself, the Tribunal provided some guidance as to what was expected of solicitors acting for claimants in the miners' compensation cases:

> 'The Tribunal had no doubt that it was part of Beresfords' retainer for them to read the agreement and comment on it to ensure that the miners fully understood what they had agreed to and to indicate to them that there was some uncertainty about the agreement and therefore about the deductions from their compensation.'[2]

1   *Beresford and Smith v SRA* [2009] EWHC 3155 (Admin).
2   9666-2007, SDT at para 156.

4.78

After its success in the *Beresford* case, the SRA prosecuted four separate sole practitioner solicitors who had accepted work from Justice Direct, an organisation that charged a hefty slice of a client's damages for doing little more than finding a solicitor for the client. All four admitted the allegations, and the Tribunal followed its approach in *Beresford* by agreeing that the failure to alert the clients to the disadvantageous nature of the Justice Direct contract amounted to professional misconduct. In the first such case, *Tilbury*,[1] the Tribunal stated:

> 'The Tribunal was satisfied that by entering into the agreement with Justice Direct, the Respondent effectively disabled himself from advising his clients as to the desirability of the client becoming liable to pay 25% of any recoverable damages to Justice Direct in return for an introduction to the solicitor. The benefits to the client of entering into the Purchase Order were claimed to be some initial screening of the claim and introduction of a suitably qualified solicitor. Neither in the Tribunal's view could justify the payment to Justice Direct of so disproportionate a share of the damages awarded to the client and the Tribunal considered that no competent solicitor rendering advice in the best interests of the client could recommend the client to enter into such an agreement.'

Both the Justice Direct cases and *Beresford* are therefore consistent with a duty to advise in relation to a pre-existing contract, if on the facts there is something obviously inaccurate or uncertain, or a fee that is apparently wholly unreasonable and disproportionate. The question remains open as to what, in the case of a lawful contract, which is unreasonable and unfair, but not unconscionable and liable to be set aside, solicitors are expected to advise. They may find themselves in an unenviable position, in breach of regulatory duty if they stay silent, and at risk of committing the tort of inducing a breach of contract, or being informed by the client that the cost of the advice is outside the scope of the retainer, if they advise in detail. It may not be very constructive, but it would be compliant, for solicitors to 'advise' that the client would have been better not to have entered into the agreement, but that nothing can now be done about it.

If a solicitor enters into or continues an arrangement with an introducer in order to generate fee income, in circumstances where the solicitor is aware that the introducer is entering into unfair agreements with the clients, he or she is at risk of allegations of lack of integrity as well as a breach of paragraph 5.1(e).[2]

1   9880-2008, SDT.
2   See also **4.65** and **4.128**.

Involvement of the introducer after the case has been referred to the solicitor

4.79

One of the legitimate concerns of the SRA in policing referral fee arrangements is that solicitors may develop an unhealthy dependence upon a flow of work from a particular introducer, and then permit the introducer an inappropriate degree of control over how the solicitor carries out the work. An introducer has a legitimate interest in ensuring that the chosen solicitor carries out the work to a reasonable standard, as the introducer has entrusted the client to the solicitor. It is commonplace to see agreements between solicitors and introducers by which the introducer has the right to audit the work of the solicitor. However, unless dealt with in the agreement between introducer and client and/or the retainer letter between solicitor and client, such a right of audit may cut across the confidentiality that is owed by the solicitor to the client. Appropriate contractual provisions can reduce or eliminate any regulatory concern on that front, but solicitors should be aware that the SRA remains very concerned at the ability of introducers to weaken the independence of solicitors' advice to their clients.

Fee sharing

4.80

The rule against solicitors fee sharing with non-solicitors was traditionally based upon the risk of a non-solicitor having an inappropriate amount of influence over a solicitor in the handling of a claim for a client. It was steadily eroded over the years. Historically, there was an absolute prohibition, but that was relaxed in March 2004 to permit fee sharing with those who introduced capital or services into a firm. Rule 8.02 of the 2007 Code maintained this exception. Because the former Practice Rules (and therefore the Code for Individuals) had the effect of subordinate legislation enacted for the protection of the public,[1] the rule against fee sharing with non-solicitors rendered an agreement to share fees in breach of the rule illegal and unenforceable.[2]

The advent of ABSs meant that the old objection to fee sharing between solicitors and non-solicitors had fallen away. The whole purpose of the reforms was to permit non-lawyers to share profits with solicitors. Fee sharing is inevitable where, for instance, a company merges with a firm of solicitors to create an ABS, or sets up an

SRA-regulated subsidiary to provide legal services to existing clients. As fee sharing had become permissible *within* one overall corporate structure, there was no logical reason why fee sharing *between* two independent corporate structures should be outlawed. Paragraph 5.1 confirms that there is no objection in principle to fee sharing.

1   *Swain v Law Society* [1983] 1 AC 598, HL.
2   *Mohamed v Alaga & Co (a firm)* [1999] 3 All ER 699, CA; *Westlaw Services Limited v Boddy* [2010] EWCA Civ 929.

4.81

If a solicitor enters into a fee sharing arrangement with a third party, the solicitor has to (a) be transparent to clients about arrangements with fee sharers; (b) ensure that the fee sharing agreement is in writing; (c) ensure that there is no sacrifice of the solicitor's independence (ie permitting the fee sharer inappropriate influence); and (d) ensure that the best interests of clients remain paramount.

Referrals to financial advisers

4.82

The 2019 Codes do not contain specific rules relating to referrals to financial advisers. That is consistent with the SRA's aim of producing regulatory arrangements which are not prescriptive and focus on overarching values and behaviours.[1] On any referral to any third party solicitors should have regard to principle 3 (acting with independence) and principle 7 (acting in the best interests of each client).[2]

1   For the SRA's approach to the 2019 Codes see, for example, 'Application for the approval of regulatory arrangements', issued by the SRA in August 2018, paras 12–26.
2   If the referral relates to a personal injury case, the solicitor also needs to take into account section 56(2) of LASPO 2012. See **4.55**.

Paragraph 5.2

4.83

Paragraph 5.2 relates to LASPO 2012. The SRA Glossary states that 'referral fee' means 'a referral fee as defined within section 57(7) of [LASPO 2012]'. The definition in section 57(7) of LASPO 2012 relates to referral fees for legal services concerning a claim or potential claim for damages for personal injury or death, or for other prescribed legal business.[1]

By section 57(8) of LASPO 2012, the SRA may make rules which provide that, where it appears to the SRA that a payment made to or by a regulated person may be a referral fee prohibited by LASPO 2012, the payment is to be treated as a referral fee unless the regulated person shows that the payment was made (a) as consideration for the provision of services or (b) for another reason, and not as a referral fee. Paragraph 5.2 is a rule made by the SRA pursuant to section 57(8) of LASPO 2012.

1   At present there is no other prescribed legal business; other prescribed legal business is 'business of a description specified in regulations made by the Lord Chancellor' (section 56(4) of LASPO 2012) and no regulations have been made.

Paragraph 5.3

4.84

Since 1 November 2015 solicitors have been permitted to own and/or actively participate in a separate unregulated business which provided legal services of all kinds except for reserved legal activities.[1]

If a solicitor owns or actively participates in a separate business[2] which is not authorised by the SRA or another approved regulator, and if the solicitor wishes to refer the client or part of the client's work to the separate business, the client's informed consent is needed. Clients should in particular be informed that their work is no longer being carried out by a solicitors' firm in a regulated environment, as the client initially decided to instruct a firm which provided the client with the protections arising from regulation.

On 21 October 2015 the SRA published guidance on the information to supply to clients who instruct a solicitors' firm and a separate business.[3] Although part of the guidance is now obsolete, it continues to be of assistance on the information to be supplied on the regulatory protection obtained by instructing a solicitors' firm as well as factors to take into account when deciding on the amount of information to provide on the division of work between regulated and unregulated businesses. For further information on the guidance see **4.140**.

1   The rules were introduced into Chapter 12 of the 2011 Code and were called the separate business rules. There were separate business rules before 1 November 2015 which allowed solicitors to have interests in businesses which did not provide legal services, but the earlier separate business rules prevented solicitors from hiving off unreserved legal services.
2   The SRA Glossary states that separate business
     'means where you own, manage or are employed by an authorised body, a separate business:
     (a)   which you own;
     (b)   which you are owned by;
     (c)   where you actively participate in the provision of its services, including where you have any direct control over the business or any indirect control over the business through another person, or
     (d)   which you are connected with,
     and which is not an authorised body, an authorised non-SRA firm or an overseas practice'.
3   See 'Chapter 12 of the SRA Code of Conduct 2011 – the separate business rule (SBR)', issued 21 October 2015.

Other business requirements

4.85

> 5.4   You must not be a *manager, employee, member* or *interest holder* of a business that:
>
> (a)   has a name which includes the word 'solicitors'; or
>
> (b)   describes its work in a way that suggests it is a *solicitors'* firm;
>
> unless it is an *authorised body*.
>
> 5.5   If you are a *solicitor* who holds a practising certificate, an *REL* or *RFL*, you must complete and deliver to the *SRA* an annual return in the *prescribed* form.

CHAPTER 4
SRA CODE OF CONDUCT FOR
SOLICITORS, RELS AND RFLS

> 5.6   If you are a *solicitor* or an *REL* carrying on *reserved legal activities* in a *non-commercial body*, you must ensure that:
>
> (a)   the body takes out and maintains indemnity insurance; and
>
> (b)   this insurance provides adequate and appropriate cover in respect of the services that you provide, or have provided, whether or not they comprise *reserved legal activities*, taking into account any alternative arrangements the body or its *clients* may make.

4.86

Paragraphs 5.4 and 5.5 speak for themselves.

A 'non-commercial body' is defined by the SRA Glossary to mean 'a body which falls within section 23(2) of the LSA'. The bodies falling within section 23(2) of LSA 2007 are: (a) a not for profit body; (b) a community interest body; and (c) an independent trade union. Those bodies are entitled to carry out reserved legal activities despite the fact that they are not regulated by an approved regulator.[1] A solicitor conducting litigation in, for example, a trade union must ensure that the trade union has professional indemnity (PI) cover for all of the solicitor's work.

1   By section 23(3) of LSA 2007, the right to carry out the reserved legal activities continues during a transitional period from the date on which the relevant part of LSA 2007 relating to reserved legal activities came into force to a date to be appointed by the Lord Chancellor. See also **4.48**.

Conflict, confidentiality and disclosure

Conflict of interests

4.87

> 6.1   You do not act if there is an *own interest conflict* or a significant risk of such a conflict.
>
> 6.2   You do not act in relation to a matter or particular aspect of it if you have a *conflict of interest* or a significant risk of such a conflict in relation to that matter or aspect of it, unless:
>
> (a)   the *clients* have a *substantially common interest* in relation to the matter or the aspect of it, as appropriate; or
>
> (b)   the *clients* are *competing for the same objective*,
>
> and the conditions below are met, namely that:
>
> (i)   all the *clients* have given informed consent, given or evidenced in writing, to you acting;
>
> (ii)   where appropriate, you put in place effective safeguards to protect your *clients'* confidential information; and
>
> (iii) you are satisfied it is reasonable for you to act for all the *clients*.

Own interest conflict

4.88

An 'own interest conflict' is defined in the SRA Glossary to mean 'any situation where your duty to act in the best interests of any client in relation to a matter conflicts, or there is a significant risk that it may conflict, with your own interests in relation to that or a related matter'.

The prohibition on acting in an 'own interest conflict' is absolute. While it could be said that this has always been so, there has also always been an understanding that not every dealing between solicitor and client which has the potential for conflict, in fact involves a conflict or a significant risk of one. Examples are an unsecured interest-free loan from solicitor to client, as an act of humanity; or bridging finance on standard terms; or a modest gift to a solicitor by a client in a will, as distinct from a gift which is 'significant'.

Guidance to the equivalent rule in the 2007 Code made it clear that solicitors could take security for their costs by a charge over the client's property, and that independent legal advice 'would not normally be essential unless the terms of the proposed charge are particularly onerous or would give you some unusual benefit or profit'. So was that not a conflict, or was it a conflict that was exceptionally permitted? It would be difficult to argue that it was not, strictly speaking, a conflict of interests (what were the terms of the legal charge to be?).

Similarly, rule 3.04 of the 2007 Code made it clear that a solicitor could accept a lifetime gift or a gift on death from a client who was not a family member without requiring the client to take independent advice unless the gift was 'significant' either in itself or having regard to the size of the client's estate and the reasonable expectations of prospective beneficiaries.

Are these historic indications still valid? In our view they are. The SRA's position may be gauged from its policy statements. In relation to the 2011 Code the SRA said:[1]

> 'The position under OFR is that we now expect firms to exercise their own judgement as to whether it would be proper to act in a particular situation, rather than the Handbook specifying the circumstances where it is appropriate to do so.'

In relation to the 2019 Codes the SRA said:

> 'Our new approach is to describe the standards to be achieved and give flexibility as to how these apply in any given situation. In doing so, we recognise that what is appropriate ... will depend on the circumstances and will, as a rule, best be judged by the solicitor or firm involved'.[2]

That suggests not a change in 'the rules', as such, but a change in the form of regulation, placing the onus on practitioners, in effect, to think and make judgements. That is indeed the outcomes-focused regulation (OFR) approach, and in our view in the situations described above by way of historic example there would be no failure to comply with the 2019 Codes, because there would be perceived to be no genuine 'own interest conflict'.

Where, however, there is a genuine 'own interest conflict', the prohibition against a solicitor acting where his or her personal interests actually conflict with those of a client is absolute. Many solicitors continue to believe that merely informing a client that independent advice should be taken is sufficient to discharge their duties to the client. This is not so and normally, if the client does not in fact take independent advice, the solicitor must not proceed with the transaction (whether it be the purchase of an asset from the client, the drafting of a will containing a significant bequest in favour of the solicitor, etc).

1   SRA, 'Policy statement on our October 2010 Consultation', March 2011, para 75.
2   'Application for approval of regulatory arrangements', issued by the SRA in August 2018, para 82.

4.89

Solicitors providing services to the public as an employee of an unregulated organisation need to take account of conflicts between the interests of their clients and their employer. In a guidance note, the SRA has said that it will normally assume that where a client's interests conflict with an employer's interests, then they will also conflict with the solicitor's interests, and the solicitor should not therefore act. That is because there will be a clash between the potential pressure on the solicitor in terms of his or her employment contract and the duty to act in the client's best interests.[1]

1   SRA guidance, 'Unregulated organisations – conflict and confidentiality', 23 July 2019, updated 25 November 2019.

4.90

On 25 November 2019 the SRA published a guidance note on the circumstances in which a solicitor can continue to act after making a mistake on a client's case. The guidance note states that not all occasions where things go wrong give rise to a risk of conflict. It is for the solicitor to decide, as a matter of professional judgement, whether personal interests interfere with the ability to act in the client's best interests when taking remedial action. Minor remediable errors such as missed time limits in litigation or defects in title which can be protected by purchase of an indemnity policy may not give rise to a risk of conflict. It may be possible to mitigate the risk of conflict arising from more serious errors by arranging for another firm to provide independent advice on a client's options on terms that the solicitor carries out the remedial work if that option is selected. The client should be informed promptly about what has happened in an open way, informed consent should be obtained for any remedial action and the solicitor should keep a detailed record of the decision-making process to justify the assessment of the risks.[1]

1   SRA guidance, 'Putting matters right when things go wrong, and own interest conflicts', 25 November 2019. This followed criticism of the decision in *Howell Jones*,11846-2018, SDT. See Treverton-Jones, 'Penalised for putting things right', *Gazette* [2019] 6 May.

Client conflict

4.91

A 'conflict of interest' is defined in the SRA Glossary to mean 'a situation where your separate duties to act in the best interests of two or more clients conflict'.

As to 'client conflicts', *The Guide to the Professional Conduct of Solicitors* (8th edn) contained a valuable commentary which remains valid and the substance of which is reproduced here: where a solicitor is acting for two or more clients, whether they are husband and wife, business partners or companies embarking on a joint venture, the solicitor always owes a duty to each individual person or body and he or she must advise each individual in accordance with that individual's interests. A practical initial test to apply to assist in identifying whether a conflict exists is to ask: what would occur if the solicitor was only acting for one of the parties? In particular, would any advice be different?

A conflict between clients can only arise if the solicitor is currently acting for two or more clients; it must involve current retainers from two or more relevant clients.

Paragraph 6.2 does not prohibit a solicitor from acting for a client against a former client. In this situation, paragraph 6.3 will be in play in relation to any confidential information that may be held about the former client. Paragraph 6.2 does not permit a client to consent to a solicitor acting in a conflict of interests situation unless one of the specified exceptions applies. It is not possible to erect an information barrier (or Chinese wall) to 'cure' a client conflict unless one of the exceptions applies.

4.92

A solicitor can only rely on one of the exceptions in paragraph 6.2 if it is in the best interests of all the clients for the solicitor to act and if the three conditions mentioned in paragraph 6.2 are met (ie (i) all clients have given informed written consent; (ii) there are effective safeguards when appropriate; and (iii) it is reasonable to act).[1]

1   It is intended that the three conditions apply to both exceptions – see SRA guidance, 'Conflicts of interest', 29 October 2019, updated 2 March 2020.

4.93

The phrase 'substantially common interest' is defined in the SRA Glossary as:

> 'a situation where there is a clear common purpose between the clients and a strong consensus on how it is to be achieved.'

The phrase 'competing for the same objective' is also defined in the SRA Glossary:

> 'any situation in which two or more clients are competing for an "objective" which, if attained by one client, will make that "objective" unattainable to the other client or clients and "objective" means an asset, contract or business opportunity which two or more clients are seeking to acquire or recover through a liquidation (or some other form of insolvency process) or by means of an auction or tender process or a bid or offer but not a public takeover.'

4.94

If clients are competing for the same objective, the clients are likely to need to keep at least some information confidential from each other. That in turn means that the exception can normally only be relied on if separate lawyers (or teams) act for each bidder and there are effective safeguards in place to protect confidential information. The test for an effective information barrier is high and requires an established structural separation within the firm (see **4.109–4.111**).

An SRA guidance note on conflicts of interests states that structural information barriers may not be needed if the clients consider it desirable for the same lawyer to

CHAPTER 4
SRA CODE OF CONDUCT FOR
SOLICITORS, RELS AND RFLS

represent them and they agree what information can and cannot be shared between the clients. The lawyer must be satisfied that the clients understand what type of information cannot be disclosed to them, that the clients are providing informed consent and that it is in the best interests of the clients to proceed on that basis.[1]

When a solicitor is deciding whether it is reasonable to rely on one of the exceptions in paragraph 6.2, factors to take into account include any particular benefits to the clients (such as niche specialist knowledge, speed, convenience and lower cost) and (in the case of the common interest exception), the respective knowledge and bargaining power of the clients, the extent to which there will need to be negotiations between the clients and whether a client who is vulnerable needs independent advice.[2]

1   SRA guidance, 'Conflicts of interest', 29 October 2019, updated 2 March 2020.
2   See the examples in SRA guidance, 'Unregulated organisations – conflict and confidentiality', 23 July 2019 and SRA guidance, 'Conflicts of interest', 29 October 2019, updated 2 March 2020.

4.95

It is possible to avoid a significant risk of a conflict by acting for joint clients on a limited retainer which confines the work to areas where a conflict is not likely to arise. For example a solicitor could carry out work on the administration of an estate for two personal representatives with competing claims to the beneficial interests in the estate, on terms that the work does not extend to representation on the claims.[1]

1   It must be in the best interests of the clients to act on the limited retainer. The SRA guidance, 'Conflicts of interest', updated 2 March 2020, contains examples of limited retainers, and the conduct issues which need to be considered when deciding whether to act.

The importance of making a judgement

4.96

As noted above, the 2019 Codes challenge solicitors to make judgements, rather than setting out in prescriptive rules how they must behave. The exercise of judgement is nowhere more important than in a solicitor's assessment of whether it is proper to act in a situation where there may be a conflict of interests. If the matter is properly and conscientiously addressed by the solicitor, an error of judgement will not amount to professional misconduct.[1] However, this does not mean that a solicitor's professional obligations are discharged merely by giving careful thought to the matter. If a solicitor does not honestly and genuinely address the matter, he may be guilty of a disciplinary offence. And if his decision is one that no reasonably competent solicitor could have made, it may be inferred that he had not (or could not have) properly addressed the issue. This inference may well be appropriate where the reason given for the solicitor's professional decision is manifestly unsustainable.

1   See *Connolly v Law Society* [2007] EWHC 1175 (Admin) at [62].

Conveyancing

4.97

The 2019 Codes do not contain any conflict rules which specifically relate to conveyancing. That is consistent with the SRA's intention that the firm should exercise its own judgement depending on the circumstances. The SRA has stated in relation to the 2019 Codes:

'Our new approach is to describe the standards to be achieved and give flexibility as to how these apply in any given situation. In doing so, we recognise that what is appropriate ... will depend on the circumstances and will, as a rule, best be judged by the solicitor or firm involved'.[1]

1   'Application for the approval of regulatory arrangements', issued by the SRA in August 2018, para 82.

4.98

The SRA's guidance note on conflicts of interest[1] contains the following limited guidance on conveyancing transactions:

'Other less direct examples of circumstances that can give rise to a conflict of interest or significant risk of one include:

● Two clients seeking separately to purchase a particular asset or to be awarded a particular contract.

● Acting for an investor and the scheme in which they will be investing.

● One client selling or leasing an asset to another client.

● Agreeing a commercial contract between two clients.

Although you should not normally act for two or more clients in these scenarios, this does not mean that you can never do so, if on the facts, there is no significant risk of a conflict arising.

This may be the case if for example, the clients are already agreed on all of the relevant terms and all of the relevant information relating to the transaction can be shared openly between them. However, if you foresee the need for substantive negotiations between the clients, then you should not act unless one of the exceptions under paragraph 6.2 applies ... This is because it is likely that a conflict will arise.

You may also need to consider if there would be disclosure concerns if all information material to their matter cannot be disclosed to each client and they have not agreed an appropriate waiver on an informed basis.

You must always be sure that it is in each client's best interests for you to act. Bear in mind that if you were acting for just one client, you normally would be negotiating their position and putting forward solutions that favour their interests over the other client. So by acting for both, you may be limiting the service that you would provide.'

1   SRA guidance, 'Conflicts of interest', 29 October 2019, updated 2 March 2020.

4.99

The Law Society has produced the following guidance:[1]

'Acting for a buyer and a seller

There is a high risk of a conflict of interest if you act for both a buyer and a seller. You'll need to decide whether there is a conflict in the circumstances. If there is, then you should not act for both clients.

The SRA's exception for circumstances where the two clients have a "substantially common interest" does not apply to a property purchase. Although both clients will have a common interest in completing the sale, they also have different interests, since one is buying and one is selling.

There may be limited circumstances where it is appropriate for you to act for both parties. If you do this, you should make sure that your decision is in the best interests of both clients. You'll also need to be able to justify your decision to the SRA. Record your decision and your reasoning.

Acting for a lender and a borrower

You should only act for both the lender and the borrower on the grant of a mortgage if there is no conflict of interest between the two, and no risk of a conflict.

The risk of a conflict is high if:

- the mortgage is not a standard mortgage (such as one provided in the normal course of the lender's activities, where a significant part of the lender's activities consists of lending and the mortgage is on standard terms) of property to be used as the borrower's private residence

- the mortgage is a standard mortgage but you do not use the approved certificate of title

Even if these criteria do not apply, you should still consider each case to make sure there's no conflict of interest.

Buy-to-let mortgages

If the property will be used as a buy to let, this will not meet the criterion for a standard mortgage that the property is used as the borrower's private home.

If you're considering acting for both lender and borrower in a buy-to-let purchase, you may want to:

- assess each case individually

- consider the risk of a conflict arising

- document your reasoning if you choose to act for both borrower and lender

- check the lender's position on whether you should act for both parties

- have separate files for the lender and the borrower

Confidentiality and disclosure

You should think carefully about confidentiality issues when considering acting for clients who are the lender and borrower, or buyer and seller. Your duties of confidentiality and disclosure may create a conflict of interest.'

1   Law Society, 'Conflict of interests in conveyancing', 18 June 2020.

4.100

In the absence of extensive guidance on conflicts in relation to the 2019 Codes, the indicative behaviours in the 2011 Code provide some further assistance. The SRA has stated that they were excluded from the 2019 Codes because they were being misinterpreted as rigid requirements rather than indicators.[1] As that is why they were excluded, and as the substantive rules on conflicts have not changed from those in the 2011 Code, they do provide some guidance on the SRA's expectations. The main provisions concerning conflicts were indicative behaviours 3.3 to 3.7, which provided that acting in the following way(s) may tend to show that you have achieved these outcomes and therefore complied with the Principles:

IB(3.3) declining to act for *clients* where you may need to negotiate on matters of substance on their behalf, for example negotiating on price between a buyer and seller of a property;

IB(3.4) declining to act where there is unequal bargaining power between the *clients*, for example acting for a seller and buyer where a builder is selling to a non-commercial *client*;

IB(3.5) declining to act for *clients* under Outcome 3.6 (*substantially common interest*) or Outcome 3.7 (*competing for the same objective*) where the *clients* cannot be represented even-handedly, or will be prejudiced by lack of separate representation;

IB(3.6) acting for *clients* under Outcome 3.7 (*competing for the same objective*) only where the *clients* are sophisticated users of legal services;

IB(3.7) acting for *clients* who are the lender and borrower on the grant of a mortgage of land only where:

(a)   the mortgage is a standard mortgage (i.e. one provided in the normal course of the lender's activities, where a significant part of the lender's activities consists of lending and the mortgage is on standard terms) of property to be used as the borrower's private residence;

(b)   you are satisfied that it is reasonable and in the *clients'* best interests for you to act; and

(c)   the certificate of title required by the lender is in the form approved by the *Society* and the Council of Mortgage Lenders.

1   'Application for the approval of regulatory arrangements', issued by the SRA in August 2018, para 91.

4.101

Property lawyers, and firms, can take the safest line and simply not act for buyer and seller, or can decide that transactions will be assessed individually on a case-by-case basis. If the latter course is taken and the solicitor decides to act on both sides of the transaction, he or she will be well advised to make a contemporaneous documentary record of why that decision was taken.

A problem arises from the SRA's 'default position', that normally there will be a conflict of interests. A property lawyer who genuinely believes that in a particular case there is no conflict, but that there is nothing out of the ordinary about the transaction, may struggle to convince the SRA that it is in the narrow category where it is proper to act.

Regard must also be had to the Code for Firms: firms of all sizes must be able to demonstrate appropriate systems and controls, including staff training, to identify and assess potential conflicts.

Confidentiality and disclosure

4.102

> 6.3 You keep the affairs of current and former *clients* confidential unless disclosure is required or permitted by law or the *client* consents.
>
> 6.4 Where you are acting for a *client* on a matter, you make the *client* aware of all information material to the matter of which you have knowledge, except when:
>
> (a) the disclosure of the information is prohibited by legal restrictions imposed in the interests of national security or the prevention of crime;
>
> (b) your *client* gives informed consent, given or evidenced in writing, to the information not being disclosed to them;
>
> (c) you have reason to believe that serious physical or mental injury will be caused to your *client* or another if the information is disclosed; or
>
> (d) the information is contained in a privileged document that you have knowledge of only because it has been mistakenly disclosed.
>
> 6.5 You do not act for a *client* in a matter where that *client* has an interest adverse to the interest of another current or former *client* of you or your business or employer, for whom you or your business or employer holds confidential information which is material to that matter, unless:
>
> (a) effective measures have been taken which result in there being no real risk of disclosure of the confidential information; or
>
> (b) the current or former *client* whose information your business or employer holds has given informed consent, given or evidenced in writing, to you acting, including to any measures taken to protect their information.

4.103

The fiduciary relationship between a solicitor and client gives rise to a number of duties including a duty not to disclose confidential information to others unless there is a clear obligation or principle overriding that duty, such as fraud on the part of the client or disciplinary proceedings.[1] The duty of confidentiality continues beyond the end of the retainer, and is owed to former clients as well as current clients.

The fiduciary relationship also gives rise to a duty to disclose information material to a retainer. In *Hilton v Barker Booth & Eastwood*[2] Lord Scott observed that the duty was 'both contractual and fiduciary, the content of the contractual duty of full disclosure being rooted in the fiduciary relationship between solicitor and client'.

The SRA Glossary defines client to mean 'the person for whom you act and, where the context permits, includes prospective and former clients'.

In practice, if a confidentiality issue arises in relation to two or more *current* clients, the principles on conflicts of interest in paragraph 6.2 are also likely to be applicable.

1   See *Finers v Miro* [1991] 1 WLR 35 and *Parry-Jones v Law Society* [1968] Ch 195.
2   [2005] UKHL 8.

4.104

A solicitor facing the conflicting duties of disclosure and confidentiality may have to cease acting on the grounds of a conflict of interest (see paragraphs 6.1 and 6.2) and may be liable to compensate a client who is not supplied with information.[1]

A decision not to supply a client with information, on the ground that the information is confidential to another current or former client, could also lead to a professional complaint. In a guidance note, the SRA has stated:

> '[You could] find yourself in a position where your duty of confidentiality to another current or former client (A) prevents you from disclosing evidence that you obtained in relation to A's case to your new client (B). The fact that you cannot meet your obligations to B because of your obligation to A will be no defence in those circumstances either to a claim against you by B or in relation to a breach of your obligations under paragraph 6.4.'[2]

It is therefore important to consider whether the duty of disclosure owed to a new client could lead to a conflict between the competing duties of disclosure and confidentiality before agreeing to take on the new work.[3] Once the work is taken on, it may be too late to prevent a civil claim or a professional complaint.

1   See *Hilton v Barker Booth & Eastwood* [2005] UKHL 8. It is important to note that outcome 4.3 of the 2011 Code (which provided that, where a duty of confidentiality to one client comes into conflict with a duty of disclosure to another client, the duty of confidentiality takes precedence) has not found its way into the 2019 Codes. The question whether one duty takes priority over the other needs to be considered with care.
2   SRA guidance, 'Unregulated organisations – conflict and confidentiality', 23 July 2019, updated 25 November 2019. Although the guidance note relates to solicitors working in unregulated organisations, the risk of conflict between the competing duties of disclosure and confidentiality applies to all solicitors.
3   The competing duties could be resolved by information barriers and informed consent; see **4.106**.

Inadvertent disclosure of privileged material

4.105

Privileged documents inadvertently disclosed in civil proceedings will in some circumstances have to be returned to the opponent, and not disclosed to the client. The test for deciding whether the documents have to be returned is set out in *Al-Fayed v Commissioner of Police for the Metropolis:*[1]

> 'The court may grant an injunction if the documents have been made available for inspection as a result of an obvious mistake. A mistake is likely to be held to be obvious ... where the documents are received by a solicitor and (a) the solicitor appreciates that a mistake has been made before making some use of the documents or (b) it would be obvious to a reasonable solicitor in his position that a mistake has been made; and in either case there are no other circumstances which would make it unjust or inequitable to grant relief.'

Where a mistake is obvious, lawyers on both sides should co-operate to resolve the matter as soon as possible. Both parties are subject to a duty of honesty and it should not be necessary to involve the court.[2]

1 [2002] EWCA Civ 780.
2 *Atlantisrealm Ltd v Intelligent Land Investments (Renewable Energy) Ltd* [2017] EWCA Civ 1029.

Informed consent and information barriers

4.106

There are exceptional circumstances in which it is possible to act for one client, to whom a duty would be owed to disclose material information, when there is a contemporaneous duty of confidentiality to a second client (or former client) which would prevent such disclosure. It is possible to continue to act, provided that (a) effective measures have been taken which result in there being no real risk of disclosure of confidential information or (b) the client or former client has given informed consent, given or evidenced in writing, to the solicitor acting, and to any measures taken to protect the information. It is important to recognise that this is an exception to the normal absolute rule that continuing to act in these circumstances would be bound to put a solicitor, the managers or the firm in breach of duties owed to one or other of the clients, and therefore impossible.[1]

If the matter relates to two clients, and there is a conflict of interest, the solicitor must also comply with paragraph 6.2.

1 See eg *Hilton v Barker Booth & Eastwood (a firm)* [2005] UKHL 8, [2005] 1 WLR 567.

4.107

As for informed consent from the client or former client entitled to confidentiality, solicitors will need to justify their approach should questions be raised by the SRA or the courts. A detailed written record of all aspects of the matter relating to obtaining the informed consent will therefore be all but essential. Particular caution should be exercised where the clients or former clients are not sophisticated users of legal services.

In its guidance note, the SRA has stated that, for there to be informed consent, a client or former client must have an understanding of any possible prejudice which could occur. That means that the person seeking the consent must be someone other than the person proposing to carry out the work for the new client, as the confidential information of the client or former client would have to be disclosed to the person obtaining consent to ensure the client or former client understands the possible prejudice.[1]

1   SRA guidance, 'Unregulated organisations – conflict and confidentiality', 23 July 2019, updated 25 November 2019.

4.108

Paragraph 6.5 does not contain an express requirement to obtain informed consent to an information barrier from the client to whom the duty of disclosure is owed. Practitioners should consider whether there is an underlying fiduciary obligation giving rise to a firm's need for consent, even if that is not required under the 2019 Codes.[1] See **4.111**.

1   Outcome 4.4(a) of the 2011 Code included a requirement to obtain informed consent from the client to whom the duty of disclosure is owed, but that requirement has not been included in the 2019 Codes. Under paragraph 6.4 of the Code for Individuals and paragraph 6.4 of the Code for Firms, there is an obligation on the individual acting for that client to make the client aware of all information material to the matter of which the individual has knowledge. That would include the existence of the information barrier.

4.109

To set up information barriers (which are also known as Chinese walls or ethical walls) an understanding of the law is required. The leading case, which relates to an information barrier between a client and a former client, is *Bolkiah v KPMG*,[1] particularly the speech of Lord Millett. The principles are helpfully extracted and summarised in *Koch Shipping Inc v Richards Butler*,[2] in the following terms (at [24]):[3]

'(1)   The Court's jurisdiction to intervene is founded on the right of the former client to the protection of his confidential information (per Lord Millett at p.234).

(2)   The only duty to the former client which survives the termination of the client relationship is a continuing duty to preserve the confidentiality of information imparted during its subsistence (per Lord Millett at p.235).

(3)   The duty to preserve confidentiality is unqualified. It is a duty to keep the information confidential, not merely to take all reasonable steps to do so (per Lord Millett at p.235).

(4)   The former client cannot be protected completely from accidental or inadvertent disclosure, but he is entitled to prevent his former solicitor from exposing him to any avoidable risk. This includes the increased risk of the use of the information to his prejudice arising from the acceptance of instructions to act for another client with an adverse interest in a matter to which the information may be relevant (per Lord Millett at pp.235–236).

(5)   The former client must establish that the defendant solicitors possess confidential information which is or might be relevant to the matter

CHAPTER 4
SRA CODE OF CONDUCT FOR SOLICITORS, RELS AND RFLS

and to the disclosure of which he has not consented (per Lord Millett at pp.234–235).

(6)   The burden then passes to the defendant solicitors to show that there is *no risk* of disclosure. The court should intervene unless it is satisfied that there is no risk of disclosure. The risk must be a real one, and not merely fanciful or theoretical, but it need not be substantial (per Lord Millett at p.237).

(7)   It is wrong in principle to conduct a balancing exercise. If the former client establishes the facts in (5) above, the former client is entitled to an injunction unless the defendant solicitors show that there is no risk of disclosure.

(8)   In considering whether the solicitors have shown that there is no risk of disclosure, the starting point must be that, unless special measures are taken, information moves within a firm (per Lord Millett at p.237). However, that is only the starting point. The Prince Jefri case does not establish a rule of law that special measures have to be taken to prevent the information passing within a firm: see also *Young v Robson Rhodes* [1999] 3 All ER 524, per Laddie J at p.538. On the other hand, the courts should restrain the solicitors from acting unless satisfied on the basis of clear and convincing evidence that all effective measures have been taken to ensure that no disclosure will occur (per Lord Millett at pp.237–238, where he adapted the test identified by Sopinka J in *MacDonald Estate v Martin* (1991) 77 DLR (4th) 249 at p.269). This is a heavy burden (per Lord Millett at p.239).'

And at [25]:

'It is to my mind important to emphasise that each case turns on its own facts.'

In *Gus Consulting GmbH v LeBoeuf Lamb Greene & Macrae*[4] (a case involving a current client and a former client) the 'ethical wall' involved three main steps: software preventing access to any electronic documents relating to restricted matters; allocation of a matter number used in archive management software to prevent given lawyers from being able to retrieve any files; and the files were physically stamped as being restricted. In addition, instructions were disseminated internally to draw attention to the importance of the confidential material not coming to the attention of anybody, particularly those in the team working on the arbitration. The sensitive material related to transactions which had taken place and been concluded some years previously. It was only upon the basis of these arrangements and the undertakings that the court was persuaded not to restrain the firm from acting by injunction.

In *Georgian American Alloys Inc v White & Case*[5] (a case involving two current clients) the firm used industry standard software to build an electronic 'ethical screen' between the teams of individuals on the opposite sides. The software automatically added a fee earner and his or her secretary to one side of the ethical screen as soon as any relevant documents relating to that side of the ethical screen were accessed, and the individuals on one side of the ethical screen could not access documents which related to the client on the other side of the ethical screen. The High Court granted an injunction restraining White & Case from continuing to act in circumstances where the ethical screen was not put in place until ten months after the work started, the firm had not produced evidence to show that all the fee earners, including those who had left, had not accessed confidential information from the other side of the ethical screen and the ethical screen did not prevent disclosure by telephone or on a face-to-face basis in circumstances where some members of the opposing side shared the same office or could meet for events organised by the firm.

1   [1999] 2 AC 222, HL. See also *Marks & Spencer plc v Freshfields* [2004] EWCA Civ 741.
2   [2002] EWCA Civ 1280, [2003] PNLR 11.
3   A useful example of the practical measures necessary to be taken can be seen from the undertakings given by the solicitors in *Gus Consulting GmbH v LeBoeuf Lamb Greene & Macrae* [2006] EWCA Civ 683, [2006] PNLR 32 at [20].
4   [2006] EWCA Civ 369.
5   [2014] EWHC 94 (Comm).

4.110

It follows that every case will remain fact sensitive, and unless the arrangements are effective, it would not be lawful for a firm to continue acting, unless it were to be possible – on the basis of informed consent by the affected client – to impose safeguards which were less than is required by the common law.

In its guidance note, the SRA states:

> 'Examples of effective measures … could … include a combination of:
>
> ● Systems that identify the potential confidentiality issue
>
> ● Separate departments handling the cases
>
> ● Separate servers so that information cannot be cross accessed
>
> ● Information being encrypted, and password protected
>
> ● Relevant individuals in the firm being aware of the "information barrier" and knowing not to cross it
>
> ● Appropriate organisational policies and training for staff …'[1]

In practice it is likely to be difficult to implement effective safeguards and information barriers if the firm is small, if the physical structure or layout of the firm means that it will be difficult to preserve confidentiality or if the clients are not sophisticated users of legal services. While this is not a 'City firm only' rule or '20+ partner only' rule, in reality it is unlikely in the extreme that any small firm would be able to achieve an effective barrier.

1   SRA guidance, 'Unregulated organisations – conflict and confidentiality', 23 July 2019, updated 25 November 2019. Although the guidance note relates to solicitors working in unregulated organisations, the standards for effective safeguards are required as a matter of law and the same high standards apply to all organisations whether they are regulated or unregulated.

A practical checklist

4.111

The 2019 Codes do not address the obligations owed to the new client for whom the firm will act if the information barrier is put in place. If a solicitor wishes to use the exception provided by paragraph 6.5(a) the following checklist may assist (where A is a new client who would be interested in receiving information, and B is a client or former client whose right to confidentiality is in play):

- Would it be reasonable, in principle, for the firm to act for A if effective safeguards to protect B could be put in place? Would this be in A's interests? One could envisage a situation in which those acting for A within the firm might have been compromised by learning of the confidential information so that, as a minimum, a new team would have to take over immediately, and it might on balance be better if A instructs a different firm. There may also be situations in which there is a risk that B will apply for an injunction against the firm and obtain an order restraining the firm from continuing to act. If so, is it in A's interest for that risk to be taken? If the answers to those questions are yes:

- A must give informed consent; that is, A must be informed that the firm has information of potential value that it cannot disclose. The firm would almost certainly not be in a position to identify B as the source of that information or to say anything more about it, although, for example, as a result of a protest by B, A may otherwise learn something of this. A must be content, without knowing more, for the firm to continue acting on the basis that the information will never be disclosed. This would require a sophisticated thought process and an enlightened individual or body, well able to understand among other things that there will be 'no cheating'. A should also be warned of the risk of an application for an injunction, and the consequences of an injunction, if there is such a risk. If A does give informed consent, either:

- B is consulted, agrees that the firm may continue to act and agrees the safeguards to be put in place to protect the confidential information, which could be to a standard sufficient to meet the common law requirements, or something less; or

- In the absence of B's informed consent, effective barriers are put in place to meet the firm's obligations under the 2019 Codes and at law.

Co-operation and accountability

4.112

7.1 You keep up to date with and follow the law and regulation governing the way you work.

7.2 You are able to justify your decisions and actions in order to demonstrate compliance with your obligations under the *SRA's regulatory arrangements*.

7.3 You cooperate with the *SRA*, other regulators, ombudsmen, and those bodies with a role overseeing and supervising the delivery of, or investigating concerns in relation to, legal services.

7.4 You respond promptly to the *SRA* and:

    (a) provide full and accurate explanations, information and documents in response to any request or requirement; and

    (b) ensure that relevant information which is held by you, or by third parties carrying out functions on your behalf which are critical to the delivery of your legal services, is available for inspection by the *SRA*.

7.5 You do not attempt to prevent anyone from providing information to the *SRA* or any other body exercising regulatory, supervisory, investigatory or prosecutory functions in the public interest.

7.6 You notify the *SRA* promptly if:

(a) you are subject to any criminal charge, conviction or caution, subject to the Rehabilitation of Offenders Act 1974;

(b) a *relevant insolvency event* occurs in relation to you; or

(c) if you become aware:

(i) of any material changes to information previously provided to the *SRA*, by you or on your behalf, about you or your practice, including any change to information recorded in the *register*; and

(ii) that information provided to the *SRA*, by you or on your behalf, about you or your practice is or may be false, misleading, incomplete or inaccurate.

7.7 You report promptly to the SRA or another *approved regulator*, as appropriate, any facts or matters that you reasonably believe are capable of amounting to a serious breach of their regulatory arrangements by any *person* regulated by them (including you).

7.8 Notwithstanding paragraph 7.7, you inform the *SRA* promptly of any facts or matters that you reasonably believe should be brought to its attention in order that it may investigate whether a serious breach of its *regulatory arrangements* has occurred or otherwise exercise its regulatory powers.

7.9 You do not subject any *person* to detrimental treatment for making or proposing to make a report or providing or proposing to provide information based on a reasonably held belief under paragraph 7.7 or 7.8 above, or paragraph 3.9, 3.10, 9.1(d) or (e) or 9.2(b) or (c) of the SRA Code of Conduct for Firms, irrespective of whether the *SRA* or another *approved regulator* subsequently investigates or takes any action in relation to the facts or matters in question.

7.10 You act promptly to take any remedial action requested by the *SRA*. If requested to do so by the *SRA* you investigate whether there have been any serious breaches that should be reported to the *SRA*.

7.11 You are honest and open with *clients* if things go wrong, and if a *client* suffers loss or harm as a result you put matters right (if possible) and explain fully and promptly what has happened and the likely impact. If requested to do so by the *SRA* you investigate whether anyone may have a claim against you, provide the *SRA* with a report on the outcome of your investigation, and notify relevant persons that they may have such a claim, accordingly.

7.12 Any obligation under this section or otherwise to notify, or provide information to, the *SRA* will be satisfied if you provide information to your firm's *COLP* or *COFA*, as and where appropriate, on the understanding that they will do so.

4.113

Section 7 stands out because of the prescriptive nature of its rules. The clear message for solicitors is that all of those regulated by the SRA must co-operate in all respects with their regulator.

For the most part, the contents of section 7 speak for themselves.

4.114

The SRA has stated that paragraph 7.1 has been included in the Code for Individuals so that there is a provision 'requiring solicitors or authorised firms (or their managers and employees) to stay up to date with legal developments and the regulatory framework linked to their area of work which reflects the principles of continuing competence'.[1]

1 'Looking to the future – flexibility and public protection', issued by the SRA in June 2016, Annex 4, p 11.

Information held by third parties

4.115

By paragraph 7.4(b) a solicitor must ensure that information held by third parties carrying out functions on behalf of the solicitor which are critical to the delivery of legal services is available for inspection by the SRA.

In order to be able to comply with paragraph 7.4, it is advisable to include a term in contracts with third parties which requires the third party to produce records and other information on demand, coupled with a provision that the term continues after termination of the services supplied under the contract.

Non-disclosure agreements

4.116

By paragraph 7.5 a solicitor must not attempt to prevent anyone from providing information to anybody exercising a regulatory, supervisory, investigatory or pros-ecutorial function in the public interest.

Paragraph 7.5 is very wide. In July 2018 the Women and Equalities Committee (WESC) published a report on the prevalence of sexual harassment in the work-place, which was critical of solicitors who improperly use settlement agreements to silence victims of sexual harassment, and critical of regulators who do not do enough.[1] Paragraph 7.5 prevents managers in law firms who are dealing with internal complaints of sexual harassment from entering into non-disclosure agree-ments (NDAs) which prevent victims from reporting the matter to the police as well as the SRA. It also prevents employment lawyers dealing with sexual harassment cases for employers in any sector from imposing similar NDAs on victims. In sexual harassment cases, paragraph 7.5 should be considered in conjunction with the SRA warning notice on NDAs which recognises that NDAs can be used to protect commercial interests but makes it clear that the confidentiality clause in an NDA must have exceptions permitting the victim to report the matter to regulators and law enforcement agencies.[2]

1   WESC, 'Sexual harassment in the workplace', issued 25 July 2018.
2   SRA warning notice, 'Use of non-disclosure agreements', issued 12 March 2018, updated 12 November 2020. See also **4.11**.

Criminal charges, convictions and cautions

4.117

Under paragraph 7.6(a) a solicitor has to notify the SRA of any criminal charge, conviction or caution (subject to the Rehabilitation of Offenders Act 1974).

The SRA's Enforcement Strategy states that the SRA will always investigate criminal convictions or cautions, whether or not they relate to the individual's practice. The regulator is unlikely to be concerned about behaviour which is low level in terms of seriousness, such as minor motoring offences, but will take seriously convictions for drink driving, assault and other offences against the person, and property offences.[1] The guidance notes published by the SRA relating to the 2019 Codes include a topic guide on drink driving convictions and a topic guide on criminal offences. The topic guide on drink driving states that one-off offences with good mitigation are likely to result in a warning, whereas serious cases with, for example, a history of drink driving will be referred to the Tribunal.[2] The topic guide on criminal convictions states that the SRA will not generally look behind a criminal conviction and points out that a person who accepts a caution admits that an offence has been committed.[3]

1   SRA Enforcement Strategy, issued February 2019, updated 25 November 2019.
2   SRA topic guide, 'Driving with excess alcohol convictions', 7 February 2019, updated 25 November 2019.
3   SRA topic guide, 'Criminal offences outside of practice', 7 February 2019, updated 25 November 2019.

Financial difficulty

4.118

Paragraph 7.6(a) requires a solicitor to notify the SRA when a 'relevant insolvency event' occurs in relation to the solicitor. The definition of 'relevant insolvency event' in the SRA Glossary relates to insolvency events concerning the firm or regulated entity, and not the individual. That may have been unintentional, as personal insolvency is relevant to questions of whether an individual should act as a manager and hold client money.

There is a strong emphasis on informing the SRA when financial difficulties arise in a regulated entity (see **5.32**).

Self-reporting and reporting others

4.119

Paragraphs 7.7 and 7.8 impose reporting obligations relating to a 'serious' breach of the regulatory arrangements. The 2019 Codes and the SRA Glossary do not define a 'serious' breach. There was a similar lacuna in the 2011 Code, and that led to widespread uncertainty and confusion in the profession as to what should be reported.

The reporting obligations under paragraphs 7.7 and 7.8 are wide. Paragraph 7.7 requires a solicitor to report any facts or matters which the solicitor reasonably believes are capable of amounting to a serious breach by any regulated person (including the solicitor) of their regulatory arrangements to that person's approved regulator.[1] For example, a serious breach by a chartered legal executive would have to be reported to the Chartered Institute of Legal Executives (CILEx). A solicitor who is also a notary would have to self-report a serious breach to the Master of Faculties as well as the SRA.

Paragraph 7.8 requires a solicitor to report to the SRA any facts or matters which the solicitor reasonably believes should be brought to the SRA's attention so that it may investigate whether a serious breach of the SRA's regulatory arrangements has occurred. Paragraph 7.8 also requires a solicitor to report to the SRA any facts or matters which should be brought to its attention in order that it may otherwise exercise its regulatory powers. The SRA's regulatory powers include intervention, the imposition of conditions on a firm's authorisation, the withdrawal of approval of the compliance officer for legal practice (COLP) or compliance officer for finance and administration (COFA) and the imposition of conditions on practising certificates.

The requirement in paragraphs 7.7 and 7.8 to report facts or matters which could comprise a serious breach was introduced into the 2019 Codes by a late amendment to the regulatory arrangements approved by the LSB on 9 May 2019. When applying for approval for the amendments, the SRA said that some solicitors thought they only had to make a report if they had carried out an investigation which conclusively proved that there was a serious breach. The amendment is designed to ensure that reports are made at an earlier stage.[2]

The SRA has stated that the test for making a report combines a subjective element (what the person making a report believes) with an objective element (the belief was reasonable bearing in mind the circumstances, information and evidence available to the decision-maker). That serves to avoid a reporting of mere allegations and suspicions and provides a balance on the spectrum between that on the one hand and fully investigated findings on the other.[3]

Paragraph 7.9 prohibits the detrimental treatment of persons who make reports. The SRA has stated that paragraph 7.9 is designed to ensure that those who make reports are supported in making what can sometimes be difficult decisions, and that solicitors are clear that they should not subject anyone making or intending to make a report to detrimental treatment for doing so.[4]

Paragraph 7.12 states that an obligation to report to the SRA is satisfied if the information is provided to the firm's COLP or COFA on the understanding that they will then make a report to the SRA. That relates only to the SRA; the solicitor still has to personally make a direct report to any other approved regulator.

1   The SRA Glossary defines 'approved regulator' to mean 'any body listed as an approved regulator in paragraph 1 of Schedule 4 to the LSA or designated as an approved regulator under paragraph 17 of that Schedule'. In shorthand, that means the regulators approved by the LSB.

2   See the LSB final decision notice dated 9 May 2019.
3   See SRA application to the LSB dated 18 April 2019 for the approval of amendments to introduce
     new SRA Regulatory Arrangements (Reporting Concerns) (Amendment) Rules, and paragraph 7
     of the LSB final decision notice dated 9 May 2019.
4   As above, see SRA application to the LSB dated 18 April 2019 and paragraph 7 of the LSB final
     decision notice dated 9 May 2019.

Schemes of redress

4.120

Paragraph 7.11 effectively permits the SRA to require solicitors to *investigate* whether any person may have a claim for redress; to *report* the outcome of the investigation; and to *notify* persons that they may have a right of redress. The standard also requires the solicitor to 'put matters right (if possible)' if 'things go wrong' and a client suffers loss or harm.

However, solicitors should have in mind section 157(1) of LSA 2007, which provides:

> 'The regulatory arrangements of an approved regulator must not include any provision relating to redress.'

Section 158 provides, so far as relevant:

> '(1) Section 157 does not prohibit the regulatory arrangements of an approved regulator from making provision requiring, or authorising the approved regulator to require, a relevant authorised person –
>
> (a) to investigate whether there are any persons who may have a claim against the relevant authorised person in relation to a matter specified by the approved regulator;
>
> (b) to provide the approved regulator with a report on the outcome of the investigation;
>
> (c) to identify persons ("affected persons") who may have such a claim;
>
> (d) to notify affected persons that they may have such a claim;'

LSA 2007 does not authorise the SRA to require solicitors to write letters in a particular form drafted by the SRA, or to require solicitors to provide redress, as happened prior to LSA 2007 in, for example, the miners' compensation cases. The clear legislative intention is that regulators should *not* be involved in the provision of redress. The role of the regulator, as circumscribed by Parliament, is simply to require solicitors to carry out investigations, identify potential claimants, and then to notify potential claimants that they may have a claim. It is no longer part of the regulator's function effectively to organise a widespread compensation scheme for a solicitor's former clients. That is the function, if appropriate, of LeO.

When you are providing services to the public or a section of the public

4.121

Client identification

8.1   You identify who you are acting for in relation to any matter.

Complaints handling

8.2   You ensure that, as appropriate in the circumstances, you either establish and maintain, or participate in, a procedure for handling complaints in relation to the legal services you provide.

8.3   You ensure that *clients* are informed in writing at the time of engagement about:

   (a)   their right to complain to you about your services and your charges;

   (b)   how a complaint can be made and to whom; and

   (c)   any right they have to make a complaint to the *Legal Ombudsman* and when they can make any such complaint.

8.4   You ensure that when *clients* have made a complaint to you, if this has not been resolved to the *client's* satisfaction within 8 weeks following the making of a complaint they are informed, in writing:

   (a)   of any right they have to complain to the *Legal Ombudsman*, the time frame for doing so and full details of how to contact the *Legal Ombudsman*; and

   (b)   if a complaint has been brought and your complaints procedure has been exhausted:

      (i)   that you cannot settle the complaint;

      (ii)   of the name and website address of an alternative dispute resolution (ADR) approved body which would be competent to deal with the complaint; and

      (iii) whether you agree to use the scheme operated by that body.

8.5   You ensure that complaints are dealt with promptly, fairly, and free of charge.

Client information and publicity

8.6   You give *clients* information in a way they can understand. You ensure they are in a position to make informed decisions about the services they need, how their matter will be handled and the options available to them.

8.7   You ensure that *clients* receive the best possible information about how their matter will be priced and, both at the time of engagement and when appropriate as their matter progresses, about the likely overall cost of the matter and any *costs* incurred.

8.8   You ensure that any *publicity* in relation to your practice is accurate and not misleading, including that relating to your charges and the circumstances in which *interest* is payable by or to *clients*.

8.9   You do not make unsolicited approaches to members of the public, with the exception of current or former *clients*, in order to advertise legal services provided by you, or your business or employer.

8.10   You ensure that *clients* understand whether and how the services you provide are regulated. This includes:

(a)   explaining which activities will be carried out by you, as an *authorised person*;

(b)   explaining which services provided by you, your business or employer, and any *separate business* are regulated by an *approved regulator*; and

(c)   ensuring that you do not represent any business or employer which is not authorised by the *SRA*, including any *separate business*, as being regulated by the *SRA*.

8.11   You ensure that *clients* understand the regulatory protections available to them.

Client identification

4.122

The SRA has stated that the paragraph 8.1 requirement to properly identify clients has been included because of the increase in identity theft, fraud and cybercrime affecting legal businesses.[1] See also paragraph 3.1 and **4.27**.

1   SRA consultation, 'Looking to the future – flexibility and public protection', issued in June 2016.

Complaints handling

4.123

Paragraphs 8.2 to 8.4 relate to the requirement for a complaints handling procedure, and for information to be supplied to clients about complaints procedures. The obligation to set up or participate in a complaints system applies to all solicitors including solicitors working in unauthorised bodies.[1]

Paragraph 8.3 imposes a requirement that all clients are informed at the time of engagement, in writing, of their right to complain to the solicitor about their services and charges and how to do so, and of any right to complain to LeO and when to do so. It relates to all clients, including repeat clients and sophisticated clients who may not think it is necessary to be informed or reminded at the time of each engagement. However, the compulsory elements are limited to the information set out in paragraph 8.3, and so to be compliant, the relevant section of a client care letter could be very limited.

Firms need to adapt their standard documentation to match their client base and the specific needs of clients. Many clients have no right to complain to LeO. In general terms, only individuals and small businesses may do so. Larger corporate clients have no such remedy.[2] In some cases it might be that solicitors would not know at the outset, or even at the conclusion of the retainer, whether a business client is able to complain to LeO, because this is a question determined by the number of staff, turnover, balance sheet value, net asset value or annual income. In those cases it will be necessary to inform the client of the possibility of the existence of a right to complain to LeO, with the relevant time limits and contact details, subject to the client being within the LeO Scheme Rules.

Paragraph 8.3 includes a requirement to inform clients about their statutory rights to challenge bills.

Paragraph 8.4(b) was added to the 2019 Codes to take account of the EU Directive on consumer alternative dispute resolution.[3] The EU Directive was introduced to improve consumer access to ADR in the EU. By paragraph 8.4(b), if a client makes a complaint to a firm which cannot be settled to the client's satisfaction within eight weeks under the complaints handling procedure, the solicitor must inform the client in writing of not only (a) any right to complain to LeO but also (b) the name of an ADR approved body which would be competent to deal with the complaint, and whether the solicitor agrees to use the scheme operated by that body.

1   Solicitors working in unauthorised bodies are also required to inform clients of their right to complain to LeO about the service the solicitor, but not the employer, is providing – see SRA guidance, 'Giving information to clients of businesses that are not authorised by a legal services regulator', issued in August 2018.
2   See rules 2.1–2.5 of LeO Scheme Rules (**Appendix 14**), and **Chapter 14**.
3   EU Directive on Consumer Alternative Dispute Resolution (2013/11/EU), implemented by the Alternative Dispute Resolution for Consumer Disputes (Competent Authorities and Information) Regulations 2015 (SI 2015/542). SI 2015/542 was revoked in part by the Consumer Protection (Amendment etc) (EU Exit) Regulations 2018 (SI 2018/1326).

Client information and client care letters

4.124

There is no express provision in the 2019 Codes which requires a solicitor to send the client a 'client care letter'. However, paragraphs 8.1–8.11 of the Code for Individuals contain a number of rules on information which must be provided to clients and it makes sense to provide a client with all the relevant information in one letter.

The following provisions in section 8 refer to information which is relevant to client care letters:

- information about the complaints handling procedure (paragraph 8.2);
- the client's right to complain about services and charges (paragraph 8.3(a));
- how a complaint can be made and to whom (paragraph 8.3(b));
- any right to make a complaint to LeO and when such a complaint can be made (paragraph 8.3(c));
- information on how the matter will be handled (paragraph 8.6);
- the best possible information about how the matter will be priced and the likely overall cost of the matter (paragraph 8.7);

- explanation as to which activities will be carried out by the solicitor as an authorised person (paragraph 8.10(a));

- explanation as to which services are regulated by an approved regulator (paragraph 8.10(b));

- ensuring any separate business is not represented as being regulated by the SRA (paragraph 8.10(c));

- ensuring clients understand the regulatory protections available to them (paragraph 8.11).

The regulatory protections available to clients instructing SRA authorised firms vary according to the type of client and the services supplied by the firm. Typical regulatory protections include PI cover, resort to the Compensation Fund, the right to complain to LeO, the right to complain to the Information Commissioner's Office (ICO), the right to use other available regulatory redress schemes such as those of the Office of the Immigration Services Commissioner (OISC) and the FCA, and the right to assessment of costs under Part III of the Solicitors Act (SA) 1974.[1]

CHAPTER 4
SRA CODE OF CONDUCT FOR SOLICITORS, RELS AND RFLS

Other information which can be included in a client care letter varies according to the type of client and the services supplied by the firm. Practitioners dealing with consumers should consider in particular the Consumer Contracts (Information, Cancellation and Additional Charges) Regulations 2013,[2] which require legal services providers to give consumers[3] prescribed information including the main characteristics of the service, the firm's name, geographical address and telephone number, the best possible information about the likely overall cost of the matter, the length of the contract, or if it is of indeterminate duration the conditions for cancelling it, and (in the case of contracts entered into off-premises) the cancellation rights during a 14-day cancellation period.

Practitioners should also consider whether to include in a client care letter information which must be provided to recipients of services under the Provision of Services Regulations 2009.[4] See **4.130**.

An SRA guidance note on client care letters states that it is important that the client care letter is easy to understand and that one of the most common complaints is about a lack of clarity on costs.[5]

It is relevant to note that LeO has reported that costs are the single largest reason for client dissatisfaction, an indication that the profession could do much more to keep clients informed, particularly as the matter progresses and circumstances change, so that initial information needs to be updated. Most firms are well organised in giving adequate information at the outset; it is much more difficult to manage the situation and to keep clients informed about changes in costs estimates as matters proceed, frequently at a fast pace.

1   For information to be provided to clients by solicitors working in unregulated organisations see SRA guidance, 'Unregulated organisations giving information to clients', 23 July 2019, updated 25 November 2019. See also **4.136**.
2   SI 2013/3134.
3   A 'consumer' is defined as 'an individual acting for purposes which are wholly or mainly outside that individual's trade, business, craft or profession' by regulation 4 of the Consumer Contracts (Information, Cancellation and Additional Charges) Regulations 2013.
4   SI 2009/2999.
5   SRA guidance, 'Client care letters', 19 July 2019, updated 25 November 2019.

Costs – contingency fees

4.125

There is no reference in the 2019 Codes, at all, to contingency fees, either in relation to the solicitor/client retainer, or in relation to associations with other organisations who charge such fees. The closest provision is paragraph 8.6: 'You ensure [clients] are in a position to make informed decisions about the services they need, how their matter will be handled and the options available to them.' In other words, to the extent that contingency fees are lawful, they no longer raise any regulatory concern per se (but suitability and the best interests of the client need still to be considered).

The provisions of the 2019 Codes follow the law without any 'add-on' obligation or constraint. The relevant law can be summarised as follows.

Contingency fees in non-contentious work

4.126

It has always been lawful for solicitors to charge contingency fees in non-contentious work. This is currently enshrined in section 57 of SA 1974.[1] Solicitors can (and always have been able to) enter into a retainer in respect of non-contentious business whereby the solicitor can be remunerated by way of a cut of any spoils, or conditional on the result. To be enforceable a non-contentious business agreement must be in writing and signed by the person to be bound by it 'or his agent in that behalf' (section 57(3)). Section 87 of SA 1974 defines contentious business:

> '"contentious business" means business done, whether as solicitor or advocate, in or for the purposes of proceedings begun before a court or before an arbitrator, not being business which falls within the definition of non-contentious or common form probate business contained in section 128 of the Senior Courts Act 1981.'

Any business that is not within that definition is non-contentious. In order to fall within the definition, proceedings must actually have been commenced before a court or an arbitrator. Thus, work undertaken in relation to a claim which might be litigated, but which is in fact resolved without the issue of proceedings, remains outside the definition of contentious business.

Similarly, in 'proceedings' which bear all the attributes of contentious work, such as those in employment tribunals, but which are not proceedings before a court or an arbitrator, solicitors have been able to charge clients on a contingency fee basis. Contingency fee agreements in relation to employment and other matters are now subject to express regulation.[2]

Otherwise there is no statutory or regulatory limit on what a solicitor may charge by way of a contingency fee in non-contentious work. The Principles and paragraph 7.1 of course require not only that the fee agreement is legal, but also that it takes account of the client's best interests. It has, in short, to be fair.

Paragraph 8.3 requires that clients are informed about their right to challenge or complain about bills, and, where applicable, their right to complain to LeO. Costs due under a non-contentious business agreement are liable to detailed assessment and the costs judge/officer may enquire into the facts and if appropriate certify for the court that the agreement should be set aside or the amount payable reduced, and the court may so order.[3]

Solicitors need also to have one eye on the doctrine of unconscionable bargain,[4] although there is no reported example of a contingency fee agreement in non-contentious work between solicitor and client being struck down as unconscionable. If such an agreement were found to be an unconscionable bargain, not only would the agreement be unenforceable, but the solicitor would be at risk of a finding of a breach of principle 2, which requires him or her to act 'in a way that upholds public trust and confidence in the solicitors' profession and in legal services provided by authorised persons'.

1   '(1) Whether or not any order is in force under section 56, a solicitor and his client may, before or after or in the course of the transaction of any non-contentious business by the solicitor, make an agreement as to his remuneration in respect of that business. (2) The agreement may provide for the remuneration of the solicitor by a gross sum or by reference to an hourly rate, or by a commission or percentage, or by a salary, or otherwise ...'
2   Section 58AA of the Courts and Legal Services Act (CLSA) 1990 (introduced into that Act by section 154 of the Coroners and Justice Act 2009) and the Damages-Based Agreements Regulations 2013 (SI 2013/609).
3   Section 57(5) of SA 1974.
4   See **4.52**.

Contingency fees in contentious work: CFAs and DBAs

4.127

For centuries, contingency fees in contentious work were outlawed on public policy grounds as offending the rule against champerty. The scope of the law of champerty has become attenuated in the light of shifting public policy perceptions.[1] The funding revolution of the 1990s brought an end to the absolute prohibition by permitting conditional fee agreements (CFAs), and CFAs are now permitted in all types of proceedings save for family and criminal proceedings,[2] provided that they comply with formalities imposed by delegated legislation.

Following the coming into force of the relevant provisions of LASPO 2012 on 1 April 2013, the law relating to CFAs fundamentally changed again. Thenceforth, the success fee was no longer recoverable from the losing party, and a cap was imposed upon the amount of the success fee that the client would have to yield up to the solicitor out of damages in personal injury cases. At the same time, DBAs became lawful in a wide range of cases (hitherto, they had been restricted to employment law cases). These are true contingency fees, the solicitor's remuneration ordinarily being calculated as a percentage of the client's damages, subject to statutory maxima.

A detailed consideration of the legal framework for CFAs and DBAs is beyond the scope of this book.

1   See *R v Secretary of State for Transport, ex p Factortame* [2003] QB 381, CA. The issue of contingency fees and the reach of the modern law on champerty was revisited by the Court of Appeal in *Sibthorpe and Morris v Southwark LBC* [2011] EWCA Civ 25.
2   For the proceedings which cannot be subject to an enforceable CFA, see section 58A of CLSA 1990.

CHAPTER 4
SRA CODE OF CONDUCT FOR SOLICITORS, RELS AND RFLS

Introducers operating on a contingency fee basis

4.128

Practitioners who receive personal injury referrals from introducers need to be aware of the SRA's concerns relating to fees charged by introducers. In order to be able to understand and perhaps more importantly answer SRA concerns, it assists to have a broad knowledge of the historical background and the rules which the SRA has abolished in the past on the grounds that they are no longer appropriate.

The 2011 Code abolished a rule that had caused difficulty and controversy for many years. Rule 9.04 of the 2007 Code re-enacted rule 9 of SPR 1990 and provided that:

> 'You must not, in respect of any claim arising as a result of death or personal injury, either: (a) enter into an arrangement for the referral of clients with; or (b) act in association with, any person whose business, or any part of whose business, is to make, support or prosecute (whether by action or otherwise, and whether by a solicitor or agent or otherwise) claims arising as a result of death or personal injury, and who, in the course of such business, solicits or receives contingency fees in respect of such claims.'

The controversy arose from the fact that the 2007 Code, in all its draft forms up to the beginning of 2007, did not contain any such provision. The policy decision had been made to abolish the rule, not least because claims management companies were to become regulated under the Compensation Act 2006. In the event, the provision was saved, and became rule 9.01(4) of the 2007 Code, until its abolition in 2011.

Many solicitors found themselves before the SDT as a result of arrangements made with introducers who charged on a contingency fee basis in both contentious and non-contentious work. A large number of solicitors handling miners' compensation cases under the claims handling agreements relating to vibration white finger and pulmonary disease claims were disciplined between 2006 and 2010 because introducers (whether commercial entities or trades unions) had agreed to take a slice of the miners' compensation. The courts eventually ruled that these were contentious proceedings.[1] There was also a handful of successful prosecutions arising out of solicitors' arrangements with an organisation known as Justice Direct, which introduced employment tribunal and personal injury claims to solicitors in return for a 'broker's fee' calculated as 25 per cent of any sum recovered plus a percentage of the fees charged by its panel solicitors.[2]

Finally, in 2011, the rule was abolished. That is not the end of the matter, however. The focus now is upon whether the solicitor can properly maintain independence if he or she has an arrangement with an introducer, and whether the agreement between the introducer and the client is in the client's best interests. The Tribunal decision in *Tilbury* remains highly relevant, and solicitors must ask themselves when taking on a new client whether an arrangement between the client and the introducer was an unconscionable bargain or otherwise not in the best interests of the new client. This is considered in greater detail in relation to the requirements of section 5 of the Code for Individuals and paragraph 5.1(e); see **4.65** and **4.76–4.78**.

1   *Beresford and Smith v SRA* [2009] EWHC 3155 (Admin).
2   *Tilbury*, 9880–2008, SDT; *Kelsall*, 10352–2009, SDT.

Information on disbursements

4.129

In 2008 there were widespread problems over the misdescription of telegraphic transfer fees. The problem was that firms developed a practice of making a charge for undertaking routine telegraphic transfers in conveyancing. There was nothing wrong with that, but what tended to happen was that if the bank charged the firm, say, £10, the firm would make a charge to the client of £20 – but still describe the fee as a disbursement, as if it had all been paid to the bank. The mischief was neither in passing on the bank's charge, nor in charging a fee for the work entailed, but rather in misdescribing a charge as a disbursement. This misled the client and hid the fact that the firm was making an extra modest profit.

The SRA concerns on the description of disbursements should not be forgotten or overlooked. The principle continues to apply to bank charges. A similar principle applies to charges for internal photocopying, which should not normally be described as a disbursement.

Provision of Services Regulations 2009

4.130

It is convenient to deal with the Provision of Services Regulations 2009[1] at this point because they require certain information to be provided to clients, but these requirements go beyond what is required by the 2019 Codes: specifically, the firm's VAT number, details of compulsory PI insurance cover, details as to how to access the professional rules and detailed information on complaint resolution procedures, and measures to avoid conflicts of interest.[2]

Not all the information has to be provided in the same way. The VAT number and insurance information – which must include the contact details of the insurers and the territorial coverage of the insurance – may optionally be given in writing at the outset, in a client care letter or terms of business, or made easily accessible to clients in hard copy at the firm's offices or on the firm's website.

Information about professional rules, which requires a reference to the professional rules and how to access them and details of the SRA Codes of Conduct and the address at which those codes may be consulted by electronic means must be provided on request. Information on other activities undertaken by the firm which are directly linked to the service in question and on the measures taken to avoid conflicts of interest must be included in any information document in which the firm gives a detailed description of the service and must also be provided on request.[3]

Information about complaint resolution procedures involves telling clients about the role of LeO and where further information can be obtained. This must be provided in a clear and unambiguous manner in good time before the conclusion of the contract or, if there is no written contract, before the service is provided, but must also be provided in any information document in which the firm gives a detailed description of the service provided. This could therefore also be provided through a website and/or the client care letter. However, LeO provides a service only to individuals and small businesses (see **CHAPTER 14**), so that telling all clients including large corporate clients that there is a complaint resolution service through LeO when they will not, in fact, be able to take advantage of it, would be misleading and unhelpful.

1   SI 2009/2999.
2   Regulation 8(1)(g) covers VAT; 8(1)(n), insurance; 9(1)(c), conflicts of interest; 9(1)(d), professional rules; 10, complaint resolution; and 11, manner of providing information. The Provision of Services Regulations 2009 also prescribe other information to be made available to recipients of services including information on the price and main features of the service and the provider's name, legal status, geographic address, and general terms and conditions, including any terms concerning competent courts and applicable law.
3   Regulation 9(1)(c) and (2).

Publicity

4.131

In the SRA Glossary, publicity is comprehensively defined as including:

> 'all promotional material and activity, including the name or description of your firm, stationery, advertisements, brochures, websites, directory entries, media appearances, promotional press releases, and direct approaches to potential clients and other persons, whether conducted in person, in writing, or in electronic form, but does not include press releases prepared on behalf of a client.'

Paragraph 8.8 shows that one of the SRA's two concerns about publicity is that it is not misleading.

The second concern is set out in paragraph 8.9, which states that a solicitor must not make unsolicited approaches to members of the public, with the exception of current or former clients, in order to advertise legal services. An SRA guidance note[1] clarifies and to a certain extent narrows the construction of that rule by stating that advertising to the public is permitted provided it is done in a non-intrusive and non-targeted way. The guidance note states:

> '... advertising to the public is permitted, subject to certain conditions ...

> Paragraphs 8.9 and 7.1(c) of the Standards and Regulations prohibit unsolicited approaches to members of the public which, even if permitted by law, may feel unwelcome or intrusive ...

> This means you cannot make direct or specifically targeted "approaches" to members of the public in person, by phone or via other means which target them individually ...

> Specifically, you are allowed to advertise your services to the public so long as this is done in a non-intrusive and non-targeted way.

This means, for example, that you may place an advert on the radio or TV, on billboards, in a local newspaper, online or on a social media platform. None of these would be considered to be intrusive as they do not constitute approaching members of the public on a targeted or individual basis.

Sending leaflets to people's homes is allowed, but only under specific circumstances whereby the distribution could not be considered to be targeted – for example you may send leaflets to all homes within a large geographic area, but may not selectively distribute leaflets to only specific homes or individuals based on wider information you know about them.'

1   SRA guidance, 'Unsolicited approaches (advertising) to members of the public', 16 December 2019.

The Transparency Rules

4.132

On 1 December 2018 the SRA introduced the SRA Transparency Rules 2018, which relate to costs, complaints and regulatory information.[1] The rules apply to all regulated firms and the information must be published in a prominent location on the firm's website. If there is no website the information must be made available to any member of the public on request.

Costs information must be publicised for specified categories of work carried out for individuals and businesses. For individuals, costs information is required for residential conveyancing (including remortgages), uncontested probate, immigration applications and Tribunal appeals (excluding asylum cases), summary only road traffic offences and Employment Tribunal claims for unfair and wrongful dismissal. For businesses, costs information is required for Employment Tribunal claims for unfair and wrongful dismissal, debt recovery up to £100,000 and licensing applications. There are detailed requirements on the content of the published costs information (see the SRA Transparency Rules at **APPENDIX 5**). Those details include information on the fee earners carrying out and supervising the work, the basis of their charges and the total cost for the service (or, where that is not practicable, the average costs or range of costs).

The website must also include the firm's SRA number, the SRA's digital badge and details of the firm's complaints handling procedure (including details of how and when complaints can be made to LeO and the SRA).

The SRA Transparency Rules also state that the firm's letterhead and emails must contain the firm's SRA number and the words 'authorised and regulated by the Solicitors Regulation Authority'.[2]

The SRA Transparency Rules contain provisions for solicitors who are not working in authorised bodies to give clients information on the availability of any PI cover and any inability to make claims against the Compensation Fund; see **4.137**.

1   The rules are supplemented by detailed SRA guidance, 'Transparency in price and service', 2 October 2018, updated 3 August 2021.
2   Rule 4.2 of the SRA Transparency Rules 2018.

Information on regulated services, unregulated organisations and separate businesses

4.133

A working knowledge of the provisions of LSA 2007 relating to reserved legal activities is needed in order to understand the different practice models permitted by the 2019 regulatory arrangements, and in turn the information which needs to be supplied to clients on the regulatory protections available under each different practice model.

Under LSA 2007, subject to a small number of exceptions,[1] a person (or an entity) is only entitled to carry on a reserved legal activity if that person is authorised to do so by an approved regulator or licensing authority.[2] The approved regulators are the Law Society (acting through the SRA), the Bar Council (through the Bar Standards Board), CILEx, the Council for Licensed Conveyancers (CLC), the Chartered Institute of Patent Attorneys (CIPA), the Chartered Institute of Trade Mark Attorneys (CITMA), the Association of Costs Lawyers (ACL), the Institute of Chartered Accountants of England and Wales (ICAEW), the Association of Chartered Certified Accountants (ACCA), the Master of Faculties and the Institute of Chartered Accountants of Scotland. Some of those approved regulators, such as the Law Society (acting through the SRA), are also licensing authorities, which means that they can license ABSs that provide reserved legal activities.

The reserved legal activities are listed in section 12(1) of LSA 2007 as follows:

'(a) the exercise of a right of audience;

(b) the conduct of litigation;

(c) reserved instrument activities;

(d) probate activities;

(e) notarial activities;

(f) the administration of oaths.'

Schedule 2 to LSA 2007 (see **APPENDIX 21**) contains detailed provisions about what constitutes each of the reserved legal activities. A significant feature of the provisions is that the scope of the reserved instrument activities and the probate activities is very limited. For example, 'probate activities' means 'preparing any probate papers … [relating to England and Wales] … on which to found or oppose a grant of probate or a grant of letters of administration'. In consequence, a person who is not authorised under LSA 2007 can provide legal services relating to the administration of an estate, apart from the application for the grant.

None of the approved regulators has power to authorise all of the reserved legal activities. For example, the Master of Faculties is the only approved regulator with power to authorise notarial activities. The Law Society (acting through the SRA) has power to authorise all of the reserved legal activities apart from notarial activities. The ICAEW and the ACCA only have power to authorise probate activities.

---

1   The main exceptions relate to the provision of immigration services under the Immigration and Asylum Act 1999 and to the exemptions specified in Schedules 3 and 5 to LSA 2007.
2   Section 13(2) of LSA 2007.

4.134

In 2011, at the time of introduction of the 2011 Code, solicitors providing any type of legal services to members of the public generally had to provide the services within an authorised entity, regardless of whether the legal service was a reserved legal activity or an unreserved legal service. There were exceptions, such as solicitors practising in law centres and in-house solicitors permitted to provide pro bono work to third parties, but those exceptions were limited.

On 1 November 2015 the SRA introduced new rules on separate businesses, known as the 'separate business rules', which permitted solicitors to own and/or actively participate in a separate unregulated business which provided legal services of all kinds except for reserved legal activities.[1] That was a significant deregulatory measure because the categories of reserved legal activities are comparatively narrow and it allowed solicitors to manage or work in legal businesses which were not regulated by the SRA. The separate business rules were, however, restrictive in the sense that the solicitor could not hold himself out as practising as a solicitor in the separate business.

The 2019 regulatory arrangements relaxed the old rules even further, and allowed solicitors to work as solicitors in legal businesses which are not regulated by any approved regulator. The SRA explained the rationale for the change as follows:

> 'Our key aim is to allow bodies that previously would not have done so to employ solicitors to provide services to the public. While there are many individuals who qualified as solicitors working for non-LSA regulated businesses currently, they must give up their practising certificate and therefore regulation to do so, or act as an in-house solicitor and supervise or advise others. On the other hand, individuals without any qualifications are permitted to provide this service. We no longer think that these restrictions … can be justified … nearly any body but solicitors can deliver unreserved services outside of LSA regulated firms. …
>
> The removal in 2015 of the restrictions on solicitors owning or participating in separate businesses that are not regulated under the LSA … was a first step towards allowing solicitors to practise in a non-LSA regulated business …'[2]

At the same time, under the 2019 regulatory arrangements, the SRA relaxed the rules on authorisation of sole practitioners to permit some individuals working on their own ('freelance lawyers') to carry out unreserved legal activities and, subject to certain conditions, reserved legal activities. The rationale for that change was explained by the SRA as follows:

> 'We will allow individual self-employed solicitors and RELs that are working alone as freelancers to provide reserved legal services to the public under their individual authorisation. They would not be required to have their practice authorised as a recognised sole practice … These freelance solicitors would have to:
>
> ● act as an individual; without any employees or partners and not work through a service company
>
> ● be engaged directly by the client

- not hold client money (except for payments on account of costs and disbursements for which the freelancer is responsible).

… we recognised that by not allowing … freelance lawyers, we might be unnecessarily restricting models of practice …'[3]

1   Chapter 12 of the 2011 Code. There were separate business rules before 1 November 2015 which allowed solicitors to have interests in business which did not provide legal services, but the earlier separate business rules prevented solicitors from hiving off unreserved legal services.
2   'Application for the approval of regulatory arrangements', issued by the SRA in August 2018, paras 117–125.
3   'Application for the approval of regulatory arrangements', issued by the SRA in August 2018, paras 199–204.

4.135

The changes to models of practice introduced under the 2019 regulatory arrangements mean that there are risks that consumers will not have a clear understanding of the differing services which can be provided by differing business models or the regulatory protections (such as PI cover) available under the business model. For example, a consumer instructing a solicitor working in a non-authorised firm may assume incorrectly that the solicitor can conduct litigation or apply for a grant of probate. Equally, the consumer may assume incorrectly that the non-authorised firm must have compulsory insurance cover.

To avoid confusion of that type, paragraphs 8.10 and 8.11 require solicitors to ensure that clients understand how the services are regulated and what the regulatory protections are. In 2018 the SRA explained the rationale for the standards as follows:

'We are introducing very clear mandatory information requirements that will apply to all solicitors. We will require solicitors working in businesses that are not regulated by us, or another legal regulator, to be clear with prospective service users about the protections in place. That means that before they begin working with a client, they will need to explain their insurance arrangements position and be clear that their client will not be eligible to submit a claim to the SRA Compensation Fund if things go wrong …

… Our Code … will place responsibility on the solicitor to explain to clients which services are provided by the solicitor as an authorised person and which are provided by others, and whether those persons are authorised or not … This will help to mitigate the risk of consumer confusion under the new regulatory arrangements and also address the current position where consumers do not know what protections come with different types of providers including solicitors'.[1]

1   'Application for the approval of regulatory arrangements', issued by the SRA in August 2018, paras 145–146.

4.136

From a regulatory point of view, the main protections available to clients instructing a solicitor who is practising in an SRA authorised firm are:

- compulsory PI cover;

- resort to the Compensation Fund;

- the right to complain to LeO;

- money on account of costs held on client account subject to the SRA Accounts Rules; and

- legal professional privilege.

Not all of those protections are available to a client who instructs a solicitor who is practising under a different business model. For example, if a client instructs a solicitor working in a non-authorised firm:

- neither the solicitor nor the firm are required to have compulsory PI cover;

- clients cannot make a claim on the Compensation Fund;

- the client can complain to LeO but only about the work provided by the solicitor;

- there is no regulated client account; and

- there are arguments that legal professional privilege does not apply.

4.137

On the introduction of the 2019 regulatory arrangements, the SRA Transparency Rules 2018 were amended to include new rules 4.3 and 4.4 relating to information on PI cover and the Compensation Fund, which must be provided to clients in many circumstances by solicitors who are not working in authorised firms.

By rule 4.3 of the SRA Transparency Rules 2018, a solicitor who is providing legal services to the public or a section of the public other than through a firm that is regulated by the SRA must (a) where they are not required to have compulsory PI cover inform all clients of that fact before engagement and specify that alternative insurance arrangements are in place if that is the case (together with information about the cover provided if requested) and (b) where applicable inform the client that they will not be eligible to apply for a grant from the SRA Compensation Fund.

By rule 4.4 of the SRA Transparency Rules 2018, rule 4.3 does not apply to a solicitor working in an authorised non-SRA firm (such as a firm authorised by the ACCA) or a 'non-commercial body'.[1]

1　Section 23(2) of LSA 2007 and the SRA Glossary define non-commercial body to mean an independent trade union, a not-for-profit body or a community interest company.

4.138

In July 2019 the SRA produced a guidance note for solicitors working in unauthorised firms on information to supply to clients.[1] The guidance note includes the following:

'You will be providing [a] service on behalf of an employer that is not authorised and regulated to provide legal services, and it will be important for clients to understand this. [...]

Complying with paragraphs 8.10 and 8.11 will include explaining to the client:

- which services are provided by you as ... [a solicitor] ...

- which services are provided by others ...

- the consequences of this in terms of the different protections available if the activities are subject to our jurisdiction and that of the Legal Ombudsman.

The client [needs to be told] who will be carrying out the work on their behalf. It might be the case … that they chose to instruct the firm because they particularly wanted to use your services as a solicitor. […]

[You should explain] that we require the firms that we regulate to have compulsory minimum levels of insurance to protect clients in case something goes wrong and what these are … [b]ut that these arrangements do not apply to the firm you are in because we do not regulate it … [and you should explain] [w]hether … your work is covered by professional indemnity insurance …

[You should tell clients] [t]hat they will not be able to make a claim on the SRA Compensation Fund …

[Y]ou must set up or participate in a complaints procedure and give clients information about how to complain under that procedure. […]

Paragraphs 8.3 and 8.4 set out your obligations to inform clients of their right to complain to the Legal Ombudsman …

You should make sure that clients understand that while they … have … [a] … right to complain to [LeO and the SRA about you] … they will have no such rights in relation to your employer …'

1   SRA guidance, 'Unregulated organisations giving information to clients', 23 July 2019, updated 25 November 2019.

4.139

When providing information to clients, the solicitor working in an unauthorised organisation should bear in mind the SRA Principles, and consider whether it is in the client's best interests to instruct an organisation without regulatory protection. The solicitor should also bear in mind the standards in the Code for Individuals including, for example, the obligation to ensure that clients receive proper information on referrals (paragraph 5.1) and costs (paragraph 8.7).

4.140

As regards clients who instruct a solicitors' firm and a separate business, the SRA published guidance on 21 October 2015 on the information to supply to the clients.[1] Although part of the guidance is now obsolete, the following extracts remain helpful in setting out factors to take into account when deciding on the amount of information to provide on the division of work between regulated and unregulated businesses:

'5.   You will always be responsible for your own services and publicity to clients and for the extent to which you refer clients to separate business or divide cases with them, and you must always act in the client's best interests. There may be some circumstances where it would be appropriate for you to consider terminating your links with the separate business altogether as it may be impossible otherwise for you to comply with your obligations; for example where you consider that the separate business lacks integrity or lacks competence to deal with the cases that it is taking on. [...]

7.   The extent of the information to be provided ... will depend on the likelihood of the confusion arising.

8.   The more obviously "separate" the business, and the further away its activities are from legal activities that consumers might expect to be provided by a lawyer, then the less detail will need to be provided.

[...]

15. If a matter is divided with a separate business or the referral is for the primary purpose of the separate business carrying on legal activity, then it is important for the client to be made aware of the differences in regulatory protection and of redress between the two businesses. The concept of informed consent includes the client understanding the consequences of these differences, not just the facts of them. [...]

16. In these circumstances, the information will need to be at an appropriate level of detail and it is likely to be necessary to explicitly draw it to the client's attention, for example in a client care letter, rather than the information just being contained in terms and conditions of engagement.

17. The starting point is that clients should be informed that the work carried out by the separate business will not be regulated by the SRA and that:

●   there will be no right to complain to the Legal Ombudsman,

●   there will be no right to apply for a grant to be made out of the Compensation Fund,

●   the work will not be covered by compulsory professional indemnity insurance (PII) (you may explain what insurance arrangements the separate business has in place),

●   the work will not be covered by legal professional privilege,

●   the protections in the SRA Accounts Rules 2011 in relation to client money will not apply.

18. This is only a starting point – the test is whether the client has actual understanding of the differences in regulation and redress and the potential consequences and it is your responsibility to ensure that this is the case.

19. Where there are factors increasing vulnerability, it may well be necessary to explain these issues in more detail to ensure that the client understands the potential consequences.'

1   See 'Chapter 12 of the SRA Code of Conduct 2011 – the separate business rule (SBR)', issued on 21 October 2015.

CHAPTER 5

The SRA Code of Conduct for Firms

Introduction

5.1

The 2019 regulatory arrangements contain two codes: the SRA Code of Conduct for Solicitors, RELs and RFLs 2019 (the 'Code for Individuals') and the SRA Code of Conduct for Firms 2019 (the 'Code for Firms'). Although firm regulation became the standard from 2009, a separate code for entities did not exist prior to November 2019. In the application to the Legal Services Board (LSB) for approval of the two codes, the SRA explained its reasoning for two separate codes as follows:

> 'By introducing two separate codes, we will make the distinction clearer between what is expected of an individual solicitor and SRA regulated firms (and by extension, to their managers and employees and compliance officers). Separate codes will ensure that enforcement is similarly targeted. By adopting a structure that distinguishes between individual and firm regulation, we have also significantly reduced the overall requirements on firms and individuals …
>
> We have sought to differentiate as clearly as possible between the two codes – the systems and procedures that a firm would need to have in place, and the ethical and behavioural standards required of individual solicitors, RELs and RFLs.'[1]

The distinction between individual and firm obligations is drawn out in the introductions to the two codes. The introduction to the Code for Individuals states that the Code for Individuals sets out the 'standards of professionalism' that are expected from individuals and comprises 'a framework for ethical and competent practice'. In contrast the introduction to the Code for Firms (which is set out in full below) sets out the 'standards and business controls' that are expected in firms, and which 'aim to create and maintain the right culture and environment for the delivery of competent and ethical legal services'.

1   'Application for the approval of regulatory arrangements', issued by the SRA in August 2018, paras 87 and 92.

5.2

Although the 2019 regulatory arrangements have two codes, there are in fact five categories of persons or entities facing obligations under the 2019 Codes (individual lawyers, firms, managers, employees and compliance officers) and the Code for Firms contains the obligations imposed on the managers and compliance officers as well as employees in the firm. The managers and compliance officers are responsible for a firm's systems and controls, and it is readily understandable why their responsibilities are included in the Code for Firms. The employees, however, are not directly responsible for the firm's systems and controls and the inclusion of obligations on employees in the Code for Firms blurs the distinction between the two codes, and sometimes makes it difficult to understand which obligations are imposed on the employees.

5.3

In this chapter, we examine the 2019 Code for Firms section by section.

Firms will continue to be prosecuted for breaches of the 2011 Principles and Code (or even earlier arrangements) as misconduct will always be assessed by reference to the rules in force at the time of the alleged misconduct. There is no limitation period applicable to allegations of misconduct and prosecutions may well relate to conduct under earlier regulatory regimes. If a commentary on the 2011 Principles and Code is needed, it can found in *The Solicitor's Handbook 2017*.

5.4

The introduction to the Code for Firms is as follows:

> This Code of Conduct describes the standards and business controls that we, the SRA, and the public expect of firms (including sole practices) authorised by us to provide legal services. These aim to create and maintain the right culture and environment for the delivery of competent and ethical legal services to clients. These apply in the context of your practice: the way you run your business and all your professional activities (subject, if you are a licensed body, to any terms of your licence).
>
> Paragraphs 8.1 and 9.1 to 9.2 set out the requirements of managers and compliance officers in those firms, respectively.
>
> A serious failure to meet our standards or a serious breach of our regulatory requirements may lead to our taking regulatory action against the firm itself as an entity, or its managers or compliance officers, who each have responsibilities for ensuring that the standards and requirements are met. We may also take action against employees working within the firm for any breaches for which they are responsible. A failure or breach may be serious either in isolation or because it comprises a persistent or concerning pattern of behaviour.
>
> In addition to the regulatory requirements set by us in our Codes, Principles and our rules and regulations, we directly monitor and enforce the requirements relating to referral fees set out in section 56 of the Legal Aid, Sentencing and Punishment of Offenders Act 2012, and provisions relating to anti money laundering and counter terrorist financing, as set out in regulations made by the Treasury as in force from time to time.
>
> All of these requirements are underpinned by our Enforcement Strategy, which explains in more detail our views about the issues we consider to be serious, and our approach to taking regulatory action in the public interest.

5.5

The Code for Firms applies to all entities authorised by the Solicitors Regulation Authority (SRA), including alternative business structures (ABSs), limited liability partnerships (LLPs), limited companies, traditional firms and recognised sole practices. It does not apply to separate businesses,[1] freelance solicitors providing legal services under their individual authorisation, firms which employ solicitors but are 'authorised non-SRA firms'[2] or businesses which employ solicitors but are not authorised by a legal services regulator.[3]

The Code for Firms also applies to managers and compliance officers of entities authorised by the SRA and employees of regulated entities.[4]

1   The SRA Glossary states that 'separate business':
      'means where you own, manage or are employed by an authorised body,
      a separate business
      (a)   which you own;
      (b)   which you are owned by;
      (c)   where you actively participate in the provision of its services, including where you have any direct control over the business or any indirect control over the business through another person, or
      (d)   which you are connected with,
      and which is not an authorised body, an authorised non-SRA firm, or an overseas practice'.
2   The SRA Glossary defines an authorised non-SRA firm to mean 'a firm which is authorised to carry on legal activities as defined by section 12 of the LSA by an approved regulator other than the SRA'.
3   The SRA has produced guidance for businesses which employ solicitors but are not authorised by an approved regulator. See SRA guidance, 'Unregulated organisations for employers of SRA regulated lawyers', 23 July 2019, updated 25 November 2019.
4   See paragraphs 8.1, 9.1 and 9.2. See also **5.2** and **5.6**.

5.6

As regards employees, the introduction to the Code for Firms states that the SRA may take action against employees working within the firm, including employees who are not solicitors, for any breaches for which they are responsible. If an employee who is not a solicitor breaches the Code for Firms, the SRA has a range of disciplinary and regulatory powers which can be levelled against the employee. The main powers include a power to make an order under section 43 of the Solicitors Act (SA) 1974 prohibiting any firm from employing the employee except with the permission of the SRA (a 'section 43 order'), powers to fine employees[1] and power to refer employees to the Solicitors Disciplinary Tribunal (the Tribunal or SDT), so that the Tribunal can then fine the employee or impose an order under section 43 of SA 1974.[2] The power to fine is infrequently used in practice against employees, apart from a power to fine senior managers of ABSs, and the SRA normally seeks to control the conduct of an employee by obtaining a section 43 order. On occasion, the SRA has sought to impose both a section 43 order and a fine. See **CHAPTER 18**.

1   See section 44D of SA 1974 and section 95 of the Legal Services Act (LSA) 2007.
2   Sections 34A(2) and 47(2E) of SA 1974.

5.7

The introduction to the SRA Principles states that the Principles apply to all those regulated by the SRA, including firms. It is difficult to see how principles which are based on a state of mind, such as the duty to act with honesty, apply to firms.[1] However, other principles can clearly apply to firms, including in particular principle 6, which is the duty to act in a way which encourages equality, diversity and inclusion. Care needs to be taken to ensure that proper systems are in place to comply with that duty.[2]

1   It is also difficult to see how a corporate entity can behave with a lack of integrity, although this has been conceded in the Tribunal on at least one occasion; see *SRA v Locke Lord*, 11717-2017, SDT.
2   See **3.20** for commentary on principle 6.

5.8

When applying for LSB approval of the 2019 Codes, the SRA said that it intended to shorten the rules and remove duplication. For that reason the SRA also said that, when the same standards applied to firms and individuals, it would set out the standards in the Code for Individuals and simply include cross-references to those standards in the Code for Firms.[1] That has happened to a certain extent, as there are cross-references in the Code for Firms to the standards in the Code for Individuals relating to the courts, referrals and (loosely speaking) 'client care'.[2] However, somewhere along the way, the idea of removing all the duplication was dropped, and there are a number of standards in the Code for Firms which simply replicate the matching standard in the Code for Individuals.

In this edition of *The Solicitor's Handbook*, when standards in the Code for Firms are simply replicated in the Code for Individuals, cross-references are provided for the commentary on the matching standards in the Code for Individuals.

1   'Looking to the future – flexibility and public protection', issued by the SRA in June 2016, Annex 4, pp 3 and 9.
2   See paragraph 7.1 of the Code for Firms.

Businesses which employ solicitors and are not authorised by a legal services regulator

5.9

Businesses that employ solicitors and are not authorised by a legal services regulator are not under an obligation to comply with the Code for Firms, or any other regulatory arrangements of the SRA.

The managers of the business need to ensure that the business does not breach any of the provisions of LSA 2007 or other statutes regulating legal services. In particular, the business should not be held out to be regulated by the SRA, or any other approved regulator, and should not supply legal services to external clients which fall within the categories of reserved legal activities,[1] immigration work (unless authorised by the Office of the Immigration Services Commissioner) and claims management services (unless authorised by the Financial Conduct Authority (FCA)).

The solicitors who are employed by the businesses are under an obligation to comply with the SRA Principles, the Code for Individuals and all other regulatory arrangements which apply to them. In practice, the managers of the business will therefore need to be satisfied that suitable arrangements are in place to ensure that the employed solicitors can comply with their regulatory obligations. Important factors to take into account include the rules that the solicitor should hold a practising certificate, should not hold client money in his or her own name, must act with independence and in the best interests of clients, owes a duty of confidentiality to the client and must establish, maintain or participate in a complaints service.[2] The SRA published express guidance for solicitors working for such employers which includes specific consideration of conflicts and confidentiality.

Solicitors are encouraged to familiarise their employers with relevant guidance and to check the terms of employment of staff in relation to ensuring confidentiality and addressing conflicts of interest as well as the provision of information to clients.[3]

The retainer with the client may need contractual provisions which permit the solicitor to comply with his or her professional obligations and which also permit the business to comply with SRA requests for information. If the SRA decides to investigate the conduct of a solicitor relating to a client matter, the SRA is likely to ask for production of the client file, and can apply to the High Court for an order for a third party to produce the file under section 44BB of SA 1974. If the retainer does not permit the business to produce the client file, the business may owe a contractual duty of confidentiality to the client which prevents it from complying with the SRA request unless the client consents or the SRA takes court proceedings against the business and obtains a production order.

1   See the commentary on paragraph 8.10 at **4.135**.
2   See also the SRA guidance, 'Unregulated organisations for employers of SRA regulated lawyers', 23 July 2019, updated 25 November 2019.
3   SRA guidance, 'Unregulated organisations – conflict and confidentiality', issued 23 July 2019, updated 25 November 2019; and SRA guidance, 'Unregulated organisations giving information to clients', issued 23 July 2019, updated 25 November 2019.

Maintaining trust and acting fairly

5.10

1.1   You do not unfairly discriminate by allowing your personal views to affect your professional relationships and the way in which you provide your services.

1.2   You do not abuse your position by taking unfair advantage of *clients* or others.

1.3   You perform all *undertakings* given by you and do so within an agreed timescale or if no timescale has been agreed then within a reasonable amount of time.

1.4   You do not mislead or attempt to mislead your *clients*, the *court* or others, either by your own acts or omissions or allowing or being complicit in the acts or omissions of others (including your *client*).

1.5   You monitor, report and publish workforce diversity data, as *prescribed*.

5.11

Paragraphs 1.1 to 1.4 are identical to paragraphs 1.1 to 1.4 of the Code for Individuals. For general commentary on those standards see **4.7–4.15**.

Entities may specifically wish to take note of the Supreme Court decision in *Harcus Sinclair LLP v Your Lawyers Ltd*[1] in which the Supreme Court confirmed that undertakings given on behalf of corporate entities are not subject to the inherent supervisory jurisdiction of the High Court. While this does not affect the SRA's powers to treat a failure to comply with an undertaking as misconduct, the fact that an undertaking is not summarily enforceable in civil proceedings may be a relevant factor in assessing the nature and extent of misconduct on the part of the person who gave it.

1   [2021] UKSC 32.

5.12

Entities are also more likely to need to have particular regard to their statutory obligations under the Equality Act as employers and service providers. Paragraph 1.1 prohibits unfair discrimination. Under the Equality Act (EqA) 2010, discrimination can be direct or indirect, and the protected characteristics are age, disability, gender reassignment, marriage and civil partnership, pregnancy and maternity, race, religion or belief, and sex or sexual orientation.[1]

Direct discrimination is defined in EqA 2010 as follows: 'A person (A) discriminates against another (B) if, because of a protected characteristic, A treats B less favourably than A treats or would treat others'. There are detailed statutory provisions in EqA 2010 which qualify or extend the statutory definition in differing ways for differing protected characteristics. For example, in relation to age, direct discrimination can be justified if it is a proportionate means of achieving a legitimate aim. Direct discrimination also covers a situation where someone is treated less favourably than another person because they are thought to have a protected characteristic or because they associate with someone who has a protected characteristic.[2]

Indirect discrimination under EqA 2010 is defined as follows: 'A person (A) discriminates against another (B) if A applies to B a provision, criterion or practice which is discriminatory in relation to a relevant protected characteristic of B's.' Indirect discrimination can only be justified if it can be shown that the policy, criterion or practice is a proportionate means of achieving a legitimate aim. Indirect discrimination does not apply to pregnancy or maternity.[3]

The use of the phrase 'unfairly discriminate' rather than 'unlawfully discriminate' in paragraph 1.1 could extend the standard to behaviour beyond the discrimination prohibited by EqA 2010.

1   Section 4 of EqA 2010.
2   See sections 13 to 18 of EqA 2010.
3   Section 19 of EqA 2010.

5.13

Paragraph 1.5 imposes a specific obligation on firms to monitor, report and publish workforce diversity data 'as prescribed'. The SRA Glossary states that 'prescribed' means 'prescribed by the SRA'. At the date of this edition of *The Solicitor's Handbook*, the SRA has not prescribed any formal rules, although it does issue regular diversity questionnaires which are to be completed via mySRA. Guidance on what information should be collected, how it should be reported and how it should be published may be found on the SRA website.

Principle 6 of the SRA Principles states that you must act in a way which encourages equality, diversity and inclusion, and paragraphs 1.5 (workforce diversity data) and 1.1 (unfair discrimination) are facets of principle 6. For commentary on principle 6 see **3.20**.

5.14

The SRA published case studies on discrimination in July 2019 to supplement the 2019 Codes.[1] The case studies make it clear that the SRA regards discrimination as a serious matter which undermines the public trust and confidence in the profession. If the SRA receives a compliance officer for legal practice (COLP) report on discrimination by an employee, the SRA may look at the firm's systems and controls relating to equality, diversity and inclusion to see whether they were effective, and may also expect the firm to implement additional training for everyone in the firm.[2]

1 SRA case studies, 'Unfair discrimination', issued in July 2019.
2 See www.sra.org.uk/solicitors/resources/diversity-toolkit/your-data.

5.15

Section 1 signposts a firm's need for appropriate policies and records for undertakings and policies and procedures relating to equality, diversity and inclusion.[1]

1 For policies on equality diversity and inclusion, see SRA guidance, 'The SRA's approach to equality, diversity and inclusion', issued 17 July 2019, updated 25 November 2019.

Compliance and business systems

5.16

> 2.1 You have effective governance structures, arrangements, systems and controls in place that ensure:
>
> (a) you comply with all the *SRA's regulatory arrangements*, as well as with other regulatory and legislative requirements, which apply to you;
>
> (b) your *managers* and employees comply with the *SRA's regulatory arrangements* which apply to them;
>
> (c) your *managers* and *interest holders* and those you employ or contract with do not cause or substantially contribute to a breach of the *SRA's regulatory arrangements* by you or your *managers* or employees;
>
> (d) your *compliance officers* are able to discharge their duties under paragraphs 9.1 and 9.2 below.
>
> 2.2 You keep and maintain records to demonstrate compliance with your obligations under the *SRA's regulatory arrangements*.
>
> 2.3 You remain accountable for compliance with the *SRA's regulatory arrangements* where your work is carried out through others, including your *managers* and those you employ or contract with.
>
> 2.4 You actively monitor your financial stability and business viability. Once you are aware that you will cease to operate, you effect the orderly wind-down of your activities.
>
> 2.5 You identify, monitor and manage all material risks to your business, including those which may arise from your *connected practices*.

5.17

The responsibility for the management of the business in the broadest sense rests with the managers. The managers should determine what arrangements are appropriate to comply with legislation and the SRA's rules, to manage all material risks to the business, and to monitor financial stability and business viability.

5.18

Whereas paragraphs 2.1 to 2.3 require systems that are designed to ensure compliance, paragraphs 2.4 and 2.5 require firms to identify and monitor 'all material risks' to the business including risks to compliance and financial stability, and to take steps to manage and address issues identified.

When considering compliance with paragraphs 2.4 and 2.5, a standard question from the SRA to a firm might be: 'What are the major risks to compliance and the financial viability of your firm that you have identified, and what steps have you taken to address them?'.

This question would obviously cover the relatively traditional matters – the risk of misappropriation of funds by accounts staff, and the checks and balances established to minimise those risks – but would also relate to larger issues, such as an over-dependence on work of a particular kind, which could dry up or be lost to competition, or an over-dependence on one or a small number of sources of work the withdrawal of which would threaten the viability of the business.

The SRA publishes a Risk Outlook on an annual basis which identifies risks regarded by the SRA to be of central importance to the profession. The business risks identified in the Risk Outlook for 2020/2021 included money laundering and misuse of client money, diversity, information and cyber security, integrity and ethics, meeting legal needs and standards of service. The main focus of the 2020/2021 Risk Outlook was on the uncertain situations developing due to Covid-19 and Brexit. Many of the main risks derive from the impact of these issues, such as the prospect of severe economic downturn and the backlog in the court system.[1]

1   SRA Risk Outlook 2020/2021.

5.19

Section 2 cannot be considered in isolation, in terms of the responsibilities associated with running a business authorised by the SRA. Paragraph 8.1 imposes an obligation on all managers to ensure compliance with the Code for Firms, including all the obligations in section 2. There is a fundamental obligation on all firms including recognised sole practitioners to have a COLP and a compliance officer for finance and administration (COFA) who must be approved in these roles by the SRA, and are under a duty to ensure compliance with the regulatory arrangements.[1] In small firms the same individual may perform both roles, and a sole practitioner may be his or her own COLP and COFA, provided approval is obtained.

For a full review of the relevant rules and the responsibilities of the COLP and COFA see **CHAPTER 7**.

1   See paragraphs 9.1(b) and 9.2(a) of the Code for Firms.

Financial stability

5.20

The recession which followed the financial crisis in 2008 had a substantial impact upon the legal profession. The financial stability of many firms was called into question, and there were a number of high-profile failures of law firms. Much of the SRA's focus and resources during 2012–13 were devoted to this issue, demonstrating the central importance that financial management now has in the regulation of the profession.

It is in this area of regulation that the greatest impact of outcomes-focused regulation (OFR) has been felt, because of its focus on risk and risk avoidance. For example, a firm in which no partner or employee has ever been guilty of misconduct in the traditional sense, which has complied meticulously with the Accounts Rules and to whom any breach of the rules of conduct would be anathema, may nevertheless feel the full force of regulatory interest and supervision if it constantly struggles to stay within its overdraft limit, and to pay the VAT, PAYE and rent on time. For these are indications that the firm may not be viable, or that the partners are imprudent in terms of the level of drawings.

Not long ago, if the question were to be asked: 'Is it professional misconduct to fail to pay the office rent?' the answer would have been that the regulator was not a debt collection agency and business debts did not raise issues of conduct, although this might trigger a precautionary inspection of the firm's accounts because of the enhanced risk that money might be 'borrowed' from the client account in such circumstances.

The modern view is that the same facts could amount to a breach of paragraph 2.5 – which requires a firm to manage all risks including financial stability.

Paragraph 3.6 requires that firms notify the SRA promptly of indicators of serious financial difficulty, insolvency events or an intention to stop operating as a legal business. See **5.30** and **5.32**.

5.21

During a period of intense focus on financial stability in 2012/2013, the SRA published a non-exhaustive list of 'poor behaviours' and 'good behaviours' drawn from its experience of firms that had suffered severe financial difficulties. Although further guidance has subsequently been issued, that list remains informative.

The 'poor behaviours' are:

- drawings exceeding net profits;
- high borrowing to net asset ratios;
- increasing firm indebtedness by maintaining drawing levels;
- firms controlled by an inner circle of senior management;
- key financial information not shared with rank and file partners;
- payments made to partners irrespective of cash at the bank figure;
- all net profits drawn with no reserve capital pot retained;
- short-term borrowings to fund partners' tax bills;
- VAT receipts used as cash received;
- partners out of touch with office bank account balances; and
- heavy dependence on high overdraft borrowings.

The 'good behaviours' are:

- all partners regularly receive full financial information including office account bank balances;

- drawings are linked to cash collection targets and do not exceed profits;

- provision is made to fund partners' tax from income received;

- a capital element is retained from profit, and a capital reserve account built up;

- premises costs are contained; and

- profitability levels are tested and unprofitable work is (properly) dropped.

5.22

If a firm reports serious financial difficulties to the SRA, the firm is likely to be assigned to a member of the SRA's supervision team, who will assess the difficulties and consider the matter from a regulatory perspective. The SRA has stated that its concern is to protect clients and the wider public interest.[1] Financial advice is not provided. Possible actions which may be taken are the creation of a compliance plan in conjunction with the SRA, or an acceptance that the business has become unviable and that a plan for the orderly closure of the practice is required, under the SRA's supervision. In some cases, it may be necessary for the SRA to visit the practice and conduct an investigation. In cases where the SRA considers that clients' interests are at serious risk, it may exercise its powers of intervention.

1   SRA guidance, 'Firm closures due to financial difficulties', 5 August 2020.

Outsourcing

5.23

Paragraph 2.3 states that the firm remains accountable for compliance with the regulatory arrangements where work is carried out through others, and paragraph 2.1(c) requires the firm to have effective arrangements in place to ensure that third parties contracted by the firm do not cause or substantially contribute to a breach of the regulatory arrangements.

5.24

Traditionally, firms have always outsourced work to specialists who can provide assistance on client matters such as counsel, medical experts, tax and accountancy experts, costs lawyers and process servers. Over the past ten years, outsourcing has increased and it now embraces a wide range of other activities.

In 2011, the SRA published a non-exhaustive list of other activities that are outsourced:

- activities which would normally be conducted by a paralegal;

- initial drafting of contracts;

- legal secretarial services – digital dictation to an outsourced secretarial service for word processing or typing;

- proofreading;

- research;

- document review;

- Companies House filing;

- due diligence (for example, in connection with the purchase of a company);

- IT functions which support the delivery of legal activities; and

- business process outsourcing.[1]

1   'Q&A – Outsourcing', SRA, 10 October 2011.

5.25

In practice, those who provide traditional specialist services, such as counsel and experts instructed in litigation, are ordinarily aware of a solicitor's regulatory obligations affecting the service they provide, and are often regulated themselves, so that it is not normally necessary for any formal arrangements to be put in place to protect matters such as client confidentiality beyond standard retainers. However, firms should have regard to the need to comply with paragraph 3.3(b) of the Code for Firms which requires that information held by third parties which is critical to the firm's delivery of legal services must be made available to the SRA for inspection. See **5.31**.

When instructing a specialist such as counsel, the firm cannot ignore its responsibilities for ensuring the client is provided with a competent service. The firm would remain 'responsible' for the service overall, including the choice of counsel, and would (perhaps jointly) be liable for any mistakes in the sense that counsel's advice or drafts could not be uncritically passed on.[1]

Reserved legal activities should not be outsourced to a person who is not authorised to conduct such activities (since to conduct unauthorised reserved legal activities is unlawful).[2]

1   See *Davy-Chiesman v Davy-Chiesman* [1984] 2 WLR 291, CA per May LJ at 303: 'a solicitor is in general entitled to rely on the advice of counsel properly instructed. However, this does not operate so as to give a solicitor an immunity in every such case. A solicitor is highly trained and rightly expected to be experienced in his particular legal fields. He is under a duty at all times to exercise that degree of care, to both client and the court, that can be expected of a reasonably prudent solicitor. He is not entitled to rely blindly and with no mind of his own on counsel's views',
2   Section 14 of LSA 2007 For a summary of the reserved legal activities see **4.133**.

5.26

The SRA appears to have two main aims on outsourcing: (i) to ensure that outsourcing does not take matters outside the ability of the SRA to regulate, and (ii) the basic requirement that any practitioner would appreciate: protection of the clients' interests.

When deciding which services to outsource, and to whom, the firm should in particular bear in mind the duties to act transparently (paragraph 6.4); act in the clients' best interests (principle 7); provide a competent service (paragraph 4.2); protect client confidentiality (paragraph 6.3); protect data (see paragraphs 3.1 and 5.2); and avoid conflicts of interest (paragraphs 6.1 and 6.2). The firm should also take account of the obligation to identify, monitor and manage all material risks to a business (paragraph 2.5); the need to maintain records to demonstrate compliance with the regulatory arrangements (paragraph 2.2); and the requirement for arrangements that ensure third parties do not cause or substantially contribute to a breach of the regulatory arrangements (paragraph 2.1(c)), as well as the fact that the firm remains accountable to the SRA for work carried out through others (paragraph 2.3).

Despite the multiplicity of standards which need to be considered, outsourcing should not be regarded as something to be avoided at all costs. In relation to IT innovation, which almost inevitably involves outsourcing, the SRA has said: 'We are committed to helping solicitors and law firms develop their businesses in new ways. An innovative legal sector is essential for delivering the efficient, affordable services the public needs'.[1]

1   SRA, 'IT and innovation', issued in March 2016.

5.27

The Principles and standards should be taken into account when deciding whether to outsource an activity, including the questions of whether outsourcing is in the client's interest and what risks the firm faces if the activity is outsourced.

Once a decision has been made to outsource, the first issue is the repute of the outsourcing company. This is a growth field and new entrants to the market are to be expected. It is necessary to investigate the background of the company and to establish reputation by suitable enquiry, including the taking of references if necessary, review of the company's systems for security of data, the control of conflicts, and the protection of client confidentiality. Assurances are required as to the qualifications and competence of those who will be undertaking the work and their supervision, and also as to their ethical standards which can vary by reference to local *mores*. The supplier's data protection policies need to be aligned with the firm's policies. There need to be systems for review of the quality of the work undertaken; how problems are rectified and disputes resolved; and what records the outsourcing company is required to keep.

There should be a written contract to control, where appropriate, matters such as the protection of data; the protection of client confidentiality; the ability to audit and check the quality of the supplier's work; the supply of records to the firm and, if necessary, the SRA; and the delivery up of data and confidential information on insolvency of the supplier or termination of the contract.

5.28

When outsourcing a service, the firm needs to consider whether clients need to be informed that the service is being outsourced and whether the client's consent is needed for the supply of confidential information or data to a third party. It is difficult to see how confidential information can be passed to a third party without the client's informed consent.

If outsourcing is driven by clients, particularly sophisticated clients who may themselves be outsourcing business processes, the clients may demand reduced legal costs on the basis of similar efficiencies. The clients need to be informed of any enhanced risks arising from outsourcing. There should also be openness in charging. There is no reason why a firm cannot take a profit from outsourcing, just as it takes a profit from the product of its own employees.[1] There is no obligation to charge clients for the outsourced services at cost, any more than there is an obligation to charge for the work of employed staff at no more than their overhead cost to the firm, but equally clients will expect savings to be made and that charging policies are clear and fair.

1   See eg *Crane v Canons Leisure Centre* [2008] 1 WLR 2549, CA.

5.29

The SRA has published a report on cloud computing (which is the storing, accessing and processing of information on a network of remote servers managed by a third party and accessed over the internet). That is a form of outsourcing.

The report recognises that there are advantages of cloud computing, including cost and flexibility (it is easy to scale cloud computing resources up or down to meet requirements) and mobility (it is easy to access facilities when out of the office). However, the report also states that there are risks which must be managed:

- it is hard for the firm to see whether the outsourcer is acting compliantly;

- firms must meet their legal obligations including data protection duties, and it is important to ensure the chosen provider can meet those requirements;

- no IT system is guaranteed to work all the time and the firm should check the provider's service level agreement, contingency plans and reliability;

- firms should be sure they know what will happen if the supplier becomes insolvent;

- firms should be sure of the exit terms, including how they retrieve their data;

- firms should check the security of access arrangements; and

- sending data to an outsourcer does not remove the duty of confidentiality – it is reasonable to expect the highest standards from IT providers.[1]

1   SRA, 'IT security: keeping information and money safe', issued in December 2016.

Co-operation and accountability

5.30

3.1   You keep up to date with and follow the law and regulation governing the way you work.

3.2   You cooperate with the *SRA*, other regulators, ombudsmen and those bodies with a role overseeing and supervising the delivery of, or investigating concerns in relation to, legal services.

3.3   You respond promptly to the *SRA* and:

    (a)   provide full and accurate explanations, information and documentation in response to any requests or requirements;

    (b)   ensure that relevant information which is held by you, or by third parties carrying out functions on your behalf which are critical to the delivery of your legal services, is available for inspection by the *SRA*.

3.4   You act promptly to take any remedial action requested by the *SRA*.

3.5   You are honest and open with *clients* if things go wrong, and if a *client* suffers loss or harm as a result you put matters right (if possible) and explain fully and promptly what has happened and the likely impact. If requested to do so by the *SRA* you investigate whether anyone may have a claim against you, provide the *SRA* with a report on the outcome of your investigation, and notify relevant persons that they may have such a claim, accordingly.

3.6   You notify the *SRA* promptly:

(a)   of any indicators of serious financial difficulty relating to you;

(b)   if a *relevant insolvency event* occurs in relation to you;

(c)   if you intend to, or become aware that you will, cease operating as a legal business;

(d)   of any change to information recorded in the *register*.

3.7   You provide to the *SRA* an information report on an annual basis or such other period as specified by the *SRA* in the *prescribed* form and by the *prescribed* date.

3.8   You notify the *SRA* promptly if you become aware:

(a)   of any material changes to information previously provided to the *SRA*, by you or on your behalf, about you or your *managers*, *owners* or *compliance officers*; and

(b)   that information provided to the *SRA*, by you or on your behalf, about you or your *managers*, *owners* or *compliance officers* is or may be false, misleading, incomplete or inaccurate.

3.9   You report promptly to the *SRA* or another *approved regulator*, as appropriate, any facts or matters that you reasonably believe are capable of amounting to a serious breach of their *regulatory arrangements* by any *person* regulated by them (including you) of which you are aware. If requested to do so by the *SRA* you investigate whether there have been any serious breaches that should be reported to the *SRA*.

3.10   Notwithstanding paragraph 3.9, you inform the *SRA* promptly of any facts or matters that you reasonably believe should be brought to its attention in order that it may investigate whether a serious breach of its *regulatory arrangements* has occurred or otherwise exercise its regulatory powers.

3.11   You do not attempt to prevent anyone from providing information to the *SRA* or any other body exercising regulatory, supervisory, investigatory or prosecutory functions in the public interest.

3.12   You do not subject any *person* to detrimental treatment for making or proposing to make a report or providing, or proposing to provide, information based on a reasonably held belief under paragraph 3.9 or 3.10 above or 9.1(d) or (e) or 9.2(b) or (c) below, or under paragraph 7.7 or 7.8 of the SRA Code of Conduct for Solicitors, RELs and RFLs, irrespective of whether the *SRA* or another *approved regulator* subsequently investigates or takes any action in relation to the facts or matters in question.

5.31

All of the standards in section 3 are comparable to standards in section 7 of the Code for Individuals apart from paragraphs 3.6 to 3.8. For commentary on the comparable standards see **4.113–4.120**.

5.32

Paragraphs 3.6(a) and (b) impose requirements on firms to notify the SRA when firms are in financial difficulty. There is a strong emphasis on informing the SRA when financial difficulties arise in a regulated entity. This was a direct result of the recession and the difficult trading conditions faced by solicitors after 2008. It can also be seen as a corollary of the obligations concerning the management of the business, and the identification and management of the risks to financial stability. The SRA is anxious to ensure the orderly wind-down of law firms where the business is failing, so as to avoid the financial costs and human distress of an intervention. The sooner that the SRA is informed about an entity's financial problems, the greater will be the opportunity to avoid an intervention. Costs of interventions tend to be very high, and to fall for the most part upon the profession rather than the intervened-upon solicitor, who rarely has the funds to discharge the obligation to pay those costs.[1]

The SRA Glossary states (in summary) that a 'relevant insolvency event' occurs in relation to an entity if there is a resolution for voluntary winding up without a declaration of solvency, the body enters into administration, an administrative receiver is appointed, a meeting of creditors is held under section 95 of the Insolvency Act 1986, a court order is made for winding up, all of the managers of an unincorporated body are made bankrupt or the body is an overseas company subject to an analogous event. The SRA Glossary does not define what is meant by 'indicators of serious financial difficulty'. The difficulty would have to relate to the firm rather than any individual in the firm, and paragraph 8.1 imposes the responsibility for deciding whether such an event has occurred on all the managers, as well as the relevant compliance officer.

The COLP is responsible for reports relating to financial stability (see paragraph 9.1 of the Code for Firms and see **CHAPTER 7** on COLPs and COFAs).

1 The costs of an intervention are recoverable from an intervened-upon solicitor as a debt by virtue of paragraph 13 of Schedule 1 to SA 1974, and the costs of an intervention into a firm can be recoverable by court order from managers of the firm under Schedule 2 to the Administration of Justice Act (AJA) 1985 and Schedule 14 to LSA 2007.

5.33

Paragraph 3.6(c) imposes an obligation to notify the SRA promptly if the firm intends to cease operating as a legal business, or managers become aware that it will cease operating. This provision emphasises the need for early notification as soon as managers know the firm will close. The notification obligation relates to mergers and other business transfers, as well as situations in which the business is closed down. The SRA's primary concern relates to disorderly business closures rather than transfers. The SRA may appoint a supervisor to oversee and advise on closure issues and ensure that suitable arrangements are in place for matters such as storage and return of client files, transfer of current cases, closure of the client account and run-off cover. If proper arrangements are not put in place and clients' interests are at risk, the SRA may intervene. See **CHAPTER 17** on intervention and orderly closure.

5.34

The reporting obligations in paragraphs 3.6(d) to 3.8 essentially require firms to ensure that the details held by the SRA about the firm and its staff are up to date and accurate. The SRA Glossary definition of 'register' states 'register includes the roll and the register of solicitors with practising certificates kept under Part I of the SA, the register of European lawyers, the register of foreign lawyers and the register of authorised bodies kept under the AJA and the LSA'.

Service and competence

5.35

> 4.1   You only act for *clients* on instructions from the *client*, or from someone properly authorised to provide instructions on their behalf. If you have reason to suspect that the instructions do not represent your *client's* wishes, you do not act unless you have satisfied yourself that they do. However, in circumstances where you have legal authority to act notwithstanding that it is not possible to obtain or ascertain the instructions of your *client*, then you are subject to the overriding obligation to protect your *client's* best interests.
>
> 4.2   You ensure that the service you provide to *clients* is competent and delivered in a timely manner, and takes account of your *client's* attributes, needs and circumstances.
>
> 4.3   You ensure that your *managers* and employees are competent to carry out their role, and keep their professional knowledge and skills, as well as understanding of their legal, ethical and regulatory obligations, up to date.
>
> 4.4   You have an effective system for supervising *clients'* matters.

5.36

Section 4 of the Code for Firms is comparable to section 3 of the Code for Individuals. Paragraphs 4.1 and 4.2 contain similar provisions to paragraphs 3.1, 3.2 and 3.4 of the Code for Individuals. For general commentary on those standards see **4.27–4.40** and **4.42**.

5.37

In the 2018 application to the LSB for approval of the new regulatory arrangements, the SRA stated that the obligations in the Code for Firms on obtaining instructions (paragraph 4.1) and identifying your client (paragraph 7.1(c)) have been added because of the reported increase in identity theft, fraud and cybercrime.[1]

In relation to cybercrime, the SRA has said that the most commonly reported issue on fraudulent instructions is email modification fraud where a rogue hacks a client's email account and sends an email to the firm diverting completion monies to the rogue's bank account.[2] For the type of action the SRA recommends that firms should take to combat cybercrime see **5.43**.

1   'Looking to the future – flexibility and public protection', issued by the SRA in June 2016, Annex 4, p 11.
2   SRA, 'IT security: keeping information and money safe', issued in December 2016.

5.38

Firms carrying out claimant personal injury work should take account of the SRA warning notice of March 2016 (updated 25 November 2019) on personal injury claims when deciding what systems are needed to comply with paragraph 4.1. The warning notice states that the role of referral organisations in the sector means that solicitors should take extra caution to ensure that they are acting on valid instructions and that they are likely to have to take instructions from, or check them directly with, the client throughout the course of the case, particularly in relation to significant decisions such as whether to settle and, if so, for how much.[1]

1   SRA warning notice, 'Risk factors in personal injury claims', issued 21 March 2016, updated 25 November 2019.

5.39

Paragraph 4.3 relates to continuing competence obligations. On 1 November 2016 the SRA replaced the continuing professional development (CPD) programme with continuing competence. Under continuing competence, every solicitor with a practising certificate should reflect on their practice to identify learning needs, plan how to address those needs, complete the planned activities, record the process and make an annual declaration when applying for renewal of their practising certificate that they have reflected on their practice and addressed any identified learning and development needs. The SRA's guidance note on competence and standards of service states that a failure to consider or address training needs will be treated as an aggravating feature in professional issues relating to standard of service.[1]

1   SRA topic guide, 'Competence and standard of service', issued August 2018, updated 25 November 2019.

5.40

Paragraph 4.4 states that a firm must have an effective system for supervising client matters. The general nature of that obligation is consistent with the general tenor of the 2019 Codes, which avoid prescriptive drafting and provide flexibility, so that managers of firms can use their own judgement when applying the Code for Firms to their practice.[1] The regular checking of the quality of the work by suitably competent and experienced people is likely to be a core requirement of any system of supervision.

Rule 9.4 of the SRA Authorisation of Firms Rules 2019 states that an authorised body must have at least one manager or employee, or must procure the services of an individual who is a lawyer of England and Wales and has practised as such for a minimum of three years and who supervises the work undertaken by the authorised body (or if the body is a licensed body, the work undertaken by the body that is regulated by the SRA).

LSA 2007 has provisions relating to supervision which affect firms. If a firm carries out reserved legal activities, employees who are not authorised to carry out reserved legal activities (such as trainees and legal executives) can only carry out reserved instrument activities and probate activities at the direction of and under the supervision of a person who is entitled to carry out the activity (such as a solicitor). An employee can exercise a right of audience in proceedings heard in chambers (apart from reserved family proceedings), provided the employee's work includes assisting in the conduct of litigation and the employee is assisting under instructions given by the solicitor and under the supervision of the solicitor.[2] The employee cannot, however, conduct the litigation. If the employee carries out the permitted reserved legal activities without supervision, or if the employee conducts the litigation, the firm could commit an offence.[3] The Immigration and Asylum Act 1999 also has provisions requiring an unauthorised employee who provides immigration advice or immigration services to be supervised by a person who is qualified to provide the immigration advice and services.[4]

1   'Looking to the future – flexibility and public protection', issued by the SRA in June 2016, Annex 4, p 13.
2   See section 13(2)(b) of and Schedule 3 to LSA 2007.
3   Section 16(2) of LSA 2007.
4   Section 84 of the Immigration and Asylum Act 1999.

Client money and assets

5.41

> 5.1   You properly account to *clients* for any *financial benefit* you receive as a result of their instructions, except where they have agreed otherwise.
>
> 5.2   You safeguard money and *assets* entrusted to you by *clients* and others.

5.42

Section 5 of the Code for Firms is comparable to section 4 of the Code for Individuals. Paragraphs 5.1 and 5.2 are identical to paragraphs 4.1 and 4.2 of the Code for Individuals. For general commentary on those standards see **4.45–4.48**.

Cybercrime

5.43

The SRA has said that cybercrime is a priority risk and that firms should have robust procedures in place to combat it.[1]

In December 2016 the SRA published a report on cybercrime which stated that emails are the medium of choice for cybercriminals and that the majority of cyber-crimes reported to the SRA are email modification scams. In a typical email modification scam a rogue hacks into a client's email system and sends an email to a conveyancing solicitor which appears to be from the client but redirects the completion funds to the rogue's bank.[2] Other scams have included bogus law firms impersonating genuine law firms in an attempt to steal mortgage redemption monies,[3] and the 'CEO fraud' in which a rogue impersonates a senior partner or director and instructs a junior staff member to transfer money. Ransomware programs can be introduced into a firm's system by attachments to emails which when opened encrypt files and demand a ransom in return for decrypting the files.[4] In 2016 and 2017 there was a series of frauds in which fraudsters impersonated members of a bank's fraud department in order to obtain firms' pin codes for electronic transfers. The pin codes were then used to withdraw money from the client accounts.

In the wake of the Covid-19 pandemic, concerns over the increasing scale of cyber-crime intensified. The SRA 2020/2021 Risk Outlook states:

> 'The lockdowns have made firms more dependent than ever on tech-nology. Many firms needed to adjust in a hurry. This means that some systems are more vulnerable to attack. And, the threats have grown. For

example, there was a 337% rise in phishing scams in the first two months of the first national lockdown.'

The SRA and the National Cyber Security Centre (NCSC) have each issued guidance on risks arising from remote working and video meetings. The NCSC has a further suite of guidance on 'bring your own devices' policies, recognising phishing scams and vulnerabilities of cloud-based systems.[5] Firms should keep up to date with the latest guidance since this is a fast moving area which presents high risks to firms.

The SRA has stated that it is important for a firm to take protective steps in relation to the IT system, which need not be complex, such as using an up-to-date antivirus system, using encryption on mobile devices, backing up files on a regular basis and setting up access controls. Backups can, for example, defeat most ransomware attacks provided the backup is not routinely connected to the main system.[6] It is also important to ensure only approved staff can transfer money. Most cybercrimes target people rather than systems and the best defence is staff training, including training to recognise common scams such as CEO fraud and email modification fraud, to not open unsolicited emails, to avoid using unapproved connection devices such as personal USBs, and to ensure passwords are not used in public spaces and are changed regularly. There should also be a robust process to confirm any requests to change bank details for payments to clients or third parties.[7] Firms should also have procedures to deal with attacks when they occur, such as knowing in advance whom to contact at the bank to try to stop payments going through.[8] It may also be necessary to report an attack to the firm's insurer, the SRA and the police. Firms should also consider whether their standard PI policy covers all loss from client account and whether additional insurance is needed to cover the firm's own losses from cybercrime.

1   'Cybercrime issues continue', SRA news release, 28 March 2017.
2   'IT security: keeping information and money safe', SRA risk publication, December 2016.
3   See SRA warning notice, 'Bogus law firms and identity theft', 26 March 2012.
4   SRA Risk Outlook 2018/19.
5   See for example SRA, 'Information and cyber security', 23 November 2020 and National Cyber Security Centre, 'Device security guidance', 29 June 2021.
6   See 'IT and innovation', SRA risk publication, March 2016, p.12.
7   'IT security: keeping information and money safe', SRA risk publication, December 2016.
8   'Cybercrime issues continue', SRA news release, 28 March 2017.

5.44

For the firm's obligations relating to data protection see **Chapter 29**.

Conflict of interests

5.45

> 6.1   You do not act if there is an *own interest conflict* or a significant risk of such a conflict.
>
> 6.2   You do not act in relation to a matter or a particular aspect of it if you have a *conflict of interest* or a significant risk of such a conflict in relation to that matter or aspect of it, unless:

(a)   the *clients* have a *substantially common interest* in relation to the matter or the aspect of it, as appropriate; or

(b)   the *clients* are *competing for the same objective,*

and the conditions below are met, namely that:

(i)   all the *clients* have given informed consent, given or evidenced in writing, to you acting;

(ii)   where appropriate, you put in place effective safeguards to protect your *clients'* confidential information; and

(iii)   you are satisfied it is reasonable for you to act for all the *clients*.

Confidentiality and disclosure

5.46

6.3   You keep the affairs of current and former *clients* confidential unless disclosure is required or permitted by law or the *client* consents.

6.4   Any individual who is acting for a *client* on a matter makes the *client* aware of all information material to the matter of which the individual has knowledge except when:

(a)   the disclosure of the information is prohibited by legal restrictions imposed in the interests of national security or the prevention of crime;

(b)   the *client* gives informed consent, given or evidenced in writing, to the information not being disclosed to them;

(c)   the individual has reason to believe that serious physical or mental injury will be caused to the *client* or another if the information is disclosed; or

(d)   the information is contained in a privileged document that the individual has knowledge of only because it has been mistakenly disclosed.

6.5   You do not act for a *client* in a matter where that *client* has an interest adverse to the interest of another current or former *client* for whom you hold confidential information which is material to that matter, unless:

(a)   effective measures have been taken which result in there being no real risk of disclosure of the confidential information; or

(b)   the current or former *client* whose information you hold has given informed consent, given or evidenced in writing, to you acting, including to any measures taken to protect their information.

5.47

Section 6 of the Code for Firms is comparable to section 6 of the Code for Individuals. The standards in both codes are virtually identical and there are no significant differences. For commentary on the standards see **4.88–4.111**.

Applicable standards in the **SRA** Code of Conduct for Solicitors, RELs and RFLs

5.48

> 7.1 The following paragraphs in the SRA Code of Conduct for Solicitors, RELs and RFLs apply to you in their entirety as though references to 'you' were references to you as a firm:
>
> (a) dispute resolution and proceedings before courts, tribunals and inquiries (2.1 to 2.7);
>
> (b) referrals, introductions and *separate businesses* (5.1 to 5.3); and
>
> (c) standards which apply when providing services to the public or a section of the public, namely client identification (8.1), complaints handling (8.2 to 8.5), and client information and publicity (8.6 to 8.11).

5.49

For commentary see the following paragraphs of **Chapter 4**:

(a) dispute resolution and proceedings: **4.16–4.25**;

(b) business requirements: **4.50–4.84**;

(c) client identification, client care and publicity: **4.122**, **4.124** and **4.131**.

Managers in **SRA** authorised firms

5.50

> 8.1 If you are a *manager*, you are responsible for compliance by your firm with this Code. This responsibility is joint and several if you share management responsibility with other *managers* of the firm.

5.51

Paragraph 8.1 imposes a responsibility on every partner (or manager[1]) of a firm to ensure that the firm's obligations are complied with. In almost all firms, different responsibilities have to be delegated to different partners, as client work cannot be carried out effectively without delegation. However, under paragraph 8.1 delegation by one partner does not absolve the other partners of their responsibilities to ensure the standards are achieved. The SRA has not produced any guidance on the steps the other partners should take properly to delegate managerial functions. The other partners should at least satisfy themselves that the delegatee is suitably qualified to carry out the role and that the delegatee's work is subject to appropriate oversight, review and reports. In practice the SRA and the SDT have historically expected a greater degree of direct oversight in small firms than in large ones, and have expected a partner in a two-partner firm to have far greater knowledge and control over the managerial activities of the co-partner than that expected from a partner in a larger firm.

---

1 The SRA Glossary defines manager to mean 'the sole principal in a recognised sole practice, a member of a LLP, a director of a company, a partner in a partnership or in relation to any other body a member of its governing body'.

Compliance officers

5.52

9.1   If you are a *COLP* you must take all reasonable steps to:

(a)   ensure compliance with the terms and conditions of your firm's authorisation;

(b)   ensure compliance by your firm and its *managers*, employees or *interest holders* with the *SRA's regulatory arrangements* which apply to them;

(c)   ensure that your firm's *managers* and *interest holders* and those they employ or contract with do not cause or substantially contribute to a breach of the *SRA's regulatory arrangements*;

(d)   ensure that a prompt report is made to the *SRA* of any facts or matters that you reasonably believe are capable of amounting to a serious breach of the terms and conditions of your firm's authorisation, or the *SRA's regulatory arrangements* which apply to your firm, *managers* or employees;

(e)   notwithstanding sub-paragraph (d), you ensure that the SRA is informed promptly of any facts or matters that you reasonably believe should be brought to its attention in order that it may investigate whether a serious breach of its *regulatory arrangements* has occurred or otherwise exercise its regulatory powers,

save in relation to the matters which are the responsibility of the *COFA* as set out in paragraph 9.2 below.

9.2   If you are a *COFA* you must take all reasonable steps to:

(a)   ensure that your firm and its *managers* and employees comply with any obligations imposed upon them under the SRA Accounts Rules;

(b)   ensure that a prompt report is made to the *SRA* of any facts or matters that you reasonably believe are capable of amounting to a serious breach of the SRA Accounts Rules which apply to them;

(c)   notwithstanding sub-paragraph (b), you ensure that the *SRA* is informed promptly of any facts or matters that you reasonably believe should be brought to its attention in order that it may investigate whether a serious breach of its *regulatory arrangements* has occurred or otherwise exercise its regulatory powers.

5.53

For the responsibilities of COLPs and COFAs see **CHAPTER 7**.

PART 3
Other rules

CHAPTER 6

The SRA Accounts Rules

Introduction to the applicable rules

6.1

The current applicable rules, the SRA Accounts Rules 2019[1] are much shorter than their predecessors,[2] reduced from 70 pages to little over six pages.

When introducing these rules the Solicitors Regulation Authority (SRA) stated that there were three main changes:

- the rules are simpler (and shorter) and easier to understand;
- they provide the option for firms to hold limited types of client money outside client account; and
- they provide an alternative to the holding of client money through the use of third party managed accounts (TPMAs).

The SRA's explanation for the changes is that the old Accounts Rules, which had not changed significantly for many years, were prescriptive and restrictive, that many firms were finding themselves in technical breach of the Accounts Rules when there was no real risk to client money, and that the complexity and resultant technical breaches were resulting in confusion, cost and non-compliance rather than good practice.[3]

1   In force from 25 November 2019.
2   The SRA Accounts Rules 2011.
3   SRA, 'Application for the approval of regulatory arrangements', August 2018, pages 56–57.

6.2

The SRA also stated that the changes to the Accounts Rules, in force from 25 November 2019, did not mean that firms had to change their accounts systems:

> 'We expect that many firms, at least at first, will continue to operate as they do under the current rules and in doing so will remain compliant with the new Accounts Rules.'[1]

That reflects the fact that, despite the radical reduction in length, the following underlying principles remain the same, are straightforward, and are well known to all practitioners – even if they may not be familiar with all the detail:

- keep other people's money in a client account, and separate from your own money;
- use only each client's or trust's money for that client's or trust's matters;

- have a proper accounts system and proper internal controls over it;
- keep accounting records to show money held for each client or trust;
- pay interest when appropriate;
- co-operate with regulatory checks and inspections by the SRA; and
- obtain an annual accountant's report when appropriate.

1 'Application for the approval of regulatory arrangements', issued by the SRA in August 2018, para 255.

6.3

The SRA Accounts Rules 2019 are accompanied by a range of SRA guidance notes. In addition to an updated warning notice and a case studies page on the improper use of client account as a banking facility (**APPENDIX 8**), the SRA has posted to its website nine further or updated topic guides, headed 'Guidance'.[1] Historically, some SRA guidance on Accounts Rules has acquired the status of prescriptive rules over time, and the eventual status and effect of any new guidance could for that reason be uncertain to the profession for a number of years.[2]

There is also scope for uncertainty arising from the substitution of words such as 'promptly', 'fair' and 'appropriate' in place of prescriptive time limits and other requirements found in the SRA Accounts Rules 2011. Those words are intended to give practitioners more flexibility, but it is unclear whether the SRA will take a restrictive approach to interpretation of those provisions over time.

1 See www.sra.org.uk for the nine guidance topics, which are: 'Accountant's report and the exemption to obtain one', updated 25 November 2019; 'Do I need to operate a client account?', updated 25 November 2019; 'Helping you keep accurate client accounting records', updated 25 November 2019; 'Joint accounts and record keeping', updated 25 November 2019; 'Third-party managed accounts', updated 25 November 2019; 'Statement of our position regarding firms operating a client's own account', updated 25 November 2019; 'Planning for and completing an accountant's report', updated 14 September 2020; 'Taking money for your firm's costs', issued 14 September 2020; and 'Granting authority to withdraw residual client balances', updated 8 October 2020.
2 In 2017 the SRA prosecuted a number of solicitors for breach of guidance note (ix) to rule 15 of the Solicitors' Accounts Rules 1998. The note provided guidance on use of a client account as a banking facility before the introduction of a rule against banking facilities in the SRA Accounts Rules 2011 – see *Langford, Howard Kennedy*, 11686-2017, SDT.

6.4

The SRA Accounts Rules 2019 comprise an introduction and a further four parts:

- Part 1 (rules 1.1 to 1.3) is concerned with to whom the rules apply and who has responsibility for them.
- Part 2 (rules 2.1 to 8.4) concerns the definition of client money, its proper handling, the correct operation of client account, interest, and accounts systems and controls.
- Part 3 (rules 9.1 to 11.2) concerns dealing with other money belonging to clients or third parties not held in a firm's client account.
- Part 4 (rules 12.1 to 13.1) is concerned with accountants' reports and the retention of accounting records.

6.5

The SRA Accounts Rules 2011, which came into force on 6 October 2011, will continue to apply to compliance obligations for accounting transactions and entries during the period from the date the SRA Accounts Rules 2011 came into force (6 October 2011) to the date of introduction of the SRA Accounts Rules 2019 (25 November 2019). The SRA Accounts Rules 2011 will therefore continue to be relevant to any SRA investigation relating to that period. The SRA Accounts Rules 2011, and commentary on them, can be found in *The Solicitor's Handbook 2017*.

Introduction and rule I

6.6

Introduction

These rules set out our requirements for when firms (including sole practices) authorised by us receive or deal with money belonging to clients, including trust money or money held on behalf of third parties. The rules apply to all firms we regulate, including all those who manage or work within such firms.

Firms will need to have systems and controls in place to ensure compliance with these rules and the nature of those systems must be appropriate to the nature and volumes of client transactions dealt with and the amount of client money held or received.

PART I: GENERAL

Rule I: Application section

1.1 These rules apply to *authorised bodies*, their *managers* and employees and references to 'you' in these rules should be read accordingly.

1.2 The *authorised body's managers* are jointly and severally responsible for compliance by the *authorised body*, its *managers* and employees with these rules.

1.3 In relation to a *licensed body*, the rules apply only in respect of activities regulated by the *SRA* in accordance with the terms of its licence.

Application and scope of the Accounts Rules

6.7

The SRA Accounts Rules 2019 apply to authorised bodies, their managers and employees.[1] The SRA Glossary defines 'authorised body' to mean '(a) a body that has been authorised by the SRA to practise as a licensed body or a recognised body, or (b) a sole practitioner's practice that has been authorised by the SRA as a recognised sole practice'. Traditional firms and limited liability partnerships (LLPs) are recognised bodies. Alternative business structures (ABSs) are licensed bodies.

In the case of an ABS or a licensed body, the SRA Accounts Rules 2019 only apply in respect of activities regulated by the SRA in accordance with the terms of its licence.[2] ABSs may be supplying both regulated and unregulated services (through multi-disciplinary practices (MDPs)). In relation to MDPs the rules apply only in respect of those activities for which the practice is regulated by the SRA, and are concerned only with money handled by the practice which relates to those regulated activities.

1   Rule 1.1 of the SRA Accounts Rules 2019.
2   Rule 1.3 of the SRA Accounts Rules 2019.

6.8

As indicated above rule 1.1 provides that the Accounts Rules also apply to all employees of authorised bodies. The SRA Glossary 2019 defines the term 'employee' to include just about all persons working for an authorised firm, that is, whether they are a solicitor or not, and whether employed under a contract of or for services, or through an umbrella or service company. The introduction to the rules, which does not form part of the rules, indicates that the rules apply to all those that work within an authorised firm.

If an employee who is not a solicitor breaches the SRA Accounts Rules 2019, the SRA has a range of disciplinary and regulatory powers which can be applied against the employee – see **CHAPTER 18**.

6.9

The SRA Accounts Rules 2019 do not apply to solicitors who practise outside an authorised body. These include traditional in-house solicitors, freelance solicitors, solicitors practising in authorised non-SRA firms (such as firms regulated by the Council for Licensed Conveyancers), solicitors practising in firms which are not authorised by a legal services regulator and solicitors working in non-commercial bodies.

The circumstances in which a solicitor practising outside an authorised body can hold client account money are governed by paragraph 4.3 of the SRA Code of Conduct for Solicitors, RELs and RFLs 2019 (the 'Code for Individuals'). By paragraph 4.3 a solicitor must not personally hold client money unless:

- the solicitor works in an authorised body;

- the solicitor works in a 'prescribed' organisation; or

- the solicitor is a 'freelance solicitor' permitted to hold client money under regulation 10.2(b)(vii) of the SRA Authorisation of Individuals Regulations 2019.

At the date of this edition of *The Solicitor's Handbook*, the only prescribed organisation is a 'non-commercial body', as defined by section 23(2) of the Legal Services Act (LSA) 2007. Solicitors working in such a body are permitted to hold client money in their own name on the terms set out in the SRA's undated 'Statement of prescribed organisations' available on its website.[1] Section 23(2) of LSA 2007 was intended to provide transitional protection for non-commercial bodies to continue to undertake reserved legal activities. As non-commercial bodes are subject to transitional status, we do not address the prescribed rules in detail, save that it may be noted that the rules prescribed for these bodies are broadly as set out in rules 2–8, 12.4–12.8 and 13 of the SRA Accounts Rules 2019, commentary on which is provided below. Solicitors wishing to hold client money working in such bodies should have regard to the precise wording of the rules set out in the SRA's statement of prescribed organisations.

Regulation 10.2(b)(vii) of the SRA Authorisation of Individuals Regulations 2019 is one of seven conditions that must be met by an individual who wishes to practise as a 'freelance solicitor' (a self-employed solicitor trading in their own name and thus not working through an authorised or other body), providing reserved legal services, without seeking authorisation as a recognised sole practice. Paragraph 4.3 of the Code for Individuals refers to this regulation as a 'permission'. Therefore, the regulation permits such an individual to hold client money on account of fees and unpaid disbursements before delivery of a bill,[2] provided that (a) any money held for disbursements relates to costs or expenses incurred by the solicitor on behalf of the client and for which the solicitor is liable and (b) the solicitor has informed the client in advance of where and how the money is to be held.

Presumably, although it is not clear, a freelance solicitor not providing reserved legal services is also able to hold client money in this way.

To the extent that client money is held pursuant to the 'permission' in regulation 10.2(b)(vii), that person does not have to comply with the SRA Accounts Rules 2019 but will nevertheless be required to safeguard money and assets entrusted to them by clients and others.[3]

1   The statement is entitled, 'The prescribed organisations and terms under which Solicitors, RELs and RFLs are allowed to hold client money in their own name'.
2   That is client money falling within rule 2.1(d) of the SRA Accounts Rules 2019.
3   Paragraph 4.2 of the Code for Individuals.

Systems and controls

6.10

The introductory sections of the SRA Accounts Rules 2011 set out lengthy lists of principles and outcomes which related to client accounts and had to be achieved. In contrast the introduction to the SRA Accounts Rules 2019 simply states that:

> 'Firms will need to have systems and controls in place to ensure compliance with these rules and the nature of those systems must be appropriate to the nature and volumes of client transactions dealt with and the amount of client money.'

While it may be comforting to smaller firms to read that the SRA's expectations of the systems employed will be proportionate to the client work and money handled, in practice, if a breach occurs, and if the breach is investigated by the SRA, the onus will rest with the firm to demonstrate that its systems were appropriate, which is often difficult.

However, the SRA has said that the new regulatory arrangements will be targeted at cases where action is needed. The new rules remove unnecessary prescription to focus on the most important aspects of client money.[1] The SRA has also commented upon the 2019 regulatory arrangements:

> 'It is our view that we need to put more trust in solicitors' professional judgement. We do not need pages and pages of prescriptive rules for a solicitor or firms to do the right thing and maintain professional standards … For instance, all good solicitors know that they should not steal money belonging to their clients. We do not think they need – or benefit – from more than 40 pages of detailed Accounts Rules setting out how to avoid stealing.'[2]

For commentary on systems and controls and the requirement for five-weekly reconciliations, see **6.47–6.49**.

1   SRA, 'Application for the approval of regulatory arrangements', August 2018, page 76.
2   SRA, 'Our response to consultation: Accounts Rules review', June 2017.

6.11

Paragraph 9.2 of the SRA Code of Conduct for Firms 2019 (the 'Code for Firms') requires the compliance officer for finance and administration (COFA) to take all reasonable steps to ensure that the firm and its managers and employees comply with any obligations imposed on them under the SRA Accounts Rules 2019. That places an obligation on the COFA to ensure that proper accounting systems and controls are in place.

The responsibilities are not limited to the COFA. Under the Code for Firms, the firm must have effective arrangements in place to ensure that compliance officers can discharge their duties,[1] and the firm is also required to have effective systems and controls in place to ensure that the firm complies with all of the regulatory arrangements.[2]

The SRA has reinforced the message in a guidance note:[3]

> 'We … expect you to have in place systems and procedures which help achieve the objective of safeguarding money and assets entrusted to you. These obligations apply regardless of the size and makeup of your firm. The effective controls and procedures a firm has in place should act as an assurance for consumers and give them confidence that money that they have entrusted to you will be kept safe.'

By paragraph 8.1 of the Code for Firms, all of the partners in a firm are responsible for ensuring that the firm complies with those obligations. Reinforcing this message, in the same guidance note referred to above, the SRA comments:

> 'In many firms those responsible for compliance with the Accounts Rules might sit in a finance team that focuses solely on compliance with the Accounts Rules. All those in a firm that are responsible for dealing with money and assets entrusted to a firm must understand their wider obligations as set out in the Principles and the codes of conduct as well as ensuring compliance with the Accounts Rules.'

1   Paragraph 2.1(d) of the Code for Firms.
2   Paragraph 2.1(a) of the Code for Firms.
3   SRA, 'Taking money for your firm's costs', 14 September 2020.

Liability for breaches

6.12

Rule 1.2 provides that the managers of a firm are jointly and severally responsible for compliance by the firm, its managers and employees. The word 'manager' is defined by the SRA Glossary to include the sole principal in a recognised sole practice, a member of a LLP, a director of a company, a partner in a partnership, or, in relation to any other body, a member of its governing body, and thus such liability extends to all such managers, and not simply those closely involved in the day-to-day management of the firm.

The comparable provision in the SRA Accounts Rules 2011 stated that all principals of the firm 'must ensure compliance with the rules by the principals themselves and by everyone employed in the firm'.[1] That provision was treated as a rule imposing strict liability on the principals for all breaches. As 'account rule breaches' allegations at the Solicitors Disciplinary Tribunal (the Tribunal or SDT) are still by and large addressing cases relating to pre-25 November 2019 rules, it still remains to be seen whether the SRA and the Tribunal will say that the new wording (which has changed from 'principals ... must ensure compliance' to 'managers ... are ... responsible for compliance') also imposes strict liability on all managers.

It is commonplace for solicitors to be unaware that breaches have occurred until well after the event (because the accounts function is usually delegated to non-solicitors), but the managers will still be responsible for compliance. The lack of knowledge or complicity on the part of the ignorant individual does not mean that a breach could not have occurred: he or she is responsible for compliance. That is why robust systems and hands-on involvement and oversight at partnership or management level are essential.

Failure to comply with any of the SRA Accounts Rules 2019 may be the subject of a complaint to the SDT[2] or an internal SRA disciplinary finding and sanction. Whether a breach results in an SRA finding, sanction, or referral to the SDT, and the severity of any sanction applied, will depend on factors such as the seriousness of the breach and the systems and controls adopted to avoid it.[3]

1 Rule 6.1 of the SRA Accounts Rules 2011.
2 Section 32(3) of SA 1974.
3 In the period of June 2012 to December 2013, more than 4,500 firms delivered a qualified accountant's report and yet only 179 were referred for consideration for further regulatory action – see 'Application for the approval of regulatory arrangements', issued by the SRA in August 2018.

6.13

Under the SRA Accounts Rules 2011, the COFA was under a duty to ensure compliance with the Accounts Rules. That has changed under the SRA Accounts Rules 2019, which do not impose any obligations on the COFA. The SRA has made the following comment on that change:

> 'We reflected on feedback that ... [making] ... the COFA directly responsible for compliance with the rules ... would place an unreasonable burden on the COFA ... [Rule 1.2] now emphasises that the Accounts Rules create obligations on the firm and its managers, not on the COFA. The COFA's obligations ... under the Code of Conduct to take all reasonable steps to ensure compliance with the Accounts Rules ... will still apply.'[1]

1 SRA, 'Application for the approval of regulatory arrangements', issued in August 2018, page 60.

6.14

The Codes of Conduct also impose obligations on individual solicitors and the firm to safeguard client money. Paragraph 4.2 of the Code for Individuals provides that 'You safeguard money and assets entrusted to you by clients and others' and there is an identical provision in paragraph 5.2 of the Code for Firms.

Rule 2: Client money

6.15

Rule 2: Client money

2.1   '*Client money*' is money held or received by you:

(a)   relating to *regulated services* delivered by you to a *client*;

(b)   on behalf of a third party in relation to *regulated services* delivered by you (such as money held as agent, stakeholder or held to the sender's order);

(c)   as a trustee or as the holder of a specified office or appointment, such as donee of a power of attorney, Court of Protection deputy or trustee of an occupational pension scheme;

(d)   in respect of your *fees* and any unpaid *disbursements* if held or received prior to delivery of a bill for the same.

2.2   In circumstances where the only *client money* you hold or receive falls within rule 2.1(d) above, and:

(a)   any money held for *disbursements* relates to costs or expenses incurred by you on behalf of your *client* and for which you are liable; and

(b)   you do not for any other reason maintain a *client account*; you are not required to hold this money in a *client account* if you have informed your *client* in advance of where and how the money will be held. Rules 2.3, 2.4, 4.1, 7, 8.1(b) and (c) and 12 do not apply to *client money* held outside of a *client* account in accordance with this rule.

2.3   You ensure that *client money* is paid promptly into a *client account* unless:

(a)   in relation to money falling within 2.1(c), to do so would conflict with your obligations under rules or regulations relating to your specified office or appointment;

(b)   the *client money* represents payments received from the Legal Aid Agency for your *costs*; or

(c)   you agree in the individual circumstances an alternative arrangement in writing with the *client*, or the third party, for whom the money is held.

2.4   You ensure that *client money* is available on demand unless you agree an alternative arrangement in writing with the *client*, or the third party for whom the money is held.

2.5   You ensure that *client money* is returned promptly to the *client*, or the third party for whom the money is held, as soon as there is no longer any proper reason to hold those funds.

Client money or office money?

6.16

Keeping your own money and that of other people separate should create no problems of interpretation, but solicitors still have problems with this issue from time to time. All money held or received in the course of practice is 'client money' (held or received for a client or as trustee) or 'office money' (which belongs to the practice).

The simplest approach is to ask the question: does this money belong, now, unconditionally and exclusively, to the firm? If the answer is 'yes', the money is office money and must be paid into office account. If the answer is 'no', it is client money.

The word 'unconditionally' is used to emphasise the fact that if a condition has to be satisfied in order for the firm to be entitled (such as the delivery of a bill), it is client money. The word 'exclusively' is used to emphasise that if someone else has an interest in the money, it is client money.

Regulated services

6.17

The SRA Glossary defines 'regulated services' to mean 'the legal and other professional services that you provide that are regulated by the SRA and includes, where appropriate, acting as a trustee or as the holder of a specified office or appointment'. That is a very wide definition, which ensures that all money received in the course of practice falls within the definition of 'client money' under rule 2.1 if it does not belong to the firm.[1]

1   The first draft of the SRA Accounts Rules 2019 used the phrase 'legal services'. That was changed following the consultation process to 'regulated services' to avoid the possibility that money received from a client might not fall within the definition of client money if the service supplied to the client was not a legal service. See 'Application for the approval of regulatory arrangements', SRA, August 2018, para 250.

Partners' money

6.18

Under rules 12.1 and 12.8 of the SRA Accounts Rules 2011, money which belonged to a partner in a firm was always office money, even if the partner was a client of the firm. If the firm was acting for a partner purchasing a property, and received a deposit in preparation for exchange, the deposit had to be paid into office account. The position under the current Accounts Rules is different. If the firm is acting for a partner, the partner is a client[1] and the money held or received relating to the service supplied to the partner is client money under rule 2.1.

1   The SRA Glossary defines 'client' to mean 'the person for whom you act and, where the context permits, includes prospective and former clients'.

Costs

6.19

When a firm is paid on account of costs for work that has not yet been billed, that money still belongs to the client and must be paid into client account.

Firms may legitimately transfer money held on account of costs from client account to office account for the payment of their fees, but only if a bill or other written notification of costs has been sent to the client.

There may be thought to be an inconsistency in the Accounts Rules between rule 2.1(d) and rule 4.3(a). Rule 2.1(d) states that money held on account of costs is client money while it is held 'prior to delivery of a bill'. Rule 4.3(a) provides that money held on client account on account of costs can be transferred after 'you … give a bill of costs, or other written notification of the costs incurred, to the client or the paying party'. It is submitted that rule 4.3(a) prevails, as that specifically relates to transfers of costs, and that money on account of costs can be transferred after giving written notification of costs, even if the bill has not yet been delivered. That practice is consistent with the position under the SRA Accounts Rules 2011 (rule 17.2 of the SRA Accounts Rules 2011 permitted transfers after written notification of costs). SRA guidance appears to confirm that rule 4.3(a) prevails.[1] However, it would be prudent simply to issue a bill, whether on an interim, interim statute or final basis, rather than rely upon the uncertainty of what constitutes a valid notification of costs.

For commentary on payment of costs out of money which is not expressly held on account of costs, see **6.36**.

The Tribunal's records are packed with cases involving solicitors who transferred money to which they considered they were fully entitled, because they had done the work, but where they had 'not got around to sending a bill'. Similar numbers of cases have involved the improper practice of 'tidying up the accounts' by sweeping old and small balances from client to office account on the basis of 'dummy bills' or 'accounts only bills' (meaning pieces of paper that were never intended to be delivered to the clients whose money was being taken).

1   SRA, 'Taking money for your firm's costs', 14 September 2020.

Agreed fees

6.20

Under rule 17.5 of the SRA Accounts Rules 2011, a payment for an 'agreed fee' had to be paid into office account. For the purpose of rule 17.5, an 'agreed fee' was narrowly defined to be one that was fixed, which could not be varied upwards or downwards, was not dependent on the transaction being completed and was evidenced in writing. The narrow definition led to confusion, as some practitioners mistakenly thought that all agreed fees could be paid into office account. The rule has now gone. Under rule 2.1(d) of the SRA Accounts Rules 2019, all money received in respect of fees is client money prior to delivery of a bill. The SRA has confirmed this position in a guidance note.[1]

1   SRA, 'Taking money for your firm's costs', 14 September 2020.

Billing in advance for costs

6.21

SRA guidance suggests that in certain circumstances it is permissible to bill in advance for costs, that is, in respect of work not yet undertaken, and disbursements not yet incurred.[1]

Upon being billed, such money is no longer client money.[2] However, the guidance indicates that when a bill is delivered in this way, any money transferred from client to office account remains subject to the obligation in the Code for Firms to 'safeguard money and assets entrusted to you'.[3]

Before adopting such a billing practice for a particular client, firms will need to justify why that is in the client's best interests and ensure that clients are fully informed and understand the potential risks of such practice as well as the options available to them.[4] The guidance suggests that the business's cashflow requirements will not be a good reason to bill in advance in this way.

The SRA guidance implies that firms should offer the alternative option to clients, to permit the firm to take costs only in respect of bills for work done and disbursements for which the firm is liable and which it has incurred.

The guidance note lists a number of risks, which it would be prudent to inform the client of if such a billing practice is being considered, including:

- in the event that the work is not undertaken, for example, where a transaction does not proceed, or a client terminates the retainer before the work is undertaken in full, giving rise to a refund, the firm may not have the resources available to make such a payment;

- where the firm suddenly has to close due to incapacity or the death of the sole practitioner, those dealing with that closure may not be in a position to immediately repay the client; and

- where the firm becomes subject to an insolvency event, and the client's money is absorbed into the insolvent's estate as it is not held in a ringfenced client account, the insolvency practitioner may refuse to repay the client's money because it is held in the firm's business account.

Reporting accountants are asked by the SRA to assess whether there have been failures by a firm to inform clients of the risk of money being paid into the business account for costs that have not been incurred and exercise judgement as to whether this should result in a qualified report to be delivered to the SRA – see commentary at **6.57**.

The SRA guidance indicates that the SRA would consider it improper, a breach of the SRA Standards and Regulations, and possibly indicative of a lack of integrity for firms to bill in advance for disbursements that the client will remain liable to pay for such as stamp duty land tax, and to receive such money into the firm's business account.

In light of the SRA guidance and obligations occasioned by the SRA Standards and Regulations, the circumstances in which billing in advance for costs will be in a client's best interests are likely to be limited. Such a practice may be in a client's best interests when it ringfences a fund required for the legal service, for example, to fund litigation, where there are potential third party claims upon it. However, firms will need to consider the situation carefully to ensure that it is proper to move such funds beyond the reach of third parties in this way, and whether in fact such a procedure achieves the aim.

Where a reporting accountant finds that a firm has engaged in the systematic billing for fees and any disbursements that have not been incurred with payments in respect of that bill being made into the business account, it is guided by the SRA to consider this to be a serious factor likely to lead to a qualified accountant's report – see **6.57**.

1   SRA, 'Taking money for your firm's costs', 14 September 2020.
2   Rule 2.1(d) of the SRA Accounts Rules 2019.
3   Paragraph 5.2 of the Code for Firms.
4   Paragraph 8.6 of the Code for Individuals; paragraph 7.1 of the Code for Firms.

Professional disbursements

6.22

It is common and proper to bill a client for costs and disbursements, including counsel's fees that have been incurred but are yet to be paid (which should be marked on the bill as unpaid[1]). It is permissible to pay the whole sum received in payment of such a bill into office account before the firm discharges its liability to pay the amount due to third parties in respect of the disbursements.[2]

There is no rule in the SRA Accounts Rules 2019 governing the timing of the firm's payment of professional disbursements out of office account. However, improper delays in payment of professional disbursements, such as counsel's fees after the client has paid the amount due to the firm, could be treated as a breach of principle 2 (not upholding public trust and confidence in the profession) and paragraph 1.2 of the Code for Firms (taking unfair advantage of others). A serious case could lead to an allegation of breach of principle 5 (lack of integrity).

Additionally, firms will remain responsible for safeguarding money paid by clients to meet disbursements. As discussed at **6.21**, there are risks to clients where a firm bills and takes payment for disbursements for which the firm is liable, but as yet remain unpaid by the firm. Therefore, if the disbursement is not to be paid from client account, and is instead transferred to office account, it would be prudent to pay the disbursement immediately upon transfer to office.

It is a well-known but wholly improper practice to withhold payment of unpaid professional disbursements for a lengthy period of time so that the office overdraft is reduced by the amount owed to counsel and others, possibly many thousands or tens of thousands of pounds. A slightly more sophisticated version of this practice is to write cheques to those entitled, which when entered on the accounts appear to show prompt payment, but the cheques are not sent and, rather, accumulate in the top left-hand drawer of the principal's or bookkeeper's desk, or comparable location. This would be regarded very seriously.[3]

SRA guidance indicates that when a bill includes disbursements that have not yet been incurred, it is permissible to leave funds in client account associated with those anticipated disbursements until such time as they have been paid.[4] As by rule 2.1(d), unpaid disbursements (the term also incorporates those not incurred) are no longer client money once billed, this is a category of non-client money that may be kept in client account. See commentary at **6.21** regarding the practice of transferring money from client to office account in respect of disbursements not yet incurred.

1 Section 67 of SA 1974.
2 Rules 2.1(d), 4.3(a) of the SRA Accounts Rules 2019.
3 See, for example, *SRA v Wingate* [2016] EWHC 3455 (Admin), per Holman J at [133]–[139]; this part of the decision was not affected by the subsequent appeal to the Court of Appeal.
4 SRA, 'Taking money for your firm's costs',14 September 2020.

Rule 2.2 payments on account of costs which do not have to be placed in client account

6.23

Under rule 2.2 payments on account of costs do not have to be placed in a client account if:

(1)   the only client money the firm holds or receives is money held or received for fees and unpaid disbursements prior to delivery of a bill;

(2)   any money held for disbursements relates to costs or expenses incurred by the firm on behalf of the client for which the firm is liable;

(3)   the firm does not maintain a client account for any other reason; and

(4)   the firm has informed the client in advance of where and how the money will be held.

If a firm relies on the rule 2.2 exemption, the money held on account of costs can be paid into the firm's office account. It is not subject to rule 2.3 (pay money promptly into a client account), rule 2.4 (ensure client money is available on demand), rule 4.1 (keep client money separate from office money), rule 7 (account for interest on client money), rule 8.1(b) and (c) (maintain a running total of all client ledger balances and a cash book showing a running total of all transactions through client account), and rule 12 (accountants' reports).

The other rules which relate to 'client money' (as opposed to the 'client account') will continue to apply to the money held on account of costs. In particular, there is a continuing obligation to return the money promptly to the client if there is no longer any reason to hold the funds (rule 2.5), to provide a bill of costs or other notification of costs (rule 4.3), to keep a client ledger recording receipts, payments and bills of costs (rule 8.1(a)), to obtain bank statements for the business account holding the money at least every five weeks (rule 8.2), to keep a central record of bills and notifications of costs (rule 8.4), and to keep the accounting records for at least six years (rule 13.1).

Firms relying on the rule 2.2 exemption will continue to need a COFA, who will be responsible for ensuring compliance with the obligations in the SRA Accounts Rules 2019 that apply if payments on account of costs are placed in an office account. The COFA will also be responsible for checking whether there is a need to operate a client account for any other reason (which would mean that the right to rely on the rule 2.2 exemption is then lost).

The partners in the firm will be under an obligation to comply with the Principles and the Code for Firms. The partners will have to ensure that clients are in a position to make informed decisions about the options available to them and the regulatory protections arising from use of a client account (paragraph 7.1(c) of the Code for Firms). If there is any risk of insolvency, and if money on account of costs is placed into office account, the partners are at risk of allegations that they have breached SRA principle 3 (act with independence), principle 5 (act with integrity), principle 7 (act in the best interests of each client) and paragraph 5.2 of the Code for Firms (safeguard money entrusted to you by clients).

The SRA has commented that 'clients should be clearly informed that the money is not being held in a client account and agree to this in the knowledge of what it means'.[1]

The rule 2.2 exemption applies to disbursements only if the expense has been incurred by the firm on behalf of the client and if the firm is liable for the expense. That appears to have been added to prevent firms from obtaining payments on account for payment of stamp duty land tax and placing them in office account under rule 2.2.[2] However, it also means firms cannot rely on rule 2.2 if money is obtained on account for payment of counsel's fees before counsel is instructed (or perhaps before the brief is deemed, as an instruction does not always give rise to an immediate liability).

The SRA Glossary definition of disbursements needs to be borne in mind. 'Disbursements' are defined to mean 'any costs or expenses paid or to be paid to a third party on behalf of the client or trust (including any VAT element) save for office expenses such as postage and courier fees'. A firm wishing to rely on the rule 2.2 exemption cannot obtain money on account for courier fees (or postage).

It is open to a firm to combine the rule 2.2 exemption with the use of a TPMA or an agreement with a client under rule 2.3(c) for an alternative arrangement for client money. A TPMA could enable a firm, for example, to carry out property work without the need to operate a client account. In the application to the Legal Services Board (LSB) for approval of the SRA Accounts Rules 2019, the SRA said:

> '[The rule 2.2 exemption] ... does not enable firms to hold other types of client money (such as a house deposit or stamp duty) outside of client account. Firms that handle these categories of client money will still be required to hold the money in client account or a TPMA unless otherwise agreed with the client (as is currently permitted for all firms).'[3]

The rule 2.2 exemption has been included to avoid the need for firms who do not hold other categories of client money from operating a client account. The expressed aim is to reduce overheads. There will be no need to invest in client account software, to employ cashiers to operate the client account or to pay for reporting accountants to prepare an accountant's report. The professional indemnity (PI) insurance premium may also be cheaper.

It is important to note that firms are not permitted to adopt a 'pick and mix' approach to payments on account of costs; if a firm operates a client account for any other reason, it will need to keep this category of client money in client account, and not, for example, use it to keep office account within an overdraft limit. For that reason, the SRA has said:

'All fees and disbursements paid in advance are considered client money until the point at which they are billed. These payments must therefore be held in a client account, unless they are the only categories of client money held by the firm and the firm takes advantage of the exemption (in new rule 2.2).'[4]

1   SRA, 'Our response to consultation: Accounts Rules review', June 2017.
2   SRA, 'Application for the approval of regulatory arrangements', August 2018, para 271.
3   SRA, 'Application for the approval of regulatory arrangements', August 2018, para 271.
4   SRA, 'Application for the approval of regulatory arrangements', August 2018, para 272.

Legal aid

6.24

The power to receive Legal Aid Agency (LAA) payments for costs into office account is retained by rule 2.3(b). Costs are defined by the SRA Glossary as fees and disbursements. There is no longer a requirement, after a specified time period, to transfer sums representing unpaid disbursements to client account, but practitioners should be particularly careful not to delay the payment of such disbursements, otherwise they risk being accused of propping up the office account. A failure to pay within a reasonable time could lead to allegations of breach of principle 2 (upholding public trust and confidence in the profession), principle 5 (integrity) and paragraph 1.2 of the Code for Firms (not taking unfair advantage of others).

Alternative arrangements – rule 2.3(c)

6.25

Alternative arrangements agreed under rule 2.3(c) should be adopted cautiously, and only where the client's interests are better served by such an alternative arrangement.

The SRA Glossary states that 'client account' has 'the meaning given to it in the SRA Accounts Rules'. The SRA Accounts Rules 2019 do not define 'client account', but rule 3.1 restricts client accounts to accounts at a branch or the head office of a bank or building society in England and Wales. Rule 2.3(c) allows firms to make arrangements for holding client money outside accounts of that type.

The power is not in fact new. Rule 2.3(c) effectively replaces rule 15.1 of the SRA Accounts Rules 2011. Rule 15.1 gave the following examples of appropriate circumstances in which alternative arrangements might be agreed: retaining money in the firm's safe in the form of cash;[1] placing money in an account in the firm's name which is not a client account, such as an account outside England and Wales; placing the money in a bank, building society or other financial institution opened in the name of the client or of a person designated by the client.

None of the other provisions of SRA Accounts Rules 2019 relating to client money are excluded if an alternative arrangement is agreed under rule 2.3. That means, for example, that the client money must be kept separate from the firm's money (rule 4.1) and there are obligations to account for interest (rule 7), to keep accounting records to the extent that they relate to client money rather than the client account (rule 8) and to obtain accountants' reports when appropriate (rule 12).

Similarly, none of the provisions of the Code for Firms are excluded, such as the obligation to safeguard client money (paragraph 5.2), and the partners in the firm continue to hold the client money subject to the Principles, including the duty to act in the client's best interests (principle 7).

1 The handling of some cash such as small amounts of foreign currency travel money received at the start of the administration of an estate would not lead to a risk of breaching the anti-money laundering (AML) legislation.

Designated deposit accounts

6.26

Rule 2.4 permits firms to reach an agreement with clients and third parties that client money held for them should not be available on demand. That enables such funds to be placed in designated deposit accounts paying a higher rate of interest. The arrangement has to be agreed in writing, and that would presumably be satisfied by an exchange of emails on the terms of the deposit account.

Obligation to return funds

6.27

Rules have been in force since 14 July 2008 to deal with the substantial problem caused by dormant accounts or 'residual balances'. The problem is now addressed by rule 2.5. There is an obligation to return funds to the client or other person entitled promptly, as soon as there is no longer any proper reason to retain them.

SRA guidance advises firms to have:

- checks and controls to make sure client files are closed promptly, and the prompt payments back to clients of any residual balances; and

- systems which make sure clients (or other people on whose behalf money is held) are kept regularly informed when funds are retained for a specified reason (which should be in respect of the delivery by you of regulated services) at the end of a matter or the substantial conclusion of a matter. This should help ensure that your client account is not being used as a banking facility when there is no need for you to hold on to monies.[1]

For the position on how to withdraw 'dormant' or 'residual' balances from client account see commentary at **6.36**.

The SRA has additionally produced a guidance note on compliance with rule 2, in a question and answer format.[2]

1 SRA guidance, 'Helping you keep accurate client accounting records', updated 25 November 2019.
2 SRA guidance, 'Do I need to operate a client account?', updated 25 November 2019.

Rule 3: Client account

6.28

Rule 3: Client account

3.1 You only maintain a *client account* at a branch (or the head office) of a *bank* or a *building society* in England and Wales.

3.2 You ensure that the name of any *client account* includes:

  (a) the name of the *authorised body*; and

  (b) the word 'client' to distinguish it from any other type of account held or operated by the *authorised body*.

3.3 You must not use a *client account* to provide banking facilities to *clients* or third parties. Payments into, and transfers or withdrawals from a *client account* must be in respect of the delivery by you of *regulated services*.

6.29

Rules 3.1 and 3.2 are self-explanatory.

For commentary on holding client money outside a bank or building society account in England and Wales, see **6.25**.

Banking facilities

6.30

Since 2011, the SRA has focused increasingly on concerns that firms should not provide a 'banking facility' for clients or third parties, and has prosecuted solicitors for alleged breaches of some antiquity.[1]

The rule against banking facilities first appeared in the Accounts Rules in 2011, as rule 14.5 of the SRA Accounts Rules 2011.[2] The wording of the current rule is different from the wording of the former rule 14.5, and it is worthwhile comparing the two rules.

Rule 14.5 of the SRA Accounts Rules 2011 provided:

> '*You* must not provide banking facilities through a *client account*. Payments into, and transfers or withdrawals from, a *client account* must be in respect of instructions relating to an underlying transaction (and the funds arising therefrom) or to a service forming part of *your* normal regulated activities.'

In contrast rule 3.3 of the SRA Accounts Rules 2019 provides:

> 'You must not use a *client account* to provide banking facilities to *clients* or third parties. Payments into, and transfers or withdrawals from a *client account* must be in respect of the delivery by you of *regulated services*.'

The main difference is in the second sentence. The references to 'underlying transaction' and 'normal regulated activities' have been removed, and replaced by a rule that client account transactions must be 'in respect of the delivery by you of regulated services'. The SRA Glossary defines 'regulated services' to mean:

> 'the legal and other professional services that you provide that are regulated by the SRA and includes, where appropriate, acting as a trustee or as the holder of a specified office or appointment.'

The change in the wording has removed a number of difficulties which arose on the interpretation of rule 14.5. It was, for example, unclear from rule 14.5 whether a client account transaction had to be connected to underlying legal work carried out by the firm, or whether the existence somewhere else of an underlying transaction was enough. The uncertainties led to two High Court cases which involved disputes on the construction of rule 14.5,[3] and the profession did not have any very clear idea of how the SRA interpreted rule 14.5 until a warning notice was published in December 2014, more than three years after introduction of the rule.

Rule 3.3 is consistent with the interpretation set out in the warning notice. The warning notice was last updated on 25 November 2019, and a copy of the updated warning notice is at **APPENDIX 8**.

The warning notice includes the following guidance on the purpose and construction of the rule:

> 'it is not a proper part of a solicitor's everyday business or practice to operate a banking facility for third parties, whether they are clients of the firm or not …
>
> … You must therefore only receive funds into your client account where there is a proper connection between receipt of the funds and the delivery by you of regulated services. It is not sufficient that there is simply an underlying transaction if you are not providing any regulated services, or if the handling of money has no proper connection to that service …
>
> … The rule is not intended to prevent usual practice in traditional work undertaken by solicitors such as conveyancing, company acquisitions, the administration of estates or dealing with formal trusts. So it does not affect your ability to make usual and proper payments from client account when they are related to the transaction (such as the payment of estate agents' fees in a conveyancing transaction).'

Active consideration (and record) is required by firms and practitioners before receiving or making any payment. The warning notice provides:

> 'You need to think carefully about whether there is any justification for money to pass through your client account when it could be simply paid directly between the clients.'

The warning notice highlights the questions that practitioners (and accounts personnel) should ask themselves, on a rolling basis during a retainer, when considering whether the rule is engaged:

> '● Throughout the retainer, you should question why you are being asked to receive funds and for what purpose. The further the details of

the transaction are from the norm or from the usual legal or professional services a solicitor provides, the higher the risk that you may breach rule 3.3.

- You should always ask why you are being asked to make a payment or why the client cannot make or receive the payment directly themselves. The client's convenience is not a legitimate reason, nor is not having access to a bank account in the UK. Risk factors could involve the payment of substantial sums to others, including family members, or to corporate entities, particularly overseas, if there is no reason why the client could not receive the money into their own account and transfer it from there.

- You have a separate obligation to return client money to the client or third party promptly, as soon as there is no longer any proper reason for you to hold those funds (rule 2.5 of the Accounts Rules). If you retain funds in client account after completion of a transaction, there is risk (depending on how long you hold the money) of breaching both rule 2.5 and 3.3.'

The warning notice and an SRA Case Studies web page, which set out a number of examples of cases which breach the rule and cases which do not, document the change in regulatory approach over the years,

'Historically, some solicitors have held funds for clients to enable them to pay the client's routine outgoings. This has been mainly for the clients' convenience such as where they are long term private clients or based abroad. In view of technological change, such as the ease of internet and telephone banking, we consider that allowing client account to be used in this way is no longer justifiable and a breach of rule 3.3.'[4]

The warning notice also requires firms and practitioners to make sure that they are fully aware of the relevant case law including the cases of *Fuglers*, *Patel* and *Zambia*.[5]

The warning notice also highlights that allowing a client account to be used as a banking facility carries with it the additional risk that you may assist money laundering. The original warning notice of December 2014 stated that risk factors of money laundering included the payment of substantial sums to others, including family members, or to corporate entities, particularly overseas, since there is no reason why the client could not receive the money into its own account and transfer it from there.

In a publication, 'Solicitors and investment fraud' of December 2016, the SRA notified the profession of its concern that use of a client account as a banking facility may be a hallmark of fraudulent or otherwise dubious investment schemes. Similarly, in a 2017 warning notice on investment schemes, the SRA warned that breaches of the rule prohibiting banking facilities can provide fraudsters with credibility and the facility to transfer investors' money through a bank account.[6] Solicitors have received significant fines at the SDT for agreeing to act as facilitator to dubious schemes.

The current warning notice highlights that compliance with 'rule 3.3 offers an important "first line of defence" against clients or others who seek to use your client account to launder money'. It remarks that:

> '● Any impropriety may be distant from the movement of money through a client account. ... the movement through a client account may be the third or fourth stage of laundering the proceeds of a distant crime. But every stage contributes to the effectiveness of the laundering process.'

The SRA notice adds that:

> 'It is no defence to, or mitigation, of a breach of rule 3.3 that there was no evidence of actual laundering. Indeed, such arguments indicate a lack of insight into the reasons for rule 3.3 and the risks it addresses.'

The notice also obligates firms and practitioners to actively consider whether there are any risk factors suggesting that the transaction subject of the firm's retainer is not genuine or is suspicious, even if it appears to be the normal work of a solicitor.[7]

In a nutshell, practices which were unremarkable a decade or two ago (eg the use of client account to settle commercial debts owed by the client to third parties) may well now fall foul of the rule. Practitioners should prudently repay client funds as soon as possible following completion of a retainer, and consider whether to do so during a hiatus in instructions. A delay in returning funds promptly could be a breach of rule 3.3 as well as a breach of the rule 2.5 requirement for prompt payment out of client money at the end of a case. Likewise, solicitors should be very cautious about paying client money out of client account to anyone other than the client (being careful to distinguish between individual and corporate clients when identifying who the client is). Similarly, solicitors should be careful to ensure that funds are received from the client, and not, for example, a 'non-client' corporate entity, whether associated with the client or not. If in doubt, specialist advice should be taken as the risks in this area are considerable. In light of the moving interpretation of the rule over the years, firms should ensure that both their accounts personnel and all employees receive regular updates to their training on the rule. Firms are advised to adapt their procedures to encourage active consideration and record.

1   See, for example, *Langford, Howard Kennedy*, 11686-2017, SDT.
2   The Solicitors' Accounts Rules 1998, which continued in force until October 2011, contained no original provision about a 'banking facility'. In 2004 in *SRA v Wood and Burdett* the SDT imposed severe sanctions on the two partners in a firm that was using its client account to offer a cheque-cashing service to all and sundry in Merseyside, clients and non-clients, to 'diversify' the business. In consequence, within a short time a guidance note was added to the 1998 Rules making express reference to *Wood and Burdett* and stating for the first time that: 'Solicitors should not ... provide banking facilities through a client account'. The 1998 Rules were to be 'interpreted in the light of the notes' so there remained no specific rule until October 2011. The reference to *Wood and Burdett* meant that the facts which might be regarded by practitioners to involve the provision of a banking facility were fairly extreme.
3   *Patel v SRA* [2012] EWHC 3373 (Admin) and *Fuglers v SRA* [2014] EWHC 179 (Admin).
4   See the SRA's warning notice, 'Improper use of client account as a banking facility', updated 25 November 2019 (at **Appendix 8**) and case studies, 'Improper use of client account as a banking facility', updated 25 November 2019. The examples in the case studies and warning notice are fact specific and should be read in full before making any decisions on rule 3.3 on the basis of comparisons with them. See also *Fuglers v SRA* [2014] EWHC 179 (Admin).
5   *Fuglers v SRA* [2014] EWHC 179 (Admin); *Patel, Premji Naram Patel v SRA* [2012] EWHC 3373 (Admin); and *Zambia (Attorney General of Zambia v Meer Care & Desai* [2008] EWCA Civ 1007.
6   SRA warning notice, 'Investment schemes including conveyancing', 23 June 2017, updated 17 August 2020.
7   In addition to SRA regulatory sanction, the warning notice also addresses other risks.

Rule 4: Client money must be kept separate

6.31

> ## Rule 4: Client money must be kept separate
>
> 4.1   You keep *client money* separate from money belonging to the *authorised body*.
>
> 4.2   You ensure that you allocate promptly any funds from *mixed payments* you receive to the correct *client account* or business account.
>
> 4.3   Where you are holding *client money* and some or all of that money will be used to pay your *costs*:
>
> (a)   you must give a bill of *costs*, or other written notification of the *costs* incurred, to the *client* or the paying party;
>
> (b)   this must be done before you transfer any *client money* from a *client account* to make the payment; and
>
> (c)   any such payment must be for the specific sum identified in the bill of *costs*, or other written notification of the *costs* incurred, and covered by the amount held for the particular *client* or third party.

Keeping office and client money separate

6.32

The rule 4.1 requirement to keep office and client money in separate accounts does not apply if the only client money which a firm holds is money on account of costs and the firm relies on the exception in rule 2.2. For commentary on rule 2.2 see **6.23**.

Mixed payments

6.33

The SRA Glossary defines a 'mixed payment' as 'a payment that includes both client money and non-client money'.

By rule 4.2, the detailed requirements on initial allocation of, and time limits for separation of, mixed payments previously seen in the SRA Accounts Rules 2011 are removed and are replaced with: 'you allocate promptly … to the correct client account or business account'.

Rule 4.2 does not prevent mixed payments from initially being placed in an office account. In the application to the LSB for approval of the new regulatory arrangements, the SRA said:

> 'We did receive objections to this proposal, which were concerned about this being an unnecessary removal of client protection and about the risk that firms will use client funds to manipulate their cash position. However we were not persuaded. If a firm were to use client money to manipulate its cash position, it is likely it would be in breach of our rules. Firms will still

be required to move money between accounts promptly and comply with all our other rules. This includes the requirement to act in a client's best interest to not retain funds for longer than necessary and to act with honesty and integrity.'[1]

Under the Solicitors' Accounts Rules 1998, some legal aid practitioners faced disciplinary proceedings in circumstances where the firm operated its office account beyond an agreed overdraft limit. LAA payments for costs including counsel's fees had to be paid into office account under those rules, and the bank enforced the overdraft limit after receipt of the LAA costs and refused to permit the practitioners to pay counsel's fees. The SRA then prosecuted the solicitors for failure to pay counsel's fees.[2] A similar problem could occur under rule 4.2. If a firm operates its office account beyond an agreed overdraft limit, and places a mixed payment into office account, there is always a risk that the bank will enforce the overdraft limit and refuse to transfer the whole of the client element of a mixed payment out of the overdrawn office account. In such circumstances, a decision to place a mixed payment in office account could not be in the client's best interests, and would carry the risk of disciplinary proceedings.

1   'Application for the approval of regulatory arrangements', SRA, August 2018, para 244.
2   See for example *SRA v Dhaliwal*, 9397-2005, SDT.

Payment of costs out of client account

6.34

By rule 4.3 it is obligatory to deliver a bill of costs or other written notification of costs incurred before transferring money from client account to office account in respect of costs (that is, fees and/or disbursements).[1]

Rule 4.3(c) provides that a firm may only transfer 'the specific sum identified in the bill' and 'covered by the amount held for the particular client or third party'. That appears to suggest that the firm can only transfer the exact sum due as identified in the bill, and not a lesser sum, even if the firm holds some funds that could be applied towards payment. In light of the SRA's expressed intention to provide flexibility, that cannot have been intended. An SRA guidance note implies that part payments may be acceptable, indicating that it is permissible to 'leave' in client account money paid for billed disbursements not yet incurred.[2]

The words 'covered by the amount held' mean that sufficient funds must be held for the client, and that the funds are held for the purposes of payment of costs. Costs cannot be paid out of client money held for a specific purpose unrelated to a firm's costs.

It is not uncommon for solicitors to face disciplinary proceedings for making 'round sum transfers' from client account to office account at month end to pay salaries, in the hope that the round sum transfer can then be allocated to month end bills which are in the course of being issued, or bills which could be issued at some time in the future to cover the amount transferred. Rule 4.3 makes it clear that this practice is unacceptable, and that any transfer must directly correlate to a specific sum payable by a specific client after the client has received notice of the amount payable.

When transferring costs, a firm must take into account rule 5.1. Rule 5.1 states that a firm can only withdraw client money from a client account 'for the purpose for which it is being held', or following receipt of instructions or receipt of SRA authorisation, or in prescribed circumstances – see **6.36** for the prescribed circumstances. It is possible that a number of different types of client receipts which have traditionally been used to pay costs, such as completion monies on a property sale and damages obtained on a settlement, are not (in the client's eyes at least) held for the purpose of payment of costs.

SRA guidance indicates that where a firm has paid a disbursement on behalf of a client, then rule 5.1(a) acts as authority for the firm to transfer the equivalent sum from client to office account, without having to deliver a bill or written notification of costs (as would seem to be required by rule 4.3(a)). The guidance indicates that when a firm avails itself of this provision, the SRA expects the firm to explain to its client how and when payments might be made on their behalf from the firm's business account and that the firm will then be seeking a reimbursement from the client account in accordance with rule 5. The guidance indicates that such information can be provided in a firm's client care letter, terms of engagement or in other communication with the client, but the client must understand how their money will be used and have confirmed their instructions. The guidance refers to examples of HM Land Registry search or court fees paid from the firm's own money (including by way of a direct debit from the firm's business account) when such a procedure would be permissible. The guidance indicates that such a procedure should not be used where the disbursements have not yet been incurred or have not been paid by the firm.

The SRA Accounts Rules 2019 do not contain any specific rules on the timing of costs transfers from client account to office account after delivery of a bill. That contrasts with the SRA Accounts Rules 2011, which contained a mandatory requirement that money earmarked for costs had to be transferred out of client account within 14 days.[3] The removal of that mandatory 14-day period does not mean that there can be delays in making transfers. Money held for costs ceases to be client money (and becomes office money) after a bill has been delivered (see rule 2.1(d)), and money belonging to the firm must be kept separate from client money (see rule 4.1). In a busy office with a large number of month end bills it can be a time-consuming task for cashiers to have to identify quickly the bills which have to be paid out of money held on account, and in a large office the COFA needs to ensure cashiers have sufficient time to carry out that task. The removal of the 14-day time period means that it is now uncertain how quickly the task needs to be carried out.

For delays in payment of counsel's fees after the fees have been transferred to the office account, see the commentary at **6.22**.

1 See **6.19** for commentary on the inconsistency with rule 2.1.
2 SRA, 'Taking money for your firm's costs', 14 September 2020.
3 Rule 17.3 of the SRA Accounts Rules 2011.

Rule 5: Withdrawals from client account

6.35

Rule 5: Withdrawals from client account

5.1 You only withdraw *client money* from a *client account*:

(a) for the purpose for which it is being held;

> (b)   following receipt of instructions from the *client*, or the third party for whom the money is held; or
>
> (c)   on the *SRA's* prior written authorisation or in *prescribed* circumstances.
>
> 5.2   You appropriately authorise and supervise all withdrawals made from a *client account*.
>
> 5.3   You only withdraw *client money* from a *client account* if sufficient funds are held on behalf of that specific *client* or third party to make the payment.

Authorisation for withdrawals

6.36

Rule 5.1 sets out the circumstances in which money can be withdrawn from client account.

Firms should be careful to record and confirm with clients and third parties the purpose for which client money is being held (rule 5.1(a)), for example, by ensuring that its engagement letter sets out the circumstances when client money can be drawn upon to pay fees and disbursements, and there is a written record in respect of any occasional transactions.

Receipt of instructions (rule 5.1(b)) will not alone be a sufficient defence to an allegation of having allowed client to be used as a banking facility – see **6.30**.

For commentary on the entitlement to pay costs out of client account see **6.34**.

Residual balances not exceeding £500

6.37

The SRA Accounts Rules 2011 contained rules permitting firms to dispose of minor residual balances not exceeding £500 to charity without obtaining the specific consent of the SRA and to dispose of larger residual balances with the permission of the SRA.[1]

The SRA Accounts Rules 2019 do not include a parallel provision for disposal of minor residual balances not exceeding £500, but rule 5.1(c) states that withdrawals can be made with the SRA's prior written authorisation or in prescribed circumstances.

'Prescribed' means prescribed by the SRA.[2] The SRA has, since the last edition of *The Solicitor's Handbook*, prescribed rules for disposing of minor residual balances not exceeding £500 to charity without the need for written authorisation from the SRA. The prescribed rules are:

> 'You may withdraw residual client balances of £500 or less on any one client matter from a client account provided:
>
> 1   the balance is paid to a charity of your choice

2   you have taken reasonable steps to return the money to the rightful owner. The reasonableness of such steps will depend on:

    i   the age of the residual balance;

    ii   the amount of the residual balance;

    iii   if you have access to the client's most up to date contact details;

    iv   if not, the costs associated with tracing your client.

    We expect you to make more intensive efforts to locate the rightful owner for larger or more recent residual balances or for balances where more details are held about the client.

3   you record the steps taken to return the money to the rightful owner and retain those records, together with all relevant documentation for at least six years;

4   you keep appropriate accounting records, including:

    i   a central register which records the name of the rightful owner on whose behalf the money was held, the amount, name of the recipient charity (and their charity number) and the date of the payment; and

    ii   all receipts from the charity and confirmation of any indemnity provided against any legitimate claim subsequently made for the sum they have received.

5   you do not deduct from the residual balance any costs incurred in attempting to trace or communicate with the rightful owner.

The records referred to in points 3 and 4 above may be requested by your reporting accountant who will look at whether you have followed these prescribed circumstances.

For amounts over £500 you will need our authority before removing this money from the client account. Please use our application form.'

The SRA has also issued the following guidance:

'You may choose to pay the money to a charity that does not offer you an indemnity but if it does not, you will be liable to pay the money to the client if they contact you later to claim it.

Some ways in which you may be able to trace your client include:

- making use of social media

- making a search of Companies House and/or the Probate Registry

- making use of the Department of Work and Pensions' letter forwarding service

- undertaking any free searches on the internet.'

1   Rules 20.1 and 20.2 of the SRA Accounts Rules 2011.
2   SRA Glossary 2019.

Residual balances exceeding £500

6.38

Withdrawals of residual balances exceeding £500 will require the SRA's prior written authorisation.[1] The SRA has issued a guidance note in this respect.[2]

The guidance gives examples of the occasions when a firm may not be in a position to return client money in accordance with rule 2.5 (see **6.27**).

The guidance indicates that requests to the SRA for authority should be made in writing but can be made by anyone on behalf of the firm, including the firm's accountant.

Before granting authority the SRA will consider whether the applicant firm has made adequate attempts to trace and repay the rightful owner having regard to evidence of steps taken.

The larger the sum involved, the greater attempts the SRA would expect to be made, but the costs of tracing the client or third party need not be disproportionate to the sum held.

Steps the SRA may expect firms to have taken, where proportionate, include use of the Department for Work and Pensions (DWP) letter forwarding service, free searches on the internet, social media, placing an advert in newspapers, local or national, tracing services, use of an investigator, and, where appropriate, making a search of Companies House and/or the Probate Registry.

Where the SRA is satisfied that adequate attempts have been made to trace and repay the owner, but the owner cannot be found or does not accept the money, it will grant the authority requested, recording the amount of money and the name of the party to whom the money is owed, and will usually impose a condition on the firm to pay the balance, plus accrued interest, to a charity of the firm's choice.

The condition attached to the decision will include a requirement for the firm to obtain an indemnity from the charity that is not time limited. The indemnity will need to provide for reimbursement of the money to the firm or the owner of the funds should the owner come forward at a later date. This indemnity protects both the client/owner and the firm, particularly where the firm has closed.

The guidance note indicates that firms have no legal authority to deduct from client money any costs incurred in attempting to trace or communicate with the client. However, the SRA indicates that it can take into account any reasonable out-of-pocket expenses when granting authority to pay the monies to charity and permit these to be paid to the firm, for example, DWP fees, and the cost of an advert or tracing agent, but this will not include the cost of correspondence or telephone calls. Any such expenses should not be deducted from the money held until the SRA has granted authorisation. The firm should pay expenses such as the DWP or tracing agent's fees from its own funds. Even if the SRA grants authority for a firm to reimburse such expenses the firm will remain liable to the client for the full sum owed and, should the client reappear, will have to reimburse the client for the full sum including all expenses deducted.

The SRA also indicates that it will not be able to authorise a withdrawal from client account in respect of money held for a dissolved company in England and Wales, or for an estate, where the firm is acting on behalf of executors.

1   Rule 5.1(c) of the SRA Accounts Rules 2019.
2   SRA, 'Granting authority to withdraw residual client balances', updated 8 October 2020.

Internal procedures for withdrawals from client account

6.39

Rule 5.2 requires firms to authorise and supervise appropriately all withdrawals from client account. That is a brief rule which is consistent with the SRA's aim of providing firms with the flexibility to manage their accounts systems in a manner which is suitable for the firm's particular practice. All responsible firms will already have addressed these issues in detail, and decided who is best suited and qualified to authorise and supervise withdrawals from client account.

SRA guidance[1] advises firms to have:

- '• established clear systems and controls for ensuring that persons permitted to authorise the withdrawal of client money from a client account have an appropriate understanding of the requirements of the Accounts Rules and sufficient seniority within the firm.

- • persons nominated to authorise payments. That person should ensure that there is evidence which supports the reason for each payment, and that this is recorded together with the date of the payment.

- • procedures for ensuring that sufficient money is held for a particular client before any withdrawals are made for that client. Your controls should be adequate to prevent a debit balance arising but if one does, the controls should make sure that it is identified and rectified promptly.

- • systems for the transfer of costs from a client to a business account. Normally transfers should be made only after issuing a bill or other written notification of costs. Rule 8.4 requires you to keep a readily accessible central record of all bills or other written notifications of costs given by you.'

When considering withdrawal authorisations, firms should bear in mind the risk of cybercrime. The SRA has issued a series of notices warning firms that cybercrime is a priority risk.[2] It is advisable for firms to review their systems for client account withdrawals periodically, taking account of the publications issued by the SRA and the Law Society highlighting the cybercrime risks faced by the profession. Staff training is also an important part of the authorisation system. In a publication on IT security and keeping money safe, the SRA stated that most cybercrimes target people rather than systems and that the best defence is to learn, and to train staff to recognise common scams.[3]

All of the partners (as well as the firm) are responsible for ensuring that appropriate systems are in place (see rule 1.2) and the COFA must take all reasonable steps to ensure the partners and the firm comply with that obligation.[4]

1   SRA guidance, 'Helping you keep accurate client accounting records', updated 25 November 2019.
2   See, for example, SRA, 'Cybercrime', 23 November 2020.
3   SRA, 'IT security: keeping information and money safe', December 2016.
4   Paragraph 9.2 of the Code for Firms.

Teeming and lading – rule 5.3

6.40

Using a client's money only for that client's purposes is a fundamental requirement. The Tribunal's caseload is materially increased by those solicitors who, when something goes wrong (either by miscalculation or through a transactional problem), and more money is needed for the client than is available, simply overdraw that client's individual ledger, using the substantial balance available in the general client bank account. This invariably means that the funds of one or more clients are being used, without their knowledge, for someone else's benefit. Effecting transfers between the clients' ledgers in these circumstances to 'cover' the shortage is a breach of rule 5.3. This is teeming and lading – robbing Peter to pay Paul. It does not overcome the fundamental problem – that there is an overall shortage of client funds. It is not uncommon to see this practice begin on a small scale before being repeated at ever reducing intervals such that it becomes very difficult to keep accurate books of account and remedy the issues. The client account shortfall tends to increase. Using client money in this way may lead to allegations of acting without integrity or dishonesty, intervention by the SRA, and amount to a criminal offence.

Rule 30 of the Solicitors' Accounts Rules 1998 (replaced by rule 27 of the SRA Accounts Rules 2011) was introduced in an attempt to inhibit this practice: it was not permissible to make a private (ie non-institutional) loan of one client's funds to another, even by means of a paper transfer between ledgers, except with the prior written authority of both clients. That rule has now gone.

Although the rule has been removed, it would be prudent to ensure that, before any private loan is made of one client's funds to another, there is prior written authority from both clients, that both clients have first taken independent legal advice and that the independent advice is documented. It would also be prudent to consider whether a client-to-client transfer in respect of the loan would breach rule 3.3 relating to banking facilities.[1]

SRA guidance on the topic[2] advises that firms should have 'systems which help to control and record accurately any transfers between different clients of the firm. Where these arise as a result of loans between clients, the written authority of both the lender and borrower should be obtained and retained on the file'.

1   For rule 3.3 and banking facilities see **6.30**.
2   SRA guidance, 'Helping you keep accurate client accounting records', updated 25 November 2019.

Rule 6: Duty to correct breaches upon discovery

6.41

Rule 6: Duty to correct breaches upon discovery

6.1   You correct any breaches of these rules promptly upon discovery. Any money improperly withheld or withdrawn from a *client account* must be immediately paid into the account or replaced as appropriate.

6.42

Rule 6.1 upgrades the previous rule 7 of the SRA Accounts Rules 2011, by requiring client account shortfalls to be remedied immediately, rather than promptly. Any other breach of the Rules must be remedied promptly upon discovery.

The rule requires the replacement of effectively any client account shortfall howsoever caused, using a partner's own money if necessary. This duty falls on all partners in the practice, and not just on the individual causing the breach or who was, for example, the partner responsible for supervising the person at fault.[1]

For this reason, the Accounts Rules effectively require all partners to know what is going on in their own accounts department; they will be personally responsible for putting right any problem, with their own money. While accounting functions are invariably delegated to non-solicitors in all but the tiniest practices, the Accounts Rules require effective oversight at management level, for example, in checking client balances; that the five-weekly (monthly in practice) reconciliation has been carried out, and is understood; and that any information given by it which prompts action is acted upon. In practice, the larger the firm, the less likely it is that the SRA will, upon discovery of a sanctionable breach, take regulatory action against all of its partners, preferring instead to sanction the firm and those that it deems are most culpable. Additionally, early remediation of a breach may be a significant factor in the SRA's decision whether to commence disciplinary action at all.

1   For commentary on when client account shortfalls are indemnified see **CHAPTER 11**.

Rule 7: Payment of interest

6.43

Rule 7: Payment of interest

7.1   You account to *clients* or third parties for a fair sum of *interest* on any *client money* held by you on their behalf.

7.2   You may by a written agreement come to a different arrangement with the *client* or the third party for whom the money is held as to the payment of *interest*, but you must provide sufficient information to enable them to give informed consent.

6.44

Rule 7.1 imposes a general requirement to account to clients and third parties for a fair sum of interest on money held on client account.

Rule 7.2 enables a firm to agree with its client not to account for interest, but the client must have sufficient information to give informed consent and the agreement must be in writing. When entering into such an agreement, the managers must have regard to the Principles, including the duties to act with independence (principle 3) and in the client's best interests (principle 7). As regards the informed consent, the SRA has stated:

> 'The level of information that will be sufficient will depend on the circumstances. It is for a firm to satisfy themselves that they have given the client the opportunity to give informed consent. The prominence and the ease of access to the information will be important in determining this.'[1]

1   SRA, 'Application for the approval of regulatory arrangements', August 2018, para 246.

6.45

The SRA Accounts Rules 2011 required a firm to have a policy for payment of interest. Rule 22.3 of the SRA Accounts Rules 2011 provided:

> '*You* must have a written policy on the payment of *interest*, which seeks to provide a fair outcome. The terms of the policy must be drawn to the attention of the *client* at the outset of a retainer, unless it is inappropriate to do so in the circumstances.'

That rule has been removed from the SRA Accounts Rules 2019. However, that does not mean that there is no longer a requirement for an interest policy. Paragraph 8.8 of the Code for Individuals and paragraph 7.1(c) of the Code for Firms require publicity relating to circumstances in which interest is payable to clients to be accurate and not misleading. Although it is not apparent from the wording of those rules, SRA commentary assumes that the rules impose an obligation to have a clear interest policy. The SRA has said:

> 'We have removed the requirement [in the Accounts Rules] to have a published interest policy. This duplicates with the new standard 8.8 in the code for individuals and does not comprise a change in policy. Firms are still required to have a clear interest policy in place. The requirement to have an interest policy also applies to firms through rule 7.1(c) in the Code of Conduct for Firms'.[1]

Rules 24 and 25 of the Solicitors' Accounts Rules 1998 contained detailed provisions on the circumstances in which interest should be paid, and the amount of the interest, including a £20 *de minimis* provision.[2] There is no reason why firms should not adopt a policy which bears a close resemblance to those rules if that is fair having regard to the nature of the practice.

1   SRA, 'Application for the approval of regulatory arrangements', August 2018, para 245.
2   The Solicitors' Accounts Rules 1998 are available on the internet.

Rule 8: Client accounting systems and controls

6.46

Rule 8: Client accounting systems and controls

8.1 You keep and maintain accurate, contemporaneous, and chronological records to:

   (a) record in client ledgers identified by the *client's* name and an appropriate description of the matter to which they relate:

      (i) all receipts and payments which are *client money* on the client side of the client ledger account;

      (ii) all receipts and payments which are not *client money* and bills of *costs* including transactions through the *authorised body's* accounts on the business side of the client ledger account;

   (b) maintain a list of all the balances shown by the client ledger accounts of the liabilities to *clients* (and third parties), with a running total of the balances; and

   (c) provide a cash book showing a running total of all transactions through *client accounts* held or operated by you.

8.2 You obtain, at least every five weeks, statements from *banks, building societies* and other financial institutions for all *client accounts* and business accounts held or operated by you.

8.3 You complete at least every five weeks, for all *client accounts* held or operated by you, a reconciliation of the *bank* or *building society* statement balance with the cash book balance and the client ledger total, a record of which must be signed off by the *COFA* or a *manager* of the firm. You should promptly investigate and resolve any differences shown by the reconciliation.

8.4 You keep readily accessible a central record of all bills or other written notifications of *costs* given by you.

6.47

The obligation to have and to maintain proper accounting systems generally needs no explanation. Firms should periodically review their systems, engaging external support where necessary. External support, for example, in the development and maintenance of systems may help to demonstrate compliance, or at least avoid a finding of culpability.

The general obligation is not expressly referred to in the Accounts Rules. It is set out in paragraph 2.1 of the Code for Firms, which requires the firm to have effective governance structures, arrangements, systems and controls in place to ensure that the firm complies with all the regulatory arrangements including the Accounts Rules. It is also reflected in the obligation on the COFA under paragraph 9.2 of the Code for Firms to take all reasonable steps to ensure that the firm, its managers and employees comply with the obligations imposed on them by the Accounts Rules. The general obligation is also referred to in the introduction to the SRA Accounts Rules 2019.

It is important not to overlook the requirement for internal controls. Firms should periodically audit compliance with their systems, not only examining the firm's books of account, but additionally checking that staff are following procedures. Evidence of such audits being carried out should be retained to demonstrate to the SRA that controls are in place to limit the risk of systemic breaches.

The SRA has produced a guidance note to assist firms in keeping accurate client accounting records.[1]

1   SRA guidance, 'Helping you keep accurate client accounting records', updated 25 November 2019.

6.48

One issue, which is both a requirement of the SRA Accounts Rules 2019 and a matter of business management, deserves special mention: it is accepted that errors will occur in the best ordered systems and one of the most effective controls in ensuring that mistakes are identified is a bank reconciliation that satisfies rule 8.3. This compares the total of all individual client ledger balances with the client cashbook and the amount shown on the bank statement or statements, shows any difference between any one of those three components and any other, and reconciles that difference. If this is done properly, most significant errors will be identified – certainly most types of client account shortage should be immediately spotted. The bank reconciliation is important; it is not a tedious bureaucratic requirement, but an essential management tool designed to enable principals who are not concerned with the day-to-day minu-tiae of the accounts to be informed of any serious underlying problems.

Managers should check reconciliation statements and their supporting documents carefully,[1] investigating any references to 'balancing items' or to a 'suspense account'.[2] If unexplained differences cannot be reconciled swiftly, a protective payment into client account may be necessary, along with an entry in the firm's risk register, and a self-report to the SRA.

Perhaps surprisingly, it is not uncommon during an SRA forensic investigation to discover that reconciliations are not being performed correctly. Some reporting accountants appear to believe that they are doing firms a favour by not pointing out errors. Errors can and will occur; the key to avoiding regulatory action is spotting them swiftly and taking appropriate remedial action.

The SRA Accounts Rules 2019 continue to require regular reconciliations and the importance of this is emphasised by a new provision (rule 8.3) that every reconcilia-tion must be 'signed off' by a manager or the COFA.

The importance of the monthly reconciliations is also emphasised by the SRA's explanation for retaining the rule in the Accounts Rules, despite the drive to simplify them and reduce their length:

> 'We have retained the requirement to obtain bank statements and do reconciliations every five weeks (at a minimum) as we consider that both are important mechanisms to ensure firms, their reporting accountants and our supervisory and enforcement functions can check compliance'.[3]

1   The firm must maintain a list of all individual client ledger balances under rule 8.1(b). The indi-vidual balances, which will be included in the supporting documents, as well as the running total

need to be checked. It is not permissible to offset a credit balance (money held) for one client against a debit balance (money owed) for another client.

2 Temporary use of a suspense account is acceptable, and is required to record unidentified receipts, but it would be imprudent to retain unallocated items on a suspense account for successive reconciliation periods unless exceptional circumstances apply and are documented. The SRA's guidance to reporting accountants suggests that a suspense account that has been used for 30 working days would be acceptable – SRA guidance, 'Planning for and completing an accountant's report', updated 14 September 2020.

3 SRA, 'Application for the approval of regulatory arrangements', August 2018, para 242.

6.49

Rule 8.1 introduced a new phrase which states the firm's records must be 'accurate, contemporaneous and chronological'. The SRA has not offered guidance to smaller firms on how often postings should be updated. The greater the level of transactions passing through client account, the more likely it will be deemed that records should be updated daily.

Rules 9 to 11: Operation of joint accounts, operation of a client's own account and TPMAs

6.50

PART 3: DEALING WITH OTHER MONEY BELONGING TO CLIENTS OR THIRD PARTIES

Rule 9: Operation of joint accounts

9.1 If, when acting in a *client's* matter, you hold or receive money jointly with the *client* or a third party, Part 2 of these rules does not apply save for:

(a) rule 8.2 – statements from *banks, building societies* and other financial institutions;

(b) rule 8.4 – bills and notifications of *costs*.

Rule 10: Operation of a client's own account

10.1 If, in the course of practice, you operate a *client's* own account as signatory, Part 2 of these rules does not apply save for:

(a) rule 8.2 – statements from *banks, building societies* and other financial institutions;

(b) rule 8.3 – reconciliations;

(c) rule 8.4 – bills and notifications of *costs*.

Rule 11: Third party managed accounts

11.1 You may enter into arrangements with a *client* to use a *third party managed account* for the purpose of receiving payments from or on behalf of, or making payments to or on behalf of, the *client* in respect of *regulated services* delivered by you to the *client*, only if:

CHAPTER 6
SRA ACCOUNTS RULES

(a)   use of the account does not result in you receiving or holding the *client's* money; and

(b)   you take reasonable steps to ensure, before accepting instructions, that the *client* is informed of and understands:

(i)   the terms of the contractual arrangements relating to the use of the *third party managed account*, and in particular how any *fees* for use of the *third party managed account* will be paid and who will bear them; and

(ii)   the *client's* right to terminate the agreement and dispute payment requests made by you.

11.2   You obtain regular statements from the provider of the *third party managed account* and ensure that these accurately reflect all transactions on the account.

Operation of joint accounts and a client's own account

6.51

Rules 9 and 10 are self-explanatory.

In relation to rule 9, the operation of joint accounts, the SRA has issued a guidance note.[1] The note indicates that while a joint account is not a client account, money held in a joint account is still client money.

It suggests that such an account might be operated by a firm with a client, another law firm or a third party, for example, where a firm's solicitor is named as joint executor with a lay person with regard to the administration of an estate.

The note suggests that the 'risks' of a joint account could be higher than those relating to a client account, as the firm does not have sole control of the account, and thus firms will need to consider in each case the risks to the client's money and any actions that could be taken to mitigate those risks – for example, ensuring that there is a joint signature mandate unless this is not possible.

The note acts as a reminder that the obligation to perform reconciliations, keep readily accessible a central record of all bills or other written notifications of costs given by the firm, and, where applicable, obtain (and deliver) an accountant's report, and keep records securely for at least six years, all apply to joint accounts.

The note recommends that firms keep a central register of joint accounts as the most practical way of keeping a record of all these accounts.

The note also indicates that a client's money should not be kept in a joint account that does not cater for the provision of the relevant statements, and that firms should have access to the original or duplicate statements.

In relation to rule 10, the operation of a client's own account, the SRA has commented that it is aware of concerns expressed about the obligations imposed on law firms by the rule, and has issued a guidance note.[2]

As indicated in the note:

> 'Law firms and solicitors might operate a client's own account in a number of scenarios. The most common is likely to be when a solicitor in a firm has been appointed as a Deputy (Court of Protection) or Attorney (under a Power of Attorney). In these matters the solicitor will have access to the client's own account and will make/receive payments directly from/into that account. There is no need for the client's money to be transferred into the law firm's client account.'

The SRA clarifies that firms' primary obligations in these circumstances are to:

- obtain statements from banks, building societies or other financial institutions at least every five weeks for these accounts;
- carry out reconciliations of each account every five weeks;
- keep a record of their bills and other notifications of their costs; and
- obtain an accountant's report.

However, the guidance notes that not all law firms will keep ledgers for a client's own account and will not have access to monthly bank statements in order for reconciliations to be carried out at least every five weeks. In those circumstances, the note indicates that:

> 'If you are unable to meet these requirements, we will not regard you as being in breach of the SRA Accounts Rules if you take reasonable steps to record – and satisfy yourself – that the client's money is not at risk and to record the position.

> Therefore, we would expect you to keep a:

> i   central register of the client own accounts that you operate,

> ii   separate record of the transactions carried out by you or on your behalf in respect of the client's own account, and

> iii record of your bills and other notification of costs relating to that client's matter.

> This information should be made available to your reporting accountant as and when required. We might also ask for this information.'

1   SRA guidance, 'Joint accounts and record keeping', updated 25 November 2019.
2   SRA guidance, 'Statement of our position regarding firms operating a client's own account', updated 25 November 2019.

Third party managed accounts

6.52

The SRA has defined a TPMA as follows: 'We define a TPMA as an account where a third party (a payment service[s] provider) holds money … [for] two … transacting parties, … a law firm and their client'.[1] In conveyancing (for example), on the purchase of a property, the payment services provider would open an account for the client, receive the purchase monies from the client (or the client's mortgagee), obtain authority from the client to operate the account on the basis of the solicitor's instructions and pay the deposit and completion monies to the vendor when directed to do so by the solicitor.

A TPMA provides an opportunity to carry out work such as conveyancing without the need to operate a client account. That would reduce the firm's overheads and avoid the regulatory risks of operating a client account. If a client account is not operated, a firm could rely on the rule 2.2 exemption to pay money on account of costs into office account.[2] Alternatively a TPMA may be used in particular transactions, notwithstanding that a firm has a general client account.

1   SRA, 'Application for the approval of regulatory arrangements', August 2018, para 293.
2   For the rule 2.2 exemption relating to money on account see **6.23**.

6.53

There was nothing in the 2011 rules to prevent the use of a TPMA and, as money placed by a client into a TPMA operated by a payment services provider is not client money (as it is not received by the firm or the solicitor), there were no professional rules directly controlling the use of TPMAs. The SRA produced a guidance note in December 2017, updated 25 November 2019, 'Third party managed accounts' on the use of TPMAs and rule 11 has been introduced to control the manner in which firms use TPMAs. Firms and solicitors will also remain subject to the requirement to protect client money and assets[1] and act in the best interests of each client.[2]

1   Paragraph 4.2 of the Code for Individuals; paragraph 5.2 of the Code for Firms.
2   Principle 7.

6.54

The obligations arising on the use of a TPMA include the following:[1]

- The solicitor should make sure the payment services provider who operates the TPMA is regulated by the Financial Conduct Authority (FCA) either as an authorised/European Economic Area (EEA) authorised payment institution or as a small payment institution with equivalent safeguarding arrangements.

- The TPMA must be an account held at a bank or building society operated as an escrow account (the third party receives and disburses money on your and your client's behalf).

- The monies in the TPMA must be owned beneficially by the third party and the use of the TPMA by the firm does not result in it receiving or holding the client's money.

- The solicitor should take reasonable steps to make sure that the client understands the arrangement with the payment services provider before it is entered into,[2] including in particular:

    - how the money will be held and how the transaction will work;

    - the terms of the contractual arrangements (the client's rights and obligations) and what the use of the TPMA means in their case, including whether they are required to authorise payments, any charges or fees that are applicable and any liability they have to pay them;[3]

- their right to terminate the agreement and dispute payment requests by the solicitor;[4] and

- the fact that complaints should be made to the FCA in accordance with their complaints procedure, and that the regulatory protections that apply to TPMAs are different from those that apply to client money held in a firm's client account.[5]

- The solicitor should also comply with the obligations to safeguard client money and have suitable arrangements in place for the use and monitoring of TPMAs, including monitoring the transactions on the account and keeping appropriate records.

- SRA permission is not required, but the SRA expects to be notified when a firm enters into an arrangement with, or ceases to use, a TPMA provider, and has produced a form for this purpose, FA9, a link to which is provided in the guidance note.[6]

- The solicitor should obtain regular statements and ensure that these reflect the transactions on the account correctly, and make sure that the funds in the TPMA are only used for their designated purpose.

1   See rule 11 of the Accounts Rules and SRA guidance, 'Third party managed accounts', updated 25 November 2019.
2   Paragraph 8.6 of the Code for Individuals.
3   Rule 11.1(b)(i) of the Accounts Rules and SRA guidance, 'Third party managed accounts', updated 25 November 2019.
4   Rule 11.1(b)(ii) of the Accounts Rules.
5   Paragraph 8.11 of the Code for Individuals.
6   SRA guidance, 'Third party managed accounts', updated 25 November 2019.

6.55

Rule 11.1 does not expressly state that the payment services provider must be regulated by the FCA as an authorised/EEA authorised payment institution or a small payment institution. Rule 11.1 is instead permissive. It states that the firm may use a TPMA; 'third party managed account' is defined in the SRA Glossary as 'an account held at a bank or building society in the name of a third party which is an authorised payment institution, [or] a small payment institution that has chosen to implement safeguarding arrangement[s] in accordance with the Payment Services Regulations or an EEA authorised payment institution (as each [is] defined in the Payment Services Regulations) regulated by the FCA, in which monies are owned beneficially by the third party, and which is operated upon terms agreed between the third party, you and your client as an escrow payment service'.

Despite the permissive nature of rule 11.1, the SRA has made the following comments on rule 11, which make it clear that the SRA expects firms to only use TPMAs which fall within the Glossary definition:

'Our approach is to allow firms to use a TPMA if:

- The TPMA is either an authorised payment institution … and, as a result has mandatory safeguarding arrangement[s], or is a small payment institution … which has adopted voluntary safeguarding arrangements

- The firm can demonstrate that it has suitable arrangements for the implementation, use and monitoring of TPMAs. For example that appropriate information is provided to clients and appropriate internal controls are in place …

… We will restrict the use of TPMAs to those operated by payment services providers that are regulated by the FCA under the Payment Services Regulations 2017'.[1]

The SRA has also stated that it does not intend to restrict the type of legal services which can be carried out with TPMAs but that it expects firms to carry out an assessment of the suitability of the provider's product for the client in the circumstances of the case.[2]

1   SRA, 'Application for the approval of regulatory arrangements', August 2018, paras 300 and 303.
2   SRA, 'Application for the approval of regulatory arrangements', August 2018, para 311.

Rule 12: Obtaining and delivery of accountants' reports

6.56

PART 4: ACCOUNTANTS' REPORTS AND STORAGE AND RETENTION OF ACCOUNTING RECORDS

Rule 12: Obtaining and delivery of accountants' reports

12.1   If you have, at any time during an *accounting period*, held or received *client money*, or operated a joint account or a *client's* own account as signatory, you must:

(a)   obtain an accountant's report for that *accounting period* within six months of the end of the period; and

(b)   deliver it to the *SRA* within six months of the end of the *accounting period* if the accountant's report is qualified to show a failure to comply with these rules, such that money belonging to *clients* or third parties is, or has been, or is likely to be placed, at risk.

12.2   You are not required to obtain an accountant's report if:

(a)   all of the *client money* held or received during an *accounting period* is money received from the Legal Aid Agency; or

(b)   in the *accounting period*, the statement or passbook balance of *client money* you have held or received does not exceed:

(i)   an average of £10,000; and

(ii)   a maximum of £250,000,

or the equivalent in foreign currency.

12.3   In rule 12.2 above a 'statement or passbook balance' is the total balance of:

(a)   all *client accounts* held or operated by you; and

(b)　any joint accounts and *clients'* own accounts operated by you,

as shown by the statements obtained under rule 8.2.

12.4　The *SRA* may require you to obtain or deliver an accountant's report to the *SRA* on reasonable notice if you cease to operate as an *authorised body* and to hold or operate a *client account*, or the *SRA* considers that it is otherwise in the public interest to do so.

12.5　You ensure that any report obtained under this rule is prepared and signed by an accountant who is a member of one of the *chartered accountancy bodies* and who is, or works for, a registered auditor.

12.6　The *SRA* may disqualify an accountant from preparing a report for the purposes of this rule if:

(a)　the accountant has been found guilty by their professional body of professional misconduct or equivalent; or

(b)　the *SRA* is satisfied that the accountant has failed to exercise due care and skill in the preparation of a report under these rules.

12.7　The *SRA* may specify from time to time matters that you must ensure are incorporated into the terms on which an accountant is engaged.

12.8　You must provide to an accountant preparing a report under these rules:

(a)　details of all accounts held or operated by you in connection with your practice at any *bank, building society* or other financial institution at any time during the *accounting period* to which the report relates; and

(b)　all other information and documentation that the accountant requires to enable completion of their report.

12.9　The accountant must complete and sign their report in the *prescribed* form.

CHAPTER 6
SRA ACCOUNTS RULES

6.57

Rules 12.1 to 12.3 set out the circumstances in which a firm must obtain an accountant's report, and if necessary deliver it to the SRA, noting that when the obligation arises, it is the firm's obligation to deliver the report, but the obligation may be satisfied by the accountant so delivering it.

Rule 12.2 exempts firms from the obligation to obtain an accountant's report where, during an accounting period:

● all of the client money held or received is money received from the LAA; or

● the average balance on client account does not exceed £10,000 and the maximum balance does not exceed £250,000. SRA guidance[1] indicates that these thresholds are to be assessed based on the reconciliations undertaken over the accounting period.[2]

Where a firm changes legal status, subject to the exemptions indicated above, it should obtain separate accountant's reports for both entities. For example, where a firm changes status from being a recognised sole practice to a partnership, it will require a report for the sole practice up to the exact date on which the firm held client money as a sole practice, and a separate first report for the partnership for the period commencing the following day.[3]

Under the SRA Accounts Rules 2011, all qualified reports were required to be delivered to the SRA. In contrast, by rule 12.1(b) of the SRA Accounts Rules 2019, firms are only required to deliver qualified reports which 'show a failure to comply with these rules, such that money belonging to clients or third parties is, or has been, or is likely to be placed, at risk'. However, this condition appears to be illusory as reporting accountants are expected to qualify reports only where there has been a significant breach of the Accounts Rules, such that money belonging to clients or third parties is, has been or may be placed at risk.[4] While a firm may disagree with an accountant's decision to qualify a report, it would be prudent to deliver all qualified reports. Further SRA guidance[5] states: 'The report should only be delivered to us if it is qualified.'

Additionally, an accountant's report must be delivered to the SRA regardless of its qualification if:

- such an obligation arises by way of a condition imposed upon a solicitor's practising certificate or firm authorisation; or

- the firm has ceased to operate as an authorised body and to hold or operate a client account and has been asked to obtain and deliver a final report under rule 12.4 – see **6.58**.

The SRA has produced a guidance note, last updated on 14 September 2020, 'Planning for and completing an accountant's report'. The note indicates that the guidance is designed to help 'plan what work might need to be undertaken and how to assure that client money is properly safeguarded' and to 'assess what factors might lead the accountant to decide that the report should be qualified and therefore submitted to us for further consideration of the risks posed', but indicates that reporting accountants should exercise their professional judgement when deciding whether a report needs to be qualified.[6]

The accountant is under a statutory duty to make an immediate report to the SRA if the accountant discovers evidence of fraud or theft in relation to the client account or another account operated by the firm, or if the accountant obtains information which is likely to be of material significance in determining whether a solicitor is a fit and proper person to hold client money.[7]

Subject to the statutory duty, the SRA has issued the following guidance on when it expects a report to be qualified and delivered:[8]

- It only expects reports to be qualified where there has been a significant breach of the Accounts Rules, such that money belonging to clients or third parties is, has been or may be placed at risk.

- Breaches from administrative errors are not likely to be significant, but still could be if they are persistent, derive from a lack of controls or breakdown of existing controls, and have put client money at risk.

- If the reporting accountant considers that their work has been limited in scope to the extent that they feel unable to make the declarations required on the accountant's report form, then they should qualify the report on that basis and make a report.

- When exercising their professional judgement, the accountant's assessment should be based on an understanding of the seriousness of all the risks posed in the context of the firm's size and complexity, areas of work, systems and controls, compliance history and the likely impact on the firm and its clients if money were to be misused or not accounted for.

- The presence of one or more serious factors is likely to lead to a qualification, including a significant and/or unreplaced shortfall, systematic billing for fees and any disbursements that have not been incurred and payments in respect of that bill being made into the business account, evidence of disregard for the safety of client money and assets, actual or suspected fraud or dishonesty by the managers or employees of the firm that may have an impact upon the safety of money belonging to clients or third parties, accounting records unavailable or significantly deficient, bank accounts/ledgers lacking reference to a client, failing to provide documentation requested by the accountant, client account bank reconciliations not carried out, client account improperly used as a banking facility and any other significant breaches not already reported to the SRA by firms and their compliance officers.

- The presence of one or more moderate factors may lead to a qualification depending upon context, including a significant, fully replaced client money shortfall, actual or suspected fraud by third parties that have had or may have an impact on the safety of client money, unreported serious breaches, failures to inform clients of the risk of money being paid into the business account for costs that have not been incurred, accounting records that are insufficient, unreliable or not retained for six years, client account bank reconciliations not regularly carried out at least every five weeks, poor control environment, inadequate performance or review of client account bank reconciliations, longstanding residual balances due to clients and improper use of suspense accounts.

The SRA's guidance note also schedules a large number of 'key risk areas' for checking by the reporting accountants.

When deciding whether to deliver a qualified report, it would be prudent to err on the side of caution, and, if in doubt, to deliver.

Firms should ensure that any qualifications noted on an accountant's report are investigated swiftly, and any breaches remedied.

The SRA also expects reporting accountants to report to it the termination of an accountant's appointment where this is based on the accountant's intention to issue a qualified accountant's report or if the accountant discovers, after making checks with the SRA, that the firm has failed to submit a qualified accountant's report.[9]

1   SRA guidance, 'Accountant's report and the exemption to obtain one', updated 25 November 2019.
2   A maximum balance of £250,000 would require at least 25 reconciliations in the accounting period to avoid exceeding an average of £10,000. As the maximum accounting period is 18 months – equivalent to 78 weeks – reconciliations in this example would have needed to have been performed around every three weeks; therefore the maximum single reconciliation threshold is unlikely to be relevant.
3   SRA guidance, 'Accountant's report and the exemption to obtain one', updated 25 November 2019.
4   SRA guidance, 'Planning for and completing an accountant's report', updated 14 September 2020.
5   SRA guidance, 'Accountant's report and the exemption to obtain one', updated 25 November 2019.
6   Ibid.
7   Section 34(9) of SA 1974.
8   SRA guidance, 'Planning for and completing an accountant's report', updated 14 September 2020.
9   Ibid.

CHAPTER 6
SRA ACCOUNTS RULES

6.58

There is no longer a positive requirement to deliver an accountant's report on ceasing to hold client money.[1] However, rule 12.4 empowers the SRA to require a firm to deliver an accountant's report on reasonable notice if a firm ceases to operate as an authorised body and to hold or operate a client account, or the SRA considers that it is otherwise in the public interest to do so.

The 'cease to hold' rule was changed because the old rule unnecessarily required a firm to file a cease to hold accountant's report when the firm changed its legal status from one form to another without cessation of the provision of legal services. It is not yet known whether the SRA will routinely ask for cease to hold reports whenever the underlying business is closed down. The SRA has commented that it will require a cease to hold report for client money if it believes it 'necessary', and has given the example of 'when a firm shuts down and closes its client account on a case-by-case basis'.[2]

1   Rule 33.5 of the SRA Accounts Rules 2011 required 'cease to hold' reports.
2   SRA, 'Application for the approval of regulatory arrangements', August 2018, para 254.

6.59

Rule 12.5 restricts those who may prepare reports to members of various accountants' professional bodies who are also registered auditors, or their employees.

Before engaging an accountant, a firm can check with the SRA whether the accountant has been disqualified from preparing a report. Rule 12.6 empowers the SRA to disqualify an accountant from preparing a report in certain circumstances. If the SRA is aware of a firm which has recently obtained an accountant's report from an accountant who is disqualified, there is a risk that the SRA will require delivery of an accountant's report under rule 12.4 and that the firm undergoes an SRA forensic investigation.

6.60

The stringent provisions of rule 12.8 govern the information and documents the firm must provide, including details of all accounts held at banks, building societies and other financial institutions operated by the firm during the relevant accounting period, and any other information the accountant requires for completion of the report.

Rule 13: Storage and retention of accounting records

6.61

Rule 13: Storage and retention of accounting records

13.1   You must store all *accounting records* securely and retain these for at least six years.

6.62

The SRA Glossary defines 'accounting records' to mean 'all reconciliations, bank and building society statements (paper or electronic), original passbooks, signed letters of engagement with reporting accountants, the accountants' reports (whether qualified or not), any client's written instructions to hold client money other than in accordance with these rules, records and documents, including electronic records, relating to any TPMAs and any other records or documents necessary to show compliance with the SRA Accounts Rules'.

CHAPTER 6
SRA ACCOUNTS RULES

CHAPTER 7

Compliance officers (COLPs and COFAs)

7.1

Compliance officers for legal practice (COLPs) and compliance officers for finance and administration (COFAs) have their origins in the Legal Services Act (LSA) 2007 which requires alternative business structures (ABSs) licensed under Part 5 of that Act to have individuals to fulfil the roles and to perform the duties of Head of Legal Practice (HOLP) and Head of Finance and Administration (HOFA).[1]

The Solicitors Regulation Authority (SRA) elected to extend the concept to all firms, and to create the roles of COLP and COFA with effect from 1 January 2013. Since then all SRA-regulated practices, whether licensed as an ABS or not, must have a COLP and a COFA (who may be the same person, and thus a sole practitioner may fulfil both roles).

1   Sections 91 and 92 of LSA 2007.

The appointment of compliance officers

The business organisations which need compliance officers

7.2

The requirement to appoint compliance officers is set out in rule 8.1 of the SRA Authorisation of Firms Rules 2019 (the 'Firm Rules'). Rule 8.1 states:

> '8.1 An *authorised body* must at all times have an individual who is designated as its *COLP* and an individual who is designated as its *COFA*, and whose designations the *SRA* has approved.'

The SRA Glossary defines 'authorised body' to mean '(a) a body that has been authorised by the SRA to practise as a licensed body or a recognised body or (b) a sole practitioner's practice that has been authorised by the SRA as a recognised sole practice'.

In contrast, both 'freelance solicitors', that is, those solicitors who practise on their own without applying for entity authorisation[1] and solicitors who practise in a business which is not authorised by the SRA do not need to appoint a COLP or COFA.

1   For the right of solicitors to practise on their own without authorisation, see regulation 10.2 of the SRA Authorisation of Individuals Regulations 2019.

Who is eligible to be appointed?

7.3

The requirement for a COFA[1] is that he or she:

(1)   should not be disqualified from acting as a HOLP or HOFA under section 99 of LSA 2007;[2]

(2)   has consented to act;

(3)   is approved by the SRA; and

(4)   is either:

    (a)   a manager or an employee of the authorised body; or

    (b)   a current compliance officer and manager or employee of a related authorised body.

Two authorised bodies are related if they have a common manager or owner.[3]

The COLP must fulfil all the above requirements and must also be either a solicitor or another individual who is authorised to carry on reserved legal activities by an approved regulator.[4]

1   Rules 8.1–8.3 of the Firm Rules.
2   For HOLPs and HOFAs see **7.1** and **7.12**.
3   Rule 8.3 of the Firm Rules.
4   Rule 8.2(d) of the Firm Rules.

Selection of compliance officers by the firm

7.4

In small firms, and sole practices in particular, one person may fulfil all roles, and there is no requirement that it should be otherwise.

Larger firms will face difficult questions: should the COLP be the managing partner, or would that create an unmanageable conflict for someone with the primary role of driving the business? Or should it be the general counsel, but would that not create a conflict with that person's role in being able to give advice in privileged circumstances?

If the compliance officer is not in the top echelon in the firm, what protections, beyond those provided in the Codes of Conduct, will it be necessary to provide to someone who may have the role of a whistle-blower, against the wishes of senior partners or managers?[1]

What level of access to information, at board level for example, must a compliance officer have? The likely inference and position of the SRA is that he/she must have access to everything. Will that mean that a COLP will have to be a partner/manager, or is the situation capable of being regulated by contract?

Early SRA guidance stated that, 'Whilst some senior or managing partners might wish to take on these roles, firms, particularly larger firms, need to consider whether senior or managing partners will be able to devote the time necessary to the role'.[2]

Guidance issued upon the SRA's 2019 regulatory arrangements coming into force indicated, 'In larger firms, or where the COLP and COFA are employees, as well as the right governance, the compliance officers must have clear reporting lines that empower them sufficiently to fulfil their roles. This is to make sure the COLP and COFA are able to implement changes or introduce new procedures to ensure compliance and good risk-management.'[3]

At the same time, the firm should take into account rule 2.3 of the SRA Assessment of Character and Suitability Rules 2019 (the 'Suitability Rules'). Rule 2.3 states that, when assessing suitability, the SRA will consider whether the applicant is of sufficient seniority and in a position of sufficient responsibility to fulfil the requirements of the role.

There is a sense that in a small number of firms, the role is viewed as a poisoned chalice, and that salaried partners without sufficient seniority or responsibility (or skills and experience) have been appointed. Managers remain responsible for compliance and such an approach is unlikely to avoid regulatory action for the managers in the event of serious breach. Changes seen in the 2019 Codes and the Accounts Rules emphasise the continuing nature of the managers' responsibilities.

Furthermore, systemic regulatory failures could be catastrophic for the firm, rendering it liable to SRA intervention, uninsurable, or cause a loss of income by reason of reputational damage.

1 Paragraphs 3.11 and 3.12 of the SRA Code of Conduct for Firms 2019 (the 'Code for Firms'); paragraph 7.9 of the SRA Code of Conduct for Solicitors, RELs and RFLs 2019 (the 'Code for Individuals').
2 SRA, 'Question of ethics: nominating your COLP and COFA', May 2012.
3 SRA guidance, 'Responsibilities of COLPs and COFAs', 25 November 2019.

Making the application for appointment

7.5

The approval of compliance officers for new entities is part of the authorisation process, and any application for authorisation as an ABS, or as a new non-ABS practice, must therefore name the proposed compliance officers whenever the application is first made.

Applications for appointment of new compliance officers in existing firms are made online by completing an SRA application form, which is available on the SRA website, unless the new nominee is automatically appointed under the deeming provisions. For the procedure if the deeming provisions apply see **7.7**.

Temporary emergency applications

7.6

If a firm (traditional or ABS) ceases to have a compliance officer of either class it must notify the SRA promptly.[1]

An application can be made for temporary emergency approval of a new compliance officer within seven days of the former compliance officer ceasing to act. The SRA will only grant a temporary approval if the SRA is satisfied that a substantive application could not reasonably have been commenced in advance, and the SRA has no reason to believe that the new appointee in not a fit and proper person to act as a compliance officer.[2]

A grant of temporary approval will be for an initial period of 28 days. It may be granted effective from the date when the former compliance officer ceased to act, so that the firm is not in default, but the temporary approval does not guarantee that a substantive application for approval will be granted, or granted without conditions. The temporary approval can be granted subject to such conditions as the SRA considers appropriate in the public interest. The initial 28-day period can be extended for such period as the SRA thinks fit, and will be extended pending determination of a substantive application if the substantive application is made within the initial 28-day period. The temporary approval, and any extension, may be revoked if the SRA considers it appropriate to do so in the public interest.[3]

1 Paragraph 3.8(a) of the Code for Firms.
2 Rule 15.2 and 15.3 of the Firm Rules.
3 Rule 15.4 of the Firm Rules.

SRA approval

7.7

The SRA may approve an individual to act as a compliance officer if it is satisfied that the individual is fit and proper to undertake the role.[1]

An individual is deemed to be fit and proper to act as a compliance officer if: (1) the individual is a lawyer[2] and a manager of the authorised body; (2) the authorised body has an annual turnover of no more than £600,000; (3) the individual is not a compliance officer of any other authorised body; and (4) the individual is not subject to a regulatory or disciplinary investigation or adverse finding or decision of the SRA, the Solicitors Disciplinary Tribunal (the Tribunal or SDT) or another regulatory body. If those deeming provisions apply, the authorised body must notify the SRA promptly on a prescribed form of the identity of the compliance officer and the SRA will then approve the appointment.[3]

If the deeming provisions do not apply, the SRA will make a decision whether the individual is fit and proper to undertake the role on the basis of the Suitability Rules.

Under the Suitability Rules, the SRA will consider whether the applicant is of sufficient seniority and in a position of sufficient responsibility to fulfil the requirements of the role. The SRA will also consider past conduct and behaviour, including criminal convictions, cautions, regulatory and disciplinary findings, any evidence of insolvency or financial mismanagement and any other available information relating to the applicant's character and suitability for the role. The applicant will be under a duty to disclose all relevant matters and must provide a certificate from the Disclosure and Barring Service and any further information the SRA may request. When making the decision the SRA will take into account the need to protect the public and maintain trust and confidence in the provision of legal services.[4]

Approval takes effect from the date of the decision, unless otherwise stated. It remains effective only if the individual takes up the role within the period specified in the notice of approval, or one year if no period is specified. The approval expires when the individual ceases to act as a compliance officer.[5]

The roles of COLP and COFA are not interchangeable. Someone already approved as a COLP cannot step into the role of a COFA without going through a further process of approval. Equally someone approved as a COLP for one entity cannot automatically step into the role of COLP for another entity.

The SRA has produced a guidance note.[6]

1   Rule 13.1 of the Firm Rules.
2   Defined in the SRA Glossary 2019 to mean '... a member of one of the following professions, entitled to practise as such: (a) the profession of solicitor, barrister or advocate of the UK; (b) an authorised person other than one authorised by the SRA; (c) any profession approved by the SRA for RFL status; and (d) any other regulated legal profession specified by the SRA for the purpose of this definition'.
3   Rules 13.5 and 13.6 of the Firm Rules.
4   See the Suitability Rules.
5   Rule 13.7 of the Firm Rules.
6   SRA, 'Approval of role holders', updated 12 March 2021.

Conditions

7.8

When granting approval the SRA has power to impose conditions on the individual's approval if it considers that there are risks to the public or the public interest which can be addressed by the imposition of condtions.[1] The SRA also has the power to impose conditions on the firm's authorisation if it is in the public interest to do so and if the SRA is satisfied that a compliance officer, or the authorised body, its managers, employees, owners, or interest holders, is unsuitable to engage in certain practising arrangements, is likely to put the interests of clients or third parties at risk, requires monitoring of compliance with the regulatory arrangements or should take steps conducive to the regulatory objectives.[2]

1   Rule 2.4 of the Suitability Rules.
2   Rules 3.1 and 3.2 of the Firm Rules.

Notification obligations

7.9

After appointment a compliance officer is under a duty to notify the SRA promptly of any information concerning the compliance officer which would be relevant to an assessment of the individual's fitness and propriety to act. The SRA can require a compliance officer to make a self-declaration as to their continuing fitness and propriety to act.[1]

A compliance officer whose appointment is based on an SRA assessment under the Suitability Rules (rather than the deeming provisions)[2] also has an ongoing obligation under the Suitability Rules to tell the SRA promptly about anything which raises a question as to his or her suitability and character, or any change to information which has previously been disclosed to the SRA in support of the application for approval.[3]

Those reporting obligations place compliance officers in a position where they will need to report to the SRA if they are unable to fulfil their roles, whether as a result of lack of time or ability, or lack of assistance from the firm.

The firm has an obligation to notify the SRA promptly if it becomes aware that information provided to the SRA by or on behalf of the firm about its compliance officers may be false, misleading, incomplete or inaccurate, or if there have been any material changes to any such information,[4] or if it becomes aware of any facts or matters that it reasonably believes are capable of amounting to a serious breach (by the compliance officer) of their regulatory arrangements.[5]

1 Rule 13.10 of the Firm Rules.
2 See **7.7**.
3 Rule 6.5 of the Suitability Rules.
4 Paragraph 3.8 of the Code for Firms.
5 Paragraphs 3.9 and 3.10 of the Code for Firms – see **7.27** for further commentary.

Withdrawal of approval

7.10

Under rule 13.9 of the Firm Rules, the SRA may withdraw approval of a compliance officer at any time if it is not satisfied that he or she is fit and proper to undertake the designated role.

Withdrawal of approval of a COLP or COFA could be terminal for a practice. If for any reason a firm ceases to have an approved COLP and COFA it must notify the SRA promptly and designate a replacement and ensure an application is made for the replacement; temporary emergency approval, if sought within seven days, may be granted pending determination of the substantive application (see **7.6**).

Larger firms may find it desirable to have more than one potential compliance officer of each class in a position to take over the role in the event of unforeseen circumstances, although as things stand there is no mechanism by which approval can be sought other than by the formal process of approval of the appointment (there is no process whereby one can obtain approval of someone with a view to later appointment).

The powers of the SRA to disqualify a HOLP or HOFA of an ABS are considered in **Chapter 26**.

Reviews and appeals

7.11

An individual has a right to apply for an internal review of an SRA decision to refuse approval of the person's designation as a compliance officer, or an SRA decision to withdraw approval of the person's designation as a compliance officer. The application must be made within 28 days from notice being given of the decision, and the review is decided on the papers.[1]

In the case of COLPs and COFAs of ABSs, the individual affected has a right of appeal to the Tribunal against the SRA's refusal of an application for approval and a decision to withdraw approval. The appeal must be made within 28 days of the decision taking effect. If there has been a prior on-time application for review, that 28-day period runs from the date the review is determined. For appeals to the Tribunal see **CHAPTER 23**.

Where a COLP or COFA is appointed within a non–ABS authorised practice, such as a traditional firm, there is no right of appeal to the Tribunal. There is a right to appeal a decision to withdraw the individual's designation as compliance officer to the High Court, but there is no right of appeal to the High Court in respect of a decision to refuse approval of an individual's designation as a compliance officer.

Because every practice must have an approved COLP and COFA, and a refusal to approve the appointment of a particular individual could mean that a practice has to close, it is not entirely satisfactory that one kind of authorised practice has a right of appeal to the Tribunal, with possible costs consequences if the SRA got it wrong, and another kind of authorised practice bound by exactly the same set of SRA rules has no external right of appeal, so that the only remedy is litigation, by judicial review. Judicial review does not generally entail a full review of the merits of the original decision and is consequently an unsatisfactory remedy.

1   The rights of internal review and external appeal are contained in the SRA Application, Notice, Review and Appeal Rules 2019.

Disqualification

7.12

Within the ABS regime, the licensing authority has the power under section 99 of LSA 2007 to disqualify a person from being a HOLP, a HOFA, or a manager or an employee of any licensed body. Disqualification by the SRA, as licensing authority, may render the individual unemployable in the regulated legal community.

For these powers and associated rights of appeal see **CHAPTERS 26** and **23** respectively.

These are powers which are specific to ABSs and do not apply to COLPs and COFAs of other kinds of authorised practices.

Duties of a COLP and COFA

Paragraph 9 of the Code for Firms

7.13

The compliance officers' duties are set out in paragraphs 9.1 and 9.2 of the Code for Firms, which are reproduced below.

> 9.1   If you are a *COLP* you must take all reasonable steps to:
>
> (a)   ensure compliance with the terms and conditions of your firm's authorisation;

(b)   ensure compliance by your firm and its *managers*, employees or *interest holders* with the *SRA's regulatory arrangements* which apply to them;

(c)   ensure that your firm's *managers* and *interest holders* and those they employ or contract with do not cause or substantially contribute to a breach of the *SRA's regulatory arrangements*;

(d)   ensure that a prompt report is made to the *SRA* of any facts or matters that you reasonably believe are capable of amounting to a serious breach of the terms and conditions of your firm's authorisation, or the *SRA's regulatory arrangements* which apply to your firm, *managers* or employees;

(e)   notwithstanding sub-paragraph (d), you ensure that the *SRA* is informed promptly of any facts or matters that you reasonably believe should be brought to its attention in order that it may investigate whether a serious breach of its *regulatory arrangements* has occurred or otherwise exercise its regulatory powers,

save in relation to the matters which are the responsibility of the *COFA* as set out in paragraph 9.2 below.

9.2   If you are a *COFA* you must take all reasonable steps to:

(a)   ensure that your firm and its *managers* and employees comply with any obligations imposed upon them under the SRA Accounts Rules;

(b)   ensure that a prompt report is made to the *SRA* of any facts or matters that you reasonably believe are capable of amounting to a serious breach of the SRA Accounts Rules which apply to them;

(c)   notwithstanding sub-paragraph (b), you ensure that the *SRA* is informed promptly of any facts or matters that you reasonably believe should be brought to its attention in order that it may investigate whether a serious breach of its *regulatory arrangements* has occurred or otherwise exercise its regulatory powers.

The COFA's duties

7.14

The COFA's duties under paragraph 9.2 of the Code for Firms are limited to two duties: (1) a duty to take all reasonable steps to ensure compliance with the Accounts Rules, that is to ensure appropriate systems and controls are in place; and (2) a duty to report (for the duty to report see **7.27**).

The COFA's duties relating to accounts under the Code for Firms are narrower than the duties imposed on the COFA under the 2011 rules because there have been the following three changes:

- Under the 2011 rules, the COLP and COFA were both under a duty to monitor and control the firm's financial stability. That duty now falls on the COLP alone.

- Under the 2011 rules, the COFA was directly responsible for breaches of the SRA Accounts Rules (as well as the systems and controls relating to the Accounts Rules). That direct responsibility for breaches has gone.

• There is no longer an express duty to record failures to comply with the SRA Accounts Rules and make the records available to the SRA on request (but see below).

Those changes are considered in further detail in the next three sections.

7.15

As regards financial stability, the COFA's duties are now in line with the duties of a HOFA under LSA 2007. When originally envisaged the role of the COFA was expected to be quite narrow. Despite the title and the references to 'finance' and 'administration' the origins of the role are found in section 92(1) of LSA 2007 in relation to ABSs:

'The Head of Finance and Administration of a licensed body must take all reasonable steps to ensure compliance with licensing rules made under paragraph 20 of Schedule 11 (accounts)'

and in the quoted paragraph of Schedule 11:

'The licensing rules must make provision as to the treatment of money … and the keeping of accounts in respect of such money.'

The 'money' in question is 'money (including money held on trust) which is received, held or dealt with by the licensed body, its managers and employees for clients or other persons'. Thus the role of the HOFA under LSA 2007 is very specific: responsibility for the correct treatment of client and trust money and the keeping of accounts. It does not entail any wider responsibility for running the business.

There was a considerable amount of 'regulatory creep' under the SRA's 2011 rules. The SRA Authorisation Rules 2011 required the COFA to take all reasonable steps to ensure the firm complied with the Accounts Rules. Rule 1.2 of the SRA Accounts Rules 2011 said: 'You must comply with the Principles set out in the Handbook, and the outcomes in Chapter 7 of the SRA Code of Conduct in relation to the effective financial management of the firm …'. Chapter 7 included the obligation to 'maintain systems and controls for monitoring the financial stability of your firm and risks to money and assets entrusted to you by clients and others, and … take steps to address issues identified' (outcome 7.4). By that means the SRA asserted that the COFA had a role in relation to financial stability. The COLP also had a direct responsibility to take all reasonable steps to ensure that the firm complied with outcome 7.4, and the COLP and the COFA therefore had overlapping responsibilities relating to financial stability.

The overlapping responsibility has now gone, and the COLP alone has responsibilities in relation to financial stability, as the SRA Accounts Rules 2019 do not include any obligations relating to financial stability of the firm.

7.16

As regards direct responsibility for compliance with the Accounts Rules, rule 6.1 of the SRA Accounts Rules 2011 stated that the COFA and all principals in the firm must ensure compliance with the rules. In contrast, rule 1.2 of the SRA Accounts Rules 2019 (the comparable provision in the SRA Accounts Rules 2019) states that the authorised body's managers are jointly and severally responsible for compliance with the Accounts Rules. The SRA has said that wording which makes the COFA directly responsible for compliance with the Accounts Rules 'would place an unreasonable burden on the COFA', and that:

> 'The rule now emphasises that the Accounts Rules create obligations on the firm and its managers, not on the COFA. The COFA's obligations under the Code of Conduct to take all reasonable steps to ensure compliance with the Accounts Rules and report any concerns from a position of independence will still apply'.[1]

1   SRA, 'Application for the approval of regulatory arrangements', August 2018, para 249.

7.17

As regards record keeping, rule 8.5(e)(i)(B) of the SRA Authorisation Rules 2011 stated that the COFA must take all reasonable steps to record any failure to comply with any obligations imposed under the SRA Accounts Rules, and make such records available on request to the SRA. That express duty has been removed from the 2019 regulatory arrangements (see paragraph 9.2 of the Code for Firms at **7.13**). However that does not mean that record keeping can be abandoned. The SRA has frequently said that records of breaches are needed to monitor a firm's systems and to identify any patterns of breaches which, when viewed cumulatively, constitute a material or serious reportable breach. In other words, record keeping is an integral part of the firm's systems and controls, as well as the reporting obligations, and the COFA needs to keep records of breaches of the SRA Accounts Rules 2019 to comply with paragraph 9.2 of the Code for Firms. Furthermore, paragraph 2.2 of the Code for Firms obligates the firm to keep and maintain records to demonstrate compliance with its obligations under the SRA's regulatory arrangements and the SRA has issued guidance to indicate that it expects compliance officers to keep a record of all breaches that occur.[1]

The records which the COFA needs to keep under paragraph 9.2 of the Code for Firms are less extensive than the records which had to be kept under the 2011 rules because there is no longer a need for the COFA to keep any records relating to financial stability.

1   SRA guidance, 'Responsibilities of COLPs and COFAs', 25 November 2019.

The COLP's duties

7.18

The role of the COLP under paragraph 9.1(a) to (c) of the Code for Firms is very wide indeed.

There is an obligation to 'take all reasonable steps' to ensure that the firm, its managers, employees and interest holders comply with all of their obligations under the SRA's regulatory arrangements (except for the obligations under the Accounts Rules) and that they do not 'cause or substantially contribute to' any breaches of those obligations.

There is also an obligation to take all reasonable steps to ensure that those whom the firm's managers or interest holders contract with do not cause or substantially contribute to a breach of the SRA's regulatory arrangements.

The SRA Glossary states 'regulatory arrangements' has 'the meaning given to it by section 21 of the LSA'. Section 21 of LSA 2007 defines 'regulatory arrangements' as including all rules, regulations and arrangements which apply in relation to a regulated person.

The COLP's obligations therefore extend to all of the rules in the SRA regulatory arrangements and all legislation which has to be complied with under those rules, apart from the Accounts Rules.

SRA guidance indicates that sole practitioners acting as COLP and COFA are additionally duty-bound to review their own performance in the roles.[1]

The next seven sections comment on changes introduced by the Code for Firms to the scope of the COLP's obligations relating to: (1) control of the firm's work; (2) solicitors' conduct in their private lives; (3) contracts with third parties; (4) training; (5) client instructions; (6) financial stability; and (7) record keeping.

1   SRA guidance, 'Responsibilities of COLPs and COFAs', 25 November 2019.

7.19

Rule 6.1 of the Firm Rules places a duty on COLPs to monitor and control the scope of a firm's business, including the scope of the fee earning and other income producing work.

> 6.1   If you are a recognised body or *recognised sole practice*, your business may consist only of the provision of:
>
> (a)   professional services of the sort provided by individuals practising as *solicitors* and/or *lawyers* of other jurisdictions; and
>
> (b)   the services set out in annex 2 (whether or not they are also included in paragraph (a)),
>
> and if you have a notary public as a *manager* or *employee*, then professional services of the sort provided by notaries public.

Annex 2 to the Firm Rules lists 12 categories of business which can be carried on, ranging from alternative dispute resolution (ADR) and company secretarial services to estate agency, authorship and publishing. The COLP will have to take reasonable steps to ensure that the firm's business activities fall within the scope of rule 6.1 and Annex 2.

Rule 6.1 does not apply to ABSs. The scope of work carried out by an ABS is defined by its licence and any conditions or waivers attached to the licence. The COLP of an ABS was under a duty to take all reasonable steps to ensure that the ABS complies with the terms of its authorisation under the 2011 rules[1] and that duty has been carried into the 2019 arrangements by paragraph 9.1(a) of the Code for Firms.

1   Rule 8.5(c)(i)(A) of the SRA Authorisation Rules 2011.

7.20

Paragraph 9.1(b) of the Code for Firms places COLPs under a duty to take reasonable steps to ensure managers and employees do not breach any of the regulatory arrangements relating to them. Managers and employees who are solicitors are under a duty to adhere to the Principles which extend to an individual's private life. The guidance published by the SRA in August 2018 to accompany the SRA's 2019 regulatory arrangements included topic guides on criminal offences outside practice (including fixed penalty notices), driving with excess alcohol convictions and the use of offensive comments on social media. The extent of the COLP's duty to control adherence to the Principles in private life is unclear. It may, for example, require new provisions in employment contracts and firm manuals on behaviour outside the office. In *Senior*[1] allegations were additionally brought against a firm of solicitors arising out of its investigation processes concerning alleged sexual harassment by a partner of a junior employee. The Tribunal found that 'there should have been a clearer and more independent process for dealing with issues such as this'[2] but did not find that this failure amounted to professional misconduct.

1   11976-2019, SDT.
2   At paragraph 35.28.

7.21

Paragraph 9.1(c) of the Code for Firms places an obligation on COLPs to monitor contractual arrangements with third parties to ensure they do not cause or substantially contribute to a breach of the SRA's regulatory arrangements.

The obligation in paragraph 9.1(c) relates to third parties with whom the managers and interest holders contract. It is not immediately clear why the obligation relates to contracts with the managers and interest holders rather than with the firm. It is possible that the provision is intended, or will be interpreted by the SRA, so as to regulate the relationship between corporate managers and interest holders and those they employ or contract with. Alternatively, it may be construed as referring to the firm's contracts with third parties (on the basis that the managers can be said to be contracting on behalf of the firm) and the standard emphasises the need to set up systems to monitor outsourcing arrangements, as well as arrangements with, for example, claims management companies and medical agencies in personal injury work.[1] The monitoring may need to cover issues such as data protection, confidentiality, and cold calling.

1   For outsourcing see **5.23**.

7.22

Paragraph 7.1 of the Code for Individuals introduced a new standard requiring solicitors to keep up to date with the law. An identical provision has been added to the Code for Firms (paragraph 3.1), and the inclusion of that standard in the Code for Firms shows that the SRA expects firms to ensure that individual solicitors in the firm keep up to date with the law. That may require COLPs to introduce new systems to monitor continuing competence.

7.23

Paragraph 3.1 of the Code for Individuals introduced a new standard requiring solicitors only to act on instructions from the client, or someone with authority to provide instructions on the client's behalf. An identical standard has been added to the Code for Firms. The SRA introduced those standards to combat the increasing prevalence of identity frauds and cybercrime.[1] The new standards may require COLPs to introduce systems to keep up to date with reports on new cybercrime scams affecting law firms and to review the firm's systems on a frequent basis to keep up to date with the ever-changing nature of cybercrime fraud.

1   SRA, 'Application for the approval of regulatory arrangements', August 2018, para 104.

7.24

Under the Code for Firms, the compliance officer duties relating to financial stability now fall on the COLP alone. Under the 2011 rules, the COLP and COFA were both responsible for financial stability. See **7.15**.

7.25

The express duty on the COLP under the 2011 rules to keep records of breaches has not been carried over to the new rules. However the COLP should continue to keep records. See **7.17**.

The responsibilities of the managers

7.26

It is important to appreciate the distinction between the responsibilities of compliance officers and managers. The COLPs and COFAs are responsible for *systems*, and for recording and reporting compliance failings. The obligation to 'ensure compliance' does not mean, in our view, that the compliance officer is personally liable if there is non-compliance. He or she can expect to face disciplinary consequences if there are no adequate systems in place to minimise risks or to monitor the effectiveness of controls, or if there is a failure to keep adequate records, or a failure to report to the SRA when it was appropriate to do so.

In contrast, the managers can be responsible for specific breaches. Paragraph 8.1 of the Code for Firms states that the managers are responsible for compliance with the Code for Firms by the firm, and rule 1.2 of the SRA Accounts Rules states that the managers are jointly and severally responsible for compliance with the Accounts Rules by the firm, its managers and employees.

The managers are also responsible for ensuring that the firm has effective governance structures, arrangements, systems and controls in place to ensure that compliance officers are able to discharge their duties.[1] There can be expected to be consequential tensions between COLPs and COFAs and managers. If a compliance officer is not provided with adequate facilities and resources that will be the responsibility of the managers, but that in itself will be a failure of compliance which is likely to mean that the compliance officer cannot carry out his/her duties, which would trigger an obligation for the compliance officer to report.

SRA guidance indicates that 'it is up to the management of the firm to review the effectiveness of its COLP or COFA'.[2]

1   Paragraph 2.1(d) of the Code for Firms.
2   SRA guidance, 'Responsibilities of COLPs and COFAs', 25 November 2019.

Reports – when to report to the SRA

7.27

The Code for Firms requires COLPs and COFAs to:

- report to the SRA promptly any facts or matters they reasonably believe are capable of amounting to a serious breach of:

    – for COLPs, the terms and conditions of the firm's authorisation, or the SRA's regulatory arrangements that apply to the firm, managers or employees, excluding potential breaches of the SRA Accounts Rules 2019;[1] and

    – for COFAs, the SRA Accounts Rules 2019 that apply to the firm;[2] and

- inform the SRA promptly of any facts or matters they reasonably believe should be brought to its attention in order that it may investigate whether a serious breach of its regulatory arrangements has occurred, or otherwise exercise its regulatory powers.[3]

This represents a significant change from the 2011 rules, which required COLPs and COFAs to report breaches by the firm or its personnel of rules, deemed to be 'material'. While there is no practical difference between a 'material' breach and a 'serious' breach, the reporting threshold has been lowered in a number of respects:

- Compliance officers are no longer required to determine whether a breach by the firm is serious; there is an obligation is to report facts or matters *capable* of amounting to a serious breach by the firm. The SRA has commented that this mirrors the threshold it applies when deciding whether to open an investigation.[4]

- There is an obligation on both COLPs and COFAs to report facts and matters, whether relating to the firm or not, which warrant *an investigation* whether a serious breach has occurred.

- There is an obligation on both COLPs and COFAs to report facts or matters, whether relating to the firm or not, which should be brought to the SRA's attention so that it may otherwise exercise its regulatory powers. Matters that might otherwise warrant the exercise of regulatory powers could include knowledge of other regulated entities' and persons' dealings that could lead to, for example, intervention, or a decision not to approve a compliance officer or to impose conditions on a practising certificate.

1 Paragraph 9.1(d) of the Code for Firms.
2 Paragraph 9.2(b).
3 Paragraphs 9.1(e) and 9.2(c).
4 SRA, 'Reporting concerns: our post-consultation position', January 2019.

Reports – seriousness

7.28

One of the most vexing problems faced by compliance officers on a daily basis is whether to report. As the SRA has commented, 'a mere breach is not in and of itself reportable: it must be "serious"'.[1]

The most cogent guidance on what constitutes a serious breach appears in the Codes of Conduct and the SRA Enforcement Strategy.

In the introduction to each Code of Conduct it is stated that 'A failure or breach may be serious either in isolation or because it comprises a persistent or concerning pattern of behaviour.'

The definition found in the SRA Enforcement Strategy[2] is similar but slightly different, indicating that facts and matters can be serious:

- in isolation; or
- because they demonstrate a persistent failure to comply, or a concerning pattern of behaviour.

The SRA Enforcement Strategy sets out the factors which affect the SRA's view of seriousness, including:[3]

(a) Past behaviour.

(b) Future risk – taking into account expressions of apology and remorse, and whether the conduct has been repeated.

(c) The systems in place and environment in which the events took place – eg assessing whether stressful circumstances and ill health might have affected the solicitor's judgement.

(d) The responsibility or control the individual had over the matters in question.

(e) The nature of the allegation. Allegations of abuse of trust, taking unfair advantage of clients or others, the misuse of client money, sexual and violent misconduct, dishonest and criminal behaviour will be treated as inherently more serious. Information security breaches may also be treated as being serious.

(f) Intent/motivation. Questions to be asked under this head include: Was the conduct planned or premeditated, persistent, repeated or concealed? Was an advantage gained? What remedial action been taken? Was there a deliberate or reckless disregard for obligations?

(g) Competence. Serious or persistently poor levels of competence – aggravated if the solicitor knowingly acted outside his or her competence or failed to update knowledge and skills. Genuine mistakes will not generally result in action (and thus not be serious) unless the failure arises from a lack of knowledge which the individual could reasonably be expected to have acquired, or there is a concerning lack of judgment.

(h) Harm and impact – including potential harm even if not materialised.

(i) Vulnerability of the client.

(j) Role, experience and seniority of the solicitor.

SRA warning notices can also provide assistance in deciding whether a breach is serious. Generally speaking, warning notices are only issued to address perceived serious misconduct, and warning notices can contain examples of the type of conduct which is permitted and the type of misconduct which is serious.

The SRA has additionally produced a guidance note on the topic of notifications, mostly addressing tangential issues,[4] a case studies page with limited examples[5] and topic guides for anti-money laundering, competence and standard of service, criminal offences outside practice, driving with excess alcohol convictions, the SRA Transparency Rules, use of social media and offensive communications and a guide to the application of principle 1, that is, the requirement to act in a way that upholds the constitutional principle of the rule of law, and the proper administration of justice.

Ultimately compliance officers will need to make an assessment of the seriousness of an issue. In this regard, the SRA has commented that, 'these matters should be for the professional judgment of the decision maker. And that this should combine a subjective element (what they believe) with an objective element … that this belief was reasonable bearing in mind the circumstances, information and evidence available to the decision-maker … This serves to avoid the reporting of mere allegations or suspicions, and provides a balance on the spectrum between this on the one hand, and fully investigated findings on the other … We believe this also provides support for appropriate reflection, investigation and professional judgment.'[6]

1   SRA, 'Reporting concerns: our post-consultation position', January 2019.
2   7 February 2019, updated 25 November 2019.
3   Paragraph 2.2.
4   SRA guidance, 'Reporting and notification obligations', 25 November 2019.
5   SRA case studies, 'Reporting and notification obligations', 25 November 2019.
6   SRA, 'Reporting concerns: our post-consultation position', January 2019.

Reports – other factors

7.29

The rules refer to the reasonable belief of the decision-maker. The SRA has indicated that it does not consider it appropriate to seek to define reasonableness.[1]

The duty to report extends beyond those matters that the firm has made a final determination on. The SRA had commented that, 'It is not the role of a Compliance Officer to make a final determination as to whether or not an act or omission amounts to a breach of the Code of Conduct … we require reporting of facts or matters which could comprise a serious breach, rather than allegations identifying specific and conclusively determined breaches.'[2]

There is a difference between a firm (a) making a final determination and (b) conducting its own investigation. The SRA has commented, 'This is not to suggest that firms shouldn't investigate matters nor that compliance officers shouldn't exercise their judgment in deciding whether a potential breach has occurred – indeed we want to encourage firms to resolve and remedy issues locally where they can.'[3]

However, there will be occasions when the SRA is in a better position to investigate. The SRA has commented that it is its responsibility to investigate and that it may be in a better place to do so: '… it is our job to investigate those concerns that are capable, if proven, of amounting to a serious breach of our requirements … and although a firm itself, having identified a breach may be best placed to gather evidence, this will not always be the case – for example where this sits in another firm or with a client.'[4]

Finally, the SRA Enforcement Strategy indicates that, '[i]f you are unsure about whether to make a report, you should err on the side of caution and do so' and sign-posts users to its Professional Ethics helpline for help in reaching a decision. External advice can be useful, both to address when the requirement has been triggered, but additionally, to offer independent advice on rectification and improvement of systems.

1   SRA, 'Reporting concerns: our post-consultation position', January 2019.
2   Ibid.
3   Ibid.
4   Ibid.

Financial services regulation

8.1

The statutory framework for financial services regulation is provided by the Financial Services and Markets Act (FSMA) 2000. Section 19(1) of FSMA 2000 provides that no person may carry on a regulated activity in the United Kingdom or purport to do so unless he is (a) an authorised person or (b) an exempt person. This is referred to as the general prohibition. A breach of this requirement is a criminal offence with a maximum penalty of two years' imprisonment.

Regulated activities are defined by the Financial Services and Markets Act 2000 (Regulated Activities) Order 2001 (RAO 2001) as amended.[1] Activities are regulated if an *activity* of a specified kind is carried on *by way of business* in relation to an *investment* of a specified kind. The Financial Services and Markets Act 2000 (Carrying on Regulated Activities by Way of Business) Order 2001[2] makes provision as to when a person is or is not to be regarded as carrying on a regulated activity by way of business. We are dealing with solicitors acting in the course of their professional practice and will assume that this requirement will be met.

1   SI 2001/544.
2   SI 2001/1177.

Activities

8.2

The specified *activities* are:

- accepting deposits;[1]

- issuing electronic money;

- effecting and carrying out contracts of insurance;

- transformation of insurance risk by transformer vehicles;

- dealing or arranging deals in investments;

- bidding in emissions auctions;

- credit broking;

- operating an electronic system in relation to lending;

- managing investments;

- assisting in the administration and performance of a contract of insurance;

- activities in relation to debt: debt adjusting, debt counselling, debt collection and debt administration;

- safeguarding and administering investments;

- sending dematerialised instructions;[2]

- specified involvement in collective investment schemes;

- the like involvement in pension schemes;

- providing basic advice on stakeholder products;

- advising on investments;

- various forms of activity at Lloyd's;

- providing funeral plan contracts;

- specified involvement in regulated credit agreements, regulated consumer hire agreements, regulated mortgage contracts, regulated home reversion plans, regulated home purchase plans and regulated sale and rent back agreements; and

- claims management activities.

There are exclusions applicable to the various categories of activity.

With effect from 1 April 2014 consumer credit activity was added as a new category of regulated activity.[3] It was formerly regulated by being licensed by the Office of Fair Trading, and the solicitors' profession enjoyed the benefits of a group licence. The consequences are considered in further detail below.

1   A sum is not a deposit for these purposes if it is received by a practising solicitor acting in the course of his profession: article 7 of RAO 2001. A 'practising solicitor' includes recognised bodies, registered European lawyers (RELs) and registered foreign lawyers (RFLs).
2   See the Uncertificated Securities Regulations 2001 (SI 2001/3755) – essentially the process whereby shares and other investments can be held in electronic form on computer systems.
3   Financial Services and Markets Act 2000 (Regulated Activities) (Amendment) (No 2) Order 2013 (SI 2013/1881).

Investments

8.3

The specified *investments* are:

- deposits;
- electronic money;
- rights under a contract of insurance;
- shares;
- debt instruments (debentures, loan stock, bonds, certificates of deposit);
- alternative finance investment bonds;
- government and public securities (gilts);

- warrants and other instruments giving entitlement to investments;

- certificates representing certain securities (conferring contractual or property rights in shares, debentures, etc);

- units in a collective investment scheme;

- rights under a pension scheme;

- emission allowances;

- options;

- futures;

- contracts for differences (for example, trading on the expected performance of a share or other index);

- Lloyd's syndicate capacity and syndicate membership;

- rights under a funeral plan contract, regulated mortgage contract, regulated home reversion plan or regulated home purchase plan, regulated sale and rent back agreements;

- credit agreements;

- consumer hire agreements; and

- rights to or interests in investments.

8.4

This book does not attempt to deal with the requirements imposed by the Financial Conduct Authority (FCA) on those authorised and regulated by that Authority. Solicitors and their practices may become involved in mainstream investment business and be required to be authorised by the FCA, but the vast majority of the profession take advantage of Part XX of FSMA 2000 which allows persons who are regulated by designated professional bodies (of which the Law Society/ Solicitors Regulation Authority (SRA) is one) to undertake regulated activities without being authorised by the FCA, provided that they comply with rules made by their own professional body. Solicitors and others regulated by the SRA complying with their own professional rules will be carrying on 'exempt regulated activities'.[1]

The rules applicable to solicitors and their practices; any form of 'authorised body', traditional firm, legal disciplinary partnership, alternative business structures (ABSs) or authorised sole practitioner, are the SRA Financial Services (Scope) Rules 2019[2] and the SRA Financial Services (Conduct of Business) Rules 2019,[3] which in this chapter will be referred to as the 'Scope Rules' and the 'COB Rules'.

The Scope Rules specify the regulated activities which solicitors and others regulated by the SRA may and may not undertake if they are to take advantage of the Part XX exemption, and the conditions that must be satisfied. The COB Rules regulate the manner in which exempt regulated activities may be carried on by solicitors and their practices.

1   Section 327 of FSMA 2000.
2   Formerly the SRA Financial Services (Scope) Rules 2001.
3   Formerly the SRA Financial Services (Conduct of Business) Rules 2001.

CHAPTER 8
FINANCIAL SERVICES
REGULATION

The Scope Rules

8.5

The Scope Rules, read with section 327 of FSMA 2000, require that certain basi conditions be met. These are primarily:

(1)   that the regulated activities arise out of, or are complementary to, the provi sion of a particular professional service to a particular client;[1]

(2)   that the provision of any service relating to regulated activities is incidental t the provision of professional services (this would, for example, therefore cove the arrangement of after the event insurance which is incidental to the mai purpose of the retainer, ie the pursuit of a claim for damages);[2]

(3)   that the firm accounts to the client for any pecuniary reward or other advan tage which the firm receives from a third party;[3] and

(4)   that the firm does not carry on or hold itself out as carrying on any regulate activity that is not permitted under the Scope Rules.[4]

As to whether the regulated activity is incidental, it is necessary to consider the scal of regulated activity in proportion to other professional services provided; whethe and to what extent activities that are regulated activities are held out as separat services; and the impression given as to how the firm provides regulated activities for example, through its advertising of its services.

As to accounting for commission and other financial benefits see paragraph 4.1 of th SRA Code of Conduct for Solicitors, RELs and RFLs 2019, paragraph 5.1 of th SRA Code of Conduct for Firms 2019 (the 'Code for Firms'),[5] and the commentar in **CHAPTER 4** (see **4.45**). Notes to the former version of the Scope Rules also encour aged practitioners at the outset, in advance of the arrangement or the provision of th financial service, to inform clients of their rights to any commission; to inform client that the arrangement and/or provision of the service is not dependent on their agree ment to waive their right to any commission; and to seek and to record clien agreement as to whether any commission should be passed to the client, retained b the firm to offset fees, or retained by the firm with the client waiving their right to it While these notes are not reproduced in the 2019 Scope Rules, the requirement t account for any commission remains, and providing clear advance information t clients regarding the issue remains an obviously prudent course.

This is consistent with the FCA guidance to the Council for Licensed Conveyancer (CLC) on the same subject; see **13.8**.

1   Rule 2.1(b).
2   Section 327(4) of FSMA 2000.
3   Section 327(3) of FSMA 2000.
4   Section 327(5) of FSMA 2000.
5   Previously outcome 1.15 of the SRA Code of Conduct 2011.

Prohibited activities

8.6

Activities from which solicitors are prohibited under the Scope Rules may b divided into two parts.

Those prohibited by orders made under section 327(6) of FSMA 2000:[1]

- accepting deposits;

- issuing electronic money;

- buying, selling, subscribing for or underwriting securities or contractually based investments (other than investments specified by article 87 or article 89 of RAO 2001) as principal;

- dealing in investments as agent or arranging deals in investments in so far as it relates to a transaction for the sale or purchase of rights under a contract of insurance and is carried on by a person not included in the record of insurance intermediaries;

- managing investments in so far as it consists of buying or subscribing for a security, contractually based investment or structured deposit;[2]

- advising on investments where such advice falls within article 6 of the Financial Services and Markets Act 2000 (Professions) (Non-Exempt Activities) Order;

- establishing, operating or winding up a stakeholder pension scheme or a personal pension scheme;

- providing basic advice on stakeholder products;

- effecting and carrying out contracts of insurance as principal;

- assisting in the administration and performance of a contract of insurance if it is carried on by a person who is not included in the record of insurance intermediaries;

- bidding in emissions auctions;

- specified activities in relation to collective investment schemes;

- managing the underwriting capacity of a syndicate as a managing agent at Lloyd's;

- advising a person to become a member of a particular Lloyd's syndicate;

- entering as provider into a funeral plan contract;

- administering a benchmark;

- advising on regulated mortgage contracts where such advice consists of a recommendation to an individual to enter into a regulated mortgage contract as borrower and, by doing so, that person would be carrying on an activity specified in article 61 of RAO 2001;[3]

- advising on regulated home reversion plans where such advice consists of a recommendation to an individual to enter into a regulated home reversion plan with a particular person and, by doing so, that person would be carrying on an activity specified in article 63B(1) of RAO 2001;[4]

- advising on regulated home purchase plans where such advice consists of a recommendation to an individual to enter into a regulated home purchase plan with a particular person and, by doing so, that person would be carrying on an activity specified in article 63F(1) of RAO 2001;[5]

- advising on regulated sale and rent back agreements where such advice consists of a recommendation to an individual to enter into a sale and rent back agreement with a particular person and, by doing so, that person would be carrying on an activity specified in article 63J(1) of RAO 2001;[6]

- entering into:

  - a regulated mortgage contract as lender or administering a regulated mortgage contract;

  - a regulated home purchase plan as a provider or administering a regulated home purchase plan;

  - a regulated home reversion plan as a provider or administering a regulated home reversion plan; and

  - a regulated sale and rent back agreement as an agreement provider or administering a regulated sale and rent back agreement,

  unless in the firm's capacity as a trustee or personal representative and the borrower, home purchaser, reversion seller or agreement seller is a beneficiary of the trust, will or intestacy.

Those directly prohibited by the Scope Rules:[7]

- entering into a regulated credit agreement as lender except where the regulated credit agreement relates exclusively to the payment of disbursements or professional fees due to you;

- exercising, or having the right to exercise, the lender's rights and duties under a regulated credit agreement except where the regulated credit agreement relates exclusively to the payment of disbursements or professional fees due to you;

- entering into a regulated consumer hire agreement as owner;

- exercising, or having the right to exercise, the owner's rights and duties under a regulated consumer hire agreement;

- operating an electronic system in relation to lending within the meaning of article 36H of RAO 2001;

- providing credit references within the meaning of article 89B of RAO 2001;

- insurance distribution activities in relation to insurance-based investment products; or

- creating, developing, designing or underwriting a contract of insurance.

All relevant definitions are contained in the SRA Glossary or RAO 2001.

1   Financial Services and Markets Act 2000 (Professions) (Non-Exempt Activities) Order 2001 (SI 2001/1227).
2   See article 5(2) of SI 2001/1227 for limitations.
3   See article 6A of SI 2001/1227. Note that endorsing the recommendation of an authorised or exempt person is not caught (see article 6A(3)).
4   See article 6C of SI 2001/1227. Note that endorsing the recommendation of an authorised or exempt person is not caught (see article 6C(3)).

5   See article 6C of SI 2001/1227. Note that endorsing the recommendation of an authorised or exempt person is not caught (see article 6E(3)).
6   See article 6C of SI 2001/1227. Note that endorsing the recommendation of an authorised or exempt person is not caught (see article 6G(3)).
7   Rule 3.1 of the Scope Rules.

8.7

There are other restrictions relating to corporate finance. Firms must not act as a sponsor to an issue of securities to be admitted for dealing on the London Stock Exchange or as nominated adviser to an issue of securities to be admitted for dealing on the Alternative Investment Market of the London Stock Exchange or as corporate adviser to an issue in respect of securities to be admitted for dealing on the PLUS Market.[1]

1   Rule 4.1 of the Scope Rules.

Insurance distribution activities

8.8

Firms may only carry on insurance distribution activities as an ancillary insurance intermediary.[1] Firms must not carry on any insurance distribution activities unless they are registered in the FCA Financial Services register and have appointed an insurance distribution officer who will be responsible for those activities.[2]

The 2019 rules were updated to abandon (for the most part) the phrase 'insurance mediation' which caused much confusion, not least because of the use of the word 'mediation'. The term used in the Scope Rules is 'insurance distribution' as defined in the FCA Handbook. 'Insurance distribution activity' is defined in the SRA Glossary and involves dealing as an agent in contracts of insurance and/or rights to or interests in a life policy, arranging deals in contracts of insurance and/or rights to or interests in a life policy, making arrangements with a view to a person entering into a contract of insurance and/or involving rights to or interests in a life policy, assisting in the administration or performance of a contract of insurance and/or rights to or interests in a life policy, advising on the merits of buying or selling a contract of insurance and/or rights to or interests in a life policy, or agreeing to do any of the above.

Most insurance contracts are now regulated investments, including life and pension policies, defective title and missing beneficiary indemnity policies, household and building insurance, long-term care insurance and after the event legal expenses insurance.

In practice, therefore, most of the profession will be likely to become involved in insurance distribution activities, even if only by advising on or arranging a title indemnity policy or after the event insurance. The process of being registered with the FCA for these purposes is arranged through the SRA (usually by completing the question on the annual application for practising certificates or recognition renewal to confirm that the firm does carry out this activity) or by informing the SRA separately if this has not been done or if the circumstances have changed since certificates or recognitions were renewed.

It seems that many firms have made mistakes in this respect. All that is required is that the person filling in the firm's annual application forms does not appreciate that 'insurance distribution' has a special meaning and ticks the box for 'No' as to whether the firm engages in that activity. In consequence the firm will not be registered with the FCA and there will be criminal offences committed every time the firm arranges an after the event legal expenses policy or title indemnity insurance. In addition, all managers and the firm's compliance officer for legal practice (COLP) may be in breach of requirements in the SRA Codes of Conduct if such a mistake arises due to a lack of understanding of legal, ethical or regulatory obligations such as to amount to a breach of the requirement at paragraph 4.3 of the Code for Firms.

1   Rule 5.1 of the Scope Rules.
2   Rule 5.2 of the Scope Rules.

Regulated mortgages and other property plans

8.9

Firms must not recommend that a client enters into a regulated mortgage contract as a borrower, but can endorse a recommendation given by a person who is regulated by the FCA for this purpose or who is exempt from the general prohibition.[1]

A regulated mortgage contract is one where the borrower is an individual or trust, the lender takes a first legal charge over property in the United Kingdom and at least 40 per cent of the property is occupied or intended to be occupied by the borrower as a dwelling or, in the case of a trust, by a beneficiary, or (in either case) by that person's spouse (or someone, whether or not of the opposite sex, whose relationship with the borrower or beneficiary has the characteristics of the relationship between husband and wife) or that person's parent, brother, sister, child, grandparent or grandchild (article 61(3) of RAO 2001).

Firms must not recommend that a client, as a purchaser, enters into a regulated home purchase plan or a regulated home reversion plan or, as a seller, a regulated sale and rent back agreement with a particular person but can endorse a recommendation given by a person who is regulated by the FCA or who is exempt from the general prohibition.[2]

A regulated home purchase plan is an arrangement under which a 'home purchase provider' buys all or part of a freehold or leasehold interest which provides for a home purchaser to buy the provider's interest during the course of or at the end of a specified period and the purchaser or a related person is entitled to occupy at least 40 per cent of the land as a dwelling and intends to do so (article 63F(3) of RAO 2001).

A regulated home reversion plan is an arrangement whereby a person, the reversion provider, buys all or part of a freehold or leasehold interest from an individual or trustees (the reversion occupier), and the reversion occupier or a related person is entitled to occupy at least 40 per cent of the land as a dwelling and intends to do so, and the arrangement specifies that the entitlement to occupy will end in specified circumstances (article 63B(3) of RAO 2001).

A regulated sale and rent back agreement is an arrangement whereby a provider buys all or part of a freehold or leasehold interest on terms that the seller or a related person is entitled to occupy at least 40 per cent of the land as a dwelling and intends to do so, but which is not a home reversion plan (article 63J(3)(a) of RAO 2001).

1 Article 6A of the Financial Services and Markets Act 2000 (Professions) (Non-Exempt Activities) Order 2001 (SI 2001/1227).
2 Articles 6C, 6E and 6G of SI 2001/1227.

Consumer credit activity

8.10

On 1 April 2014 consumer credit activity became a mainstream financial services activity regulated by the FCA. The categories of activity listed in rule 3.1(c)–(h) of the Scope Rules and set out at **8.6** are prohibited consumer credit activities. Solicitors may only carry out consumer credit activities:

- if they are fully FCA-authorised, or had previously been granted interim permission to continue to do so, for which application had to be made by 31 March 2014 (and which will not therefore be considered);

- if they have the benefit of the Part XX exemption (see **8.4**) though this may be more problematic in its application than in relation to other regulated activities; or

- if they are acting in the course of contentious business as defined in section 87 of the Solicitors Act (SA) 1974 (which must involve proceedings before a court or arbitrator, excluding non-contentious probate business). It is important to note that this therefore only applies where proceedings have been commenced, and not to any activity carried out before proceedings have been issued.[1]

Regulated consumer credit activities include:

- credit broking;
- operating an electronic system in relation to lending;
- debt adjusting;
- debt-counselling;
- debt-collecting;
- debt administration;
- entering into a regulated credit agreement as lender;
- exercising or having the right to exercise lender's rights under a regulated consumer credit agreement;
- entering into a regulated consumer hire agreement as owner;
- exercising or having the right to exercise owner's rights under a regulated consumer hire agreement;
- providing credit information services;
- providing credit references; and
- agreeing to carry on any of the above.

Each of the listed activities has exemptions specific to the relevant activity and those firms likely to be undertaking these activities as a mainstream activity (to which this book is not addressed) need to consider RAO 2001 in detail, as amended by the Financial Services and Markets Act 2000 (Regulated Activities) (Amendment) (No 2) Order 2013.[2]

Of greater relevance to most solicitors' firms will be the Part XX exemption, which is available where the activity arises out of, or is complementary to, the provision of a particular professional service to a particular client; the manner of the provision of any service in the course of carrying on the activities is incidental to the provision of professional services; the firm accounts to a client for any pecuniary reward or other advantage which the firm receives from a third party; and the firm does not carry on any activities regulated by the FCA other than those permitted under Part XX of FSMA 2000, or in relation to which the firm is an exempt person.

The 'incidental' test must be applied on a case-by-case basis and it is unlikely that firms specialising in debt collection to any substantial extent would be able to avoid being regulated by the FCA.

Rule 6 of the Scope Rules sets out the relevant limitations:

Rule 6: Credit-related regulated financial services activities

6.1   You must not enter into any transaction with a *client* in which you:

    (a)   provide the *client* with credit card cheques, a credit or store card, *credit tokens*, *running account credit*, a current account or *high-cost short-term* credit;

    (b)   hold a *continuous payment authority* over the client's account; or

    (c)   take any article from the *client* in *pledge* or *pawn* as security for the transaction.

6.2   You must not:

    (a)   enter into a *regulated credit agreement* as lender; or

    (b)   exercise, or have the right to exercise, the lender's rights and duties under a *regulated credit agreement*,

    which is secured on land by a *legal or equitable mortgage*.

6.3   You must not:

    (a)   enter into a *regulated credit agreement* as lender; or

    (b)   exercise, or have the right to exercise, the lender's rights and duties under a *regulated credit agreement*,

    which includes a variable rate of interest.

6.4   You must not provide a *debt management plan* to a *client*.

6.5   You must not charge a separate fee for, or attribute any element of your fees to, *credit broking* services.

---

1   For example articles 36F(1)(b) and 39K(1)(b) of RAO 2001 as amended.
2   SI 2013/1881.

The COB Rules

8.11

As explained above, the COB Rules govern the manner in which solicitors' firms may carry out regulated activities that they are permitted to carry out under the Scope Rules. The Rules apply to licensed bodies (ABSs) only in respect of that part of their business which is regulated under the Legal Services Act (LSA) 2007: in other words, to the provision of legal services as opposed to any other services that the business may be providing (such as funeral services). They apply, with one exception, to firms that are not regulated by the FCA and to firms that are regulated by the FCA but only in relation to non-mainstream regulated activities and to managers and employees of those firms.

Status disclosure

8.12

The exception is rule 2, which relates to status disclosure and which applies only to firms that are *not* regulated by the FCA. Before such a firm provides any service which includes a regulated financial services activity it must give the client the following information in writing, in a manner that is clear, fair and not misleading:

- a statement that the firm is not authorised by the FCA;
- the name and practising address of the firm;
- the nature of the regulated financial services activities carried on by the firm and the fact that they are limited in scope;
- a statement that the firm is authorised and regulated by the SRA; and
- a statement explaining that complaints and redress mechanisms are provided through the SRA and the Legal Ombudsman (LeO).[1]

The following words are not compulsory but are in an acceptable form when combined with the other specific requirements listed above:

> 'The Law Society is a designated professional body for the purposes of the Financial Services and Markets Act 2000 but responsibility for regulation and complaints handling has been separated from the Law Society's representative functions. The Solicitors Regulation Authority is the independent regulatory body of the Law Society.'

Where you are providing services which include the carrying on of insurance distribution activity, the following specific written disclosure must be provided to the client in good time before the conclusion of a contract of insurance, along with confirmation that you are an ancillary insurance intermediary:

> '[This firm is] [We are] not authorised by the Financial Conduct Authority. However, we are included on the register maintained by the Financial Conduct Authority so that we can carry on insurance distribution activity, which is broadly the advising on, selling and administration of insurance contracts. This part of our business, including arrangements for complaints

CHAPTER 8 FINANCIAL SERVICES REGULATION

or redress if something goes wrong, is regulated by the Solicitors Regulation Authority. The register can be accessed via the Financial Conduct Authority website at www.fca.org.uk/firms/financial-services-register.'

There is no reason why the required disclosures cannot be incorporated in the firm's standard client care material, but they can be provided separately. It is not necessary to tailor the disclosure to the needs of the specific client, although the Solicitors (Disciplinary Proceedings) Rules 2019 (SI 2019/1185) (the '2019 Rules') require that the disclosure be provided in a way which is clear, fair and not misleading.[2] Since LeO's service is available not to all clients, but only to individuals and small businesses (see **CHAPTER 14**), care should be used in making reference to the availability of a redress mechanism in the very generic terms required by the SRA.

1   Rule 2.1 of the COB Rules.
2   Rule 2.2 of the COB Rules, and associated guidance notes.

Other requirements

8.13

Firms must ensure that when it has been decided or agreed to effect a transaction they do so as soon as possible, unless it is reasonably believed that it is not in the best interests of the client to do so.[1]

The COB Rules contain provisions requiring specified records to be kept of transactions, commissions received, how the firm accounted for commission to the client, and as to the safekeeping of clients' investments.[2] As to the principles involved in accounting for commission, see **8.5**.

If a firm arranges any transaction for a client involving a retail investment product on an execution-only basis, the firm must send written confirmation to the client that, as the case may be, no advice had been sought from or given by the firm, or advice had been given but the client nevertheless persisted in requiring the transaction to be effected – and in either case that the transaction is effected on express instructions.[3]

There are additional detailed requirements where firms engage in insurance distribution activities. These are primarily concerned with the disclosure of information and the extent to which a comparative market analysis has been carried out, with the need to establish by reasonable steps that the recommended policy is suitable for the client's demands and needs, and with the obligation to provide a 'demands and needs statement' before the contract is finalised (among other things explaining any recommendation made). Specific rules also govern the use of intermediaries, remuneration and fee disclosure, cross-selling requirements where insurance is the ancillary product and organisation requirements, including the obligation to ensure that the firm and its employees possess appropriate knowledge and ability in order to complete their tasks and perform duties adequately and all managers and persons directly involved in insurance distribution activities are of good repute. 'Good repute' essentially involves not being convicted of crimes involving property or financial activities and not being bankrupt – in either case, unless rehabilitated.[4] In practice, it is the latter which is most likely to be of concern to firms. Should any manager of a firm be declared bankrupt, this may have an impact on the firm's ability to lawfully conduct insurance distribution activity.[5]

1   Rule 3.1 of the COB Rules.
2   Rules 4, 5 and 6 of the COB Rules.
3   Rule 7 of the COB Rules.
4   Rule 20.2 of the COB Rules.
5   Part 3 of the COB Rules.

8.14

In relation to consumer credit activities firms must comply with Part 4 of the COB Rules:

Rule 23: Disclosure of information

23.1   Where you undertake *credit-related regulated financial services activities* for a *client*, you must ensure that information in connection with such activities and any agreements to which they relate are communicated to the *client* in a way that is clear, fair and not misleading.

23.2   Where you carry on the activity of *credit broking*, you must indicate in any advertising and documentation intended for consumers or *clients* the extent and scope of your *credit broking* activities, in particular whether you work exclusively with one or more lenders or as an independent broker.

Rule 24: Regulated credit agreements

24.1   Where you carry on a *credit-related regulated financial services* activity involving a proposed *regulated credit agreement*, you must;

    (a)   provide adequate explanations to the *client* in order to enable the *client* to assess whether the proposed *regulated credit agreement* is suitable to the *client's* needs and financial situation; and

    (b)   when providing such explanations, comply with the requirements of the *FCA* Consumer Credit sourcebook 4.2.5R.

24.2   Before entering into a *regulated credit agreement* as lender, you must assess the *client's* creditworthiness on the basis of sufficient information to enable you to make the assessment, where appropriate such information will be obtained from the *client* and, where necessary, from a credit reference agency.

24.3   After entering into a *regulated credit agreement* where you are the lender, if the parties agree to change the total amount of credit, you must update the financial information you hold concerning the *client* and assess the *client's* creditworthiness before any significant increase in the total amount of credit.

24.4   In the event of you assigning to a third party your rights as lender in relation to a *regulated credit agreement*, you must inform the *client* of the assignment.

Rule 25: Appropriation of payments

25.1   Where you are entitled to payments from the same *client* in respect of two or more *regulated credit agreements*, you must allow the *client* to put any payments made, in respect of those agreements, towards the satisfaction of

> the sum due under any one or more of the agreements in such proportions as the *client* thinks fit.

Rule 26: Consumer credit guidance

26.1 Where you undertake *credit-related regulated financial services activities*, you must have regard to any guidance issued by the *SRA* from time to time relating to such activities.

Financial promotions

8.15

There is a second separate strand of regulation under FSMA 2000 of which practitioners should be aware. Under section 21 of FSMA 2000, you are prohibited from, in the course of business, communicating an invitation or inducement to engage in investment activity unless this is done by an authorised person, or the content of the communication is approved by an authorised person. Solicitors' practices are not authorised persons but can take advantage of an exemption to undertake exempt regulated activities as explained above, for the purposes of RAO 2001. This regime does not, however, apply to financial promotions, which are covered by the Financial Services and Markets Act 2000 (Financial Promotion) Order 2005 (FPO 2005).[1] Regulated activities for the purposes of RAO 2001 are not precisely the same as (though are very similar to) controlled activities for the purposes of FPO 2005.

If a firm, therefore, does communicate invitations or inducements to engage in an investment activity, it must, if it is regulated by the SRA rather than the FCA, be able to rely on an exemption within FPO 2005. Fortunately, there are exemptions specifically in favour of members of professions. Under article 55 of FPO 2005, the financial promotion restriction does not apply to a real time communication (whether solicited or unsolicited) which is made by a person who carries on a regulated activity to which the general prohibition does not apply by virtue of section 327 of FSMA 2000 (in other words those carrying out exempt regulated activities and who are regulated by their own professional body); and which is made to a recipient who has, prior to the communication being made, engaged that person to provide professional services, and where the activity to which the communication relates is (in short) for the purposes of, and incidental to, the provision of professional services to or at the request of the recipient.

A real time communication is any communication made in the course of a personal visit, telephone conversation or other interactive dialogue.[2] Note that this exemption applies to communications with existing clients, but can be solicited or unsolicited.

The article 55 exemption does not apply to non-real time communications, including letters, emails and material in a publication such as a brochure. Article 55A provides an exemption for members of a profession in relation to non-real time communications if the stated conditions are satisfied. The financial promotion restriction does not apply to a non-real time communication which is made by a person who carries on Part XX activities (that is, again, those who are carrying out exempt regulated activities and who are regulated by their own professional body) and which is limited to a communication expressly provided for in article 55A: that is, one that promotes an activity that is within Part XX of FSMA 2000 (in other words, one that is not prohibited by the Scope Rules). The communication must contain the following:

> 'This [firm/company] is not authorised under the Financial Services and Markets Act 2000 but we are able in certain circumstances to offer a limited range of investment and consumer credit-related and claims management-related services to clients because we are members of [relevant designated professional body]. We can provide these investment and consumer credit-related services if they are an incidental part of the professional services we have been engaged to provide.'[3]

Note that this is similar to but not identical with the notice that is required by the COB Rules for insurance mediation activities (see **8.12**).

Firms can therefore communicate an invitation or inducement in writing provided the promoted activities fall within the scope of exempt regulated activities and the invitation or inducement is accompanied by the specified notice and compliant with article 55A of FPO 2005.

1   SI 2005/1529.
2   Article 7 of FPO 2005.
3   Article 55A(2) of FPO 2005.

CHAPTER 9

Property selling

9.1

The Property Selling Rules were a part of the 2011 Handbook. They were relatively prescriptive in that they were required to mirror the statutory provisions of the Estate Agents Act 1979. The SRA's approach in the 2019 regulatory arrangements is to not include specific provisions which are adequately covered by statute or more generic requirements. There is no replacement for the Property Selling Rules 2011 in the 2019 arrangements.

Firms engaged in property selling should ensure compliance with the information requirements at section 8 of the SRA Code of Conduct for Solicitors, RELs and RFLs 2019 (the 'Code for Individuals') discussed at **4.121–4.132**.

Solicitors engaged in property selling should pay particular attention to the requirement of paragraph 8.6 of the Code for Individuals: to ensure that clients are in a position to make informed decisions about the services they need, how their matter will be handled and the options available to them. While there are no longer any express requirements relating to property selling in the 2019 regulatory arrangements, any failure to provide information which would be required pursuant to the Estate Agents Act 1979 could well amount to a breach of this requirement.

CHAPTER 10

Overseas and European cross-border practice

10.1

Overseas and European cross-border practice is governed by the SRA Overseas and Cross-border Practice Rules 2019 ((the 'Overseas Rules' or 'OCB Rules')). The OCB Rules disapply the SRA Principles and the Codes of Conduct and replace them with modified requirements for the purposes of regulating practice outside England and Wales. Individual solicitors practising outside England and Wales may nevertheless be subject to the SRA Principles and SRA Code of Conduct for Solicitors, RELs and RFLs 2019 if their practice predominantly comprises the provision of legal services to clients in England and Wales or in relation to assets located in England and Wales.[1] This provision is intended to ensure that solicitors do not seek to circumvent regulation by the Solicitors Regulation Authority (SRA) by physically moving out of the jurisdiction but conducting their practice remotely.

Overseas practice involves a branch office, subsidiary company or undertaking or entity otherwise owned or managed in fact and law by an authorised body established outside England and Wales and providing legal services as well as an individual so established acting as a representative of an authorised body, or sole principal so established whose business management or ownership is controlled in fact or law by an authorised body.

The OCB Rules modify the SRA Principles very slightly to make it clear that it is the administration of justice in England and Wales and public trust in the profession in England and Wales which are within the ambit of principles 1 and 2 respectively and to constrain the requirement to encourage equality, diversity and inclusion (principle 6) by reference to the legal, regulatory and cultural contexts where your practice is located.

Other requirements for cross-border practice are designed to ensure proper stewardship of client funds[2] and to ensure proper co-operation with the SRA and regulatory bodies (including the Legal Ombudsman (LeO)).[3] The reporting requirements are less onerous than those imposed in respect of practice in England and Wales but nevertheless require full and accurate explanations, information and documentation to be provided in response to any request made by the SRA.[4]

The OCB Rules are very short and little is added by commenting in further detail.

European cross-border practice involves professional activity regulated by the SRA in a CCBE state (see **10.2**) other than the United Kingdom, whether or not the practitioner or firm is physically present in that state, and any professional contact of a kind that is regulated by the SRA with a lawyer of a CCBE state other than the United Kingdom. Contacts and activities within a firm or in-house legal department are not within the definition.[5]

1   Rule 1.3 of the OCB Rules.
2   Rule 3.1 of the OCB Rules.
3   Rule 4.1 of the OCB Rules.
4   Rule 4.4(a) of the OCB Rules.
5   See the SRA Glossary.

10.2

CCBE is the recognised abbreviation for the Council of the Bars and Law Societies of Europe and was originally the Commission Consultative des Barreaux d'Europe. Its correct current French title is 'Conseil des Barreaux Européens'. The Council's principal object is to study all questions affecting the legal profession in the member states of the European Union and the European Economic Area (EEA) and to formulate solutions designed to co-ordinate and harmonise professional practice. It has set up a Council for Advice and Arbitration to assist in resolving complaints between lawyers in different member states.

The CCBE has published a Code of Conduct for European Lawyers (in October 1988; most recently updated in May 2006) for the purposes of regulating the conduct of lawyers within the Community concerned in cross-border activities.

There are 31 full member states of the CCBE, five associate members and eight observer members. The United Kingdom is currently the sole affiliate member as a result of Brexit. The CCBE Code of Conduct applies to all of them without distinction.

The full members are:

Austria	Greece	Poland
Belgium	Hungary	Portugal
Bulgaria	Iceland	Romania
Croatia	Ireland	Slovak Republic
Cyprus	Italy	Slovenia
Czech Republic	Latvia	Spain
Denmark	Liechtenstein	Sweden
Estonia	Lithuania	Switzerland
Finland	Luxembourg	The Netherlands
France	Malta	
Germany	Norway	

The associate members are:

Montenegro
Serbia
Turkey
Albania
North Macedonia

The observer members are:

Andorra	Georgia	San Marino
Armenia	Moldova	Ukraine
Bosnia and Herzegovina	Russia	

10.3

The sole requirement of the provisions in the OCB Rules relating to European cross-border practice is that solicitors engaged in European cross-border practice comply with the CCBE Code of Conduct for European Lawyers. The CCBE Code is included at **APPENDIX 11**.

10.4

There are some aspects of the CCBE Code which may be sufficiently dissimilar to requirements applicable in England and Wales to warrant mention and which were formerly mentioned expressly in the SRA European Cross-Border Practice Rules 2011:

- occupations considered incompatible with legal practice, which is an issue to be determined by reference to the rules of the CCBE state in question (rule 2.5 of the CCBE Code);

- fee sharing with non-lawyers (rule 3.6 of the CCBE Code);

- co-operation between lawyers of different CCBE states (rule 5.2 of the CCBE Code);

- considerations arising from correspondence between lawyers of different CCBE states, because 'confidential' and 'without prejudice' may be interpreted differently (rule 5.3 of the CCBE Code);

- a prohibition on payment of referral fees to non-lawyers (rule 5.4 of the CCBE Code);

- the proper procedure in the event of a dispute between lawyers (rule 5.9 of the CCBE Code); and

- obligations in relation to fees when other lawyers are instructed (rule 5.7 of the CCBE Code).

10.5

Rule 2.5 provides that if you act in legal proceedings or proceedings before public authorities in a CCBE state other than the United Kingdom, you must, in that state, comply with any rules regarding occupations incompatible with the practice of law, as if you were a lawyer of that state, whether or not you are based at an office in that state; and if you are a solicitor based at an office in a CCBE state other than the United Kingdom, you must respect any rules regarding participation in commercial or other activities not connected with the practice of law, as they are applied to lawyers of that state.

Rule 3.6 provides that lawyers must not share fees with non-lawyers, save as permitted by the professional rules to which that lawyer is subject. That does not prevent payment to a deceased lawyer's heirs or to a retiring lawyer in respect of taking over the deceased or retiring lawyer's practice.

Rule 5.2 imposes an obligation to provide reasonable co-operation to other lawyers. It requires that if you are approached by a lawyer of a CCBE state other than the United Kingdom to undertake work which you are not competent to undertake, you must assist that lawyer to obtain the information necessary to find and instruct a lawyer capable of providing the service requested. When co-operating with a lawyer of a CCBE state other than the United Kingdom you must take into account the differences which may exist between the respective legal systems and the professional organisations, competencies and obligations of lawyers in their respective states.

10.6

Rule 5.3 seeks to avoid misunderstandings in professional correspondence when communications are intended to be 'confidential' or 'without prejudice'. Before sending the communication you must clearly express your intention in order to avoid misunderstanding, and ask if the lawyer is able to accept the communication on the intended basis. When you send the communication you must express your intention clearly at the head of the communication or in a covering letter. If you are the intended recipient of a communication from a lawyer in another CCBE state which is stated to be 'confidential' or 'without prejudice', but which you are unable to accept on the basis intended by that lawyer, you must inform the sender accordingly without delay. If the communication has already been sent you must return it unread without revealing the contents to others. If you have already read the communication and you are under a professional duty to reveal it to your client you must inform the sender immediately.

10.7

Under rule 5.4 the payment of referral fees to non-lawyers is prohibited if the non-lawyer is situated in a CCBE state other than the United Kingdom or if you are practising from an office in a CCBE state other than the United Kingdom, whether or not you are physically present at that office. The rule applies to any fee, commission or any other compensation as a consideration for referring a client.

Under rule 5.7, unless agreed to the contrary, you are under a professional obligation to pay the fees of a lawyer or legal business in another CCBE state instructed by you even if the underlying client becomes insolvent or unable to pay you, subject to specified exceptions including an express disclaimer. This does not apply where your involvement goes no further than a recommendation to instruct the lawyer or legal business.

By virtue of rule 5.9, if you consider that a lawyer in a CCBE state other than the United Kingdom has acted in breach of a rule of professional conduct you must draw the breach to the other lawyer's attention and, before commencing any form of proceedings against the other lawyer, you must inform the Law Society and the other lawyer's bar or law society in order to allow them an opportunity to assist in resolving the matter.

Professional indemnity insurance

Obligation to insure

11.1

The compulsory requirement that solicitors should be insured against professional risks dates from 1976, when the Law Society made indemnity rules under the powers provided by section 37 of the Solicitors Act (SA) 1974. From then until 1987 the Law Society negotiated the terms of a master policy with the insurance industry year by year. In 1987 the Solicitors Indemnity Fund (SIF) was established to replace the master policy scheme.

In 2000 the requirement that all solicitors be insured through the SIF was abolished and solicitors became free to negotiate their professional indemnity (PI) insurance on the open market.

Save for three recent exceptions,[1] since 2000 there have been two stipulations within what is otherwise a free market:

(1) the insurer must be a participating insurer, that is an authorised insurer (essentially any insurer authorised to carry out that class of business under the Financial Services and Markets Act (FSMA) 2000)[2] which has entered into a participating insurers agreement with the Solicitors Regulation Authority (SRA)[3] which remains in force for the purposes of underwriting new business at the date of the insurance contract; and

(2) the terms of the insurance cover must meet the 'minimum terms and conditions' (MTC) set by the current indemnity insurance rules.[4]

Qualifying insurance may be underwritten by more than one insurer provided that, collectively, the MTC are satisfied and that one insurer is identified as the lead insurer.[5] A list of participating insurers can be found on the SRA website.

Until 30 September 2013 all insurance policies ran for one year from 1 October in each year. Since 1 October 2013 insurers have been free to issue policies with variable renewal dates. Policies may be for periods of any length.

The obligation to effect insurance and ancillary rules are:

- for SRA authorised firms, set out in the SRA Indemnity Insurance Rules 2019 (SIIR 2019);

- for freelance solicitors, set out in the SRA Authorisation of Individuals Regulations 2019;[6] and

- for solicitors providing reserved legal services from non-commercial bodies, set out in the SRA Code of Conduct for Solicitors, RELs and RFLs 2019 (the 'Code for Individuals').[7]

Commentary on key changes is provided at **11.2**, SIIR 2019 are addressed at **11.4–11.11**, and commentary on the obligations of non-SRA firms, freelance solicitors and solicitors practising in non-commercial bodies is at **11.12**.

1   SIIR 2019 do not apply to solicitors providing unreserved legal services from a non-SRA firm, freelance solicitors, or solicitors providing reserved legal services through a non-commercial body: see **11.12**.
2   See the Participating Insurers Agreement 2021, being the latest available at the time of writing.
3   Formerly with the Law Society.
4   Annex 1 to SIIR 2019.
5   Clause 2.6 of Annex 1 to SIIR 2019.
6   Regulation 10.2(b)(vi).
7   Paragraph 5.6.

Key changes

11.2

In the last edition of this book we reported on proposed sweeping and controversial changes to the rules that were being considered by the SRA including reducing the compulsory layer of insurance to £500,000, or £1 million for firms providing conveyancing services, and capping run-off at £1.5 million, or £3 million for firms providing conveyancing services. In June 2018 the SRA closed a consultation on the proposed changes, the most controversial of which were not included in SIIR 2019. The SRA had indicated that the proposals remained under consideration. On 19 December 2019, the SRA announced that it would not be proceeding with any of the proposed changes, save that it would continue its work in three key areas in relation to insurance:

- How it can make it easier for firms to close in an orderly way, including reviewing the SRA successor practice definition.

- What should be in the scope of cybercrime cover and working with insurers to support the development of products. See **11.15**.

- Introducing an improved participating insurers agreement (PIA) for the 2020/2021 indemnity year.

At the time of writing there have been no changes to the SRA successor practice definition – see commentary at **11.9**.

The principal changes introduced in the 2020 PIA, and maintained in the 2021 PIA, relate to the insurer's reporting obligations to the SRA. In the 2018 PIA insurers were obliged only to report a material inaccuracy in a proposal form; any matter that, but for the 'No avoidance or repudiation' clause in the minimum terms and conditions, would have resulted in the insurer repudiating the contract; dishonesty or fraud; or a wilful refusal to pay any sum due to the insurer. In addition to these categories, since the 2020 PIA insurers have been obligated to report:

- a failure by an authorised body (and/or any principal of the said body), whether wilful or not, to:

  – pay any sum required by SIIR 2019 (eg the insurance premium); or

  – reimburse the insurer of any amount falling within a policy excess which has been paid out by a participating Insurer to a claimant;

- where the insurer is aware that an authorised body has operated or is operating without qualifying insurance; and

- where the insurer becomes aware of any claim of inadequate professional services made against the authorised body or any insured of that body (and therefore including all employees and consultants).[1]

---

1 Until the relevant sections were repealed by the Legal Services Act (LSA) 2007, 'inadequate professional services' were addressed by SA 1974. The term is not defined in the SRA Glossary or otherwise by statute. Presumably this is intended to refer to a service-style complaint within the jurisdiction of the Legal Ombudsman (LeO).

Solicitors Indemnity Fund

11.3

The SIF remains relevant to current regulatory requirements in that it provides run-off cover for new claims against firms, where there is no successor practice, which:

- ceased before 1 September 2000; or

- have ceased since 1 September 2000, but only where:

  – the run-off cover period provided by qualifying insurers has expired; and

  – the claim was or is first notified to the SIF on or before 30 September 2022.

Qualifying insurers are obligated to provide run-off cover for a period of at least six years under the MTC.

SIF-backed 'run-off' cover beyond firms' six years' commercial run-off cover was slated to close in 2017. That deadline was postponed first to September 2020, then again to 30 September 2021 and then, under considerable pressure from the Law Society, and the profession at large, on 15 June 2021, it was extended once further, to 30 September 2022.

Consequently, firms will need to consider their insurance arrangements carefully when planning closure, succession and merger.

Solicitors are currently subject to four sets of indemnity rules: the SRA Indemnity Rules 2012, which regulate the relationship between the profession and the SIF, SIIR 2019, which set out the requirements for SRA authorised firms to obtain qualifying insurance on the open market, the SRA Authorisation of Individuals Regulations 2019,[1] and the Code for Individuals,[2] the latter two of which set out the requirement for freelance solicitors and solicitors providing reserved legal services in non-commercial bodes to obtain 'adequate and appropriate' insurance.

With the closure of the largest part of the SIF's work anticipated to have occurred by 30 September 2022, it is expected that the SRA Indemnity Rules 2012 will only be relevant in practice to the mechanisms for dealing with an increasingly small number of potential claims capable of being indemnified under the run-off arrangements. These issues are likely to be of minimal significance and will therefore not be considered.

1   Regulation 10.2(b)(vi).
2   Paragraph 5.6.

The SRA Indemnity Insurance Rules 2019 – the basic requirements

11.4

The rules only apply to SRA authorised firms[1] and their principals[2] and thus do not apply to solicitors providing unreserved legal services[3] from a body that is not authorised by the SRA, freelance solicitors – whether providing reserved legal services or not, or solicitors providing reserved legal services from a non-commercial body (see **11.12**).

Every SRA authorised firm must arrange insurance with one or more qualifying insurer that must comply with the MTC set out in Annex 1 to SIIR 2019; the obligation is imposed both on the firm and on every principal.[4] Licensed bodies (alternative business structures, ABSs) must have qualifying insurance in relation to their regulated activities, where they undertake both regulated and unregulated activities, and SIIR 2019 apply to licensed bodies generally only in relation to their regulated activities.

SIIR 2019 enable the SRA to require the production of information and evidence that qualifying insurance is in place.[5]

The rules do not apply to overseas practice.

The sum insured for any one claim (exclusive of defence costs) must be, where the insured firm is a relevant recognised body or a relevant licensed body (in respect of activities regulated by the SRA in accordance with the terms of the body's licence), at least £3 million, and in all other cases, at least £2 million.[6] A 'relevant recognised body', excludes, in most cases, conventional (unincorporated) partnerships.

In any event, firms are obligated to effect a higher level of cover if the minimum level fails to provide 'adequate and appropriate cover'.[7] Thus, if a firm regularly conducts transactions of a value exceeding the compulsory layer, if it fails to provide adequate cover for claims that might arise, the firm and its senior managers lay themselves open to allegations of a breach of the SRA's regulatory arrangements.

Firms must take into account current and past practice, as well as any alternative arrangements the firm or its clients make.[8] Past practice is relevant, as cover is provided on a 'claims made' basis, that is, cover is provided by the insurer, subject to the terms for the insurance period in which a claim is first made (unless a 'circumstance' has been notified to an insurer in an earlier period) and which, for example, may relate to a negligent act in earlier years. The 'adequate and appropriate cover' rule necessitates careful consideration, and communication with a firm's insurer, before the acquisition of another firm is completed. Any excess layer above and beyond that complying with the MTC need not be with participating insurers, but the terms of cover will need to be adequate and appropriate.

The SRA has indicated that it expects firms to carry out a reasonable and rational assessment to consider whether the minimum level and terms of cover are sufficient. The SRA has produced guidance on the factors to take into account.[9]

Even if it is not required to satisfy the 'adequate and appropriate cover' rule, firms are free to arrange cover in excess of the minimum levels and may do so with insurers which are not participating insurers.

Firms and insurers are free to negotiate the level of any excess which the firm may elect to meet in respect of claims – see **11.6**.

Firms must ensure that clients have the benefit of the indemnity insurance required by the rules, and must not exclude or attempt to exclude liability below the minimum level of cover required under these rules.[10] The SRA has since clarified that 'minimum level of cover' in this rule means the cover required under the minimum terms and conditions,[11] and thus £2 million or £3 million, as is applicable, rather than any higher level deemed appropriate and adequate,[12] as required by the rules, if that is higher than the minimum level of cover requirement. Nevertheless, despite the limitation to this prohibition, firms should consider carefully whether it would be appropriate to cap liability at this minimum level of cover, particularly if they have excess layer cover.

A minimum of six years' run-off cover is required if the firm ceases to practise during an indemnity period.[13] Run-off cover is not required if there is a successor practice. In that event the qualifying insurance will be that of the successor practice.

If the insurer suffers an insolvency event, then, subject to any waiver granted by the SRA, the firm and its principals must ensure that alternative qualifying insurance is arranged within four weeks of the insolvency event.[14]

Version 19 of the SRA Handbook 2011, released on 1 October 2017, amended the MTC to remove the obligation on firms which transfer between regulators to obtain run-off cover, as opposed to arranging insurance meeting the requirements of the other regulator. It had been a significant barrier for conveyancing firms wishing to be regulated by the Council for Licensed Conveyancers (CLC) that the SRA formerly treated the firm as 'closing', triggering the need for run-off cover. The removal of the obligation to obtain run-off cover in these circumstances is conditional upon the firm becoming an authorised non-SRA firm, as now defined in the SRA Glossary, and the authorised non-SRA regulator being a signatory to a protocol on terms agreed by the SRA which relates to switching between approved regulators.[15]

In the last edition of *The Solicitor's Handbook* we highlighted that in bringing into force SIIR 2019 the SRA had signalled its intention to withdraw its power to direct an insurer, in the event of a coverage dispute, to conduct a claim, advance defence costs and compromise and pay a claim. This power[16] was an important safeguard for small firms, unable to finance a claim against a large commercial insurer following a declinature, and its omission would have been regrettable. The SRA had decided to withdraw this power despite acknowledging in its consultation that the positions taken by insurers can be controversial. At the time of writing this power has been reinstated as clause 4.8A of the minimum terms and conditions of insurance.[17]

A firm, and any principal, is required to provide details of its qualifying insurance to any person who asserts a claim apparently covered by the policy, and to anyone who is insured under the policy, upon request.[18] The Provision of Services Regulations 2009[19] also obligate firms to provide contact details for the insurer and the territorial coverage,[20] which in the case of the MTC, is worldwide. The requirements can be met by a notice in the firm's reception area.

1 Licensed bodies, recognised bodies and recognised sole practices.
2 Rule 1.1 of SIIR 2019.
3 The reserved legal activities are those falling within the definition at section 12(1) of LSA 2007.
4 Rule 4.1.
5 Rule 6.1.
6 Clause 2.1 of Annex 1 to SIIR 2019.
7 Rule 3.1.
8 Rule 3.1.
9 See SRA guidance, 'Adequate and appropriate indemnity insurance', 25 November 2019 as well as Application to the Legal Services Board (LSB) for approval of changes to regulatory arrangements relating to the SRA's PI insurance requirements, 5 March 2019.
10 Rule 3.2.
11 Clause 2.1 of Annex 1 to SIIR 2019.
12 SRA guidance, 'Adequate and appropriate indemnity insurance', 25 November 2019.
13 Clause 5.4(d) of Annex 1 to SIIR 2019.
14 Rule 5.1.
15 Clause 5.7 of Annex 1 to SIIR 2019.
16 Previously clause 4.10 of Appendix 1 to SIIR 2013.
17 Annex 1 to SIIR 2019.
18 Rule 9.2.
19 SI 2009/2999.
20 Regulation 8(1)(n).

The extended policy period and the cessation period

11.5

Until 30 September 2013 there was an expensive safety net for firms which were unable to acquire insurance on the open market: the Assigned Risks Pool (ARP). For an analysis of this system see Chapter 10 of *The Solicitor's Handbook 2013*.

From 1 October 2013 the ARP was abolished save in respect of run-off cover. With the ARP's closure, the situation whereby firms were able to continue in practice without being able to obtain insurance on the open market and without (in many cases) paying the ARP premium has been brought to an end.

The position since 1 October 2013 has been that, if a firm is unable to renew its existing policy or to obtain insurance from another participating insurer on or by the renewal date it has 30 days within which to obtain cover,[1] during which its existing insurer will continue to insure (the 'extended policy period', formerly known as the 'extended indemnity period').[2]

If no qualifying insurance is found in that 30-day period the firm must cease practice promptly, and in any event no later than a further 60 days (the 'cessation period'), unless qualifying insurance can be found within the cessation period which will be effective from the renewal date.[3] The existing insurer will also provide cover during the cessation period.[4]

During the cessation period (after the extended policy period has expired) the firm and every principal must ensure that the firm, every principal and every employee undertakes no work in relation to private legal practice and accepts no instructions save to the extent that the work or the instructions are necessary to discharge obligations within the scope of the firm's existing instructions.[5]

In short, from the date of renewal, the firm has 30 days to find cover during which it may continue to work normally, but from that point on, although it may still try to find insurance for a further 60 days, it is obliged to work towards an orderly close down, accepting no new work.

The insurer providing cover for the previous insurance period must extend cover for the whole of the 90 days, unless another participating insurer steps in.

The MTC permit insurers to require reimbursement, to the extent that it is just or equitable having regard to the prejudice caused to the insurer's interests, where the firm undertakes work in the cessation period contrary to rule 4.2 of SIIR 2019.[6]

A firm must notify the SRA and its insurer as soon as reasonably practicable, and in any event within five business days, after entering the extended policy period, and after entering the cessation period, and must also notify both parties if qualifying insurance is obtained within either period, with the details of the participating insurer and policy.[7]

1 Rule 2.3 of SIIR 2019.
2 Clause 5.1 of Annex 1 to SIIR 2019.
3 Rule 2.4.
4 Clause 5.2 of Annex 1 to SIIR 2019.
5 Rule 4.2.
6 Clause 7.2(b) of Annex 1 to SIIR 2019.
7 Rule 8.1.

The minimum terms and conditions

11.6

The MTC are set out in Annex 1 to SIIR 2019. Some aspects have already been mentioned, namely the minimum level of cover at £2 million or £3 million for relevant recognised bodies or relevant licensed bodies for each claim.[1]

The insurance must indemnify against civil liability to the extent that it arises from private legal practice[2] in connection with the insured firm's practice, on a 'claims made' basis; that is, claims are covered if made:

- within the period of insurance; or
- after the period of insurance, if arising from 'circumstances' first notified during the period of insurance.

Consistent with earlier rules, included within the definition of 'claim'[3] is an obligation on an insured to remedy a breach of the prevailing accounts rules.[4] See **11.11**.

The insurance must indemnify against any amount paid or payable in accordance with the recommendation of the Office for Legal Complaints (including LeO) or any other regulatory authority to the same extent as it indemnifies the insured against civil liability, but not in respect of any determination requiring the firm to refund fees.[5]

Defence costs[6] must also be covered without limit.[7] Where a claim exceeds the sum insured, the insurer may limit its liability for defence costs to the proportion that the sum insured bears to the total amount paid or payable to dispose of the claim.[8]

As already mentioned, firms are free to negotiate the level of excess to be applied – meaning firms can elect to self-insure to a substantial extent without regard to the minimum terms.[9] Protection for the public is partially maintained as, if the insured fails to pay the amount of any excess to the claimant within 30 days, then following notification by the claimant, the insurer must make good the sum, reclaiming it from the insured as necessary.[10] While the amount of any excess agreed between insurer and the insured does not reduce the total limit of the insurer's liability,[11] if the insurer, upon being required to do so,[12] makes a payment to a claimant in default of an insured paying an excess, the insurer may stipulate that such payment (remedying the default) erodes the sum insured.[13] In contrast with previous rules, an excess must not apply to defence costs.[14] The insurance may provide for multiple claims to be treated as one claim for the purpose of calculating any excess, on terms that may be agreed between insurer and insured.[15]

The insurance may, for the purposes of determining the limit of the indemnity cover, and as set out in the MTC,[16] make provision such that more than one claim made against an insured may be treated as 'one claim'. This is known as 'aggregation'; it has been a thorny issue, subject of recent litigation and we provide commentary at **11.7**.

The most important element of the MTC consists of the restrictions they impose on insurers for the purpose of ensuring that members of the public are not deprived of the benefits of compulsory PI insurance as a result of matters which, in other circumstances, might enable an insurer to disclaim or avoid liability. These are referred to in Annex 1 to SIIR 2019 as 'special conditions' and are addressed at **11.8**.[17]

1   Clause 2.1 of Annex 1 to SIIR 2019.
2   Annex 1, clause 1.1.
3   SRA Glossary 2019.
4   SRA Accounts Rules 2019, or any rules which replace them in whole or in part.
5   Annex 1, clause 1.4.
6   See definition at **11.11.**
7   Annex 1, clauses 1.2 and 2.2.
8   Annex 1, clause 2.3.
9   Annex 1, clause 3.1.
10   Annex 1, clause 3.4.
11   Annex 1, clause 3.2.
12   Annex 1, clause 3.4.
13   Annex 1, clause 3.4.
14   Annex 1, clause 3.3.
15   Annex 1, clause 3.5.
16   Annex 1, clause 2.5.
17   Annex 1, clause 4.

Aggregation

11.7

One of the most important things that a solicitor needs to know is whether his or her insurance cover is going to be sufficient, and thus whether to purchase top-up cover. When applicable, 'aggregation' (treating a number of claims as one claim) can have serious ramifications for a firm's and thus a client's cover. It is highly contentious and has been the subject of recent litigation as detailed below.

As described in the preceding section, the insurance may make provision as to the meaning of 'one claim' for the purposes of determining the limit of indemnity and, in particular, may provide that all claims against any one or more insured will be regarded as one claim when arising from:

(a)   one act or omission;

(b)   one series of related acts or omissions;

(c)   the same act or omission in a series of related matters or transactions; or

(d)   similar acts or omissions in a series of related matters or transactions; and

(e)   all claims against one or more insured arising from one matter or transaction.[1]

Where there are a number of high value claims, each below the level of insurance for 'one claim' but collectively exceeding it, insurers will benefit from aggregation in that their total exposure will be capped at the level for a single claim. Where there are a number of low level claims, collectively within the insured limit, the insured firm will benefit from aggregation, because there will then be only one deductible or excess, rather than a multiple.

In light of the decision in *Lloyds TSB General Insurance Holdings Ltd v Lloyds Bank Group Insurance Co Ltd*[2] and in response to market pressures by PI insurers, the Law Society amended clause 2.5 by adding sub-clauses (iii) and (iv) (set out at (c) and (d) above).

AIG Europe Ltd v Woodman[3] concerned the interpretation of clause 2.5(a)(iv) of the MTC[4] – ie what amounts to 'similar acts or omissions, in a series of related matters or transactions' (at (d) above). The Supreme Court held that the word 'related' implied some interconnection between the matters or transactions that were individually the subject of claims.

The SRA intervened in the case of *Lord Bishop of Leeds v Dixon Coles and Gill (A Firm)*[5] which concerned the interpretation of clauses 2.5(a)(i) and (ii) of the MTC[6] – ie what amounts to 'one act or omission' and 'one series of related acts or omissions' (at (a) and (b) above), and additionally what amounted to 'one claim'.

The firm had made a claim upon its insurer for an indemnity in respect of the sum required to rectify a shortfall on client account, in respect of about £4 million of client funds dishonestly withdrawn over a number of years by a partner.

'Claim' is defined to include an obligation to remedy a breach of the SRA Accounts Rules.[7]

The Court of Appeal, upholding the decision of the High Court (which had found both that the partner's thefts were separate acts, and that each client shortfall gave rise to a separate duty to remedy), also found that the partner's dishonesty was not a sufficient unifying factor to constitute a series of related acts and thus the claims were not aggregated.[8]

The Court of Appeal had regard to the primary purpose of the obligation to insure being the protection of the public[9] commenting that:

'an ordinary member of the public ... who proposed instructing a firm ... could, if prudent, inquire about the level of insurance cover carried by the firm and, on being told that the minimum was £2m per claim, take comfort from the fact that the value of his transaction to be effected with them would be well under this limit ... however ... he could find that his claim was aggregated with those of many other clients of the firm, stretching back over many years, of whom he knew, and could know, nothing.'[10]

In light of the court's observations, it would be prudent for practitioners, when providing information to clients to enable them to make informed decisions,[11] to draw to their attention that there are potential limitations to the firm's publicised insurance cover, and additionally, that any claim that arises would fall due to be considered, not necessarily under the firm's current policy of insurance, but under the policy in force at the time that the claim is deemed to have been intimated or made, the terms and limit of cover for which may be different.

In *obiter* remarks, Lord Justice Nugee also cast doubt on the SRA's practice of treating a false entry posted to a client ledger, which causes the ledger at least to suggest there is a client account deficit, as being evidence of money owed to that client:

'when the money is in a mixed account it is not so obvious whose money has been stolen each time there is a theft ... the fraudulent solicitor will need to cover their tracks by making an entry in one of the client ledgers so that the totals still reconcile. This can be done for example by creating an entry in a client ledger showing a fictitious payment out. We were told that where this is done, the practice is to regard that particular theft as allocated to that client. I have some doubts about this, as it seems surprising that a solicitor stealing client money from a mixed account can decide for him or herself which client to allocate the loss to ...'[12]

1   Clause 2.5 of Annex 1 to SIIR 2019, the final example listed as 2.5(b).
2   [2003] 4 All ER 43, HL.
3   [2017] UKSC 18.
4   Appendix 1 to the SRA Indemnity Insurance Rules 2013 (SIIR 2013).
5   [2021] EWCA Civ 1211 on appeal from [2020] EWHC 2809 (Ch). The matter also came back before the court on a separate point resulting in a judgment on 20 July 2021, [2021] EWCA Civ 1097, where the court found that claims against the 'innocent partners' were subject to a six-year limitation period. This may have ramifications for insurance premiums.
6   Appendix 1 to SIIR 2013.
7   SRA Glossary 2019 and a similar provision was contained in the SRA Glossary 2012.
8   At [53] and [72].
9   *Swain v The Law Society* [1983] 1 AC 598.
10 At [86].
11 Paragraph 8.11 of the Code for Individuals.
12 At [81].

Restrictions on insurers – the 'special conditions'

11.8

Insurers are not entitled to:

- Avoid or repudiate insurance on any grounds whatsoever, including any breach of the duty to make a fair presentation of the risk or misrepresentation (fraudulent or otherwise).

- Reduce or deny their liability on any grounds whatsoever, including any breach of any term or condition of the insurance, other than if one of the specified exclusions applies (see further below).

- Cancel the insurance unless agreed by the insured firm, and then only where either there is alternative qualifying insurance in place (for example, in the event of a merger of firms), or the insured firm is no longer required to carry qualifying insurance. Additionally, cancellation must not affect rights and obligations that accrued prior to the cancellation.

- Set off any amounts due from the insured, such as any premium or reimbursement that may be due, against any amount payable to a claimant.

- Reduce or exclude liability by reason of the existence or availability of other insurance (except (i) where the claim was first intimated or made in an earlier qualifying insurance period, or (ii) where the insured, having entered the extended policy period or cessation period, obtains a policy of qualifying insurance that incepts from and with effect from the expiration of the policy period.

- Exclude or limit liability because relevant matters occurred before a specified date.[1]

The insurance may provide that, if the insured firm's practice is succeeded during the period of insurance and, as a result, a situation of 'double insurance' exists between two or more insurers of the successor practice, contribution between insurers is to be determined in accordance with the relative numbers of principals of the owners of the constituent practices immediately prior to succession.[2]

The insurance must provide that:

- If there is a dispute as to whether a practice is a successor practice, all parties involved are required to take all reasonable steps to resolve it, including, if appropriate, referring the dispute to arbitration.

- Pending resolution of any coverage dispute and without prejudice to any issue in dispute, the insurer will, if so directed by the SRA, conduct any claim, advance defence costs and, if appropriate, compromise and pay the claim. The SRA may, in its absolute discretion, make such a direction where it is satisfied that:

  - the party requesting the direction has taken all reasonable steps to resolve the dispute with the other party/ies;

  - there is a reasonable prospect that the coverage dispute will be resolved or determined in the insured's favour; and

  - it is fair and equitable in all the circumstances for such direction to be given.

- Insurers will meet defence costs (in so far as they are within the scope of insurance) as and when they are incurred unless and until the insured admits that he or she has committed or condoned dishonesty or a fraudulent act or omission, or a court or other judicial body finds that the insured was guilty of such dishonesty or fraudulent act or omission.

- The insurer will vary the terms of the insurance to give effect to any variation in the SIIR (including the Glossary and MTC), to be implemented on the earliest of: renewal, replacement, or extension of the policy, or 18 months from the commencement of the policy period (although not if the 18-month period falls within the extended policy or cessation periods).

- The insurance is to be construed or rectified so as to comply with the require-ments of the MTC (including any variation required to be implemented), and any inconsistent provision must be severed or rectified to be compliant.[3]

1   Clauses 4.1 to 4.6 of Annex 1 to SIIR 2019.
2   Annex 1, clause 4.7.
3   Annex 1, clauses 4.8 to 4.11.

Run-off and successor practices

11.9

Clause 5 of Annex 1 to SIIR 2019 deals with the extended indemnity period, the cessation period (see **11.5**), and run-off cover.

As described at **11.4**, run-off cover must be for a minimum period of six years. Subject to the rules on succession (see below), it runs from cessation, which may be during the policy, extended policy or cessation periods, or at the expiration of the policy or cessation periods.

Additionally, a practice shall be regarded as ceasing if and when it becomes a 'non-SRA firm' (that is, a firm authorised or capable of being authorised to practise by another approved regulator; or not capable of being authorised to practise by any approved regulator) save where (a) the insured firm becomes an 'authorised non-SRA firm' (a firm which is authorised to carry on legal activities as defined in section 12 of LSA 2007 by an approved regulator other than the SRA), and (b) provided that the approved regulator, by which the non-SRA firm is authorised, is a signatory to a protocol on terms agreed by the SRA which relates to switching between approved regulators – see **11.4** for additional commentary.

What is or is not a successor practice is a very material consideration because the insurers of a successor practice will become liable for any claims, first intimated or made during the successor practice's policy period, arising from the private legal practice of the former practice. This term has its own definition in the SRA Glossary and is reproduced here for convenience.

successor practice

    (a)   means a *practice* identified in this definition as 'B', where:

        (i)   'A' is the *practice* to which B succeeds; and

        (ii)   'A's owner' is the owner of A immediately prior to transition; and

        (iii) 'B's owner' is the owner of B immediately following transition; and

        (iv) 'transition' means merger, acquisition, absorption or other transition which results in A no longer being carried on as a discrete legal *practice*.

    (b)   B is a successor practice to A where:

        (i)   B is or was held out, expressly or by implication, by B's owner as being the successor of A or as incorporating A, whether such holding out is contained in notepaper, business cards, form of electronic communications, publications, promotional material or otherwise, or is contained in any statement or declaration by B's owner to any regulatory or taxation authority; and/or

(ii) (where A's owner was a *sole practitioner* and the transition occurred on or before 31 August 2000) – the *sole practitioner* is a *principal* of B's owner; and/or

(iii) (where A's owner was a *sole practitioner* and the transition occurred on or after 1 September 2000) – the *sole practitioner* is a *principal* or *employee* of B's owner; and/or

(iv) (where A's owner was a *recognised body* or a *licensed body* (in respect of an activity regulated by the SRA in accordance with the terms of the body's licence)) – that body is a *principal* of B's owner; and/or

(v) (where A's owner was a *partnership*) – the majority of the *principals* of A's owner have become *principals* of B's owner; and/or

(vi) (where A's owner was a *partnership* and the majority of *principals* of A's owner did not become *principals* of the owner of another legal *practice* as a result of the transition) – one or more of the *principals* of A's owner have become *principals* of B's owner and:

(A) B is carried on under the same name as A or a name which substantially incorporates the name of A (or a substantial part of the name of A); and/or

(B) B is carried on from the same premises as A; and/or

(C) the owner of B acquired the goodwill and/or *assets* of A; and/or

(D) the owner of B assumed the liabilities of A; and/or

(E) the majority of staff employed by A's owner became *employees* of B's owner.

(c) notwithstanding the foregoing, B is not a successor practice to A under paragraph (b) (ii), (iii), (iv), (v) or (vi) if another *practice* is or was held out by the owner of that other *practice* as the successor of A or as incorporating A, provided that there is insurance complying with the *MTC* in relation to that other *practice*.

In brief, most circumstances involving the partners or other owners of a practice (or a majority of them) being absorbed into another firm – or even a minority in certain circumstances, or anything done or said which holds out expressly or impliedly that the second firm is succeeding to or incorporating the first firm – will result in the second firm being a successor practice. The definition focuses on people and ownership, rather than on cases and clients, so that if a firm does not hold itself out as a successor practice and acquires the clients and files of a firm that closes (for example) but does not take on its owners, either as principals or as employees, it will not be a successor practice. Firms should be particularly careful, if they wish to avoid successor practice status, when employing a solicitor who previously traded as a sole practitioner, to ensure that the sole practitioner, prior to cessation, both elected to pay, and paid, the premium for run-off cover.

A firm which is about to close and to which there would be a successor practice for the purpose of SIIR 2019 has an option. It may allow that situation to occur, or it may, before the cessation of its business, elect to trigger its own run-off cover and pay the premium. In that event, there is no successor practice. If, prior to cessation, either the election is not made, or the run-off premium is not paid, the option is lost and the normal rules on succession will apply.[1] SIIR 2013 stipulated that notice must be given to the SRA by the insurer within seven days of receipt of notice of the election – this requirement is not replicated in SIIR 2019.

When a firm enters a run-off period but restarts practice (which might happen inadvertently), the insurer may cancel run-off cover provided that there is qualifying insurance in place, and it gives notice to the insured, and any other interested insurer, that it is providing qualifying insurance for the current indemnity period as a continuation of the insured firm's practice prior to cessation, and that it is liable for claims against the insured firm arising from circumstances which occurred prior to cessation.[2]

The successor practice rule was designed to provide clarity on which insurer was obliged to indemnify a claim following a merger or takeover; it has no effect on the underlying liability. In *Cohen v Lorrells LLP*[3] the claimant sought a declaration that the second defendant, a firm of solicitors, was a successor practice. The second defendant applied to strike out the claim. Master Cook, in deciding that he would have struck out the claim, but for it being proportionate to allow the claimant the chance to apply to amend its claim, so as to direct the application against the second defendant's insurer, found that:

> 'The important point to grasp is that the insurance arrangements, whatever they may be, do not transfer the liability of the first defendant to the second defendant' and 'a declaration in the form currently sought will not bind … the insurer who is potentially liable to pay the claim.'[4]

1   Clause 5.5 of Annex 1 to SIIR 2019.
2   Annex 1, clause 5.6.
3   [2019] EWHC 32 (QB).
4   Ibid at [40] and [43].

Permitted exclusions

11.10

The MTC specify the grounds upon which an insurer may exclude or limit liability in respect of any claim (including for defence costs cover).[1]

Most significantly, insurers may exclude liability (and always do) where any civil liability or related defence costs arise from the dishonesty of or a fraudulent act or omission committed or condoned by an individual insured. Insurance must nonetheless cover each other insured and must provide that no dishonesty, act or omission can be imputed to a body corporate unless it was committed or condoned by all directors of a company or members of a limited liability partnership (LLP).[2]

Following the Supreme Court decision in *Ivey v Genting Casinos*,[3] there should no longer be scope for significant disagreement on the test for dishonesty as there had been before that decision.

The other grounds, in summary, are:

- claims where cover is provided under insurance for a prior period;

- liability for death or bodily injury, except psychological injury and emotional distress arising from an insured breach of duty (that is, in the performance of or failure to perform legal work);

- liability for damage or loss to, or destruction of, property – unless it is property in the care of the insured in connection with the insured firm's practice, or where the damage or loss arises from an insured breach of duty;

- claims arising from partnership disputes within the firm or the like;

- claims in the nature of employment disputes about dismissal, harassment or discrimination and the like, including any training agreements;

- personal debts and trading liabilities (excluding HM Land Registry fees);

- claims in relation to guarantees, indemnities or undertakings in connection with the provision of financial or other benefits for the personal advantage of the insured;

- any fine or penalty or order for costs in relation to a professional conduct complaint;

- punitive or exemplary damages awarded under US or Canadian law, other than in defamation;

- company directors' or officers' liability, in that capacity (unless it arises from an insured breach of duty); and

- claims arising from terrorism, war and other hostilities, and asbestos-related injury or damage (unless arising from an insured breach of duty).

Additionally, the insurer shall be deemed not to provide cover to the extent that it would expose the insurer to any sanction, prohibition or restriction under United Nations resolutions or the trade or economic sanctions, laws or regulations of the European Union, United Kingdom, Australia or United States of America.

1   Clause 6 of Annex 1 to SIIR 2019.
2   Annex 1, clause 6.8.
3   [2017] UKSC 67.

Definitions of 'claim' and 'defence costs'

11.11

A claim includes:

- any civil claim for damages or compensation or an intimation of the same; and

- an obligation on the insured to remedy any breach of the SRA Accounts Rules, or any rules that replace them, even if no individual has made any claim or given any intimation of a claim in relation to such breach.[1]

With regard to the second limb above, the definition of 'claim' refers only to 'the SRA Accounts Rules, or any rules which replace them'. The current SRA Accounts Rules are the 2019 rules. The definition does not, as it did in the SRA Glossary

2012, refer to earlier sets of rules.[2] However, the claim being indemnified is the obligation to remedy, which exists immediately upon a breach existing,[3] whether or not a person makes a claim for compensation. Thus, any indemnity required should be covered by the insurer for the insurance year in which the breach first existed, the SRA Glossary 2012 definition being consistent to this extent.

Defence costs[4] include legal costs and disbursements (including investigative and related expenses) reasonably and necessarily incurred with the consent of the insurer in:

- defending any proceedings relating to a claim;

- conducting any proceedings for indemnity, contribution or recovery relating to a claim;

- investigating, reducing, avoiding or compromising any actual or potential claim; and

- acting for any insured in connection with any investigation, inquiry or any disciplinary proceeding (save in respect of any disciplinary proceeding under the authority of the SRA or the Solicitors Disciplinary Tribunal (the Tribunal or SDT)).

Defence costs do not include any internal or overhead expenses of the insured firm or the insurer or the cost of the insured firm's time.

The costs of disciplinary proceedings were formerly required to be covered, with some limitations, but this obligatory aspect of cover was removed from 1 October 2010.

1   SRA Glossary 2019.
2   SRA Glossary 2012 expressly referred to the Solicitors' Accounts Rules 1998 and any rules that replace them including the SRA Accounts Rules – the SRA Accounts 2011 replaced them.
3   Or at least 'promptly' – rule 7.1 of the SRA Accounts Rules 2011.
4   SRA Glossary 2019.

Non-SRA firms, freelance solicitors and non-commercial bodies

11.12

As described above, SIIR 2019 apply only to SRA authorised bodies and their principals; thus they do not apply to solicitors practising in non-SRA firms (ie those providing unreserved legal services[1] from bodies not authorised by the SRA), freelance solicitors or solicitors providing reserved legal services in non-commercial bodies.[2]

The SRA does not require non-SRA firms to carry PI insurance; thus, for example, the SRA permits solicitors practising in-house to provide unreserved legal services to members of the public without insurance. However, non-SRA firms may otherwise be obliged to carry such insurance, for example as may be required by another regulator.

Freelance solicitors that conduct reserved legal activities are obliged to 'take out and maintain indemnity insurance that provides adequate and appropriate cover in respect of the services that you provide or have provided, whether or not they comprise reserved legal activities, taking into account any alternative arrangements you or your clients may make'.[3] Thus freelance solicitors who do not undertake reserved legal activities are not required to carry insurance, but those that do undertake reserved legal activities are required to carry insurance for all of their work, that is, both the reserved and unreserved legal activities.

Solicitors (and registered European lawyers – RELs) carrying on reserved legal activities in a non-commercial body must ensure that '(a) the body takes out and maintains indemnity insurance; and (b) this insurance provides adequate and appropriate cover in respect of the services that you provide or have provided, whether or not they comprise reserved legal activities, taking into account any alternative arrangements the body or its clients may make.'[4]

'Adequate and appropriate cover' is not defined, but the SRA has produced guidance[5] – see commentary at **11.4**. If the SRA had intended that adequate and appropriate cover should mean cover equivalent to the MTC, it would have imposed a duty upon solicitors caught by the rule to procure such cover. In its application to the LSB, the SRA commented: 'only SRA authorised firms will be required to have insurance that meets our MTCs'.[6] Thus, adequate and appropriate cover may fall short of the MTC. One of the important protections of the MTC is that the cover cannot be avoided in the same way that commercial insurance can. Freelancers and solicitors providing reserved legal services in non-commercial bodies may need to take particular care when considering the terms of insurance including any avoidance provisions.

When considering what insurance cover is adequate and appropriate, both freelancers and solicitors providing reserved legal services in non-commercial bodes are obliged to address past practice, as authorised bodies are obliged to do.

As these categories of practitioner and practice are not subject to SIIR 2019, the obligations set out therein not to exclude liability below the minimum level of cover, and to procure run-off cover, are not applicable to them. Freelancers providing reserved legal services, and solicitors providing reserved legal services in non-commercial bodies, should proceed cautiously when seeking to exclude liability, and have regard to general consumer laws, including fairness of contract, and the requirements upon them to provide adequate and appropriate cover, act in a client's best interests, not take unfair advantage of clients, and ensure that clients understand the impact of the limitation of liability.

The SRA has produced guidance[7] for such practitioners considering capping liability, referencing the duties:

- not to abuse your position by taking unfair advantage of clients (see paragraph 1.2 of both the Code for Individuals and the SRA Code of Conduct for Firms 2019 (the 'Code for Firms')); and

- to give clients information in a way they can understand and ensure they are in a position to make informed decisions about the services they need, how their matter will be handled and the options available to them (see paragraph 8.6 of the Code for Individuals and paragraph 7.1 of the Code for Firms).

The guidance also provides that any cap should therefore: be fair and reasonable in the particular circumstances of the client and the case; reflect the balance of power and knowledge between the solicitor, REL or firm and that client and take into account the best interests of that client (SRA principle 7). It must also be communicated to the client in a way that they can understand the impact.

The guidance indicates that the SRA would not expect to see caps put on liability to clients as a matter of routine. The guidance does not specifically suggest that adequate and appropriate cover requirement extends to run-off cover.

Freelancers are required to inform their clients, before engagement, that they are not subject to the requirement to purchase qualifying insurance on the SRA's MTC and, where applicable, that alternative arrangements are in place. The freelancer will also, upon request, need to provide information about the cover provided.[8]

1 The reserved legal activities are those falling within the definition at section 12(1) of LSA 2007.
2 As permitted by section 23(1) of LSA 2007 and as defined by section 23(2).
3 Regulation 10.2(b)(vi) of the SRA Authorisation of Individuals Regulations 2019 as amended by the SRA Regulatory Arrangements (Indemnity Insurance) (Amendment) Rules 2018.
4 Paragraph 5.6 of the Code for Individuals as amended by the SRA Regulatory Arrangements (Indemnity Insurance) (Amendment) Rules 2018.
5 SRA guidance, 'Adequate and appropriate indemnity insurance', 25 November 2019.
6 Application 5 March 2019.
7 SRA guidance, 'Adequate and appropriate indemnity insurance', 25 November 2019.
8 Rule 4.3 of the SRA Transparency Rules 2018.

The Insurance Act 2015

11.13

The Insurance Act 2015, in force since 12 August 2016, imposes a duty on the insured to make a 'fair presentation of the risk' to insurers when taking out insurance (including renewals and variations) (section 3(1)). This requires disclosure of material circumstances that it knows of, those that it ought to know of and sufficient information to make further enquiries for the purpose of revealing those material circumstances.

Section 4(6) of the Act provides that:

> '… an insured ought to know what should reasonably have been revealed by a reasonable search of information available to the insured (whether the search is conducted by making enquiries or by any other means).'

It would be prudent for firms to err on the side of caution, to avoid allegations of a breach of this duty, which might lead to a claim for an increased premium or excess, or reimbursement, as the policy may provide.

Dealing with claims

11.14

Paragraph 3.5 of the Code for Firms and paragraph 7.11 of the Code for Individuals require that: 'You are honest and open with clients if things go wrong and if a client suffers loss or harm as a result you put matters right (if possible) and explain fully and promptly what has happened and the likely impact.'

Prior to 25 November 2019, firms on notice of a potentially negligent error were required only to advise clients to seek independent legal advice.[1] The current rule imposes a positive obligation to:

- be open and honest with the client where things have gone wrong, and

- if a client suffers loss or harm as a result, to:
    - put matters rights (where possible), and
    - provide a full and prompt explanation of what has happened and the likely impact.

In addition to the obligation to notify a PI insurer of a 'circumstance' (see **11.6**), most policies obligate an insured not to admit liability without the prior written consent of the insurer. Early contact with the firm's insurer will be key to ensuring that the full and prompt explanation does not prejudice the firm's insurance cover.

The SRA has published guidance on how to deal with matters when meeting these obligations presents a risk of an own interest conflict.[2] The guidance, which makes it clear that the obligation to 'put matters right' is subject to the obligation not to act where there is an own interest conflict, indicates that it will be a matter of professional judgement in all the circumstances whether an own interest conflict arises.

In a Tribunal judgment[3] on an application for an agreed outcome, pre-dating the introduction of the Code for Firms, a firm was found to have acted improperly in seeking to 'put matters right', in light of an own interest conflict.

It is difficult to envisage many situations where an error does not give rise to at least the risk of an own interest conflict. Firms should communicate with their insurers at an early stage, but, given the potentially conflicting duties, on the one hand to disclose and where possible, to remedy, and on the other hand, to maintain PI insurance, and in certain situations, not to act (and therefore not to remedy), it may be prudent to seek specialist advice.

1 Outcome 1.16 of the SRA Code of Conduct 2011 provided that, 'you inform current clients if you discover any act or omission which could give rise to a claim by them against you'.
2 SRA guidance, 'Putting matters right when things go wrong, and own interest conflicts', 25 November 2019.
3 *SRA v Howell Jones LLP*, 11846-2018, SDT. This decision was criticised by one of the authors of this book – see Treverton-Jones, 'Penalised for putting things right', *Gazette* [2019] 6 May.

Cybercrime cover

11.15

Following consultation the SRA has applied to the LSB for approval of changes to the MTC (see **11.6**) in relation to cyber risks. In summary the changes seek to make it explicit that the consumer protection under its PI insurance arrangements applies equally if the loss results from a cyber-attack/event.

It is proposed that the permitted exclusions at clause 6 of the MTC (see **11.10**), will be extended to an insurer's right to exclude:[1]

'by way of an exclusion or endorsement, the liability of the *insurer* to indemnify any *insured* in respect of, or in any way in connection with:

    (a) a *cyber act*

    (b) a partial or total failure of any *computer system*

    (c) the receipt or transmission of malware, malicious code or similar by the *insured* or any other party acting on behalf of the *insured*

    (d) the failure or interruption of services relating to *core infrastructure*

    (e) a breach of Data Protection Law

provided that any such exclusion or endorsement does not exclude or limit any liability of the *insurer* to indemnify any *insured* against:

    (i) civil liability referred to in clause 1.1 (including the obligation to remedy a breach of the SRA Accounts Rules as described in the definition of *claim*)

    (ii) *defence costs* referred to in clause 1.2 that would have been covered under the insurance even absent an event at 6(a) to 6(e) detailed above

    (iii) any award by a regulatory authority referred to in clause 1.4

In addition, any such exclusion or endorsement should not exclude or limit any liability of the *insurer* to indemnify any *insured* against matters referred to at (i) (ii) and (iii) above in circumstances where automated technology has been utilised.'

As any exclusion or endorsement may not exclude or limit the insurer's liability to indemnify an insured for civil liability, defence costs or an award by a regulatory authority (all as defined by MTC), the proposed change appears to have no practical effect on the current MTC. During consultation, the SRA indicated that the change amounts to no more than a clarification of existing cover (and thus should not affect premiums).

The SRA indicates that the last paragraph of the proposed new clause is intended to cover scenarios where third party losses arise following the use of technology in the provision of advice. The SRA indicates that examples could include Stamp Duty Land Tax calculators or auto-generated advice. The SRA makes clear that such losses should be covered by the PII policy.

New definitions are proposed for 'cyber act', 'computer system', 'core infrastructure' and 'Data Protection Law'.

1   Annex 1 to the SRA's 'Application to LSB for the approval of alterations to regulatory arrangements to minimum terms and conditions (MTCs) for professional indemnity insurance (PII) in relation to cyber risks', 20 October 2021.

CHAPTER 12

Registered European lawyers and registered foreign lawyers

12.1

A registered European lawyer (REL) is an individual registered with the Solicitors Regulation Authority (SRA) under regulation 17 of the European Communities (Lawyer's Practice) Regulations 2000[1] (the '2000 Regulations').[2] Since implementation period completion day (or Brexit), only a very limited category of RELs remain under transitional provisions prescribed by the Services of Lawyers and Lawyer's Practice (Revocation etc.) (EU Exit) Regulations 2020.[3] The SRA's guidance note 'European lawyers practising in the UK' describes this group as a 'defined group of Swiss lawyers'.[4] The majority of RELs were obliged to make alternative practising arrangements if they wished to continue practising within the jurisdiction after 31 December 2020; those who met the requirements of Part V of the 2000 Regulations and character and suitability requirements were entitled to qualify as solicitors pursuant to regulation 4.1 of the SRA Authorisation of Individuals Regulations.

A registered foreign lawyer (RFL) is an individual registered with the SRA under section 89 of the Courts and Legal Services Act (CLSA) 1990: see **APPENDIX 20**.

By virtue of their registration, both RELs and RFLs become subject to regulation by the SRA and are subject to the same rules of professional conduct and the whole regulatory and disciplinary regime that is in place for solicitors, with very little modification or exception. Further, as a result of the move to entity-based regulation, RELs and RFLs are liable for compliance with all relevant professional rules, including the 2019 regulatory arrangements, as managers or employees of regulated practices (see **CHAPTER 2**).

1 SI 2000/1119.
2 Note that primary legislation in the form of the Professional Qualifications Bill is expected to address cross-border recognition of professional qualifications and replace the current transitional arrangements.
3 SI 2020/1342.
4 SRA guidance, 'European lawyers practising in the UK', issued 22 April 2016, updated 25 March 2021.

12.2

RELs (in so far as they still exist) may practise, for all practical purposes, as if they are solicitors, and subject to the same restrictions, in that they can practise on their own account (but only if they are authorised to do so as a recognised sole practice, as solicitors are required to be under the SRA Authorisation of Firms Rules 2019), or as employees or managers of authorised bodies in accordance with the SRA Authorisation of Firms Rules 2019.

There are some limitations on the practising rights of RELs set out in regulations 9.2 and 9.3 of the SRA Authorisation of Individuals Regulations 2019. These require:

(i) that RELs conducting litigation before a court, preparing court documents or exercising rights of audience may only do so in conjunction with a solicitor or barrister authorised to do so;[1]

(ii) that RELs may only prepare and/or lodge instruments transferring or charging land for remuneration if they have a home title listed under regulation 12 of the 2000 Regulations;[2] and

(iii) that RELs may only carry on probate activities for remuneration if they have a home professional title listed under regulation 13 of the 2000 Regulations.[3]

The provisions permitting RELs to operate within England and Wales without necessarily needing to do so through an SRA authorised body, by practising through an Exempt European Practice (EEP) as defined in the SRA Handbook Glossary 2012, have not been replicated in the 2019 regulatory arrangements. This is presumably because the SRA has instead advocated a revised approach permitting practice as a solicitor, REL or RFL in unregulated firms – provided that no reserved activities are provided to the public. This revised approach removes any need for the specific provisions of the EEP regime.

RELs working in unregulated firms, including firms which may have been EEPs, will still be required to comply with the SRA Code of Conduct for Solicitors, RELs and RFLs 2019 (the 'Code for Individuals').

Following Brexit, those who are no longer eligible to become or practise as RELs have the following options as explained by the SRA's guidance note 'European lawyers practising in the UK':[4]

- practising your home law and/or EU law under your home professional registered title. This does not entitle you to undertake reserved work or specifically authorised work such as immigration and claims management and does not require registration with the SRA;

- acting as an employee of a regulated firm (on the same basis as unadmitted employees);

- becoming a manager or an interest holder in a regulated firm as either an RFL or an approved manager or interest holder in an ABS;

- registering as an RFL (with the attendant restrictions on practice – see below); and

- qualifying as a solicitor via the Qualified Lawyers Transfer Scheme (or, from 1 September 2021, the Solicitors Qualifying Exam).

1 Regulation 9.2.
2 Regulation 9.3(a).
3 Regulation 9.3(b).
4 SRA guidance, 'European lawyers practising in the UK', issued 22 April 2016, updated 25 March 2021.

12.3

RFLs, in contrast, are more restricted in the way they can practise. The main purpose of being registered as an RFL is to enable the individual to practise in a recognised body with a solicitor or solicitors, or an REL or RELs or a combination of the two – that is, as a manager, member or owner of a recognised body.[1] There is no requirement on a foreign lawyer to become an RFL for the purposes of being employed by a recognised body or a sole practitioner, or to be an owner, manager or employee of a licensed body. Registration does not permit an RFL to practise as a sole practitioner or an in-house RFL.[2]

Limitations on practising requirements for RFLs have largely been removed in the 2019 regulatory arrangements. The express requirements have been replaced by general information requirements in the Code for Individuals, in particular at paragraph 8.10 (as discussed at **4.135**).

RFLs are not permitted to undertake reserved activities in the same way that solicitors and RELs are. Regulation 9.4 of the SRA Authorisation of Individuals Regulations 2019 provides that RFLs may only:

'(a)   undertake advocacy in chambers in England and Wales under instructions given by a person who is authorised to do so;

(b)   under the direction and supervision of a person qualified to supervise:

(i)   prepare *court* documents;

(ii)   prepare instruments and the lodging of documents relating to the transfer or charge of land;

(iii)   prepare papers on which to found or oppose a grant of probate, or a grant of letters of administration;

(iv)   prepare trust deeds disposing of capital if you also are eligible to act as a *lawyer of England and Wales*;

(c)   in relation to *immigration work*:

(i)   undertake advocacy before immigration tribunals;

(ii)   have conduct of, and prepare documents for, immigration tribunal proceedings.'

where immigration work may only be undertaken through an authorised body, an authorised non-SRA firm which is a qualified person for the purposes of the Immigration and Asylum Act 1999 or a body regulated by the Office of the Immigration Services Commissioner.[3]

RFLs are otherwise not permitted to undertake any reserved activities.

1   See rules 1.1(b) and 13.2 of the SRA Authorisation of Firms Rules 2019. RFLs are within the definition of 'legally qualified' pursuant to section 9A(6)(b) of the Administration of Justice Act (AJA) 1985.
2   Rule 1.1(c) of the SRA Authorisation of Firms Rules 2019.
3   Regulation 9.5 of the SRA Authorisation of Individuals Regulations 2019.

12.4

Under Schedule 4 to the 2000 Regulations most of the statutory regime applying to solicitors through the Solicitors Act (SA) 1974 is extended to RELs, including provisions relating to:

●   regulation through practising certificates (section 28 of SA 1974);

●   all the rule-making powers in relation to professional conduct, accounts and insurance (sections 31, 32, 33A, 34 and 37 of SA 1974);

- the SRA's investigative and disciplinary powers (sections 44B, 44BA, 44BC, 44C and 44D of SA 1974);

- the control of the employment of disqualified persons, equally applicable to RELs as employers and employees (sections 41 to 44 of SA 1974);

- the powers of the Solicitors Disciplinary Tribunal (the Tribunal or SDT) and the High Court (sections 46 to 53 of SA 1974); and

- the powers of intervention (section 35 of and Schedule 1 to SA 1974).

This is not intended to be an exhaustive list.

The statutory regime governing RFLs is to be found in Schedule 14 to CLSA 1990 (see **Appendix 20**). This makes provision for applications for registration, registration subject to conditions, the renewal of registration, and for appeals to the High Court against a refusal to register, refusal to renew registration, and the imposition of conditions.

The Schedule also provides for contributions to the Compensation Fund (and this also is extended to RELs by the 2000 Regulations), imposes a requirement to provide accountants' reports, provides for the effect of bankruptcy and for the effect of disciplinary action leading to the RFL being dealt with in his or her home jurisdiction in a way that is equivalent to being struck off or suspended, and extends the jurisdiction of the Tribunal to RFLs.

CHAPTER 13

Regulation by other approved regulators

13.1

As pointed out in **CHAPTER 2**, in any analysis of the regulation of solicitors it is no longer possible to consider only the rules and regulations promulgated by the Solicitors Regulation Authority (SRA). From 31 March 2009, a solicitor could be individually regulated by the SRA, but employed by or a manager of a business entity supplying legal services that is regulated by another approved regulator. In that situation, the solicitor, in his professional dealings, must comply with the rules of the business's regulator, because the Legal Services Act (LSA) 2007 specifies that if there is a conflict between the regulation of the entity and the regulation of the individual, the regulation of the entity takes precedence.[1]

Currently, there are no fewer than five approved regulators able to authorise and regulate entities in which solicitors could be employees or partners (or equivalent): the SRA, the Council for Licensed Conveyancers (CLC), the Bar Standards Board (BSB), the Institute of Chartered Accountants in England and Wales (ICAEW), and CILEx Regulation.

At present, the CLC (although a licensing authority for the purposes of LSA 2007) regulates only conveyancing, probate and will writing activity. As of April 2017, the BSB was authorised as a licensing authority for all reserved activities; however, its expressed focus is on litigation and advocacy before a court as it considers those matters to be reflective of its areas of expertise. CILEx Regulation's application for approval as a licensing authority was approved by the Legal Services Board (LSB) in July 2018 and a statutory instrument giving effect to that decision came into force on 1 April 2019. Roughly a third of the 22 firms currently authorised by CILEx Regulation have one or more managers who are solicitors.

Following changes to professional indemnity (PI) insurance requirements which made it easier to change regulators, evidence began to emerge of firms electing to move away from regulation by the SRA to other regulators, principally the CLC. On the information currently available, the CLC has been selected as the primary alternative regulator of choice, although this position may have been driven by the comparatively belated approval of the other potential regulators. For the purposes of this edition of *The Solicitor's Handbook*, a brief consideration of the CLC rules is justified; however, this is not intended to be exhaustive.

---

1   Section 52(4) of LSA 2007.

Conduct rules

13.2

The CLC has its own 'Handbook' comprising principles, a Code of Conduct, and a series of supplementary codes dealing with accounts, anti-money laundering (AML) and combating terrorist financing, complaints, conflicts of interest, continuing professional development (CPD), dealing with non-authorised persons, disclosure of profits and advantages, equality, estimates and terms of engagement, management and supervision, notification requirements, PI insurance, transaction files, undertakings, acting as ancillary insurance intermediaries and acting for lenders and prevention and detection of mortgage fraud. There are also codes relating to the governance and operation of recognised bodies and licensed bodies.

The CLC has, like the SRA, embraced outcomes-focused regulation (OFR). It has its own six 'overriding principles' (compared with the SRA's seven (formerly ten)):

'1. Act with independence and integrity;

2. Maintain high standards of work;

3. Act in the best interests of your Clients;

4. Comply with your duty to the court;

5. Deal with regulators and ombudsmen in an open and co-operative way;

6. Promote equality of access and service.'

13.3

The whole of the CLC Code of Conduct is contained within some nine pages at **Appendix 12**.

Whereas the SRA Principles sit alongside the SRA Codes of Conduct, which deal with specific requirements, the CLC Code of Conduct is in six parts, each developing and expanding one of the six overriding principles by stating required outcomes, principles underlying the outcomes and specific requirements associated with the overriding principle. Stylistically, they are readily interpreted as rules, with little that is vague or uncertain.

Conflicts of interest – acting for buyer and seller

13.4

Perhaps the most stark variation between the approach of the CLC and the SRA is in this aspect of the regulation of conveyancing practice. It is notable that the attitude of the CLC to conflicts of interest in conveyancing is in vivid contrast to that of the SRA – in acting for buyer and seller the SRA considers that a conflict of interests is almost inevitable, and that solicitors should not generally act for both parties (although there is no longer any express requirement in the new Codes of Conduct to replicate indicative behaviour 3.3 of the SRA Code of Conduct 2011). The CLC's requirement is: 'Where the entity represents parties with different interests in any transaction each party is at all times represented by different Authorised

Persons conducting themselves in the matter as though they were members of different entities'.[1]

Further guidance is given in the CLC's Conflicts of Interest Code:

'7. Before or when accepting instructions to act for a second Client you inform each Client in writing that the body has been asked to act for another Client in the same matter and you explain the relevant issues and risks to them.

8. You only act for both Clients if each Client has provided informed written consent that you may act for another Client in the matter.

9. You do not act, or do not continue to act, for a Client where your ability to give independent advice is in any way restricted. This may arise if:

(a) you owe separate duties to act in the best interests of two or more clients in relation to the same or related matters, and those duties conflict, or there is a significant risk that those duties may conflict; or

(b) your duty to act in the best interests of any client in relation to a matter conflicts, or there is a significant risk that it may conflict, with your own interests in relation to that or a related matter.

10. If a conflict arises which was or should have been foreseen, you do not charge either Client a fee for the work undertaken (other than for disbursements properly incurred).'[2]

1   CLC Code of Conduct, overriding principle 3 (client's best interests), specific requirement (n).
2   CLC Conflicts of Interest Code, specific requirements 7 to 10.

13.5

The CLC also expressly permits sole practitioners (or businesses where there is only one authorised person) to act for buyer and lender in the same transaction, if the lender is providing mortgages in the normal course of its business activities, without additional obligations.[1]

The guidance to the Conflicts of Interest Code includes references as to the nature and significance of transactions that are not at arm's length, and as to the need for additional caution when the selling client is a developer or builder, or a lessor granting a lease.[2]

1   CLC Conflicts of Interest Code, specific requirement 11.
2   CLC Conflicts of Interest Guidance.

Referrals and commission

13.6

The CLC's regulatory requirements in these areas are succinct and straightforward. Referral arrangements and fees are dealt with primarily within overriding principle 3 (the requirement to act in the client's best interests): that clients have the information they need to make informed decisions; clients are aware of any referral arrangements and that they are consistent with the practitioner's responsibilities both to them and to the CLC; and clients are informed promptly in writing of the existence and amount of any sum payable directly or indirectly as a result of receipt of the client's instructions.[1]

All referral arrangements between the CLC practice and a third party including any fee sharing arrangement must be in writing, and referral arrangements must be periodically reviewed to ensure that they deliver the appropriate outcomes to clients. Practitioners must inform clients in writing of the existence of the arrangement no later than when receiving instructions (or when introducing the client to another person). Clients should be advised that they have a choice of provider, and informed of the nature of the arrangement (including any payment made), with whom it is made, and any impact (including any legal costs they are charged).[2]

The CLC requirement in relation to payments received by the practitioner or business when the client is introduced to another party is found in principle 3 of the Code of Conduct, specific requirement (s): 'You promptly inform the Client in writing of the existence and amount of any sum payable (whether directly or indirectly) as a result of receipt of that Client's instructions.'

It may be noted that the requirement is to inform, not to account. However, as discussed at **4.103**, the obligation to account arises from the fiduciary relationship between the professional person and the client and is a matter of law independent of any professional rule. The CLC Code of Conduct, overriding principle 1: acting with independence and integrity, includes a compulsory outcome that clients receive an honest and lawful service,[3] and compliance with the law would require the client's informed consent if the sum is to be retained. However, it can be said that the CLC regulations follow the law, with no further complications, and the issue could be dealt with by standard terms and conditions of business if there is sufficient clarity.

Moreover, in relation to financial services, the CLC position also follows the law precisely. If commission is earned in relation to services regulated under the Financial Services and Markets Act (FSMA) 2000, there is an obligation to account to the client for any pecuniary award or other advantage received other than from the client.[4] See further at **8.5**.

1   CLC Code of Conduct, overriding principle 3, outcomes 3.3 and 3.4 and specific requirement (s).
2   CLC Disclosure of Profits and Advantages Code, specific requirements 12 to 16.
3   CLC Code of Conduct, overriding principle 1, outcome 1.2.
4   Section 327(3) of FSMA 2000 and specific requirement 43 of the CLC Acting as Ancillary Insurance Intermediaries Code.

Accounts and financial services

13.7

Solicitors familiar (historically) with the Solicitors' Accounts Rules 1998 and the SRA Accounts Rules 2011 will not encounter any difficulties in complying with the CLC's Accounts Code and accompanying Guidance. The latter are a rather less complex set of rules but directed to the same ends.

The Accounts Code is split into parts, comprising basic rules on the definition and treatment of client money, the obligation to maintain proper accounting records, accountant's reports, and third party managed accounts (TPMAs). There is separate guidance on aged balances.

Rule 1 of the CLC Accounts Code contains general provisions as follows:

'1.1 The requirements of the Accounts Code apply to all CLC Lawyers and practices who receive or deal with money belonging to a Client.

1.2 Each Manager of a CLC Practice is jointly and severally responsible with any other Manager of that CLC Practice for compliance with the Accounts Code by the CLC Practice and its employees.

1.3 Managers must maintain proper governance, management and super-vision of the CLC Practice and ensure appropriate systems, procedures, processes and internal controls are in place to comply with the Accounts Code.

1.4 To monitor compliance with the Accounts Code, the CLC may at any time request information which must be delivered at the time and place and in the format requested by the CLC.

1.5 The CLC is entitled to seek verification of information from clients, staff, service providers and banks. If requested, the CLC Practice will provide written permission to facilitate the provision of this information.

1.6 CLC Practices must comply with anti–money laundering and counter-terrorist financing legislation.'

Rules 2 and 3 of the Accounts Code define client account and client money respec-tively. Provisions worthy of particular note include:

- rule 2.2 confirms that client accounts must not be used to offer clients a banking facility;

- rule 2.3 confirms that both office account and client account may be used only in connection with services regulated by the CLC. As regards office account, this is potentially more restrictive than SRA requirements;

- rule 3.3 confirms that client funds must be kept immediately available to be applied in accordance with client instructions;

- rule 3.7 provides that funds must be paid into client account if there is any doubt that funds received are wholly office money;

- rule 3.9 requires notification of discovery of misappropriation to the CLC without delay, and rectification from office account without delay. The prescribed rectification being from office account is again somewhat more restrictive than SRA requirements; and

- rule 3.10 requires that interest earned must be credited to client ledgers unless the written consent of the client is obtained for some other course.

Rule 4 details the circumstances in which funds may be withdrawn from client account and the mechanisms for doing so. Broadly, funds may be withdrawn: where they are required for payments to or on behalf of the client (rule 4.1(a)), to pay fees and disburse-ments (4.1(b) and (c)), where funds were paid in to client account in error (4.1(d)), upon transfer to another client account (4.1(e)) and in circumstances specified under rule 4.4.

Rule 4.4 allows funds to be withdrawn where there has been no movement on the ledger for 12 months and attempts to pay the rightful recipient of the funds have failed. By rule 4.5, such funds to a value of £50 may be paid to a charity, to office account or to the CLC subject to the requirement of reimbursement to the rightful recipient by the firm or the CLC if funds were paid to the CLC.

By rule 4.7, any such balance in excess of £50 must be paid to the CLC which then becomes liable to pay the funds to the rightful recipient upon demand.

Rule 5 contains specific provisions regarding accounting records, including, at rule 5.3 a requirement that accounting records be compiled by a person with appropriate skill and experience. Rules 5.5 and 5.6 require monthly client account reconciliations. Rule 5.8 imposes monitoring obligations where accounting functions are outsourced and rule 5.9 requires that accounts records be kept for six years.

Rule 6 contains detailed provision as to accountant's reports and rule 7 permits the use of TPMAs with CLC permission.

The guidance on aged balances is in two parts: the first part concentrates on mechanisms and systems designed to avoid the problem occurring. The CLC arrangements for withdrawing aged balances are in two bands, sums not exceeding £50 and sums exceeding £50. In the first category the firm may withdraw the funds upon its own certification that the requirements of rule 4.4 of the Accounts Code have been met. The CLC may, upon application, give permission for larger sums to be paid to the CLC's Compensation Fund and the Aged Balances Guidance contains specific details as to what such an application should contain and what steps would be considered reasonable to try and trace a rightful recipient before such application is made.[1]

1   CLC Accounts Guidance, Aged Balances Guidance, paragraphs 13–15.

13.8

The CLC has issued the Acting as Ancillary Insurance Intermediaries Code and accompanying Guidance to regulate the supply of services under Part XX of FSMA 2000 by bodies regulated by the CLC enabling firms to provide specified financial services that are incidental to conveyancing or other services regulated by the CLC.

The obligation to account for commission related to the supply of services regulated under FSMA 2000 has been mentioned above; see **13.6**. The CLC clarified the position with the Financial Services Authority (as it then was) and has offered further guidance, updated to reflect the replacement of the Financial Services Authority by the Financial Conduct Authority (FCA):

'The FCA considers that, in order for a Client to be accounted to for the purposes of s.327(3) FSMA, you must treat any commission or other pecuniary benefit received from third parties and which results from Regulated Activities carried on by the body, as held to the order of the Client. You will not be accounting to the Client simply by telling them that you receive commission. Unless the client agrees to you keeping it, the commission belongs to them and must be paid to them. There is no de minimis below which you may retain the sum. In the FCA's opinion, the condition would be satisfied if you pay over to the Client any third party payment received. Otherwise, it would be satisfied by informing the Client of the payment received and advising the Client that they have the right to require the body to pay them the sum concerned. This could then be used to offset fees due from the Client in respect of Professional Services provided or in recognition of other services provided. However, it does not permit retention of third party payments by seeking the Client's agreement through standard terms and conditions. Similarly, a mere notification to the Client that a particular sum has been received coupled with your request to retain it does not satisfy the condition.'[1]

1   Paragraph 9 of the CLC's Acting as Ancillary Insurance Intermediaries Guidance.

PART 4
The regulatory system in practice

CHAPTER 14

The Legal Ombudsman

Statutory authority

14.1

On 6 October 2010 another major milestone was reached on the road to the transformation of the regulation of legal services brought about by the Legal Services Act (LSA) 2007: the Legal Ombudsman (LeO) opened for business. LeO is the brand adopted by the Office for Legal Complaints, a body corporate established by section 114 of LSA 2007.

Since that date all consumer complaints about the quality of service provided by any regulated legal professional[1] (or 'authorised person' to use the terminology of LSA 2007) have been made to LeO. The previous fragmented system, whereby complaints about barristers went to the Bar Standards Board (BSB), those about solicitors went to the Legal Complaints Service (LCS) of the Law Society, and those about licensed conveyancers went to the Council for Licensed Conveyancers (CLC), has been replaced with a single complaints body. A typical consequence is that a litigation client who knows or believes that something has gone wrong, but does not know whether it is the fault of his solicitor or barrister, does not have to guess to whom he or she should complain, in the expectation of choosing the wrong one first. LeO has the task of establishing whether anything did go wrong and, if so, who should provide redress.

LeO started with a clean slate; it did not take over any complaints which were already in the hands of the former organisations.

1 Between January 2015 and April 2019 LeO also took responsibility for claims management complaints.

The remit and the approach

14.2

LSA 2007 does not contain any words which are the equivalent of 'inadequate professional services' as used in Schedule 1A to the Solicitors Act (SA) 1974.[1] LeO has jurisdiction in relation to complaints made by clients (and limited other categories) about acts or omissions of authorised persons; the only threshold or test to be satisfied for an award or direction to be made is that it is fair and reasonable in all the circumstances of the case.

In practice, similarly to predecessor regimes, LeO has continued to focus on 'poor service', rather than 'misconduct', the latter being within the jurisdiction of the SRA.[2]

LeO concentrates on what the client is actually complaining about, and in particular what would put it right. A LeO guidance note[3] indicates that five questions will be asked:

'1. Has there been poor service?

2. If yes, has the poor service led to any specific loss or disadvantage to the customer?

3. Has the poor service had an emotional impact on the individual?

4. Can we take steps that will put the customer back in the position they would have been in, if the service had been reasonable?

5. What kind of outcome would be appropriate in the circumstances (e.g. an apology, some compensation, the service provider carrying out more work)?'

If LeO determines that poor service has had an impact upon a client, the outcome may be as simple as an acknowledgement that something had gone wrong, and an apology or a modest amount of money awarded to recognise non-economic or non-quantifiable loss for inconvenience, annoyance and distress, but may also be the equivalent of common law damages (in amount) for real financial loss.

The investigative approach is inquisitorial, not adversarial: a fact-gathering exercise. LeO examines what happened, and what if anything went wrong. To establish this, it requests information and documents from the parties, including evidence of how the authorised person addressed the complaint internally. The flow of information follows targeted requests, and the ping-pong of charge and counter-charge is avoided so far as possible. With that in mind there is no automatic exchange of documents containing complaints and explanations. LeO sends a summary of a complaint to the lawyer and will collect evidence *at the same time* from both complainants and lawyers. This is regarded as good investigative practice and meets the statutory test of dealing with matters quickly and with minimum formality. LeO considers carefully whether there is a need to share evidence before everything is gathered in from both parties and if that could adversely affect an investigation.

The existence or otherwise of rule breaches is not a central consideration; after all, a clear, helpful and comprehensive client care letter may be followed by appalling service, and an excellent service might be provided despite muddled initial correspondence. Rule breaches are primarily matters for the regulator, not LeO.

Nor is the degree of fault the measure of compensation – a very bad error could have negligible consequences, and a small mistake could be very costly; redress will relate to the consequence of the failing, and is designed to put the complainant so far as possible in the position he or she should have been in; but it is not a penalty imposed on the professional for a more or less serious mistake.

Sometimes, in what they see as 'nuisance' complaints, solicitors are prepared to offer a small sum on an *ex gratia* and without prejudice basis to the disaffected client in order to retain goodwill and save the time and effort involved in dealing with complaints. We understand that LeO has no objection in principle to such proposals, and that if the offer is rejected, this will not be held against the solicitor who made it, or regarded as an admission. Any subsequent complaint would be dealt with on its merits. If such an offer is accepted, but the client nevertheless makes a complaint to LeO, the acceptance of the offer would be seen as an important factor in LeO's consideration of the case.

1 LSA 2007 repealed the relevant sections of SA 1974, eg Schedule 16, Part 2, paragraph 39 repealed section 37A of SA 1974. However the term is used at clause 6.1.4 of the Participating Insurers Agreement 2020 – see **11.1**.
2 See LeO guidance, 'Our approach to putting things right', 2020.
3 LeO, 'Our approach to putting things right' 2020'.

Duty to co-operate

14.3

SRA-regulated firms and individuals are obligated to co-operate with LeO's investigation.[1]

Bar Standards Board v Smith[2] involved a Bar disciplinary hearing, in which the barrister was acquitted of professional misconduct for failing to co-operate with LeO. The disciplinary tribunal held that although the barrister was in breach of the rules requiring him to co-operate, the breach did not amount to professional misconduct because he 'could be forgiven, if not justified in taking the stance that he did' in declining to co-operate when LeO refused to release material supplied by the complainant on which the LeO investigator intended to rely, until after she had reached her conclusion, albeit that her conclusion would not at that stage be binding. The tribunal added: 'A barrister could not reasonably or necessarily be expected to co-operate with the Ombudsman in that situation'. The consequence of the non-co-operation, however, was that the complaint to LeO by the client was inevitably upheld.

Following *Bar Standards Board v Smith*, LeO reviewed its evidence guidance and changed the reference to sharing evidence to make it clear how evidence would be shared, even if not asked for. The internal guidance for LeO investigators, extracts of which LeO has been kind enough to disclose to us, now states:

> 'We must ensure that any documentary evidence that we have relied upon to form a view or make a recommendation has been seen by both sides, and we should share it at the earliest appropriate opportunity. Ordinarily, this will be at the informal resolution stage as you can refer to the evidence to support the conclusions you have drawn and the recommendation you are making to resolve the complaint.
>
> However, it may be that sharing a piece of evidence early on in the investigation can help to facilitate a timely resolution if, for example, it proves or disproves an issue of complaint.'

1 Paragraph 7.3 of the SRA Code of Conduct for Solicitors, RELs and RFLs 2019 (the 'Code for Individuals') and paragraph 3.2 of the SRA Code of Conduct for Firms 2019 (the 'Code for Firms').
2 PC 2013/0193.

The process in outline

14.4

Upon receipt of a complaint, and prior to accepting jurisdiction (more about this below), LeO will write to the regulated legal professional to inform them of the complaint and let them know the details. LeO's website suggests that this early notice allows the professional, first, to revisit the complaint and consider whether there is anything else they can do to resolve it, and secondly, to inform LeO if the professional considers that the complaint falls outside LeO's jurisdiction.

When LeO is clear that the complaint falls within its jurisdiction, an investigator will discuss the complaint with both parties, to understand their point of view and consider ways in which the complaint may be resolved.

If early resolution is not possible, the investigator will advise which aspects of the complaint will be investigated, and will request that evidence be provided by a certain date. That evidence will include the firm's complaints handling file, as LeO will also decide whether the complaint was reasonably handled.[1]

LeO has wide powers to gather and use evidence, including compelling both the complainant and the legal professional to produce evidence,[2] and to rely on evidence inadmissible in a court.[3] Exceptionally, an investigator may decide to conduct an oral hearing, including by telephone, that is, if it is decided that the complaint cannot be fairly determined without one.[4]

Having investigated, the investigator will share their 'assessment' of the complaint with both parties with a view to reaching an 'agreed outcome'. If an agreed outcome is not reached, the investigator will make a case decision (described in LSA 2007 as an 'assessment'). If both parties accept the case decision, the matter is resolved on that basis; if either party demurs, the matter is referred to an ombudsman for a 'final decision' (described in LSA 2007 as a 'determination').

It is open to the complainant (only) to accept or reject an ombudsman's final decision. If it is accepted by the complainant, it is binding on all parties and final.[5] If it is rejected, the role of LeO is concluded and the complainant is free to pursue other remedies.

There is no appeal from an ombudsman's determination, so that judicial review is the only available mechanism for challenge. However, if it is clear that an obvious mistake has been made, an ombudsman might well be prepared voluntarily to reconsider the matter.

1   Since April 2020 in each published decision LeO has indicated whether the first-tier complaint handling was reasonable.
2   Rules 5.25 and 5.26 of the LeO Scheme Rules.
3   Rule 5.24(d).
4   Rule 5.33.
5   Section 140(4) of LSA 2007.

The overlap with negligence

14.5

The limit of compensation available through LeO is £50,000 (considered in more detail below), plus a reduction in costs in a theoretically unlimited amount, capped only by the amount of the costs that has been charged. This is sufficiently large to attract many cases which might otherwise have been pursued as negligence claims. A complaint to LeO involves no expense and no adverse costs risk for a complainant.

LeO does not reject complaints simply because they could be pursued as negligence claims. However, neither are they considered as if they were negligence claims. As in all matters, the question is whether it is fair and reasonable for redress to be provided in all the circumstances, in consequence of an act or omission by an authorised person. Awards may be made by LeO whether or not the complainant may have a cause of action against the authorised person in negligence.[1]

It must follow that there can be circumstances in which complainants might achieve a higher award of damages by court action than could be directed by LeO, and in accepting an award capped at £50,000, might lose what might have been available in another jurisdiction. If a LeO award is accepted and becomes binding, it is in full satisfaction; no further proceedings may be taken in relation to the subject matter (see **14.17**) and the potential for a higher award of damages will be lost. On the other hand, litigation is risky and expensive. Subject to what is said below, it is essentially a choice for the complainant.

Where a complaint is about professional negligence or judgement, LeO will consider (on a case-by-case basis) whether the issue is one that it can deal with or whether the issue would be better dealt with in court. If it decides that it would be more suitable for the issue to be dealt with by a court or by arbitration, it may dismiss or discontinue all or part of the complaint.[2]

Amounts paid or payable following a determination by LeO are insured under the SRA Minimum Terms and Conditions of Professional Indemnity Insurance[3] (except in respect of orders to refund fees) and thus a notification of a complaint to LeO should be reported by a firm to its insurer.

1 Section 137(5) of LSA 2007.
2 Rule 5.7(g) and note 43 of the LeO Scheme Rules.
3 Clause 1.4, Annex 1 to the SRA Indemnity Insurance Rules 2019 (SIIR 2019).

Fee structure

14.6

No fee is payable by the complainant to LeO. A fee, called a case fee, is payable by the authorised person for every potential chargeable complaint[1] when it is closed, unless two conditions are satisfied: first, that the complaint is either (a) abandoned or withdrawn or (b) settled, resolved or determined in favour of the authorised person; and, second, that LeO is satisfied that the authorised person took all reasonable steps to try to resolve the complaint under his or her own complaints handling system.

In all other cases, the authorised person is liable to pay the case fee, currently £400 for each complaint.[2]

1 Defined at rule 6.1 of the LeO Scheme Rules.
2 Rules 6.1 to 6.3.

Publicity

14.7

LSA 2007 empowers LeO to publish a report of its investigation, consideration and determination if it considers it appropriate to do so in any particular case.[1] In determining what is appropriate, LeO is guided by the regulatory objectives of LSA 2007, in particular, protecting and promoting both the public interest and the interests of the consumer, and encouraging an independent, strong, diverse and effective legal profession. LeO states that it aims to strike a balance between being open and transparent without having a disproportionate impact on the profession.[2]

The extent to which decisions of LeO are published in a manner which will identify the lawyers involved has proved to be a vexed question. LeO conducted two full consultations on the subject. The Legal Services Consumer Panel,[3] and others broadly representing consumer interests, favoured naming and shaming by the publication of awards and directions. Others are more cautious as to whether this is ultimately in the interests of consumers, if it discourages solicitors from taking on work associated with high levels of sometimes ill-informed complaint, or encourages the settlement of undeserving and unmeritorious complaints because of the perceived commercial consequences of publicity. Ultimately LeO is there to provide redress, not to impose penalties on lawyers, and publicity has a direct and effectively penal consequence. If there are 'season ticket holders' in terms of complaint generation, it may be a matter for the regulator, rather than LeO.

Anonymised case studies are published to give assistance in identifying trends and to offer guidance as to how typical cases are resolved. Since the summer of 2011 anonymised summaries of all formal decisions by ombudsmen have been published.

Following the completion of the consultation process and the tracking of data the decision was finally made to publish the names of lawyers in two circumstances.

First, there may be discretionary publication of cases (described as Category 1 cases) where a pattern of complaints raises sufficient concerns that the public interest requires publication as a warning to consumers and potential consumers; this has so far been done in only one case, within LeO's jurisdiction in respect of lawyers,[4] in December 2014 involving a barrister, where 25 complaints had been upheld in a two-year period involving total awards of over £8,000.

Second, in Category 2 cases, on a quarterly basis, all final decisions made by ombudsmen within the previous 12 months are published, even where the decision is favourable to the lawyer and no action by LeO was necessary. Information relating to decisions that were made before the earliest published decision can be requested under the Freedom of Information Act 2000. The first list was published on 17 September 2012.

In Category 2 cases, LeO publishes the name of each service provider, the number of decisions made against that provider in the previous 12 months, the date of the decision, the area of law, the remedy required, the type of complaint, if evidence of poor service was found, and since April 2020, whether the firm's internal (described as 'first-tier') complaints handling was found to be reasonable.

Therefore, save potentially in Category 1 cases, cases which do not progress to a final decision will not be published. If a complainant insists on an ombudsman's decision, as is his or her right, the firm's name will appear on the list even though no fault may be found.

The information publicised has been criticised for lacking context. As LeO does not know how many clients a firm may have it cannot say whether the number of complaints is comparatively large or a tiny percentage of the firm's cases. This is a point LeO makes on its website.[5]

1   Section 150 of LSA 2007, rule 5.55 of the LeO Scheme Rules.
2   LeO, 'Policy statement – publishing our decisions'.
3   An independent arm of the Legal Services Board (LSB), created by LSA 2007.
4   Between January 2015 and 1 April 2019 LeO had, in addition to its jurisdiction in respect of lawyers, power to hear complaints against claims management companies (CMCs), and has published decisions in respect of a CMC. By the Financial Guidance and Claims Act 2018, the regulation of CMCs transferred to the FCA, effective from 1 April 2019.
5   LeO, 'Ombudsman decision data'.

The Scheme Rules in more detail

Who can complain?[1]

14.8

A complainant must be an individual, or any of the following:

- a small business: a micro-enterprise as defined in European Recommendation 2003/361/EC of 6 May 2003 (broadly, an enterprise with fewer than ten staff and a turnover or balance sheet value not exceeding €2 million);

- a charity with an annual net income less than £1 million;

- a self-managed club, association or organisation with an annual net income less than £1 million;

- a trustee of a trust with a net asset value less than £1 million; or

- a personal representative or the beneficiary of an estate where a person with a (potential) complaint died before referring it to the ombudsman scheme.

If a complainant who has referred a complaint to LeO dies or is otherwise unable to act, the complaint may be continued by anyone authorised by law (for example, the executor of a complainant who has died or someone with a lasting power of attorney from a complainant who is incapable or the residuary beneficiaries of the estate of a complainant who has died).

A complainant must not have been, at the time of the act or omission to which the complaint relates, a public body (or acting for a public body) in relation to the services complained about, or an authorised person who procured the services complained about on behalf of someone else. For example, where the complaint is about a barrister who was instructed by a solicitor on behalf of a consumer, the consumer may complain but the solicitor may not.

A complainant may authorise someone else in writing (including an authorised person) to act on behalf of the complainant in pursuing a complaint, but LeO remains free to contact the complainant direct where it considers that to be appropriate.

1   See rules 2.1 to 2.5 of the LeO Scheme Rules.

CHAPTER 14
THE LEGAL OMBUDSMAN

What can be complained about?[1]

14.9

There are no categories of complaint that are excluded. The complaint must relate to an act or omission by someone who was an authorised person at the relevant time. An act or omission by an employee is usually treated as an act or omission by the employer, whether or not the employer knew or approved. An act or omission by a partner is usually treated as an act or omission by the partnership, unless the complainant knew (at the time of the act or omission) that the partner had no authority to act for the partnership.[2]

The act or omission does not have to relate to a reserved legal activity, nor to have occurred after LSA 2007 came into force.[3] The complaint must relate to services which the authorised person provided to the complainant or to another authorised person who procured them on behalf of the complainant, or to – or as – a personal representative or trustee where the complainant is a beneficiary of the estate or trust. However, a complaint may also be made about services which an authorised person offered or refused to provide to the complainant. This jurisdiction is not likely to be employed frequently. It would cover circumstances in which, for example, a lawyer refused to accept instructions for an unlawfully discriminatory reason, and would also be appropriate where a lawyer agrees to look at papers with a view to representing the complainant at a forthcoming court hearing, for example, but later decides not to accept instructions, leaving the complainant unrepresented with no adequate notice.

A complaint is not affected by any change in the composition of a partnership or other unincorporated body. Where a firm or business closes and another business succeeds to the whole of it, or substantially the whole of it, the successor body becomes responsible for the acts and omissions of and complaints against the original firm[4] unless an ombudsman decides that this is not fair and reasonable in all the circumstances.[5]

1   Rules 2.6–2.10 of the LeO Scheme Rules.
2   Section 131 of LSA 2007.
3   Although the Scheme Rules provide that the act or omission, or when the complainant should reasonably have known there was cause for complaint, must have been after 5 October 2010 – see **14.10**.
4   Section 132 of LSA 2007.
5   Rule 2.10 of the LeO Scheme Rules.

Jurisdiction and time limits

14.10

Ordinarily, a complainant cannot complain to LeO unless the complainant has first used the authorised person's complaints procedure.[1] However, this does not apply if the complaint has not been resolved to the complainant's satisfaction within eight weeks of being made to the authorised person, or if an ombudsman considers that there are exceptional reasons to consider the complaint sooner, or without it having been made first to the authorised person, or where in-house resolution is not possible due to irretrievable breakdown in the relationship between the lawyer and the person making the complaint. For example, an ombudsman may decide that the ombudsman service should consider the complaint where the authorised person has refused to consider it, or where delay would harm the complainant.[2]

Ordinarily, a complainant must refer a complaint to LeO within six months of the date of the authorised person's written response (within the firm's complaints handling system), but only if that written response prominently included an explanation that the LeO service was available if the complainant remained dissatisfied and full contact details for LeO were given, together with a warning that the complaint must be referred to LeO within six months.[3]

A complainant must also generally refer a complaint to LeO no later than six years from the act or omission complained of, or three years from the point at which the complainant should reasonably have known that there was cause for complaint.[4] Ordinarily the act or omission, or when the complainant should reasonably have known there was cause for complaint, must also have occurred after 5 October 2010.[5] In the case of a complaint made by a personal representative or beneficiary of the estate of a person who had not complained before he or she died, the period runs from the point at which the deceased should reasonably have known that there was cause for complaint.

If an ombudsman considers that there are exceptional circumstances (for example, a delay caused by illness), he or she may extend any of these time limits to the extent that he or she considers fair.[6] An ombudsman is likely to extend a time limit where the time limit had not expired when the complainant raised the complaint with the authorised person.[7]

1   Section 126 of LSA 2007.
2   Rules 4.1–4.3 and 5.3 of the LeO Scheme Rules.
3   Rule 4.4.
4   Rule 4.5.
5   Rule 4.5.
6   Rules 4.7 and 4.8.
7   Rule 4.8(b).

Preliminary consideration and summary dismissal

14.11

If an ombudsman considers that all or part of the complaint is not within LeO's jurisdiction, or is out of time, or may be one that should be dismissed without considering its merits, the ombudsman will give the complainant an opportunity to make representations before deciding. If an authorised person challenges the complaint on the same grounds, the ombudsman will give all parties an opportunity to make representations. In either case, the ombudsman will then make a decision and give reasons.[1]

An ombudsman may (but does not have to) dismiss all or part of a complaint without considering its merits if, in his or her opinion:

- the complaint does not have any reasonable prospect of success, or is frivolous or vexatious;

- the complainant has not suffered (and is unlikely to suffer) financial loss, distress, inconvenience or other detriment;

- the authorised person has already offered fair and reasonable redress in relation to the circumstances alleged by the complainant and the offer is still open
for acceptance;

- the complainant has previously complained about the same issue to LeO or a
predecessor complaints scheme (unless the ombudsman considers that material new evidence, likely to affect the outcome, only became available to the
complainant afterwards);

- a comparable independent complaints (or costs–assessment) scheme or a court
has already dealt with the same issue;

- a comparable independent complaints (or costs–assessment) scheme or a court
is dealing with the same issue, unless those proceedings are first stayed, by
the agreement of all parties or by a court order, so that LeO can deal with the
issue;

- it would be more suitable for the issue to be dealt with by a court, by arbitration or by another complaints (or costs–assessment) scheme;

- the issue concerns an authorised person's decision when exercising a discretion under a will or trust;

- the issue concerns an authorised person's failure to consult a beneficiary before
exercising a discretion under a will or trust, where there is no legal obligation
to consult;

- the issue involves someone else who has not complained and the ombudsman
considers that it would not be appropriate to deal with the issue without that
person's consent;

- it is not practicable to investigate the issue fairly because of the time which has
elapsed since the act or omission;

- the issue concerns an act or omission outside England and Wales and
the circumstances do not have a sufficient connection with England and
Wales;

- the complaint is about an authorised person's refusal to provide a service and
the complainant has not produced evidence that the refusal was for other than
legitimate or reasonable reasons; or

- there are other compelling reasons why it is inappropriate for the issue to be
dealt with under the ombudsman scheme.[2]

Exceptionally, an ombudsman may refer a discrete legal question to a court if the
resolution of the question is necessary to resolve the matter, but it is not more suitable for the court to deal with the whole dispute. The authorised person may request
that a matter be considered as a test case by a court and an ombudsman may accom-
modate that request by dismissing the complaint to enable proceedings to be taken,
but only on an undertaking that the authorised person will pay the complainant's
costs and on such other terms as the ombudsman considers appropriate.[3]

An ombudsman may also refer the complaint to another complaints scheme in
appropriate circumstances, and if the complainant agrees.[4]

1   Rules 5.4–5.6 of the LeO Scheme Rules.
2   Rule 5.7.
3   Rules 5.8–5.11.
4   Rule 5.12.

Procedure, evidence and hearings

14.12

LeO may request the assistance of others, including approved regulators, in the investigation and consideration of complaints.[1] LeO is not restricted by the terms of the complaint as to who is to be investigated. If appropriate LeO will investigate another authorised person as a joint respondent.[2]

Efforts will be made to resolve all complaints at the earliest possible stage by any appropriate means, including informal resolution.[3] If an investigation is necessary, after both parties have been given an opportunity to make representations, a case-worker will send the parties a preliminary decision (referred to in the Scheme Rules as a case decision) and will set a time limit for response. If no party disagrees within the specified time limit, the complaint may be treated as resolved by the preliminary decision. If any party disagrees, the matter is referred to an ombudsman for final decision.[4]

1   Rule 5.14 of the LeO Scheme Rules.
2   Rules 5.15 and 5.16.
3   Rule 5.17.
4   Rules 5.19 and 5.20.

14.13

An apology will not of itself be treated as an admission of liability.[1] An ombudsman cannot require anyone to produce any information or document which that person could not be compelled to produce in High Court civil proceedings. Subject to this, an ombudsman may:

- give directions as to the issues on which evidence is required and the way in which evidence should be given;

- take into account evidence from approved regulators or the LSB or from other third parties;

- treat any finding of fact in disciplinary proceedings against the authorised person as conclusive;

- include or exclude evidence that would be inadmissible or admissible in court;

- accept information in confidence where he or she considers that this is both necessary and fair;

- make a determination on the basis of what has been supplied;

- draw inferences from any party's failure to provide information requested; and

- dismiss a complaint if the complainant fails to provide information that has been requested.[2]

An ombudsman may require a party to attend to give evidence and produce documents at a specified time and place. An ombudsman may require a party to produce any information or document that the ombudsman considers necessary for the determination of a complaint; may specify the time within which this must be done; may specify the manner or form in which the information is to be provided; and may require the person producing the document to explain it. If the document is not produced, an ombudsman may require the relevant party to say, to the best of his or her knowledge and belief, where the document is.

If an authorised person fails to comply with a requirement to produce information or a document, the ombudsman will tell the relevant approved regulator and may require that approved regulator to tell the ombudsman what action it will take (and may report any failure by the approved regulator to the LSB). If any party fails to comply with a requirement to produce information or a document, the ombudsman may also enforce the requirement through the High Court, and if the failure occurs without reasonable excuse, it may be treated as contempt.[3]

An ombudsman may fix (and may extend) a time limit for any stage of the investigation, consideration and determination of a complaint. If any party fails to comply with such a time limit, the ombudsman may proceed with the investigation, consideration and determination, and draw inferences from the failure. Where the failure is by the complainant, the ombudsman may dismiss the complaint; or where the failure is by the authorised person, the ombudsman may include compensation for any inconvenience caused to the complainant in any award.[4]

1   Although the SRA may do so if also investigating a potential regulatory breach arising from the same matter.
2   Rules 5.21–5.24 of the LeO Scheme Rules.
3   Sections 147 to 149 of LSA 2007; rules 5.25 to 5.30 of the LeO Scheme Rules.
4   Rules 5.31 and 5.32 of the LeO Scheme Rules.

14.14

An ombudsman will only hold an oral hearing where he or she considers that the complaint cannot be fairly determined without one. In deciding whether (and how) to hold a hearing, the ombudsman will take account of Article 6 of the European Convention on Human Rights. A party who wishes to request a hearing must do so in writing setting out the issues he or she wishes to raise and (if appropriate) any reasons why the hearing should be in private. The ombudsman will consider whether the issues are material, whether a hearing should take place and whether any hearing should be in public or private. A hearing may be held by any means the ombudsman considers appropriate in the circumstances, including (for example) by telephone.[1]

1   Rules 5.33–5.35 of the LeO Scheme Rules.

Determinations and awards

14.15

An ombudsman will determine a complaint by reference to what is, in his or her opinion, fair and reasonable in all the circumstances of the case. In determining what is fair and reasonable, the ombudsman will take into account (but is not bound by) what a court might decide, the relevant approved regulator's rules of conduct at the time of the act or omission, and what the ombudsman considers to have been good practice at the time.[1]

A LeO guidance note describes common factors which may influence its decision on what is fair and reasonable, including:

- the characteristics of the customer, for example, their vulnerability and level of experience;

- the expertise of the service provider/firm, for example the standard of service expected of a firm that holds itself out as an expert;

- promises, assurances and service level agreements and how circumstances might mean that a provider needs to go beyond their stated agreements; and

- reliance on the advice of others, and the expectation that service providers will use their own expertise to assess the work of others, for example the duty to consider any advice received from counsel.[2]

Awards and determinations may include any one or more of the following directions to the authorised person in favour of the complainant:

- to apologise;

- to pay compensation of a specified amount for loss suffered;

- to pay interest on that compensation from a specified time;

- to pay compensation of a specified amount for inconvenience or distress caused;

- to ensure (and pay for) putting right any specified error, omission or other deficiency;

- to take (and pay for) any specified action in the interests of the complainant;

- to pay a specified amount for costs incurred by the complainant in pursuing the complaint (however, as the Scheme Rules state, a complainant does not usually need assistance to pursue a complaint with LeO, so awards of costs are likely to be rare);[3] or

- to limit the authorised person's fees to a specified amount.[4]

If the determination contains a direction to limit fees to a specified amount, it may also require the authorised person to ensure that: all or part of any amount paid is refunded; interest is paid on that refund from a specified time; all or part of the fees are remitted; the right to recover the fees is waived, wholly or to a specified extent; or any combination of these.[5]

An ombudsman may set a time limit for the authorised person to comply with a determination, and may set different time limits for different parts of a determination. Any interest payable under the determination will be at the rate specified in the determination or, if not specified, at the rate payable on High Court judgment debts.[6]

1 Section 137 of LSA 2007; rules 5.36 and 5.37 of the LeO Scheme Rules.
2 LeO, 'Our approach to determining complaints', January 2019.
3 Rule 5.39 of the LeO Scheme Rules.
4 Rules 5.38 and 5.39.
5 Rule 5.40.
6 Rules 5.41 and 5.42.

14.16

There is a limit of £50,000 on the total value that can be awarded on the determination of a complaint in respect of the total of: compensation for loss suffered; compensation

CHAPTER 14
THE LEGAL OMBUDSMAN

for inconvenience or distress caused; the reasonable cost of putting right any error, omission or other deficiency; and the reasonable cost of any specified action in the interests of the complainant. If (before or after the determination is issued) it appears that the total value will exceed £50,000, an ombudsman may direct which part or parts of the award are to take preference.[1]

Compensation for non-financial loss (distress and inconvenience) (which is cumulated with other heads of loss as described above, forming part of the £50,000 limit) is in modest amounts: a LeO guidance note indicates three bands, modest awards of between £50 and £250, significant awards of between £250 and £750, and exceptional awards of between £750 and £1,000.[2]

The £50,000 limit does not apply to: an apology; interest on specified compensation for loss suffered; any specified amount for costs the complainant incurred in pursuing the complaint; the financial consequences of limiting fees to a specified amount; or interest on fees to be refunded.[3]

1   Section 138 of LSA 2007; rules 5.43 and 5.44 of the LeO Scheme Rules.
2   LeO, 'Our approach to putting things right', 2020.
3   Rule 5.45 of the LeO Scheme Rules.

14.17

The determination is in writing, signed by the ombudsman. It must give reasons and require the complainant to notify the ombudsman, before a specified time, whether the complainant accepts or rejects the determination. The ombudsman may require any acceptance or rejection to be in writing, but will have regard to any reason why the complainant may be unable to communicate in writing. The ombudsman will send copies of the determination to the parties and the relevant approved regulator. If the complainant tells the ombudsman that he or she accepts the determination it is binding on the parties and final.[1]

Once a determination becomes binding and final, neither party may start or continue legal proceedings in respect of the subject matter of the complaint.[2]

If the complainant does not tell the ombudsman, before the specified time, that he or she accepts the determination, it is treated as rejected. But if the complainant later tells the ombudsman that he or she accepts the determination, and the complainant has not previously told the ombudsman that he or she rejects the determination, and if the ombudsman is satisfied that there are sufficient reasons why the complainant did not respond in time, the determination will be treated as accepted, final and binding. If the complainant does not respond before the specified time, the ombudsman will notify the parties and the relevant approved regulator of the outcome, describing the provisions concerning late acceptance. Whether the complainant accepts or rejects the determination, the ombudsman will notify the parties and the relevant approved regulator of the outcome.[3]

If a determination is rejected (or treated as rejected) by the complainant, it has no effect on the legal rights of any party.[4]

1   Section 140(1)–(4) of LSA 2007; rules 5.46 to 5.49 of the LeO Scheme Rules.
2   Section 140(11) of LSA 2007; rule 5.50 of the LeO Scheme Rules.
3   Rules 5.51–5.53 of the LeO Scheme Rules.
4   Rule 5.54.

Enforcement and misconduct

14.18

A binding and final determination can be enforced through the High Court or a county court by the complainant. LeO may also enforce a determination through the courts if the complainant agrees and LeO considers it appropriate in all the circumstances. In 2016, on the application of LeO, a circuit judge sitting in Cardiff County Court made a suspended committal order against a solicitor who had failed to comply with a court order enforcing a LeO final decision. A court which makes an enforcement order must inform LeO and LeO will then inform the relevant approved regulator, may require the approved regulator to tell LeO what action it will take, and may report any failure by the approved regulator to the LSB.[1]

At any stage after LeO receives a complaint, if LeO considers that the complaint discloses any alleged misconduct about which the relevant approved regulator should consider action against the authorised person, or if LeO considers that an authorised person has failed to co-operate with LeO, LeO will tell the relevant approved regulator, may require the approved regulator to tell LeO what action it will take, and may report any failure by the approved regulator to the LSB. If an approved regulator is informed about a matter involving potential misconduct, LeO will tell the complainant that this has been done.[2] The duty to report potential misconduct is not affected by any withdrawal or abandonment of the complaint.

LeO will disclose to an approved regulator any information that the regulator requests to enable it to investigate alleged misconduct or to fulfil its regulatory functions, if LeO considers that the information is reasonably required, and the approved regulator has regard to any right of privacy of any complainant or third party involved.[3]

1 *Legal Ombudsman v Cory* [2016] EW Misc B36 (CC) (3 November 2016).
2 Sections 141 and 142 of LSA 2007; rules 5.56 to 5.58 of the LeO Scheme Rules.
3 Rule 5.61 of the LeO Scheme Rules.

Judicial review

14.19

As mentioned above, there is no appeal from an ombudsman's determination, so that judicial review is the only available mechanism for challenge.

Although LeO has been threatened with judicial review on a fairly regular basis only five cases have yet reached a hearing. Four have been decided on a fact-sensitive basis (two in favour of LeO[1] and two against[2]). The courts have emphasised that LeO has a wide discretion within a statutory framework which is itself drawn in very broad terms – ie what is fair and reasonable in all the circumstances of the case.[3] Two successful challenges have involved an obvious misinterpretation of the facts,[4] a result influenced by the failure of LeO to file evidence which might have led to a different conclusion,[5] something that is unlikely to be repeated.

In *Stenhouse v Legal Ombudsman*,[6] LeO was sharply criticised for exceeding its jurisdiction and acting in breach of natural justice. LeO had concluded that a barrister was open to criticism for issuing proceedings to recover his fees. Those proceedings were stayed pending LeO's determination and pending the result of the subsequent judicial review. The ombudsman decided that the barrister should pay compensation in the amount of costs incurred by the complainant in defending that claim to date, amounting to more than £2,000. Among the difficulties in this respect were that no complaint had been made as to this; the barrister had not known it was in issue until after the determination had been made; the criticisms of the barrister in relation to his commencement of the proceedings were irrational, and the award, relating to court proceedings, could not have been made by the court itself, as no part of the proceedings had been concluded. Although an award of compensation for distress arising from the aggressive and discourteous behaviour of the barrister was upheld (not without criticism of LeO for 'sloppy' drafting of key documents), that part of the determination relating to the complainant's costs was quashed.

A decision by LeO was most recently, unsuccessfully, challenged by the complainant in an application for permission for judicial review, in the matter of *R (Mottler) v The Legal Ombudsman*.[7] The application serves as a reminder of the difficulty in achieving a successful judicial review of a LeO determination:

> '... the court will be slow to interfere with the Defendant's decision where it is challenged on rationality grounds and ... the threshold is a high one. That is because Parliament has entrusted it to the Defendant, first and foremost, to decide what is fair and reasonable'.[8]

The complainant had also sought an award in respect of 'consequential loss'. The court found that LeO does not have a general power to direct compensation.[9]

However, the courts have more recently been prepared to interfere with decisions of other ombudsmen[10] and such rulings may have an impact upon meritorious future challenges of LeO decisions.

LeO's decisions may be more difficult to challenge as both case and final decisions are narrative in form and seek to avoid the black and white concepts which involve 'upholding' the complaint or the opposite. It may be difficult or inappropriate to say whether a multiple complaint, of which one element was found to justify criticism, was 'upheld'. Rather, the decision recites what the caseworker or ombudsman has considered to have gone wrong and what the redress should be.

1   *Layard Horsfall Ltd v Legal Ombudsman* [2013] EWHC 4137 (QB) and *R (Rosemarine) v Office for Legal Complaints* [2014] EWHC 601 (Admin).
2   *R (Crawford) v Legal Ombudsman* [2014] EWHC 182 (Admin) and *R (Hafiz & Haque Solicitors) v Legal Ombudsman* [2014] EWHC 1539 (Admin).
3   Section 137(1) of LSA 2007.
4   *Crawford* supra.
5   *Hafiz & Haque* supra.
6   [2016] EWHC 612 (Admin).
7   [2021] EWHC 1656 (Admin).
8   At [18].
9   At [20].
10 *Miller v Health Service Commissioner for England* [2018] EWCA Civ 144; *R (TF Global Markets (UK) Limited (trading as Thinkmarkets)) v Financial Ombudsman Service Limited* [2020] EWHC 3178 (Admin).

CHAPTER 15

SRA investigations

Rules and objectives

15.1

The rules which govern SRA investigations are the SRA Regulatory and Disciplinary Procedure Rules 2019 (the 'Disciplinary Rules 2019').[1]

The SRA describes its role as to 'set, promote and secure in the public interest, standards of behaviour and professional performance necessary to ensure clients receive a good standard of service and the rule of law is upheld'.[2]

Investigations are conducted to uphold levels of competence, and compliance with the SRA Standards and Regulations 2019. The SRA has regard to solicitors' respected position in society, their privileged access to confidential information, and the relationship of trust that exists with clients, some of whom may be very vulnerable.[3]

1   Section 31 of the Solicitors Act (SA) 1974 confers authority upon the SRA to make rules, to ascertain whether its rules and guidance have been complied with.
2   SRA, 'Investigation and enforcement', 25 November 2019.
3   SRA guidance, 'Making decisions to investigate concerns', updated 25 November 2019.

The decision to investigate

15.2

The SRA receives information and complaints, more commonly referred to as 'reports', from the firms and individuals it regulates, their clients, other members of the public, courts, the police, MPs and other regulators.

Reports received by the SRA are directed to the SRA's 'Investigations and Supervision' function, 'Supervision' deciding whether to open an investigation.[1]

The SRA is required by its rules to assess all reports received that include 'allegations' that raise a question whether a regulated individual or entity:

- has committed professional misconduct – see commentary at **CHAPTER 19**;

- has committed or been responsible for a serious breach of any regulatory obligation placed on them by the SRA's regulatory arrangements, section 56 of the Legal Aid, Sentencing and Punishment of Offenders Act (LASPO) 2012, or the Money Laundering, Terrorist Financing and Transfer of Funds (Information on the Payer) Regulations 2017[2] (MLR 2017), the Financial Guidance and

Claims Act 2018 or any equivalent legislative requirements that may succeed the same;

- as a manager or an employee of an authorised body, is responsible for a serious breach by the body of any regulatory obligation placed on it by the SRA's regulatory arrangements;

- not being a solicitor, has been convicted of a criminal offence, or been involved in conduct related to the provision of legal services, of a nature that indicates it would be undesirable for them to be involved in legal practice;

- in relation to its activities as a licensed body, has committed or substantially contributed to a serious breach of any regulatory obligation of a nature that indicates it is undesirable for them to carry out activities as a Head of Legal Practice (HOLP), Head of Finance and Administration (HOFA), manager or employee of an authorised body; or

- has otherwise engaged in conduct that indicates they should be made subject to a decision (under rule 3.1 of the Disciplinary Rules 2019), namely to impose a sanction, make an application to the Solicitors Disciplinary Tribunal (the Tribunal or SDT), or otherwise exercise its regulatory powers – see CHAPTER 20.[3]

Whether reports are received in the form of a complaint or not, the SRA's approach is the same, and thus complaints are treated simply as information upon which the SRA determines whether to conduct an investigation in accordance with its rules. The public-facing section of the SRA's website differentiates between 'Complaints' which are made to firms, and to the Legal Ombudsman (LeO), and 'Reports' which are made to the SRA.[4] Therefore, resolving a complaint that has been drawn to the attention of the SRA may not prevent an investigation from proceeding.

The SRA adopts a risk-based approach, focusing on misconduct most likely to harm the public interest while ensuring that any decision to investigate is proportionate, balancing the public interest with the interests of the individual or firm whose conduct or behaviour has been called into question.[5] The SRA acknowledges its statutory obligation to have regard to 'the principles under which regulatory activities should be transparent, accountable, proportionate, consistent and targeted only at cases in which action is needed'.[6]

The SRA applies a three-stage 'Assessment Threshold Test' to the information received to determine whether to open an investigation. The test is:

1. Does the information raise a question that there has been a breach of the SRA Standards and Regulations or that there is a risk to clients, the public or the wider public interest?

2. Is the potential breach or risk sufficiently serious that we would take action?

3. Is the breach or risk capable of being evidenced to the required standard of proof?[7]

A report will only pass the Assessment Threshold Test, and be investigated further, where the SRA believes the answer to all three stages of the test is 'yes'. Sometimes, initial investigation is required in order to have sufficient information to apply the test. The SRA is empowered to exercise any of its investigative powers, as it considers appropriate to identify whether a matter is one that it is obliged to investigate.[8]

SRA guidance[9] indicates that in answering the three questions of the Assessment Threshold Test the SRA will:

- exercise judgement in respect of the information received;

- assess the seriousness of the alleged act or omission in isolation, or alternatively will consider whether it forms part of a persistent failure to comply or a pattern of behaviour, taking into account any aggravating and mitigating features; and

- only consider matters already investigated by the SRA where the earlier investigation was closed without a formal decision on the facts, and the new report raises substantively new information or suggests a pattern of similar concerns.

The SRA Enforcement Strategy (see **15.12**) underpins how the SRA decides what is serious and as such is used to support the Assessment Threshold Test.

Where the concerns appear to relate solely to poor service, complainants are directed to LeO – see **CHAPTER 14**.

Unless there is a good reason not to do so, the source of the report will be advised of the outcome of the test, and if an investigation is not to proceed, why not.

1   SRA, 'Supervision', at www.sra.org.uk/solicitors/supervision.
2   SI 2017/692.
3   Rules 1.1 and 1.2 of the Disciplinary Rules 2019.
4   SRA, 'Problems and complaints', at www.sra.org.uk/consumers/problems.
5   Ibid.
6   Section 28 of the Legal Services Act (LSA) 2007.
7   SRA guidance, 'Making decisions to investigate concerns', issued 8 August 2016, updated 25 November 2019.
8   Rule 2.1 of the Disciplinary Rules 2019.
9   SRA guidance, 'Making decisions to investigate concerns', updated 25 November 2019.

Notification of an investigation

15.3

As soon as reasonably practicable after commencing an investigation the SRA will, unless and to the extent that it considers that it would not be in the public interest to do so, inform the subject of the investigation, and if it is an individual, their employer too, of the decision to investigate.[1] In most cases, the SRA will make this initial contact by telephone or email, explaining the nature of the allegations being investigated and what will happen next.[2] The SRA's current template letter for notifying employers provides that, 'We are concerned that [solicitor] has [eg acted dishonestly]', and as such may cause an employer to believe that a regulatory decision has already been made.

The SRA will also inform the informant, and may inform any other relevant regulator of the decision to investigate, as well as others who may hold relevant evidence.[3]

1   Rule 2.2 of the Disciplinary Rules 2019.
2   SRA guidance, 'If we are investigating you', 25 November 2019.
3   Ibid.

Conduct of an investigation

15.4

Investigations may be desk-based, involve an on-site investigation (known as an 'inspection' or a 'forensic investigation') (see **15.6**), or comprise both.[1]

The investigator will seek to gather evidence to try and establish the facts and form a view on whether the SRA needs to take action. While the SRA may formally request an explanation of documents or conduct, it is prudent to consider whether to volunteer an explanation at an early stage. In any event, individuals and firms being investigated are duty-bound to co-operate with the SRA.[2]

The SRA has recently commenced providing the subject of the investigation with a target date for the provision of an update on the progress of the investigation. A substantive response should not be expected within this timeframe; these deadlines are frequently extended.

1   SRA guidance, 'On-site investigations (inspections)', updated 25 November 2019.
2   Paragraph 7.3 of the SRA Code of Conduct for Solicitors, RELs and RFLs 2019 (the 'Code for Individuals') and paragraph 3.2 of the SRA Code of Conduct for Firms 2019 (the 'Code for Firms').

Investigatory powers

15.5

The SRA has a number of investigatory powers including:

- the right to see information even if it is confidential or subject to a client's legal professional privilege,[1] or subject to a firm's lien;[2]

- to require the production of full and accurate explanations, information and documentation (paper and electronic), by way of what is commonly known as a production notice or order,[3] including, upon application to the High Court, from third parties;[4]

- to make sure that relevant information held by a subject of an investigation, or by a third party carrying out functions on their behalf which are critical to the delivery of their legal services, is available for inspection;[5] and

- the right to conduct interviews.[6]

In *Rocha v Law Society of England and Wales (SRA)*[7] the Chancery Division upheld a Master's order requiring the solicitor to disclose to the SRA documents relating to his dealings with a former client's wife. The solicitor argued that as the documents related to private work not conducted as a solicitor, the court did not have jurisdiction or the production order otherwise breached his rights under Article 8 of the European Convention on Human Rights. The Chancery Division held that the evidence showed a clear link or nexus between the solicitor's practice as a solicitor and the concerns being investigated, that there was no hard and fast distinction between the appellant's role as a solicitor and his private business, and if there was some interference with the appellant's Article 8 rights, it was justified.

It is a criminal offence for anyone:

- who knows, or suspects, that an investigation is happening (or likely to happen) to falsify, conceal, destroy or dispose of a document they know to be or believe to be relevant (or cause such an act). It will be a defence if they can show they had no intention of concealing facts;

- in receipt of an SRA production order[8] to knowingly or recklessly provide false or misleading information.[9]

A failure to provide information in an organised way may be treated as a failure to co-operate, or to comply with a production order.[10]

The SRA may in exceptional circumstances consider paying actual costs incurred in complying with the SRA's requirements to produce documents, or attend an interview, for example, where to do so will cause significant financial hardship.[11]

Time limits imposed by a production order should be strictly observed. If additional time is required for compliance, early contact should be made with the SRA to explain why and seek agreement.

1   *Parry-Jones v Law Society* [1969] 1 Ch 1 and Lord Hoffmann's comments on that decision in *R (Morgan Grenfell & Co Ltd) v Special Commissioners of Income Tax* [2002] UKHL 21 although the recent decision in *Sports Direct International plc v The Financial Reporting Council* [2020] EWCA Civ 177 may create some uncertainty.
2   *Law Society of England & Wales (SRA) v Sophie Khan and Co Ltd* [2021] EWHC 2 (Ch) and section 44B(7) of and paragraph 12 of Schedule 1 to SA 1974.
3   Paragraph 7.4 of the Code for Individuals, paragraph 3.3 of the Code for Firms, sections 44B and 44BA of SA 1974, section 93 of LSA 2007. See also 'limited intervention' at **17.27** and **APPENDIX 18** for the statutory provisions.
4   Section 44BB of SA 1974, article 5 of the Legal Services Act 2007 (Designation as a Licensing Authority) (No 2) Order 2011 (SI 2011/2866).
5   Paragraph 7.4 of the Code for Individuals and paragraph 3.3 of the Code for Firms.
6   Section 44BA of SA 1974, section 93(4) of LSA 2007.
7   [2021] EWHC 1666 (Ch).
8   Issued under sections 44B, 44BA or 44BB of SA 1974.
9   Section 44BC of SA 1974.
10 SRA guidance, 'How we gather evidence in our regulatory and disciplinary investigations', 25 November 2019.
11 Ibid.

The decision whether to conduct an 'on-site' or 'forensic' investigation

15.6

On-site investigations, particularly those involving an in-depth inspection of a firm's activities, are conducted by an SRA Forensic Investigation Officer. Alternatively, on occasion, an SRA Investigation Officer may seek an attendance. An on-site investigation is never random; the investigator(s) will have specific concerns or specific reasons for their visit.

When deciding whether it is necessary to conduct an on-site investigation, the SRA will take into account a range of factors which may include the following:

- the seriousness of its concerns;

- the most efficient way of investigating, having regard to the volume of paper and electronic documentation, to avoid disruption; and/or

- a decision to interview individuals, for example where the issues are sensitive or complex, or where the SRA wishes to test credibility.[1]

1 SRA guidance, 'On-site investigations (inspections)', updated 25 November 2019.

Notice of an on-site or forensic investigation

15.7

While the SRA usually gives written notice of an on-site investigation, it may not do so:

- where the concerns are very serious, for example, where intervention is contemplated (see **Chapter 17**);

- if there is a risk that those under investigation may destroy evidence, seek to influence witnesses, default, or abscond if the SRA sends notice of the inspection;

- if notification would cause the SRA to commit a criminal offence, such as a tipping off offence about possible money laundering; and/or

- if notification would otherwise prejudice or frustrate an investigation or prosecution by another body, or other regulatory action that the SRA may wish to take.

In any of the above examples, an SRA (Forensic) Investigation Officer may arrive at a firm's premises to conduct an inspection without advance notice.

When advance notice of an inspection is provided, typically, the SRA gives a brief statement of the reasons, but it may not. The quantity and quality of the information will depend on the SRA's perception of the risk of providing it. Despite claims to transparency in relation to this process the reasons that are given are frequently opaque, such as 'concerns in respect of business management'. Upon receipt of a notice, it would be prudent for firms to attempt to ascertain the cause of the investigation, and if a problem is discovered, either demonstrably resolve it, or if that is not possible in the timeframe before the on-site visit commences, put in place an action plan to do so.

The notice invariably appends a long list of documents and materials required to be produced at the commencement of the investigation, typically accompanied by a production notice,[1] as well as a questionnaire to be completed, sometimes by all fee earners at the firm. Firms are likely to be requested to provide consents and permissions necessary for investigators to seek verification from clients, staff, banks, building societies or other financial institutions, and to comply with requests for the supply of copies of documents or documents in electronic form.[2]

1 Sometimes referred to as a section 44B notice, with reference to the relevant section of SA 1974.
2 Paragraph 7.4(a) of the Code for Individuals and paragraph 3.3(a) of the Code for Firms.

The conduct of an on-site investigation

15.8

On-site investigations usually take place at the main practice address, with one or more investigators in attendance. During the Covid-19 pandemic, many investigations that would usually have been conducted on site have involved a hybrid procedure, with video conferencing software used for interviews, and either cloud-based software for the uploading of large volumes of documentation, or personal collection arranged. Some on-site investigations or face-to-face interviews in neutral locations have continued. It remains to be seen whether the SRA's experience during the pandemic will influence the future conduct of its investigations.

The SRA does not have a right of entry into a place of business it regulates, but a failure to produce documents or co-operate, as mentioned above, whether deliberate or not, is likely to lead to regulatory action.

Other than in the most extreme case of obvious dishonesty, when an urgent intervention will occur after a very brief inspection, the inspection usually commences with an interview with the compliance officer for legal practice (COLP) or a senior manager to obtain basic details of the firm's practice and partners/managers. If the reason for the inspection has not already been deduced, some of the questions may identify it. The initial interview usually concludes by the investigation officer enquiring whether there is any other information the individual wishes to disclose – this is an opportunity to self-report any other issues the individual or firm is experiencing. A failure to report a known issue may itself amount to a breach of a rule,[1] or otherwise be taken into consideration in the SRA's inspection, for example, when assessing a firm's or an individual's explanation, or in assessing competence or risk management. This final question highlights the importance of conducting a full audit upon receipt of a notice of investigation.

Following the initial interview, typically, the investigation officer will ask to be provided with the documents as required to be produced in the original notice of investigation. Where advance notice of the investigation has been given, the materials should have been collated ready for inspection. Often, the investigation officer will also ask to be provided with a place from which to work and for use of the firm's photocopier.

Typically, the SRA officer will inspect the firm's books of account, office systems and business arrangements (such as agreements with introducers) and relevant client files over a period of time, requests being made for further information and explanation as matters arise.

When on site, the SRA is not restricted to investigating only those issues referred to in the reasons given. Sometimes additional issues are identified during an inspection.

While most on-site investigations involve only one or two days of attendance, in complex cases, investigations can take days, weeks or months, with investigators staying for many days at a time. Typically, at the end of the first day the investigation officer will provide some feedback on the reason for the inspection and what has been found. Copies of documents may be taken away.

Requests for further documents and explanations may be made at any time during an investigation.

**CHAPTER 15
SRA INVESTIGATIONS**

Solicitors are under an obligation to co-operate with the SRA at all times during the inspection.[2] Refusal to co-operate either generally or in relation to specific requests is most unwise, at least in the absence of strong expert advice that the investigators are exceeding their powers or otherwise acting unlawfully. The SRA has the ultimate deterrent: if there is a failure to comply with any rule made by the SRA regulating, for example, professional practice, conduct, and accounts,[3] the powers of intervention will have arisen. Solicitors and firms should also bear in mind that, in the event that SDT proceedings follow, the SRA will almost certainly seek to recover the costs of the investigation, on a 'time spent/hourly rate' basis. These costs can, and often do, run into the tens of thousands of pounds and often exceed any fine ordered by the Tribunal; therefore co-operation, which typically obligates the practitioner to provide information, should be forthcoming, and that information should be coherent and concise.

However, an obligation to provide information promptly is not an obligation to do so instantly, or without proper consideration or advice (if appropriate); nor is it unreasonable in a situation of complexity or apparent seriousness to obtain clarification of requests by seeking them in writing. Investigators are fully aware of this and should not object. In an exceptional case, however, where the facts appear clear and the investigators consider that such requests amount to evasion and prevarication, rather than proper caution, the request may be declined and the investigation concluded without further response from the person investigated.

The investigation concludes with a final interview at which the investigator will summarise all matters identified as causing apparent concern, if any, and on which they require a more formal response.

If there are matters of concern, the interview will have a greater degree of formality and will be recorded. The interview is not conducted under caution; there is no obligation to give a caution, as this is not a criminal investigation. However, it has some of the characteristics of a police interview in that it can be expected to be searching, challenging and potentially hostile in terms of the style of questioning. Admissions that rules have been broken may be expressly invited.

The investigator is unlikely to be drawn on the question that virtually every solicitor will ask: 'What is going to happen?'. They may indicate an intention to submit a report (internally to the SRA) who will decide what happens next.

Following the conclusion of the on-site investigation the investigator may proceed with a desk-based investigation with a view to preparing a report to be submitted internally to Supervision. While Supervision will determine whether to send the report to the subject of the investigation, the decision is in effect determined by the content of the report.

1　Paragraph 7.7 of the Code for Individuals and paragraph 3.9 of the Code for Firms.
2　Paragraph 7.3 of the Code for Individuals and paragraph 3.2 of the Code for Firms.
3　Paragraph 1(1)(c) of Schedule 1 to SA 1974.

The report stage

15.9

At the conclusion of the investigation process, whether desk-based, or on site, the supervisor has several options.

If the SRA does not intend to commence a disciplinary process, the subject of the investigation will be informed that the investigation is not proceeding, or that 'no further action' is to be taken and that the SRA's file is being closed. Recently, the SRA has commenced providing a narrative explanation for its decision. Typically, the closure notice will indicate that if the SRA were to receive new evidence, or similar reports, it may review the position.

Alternatively, the supervisor may decide that although there have been errors or rule breaches, no sanction is required. In this event a 'letter of advice' or 'warning regarding future conduct' will be sent, which identifies the fault found and advises against repetition, but confirms that there is no sanction. Before the SRA issues such a decision, the subject of the investigation must receive written notice of the allegations and evidence in support.[1] Such a result will remain on the 'record' of the individuals affected in case it should ever be relevant in the future. Items on a solicitor's record are never 'spent'; they remain forever, but can of course become irrelevant in practice due to lapse of time.

Where an investigation is closed without further action, or with a letter of advice or warning as to future conduct, unless it is not in the public interest to do so,[2] the SRA must give notice of the decision with reasons to:

- if already on notice of the investigation, the subject of the investigation's employer; and

- where practicable, the complainant.[3]

If the matter is to be considered for sanction, the supervisor will 'give notice' to the subject of the investigation. Typically this will be in the form of a report, additionally setting out the allegations, a brief statement of the SRA's understanding of the facts, a summary of any relevant regulatory history of the subject being investigated, and a recommendation (to the authorised decision-maker) of the appropriate sanction and costs award. Enclosed with the report will be the evidence relied upon by the SRA in support (which, if there has been an on-site investigation, will typically include the (usually lengthy) report of that investigator, described as an SRA Forensic Investigation Report).

The SRA will allow a minimum period of 14 days for a response.[4] It is often a considerable undertaking to respond to such a report and evidence, typically being significant in length, and often not adequately cross-referenced to the supporting evidence, which evidence itself is rarely presented in chronological order.

The SRA may dispense with giving notice to the subject of the investigation if:

- the allegations to be raised are simply further allegations in a matter already subject to an application or ongoing proceedings before the Tribunal;

- it intends to make an application to the Tribunal in a case in which it is exercising its powers of intervention as a matter of urgency; or

- it is otherwise in the public interest to do so.[5]

The solicitor may agree with the recommended sanction in the notice, in which circumstances the SRA will either impose it, or record the agreement in what is known as a regulatory settlement agreement.[6]

If agreement is not reached, and the SRA determines that it is not appropriate to use the fast track procedure and decides not to refer the matter for adjudication (see below and **CHAPTER 20**), it will go on to make a decision applying the civil standard of proof.[7] Supervisors are authorised by the SRA to make disciplinary decisions.

The SRA has the option to refer consideration of the allegation to a single adjudicator or a panel of adjudicators. SRA adjudicators may have a legal or lay background. Their function forms part of the SRA decision-making process, it is not an independent review. The current Chief SRA Adjudicator has said that, generally speaking, the SRA refers decisions to adjudicators in complex cases.

Whether referred for adjudication or not, the supervisor's recommendations are not binding on the decision-maker but give a clear indication to the subject of the investigation, as to what sanction they face so that focused representations can be made on the report.

At any stage after notice is given, the SRA may, even before a final decision is made, impose interim conditions on the practising certificate of a solicitor, the registration of an REL or a registered foreign lawyer (RFL) or the authorisation of a body, where satisfied it is necessary for the protection of the public or in the public interest to do so.[8]

1   Rule 2.4 of the Disciplinary Rules 2019.
2   Rule 2.5(c).
3   Rule 2.6.
4   Rule 2.3.
5   Rule 2.5.
6   Rule 8.2 expressly permits such agreements; for commentary on regulatory settlement agreements see **20.18**.
7   Rule 8.7.
8   Rule 3.2(a).

The decision

15.10

On finding that an allegation is proved, an authorised decision-maker may exercise any of a number of regulatory powers, or make an application to the Tribunal – SRA-imposed sanctions, including adjudication powers and procedures are discussed at **CHAPTER 20**, and the disciplinary powers of the SRA in relation to alternative business structures (ABSs) at **CHAPTER 26**). In summary however, if the decision-maker believes that the appropriate sanction exceeds the SRA's powers, ie save in respect of licensed bodies and their employees (see **CHAPTER 26**), the appropriate sanction is a fine greater than £2,000, or that the solicitor should be suspended or struck off the roll of solicitors, the matter will be referred for SRA prosecution at the Tribunal.

Generally, as soon as reasonably practicable, the SRA must give notice to the relevant person of any decision made, together with reasons, and will inform the person of any right they may have to apply for a review or appeal of the decision (see **20.15**).[1]

However, a supervisor can report direct to the SRA's legal department if it is considered appropriate to refer the matter to the Tribunal without further formality. The formal process of adjudication, involving disclosure of a report with recommendations, can be bypassed, with the result that a decision to refer the solicitor's conduct to the Tribunal can be made after a solicitor's explanation is received, but otherwise without notice and without any right of appeal.[2]

The more serious the allegation of misconduct, and the clearer the evidence, the more likely that this 'fast track' system will be employed. Many cases involve a fine judgement as to whether the matter requires referral to the Tribunal or can proportionately be dealt with by a rebuke and financial penalty.

Solicitors finding themselves in this situation, with a belief that the decision is wrong, should not hesitate to make further representations voluntarily, in the hope that the SRA or any external advocate retained will review the evidence and give appropriate advice if necessary.

1   Rule 3.3 of the Disciplinary Rules 2019.
2   Rules 2.5 and 3.1(g).

Firm or individual?

15.11

The SRA may commence an investigation into the activities of the firm, the individual or both. An understanding of the history of entity-based regulation, alongside the provisions of the SRA's current Enforcement Strategy, will indicate the factors the SRA will take into consideration in determining who to investigate, and the outcomes of such an investigation.

Since 1986, when it became possible to practise through a corporate structure as a recognised body, the SRA (formerly the Law Society) has been able to exercise direct control over a business entity (see **21.9**).

The SRA attempted to shift primary responsibility to the entity in 2009. The opening words of its 2009 guidance were, 'The primary responsibility for ensuring compliance with a firm's regulatory obligations rests with the firm itself'.

This was capable of being misconstrued. The firm's obligations are those of the business to comply with the SRA regulatory requirements. If an employee or a partner fails to act with integrity, it does not mean that the firm as a whole has done so. Entity regulation is not a means of imposing vicarious liability on the firm or the principals for everything that happens in it. Rather it is the responsibility of the firm to manage, in order to avoid regulatory risks as far as possible. The firm can be held to account for deficient management and systems, but there is no vicarious liability in conduct.[1]

In September 2011 the SRA reviewed this guidance. The opening was subtly altered: 'Firms are responsible for delivering outcomes and for all aspects of compliance within the firm. Action may be taken against the firm only, individuals or both'.

In 2019 the SRA introduced separate codes of conduct for firms and for solicitors. Thus the standards required of each are somewhat differentiated. Additionally, the

SRA published a new Enforcement Strategy,[2] a link to which is provided in the introduction to the Disciplinary Rules 2019 which states that:

> 'We would take action against an individual where they were personally responsible … However, we will usually take action against a firm alone, or in addition to taking action against an individual, where there is a breach of the code of conduct for firms or of our other requirements.'

The SRA Enforcement Strategy provides examples of when action will be taken against a firm:

- to mark the firm's responsibility and to hold it to account for the breach, especially where it is not possible or proportionate to establish individual responsibility.

- when the events demonstrate a failure which relates to the culture, systems, supervision arrangements or processes for which the firm, as a whole, should be held accountable.

- to encourage a culture of compliance and management of future risk.

- when firm-specific action is appropriate. This might include a fine to remove the benefit obtained from the wrongdoing, suspension or revocation of the firm's authorisation, or firm-based conditions or compliance plans. Examples of the latter might include: requirements relating to the firm's governance or oversight arrangements, mandatory remedial action such as establishing compliance systems or reporting to us of accounting records, or restrictions to prevent certain work being carried out or funds being held.'

Thus, if a breach of a principle or rule, by an individual or individuals, could or should have been prevented by adequate systems and controls, both the individual and the firm could face regulatory action. Whether regulatory action will be taken will depend on the perceived risk to the public interest.

Entity-based regulation has raised the question of the extent to which a sanction against a firm binds its principals. The SRA Enforcement Strategy states that, 'A finding against a firm is not a finding of personal misconduct against the partners or other managers.' However, the SRA will take action against individuals, 'to ensure that they cannot avoid accountability and/or repeat similar behaviour simply by moving firms.'

The decision whether to sanction the firm or the individual can have significant consequences. Managers, teams and their work can transfer from one firm to another with relative ease. There is a risk that if a public record hangs over the firm as a whole as a result of the enforcement action, the break-up of firms could follow, as partners or practice groups leave to avoid having to declare an entity sanction in their continuing client acquisition (tendering for example), or in relation to PI insurance. On the other hand in this reputation-sensitive era, a publicised minor regulatory sanction of an individual can be disastrous for that individual, for example, in respect of their employment relationship (for example, having regard to risk of reputational damage, disqualification from membership of accredited bodies, or precluding the winning of client work, where there is a requirement to disclose regulatory history in a pass/fail tendering process). Thus, conflict can arise between the entity and the individual when responding to an SRA investigation.

A further issue that may arise is that a financial penalty could fall on a firm and all its partners despite a change in composition and the departure of the person or persons who caused the problem.

In response, the SRA's Enforcement Strategy has developed to provide that, 'firms may cease to exist, deliberately or otherwise, and therefore where an individual is directly culpable, we will generally proceed against them in order to mitigate that risk. This is more likely where the practice is small and may, in effect, have no separation from its principal or partners.'

The SRA will also consider which individuals within a firm are liable – is the case handler to blame or management? The SRA Enforcement Strategy provides that, 'Generally, we will only hold managers to account for the actions of the firm (as opposed to their own conduct or behaviour) where they had a responsibility for – or should have known about and should have intervened into – the relevant events.'

For further commentary see **19.20**.

1   *Akodu v SRA* [2009] EWHC 3588 (Admin).
2   SRA Enforcement Strategy, 7 February 2019, updated 25 November 2019.

When is a matter sufficiently serious for the SRA to take action?

15.12

As described at **15.2**, the SRA applies a 'seriousness' threshold before opening an investigation. The same threshold applies to its decision-making:

> 'we will take action in relation to breaches which are serious, either in isolation or because they demonstrate a persistent failure to comply or a concerning pattern of behaviour.'[1]

The introductions to the 2019 Codes of Conduct make express reference to 'seriousness'. The introduction to the Code for Individuals contains this:

> 'A serious failure to meet our standards or a serious breach of our regulatory requirements may result in our taking regulatory action against you. A failure or breach may be serious either in isolation or because it comprises a persistent or concerning pattern of behaviour.'

While the introduction to the Code for Firms provides that:

> 'A serious failure to meet our standards or a serious breach of our regulatory requirements may lead to our taking regulatory action against the firm itself as an entity, or its managers or compliance officers, who each have responsibilities for ensuring that the standards and requirements are met. We may also take action against employees working within the firm for any breaches for which they are responsible. A failure or breach may be serious either in isolation or because it comprises a persistent or concerning pattern of behaviour.'

The addition of the phrase 'concerning pattern of behaviour', which was not included in the original draft of the proposed new rules, indicates that the SRA will consider a failure or breach to be serious where it is neither an isolated event nor a persistent breach, but nevertheless is concerning.

The SRA Enforcement Strategy suggests that the SRA will subjectively determine seriousness according to a series of stated criteria.[2]

The Enforcement Strategy provides a narrative description of factors the SRA will take into account when assessing seriousness including: past behaviour, future risk, systems in place and environment in which the events took place, the responsibility or control the individual had over the matters in question, the nature of the allegation, intent and motivation, whether an advantage was gained, whether remedial action has been taken, whether there was a deliberate or reckless disregard for obligations, competence, a concerning lack of judgement, harm and impact (including potential harm), vulnerability of the client and the role, experience and seniority of the solicitor.

The factors indicate that more or less any breach might in the given circumstances be considered serious.

Despite the SRA's subjective evaluation of seriousness, the Tribunals and courts have applied an objective test when determining whether an act of misconduct should be sanctioned.

Historically, disciplinary action, particularly an application to the Tribunal, would follow where there was statutory misconduct, eg a breach of SA 1974, or non-statutory 'misconduct', typically described as 'professional misconduct' or 'conduct unbefitting a solicitor'. Misconduct was not defined by SA 1974, so that it was taken to mean that which the Tribunal and judges from time to time considered it to be.

Three cases highlighted the approach. In *Ridehalgh v Horsefield*[3] it was said,

> 'Conduct which would be regarded as improper according to the consensus of professional (including judicial) opinion can be fairly stigmatised as such whether or not it violates the letter of a professional code.'

In *Re A Solicitor*[4] it was said that, 'Negligence may be misconduct if is sufficiently reprehensible or "inexcusable and such as to be regarded as deplorable by his fellows in the profession".' In *Re A Solicitor*[5] it was said that,

> 'What constitutes conduct unbefitting a solicitor is best judged, in my view, by his professional colleagues, applying their undoubted experience of what is to be properly expected of a solicitor in his practice, when they are sitting formally as part of a disciplinary tribunal in judgment of one of them.'

Thus, Tribunals would apply their expertise to determine whether the conduct would be regarded as serious (and reprehensible) by the respondent solicitor's peers (ie competent and responsible solicitors).

The steady change over the years to a principle- and rule-based system initially led to uncertainty regarding whether all rule breaches were matters that should result in disciplinary action. The SDT's view is that they are not.[6] In *SRA v Leigh Day*[7] the Administrative Court took the same view, when commenting as follows:

'156. As we have had cause to ask rhetorically before in this judgment: what was this particular allegation doing before the Tribunal if it was not a matter of professional misconduct? In truth, if such an allegation under Principle 5 is to be pursued before a tribunal then it ordinarily needs to have some inherent seriousness and culpability. It no doubt can be accepted that negligence may be capable of constituting a failure to provide a proper standard of service to clients. But even so, questions of relative culpability and relative seriousness surely still come into the equation under this Principle if the matter is to be the subject of disciplinary proceedings before a tribunal. We do not, we emphasise, say that there is a set standard of seriousness or culpability for the purposes of assessing breaches of the core principles in tribunal proceedings. It is a question of fact and degree in each case. Whether the default in question is sufficiently serious and culpable thus will depend on the particular core principle in issue and on the evaluation of the circumstances of the particular case as applied to that principle. But an evaluation of seriousness remains a concomitant of such an allegation.

157. If authority be needed for such an approach, then it can be found not only in the observations of Jackson LJ (in the specific context of Principle 6) in Wingate and Evans (cited above) but also in the decision of the *Court of Session in Sharp v The Law Society of Scotland* [1984] SC 129. There, by reference to the applicable Scottish legislation and rules, it was among other things held that whether a breach of the rules should be treated as professional misconduct depended on whether it would be regarded as serious and reprehensible by competent and responsible solicitors and on the degree of culpability: see the opinion of the court delivered by the Lord President (Lord Emslie) at page 134.

158. We consider that, though the statutory schemes are by no means the same, the like approach is generally appropriate and required for the English legislative and regulatory regime in the treatment of alleged breaches of the core principles. We appreciate that there may be some breaches of some rules – for instance, accounts rules: see, for example, *Holden v Solicitors Regulation Authority* [2012] EWHC 2067 (Admin) – which can involve strict liability. But that cannot be said generally with regard to all alleged breaches of the core principles coming before the Tribunal; which in our view ordinarily will involve an evaluative judgment and an assessment of seriousness to be made. All that said, in the present case, we repeat that this debate under Principle 5 is particularly sterile, given that the evaluation of the majority was that AC had not even been proved to be personally negligent, let alone that the negligence was such that it constituted professional misconduct (paragraph 145.34).'

Observations by the Divisional Court in *Beckwith v SRA*[8] may be difficult to reconcile with the judgment in *SRA v Leigh Day*[9] – see commentary at **CHAPTER 19** – albeit, the SRA's own rules imply that not all breaches of rules will amount to professional misconduct and will thus be actionable by them.[10]

1   SRA Enforcement Strategy, updated 25 November 2019.
2   SRA Enforcement Strategy, updated 25 November 2019.
3   [1994] Ch 205, [1994] 3 All ER 848.
4   [1972] 2 All ER 811 at 815.
5   [1991] unreported, per Watkins LJ; cited with approval in *Re A Solicitor* (1995), unreported per Taylor J.
6   See eg *Pabla and Pabla*, 10376-2009.
7   [2018] EWHC 2726 (Admin).
8   [2020] EWHC 3231 (Admin).
9   [2018] EWHC 2726 (Admin).
10 Rule 1.2 of the Disciplinary Rules 2019.

Publicity during investigations

15.13

Generally, no publicity is given to investigations and matters remain confidential as between the solicitor and the SRA, but rule 9.1 of the Disciplinary Rules 2019 gives the SRA a discretion to publish information if it considers that it is in the public interest to do so, for example, where there is an investigation giving rise to significant public concern. The SRA may disclose how the investigation is progressing or that it has been concluded without an adverse finding against the solicitor.

Although matters of this nature are treated as confidential as between the SRA and the solicitor, nothing prevents the complainant, if informed, from disclosing the result.[1]

For publication of SRA-imposed fines and rebukes see **CHAPTER 20**.

1   *Napier v Pressdram Ltd* [2009] EWCA Civ 443, [2010] 1 WLR 934.

Length of the investigation

15.14

The SRA aims to complete 93 per cent of its investigations within 12 months.[1] In the latest statistics available at the time of writing, the SRA reported that in 2019/2020, 9,642 reports were received, in 6,021 cases it did not investigate, in 2,279 it completed an investigation, and on average during that period 1,983 remained ongoing.[2] The report indicated a downward trend in the number of reports being received.

The SRA is statutorily obliged to encourage an independent, strong, diverse and effective legal profession[3] and, arguably, to carry out its activities in a way that supports those it regulates to comply and grow.[4] In partial recognition of that obligation, the SRA has committed itself to carefully balancing the public interest with the interests of individual solicitors (see **15.2**). Despite those obligations, investigations are often tortuously slow.

Regulated individuals and firms may face a number of adverse consequences of a lengthy investigation including:

- increased PI insurance premiums, or refusal, on renewal;

- reputational damage upon publication;

- loss of tender work, eg where it is a requirement not to be subject of a regulatory investigation;

- ill health – the SRA acknowledges that the regulatory process can be stressful and may trigger health issues. The SRA accepts responsibility in such situations, as 'a responsible regulator' of the 'need to balance carefully the public interest against the interests of the individual'.[5]

- loss of management and fee earning time;

- cost of representation; and

- inability to merge, acquire or dispose of the firm, or for individuals to obtain employment elsewhere.

In *Aaron v The Law Society*, Auld J said,

> 'those responsible administratively and judicially for regulation of the solicitors' profession should now have the reasonable time requirement of Article 6 in the forefront of their minds in any disciplinary process for which they are responsible … Disciplinary proceedings before the Solicitors' Disciplinary Tribunal are analogous to criminal proceedings. The uncertainty that springs from and festers with unnecessary and unreasonable delay can, in itself, cause great injustice to practising solicitors, whose livelihood and professional reputations are at stake. Nor does such delay serve the solicitors' profession as a whole. It is in their interest and that of the members of public whom they serve that their regulatory body and the Tribunal should be prompt, as well as otherwise effective, in the enforcement of the high standards of their profession.'[6]

1 SRA guidance, 'If we are investigating you', 25 November 2019.
2 SRA, 'Upholding professional standards 2019/2020', 22 July 2021.
3 Sections 28 and 1(1)(f) of LSA 2007.
4 Better Regulation Delivery Office of the Department for Business, Innovation & Skills, 'Regulators' code', April 2014.
5 SRA guidance, 'SRA investigations: health issues and medical evidence', August 2020.
6 [2003] EWHC 2271 (Admin) at [84].

Other regulatory powers

15.15

The SRA may also in effect require solicitors and law firms to investigate themselves. By virtue of paragraphs 7.10 and 7.11 of the Code for Individuals and paragraphs 3.4 and 3.5 of the Code for Firms, if the SRA gives notice requiring such action to be taken in relation to a matter specified in the notice, you must:

- investigate whether anyone may have a claim against you;

- provide the SRA with a report on the outcome of your investigation;

- notify relevant persons that they may have such a claim; and

- act promptly to take any remedial action requested by the SRA.

This provision was designed, during the course of the Legal Services Bill through Parliament, to give the SRA additional powers to deal with firms caught up in the miners' compensation scheme in a manner thought to justify criticism. It enables the SRA to direct firms to act in a way which may result in an identified class of client being compensated *en masse*, although it would not be the SRA which imposes the obligation to provide the compensation. The SRA can only compel the firm to treat that class of client as if they had made a complaint. It cannot compel, even indirectly, the payment of compensation or redress, because of an express statutory provision.

Section 157 of LSA 2007 provides that 'The regulatory arrangements of an approved regulator must not include any provision relating to redress' – the clear legislative intent being that this is now exclusively a matter for LeO.

Representation during investigations

15.16

There is no doubt that regulatory investigations can be exceptionally demanding and stressful, and may well interfere materially with an individual's or a firm's ability to carry on with their practice. Specialist advice and representation can assist, both in ensuring that efforts are appropriately targeted, and in ensuring balance and objectivity.

CHAPTER 16

Practising certificate controls and removal of a solicitor's name from the roll

Requirement to hold a practising certificate

16.1

Every solicitor must at all times hold a valid practising certificate in order to practise as such.[1] Accordingly, the power to impose conditions on a solicitor's practising certificate represents a very powerful regulatory control in the hands of the Solicitors Regulation Authority (SRA).

The obligation to hold a valid practising certificate extends to a person on the roll of solicitors, but not working as such, where still employed in connection with the provision of any legal services:

(a)   by any person who is qualified to act as a solicitor;

(b)   by any partnership at least one member of which is so qualified;

(c)   by a body recognised under section 9 of the Administration of Justice Act (AJA) 1985 (incorporated practices);

(d)   by any other person who, for the purposes of the Legal Services Act (LSA) 2007, is an authorised person in relation to an activity which is a reserved legal activity (within the meaning of that Act).[2]

Therefore, for example, a person employed by a firm as a paralegal,[3] whose name is on the roll of solicitors, will require a practising certificate.

1   Section 1 of the Solicitors Act (SA) 1974.
2   Section 1A of SA 1974.
3   Not uncommon in times when there is a shortage of available positions.

Applicable rules

16.2

The applicable rules are those contained in the SRA Authorisation of Individuals Regulations 2019.[1]

The SRA's powers to refuse to issue, or impose conditions on, practising certificates, derive from statutory powers arising under Part 1 of SA 1974. Until 2009, the circumstances in which the powers could be exercised were prescribed by section 12 of SA 1974. The whole regulatory system in relation to practising certificates changed on 1 July 2009, when section 12 of SA 1974 and associated provisions were repealed and replaced by provisions that the powers could be exercised in circumstances prescribed by the SRA. In consequence, the control of practising certificates is now a rule-based system (subject to the overriding 'umbrella' of Part 1 of SA 1974).

Although the circumstances in which the powers can be exercised are now prescribed by SRA regulations, rather than the old section 12, there have been no material changes in the processes of investigation and adjudication, or in the principles applied. Past decisions by the Master of the Rolls on practising certificate appeals under the former statutory regime have been accepted by the SRA to be relevant and binding.[1]

1 See also rules 1.1, 1.2(f) and 3.1(e) of the SRA Regulatory and Disciplinary Procedure Rules 2019 (the 'Disciplinary Rules 2019'); disciplinary procedures are addressed at **CHAPTERS 15** and **20**.

Eligibility for practising certificates

16.3

An individual can apply for a practising certificate if the individual's name is on the roll and the individual has sufficient knowledge of written and spoken English or Welsh and has not been suspended from practice as a solicitor.[1]

1 Regulation 6.2 of the SRA Authorisation of Individuals Regulations 2019.

Refusal of practising certificates

16.4

On an initial application for a practising certificate, or on an application for its renewal, the SRA must refuse the application if it considers it to be in the public interest to do so.[1]

1 Regulation 7.1(a) of the SRA Authorisation of Individuals Regulations 2019. See also section 10(3) of SA 1974.

The practising certificate year

16.5

Practising certificates may be issued at any time during a year, but, if not renewed, will, unless the deadline is extended by the SRA,[1] expire on 31 October.[2] The renewal deadline should be strictly observed.

Individuals may 'opt in' to their firm's bulk renewal application, but responsibility rests with the individual to check. Individual solicitors can opt in or out using their 'mySRA' account, and therefore firms should be careful to check that all solicitors working under their authorisation are either included in the bulk renewal process, or otherwise have made a timely renewal application.

Practising without a certificate may amount to a criminal offence[3] as well as attracting regulatory sanctions. Firms that fail to spot a solicitor working under their authorisation without a practising certificate, including those not employed as a solicitor (see **16.1**), may also face regulatory sanction.

The fee payable upon an application for a practising certificate depends on the date of application, reducing quarterly through the year.

If a solicitor does not wish to renew their practising certificate but wishes to remain on the roll of solicitors, they should complete a notification of non-renewal (NNR) form.

1   The SRA extended the renewal deadline for 2021 to 20 November 2021 caused by IT issues.
2   Regulation 8.2 of the SRA Authorisation of Individuals Regulations 2019.
3   Section 20 of SA 1974.

Imposition of conditions

16.6

The provisions governing the power to impose conditions, and the nature of the conditions, are contained in regulations 7.1 to 7.3 of the SRA Authorisation of Individuals Regulations 2019, and those are set out below.

7.1   If the *SRA* considers it to be in the public interest to do so, it must:

   (a)   refuse your application for a practising certificate, or your application for registration or renewal of registration, in the *register of European lawyers* or the *register of foreign lawyers*; or

   (b)   at any time, whether on grant of such an application or at the end of a period of suspension of a practising certificate or registration, or otherwise, impose such conditions on your certificate or registration as it thinks fit in accordance with regulations 7.2 and 7.3.

7.2   The *SRA* may impose conditions under regulation 7.1(b) if it is satisfied that you:

   (a)   are unsuitable to undertake certain activities or engage in certain business or practising arrangements;

   (b)   are putting, or are likely to put, at risk the interests of *clients*, third parties or the public;

   (c)   will not comply with the *SRA's regulatory arrangements* or require monitoring of compliance with the *SRA's regulatory arrangements*; or

   (d)   should take specified steps conducive to the *regulatory objectives*.

7.3   The conditions imposed by the *SRA* under regulation 7.1(b) may:

   (a)   specify certain requirements that must be met or steps that must be taken;

   (b)   restrict the carrying on of particular activities or holding of particular roles; or

   (c)   prohibit the taking of specified steps without its approval.

16.7

The purposes for which the SRA may impose conditions, either on renewal or on a current certificate, are spelled out in regulation 7.2, but it remains, as affirmed by the Administrative Court (see **16.14**) primarily a question as to what is necessarily and proportionately required for the protection of the public.

16.8

The SRA may also vary or revoke any conditions on a practising certificate.[1] The SRA Authorisation of Individuals Regulations 2019 do not specify that the power to vary is only exercisable if one or more of the circumstances set out in regulation 7.2 applies. Section 13A of SA 1974 (as amended by LSA 2007) provides that conditions may be imposed on a current practising certificate if it appears to the SRA that the case is of a 'prescribed description' and 'prescribed' means prescribed by the relevant regulations.[2] It is likely that the SRA Authorisation of Individuals Regulations 2019 are intended to be read so as to mean that the prescribed circumstances for the imposition of new varied conditions are those set out in regulation 7.2.

1   Regulation 7.4 of the SRA Authorisation of Individuals Regulations 2019.
2   Sections 13A and 28 of SA 1974.

16.9

If a condition is to be imposed or varied, the SRA must give 28 days' notice of its intention to do so, inviting representations regarding the issues giving rise to the proposed conditions. The SRA may shorten or dispense with the 28-day period where conditions are imposed on grant of a practising certificate, or otherwise if it is satisfied that it is in the public interest to do so.[1]

1   Regulations 7.5 and 7.6 of the SRA Authorisation of Individuals Regulations 2019.

Revocation of practising certificates

16.10

By regulation 8.4, the SRA may revoke a practising certificate at any time, if it is satisfied that it was granted or renewed as a result of error, misleading or inaccurate information or fraud; if the replacement or renewal date has passed and the SRA has not received an application for renewal of the certificate; or if a solicitor has failed to pay the prescribed fee.[1]

The SRA must revoke a practising certificate on the application of the person concerned unless the solicitor is subject to any proceedings, investigation or consideration of their conduct by the SRA or the Solicitors Disciplinary Tribunal (the Tribunal or SDT).[2] In those circumstances the SRA may refuse the application.[3]

If the SRA decides to revoke a practising certificate, it must give the person concerned 28 days' notice of its intention to do so, inviting representations regarding the issues giving rise to the proposed revocation.[4]

1   Regulation 8.4(a)–(c) of the SRA Authorisation of Individuals Regulations 2019. SA 1974 does not confer an express power on the SRA to revoke practising certificates on its own motion, and it is unclear whether the SRA has statutory jurisdiction to do so. For the statutory power to suspend a practising certificate under section 13B of SA 1974, see **16.11**.

2   Regulation 8.6 of the SRA Authorisation of Individuals Regulations 2019.
3   For rules on removal from the roll during pending proceedings before the Tribunal see **16.23** and **16.24**.
4   Regulation 8.5 of the SRA Authorisation of Individuals Regulations 2019.

Suspension of practising certificate

16.11

Under SA 1974, a practising certificate may be suspended with immediate effect in the following circumstances:

- where the solicitor has been convicted of an offence involving dishonesty or deception, or an indictable offence, *and* the SRA has made an application to the Tribunal with respect to him. The SRA may suspend his practising certificate for up to six months, and may renew that suspension once for a maximum of a further six months;[1]

- where an order has been made for the suspension of a solicitor from practice by a court or the Tribunal, or the court has made a bankruptcy order against a solicitor. These operate as an automatic suspension of the practising certificate[2] – from any date specified by the court or Tribunal in the case of a suspension from practice, and immediately on an adjudication of bankruptcy;

- where there is an intervention on the grounds of suspected dishonesty, or breaches of the SRA Accounts Rules, or breaches of any rules made under section 31 of SA 1974 (which include the SRA Codes of Conduct), or because the solicitor has been committed to prison in criminal or civil proceedings. This also automatically suspends the solicitor's practising certificate, unless the adjudicator or adjudication panel which resolves to intervene directs otherwise.[3] The additional provision relating to rules made under section 31 (the successive Practice Rules and Codes of Conduct, in addition to the Accounts Rules, made under section 32), which was effected by amendment of SA 1974 by LSA 2007, means that in practical terms the practising certificate can be expected to be suspended on every intervention unless the decision-maker directs otherwise.

1   Section 13B of SA 1974.
2   Section 15(1).
3   Section 15(1A) and (1B).

16.12

When a practising certificate is suspended on intervention or by reason of bankruptcy the solicitor may apply to the SRA to terminate the suspension.[1]

It is a common and erroneous belief that bankruptcy is the equivalent of being struck off. It is not; indeed, when a solicitor knows that he or she will be made bankrupt, or is very likely to be, it used to be possible to apply to the SRA in advance of the date on which the adjudication is expected for the inevitable and automatic suspension to be terminated either conditionally or unconditionally. At present, the SRA declines to do this and will not begin to process the application until a bankruptcy order is produced. The same principles as to necessity and proportionality apply as they do to any decision to impose conditions (see **16.14**).

For the situation that arises following interventions, see **17.11**.

1   Section 16(3) and (4) of SA 1974.

16.13

If a practising certificate is suspended, it expires on its replacement date, or if the replacement date has passed, 14 days after the suspension took effect.[1]

1   Regulation 8.7(e) of the SRA Authorisation of Individuals Regulations 2019; see also section 16(1) of SA 1974.

The test to be applied by the SRA when imposing conditions

16.14

Practising certificate conditions are imposed primarily to manage risk to the public.[1]

The events listed in regulation 7.2 of the SRA Authorisation of Individuals Regulations 2019 are situations in which a solicitor may be regarded as representing an increased risk.

In *Moosavi v SRA*[2] Mrs Justice Whipple reiterated the longstanding reasons for imposing conditions, and the test to be applied:

> 'The test to be applied by the SRA is set out in *Odunlami v Law Society* [2008] EWCA Civ 1598 at [21]:
>
> "… regulatory conditions are imposed where they are necessary in the interests of the public and the reputation of the profession. They must not only be necessary but also reasonable and proportionate".'

Conditions imposed by the SRA must be targeted at a specific, identified, risk.[3]

In *Razeen (No 15 of 2008)*[4] the Master of the Rolls stated:

> 'Reference to reputation of the profession is really an incident of the protection of the public interest'.

While in *Bryant v SRA*[5] Mr Justice Eady stated:

> '… it is hardly surprising that the SRA should wish to impose conditions at least partly with a view to assisting rehabilitation (obviously assuming that employment opportunities are available). As I have already noted, there are other important considerations. These are the closely related needs to protect the public and to maintain or restore confidence in the profession.'

Thus, while conditions are imposed primarily to protect the public, the SRA will also take into account other closely related factors such as the reputation of the profession, and the rehabilitation of the solicitor. Often, it is by the solicitor demonstrating rehabilitation that the SRA is satisfied that there is no further need for the conditions.

The correct approach to the imposition of conditions is therefore:

(1)   to identify the risk;[6]

(2)   to identify a mechanism to manage and control the risk to minimise its consequences; and

(3)   to determine whether the proposed mechanism is necessary, reasonable and proportionate to the risk.[7]

The conditions need not completely eliminate the risk to the public; additional SRA or peer oversight may be deemed sufficient to meet the necessary, reasonable and proportionate test.

In *Re a Solicitor, No 6 of 1993*[8] the Master of the Rolls stated:

'The purpose of a condition on a practising certificate … is intended to ensure that a solicitor who has run into trouble in a professional capacity is subject to a degree of oversight in the conduct of his professional life at least until he has demonstrated over a period that he is not in need of any such supervision to protect the public'.

In *Akodu v SRA*[9] Moses LJ stated:

'There are strong arguments for thinking that, having regard to the whole history of this matter, the public interest does require that Mr Akodu be supervised, in the sense of having to work either in employment or in another partnership so as to avoid similar defects in the way he conducts his practice occurring in the future.'

1   'Our primary concern is to protect the interests of the public.' SRA, 'Conditions on practising certificates and registration', updated 25 November 2019.
2   [2016] EWHC 1821 (Admin) at [29].
3   *Moosavi v SRA* [2016] EWHC 1821 (Admin) at [30] citing *Razeen* [2008] EWCA Civ 1220.
4   [2008] EWCA Civ 1220.
5   [2012] EWHC 1475 (Admin).
6   *Razeen* supra.
7   *Moosavi v SRA* [2016] EWHC 1821 (Admin). See also *Brandon* [2008] EWCA Civ 967 at [32] and *Odunlami* [2008] EWCA Civ 1598 at [21].
8   23 July 1993, CA
9   [2009] EWHC 3654 (Admin) at [13].

Common conditions on practising certificates

16.15

In cases where firms have not kept accurate books of accounts such that there have been breaches of the Accounts Rules, the SRA has typically imposed a condition requiring the delivery of additional (usually half-yearly) accountants' reports. The condition does not eliminate the risk, but allows the SRA greater oversight.

Where serious errors of judgement have occurred, and there is a risk of repetition, or where there have been serious administrative failings, a condition requiring a solicitor to practise only in an approved partnership or, in extreme cases, approved employment, could be appropriate. In this way the SRA can be assured that the

CHAPTER 16
PRACTISING CERTIFICATE
CONTROLS

solicitor is working under the supervision of a solicitor, on notice of the previous issues encountered.

The precise content of conditions will depend upon the regulatory concerns of the SRA, and as to how the public can best be protected. For instance, the solicitor may be excluded from carrying out specified work of a particular kind, such as probate, or may be required to attend a particular type of training course on solicitors' accounting procedures or practice management. The SRA may take into account, when imposing conditions, that an application has been made against the solicitor to the Tribunal if the allegations are sufficiently serious, even though those allegations have not yet been adjudicated upon.[1]

The decision to impose conditions is regulatory[2] and not punitive[3] but this may be the effect. For example, a condition requiring a firm to produce half-yearly accountants reports will be expensive, and a condition permitting the solicitor to practise only in approved employment will force a sole practitioner to close or dispose of the practice, and seek employment, which may not be available, particularly having disclosed the conditions imposed.

1   *Burdett (No 8 of 2002)* [2002] EWCA Civ 1194; *Awan v Law Society* [2003] EWCA Civ 1969; *Walker (No 13 of 2001)* [2001] EWCA Civ 1596.
2   *Lebow (No 13 of 2007)* [2008] EWCA Civ 411 at [23].
3   *Re A Solicitor (No 6 of 1993)*; see also *Brandon* [2008] EWCA Civ 967 at [31].

Duration of conditions

16.16

A condition is generally imposed for the duration of the practising certificate and therefore, unless varied or revoked, will have force until 31 October following imposition. However, upon each renewal application, the SRA will review the position to decide whether to 'relax, lift or leave in place any conditions'.[1]

As the SRA indicates in its website advice, it is not uncommon for conditions to be reimposed for two or three years, possibly longer.[2] The more serious the risk which gave rise to the condition, the longer the solicitor can expect conditions to be imposed for, although the precise conditions may vary from year to year. For example, if conditions are imposed following misconduct which resulted in a Tribunal fine, or upon expiry of a period of suspension imposed by the Tribunal, conditions are likely to be imposed for at least three or four years. There is, however, no hard and fast rule to this effect and it may well be possible for the solicitor to secure an unconditional certificate if it can clearly be demonstrated that the problem period is over, and there is no continuing cause for concern or the need for any additional safeguard.

If the condition was imposed by reason of a set of circumstances which by their nature continue (for example, the existence of judgment debts), the solicitor can expect the condition to continue until the underlying cause is removed (for example, by the discharge of those debts).[3]

The SRA's decision whether to vary the conditions or grant a practising certificate free of conditions will depend upon whether the SRA considers that conditions remain necessary in the public interest.[4]

1   SRA, 'Conditions on practising certificates and registration', updated 25 November 2019.
2   Ibid.
3   Comments by Lord Donaldson MR in *No 6 of 1990* (unreported).
4   SRA, 'Conditions on practising certificates and registration', updated 25 November 2019.

Procedure

16.17

Generally, the procedure followed is the same as that used for making a 'decision' on matters of conduct[1] (see **CHAPTERS 15** and **20**), by the production of a report by the relevant SRA officer which contains recommendations on which the solicitor has the opportunity to comment, usually within 14 days. If the solicitor does not oppose the recommended course or does not respond, the provisional decision becomes final (subject to appeal).

If the proposed course is not accepted and representations are made, the matter is adjudicated upon, but the level and seniority of the decision-maker can vary.[2]

Similar procedures are followed where, for example, there is an existing practising certificate condition requiring approval of any proposed partnership or employment, and application is made for approval.

The decision will take effect on the earliest of 28 days after the decision is made, the determination or discontinuation of a review (see **16.18**), or following a decision that the conditions should have immediate effect in the public interest.[3]

1   Rules 1.1, 1.2(f) and 3.1(e) of the Disciplinary Rules 2019.
2   The full list of those to whom authority to make decisions is delegated in set out at www.sra.org.uk/sra/decision-making/schedule-delegation.
3   Rules 6.1 and 6.2 of the SRA Application, Notice, Review and Appeal Rules 2019.

Internal reviews

16.18

A solicitor has a right to an internal review of a decision to refuse an application for a practising certificate, impose conditions on or revoke the practising certificate.[1] The application for review must be made within 28 days of notice being given of the decision (or reasons for the decision if later) and must explain the grounds of review and provide reasons and any evidence in support. The review will likely be considered by an adjudicator or an adjudication panel[2] and on the papers alone.[3]

If an application is made for a review before expiry of the 28-day time period, the decision takes effect on determination or discontinuation of the review, unless the SRA directs, in the public interest, that the decision is to take effect immediately.[4]

1   Rule 3.2 of and Annex 1 to the SRA Application, Notice, Review and Appeal Rules 2019.
2   Rule 3.5 of the SRA Application, Notice, Review and Appeal Rules 2019.
3   Rule 4.1.
4   Rules 6.1 and 6.2.

Appeals to the High Court

16.19

All the decisions of the SRA set out above can be contested by way of appeal to the High Court (rather than to the Master of the Rolls as was the case prior to LSA 2007).[1] Previous decisions of successive Masters of the Rolls have continued to be binding on the SRA, and cited in the High Court since – see **16.14**.

Initially, following transfer of jurisdiction, the High Court acknowledged its inexperience in such matters, for example, in *Akodu v SRA*,[2] Moses LJ remitted the issue of practising certificate conditions back to an SRA adjudicator, stating:[3]

> 'I would, for my part, underline that which Mr Barton [for the SRA] urged, namely, that in the normal case, this court should deal with these questions rather than remitting them. No doubt, as the body of experience expands, confined as it will be to a number of nominated judges as we were told, it will not be necessary to adopt the course I have reluctantly decided should be adopted.'

However, it did not take long for the High Court to consider itself competent to determine such appeals.[4]

Although the High Court has an unfettered discretion in hearing such appeals, it must give weight to the decision of the primary decision-maker.[5] First instance decisions may now be taken by investigation staff.[6]

The SRA encourages solicitors to utilise its internal review procedure (see **16.18**) before exercising their statutory rights of appeal (historically the Master of the Rolls took the same view). Reviews are likely to be considered by an SRA Adjudicator.[7] Although SRA Adjudicators form part of the SRA decision-making process, they stand independent from Supervision and Investigation Officers.

The High Court has power to make such order as it thinks fit. On costs, the High Court applies traditional costs principles to practising certificate appeals, so that costs will ordinarily follow the event.

The Master of the Rolls emphasised the importance of appeals being held in public save in exceptional circumstances.[8] Appeals to the High Court are heard in public in the usual way.

If and when the SRA makes rules to this effect, appeals may lie to the Tribunal rather than the High Court.[9] There is no sign that the SRA has any current intention of making such rules.

1   Sections 13, 13A(6), 13B(7) and 16(5) of SA 1974.
2   [2009] EWHC 3588 (Admin).
3   At [14].
4   See *Bryant v SRA* [2012] EWHC 1475 (Admin) and *Moosavi v SRA* [2016] EWHC 1821 (Admin) also discussed at **16.14**.
5   *Moosavi v SRA* [2016] EWHC 1821 (Admin) at [31] citing *Lebow (No 13 of 2007)* [2008] EWCA Civ 411 at [23] and *Bryant v SRA* [2012] EWHC 1475 (Admin) at [15].
6   See www.sra.org.uk/sra/decision-making/schedule-delegation.
7   See www.sra.org.uk/sra/decision-making/schedule-delegation.

8   *L v Law Society (No 13 of 2008)* [2008] EWCA Civ 811. This appeal concerned the revocation of a student's membership on the grounds of fitness for admission to the roll, but considered the principles of public and private hearings generally.
9   Section 49A of SA 1974.

SDT restriction orders

16.20

While the Tribunal has no specific power itself to impose conditions on a practising certificate, it can make recommendations to the SRA and, because it can make 'such order as it may think fit',[1] it can also make orders in the form of restrictions upon the way in which a solicitor continues to practise, either for a finite period or indefinitely with liberty to apply. These are commonly known as restriction orders.

The Divisional Court first encouraged the Tribunal to use, and subsequently stated that the Tribunal should use, such a power, where it considers it to be in the public interest to do so, rather than to leave such future considerations to the SRA.[2]

In *Olufeku (No 7 of 2007)* and *Brandon (No 12 of 2008)*,[3] the Master of the Rolls, when considering the overlapping jurisdictions of the SRA and the Tribunal in such matters, suggested that whereas decisions of the Tribunal are punitive and disciplinary, those of the SRA are regulatory and not punitive. Additionally, in *SRA v Kadurugamuwa*[4] the Administrative Court, in dismissing an SRA appeal against sanction, rejected the SRA's argument that only the 'fine' element of an SDT's order comprised the 'sanction', finding that the fine and restrictions on practice combined represented the SDT sanction.

However, while the SDT's Guidance Note on Sanctions[5] lists restriction order as a particular type of 'sanction' that it may impose, rather than a 'power',[6] its guidance suggests a regulatory approach. The test now adopted by the SDT, when considering whether to make such an order, is very similar to that discussed at **16.14**.

Since the decision in *Ebhogiaye v SRA*[7] the Tribunal has regularly made such orders, which can constitute the entirety of a sanction against a solicitor, or part thereof. If the SDT makes such an order for an indefinite period, it will specify as part of the order that the respondent may apply to the Tribunal to vary or rescind the restrictions either at any time or after the lapse of a defined period[8] against such orders would be made to the Administrative Court.

Following the decision in *Manak v SRA*,[9] the Tribunal will need to allow a respondent solicitor the chance to make representations regarding any proposed restriction order, give reasons for any order imposed and consider the length of any such restrictions. In *Manak*, the court quashed three restriction orders, observing that the Tribunal gave no reason for its decision that some continuing restrictions on practice were necessary and appropriate, and no reason for its decision that these particular restrictions were necessary and appropriate. The court found that:

> 'factors leading to an adverse adjudication in respect of past events do not necessarily, and without more, justify the imposition of a continuing restriction in the future. There must be some basis for concluding that a defaulting solicitor, having paid the appropriate penalty by way of reprimand, fine or

suspension, must be subject to restrictions on his or her practice in the future ... a Tribunal contemplating the imposition of continuing restrictions should hear submissions about it from the solicitor concerned or his representative ... The Tribunal gave no reason why they were all regarded as necessary and appropriate ... if restrictions were regarded as necessary and appropriate, the Tribunal had to determine whether they must be indefinite or be limited in time ... If no explanation is given of why a restriction is necessary or appropriate, there is no yardstick against which anyone considering a future application to vary or lift the restriction can measure the subsequent conduct of the solicitor.'[10]

The court also had regard to the effect of the conditions on Mr Manak's employability when considering whether they were proportionate:

'it was disproportionate to impose restrictions which will make it very difficult for Mr Manak to obtain employment as an assistant solicitor. ... the terms of the restrictions ... are likely to be regarded by prospective employers as implying some form of misappropriation of funds. Those restrictions in our judgment went beyond what was necessary and appropriate in the circumstances of this case, and should be lifted. If that is done, it seems to us that the remaining restrictions on practice can properly continue to be of indefinite duration, with any variation being a matter for future consideration if and when Mr Manak makes an appropriate application.'[11]

The court also commented that Mr Manak's post-suspension experience would be relevant to a further application to lift the remaining restrictions:

'In the light of our decision, both he and those who may have to consider any such application will be able to have regard to his post-suspension work as a solicitor.'[12]

If the Tribunal makes a restriction order, the SRA may inform the solicitor that it intends to impose matching or more restrictive practising certificate conditions. See **22.11** for further discussion.

1   Section 47(2) of SA 1974.
2   *Camacho v Law Society* [2004] 33 LS Gaz R 37; *Taylor v Law Society* [2005] EWCA Civ 1473; *Ebhogiaye v SRA* [2013] EWHC 2445 (Admin).
3   [2007] EWCA Civ 840 and [2008] EWCA Civ 967, respectively. Also see *Ebhogiaye v SRA* [2013] EWHC 2445 (Admin).
4   [2017] EWHC 2245 (Admin).
5   Republished from time to time, currently eighth edition, December 2020 at page 14.
6   The latter being the terminology adopted by section 47(2) of SA 1974.
7   [2013] EWHC 2445 (Admin).
8   Guidance Note on Sanctions, December 2020 at para 35.
9   [2018] EWHC 1958 (Admin).
10 At [62].
11 At [63].
12 At [63].

Publicity

16.21

The SRA is required by its rules to publish all practising certificate conditions and SDT restriction orders imposed, unless it is in the public interest not to do so.[1]

SRA guidance states that:

- It will publish controls on practising certificates unless it considers the particular circumstances outweigh the public interest in publication. Examples provided of circumstances that may outweigh the public interest include where publication would disclose someone's confidential or legally privileged information, prejudice other investigations or legal proceedings, or where in all the circumstances the impact of publication on the regulated person would be disproportionate (in particular, considering Article 8 of the European Convention on Human Rights and the need to balance the right to a private life with the legitimate aim of publication).

- Publication is effected by means of an entry on the SRA's website. Published information will usually be limited to a short statement as to the decision and the reasons for it.

- Generally, the solicitor is afforded the opportunity to comment in advance about whether the decision should be published.

- Publications may be amended or removed where the SRA considers that publication is no longer necessary in the public interest, or to correct or update the information.

- Generally, the SRA will automatically remove decisions from its website three years after the date of publication, unless it considers that exceptionally it is not in the public interest to do so.

- If asked to remove a publication within a three-year period because of new information or a change in circumstances, the SRA will consider whether this is appropriate, having regard to all the circumstances.[2]

Save where the SRA determines it to be in the public interest to publish a decision immediately, a decision to publish takes effect:

- if no application for a review or appeal is made, on the expiry of the date for bringing such an application under the rules; and

- if an application for a review or an appeal is made, on the date any review or appeal has been determined or discontinued.

Under section 17(1) of SA 1974, the SRA must forthwith publish suspensions to practising certificates arising as a result of an order made by the High Court on appeal or a bankruptcy order.

1   Rules 5.1 and 5.2 of the SRA Roll, Registers and Publication Regulations.
2   SRA guidance, 'Publishing regulatory and disciplinary decisions', see www.sra.org.uk/sra/decision-making/guidance/disciplinary-publishing-regulatory-disciplinary-decisions.page.

Regulatory settlement agreements

16.22

In *Bryant v SRA*[1] Mr Justice Eady found no reason for bypassing the statutory regime relating to the imposition of conditions on practising certificates, and addressing the regulator's legitimate concerns by way of undertakings. He found that:

CHAPTER 16
PRACTISING CERTIFICATE
CONTROLS

'Either they would make no difference or they would be less effective in serving the SRA purposes of protecting the public and maintaining confidence in the profession.'

Times have changed and the SRA has acknowledged the good public policy arguments for regulatory settlement agreements (RSAs) and the use of undertakings. SRA guidance indicates that:

'An RSA is an agreement to end disciplinary proceedings in whole or in part. RSAs allow us to protect both consumers and the public interest by reaching appropriate outcomes swiftly, efficiently and at proportionate cost.'[2]

The guidance note continues:

'We may consider entering into an RSA if the … individual we are investigating agrees with our proposed … control. They are flexible to ensure that we can reach the best possible outcome in the public interest. They … may include practising certificate restrictions … or undertakings given by the individual …'

The guidance note indicates that undertakings have the equivalent effect of an imposed sanction:

'In all cases where a sanction is agreed in an RSA, it has the same effect and status as one imposed by a decision maker such as one of our adjudicators.'

Thus the SRA may be prepared to enter into a regulatory settlement agreement and its guidance sets out when such agreements may be appropriate (for regulatory settlement agreements generally, see **20.18**).

Therefore such agreements may enable undertakings to be given, for example:

- not to engage in a particular form of work, such as conveyancing, acting for lenders or in litigation;

- to practise only as an employee after a specified date, pending the outcome of an investigation; or

- to provide independent evidence that accounts are in compliance, or of a return to physical or mental good health.

The SRA usually requires that regulatory settlement agreements are publicised on its website.

1   [2012] EWHC 1475 (Admin) at [28].
2   SRA guidance, 'Agreeing regulatory and disciplinary outcomes', 25 November 2019.

The roll

16.23

A solicitor may keep his or her name on the roll without holding a practising certificate, but as explained above the circumstances in which a solicitor may practise or be held out as a solicitor without a practising certificate are now very few. A solicitor without a practising certificate may nevertheless be described as a 'solicitor – not practising'.

Removal from the roll

16.24

Until 2011, the SRA wrote every year during March or April to every solicitor whose name was on the roll but who did not have a practising certificate enquiring whether he or she wanted to remain on the roll. The process was changed and letters were written to all in this category in August 2011 with a requirement to register online. The current situation is that the SRA may enquire at intervals of its own choosing whether an individual wishes his or her name to remain on the roll: 'The SRA will write to you at the last notified version of your postal or email address to ask you whether you wish your name to remain on the roll at appropriate intervals as prescribed if you do not hold a practising certificate'.[1] Anyone who either replies asking to be removed from the roll, or fails to reply and to pay the required fee within eight weeks, may have his or her name removed from the roll.

A solicitor may also apply to have his or her name removed from the roll at any time.[2] The application can be made using the solicitor's 'mySRA' account. Removal is not automatic, for the rules provide that the SRA:

- may refuse to remove the application where the solicitor is subject to any proceedings, investigation, or consideration of their conduct or practice by the SRA; and

- must not remove a solicitor's name from the roll if they are the subject of disciplinary proceedings (either in progress or pending) before the senior courts or the Tribunal.[3]

If there are no pending proceedings before the Tribunal, the SRA will consider entering into a regulatory settlement agreement, where it is in the interests of the public to do so, agreeing to the solicitor under investigation being removed from the roll.[4]

Such an agreement will likely cite the relevant allegations of misconduct, admissions, background facts and the reasons why the agreement is in the public interest. It is likely that undertakings will be required not to apply to be restored to the roll, not to work in a solicitors' practice without the written permission of the SRA, and to make full and frank disclosure to any prospective employer of the agreement that has been reached.

A person whose name has been removed from the roll may apply to the SRA for it to be restored. On receipt of such an application, the SRA is entitled to assess the character and suitability of any applicant, so the process is not automatic.[5] The SRA may refuse to restore the name of a solicitor to the roll if there are outstanding complaints.

There is a right of appeal to the High Court for persons aggrieved by decisions of the SRA to remove (without consent), refuse to remove, or refuse to restore, a name to the roll. There is also a right to apply for an internal review of such decisions before appealing to the High Court.[6]

1   Regulation 5.4 of the SRA Authorisation of Individuals Regulations 2019.
2   Regulation 5.6(b).
3   Regulation 5.10.
4   SRA guidance, 'Agreeing regulatory and disciplinary outcomes', 25 November 2019; see also **20.18**).
5   Regulation 5.9 of the SRA Authorisation of Individuals Regulations 2019. This does not, of course, apply if the solicitor has been struck off or the Tribunal has ordered that the solicitor may not be restored to the roll other than by order of the Tribunal.
6   Section 8(4) of SA 1974, and rule 3.2 of the SRA Application, Notice, Review and Appeal Rules 2019. Applications for internal review must be made within four weeks of the relevant decision. Rule 5.1 of the SRA Application, Notice, Review and Appeal Rules 2019 specifies a 28-day period for appeals to the High Court (which runs from the date of determination of the internal review, if the application for review is made in time), unless otherwise provided in rules of court. The relevant rules of court are CPR, Part 52 and the practice directions to CPR, Part 52.

Intervention and orderly closure

Introduction

17.1

The Solicitors Regulation Authority (SRA)[1] is empowered in prescribed circumstances to 'intervene' into the practice of an SRA-regulated firm or individual.[2] As the etymology of the word suggests, when resolving to intervene the SRA will come between the firm as an entity, and its practice as a firm of solicitors, exercising various powers, such that the firm's practice no longer exists as a viable entity, and is almost certainly forced to close.[3]

Upon SRA intervention, all money held by the firm, that is, in both client and office account, legally vests in the SRA, and the SRA will take possession of all the firm's files and documents. The SRA will not become the owner of the firm, leaving its management with responsibility for what is almost certain to be the closure of an empty shell.

Thus, involving the almost certain destruction of the firm and/or an individual's practice within it, intervention represents the most powerful regulatory weapon available to the SRA. In recognition of the punitive impact upon a firm, the statutory provisions have been described as a 'draconian' jurisdiction, necessary to protect the public interest, but balanced, at least in theory, by the right to apply to the court for relief.[4]

Despite its destructive impact, an intervention is a regulatory rather than a disciplinary measure, which the SRA describes as being a protective step taken to safeguard money and documents, driven by the need to protect clients and the public from risks posed by individuals or firms. It prevents further harm being caused by the individual or firm and preserves evidence for future disciplinary action.[5] Additionally, courts have indicated that the power helps preserve public confidence in the profession and reduces claims on the Compensation Fund.[6]

A firm or an individual that is the subject of an SRA intervention may, within a short and strict time limit – see **17.16** apply to the High Court for 'relief' from the intervention. If the court determines that grounds for intervention exist, it must carry out a balancing exercise between the interests of protecting the public, and the consequences to the firm and or individual if the intervention were to continue.[7] However, in the many decades since the introduction of the intervention regime,[8] there have been only a handful of successful statutory challenges to interventions,[9] and in those cases the Law Society did not oppose the withdrawal of the intervention. The claimant in *Sheikh v Law Society* succeeded in a contested challenge at first instance,[10] but the decision was reversed by the Court of Appeal.[11]

1 The power granted to the Law Society is exercised by the SRA.
2 Schedule 1 to the Solicitors Act (SA) 1974, Schedule 14 to the Courts and Legal Services Act (CLSA) 1990, Schedule 2 to the Administration of Justice Act (AJA) 1985, Schedule 14 to the Legal Services Act (LSA) 2007.
3 Save in the case of limited interventions – see **17.27**.
4 See *Holder v Law Society* [2003] EWCA Civ 39 at [14]; *Buckley v Law Society (No 2)* [1984] 3 All ER 313, ChD; *Giles v Law Society* (1996) 8 Admin LR 105 at 116D–E, CA, per Ward LJ.
5 SRA guidance, 'How we approach decisions to intervene', 25 November 2019.
6 See *Buckley v Law Society (No 2)* [1984] 1 WLR 1101, ChD at 1105–6, per Sir Robert Megarry VC; *Sritharan v Law Society* [2005] EWCA Civ 476 at [17] and [18], [2005] 1 WLR 2708 at 2714A–D; and *Sheikh v Law Society* [2006] EWCA Civ 1577, [2007] 3 All ER 183.
7 See *Holder v Law Society* [2003] EWCA Civ 39 at [15].
8 Introduced by the Solicitors Act 1941.
9 See *Yogarajah v Law Society* (1982) 126 Sol Jo 430; *Patel v Law Society* [2008] EWHC 3564 (Ch); *Khan v SRA* (18 May 2012, unreported); and *Williams v SRA* [2015] EWHC 2302 (Ch), [2015] 1 WLR 4982. In each of these cases, the Law Society/SRA either consented to, or did not oppose, the setting aside of the intervention.
10 [2005] EWHC 1409 (Ch), [2005] 4 All ER 717.
11 [2006] EWCA Civ 1577, [2007] 3 All ER 183.

Grounds for intervention

17.2

The grounds upon which the SRA is entitled to intervene into the practice of an SRA-regulated firm or individual are contained in Schedule 1 to SA 1974 as amended by LSA 2007.[1] Essentially, these are designed to permit intervention when a solicitor cannot run (through ill health, imprisonment, bankruptcy and the like), or alternatively cannot be trusted to run, a solicitor's practice so as to ensure that clients' monies are secure. The statutory grounds are the following:[2]

- The SRA has reason to suspect dishonesty on the part of the solicitor, an employee of the solicitor or the personal representatives of a deceased solicitor, in connection with that solicitor's practice or former practice, or in connection with any trust of which that solicitor is or formerly was a trustee or that employee is or was a trustee in his capacity as such an employee (para 1(1)(a) of Schedule 1).

- The SRA has reason to suspect dishonesty on the part of a solicitor in connection with (i) the business of any body of which the solicitor is or was a manager or (ii) any business carried on by the solicitor as a sole trader (para 1(1)(aa) of Schedule 1).

- The SRA considers that there has been undue delay on the part of the personal representatives of a deceased solicitor who immediately before his death was practising as a sole solicitor, in connection with that solicitor's practice or in connection with any trust (para 1(1)(b) of Schedule 1).

- The SRA is satisfied that the solicitor has failed to comply with rules made by virtue of sections 31, 32 or 37(2)(c) of SA 1974. Section 31 refers to rules of professional practice, conduct, fitness to practise and discipline of solicitors, section 32 to accounts rules and section 37 to rules in relation to professional indemnity (PI) insurance. In essence any breach of any part of the 2019 regulatory arrangements, or their statutory predecessors, will suffice.

- The solicitor has been made bankrupt or has made a composition or arrangement with his creditors (para 1(1)(d) of Schedule 1).

- The solicitor has been committed to prison in any civil or criminal proceedings (para 1(1)(e) of Schedule 1).

- The SRA is satisfied that a sole solicitor is incapacitated by illness, injury or accident to such an extent as to be unable to attend to his practice (para 1(1) (ee) of Schedule 1).

- The solicitor lacks capacity within the meaning of the Mental Capacity Act 2005 to act as a solicitor and powers under sections 15 to 20 or section 48 of that Act are exercisable in relation to him (para 1(1)(f)) of Schedule 1).

- The name of a solicitor has been removed from or struck off the roll or a solicitor has been suspended from practice (para 1(1)(g) of Schedule 1).

- The SRA is satisfied that a sole solicitor has abandoned his practice (para 1(1) (h) of Schedule 1).

- Any power conferred by Schedule 1 to SA 1974 has been exercised in relation to a sole solicitor by virtue of sub-paragraph (1)(a) (reason to suspect dishonesty) and he has acted as a sole solicitor within the period of 18 months beginning with the date on which it was so exercised (para 1(1)(j) of Schedule 1).[3]

- The SRA is satisfied that a person has acted as a solicitor at a time when he did not have a practising certificate which was in force (para 1(1)(k) of Schedule 1).

- The SRA is satisfied that the solicitor has failed to comply with any condition, subject to which his practising certificate was granted or otherwise has effect, to the effect that he may act as a solicitor only in employment which is approved by the SRA in connection with the imposition of that condition, or as a member of a partnership which is so approved, or as a manager of a body recognised by the SRA under section 9 of AJA 1985 and so approved – or in any specified combination of those ways (para 1(1)(l) of Schedule 1). The word 'manager' has the same meaning as in LSA 2007 (see section 207 of LSA 2007).[4]

- The SRA is satisfied that it is necessary to exercise the powers of intervention, or any of them, to protect the interests of clients, or former or potential clients, of the solicitor or his firm, or the interests of the beneficiaries of any trust of which the solicitor is or was a trustee (para 1(1)(m) of Schedule 1).

1   Section 9(2)(f) of AJA 1985 and paragraphs 32–35 of Schedule 2 thereto, as amended, provide for rules made under SA 1974, and the powers of intervention, to have effect in relation to recognised bodies and section 102 of and Schedule 14 to LSA 2007 confer similar powers in relation to alternative business structures (ABSs).
2   The statute refers to 'the Society' but in practice the powers are exercised by the SRA.
3   This is an anachronism – it has been superseded by the provision for the automatic suspension of the solicitor's practising certificate when an intervention occurs by reason of a suspicion of dishonesty. Before this power was acquired (by section 15(1A) of SA 1974, inserted by CLSA 1990) a solicitor who was the subject of an intervention could theoretically immediately set himself up in practice again and encourage all his clients to reinstruct him.
4   Paragraph 1(1A) of Schedule 1 to SA 1974.

17.3

It is arguable that the ground for intervention, paragraph 1(1)(m) of Schedule 1, introduced by LSA 2007, is so widely drawn that all other grounds are obsolete, but it is anticipated that reliance will continue to be placed on the traditional grounds, if only because there will be an obligation to explain why the SRA considered it 'necessary' to intervene.

Another ground added by LSA 2007 is paragraph 1(1)(aa) of Schedule 1, which envisages intervention when there is suspected dishonesty on the part of a solicitor in connection with a business that is not a solicitor's practice; that is, a business (not being a solicitor's practice or trust) of which the solicitor is the sole proprietor, or of which he or she is an employee or manager. This is intended to deal with the situation in which a solicitor has a legal practice but is also involved in another business, for example, one that provides financial services, where there is reason to suspect dishonesty in relation to that separate business. One could see that if the Financial Conduct Authority (FCA) (using the same example) took action against such a business in circumstances where a suspicion of dishonesty arose, there could be a need to intervene in the solicitor's practice, as the same person could be seen to pose a risk to clients.

It was the case that the powers of intervention could only be exercised after specific notice had been given to the solicitor if they were to be exercised under sub-paragraph (1)(c) – breaches of specified rules relating to professional practice, conduct and discipline of solicitors.[1] The solicitor had to be given notice in writing that he had failed to comply with the rules specified in the notice and also (at the same or any later time) notice that the powers of intervention were accordingly exercisable, but this provision was repealed by LSA 2007.

Intervention can therefore occur with no notice at all, and the solicitor may have no opportunity to make any representations on his or her own behalf before the decision to intervene is made.

1   Paragraph 1(2) of Schedule 1 to SA 1974 was repealed by para 77(2)(k) of Schedule 16 to LSA 2007.

The adjudication process

17.4

The resolution to intervene may be made by two or more adjudicators, including members of the adjudication panel and employed adjudicators, save that one adjudicator may so resolve in cases of 'severe and imminent risk to the public'.[1] Accordingly, an intervention into a solicitor's practice can be authorised by a single employee of the SRA. Typically the adjudicators will consider a Forensic Investigation Report, any representations the solicitor may have made in answer to that report, and the recommendations of an SRA officer contained in his or her own report which will summarise the facts and issues. The recommendation of an SRA officer is in no sense binding upon the panel; in *Sheikh v Law Society*,[2] the supervisor had recommended against intervention but the adjudication panel nevertheless resolved to intervene.

In cases of clear suspected dishonesty or where it is intended that the intervention should occur without notice, the SRA officer's report will not be disclosed to the solicitor. Indeed, in the most serious cases, usually involving an obvious and substantial client account shortfall in circumstances amounting to theft, the procedure may involve a brief visit from an investigating officer, a report by way of a one-page memorandum and an intervention as soon as the necessary practical arrangements have been made. In its latest guidance the SRA has indicated that, 'If we think it is important to intervene in the public interest at an early stage, we may not give notice'.[3]

1   SRA, 'Schedule of delegation', 25 November 2019.
2   [2006] EWCA Civ 1577, [2007] 3 All ER 183.
3   SRA guidance, 'How we approach decisions to intervene', 25 November 2019.

Natural Justice and Human Rights Act 1998 implications

17.5

Solicitors who are the subject of interventions have challenged the exercise of this powerful and terminally damaging regulatory weapon without any requirement for notice, and/or reasoning, on the grounds that it is in breach of the common law rules of procedural fairness (also referred to as the principles of natural justice) and that it is incompatible with the rights protected by the Human Rights Act (HRA) 1998. All such challenges have failed. The natural justice arguments were rejected in *Giles v Law Society*,[1] most recently confirmed in *Neumans LLP v Law Society*[2] and the HRA 1998 arguments failed in *Holder v Law Society*.[3] In the latter case, the Court of Appeal held that the statutory regime as a whole did not offend HRA 1998, although it remained open to a solicitor to assert that an intervention in a particular case breached the rights protected by the European Convention.

However, while the intervention scheme itself has been held not to breach the common law rules of procedural fairness, in *Neumans*,[4] Singh LJ, commenting on the possibility that it may apply in individual cases, held that:

> 'the [SRA] submits that the law should not impose a duty of procedural fairness in this context, where speed and sometimes secrecy are of the essence in order to protect the public interest. Yet, on the facts of this case, the [SRA] *did* afford the opportunity to make representations before intervention took place. That at least suggests that it is possible, depending on the facts of a particular case, to comply with the normal requirements of procedural fairness and so it may not be necessary to have an absolute rule that those requirements never apply before an intervention can take place. In other contexts public law has not shied away from imposing the duty of procedural fairness as a matter of principle, while recognising that (where appropriate, depending on the facts of the individual case) it may not be possible to comply with that duty in advance of a decision, for example because there is a need for speed or secrecy.'

1   (1996) 8 Admin LR 105, CA. See also *Yogarajah v Law Society* (1982) 126 Sol Jo 430; and *Buckley v Law Society* (9 October 1985, unreported).
2   [2018] EWCA Civ 325.
3   [2003] EWCA Civ 39, [2003] 3 All ER 62, [2003] 1 WLR 1059.
4   [2018] EWCA Civ 325 at [46].

The extent of the powers

17.6

The mechanism selected by Parliament to permit the Law Society to achieve intervention in a solicitor's practice is, in essence, to exercise powers to vest the solicitor's practice monies in the Society, and to require the solicitor to yield up the practice documents. These powers have been delegated to and are exercised by the SRA.

CHAPTER 17
INTERVENTION AND
ORDERLY CLOSURE

Money

17.7

The intervention resolution will vest in the SRA all sums of money held by, or on behalf of, a solicitor or his firm in connection with his practice, and the right to recover or receive those sums.[1] In short, the SRA takes control of office and client accounts. Where the intervention is solely by reason of the death of a sole practitioner, only client account is affected.[2] The SRA may also resolve to vest in itself the right to recover or receive debts due to the solicitor or his firm in connection with his practice or former practice.[3]

Schedule 1 to SA 1974 also provides the court with specific powers to assist the SRA, upon application, in gaining control of the practice monies. The court may order that no payment shall be made without the leave of the court by any person (whether or not named in the order) of any money held by him (in whatever manner and whether it was received before or after the making of the order) on behalf of the solicitor or his firm.[4] The court may require a person suspected of holding money on behalf of the solicitor or his firm to provide information to the SRA as to such money and the accounts in which it is held.[5]

The SRA holds the money on trust for the purposes of the intervention and 'subject thereto … upon trust for the persons beneficially entitled to them'.[6] What this means in practice is that the SRA holds client money on trust for the clients, and office money (if any) in circumstances where the solicitor is likely to be in substantial debt, (a) to his clients in the event of any client account shortfall and (b) to the SRA in respect of the intervention costs (more of which below: see **17.14**). While the solicitor is 'beneficially entitled' to anything that might be left, frequently, there is nothing left.

In terms of practice, the SRA deals with the money in accordance with the SRA Statutory Trust Rules 2019.

The extent of the statutory trust was considered in *Williams v SRA*,[7] in which the SRA had agreed to set aside an intervention. An issue later arose as to whether a sum of money which the SRA had received from the Legal Aid Agency (LAA), which the claimant said represented work carried out by him while an earlier partnership than the one that was the subject of the notice of intervention was still in being, was within the scope of the statutory trust. Sir William Blackburne held that:

- 'practice' for the purposes of paragraph 6(2) of Schedule 1 to SA 1974 meant the activities of a solicitor so far as carried out in that capacity, in contrast to the named organisation or structure though which the solicitor practised;

- the claimant's 'former practice' for the purposes of paragraph 6(2)(a) therefore included his practice while a partner of the earlier partnership, namely the activities he had carried on as a solicitor during that time, even though the earlier partnership had not been named in the intervention resolution; and

- accordingly, in so far as it derived from the solicitor's 'practice' while a member of the earlier partnership, the LAA payment fell within the scope of the statutory trust.

The extent of the statutory trust was considered again by the Court of Appeal in *Law Society of England and Wales v Pathania*.[8] Sir Geoffrey Vos, giving the leading judgment, reversed the decision of the High Court when it held that loans made by the solicitor from client account, in breach of trust/fiduciary duty, prior to the resolution to intervene, were not sums, 'held by or on behalf of the solicitor or his firm'.[9] This was so, as the funds the loans represented were, by their nature, not 'held' but had been paid away. The Law Society had not issued a resolution exercising the 'right to recover or receive debts due to the solicitor or his firm in connection with his practice or former practice'.[10]

The Court of Appeal held that while the solicitor 'is obliged to account to the client for the monies he has paid away on the footing of wilful default, and would be held liable to pay equitable compensation to the client for his breach of fiduciary duty' (at [72]), as the solicitor held no funds, the claims (against the debtors) arising from the money improperly paid away did not vest in the Law Society by virtue of the resolution made.[11]

Sir Geoffrey Vos held that historically,[12] the legislation[13] intended to cover monies actually held (bank deposits treated as being held despite the creditor/debtor relationship), or subsequently received, as well as monies held in a bare trust for the solicitor (eg where paid away to avoid the effects of an intervention). Thus he concluded (at [83]) that:

> 'paragraph 6(2)(a) does not cover monies wrongfully paid out of client account before the Intervention where there is no specific fund held by or on the solicitor's behalf to which the solicitor's obligation to replace the monies can directly attach. It is not enough that the borrower has an obligation to repay the monies under the terms of a loan agreement.'

Sir Geoffrey Vos also held that the solicitor was not required to account to the Law Society in respect of his past defaults; rather he was liable to account to his clients for his breaches. He added, however, that when the loans are repaid, they will be caught by the statutory trusts.

The court also commented (at [86]) that:

> 'the outcome is undesirable from the Law Society's point of view … the Law Society has not historically made use of paragraph 6A. It may wish to do so in future …'.

In *Law Society of England and Wales v Dua*[14] the SRA, seeking to recover the costs of its intervention, failed to obtain orders for sale in respect of two properties held in trust by the intervened solicitor for her children. The SRA claimed, among other things, that in circumstances in which the solicitor could reappoint herself as a beneficiary of the trust, her position in relation to it was 'indistinguishable to that of ownership'.[15] The court did not agree, citing, amongst other things, the fiduciary responsibility of the solicitor in relation to the trust. However in its concluding remarks, the court implied that the SRA could still put its theory of control to the test, when commenting:

> 'it is a matter for the trustees … to decide what provision should be made for Mrs Dua if the Law Society concludes its only other enforcement route is bankruptcy.'[16]

CHAPTER 17
INTERVENTION AND
ORDERLY CLOSURE

1   Paragraph 6 of Schedule 1 to SA 1974.
2   Paragraphs 2 and 6(2)(b) of Schedule 1.
3   Paragraph 6A of Schedule 1. This was added by LSA 2007 and puts on an express statutory footing that which had been held in *Dooley v Law Society (No 2)* [2001] All ER (D) 362, *Times*, 16 January 2002, ChD to be the case as a matter of proper interpretation of the statute prior to its amendment.

4   Paragraph 5(1) of Schedule 1 to SA 1974.
5   Paragraph 8 of Schedule 1.
6   Paragraph 6(1) of Schedule 1.
7   [2015] EWHC 2302 (Ch), [2015] 1 WLR 4982.
8   [2019] EWCA Civ 517.
9   Paragraph 6(2)(a) of Schedule 1.
10   Paragraph 6A of Schedule 1.
11   Resolution under paragraph 6(2)(a) of Schedule 1.
12   Prior to the introduction of paragraph 6A of Schedule 1.
13   Paragraph 6 of Schedule 1.
14   [2020] EWHC 3528 (Ch).
15   At [154].
16   At [205].

Practice documents

17.8

The intervention resolution results in a notice to the solicitor or his firm requiring the production or delivery to any person appointed by the SRA of all documents in the possession of the solicitor or his firm in connection with his practice.[1] Failure or refusal to comply with the notice is a criminal offence.[2] The High Court has power to order the production or delivery of documents by the solicitor and/or by any person suspected of being in possession of relevant documents.[3] Once possession has been taken of the documents, the SRA must serve on the solicitor a notice that possession has been taken by the person appointed on its behalf.[4]

1   Paragraph 9 of Schedule 1 to SA 1974.
2   Paragraph 9(3) of Schedule 1.
3   Paragraph 9(4) and (5) of Schedule 1.
4   Paragraph 9(7) of Schedule 1.

Recovery of costs

17.9

The SRA's intervention costs, which can amount to £100,000 or more,[1] are a liqui-dated[2] debt due from the solicitor or his estate, unless the High Court orders otherwise.[3] Such costs, which invariably include the costs of the SRA's intervention 'agent', that is, a firm of solicitors engaged by the SRA to manage its administration, and may include various disbursements including external accountancy advice and reports, are, upon application, subject to detailed assessment.[4]

In *The Law Society (acting through the SRA) v Blavo*[5] the Court of Appeal, overturning the decision of the High Court, found that the SRA's costs on intervention are for a 'liquidated sum', and thus declined to set aside the SRA's statutory demand. The court decided that a solicitor's right to seek a detailed assessment of the SRA's inter-vention costs[6] did not result in the SRA's claim being for an unliquidated sum, as, relying on *McGuinness v Norwich & Peterborough Building Society*[7] the costs were a 'pre-ascertained liability … where the amount due is to be ascertained in accord-ance with a contractual formula or contractual machinery which, when operated will produce a figure',[8] in this case, SA 1974 providing the machinery. The court noted that the position contrasts with solicitors' costs generally, that is, save where costs are expressly agreed, a claim by a solicitor for his charges is for an unliquidated sum, as it is 'analogous to one … for an unquantified sum' with the solicitor being entitled to 'reasonable and fair remuneration for the work they have done'.[9]

The High Court may, on the application of the SRA, order a former partner of the solicitor to pay a specified proportion of the intervention costs otherwise payable by the solicitor if it is satisfied that the conduct of the solicitor that led to the intervention was carried on with the consent or connivance of, or attributable to any neglect on the part of, the former partner.[10] Since the power was first introduced by LSA 2007, only one application has ever been made to the court for such an order. In *SRA v Robinson*,[11] the court made such an order, finding that, despite the solicitor having ceased to be a partner some 17 months before the intervention (by reason of suspension and then practising certificate conditions), in fact he remained in practice controlling the operation of the practice at all times. The court ordered that the former partner be responsible for a percentage, in this case 100 per cent.

1 For example, as reported in *The Law Society (acting through the SRA) v Blavo* [2018] EWCA Civ 2250 the SRA's costs of intervention were almost £800,000.
2 *The Law Society (acting through the SRA) v Blavo* [2018] EWCA Civ 2250.
3 Paragraph 13 of Schedule 1 to SA 1974.
4 *Pine v Law Society (No 2)* [2002] EWCA Civ 175, [2002] 2 All ER 658].
5 [2018] EWCA Civ 2250.
6 *Pine v Law Society (No 2)* [2002] EWCA Civ 175, [2002] 2 All ER 658.
7 [2012] 2 All ER (Comm) 265.
8 *McGuinness* at [36] (quoted by the Court of Appeal in *Blavo* at [86]).
9 *Thomas Watts & Co v Smith* [1998] 2 Costs LR 59 at 73.
10 Paragraph 13A of Schedule 1 to SA 1974.
11 [2019] EWHC 3223 (Ch).

Other powers

17.10

The High Court may also make orders permitting forcible entry to premises to search for and seize documents,[1] for the redirection of mail, telephone and electronic communications[2] and for the appointment of a new trustee in substitution for the solicitor as trustee of any trust.[3]

The SRA's statutory powers in relation to money and documents take precedence over any lien or other right to possession in any other person.[4] These powers continue to be exercisable after a solicitor's death, or after his name has been removed from or struck off the roll.

1 Paragraph 9(6) of Schedule 1 to SA 1974 and as ordered in *SRA v Soophia Khan (1) and Sophie Khan & Co Ltd (2)* [2021] EWHC 2721 (Ch).
2 Paragraph 10 of Schedule 1 and as ordered in *SRA v Soophia Khan (1) and Sophie Khan & Co Ltd (2)* [2021] EWHC 2721 (Ch).
3 Paragraph 11 of Schedule 1.
4 Paragraph 12 of Schedule 1.

Practising certificate

17.11

Where an intervention is authorised because of a suspicion of dishonesty on the part of the solicitor, breaches of the SRA Accounts Rules 2019, breaches of any other rule or provision made under section 31 of SA 1974, including the SRA Codes of Conduct, or the solicitor's committal to prison, any practising certificate of the solicitor then in force is immediately suspended,[1] unless the adjudicator or adjudication panel authorising the intervention directs otherwise.[2]

The solicitor may (at any time before the certificate expires) apply to the SRA to terminate the suspension and the SRA may terminate the suspension conditionally or unconditionally or refuse the application.[3] If the SRA refuses the application, or the solicitor is aggrieved at the conditions imposed he or she may appeal to the High Court.[4]

In practice, the SRA is usually prepared to restore a solicitor's practising certificate subject to stringent conditions, commonly a requirement that the solicitor may only practise in employment approved by the SRA, and on condition that he or she has no access to clients' money.

1   Section 15(1A) of SA 1974, inserted by section 91(2) of CLSA 1990.
2   Section 15(1B) of SA 1974.
3   Section 16(3) and (4).
4   Section 16(5).

The practical reality

17.12

The legal department of the SRA, which manages interventions, appoints an intervening agent, a solicitor who is a member of the SRA's Intervention Panel practising in the relevant area, who will take direct responsibility for (in particular) client files. Provisional arrangements may be made in advance of the intervention resolution when it can reasonably be expected to occur. Notice of the intervention will not be given to the solicitor (even if the Panel has resolved on the intervention some days before) until the agents are ready to act and the solicitor's bank has received notice. The solicitor will therefore not know of the intervention until after his or her bank accounts are frozen. The first that a solicitor will typically hear of the decision will either be by a cryptic telephone call from the SRA requesting him to expect an email, or an email with the resolution to intervene. Depending upon the risk profile of the firm and individuals involved, and the resources available at the time, the SRA's intervention agent may attend the firm's premises immediately, the next day or within a few days.

The intervening agents attend at the solicitor's address and take possession of the practice documents which in most cases are removed without delay. Matters which are urgent and require prompt action are identified and (hopefully, assuming the solicitor's co-operation) discussed. Practice monies are transferred to a bank account under the control of the intervening agents. The intervening agents attempt to bring the practice's accounting records into proper order.

Clients will receive a standard letter informing them that the SRA has been obliged to exercise its statutory powers and inviting them to nominate successor solicitors or, if appropriate, to accept delivery of the papers themselves.

If claims in professional negligence or breach of fiduciary duty are made against the solicitor, the solicitor's PI insurers may wish to see the files seized by the SRA to seek to discover grounds for declining indemnity cover. However, the SRA refuses to provide insurers with the files in those circumstances unless the lay client has provided consent, and this refusal was upheld by the Court of Appeal in *Quinn Direct Insurance Ltd v Law Society*[1] on the ground that privilege and confidentiality in the documents remain after intervention, and there is no room for implying into the statutory scheme any entitlement in insurers to see the documents.[2]

1 [2010] EWCA Civ 805.
2 At [29].

17.13

The intervening agents do not in any sense take over or run the practice. They seek to ensure that all clients are informed of the intervention and find alternative solicitors, and that the practice monies are distributed properly; they may have to seek directions from the court to achieve this. They are likely to have to take urgent and protective steps in circumstances where it is necessary to guard the interests of clients, but it is not their function to take over client matters in any other sense or for any other purpose.

The description of intervention as striking a mortal blow to the practice[1] is, if anything, an understatement. Quite apart from the automatic suspension of the practising certificate, the solicitor loses control of the practice's bank accounts and the practice's documentation. It instantly becomes impossible to service any bank overdraft. Unless the intervention is rapidly reversed by the court, the solicitor's practice is lost without any compensation, and the solicitor faces almost inevitable financial ruin.

1 *Giles v Law Society* (1996) 8 Admin LR 105, CA.

17.14

Many practices have little in the way of measurable assets – offices are rented, equipment and cars leased, and the office account is likely to be in substantial overdraft. Assets represented by goodwill suddenly become worthless and there are difficulties in gaining access to files to render invoices for work in progress. In addition, as has been said, the solicitor is liable for the costs of intervention, recoverable as a debt due to the SRA.[1] As already indicated, these costs can be very substantial. Unless the solicitor has private wealth there will often be nothing left. Intervention and subsequent bankruptcy commonly go hand in hand.

Although, in theory, a solicitor subject to an intervention is entitled to payment for work in progress at the time of the intervention, this entitlement is more apparent than real. The successor solicitor taking over an individual file will have to extract such payment from the client, and will often doubtless be met by an argument from the lay client that he or she should not be liable for two sets of fees in respect of the same legal work. The intervened solicitor has no means of compelling anyone to recover outstanding costs. The SRA is under no obligation to do so.[2] Any payments recovered in respect of work in progress will first be set off against the solicitor's liability for the intervention costs.[3] Further, the SRA may have vested in itself the right to recover debts due to the practice, including outstanding bills and the value of work in progress.

Ownership of the solicitor's other assets, such as office furniture, computer equipment and the like is not affected by the intervention. Only practice monies and documents are affected (save that the SRA may require possession of computer equipment necessary to access documents held only in electronic form).[4] Similarly, the solicitor's contractual obligations are unaffected – the intervention does not have the effect of dismissing employees or in itself making them redundant.[5]

1 Paragraph 13 of Schedule 1 to SA 1974. The solicitor may require the detailed assessment of the costs: *Pine v Law Society (No 2)* [2002] EWCA Civ 175, [2002] 2 All ER 658.
2 *Dooley v Law Society (No 2)* [2001] All ER (D) 362, *Times*, 16 January 2002. Under LSA 2007, the SRA acquired the right to recover sums due to the solicitor and may therefore elect to pursue outstanding costs and work in progress to meet client liabilities or intervention costs.
3 *Dooley v Law Society (No 2)* [2001] All ER (D) 362, *Times*, 16 January 2002.
4 Paragraph 9(5A) and (6)(b) of Schedule 1 to SA 1974.
5 *Rose v Dodd* [2005] EWCA Civ 957, [2006] 1 All ER 464.

17.15

Essentially, therefore, an intervention means the total destruction of a solicitor's practice. The solicitor is unable to sell that practice to a willing purchaser. The practice's clients have to find new solicitors. The practice's employees have to find new jobs. And the solicitor has to apply for the suspension of the practising certificate to be lifted if he or she is to resume any sort of practice as a solicitor. The solicitor will only be able to practise at all by finding a willing employer.

Ordinarily, at the time of making the resolution to intervene, the adjudication panel will also refer the solicitor's conduct to the Solicitors Disciplinary Tribunal (the Tribunal or SDT).

Because all the statutory provisions refer to a solicitor, and a solicitor's practice, it is possible (and it does occur) that interventions are authorised into the practice of a solicitor who may be a partner in a firm, rather than a sole practitioner. In that event only the client funds, client documents and any practice funds and papers personal to that solicitor are subject to the intervention. Inevitably this has the potential to be highly disruptive for the remaining partners, but they are not directly affected by the exercise of the statutory powers.

Challenging an intervention[1]

17.16

The SRA must serve on the solicitor or his or her firm, and on any other person having possession of sums of money caught by the intervention, a certified copy of the intervention resolution and a notice prohibiting the payment out of any such sums of money.[2] Within eight days of the service of that notice, the solicitor, on giving not less than 48 hours' notice in writing to the SRA, may apply to the High Court for an order directing the SRA to withdraw the notice.[3]

Likewise, where the SRA has taken possession of practice documents following service of a notice,[4] the solicitor may apply to the High Court (again, within eight days of the service of the notice) for an order directing the SRA to deliver the documents to such person as the solicitor claimant may require.[5]

If the court makes an order in favour of the solicitor, it shall have power also to make such other order as it may think fit.[6]

The eight-day time limit is mandatory, and cannot be extended by the court or by the consent of the parties.[7] The proceedings are assigned to the Chancery Division and are governed by CPR Part 8 and rule 67.4. If the proceedings are not litigated expeditiously by the solicitor, so that they eventually become academic as a result of the destruction of his practice, they may be struck out as an abuse of process.[8]

There is no power for the SRA to withdraw an intervention once it has been put in place. If it is rapidly concluded that the decision was lawful but not justified or was ill advised, the solution is a consent order of the High Court.[9]

1   This term is used as there is no 'appeal' against an intervention – the remedy is an application to the High Court for an order directing the withdrawal of the intervention.
2   Paragraph 6(3) of Schedule 1 to SA 1974.
3   Paragraph 6(4) of Schedule 1. The eight-day limitation period should be seen as a strict requirement: as to whether the courts may be able to apply any flexibility, see *Gadd v SRA* [2013] EWCA Civ 837.
4   Paragraph 9(7) of Schedule 1.
5   Paragraph 9(8) and (9) of Schedule 1.
6   Paragraphs 6(5) and 9(11) of Schedule 1.
7   *Re a Solicitor* [1994] Ch 1994 B 4973.
8   *Virdi v Law Society* [1999] 29 LS Gaz R 29. Mr Virdi's appeal to the Court of Appeal was dismissed, but this is unreported.
9   *Patel v Law Society* [2008] EWHC 3564 (Ch). Norris J commented in approving a consent order that the parties were right to seek such an order as there was no power provided to the SRA by the statute to reverse its own decision.

17.17

As has been seen, it has proved to be almost impossible to challenge an intervention successfully. This is at least in part because of the financial consequences of an intervention described above. The solicitor is in a quandary – does he or she recognise the likely reality that the only way in which family and personal financial commitments can be met is if he or she finds a job with a willing employer? If so, the solicitor must recognise also that the original practice will not survive; the conditions on his or her practising certificate will prevent recovery of the remnants of that practice, even if the challenge is successful. There is the additional risk that the proceedings will be struck out as an abuse as they will no longer have any practical purpose.

Alternatively, does the solicitor fight on, without employment or other income, with mounting and unserviceable debts, probably without funds to pay for the needed specialist assistance, and with no prospect of obtaining public funding, against an opponent with unlimited resources?

If a solicitor believes that he or she is at risk of intervention, it is wise to take precautions (such as putting another solicitor in funds) to ensure that a rapid statutory challenge can be mounted if so advised. Once the intervention has commenced, it will be impossible to draw upon office account. Any attempt to put funds beyond the reach of the SRA after the intervention has commenced may well be taken into account against the solicitor at the High Court hearing.[1]

It is highly doubtful whether the courts have jurisdiction to provide interim relief by 'unscrambling' the intervention and/or reversing the suspension of the solicitor's practising certificate pending the full hearing. Where the solicitor challenges the intervention, the SRA will ordinarily be prepared to co-operate in slowing down the practical effect of the intervention (ie by not informing clients of the intervention unless the particular matter is urgent).

However, the problem will remain as to what is to be done for those clients whose matters are not particularly pressing but who cannot be ignored. The solicitor who is the subject of the intervention cannot continue to act; he or she has no practising certificate. It is possible, if there is a suitable and willing person and the solicitor can afford to remunerate him or her (allowing for the fact that money coming in to the practice will vest in the SRA), for the solicitor to appoint another solicitor with an unconditional practising certificate as practice manager; this might be an existing employee or someone brought in for the purpose. Such arrangements will in practice require the co-operation of the SRA but will provide a mechanism for maintaining the status quo where a challenge is credibly made and expeditiously pursued.

1   See *Sheikh v Law Society* [2006] EWCA Civ 1577, [2007] 3 All ER 183.

17.18

The solicitor mounting a statutory challenge will be well advised to make an early application for directions to ensure that the case is brought on speedily for trial, and that the essential issues are identified at the outset.

The statutory challenge provided for by paras 6 and 9 of Schedule 1 to SA 1974 is the only manner in which an intervention can be challenged.[1] Any issues under HRA 1998 can be considered within the statutory proceedings.

1   *Hedworth v Law Society* (1994, unreported); *Miller v Law Society* [2002] EWHC 1453 (Ch), [2002] 4 All ER 312.

The proceedings and the test to be applied

17.19

In providing an extremely short mandatory limitation period (see **17.16**), Parliament clearly envisaged a swift summary procedure. One reason for the lack of successful challenges to interventions may be that this laudable aim has become lost in the complexities of High Court litigation. The tortuous course of the proceedings in *Sheikh v Law Society*[1] indicated that the statutory remedy was not working efficiently. The claimant's application to set aside the intervention did not come on for hearing for four months, and occupied eight days of court time. The judgments at first instance and of the Court of Appeal each ran to 70 pages of single-spaced typescript.

In most cases, the reasons for intervention will be obvious to all. However, this is not invariably so, and unless the reasons are properly identified at an early stage, there is a danger that the solicitor will be denied the effective summary remedy that Parliament intended to provide.

The burden of proof to justify the continuation of the intervention rests on the SRA – the solicitor, though nominally the claimant, is in reality the defendant.[2] Accordingly, unless the parties agree otherwise, the SRA will present its case first.

The traditional approach to the statutory challenge was the 'two-stage test' propounded by Neuberger J in *Dooley v Law Society*[3] approved by the Court of Appeal in *Holder v Law Society*:[4]

'The court's decision is a two-stage process. First it must decide whether the grounds under paragraph 1 are made out; in this case, primarily, whether there are grounds for suspecting dishonesty. Secondly, if the court is so satisfied, then it must consider whether in the light of all the evidence before it the intervention should continue. In deciding the second question, the court must carry out a balancing exercise between the need in the public interest to protect the public from dishonest solicitors and the inevitably very serious consequences to the solicitor if the intervention continues.'

1   [2006] EWCA Civ 1577, [2007] 3 All ER 183.
2   See *Giles v Law Society* (1996) 8 Admin LR 105 at 114F–G, CA, per Nourse LJ.
3   (2000) HC Transcript 0002868.
4   [2003] EWCA Civ 39, [2003] 3 All ER 62.

17.20

That must now be considered in the light of the more subtle approach suggested by the Court of Appeal in *Sheikh v Law Society*.[1] The court may need to decide whether, at the time of the resolution to intervene, the statutory ground relied upon by the SRA actually existed – for example, whether there was, at that time, reason to suspect dishonesty on the basis of the information available to the SRA. It has not been conclusively decided whether, if no such ground existed, the solicitor is entitled to have the notices of intervention withdrawn for that reason alone, but it seems likely that in that event the resolution will have been fundamentally flawed and liable to be set aside. On the other hand, such a circumstance is likely to be very rare.

In *Neumans LLP v The Law Society*[2] the Administrative Court rejected the appellant's argument that the SRA may not intervene on the ground of suspected dishonesty, if the manager so suspected is no longer a manager at the date of intervention.[3]

If there is no challenge to the validity of the resolution or to the service of the intervention notices, the single issue for the court is whether the notices should be withdrawn. In considering this, the court is exercising its own judgement and is entitled to take into account material that was not available to the SRA when resolving to intervene, but which is available to the court. Moreover, the court will also take into account the views of the SRA as a relevant evidential factor, although it is unclear how these views are ascertained in practice – save through the mouths of the advocates representing the SRA at the hearing of the application to withdraw the intervention notices. This is an unsatisfactory 'evidential' basis upon which to ask a court to make decisions.

As noted above, the intervention regime is in principle compliant with the requirements of natural justice and HRA 1998, but is capable of being operated unfairly in an individual case.

1   [2006] EWCA Civ 1577, [2007] 3 All ER 183.
2   [2017] EWHC 2004 (Ch).
3   The appellant went on to appeal to the Court of Appeal on other grounds – which failed.

17.21

If the challenge is successful the statute envisages an order requiring the withdrawal of the paragraph 6(3) notice[1] so as to return control of practice monies to the solicitor, and an order directing the SRA to deliver the practice documents to such person as the solicitor claimant may require. In addition, the court probably has jurisdiction to restore the suspended practising certificate to the solicitor,[2] and in *Sheikh v Law Society*,[3] the judge at first instance imposed a condition on the successful claimant's practising certificate.

The statutory scheme set out in Schedule 1 to SA 1974 cannot be replaced by a judge-made scheme. There is no 'half-way house': the court must either direct or decline to direct withdrawal of the intervention[4] (although the court's power to make consequential orders should enable it to ensure that the SRA is able to exercise proper regulatory control over the solicitor in the light of the facts found by the court).

There is no statutory entitlement to damages at the suit of the successful solicitor if the challenge succeeds. Whether damages may be awarded at common law, under SA 1974 or under HRA 1998, has not been decided and may well depend upon the court's view as to whether the decision to intervene was justified at the time it was made.

1   *Holder v Law Society* [2003] EWCA Civ 39, [2003] 3 All ER 62; *Sritharan v Law Society* [2005] EWCA Civ 476, [2005] 4 All ER 1105.
2   *Sritharan v Law Society* [2005] EWCA Civ 476, [2005] 4 All ER 1105.
3   [2006] EWCA Civ 1577, [2007] 3 All ER 183.
4   *Sritharan v Law Society* [2005] EWCA Civ 476, [2005] 4 All ER 1105.

Alternatives to intervention

17.22

In recent years the SRA has increasingly sought to find alternatives to intervention, principally because the cost of intervention is high and recovery of this from the solicitor is uncertain. The SRA is more willing than hitherto to achieve tight regulatory control over a solicitor who would otherwise have been subject to an intervention by means of the imposition of stringent conditions on his practising certificate. Alternatively, the SRA may permit the orderly disposal of the practice. The SRA may be prepared to enter into a regulatory settlement whereby the solicitor agrees to close his firm within a set period, or to correct errors in the firm's accounts and provide independent evidence of the accounts being compliant, or to seek medical treatment and provide independent evidence, for example, as to an addiction being overcome (see **20.18** as to regulatory settlements generally).

Orderly closure

17.23

There are a number of instances when a practice may be required to close, for example:

● retirement;

● ill health or death of a sole practitioner (where there is no special executorship clause in a will);

● financial restructure;

- compulsory PI insurance cannot be obtained; or

- to avoid an intervention by the SRA because:

  - the practice is not financially viable; or

  - the practice is no longer authorised by the SRA, for example as a result of a decision to revoke authorisation or following restrictive practising certificate conditions.

For regulatory and insurance purposes closure takes place when a regulated entity ceases to conduct work for clients. This is not the same as revocation of SRA authorisation – see **17.26** or the winding up of the entity. There is likely to be a lapse of time between the practice ceasing to engage in fee earning work, revocation of authorisation, and the winding up of the entity.

From the point of closure, the practice cannot engage in fee earning work and its activities are restricted to recovery of fees and effecting a closure programme. Failure to adhere to the restriction on undertaking client work will revoke the practice's run-off insurance provision and imposes an obligation to obtain a new PI insurance policy. Even responding to a query from HM Land Registry is likely to constitute practice and thus be an insurable activity. Therefore it is important to plan ahead for closure.

It is prudent to consider the possibility of selling the practice rather than closing. It is often cheaper to do so, not least as a result of the impact of liability for run-off indemnity insurance; and it is less disruptive for staff and clients. However, the very same insurance factor will inhibit potential purchasers; if they become a successor practice (see **11.9** including commentary on how this can be avoided), the acquiring firm's insurers are liable for any possible negligence claims of the prior practice.

When planning ahead for closure the practice will need to consider how best it can service its creditors at a time when the only income will be payment for work undertaken prior to closure. The advice of an insolvency practitioner may be required. It will be necessary to control overheads and manage redundancies, among other things. If the firm is a legal aid practice the LAA should become involved at an early stage, to manage both the transfer of cases and payments on account.

The procedure to be followed upon closure varies from practice to practice, reflecting factors such as the regulated entity's legal status (limited liability company, limited liability partnership (LLP) or traditional partnership), the complexity of the structure of the practice, the practice's relationships with third parties and its obligations to clients. No two practices are the same and each closure will have its challenges.

Informing the SRA

17.24

When a practice becomes aware of an intention to close, or that it will close, it is required to inform the SRA promptly.[1] Currently, notice takes the form of an application to be made using the firm's mySRA account. In an acquisition or merger, the form asks for details of each of the authorised bodies which have taken over the practice and a manager whom the SRA can contact; and in any event, the date the firm or authorised body has stopped or will stop holding or receiving client money, the firm's plans to distribute current client files, the details of residual balances and outstanding undertakings, the number of closed client files, wills and deeds and storage details, details of any other authorised body where files will be stored and details of a manager whom former clients or third parties can contact in relation to files.[2]

If the firm is the subject of an SRA investigation, it is best practice to write to the SRA officer setting out a fuller closure programme, addressing procedures for remedying any breaches of Accounts Rules or other rules, and otherwise for dealing with current client matters, the client bank account, accounting requirements, relationships with third parties and the storage of archived files. The SRA may accept this but may also seek to impose its own terms, as above. If the programme is accepted (with or without amendments) the SRA will expect to receive regular reports on progress.

Indeed, whether there is an investigation or not, the SRA may impose obligations on a closing firm in the form of a 'compliance plan', and can insist on its terms with a threat of intervention as an alternative. Although the circumstances in which this will occur will inevitably be fraught and pressured, it is extremely important that the terms of the required plan are considered with care. The terms are likely to incorporate undertakings, express or implied, as to the achievement of targets, for example to reduce the client account to a nil balance. A failure to achieve a target has been treated by the SRA as a breach of undertaking and potentially a disciplinary matter. It is important only to accept obligations which are achievable. If necessary it may be desirable to seek specialist advice. Indeed anyone facing pressure to close a solicitors' practice is likely to benefit from specialist advice.

1   Paragraph 3.6(c) of the SRA Code of Conduct for Firms 2019 (the 'Code for Firms'); note also that paragraph 7.6(c)(i) of the SRA Code of Conduct for Solicitors, RELs and RFLs 2019 (the 'Code for Individuals') also requires ceasing freelancers to notify the SRA.
2   www.sra.org.uk/solicitors/firm-based-authorisation/firm-closures.

The closure process

17.25

Clients must be contacted promptly with information as to the proposed closure, and to make arrangements concerning the collection of their files, stored documents and client funds or their transfer to another practice.[1] This may be stressful for clients and the firm will have to determine how this is best done bearing in mind the nature of its clients, their degree of vulnerability and their chosen method of communication. Clients must be advised that they are free to choose a solicitor of their choice although it is permissible to indicate that a client would be welcome to join principals or fee earners in any new practices they may have joined, save that if that firm is not regulated by the SRA, the closing firm must ensure that the client is able to make an informed decision, for example, by explaining the differences in regulatory protection. Clients' consent is required before their files (and any money held for clients) are transferred to another firm.

Client account balances need to be returned or transferred as instructed. If the practice has historical dormant balances any gradual process being followed to deal with such matters will have to be accelerated. Every effort should be made to reduce the client account to a nil balance, and this should receive priority as soon as a decision is made to close (as to dealing with dormant balances see **6.27**). Client money received after closure must be dealt with in accordance with rule 2.5 of the SRA Accounts Rules 2019 – see **CHAPTER 6**.

SRA guidance[2] notes that the court has accepted that solicitors who do not have a practising certificate may sign a bill of costs for work done when they did have such a certificate, but this must be made clear on the bill.[3]

Archived files can be returned to clients, stored or, where permitted, destroyed. If files are stored then the SRA must be advised of their whereabouts – therefore, if the address provided on application changes, the new address should be communicated to the SRA. There have been situations where intervention has taken place in respect of archived files alone, which remain client property pending their destruction. Firms should bear in mind that the security of client confidential information is paramount. Firms should also consider their data protection obligations.

Upon closure the practice must accurately indicate its new status. The practice's letterhead, website, emails and all other material will need to be adapted. Incoming telephone calls should be greeted with a message indicating the closure and who can be contacted for guidance. A notice of closure should be advertised in the *London Gazette* and a local newspaper. All regulated persons should make necessary amendments to their 'mySRA' account.

The practice must inform its PI insurer of the intended closure as closure triggers the run-off provisions in its contract of insurance. The practice must pay the contractual run-off premium as set out in the schedule of insurance. The practice's insurer is often the largest creditor in a solvent closure. If the practice is not in a financial position to make the payment, it is sometimes possible to negotiate a reduced premium. This is an area in which specialist advice can be sought. For commentary on the insurance obligations of a closing firm see **CHAPTER 11**.

Unless the firm is exempt from the requirement to obtain an accountant's report under rule 12.2 of the SRA Accounts Rules 2019, it must continue to obtain (and, if required under rule 12.1(b), to deliver) yearly accountant's reports until such time as it ceases to hold client money (rule 12.1 of the Accounts Rules).

The SRA should be notified of the date upon which the firm ceases to hold all client money. SRA guidance indicates that in most cases, the firm will not be expected to obtain or deliver a final report; however the power to require one to be obtained and delivered arises under rule 12.4 of the Accounts Rules.

The process of closure and the examination of all files in the practice not infrequently gives rise to the discovery of problems not previously identified which will need to be reported to insurers and possibly to the SRA by either the compliance officer for legal practice (COLP) or the compliance officer for finance and administration (COFA), who will retain their responsibilities throughout (see **CHAPTER 7**). Some level of complaint from clients, including opportunistic complaints, should be anticipated. Principals may continue to be liable in respect of awards by the Legal Ombudsman (LeO) despite closure of the practice (see **14.9**).

Responsibility for compliance with undertakings does not cease with the closure of a practice and the firm and its relevant individuals will continue to be liable in respect of any undertakings given.

The practice should consider the existence of any laws and regulations requiring certain documents to be retained for specified periods. For example, as noted in SRA guidance, there are obligations under rule 8.1 of the Financial Services (Conduct of Business) Rules and rule 13.1 of the Accounts Rules to retain records for a period of at least six years, the Money Laundering, Terrorist Financing and Transfer of Funds (Information on the Payer) Regulations 2017[4] (MLR 2017), and for VAT purposes. Additionally, the SRA recommends retaining evidence of clients' consent to the retention of commission (presumably beyond the minimum periods for retention of client files).

The SRA's guidance[5] also includes checklists of persons to notify, and actions to take.

1   Paragraphs 8.6 and 8.11 of the Code for Individuals.
2   SRA guidance, 'Closing down your practice', updated 25 November 2019.
3   *Connolly v Liverpool City Council; SRA intervening* Liverpool County Court, HH Judge Stewart QC Claim No 7LV11622 (Appeal No 185/08) 20 August 2009.
4   SI 2017/692.
5   SRA guidance, 'Closing down your practice', updated 25 November 2019.

Revocation of SRA authorisation

17.26

Post notification of closure, a firm ceases to be authorised by the SRA when its authorisation is revoked. Application for revocation is made to the SRA on the prescribed form in the firm's 'mySRA' account, under rule 4.3(e) of the SRA Authorisation of Firms Rules. The SRA may refuse the application if the applicant is subject to any proceedings, investigation or consideration of their conduct or practice by the SRA or the Tribunal. When applying for revocation, the principals will normally be winding up the entity, although there is nothing to prevent the entity, following such revocation, subject to compliance with other obligations (for example, transparency), to continue in existence, with the same employed solicitors, without undertaking regulated legal activities.

Limited intervention

17.27

This form of intervention is of a very different character and for very different purposes and is almost entirely unrelated to the matters discussed above.

It is designed solely to recover from a solicitor a file or files relating to specific matters, either for the purposes of the file(s) being handed to clients or for the purposes of inspection by the SRA to assist in the investigation of complaints or regulatory concerns, respectively.

It may occur in two circumstances. The first is concerned exclusively with delay, and is somewhat convoluted. If the SRA is satisfied that there has been undue delay in connection with any matter in which the solicitor or his firm is or was acting on behalf of a client or with any trust, or by any employee of a solicitor in connection with a trust of which the employee is or was a trustee in his capacity as such an employee, and the solicitor has been invited to give an explanation in answer to the complaint within a specified period[1] and:

- the solicitor fails within that period to give an explanation which is regarded as satisfactory;

- notice has been given to the solicitor of the fact that he has failed to give a satisfactory explanation; and

- either then or later a notice is given that the powers of intervention are exercisable for those reasons

the SRA may 'intervene' in the solicitor's practice for the limited purpose of recovering the file or files in question, and for that purpose only.[2] In this event the file(s) will be obtained and handed to the client or to successor solicitors appointed by the client, so that the problems encountered as a result of the unexplained delays are overcome.

The second circumstance arises if a decision is made to require the solicitor to produce a file or files for inspection by the SRA for the purposes of an investigation;[3] the powers of intervention can be employed to compel the delivery up of such file(s).[4] The documents required in these circumstances will be all the documents in the possession of the solicitor or his firm relevant to the matter under investigation.

In either event the procedure is the same: an agent of the SRA is appointed, usually a solicitor on the SRA's Intervention Panel or a member of the staff of the SRA. The solicitor is given notice of the time and date on which the agent will attend at his offices for the purposes of collecting the file or files, and the agent is instructed to collect the file or files accordingly. Such limited interventions generally occur only after an unsuccessful attempt has been made to persuade the solicitor to deliver up the file(s) voluntarily.

Because these powers are part of the intervention regime the statutory powers of the High Court are available and in the event of non-co-operation on the part of the solicitor an application could be made by the SRA for an order to compel delivery. One would naturally expect this to be an extremely rare occurrence.[5]

1   Paragraph 3 of Schedule 1 to SA 1974 requires not less than eight days' notice.
2   Paragraph 3 of Schedule 1 to SA 1974.
3   Section 44B(1) of SA 1974.
4   Section 44B(6).
5   *Stevenson*, 7814–1999, SDT details an example of its use. See also *Law Society of England & Wales (SRA) v Sophie Khan and Co Ltd* [2021] EWHC 2 (Ch) for an SRA application to court seeking enforcement of a production order issued pursuant to section 44B of SA 1974 and *SRA v Soophia Khan (1) and Sophie Khan & Co Ltd (2)* [2021] EWHC 2721 (Ch) for an SRA application (1) to search and seize relevant practice documents and (2) redirect to the SRA communications addressed to the defendant.

Control of solicitors' employees and consultants

18.1

Originally through the Solicitors Act (SA) 1974 and its predecessors, Parliament provided regulatory powers to the Law Society and the Solicitors Disciplinary Tribunal (the Tribunal or SDT) to enable the control of non-solicitors who work in solicitors' firms, and who may abuse their position. The rationale for the existence of these powers is the need to protect those who deal with solicitors, and to safeguard the reputation of the profession. The Legal Services Act (LSA) 2007 promotes the concept of firm- or business entity-based regulation so that all managers and employees of regulated practices are now subject to personal regulation by virtue of their employment, whether or not they are legally qualified. In consequence, regulation of solicitors' employees now takes four forms: (1) statutory restrictions on the employment of certain disqualified persons, for example, former solicitors who have been struck off (see **18.2** and **18.3**); (2) the making of orders that control the employment of non-solicitors guilty of material misconduct (see **18.4–18.10** and **18.12**); (3) direct disciplinary control of employees of regulated practices (see **18.11**); and (4) other regulatory powers **18.13**.

Restriction on employment of persons struck off or suspended

18.2

Solicitors may not, in connection with their practice as a solicitor, employ or remunerate persons who to their knowledge have been disqualified from acting as solicitors through being struck off or suspended from practice, save with the written permission of the Solicitors Regulation Authority (SRA). The SRA may grant permission for such period and subject to such conditions as it thinks fit.[1]

Until 31 March 2009, section 41(4) of SA 1974 provided a mandatory penalty of suspension or striking off for any solicitor found to have acted in breach of this prohibition. There were originally two offences attracting a mandatory penalty: acting as an agent for an unqualified person in court proceedings (section 39 of SA 1974 which was repealed in full in 1991, so removing the statutory offence as well as the mandatory penalty); and employing or remunerating a struck off or suspended solicitor without written permission. LSA 2007 retained the statutory offence but removed the mandatory penalty. In *Re a Solicitor (Rosen)*,[2] the Divisional Court requested and was provided with a schedule of penalties imposed upon solicitors for breaches of section 41. There was a wide range, some suspensions being for a few days only, sometimes being timed to coincide with holidays already arranged by the solicitor concerned or (in the case of a number of partners all requiring to be sentenced) being staggered so as to minimise disruption to the practice concerned.[3]

In these instances, the Tribunal had plainly felt that little or no moral blame attached to the solicitors in question, and would not have suspended them in the absence of the mandatory provision. At the other end of the spectrum were solicitors who had been struck off for deliberately flouting the statutory provisions. The removal of the mandatory penalty enables the Tribunal more effectively to tailor the penalty to the breach.

It is important to appreciate that a breach of section 41 is a strict liability offence. All that is required is (1) that the solicitor knows the true status of the employee, namely that he or she has been struck off or suspended; and (2) that, as a matter of fact, the written permission of the Law Society/SRA has not been obtained (or that conditions imposed on the grant of permission have not been met). It does not provide a defence, for example, to show that one partner had responsibility for making the employment arrangements and reassured all other partners that there was no compliance issue, and they reasonably relied on that reassurance.[4] It has even happened that a struck off solicitor has forged the permission; the employing solicitor was still guilty of the offence.[5] Indeed, this serves to reinforce the point that the employer, and not the proposed employee, must obtain the necessary SRA permission.

1 Section 41 of SA 1974.
2 [2004] EWHC 907 (Admin).
3 Cases in which this sort of leniency was shown include *McMillan*, 5740-1989, SDT; *Cunnew*, 6134-1992, SDT; and *Coxall*, 8401-2001, SDT.
4 *Coxall*, 8401-2001, SDT.
5 *Awoloye-Kio*, 8940-2003, SDT.

18.3

The Tribunal has also emphasised that an employer's wilful ignorance of the true status of the employee could lead to a breach of this provision:

> 'The Tribunal take the view that a solicitor can only claim not to have knowledge of a striking off order if he has first made appropriate enquiries. Total ignorance as a result of a total failure to make the enquiries which a prudent solicitor employer would make is not a state of knowledge but a state of deliberate ignorance.'[1]

As this is a statutory offence to be construed by reference to the precise words of the section this conclusion must be open to some doubt. Nevertheless, it is apparent that the Tribunal will strive to give a purposive construction to the section to meet the perceived mischief:

> 'The Tribunal accept that the mischief which section 41 seeks to avert is the handling of clients' affairs in a solicitors office by a struck off solicitor except in circumstances where he is subject to strict controls. It is clear that the constraints are imposed to protect the interests of the public and maintain the good name of the solicitors' profession.'[2]

The Tribunal's interpretation and purposive construction of the rule was endorsed in *Ramasamy v SRA:*[3]

> 'It is necessary for the protection of the public and for public confidence in the solicitors' profession that a struck off solicitor should not be enabled to provide (or to purport to provide) legal services to the public by reason of an apparent association with a legitimate firm of solicitors.'[4]

The words 'employ or remunerate' have been construed widely. In *Cunnew*, 'keeping busy' or 'occupied' and the payment of expenses were deemed sufficient:

> 'The Tribunal consider that "employment" should be construed in the wider sense of "keeping busy" or "keeping occupied". It follows from that that payment of a wage is not essential to establish employment. The intention of section 41 is that struck off solicitors be kept out of solicitors offices save in exceptional and closely regulated cases. Although not argued before them, the Tribunal believe it is useful to add that in its view the word "remunerate" should also be interpreted in its widest sense so that it not only means "to reward" or "to pay for services" but also "to provide recompense for". The payment of out of pocket expenses by the respondent was therefore remuneration.'[5]

In *Ramasamy v SRA*,[6] it was held that being afforded the facility to provide services was sufficient, even though there was no direct financial remuneration and the individual was not employed by the firm:

> 'A struck off solicitor who is afforded facilities at such a firm which enables or assists him to provide such services, apparently on behalf of the firm in question, can properly be regarded as employed by the firm even in the absence of a contract of employment. He can properly be regarded as remunerated by the firm if the provision of such facilities represents a benefit to him even if he receives no financial payment.'

Section 41 has been deployed by the SRA in one additional and highly unusual situation, against a former solicitor involved in a solicitors' practice, rather than against an employer. In *Law Society v Shah*[7] the defendant was a struck off former solicitor who continued to involve himself in solicitors' firms and there were non-conclusive indications that he continued to hold himself out as a solicitor. He was regarded as particularly dangerous, having allegedly misappropriated over £8 million in client funds and having served a term of imprisonment for mortgage fraud. The SRA sought an injunction on a *quia timet* basis to prevent him continuing to associate with solicitors' firms. It was held that section 41(4)(c) (which allowed the SDT or the High Court to 'make such other order in the matter as it thinks fit') was sufficiently widely drawn as to enable the court to grant the requested injunction.

1   *Cunnew*, 6134-1992, SDT.
2   *Cunnew*, 6134-1992, SDT.
3   [2018] EWHC 117 (Admin).
4   At [29].
5   *Cunnew*, 6134-1992, SDT.
6   [2018] EWHC 117 (Admin) at [29].
7   [2014] EWHC 4382 (Ch).

Control of solicitors' employees and consultants

18.4

Naturally, unadmitted employees and consultants involved in legal practice do not have practising certificates. The SRA's ability to control (or prevent) the employment in legal practice of such individuals is limited to situations where it (or, upon application, the Tribunal) finds, in certain circumstances, that it is 'undesirable' for them to be involved in a legal practice. If such a finding is made, they can be made the subject of one or more of the orders set out in section 43(2) of SA 1974. Such orders are commonly known as section 43 orders).[1]

Following a finding of 'undesirability' of the individual concerned, the order prevents all solicitors from employing or remunerating, in connection with their practice as solicitors, the individual in question (except in accordance with permission in writing granted by the SRA for such period and subject to such conditions as the SRA may think fit). The order can also prevent any employee of a solicitor from employing or remunerating the individual in relation to legal practice, and can prevent an individual from being a manager of or having an interest in a legal practice.[2]

Such orders, whether made by the SRA or the Tribunal, are deemed regulatory rather than disciplinary in nature, and despite the apparent 'undesirability' of their involvement, will not act to prohibit the individual from working for a solicitor.[3] In *Gregory*,[4] Treacy J stated that:

> 'Section 43 is not punitive in nature. It is there to protect the public, to provide safeguards and to exercise control over those who work for solicitors, in circumstances where there is necessity for such control shown by their past conduct. Its purpose is to maintain the good reputation of, and maintain confidence in, the solicitors' profession. An order made under section 43 does not prohibit a person from working for a solicitor. The requirement is that the Law Society's permission should be obtained so that they can scrutinise the circumstances in which such a person is to be employed.'

In practice, and in the absence of other direct powers of control over such individuals, this rather blunt instrument is seemingly now employed whenever the SRA deems that an unadmitted employee of a legal practice should face some regulatory control. In *SRA v Green & Bishop*,[5] the misconduct did not make it undesirable for the unadmitted first respondent to be involved in legal practice, and the Tribunal declined to make such an order (despite a number of allegations being admitted and found proven). The Tribunal's alternative powers were limited to imposing a fine or otherwise requiring the SRA to consider taking certain steps[6] and it ordered that the SRA should consider issuing the unadmitted first respondent with a rebuke.[7]

It seems that the SRA will consider it appropriate to make the order itself at the authorised decision stage if there has been a conviction or there is no dispute as to the facts, and will make an application to the Tribunal for an order when there is likely to be a dispute of fact or other factor justifying an oral hearing, or when the employing solicitor also faces Tribunal proceedings arising from the same facts. In either event, an appeal lies to the Tribunal by way of review (see **18.10**).[8]

---

1   By section 43(1A)(e) and (f) of SA 1974 such orders may also be made in respect of a manager of a recognised body, and a person that has or intends to acquire an interest in such a body.
2   Section 43(2).
3   *Gregory v The Law Society* [2007] EWHC 1724 (Admin), and *SRA v Ali* [2013] EWHC 2584 (Admin).
4   *Gregory v The Law Society* [2007] EWHC 1724 (Admin) at [18].
5   12105-2020, SDT.
6   Section 47(2E) of SA 1974.
7   The SRA is empowered to do so by section 44D of SA 1974.
8   Section 43(3).

The statutory grounds for an order

18.5

There are two statutory grounds for making a section 43 order: (a) criminal convictions, and (b) certain acts or defaults while working in a legal practice.

Criminal convictions

18.6

The order may be made when the person concerned has been convicted of a criminal offence which is such that, in the opinion of the SRA, it would be undesirable for him to be involved in legal practice.[1]

SRA guidance indicates that it will not always decide that it is necessary to impose a section 43 order on the basis of a conviction, acknowledging the duty to decide whether, as a result of the conviction, it is undesirable for the individual to be involved in legal practice in the future. The term 'undesirable' is not defined and the guidance indicates that the SRA will apply its natural meaning, exercising its judgement in deciding whether the order is appropriate. In doing so, it offers the following guidance on factors that it will take into account:

'● The type of offence. If it involves dishonesty, of any sort, we are likely to consider a s43 Order is appropriate. This is because of the risk the behaviour will be repeated in the workplace, causing harm to clients. However, we may also impose a s43 Order for other types of criminal offences such as a conviction for causing Grievous Bodily Harm. We might do this if we consider that either there is risk of repetition of such conduct in the workplace, or if the conviction is likely to damage public confidence in the delivery of legal services.

● The seriousness of the criminal offence. As above, we will consider whether the offence is likely to damage public confidence in the delivery of legal services. In deciding the level of seriousness, we look at the sentence given, such as whether a custodial sentence was imposed, and any sentencing remarks given by the judge.

● The circumstances in which the offence took place. For example, we are likely to consider it more undesirable for you to be involved in a law firm we regulate if the victim of the offence was vulnerable. This is because of the damage such an offence would cause to public confidence and the risk of you abusing any position of trust by working in a law firm or with a solicitor in the future.'[2]

1 Section 43(1)(a) of SA 1974.
2 SRA guidance, 'How we regulate non-authorised persons', 25 November 2019.

Acts or defaults while working in a legal practice

18.7

The order may also be made when the person concerned has 'occasioned or been a party to, with or without the connivance of a solicitor, an act or default in relation to a legal practice which involved conduct on his part of such a nature that in the opinion of the [SRA] it would be undesirable for him to be involved in a legal practice'.[1]

This somewhat convoluted subsection requires the SRA or the Tribunal to answer two essential questions:

(1)   Has the person concerned occasioned an act or default which involved conduct on their part of such a nature that it would be undesirable for them to be involved in a legal practice?

(2)   If so, was that act or default occasioned in relation to a legal practice?

The two subsections must be construed independently of each other. Section 43(1)(a) requires there to have been a criminal conviction, but subsection (b) does not require similar or equivalent conduct. An order under section 43(1)(b) can be founded upon foolishness, recklessness or errors of judgement if the consequence is that it is undesirable for the individual concerned to work in a legal practice.[2]

However, conduct that warrants the issue of a rebuke may not be sufficient for the Tribunal to make such an order.[3]

The statutory jurisdiction did not (as originally enacted) extend to a situation in which the party alleged to be at fault remunerated himself, purporting to be an employee of a solicitor but in fact being his own employer in a sham arrangement;[4] however, the section as amended by LSA 2007 is probably sufficiently wide to overcome this difficulty.

It is noteworthy that the individual's conduct in his or her private life, unconnected with legal practice, which does not result in a criminal conviction, cannot be relied upon to make a section 43 order. The SRA has acknowledged this position in guidance.[5] The guidance indicates that it will take into account conduct that calls into question the individual's character and ethics, including behaviour which:

'●   is unacceptable in view of a client's expectation of a trustworthy and reliable service

●   demonstrates a serious lack of judgment given your position or role

●   brings into doubt your ability to make sound and competent decisions in a client's best interests

●   demonstrates impropriety or unethical behaviour.'

The SRA and the Tribunal have, respectively, the power to make orders for costs when exercising this jurisdiction.[6]

---

1   Section 43(1)(b) of SA 1974.
2   See *Ojelade v Law Society* [2006] EWHC 2210 (Admin); and, particularly, *Gregory v Law Society* [2007] EWHC 1724 (Admin).
3   *SRA v Green & Bishop*, 12105-2020, SDT – see **18.4**.
4   *Izegbu and Okoronkwo v Law Society* [2008] EWHC 1043 (Admin).
5   SRA guidance, 'How we regulate non-authorised persons', 25 November 2019.
6   Section 43(2A) and (4) of SA 1974.

The procedure

18.8

The SRA may make an order under section 43 to control the person's activities in connection with legal practice or decide to make an application to the Tribunal for the allegation to be considered by the Tribunal.[1] The SRA also has power to apply a range of other disciplinary and regulatory sanctions against employees including rebukes, fines and disqualifications (see **18.11**).[2] The SRA may disclose or publish information relating to an investigation where the public interest outweighs other circumstances[3] and may impose a charge of up to £1,350 for the first 16 hours of its investigation, and further charges at the rate of £75 per hour thereafter for such further time rounded up or down to the nearest half-hour.[4]

Before deciding to apply to the Tribunal for an order in respect of an unadmitted employee (or indeed a solicitor), the SRA must determine whether there is a realistic prospect of the Tribunal making an order.[5]

1 Rule 3.1(d) and (g) of the SRA Regulatory and Disciplinary Procedure Rules 2019 (the 'Disciplinary Rules 2019').
2 Rule 3.1(a)–(c) of the Disciplinary Rules 2019.
3 Rules 9.1 and 9.2. Currently, the SRA publishes decisions against unadmitted individuals on the 'Check a solicitor's record' page of its website.
4 Rule 10.1 of and Schedule 1 to the Disciplinary Rules 2019.
5 Rule 6.1. It must also be in the public interest to make an application.

The standard of proof

18.9

The Disciplinary Rules 2019 provide that the SRA will apply the civil standard of proof[1] to the exercise of its powers under section 43 of SA 1974.[2] The SDT will also apply the civil standard in respect of all proceedings considered under its Rules,[3] that is, those in respect of applications made on or after 25 November 2019.[4]

For applications that were made to the Tribunal prior to 25 November 2019, the civil standard applied to reviews of SRA-made section 43 orders,[5] whereas the criminal standard applied to applications to the Tribunal where the SRA had not made a section 43 order.[6]

In the past the Tribunal had held that the standard of proof should be the criminal standard, whoever makes the decision. That position was no longer sustainable in so far as it concerned decisions made by the SRA rather than the Tribunal, following *SRA v Solicitors' Disciplinary Tribunal, Arslan Interested Party*,[7] when the SRA appealed to the High Court against decisions made by the SDT in respect of a Mr Arslan. An SRA adjudicator had made a section 43 order against, and imposed a fine upon, Mr Arslan: both decisions had been quashed on appeal by the SDT. Whereas the adjudicator had adopted the civil standard of proof in accordance with the SRA Disciplinary Procedure Rules 2011, the SDT had adopted the criminal standard of proof in accordance with its own long-standing practice, when dealing with the appeals.

On the further appeal to the High Court, the court held that it had been plainly appropriate for the SRA adjudicator to have adopted the civil standard in accordance with the 2011 Rules which had statutory effect, and that in carrying out a review on the appeal (which should not involve the finding of any facts by the Tribunal), the SDT was not entitled to apply its own, different, standard of proof. Although the court was invited by the SRA to give an opinion as to the standard of proof which the SDT should apply in cases in which it is the primary fact-finder, the court declined to do so. Both judges (Sir Brian Leveson P and Leggatt J) considered that the authorities which supported adoption of the criminal standard by the SDT when it sits in its fact-finding capacity were ripe for reconsideration.[8] As indicated above, since 25 November 2019, the SDT has adopted the civil standard.

1   Rule 8.7 of the Disciplinary Rules 2019.
2   Rules 1.2(d) and 3.1(d) of the Disciplinary Rules 2019.
3   Rule 5 of the Solicitors (Disciplinary Proceedings) Rules 2019 (SI 2019/1185) (the '2019 Rules').
4   Rule 51 of the 2019 Rules.
5   Rule 3.1(d) of the Disciplinary Rules 2019.
6   Rule 3.1(g) of the Disciplinary Rules 2019.
7   [2016] EWHC 2862 (Admin).
8   See at [49] (Leggatt J) and [73] (Sir Brian Leveson P).

Appeals and reviews

18.10

The SRA and the Tribunal can revoke their own decision to make a section 43 order,[1] for example, because it is no longer required as the individual has been employed in the profession without further fault for an appropriate period of time. The Disciplinary Rules 2019 state that an application may be made to the SRA for a section 43 order to cease to apply 'where there has been a material change in circumstances'.[2]

If the order was made by the Tribunal any application for revocation is made to the Tribunal.[3] As indicated at **18.4**, a person aggrieved by an order made by the SRA can apply to the Tribunal for a review of that order and the Tribunal can quash it, vary it or confirm it.[4] An order made by the Tribunal can be appealed to the High Court.[5] The High Court has power to make such order on an appeal as it thinks fit. Any decision of the High Court is final and there is no further appeal.[6]

In *SRA v Ali*[7] a decision by the SDT to revoke an order was overturned because the Tribunal had wrongly focused its attention upon the individual's (unsuccessful) attempts to obtain the necessary experience of working directly under supervision so as to rehabilitate himself, whereas it ought to have asked itself whether the order remained necessary to safeguard the public and the reputation of the profession.

1   Section 43(3)(b) of SA 1974.
2   Rule 7.1 of the Disciplinary Rules 2019.
3   Section 43(3) of SA 1974.
4   Section 43(3A).
5   Section 49(1).
6   Section 49(6).
7   [2013] EWHC 2584 (Admin) at [41].

Disciplinary control of employees

18.11

LSA 2007 amended SA 1974 by adding sections 34A, 44D, 44E and subsection 47(2E).

Section 34A enables the SRA to provide that the rules of professional conduct 'have effect in relation to employees of solicitors with such additions, omissions or other modifications as appear to the [SRA] to be necessary or expedient'. With effect from 31 March 2009 the SRA amended the Solicitors' Code of Conduct 2007 and other professional rules (including the Solicitors' Accounts Rules 1998) to make clear that it regulates not only solicitors but also the employees of solicitors, registered European lawyers (RELs) and their employees, registered foreign lawyers (RFLs), recognised bodies (including authorised sole practitioners) and their managers and employees. The 2011 SRA Handbook and the 2019 regulatory arrangements have maintained this position.

The extension of such regulatory arrangements to employees of solicitors means that, in certain circumstances, the conduct of such individuals in their private life, unconnected with legal practice, may be sanctioned by the SRA. This contrasts with the SRA's powers to make a section 43 order. The SRA has acknowledged this in guidance.[1]

Section 44D enables the SRA to impose a written rebuke or a fine not exceeding £2,000[2] on an employee of a solicitor who has failed to comply with a requirement imposed by or by virtue of SA 1974 or any rules made by the SRA,[3] and, where it is in the public interest to do so, may publish such a decision.[4] Any fine imposed does not become payable, and the SRA may not publish decisions, until the earliest of the expiry of the time limit for an appeal, determination or withdrawal of an appeal.[5]

Obligated by section 44D(7) of SA 1974, the SRA introduced rules to regulate these powers. The current rules are the Disciplinary Rules 2019,[6] which we address in **Chapters 15** and **20**.

By section 44E(1), an employee of a solicitor who is the subject of a decision made pursuant to section 44D may appeal to the Tribunal against an SRA rebuke (but only if a decision is also made to publish details of it), a penalty (or the amount of it), and/or a decision to publish a section 44D sanction. On appeal, the Tribunal has power to make such order as it thinks fit, and such an order may, in particular, affirm or revoke the decision of the SRA, vary the amount of the penalty, make an order under section 47(2E) – see below, or make such provision as the Tribunal thinks fit as to payment of costs.[7]

Section 47(2E) of SA 1974 extends the Tribunal's jurisdiction to the employees of solicitors. LSA 2007 also amended Schedule 2 to the Administration of Justice Act (AJA) 1985 (which relates to incorporated practices or 'recognised bodies') to give the same powers to the Tribunal in relation to managers and employees of recognised bodies.

In relation to managers and employees, the Tribunal may:

- impose a fine, unlimited in amount, payable to the Treasury;[8]

- require the SRA to take such steps in relation to the relevant person as the Tribunal may specify;[9]

- control the employment of the relevant person under section 43 of SA 1974;[10] and/or

- order the SRA to refer the conduct of the relevant person to an appropriate regulator.[11] An 'appropriate regulator' would be the relevant approved regulator authorised under LSA 2007 if the manager or employee is an authorised person in relation to a reserved legal activity (eg a barrister or licensed conveyancer) or any body which regulates the activities actually undertaken by the person concerned, if he or she was not an authorised person for LSA 2007 purposes.[12]

Appeals from the Tribunal are made to the High Court. Upon such an appeal, the court has power to make such order as it thinks fit, and the court's decision is final.[13]

The definition of 'employee' was considered in *Solicitors Regulation Authority v Solicitors' Disciplinary Tribunal, Arslan Interested Party*.[14] Mr Arslan was a consultant to a firm of solicitors; he was not employed by them. The SRA imposed upon him a written rebuke and fine of £500. Upon Mr Arslan's appeal, the Tribunal revoked the rebuke and fine, finding that unadmitted consultants working in legal practice, as distinct from employees, did not fall within the SRA's disciplinary powers. The SRA, whose rules defined the term 'employee' so as to include consultants, appealed to the High Court. Leggatt J in upholding the decision of the Tribunal, found that it was not permissible to use delegated legislation to define the scope of primary legislation. He found it instructive that whereas section 43 of SA 1974 referred to both 'solicitors' employees and consultants', section 44D referred only to 'employees of solicitors'. Additionally, Leggatt J acknowledged the consequent gap in protection, but found that this was intended by Parliament, and that given the powers available under section 43 of SA 1974, it was not significant.[15]

The SRA has since acknowledged this position in guidance, adding that it does not have the power to discipline unadmitted employees of a freelance solicitor delivering only non-reserved legal activities and so operating under regulation 10.2(a) of the Authorisation of Individuals Regulations.[16]

---

1   SRA guidance, 'How we regulate non-authorised persons, 25 November 2019.
2   Section 44D(2) of SA 1974.
3   Section 44D(1).
4   Section 44D(3).
5   Section 44D(5) and (6).
6   See rules 1.2(c), 3.1(a), (b) in particular concerning employees of solicitors.
7   Section 44E(4) of SA 1974.
8   Section 47(2E)(a) of SA 1974; para 18A(2)(a) of Schedule 2 to AJA 1985.
9   Section 47(2E)(b) of SA 1974; para 18A(2)(b) of Schedule 2 to AJA 1985.
10 Section 47(2E)(c) of SA 1974; para 18A(2)(c) of Schedule 2 to AJA 1985.
11 Section 47(2E)(d) of SA 1974; para 18A(2)(d) of Schedule 2 to AJA 1985.
12 Section 47(2H) of SA 1974; para 18A(7) of Schedule 2 to AJA 1985.
13 Section 44E(6)–(8).
14 [2016] EWHC 2862 (Admin).
15 At [25]–[37].
16 SRA guidance, 'How we regulate non-authorised persons', 25 November 2019.

Licensed bodies

18.12

Section 99 of LSA 2007 gives the SRA power to disqualify an individual from being an employee or a licensed body (an ABS), or from taking up certain activities, such as acting as a manager, the Head of Legal Practice (HOLP) or the Head of Finance and Administration (HOFA), where (a) the disqualification condition is satisfied and (b) it is deemed undesirable for the person to engage in that activity or those activities.[1]

The disqualification condition is satisfied in relation to a person if, in relation to a licensed body, the person (intentionally or through neglect) (a) breaches a relevant duty to which the person is subject, or (b) causes, or substantially contributes to, a significant breach of the terms of the licensed body's licence. The duty of a non-authorised person who is an employee or a manager of a licensed body, or has an interest or an indirect interest, or holds a material interest, in a licensed body, is not to do anything which causes or substantially contributes to a breach by (a) the licensed body, or (b) an employee or manager of the licensed body who is an authorised person in relation to an activity which is a reserved legal activity, of the duties imposed on them.[2]

SRA guidance gives examples of conduct when it may be satisfied to make such a disqualification order:

'• has caused significant loss or harm

• involved an abuse of trust

• has caused harm to or to the interests of a vulnerable person

• was motivated by any form of discrimination

• was deliberate, pre-meditated, repeated or reckless

• has put the public confidence in the regulation of the profession at risk; or

• indicates you are unsuitable for the role being undertaken.'

The guidance indicates that the following factors might support a decision not to disqualify the individual:

'• the misconduct was committed as a result of a genuine mistake or misunderstanding

• you have cooperated fully with the SRA

• the conduct was trivial; or

• there is a low likelihood of repetition of the conduct.'

The guidance adds that the SRA may consider a fine in addition to or in place of disqualification.[3]

Upon disqualification, the Legal Services Board (LSB) is notified.[4]

CHAPTER 18
SOLICITORS' EMPLOYEES AND
CONSULTANTS

A material change in circumstance is required before an individual who has been disqualified may apply to the SRA seeking a decision that the disqualification should cease to be in force.[5] An authorised decision-maker may decide that a disqualification should cease to be in force if they are satisfied that it is no longer undesirable for the disqualified person to engage in the relevant activity or activities.[6]

1   See also rule 3.1(c) of the Disciplinary Rules 2019.
2   Section 90 of LSA 2007.
3   SRA guidance, 'How we regulate non-authorised persons', 25 November 2019.
4   Rule 9.3(a) of the Disciplinary Rules 2019.
5   Rule 7.1.
6   Rule 7.2.

Other regulatory powers

18.13

Solicitors' employees and consultants may become compliance officers, managers and owners. In addition to other regulatory requirements, in most cases, they must be approved by the SRA as suitable to take up their role.[1]

There are mechanisms for the control of compliance officers for legal practice and compliance officers for finance and administration (COLPs and COFAs) including the power to disqualify, which could have the effect of rendering the individual unemployable in the legal services market. While COLPs and COFAs may be principals in the firm, partners, members or directors, they may also be employees. These powers are considered in detail in **Chapter 7**.

Employees of solicitors and employees or managers of,[2] or a person with an interest in,[3] an authorised body may be compelled to produce documents and explanations to, and be interviewed in respect of them by, the SRA.[4] These powers are considered in detail in **Chapter 15**.

1   Rules 8.1 and 9.1 of the SRA Authorisation of Firms Rules 2019.
2   In the case of a licensed body, by section 93(2)(b) of LSA 2007 also former managers or employees.
3   In the case of a licensed body, by section 93(2)(c) also an indirect interest.
4   Sections 44B, 44BB of SA 1974 and section 93 of LSA 2007.

PART 5

The disciplinary system in practice

CHAPTER 19

Professional misconduct, its forms and formulation

19.1

Historically, there have been two types of professional misconduct by solicitors:

(1) statutory misconduct, consisting of breaches of provisions of the Solicitors Act (SA) 1974 (for example, in relation to the obligation to deliver accountants' reports) or of rules made by virtue of that Act (such as, in their time, the Solicitors' Accounts Rules 1998 or the successive Solicitors' Practice Rules (SPR)); and

(2) non-statutory misconduct – what could be called the common law of conduct, which covered anything and everything that could bring the individual or the profession into sufficient disrepute so as to engage the risk of disciplinary sanction, but which was not covered by any specific rule.

In the Solicitors Disciplinary Tribunal (the Tribunal or SDT), any action, failing or course of conduct that offended the common law of conduct was alleged to be 'professional misconduct', until the late 1950s when the phrase 'conduct unbefitting a solicitor' was substituted. The latter formulation enabled the point to be made as necessary that misconduct outside a solicitor's professional practice, in his or her private life, could have disciplinary consequences.

On 1 July 2007 the Solicitors' Code of Conduct 2007 came into force. The 2007 Code was designed to be an all-embracing and codified system of professional regulation. Accordingly, prosecutors in the Tribunal started to allege a breach of a rule *simpliciter* (rather than conduct unbefitting) against solicitors whose conduct had been referred to the Tribunal.

On 6 October 2011, the 2011 SRA Principles and Code came into force, based upon the principles of outcomes-focused regulation (OFR). Since then, the practice has been for prosecutors to allege breaches of either the Principles or the mandatory outcomes (or both), and allegations of conduct unbefitting a solicitor have fallen into disuse. Where prescriptive rules, such as the SRA Accounts Rules, are alleged to have been breached, the relevant allegation should make that clear.

The concept of 'professional misconduct'

19.2

As the use of the phrase 'conduct unbefitting' faded away after the introduction of the 2007 Code of Conduct, the SDT had to grapple with the issue of whether *any* breach of any principle or rule justified a finding against a solicitor, or whether such a finding should only be made where the conduct of the solicitor was sufficiently serious to justify a public finding against him or her. In *Pabla and Pabla*,[1] the SDT dismissed allegations against solicitors even though breaches of the provisions concerning the introduction and referral of clients in the 2007 Code of Conduct had been admitted. The Tribunal held the breaches to be too trivial to justify a finding against the solicitors.

The correctness of the Tribunal's approach was underlined by the Divisional Court in the *Leigh Day* case,[2] in which Davis LJ stated at [156]–[158]:

'156. As we have had cause to ask rhetorically before in this judgment: what was this particular allegation doing before the Tribunal if it was not a matter of professional misconduct? In truth, if such an allegation under Principle 5 is to be pursued before a tribunal then it ordinarily needs to have some inherent seriousness and culpability. It no doubt can be accepted that negligence may be capable of constituting a failure to provide a proper standard of service to clients. But even so, questions of relative culpability and relative seriousness surely still come into the equation under this Principle if the matter is to be the subject of disciplinary proceedings before a tribunal. We do not, we emphasise, say that there is a set standard of seriousness or culpability for the purposes of assessing breaches of the core principles in tribunal proceedings. It is a question of fact and degree in each case. Whether the default in question is sufficiently serious and culpable thus will depend on the particular core principle in issue and on the evaluation of the circumstances of the particular case as applied to that principle. But an evaluation of seriousness remains a concomitant of such an allegation.

157. If authority be needed for such an approach, then it can be found not only in the observations of Jackson LJ (in the specific context of Principle 6) in *Wingate and Evans* (cited above) but also in the decision of the Court of Session in *Sharp v The Law Society of Scotland* [1984] SC 129. There, by reference to the applicable Scottish legislation and rules, it was among other things held that whether a breach of the rules should be treated as professional misconduct depended on whether it would be regarded as serious and reprehensible by competent and responsible solicitors and on the degree of culpability: see the opinion of the court delivered by the Lord President (Lord Emslie) at page 134.

158. We consider that, though the statutory schemes are by no means the same, the like approach is generally appropriate and required for the English legislative and regulatory regime in the treatment of alleged breaches of the core principles. We appreciate that there may be some breaches of some rules – for instance, accounts rules: see, for example, *Holden v Solicitors Regulation Authority* [2012] EWHC 2067 (Admin) – which can involve strict liability. But that cannot be said generally with regard to all alleged breaches of the core principles coming before the Tribunal; which in our view ordinarily will involve an evaluative judgment and an assessment of seriousness to be made …'

1   10376-2009, SDT.
2   *SRA v Day* [2018] EWHC 2726 (Admin).

19.3

At the time, this passage was not considered to be controversial. However, observations by the Divisional Court in *Beckwith v SRA*[1] may be difficult to reconcile with it. In *Beckwith*, which concerned a consensual sexual encounter away from the office and which is dealt with in detail below (see also **3.13**, **19.4**, **19.6** and **22.24**), the Divisional Court stated:

> '14. … On the Appellant's submission the notion of professional misconduct provides both a threshold requirement to weed out complaints concerning matters that are insufficiently serious to be the subject of regulatory sanctions, and also provides a boundary to mark the limits of regulatory incursion into conduct that occurs outside work or otherwise in the course of professional life.
>
> 15. Although we agree that such limits to the scope of professional regulation by the SRA do exist, we do not consider it is appropriate to identify where those limits are by reference to a notion of "professional misconduct". The notion that the Tribunal should only deal with allegations which amount to "professional misconduct" has superficial attraction. But on closer consideration, this notion disintegrates. What is or is not professional misconduct depends on the rules of the scheme that applies to the profession in hand. Some schemes may describe prohibited conduct by reference to the phrase "professional misconduct" or other similar words – see, for example, the cases referred to below at paragraphs 19 – 22. In such cases, the relevant regulator or tribunal does have to decide whether the conduct alleged can be described as professional misconduct. But other schemes for regulation may not be formulated in this way; they may describe prohibited conduct in other ways. Where that is so, the only question for the relevant regulator or tribunal is whether or not such conduct has occurred, and if so, what penalty should be imposed. One might describe the product of that process as a finding of "professional misconduct", but that phrase will be no more than descriptive; it will not identify the relevant standard of behaviour which has caused the penalty to be imposed.
>
> 16. Put another way, whether or not a notion of "professional misconduct" has any part to play in any particular regulatory scheme will depend on the terms in which that scheme has been made. There is no universal principle.'

1   [2020] EWHC 3231 (Admin).

19.4

The court in *Beckwith* went on to hold that certain allegations of breach of the SRA Principles, particularly allegations of lack of integrity and failing to behave in a way that upholds public trust and confidence in the profession, should be tethered to allegations of breaches of particular rules. The difficulty with this approach is that no suite of detailed rules can ever hope to capture every example of misconduct (whether it is described as 'professional misconduct' or something else). This is where the 2007 Code of Conduct, which sought to be an all-encompassing prescriptive code, came unstuck. In *R (on the application of the British Bankers Association) v Financial Services*

Authority[1] Ouseley J said (about the relationship between the Financial Services Authority (now the Financial Conduct Authority) Principles and the Insurance: Conduct of Business Sourcebook (ICOBS) rules) at [161]–[162]:[2]

> '161. I turn to the substance, dealing first with the general approach. In my judgment, and fundamentally, the BBA analysis rather puts the issue the wrong way round when it contends that the Principles cannot be used to contradict or augment the specific rules. The relationship between them has to be determined by understanding the true role of the Principles. The Principles are the overarching framework for regulation, for good reason. The FSA has clearly not promulgated, and has chosen not to promulgate, a detailed all-embracing comprehensive code of regulations to be inter-preted as covering all possible circumstances. The industry had not wanted such a code either. Such a code could be circumvented unfairly, or contain provisions which were not apt for the many and varied sales circumstances which could arise. The overarching framework would always be in place to be the fundamental provision which would always govern the actions of firms, as well as to cover all those circumstances not provided for or adequately provided for by specific rules.
>
> 162. The Principles are best understood as the ever present substrata to which the specific rules are added. The Principles always have to be complied with. The specific rules do not supplant them and cannot be used to contradict them. They are but specific applications of them to the particular require-ments they cover. The general notion that the specific rules can exhaust the application of the Principles is inappropriate. It cannot be an error of law for the Principles to augment specific rules.'

1   [2011] EWHC 999 (Admin).
2   The same approach had been taken by the High Court in *Henneberry v Law Society* (2000, unreported).

Conduct, including sexual conduct, away from work

19.5

The issues considered above have particular relevance where the alleged misconduct occurred away from the workplace. It may be no defence to an allegation of profes-sional misconduct that the act took place away from work, and had nothing to do with the respondent's practice as a solicitor. The reputation of the profession can be damaged by a solicitor's conduct away from the workplace. The most obvious example is serious criminal conduct. Any conviction for an offence of dishonesty by a practising solicitor is likely to lead to the termination of the right to practise, even where the offence had nothing to do with the solicitor's legal practice. Solicitors must also be careful in their use of social media. In *Mahmood*,[1] a solicitor was found to have posted antisemitic comments on a Facebook page, and was severely dealt with by the Tribunal.[2]

1   11625-2017, SDT.
2   On 7 February 2019, the SRA issued a topic guide entitled 'Use of social media and offensive communications'.

19.6

As for sexual conduct, since the #MeToo movement came to public attention in the wake of revelations about Harvey Weinstein in 2017, professional regulators have faced difficult decisions as to how to deal with allegations of inappropriate sexual conduct in the workplace or between colleagues. The scandal highlighted the unacceptable treatment by men of women, and the extent to which women have had to deal with harassment or worse from men in positions of power over them. One of the results was that there was a considerable increase in complaints of harassment and the like to the SRA.

In *Beckwith*, an unspecified but consensual sexual encounter took place between the respondent, a partner in Freshfields, and an associate, who was working out her notice and was due to leave her employment within a few days. The SDT found that there was no abuse of the respondent's position, but found nevertheless that his conduct, which it described as 'inappropriate', constituted a breach of SRA principles 2 ('you must act with integrity') and 6 ('You must behave in a way that maintains the trust that the public places in you and in the provision of legal services').

In allowing the appeal, the Divisional Court sought to restrict the use of the 2011 SRA principles 2 (integrity) and 6 (trust in the profession). It held that the requirement to act with integrity must comprise identifiable standards and that the SDT could not have *carte blanche* to decide what the requirement means. Therefore, the requirement to act with integrity and to uphold trust in the profession must be tethered to other rules in the Handbook.

The facts were unusual in *Beckwith* in that there was, on the findings of fact made by the SDT, no lack of consent by person A or abuse of position by Mr Beckwith. A number of other cases brought before the SDT have resulted in adverse findings against solicitors (see **22.24**). There is no reason why many sexual misconduct cases need give rise to difficulties. If the conduct amounts to a sexual assault, or harassment as defined in the Equality Act (EqA) 2010, there is a clear basis for a successful prosecution. Where there is consent and no significant abuse of position by the respondent solicitor, in the light of *Beckwith*, a Tribunal is likely to take the view that such conduct is none of the regulator's business. There will be cases close to the line which will have to be dealt with on a case-by-case basis.

Dishonesty

19.7

For any solicitor to behave dishonestly strikes at the heart of the reputation of the profession, and will almost inevitably lead to an order striking that solicitor off the roll.[1] Until the autumn of 2017, the test for dishonesty was stated to be the mixed subjective/objective test, deriving from the criminal law (*R v Ghosh*[2]) and adopted in disciplinary proceedings against solicitors in *Bultitude v Law Society*[3] and *Bryant and Bench v Law Society*.[4] The twin test was expressed thus by Lord Hutton in *Twinsectra Ltd v Yardley*[5] (at [27]):

> 'before there can be a finding of dishonesty it must be established that the defendant's conduct was dishonest by the ordinary standards of reasonable

and honest people and that he himself realised that by those standards his
conduct was dishonest.'

1   See **CHAPTER 16**.
2   [1982] QB 1053.
3   [2004] EWCA Civ 1853.
4   [2009] 1 WLR 163.
5   [2002] UKHL 12.

19.8

This twin test created uncertainty, and was criticised in a line of cases concerned
with the liability of accessories for breach of trust. On 25 October 2017, the Supreme
Court handed down its judgment in *Ivey v Genting Casinos*,[1] and in doing so swept
away 35 years of confusion about the correct test for dishonesty. In his judgment,
Lord Hughes JSC laid bare the unnecessary difficulties which the *Ghosh/Twinsectra*
twin test had created, among which was the unintended effect of the *Ghosh* decision
that the more warped a defendant's standards of honesty, the less likely he was to be
convicted of dishonest behaviour. Crucially, however, his Lordship pointed out that
the twin test was not necessary to preserve the principle that dishonesty must depend
upon the actual state of mind of the defendant. He made clear that the courts do not
need to invent a two-stage test in order to ensure that an accused's state of mind is
taken into account in assessing whether he has been dishonest. Two passages from
his judgment set out what must now be seen as the correct test, although they are
technically *obiter*:

> '60 It is plain that in Ghosh the court concluded that its compromise
> second leg test was necessary in order to preserve the principle that
> criminal responsibility for dishonesty must depend on the actual
> state of mind of the defendant. It asked the question whether "dishon-
> estly", where that word appears in the Theft Act, was intended to
> characterise a course of conduct or to describe a state of mind. The
> court gave the following example, at p 1063, which was clearly central
> to its reasoning:
>
> "Take for example a man who comes from a country where public
> transport is free. On his first day here he travels on a bus. He gets off
> without paying. He never had any intention of paying. His mind is
> clearly honest; but his conduct, judged objectively by what he has
> done, is dishonest. It seems to us that in using the word 'dishonestly' in
> the Theft Act 1968, Parliament cannot have intended to catch
> dishonest conduct in that sense, that is to say conduct to which no
> moral obloquy could possibly attach."
>
> But the man in this example would inevitably escape conviction by
> the application of the (objective) first leg of the Ghosh test. That is
> because, in order to determine the honesty or otherwise of a person's
> conduct, one must ask what he knew or believed about the facts
> affecting the area of activity in which he was engaging. In order to
> decide whether this visitor was dishonest by the standards of ordinary
> people, it would be necessary to establish his own actual state of
> knowledge of how public transport works. Because he genuinely
> believes that public transport is free, there is nothing objectively
> dishonest about his not paying on the bus. The same would be true of
> a child who did not know the rules, or of a person who had innocently
> misread the bus pass sent to him and did not realise that it did not

operate until after 10.00 in the morning. The answer to the court's question is that "dishonestly", where it appears, is indeed intended to characterise what the defendant did, but in characterising it one must first ascertain his actual state of mind as to the facts in which he did it. It was not correct to postulate that the conventional objective test of dishonesty involves judging only the actions and not the state of knowledge or belief as to the facts in which they were performed. What is objectively judged is the standard of behaviour, given any known actual state of mind of the actor as to the facts.'

The second passage from the judgment, at [74], also merits quotation:

'When dishonesty is in question the fact-finding tribunal must first ascertain (subjectively) the actual state of the individual's knowledge or belief as to the facts. The reasonableness or otherwise of his belief is a matter of evidence (often in practice determinative) going to whether he held the belief, but it is not an additional requirement that his belief must be reasonable; the question is whether it is genuinely held. When once his actual state of mind as to knowledge or belief as to facts is established, the question whether his conduct was honest or dishonest is to be determined by the fact-finder by applying the (objective) standards of ordinary decent people. There is no requirement that the defendant must appreciate that what he has done is, by those standards, dishonest.'

1   [2017] UKSC 67.

19.9

It should be noted that the 2019 Principles impose for the first time an explicit obligation upon a solicitor to act with honesty as well as with integrity.

Lack of integrity

19.10

It has long been required of solicitors by their professional rules that they behave with integrity. Rule 1 of the Solicitors' Practice Rules 1990 (SPR 1990) provided:

'**(Basic principles)** A solicitor shall not do anything in the course of practising as a solicitor, or permit another person to do anything on his or her behalf, which compromises or impairs or is likely to compromise or impair any of the following: (a) the solicitor's independence or integrity ...'

As noted above, the introduction of the 2007 Code (which set out in rule 1 a number of 'core duties' including at 1.02: Integrity, 'You must act with integrity') led to a change of practice. Henceforth, the SRA tended to charge breaches of specific core duties and rules, rather than the more general 'conduct unbefitting'. Prior to the adoption of the 2007 Code, the SRA and its predecessors had been content to charge 'conduct unbefitting', and to leave the SDT to determine the gravity of the conduct, if proved. 'Lack of integrity' was rarely, if ever, specifically charged. From 2007 onwards, however, it became common for disciplinary charges to make a specific allegation of lack of integrity. The 2011 Handbook reinforced this change of practice: Principle 2 required that you must 'act with integrity', and for the first time reference was made to this requirement binding solicitors outside their practice in the notes to the Principles:

'5.   Application of the SRA Principles outside practice

5.1 In relation to activities which fall outside practice, whether undertaken as a lawyer or in some other business or private capacity, Principles 1, 2 and 6 apply to you if you are a solicitor …'

19.11

Just as had been the case with the meaning of dishonesty, the concept of lack of integrity gave rise to considerable judicial confusion and disagreement. The difficulties centred upon two issues: (a) what, if any, was the essential difference between honesty and integrity?; and (b) what is the relevance of the solicitor's state of mind to whether he or she had acted with a lack of integrity?

As for the first issue, the meaning of 'integrity' is somewhat elusive, and was explored in a series of cases arising out of the provision of financial services. The most frequently cited case was *Hoodless & Blackwell v FSA*[1] (3 October 2003), in which the Financial Services and Markets Tribunal described it as such:

'In our view "integrity" connotes moral soundness, rectitude and steady adherence to an ethical code. A person lacks integrity if unable to appreciate the distinction between what is honest or dishonest by ordinary standards. (This presupposes, of course, circumstances where ordinary standards are clear. Where there are genuinely grey areas, a finding of lack of integrity would not be appropriate.)'

Attempts by the SRA to persuade the courts to expand upon the meaning of integrity were not initially successful. Like the proverbial elephant, it seems that integrity was easier to recognise than to define. In *SRA v Chan*,[2] Davis LJ said the following at [48]:

'As to want of "integrity", there have been a number of decisions commenting on the import of this word as used in various regulations. In my view, it serves no purpose to expatiate on its meaning. Want of integrity is capable of being identified as present or not, as the case may be, by an informed tribunal or court by reference to the facts of a particular case.'

1   [2003] FSMT 007.
2   [2015] EWHC 2659 (Admin).

19.12

As for the mental element involved in lack of integrity, the analysis which generally held sway before the Supreme Court decision in *Ivey* was that whereas dishonesty involved a twin subjective/objective test, the test for lack of integrity was objective only. Then in *Malins v SRA*[1] Mostyn J stated that honesty and integrity were synonymous and interchangeable concepts. He disagreed with the judgment of Holman J in *SRA v Wingate*[2] in which the judge had held that there was a clear distinction between the two concepts. But Mostyn J's view in turn was disapproved in *Williams v SRA*[3] by a strong Divisional Court (Sir Brian Leveson P and Carr J), who, for the first time, aligned the meaning of 'integrity' with adherence to high professional standards. Sir Brian Leveson observed at [130]:

'... in the absence of compelling justification, I would reject Mostyn J's description of the concept of want of integrity as second degree dishonesty. Honesty, i.e. a lack of dishonesty, is a base standard which society requires everyone to meet. Professional standards, however, rightly impose on those who aspire to them a higher obligation to demonstrate integrity in all of their work. There is a real difference between them.'

1   [2017] EWHC 835 (Admin).
2   [2016] EWHC 3455 (Admin).
3   [2017] EWHC 1478 (Admin).

19.13

In due course, in February 2018, the matter came before the Court of Appeal in the SRA's appeal against Mostyn J's judgment in *Malins* and the solicitors' appeal against Holman J's judgment in *Wingate*. In his judgment,[1] Rupert Jackson LJ upheld the traditional analysis that the concepts of honesty and integrity are distinct, and sought to provide some guidance as to the meaning of lack of integrity:

'96   Integrity is a more nebulous concept than honesty. Hence it is less easy to define, as a number of judges have noted.

97   In professional codes of conduct, the term "integrity" is a useful shorthand to express the higher standards which society expects from professional persons and which the professions expect from their own members. See the judgment of Sir Brian Leveson P in *Williams* at [130]. The underlying rationale is that the professions have a privileged and trusted role in society. In return they are required to live up to their own professional standards.

[...]

100   Integrity connotes adherence to the ethical standards of one's own profession. That involves more than mere honesty. To take one example, a solicitor conducting negotiations or a barrister making submissions to a judge or arbitrator will take particular care not to mislead. Such a professional person is expected to be even more scrupulous about accuracy than a member of the general public in daily discourse.

101   The duty to act with integrity applies not only to what professional persons say, but also to what they do. It is possible to give many illustrations of what constitutes acting without integrity. For example, in the case of solicitors:

(i)   A sole practice giving the appearance of being a partnership and deliberately flouting the conduct rules (*Emeana*);

(ii)   Recklessly, but not dishonestly, allowing a court to be misled (*Brett*)

(iii)   Subordinating the interests of the clients to the solicitors' own financial interests (*Chan*);

(iv)   Making improper payments out of the client account (*Scott*);

(v)   Allowing the firm to become involved in conveyancing transactions which bear the hallmarks mortgage fraud (*Newell-Austin*);

(vi)   Making false representations on behalf of the client (*Williams*).

102 Obviously, neither courts nor professional tribunals must set unrealistically high standards, as was observed during argument. The duty of
integrity does not require professional people to be paragons of virtue.
In every instance, professional integrity is linked to the manner in
which that particular profession professes to serve the public.'

1   [2018] EWCA Civ 366. See also *Zivancevic v SRA* [2019] EWHC 1950 (Admin).

19.14

Difficulties, however, remain. The important question that the Court of Appeal left
unanswered in *Wingate* is what differentiates 'ordinary' professional misconduct
from professional misconduct which involves a lack of integrity. All proven or
admitted instances of professional misconduct are serious, save those rare cases in
which the SDT imposes no sanction, and therefore involve a departure from the
high professional standards expected of solicitors. What then is the additional ingre-
dient which merits the description 'lack of integrity'? Perhaps it is the scale of the
departure from the standards imposed by the relevant rules, perhaps it is the mindset
of the solicitor (intentional or reckless breaches of professional standards being more
serious than inadvertent breaches), or perhaps it is both. In any event, even following
the decision in *Wingate* it seems that lack of integrity, like an elephant, remains
easier to recognise than to define. Secondly, the Divisional Court judgment in
Beckwith, which ruled that allegations of lack of integrity should be tethered to allegations of breaches of specific rules as discussed above, may be difficult to apply
where the alleged misconduct occurs away from the workplace and outside the
solicitor's practice.

Recklessness

19.15

The SRA sometimes alleges that breaches of principles or outcomes have been
committed recklessly. This is plainly less serious professional misconduct than
dishonesty, but is likely to be regarded as more serious than misconduct arising out of
negligence/manifest incompetence. Recklessness is defined as a matter of law, and
the definition has been applied by the SDT; see *Lawson*[1] and *Fuglers*[2] (undisturbed by
the High Court on appeal). The following quotations, paraphrasing *R v G*,[3] were
cited by the SDT in each of those cases:

'Recklessness means the taking of an unreasonable risk of which the risk-
taker is aware: a person acts "recklessly" with respect to a circumstance when
he is aware of a risk that did or would exist, and acts recklessly with respect to
a consequence when he is aware of a risk that it will occur, and in either case,
it is, in the circumstances known to him, unreasonable to take the risk.'

'… it had to be shown that the defendant's state of mind was culpable in
that he acted recklessly in respect of a circumstance if he was aware of a
risk which did or would exist, or in respect of a result if he was aware of a
risk that it would occur, and it was, in the circumstances known to him,
unreasonable to take the risk.'

In the context of professional conduct, the concept of recklessness is best encapsu-
lated by an assertion that the solicitor could not care less about the professional rules

concerned. Although perhaps not breaching rules intentionally, the solicitor will have demonstrated a 'couldn't care less' attitude to the relevant ones, which renders the misconduct potentially very serious.

1   11048-2012, SDT.
2   10917-2012, SDT.
3   [2004] 1 AC 1034, HL.

Negligence and manifest incompetence

19.16

All lawyers make mistakes during the course of their professional careers. It has always been the case that solicitors were not penalised for making mistakes – 'generally the honest and genuine decision of a solicitor on a question of professional judgment does not give rise to a disciplinary offence'.[1] Equally, there is some professional negligence that is so serious that it calls into question a solicitor's fitness to practise, and needs to be marked with a sanction – not merely dealt with by way of a civil action leading to compensation. This is because the public is entitled to expect a basic level of competence from the lawyers whom they instruct, and because the reputation of the profession is bound to suffer where a solicitor exhibits an unacceptable level of professional competence.

In *Iqbal v SRA*,[2] the appellant solicitor had incorrectly held out individuals as his partners who were not, in law, his partners (it was alleged that he had done this in order for his firm to be eligible for membership of mortgagee lenders' panels of solicitors, for which membership is not available for sole practitioners). Acquitted of dishonesty, he was nevertheless struck off the roll, and his appeal to the High Court failed. Sir John Thomas, President of the Queen's Bench Division at the time, said at [23]:

> 'It seems to me that trustworthiness also extends to those standards which the public are entitled to expect of a solicitor, including competence. If a solicitor exhibits manifest incompetence, as, in my judgment, the appellant did, then it is impossible to see how the public can have confidence in a person who has exhibited such incompetence. It is difficult to see how a profession such as the medical profession would countenance retaining as a doctor someone who had showed himself to be incompetent. It seems to me that the same must be true of the solicitors' profession. If in a course of conduct a person manifests incompetence as, in my judgment, the appellant did, then he is not fit to be a solicitor. The only appropriate remedy is to remove him from the roll. It must be recalled that being a solicitor is not a right, but a privilege. The public is entitled not only to solicitors who behave with honesty and integrity, but solicitors in whom they can impose trust by reason of competence.'

1   *Connolly v Law Society* [2007] EWHC 1175 (Admin).
2   [2012] EWHC 3251 (Admin).

19.17

Where then is the line to be drawn between 'mere negligence' and manifest incompetence deserving of sanction? In *Re a Solicitor*[1] at [815] Lord Denning MR stated:

'In my opinion, negligence in a solicitor may amount to a professional misconduct if it is inexcusable and is such as to be regarded as deplorable by his fellows in the profession'.

In his judgment in *Wingate* (supra), Rupert Jackson LJ sounded a note of warning (at [106]):

'In applying Principle 6 it is important not to characterise run of the mill professional negligence as manifest incompetence. All professional people are human and will from time to time make slips which a court would characterise as negligent. Fortunately, no loss results from most such slips. But acts of manifest incompetence engaging the Principles of professional conduct are of a different order.'

1   [1972] 2 All ER 811, CA.

19.18

It is undesirable to attempt a comprehensive definition. The issue, as with all professional misconduct, is best decided on a case-by-case basis by the expert Tribunal charged by Parliament with the task of sitting in judgment upon solicitors:

'The suggestion was that the phrase "moral turpitude" is analogous to conduct unbefitting. My response to that is that it may be in some circumstances, but not in all. Allegations against professional men vary infinitely in gravity. What constitutes conduct unbefitting a solicitor is best judged, in my view, by his professional colleagues, applying their undoubted experience of what is to be properly expected of a solicitor in his practice, when they are sitting formally as part of a disciplinary tribunal in judgment of one of them. I should be most reluctant to attempt to provide any kind of definition of a term which is used, the words being slightly different here and there, in many professions, including the armed forces'.[1]

1   *Re a Solicitor*(1991, unreported), per Watkins LJ; cited with approval in *Re a Solicitor* (1995, unreported), per Lord Taylor CJ.

19.19

In *Wingate* one of the solicitors (Evans) had been acquitted by the SDT of professional misconduct: it had been alleged by the SRA that he ought to have checked a contract for the provision of finance which had been negotiated and signed by his partner. On the SRA's appeal to the Divisional Court, Holman J had reversed this acquittal, and found that the solicitor had been guilty of manifest incompetence. Evans appealed successfully to the Court of Appeal, Rupert Jackson LJ observing at [130]:

'The judge has held that Mr Evans' failure to obtain and read the funding agreement was manifest incompetence. I agree that Mr Evans was imprudent in that regard. But on the facts presented to Mr Evans, it was obviously advantageous to take a loan from Axiom and to repay the HBOS debt, which he had personally guaranteed. Mr Evans was hard pressed with other matters and he trusted Mr Wingate to deal with the finances. Mr Evans' failure to read the funding agreement and then to challenge his partner may be characterised as carelessness or negligence, but it did not amount to "manifest incompetence", engaging the Principles of professional conduct. In my view, the judge's decision in that regard is a bridge too far.'

Vicarious liability

19.20

In recent years there has been some confusion as to whether partners who have not known of or directly participated in a decision that breached a regulatory rule should face disciplinary action as a result. It was felt by the SRA that if, for instance, an equity partner benefited financially from a breach of the prohibition against referral fees, that partner should face disciplinary proceedings. It is submitted that the better view is that unless a disciplinary offence is truly one of strict liability (such as an Accounts Rules breach), a solicitor should only face disciplinary consequences if he or she is believed to be in some way culpable.

This had been the general approach of the Tribunal.[1] The concept of conduct unbefitting a solicitor, which was the method of charging before 2007, carried with it some degree of moral culpability: the Tribunal had held that partners should not be required to supervise or monitor the work of other partners, and that a partner was not guilty of professional misconduct merely because he is the partner of a solicitor who is guilty of professional misconduct.[2]

This general approach has been approved by the Divisional Court in *Akodu v SRA*[3] per Moses LJ (at [10]):

> 'there is no other reasonable conclusion that can be reached other than that the basis upon which he had been found guilty was merely on the basis that he was a partner of the firm. If that was the only basis, then there has been no argument advanced on behalf of the Law Society to suggest that that was a lawful basis upon which any solicitor can be found guilty of conduct unbefitting his profession. If authority is needed for the proposition, it can be found in *Cordery on Solicitors* at J 2225. Some degree of personal fault is required.'

1   See *Pabla and Pabla*, 10376-2009, SDT. See also *SRA v Day* [2018] EWHC 2726 (Admin) at [156]–[158].
2   *Ali and Shabir*, 9339-2005, SDT; *Aziz and Saunders*, 9032-2004, SDT; *Ross*, 10002-2008, SDT; and *Bagri*, 10229-2009, SDT.
3   [2009] EWHC 3588 (Admin).

19.21

For the same reason, the fact that something has gone seriously wrong in a regulated entity will not be enough to establish professional misconduct against a solicitor or the entity. It is not unknown for a rogue employee, or sometimes even a rogue partner, to engage in fraudulent activity under the noses of his or her colleagues, but without their knowledge. In order for individual solicitors in the firm (or the entity itself) to be liable in conduct in such circumstances, there must be some culpable failure by them, most typically a failure of supervision. However, in order to succeed with such a prosecution, the SRA must be able to point to something concrete that the respondent solicitor (or the entity) did that ought not to have been done, or failed to do that ought to have been done. If this cannot be proved to the requisite standard, the prosecution will fail.[1] Sadly, no system of oversight or supervision will always be proof against a determined and resourceful fraudster.

1   See *Bass and Ward v SRA* [2012] EWHC 2457 (Admin), especially at [24]; *Wilson and Carroll*, 10767-2011, SDT; and *Barber and Bagas*, 11631-2017, SDT.

CHAPTER 20

SRA-imposed sanctions

The statutory provisions

20.1

Until the summer of 2010 the only regulatory 'sanction' that the Solicitors Regulation Authority (SRA) could impose upon a solicitor was a reprimand or severe reprimand. This was generally kept confidential as between the solicitor and the SRA though if there was a third party complainant or informant involved that party would be informed, and was free to disclose it.[1] The Legal Services Act (LSA) 2007 introduced a new section 44D into the Solicitors Act (SA) 1974. This provided a statutory power for the SRA to impose fines of up to £2,000, or a written rebuke, upon solicitors. A parallel power in relation to recognised bodies, their managers and employees, was inserted in the Administration of Justice Act (AJA) 1985 as paragraph 14B of Schedule 2. Parliament's intention was to remove the less serious cases from the Solicitors Disciplinary Tribunal (the Tribunal or SDT), and to allow the SRA to deal with them more speedily and cheaply instead. The worrying feature for solicitors was that the confidentiality of the process was removed. The SRA may itself publish details of any action it has taken under section 44D if it considers this to be in the public interest.

The new statutory powers could not be exercised until the SRA had made rules in accordance with the terms of section 44D, which also required consultation with the Tribunal about the content of the rules. There was considerable delay in the promulgation of the rules, caused largely by disagreement over the standard of proof to be adopted by the SRA in making disciplinary decisions. Eventually the SRA (which wanted to use the civil standard against the wishes of the Tribunal and the Master of the Rolls) prevailed, and the Legal Services Board (LSB) approved the SRA (Disciplinary Procedure) Rules 2010, which commenced on 1 June 2010. Those rules were short-lived and were replaced on 6 October 2011 by the SRA Disciplinary Procedure Rules 2011 (the 'Disciplinary Rules 2011'). The Disciplinary Rules 2011 were then replaced on 25 November 2019 by the SRA Regulatory and Disciplinary Procedure Rules 2019 (the 'Disciplinary Rules 2019').

1 *Napier v Pressdram Ltd* [2009] EWCA Civ 443, [2010] 1 WLR 934.

20.2

By section 44D(10) of SA 1974, the Lord Chancellor may by order increase the £2,000 limit to such other amount as may be specified in the order. The SRA is anxious to secure an increase, in part at least to reduce the disparity between its powers in relation to traditional law firms and those who work in them, and its powers in relation to alternative business structures (ABSs) and those who work in them: the SRA has a power to impose huge fines upon ABSs. For the more extensive powers of the SRA to take disciplinary action against ABSs see **CHAPTER 26**.

20.3

The issue of publicity is a vexed one. On the one hand, as a statutory regulator, regulating in the public interest, the SRA wishes to operate in an open and transparent manner. On the other, the effect of publicity for the individual solicitor may be wholly disproportionate to the regulatory breach that occurred. In the internet age, such information is easily obtained by a prospective client, and is bound to have a deterrent effect upon the prospective client's intention to instruct the solicitor in question.

20.4

Section 44E of SA 1974 confers a right of appeal upon a solicitor who is fined or rebuked under section 44D if, in the case of a rebuke, a decision has been made to publish the rebuke. The appeal lies to the Tribunal. For a consideration of this and other appellate jurisdictions of the Tribunal see **Chapter 23**.

Letters of advice and warnings

20.5

The SRA can close an investigation on terms that the solicitor is provided with a letter containing advice and a warning regarding future conduct and behaviour. Before issuing the letter the SRA must give the person under investigation notice of the allegations and facts in support and an opportunity to make representations in response.[1] The letter is used for minor regulatory breaches which are not sufficiently serious to justify a rebuke, fine or restriction on the ability to practise, and the decision to issue the letter can be taken by supervision staff.[2] The letter does not amount to a disciplinary finding against the solicitor, and need not ordinarily be reported to insurers unless an unusual term in the contract of insurance provides for this.

Breaches which are more serious are referred either to adjudication or directly to the Tribunal.

1   Rule 2.4 of the Disciplinary Rules 2019.
2   SRA Enforcement Strategy, 25 November 2019. See also the SRA Schedule of Delegation.

The powers of the adjudicator and adjudication panels

20.6

By rule 3.1 of the Disciplinary Rules 2019, an adjudicator or an adjudication panel can impose a rebuke or fine or refer a matter to the Tribunal.

20.7

A rebuke is a less serious sanction than a fine, and the SRA Enforcement Strategy states that the decision-maker will consider available sanctions and controls in turn, starting with the least restrictive.

The Disciplinary Rules 2019 do not specify the circumstances in which a rebuke is appropriate. The SRA Enforcement Strategy states that a rebuke is appropriate where the issues are only of moderate seriousness, and that the following factors favour a rebuke:

- no lasting significant harm to consumers or third parties;

- conduct or behaviour reckless as to risk of harm/regulatory obligations;

- breach rectified/remedial action taken, but persisted longer than reasonable/ only when prompted;

- low risk of repetition; or

- some public sanction required to uphold public confidence in the delivery of legal services.[1]

1 Appendix A to the SRA Enforcement Strategy, 25 November 2019.

20.8

By rule 4.1 of the Disciplinary Rules 2019, a fine can be imposed where it is appropriate to:

(a) remove any financial or other benefit arising from the conduct;

(b) maintain professional standards; or

(c) uphold public confidence in the profession and in legal services provided by authorised persons.

The SRA Enforcement Strategy states that a fine is appropriate where there is a serious breach but protection of the public does not require suspension or striking off, and that the following factors favour a fine:

- conduct/behaviour caused/had potential to cause significant harm;

- direct control/responsibility for conduct/behaviour;

- conduct planned/premeditated;

- wilful or reckless disregard of risk of harm/regulatory obligations;

- breach rectified/remedial action taken, but persisted longer than reasonable/ only when prompted; or

- fine appropriate to remove financial gain or other benefit as a consequence of the breach.[1]

1 Appendix A to the SRA Enforcement Strategy, 25 November 2019.

20.9

The decision may be made by an adjudicator or an adjudication panel consisting of at least two members. Any evidence which the adjudicator or adjudication panel considers to be fair and relevant can be admitted whether or not the evidence would be admissible in court.[1] By rule 8.7 of the Disciplinary Rules 2019 the standard of proof adopted is the civil standard, and decisions of an adjudication panel are made by a simple majority.

Any decision may also be taken by agreement with the regulated person.

1 Rule 8.8 of the Disciplinary Rules 2019.

Setting the level of fine

20.10

The Disciplinary Rules 2019 do not specify the criteria which should be taken into account when deciding the level of the fine. The SRA Enforcement Strategy states that the factors which affect the SRA's view on seriousness include the nature of the misconduct, whether the conduct was deliberate or inadvertent, whether proper management systems were in place, whether any harm has been caused and if so the impact on the victim, whether an affected person is vulnerable, whether the regulated person had responsibility or control over the matters in question, whether there are patterns of repeated misconduct, whether there is remorse or insight or a poor regulatory history and whether any remedial action has been taken.

The SRA has issued a guidance note which sets out a three-stage process for determining the level of a fine.[1] Subject to the limits to the SRA's fining powers, the level is decided by (1) identifying the appropriate base penalty having regard to the seriousness of the misconduct and, in the case of a regulated entity, the size of the turnover; (2) taking any mitigation into account; and (3) adjusting the level to eliminate any financial benefit obtained by the misconduct.

The two main criteria that are likely to affect the high levels of fines which can be imposed on ABSs (a maximum of £250 million for a licensed body and £50 million for a manager or employee; see **CHAPTER 26**) are the linking of the base penalty to turnover (under the guidance note the base penalty can be up to 2.5 per cent of annual domestic turnover) and the adjustment of the base penalty to eliminate any financial gain obtained from the misconduct.

If a financial penalty is in contemplation the SRA may require a statement as to the financial means of the person or body, verified by a statement of truth, within a specified time.[2]

The SRA may suspend a fine, which may have the result of making it payable only if there is a further adverse finding within the period of the suspension.[3]

Any fine is payable to the Treasury, but is not payable until the time for appealing has expired.

1 SRA guidance, 'The SRA's approach to financial penalties', 13 August 2013, updated 25 November 2019.
2 Rule 4.2 of the Disciplinary Rules 2019.
3 Rule 4.3(b) of the Disciplinary Rules 2019.

Publication of decisions

20.11

Rule 9.1 of the Disciplinary Rules 2019 states that the SRA may disclose or publish any information arising from or relating to an investigation where it considers it to be in the public interest to do so. In practice the SRA does not publicise investigations before a disciplinary decision is made and does not publish letters of advice or warnings.

Rule 9.2 of the Disciplinary Rules 2019 states that the SRA shall publish any decision to give a rebuke or impose a fine unless it considers the particular circumstances outweigh the public interest in publication. That emphasis on publication is arguably wider than the statutory provision for publication, as section 44D(3) of SA 1974 states that the SRA may publish a decision to rebuke or fine if it considers it to be in the public interest to do so.

On 10 August 2016 the SRA issued a guidance note which states that representations against publication will be taken into account.[1] The guidance note emphasises transparency, states that the SRA generally expects rebukes and fines to be published, and lists a small number of factors which may lead to a decision not to publish. The main factor is 'in all the circumstances the impact of publication on the regulated person would be disproportionate'. In practice, it is difficult to persuade the SRA not to publish.

1 SRA guidance, 'Publishing regulatory and disciplinary decisions', issued August 2016, updated 25 November 2019.

Oral hearings

20.12

Adjudication proceedings are normally conducted in private and decided on the papers. It is open to a solicitor to request an oral hearing. Rule 8.5 of the Disciplinary Rules 2019 states that an adjudication panel may decide to conduct a hearing, which could be held in public, if it considers it in the interests of justice to do so. That is a relatively new rule, because there was no provision for oral hearings under the Disciplinary Rules 2011.

On 25 November 2019 the SRA issued a guidance note which states that, when deciding whether to hold a hearing, the SRA will consider all the circumstances. Factors in favour of a hearing include circumstances where there are important material facts in dispute which cannot fairly be determined on the documentation alone, where an explanation or mitigation needs to be heard orally to consider its credibility or where there is a possibility (which could apply to ABSs) that the decision-maker will impose a substantial fine. The guidance note also states that the hearing may be held in public if the adjudication panel considers it is in the public interest or the interests of justice to do so.[1]

Despite rule 8.5, oral hearings are very rare. By case law, in order to have any prospect of persuading the adjudicator to grant an oral hearing, the solicitor will have to demonstrate that fairness requires an oral hearing, and that the matter cannot be adequately considered on paper.[2] In order to have any prospect of success in appeals or judicial review proceedings based upon a failure to grant an oral hearing, it will be essential for the solicitor to have requested such a hearing; failure to have done so will be fatal to the application.[3]

1 SRA guidance, 'Decision-making, reviews and attendance procedures', 25 November 2019.
2 See generally *Yussouf v SRA* [2018] EWHC 211 (Admin).
3 *R (Thompson) v Law Society* [2004] 1 WLR 2522, CA. See also *R (Smith) v Parole Board (No 2)* [2004] 1 WLR 421, CA.

Costs of the investigation

20.13

The SRA has a statutory power to make regulations requiring a solicitor to pay a charge for the costs of an investigation into possible professional misconduct by the solicitor, or a failure or apprehended failure by the solicitor to comply with any regulatory requirement.[1] Rule 10.1 of the Disciplinary Rules 2019 provides that a person who is subject to a rebuke or fine can be directed to pay a charge. The current practice is to charge on a time basis in bands. If an investigation takes less than two hours' work (which would be unusual), the costs are a fixed figure of £300. If the time spent is more than two but under eight hours, the charge is £600. Between eight and 16 hours' work results in a charge of £1,350 and longer investigations are charged at £1,350 plus £75 for each hour and £37.50 for every half-hour over the 16th hour, rounded up or down to the nearest half-hour.[2] There is a discretion to charge less if it would be just to do so.

1 Section 44C of SA 1974.
2 Schedule 1 to the Disciplinary Rules 2019.

Referrals to the Tribunal

20.14

The SRA can refer a regulated person to the Tribunal if satisfied that (a) there is a realistic prospect of the Tribunal making an order in respect of the allegation and (b) it is in the public interest to make the application.[1] The referral decision can be made by some categories of legal and supervision staff as well as adjudicators, heads of functions and directors of the SRA.

The Disciplinary Rules 2019 state that the SRA can publish the referral decision unless it considers that the particular circumstances of the case outweigh the public interest in publication.[2]

1 Rule 6.1 of the Disciplinary Rules 2019.
2 Rule 9.2 of the Disciplinary Rules 2019.

Internal reviews

20.15

The powers to rebuke, fine and publicise the sanction are subject to an internal right of review.[1] The application for review must be launched within 28 days, and it is important for the applicant to provide properly reasoned arguments in support of the review. The review is dealt with on paper and can be decided by an adjudicator or an adjudication panel. On the review, the decision-maker can uphold the decision, overturn all or part of the decision, make any other decision which could have been made by the original decision-maker or remit the matter for further investigation.

There is no right of review of a decision to refer a person or body to the Tribunal.[2]

The SRA can on its own initiative for any reason apply for a review of any regulatory decision made by an adjudicator or adjudication panel, apart from a decision made on a review. The regulated person must be given notice of the review and an opportunity to provide written representations.[3]

1   Rule 3.2 of and Annex 1 to the SRA Application, Notice, Review and Appeal Rules 2019.
2   Annex 1 to the SRA Application, Notice, Review and Appeal Rules 2019.
3   Rules 3.1 and 3.6 of the SRA Application, Notice, Review and Appeal Rules 2019.

Appeals to the Tribunal

20.16

In respect of regulatory breaches occurring after 1 June 2010, there is a free-standing right of appeal to the Tribunal against a fine, against any direction for publicity, and against a rebuke only if there is a direction to publicise.[1]

1   Section 44E of SA 1974. See **Chapter 23**.

Judicial review

20.17

Judicial review continues to be theoretically available in respect of decisions by an adjudicator or an adjudication panel to impose a rebuke without publication, or a finding or warning, as there is no statutory right of appeal to the Tribunal against such decisions.[1] Ordinary public law principles would apply to such applications. Judicial review is often seen as a disproportionate response in circumstances where the decision, even if challengeable, makes little difference to the solicitor in practice, and permission can be refused on that basis alone.

As for decisions in respect of which a statutory right of appeal to the Tribunal exists, these cannot be challenged in judicial review proceedings owing to the existence of this alternative remedy.

1   See section 44E(1) of SA 1974. Annex 2 to the SRA Application, Notice, Review and Appeal Rules 2019 states that any decision to give a written rebuke can be appealed to the Tribunal. It is submitted that is incorrect, as the appellate jurisdiction of the Tribunal under SA 1974 is determined by statute and not the SRA's internal rules.

Regulatory settlements

20.18

The SRA is prepared to enter into agreements to settle regulatory and disciplinary cases. The agreement may take two forms: a settlement agreement, which will resolve the whole matter, or an issue agreement, which will resolve a particular issue within an investigation without concluding the investigation.

There is no requirement or compulsion on the SRA to consider a regulatory settlement of either kind or to enter into negotiations. If negotiations are conducted they will be on a without prejudice basis, and will not be referred to in any investigations or proceedings unless the court or the Tribunal orders otherwise. Agreements may be rescinded if there proves to have been material misrepresentation.

In practice, the SRA will not enter into a regulatory settlement agreement if the solicitor's honesty is in issue, if the SRA believes the solicitor will not comply with the agreement, if there is a history of persistent non-compliance or if the sanction sought by the SRA is more severe than the sanctions which the SRA has the power to impose.

Agreements will be in writing, state the relevant facts, identify any failings admitted by the solicitor, identify the action the solicitor has taken or intends to take, identify any sanction imposed (such as a rebuke or fine), require the solicitor to pay investigation costs and will be published by the SRA unless expressly agreed otherwise.

Any agreed course of action will be supported by professional undertakings and a breach of the agreement will be considered to be misconduct.

The investigation can be reopened if the solicitor fails to comply with the agreement or acts inconsistently with it (for example, by denying misconduct that has been admitted for the purposes of the agreement).

CHAPTER 21

Proceedings before the SDT: (1) pre-trial

Membership and constitution of the Tribunal

21.1

Members of the Solicitors Disciplinary Tribunal (the Tribunal or SDT) are appointed by the Master of the Rolls. The Tribunal consists of solicitor members who are practising solicitors of not less than ten years' standing, and lay members, who are neither solicitors nor barristers. Lay members are paid a daily stipend by the Ministry of Justice; until 2009 solicitor members were unpaid but can now be paid from the Tribunal's annual budget met by the Law Society. The President of the Tribunal is elected to the post by the Tribunal members, and must be a solicitor member.[1] The members also appoint one solicitor member and one lay member to be vice-presidents. The Tribunal has been held to be an independent and impartial tribunal for the purposes of Article 6 of the European Convention on Human Rights.[2]

1   Rule 7 of the Solicitors (Disciplinary Proceedings) Rules 2019 (SI 2019/1185) (the '2019 Rules').
2   *Pine v Law Society* (2000) DC Transcript CO 1385/2000.

The Tribunal's statutory powers

21.2

On the hearing of an application, the Tribunal has the power, in relation to solicitors, to make such order as it thinks fit, and any such order may in particular include provision for any of the following matters:[1]

'(a)   the striking off the roll of the name of the solicitor to whom the application or complaint relates;

(b)   the suspension of that solicitor from practice indefinitely or for a specified period;

(c)   the payment by that solicitor or former solicitor of a penalty, which shall be forfeit to Her Majesty;[2]

(d)   in the circumstances referred to in subsection (2A) [of the Solicitors Act 1974], the exclusion of that solicitor from criminal legal aid work (either permanently or for a specified period);

(e)   the termination of that solicitor's unspecified period of suspension from practice;

(f)   the restoration to the roll of the name of a former solicitor whose name has been struck off the roll and to whom the application relates;

> (g) in the case of a former solicitor whose name has been removed from the roll, a direction prohibiting the restoration of his name to the roll except by order of the Tribunal;
>
> (h) in the case of an application under subsection (1)(f) [of the Solicitors Act 1974], the restoration of the applicant's name to the roll;
>
> (i) the payment by any party of costs or a contribution towards costs of such amount as the Tribunal may consider reasonable.'

1 Section 47(2) of Solicitors Act (SA) 1974.
2 The former limit of £5,000 for each offence was removed by the Legal Services Act (LSA) 2007 with effect from 31 March 2009. Higher fines are now levied, particularly on recognised bodies in the context of firm-based regulation (see **Chapter 2**).

Other powers and jurisdictions

21.3

The Tribunal has jurisdiction over recognised bodies (incorporated practices registered with the Solicitors Regulation Authority (SRA)),[1] registered European lawyers (RELs),[2] registered foreign lawyers (RFLs)[3] and non-solicitors involved in legal practice.[4]

The Tribunal also has jurisdiction to disqualify solicitors from undertaking legal aid work,[5] but so far as can be established the power has never been used.

The Tribunal has jurisdiction to consider the conduct of and to impose sanctions on an individual who was not a solicitor at the time of the actions complained of but who had since been admitted as a solicitor.[6]

The Tribunal has jurisdiction over former solicitors in respect of conduct while they were solicitors.[7]

Appeal lies to the Tribunal from the imposition of fines by the SRA under section 44D of SA 1974 and/or under paragraph 14B of Schedule 2 to the Administration of Justice Act (AJA) 1985 and in respect of written rebukes by the SRA (under the same provisions) if a decision is made that the rebuke should be published, and also against any decision to publish the details of any action taken by the SRA under section 44D of SA 1974.[8] On such an appeal the Tribunal may affirm or revoke the SRA's decision, vary the amount of any fine, and also may exercise its normal jurisdiction over the appellant (to strike off, suspend, revoke a sole solicitor endorsement, fine, and so forth) as if an application had been made against that person.[9] Appeal also lies to the Tribunal from licensing decisions of the SRA concerning alternative business structures (ABSs). For the appellate jurisdiction of the Tribunal see **Chapter 23**.

Section 47(3B) of SA 1974, inserted by LSA 2007, provides that the Tribunal is not permitted to make any order requiring redress to be made in respect of any act or omission of any person. An order, for example, that a solicitor compensate a client would therefore not be permitted. The parliamentary intention is clear: that redress is not a matter for either the SRA or the Tribunal, rather it is an issue for the Legal Ombudsman (LeO) (see **Chapter 14**). This section came into force on 1 October 2011.

The SRA may also make rules, with the approval of the Tribunal, providing for appeals to the Tribunal from certain decisions of the SRA where appeal would otherwise lie to the High Court. These relate primarily to practising certificate conditions, and no such rules have yet been made.[10] It is understood that these are not in immediate contemplation.

1   Paragraphs 16 to 18A of Schedule 2 to AJA 1985.
2   Swiss lawyers are entitled to practise as RELs under the European Communities (Lawyer's Practice) Regulations 2000 (SI 2000/1119) (the '2000 Regulations') as amended by the Services of Lawyers and Lawyer's Practice (Revocation etc.) (EU Exit) Regulations 2020 (SI 2020/1342) ('the 2020 Regulations') and the Tribunal has jurisdiction over those RELs under regulation 26 of the 2000 Regulations. The rights of other European lawyers to practise as RELs were revoked by the 2020 Regulations on 1 January 2021, but under the transitional provisions of the 2020 Regulations the Tribunal continues to have jurisdiction over those former RELs in respect of disciplinary proceedings commenced before 1 January 2021. For RELs, see **CHAPTER 12**.
3   Paragraphs 15 to 17 of Schedule 14 to the Courts and Legal Services Act (CLSA) 1990.
4   Sections 43 and 47(2E) of SA 1974: see **18.4–18.13**.
5   Section 47(2A), (2B), (2C) and (2D) of SA 1974. These subsections were introduced by AJA 1985, granting the Tribunal the powers formerly vested in the Legal Aid (Complaints) Tribunal (established by the Legal Aid Act 1974, and which had dealt with two cases in its lifetime) and the Legal Aid in Criminal Cases (Complaints) Tribunal (established under the Criminal Justice Act 1967, which had dealt with one).
6   *Re a Solicitor (Ofosuhene)* (21 February 1997, unreported).
7   Section 47(1)(c) of SA 1974.
8   Section 44E(1) of SA 1974; para 14C of Schedule 2 to AJA 1985.
9   Section 44E(4) of SA 1974; para 14C of Schedule 2 to AJA 1985.
10 Section 49A of SA 1974. The matters which, subject to the rules if and when they are made, may be appealed to the Tribunal are: decisions as to restoring the name of a solicitor removed from the roll other than by order of the Tribunal (section 8(4) of SA 1974); the imposition of conditions on practising certificates or refusal to issue practising certificates or sole solicitor endorsements (sections 13A(6) and 28(3D)); decisions relating to the termination of the suspension of practising certificates (section 16(5)); decisions relating to the grant of permission to employ a struck off or suspended solicitor (section 41(3)); and decisions under the parallel jurisdiction in relation to conditions on the registration of foreign lawyers (para 14 of Schedule 14 to CLSA 1990).

The Tribunal's procedural rules, practice directions, guidance notes and application forms

21.4

The Tribunal has power to make its own rules about its procedure and practice. Any alterations to the procedural rules made after introduction of LSA 2007 are subject to the approval of the Legal Services Board (LSB), which also has the power to direct changes to the rules. The rules are made by way of statutory instrument.[1]

The Tribunal's procedures are governed by the 2019 Rules,[2] in force from 25 November 2019 onwards,[3] and the Solicitors Disciplinary Tribunal (Appeals and Amendment) Rules 2011[4] which came into force on 1 October 2011 (the 'Appeal Rules').

The 2019 Rules are set out in full in **APPENDIX 15**.

By rule 6(3) of the 2019 Rules the Tribunal has power to make practice directions, and the Tribunal has made two practice directions, one on agreed outcomes and the other on remote and hybrid hearings.

The Tribunal publishes guidance notes, policy documents and information guides. The main guidance note is a guidance note on sanctions. Other guidance notes include notes relating to adjournments, procedural applications, appeals to the Tribunal from SRA decisions, requests to give evidence by video link, applications for special measures for vulnerable witnesses, and applications relating to restoration, termination of suspension and revocation of section 43 orders.[5] The main policy documents are a judgment publication policy and a policy on the supply of documents to a non-party from Tribunal records. The information guides include guides on Caselines[6] and remote and hybrid hearings and guides for unrepresented respondents, unrepresented applicants, lay applicants and witnesses. The Tribunal has also published a protocol on the use of Caselines.

Under the 2019 Rules, there are prescribed forms for applications made by the SRA and lay persons against solicitors (rule 12), and applications for restoration and termination of indefinite suspensions (rule 17), variation or removal of conditions on practice (rule 18), review of section 43 orders made by the SRA (rule 19), procedural applications (rule 22) and rehearings (rule 37). The Tribunal also publishes forms for certificates of readiness, applications for non party disclosure,[7] applications for special measures[8] and notices of appeal to the Tribunal.

1 Section 46(9)(b) and (12) of SA 1974; section 178 of LSA 2007.
2 SI 2019/1185.
3 The 2019 Rules replace the Solicitors (Disciplinary Proceedings) Rules 2007 (the '2007 Rules') (SI 2007/3588). The 2007 Rules continue to apply after 25 November 2019 to applications made to the Tribunal before 25 November 2019, and commentary on the 2007 Rules can be found in *The Solicitor's Handbook 2017.*
4 SI 2011/2346.
5 That is an order under section 43 of SA 1974 relating to an employee or consultant of a solicitors' firm.
6 Caselines is a digital court platform which provides the Tribunal and the parties with access to all filed documents in electronic format – see **21.18**.
7 That is an application to the Tribunal for the disclosure of Tribunal documents to a third party.
8 That is an application to the Tribunal for directions for facilitating the hearing of evidence by vulnerable witnesses.

The rule 12 statement and certification of a case to answer

21.5

When an adjudicator or adjudication panel or other authorised person of the SRA resolves to refer the conduct of a solicitor to the Tribunal, the case is allocated by the Legal Directorate of the SRA either to an in-house advocate in that department or to the solicitor instructed by the SRA to prosecute cases. The in-house advocate, or the solicitor, normally drafts the originating process, which consists of an application notice under rule 12 of the 2019 Rules supported by a statement ('the rule 12 statement') which sets out the allegations and facts and matters in support and exhibits any documents relied on. Occasionally counsel is instructed to draft the documents. The solicitor facing the allegations is described as the respondent.

Selecting the respondent(s)

21.6

In many cases, the identity of the appropriate respondent(s) will be obvious to the prosecutor: the proceedings will be commenced against those members of the firm who are felt to be culpable for what has occurred. Generally, the SDT will not be prepared to find a solicitor guilty of professional misconduct unless he or she can be said to be personally culpable. One obvious exception to this relates to the Accounts Rules. The Tribunal regards liability for a breach of those Rules to be a matter of strict liability, as far as the principals of a practice are concerned, because the Accounts Rules require all the principals ('managers' in the terminology of the SRA Glossary) in a practice to ensure compliance with the Rules by themselves and by everyone else working in the practice;[1] this also applies to the firm's compliance officer for finance and administration (COFA) whether or not that individual is a manager. In Accounts Rules cases, the prosecutor must still decide how far to cast the net, ie how many 'principals' to join as respondents to the disciplinary proceedings. In this regard, partners in small firms may be less fortunate than their equivalents in the larger firms: the SRA may prosecute all of the partners in a small firm, whereas to do so in the case of a large firm would be regarded as absurd.

1   Rule 1.2 of the SRA Accounts Rules 2019.

Prosecuting 'innocent' partners

21.7

There has been confusion in recent years as to whether partners who have not known of or directly participated in a decision that breached a regulatory rule should face disciplinary action as a result. Please see the discussion of vicarious liability at **19.20**.

Prosecuting managers, COLPs and COFAs

21.8

In 2013 the SRA introduced a requirement for all firms to appoint a compliance officer for legal practice (COLP) and a COFA with responsibilities for ensuring that the firm has systems and controls in place to enable the firm, its managers, owners and employees to comply with the Accounts Rules (in the case of the COFA) and with all other regulatory requirements (in the case of the COLP).[1] Although all managers (or partners) in a practice have similar obligations to ensure there are effective systems and controls in place,[2] the additional responsibilities placed on COLPs and COFAs, which cannot properly be delegated to others, has led to prosecutions against COLPs and COFAs rather than other managers when there are faults in a firm's management systems.

1   Rule 8.5 of the SRA Authorisation Rules 2011, the guidance notes to rule 8 of the SRA Authorisation Rules 2011 and paragraphs 9.1 and 9.2 of the SRA Code of Conduct for Firms 2019 (the 'Code for Firms').
2   Chapter 7 of the SRA Code of Conduct 2011; paragraph 8.1 of the Code for Firms.

Prosecuting entities

21.9

From the point at which it became possible to practise through a corporate structure as a recognised body in 1986,[1] the Law Society as regulator has been able to exercise direct control over the business entity. Disciplinary action could be taken against the recognised body by the revocation of recognition and applications could be made to the Tribunal for disciplinary sanctions, but in practice these powers were not used. Between 1986 and 31 March 2009, only two applications were made to the Tribunal against such a body as a respondent.[2] In both cases the company was a respondent to proceedings which were primarily directed at individuals, and in one of those two cases the Tribunal accepted a submission that any sanction on the company would simply be a second sanction against the individual who owned it, for the same offence, and declined to impose any separate sanction.[3]

The growth of entity regulation since 2009 suggested that there would be a marked increase in the number of entities (as opposed to individual solicitors) prosecuted before the Tribunal. However, that did not happen, and SRA prosecutions continued to focus upon individuals rather than entities. There was no published policy by the SRA as to when it considered it appropriate to prosecute an entity as well as, or instead of, individual solicitors, but it was understood to be the 'official position' of the SRA in terms of policy that entity regulation should primarily involve 'supervision', with 'enforcement' being deployed only in two circumstances: (a) where there was a serious failure of management – something fundamentally attributable to the way that the firm is being run; or (b) where on a problem being identified the firm is unwilling or unable to work with the SRA to put things right.[4] It is submitted that such an approach is sensible.

In 2019 the SRA separated the code of conduct into two separate codes for individual solicitors and firms. The SRA also published an Enforcement Strategy[5] which states that where an individual is directly culpable, the SRA will generally proceed against the individual. However, the Enforcement Strategy also states that the SRA will usually take action against the firm where there has been a breach of the Code for Firms, and the examples in the Enforcement Strategy of occasions on which action will be taken against firms include a failure which relates to the culture, systems, supervision arrangements or processes for which the firm as a whole should be held accountable, occasions where it is not possible or proportionate to establish individual responsibility and occasions on which action against the firm is appropriate to remove the benefit of wrongdoing by a fine or to suspend, revoke or impose conditions on a firm's authorisation.

Although the prosecution of entities has become rather more common than hitherto in the last five to six years, the introduction of the Code for Firms in 2019 has not led to a noticeable change in approach or a significant increase in the number of firms prosecuted for breaches of the conduct rules.

1   Section 9 of and Schedule 2 to AJA 1985.
2   *Atikpakpa*, 8913-2004, SDT and *Le Moine*, 9048-2004, SDT.
3   *Le Moine*, 9048-2004, SDT.
4   See too SRA, 'Criteria to determine the focus of an investigation', 10 May 2012.
5   SRA Enforcement Strategy, 7 February 2019, updated 25 November 2019.

Pleading the case against the respondent(s)

21.10

Great care is required in drafting the rule 12 statement. It is the entire basis of the prosecution case, containing not only the allegations which the respondent solicitor will have to face, but also the narrative supporting those allegations. If the narrative is unclear, or does not properly reflect the allegations, the Tribunal, or the High Court on appeal, is likely to be critical. One such instance was the case of *Thaker v SRA*,[1] in which the court was highly critical of the drafting of the relevant statement (at [17]):

> 'I regret to say that both the RAS [the re-amended statement of the SRA's case] and the schedule are chaotic documents. Although these documents are formidable at first sight, when one settles down to study them it is quite impossible to understand the case which Mr Thaker was being called upon to answer. The order in which matters are set out in the RAS is neither chronological nor logical. There are many cross references which are impossible to follow up, as the reader seeks to navigate a path through the hundreds of pages which form attachments to the RAS.'

Three further passages from reported cases should be borne in mind by any prosecutor. In his judgment in *Constantinides v Law Society*,[2] Lord Justice Moses said (at [35]):

> 'We should stress that we do not consider that the allegations of dishonesty were clearly and properly made in the Rule 4 statement. The Rule 4 statement, after alleging conduct unbefitting a solicitor, should have identified that conduct and stated with precision in relation to each aspect of the allegedly guilty conduct the respects in which it was said to be dishonest. It should have alleged that when the appellant acted, despite the conflict of interest, that that conduct was dishonest by the ordinary standards of honest behaviour and that he knew that he was transgressing the ordinary standards of honest behaviour.'[3]

Likewise in *Thaker v SRA*, Jackson LJ observed:

> '64. In order to have an effective re-trial, the SRA must serve a properly drafted Rule 4 statement in respect of any of the twelve allegations which it wishes to pursue. For the avoidance of doubt a properly drafted Rule 4 statement will set out a summary of the facts relied upon. It would be helpful if those facts are set out concisely and in chronological order … It is the duty of the draftsman (not the reader) of a pleading or a Rule 4 statement to analyse the supporting evidence and to distil the relevant facts, discarding all irrelevancies.[4]
>
> 65. If the Rule 4 statement alleges that Mr Thaker knew or ought to have known certain matters, the facts giving rise to that actual or constructive knowledge should also be set out. Once the Rule 4 statement has set out the primary facts asserted, it should then set out the allegations which are made on the basis of those primary facts. The person who drafts the Rule 4 statement should heed the guidance given by this court in *Constantinides* in relation to pleading dishonesty. In a complex case such as this the Solicitors' Disciplinary Tribunal needs to have a coherent and intelligible Rule 4 statement, in order to do justice between the parties.'

In *Connolly v Law Society*[5] Stanley Burnton J (with whom Laws LJ agreed) held (at [104]):

> 'the Law Society should avoid where possible formulating charges which include "and/or" allegations, such as charge (xl) in the present case, which

comprised numerous alternatives. Where such a charge is laid, the Tribunal should make specific findings as to which allegation has been proved.'

These criticisms have to some extent fallen on deaf ears. 'And/or' allegations remain commonplace. In *SRA v Andersons*,[6] Treacy LJ observed, at [3]:

'During the course of the hearing we commented on the highly complicated structure of the charges, involving multiple allegations of breaches of rules, either cumulatively or in the alternative. Mr Dutton QC, for the SRA, acknowledged the force of this criticism. We would hope that in the future consideration would be given to a significantly clearer method of framing charges.'

Similarly, it remains commonplace to have to cross-refer to exhibits to understand the SRA's case. In *SRA v Manak* Holroyde LJ said:

'... we are surprised and disappointed that the SRA felt it appropriate to set out their case in the manner in which they did. The amended rule 5 statement is some 25 pages in length, but it incorporates by reference both FIR 2010[7] and FIR 2012, and is in places cross referenced to those reports. It follows that, in order to understand the allegations ... it is necessary to refer to documents which collectively amount to more than 900 pages ... we are left with the clear feeling that the very unhelpful way in which the amended rule 5 statement was drafted set the scene for unnecessarily protracted proceedings.'[8]

1   [2011] EWHC 660 (Admin).
2   [2006] EWHC 725 (Admin).
3   The rule 4 statement was the originating process under rule 4 of the Solicitors (Disciplinary Proceedings) Rules 1994.
4   In *SRA v Manak* [2016] EWHC 1914 (Admin), Thirlwall J observed at [23] that paragraph 64 of the *Thaker* judgment should be part of the training manual for those who draft pleadings on behalf of the SRA.
5   [2007] EWHC 1175 (Admin).
6   [2013] EWHC 4021 (Admin).
7   That is, the SRA's Forensic Investigation Report.
8   *Manak v SRA* [2018] EWHC 1958 (Admin) at [21] and [24].

Alleging breaches of the SRA Principles and the Codes of Conduct

21.11

Since 2011, the preferred method of charging disciplinary offences in matters which do not involve allegations of breaches of the Accounts Rules has been for the SRA to allege breaches of one or more of the SRA Principles, and, less universally, failure to achieve one or more of the outcomes or standards in the codes of conduct. This method of pleading has superseded allegations of conduct unbefitting a solicitor, which tended to be the norm prior to 2007.

The SRA Principles 2011 and the SRA Code of Conduct 2011 will continue to apply to breaches which occurred before introduction of the SRA Principles 2019 and the 2019 Codes of Conduct and pleadings alleging breaches of the 2011 rules will continue to be heard by the Tribunal for a number of years after introduction of the 2019 regulatory arrangements. If a course of conduct persists over a period of time, and leads to breaches of the 2011 rules as well as the 2019 regulatory arrangements, the pleadings are likely to include allegations of breaches of both sets of rules.

The Principles are deliberately couched in very wide terms. Not every breach of a principle will amount to professional misconduct. For instance, principle 5 of the SRA Principles 2011 requires solicitors to provide a proper standard of service to clients. Negligence can amount to professional misconduct, but only if it meets the test of being 'inexcusable and … such as to be regarded as deplorable by his fellows in the profession'.[1] A finding of misconduct is based on an evaluative assessment of the seriousness of the breach of the principle. The same applies to breaches of the mandatory outcomes in the 2011 Code and the standards in the 2019 Codes: while such a breach may amount to professional misconduct, it must not necessarily do so.[2]

1   *Re a Solicitor* [1972] 2 All ER 811, CA at 815 and see *Connolly v Law Society* [2007] EWHC 1175 (Admin) at [62] and *SRA v Day* [2018] EWHC 2726 (Admin) at [156] to [158]. See the general discussion of professional misconduct in **CHAPTER 19**.
2   *SRA v Day* [2018] EWHC 2726 (Admin) at [156]–[158].

Alleging dishonesty

21.12

If dishonesty is to be alleged against a solicitor, this must be pleaded with 'pitiless clarity'[1] and the allegation should be pleaded in the rule 12 statement.[2] None of the principles and outcomes in the 2011 rules expressly require a solicitor to act honestly and if the SRA considers that a solicitor's breach of any of the 2011 rules involves dishonesty, the SRA will allege a breach of the rule and add a separate allegation that the breach involved dishonesty. Principle 4 of the SRA Principles 2019 expressly requires a solicitor to act honestly, and an allegation of dishonesty relating to conduct occurring while the 2019 regulatory arrangements are in force will include an allegation that principle 4 has been breached.

Failure expressly to allege or particularise dishonesty in a document in advance of the Tribunal hearing is likely to amount to a serious procedural flaw, which may well result in any finding of dishonesty by the Tribunal being overturned.[3] In *Fish v GMC* Foskett J said:

> 'An allegation of dishonesty against a professional person … should not be made without good reason … no-one should be found to have been dishonest on a side wind or by some kind of default setting in the mechanism of the inquiry. It is an issue that must be articulated, addressed and adjudged head on.'[4]

It is not enough to make a free-standing allegation of dishonesty: such an allegation must make clear the acts or omissions that are said to be dishonest.[5]

The test for dishonesty is set out by Lord Hoffmann in *Barlow Clowes* as follows:

> 'Although a dishonest state of mind is a subjective mental state, the standard by which the law determines whether it is dishonest is objective. If by ordinary standards a defendant's mental state would be characterised as dishonest, it is irrelevant that the defendant judges by different standards.'[6]

In *Ivey* Lord Hughes confirmed that this is the test for dishonesty:

> 'The test of dishonesty is as set out by Lord Nicholls in *Royal Brunei Airlines Sdn Bhd v Tan* and by Lord Hoffmann in *Barlow Clowes* ... When dishonesty is in question the fact-finding tribunal must first ascertain (subjectively) the actual state of the individual's knowledge or belief as to the facts. The reasonableness or otherwise of his belief is a matter of evidence (often in practice determinative) going to whether he held the belief, but it is not an additional requirement that his belief must be reasonable; the question is whether it is genuinely held. When once his actual state of mind as to knowledge or belief as to facts is established, the question whether his conduct was honest or dishonest is to be determined by the fact-finder by applying the (objective) standards of ordinary decent people. There is no requirement that the defendant must appreciate that what he has done is, by those standards, dishonest.'[7]

In *SRA v Wingate*, the Court of Appeal stressed that, although the test for dishonesty is an objective test, a defendant's state of mind is relevant. Jackson LJ said:

> 'As explained most recently in *Ivey*, the test for dishonesty is objective. Nevertheless, the Defendant's state of mind as well as their conduct are relevant to determining whether they have acted dishonestly.'[8]

The Tribunal is regularly called upon to consider whether the failings of a solicitor amount to dishonesty, with an understanding that if there is a finding of dishonesty, the solicitor will almost inevitably be struck off (see **22.18** and **22.19**).

1   This memorable phrase was used by Mostyn J in *Malins v SRA* [2017] EWHC 835 (Admin).
2   *SRA v Manak* [2016] EWHC 1914 (Admin) at [26].
3   *Singleton v Law Society* [2005] EWHC 2915 (Admin); *Constantinides v Law Society* [2006] EWHC 725 (Admin); *Onibudo v Law Society* [2002] EWHC 2030 (Admin).
4   *Fish v GMC* [2012] EWHC 1269 (Admin) at [68]–[70]. See also *SRA v Prescott* [2019] EWHC 1739 (Admin) at [42].
5   See *SRA v Manak* [2016] EWHC 1914 (Admin) at [26].
6   *Barlow Clowes International Ltd v Eurotrust International Ltd* [2006] 1 WLR 1476, PC at [1479]–[1480]. See too the discussion of dishonesty in **CHAPTER 19**.
7   *Ivey v Genting Casinos (UK) Ltd* [2017] UKSC 67 at [74].
8   *SRA v Wingate; SRA v Malins* [2018] EWCA Civ 366 at [94]. See also the two-stage approach on application of the test in *Zivancevic v SRA* [2019] EWHC 1950 (Admin) at [19].

Alleging lack of integrity

21.13

Principle 2 of the SRA Principles 2011 and principle 5 of the SRA Principles 2019 require solicitors to act with integrity. Allegations of lack of integrity have become popular with the SRA since 2011, as a means of alleging serious misconduct short of dishonesty.

The meaning of the phrase 'lack of integrity' has been explored in a series of cases relating to financial services and solicitors since 2003, and was considered by the Court of Appeal in *SRA v Wingate* in 2018.[1]

The first notable case was *Hoodless & Blackwell v FSA* in 2003, in which the Financial Services and Markets Tribunal said:

'In our view "integrity" connotes moral soundness, rectitude and steady adherence to an ethical code. A person lacks integrity if unable to appreciate the distinction between what is honest or dishonest by ordinary standards. (This presupposes, of course, circumstances where ordinary standards are clear. Where there are genuinely grey areas, a finding of lack of integrity would not be appropriate.)'[2]

In *Wingate* Jackson LJ said that the observations in *Hoodless* had met with general approbation between 2003 and 2018 but that it was not possible to formulate an all-purpose, comprehensive definition of integrity.[3]

As regards integrity in professional conduct cases, Jackson LJ said:

'In professional codes of conduct, the term "integrity" is a useful shorthand to express the higher standards which society expects from professional persons and which the professions expect from their own members ... The underlying rationale is that the professions have a privileged and trusted role in society. In return they are required to live up to their own professional standards ...

Integrity connotes adherence to the ethical standards of one's own profession. That involves more than mere honesty. To take one example, a solicitor conducting negotiations ... will take particular care not to mislead. Such a professional person is expected to be even more scrupulous about accuracy than a member of the general public in daily discourse ...

The duty to act with integrity applies not only to what professional persons say but also to what they do ...

Obviously, neither Courts nor professional tribunals must set unrealistically high standards ... The duty of integrity does not require professional people to be paragons of virtue. In every instance, professional integrity is linked to the manner in which that particular profession professes to serve the public ...

A professional disciplinary tribunal has specialist knowledge of the profession to which the respondent belongs and of the ethical standards of that profession. Accordingly such a body is well placed to identify want of integrity ...'[4]

In *Wingate* the Court of Appeal did not expressly state that the test for lack of integrity is an objective test. That issue was considered by Morris J in *Newell-Austin v SRA*, who said that the test is an objective test, and that there is no requirement for the respondent to have an appreciation of the lack of integrity. However Morris J also said:

'The person's state of knowledge or intention in relation to the underlying conduct (said to demonstrate lack of integrity) is a relevant consideration in assessing whether, in carrying out such conduct, a person demonstrated a lack of integrity.'[5]

1 *SRA v Wingate; SRA v Malins* [2018] EWCA Civ 366 at [98] and [99]. See also *SRA v Chan* [2015] EWHC 2659 (Admin); *Scott v SRA* [2016] EWHC 1256 (Admin); *Newell-Austin v SRA* [2017]

EWHC 411 (Admin) and *Williams v SRA* [2017] EWHC 1478 (Admin). See generally the discussion of lack of integrity in **Chapter 19**.

2 *Hoodless & Blackwell v FSA* [2003] FSMT 007.

3 *SRA v Wingate; SRA v Malins* [2018] EWCA Civ 366 at [98] and [99].

4 *SRA v Wingate; SRA v Malins* [2018] EWCA Civ 366 at [97]–[103].

5 *Newell-Austin v SRA* [2017] EWHC 411 (Admin) at [48]–[50]; see also *SRA v Wingate; SRA v Malins* [2018] EWCA Civ 366 at [85].

Alleging recklessness

21.14

An allegation of recklessness should be pleaded.[1] Recklessness is defined as a matter of law, and the definition has been applied by the SDT; see *Lawson*[2] and *Fuglers*[3] (undisturbed by the High Court on appeal). The following quotations, paraphrasing *R v G*,[4] are from *Lawson* and *Fuglers* respectively:

> 'Recklessness means the taking of an unreasonable risk of which the risk-taker is aware: a person acts "recklessly" with respect to a circumstance when he is aware of a risk that did or would exist, and acts recklessly with respect to a consequence when he is aware of a risk that it will occur, and in either case, it is, in the circumstances known to him, unreasonable to take the risk.'

> '… it had to be shown that the defendant's state of mind was culpable in that he acted recklessly in respect of a circumstance if he was aware of a risk which did or would exist, or in respect of a result if he was aware of a risk that it would occur, and it was, in the circumstances known to him, unreasonable to take the risk.'[5]

1 *Constantinides v Law Society* [2006] EWHC 725 (Admin) at [35]; *SRA v Manak* [2016] EWHC 1914 (Admin) at [26]. But see also *Keazor v Law Society* [2009] EWHC 267 (Admin) at [14].

2 11048-2012, SDT.

3 10917-2012, SDT.

4 [2004] 1 AC 1034, HL.

5 In *SRA v Dar* [2019] EWHC 2831 (Admin) at [55] Hickinbottom LJ and May J confirmed that the correct test for recklessness in the Tribunal is the test described in *R v G*.

Certification of a case to answer

21.15

When the rule 12 statement and supporting documents are filed with the Tribunal, the papers are considered by a solicitor member of the Tribunal, who certifies whether a 'case to answer' is made out against the respondent.[1] If no such case is revealed, the papers are considered by a panel of three members, and, if all agree, the case can be dismissed without hearing any party. The respondent solicitor is not invited to make any representations as to why the Tribunal should not certify a prima facie case – indeed the solicitor will not even know that this process is taking place. If the case is dismissed the applicant must be given written reasons for the decision. If a decision is made to certify a case to answer, no reasons are given for the Tribunal's decision to certify, and indeed the affected solicitor is not even informed when and by whom this certification has been provided. It is believed that this somewhat unusual process results from the fact that any member of the public may commence disciplinary proceedings in the Tribunal against a solicitor, and that it is important to have a system by which hopeless cases can be weeded out at a very early stage. Occasionally, however, the Tribunal declines to certify a case when the proceedings have been initiated by the SRA. No statistics are available as to how often this happens.

After the case has been certified, the Tribunal serves the prescribed application form, the rule 12 statement and its exhibits on the respondent.[2]

1   See generally rule 13 of the 2019 Rules.
2   Rule 13(5) of the 2019 Rules.

The respondent's answer

21.16

Before October 2013, pre-trial procedures were governed by the 2007 Rules, and ad hoc arrangements made between the legal representatives for the parties. There were serious drawbacks in these procedures. In particular, there was no provision in the Rules for the defence case to be properly pleaded or set out for the benefit of the Tribunal unless the respondent chose to serve a defence case statement or detailed witness statement in answer to the allegations. There was no specific obligation to provide a defence case statement, and respondents often failed to serve a witness statement until the last moment or even at all.

In October 2013 the Tribunal introduced standard directions which required the respondent to serve an answer, and answers have been served as a matter of routine since then.

Rule 20(2) of the 2019 Rules states that the standard directions may specify the date by which the respondent must send to the Tribunal and serve on every party an answer to the allegations. Rule 20(4)(a) states that an answer sets out '(i) which allegations in the [rule 12] Statement are admitted and which are denied; and (ii) the reasons for denial'. The answer does not need to deal with every matter in every paragraph of the rule 12 statement, and so does not resemble a defence in civil proceedings. It can set out the respondent's case succinctly, so that the Tribunal can understand from the pleadings alone what is asserted by each party in the case.

Standard directions, Caselines, procedural applications and hearings

Standard directions

21.17

The Tribunal issues standard directions which are served on all parties at the same time as the rule 12 statement is served on the respondent.

Rule 20(2) of the 2019 Rules states that the standard directions may specify:

- the date fixed for the substantive hearing;

- the date by which a respondent must send to the Tribunal and serve on every other party an answer to the allegations;

- the date by which a respondent must send to the Tribunal and serve on every other party all documents on which the respondent intends to rely at the substantive hearing;

- the date by which all parties must send to the Tribunal and serve on every other party a list of witnesses upon whose evidence they intend to rely at the substantive hearing;

- the date by which the parties must notify the Tribunal of any intention to rely on expert evidence;

- the date on which any case management hearing will take place;

- the date by which the parties must send a statement of readiness to the Tribunal;

- the date by which hearing bundles must be sent to the Tribunal; or

- any other standard directions which the Tribunal considers appropriate.

The other standard directions which the Tribunal may well make include directions for service of witness statements[1] and any Civil Evidence Act notices,[2] a direction confirming the time by which any application for an agreed outcome should be made to the Tribunal[3] and directions specifying the time by which any statements of the respondent's means[4] or statements of costs should by served and sent to the Tribunal.

A 'statement of readiness' is a document confirming whether a party is ready for the substantive hearing, setting out what if any further directions are required and confirming the time estimate for the hearing. It is normally served and sent to the Tribunal four weeks before the substantive hearing.[5]

1 Rule 28(2) of the 2019 Rules.
2 By rule 29 of the 2019 Rules, the provisions of the Civil Evidence Act 1995 apply to Tribunal proceedings and any Civil Evidence Act notices under section 2(1) of the Civil Evidence Act 1995 must be given no later than the date for service of the witness statements.
3 By rule 25(1) of the 2019 Rules the parties may submit any application for an agreed outcome to the Tribunal up to 28 days before the substantive hearing, unless the Tribunal directs otherwise.
4 Rule 43(5) of the 2019 Rules.
5 Rule 20(4)(b) of the 2019 Rules.

Caselines

21.18

In April 2019 the Tribunal introduced Caselines, a digital court platform which dispenses with the need for paper bundles at hearings by providing the Tribunal and the parties with access to all filed documents in electronic format. Under Caselines, the parties upload any documents for service on to a master bundle on the Tribunal's platform. The master bundle can be accessed by the parties via the internet. Hearing bundles are created by transferring relevant documents from the master bundle to a hearing bundle. The hearings are then conducted without paper files by using laptops to provide access to the electronic hearing bundle.[1]

The Tribunal does not in practice require hard copies of documents when Caselines is used. However, if a hard copy of a document does need to be presented to the Tribunal, four copies are normally required – one for each of the members and one for the clerk.

1 The Tribunal has published an information guide on Caselines, a user guide for parties and advocates and a protocol on the use of Caselines which can be found on the Tribunal website at www.solicitorstribunal.org.uk.

Case management hearings

21.19

The standard directions served on the parties at the same time as the Tribunal's service of the rule 12 statement on the respondent will include a direction for a case management hearing (CMH) in cases where (a) a clerk considers a CMH is justified by reason of the time estimate provided by the SRA or (b) the clerk who reviews the application on receipt identifies issues which in the opinion of the clerk justify the holding of a CMH.[1] The SRA is required to provide a time estimate for the substantive hearing when lodging the rule 12 statement with the Tribunal,[2] and in practice the Tribunal will always hold a CMH if the time estimate is three days or more.

A CMH may also be fixed in any case at any other time before the substantive hearing by the Tribunal or a clerk.[3]

The parties are encouraged to agree directions for the management of the case going forward. The CMH can be held by telephone. Indeed in many cases, the parties will be able to agree appropriate directions in advance and obtain the Tribunal's consent to the directions on paper so that it is unnecessary for them to attend the CMH in person or by phone. General matters that may be dealt with at a CMH include:

- amending the rule 12 statement;

- ordering the SRA to provide 'further and better particulars of the rule 12 statement'; and

- variations to the standard directions.

In most cases, one CMH will suffice, but additional ones may prove necessary in the more complex cases. Other specific applications that may be made at the interlocutory stage are set out below.

1 See rule 21(1) of the 2019 Rules.
2 Rule 12(3)(b) of the 2019 Rules.
3 Rule 21(2) of the 2019 Rules.

Procedural applications generally

21.20

The Tribunal has a standard application form for procedural applications, which should be used on any interim application.[1] The application form should be sent to the Tribunal and every other party accompanied by any supporting documents. Minor applications, such as uncontroversial requests for extensions of time, are dealt with on paper by a clerk[2] or the Tribunal after the other parties have been invited to make representations on the application. Other applications are listed for hearing before the Tribunal, and in complex interim applications the Tribunal may give directions for service of evidence and exchange of skeleton arguments. The Tribunal issues written reasons for its decisions on interim applications.

There is no statutory appeal against an interim order of the Tribunal, and the only avenue of challenge is therefore an application for judicial review. In *Stokes v Law Society*,[3] Kennedy LJ observed that relief would be given only in exceptional circumstances 'and never where, as here, the error relied upon has been rectified'.

1   Rule 22(1) of the 2019 Rules.
2   For the powers of clerks on interim applications see rule 8(6) of the 2019 Rules.
3   [2001] EWHC Admin 1101.

Applications for disclosure of documents

21.21

By rule 26(1), if an application is made for disclosure, the Tribunal may make an order for disclosure where it considers that the production of the material is necessary for proper consideration of the case, unless the Tribunal considers that there are compelling reasons in the public interest not to order disclosure.[1]

An order for disclosure will only apply to material which is in the possession or under the control of a party, and will not oblige the party to produce any material which they would be entitled to refuse to produce in court proceedings.[2]

A party to Tribunal proceedings is required to disclose only (a) the documents on which the party relies; (b) any documents which (i) adversely affect that party's own case, (ii) adversely affect another party's case, or (iii) support another party's case; and (c) any documents which a party is required to disclose by a relevant practice direction.[3]

In practice, applications by respondents to the Tribunal for disclosure of documents are unusual. Applications for disclosure made by the SRA against a respondent are even rarer, and there is considerable doubt as to whether the SRA is entitled to seek disclosure during disciplinary proceedings which it has brought. There is no obligation of disclosure upon defendants in criminal proceedings, to which disciplinary proceedings bear some relationship. Moreover, the SRA will have had an opportunity during its investigation to compel disclosure of documents by the regulated individual through use of its statutory powers under SA 1974.

1   Rule 26(1) of the 2019 Rules.
2   Rule 26(2) and (3) of the 2019 Rules.
3   Rule 26(4) of the 2019 Rules. As at the date of writing, there are no relevant practice directions.

Applications for hearings to be held in private

21.22

Under the Tribunal's rules, any party to the disciplinary proceedings, or a third party who claims to be affected, may apply for all or part of the hearing to be conducted in private on the grounds of exceptional hardship or exceptional prejudice to a party, witness, or any person affected by the application.[1] Otherwise the presumption is that the case will be heard in public.[2]

The principle of open justice, and that legal proceedings should be conducted in public, is an important one.[3] The Tribunal will ordinarily depart from that to the least extent possible. As a result, in *Lee*,[4] rather than hearing the case in private, the Tribunal permitted (for the first time) a vulnerable female witness to give evidence from behind a screen about flirtatious texts sent to her by the respondent. Sometimes, however, the principle of open justice has to yield, and this will be particularly so in cases in which the lay client has not waived privilege, and to hear the case in public will necessarily involve identification of the client, and/or publication of confidential and privileged matters.[5]

The Tribunal is most unlikely to accede to any submission by or on behalf of the respondent that the case should be heard in private because of the emotional effect upon the respondent that a public hearing will have. Such an application would have to be supported by cogent and persuasive medical evidence in order to have any prospect of success, and even in such an event, the Tribunal may well feel that the desirability of open justice trumps any psychological effect upon the respondent. On the other hand, if there is compelling evidence that a public hearing might place the respondent or a witness in real physical danger, the Tribunal may be more sympathetic to an application for the case to be heard in private.

If a party or any other person wishes to apply for a hearing to be conducted in private, that person should consider whether to also apply for an order that the cause list be anonymised. Such an application should be made and served no later than 28 days before the hearing.[6] See **21.34**.

If the respondent is considering seeking a judicial review of an SRA decision to publish details of the allegations before the substantive hearing, the respondent will be well advised to apply to the Tribunal for any CMH to be heard in private, and/or that the respondent should not be identified on the Tribunal's lists for hearings.[7]

1   Rule 35(2) and (5) of the 2019 Rules.
2   Rule 35(1) of the 2019 Rules.
3   In *L v Law Society* [2008] EWCA Civ 811 at [41] (a case concerned with an appeal against a decision of the SRA to revoke student membership, but which canvassed wider issues concerning public and private hearings), the Master of the Rolls emphasised the importance of public hearings in the Tribunal in maintaining the confidence of the public in the disciplinary process. See too *SRA v Spector* [2016] EWHC 37 (Admin), [2016] 4 WLR 16 at [19]–[21].
4   11398-2015, SDT.
5   One example of the entire proceedings being held in private is *Chapman and Abramson, News UK intervening*, 11164-2013, SDT. However, the decision that the whole proceedings should be in private was based on the conclusion that there was a substantial risk of prejudice to the course of justice because of extant criminal proceedings, rather than the need to protect the client's privilege: see para 6.1.9 of the judgment.
6   Rule 34(3)(a) of the 2019 Rules.
7   See *Andersons v SRA* [2012] EWHC 3659 (Admin).

Applications to strike out the rule 12 statement as an abuse of process, etc

21.23

The Tribunal may strike out proceedings if it considers that the prosecution amounts to an abuse of process. In the criminal courts, it has long been held that applications to stay proceedings for abuse of process should only rarely be granted, and that the threshold to be surmounted by the applicant is a high one.[1] The Tribunal takes a similar approach, and successful abuse of process applications are rare. A notable example was *Heer Manak*,[2] in which the Tribunal struck out the entire case at the close of the prosecution case on the ground that the rule 5 statement (2007 Rules) was so defective that the respondents (and the Tribunal) were unable to know the case that the respondents had to meet. The SRA's appeal against this decision in so far as it related to two of the six respondents was largely successful. Although critical of the way that the matter had been pleaded, Thirlwall J held that for the most part it was possible to understand what was alleged, and therefore it could not have been an abuse of process for the Tribunal to continue to hear it.[3]

One particular area in which such applications have succeeded is where there has been inordinate delay in bringing the case before the Tribunal.[4] This may amount to an abuse of process on a traditional common law analysis, or it may breach the 'reasonable time' requirement in Article 6(1) of the European Convention on Human Rights. The Tribunal has held that time starts for this purpose when the decision to refer the solicitor to the Tribunal is made, and has struck out cases which have been inordinately delayed thereafter.[5]

The Tribunal has ruled that proceedings should generally be issued within three months of the decision to refer a respondent to the Tribunal, and that if necessary an application for further time (if needed before the matter was listed for hearing) could be considered by the Tribunal.[6] If a fair trial is possible despite delay in issuing the proceedings, it is open to the Tribunal to take the delay into account when deciding the penalty and costs.[7]

1   The leading cases are *Connelly v DPP* [1964] AC 1254, HL; *DPP v Humphrys* [1977] AC 1, HL; *R v Horseferry Road Magistrates' Court, ex p Bennett* [1994] 1 AC 42, HL; and *R v Maxwell* [2011] 1 WLR 1837, SC.
2   11165-2013, SDT.
3   *SRA v Manak* [2016] EWHC 1914 (Admin).
4   For the general approach of the courts, see *Attorney-General's Reference (No 2 of 2001)* [2004] 2 AC 72, HL; *Porter v Magill* [2002] 2 AC 357, HL; and *Dyer v Watson* [2004] 1 AC 379, PC.
5   See generally *Loomba and Loomba*, 9022-2004, SDT; *Davis*, 9017-2004, SDT; *Judge and Stanger*, 9028-2004, SDT; *Rutherford*, 9074-2004, SDT; *Fallon*, 9154-2004, SDT and *Sancheti*, 7976-2007, SDT.
6   *Nulty and Trotter*, 9871-2008, SDT – memorandum of preliminary hearing, 1 July 2008.
7   *Davis*, 9017-2014, SDT.

21.24

If the respondent considers that there is a fatal flaw in the applicant's case against him, the Tribunal may be willing to consider that as a preliminary issue with a view to saving time and expense. Accordingly, cases can be disposed of summarily at the start of the substantive hearing, and there would seem to be no reason in principle in an appropriate case why the respondent should not seek an early listing of the case to ascertain whether it can be summarily disposed of in this way.[1] It must be accepted that these situations are likely to be rare.

1   *Law Society v Adcock and Mocroft* [2006] EWHC 3212 (Admin) at [30].

Applications for adjournments

21.25

The Tribunal has published a guidance note on the subject of adjournments. An application for an adjournment should be supported by documentary evidence of the need for the adjournment.[1]

The Tribunal is generally not prepared to adjourn the disciplinary proceedings pending completion of a criminal investigation or prosecution.[2] The same applies in relation to civil proceedings.[3] The only exception is where there is a risk of 'muddying the waters of justice' but in practice this is usually either an illusory or a manageable risk.

The Tribunal is sometimes faced with applications made at the last minute by respondents who claim to be unable properly to participate in the proceedings on grounds of psychiatric illness, psychological stress, or the like. Such applications are most unlikely to succeed unless supported by cogent medical evidence, and even then may be rejected. The Tribunal is well aware that facing a disciplinary tribunal hearing is a highly stressful experience for any individual, but once the case has been listed and arrangements have been made to hear it, it is plainly important that it should proceed if at all possible. That said, it would be unjust to proceed in the absence of the respondent if a last-minute application was made on the basis of medical evidence from a sufficiently qualified practitioner who had recently examined the respondent which clearly showed that the respondent's ability to participate properly in a hearing had been affected and impaired by a medical condition.[4]

1   SDT Guidance Note on Adjournments, 6 November 2019, and rule 23 of the 2019 Rules.
2   *R v Solicitors Disciplinary Tribunal, ex p Gallagher* (1991, unreported).
3   *Lipman Bray v Hillhouse and Jacob* [1987] NLJR 171, CA.
4   *Rodriguez-Purcet v SRA* [2018] EWHC 2879 (Admin) at [42].

Applications relating to expert evidence

21.26

A party wishing to rely on expert evidence should make an application to the Tribunal for leave to adduce the evidence. No party can call an expert or rely on an expert's report at the substantive hearing without leave of the Tribunal.[1] The Tribunal may grant leave where it considers the expert evidence is necessary for the proper consideration of an issue or issues in the case,[2] although it should be noted that the Tribunal will rarely require expert assistance on matters of law or practice as it is itself an expert tribunal.

An expert's report must set out the expert's professional qualifications and the substance of the instructions provided for the report, and must contain a declaration that the expert is aware of the duty to assist the Tribunal and understands that this duty overrides any obligation to the party providing the instructions.[3]

1   Rule 30(1) of the 2019 Rules.
2   Rule 30(3) of the 2019 Rules.
3   Rule 30(6) of the 2019 Rules.

Applications by the SRA to withdraw allegations

21.27

Once proceedings have been issued, an allegation cannot be withdrawn without the consent of the Tribunal.[1] The Tribunal will often be resistant to giving that consent, because it has earlier certified a prima facie case on the papers: it has often enquired of the SRA advocate what has changed to justify withdrawal. Such an approach contrasts not only with the role of the court in criminal proceedings, but also with that of other courts or tribunals in proceedings that are similar to disciplinary proceedings: ordinarily, such courts and tribunals are discouraged from insisting that particular charges, allegations or issues be tried where the parties have agreed that they need not be tried (see eg *Secretary of State for Trade and Industry v Rogers*[2] in the context of directors' disqualification proceedings).

The origins and purposes of the principle are mentioned in the 1960 *Guide to the Professional Conduct and Etiquette of Solicitors* by Sir Thomas Lund:[3]

> '… an application made to the Disciplinary Committee cannot be withdrawn without the consent of the Committee. That is because it used to be a favourite dodge for clients to lodge an application against a solicitor alleging that moneys were unaccounted for and then, as soon as they were paid off, to withdraw the application, although probably Paul's money had been used for the benefit of Peter.'

So in historical context this provision was designed to ensure that lay applicants were not bought off, leaving a potential underlying issue disguised and undiscovered. It would appear to have no continuing relevance in the modern era when there is a statutory regulator involved.

1   Rule 24 of the 2019 Rules.
2   [1996] 1 WLR 1569, CA.
3   See page 116 and the second half of the middle paragraph.

Miscellaneous matters

Power of the Tribunal to regulate its own procedure

21.28

Rule 6(1) and (2) of the 2019 Rules confer the all-important powers on the Tribunal to regulate its own procedure subject to the Rules, and to dispense with any requirements of the Rules in respect of notices, statements, witnesses, service or time in any case where it appears to be just to do so. At the discretion of the Tribunal, the strict rules of evidence do not apply.[1]

1   Rule 38(2) of the 2019 Rules.

Witness statements and defence material

21.29

The 2019 Rules state that permission is needed for a witness to give evidence at the hearing unless a witness statement is provided to the Tribunal and the other parties on a date determined by the Tribunal which must be no less than 28 days before the hearing.[1] In practice the date determined by the Tribunal will be the date specified in the standard directions.

In the case of the respondent, it is standard practice in contested or complex cases to serve a witness statement as well as the answer (and the witness statement should be served within the time specified in the standard directions). In other cases, it has usually been accepted that the representations made to the SRA at the investigation stage can stand as the respondent's evidence.

The respondent has the option whether or not to give oral evidence, although it is unusual for him or her to elect not to do so in a contested case. In 2012 in *Iqbal v SRA* the High Court said that ordinarily the public would expect a professional man to give an account of his actions.[2] That is reflected in the 2019 Rules, which state that if a respondent fails to serve an answer, or give evidence at the substantive hearing or submit to cross-examination, the Tribunal can draw such adverse inferences as it considers appropriate.[3]

It is common to produce, without undue formality, bundles of testimonials as to the respondent's good character. This can be by way of pure mitigation but can also be directly relevant to issues of honesty and integrity. Such evidence is relevant and admissible where the disciplinary allegations brought against the solicitor impugn his or her honesty.[4]

1   Rule 28(2) and (5) of the 2019 Rules.
2   *Iqbal v SRA* [2012] EWHC 3251 (Admin) at [25].
3   Rule 33 of the 2019 Rules.
4   *Donkin v Law Society* [2007] EWHC 414 (Admin) and *Bryant and Bench v Law Society* [2007] EWHC 3043 (Admin).

Disputed facts and hearsay evidence

21.30

The nature of legal practice means that normally the case against the solicitor is largely or wholly documented. The primary evidence against the respondent in most cases is likely to be the content of his or her own accounts records and files. Serious disputes of fact relating to the underlying events in the prosecution case are comparatively rare, and often it is unnecessary for the applicant to call any oral evidence. The outcome of the case will usually depend upon the respondent's explanation for the accounts records and the documents in the files.

The applicant will normally serve a notice to admit the authenticity of the documents. Under rule 28(6) of the 2019 Rules, any party may (not later than 21 days before the date fixed for the hearing) request any other party to agree that any document may be admitted as evidence. In the absence of a counter-notice requiring authenticity to be proved, the recipient will be deemed to have admitted the document unless otherwise ordered by the Tribunal.[1]

Under rule 28(3) of the 2019 Rules each party must notify the other parties if they require any witnesses to attend for cross-examination, no later than seven days after service of witness statements. If no party requires the attendance of a witness, the Tribunal may accept the statement of the witness as evidence.[2]

As for hearsay evidence, the 2019 Rules import the hearsay provisions in the Civil Evidence Act 1995 into disciplinary proceedings before the Tribunal.[3]

Under rule 13(4) of the 2007 Rules, the applicant was entitled to serve a notice requiring the respondent to indicate within 14 days which of the facts set out in the rule 5 statement were in dispute. This was invariably done in a standard form letter at an early stage. There was no sanction for any failure to admit the facts (other than in costs). The 2019 Rules do not include a similar procedure for service of a notice to admit facts, which is a welcome omission.

1   Rule 28(6)–(8) of the 2019 Rules.
2   Rule 28(1)–(3) of the 2019 Rules.
3   Rule 29 of the 2019 Rules. See also *R (Bonhoeffer) v General Medical Council* [2011] EWHC 1585 (Admin).

Witness summonses

21.31

Either party may compel the attendance of witnesses and the production by witnesses of documents by means of witness summonses.[1] Witness summonses are issued by the Administrative Court (not the Tribunal) under CPR rule 34.4 and the summons must be compliant with the Civil Procedure Rules 1998.

1   Section 46(11) of SA 1974 and rule 28(4) of the 2019 Rules.

Findings of another court or tribunal

21.32

Findings of fact in civil proceedings by another court or tribunal are admissible as prima facie proof of those facts. Accordingly, civil judgments relevant to issues before the Tribunal can be admitted into evidence but may be rebutted. The Tribunal is free to depart from findings in civil proceedings and has done so in several cases,[1] although it will be slow to do so.[2] The situation in relation to criminal convictions is otherwise: it has been held that the Tribunal was right to refuse to hear evidence intended to show a wrongful conviction, as public policy required that, save in exceptional circumstances, a challenge to a criminal conviction should not be entertained by a disciplinary tribunal.[3] The 2019 Rules make explicit provision for these matters: findings of fact upon which a criminal conviction was based are admissible as conclusive proof of those facts save in exceptional circumstances, whereas a civil court judgment is admissible as proof but not conclusive proof of the findings of fact upon which the judgment was based.[4]

As for views formed by a judge in earlier proceedings, in *Constantinides v Law Society*,[5] Moses LJ stated at [28]–[33]:

'[28] … The judgment was admissible to prove background facts in the context of which the appellant's misconduct had to be considered. But that was the limit of its function, in the particular circumstances of this case. The judge's views as to the appellant's dishonesty and lack of integrity were not admissible to prove the Law Society's case against this appellant in these disciplinary proceedings …

[33] We ought, however, to record that we do not see why it was necessary to refer to the judgment at all. The background facts were not in dispute. Provided they were clearly set out within the Rule 4 statement there was no need to rely upon it save in so far as it emerged that the appellant disputed

those primary facts. However, the Rule 4 statement was itself a mixture of assertion of fact and argument. We would suggest that had a simple account of the facts been set out with a reference to relevant paragraphs in the judgment there would have been no further need to refer to it.'

1   See *Gold*, 6050-1991, SDT; *Brebner*, 8805-2003, SDT; *Slater*, 9619-2006, SDT; and, for the general approach, *Choudry v Law Society* [2001] EWHC Admin 633.
2   See *General Medical Council v Spackman* [1943] AC 627, HL.
3   *Re a Solicitor, Times*, 18 March 1996.
4   Rule 32 of the 2019 Rules.
5   [2006] EWHC 725 (Admin).

Pre-trial publication of disciplinary allegations

21.33

The SRA's written guidance, 'Publishing regulatory and disciplinary decisions', states that there is a public interest in being transparent and that the SRA generally expects to publish its decisions to issue proceedings before the Tribunal once the Tribunal has certified there is a case to answer. The guidance states that a decision may be made not to publish if the publication would lead to disclosure of confidential or privileged information. In addition the SRA may decide not to publish if satisfied that:

'in all the circumstances the impact of publication on the regulated person would be disproportionate. In particular, we need to consider Article 8 of the European Convention on Human Rights and balance the right to a private life with the legitimate aim of publication.'[1]

The legality of an earlier SRA publication policy was challenged unsuccessfully in *Andersons v SRA*.[2]

1   SRA guidance, 'Publishing regulatory and disciplinary decisions', 1 September 2016, updated 25 November 2019.
2   [2012] EWHC 3659 (Admin).

21.34

The Tribunal publishes a cause list of all interim and substantive hearings on its website, and a paper copy of the daily cause list is displayed in the Tribunal building. The Tribunal has a discretion to direct that a name on the cause list should be anonymised. The 2019 rules state that an application for anonymisation can be made on the grounds of exceptional hardship or exceptional prejudice to a party, a witness or any person affected by the proceedings. The application should be made no later than 28 days before the hearing.[1]

1   Rule 34 of the 2019 Rules.

Pre-trial procedure – what happens in practice

21.35

Following a decision to refer a solicitor to the Tribunal the solicitor will receive, after an interval, confirmation from the SRA that the papers have been referred to the SRA's external solicitors or to an in-house advocate. Unfortunately, it is not unusual for there to be a delay of several months before proceedings are issued. On the assumption that the Tribunal determines that there is a case to answer, the next development will be service of the papers.

Service is arranged by the Tribunal by special delivery mail. It is possible to inform the applicant in advance that papers can be served on a nominated representative. The documents served will include the rule 12 statement and any documents annexed or exhibited to it, a full set of the current Solicitors (Disciplinary Proceedings) Rules, the standard directions made in the case, a list of those most regularly appearing in the Tribunal as advocates, and details of the Solicitors' Assistance Scheme.

21.36

The Tribunal generally sits between two and three days a week, in addition to any court time needed for multi-day cases, and has four courtrooms so that long cases can be accommodated in one court while routine matters occupy the other courts in greater numbers.[1] A typical list of routine matters will have three to five applications listed for hearing. Because the Tribunal members pre-read the papers and most cases are well documented (see above), even quite substantial contests can be disposed of in less than a day.

The Tribunal expects the parties to have a sensible dialogue to refine issues and avoid unnecessary contention. The overwhelming majority of cases proceed on the basis of admissions and mitigation, or on the basis of admitted facts with argument limited to the proper interpretation of those facts and the inferences that it is proper to draw. In cases which are likely to last three days or more, there will be a case management hearing. Only infrequently, in very substantial or complex cases, is there any need to consider other interim applications. For example, even if there is a perceived need for the applicant to clarify the case the respondent has to meet, one would expect that clarification to be volunteered without the need for any formal intervention by the Tribunal.

1   In 2020 the Tribunal introduced remote hearings in response to the coronavirus outbreak. Practice Direction: Remote and Hybrid Hearings was published on 15 April 2020 and updated on 28 August 2020. A hybrid hearing is one at which some participants attend in person and some attend via a video platform.

Absence of the respondent from the substantive hearing

21.37

The Tribunal may proceed in the absence of the respondent upon proof of service of the notice of hearing.[1] This regularly occurs. Where a respondent is neither present nor represented, and the Tribunal decides the case in his absence, he may apply for a rehearing within 14 days of the filing of the order (in practice therefore within 14 days of the hearing) – which application the Tribunal may grant upon such terms as it thinks fit.[2] A solicitor who voluntarily absents himself from the hearing will ordinarily, however, receive little sympathy from the Tribunal, and is unlikely to obtain a rehearing. In *R (Elliott) v Solicitors Disciplinary Tribunal*,[3] the applicant applied for an adjournment of the substantive hearing, and then walked out when the adjournment was refused. The Tribunal heard the remainder of the case in his absence, and subsequently refused an application for a rehearing. It was held in judicial review proceedings that the rule (then rule 25 of the 1994 Rules) did not apply to such a situation.

1   Rule 36 of the 2019 Rules.
2   Rule 37 of the 2019 Rules.
3   [2004] EWHC 1176 (Admin). See also *Gurpinar v SRA* [2012] EWHC 192 (Admin).

CHAPTER 22

Proceedings before the SDT: (2) tri
sanctions, costs and appeals

The hearing

22.1

The Solicitors Disciplinary Tribunal (the Tribunal or SDT) sits in Gate House, at the south (Ludgate Circus) end of Farringdon Street, London EC4M 7LG.[1] Hearings in the Tribunal are a mixture of the formal and informal; evidence is taken on oath but, as has been seen, the strict rules of evidence do not apply. The parties conduct their advocacy seated, and the hearings are recorded. No pleas to the allegations are formally taken. The applicant is expected to have established the position in this respect and will inform the Tribunal which allegations are admitted and which require to be resolved by the Tribunal. The respondent is required to do no more at this stage, hopefully, than give a monosyllabic confirmation.

The applicant will then open the case and call his or her evidence. As has been said, only rarely is it necessary for the applicant to rely on oral evidence, and usually the applicant's case can be presented entirely by reference to documents, including the written explanations and submissions of the respondent at the investigation stage. The one witness most frequently called by applicants will be the investigating officer of the Solicitors Regulation Authority (SRA)'s Forensic Investigation Unit who undertook the original investigation of, for example, the respondent's accounts.

Factual witnesses are excluded from the hearing until their evidence has been given, unless they are parties to the proceedings, the parties agree, or the Tribunal makes an alternative direction.[2] Examination, cross-examination and re-examination of witnesses proceed as normal, following the pattern of the civil courts as to the use of any witness statement as primary evidence-in-chief.

The hearing bundle is produced in electronic format on the Tribunal's Caselines system and paper hearing bundles are no longer used.[3]

Following the conclusion of the applicant's case the respondent may make a submission of no case to answer,[4] and then will open his or her case, give evidence and call witnesses, and may make a closing submission. In contested cases it tends to be assumed that the respondent will give evidence; in cases where the respondent is accused of and denies dishonesty it would be an exceptional course to fail to do so, and the Tribunal may draw an adverse inference from such a failure.[5] Once the evidence is completed, ordinarily the defence advocate will make a closing speech. It is not usual for the applicant (usually the SRA) to make a closing speech, but exceptionally and with the permission of the Tribunal he or she may do so in a lengthy or complex case where evidence can helpfully be summarised and commented upon. The applicant does not have a right of reply save in relation to points of law or to correct mistakes.[6]

1   The Tribunal is able to hear cases remotely and introduced remote hearings in 2020 in response to the coronavirus outbreak.
2   Rule 35(7) of the Solicitors (Disciplinary Proceedings) Rules 2019 (SI 2019/1185) (the '2019 Rules').
3   For Caselines see **21.18**.
4   The Tribunal has frequently demonstrated a reluctance to accede to such a submission. There is at this stage in a contested application an understandable interest in hearing what the respondent has to say. For an exceptional case in which the Tribunal acceded to such a submission see *Cohen*, 9942-2008, SDT.
5   See *Iqbal v SRA* [2012] EWHC 3251 (Admin) and rule 33 of the 2019 Rules.
6   This should be taken to reflect current practice; there is no formal rule as to this.

Standard of proof

22.2

By rule 5 of the 2019 Rules the Tribunal applies the civil standard of proof.[1]

1   The Solicitors (Disciplinary Proceedings) Rules 2007 (the '2007 Rules') did not specify the standard of proof and the Tribunal has applied the criminal standard to cases proceeding under the 2007 Rules. The adoption of the criminal standard was supported by high authority. In *Campbell v Hamlet* [2005] UKPC 19, [2005] 3 All ER 1116, interpreting *Re a Solicitor* [1993] QB 69, it was held by the Privy Council that the standard of proof in deciding facts against a respondent solicitor in disciplinary proceedings should be the criminal standard, irrespective of whether dishonesty is alleged. In *Richards v Law Society* [2009] EWHC 2087 (Admin) the SRA sought to argue for the civil standard. The Divisional Court held that on the particular facts of the case, the issue was academic, but strongly implied that the Tribunal was bound to apply the criminal standard unless and until the Supreme Court ruled otherwise. See also *Law Society v Waddingham* [2012] EWHC 1519 (Admin), in which the SRA appealed against a finding by the Tribunal that it was not satisfied that dishonesty had been proved against two of the respondents: the High Court dismissed the appeal specifically on the basis that dishonesty had not been established to the criminal standard (at [60]). However, the regulatory tide generally was flowing in the direction of replacing the criminal standard with the civil standard in professional disciplinary proceedings, and in 2016 the High Court said the authorities were 'ripe for reconsideration': see *SRA v Solicitors' Disciplinary Tribunal, ex p Arslan* [2016] EWHC 2862 (Admin) at [49] and [73]. In July 2018 the Tribunal issued a consultation paper on its new rules questioning whether the criminal standard should continue to apply, and a decision was made to apply the civil standard. The Legal Services Board (LSB) approved the new rules adopting the civil standard on 25 July 2019. The statutory instrument for the new rules was made on 6 August 2019, with the new rules coming into force on 25 November 2019 and applying to all cases commenced on or after 25 November 2019.

Decision, mitigation and penalty

22.3

The Tribunal invariably announces its findings, together with brief reasons, at the conclusion of the hearing. If it finds any of the allegations against the respondent substantiated, the Chairman asks the Tribunal clerk whether there have been previous findings against the respondent. The respondent is permitted to make a plea in mitigation (possibly at this stage adducing testimonials as to character) and the Tribunal then determines penalty.[1] If the Tribunal decides to suspend a solicitor, it may be prepared to delay the start of that suspension to enable the solicitor to make appropriate arrangements for running his practice during the period of suspension. The Tribunal is noticeably more reluctant to delay the effect of a striking-off order although this does occasionally happen.[2] Respondents seeking a stay pending appeal must, if the Tribunal does not grant a stay, appeal and apply to the Administrative Court for a stay pending a hearing of the substantive appeal. The appeal does not operate as a stay. For further guidance on appeals, see **22.43–22.50**.

1   This summary of the practice is enshrined in rule 41 of the 2019 Rules. Rule 40(1) of the 2019 Rules contains a provision that the Tribunal may reserve its decision for announcement at a later date, but in practice the decision is announced at the conclusion of the hearing.
2   *Aaronson,* 10099-2008, SDT.

The written judgment of the Tribunal

22.4

The written judgment of the Tribunal is ordinarily delivered some weeks after the hearing. In *Virdi v Law Society*[1] a full-scale attack was made on the Tribunal's process for production of the findings, on the basis that the clerk had a role in producing a first draft of the document based, inter alia, on the oral findings and reasons given by the Chairman at the conclusion of the hearing. Although the (exceptional) delay in producing the findings in that case was the subject of criticism, the process was held to be entirely proper by both the Divisional Court and the Court of Appeal.

By section 48 of the Solicitors Act (SA) 1974, a statement of the Tribunal's findings must be filed with the Law Society and the files are open to public inspection. The Tribunal also publishes its written judgments on the Tribunal website.

The Tribunal may make directions prohibiting publication of specified information relating to the proceedings including direction for anonymisation of the names of the respondents or any other persons.[2] In 2016 in *SRA v Spector*[3] the Tribunal anonymised the identities of the respondents who had been acquitted after the case was heard in public. On appeal, the Divisional Court held that there was no legal ground upon which the principle of open justice could be disapplied: the proceedings had been freely reportable, and the public had been able to attend the public hearing of the case. There was as much legitimate public interest in an acquittal as in a disciplinary 'conviction', and the importance of open justice was such that anonymisation of acquitted respondents was impermissible.

In October 2018 the Tribunal published a judgment publication policy stating that any application for restrictions on publication will be considered on its own merits. Factors supporting publication include the principle of open justice and the need to maintain public confidence in the profession. The fact that a case has been heard in private does not mean that the Tribunal must decide that the judgment should be anonymised. The policy also specifies the time periods for different categories of judgments to remain on the website.[4]

1   [2009] EWHC 918 (Admin) (Divisional Court); [2010] EWCA Civ 100 (Court of Appeal).
2   See rule 35(9) and (10) of the 2019 Rules and the Tribunal's 'Judgment Publication Policy', October 2018, updated 6 May 2020 (available on its website).
3   [2016] EWHC 37 (Admin), [2016] 4 WLR 16.
4   The Tribunal's 'Judgment Publication Policy', October 2018, updated 6 May 2020.

The range of penalties available to the Tribunal and Tribunal guidance

22.5

From the 'bottom' upwards, where allegations are proved or admitted, the Tribunal may:

CHAPTER 22
THE SDT: (2) TRIAL, SANCTIONS, COSTS, APPEALS

- make no order – this course is followed when the Tribunal considers that it would be unfair or disproportionate to impose a sanction. It may nevertheless decide to make an order for costs against the respondent solicitor;

- impose a reprimand;

- impose an unlimited fine;

- impose a restriction order;

- suspend, either for a fixed period or indefinitely; or

- strike off.

22.6

Until the summer of 2012, the Tribunal provided no published guidance to the profession or the public as to how it exercised its disciplinary powers. This was the subject of criticism by Nicola Davies J in *Hazelhurst v SRA*[1] in which she said (at [38]):

> 'It is of note that the SDT has not published Indicative Sanctions Guidance. Such guidance identifies the purpose, parameters and range of sanctions. It permits those who appear before it to better understand the proceedings and the thinking of the SDT. It assists the transparency of the proceedings. Such guidance has been used by other regulatory bodies for some years and is a valuable reference point both for the tribunal and for those who appear in front of it, as practitioners or advocates.'

Following that criticism, a Guidance Note on Sanctions was issued by the Tribunal in late August 2012 and has since been periodically updated. The current (eighth) edition came into force in December 2020. It is reproduced in full in **Appendix 17**. It sets out the Tribunal's principles, procedure and policies in imposing sanctions.

1   [2011] EWHC 462 (Admin).

The general approach – Bolton v Law Society

22.7

In *Bolton v Law Society*,[1] the Master of the Rolls, Sir Thomas Bingham, made a general and oft-cited statement of the rationale for and purpose of punishment by the Tribunal. It merits citation here, as it provides the logical cornerstone for much of what both the Tribunal and appellate courts decide:

> 'It is required of lawyers practising in this country that they should discharge their professional duties with integrity, probity and complete trustworthiness ...
>
> Any solicitor who is shown to have discharged his professional duties with anything less than complete integrity, probity and trustworthiness must expect severe sanctions to be imposed upon him by the Solicitors Disciplinary Tribunal. Lapses from the required high standard may, of course, take different forms and be of varying degrees. The most serious involves proven dishonesty, whether or not leading to criminal proceedings and criminal penalties. In such cases the tribunal has almost invariably,

no matter how strong the mitigation advanced for the solicitor, ordered that he be struck off the Roll of Solicitors … If a solicitor is not shown to have acted dishonestly, but is shown to have fallen below the required standards of integrity, probity and trustworthiness, his lapse is less serious but it remains very serious indeed in a member of a profession whose reputation depends upon trust. A striking off order will not necessarily follow in such a case, but it may well. The decision whether to strike off or to suspend will often involve a fine and difficult exercise of judgment, to be made by the tribunal as an informed and expert body on all the facts of the case. Only in a very unusual and venial case of this kind would the tribunal be likely to regard as appropriate any order less severe than one of suspension.'

1   [1994] 1 WLR 512, CA.

Reprimands

22.8

Although it has no express statutory power to do so, the Tribunal frequently issues a reprimand to a solicitor. It has also censured a solicitor, stating that this was a more serious order than a reprimand and has directed a solicitor to pay counsels' fees (thereby making an unenforceable obligation enforceable as a High Court order).[1]

1   *Prince*, 6578-1994, SDT, unsuccessfully appealed as *Re a Solicitor*, CO 1324-1995. See also section 48(4) of SA 1974.

Fines

22.9

Since March 2009, there is no statutory limit on the amount of the fine (until then it was £5,000 per allegation). Fines are payable to the Treasury, which is responsible for enforcing payment.

The Guidance Note on Sanctions sets out five indicative fine bands ranging from fines of £2,000 or less for the lowest level of misconduct which justifies a fine rather than a reprimand (level 1) to fines over £50,000 for conduct assessed as significantly serious but falling short of conduct resulting in suspension or strike off (level 5).[1]

In practice, it is unusual for a fine against an individual to exceed £35,000, and the vast majority fall below that level. Fines against some entities are higher, but it is unusual for a fine against a firm to exceed £50,000.

A very small number of fines have been significantly higher, and the level of those high fines has increased over time. Up to 2014, the highest fine was £50,000 imposed in the case of *Fuglers v SRA*[2] upon the firm, with the two respondent partners being fined £20,000 and £5,000. In 2015 a fine of £305,000 was imposed on an individual in *Harvie*.[3] In July 2017 a fine of £250,000 was imposed on White & Case LLP under an agreed outcome,[4] and in November 2017 a fine of £500,000 was imposed on Locke Lord (UK) LLP under an agreed outcome.[5]

The general approach of the Tribunal to the level of fines was supported by the High Court in *SRA v Andersons*.[6] For the first time the SRA launched an appeal simply to obtain an increase in the fines imposed by the Tribunal. Although the High Court did order an increase in the fines (from £1,000 upon each of the individual respondents to £15,000 on one respondent and £5,000 in the others), these increases fell far below the figures contended for by the SRA. It would seem therefore, that the general approach of the Tribunal to individual solicitors is unlikely to change, unless, for instance, the Tribunal is satisfied that a solicitor has deliberately breached the rules in order to make a substantial profit. In such a case, it would be open to the Tribunal to impose a very substantial fine, as it did in *Harvie*. The position of large firms, with high turnovers, is different however, which explains some of the high six-figure fines that have been seen in recent times.

1   SDT Guidance Note on Sanctions, para 29.
2   [2014] EWHC 179 (Admin).
3   11257-2014, SDT.
4   11592-2016, SDT.
5   11717-2017, SDT.
6   [2013] EWHC 4021 (Admin).

22.10

As in the criminal courts, the financial circumstances of the respondent are highly relevant to the decision on the level of the fine. This was made clear in *D'Souza v Law Society*,[1] in which no apparent account had been taken of the admittedly parlous circumstances of Mr D'Souza, who had been ordered to pay a fine of £1,500 and costs in the order of £8,000. The total was reduced on appeal from £9,500 to £2,000: £500 by way of fine and £1,500 for costs.[2]

In imposing a financial penalty, the Tribunal should consider the respondent's overall financial liability for the fine and costs. In *Matthews v SRA*,[3] Collins J reduced a fine of £5,000 and costs of £16,000 to an overall liability of £5,000 on account of the appellant's limited means. The costs, which made up £4,500 of this sum, were not to be enforced without leave of the Tribunal.

Rule 43(5) of the 2019 Rules states that a respondent who wishes his means to be taken into account should provide a statement of means supported by documentary evidence. The time for service of the statement is normally specified in the standard directions as 28 days before the substantive hearing.[4]

1   [2009] EWHC 2193 (Admin).
2   See also *Tinkler v SRA* [2012] EWHC 3645 (Admin) and the Guidance Note on Sanctions under the heading 'Level of Fine' at **Appendix 17**. The respondent's means may also be highly relevant to the correct costs order and this is discussed at **22.38**.
3   [2013] EWHC 1525 (Admin).
4   Rule 43 of the 2019 Rules relates to costs, but the statement could be relied on in support of representations on the level of the fine. In practice it is rare for the Tribunal to take account of means when considering the level of the fine.

Restriction orders

22.11

The Tribunal has no power itself to impose conditions on a practising certificate when imposing a penalty upon a solicitor, but because it can make 'such order as it may think fit', it can also make orders requiring a solicitor not to practise in particular ways, for example as a sole practitioner.

In *Camacho v Law Society*,[1] the Tribunal had ordered the indefinite suspension of a solicitor. On the solicitor's appeal, the Divisional Court substituted a finite period of suspension but identified five conditions which it considered should be imposed in relation to the way in which the solicitor might practise. The court held that the terms of section 47(2) of SA 1974 were sufficiently wide to give the Tribunal itself power to impose restrictions on the manner in which a solicitor might practise, and that if the Tribunal considered that a period of complete suspension followed by a period of restricted practice was the appropriate sanction to protect the public, that was part of the decision it had made and – unless there were exceptional reasons – it should be for the Tribunal to make that order, rather than to make recommendations to the SRA as had been the former practice.

Where the Tribunal makes such an order for an indefinite period it should grant liberty to apply, as there is otherwise no mechanism for a solicitor subject to such an order to apply for it to be varied or reviewed.[2]

The Tribunal has on occasion refined this approach by imposing a suspension from practice for one year, but suspending that order for so long as the solicitor practised only (in substance) in employment expressly approved by the SRA without access to clients' money. The Tribunal gave guidance as to the circumstances in which an application might be made to the Tribunal to vary or revoke the terms of the restriction.[3]

Restriction orders are only made when considered necessary to protect the public or the reputation of the profession – they have no punitive function.[4] Inevitably, when the Tribunal makes such orders the SRA can be expected to impose matching or more restrictive practising certificate conditions.

---

1   [2004] EWHC 1675 (Admin), [2004] 1 WLR 3037. See too *Ebhogiaye v SRA* [2013] EWHC 2445 (Admin).
2   *Taylor v Law Society* [2005] EWCA Civ 1473. The formula substituted on appeal to the Master of the Rolls in *Taylor* was: 'In the future the petitioner may not practise as a sole practitioner but only in employment or partnership. When employed he must not operate a client account. The petitioner to have liberty to apply to the Tribunal to vary these conditions'.
3   *Bajela and Fonkwo*, 9543-2006, SDT. See also *SRA v Dar* [2019] EWHC 2831 (Admin).
4   See SDT Guidance Note on Sanctions, para 33. See also *Manak v SRA* [2018] EWHC 1958 (Admin) at [62].

Suspensions

22.12

Suspensions may be for a fixed term or for an indefinite period. The effect of a suspension for a solicitor will vary according to the size of the practice. For a middle-aged sole practitioner, suspension may in reality be equivalent to a striking off, as it may prove impossible for the solicitor to arrange cover during the period of the suspension, and/or the solicitor may face insurmountable practising certificate conditions when he or she returns to practice. For a solicitor working in a large firm, whose partners/employers have not dismissed him or her, the effect of a short suspension may be little more than an inconvenience.

Indefinite suspensions are usually imposed where there is a medical explanation for the solicitor's misconduct, or where there is truly exceptional personal mitigation. Such suspensions come within a whisker of a striking off, but the Tribunal may consider that there is a real prospect of successful rehabilitation, thus meriting an order which will not make it impossible for the solicitor to resume practice.[1]

Suspensions are normally imposed for one year or more. Where they are for a period of months (or less) it is important to note that the expiry of the suspension does not enable an automatic return to practice. The solicitor's practising certificate is not automatically restored; rather it remains suspended until the SRA terminates the suspension on the application of the solicitor (although an application may be made before the suspension expires, so minimising the consequences).[2] The termination of the suspension may be accompanied by the imposition of conditions on the practising certificate[3] and almost certainly will.

Suspensions may themselves be suspended, when accompanied by a restriction order.[4] An order of suspended suspension should make clear that the suspension will be activated if there is further misconduct during the period of suspension. As pointed out by Flaux LJ in *SRA v James, MacGregor and Naylor*[5] at [125]:

> 'There is a certain illogicality in the concept of suspension of a penalty that is itself a suspension. Suspension of striking off is easier to comprehend, since that is akin to a suspended sentence of imprisonment in criminal proceedings. However, suspended suspension is one of the range of possible sanctions available to the SDT.'

1   See para 47 of the SDT Guidance Note on Sanctions.
2   Section 16(3) of SA 1974.
3   Section 16(4).
4   See paras 41–44 of the SDT Guidance Note on Sanctions. See also *SRA v Dar* [2019] EWHC 2831 (Admin) at [93].
5   [2018] EWHC 3058 (Admin).

Striking off and restoration to the roll

22.13

A struck off solicitor can no longer describe him- or herself as a solicitor, and to do so may be a criminal offence under section 20 and/or section 21 of SA 1974. An unqualified person, as the struck off solicitor becomes, may not perform those activities which only a qualified solicitor may perform, in particular the reserved legal activities set out in the Legal Services Act (LSA) 2007. A struck off solicitor may not be employed by a solicitor without the prior consent of the SRA.[1]

1   See section 41 of SA 1974.

22.14

The Tribunal has a statutory power under section 47(1)(e) of SA 1974 to restore struck off solicitors to the roll. However, the guidance provided by the Court of Appeal in *Bolton v Law Society*[1] as to the purposes of imposing disciplinary sanctions and summarised at **22.7**, applies to applications to restore to the roll:

> 'the most fundamental [purpose] of all: to maintain the reputation of the solicitors' profession as one in which every member, of whatever standing,

may be trusted to the ends of the earth. To maintain this reputation and sustain public confidence in the integrity of the profession it is often necessary that those guilty of serious lapses are not only expelled but denied re-admission.'

1 [1994] 1 WLR 512, CA at 518.

22.15

As a result, it has hitherto proved all but impossible for former solicitors who have been struck off for disciplinary offences involving dishonesty, to persuade the Tribunal to permit restoration to the roll. The former Master of the Rolls, Lord Donaldson of Lymington said in one case:[1]

'however sympathetic one may be towards an individual member of either branch of the legal profession, if you fall very seriously below the standards of that profession and are expelled from it, there is a public interest in the profession itself in hardening its heart if any question arises of your rejoining it. Neither branch of the profession is short of people who have never fallen from grace. There is considerable public interest in the public as a whole being able to deal with members of those professions knowing that, save in the most exceptional circumstances, they can be sure that none of them have ever been guilty of any dishonesty at all.'

In his final decision as Master of the Rolls, Lord Donaldson went further, and wondered whether Parliament had ever contemplated that a solicitor who had been guilty of fraud could be restored to the roll, although he continued:[2]

'It may be that in a very exceptional case it did – something which really could be described as a momentary aberration under quite exceptional strain, the sort of strain which not everybody meets but some people do meet in the course of their everyday lives.'

To date in the modern era (that is for some three decades at least), only one solicitor who has been struck off for dishonesty has successfully applied for restoration to the roll.[3]

1 No 5 of 1987, unreported.
2 No 11 of 1990, unreported.
3 *Vane*, 8607-2002, SDT. For an example of a case in which the SRA appealed successfully against the SDT's decision to restore to the roll a solicitor who had been convicted of offences involving dishonesty, see *SRA v Kaberry* [2012] EWHC 3883 (Admin).

22.16

A former solicitor who has been struck off for less serious disciplinary offences, not involving dishonesty, may be more fortunate. In order to contemplate making an order of restoration, the Tribunal will need to be satisfied first that the former solicitor has demonstrated his or her complete rehabilitation, and secondly that restoration to the roll would not involve any damage to the reputation of the profession. Lord Donaldson encouraged the Tribunal to ask:[1]

'If this was the sort of case where, even if the back history was known (that is whatever explanation and mitigation was available to explain why the solicitor committed the original offence), and without the explanation as to what has happened subsequently, the members of the public would say "that does not shake my faith in solicitors as a whole".'

These hurdles, particularly the second, remain very difficult to surmount. Even if they are overcome, it is unlikely that the Tribunal, or the SRA, would contemplate permitting the solicitor, once restored to the roll, to practise without any form of restriction upon his or her practising certificate. Moreover, save in the most exceptional circumstances, an application for restoration to the roll within six years of the original striking off is likely to be regarded by the Tribunal as premature.

The Tribunal has published a guidance note which states that on an application for restoration the Tribunal will take account of the effect of restoration on public confidence in the profession, the period which has elapsed since the strike off, evidence of rehabilitation, the applicant's future employment intentions and the extent to which reparation has been made for any loss suffered by others as a result of the original misconduct.[2]

1   No 11 of 1990, unreported.
2   SDT Guidance Note on Other Powers of the Tribunal, December 2020, para 8.

Penalties – the approach in practice

22.17

Once again it is necessary to quote Sir Thomas Bingham in *Bolton*[1] in order to understand the rationale behind the sanctions imposed in disciplinary proceedings:

'It is important that there should be full understanding of the reasons why the tribunal makes orders which might otherwise seem harsh. There is, in some of these orders, a punitive element: a penalty may be visited on a solicitor who has fallen below the standards required of his profession in order to punish him for what he has done and to deter any other solicitor tempted to behave in the same way. Those are traditional objects of punishment. But often the order is not punitive in intention. Particularly is this so where a criminal penalty has been imposed and satisfied. The solicitor has paid his debt to society. There is no need, and it would be unjust, to punish him again. In most cases the order of the tribunal will be primarily directed to one or other or both of two other purposes. One is to be sure that the offender does not have the opportunity to repeat the offence. This purpose is achieved for a limited period by an order of suspension; plainly it is hoped that experience of suspension will make the offender meticulous in his future compliance with the required standards. The purpose is achieved for a longer period, and quite possibly indefinitely, by an order of striking off. The second purpose is the most fundamental of all: to maintain the reputation of the solicitors' profession as one in which every member, of whatever standing, may be trusted to the ends of the earth. To maintain this reputation and sustain public confidence in the integrity of the profession it is often necessary that those guilty of serious lapses are not only expelled but denied re-admission. If a member of the public sells his house, very often his largest asset, and entrusts the proceeds to his solicitor, pending re-investment in another house, he is ordinarily entitled to expect that the solicitor will be a person whose trustworthiness is not, and never has been, seriously in question. Otherwise, the whole profession, and the public as a whole, is injured. A profession's most valuable asset is its collective reputation and the confidence which that inspires.

Because orders made by the tribunal are not primarily punitive, it follows that considerations which would ordinarily weigh in mitigation of punishment have less effect on the exercise of this jurisdiction than on the ordinary run of sentences imposed in criminal cases. It often happens that a solicitor appearing before the tribunal can adduce a wealth of glowing tributes from his professional brethren. He can often show that for him and his family the consequences of striking off or suspension would be little short of tragic. Often he will say, convincingly, that he has learned his lesson and will not offend again. On applying for restoration after striking off, all these points may be made, and the former solicitor may also be able to point to real efforts made to re-establish himself and redeem his reputation. All these matters are relevant and should be considered. But none of them touches the essential issue, which is the need to maintain among members of the public a well-founded confidence that any solicitor whom they instruct will be a person of unquestionable integrity, probity and trustworthiness. Thus it can never be an objection to an order of suspension in an appropriate case that the solicitor may be unable to re-establish his practice when the period of suspension is past. If that proves, or appears likely, to be so the consequence for the individual and his family may be deeply unfortunate and unintended. But it does not make suspension the wrong order if it is otherwise right. The reputation of the profession is more important than the fortunes of any individual member. Membership of a profession brings many benefits, but that is a part of the price.'

Cases before the Tribunal vary infinitely and no analytical consideration of particular facts, individual cases or individual penalties is of material assistance. There are, however, some general principles and typical classes of case that can usefully be considered.

The Tribunal adopts the procedure used in the criminal courts when the solicitor makes admissions but there is a dispute between the parties as to the facts upon which the admissions are based. In such cases, the Tribunal will hold a *Newton* hearing.[2] Often, the Tribunal does not differentiate between individual allegations when imposing a sanction. This is particularly the case with fines – the Tribunal may impose an overall fine without distinguishing between the allegations as to how the fine is calculated.[3] This may cause difficulties for the High Court on appeal where an appeal is partially successful and the court cannot know how much of the overall fine related to the allegations that have been quashed.

The SDT Guidance Note on Sanctions sets out details of how the Tribunal assesses seriousness, and what may be seen as aggravating and mitigating factors.

1   [1994] 1 WLR 512, CA at 518–19.
2   See *R v Newton* [1983] Crim LR 198, and paras 11–14 of the SDT Guidance Note on Sanctions. For an example of the events during a *Newton* hearing being considered on appeal, see *Slater v SRA* [2012] EWHC 3256 (Admin).
3   See paras 15 and 16 of the SDT Guidance Note on Sanctions.

Dishonesty in connection with client account

22.18

Such is the importance of the principle that clients' money must be held separately from a solicitor's own funds, that any dishonest misappropriation of clients' monies will lead inevitably to a striking-off order, whether or not the misappropriation also amounts to theft. This is now seen as all but automatic.[1] In *Bultitude v Law Society*,[2] the Law Society appealed against the reduction of a striking-off order to a suspension by the Divisional Court. The appeal was allowed by the Court of Appeal, and the court was informed that there was only one known instance of dishonesty in connection with client account that had not resulted in a striking off.

1   See *Bolton v Law Society* [1994] 1 WLR 512, CA; *Weston v Law Society*, *Times*, 15 July 1998.
2   [2004] EWCA Civ 1853.

Other forms of dishonesty

22.19

It is now well established that, save in exceptional circumstances, any solicitor who is found to have acted dishonestly will be struck off the roll. In *SRA v Sharma*[1] the Divisional Court allowed an appeal by the SRA against a three-year suspension imposed upon a solicitor who had forged documents, and sent them as 'duly signed' under cover of a letter written on his firm's notepaper. The court imposed a striking-off order in place of the suspension, and Coulson J stated (at [13]):

'(a)   Save in exceptional circumstances, a finding of dishonesty will lead to the solicitor being struck off the roll, see *Bolton*[2] and *Salsbury*.[3] That is the normal and necessary penalty in cases of dishonesty: see *Bultitude*.[4]

(b)   There will be a small residual category where striking off will be a disproportionate sentence in all the circumstances: see *Salsbury*.

(c)   In deciding whether or not a particular case falls into that category, relevant factors will include the nature, scope and extent of the dishonesty itself; whether it was momentary, such as *Burrowes*,[5] or over a lengthy period of time, such as *Bultitude*; whether it was a benefit to the solicitor (*Burrowes*), and whether it had an adverse effect on others.'

And also (at [26]):

'The question for this court is whether in the light of the principles outlined above, the Tribunal's decision can be described as excessively lenient. If it can, then this court should substitute for the Tribunal's sentence, the sentence that it considers to be commensurate with these offences. If the sentence cannot be regarded as excessively lenient, even if it is not necessarily the sentence which this court would itself have imposed, the sentence should remain unchanged.'

1   [2010] EWHC 2022 (Admin).
2   *Bolton v Law Society* [1994] 1 WLR 512, CA.
3   *Law Society v Salsbury* [2008] EWCA Civ 1285.
4   *Bultitude v Law Society* [2004] EWCA Civ 1853.
5   *Burrowes v Law Society* [2002] EWHC 2900 (QB).

Exceptional circumstances

22.20

On a number of occasions, when the SDT has declined to strike off a solicitor who has been found to have acted dishonestly, the SRA has appealed. In every case save one (*SRA v Imran*;[1] see also *Burrowes v Law Society* and the cases referred to in the judgment[2] for earlier cases in which apparent dishonesty did not lead to a striking-off order), those appeals have succeeded and the High Court has substituted a striking-off order.[3] This pattern was followed in three appeals heard together in October 2018, *SRA v James, MacGregor and Naylor*.[4] All three solicitors had been found to have acted dishonestly in different cases at separate hearings, and on each occasion the SDT had declined to strike off, imposing instead a suspended suspension from practice. The SRA's appeals were successful, and striking-off orders were imposed by the High Court. In his judgment, Flaux LJ gave guidance as to what can and cannot constitute exceptional circumstances:[5]

> 'First, although it is well-established that what may amount to exceptional circumstances is in no sense prescribed and depends upon the various factors and circumstances of each individual case, it is clear from the decisions in *Sharma*, *Imran* and *Shaw*, that the most significant factor carrying most weight and which must therefore be the primary focus in the evaluation is the nature and extent of the dishonesty, in other words the exceptional circumstances must relate in some way to the dishonesty. This point was made very clearly by Dove J at [29] of *Imran*, where he said:
>
> > "… in my view it is not possible when assessing exceptional circumstances simply to pick off the individual features of the case. It is necessary, as the tribunal did, to record and stand back from all of those many factors, putting first and foremost in the assessment of whether or not there are exceptional circumstances the particular conclusions that had been reached about the act of dishonesty itself. The fact that many solicitors may be able to produce testimonials and may immediately confess the dishonest behaviour is certainly relevant to the determination of whether or not it is an exceptional case, but is not a factor that is likely to attract very substantial weight. Of far greater weight would be the extent of the dishonesty and the impact of that dishonesty both on the character of the particular solicitor concerned but, most importantly, on the wider reputation of the profession and how it impinges on the public's perception of the profession as a whole".'

Similarly, in *SRA v Siaw*[6] Flaux LJ said that: 'In considering whether there are "exceptional circumstances" in any given case, the principal focus is on the nature and extent of the dishonesty and the degree of culpability'.[7]

1   [2015] EWHC 2572 (Admin).
2   [2002] EWHC 2900 (QB) at [6], [10]–[13], [17] and [20].
3   See *SRA v Tilsiter* [2009] EWHC 3787 (Admin); *SRA v Dennison* [2011] EWHC 291 (Admin) – the solicitor's appeal to the Court of Appeal failed: [2012] EWCA Civ 421; *SRA v Rahman* [2012] EWHC 1037 (Admin); and *SRA v Spence* [2012] EWHC 2977 (Admin).
4   [2018] EWHC 3058 (Admin).
5   At [101].
6   [2019] EWHC 2737 (Admin).
7   At [65].

22.21

As for the relevance of the solicitor's mental health at the time of the dishonest act or omission, Flaux LJ observed in *SRA v James*[1] at [103]:

'Inevitably, an assessment of the nature and extent of the dishonesty and the degree of culpability will involve an examination of what Ms Morris QC termed the "mind set" of the respondent, including whether the respondent is suffering from mental health issues and the workplace environment, as part of the overall balancing exercise. However, where the SDT has concluded that, notwithstanding any mental health issues or work or workplace related pressures, the respondent's misconduct was dishonest, the weight to be attached to those mental health and working environment issues in assessing the appropriate sanction will inevitably be less than is to be attached to other aspects of the dishonesty found, such as the length of time for which it was perpetrated, whether it was repeated and the harm which it caused, all of which must be of more significance. Certainly, it is difficult to see how in a case of dishonesty, as opposed to some lesser professional misconduct, the fact that the respondent suffered from stress and depression (whether alone or in combination with extreme pressure from the working environment) could without more amount to exceptional circumstances, a matter to which I return below.'

and, at [110]:

'… I do not consider that mental health issues, specifically stress and depression suffered by the solicitor as a consequence of work conditions or other matters can, without more, amount to "exceptional circumstances", justifying a lesser sanction than striking off where the SDT has found dishonesty.'

1   [2018] EWHC 3058 (Admin).

Non-dishonest serious misconduct and lack of integrity

22.22

It should be stressed that the absence of a finding of dishonesty does not protect a solicitor from a striking-off order. To return to what was said by Sir Thomas Bingham MR in *Bolton*:[1]

'… If a solicitor is not shown to have acted dishonestly, but is shown to have fallen below the required standards of integrity, probity and trustworthiness, his lapse is less serious but it remains very serious indeed in a member of a profession whose reputation depends upon trust. A striking off order will not necessarily follow in such a case, but it may well. The decision whether to strike off or to suspend will often involve a fine and difficult exercise of judgment, to be made by the tribunal as an informed and expert body on all the facts of the case. Only in a very unusual and venial case of this kind would the tribunal be likely to regard as appropriate any order less severe than one of suspension.'

Many solicitors have been struck off in such circumstances, and an appeal mounted on the principal basis that no finding of dishonesty has been made by the Tribunal is unlikely to attract much judicial sympathy. In *Moseley v SRA*,[2] Lewis J stated at [19]:

> 'In my judgment there is no requirement or presumption that, if the conduct is independent of the discharge of professional duties, then it must involve either dishonesty or a serious criminal offence, or that there be exceptional circumstances before striking off is appropriate. Rather, where the conduct complained of is found to involve a lack of integrity and diminishes public trust in the profession it may still, depending on the particular facts, be appropriate to impose the sanction of striking off the roll. Where conduct is dishonest or criminal, it is very likely that that would be the result. But even where conduct is not dishonest or criminal and even if it is unconnected the discharge of professional duties, it may justify striking off where it involves a lack of integrity or results in a diminution in the public trust in the profession.'

1   [1994] 1 WLR 512, CA at 518.
2   [2013] EWHC 2108 (Admin); see too *Afolabi v SRA* [2012] EWHC 3502 (Admin), *Law Society (SRA) v Emeana* [2013] EWHC 2130 (Admin); *SRA v Good* [2019] EWHC 817 (Admin) at [78]–[82]; and *SRA v Lorrell* [2019] EWHC 981 (Admin) at [42].

22.23

The SRA has occasionally appealed against sanctions which it considers to have been too lenient in cases where dishonesty has not been established against the solicitor concerned. It was successful in *SRA v Uddin*[1] and *SRA v Chan and Ali*,[2] whereas it was unsuccessful in *SRA v Norman*.[3]

1   [2014] EWHC 4553 (Admin).
2   [2015] EWHC 2659 (Admin).
3   [2013] EWHC 3886 (Admin).

Sexual misconduct

22.24

There is potentially a wide spectrum of sexual misconduct cases.

At the most serious end of the spectrum are cases involving criminal convictions, where the solicitor is likely to be struck off, or at least suspended. Convictions for downloading indecent images of children will invariably lead to the solicitor being struck off. Convictions for assaults following the breakdown of a consensual affair could be less severe. In *SRA v Main* the Tribunal suspended a solicitor for a period of less than a year after he had been convicted of sexual assault and placed on the sex offenders register for five years for repeatedly smacking his former partner. The SRA appealed the sentence on the grounds that it was unduly lenient. The High Court decided that suspension was the appropriate penalty but that the suspension should last for four years while the solicitor remained on the sex offenders register, as public confidence in the profession would be damaged by a shorter suspension, particularly as it meant the solicitor would be permitted to practise while on the sex offenders register.[1]

Since 2017, and the start of the #MeToo movement, there have been a number of cases of sexual misconduct involving a male partner and a junior female employee, in which the partner's actions in the workplace are unwanted and amount to sexual harassment. The cases involve allegations that the partner has breached principle 2 (upholding public trust and confidence in the profession) and principle 5 (integrity), and if adverse findings are made the sentence is likely to be a heavy fine. The findings are normally based on a decision that the partner was in a position of responsibility and authority over the junior employee, and abused his position. An unwanted pass between two members of staff at the same level of seniority is unlikely in itself to result in disciplinary proceedings.

The partner's firm will not necessarily avoid disciplinary action. The SRA is likely to investigate the firm to decide whether appropriate policies were in place, whether the firm carried out a proper investigation once aware of the junior employee's complaint and whether the firm took appropriate remedial action against the partner.

The extent to which disciplinary action should extend into private life when the alleged misconduct occurs outside the workplace was considered by the High Court in *Beckwith v SRA*. In *Beckwith*, a sexual encounter took place between a partner in a firm and an associate, who was working out her notice and was due to leave her employment within a few days. The encounter was not a case in which there was no consent, and it took place outside work at night at the associate's flat while she was heavily intoxicated. The Tribunal decided that the partner had not abused his position of seniority but found that his conduct was 'inappropriate' and that he had breached the principles of integrity and maintaining public trust and confidence in the profession. On appeal, the Tribunal order was quashed by the High Court, which decided that the circumstances in which a solicitor should be required to act with integrity or uphold public trust and confidence in the profession should be identified by reference to the contents of the Handbook (and primarily the rules in the Code of Conduct) as the Handbook is the best guide to the occasions and contexts where solicitors should be held to the higher standards required from members of the profession.[2] The High Court also said that the decision in the case should not be treated as 'any form of permission to expand the scope of the obligation to act with integrity simply by making rules that extend ever further into personal life'.[3]

In the light of *Beckwith*, where there is no issue of consent and no significant abuse of position by the respondent solicitor, the Tribunal is likely to take the view that the conduct is none of the regulator's business. There will be cases close to the line which will have to be dealt with on a case-by-case basis. There is no reason why many sexual misconduct cases need give rise to difficulties. If the conduct amounts to a sexual assault, or harassment as defined in the Equality Act (EqA) 2010, there is a clear basis for a successful prosecution.

1   *SRA v Main* [2018] EWHC 3666 (Admin) at [30].
2   *Beckwith v SRA* [2020] EWHC 3231 (Admin). The High Court made it clear that it was considering the Handbook containing the 2011 Principles and Code of Conduct, but the decision applies equally to the 2019 regulatory arrangements. For commentary on *Beckwith* see also **3.13**, **19.3–19.4** and **19.6**.
3   *Beckwith v SRA* [2020] EWHC 3231 (Admin) at [39].

Breaches of the SRA Accounts Rules

22.25

Breaches of the Accounts Rules can range from the serious to the trivial. Improper transfers from client accounts to office accounts falling short of dishonesty may merit a striking-off order or suspension, as may a chaotic accounting system which creates risk to clients and to the public. The importance of regular reconciliations and accountants' reports cannot be overestimated, as these are the mechanisms by which problems can be detected at a relatively early stage. Other administrative failings and errors, including failure to carry out reconciliations timeously or to obtain accountants' reports at the correct time, if standing alone, are likely to be visited with a fine.

Solicitors providing banking facilities

22.26

Since 2011, the SRA has taken a vigorous approach to investigating and pursuing allegations that client accounts have been misused to provide banking facilities. There have been a number of cases in which solicitors who have provided banking facilities to clients have been fined by the Tribunal.[1]

Rule 14.5 of the SRA Accounts Rules 2011 provides:

'You must not provide banking facilities through a client account. Payments into, and transfers or withdrawals from, a client account must be in respect of instructions relating to an underlying transaction (and the funds arising therefrom) or to a service forming part of your normal regulated activities.'

The precise meaning of the 2011 rule has led to disputes on construction in the High Court. In *Patel v SRA*, Moore Bick LJ stated at [42]–[43]:

'[Counsel for the Appellant] submitted that the word "or" is to be read disjunctively and that the existence of an underlying transaction of any kind which a solicitor can lawfully undertake, including one that does not form part of a solicitor's normal professional activities, is capable of supporting the use of a client account. The tribunal, he submitted, had erred in conflating the two limbs of rule 14.5 which had led it to hold that there must be an underlying transaction of a legal nature.

In my view that argument states the position too broadly. The primary purpose of maintaining a client account is to segregate funds held for the client from the solicitor's own funds in order to provide the client with a measure of protection. One would therefore expect it to be used to hold funds which have come into the solicitor's hands in relation to services carried out for the client, to be paid out in due course to the client or in accordance with his instructions. Rule 14.5 of the SRA Accounts Rules refers to instructions relating to an underlying transaction or a service forming part of the solicitor's normal regulated activities.'

The SRA issued a warning notice in December 2014, which contained guidance on the meaning of the banking facilities. The warning notice was updated in November 2019 and this is set out in **APPENDIX 8**.[2]

Rule 3.3 of the SRA Accounts Rules 2019 amended the rule on banking facilities. Rule 3.3 provides:

'You must not use a *client account* to provide banking facilities to *clients* or third parties. Payments into, and transfers or withdrawals from a *client account* must be in respect of the delivery by you of *regulated services*.'

The guidance on the prohibition of banking facilities in the November 2019 warning notice is as relevant to the SRA Accounts Rules 2019 as it is to the SRA Accounts Rules 2011.

1   See *Wood & Burdett*, 8669-2002, SDT; *Patel v SRA* [2012] EWHC 3373 (Admin); and *Fuglers v SRA* [2014] EWHC 179 (Admin).
2   The warning notice includes SRA case studies, 'Improper use of client account as a banking facility', 25 November 2019.

Culpable or dishonest overcharging

22.27

There is potentially a wide spectrum of 'overcharging' by a solicitor. The reduction of a solicitor/own client bill or an *inter partes* bill at a detailed assessment is an everyday experience for solicitors and implies no professional misconduct of any sort. Where such a reduction is very substantial, however, the solicitor may be open to a charge of 'culpable overcharging'. As a rule of thumb, if a bill is reduced by more than 50 per cent on assessment, this may give cause for regulatory concern, and may lead to further investigation (and possible disciplinary proceedings).[1] The concept of culpable overcharging does not incorporate within it any implication or allegation of dishonesty.

At the most serious end of the spectrum is dishonest overcharging, where the solicitor has no honest belief that the sum charged is a reasonable sum for the work done. As with any form of dishonesty, a solicitor found guilty of dishonest overcharging can expect to be struck off.[2]

Unsurprisingly, therefore, penalties imposed by the Tribunal on this subject vary considerably. Particular care may be required in probate cases, where a solicitor may be the sole executor of the estate and there may be no independent scrutiny of his or her charges.[3] In *Sheikh v Law Society*, Chadwick LJ observed that evidence from a costs draftsman with suitable experience as to what he would expect to see in such cases provides a useful starting point in evaluating the issue as to whether there has been not merely culpable but possibly dishonest overcharging, in the sense that significant deviation from the norm may require explanation.[4]

1   This is consistent with article 5(1) of the Solicitors' (Non-Contentious Business) Remuneration Order 1994 (SI 1994/2616), since repealed, which required any costs judge who reduces a solicitor/client non-contentious bill by more than half on detailed assessment to report the matter to the Law Society.
2   See eg *SRA v Good* [2019] EWHC 817 (Admin) at [80], a case involving culpable overcharging in bills of costs payable by opponents in successful litigation cases.
3   See eg *Sheikh v Law Society* [2006] EWCA Civ 1577, [2007] 3 All ER 183 at [45].
4   *Sheikh v Law Society* [2006] EWCA Civ 1577, [2007] 3 All ER 183 at [64].

Conflicts of interest

22.28

Actual or potential conflicts of interests may arise in a variety of ways and those of a relatively innocent nature, such as those due to an error of judgement, will merit no more than a fine.[1] Some conflicts are infinitely more serious and involve solicitors deliberately or recklessly preferring their own interests to those of their clients, for example, by obtaining unsecured loans from clients without ensuring that the clients receive independent advice. These are likely to be regarded very seriously and can result in the solicitor being struck off.[2]

1   For example *O'Brien*, 9574-2006, SDT (the 'Freshfields Two' case).
2   Unhappily, there have been very many cases in this category. Examples are *Predko*, 7099-1996, SDT, *Austin-Olsen*, 9361-2005, SDT and *Beller v Law Society* [2009] EWHC 2200 (Admin).

Payment of referral fees

22.29

As described above (at **4.51**), until 2004, there was an outright ban on the payment of referral fees by solicitors to introducers of work. This proved difficult to enforce, and there were concerns that it might offend competition law. In 2004 the ban was abolished. Instead, the Law Society required that solicitors be transparent about the fact and amount of referral fees in a new section 2A of the Solicitors' Introduction and Referral Code. This was substantially replicated by Chapter 9 of the SRA Code of Conduct 2011, and very similar provisions are now contained in paragraph 5 of the SRA Code of Conduct for Solicitors, RELs and RFLs 2019 and paragraph 7.1 of the SRA Code of Conduct for Firms 2019 (the 'Code for Firms'). The Tribunal recognised that regulation in this area had proved to be problematic and in the past dealt with such cases by way of a fine, save where there had been a deliberate and wholesale breach of the ban.[1]

It is likely that both the SRA and the Tribunal will take a less emollient view towards breaches of the referral fee ban in the Legal Aid, Sentencing and Punishment of Offenders Act (LASPO) 2012 than in the past. The ban is imposed by an Act of Parliament rather than a somewhat controversial professional rule. The Government will expect the ban to be enforced by the regulators, and part of that enforcement is likely to involve significant penalties being imposed upon those who transgress. However, at the time of writing there have been no prosecutions arising out of the LASPO 2012 ban.

1   For example, *Mendelson*, 9212-2005, SDT. In *Barber*, 9698-2007, SDT, two solicitors were suspended for deliberate and wholesale breach of the ban, in the context of the miners' compensation cases.

Misleading the court

22.30

Solicitors have a pivotal role in the administration of justice, and owe duties to the court which can sometimes override their duties to the lay client. The courts depend upon the legal profession to discharge its duties to them in order to ensure that cases can be efficiently determined. A useful summary of an advocate's duty is set out by Lord Hoffmann in *Arthur JS Hall v Simons*:[1]

> 'Lawyers conducting litigation owe a divided loyalty. They have a duty to their clients, but they may not win by whatever means. They also owe a duty to the court and the administration of justice. They may not mislead the court or allow the judge to take what they know to be a bad point in

their favour. They must cite all relevant law, whether for or against their case. They may not make imputations of dishonesty unless they have been given the information to support them. They should not waste time on irrelevancies even if the client thinks that they are important. Sometimes the performance of these duties to the court may annoy the client. So, it was said, the possibility of a claim for negligence might inhibit the lawyer from acting in accordance with his overriding duty to the court. That would be prejudicial to the administration of justice.'

1   [2002] 1 AC 615, HL at 686.

22.31

As a result, any misleading of the court will be dealt with severely by the Tribunal. As stated by Lord Thomas CJ in *Brett v SRA*:[1]

'Every lawyer must be alive to the fact that circumstances can arise during the course of any lawyer's professional practice when matters come to his knowledge (or are obvious to him) which may have the effect of making his duty to the court his paramount duty and to act in the interests of justice. In many cases it will be clear what course the lawyer must take, either through the way in which the case is presented or by withdrawing from acting for the client. In others it may be more difficult. The lawyer may not be absolutely sure that his actions will discharge his duty to the court. In such a case, for reasons which I shall explain, a lawyer would be ill-advised if he did not put the matters before a person more senior within his firm or before independent counsel, making full and complete disclosure to such a person of all the relevant circumstances.

The reason why that is so important is that misleading the court is regarded by the court and must be regarded by any disciplinary tribunal as one of the most serious offences that an advocate or litigator can commit. It is not simply a breach of a rule of a game, but a fundamental affront to a rule designed to safeguard the fairness and justice of proceedings. Such conduct will normally attract an exemplary and deterrent sentence. That is in part because our system for the administration of justice relies so heavily upon the integrity of the profession and the full discharge of the profession's duties and in part because the privilege of conducting litigation or appearing in court is granted on terms that the rules are observed not merely in their letter but in their spirit. Indeed, the reputation of the system of the administration of justice in England and Wales and the standing of the profession depends particularly upon the discharge of the duties owed to the court.'

1   [2014] EWHC 2974 (Admin) at [110]–[111]. See also *Shaw v SRA* [2017] EWHC 2076 (Admin) in which Carr J said at [107] that the dishonest misleading of the court by a solicitor is a matter of the utmost gravity.

Improper use of litigation

22.32

In recent years there has been considerable concern expressed by the senior judiciary about the improper use of litigation by solicitors on behalf of clients about to be deported from the United Kingdom. This impropriety has tended to consist of last-minute applications in cases wholly lacking in merit, in which the solicitors have failed to make full and frank disclosure to the court in accordance with their professional duties. In *Ip v SRA*,[1] the appellant had been struck off in such circumstances. His appeal to the High Court failed, and Irwin LJ observed at [180]–[181]:

> 'The Courts well understand the vulnerability of many of those at risk of removal or deportation from the country. They can be desperate to remain. They are often prepared to grasp at straws. The Courts are also fully alive to the technicality and difficulty of immigration law, and of the Immigration Rules. These factors add to the difficulty of representing such clients. However, they also add to the responsibility of solicitors engaged for such clients.
>
> It is critical that solicitors, and others, representing such clients, are scrupulous in observing professional standards. The cost of not doing so to the system is obvious and has been emphasised many times. Spurious, or merely hopeless, applications to courts and tribunals add greatly to the burden on the system of justice, and to the costs of government. However, it should not be forgotten that such applications also cost the applicants, both financially and in engendering prolonged and unjustified expectations. In addition, poor, and where it arises unscrupulous, representation must, to some degree at least, overshadow careful and expert immigration lawyers. The Solicitors Disciplinary Tribunal is entirely justified in taking very seriously cases such as this.'

1   [2018] EWHC 957 (Admin). See also *Nazeer v SRA* [2019] EWHC 37 (Admin) for sanctions imposed on a compliance officer for legal practice (COLP) and co-partner found to have ignored warnings that a co-partner was improperly conducting litigation.

Failure to reply to correspondence from clients and/or the SRA and the Legal Ombudsman

22.33

Failures to reply to correspondence are regarded seriously by the Tribunal, as they damage the reputation of the profession. Standing alone, such failures will merit a fine – even if the original complaint, to which the respondent failed to respond, was in fact without merit.

Tribunal's reasons for imposing sanctions

22.34

Whereas cases in which a solicitor has to be struck off or suspended will usually be fairly easy to identify, as will the misconduct that justifies such a sanction, the Tribunal nevertheless must reveal proper reasoning and explanation for selecting the sanction imposed. This was made clear by Nicola Davies J in *Hazelhurst v SRA*[1] in which she said (at [36]–[37]):

> '36. … it is difficult to understand how the SDT decided that a monetary penalty was appropriate. No mention of other sanctions is made, no reason

is given for the sum imposed nor how such sum is apportioned as between the three breaches so as to permit the respondents or indeed members of the public to understand what degree of seriousness should be attached to any given breach of the professional rules.

37. The absence of any or any adequate reasoning by the SDT as to why the sanction of the financial penalty was appropriate, the amount of that penalty and specifically in respect of any breach, how much of that penalty applied, renders it impossible for this court to determine whether the considerations of the SDT which led to the financial penalty were fair and/or reasonable.'

1   [2011] EWHC 462 (Admin) especially at [30] to [31]; see also *English v Emery Reinbold & Strick Ltd* [2002] 1 WLR 2409, CA.

Agreed outcomes[1]

22.35

An agreed outcome is a settlement agreement between the SRA and a respondent to Tribunal proceedings that has been approved by the Tribunal. An agreed outcome normally contains the following terms:

- a list of the allegations which are admitted by the respondent;

- a list of any allegations which are not admitted;

- an agreement as to whether the parties intend to dispose of any allegations which are not admitted by inviting the Tribunal to withdraw them or direct that they should lie on the file;

- a detailed statement of the agreed facts;

- a description of the mitigation upon which the respondent relies;

- a sanction which the parties agree to invite the Tribunal to impose by order;

- an explanation why the sanction is appropriate having regard to the Tribunal's Guidance Note on Sanctions;

- an agreement to pay the SRA's costs; and

- a declaration signed by the parties confirming that the facts in the statement are true and that the parties agree to the outcome.

1   See also **20.18** on regulatory settlement agreements.

22.36

In practice the SRA is willing to negotiate agreed outcomes with most respondents unless dishonesty is alleged or there are other allegations which are so serious they are likely to lead to a strike-off if proved.[1] A respondent wishing to negotiate an agreed outcome should approach the SRA early in the proceedings, as negotiations with the SRA can take a long period of time and rule 25(1) of the 2019 Rules provides that any agreed outcome should be submitted to the Tribunal for approval not less than 28 days before the substantive hearing.

If an agreed outcome is submitted to the Tribunal for approval, the Tribunal will initially consider the matter on the papers, and may direct that there should be a case management hearing in private to consider submissions before making a decision. If there is more than one respondent, and the agreed outcome does not relate to all the respondents, the non-participating respondents are given an opportunity to comment before a decision is made. If the Tribunal does not approve the agreed outcome, it will give written reasons for its decision and the parties can then submit a revised proposal. If an agreed outcome is not ultimately approved the application will be treated as a without prejudice application and the substantive case will be heard before a different panel. If the agreed outcome is approved the Tribunal will make an order in the agreed terms and will announce its decision at a public hearing.[2]

1   In dishonesty cases, the SRA may exceptionally be willing to negotiate an agreed outcome if the dishonesty is admitted and the respondent agrees to a striking-off order.
2   The procedure is set out in rule 25 of the 2019 Rules and the Tribunal's Practice Direction Number 1 on Agreed Outcomes dated 6 November 2019.

Costs

Costs against the unsuccessful respondent

22.37

Rule 43(1) of the 2019 Rules states that the Tribunal can make such order as to costs as it thinks fit.

A very high percentage of applications against solicitors are successful in whole or in part and the respondent in those cases will ordinarily be ordered to pay the costs of the SRA.[1] Even if not all allegations are found proved it is the Tribunal's practice to award all the costs against the respondent if, on the facts, it was reasonable to make those allegations.[2] If there has been a substantial contest over part of the case in which the respondent has been successful, the order may be to pay a reduced percentage of the SRA's costs.

The normal order for costs in a case where there has been a forensic investigation is an order for the payment of costs 'of and incidental to the application and enquiry' to include the costs of the forensic investigation. These are usually considerable – several thousands of pounds – and can exceed the applicant's legal costs. Regrettably, there is little published material as to how these costs are calculated, and it is usually difficult or impossible for the respondent solicitor to make a meaningful challenge as to the quantum of those costs at a summary assessment by the Tribunal.

The Tribunal can endorse an agreement between the parties and make an order for fixed costs, can summarily assess the costs in appropriate circumstances, or can order that the costs be subject to detailed assessment if not agreed – with or without an interim payment of costs being directed.[3] As orders made by the Tribunal are enforceable as orders of the High Court,[4] detailed assessment is dealt with by the Supreme Court Costs Office and the Civil Procedure Rules 1998 apply to that assessment in the usual way.

When making an order for costs, the Tribunal's reasons can be shortly stated, but they should be sufficient for the paying party to know why they have been ordered to pay costs and why they have been ordered to pay the amount specified in the order.[5]

1   There is a section on costs in the SDT Guidance Note on Sanctions at paras 63–76. See **APPENDIX 17**.
2   See generally para 69 of the SDT Guidance Note on Sanctions. See also **22.41**.
3   In *Gale v SRA* [2019] EWHC 222 (Admin) Pepperall J said at [36] that rule 18 of the 2007 Rules conferred on the Tribunal a wide and unfettered discretion as to the making of a costs order, the question of referral for detailed assessment and the amount of any order made on a summary assessment. There is no significant difference between rule 18 of the 2007 Rules and rule 43(1) of the 2019 Rules; both state the Tribunal can make such order as to costs as the Tribunal thinks fit.
4   Section 48(4) of SA 1974.
5   *Shah v SRA* [2017] EWHC 3657 (Admin) at [33].

The relevance of the respondent's means

22.38

In imposing fines and making costs orders the Tribunal should take into account the means of the respondent. In particular, where a solicitor is suspended or struck off, enquiry as to the solicitor's means must be made before any decision is made.[1] These propositions were unsuccessfully attacked by the SRA in *SRA v Davis and McGlinchey*.[2] The SRA asserted that the respondent's means should be irrelevant to the making of an order for costs. This was rejected by Mitting J, who provided valuable guidance as to how the issue should be tackled in future (at [22]–[24]):

'22. … where a solicitor admits the disciplinary charges brought against him, and who therefore anticipates the imposition of a sanction upon him, it should be incumbent upon him before the hearing to give advance notice to the SRA and to the Tribunal that he will contend either that no order for costs should be made against him, or that it should be limited in amount by reason of his own lack of means. He should also supply to the SRA and to the Tribunal, in advance of the hearing, the evidence upon which he relies to support that contention. In a case in which the solicitor disputes the charges brought against him, it would be burdensome to impose an advance obligation upon him of providing information about his means.

23. … [But] once the Tribunal has found that the charges are proved, then the same obligations … will be imposed upon a solicitor arguing that he cannot meet an order for costs, or that one should be limited in amount.

24. In either of the two sets of circumstances the SRA must be afforded a reasonable opportunity to test the evidence relied upon by the solicitor, and in an appropriate case to call evidence itself on the question of the solicitor's means and of course to make submissions about the matter to the Tribunal.'

The judge's recommendations in paragraph 22 of the judgment were acted upon by the SDT introducing a standard direction which required proper disclosure of a respondent's means by service of a statement of means when the respondent wishes the Tribunal to take those means into account. That is now embodied in the 2019 Rules, and rule 43(5) states that the statement of means should include details of the respondent's assets, income and expenditure and must be supported by documentary evidence. A failure to provide documentary evidence is usually fatal.

Where the respondent is shown to be impecunious, if the Tribunal is satisfied that there is a reasonable prospect that at some time in the future his or her ability to pay a costs order will improve, it may order the respondent to pay costs, but direct that such order is not to be enforced without further leave of the Tribunal.[3] However, a respondent must think carefully whether he or she wishes to plead poverty. While to do so may well reduce the amount of the fine or costs payable, there may be other regulatory repercussions for solicitors shown to be impecunious. Since the start of the 2008 recession, the SRA has devoted considerable resources to the issue of the financial stability of solicitors and entities, because of the potential damage to the reputation of the profession caused by the uncontrolled failures of law firms.

1 See *Merrick v Law Society* [2007] EWHC 2997 (Admin) at [60]–[66], in which an order for costs in the sum of £45,000 against a suspended solicitor, who did not have the means or ability to pay, was quashed on appeal. See also *Agyeman v SRA* [2012] EWHC 3472 (Admin) and *Sharma v SRA* [2012] EWHC 3176 (Admin) – in the latter case the Divisional Court observed that the solicitor must adduce evidence of inability to pay a costs order, including independent valuations of properties. In *Matthews v SRA* [2013] EWHC 1525 (Admin), Collins J held that in imposing a financial penalty, the Tribunal should consider the respondent's overall financial liability for the fine and costs, and reduced a fine of £5,000 and costs of £16,000 to an overall liability of £5,000 on account of the appellant's limited means.
2 [2011] EWHC 232 (Admin).
3 See para 68 of the SDT Guidance Note on Sanctions and eg *Ijomantu v SRA* [2013] EWHC 3905 (Admin).

Proportionality

22.39

Legal costs claimed by the SRA against unsuccessful respondents can be very high, as the regulator has frequently instructed barristers from commercial London Chambers. As for this, a word of warning was sounded by Lord Thomas CJ in *Brett v SRA*[1] in which he stated at [114]:

> 'It is now well established that the costs of proceedings which a person may be ordered to pay must be proportionate. It may well be that in a particular case, the regulatory authority bringing proceedings will wish to instruct a person or firm who in the current state of the legal market can command high fees which the regulatory authority may be prepared to pay. However the fact that the market enables such persons or firms to command such high fees does not mean that it is proportionate to make an order for costs by reference to the rates which the legal services market enables such persons or firms to command from the regulatory authority. A tribunal must assess what is proportionate, taking into account all the material circumstances.'

1 [2014] EWHC 2974 (Admin).

22.40

It regularly occurs that the SRA succeeds in large part against the respondent solicitor, but that some of the allegations are nevertheless dismissed by the Tribunal. In such circumstances, it may be appropriate for the Tribunal to take that into account when determining costs issues, and perhaps apply a discount to reflect the fact that the SRA failed in part.[1]

1 The authorities are not consistent. No discount was applied in *Baxendale-Walker v Law Society* [2007] EWCA Civ 233, [2007] 3 All ER 330, *Beresford v SRA* [2009] EWHC 3155 (Admin) and *Levy v SRA* [2011] EWHC 740 (Admin). See now though *Broomhead v SRA* [2014] EWHC 2772 (Admin), in which the High Court applied a discount and doubted *Levy*.

Costs against a successful respondent solicitor

22.41

Rule 22 of the 1994 Rules specifically provided that an order for costs may be made by the Tribunal against the respondent without finding any allegation proved – and even if no other order is made if, having regard to his or her conduct or to all the circumstances (or both), the Tribunal thinks it fit.[1] In *Rowe v Lindsay*, the Divisional Court indicated that this rule did not justify an order for costs against a successful respondent who had been acquitted of misconduct and whose conduct in relation to the questions before the Tribunal, and since the commencement of proceedings against him, had not in the event been criticised.[2]

If intending to impose a costs sanction (either an order against a successful respondent or an order depriving a successful respondent solicitor of his costs) by reason of any fault found against the solicitor, the Tribunal is bound to consider what impact the conduct of the solicitor, of which it is critical, has had on the costs incurred. The calculation need not be exact, but there must be a reasonable and just balance between the order made and what has occurred in the proceedings. There must be a causal connection between the fault found by the Tribunal and the incurring of costs.[3]

1   This provision was not carried into the 2007 Rules or the 2019 Rules. Rule 43(1) of the 2019 Rules gives the Tribunal a wide discretion as to costs orders.
2   (2001) DC Transcript CO/4737/2000.
3   *Hayes v Law Society* [2004] EWHC 1165 (QB). In referring to depriving the successful respondent of his costs (as distinct from the possibility of an order against a successful respondent) this decision should now be considered to have been overruled by *Baxendale-Walker v Law Society* [2007] EWCA Civ 233, [2007] 3 All ER 330.

Costs orders against the Law Society/SRA

22.42

Until 2006, those appearing in the Tribunal could expect, and advise their clients to expect, that costs would probably follow the event. If a respondent were to be acquitted of all charges in the Tribunal, the successful solicitor could generally expect an order that his or her costs should be paid by the Law Society.

This state of affairs altered with the decision of the Divisional Court in *Baxendale-Walker v Law Society*,[1] which was upheld by the Court of Appeal.[2] The rationale is that the Law Society is a statutory regulator, exercising its powers in the public interest; when the Law Society/SRA is addressing the question whether there is sufficient evidence to justify an application to the Tribunal, the ambit of its responsibility is far greater than it would be for a litigant deciding whether to bring civil proceedings.

In 2020 in *CMA v Flynn Pharma*[3] (a Competition Appeal Tribunal case where the regulator was unsuccessful) the Court of Appeal recognised that it was bound by previous case law, including *Baxendale-Walker*, and Lewison LJ set out the following principles:

'The applicable legal principles to be derived from these cases are, in my judgment, as follows:

i) Where a power to make an order about costs does not include an express general rule or default position, an important factor in the exercise of discretion is the fact that one of the parties is a regulator exercising functions in the public interest.

ii) That leads to the conclusion that in such cases the starting point or default position is that no order for costs should be made against a regulator who has brought or defended proceedings in the CAT acting purely in its regulatory capacity.

iii) The default position may be departed from for good reason.

iv) The mere fact that the regulator has been unsuccessful is not, without more, a good reason. I do not consider that it is necessary to find "exceptional circumstances" as opposed to a good reason.

v) A good reason will include unreasonable conduct on the part of the regulator, or substantial financial hardship likely to be suffered by the successful party if a costs order is not made.

vi) There may be additional factors, specific to a particular case, which might also permit a departure from the starting point.'

The normal approach to costs decisions in ordinary civil litigation, that costs should follow the event, accordingly has no direct application to unsuccessful disciplinary proceedings against solicitors. The starting point is that no order for costs should be made against the SRA, but that can be departed from for good reason. A good reason will include unreasonable conduct by the regulator. Where disciplinary proceedings are held to amount to an abuse of process, have been inefficiently prosecuted or have been mounted upon inadequate evidence, the respondent solicitor will ordinarily have a powerful argument that costs should follow the event. However, even if the SRA has acted reasonably, the Tribunal should consider – in addition to any other relevant fact or circumstance – the financial prejudice to the particular respondent if an order for costs is not made in his or her favour.

The principles set out in *Baxendale-Walker* and *Flynn* do not apply to appeals from the Tribunal to the High Court. On such appeals, the costs provisions of the Civil Procedure Rules are applied, and so ordinarily costs will follow the event. An appellant who successfully challenges findings against him or her can therefore expect to be awarded the costs of the appeal.[4]

1   [2006] EWHC 643 (Admin), [2006] 3 All ER 675.
2   [2007] EWCA Civ 233, [2007] 3 All ER 330. See too *Murtagh v SRA* [2013] EWHC 2024 (Admin).
3   [2020] EWCA Civ 617 at [79]. At the date of this edition of *The Solicitor's Handbook*, the Supreme Court has given permission to appeal to Flynn Pharma, and the appeal is likely to be heard in February 2022.
4   See *Bryant and Bench v Law Society* [2007] EWHC 3043 (Admin) at [251] and *Bass and Ward v SRA* (judgment on costs) [2012] EWHC 2457 (Admin).

Appeals from the Tribunal

Statutory provisions

22.43

Either party may appeal to the High Court without permission and such appeals are governed by CPR, Part 52.[1]

The time for appealing is now 21 days from the date on which the written judgment is sent to the appellant.[2]

The court has power to make such order on an appeal as it may think fit.[3] Appeals to the High Court are heard in the Administrative Court, usually by a single judge or on occasion by a two-judge Divisional Court.

1   Section 49 of SA 1974. The one exception, which will only be relevant when rules are made to permit appeals to the Tribunal from decisions of the SRA in relation to practising certificate and comparable issues, is that the decision of the Tribunal on such appeals will be final; see section 49A(3) of SA 1974. See footnote 10 to **21.3**.
2   CPR rule 52.12(2)(b) modified by Part 52 Practice Direction 52D, para 3.3A.
3   Section 49(4) of SA 1974.

Stay pending appeal

22.44

As has been said (see **22.3**), the Tribunal does not readily grant a stay pending appeal, or any other period of grace, in cases where an order for striking off is made, still less when there has been a finding of dishonesty, and an appeal does not in itself operate as a stay.[1] It is necessary to lodge an appeal and to apply within that appeal for interim relief. The test that will be applied is set out in *Re a Solicitor*:[2]

> 'For such a submission to succeed, it would be necessary to establish not only that the applicant's appeal against striking off would have a reasonable prospect of success, but, further, that this Court would be likely to impose in substitution for the order of the Tribunal a penalty no greater than suspension from practice for some three or four months [being the period within which the substantive appeal could be expected to be heard].'

In that case, in which the application was heard in November 1998, the appeal was expected to be heard in February 1999.

It will be seen that an application for a stay pending appeal would be more likely to succeed in a case of a suspension from practice where the suspension would substantially have been served by the time the appeal came to be heard. Successful applications for a stay pending appeal where the solicitor has been struck off can be expected to be rare.

1   CPR rule 52.16.
2   16 November 1998, unreported, transcript CO/4359/98, per Rose LJ.

Approach of the courts

22.45

Until the advent of the Human Rights Act (HRA) 1998, the courts were reluctant to interfere with the decisions of the Tribunal as an expert professional disciplinary tribunal. It was stated that it would require a very strong case to interfere with sentence, because the Tribunal was best placed to weigh the seriousness of professional misconduct.[1] The modern approach of the courts in the light of the HRA 1998 has altered in this respect, and was first determined in *Langford v Law Society*.[2]

The following extracts from Lord Millett's speech in *Ghosh v General Medical Council*[3] were cited by Rose LJ in *Langford*:

> 'their Lordships wish to emphasise that their powers are not as limited as may be suggested by some of the observations which have been made in the past …
>
> … the Board will accord an appropriate measure of respect to the judgment of the committee whether the practitioner's failings amount to serious professional misconduct and on the measures necessary to maintain professional standards and provide adequate protection to the public. But the Board will not defer to the committee's judgment more than is warranted by the circumstances …'

1   See *McCoan v General Medical Council* [1964] 1 WLR 1107, PC; and *Bolton v Law Society* [1994] 1 WLR 512, CA.
2   [2002] EWHC 2802 (Admin); see particularly at [14] and [15].
3   [2001] 1 WLR 1915, PC.

22.46

The approach of the courts to appeals against Tribunal decisions on sanction was reviewed in the Court of Appeal in 2008 in *Law Society v Salsbury*.[1] Jackson LJ said that 'absent any error of law, the High Court must pay considerable respect to the sentencing decisions of the Tribunal. Nevertheless, if the High Court, despite paying such respect is satisfied that the sentencing decision was clearly inappropriate, then the court will interfere'.

The approach was considered again in 2018 by the Court of Appeal in *Bawa-Garba v General Medical Council* (an appeal relating to the Medical Practitioners Tribunal).[2] The Court of Appeal emphasised the need for particular caution in relation to evaluative decisions of specialist tribunals (including evaluative decisions relating to sanction). Lord Burnett CJ said an appeal court should only interfere with such an evaluative decision if (1) there was an error of principle in carrying out the evaluation or (2) for any other reason, the evaluation was wrong, that is to say it was an evaluative decision which fell outside the bounds of what the adjudicative body could properly and reasonably decide … As the authorities show, the addition of "plainly" or "clearly" to the word "wrong" adds nothing in this context'.

1   [2008] EWCA Civ 1285 at [30].
2   [2018] EWCA Civ 1879 at [67].

22.47

In 2019 in *SRA v Good*[1] Flaux LJ said, following the decision in *Bawa-Garba*, that the court should only interfere with a decision of the SDT as to the appropriate sanction if the court is 'satisfied that in reaching the particular decision the SDT committed an error of principle or its evaluation was wrong in the sense of falling outside the bounds of what the SDT could properly and reasonably decide'.

Flaux J also set out the legal principles for determining an appeal against a Tribunal decision on liability or sanction in further detail, having regard to the restraint to be exercised when considering a decision of a specialist disciplinary panel, as follows:

> 'The appeal is by way of review not rehearing: CPR 52.21(1), so that the Court will only allow an appeal where the decision is shown to be "wrong":

CPR 52.21(3)(a). This can connote an error of law, an error of fact or an error in the exercise of discretion ...

An appellate court should exercise particular caution and restraint in interfering with the findings of fact of a lower court or tribunal, particularly where that court or tribunal has reached those findings after seeing and evaluating the witnesses ... what matters is whether the decision under appeal is one that no reasonable judge could have reached ...

It follows that, in the absence of some other identifiable error, such as (without attempting an exhaustive account) a material error of law, or the making of a critical finding of fact which has no basis in the evidence, or a demonstrable misunderstanding of relevant evidence, or a demonstrable failure to consider relevant evidence, an appellate court will interfere with the findings of fact made by a trial judge only if it is satisfied that his decision cannot reasonably be explained or justified ...

The appropriate restraint on the part of an appellate court is still called for where the conclusion of the lower court or tribunal is not just as to the primary facts, but as to the evaluation of those facts. The appellate court should only interfere if there was an error of principle in carrying out the evaluation or for any other reason the evaluation was "wrong", in other words, was an evaluative decision which fell outside the bounds of what the court or tribunal could properly and reasonably have decided ...

The particular caution and restraint to be exercised before interfering with an evaluative judgment by a specialist tribunal, where that tribunal has made an assessment having seen and heard the witnesses, was emphasised in the context of the SDT by the Divisional Court in Day ... and in the context of the Medical Practitioners Tribunal ("MPT") by the Court of Appeal in ... *Bawa-Garba* ...

Similar restraint should be exercised by an appellate court before interfering with the sanction imposed by a specialist disciplinary tribunal for professional misconduct. That involves a multi-factorial exercise of discretion and evaluative judgment by the relevant tribunal, which is particularly well-placed to assess what sanction is required in the interest of the profession and to protect the public.'[2]

1   [2019] EWHC 817 (Admin) at [28]–[32]. See also *SRA v Dar* [2019] EWHC 2831 (Admin) at [32].
2   *SRA v Good* [2019] EWHC 817 (Admin) at [28]–[32]. See also *SRA v Dar* [2019] EWHC 2831 (Admin) at [32].

Fresh evidence

22.48

Solicitors may wish to adduce fresh evidence on appeal, often of the medical or financial variety. The *Ladd v Marshall* principles (which in any event do not hold sway to the extent that they did before the Woolf reforms) are not always applied with their full rigour in statutory appeals of this type, where the likelihood of prejudice to the regulator is minimal, and it is in the interests of both parties that the correct sanction is applied to the regulated individual.[1] Although the court may adopt a more flexible approach than in conventional civil litigation, this cannot be taken for granted.[2]

1 See *R (Adelakun) v SRA* [2014] EWHC 198 (Admin) and *R (Khan) v GMC* [2014] EWHC 404 (Admin).
2 See *Sohal v SRA* [2014] EWHC 1613 (Admin).

Costs

22.49

It has already been noted (see **22.42**) that costs in the High Court will ordinarily follow the event in accordance with CPR rule 44.2(2), and that *Baxendale-Walker* has no application to appeals from the SDT.[1] In the case of an impecunious unsuccessful appellant, the court may be prepared to order that its own costs order should not be enforced by the SRA without leave.[2]

1 See *Bryant and Bench v Law Society* [2007] EWHC 3043 (Admin) at [251] and *Bass and Ward v SRA* (judgment on costs) [2012] EWHC 2457 (Admin). See too *SRA v Wingate; SRA v Malins* [2018] EWCA Civ 366 at [133]–[136].
2 See *Webb v SRA* [2013] EWHC 2225 (Admin) and *R (Adelakun) v SRA* [2014] EWHC 198 (Admin).

Further appeal to the Court of Appeal

22.50

Further appeals require the permission of the Court of Appeal, as a second appeal governed by section 55(1) of the Administration of Justice Act (AJA) 1985 and CPR rule 52.7, and are rarely mounted. To obtain permission, the appellant needs to show a real prospect of success and that either (a) the appeal would raise an important point of principle or practice or (b) there is some other compelling reason for the appeal. Since 1994 the Law Society has appealed to the Court of Appeal on only four occasions, in each case to establish important points of principle.[1]

1 *Bolton v Law Society* [1994] 1 WLR 512, CA; *Bultitude v Law Society* [2004] EWCA Civ 1853, *Times*, 14 January 2005; *Law Society v Salsbury* [2008] EWCA Civ 1285; and *SRA v Malins* [2018] EWCA Civ 366.

CHAPTER 23

Proceedings before the SDT: (3) appeals to the Tribunal

23.1

CHAPTER 20 dealt, among other things, with the Solicitors Regulation Authority (SRA)'s powers to impose fines on practices and practitioners, to impose rebukes, and to publish its decisions; see **20.1**. Those decisions are made, so far as they relate to individual solicitors and employees, under section 44D of the Solicitors Act (SA) 1974 (see **APPENDIX 18**); and so far as they relate to recognised bodies, their managers and employees, under paragraph 14B of Schedule 2 to the Administration of Justice Act (AJA) 1985 (see **APPENDIX 19**).

CHAPTER 2 considers the powers of the SRA in relation to the authorisation of alternative business structures (ABSs) or 'licensable bodies', including the power to refuse an application, to impose conditions and to revoke or suspend an authorisation, and the power to withhold approval of individuals as managers or compliance officers and to withdraw approval; see **2.9–2.15**. CHAPTER 25 explains the process whereby ownership of ABSs is regulated. CHAPTER 26 deals with the disciplinary powers of the SRA to fine ABSs and disqualify individuals. All of those decisions are made as a licensing authority under Part 5 of the Legal Services Act (LSA) 2007 (see **APPENDIX 21**) or licensing rules. For relevant purposes the 'licensing rules' comprise the SRA Handbook and most relevantly the SRA Authorisation of Firms Rules 2019.

Appeals lie to the Solicitors Disciplinary Tribunal (the Tribunal or SDT) against decisions of the SRA:

- to impose fines on individuals or recognised bodies;[1]

- to impose a rebuke on individuals or recognised bodies, if the SRA decides to publish the rebuke, but not otherwise;[2]

- to publish a rebuke or fine imposed by the SRA;[3]

- to disqualify a person from acting as Head of Legal Practice (HOLP) or Head of Finance and Administration (HOFA) or from being a manager or employee of a licensed body;

- to refuse to bring a disqualification to an end following a review;

- to impose fines on licensed bodies or managers or employees of licensed bodies;

- to refuse an application for authorisation as a licensed body;

- to impose a condition on the authorisation of a licensed body;

- to revoke or suspend a licensed body's authorisation;

- to extend, revoke or vary the terms and conditions of authorisation of a licensed body, or to refuse an application to do so;

- not to approve a person to be a manager or compliance officer of a licensed body;

- to approve a person to be a manager or compliance officer of a licensed body subject to conditions;

- to withdraw approval of a manager or compliance officer of a licensed body;

- not to approve a person being an owner of a licensed body;

- to impose conditions on the authorisation of a licensed body in connection with the approval of an owner;

- to withdraw approval of a person as an owner of a licensed body;

- to notify the Legal Services Board (LSB) that an owner has exceeded a share or voting limit;[4]

and against a failure of the SRA to make a decision on an application for authorisation within the required period.[5]

1　Section 44E of SA 1974 and para 14C of Schedule 2 to AJA 1985.
2　Section 44E of SA 1974 and para 14C of Schedule 2 to AJA 1985.
3　Section 44E of SA 1974 and para 14C of Schedule 2 to AJA 1985.
4　The appealable decisions relating to ownership are set out in further detail in **23.6**.
5　Legal Services Act 2007 (Appeals from Licensing Authority Decisions) (No 2) Order 2011 (SI 2011/2863).

23.2

In this chapter we consider only the procedural aspects of such appeals. The appeals are governed by the Solicitors Disciplinary Tribunal (Appeals and Amendment) Rules 2011[1] (the 'Appeal Rules'). The Appeal Rules came into force on 1 October 2011 to regulate appeals to the Tribunal under SA 1974 and AJA 1985. The Appeal Rules were amended by the Solicitors Disciplinary Tribunal (Appeals) (Amendment) Rules 2011[2] to cover appeals relating to licensed bodies under LSA 2007 with effect from 23 December 2011.[3] The Tribunal publishes a guidance note on appeals which summarises the categories of appeals that can be made to the Tribunal and the orders that can be made by the Tribunal.[4]

The number of appeals heard by the Tribunal is very small. At the time of writing, only one of the appeal decisions made by the Tribunal, *Arslan*,[5] has led to a second appeal to the High Court.

In **Appendix 16** we have included the Appeal Rules, including the ABS-specific provisions.

1　SI 2011/2346. See also **Appendix 16**.
2　SI 2011/3070.
3　Minor amendments were also made to the Appeal Rules by rule 49 of the Solicitors (Disciplinary Proceedings) Rules 2019 (the '2019 Rules') with effect from 25 November 2019 to (1) change a daily time deadline for carrying out procedural steps from 5pm to 4.30pm and (2) update the cross-references to the Solicitors (Disciplinary Proceedings) Rules 2007 (the '2007 Rules') contained in the Appeal Rules to cross-references to the 2019 Rules.
4　SDT Guidance Note on Appeals, fourth edition, December 2020.
5　11356-2015, SDT; *SRA v SDT (re Arslan)* [2016] EWHC 2862 (Admin).

23.3

The Tribunal has jurisdiction to review orders made by the SRA under section 43(3) of SA 1974, relating to solicitors' employees. Applications to the Tribunal relating to section 43 orders are not regulated by the Appeal Rules.[1] For section 43 applications see **18.10**.

1   Section 43 applications commenced on or after 25 November 2019 are regulated by the 2019 Rules. Any subsisting applications commenced before that date are regulated by the 2007 Rules. See rule 1(2) of the Appeal Rules, rule 8(4) of the 2007 Rules and rule 2(a)(ii) of the 2019 Rules.

Constitution of appeal panels, delegation and general powers

23.4

The one certainty in relation to ABSs is that, however much informed opinion there may be, no one can predict reliably exactly how the market will develop, what forms new businesses will take and what degree of complexity will be involved in licensing decisions, and therefore in appeals from licensing decisions. The Tribunal has sensibly created for itself a degree of flexibility.

The 2019 Rules dealing with the historical and original jurisdiction of the Tribunal are rigid as to the constitution of the adjudicating panel; it consists of three and only three: a lay member and two solicitors.[1] In contrast, the Appeal Rules state that for the hearing of any appeal a panel will be 'at least three members of the Tribunal', and that 'Unless the President otherwise directs, the majority of the Panel members shall be solicitor members'.[2]

The lay members of the Tribunal have a wealth of expertise in a wide variety of subjects outside the law, including, for example, business management, and it could be foreseen that in appropriate cases an expanded appeal panel could draw on that experience.

1   Rule 9 of the 2019 Rules.
2   Rule 3 of the Appeal Rules.

23.5

A single solicitor member may make case management decisions and give directions under rule 9 of the Appeal Rules;[1] may waive or require a procedural failure to be remedied under rule 11; may make a direction adding, substituting or removing a party under rule 13; may deal with the prohibition of disclosure of documents under rule 14; may make orders about lead cases, rule 15, consent to the withdrawal of an appeal under rule 16, and give directions as to disclosure, evidence and submissions under rule 19(1).[2]

The Tribunal clerks have delegated authority to give case management directions under rules 9, 13 and 19(1), subject to the right of a party to apply, within 14 days, for the decision to be considered afresh by a panel or single solicitor member.[3]

The Tribunal (or a panel of Tribunal members consisting of no fewer than five members, of whom no fewer than two shall be lay members) may make general practice directions: notices or directions concerning the practices or procedures of the Tribunal, consistent with the Appeal Rules, which are to be promulgated under the authority of the President.[4]

Subject to the Appeal Rules themselves, the Tribunal may regulate its own procedure, and may dispense with any requirements of the Rules in respect of notices, statements or other documents, witnesses, service or time in any case where it appears to the Tribunal to be just so to do.[5] This does not extend, however, to the time limit for appeals from decisions of the SRA as a licensing authority relating to the ownership of ABSs; see **23.6**.

The Tribunal may consent to a witness giving, or require any witness to give, evidence on oath, and may administer an oath for that purpose.[6]

1   The detailed rules referred to in this paragraph are considered at **23.9** and **23.10**.
2   Rule 5(4) of the Appeal Rules.
3   Rule 5(1) and (3).
4   Rule 10.
5   Rule 18.
6   Rule 19(3).

Preliminary steps

23.6

The time for appeal is in all cases 28 days from notification of the decision. In relation to some ABS appeals this is a statutory time limit fixed by rules made by the LSB under its powers in paragraph 8 of Schedule 13 to LSA 2007,[1] and may not be exceeded. Neither the Tribunal nor any other party has power to waive the limit or consent to its extension.

This statutory time limit applies to appeals by licensed bodies, their managers and employees against financial penalties[2] and to appeals concerning the following SRA licensing decisions as to ownership of a licensed body:

- to approve an investor's notified interest subject to conditions, on granting a licence;

- to object to an investor's notified interest;

- to approve an investor's notifiable interest subject to conditions, after a licence has been granted;

- to object to an investor's notifiable interest;

- to impose conditions or further conditions on an existing restricted interest;

- to object to an existing restricted interest; and

- to notify the LSB that an owner has exceeded a share or voting limit.[3]

1   Rule 5 and 6 of the LSB Rules on the Prescribed Period for the Making of Appeals against Licensing Authority Decisions Relating to Ownership of Licensed Bodies, April 2018 and rule 6 of the LSB Rules on the Period for the Making of Appeals against Decisions of a Licensing Authority in Relation to Financial Penalties, April 2018.
2   Section 96(1) of LSA 2007. Particular care must be taken on the time for appealing financial penalties under LSA 2007. Section 96(8) of LSA 2007 states that the validity of a penalty is not to be

questioned by any legal proceedings whatever, except those permitted by section 96(1). Section 96(1) permits an appeal before the end of the time period prescribed by the LSB rules. The LSB rules specify a 28-day period running from 'the date on which notice of the decision of the licensing authority is given to the applicant'. If there is an internal SRA appeal, it is unclear whether time starts to run from the date of the original decision or the decision made on the internal appeal.

3   Respectively paras 17(1), 19(1), 28(1), 31(1), 33(1), 36(1) and 49(2) of Schedule 13 to LSA 2007.

23.7

Rule 6(4) of the Appeal Rules states that the notice of appeal[1] must set out:

- the name and address of the appellant;
- the name and address of the appellant's representative (if any);
- an address where documents for the appellant may be sent or delivered;
- the basis on which the appellant has standing to start proceedings before the Tribunal;
- the name and address of the respondent;
- details of the decision or act to which the proceedings relate;
- the result the appellant is seeking;
- the grounds on which the appellant relies;
- any application for a stay, if the appellant is allowed to make such an application under the licensing rules;
- a statement as to whether the appellant would be content for the case to be dealt with without a hearing if the Tribunal considers it appropriate; and
- any further information or documents required by a practice direction.

A copy of any record of the decision which is the subject of the appeal, and any statement of reasons that the appellant has or can reasonably obtain, must be supplied. Three additional copies of the notice and all accompanying documents must be filed with the Tribunal. A copy of the notice of appeal and all accompanying documents must be served on the respondent at the same time that the appellant sends or delivers the notice of appeal to the Tribunal.[2]

1   A notice of appeal form can be downloaded from the Tribunal's website.
2   Rule 6(5), (6) and (7) of the Appeal Rules.

23.8

The respondent's response to the notice of appeal must be sent or delivered to the Tribunal and the appellant within 28 days of receipt by the respondent of the notice of appeal. There is no set form but the response must include:

- the name and address of the respondent;
- the name and address of the respondent's representative (if any);
- an address where documents for the respondent may be sent or delivered;
- any further information or documents required by a practice direction or direction;
- a statement as to whether the respondent would be content for the case to be dealt with without a hearing if the Tribunal considers it appropriate; and

- a statement as to whether the respondent opposes the appellant's case and, if so, any grounds for such opposition which are not contained in another document sent or delivered with the response.

Documents relied on by the respondent in making the decision and any documents considered by the respondent to be relevant to the appeal should accompany the response, including any record of the decision under appeal or reasons if not provided by the appellant.[1]

The onus is thus placed initially on the respondent to produce all documents that are 'relevant' to the extent that they have not already been placed before the Tribunal by the appellant. This requires an exercise of judgement as the documents required are not limited simply to those upon which the respondent may wish to rely. The Tribunal's requirement for disclosure of documents which adversely affect the respondent's case or support the appellant's case under rule 26(4) of the 2019 Rules may be relevant by analogy.

Three copies of the respondent's material must be provided to the Tribunal and service must be effected contemporaneously. If the response is out of time a request for an extension of time and the reason for it must be included.

An appellant may file and serve a reply within 14 days from receipt of the respondent's response, and any additional documents intended to be relied upon. At the same time the appellant may elect to supply a list of documents intended to be relied upon that were not appended to the notice of appeal, and if requested by the respondent or the Tribunal must provide copies or make those documents available for inspection and/or copying within seven days.[2]

1   Rule 7 of the Appeal Rules.
2   Rule 8.

Case management

23.9

On the direction of the Tribunal parties may be added, substituted or removed as an appellant or a respondent.[1]

The Tribunal may give directions to:

- extend or shorten the time for complying with any rule, practice direction or direction, unless such extension or shortening would conflict with a provision of another enactment (or of any rule made under another enactment) containing a time limit;

- consolidate or hear together two or more sets of proceedings or parts of proceedings raising common issues, or treat a case as a lead case;

- hear any application for a stay;

- permit or require a party to amend a document;

- permit or require a party or another person to provide documents, information or submissions which are relevant to the proceedings to the Tribunal or a party;

- deal with an issue in the proceedings as a preliminary issue;

- hold a hearing to consider any matter, including a case management issue;

- decide the form of any hearing;

- adjourn or postpone a hearing;

- require a party to produce a bundle for a hearing;

- require a party to provide a skeleton argument;

- decide the place and time of any hearing;

- make requirements about documentation and inspection;

- stay proceedings; or

- suspend the effect of its own decision pending the determination by the High Court of an application for permission to appeal against, and any appeal of, that decision.[2]

A clerk may appoint a time and place for the review of the progress of the matter and notify the parties.[3]

1   Rule 13 of the Appeal Rules.
2   Rule 9(1) and (2).
3   Rule 9(3).

23.10

Directions may also be given by the Tribunal as to:

- the exchange between parties of lists of documents which are relevant to the appeal, or relevant to particular issues, and the inspection of such documents;

- the provision by parties of statements of agreed matters;

- issues on which it requires evidence or submissions;

- the nature of the evidence or submissions it requires;

- whether the parties are permitted or required to provide expert evidence, and if so whether the parties must jointly appoint a single expert to provide such evidence;

- any limit on the number of witnesses whose evidence a party may put forward, whether in relation to a particular issue or generally;

- the manner in which any evidence or submissions are to be provided, which may include a direction for them to be given orally at a hearing or by written submissions or witness statement; and

- the time at which any evidence or submissions are to be sent or delivered.[1]

The Tribunal may admit evidence whether or not the evidence would be admissible in a civil trial in the United Kingdom; or the evidence was available to a previous decision-maker. It may also exclude evidence that would otherwise be admissible where the evidence was not provided within the time allowed by a direction or a practice direction; or where the evidence was otherwise provided in a manner that did not comply with a direction or a practice direction; or it would otherwise be unfair, disproportionate or unnecessary in the interests of justice to admit it.[2]

The Tribunal may in its discretion proceed on the basis of written evidence subject to provisions as to service, notice, and the entitlement of the other party to object. If a witness is to be called to give oral evidence a witness statement with a statement of truth must be filed and served at least ten days before the hearing date. Five copies must be provided to the Tribunal.

By rule 11 of the Appeal Rules a failure to comply with any provision of the Rules, a practice direction or a direction does not render void either the appeal or any step taken in the appeal. The Tribunal may waive the requirement; require the failure to be remedied; exercise its power to strike the whole or part of the appeal (see further below); bar or restrict a party's participation in the appeal, but an order barring or restricting a party's participation in the appeal may not be made without giving the party an opportunity to make representations.

Where two or more appeals give rise to common or related issues one or more lead cases may be selected and other affected appeals may be stayed.[3]

1　Rule 19(1) of the Appeal Rules.
2　Rule 19(2).
3　Rule 15.

Private and public hearings

23.11

All hearings, including interlocutory hearings, are heard in public unless the Tribunal is satisfied that exceptional hardship or exceptional prejudice will be caused to a party, a witness or any other person affected by the appeal, or if a hearing would prejudice the interests of justice.[1]

The Tribunal has the power to direct that someone be excluded from any hearing if he or she is likely to prove disruptive, or for comparable reasons.[2] The Tribunal may also exclude a witness until he or she has given evidence.[3]

Under rule 14 of the Appeal Rules there is a power to prohibit the disclosure or publication of documents or other material likely to identify someone the Tribunal considers should not be identified (which is regularly if not invariably done to protect the identity of clients, by identifying them by letters of the alphabet).

Under the same rule there are more complex provisions enabling documents to be withheld from a party altogether if there is a likelihood of serious harm to someone and in the interests of justice, with appropriate safeguards. The use of such powers is likely to be highly exceptional.

1　Rule 23(1) to (4) of the Appeal Rules.
2　Rule 23(5).
3　Rule 23(6).

Listing, hearings and other methods of disposal

23.12

Appeals may be disposed of without a hearing if both parties consent and the Tribunal considers it can properly determine the issues in this way.[1] Otherwise, hearings are listed on the basis that at least 28 days' notice is given, unless all the parties agree and the Tribunal has ordered a shorter period.[2] Any party may appoint a representative, who need not be a legal representative.[3]

Appeals can be disposed of by consent if the Tribunal considers the agreement appropriate, and in this event there need not be a hearing.[4]

Either party may unilaterally withdraw – the appeal or opposition to it – but the withdrawal does not take effect until the Tribunal consents to it, which it may do on terms as to costs. A party may also apply to reinstate an appeal or opposition to an appeal. The application must be made in writing within 28 days of the withdrawal (whether that was on written notice or orally at a hearing).[5]

Under rule 12 the Tribunal may strike out the whole or part of an appeal if the appellant has failed to comply with a direction which stated that a failure to comply could lead to that result (if the appeal or part of it is struck out on this basis the appellant may apply to reinstate it, within 28 days). An appeal or part of it may also be struck out if the appellant has failed to co-operate to such an extent that the appeal cannot be dealt with fairly and justly, or if the Tribunal considers that there is no reasonable prospect of the appellant's case, or that part of it, succeeding.

The same provisions apply in relation to striking out a respondent's opposition to an appeal *mutatis mutandis*.[6]

If an appeal has been finally disposed of at a hearing at which a party neither attended in person nor was represented, that party may apply for a rehearing. The application must be made within 14 days of receipt of the Tribunal's order. It can be expected that such applications will be dealt with in no different a manner from applications made in the same circumstances under the 2019 Rules; see **21.37**.

1   Rule 21 of the Appeal Rules.
2   Rule 22.
3   Rule 28.
4   Rule 17. For disposal of an appeal by consent which varied an adjudication order see *Heselton*, 11636-2017, SDT.
5   Rule 16.
6   Rule 12(6).

Review or rehearing

23.13

The Appeal Rules do not state whether an appeal should proceed by way of review or rehearing.

In *Arslan*[1] the High Court accepted that an appeal in the Tribunal under section 44E should proceed by way of review and not a rehearing. The Tribunal's Guidance Note on Appeals states that when considering any appeal the Tribunal will carry out a review and will not rehear the original case.[2]

In *Arslan* Leggatt J said:

'It is not in dispute that the Tribunal was correct to hold that … the proper approach was to proceed by way of a review and not a rehearing. As for what such a review involves, the Tribunal accepted … that its function was analogous to that of a court dealing with an appeal from another court or from a tribunal and that it should apply by analogy the standard of review applicable to such appeals which is set out in rule 52.11 of the Civil Procedure Rules. Rule 52.11 makes it clear that a court or tribunal conducting a review should not generally receive new evidence that was not before the original decision-maker, although it may do so if justice requires it, and it should interfere with a decision under review only if satisfied that the decision was wrong or that the decision was unjust because of a serious procedural or other irregularity in the proceedings.

It follows that the Tribunal should not embark on an exercise of finding the relevant facts afresh. On matters of fact the proper starting point for the Tribunal in this case was the findings made by the adjudicator and the evidence before the adjudicator. The Tribunal had to consider whether, on that evidence, the adjudicator was justified in making the factual findings that he did.

More guidance on the proper approach to a review is given in the judgment of Clarke LJ in *Assicurazioni Generali SpA v Arab Insurance Group* [2003] 1 WLR 577 … In [the judgment] the point is made that the approach to any particular case will depend upon the nature of the issues under review. Where a challenge is made to conclusions of primary fact, the weight to be attached to the findings of the original decision-maker will depend upon the extent to which that decision-maker had an advantage over the reviewing body; the greater that advantage the more reluctant the reviewing body should be to interfere. Another important factor is the extent to which the original decision involved an evaluation of the facts on which there is room for reasonable disagreement. In such a case the reviewing body ought not generally to interfere unless it is satisfied that the conclusion reached lay outside the bounds within which reasonable disagreement is possible'.[3]

The Tribunal has adopted the principles for review referred to in *Arslan* in subsequent appeals under section 44E. For example, in *Shulman* the Tribunal stated that its role was to review the Adjudicator's decision, rather than conduct a rehearing, and that the Tribunal should interfere with the decision only if satisfied that the decision was wrong or was unjust because of a serious procedural or other irregularity. Where the original decision involved an evaluation of the facts on which there was room for reasonable disagreement, the Tribunal ought not generally to interfere unless satisfied that the conclusion reached lay outside the bounds within which reasonable disagreement was possible.[4]

The Tribunal has also adopted the principles relating to new evidence set out in *Arslan* in subsequent appeals under section 44E in *Cannon*[5] and *White*.[6] Applications to introduce new evidence were made in both cases. In *White* the Tribunal admitted some additional documents and in *Cannon* the Tribunal admitted oral evidence from a witness limited to specific issues.

1   [2016] EWHC 2862 (Admin).
2   SDT Guidance Note on Appeals, fourth edition, December 2020, para 6.
3   *SRA v SDT (re Arslan)* [2016] EWHC 2862 (Admin) at [38]–[40].

4   12138-2020, SDT; see also *Das* 12137-2020, SDT.
5   11547-2016, SDT.
6   11680-2017, SDT.

The burden of proof

23.14

The appellate jurisdiction of the Tribunal covers three areas: appeals against SRA in-house sanctions of rebukes and fines, imposed in relation to individual solicitors and traditional (non-ABS) practices; appeals against decisions of a disciplinary character involving ABSs to impose fines, revoke authorisations and disqualify individuals; and appeals against licensing decisions, such as to refuse to grant an ABS licence, to refuse to approve individual applicants in regulated positions, or to impose conditions. The first two areas relate to disciplinary matters and the third relates to licensing matters. At the time of writing there have been no known appeals to the Tribunal on licensing matters.

In *Arslan* the High Court accepted that disciplinary appeals under section 44E are analogous to appeals by way of review under CPR, Part 52.[1] That places the burden of proof on the appellant, and in subsequent disciplinary appeals the Tribunal has proceeded on the basis that the burden of proof falls on the appellant.[2]

1   *SRA v SDT (re Arslan)* [2016] EWHC 2862 (Admin) at [38]–[40].
2   For example, *Cannon*, 11547-2016, SDT; *White*, 11680-2017, SDT; *Shulman*, 12138-2020, SDT.

23.15

As regards the burden of proof in licensing appeals, the closest analogy is that of those seeking to join the solicitors' profession, and about whom there is a question over character and fitness. The general principle is that no one has the right to become a solicitor, and the burden is on the applicant to demonstrate his or her fitness.[1]

1   See *Jideofo v Law Society*, *Evans v SRA* and *Begum v SRA*: respectively No 6 of 2006, No 1 of 2007 and No 11 of 2007, unreported.

The standard of proof

23.16

In *Arslan* the High Court said that the standard of proof to apply on an appeal under section 44E of SA 1974, is the civil standard:

> 'It follows from the nature of the Tribunal's role as a review body rather than a primary decision-maker that it was not for the Tribunal to apply its own standard of proof. In relation to the standard of proof the only relevant questions for the Tribunal were to ask, first, what standard the SRA as the primary fact-finder ought to have applied; and second, whether the SRA adjudicator had properly applied that standard.
>
> There can be no doubt that, in deciding whether to take action under section 44D, the SRA was correct to apply the civil standard … It follows

that the only question for the Tribunal when hearing an appeal under section 44E is whether the SRA properly applied the civil standard of proof. There is no scope for the Tribunal to apply the criminal standard.'[1]

Paragraph 8 of the Tribunal's Guidance Note on Appeals states that the Tribunal will apply the civil standard of proof when hearing any appeal.[2]

1 *SRA v SDT (re Arslan)* [2016] EWHC 2862 (Admin) at [43]–[44].
2 SDT Guidance Note on Appeals, fourth edition, December 2020, para 8.

The Tribunal's order

23.17

The Tribunal's jurisdiction to hear appeals arises from three different statutes (SA 1974, AJA 1985 and LSA 2007) and the type of order which the Tribunal can make on appeal is dependent on the provisions of those statutes.

For appeals under SA 1974, the Tribunal can make such order as it thinks fit.[1] For appeals under AJA 1985 and LSA 2007, the Tribunal does not have a general power to make such order as it thinks fit. For appeals under AJA 1985, the Tribunal's powers are, in summary, aligned with the sanctions which can be imposed in respect of recognised bodies in first instance proceedings.[2] For appeals on financial penalties under LSA 2007, the Tribunal can quash the penalty, substitute a penalty of such lesser amount as it considers appropriate or, in the case of an appeal relating to the time for payment, substitute a different time or times.[3] For appeals relating to licensing matters under LSA 2007 the Tribunal in general terms has power to affirm or quash the decision in whole or in part, substitute another decision of the kind that could be made by the SRA or, in some circumstances, remit the matter back to the SRA.[4]

1 Section 44E of SA 1974.
2 See paras 14C, 18(2) and 18A(2)–(3) of Schedule 2 to AJA 1985.
3 Section 96(3) of LSA 2007. There is no express statutory power for the Tribunal to deal with any costs order made by the SRA at first instance.
4 See generally Schedule 13 to LSA 2007, and Legal Services Act 2007 (Appeals from Licensing Authority Decisions) (No 2) Order 2011 (SI 2011/2863).

Costs

23.18

By rule 29 of the Appeal Rules the Tribunal may make such order for costs of the appeal as it thinks fit, at any stage of an appeal, including an order disallowing costs incurred unnecessarily; and may order that costs be paid by any party judged to be responsible for wasted or unnecessary costs.

The Tribunal may order that any party bear the whole or a part or a proportion of the costs, and the amount of costs may either be fixed by the Tribunal or be subject to detailed assessment by a costs judge. The Tribunal may also make an order for costs where an appeal is withdrawn or amended.

The costs regime in relation to the normal (original as opposed to appellate) juris-diction of the Tribunal is very burdensome on successful respondents – see **22.37** and **22.42**. However, this would not seem to be relevant to an appellate jurisdiction. The same public interest considerations do not apply. Certainly, one can expect that those who appeal unsuccessfully to the Tribunal against a decision of the SRA will be ordered to pay the SRA's costs in the normal course of events, but if appellants are successful, unless there is some unusual circumstance, it will be on the basis that the SRA's decision will have been wrong.

One would expect successful appellants to be awarded their costs, and in *Hafiz and Haque*,[1] the successful appellants were awarded costs.[2] Equally, if an appeal succeeds in part there may be no order for costs: in *Das*, the solicitor succeeded in part and the Tribunal made no order for costs.[3]

There are two analogies, situations where the SRA has historically made decisions which are open to challenge by appeal: the first relates to the imposition of prac-tising certificate conditions and similar decisions; the second involves matters of character and fitness, and appeals by those seeking enrolment as students with the SRA or admission to the roll as solicitors. In both cases appeal lies to the High Court (to the Master of the Rolls before 2008). In both situations the normal consid-erations under the Civil Procedure Rules apply and the general position is that costs follow the event. If the SRA is held to be wrong to have imposed the practising certificate conditions or wrong to have refused enrolment or admission the starting point is that the appellant is entitled to his or her costs against the SRA. The same principles have been applied in relation to appeals from the Tribunal to the High Court, despite an attempt by the SRA to suggest that the principles of *Baxendale-Walker v Law Society*[4] apply not only to the original prosecution in the Tribunal but also to appeals from the Tribunal; see *Bryant and Bench v Law Society*.[5] On a purely pragmatic level, unless solicitors are to be awarded their costs if they appeal success-fully, few if any are likely to avail themselves of the ability to appeal to the Tribunal, and in that way the intention of Parliament in providing this appeal route would be neutered.

1   11253-2014, SDT.
2   In contrast, the successful appellant in *Arslan v SRA*, 11356-2015, SDT was ordered to pay £20,000 towards the SRA's costs, but that was a decision upon its own unusual facts.
3   12137-2020, SDT.
4   [2007] EWCA Civ 233, [2007] 3 All ER 330; for the principles see **22.42**.
5   [2007] EWHC 3043 (Admin) at [251]. See too *Bass and Ward v SRA* (judgment on costs) [2012] EWHC 2457 (Admin).

Further appeals

23.19

As in the case of the Tribunal's original (non-appellate) jurisdiction, appeal from the Tribunal lies to the High Court without permission,[1] save in relation to ABS appeals under LSA 2007. All appeals from decisions of the SRA as a licensing authority for ABSs, whether under Part 5 of LSA 2007 or the SRA's rules (and not only those made under Schedule 13 to LSA 2007 listed in **23.6**) are governed by the Legal Services Act 2007 (Appeals from Licensing Authority Decisions) (No 2) Order 2011.

In those cases appeal lies to the High Court only on a point of law arising from the decision of the Tribunal, and only with the permission of the High Court.[2] The time limit for appeals in that category is also a statutory limit set by the LSB and is 28 days from the date the party is given notice of the decision of the Tribunal.[3] If the Tribunal follows its normal practice of making an immediate decision but providing full written reasons on a later date it may therefore be necessary to lodge an appeal before the reasons are available.

1   Section 49 of SA 1974 and see **22.43**.
2   Article 5(3) of the Legal Services Act 2007 (Appeals from Licensing Authority Decisions) (No 2) Order 2011 (SI 2011/2863).
3   Rule 6 of the LSB Rules on the Prescribed Period for the Making of Appeals against Licensing Authority Decisions Relating to Ownership of Licensed Bodies 2018.

CHAPTER 24

Disciplinary jurisdiction of the High Court

24.1

Solicitors are officers of the Senior Courts: the court itself can discipline solicitors,[1] and may order that a solicitor's name be struck off the roll of solicitors, rather than referring the matter to the Solicitors Regulation Authority (SRA). This power is available to the High Court, the Crown Court and the Court of Appeal, or any division or judge of those courts.[2] This jurisdiction is only rarely exercised, and the relevant principles as to its exercise were summarised by Hickinbottom J in *Coll v Floreat MB*[3] in the following terms at [45]:

'(i) The court's jurisdiction over solicitors is conceptually very wide, being curtailed only to the extent that legislation limits it.

(ii) However, although now maintained by section 50 of the Solicitors Act, the jurisdiction is one which the High Court has taken to itself as part of its inherent powers in pursuit of its duty to supervise the conduct of solicitors as officers of the court. The court has, in practice, imposed boundaries on the exercise of its own jurisdiction.

(iii) The jurisdiction has both punitive and compensatory elements. However, given that solicitors are now the subject of a comprehensive and sophisticated regulatory regime through the SRA, the jurisdiction will only usually be exercised where someone has lost out as a result of the solicitor's conduct and the court is the appropriate forum to require that loss to be put right on a summary basis. The jurisdiction is therefore primarily compensatory, although in a disciplinary context. However, whilst misconduct is necessary, simply because there has been misconduct is not sufficient for the jurisdiction to be exercised. Whether the court intervenes in a particular case is always a matter for the court's discretion.

(iv) Where another forum is more appropriate than the court for the investigation of misconduct by a solicitor and the subsequent imposition of a sanction, then the court will not exercise its discretion to act against that solicitor. The SRA is appointed by Parliament to investigate and deal with allegations of misconduct by solicitors: the court will not exercise its disciplinary function over solicitors if the alleged misconduct conduct can be as, or more, appropriately dealt with by the SRA.'

A claimant applying to the High Court to exercise this jurisdiction, rather than making an application to the Tribunal, would need to show that it was reasonable to follow this exceptional course. The power has also been used in the course of other litigation, on the application of the Law Society.[4]

Applications of this kind made by litigants in person will not be entertained because the Solicitors Act (SA) 1974 preserves the court's inherent jurisdiction as it had been prior to the Supreme Court of Judicature Act 1873, and both before and after that Act it was settled law that the jurisdiction was limited in practice, in that an application could only be made if supported by counsel.[5]

Ordinarily, if a judge is concerned that a solicitor may have been guilty of professional misconduct, he will order that the matter be referred to the SRA, and a transcript made of the relevant part of the proceedings. Alternatively the judge may write to the SRA, setting out his or her concerns about the professional conduct of the solicitor in question.

1 The power to discipline solicitors is an aspect of the courts' inherent supervisory jurisdiction over solicitors as officers of the court. The history of this jurisdiction is traced by the Supreme Court in *Harcus Sinclair LLP v Your Lawyers Ltd* [2021] UKSC 32 at [93]–[98].
2 Section 50 of SA 1974; the procedure is set out in section 51.
3 [2014] EWHC 1741 (QB) – see the discussion at [36]–[45].
4 *Penna v Law Society (No 3)* (1999, unreported); and *Law Society v Young* [2002] EWHC 2962 (Admin). In each case the solicitor had been the subject of an intervention on the grounds of a suspicion of dishonesty. In *Penna*, in the subsequent proceedings by which he sought to challenge the intervention the solicitor so misconducted himself in defiance of court orders that the court on the Law Society's application used its inherent powers to strike him off, taking the facts that led to the intervention and his subsequent conduct into account. In *Young* the solicitor continued to practise as a solicitor and to hold himself out as a solicitor in court proceedings, so that there was contempt as well as continuing misconduct.
5 *Re Solicitors, ex p Peasegood* [1994] 1 All ER 298, DC.

24.2

The court's inherent jurisdiction is exercisable only over solicitors, as officers of the court; barristers are not officers of the court, nor in the context of entity or firm-based regulation, are firms of solicitors, or other forms of law firm ('recognised bodies') including alternative business structures (ABSs) ('licensed bodies'). This was the conclusion, *obiter*, of the Court of Appeal in *Assaubayev v Michael Wilson & Partners Ltd*.[1]

In *Harcus Sinclair LLP v Your Lawyers Ltd,*[2] following full argument, the Supreme Court, with considerable reluctance declined to extend the court's inherent supervisory jurisdiction over solicitors to cover incorporated law firms as well as individual solicitors. At [148], the court expressed the hope that Parliament would address the lacuna which the case had identified.

1 [2014] EWCA Civ 1491 at [47].
2 [2021] UKSC 32.

24.3

It has been held that the jurisdiction extends to those who have pretended to be solicitors; see for example *Re Hurst & Middleton Ltd*.[1] The 'keystone of the success of such an application' was, as held by Kennedy LJ:

> 'that the man has, by virtue of his assumption of the position and privilege of a solicitor, either obtained something which he ought not to have obtained (I do not desire to limit it – there may be other cases, but broadly that would be generally the case), and therefore the restitution of which is just, or done some act for which there would be a remedy in the Court if it were an act done by an officer of the Court, and if the man has done the act

or obtained the property by the assumption of the privilege and position of a solicitor. In such a case the Court will exercise the power which it would be right to exercise if the man were an officer of the Court; and in such a case the man cannot be allowed to say that he is free from the jurisdiction of the Court because he is not in fact, a solicitor, and therefore not an officer of the Court.'

1   [1912] 2 Ch 520, CA.

PART 6
The regulation of ABSs

CHAPTER 25

Alternative business structures: getting started

25.1

CHAPTER 2 deals with the authorisation of legal services bodies (traditional practices or recognised bodies – a recognised body is a legal services body that has become recognised and authorised by the Solicitors Regulation Authority (SRA)) and licensable bodies (alternative business structures (ABSs) or licensed bodies – in the same way, a licensed body is a licensable body that has become authorised).

The SRA approach to regulation is to apply the same authorisation system to all, regardless of size, label or structure. However, there are some ABS-specific considerations, principally concerned with ownership.

It is relevant to bear in mind that ABSs may vary enormously. The popular concept remains that of 'Tesco law' – in other words a large, possibly national or international, company taking control of one or more law firms or choosing to invest in them.

The main focus of the regulatory provisions of the Legal Services Act (LSA) 2007 in Part 5 and Schedules 11 to 14 is to ensure that the wrong kind of people do not end up controlling law firms, and to incorporate necessary checks and balances, including the requirement to have a lawyer as Head of Legal Practice (HOLP).

But at the other end of the spectrum, any law firm which is currently a traditional practice of, say, four partners, which chose to appoint its non-lawyer financial director as one of the four, and became designated as a legal disciplinary practice with a non-lawyer manager between March 2009 and 6 October 2011, is potentially licensable as an ABS, and will have to have become authorised as such at some point. (The end of the transitional period, when existing recognised bodies of that kind will have to convert to ABSs, is to be set by the Legal Services Board (LSB) and has not yet been set. The SRA's guidance note 'Legal Disciplinary Practices' published on 25 November 2019 confirms that position.)

An ABS, or in LSA 2007 terminology a licensable body, is a body that carries on (or wishes to carry on) reserved legal activities, and a non-authorised person[1] is a manager[2] of the body or has an interest[3] in it.[4] Alternatively, a body (B) is a licensable body if another body (A) is a manager of the body or has an interest in it and non-authorised persons are entitled to exercise, or control the exercise of, at least 10 per cent of the voting rights in A.[5] Accordingly, if a holding or parent company of a firm providing reserved legal activities is partly owned by a non-authorised person who holds less than 10 per cent of its voting rights then the firm would not need to be authorised as an ABS, but would still need to be regulated by an approved regulator in the provision of reserved legal activities.

Many firms who would not apply the 'Tesco law' label to themselves may have no option but to be regulated as ABSs.

1   The term 'person' includes a body of persons corporate or unincorporate (section 207 of LSA 2007). A non-authorised person is not defined in LSA 2007 but 'authorised person' is, and refers to a person who is authorised to provide reserved legal activities; see section 18.
2   The term 'manager' is defined in section 207. In summary, a manager will be a member of a limited liability partnership (LLP) or similar organisation, director of a company, partner in a partnership or the member of a governing body of an unincorporated association.
3   Having an 'interest' is defined as either holding shares or being entitled to exercise, or control the exercise of, voting rights in the body – section 72(4).
4   Section 72(1) of LSA 2007.
5   Section 72(2).

25.2

There is a limited but expanding choice of regulator. The SRA, the Bar Standards Board (BSB) and the Council for Licensed Conveyancers (CLC) are licensing authorities approved by the LSB; in the case of CLC, limited to businesses undertaking conveyancing and probate; so is the Institute of Chartered Accountants in England and Wales (ICAEW), in relation to probate. CILEx Regulation has been approved as a licensing authority with effect from 1 April 2019. Currently the SRA regulates the supply of all reserved legal activities apart from notarial activities, and we will confine our commentary to regulation by the SRA.

Regulation of ownership

25.3

LSA 2007 regulates ownership of an ABS by a non-authorised person where that person controls a material interest in an ABS. Broadly, a material interest is one where the non-authorised person holds at least 10 per cent of the shares of the ABS (or equivalent) or at least 10 per cent of the shares of the parent of the ABS, or is able to exercise significant influence in the management of the ABS or its parent by virtue of the shareholding.[1] The licensing authority has to be satisfied that the non-authorised person holding a material interest in the ABS does not compromise the regulatory objectives set out in section 1 of LSA 2007 (see **1.4**). It must also not compromise the duty of regulated persons employed by the ABS to fulfil their duty to comply with regulatory requirements; and the person must be fit and proper to hold the interest.[2] In determining whether the licensing authority is satisfied as to the above matters, it must have regard to the non-authorised person's probity and financial position, whether he or she is disqualified from being a HOLP, Head of Finance and Administration (HOFA) or as a manager or employee of a licensed body, under section 99 of LSA 2007, or included on the LSB's list of persons subject to objections and conditions (that is objections and conditions relating to ownership notified to the LSB by licensing authorities), and must also have regard to the person's associates.[3]

Where the ABS is owned by one or more non-authorised persons who have a less than 10 per cent interest in the ABS, these persons will not be subject to the same controls.

Where applicable, the SRA Assessment of Character and Suitability Rules 2019 (the 'Suitability Rules') will be applied to interest holders as they are to non-lawyer managers, which is essentially the same test as that which applies in relation to admission to the solicitors' profession. It is entirely logical that the character and suitability requirements for non-lawyers having a material interest in a regulated business should be identical to those applied to the lawyers. In some respects the test may need to be more onerous as LSA 2007 clearly contemplates consideration of the associates of the non-authorised owners and managers as part of the assessment process. These are widely defined to include family and other businesses related directly or indirectly to the non-authorised person.[4] There is no equivalent process for admission to one of the legal professions. The Suitability Rules are less prescriptive than the SRA Suitability Test and place the onus of providing all relevant information squarely on the applicant. There is no full definition of 'relevant information' for the purposes of the Rules, the examples specified are expressly not intended to be exhaustive.[5]

1 Paragraph 3 of Schedule 13 to LSA 2007.
2 Paragraph 6(1) of Schedule 13.
3 Paragraph 6(3) of Schedule 13.
4 Paragraph 5 of Schedule 13.
5 See rules 6.1, 6.6 and 2.2 of the Suitability Rules.

25.4

There is a requirement to identify any non-authorised person who has or is expected to have a material interest in the ABS in the application for a licence.[1] There is also an obligation to inform the licensing authority when a non-authorised person acquires a material interest in an ABS.[2] It is a criminal offence to fail to comply with either of these requirements.[3] The licensing authority may impose conditions on the approval of the non-authorised person, either in the context of an application (a notified interest) or when notification is made of a new interest in an existing licensed body (a notifiable interest).[4] If it proposes to do so it must give a warning notice as to the proposed conditions and the reasons for imposing them, and permit representations to be made before a final decision is made. The licensing authority may also object altogether to the non-authorised person's interest in the ABS, with the same limitations.[5] Where a licence has already been granted and the objection or conditions relate to a new notifiable interest, notice and the opportunity for representations may be dispensed with if it is necessary or desirable to do so for the purpose of protecting any of the regulatory objectives.[6]

It is also possible to impose conditions or further conditions on an existing interest holder, or to raise an objection to an existing interest holder, with the same limitations and exceptions.[7]

There is a right of appeal to the Solicitors Disciplinary Tribunal (the Tribunal or SDT) (if the licensing authority is the SRA) against such decisions. See **CHAPTER 23** for appeals to the Tribunal.

There is, of course, no indication at present as to what conditions could sensibly be applied to an interest holder if in all respects he or she is suitable to hold the interest.

1 Paragraph 10 of Schedule 13 to LSA 2007.
2 Paragraph 21 of Schedule 13.
3 Paragraphs 11 and 22 of Schedule 13.
4 Paragraphs 17 and 28 of Schedule 13.
5 Paragraphs 17(3) to (5), 19(2) to (4), 28(3) to (5) and 31(2) to (5) of Schedule 13.
6 Paragraphs 28(4) and 31(3) of Schedule 13.
7 Paragraphs 33 and 36 of Schedule 13.

25.5

Paragraph 38 of Schedule 13 to LSA 2007 enables licensing rules to make general provision for the limitation of the level of the shareholding, control or voting rights of non-authorised persons. The SRA's rules do not expressly provide for this, but the same effect can be achieved by imposing conditions on a case-by-case basis. There is no restriction in LSA 2007 as to the number of ABSs in which a non-authorised person can take an interest.

25.6

If a non-authorised person continues to hold an interest in an ABS in breach of conditions or despite objection the licensing authority may apply to the High Court for an order that the person be divested of the interest; see **26.8**.

Other controls

25.7

All non-lawyer managers of ABSs must also be expressly approved, as must the Heads of Legal Practice and of Finance and Administration who, within the SRA Authorisation of Firms Rules 2019, become compliance officers for legal practice (COLPs) or for finance and administration (COFAs). No distinction is drawn by the SRA between the mechanisms for approval of COLPs and COFAs or non-lawyer managers by reference to whether the body is an ABS or a traditional law practice. As to authorisation generally see **CHAPTER 2**. As to COLPs and COFAs, see **CHAPTER 7**.

CHAPTER 26

Alternative business structures: discipline and enforcement

Disciplinary powers

26.1

In this chapter we will consider only alternative business structures (ABSs) licensed by the Solicitors Regulation Authority (SRA), which is overwhelmingly the largest regulator of licensable or licensed bodies. The Council for Licensed Conveyancers (CLC), Bar Standards Board (BSB) and CILEx Regulation have together licensed fewer than 200 ABSs, whereas the SRA has licensed over 1,200. The Institute of Chartered Accountants in England and Wales (ICAEW) may only license ABSs providing probate services (at present).

For law firms in their traditional form the relationship between their practices and their regulatory and disciplinary bodies had been unchanged for decades; indeed for a century. Discipline, in the sense of penalty, including the ultimate deterrent of being struck off the roll, was the province of the court (initially exclusively, but in modern times only through a surviving inherent jurisdiction rarely used – see CHAPTER 24), and the Solicitors Disciplinary Committee (from the nineteenth century until 1975), and the Solicitors Disciplinary Tribunal (the Tribunal or SDT) from 1975.

The Law Society, and latterly the SRA, had no disciplinary powers at all; it could exercise control through the training and admission process, and by means of practising certificate conditions, and by intervention, and it could elect to prosecute solicitors before the Tribunal, but in that respect it was not a decision-maker, it was a party in adversarial proceedings.

The practice which grew up of imposing what were first called rebukes, severe rebukes and chairman's rebukes (which involved the solicitor attending at the Law Society to be told off by the chairman of the relevant committee, warned that he (or much more rarely she) had come within a whisker of being referred to the Tribunal, and cautioned not to do it again),[1] and which later changed their name to reprimands and severe reprimands (for no discernible reason) had never had any statutory origin. They were developed as a mechanism by which a solicitor could be told that something had gone wrong in circumstances in which no further action was necessary.

1   These fell into disuse in the 1990s when solicitors became more argumentative.

26.2

It all changed as a result of the Legal Services Act (LSA) 2007 and another raft of changes to the much amended Solicitors Act (SA) 1974. After some wrangling over the required procedural rules the Law Society, in the guise of the SRA, became a disciplinary body in relation to solicitors in relation to acts and omissions occurring or continuing on or after 1 June 2010 (see **CHAPTER 20**).

Those powers however, in relation to solicitors in traditional law firms, remain modest. Formal statutory and potentially public rebukes have replaced informal non-statutory and largely private reprimands, and there is a power to impose a fine not exceeding £2,000. Importantly, this was only designed to reduce the caseload of the Tribunal and remove low level cases from its jurisdiction. The Tribunal remains the primary disciplinary body, although the SRA has, from a time shortly after it acquired the power, periodically sought to increase the level of fines it can impose.

26.3

It may come as a shock to those solicitors who, instead of being partners or managers or employees of a traditional firm or recognised body, are partners or managers or employees of an ABS, to learn that their primary disciplinary body has become the SRA.

The structure of LSA 2007 is that the licensing authority is responsible for disciplinary as well as licensing decisions, with the Tribunal reverting to being an appeal body (see **CHAPTER 23**).

It is the SRA which has the power to fine the business, its managers and employees (not the Tribunal),[1] and the fine is not limited to £2,000, but extends to a maximum of £250 million, for the business, and £50 million, for an individual.[2]

Further the SRA has the power of disqualification – to disqualify any individual from being a Head of Legal Practice (HOLP) or Head of Finance and Administration (HOFA) (compliance officer for legal practice (COLP) or compliance officer for finance and administration (COFA) in SRA terminology) and from being a manager of an ABS, and from being even an employee of an ABS.[3]

A disqualification from being employed in one or more of those capacities could be as devastating in its consequences as being struck off as a solicitor.

However, although the consequences of an adverse result are infinitely more serious, the disciplinary powers in relation to ABSs and all individuals within ABSs are dealt with under the same rules and the same procedures as are applied to traditional practices (see **CHAPTERS 15** and **20**).

The SRA has not made clear whether and to what extent it will move from its present position of rarely if ever conducting oral hearings, although there is provision in the SRA Regulatory and Disciplinary Procedure Rules 2019 (the 'Disciplinary Rules 2019') for public hearings in appropriate cases.[4] It is likely to be argued that an opportunity to appeal to the Tribunal and to obtain a discretionary stay would not be sufficient to provide a fair disciplinary system. It is understood that the SRA may well accept that oral hearings and a more formal and transparent approach to decision-making will be necessary for serious or contentious matters affecting ABSs, although the factors which may inform any such acceptance have yet to become apparent in practice.

For appeals to the Tribunal against the exercise of the SRA's disciplinary powers and licensing decisions see **CHAPTER 23**.

1   Section 95 of LSA 2007.
2   Legal Services Act 2007 (Licensing Authorities) (Maximum Penalty) Rules 2011 (SI 2011/1659).
3   Section 99 of LSA 2007.
4   See rule 8.5.

Investigatory powers

26.4

The SRA's investigatory powers under sections 44B and 44BA of SA 1974 are considered in **Chapter 15** (see **15.5**). These apply to solicitors subject to the regulation of the SRA whether they are employed in ABSs or traditional firms. They do not otherwise apply to ABSs. The parallel provisions in relation to non-solicitor managers or employees of ABSs are in sections 93 and 94 of LSA 2007.

The terms of section 93 are similar to sections 44B and 44BA combined, and extend the powers of the SRA, to require information to be provided and documents to be produced, to former managers and employees of the licensed body and any non-authorised person who has an interest or an indirect interest, or holds a material interest, in the licensed body. However, the powers are not backed by criminal sanctions and the remedy for non-compliance, provided by section 94, is an application by the licensing authority to the High Court for an order to comply with the notice.

The duty to co-operate fully with the SRA in relation to any investigation (paragraph 7.3 of the SRA Code of Conduct for Solicitors, RELs and RFLs 2019 (the 'Code for Individuals') and paragraph 3.2 of the SRA Code of Conduct for Firms 2019 (the 'Code for Firms')) continues to apply to every person and body regulated by the SRA, as do paragraph 7.4 of the Code for Individuals and paragraph 3.3 of the Code for Firms imposing an obligation to supply explanations, information and documents to the SRA in response to any requests or requirements.

Other quasi-disciplinary powers

26.5

The licence of an ABS may be suspended or revoked[1] in circumstances which are regulated by paragraph 24 of Schedule 11 to LSA 2007. These are replicated in rule 4.3 of the SRA Authorisation of Firms Rules 2019.[2] The SRA may revoke or suspend an authorised body's authorisation (that is, any practice that the SRA has authorised, ABS or non-ABS) where:

- authorisation was granted as a result of error, misleading or inaccurate information, or fraud;

- the body is or becomes ineligible to be authorised or the grounds for refusal of an application are met;

- the body has failed to provide any information the SRA has reasonably requested;

- the body has failed to pay any prescribed fee to the SRA;

- a relevant insolvency event has occurred in relation to the body or a sole principal;

- the body makes an application to the SRA for its authorisation to be revoked;

- the body is subject to any proceedings, investigation or consideration of their conduct or practice by the SRA or the Tribunal;

- the SRA has decided to exercise its intervention powers in relation to the body or a solicitor's practice within the body;

- the body has failed to comply with any obligations under the SRA's regulatory arrangements;

- in the case of a licensed body (applicable to ABSs alone) the body fails to comply with the prohibition on appointing disqualified managers; or in the case of any authorised body, the body fails to comply with the prohibition on employing disqualified persons (struck off solicitors and the like) if the manager or employee concerned was disqualified as a result of breach of the duties imposed upon the manager or employee by sections 176 or 90 of LSA 2007 (the general duties imposed to comply with all regulatory arrangements for ABSs); or

- for any other reason it is in the public interest.

In the case of a *licensed* body (applicable to ABSs alone), it may revoke or suspend a body's authorisation, where a non-authorised person holds an interest in the licensed body:

- as a result of the person taking a step in circumstances where that constitutes an offence under paragraph 24(1) of Schedule 13 to LSA 2007 (whether or not the person is charged with or convicted of an offence under that paragraph) – this is failing to give notice as to the proposed or actual acquisition of a material interest in an ABS;

- in breach of conditions imposed on the owners of material interests in the ABS; or

- the person's holding of which is subject to an objection by the licensing authority.

1   Section 101 of LSA 2007.
2   This subject is also dealt with in **Chapter 2** but is repeated here for convenience.

26.6

Before the SRA can revoke or suspend an authorisation it must first give the authorised body an opportunity to make representations to it on the issues that have led the SRA to consider this course, and it must also give at least 28 days' notice of its intention to make the decision to revoke or suspend.[1]

1   Rule 4.5 of the SRA Authorisation of Firms Rules 2019.

26.7

Where an interest holder holds a material interest in an ABS in breach of conditions imposed by a licensing authority the authority may apply to the High Court for an order to secure compliance with the conditions. The licensing authority may not make an application to the court unless it has given notice of its intention to do so and, at the end of the notice period, the interest holder is still in breach of the conditions. In other words, an opportunity must be given to the interest holder to regularise the position. The notice period is to be prescribed by the Legal Services Board (LSB) and has not yet been set.

No order may be made by the court until the end of any period for appeal against the imposition of conditions and, if there is an appeal, until the appeal is disposed of.[1]

1 Paragraph 46(5) of Schedule 13 to LSA 2007.

Divestiture

26.8

Part 5 of Schedule 13 to LSA 2007 contains provisions enabling the licensing authority to apply to the High Court for an order divesting an interest holder of an interest in an ABS where the interest consists of a shareholding in a company with a share capital, if the non-authorised person holds a material interest in the licensed body either in circumstances where notice has not been given of the acquisition or intended acquisition of the interest so that an offence has been committed under paragraph 24(1) of Schedule 13, or the interest is held in breach of conditions imposed by the licensing authority or in contravention of an objection by the authority.

The licensing authority may serve a 'restriction notice' which may provide that a transfer of shares or similar arrangement is void, that no voting rights may be exercised, that no further shares be issued to the holder and that no payment may be made by the company in relation to the shares (other than in a liquidation).[1]

On an application to the High Court the court may order the sale of the shares. The licensing authority may not make an application to the court for a divestiture order unless it has given notice of its intention to do so and, at the end of the notice period, the conditions for divestiture still apply. In other words, an opportunity must be given to the interest holder to regularise the position. The notice period is to be prescribed by the LSB and has not yet been set.

No order may be made by the court until the end of any period for appeal against the imposition of conditions or the objection and, if there is an appeal, until the appeal is disposed of.[2]

1 Paragraph 44 of Schedule 13 to LSA 2007.
2 Paragraph 45(5).

Intervention

26.9

Powers of intervention are available to the licensing authority which are broadly comparable to those applying to solicitors' practices under Schedule 1 to SA 1974. They are set out in Schedule 14 to LSA 2007.

An intervention may be authorised where a licence granted to a body has expired, and has not been renewed or replaced by the relevant licensing authority, or where one or more of the intervention conditions is satisfied.

The intervention conditions are:

'(a) that the licensing authority is satisfied that one or more of the terms of the licensed body's licence have not been complied with;

(b) that a person has been appointed receiver or manager of property of the licensed body;

(c) that a relevant insolvency event has occurred in relation to the licensed body;

(d) that the licensing authority has reason to suspect dishonesty on the part of any manager or employee of the licensed body in connection with—

(i) that body's business,

(ii) any trust of which that body is or was a trustee,

(iii) any trust of which the manager or employee of the body is or was a trustee in that person's capacity as such a manager or employee, or

(iv) the business of another body in which the manager or employee is or was a manager or employee, or the practice (or former practice) of the manager or employee;

(e) that the licensing authority is satisfied that there has been undue delay—

(i) on the part of the licensed body in connection with any matter in which it is or was acting for a client or with any trust of which it is or was a trustee, or

(ii) on the part of a person who is or was a manager or employee of the licensed body in connection with any trust of which that person is or was a trustee in that person's capacity as such a manager or employee,

and the notice conditions are satisfied;[1]

(f) that the licensing authority is satisfied that it is necessary to exercise the powers conferred by this Schedule (or any of them) in relation to a licensed body to protect:

(i) the interests of clients (or former or potential clients) of the licensed body,

(ii) the interests of the beneficiaries of any trust of which the licensed body is or was a trustee, or

(iii) the interests of the beneficiaries of any trust of which a person who is or was a manager or employee of the licensed body is or was a trustee in that person's capacity as such a manager or employee.'

---

1 This only applies if the licensing authority has requested an explanation, that at least eight days have been given for a reply, and if notice has then been given that the licensing authority does not regard the response to be satisfactory and that the powers of intervention have arisen.

26.10

Essentially the same relief is available to challenge the intervention by application to the High Court as is available to solicitors' practices; see **CHAPTER 17**.

PART 7
Fraud and money laundering

CHAPTER 27

The risks of fraud

27.1

In this section it is intended to highlight certain danger areas which have resulted in guidance being given to the profession but which are not reflected in any specific rule.

There are three possible consequences of involvement in fraud. First, solicitors, even if innocent of any involvement in the fraud itself, may face regulatory or disciplinary action if they facilitate a fraud through a failure to be alert to warning signs or known red flags. Where an employee acts fraudulently, firms or managers may also be at risk of allegations of a failure to supervise or not having adequate systems in place.

Second, particularly in the context of identity fraud where funds are paid to a fraudster, solicitors may be immediately liable to replace the consequential shortage on client account. This may be true even where the fraudster is not the solicitor's own client.

Third, cyber fraud has become an enormous problem, by which criminals use technology to facilitate fraud, for example, by fooling solicitors into disclosing sensitive information and persuading them, for example, to pay client funds to the fraudster's bank account by masquerading as the client, using what appears to be the client's email address to communicate. Other forms of cybercrime such as ransom attacks are also increasing.

Mortgage fraud

27.2

The involvement, innocent or otherwise, of solicitors or licensed conveyancers is essential to all mortgage fraud, in the sense that they are required to enable the transaction to occur.

There have historically been four basic types of 'traditional' mortgage fraud, with a potentially endless selection of variations on the basic theme:

(1)   exaggeration of the borrower's income to obtain a mortgage that would otherwise be declined;

(2)   multiple purchases, where a fraudster uses false names or nominees to build up a portfolio of property through residential rather than commercial borrowing;

(3) identity theft, where money is borrowed in the name of the proprietor on a remortgage, and diverted to the fraudsters; and

(4) exaggeration of price or value, to obtain a higher mortgage than would properly be justified.

Of course, sometimes more than one element can feature in a fraudulent scheme.

More recently, identity theft as a mortgage fraud device has been extended to situations in which property is sold from under the genuine proprietor by a fraudster using the proprietor's name or situations where the fraudster sets up a bogus law firm or a bogus branch office of a legitimate firm.[1]

Solicitors should be aware of the SRA's warning notice 'Investment schemes including conveyancing'[2] (updated 17 August 2020 and considered below) as well as notices published by the SRA via its 'scam alert' service and of notices published by the Financial Conduct Authority (FCA) where it is the lender or financial adviser who has been targeted by fraudsters. The FCA maintains a warning list of unauthorised firms and a register of warnings issued by foreign regulators.

Solicitors will not generally expect to encounter false employers' references, for example, although there could well arise circumstances to put any reasonable solicitor on notice that the borrower client's means do not appear to match the lender's requirements for the amount being loaned. The extent to which a solicitor may be required to investigate the borrower client's financial position may well vary depending on the risk profile of the transaction and the firm's anti-money laundering (AML) risk assessment policies.

The obligations under the Money Laundering, Terrorist Financing and Transfer of Funds (Information on the Payer) Regulations 2017[3] (MLR 2017) of due diligence and enhanced due diligence, and the obligation to monitor business relationships and transactions as they develop (considered in detail in **CHAPTER 28**) have a direct relevance to these issues and should result in patterns being detected. Firms should always consider the totality of their relationship with their client and information relating to a client's business interests, source of wealth and source of funds, and assess the risks associated with a particular transaction against the background of all known information.

Regrettably, there have been solicitors who have been prepared to provide false references for their own employees or even to indulge in this kind of fraud for their own benefit.[4]

Solicitors are well placed to detect and prevent frauds of the second and third kinds and in some cases their active complicity, or determinedly deliberate Nelsonian blindness, is essential to the success of the frauds.

1   See the Solicitors Regulation Authority (SRA) warning notice, 'Bogus law firms and identity theft', updated 25 November 2019, and *Lloyds TSB Bank plc v Markandan & Uddin* [2012] 2 All ER 884; *Davisons Solicitors v Nationwide Building Society* [2012] EWCA Civ 1626; *Santander UK plc v RA Legal Solicitors* [2014] EWCA Civ 183; *Purrunsing v A'Court & Co* [2016] EWHC 789 (Ch).
2   At **APPENDIX 8**.
3   SI 2017/692.
4   *Re a Solicitor (Maharaj)* (1999, unreported).

27.3

In a rising market property fraud can frequently remain undetected as, if questions are asked or arrears develop, the property can be sold at a profit and the lender's concerns assuaged. It is when a sudden drop in prices occurs and there is no escape route that frauds become particularly apparent. It is for that reason that following the recession that started in about 1989 and continued into the 1990s the profession was caught up in one of its greatest scandals as the extent of widespread mortgage fraud became known, and the extent to which the negligence of solicitors, or worse, had contributed to it.

The 2008 financial crisis and subsequent recession created a similar effect in exposing mortgage fraud. The adverse effects on the buy-to-let market caused by the economic downturn provided opportunities for fraudsters in relation to the bulk refinancing/remortgaging of such borrowing. Since then, successive modifications to AML requirements and increased focus on affordability of lending have helped to reduce certain types of fraud resulting in fraudsters modifying their own tactics.

Multiple purchases

27.4

When it was the norm to meet your client in routine domestic conveyancing it was easier to spot warning signs. Now, despite the requirement for identity checks imposed by money laundering legislation, because of the development of commoditised conveyancing and online dealings, the conveyancing environment remains relatively friendly to frauds of this kind.

Individual buyers may be real people, but nominees. A common feature of this kind of fraud is a central figure through whom communications are required to be channelled. This could be a broker or a senior family member. All or most instructions are given by the key individual; solicitors may be encouraged to correspond with clients through that individual, and to send money and documents to that individual. Documents are sent to him or her to be signed by others and come back signed and witnessed. It all seems very efficient. Solicitors must nevertheless be aware of the requirement of paragraph 3.1 of the Code of Conduct for Solicitors, RELs and RFLs, which requires solicitors to be satisfied that they are acting on the basis of proper authority.

27.5

Solicitors should be alive to the fact that commercial pressures exist, and that fraudsters are highly attuned to the business community. They may be attracted to your practice, not because it has the best local reputation for efficient conveyancing, but because it is new or not apparently very wealthy, so that offers of substantial work might encourage the turning of a blind eye. Fraudsters will have their own intelligence network and will seek out those perceived to be vulnerable or susceptible to financial pressures, flattery, or occasionally coercion and blackmail. Coercion and blackmail sound like extreme scenarios, but you need to bear in mind that if a solicitor bends or breaks a rule as a 'favour' he also gives any person with knowledge of his wrongdoing power over him, including the person to whom he gave the favour ('We are now in this together ...').

A more sophisticated version of this fraud involves the fraudster instructing a panel of solicitors, without disclosing to any firm that he is using more than one. Multiple transactions become more difficult to detect. If you become aware that an individual has more than one firm acting for him in such circumstances or for unexplained reasons, be suspicious.

Mules

27.6

Experienced conveyancers are very familiar with the patterns of behaviour of purchaser clients. To most, buying a new home is a very substantial, serious and potentially stressful transaction; they will ask questions, be concerned about matters of detail, be anxious about dates and progress. If clients introduced by Mr X show a pattern of near indifference, and contact is limited and amounts to virtually no more than an exchange of documents, there are likely to be grounds for suspicion. If the attitude of Mr X appears to be that of a businessman asking questions that are consistent with a businessman's outlook, rather than the questions clients could be expected to ask, it is more likely that it is he who has the true interest in the transaction, rather than those he purports to represent.

Mules – nominees or people with false identification used as buyers of property to facilitate fraud – have none of the normal interest that buyers of property will display. They may sometimes be exposed by even casual questioning.

Identity theft

27.7

Fraudsters can steal the identity of property owners, either to remortgage the property or to sell it to a genuine buyer or a co-conspirator. Ensure you know with whom you are dealing. Be concerned if it is said that there are reasons why the seller cannot be contacted. Common features are:

- a central figure, usually a broker introducing multiple transactions to the practice. He will be the only point of contact and will deal with clients on your behalf. He will reassure you that all regulatory and professional obligations have already been attended to. You may rarely if ever meet or have direct dealings with the client;

- rushed transactions; there will be an explanation such as a family crisis or other reason for urgency;

- the only money changing hands being the mortgage advance; and

- instructions to remit funds to the client account of a named firm of solicitors (possibly the funds are urgently needed for mother's nursing home fees). The destination account may involve a bogus firm of solicitors or a ghost branch office of a genuine firm.

In the examples given in footnote 1 to **27.2**, in *Lloyds TSB Bank plc v Markandan & Uddin*,[1] the true owners of the property were unaware of the transaction, the solicitors who purported to act for the vendors did not exist and the fraudsters took the money. In *Davisons Solicitors v Nationwide Building Society*,[2] an imposter had notified the Law Society and the SRA of a false business address for an existing sole practitioner. The sole practitioner had informed the Law Society and the SRA that the information was false but they had failed to remove it from their websites. The solicitors were relieved of liability for breach of trust as they had acted reasonably in making all necessary prudent enquiries.

In *Santander UK plc v RA Legal Solicitors*,[3] the fraud was perpetrated by a firm of solicitors which pretended to act for the seller, who had no contact with the firm at all. The signature on the transfer was forged. The buyer's solicitors were not relieved of liability as, among other things, they had released the purchase monies to the fraudulent firm before any contracts had been exchanged and without any undertakings being given.

In *Purrunsing v A'Court & Co*,[4] a fraudster purported to be the owner and seller of property which he did not own; neither the conveyancers acting for him nor the solicitors acting for the buyer had taken sufficient care and they were each held liable as to one-half of the loss.

It is not only the solicitor acting on behalf of the fraudster who faces potential liability for losses arising from a fraudulent sale. The question as to division of liability between a solicitor who has acted for a fraudster and a solicitor acting for an innocent purchaser has been considered by the Court of Appeal in the joined appeals in *P&P Property Ltd v (1) Owen White & Catlin LLP (2) Crownvent Ltd; Dreamvar (UK) Limited v Mishcon De Reya*.[5] Mishcon De Reya was found to be strictly liable for at least a portion of its innocent purchaser client's losses as a result of the release of the purchase monies to a person other than the true seller. Solicitors for the fraudster shared liability on the basis of a failure to properly identify their client. The Court of Appeal observed that failure to comply with money laundering requirements may be an important factor in establishing or apportioning civil liability on the part of solicitors in cases of identity fraud.[6] This proposition was considered in the case of *Lennon v Englefield*[7] in which the court held that non-compliance with money laundering requirements did not give rise to any cause of action in negligence as between solicitor and client unless the obligation to carry out checks falls within the scope of the duty of care owed generally by solicitors to their clients. The court went on to hold that:

> 'duties are owed pursuant to regulations which are intended to protect the general public, not clients of solicitors.'[8]

1   [2012] 2 All ER 884.
2   [2012] EWCA Civ 1626.
3   [2014] EWCA Civ 183.
4   [2016] EWHC 789 (Ch).
5   [2018] EWCA Civ 1082.
6   Per Patten LJ at [31].
7   [2021] EWHC 1473 (QB).
8   At [87].

Exaggerated price or value

27.8

At its most basic this involves a friendly valuer putting too high a figure on the property and some private arrangement between buyer and seller, but in this type of fraud it is more often than not the case that the manipulation of the price is apparent to a watchful solicitor.

A solicitor should be alive to anything which could artificially inflate the price to be paid so that the amount of money that changes hands is less than the stated purchase price. Historically, this has been done by such things as mythical 'deposits paid direct' or an 'allowance on completion' operating as a substantial discount on the stated price.

Another mechanism is to introduce a third party into the chain so that the transaction proceeds as a sale and sub-sale, or a 'back-to-back' sale and resale – the first half of the transaction being at the correct price agreed to be paid to the seller and the second half involving a sale to the real buyer at the inflated price declared to the mortgagee.

The purpose is to achieve a situation in which the mortgagee lends more than 100 per cent of the true value or price so that the fraudulent buyer acquires the property and a cash bonus.

Another warning sign is a client instructing a solicitor geographically distant from the property for no good apparent reason; this limits the opportunities for personal dealing and avoids local knowledge of the housing market.

A flat property market offers limited opportunities for price leverage but sale and leaseback can be used for this purpose, for example where there is a distressed vendor (facing repossession), genuine or impersonated. A firm may be approached by a broker and offered a package of such transactions, all pre-agreed and pre-arranged.

27.9

Solicitors can become complicit by failing to identify the relevant features of the transaction for what they are, or occasionally by more active assistance. One solicitor, when faced with solicitors acting for the seller who refused to co-operate by agreeing, as requested, to an inflated contract price and an 'allowance on completion' amounting to more than 25 per cent of the true price, solved his fraudulent client's problem by acquiring an off the shelf Isle of Man company and arranging the sale to the company at the true price and immediate sale on by the company to his client at the inflated price declared to the mortgagee. He charged for both conveyancing transactions, and the services involved in arranging the company and its involvement.[1]

Solicitors will face not only civil claims from mortgagees if fraud has occurred, but also disciplinary proceedings with serious consequences – even if it is ultimately established that the solicitor was not actively complicit as a co-conspirator, but only insufficiently alert to the danger signs.

1   *Levinson,* 6942-1995, SDT. Mr Levinson explained to the Tribunal that this was not his own idea; he had copied it from his former partner, a Mr Nathan, who had in the meantime been struck off and sent to prison. Mr Levinson was struck off.

Fraud factories

27.10

Another development has involved the acquisition of law practices by fraudsters. Genuine firms facing difficulties or under financial pressure may be offered the opportunity of being taken over by a team which offers to introduce a portfolio of transactions, and conveyancing clerks to manage it. The purchaser may purport to be a solicitor, impersonating a genuine solicitor. Alternatively it may be a non-solicitor who makes the same offer, on the basis that he will become a financial controller or office manager. All such new arrivals, and their support teams, will be heavily resistant to supervision.

These arrangements are not designed to last for long, and the new owners have no interest in the success of the business; they are simply designed to obtain mortgage advances which are stolen. These 'fraud factories' may have a life of only three months, but those who control them can steal millions in that time.

A variation on the theme involves using the identity of an established firm by purporting to set up a branch office. The SRA publishes details of the misuse of solicitors' names on its website.

Solicitors as victims

27.11

Criminals, particularly international criminals, appear to have concluded that solicitors can be a soft touch by being too trusting. The National Crime Agency (NCA) has issued a warning to solicitors, particularly litigation practices which, because they may undertake little or no transactional work and may not even be subject to the Money Laundering Regulations, may be less alive to the risks. Fraudsters are approaching British firms for assistance in relation to personal injury, debt and other claims. The firms shortly receive large cheques representing purported settlements. If the solicitors are incautious enough, under pressure, to release funds without waiting for the received cheques to clear, they find that the cheques are fraudulent or stolen, leaving the firm to bear the loss.

Firms are also vulnerable to social engineering attacks – attempts by fraudsters to dupe solicitors and accounts staff into disclosing bank login details. Such attacks are characterised by attempts on the part of the fraudster to build trust by revealing some knowledge of the account or transaction.

Firms must also be aware of ways in which individuals may be targeted. Fraudsters posing as banks, HMRC or even regulators may make contact by email, text or phone and appear plausible enough for information or access to be provided which may facilitate cyber fraud attacks (see below).

Investment fraud

27.12

Investment fraud is another serious issue for the profession because, in relation to the kinds of fraud that are discussed here, solicitors are essential to their success.

The broad nature of these frauds is that they offer to be highly profitable – to the point of absurdity – while being at the same time wholly secure. The justification for this investment paradox, which defies all normal rules, is that they are reserved to the few insiders who know about them. They are also targeted at those who can afford, or at least can find, large sums to invest – commonly US$1 million or more (the medium is usually US dollars) – so that the victim may think that it is his wealth that enables him to engage in business ventures unavailable to others.

The trap

27.13

These frauds are more successful than would otherwise be expected because of the involvement of solicitors. The necessity for the involvement of solicitors is explained by an understanding of the different attitudes of the three participants – fraudster, victim and solicitor – which the fraudster exploits.

The victim will think, 'This is new to me; I have not heard of this form of investment before, but I am sure that if it was not genuine no solicitor would permit himself to be involved'.

The solicitor's attitude is, 'I do not truly understand what is going on here, but I do not have to. All I am being asked to do is to confirm that this copy document is a true copy of an original, or that I have received a particular document or a document of a particular description, or that I have received a specific sum of money. I do not have to go beyond that and I am not required to'.

The fraudster's position is, 'If I can get a solicitor involved the victim will be reassured, and the scheme given a credibility that it would not otherwise have. I am prepared to pay substantial sums for that involvement; it will be money well spent'.

The solicitor may be offered generous fees for doing very little, or the opportunity to earn interest on very large sums of money that pass through his or her client account.

The test

27.14

It is not considered to be particularly helpful to attempt to describe the range of possible kinds of fraud or the (usually highly complex and turgid) details of those that have been attempted in the past. They change and become more sophisticated as time passes and the SRA has routinely published and updated warning notices containing red flags, in the form of common phrases or features of transactions. The current warning notice 'Investment schemes including conveyancing' appears at APPENDIX 8 and was reissued on 17 August 2020, highlighting the following red flags:

- high deposits paid in instalments before exchange;
- comparatively high returns;
- complex and unfair agreement terms;
- guaranteed buy-back of a product or property for profit;

- having an interest in the scheme, eg panel firms and referrals;

- sellers ask firms to promote the scheme or appear in marketing material;

- exclusive offers on investment products that require secrecy;

- buyers are mainly from another jurisdiction to the location of the scheme;

- third party buyers do not have representation; and

- high commissions due to sellers from deposits.

Over time, the SRA has moved away from trying to identify specific details of schemes in its warning notices and has instead focused on the need properly to understand the transaction and a solicitor's role in it in considering red flags. Allegedly dubious transactions or allegedly fraudulent schemes remain a significant element of the SRA's investigative workload.

The most significant common theme which emerges from past cases is that if dubious or fraudulent schemes are carefully considered they do not make sense. They were often referred to as 'prime bank instrument' frauds, by reference to the kind of document that was used to perpetrate them; they have also been termed 'high yield investment programmes'. They were described by Neuberger J in *Dooley v Law Society*[1] in these words:

> 'Bank instrument frauds are based on documents which are full of impressive phrases, which on analysis make little sense, and which promise returns which are fantastic in both senses in which that word is used, namely fictitious and enormous. They are used by unscrupulous rogues to encourage the badly advised, the ignorant, the gullible and the greedy to part with their money, tempted by promises of the fantastically high returns. Once these investors part with their money, they are lucky if they see any of it again. Generally speaking, a man may as well burn his money for all the good it would do him. At least it would remove the false hopes and subsequent agony that such so-called investments involve.'

1   2000, unreported.

27.15

The Tribunal has dealt with many such cases. The following comments made by the Tribunal help to identify the pattern, and particularly the kind of mistake, that solicitors make:

> 'Members of the solicitors' profession had been warned about the dangers of becoming involved in prime bank instrument fraud or money laundering. The matter in which the Respondent had become involved demonstrated many of the notified hallmarks of fraud; it was entirely clear that the Respondent himself had no understanding of the investment scheme and had simply done what he was told and allowed his client account to be a repository for a huge sum of money.
>
> The Tribunal has had cause in the past to make the observation which it again makes. A solicitor is not a bank. A solicitor can have no business simply in receiving and paying out money with no purpose attached to it. If a solicitor is not more knowledgeable about the subject matter of the

cases of which he has conduct than his clients then he should not be handling such cases. A solicitor's stock-in-trade is his knowledge and expertise. If his clients are not utilising such knowledge and expertise it is likely that the solicitor is being involved in order that a spurious scheme be given a cloak of respectability.'[1]

'It is not for a client to explain the nature of a transaction to a solicitor but rather the solicitor's role is to explain the nature of a transaction to the client. It can be described as nothing other than crass stupidity to accept a role as, for example, an "escrow agent" when the solicitor cannot know what that means as, indeed, that expression has no meaning in English law. It is, in any event, serious professional misconduct for a solicitor to accept instructions to undertake work in connection with which he has no knowledge, expertise or experience and where the only reason for his involvement is to add a "cloak of respectability" and thereby induce the victims of fraud to take part. The Respondent himself accepts that he should have known or suspected that the transactions in which he became involved were not viable commercial transactions.'[2]

'The Respondent had ensured that scurrilous transactions were given a cloak of respectability by allowing his firm's name to be used in connection with what was on its face a transaction of the type against which the Law Society had issued warnings. It is in the Tribunal's opinion perhaps the most important aspect of this case that the Respondent was prepared to write letters regarding a matter in which he played no part as a solicitor. He had no knowledge of the type of transactions involved, he had no relevant experience and he did not, and indeed could not, give anybody any advice as to the legal aspects. A solicitor becomes involved in acting for a client when the client needs the solicitor's advice and expertise in the relevant area of law. The Tribunal accepts that there are rogues and fraudsters who are extremely plausible. A solicitor is unlikely to be taken in by such a person if he asks himself the question "why am I invited to become involved in this matter?" If the answer is not "because the client seeks to rely upon my legal expertise, knowledge and experience", he should not be playing any part in the matter.'[3]

'The Respondent at the relevant time had been an experienced practitioner. He had stated that he had not seen the yellow warning card issued by the Law Society. The warning card had however not changed the then existing duties on solicitors but had provided clarificatory guidance. The Respondent had clearly been asked to become involved in something which was out of his ordinary line of business involving overseas countries and huge sums of money. The Respondent had put his name to unintelligible documents and to documents drafted by his client which he had not questioned. He had distributed funds received from third parties at the direction of his client and had produced no evidence of proper authority to do so. He had written letters of comfort to banks and solicitors. He had involved himself in the transactions over a period of time. The transactions had never completed. The Respondent had expected significant personal gain from his involvement.'[4]

'The Respondent himself had come to recognise that he should not have been involved in the dubious HYI [High Yield Investment] transactions details of which had been placed before the Tribunal. The attention of members of the profession had been drawn to the proliferation of fraudulent investment schemes purporting to produce extraordinarily high returns on investments. It was recognised that a number of fraudsters sought to deprive potential investors of large sums of money by the production of bizarre schemes, spurious documentation and promises of very high returns indeed, often with the added incentive to invest provided by an assurance that monies would be used for charitable causes or humanitarian projects. It ill behoves a solicitor to use phrases and expressions that have no meaning in English law. It beggars belief that a solicitor should employ such phrases in letters that he himself has written. The question has to be asked, "how can a solicitor offer advice to any client or third party upon a scheme which is so nonsensical that he himself cannot have any useful knowledge of it?" It is well recognised that the fraudsters customarily seek to involve a member of the solicitors' profession in order that a cloak of respectability may be achieved and those defrauded are encouraged to part with large sums of money because of the comfort they derive from the fact that a solicitor is involved in the transaction. In becoming involved in the fraudulent schemes, as the Respondent did, he falsely allowed his own status and the good reputation of the solicitors' profession to be used improperly to persuade potential "investors" to make substantial investment of money. The only proper way for a solicitor to behave when invited to participate in one of these schemes, in whatever capacity, is to refuse to do so and report the approach made to him to the appropriate authorities. For a solicitor to become involved in dubious and/or fraudulent transactions of this type was not compatible with his continued membership of the profession.'[5]

1   *Wayne*, 8189-2000, SDT.
2   *Wilson-Smith*, 8772-2003, SDT.
3   *Rose*, 9067-2004, SDT.
4   *Rosling*, 9242-2005, SDT.
5   *Heath*, 9502-2006, SDT.

27.16

It will have been noted that the single strand of logical concern that permeates these cases is that the client knows more about the subject matter than the solicitor: he is not seeking legal advice and assistance; he is directing the solicitor in what he is required to do and explaining matters to the solicitor, not seeking guidance. In fact, many such schemes are constructed purely for the purposes of money laundering between individuals with a common interest, serving only to move large amounts of money into and out of a solicitor's client account. Compliance with MLR 2017[1] considered in **CHAPTER 28** is vital, and would be effective to prevent involvement in such schemes if faithfully followed.

Further, if solicitors ask themselves the questions identified by the Tribunal in *Rose* and *Heath* the precise nature of the fraudulent scheme will not matter. However much fraudsters change the language and apparent structure, and even if the consequence of such changes is that every 'common characteristic' or 'typical phrase' previously exposed or specific issue appearing in the SRA's warning notice 'Investment schemes including conveyancing'[2] is avoided, it will be a straightforward matter for solicitors to identify dubious transactions and avoid involvement. Solicitors should nevertheless be fully familiar with the SRA's warning notice and ensure that all staff are aware of the principles contained within it.

In *Bryant and Bench v Law Society*,[3] solicitors who had acted for clients in a series of 'dubious' transactions, even though not themselves dishonest, were both suspended. 'Dubious' in this context meant that the transactions bore the indicia of fraud or possible fraud, and that it was professional misconduct for the appellants to act or to continue to act in relation to them without carrying out sufficient enquiries to satisfy themselves that the transactions were not, in fact, fraudulent. The Divisional Court stated (at [199] and [239]):

> '199. In our view the appellants should have concluded that these transactions involving NIC and Mr Alonso were "dubious" in the sense described above at the very latest by the end of August 2003. But they never did so. They appeared to be naïve, uncommercial and unwilling to question matters; whereas we would have expected solicitors who had considerable experience of international clients and transactions to have developed a healthy scepticism.

> 239. ... In the case of Mr Bryant, the incompetence displayed was considerable and continued for approximately a year. In the case of Mr Bench, his culpability was far less, but, on our findings, remains significant. We accept the submission on behalf of the Law Society that such incompetence threatens the reputation of the profession for prudence as well as competence and that it puts the public at risk.'

1   SI 2017/692.
2   See **APPENDIX 8**.
3   [2007] EWHC 3043 (Admin). See also *Yildiz*, 10997-2012, SDT and the litigation which followed on the same facts: *Global Marine Drillships Ltd v La Bella* [2014] EWHC 2242 (Ch).

Land banking schemes and property investment

27.17

A further species of investment fraud, which also contains features of mortgage fraud, relates to so-called land banking schemes. These typically occur where agricultural, brownfield or other blighted land is acquired at low cost and divided into plots for sale to investors. Investors are informed that the land will soar in value once planning permission is obtained. However, as the land will usually be on a green belt or protected site, the land is unlikely to obtain planning permission or achieve the value intimated by the operator, resulting in the investor paying an inflated price for the land. Such schemes are often promoted on the basis that planning permission is imminent or that a well-known company is about to buy the land. Forged HM Land Registry letters and HM Land Registry estate plan approval letters have been used as evidence that planning permission is available when this is not the case. Also the obtaining of planning permission may be in the control of a management company which may have no intention of applying for planning permission. Operators of land banking schemes are often based overseas, making it difficult for an investor to recover funds invested in a scheme or for enforcement action to be taken against the operator. Operators may also attempt to conceal the original value of the land by inter-company transactions which inflate the original purchase price.

Some variations on this theme have emerged in recent years whereby investors purchase or lease hotel rooms, car parking spaces, rooms in care homes or units in a development yet to be built. The SRA considers these schemes to be inherently risky as they are dependent not only on the completion of the development but also on successful commercial management of the hotel/care home, etc which has then been built. The SRA warning notice indicates that there is no apparent reason why such schemes should produce intrinsically high returns and highlights a £120 million Serious Fraud Office investigation in connection with self-storage schemes.

The SRA also highlights the general risk of 'buyer led financing of a development' where investors are encouraged to release high deposits or even the full purchase price to the developer in order to fund the development. While not necessarily improper, such schemes are risky and the SRA expects solicitors to advise on the specific risks identified in the warning notice as:

'1. Buying a property not yet built or completed ie buyer-led or subject to significant refurbishment, involves a substantial risk that the developer or seller could fail, and money will be lost.

2. Promises of substantial returns can be misleading. Standard warnings in publicity about the risk of capital loss are therefore not enough to make sure that you have properly advised your client upon the risks of the transaction.'

Cyber fraud

27.18

Criminals use a variety of ever-changing and increasingly sophisticated means, electronic and/or verbal, involving impersonation or infiltration, in an attempt to obtain confidential financial information and data with the aim of stealing money from bank accounts. A firm's client account can be targeted in this way. Banks and clients can also be targeted in an attempt to defraud the client account.

To make their fraud appear credible, the criminals may use tactics such as convincingly passing themselves off as calling from a bank or referring to the details of a genuine transaction which they have acquired dishonestly. Or they may use the names of law firms, solicitors, parties to a conveyancing transaction, beneficiaries of trusts and wills or persons linked directly or indirectly to a client account, to make their activity seem credible.

Fraud mechanisms are ever-changing and more sophisticated, but the following have been known to target law firms:

- Variants on the 'CEO fraud'. Typically this occurs in commercial organisations with an email from a fraudster purporting to be a senior person in the organisation to a member of staff in an accounts or finance department, directing the urgent payment of money to a specified bank account for a credible reason. The money is sent to the fraudster's account and rapidly disappears. The email may have involved cloning a genuine email account or using an originating address which is very similar. Applied to law firms, this could involve the impersonation of a genuine CEO or equivalent, or of a client.

- 'Friday afternoon' frauds involve a late notification from someone pretending to be the client and likewise appearing to come from the client's email address, instructing the solicitor that there is a change of bank details to which to send the proceeds of sale. The new destination is the fraudster's bank account.

- Identity fraud, supported by technology (such as text messages purporting to be from a bank, HMRC or a regulator directing you to websites which appear genuine) or invoices from genuine suppliers or creditors which contain fraudulent payment details. The documentation supplied by the fraudsters will often appear to come from a genuine source but have been altered.

As technologies develop, the rise of malware (eg ransomware) is a risk against which solicitors need to be vigilant. Opening an infected attachment could lead to serious breaches of cyber security, potentially crippling a firm's systems or – perhaps more worryingly – enabling fraudsters to obtain detailed confidential information which could be used to facilitate more widespread frauds on clients and other firms.

CHAPTER 28

Money laundering

28.1

This chapter provides a brief introduction to this important and complex subject, specific guidance on the Money Laundering, Terrorist Financing and Transfer of Funds (Information on the Payer) Regulations 2017[1] (MLR 2017) and some commentary on the principal elements of the criminal law that are engaged. It does not provide an all-encompassing guide to the subject, which derives from the criminal law and is beyond the scope of this book. The focus in this chapter is on the regulation of practitioners and the warning signs.

1   SI 2017/692.

What is money laundering?

28.2

To quote the Financial Action Task Force of the Organisation for Economic Co-operation and Development:

> 'The goal of a large number of criminal acts is to generate a profit for the individual or group that carries out the act. Money laundering is the processing of these criminal proceeds to disguise their illegal origin. This process is of critical importance, as it enables the criminal to enjoy these profits without jeopardising their source.'

Money laundering is the process by which assets illegally obtained are 'cleaned' to give them apparent legitimacy to enable their subsequent use. It involves the purported legitimisation of *any asset* that is illegitimately obtained. An accumulation of small amounts obtained or retained by tax evasion would be criminal property for these purposes. Money laundering is designed to disguise the true origin of criminal proceeds. The process typically involves three stages – placement, layering and integration – but these are not clear cut distinctions and money laundering may become a seamless blend of all three.

Placement

28.3

The placement stage involves the placing in the financial/banking system of the proceeds of crime. The intention is to change the identity of the illegitimate asset. A solicitor's client account will serve this purpose.

Layering

28.4

The layering stage involves moving the asset through the financial system. The intention is to hide the origins of the illegitimate asset, making it difficult to trace and recover. Complex transactions may be used to disguise the source of funds. Sometimes the transactions may have no legitimate economic purpose, but simply result in money moving around (see the commentary on investment frauds at **27.12**).

Integration

28.5

The integration stage involves the translation of the laundered funds into a legitimate asset, such as the purchase of property through a conveyancing solicitor.

Solicitors as 'gatekeepers'

28.6

According to the Serious Organised Crime Agency (now the National Crime Agency (NCA)):

> 'Serious organised criminals have a number of options when looking to realise the proceeds of their criminal activities. These include smuggling cash or assets out of the UK; laundering the money themselves; employing "gatekeepers", such as solicitors and accountants, with access to financial facilities; corrupting or coercing bank employees; or using professional launderers.'[1]

Professionals, including solicitors, may have a lack of awareness or lack of curiosity, so allowing themselves to be used by criminals to access the banking system and to enable the conversion of criminal funds into legitimate assets.

Solicitors may assist by becoming involved in normal transactions, such as a property purchase, but in circumstances where the client's true identity or status as nominee are disguised, and/or where the source of funds cannot be ascertained or is suspicious. Solicitors may also become involved in unusual transactions with no obvious logic where large amounts of money move about without any apparent aim. Investment frauds of the kind considered in **CHAPTER 27** invariably 'fail' in the sense that nothing comes of the 'investment' but it can be that all parties to the scheme are colluding and that the only real purpose is to move money in and out of a solicitor's client account.

A derivative of investment frauds is sham litigation. Here the fraudsters collude to litigate over an original scheme which, on close analysis, may make little sense. Signs to watch for will include clients with an unusual lack of interest in the risks of litigation, and who seem reluctant to engage in the detail. Another indicator is that one party to the litigation will suddenly capitulate, submitting to judgment for the full amount, without material effort to achieve a compromise solution. Note that the conduct of litigation does not necessarily fall within the scope of MLR 2017. The Law Society's Quick Guide to the Money Laundering Regulations 2017 states:

'The MLR 2017 does not apply to:

- paying costs to a legal professional

- providing legal advice

- participation in litigation or a form of alternative dispute resolution

- will-writing, although you should consider whether any accompanying taxation advice is covered

- work funded by the Legal Services Commission

You should get legal advice if you are not certain whether the MLR 2017 apply to your work. Alternatively, you may wish to follow the MLR 2017 even if you are not performing regulated work.'[2]

The formal sector guidance issued by the Legal Sector Affinity Group (LSAG) no longer contains a similar provision, stating instead that:

'All legal practices must consider whether their business brings them into scope of The Money Laundering, Terrorist Financing and Transfer of Funds (Information on the Payer) Regulations 2017 (as amended) ("the Regulations"), through any of the qualifying activities but particularly those stated in R12.'[3]

Litigation is acknowledged to be 'generally out of scope' at section 18.8 of the LSAG guidance dealing with worktype specific red flags.

1 The Serious Organised Crime Agency, *United Kingdom Threat Assessment of Serious Organised Crime 2006/07.*
2 This was set out in the original LSAG, 'Anti-Money Laundering: Guidance for the Legal Sector', March 2018, at page 17 but has not been reproduced in the updated LSAG guidance issued in 2021.
3 See **28.10**.

Six key questions for solicitors

28.7

There is no substitute for understanding and following MLR 2017 (see **28.9**), but solicitors should always ask themselves:

- Am I confident I know who this person is and that I understand with whom I am really dealing?

- Am I confident that I know and understand the source of funds?

- Am I confident that I know and understand the transaction?

- Is there anything about the transaction which is unusual or financially illogical?

- Is the client showing an appropriate degree of interest in the transaction?

- Do I understand why this client has chosen to instruct me?

These are issues of which solicitors should be aware at the beginning of a business relationship or transaction, *and* which they should also continue to have in mind and to monitor as relationships and transactions develop.

Law Society guidance and assistance

28.8

Regulation 47(1) of MLR 2017 requires supervisory authorities (ie HM Treasury) to make up-to-date information available to those it supervises. A court must take into account any guidance approved by HM Treasury in determining whether certain offences under the Proceeds of Crime Act (POCA) 2002 and the Terrorism Act (TA) 2000 may have been committed. The guidance is also relevant to a number of obligations under MLR 2017.

HM Treasury has determined that there will only be one piece of Treasury-approved guidance across the whole legal sector. This, in its current form, is 'Anti-Money Laundering Guidance for the Legal Sector' published by the Legal Sector Affinity Group in January 2021 ('LSAG guidance'). Solicitors should be familiar with the LSAG guidance and the occasions on which they must have regard to it. See **28.10**.

The full guidance, which runs to 212 pages, can be found at www.sra.org.uk/globalassets/documents/solicitors/firm-based-authorisation/lsag-aml-guidance.pdf. In addition, the Law Society's Practice Advice Service will assist in understanding the LSAG guidance and is available to talk through any problems (tel: 020 7320 5675) although the Law Society does not give legal advice. There is also a list[1] of solicitors with relevant expertise willing to give other solicitors 30 minutes' free advice on legal issues relating to money laundering.

The Law Society also produces a bi-monthly anti-money laundering (AML) e-newsletter which provides useful information on developments in money laundering, including a section titled 'Launderers in the News', which summarises recent prosecutions.

1   See www.lawsociety.org.uk/Advice/Anti-money-laundering/AML-directory.

Money Laundering, Terrorist Financing and Transfer of Funds (Information on the Payer) Regulations 2017

28.9

MLR 2017[1] were implemented to ensure compliance with the Fourth Money Laundering Directive.[2] They came into force on 26 June 2017 and were amended to comply with the Fifth Money Laundering Directive with effect from 10 January 2020.[3]

1   SI 2017/692.
2   Directive (EU) 2015/849 of the European Parliament and of the Council of 20 May 2015 on the prevention of the use of the financial system for the purposes of money laundering or terrorist

financing, amending Regulation (EU) No 648/2012 of the European Parliament and of the Council, and repealing Directive 2005/60/EC of the European Parliament and of the Council and Commission Directive 2006/70/EC.

3   The Money Laundering and Terrorist Financing (Amendment) Regulations 2019 (SI 2019/1511).

Relevant persons

28.10

MLR 2017 (as amended) 'set out requirements which must be adhered to. These, in addition to the compliance principles [in the LSAG guidance], should be viewed as the "building blocks" for creating robust AML policies, controls and procedures.'[1]

MLR 2017 aim to limit the use of professional services for money laundering by requiring professionals to know their clients and monitor the use of their services by clients.

Regulation 8 states that MLR 2017 apply to persons acting in the course of business carried on in the United Kingdom including independent legal professionals, which do not include solicitors employed by a public authority or working in-house.

MLR 2017 only apply to certain solicitors' activities where there is a high risk of money laundering occurring, as follows:

'(a)   the buying and selling of real property or business entities;

(b)   the managing of client money, securities or other assets;

(c)   the opening or management of bank, savings or securities accounts;

(d)   the organisation of contributions necessary for the creation, operation or management of companies; or

(e)   the creation, operation or management of trusts, companies, foundations or similar structures,

and, for this purpose, a person participates in a transaction by assisting in the planning or execution of the transaction or otherwise acting for or on behalf of a client in the transaction.'[2]

The Treasury has confirmed that the following would not generally be viewed as participation in financial transactions, and therefore are not covered by MLR 2017:

- payment on account of costs to a solicitor or payment of a solicitor's bill;

- provision of legal advice;

- participation in litigation or a form of alternative dispute resolution (ADR);

- will-writing, although you should consider whether any accompanying taxation advice is covered; and

- work funded by the Legal Aid Agency (LAA).

CHAPTER 28
MONEY LAUNDERING

It is important therefore to identify whether a solicitor's work comes within the regulated sector; for example, a firm conducting exclusively claimant litigation may not come within the regulated sector .

1 LSAG guidance, page 17.
2 Regulation 12(1).

Customer due diligence and ongoing monitoring

28.11

A solicitor must conduct customer due diligence (CDD) on clients who retain the solicitor for services regulated under MLR 2017. Regulation 27 requires that CDD be conducted when:

- establishing a business relationship;[1]

  (note that a relationship where the relevant person is asked to form a company for its customer is to be treated as a business relationship for the purpose of these Regulations, whether or not the formation of the company is the only transaction carried out for that customer[2]);

- carrying out an occasional transaction that amounts to a transfer of funds within the meaning of article 3.9 of the Funds Transfer Regulation[3] exceeding €1,000;

- the solicitor suspects money laundering or terrorist financing;[4] or

- the solicitor doubts the veracity or adequacy of documents or information previously obtained for the purposes of identification or verification.[5]

A relevant person must also apply CDD measures:

- where there is a legal duty to contact a client in the course of the calendar year for the purpose of reviewing information relevant to the risk assessment of that client and relating to the beneficial ownership;[6]

- where the relevant person needs to contact an existing client to fulfil a duty under the International Tax Compliance Regulations 2015;[7]

- 'at other appropriate times to existing customers on a risk based approach';[8] and

- when a solicitor 'becomes aware that the circumstances of an existing customer relevant to its risk assessment for that customer have changed'.[9]

Customer due diligence measures are covered by regulation 28 of MLR 2017 and require that a solicitor must:

- identify the customer and verify[10] the customer's identity unless the identity of the customer is already known to and has been verified by the solicitor;[11]

- assess and, where appropriate, obtain information on the purpose and intended nature of the business relationship or occasional transaction;[12]

- in the case of a customer who is a legal person, trust or similar legal arrangement, take measures to understand the ownership and control structure of the person, trust or arrangement;[13] and

- identify, where there is a beneficial owner who is not the customer, the beneficial owner and take reasonable measures to verify his identity so that the relevant person is satisfied that he knows who the beneficial owner is, including, in the case of a legal person, trust or similar legal arrangement, measures to understand the ownership and control structure of the person, trust or arrangement.[14]

Compliance with CDD requirements must reflect the risk assessment carried out by the relevant person under regulation 18(1)[15] and the assessment of the level of risk arising in any particular case; compliance may therefore vary from case to case.[16] The assessment of the level of risk in any particular case must take account of factors including: (a) the purpose of an account, transaction or business relationship; (b) the assets involved or the size of the transaction; and (c) the regularity and duration of the business relationship.[17]

A solicitor must 'be able to demonstrate to [his] supervisory authority that the extent of the measures … are appropriate in view of the risks of money laundering and terrorist financing' with regard to the risk assessments carried out under regulation 18(1) and information made available by the supervisory authority under regulations 17(9) and 47.[18] This is required as part of both CDD measures, and ongoing monitoring. Where a relevant person has to apply CDD in the case of a trust or similar arrangement and the beneficial owner consists of a class of persons, it may not be necessary to identify all members of the class.[19]

A relevant person must keep under review every business relationship and conduct 'ongoing monitoring'. This means:

> '(a) scrutiny of transactions undertaken throughout the course of the relationship (including, where necessary, the source of funds) to ensure that the transactions are consistent with the relevant person's knowledge of the customer, the customer's business and risk profile;
>
> (b) undertaking reviews of existing records and keeping the documents or information obtained for the purpose of applying customer due diligence measures up-to-date.'[20]

1 'Business relationship' means a business, professional or commercial relationship between a relevant person and a customer, which: (a) arises out of the business of the relevant person; and (b) is expected by the relevant person, at the time when contact is established, to have an element of duration.
2 Regulation 4 of MLR 2017.
3 Regulation (EU) 2015/847 of the European Parliament and of the Council of 20 May 2015 on information accompanying transfers of funds and repealing Regulation (EC) No 1781/2006.
4 Regulation 27(1)(c).
5 Regulation 27(1)(d).
6 Regulation 27(8)(za).
7 Regulation 27(8)(zb).
8 Regulation 27(8)(a).
9 Regulation 27(8)(b).
10 Where 'verify' means 'verify on the basis of documents or information … obtained from a reliable source which is independent', per regulation 28(18).
11 Regulation 28(2)(a) and (b).
12 Regulation 28(2)(c).
13 Regulation 28(3A).
14 Regulation 28(4). Note that this does not apply where a customer is listed on a regulated market (see regulation 28(5)). Note also that it is not permissible to rely solely on the statement of significant control to comply with regulation 28(4) (per regulation 28(9)).

15 See **28.18**.
16 Regulation 28(12)(a) and (b).
17 Regulation 28(13).
18 Regulation 28(16).
19 Regulation 6(1) defines beneficial ownership as it relates to trusts and similar structures. Regulation 30(7) requires that, where CDD measures are required, they must be completed before a member of a class receives payment or exercises any vested rights under a trust, legal entity or legal arrangement.
20 Regulation 28(11).

28.12

It is important to note that, by requiring a risk-based assessment of the needs of due diligence and a full and proper understanding of transactions, the MLR 2017 impose obligations actively to monitor the way that business relationships and transactions develop, with an understanding of the aims of money laundering. This is not a box-ticking exercise so that, having obtained a copy passport and a utility bill (for example), a solicitor can consider the money laundering requirements to have been satisfied. There is an ongoing obligation for relevant persons in relation to all clients and all transactions. Many will involve minimal risk and commensurate monitoring, but the MLR 2017 require relevant persons to be watchful and thoughtful.

A client's identity must be verified before a business relationship is established or an occasional transaction is carried out[1] but the verification process may be completed during the establishment of a business relationship, if it is 'necessary not to interrupt the normal conduct of business' and 'there is little risk of money laundering or terrorist financing occurring' provided that the verification is completed as soon as practicable after contact is first established.[2]

A solicitor unable to establish a client's identity must not carry out any transaction with or for the client through a bank account; must not establish a business relationship or carry out an occasional transaction with the client; must terminate any existing business relationship with the client and must consider whether he or she is required to make a disclosure (under Part 7 of POCA 2002 or Part III of TA 2000).[3]

There is an important exception in favour of a solicitor where he is 'in the course of establishing the legal position for his client or performing his task of defending or representing that client in, or concerning, legal proceedings, including advice on the institution or avoidance of proceedings'.[4]

This exception does not apply to transactional work so solicitors should be careful to distinguish between advice and litigation work, and transactional work.

Specific provisions apply where solicitors are unable to verify the beneficial owner of a body corporate and where solicitors identify discrepancies between information held on the register and information which becomes available in the course of carrying out duties under MLR 2017 in establishing a business relationship.

By regulation 28(8), where a solicitor is unable to identify to his satisfaction the beneficial owner of a body corporate, he must keep records in writing of actions taken to establish identity and take reasonable measures to identify the senior person in the body corporate responsible for managing it and keep written records of such actions and any difficulties encountered.

By regulation 30A, a solicitor must obtain proof of registration or an excerpt from the register before establishing a relationship with:

(a) a company which is subject to the requirements of Part 21A of the Companies Act 2006 (information about people with significant control);

(b) an unregistered company which is subject to the requirements of the Unregistered Companies Regulations 2009;[5]

(c) a limited liability partnership (LLP) which is subject to the requirements of the Limited Liability Partnerships (Application of Companies Act 2006) Regulations 2009;[6] or

(d) an eligible Scottish partnership which is subject to the requirements of the Scottish Partnerships (Register of People with Significant Control) Regulations 2017.[7]

Subject to legal professional privilege, a solicitor must report to the registrar any discrepancy between the information contained in the registration details obtained and information which becomes available in the course of carrying out duties under MLR 2017 in establishing a business relationship.[8]

1 Regulation 30(2) of MLR 2017.
2 Regulation 30(3).
3 Regulation 31.
4 Regulation 31(3).
5 SI 2009/2436.
6 SI 2009/1804.
7 SI 2017/694.
8 Regulation 30A(2) and (3).

Enhanced customer due diligence

28.13

There are requirements for 'enhanced customer due diligence' and ongoing monitoring to manage and mitigate the risks arising from, among other things:

- higher risks identified as a result of risk assessments under regulation 18(1) and/or information provided by the supervisory authority under regulations 17(9) and 47;[1]

- the client being established in a high risk country or undertaking transactions with counterparties so established;[2]

- the client being a 'politically exposed person' (PEP) or a family member or known close associate of a PEP;[3]

- the client having provided false or stolen ID documents and the solicitor continuing to deal with the client;[4]

- unusually large and complex transactions, transactions forming an unusual pattern or transactions with no apparent economic or legal purpose;[5] or

- in any other situation which by its nature can present a higher risk of money laundering or terrorist financing.[6]

A PEP is an individual who is or has at any time in the preceding year been entrusted with prominent public functions other than a middle-ranking or more junior official.[7]

Enhanced due diligence may be required in the case of clients who are not physically present for identification purposes, since non-face-to-face transactions are an increased risk factor pursuant to regulation 33(6). Enhanced due diligence in the case of PEPs requires: senior management approval of the business relationship; measures to be taken to establish the source of wealth and source of funds involved in the proposed business relationship or occasional transaction; and enhanced ongoing monitoring.[8]

Enhanced due diligence measures in relation to parties established in high risk countries must include:

(a)   obtaining additional information on the customer and on the customer's beneficial owner;

(b)   obtaining additional information on the intended nature of the business relationship;

(c)   obtaining information on the source of funds and source of wealth of the customer and of the customer's beneficial owner;

(d)   obtaining information on the reasons for the transactions;

(e)   obtaining the approval of senior management for establishing or continuing the business relationship;

(f)   conducting enhanced monitoring of the business relationship by increasing the number and timing of controls applied, and selecting patterns of transactions that need further examination.[9]

Enhanced CDD measures in relation to unusual transactions must include:

(a)   as far as reasonably possible, examining the background and purpose of the transaction, and

(b)   increasing the degree and nature of monitoring of the business relationship in which the transaction is made to determine whether that transaction or that relationship appear to be suspicious.[10]

1   Regulation 33(1)(a).
2   Regulation 33(1)(b).
3   Regulation 33(1)(d).
4   Regulation 33(1)(e).
5   Regulation 33(1)(f).
6   Regulation 33(1)(g). Note the list of factors to be taken into account in assessing whether there is a higher risk set out in regulation 33(6).
7   Regulation 35(12).
8   Regulation 35(5).
9   Regulation 33(3A).
10   Regulation 33(4).

Law Society guidance on customer due diligence

28.14

Section 6 of the LSAG guidance contains comprehensive guidance on CDD. It provides detailed advice as to how to deal with the verification of individuals; clients unable to produce standard documentation; other professionals; partnerships and LLPs and corporate bodies. It also explains how to approach money laundering issues concerning other legal or quasi-legal entities such as trusts, foundations, charities, deceased persons' estates, churches, schools, clubs and pension funds.

As for ongoing monitoring, the LSAG guidance states (at paragraph 6.21):

'R28(11) requires that you conduct ongoing monitoring of business relationships. Ongoing monitoring is defined as:

- scrutiny of transactions undertaken throughout the course of the relationship, (including where necessary, the source of funds), to ensure that the transactions are consistent with your knowledge of the client, their business and their risk profile; and

- undertaking reviews of existing records and keeping the documents, or information obtained for the purpose of applying CDD, up to date.

You must also be aware of obligations to keep clients' personal data updated under the Data Protection Act 1998 and the GDPR or their equivalent.

In order to comply, you may:

- renew and re-evaluate CDD at appropriate intervals (including during the course of a given transaction), noting that as outlined in R27(8), this is mandatory in certain circumstances;

- suspend or terminate a business relationship until you have updated information or documents, though this may be excessive if you are satisfied you know who your client is, and keep under review any request you have made for information or documents; or

- use technology to aid your ongoing monitoring.

You should operate a system of regular review and renewal of CDD and take a risk-based approach to such activity. You should consider reviewing (although not necessarily redoing) the CDD upon each new matter. Where there has been a significant gap between instructions (anything above a year may be considered a significant gap in relation to those clients or transactions assessed as higher-risk), you should consider refreshing the CDD.

You must update the CDD when you become aware of any changes to the client's identification information. This would include change of name, address, beneficial owner or business.

In accordance with R27(9) you must apply (or reapply) CDD to existing clients on a risk based approach and when you become aware that the circumstances of the existing client have changed.'

Sanctions and counter-measures

28.15

Customer due diligence systems should be able to enable identification of persons subject to restrictions imposed by the UK Government. The Office of

Financial Sanctions Implementation is responsible for publishing details of such restrictions.

Customer due diligence systems should also be able to enable identification of persons subject to financial sanctions following designation by the United Nations or the European Commission. The Office of Financial Sanctions publishes one consolidated list covering restrictions imposed by the UK, the EU and the UN. The full list can be accessed at www.gov.uk/government/publications/financial-sanctions-consolidated-list-of-targets/consolidated-list-of-targets.

Reliance on third parties and outsourcing

28.16

Solicitors may rely on a third party to conduct CDD on their behalf, provided that the third party falls within specified categories;[1] and that the solicitor immediately obtains all necessary information and an arrangement is in place permitting the solicitor to obtain ID and verification data immediately upon request and ensuring that the third party keeps the records for five years.[2] The solicitor remains liable for any default by the person they relied upon.[3]

The reliance provisions are not required:

- for use of e-verification information to verify identity;
- for passporting clients between offices of the same legal practice;
- for receiving actual identity documents (including certified copies) to assist you with verification; or
- by financial institutions when applying the simplification provisions in regulation 37 to a solicitor's client account.

1   Listed in regulation 39(3); see also paragraph 6.23 of the LSAG guidance.
2   Regulation 39(2).
3   Regulation 39(1).

Record keeping

28.17

Relevant persons must keep records to demonstrate compliance with MLR 2017. In substance this requires you to keep evidence of identity and other file records of a relationship or transaction for five years from the completion of the transaction or the end of the relationship.[1] Note that this may have an impact on General Data Protection Regulation (GDPR)[2] and other data protection obligations in respect of the period for which personal data, and in particular special category data, may be retained.

1   Regulation 40.
2   Regulation (EU) 2016/679 of the European Parliament and of the Council of 27 April 2016 on the protection of natural persons with regard to the processing of personal data and on the free movement of such data, and repealing Directive 95/46/EC (General Data Protection Regulation).

Risk assessments

28.18

MLR 2017 introduced, for the first time, the requirement to undertake a practice-wide risk assessment.[1] The risk assessment must identify and assess the risk of money laundering and terrorist financing faced by a business. The LSAG guidance contains detailed consideration of the assessment of a business's risk profile at section 5, in particular, paragraphs 5.3–5.7. A risk assessment will need to take account of the nature of the business's work in the legal sector, the nature and location of its clients and their businesses and the geographic locations in which the business operates. Assessment of risk will vary between practices and it is essential to have a detailed understanding of both the generic risks facing the legal sector as a whole as discussed in the LSAG guidance, and also the specific risks which are of more immediate relevance to the specific practice.

A comprehensive and well-documented risk assessment will assist businesses in ensuring consistency in decision-making, demonstrating appropriate systems and compliance and will help to justify any decisions to law enforcement agencies, the courts and interested regulators.

1 Regulation 18(1).

Systems and training

28.19

Relevant persons must establish and maintain appropriate risk-sensitive policies and procedures to prevent activities relating to money laundering or terrorist financing. These must address:

- CDD measures and ongoing monitoring;
- reporting;
- reliance and record keeping;
- internal controls;
- risk assessment and management; and
- the monitoring and management of compliance with, and the internal communication of, such policies and procedures.[1]

Solicitors' firms must have a money laundering reporting officer (MLRO) – a 'nominated officer' for the purpose of MLR 2017 to receive and to make disclosures.[2]

Policies and procedures must include those which provide for the identification and scrutiny of:

- complex or unusually large transactions;
- unusual patterns of transactions which have no apparent economic or visible lawful purpose; and
- any other activity which the relevant person regards as particularly likely by its nature to be related to money laundering or terrorist financing.[3]

As mentioned above, the requirement to have a full and proper understanding of transactions is reinforced, and it will be seen that a responsible application of regulation 19 will avoid the involvement of solicitors in the kind of investment frauds considered in **CHAPTER 27**.

Relevant persons must take appropriate measures to ensure that all 'relevant employees' and agents are 'made aware of the law relating to money laundering and terrorist financing', and are 'regularly given training in how to recognise and deal with transactions and other activities or situations which may be related to money laundering or terrorist financing'.[4]

For the guidance on training see section 8 of the LSAG guidance. Paragraph 8.1 contains the following advice:

> 'In deciding what measures are appropriate you should consider the size and nature of the business and the areas of risk identified in, and outcomes of your Practice-Wide Risk Assessment (PWRA).
>
> You should also consider questions relevant to any other form of training including:
>
> ● How to assess the success of training, both in terms of information retention and whether training is reflected in the practices of individuals.
>
> ● How and when to review and update training.
>
> ● What the triggers for an individual redoing training are; and
>
> ● What content should there be widespread training on and where are there specialised needs.
>
> A practice should set the answers to these questions out in a written training policy, which should be reviewed and updated as needed.'

1   Regulation 19.
2   Regulation 21.
3   Regulation 19(4).
4   Regulation 24.

Compliance

28.20

The Law Society, through the SRA, is a supervisory authority with responsibility to monitor those it regulates and to take necessary measures for the purposes of securing compliance with MLR 2017.[1] A failure to comply with any of the requirements of MLR 2017 listed above is a criminal offence punishable by a term of imprisonment of up to two years.[2] No offence is committed if all reasonable steps were taken and all due diligence was exercised to avoid committing the offence.[3]

Note that the SRA usually prosecutes failure to comply with money laundering requirements through its disciplinary procedures. In 2021, the SRA fined a number of firms for failing to comply with requirements to implement practice-wide risk assessments following a significant exercise auditing compliance with MLR 2017 across a wide range of firms.

1   Regulation 7(1)(b) and Schedule 1.
2   Regulation 86(1).
3   Regulation 86(3).

Communications with clients

28.21

Although not required by MLR 2017, it may be regarded as good practice and good client relations to explain the statutory obligations to which solicitors are subject, in terms of CDD and reporting, in client care material and/or terms of business.

The verification of identity will also, of necessity, require personal data to be processed. Where biometric data is included in identity documents, it will fall within the definition of special category data. Accordingly, solicitors should consider data protection obligations when communicating with clients and, in particular, should ensure that processing is carried out on grounds which do not bring data protection obligations into conflict with the requirements of MLR 2017 to verify identity and to retain appropriate records.

The criminal law – primary offences

28.22

The primary money laundering offences are currently found in Part 7 of POCA 2002. There are also separate offences aimed at preventing the laundering of and dealing with terrorist property in Part 3 of TA 2000.

The three primary money laundering offences are those contained in sections 327, 328 and 329 of POCA 2002. These are:

- transferring, converting, concealing, disguising or removing criminal property from the United Kingdom (section 327);

- arrangements involving criminal property (section 328); and

- acquiring, using or possessing criminal property (section 329).

A prohibited arrangement involving criminal property exists if a person 'enters into or becomes concerned in an arrangement which he knows or suspects facilitates (by whatever means) the acquisition, retention, use or control of criminal property by or on behalf of another person'.[1]

Knowledge or suspicion that the property is criminal property is required for an offence to be committed. The Crown must show that the offender knew or suspected that the arrangement was an arrangement which facilitated the acquisition, retention or control of criminal property. For property to be 'criminal property' the offender must be proved to have known or suspected that the property constituted a person's benefit from criminal conduct, or that it represented such a benefit (in whole or in part, directly or indirectly).[2]

There is no statutory definition of an arrangement; the courts have only been called upon to rule as to what 'arrangements' do *not* include. In *Bowman v Fels*,[3] the Court of Appeal held that an arrangement does not include action undertaken in the context of litigation:

> 'the issue or pursuit of ordinary legal proceedings with a view to obtaining the court's adjudication upon the parties' rights and duties is not to be regarded as an arrangement or a prohibited act within ss 327–9.'[4]

The LSAG's views as to whether and in what circumstances solicitors are involved in an 'arrangement' in the light of *Bowman v Fels* are set out in the LSAG guidance at paragraph 16.3.6 in the following terms:

> '*Bowman v Fels* (2005) EWCA Civ 226 held that s328 does not cover or affect the ordinary conduct of litigation by legal professionals, including any step taken in litigation from the issue of proceedings and the securing of injunctive relief or a freezing order up to its final disposal by judgment.
>
> Dividing assets in accordance with a judgment, including the handling of the assets which are criminal property, is not an arrangement. Settlements, negotiations, out of court settlements, alternative dispute resolution and tribunal representation are also not arrangements. However, the property will generally still remain criminal property and you may need to consider referring your client for specialist advice regarding possible offences they may commit once they come into possession of the property after completion of the settlement.
>
> A victim of an acquisitive offence who is recovering their property will not be committing an offence under either s328 or s329 of the Act. However, if there is an agreement e.g.in an insolvency scenario, whereby a victim agrees to accept a lower percentage in full settlement of a claim, you may still need to consider s328.'

1   Section 328(1) of POCA 2002.
2   Section 340.
3   [2005] EWCA Civ 226, [2005] 1 WLR 3083, [2005] 4 All ER 609.
4   [2005] EWCA Civ 226, [2005] 1 WLR 3083, [2005] 4 All ER 609 at [95].

28.23

There are broadly comparable offences under TA 2000. Those most likely to be of concern to solicitors are contained in sections 17 and 18 of TA 2000. A person commits an offence if he 'enters into or becomes concerned in an arrangement as a result of which money or other property is made available or is to be made available to another', and he 'knows or has reasonable cause to suspect that it will or may be used for the purposes of terrorism';[1] and a person commits an offence if he 'enters into or becomes concerned in an arrangement which facilitates the retention or control by or on behalf of another person of terrorist property' by concealment, removal from the jurisdiction, transfer to nominees or in any other way.

It is a defence to prove that the person accused did not know and had no reasonable cause to suspect that the arrangement related to terrorist property.[2]

Although, as has been seen, MLR 2017 encourage and require a proportionate risk-based approach, this is not the test applied to the primary and secondary criminal offences, where the obligations not to engage in prohibited activities and to make disclosure when required are mandatory.

1   Section 17 of TA 2000.
2   Section 18.

Disclosure

28.24

The concept of 'disclosure' in relation to this area of the law is relevant in two respects.

The offence of non-disclosure

28.25

Section 330 of POCA 2002 applies to information received in the course of business in the regulated sector, and therefore applies to solicitors who are relevant persons for the purposes of MLR 2017. The corresponding non-disclosure offence in respect of terrorist funding is found in section 21A of TA 2000. It is a criminal offence for a person to fail to disclose information received in those circumstances where that person knows or suspects or has reasonable grounds to know or suspect that another person is involved in money laundering or terrorist funding, and is either able to identify the person concerned, or the whereabouts of any of the laundered property, or believes (or can reasonably be expected to believe) that the information will or may assist in identifying the person or the whereabouts of laundered property.

The information required to be disclosed is the identity of the person concerned if known, the whereabouts of the laundered property, so far as known, and any information leading to the identification of the person or location of the property.

Non-disclosure, tipping-off or otherwise prejudicing the course of an investigation (see further at **28.33–28.35**) are referred to as secondary offences.

It will have been noted that by introducing the concept of having 'reasonable grounds for knowing or suspecting', an objective test is applied. In the regulated sector you may be guilty of the offence under section 330 or section 331 if you should have known or suspected money laundering was taking place.

Where a solicitor has the relevant knowledge, suspicion or reasonable grounds to suspect, he or she should make a disclosure to their legal practice's nominated officer (often known as a MLRO) to avoid committing this offence.

Once the nominated officer receives such a disclosure, if he or she has the relevant knowledge, suspicion or reasonable grounds to suspect, the officer must make a disclosure to the NCA, in order to avoid committing an offence under section 331 of POCA 2002. This obligation is subject to considerations regarding privilege, see **28.30**.

If a nominated officer acting outside the regulated sector similarly has the relevant knowledge or suspicion, he or she too must make a disclosure to NCA, in order to avoid committing an offence under section 332 of POCA 2002. Again, this obligation is subject to considerations regarding privilege, see **28.30**.

Authorised disclosure – a defence

28.26

If a person is involved in an arrangement such as would be caught by section 328 of POCA 2002 (or would otherwise be dealing with criminal property contrary to section 327 or 329), it is a defence to make an authorised disclosure, and a solicitor in this position does not commit an offence of money laundering despite carrying through the transaction to completion if, having made proper disclosure, he or she is given 'appropriate consent' to continue to act. It is essential that all the statutory requirements are met. Such appropriate consent will not be a defence to any complicity in the underlying offence, such as fraud.

Timing

28.27

To constitute an authorised disclosure sufficient to amount to a defence for someone who has become involved in an activity prohibited by sections 327 to 329 of POCA 2002, disclosure must be made as soon as practicable after the information or other matter on which his or her knowledge or suspicion (or reasonable grounds for such knowledge or suspicion) was acquired.

Disclosure should be made *before* a prohibited act takes place.[1]

If disclosure is made *during* the prohibited act the solicitor must have had no relevant knowledge or suspicion when the act was started; the disclosure must be made as soon as practicable after relevant knowledge or suspicion was acquired; and the disclosure must be made on the solicitor's own initiative (that is, not for example prompted by the realisation of imminent discovery or the encouragement of another). The burden of proof will be on the accused to satisfy the court that these conditions are met, otherwise the disclosure is not an authorised disclosure and no defence is available.[2]

If disclosure is made *after* the prohibited act has taken place there must have been good reason why a disclosure was not made before the prohibited act was carried out; the disclosure must have been made as soon as practicable after the prohibited act has taken place; and the disclosure must have been made on the solicitor's own initiative. Again, the burden of proof will be on the accused to satisfy the court that these conditions are met, otherwise the disclosure is not an authorised disclosure and no defence is available.[3]

1   Section 338(2) of POCA 2002.
2   Section 338(2A).
3   Section 338(3).

Making the report

28.28

For individual solicitors an internal report may be made in any form and manner designed by the firm (there is no statutory requirement as to this) to the firm's nominated officer. Once such a report is made the reporting solicitor has no further responsibility and the onus is on the nominated officer to consider the information and, if required, to make disclosure to NCA. Because of the complicated considerations around privilege, the potential civil and criminal liability for continuing with a retainer even where consent has been given, and the need to manage different stakeholder expectations if consent is refused, it is best practice for the nominated officer or a designated deputy to make the report to NCA.

NCA has removed the need to complete and post or fax paper-based forms or other existing certification processes and reports are now primarily made online to the NCA website which is self-explanatory and very user friendly. It remains possible to submit a manual report but the website warns that it may take longer to process.

Nominated officers intending to make a report are well advised to consult the UK Financial Intelligence Unit's 'Guidance on Submitting Better Quality Suspicious Activity Reports (SARs)' updated periodically. Version 6 was published in September 2021 and contains guidance on the suspicious activity reports (SARs) regime, how to structure a SAR and tips and examples demonstrating good practice.

The more onerous responsibilities falling on nominated officers are beyond the scope of this chapter.

'Appropriate consent' to further action

28.29

In general terms, once a disclosure has been made, the disclosing party can take no further action until consent is obtained. A nominated officer may give consent, but only if he or she has obtained consent from NCA or certain time limits have expired. In reality, in a firm of solicitors, further action is determined exclusively by the reaction of NCA.[1]

There are three possibilities:

(1)   NCA may give consent to the transaction continuing.

(2)   If NCA does not reply refusing consent within seven working days starting with the first working day after disclosure is made, this is treated as appropriate consent.

(3)   NCA may reply within the same period refusing consent. This imposes a moratorium on further action which lasts for 31 days starting with the day on which notice of refusal of consent is given. If the moratorium expires without any further action being taken by NCA this is treated as appropriate consent.

The delay could of course cause prejudice to clients, and although compliance with the statutory obligation would be a defence to any claim, solicitors may be required ultimately to justify the suspicion that prompted the report and caused the delay.[2]

1   Sections 335 and 336 of POCA 2002.
2   *Shah v HSBC Private Bank (UK) Ltd* [2010] EWCA Civ 31.

Disclosure, confidentiality and privilege

28.30

The disclosure offences under sections 330 to 332 of POCA 2002 and section 21A of TA 2000 specifically exclude any obligation to disclose information received in privileged circumstances.[1] The phrase 'privileged circumstances' is a term of art defined in section 330(10) of POCA 2002 and section 21A(8) of TA 2000 and is not identical with legal professional privilege. However, the two are closely linked concepts.

As noted above, the Court of Appeal held in *Bowman v Fels* that litigation did not involve an arrangement for the purposes of sections 327 to 329 of POCA 2002. It was also held that the giving of legal advice (other than where the crime/fraud exception applies) did not constitute an arrangement and did not itself give rise to any duty of disclosure.[2]

1 Section 330(6), (7B), (10) of POCA 2002; section 21A(5) of TA 2000.
2 *Bowman v Fels* [2005] EWCA Civ 226, [2005] 1 WLR 3083, [2005] 4 All ER 609 at [63].

28.31

Solicitors must keep the affairs of clients and former clients confidential except where disclosure is required or permitted by law,[1] but confidentiality and privilege are not synonymous, and confidentiality is overridden by the statutory duties of disclosure here being considered. The duties of disclosure are express duties imposed by statute and an authorised disclosure 'is not to be taken to breach any restriction on the disclosure of information (however imposed)'.[2]

Not all confidential information is covered by legal professional privilege, the ambit of which is quite narrow. Legal advice privilege covers all communications made in confidence between solicitors and their clients for the purpose of giving or obtaining legal advice. It does not matter whether the communication is directly between the client and his legal adviser or is made through an intermediate agent of either.[3]

Litigation privilege covers oral or written communications between a person or his lawyer (on the one hand) and third parties (on the other) or other documents created by or on behalf of the client or his lawyer, which came into existence once litigation is in contemplation or has commenced, and which came into existence for the dominant purpose of obtaining information or advice in connection with, or of conducting or aiding in the conduct of, such litigation (for example, obtaining evidence to be used in litigation or information which might lead to such evidence).[4]

A characteristic of litigation privilege is that it involves dealings between a lawyer and a third party (such as a potential witness). The characteristic of legal advice privilege is that it always relates to dealings between solicitor and client.

As has already been seen, litigation will not be likely to engage any of the primary offences.

Legal advice privilege is, expressly, limited to communications 'for the purposes of giving or obtaining legal advice'. Privilege does not attach to documents which are the products of legal advice. If one considers a typical property purchase (something that could readily engage money laundering concerns), the conveyancing documents and records of the financing of the transaction are not the subject of legal professional privilege, whereas correspondence between solicitor and client is privileged if directly related to the performance of the solicitor's professional duties as legal adviser.[5]

1 Paragraph 6.3 of the SRA Code of Conduct for Solicitors, RELs and RFLs 2019 and paragraph 6.3 of the SRA Code of Conduct for Firms 2019 (the 'Code for Firms'): see **4.102**.
2 Sections 337(4A) and 338(4) of POCA 2002; see also section 21B(1) of TA 2000.
3 *Three Rivers District Council v Governor and Company of the Bank of England (No 6)* [2005] 1 AC 610 at [50].
4 *Three Rivers District Council v Governor and Company of the Bank of England (No 6)* [2005] 1 AC 610 at [102].
5 *R v Inner London Crown Court, ex p Baines* [1988] 1 QB 579, [1988] 2 WLR 549, [1987] 3 All ER 1025; and see *Three Rivers District Council v Governor and Company of the Bank of England (No 6)* [2005] 1 AC 610 at [111].

Law Society guidance on disclosure

28.32

In short, legal professional privilege in both its limbs – litigation privilege and legal advice privilege – overrides the duty to disclose. The LSAG guidance offers valuable further guidance at paragraph 13.3.1 in the following terms:

'13.3.1 Legal Advice Privilege (LAP)

Principle

Communications, whether written or oral, between a legal professional (acting in their capacity as a legal professional) and a client/the client's agent for the purpose of that communication, are privileged if they are both:

- confidential; and

- for the dominant purpose of seeking legal advice and legal assistance from a legal professional or providing it to a client.

Scope

Communications are not privileged merely because a client is speaking or writing to you. The protection applies only to those communications which directly seek or provide advice (or are part of what the Court of Appeal in *Balabel v Air India* called the "continuum of communications" resulting from seeking that advice) or are given in a legal context, that involve the legal professional using their legal skills and which are directly related to the performance of the legal professional's professional duties. The Court of Appeal summarised the key points in Balabel as follows:

> "… once a legal context is established, LAP applies, not just to those communications which expressly seek or give legal advice, but also to the 'continuum of communications' between a lawyer and client aimed at 'keeping both informed so that advice may be sought and given as required".

Advice within a transaction

All communications between a legal professional and his or her client relating to a transaction in which the legal professional has been instructed for the purpose of obtaining legal advice are covered by advice privilege, notwithstanding that they do not contain advice on matters of law and construction, provided that they are directly related to the performance by the legal professional of their professional duty as legal adviser of his or her client [*Three Rivers District Council and others v the Bank of England* [2004] UKHL 48 at 111].

This means that where you are providing legal advice in a transactional matter (such as a conveyance) the advice privilege will cover all:

- communications with,
- instructions from, and
- advice given to

the client, including any working papers and drafts prepared, if they are directly related to your performance of your professional duties as a legal adviser in providing legal advice. However, there is a limitation in that the fruits of that advice, such as a draft contract, lease, or conveyance will not be covered by LPP unless draft would reveal, or provide an indication, as to the nature of the legal advice itself. [Fruits of advice limitation?]

It is important to keep in mind four principles when deciding whether legal advice privilege applies:

14. The retainer of the lawyer must be reviewed. When a lawyer is consulted by a client, there is likely to be a relevant legal context defined in the retainer letter or terms of engagement. Whilst it is not conclusive, it does give a steer as to the nature of the legal context and the exchanges between lawyer and client for the purpose of legal advice.

15. As a result of the decision in Three Rivers (No 5) it is necessary to be clear as to the identity of the corporate client (i.e., clarify which employees are considered to be 'the client') to trigger the claim to LPP.

16. The definition of legal advice is drawn in quite a wide frame and, as established in *Balabel v Air India*, it extends to "what should reasonably and sensibly be done in a relevant legal context." In such a context, most exchanges, passing between client and lawyer will include advice on an issue from a legal perspective. That includes, as Taylor L.J. pointed out in Balabel 'Where information is passed by the solicitor or client to the other as part of the continuum aimed at keeping each other both informed so that advice may be sought and given as required, privilege will attach'.

17. The precise document, or the oral exchange, should be reviewed, not in isolation but in in light of the relevant legal context. This approach was reiterated recently as follows: "In considering whether a document is covered by LAP, the breadth of the concepts of legal advice and

continuum of communications must be taken into account" There will always be a problem in the "marginal cases where the answer is not easy," and where the relevant legal context is not clear.

13.3.2 Litigation privilege

Principle

This privilege, which is wider than legal advice privilege since it extends to communications with third parties, protects confidential communications made after litigation has started, or when it is reasonably in prospect, between any of the following:

- a legal professional and a client.
- a legal professional and an agent, whether or not that agent is a legal professional; or
- a legal professional and a third party.
- a client and a third party.

These communications must be for the sole or dominant purpose of litigation, for any of the following:

- for seeking or giving advice in relation to it.
- for obtaining evidence to be used in it; or
- for obtaining information leading to obtaining such evidence

13.3.3 Important points to consider across Legal Advice and Litigation Privilege

An original document not brought into existence for these privileged purposes and so not already privileged, very rarely becomes privileged merely by being given to a legal professional for advice or other privileged purpose. See *CAA v R(Jet2.com)* at para100 (vii).

It is important to note that where a communication, although not itself created for the purpose of seeking or providing legal advice, might realistically disclose either the advice sought or given, that communication may nevertheless be privileged: *CAA v R (Jet2.com)* at para 107. (for example, a summary of legal advice made for a board meeting).

Further, in connection with LAP, where you have a corporate client, communication between you and the employees of a corporate client may not be protected by LPP if the employee cannot be considered to be 'the client' for the purposes of the retainer. As such, some employees will be clients, while others will not. [*Three Rivers District Council v the Governor and Company of the Bank of England (no 5)* [2003] QB 1556] and more recently, *Director of the Serious Fraud Office v Eurasian Natural Resources Corporation Limited* [2018] EWCA Civ 2006. In a corporate context, particularly where in-house lawyers are involved, the privilege attached to a communication between lawyer and client may be inadvertently lost if dissemination occurs internally between a lawyer and those who would not be regarded as 'the client'. This is especially the case where the dissemination is widespread and by e-mail or other forms of electronic communication.

It is not a breach of LPP to discuss a matter with your nominated officer for the purposes of receiving advice on whether to make a disclosure.

13.4 Crime/fraud or iniquity exception

LPP protects advice you give to a client on avoiding committing a crime [*Bullivant v Att-Gen of Victoria* [1901]AC 196] or warning them that proposed actions could attract prosecution [*Butler v Board of Trade* [1971] Ch 680].

LPP does not extend to documents which themselves form part of a criminal or fraudulent act, or communications which take place in order to obtain advice with the intention of carrying out an offence [*R v Cox & Railton* (1884) 14 QBD 153].

The iniquity exception can occur in both a civil context and does not, necessarily, involve the commission of a criminal offence. For instance, see further examples in *Dubai Aluminium Co Ltd v Al Alawi* [2005] Civ 286 (attempt to cover up fraud in civil proceedings); *Kuwait Airways Corp v Iraqi Airways Co* [2005] EWCA Civ 286 (invented alibi). In *BBGP Managing General Partner Ltd & Brown Global Partners* [2010] EWHC 2176 (Ch), Norris, J stated as follows:

> "the wrongdoer has gone beyond conduct which merely amounts to a civil wrong: he has indulged in sharp practice, something of an underhand nature where the circumstances required good faith."

In *Barrowfen v Patel & others* [2020] EWHC 2536 (Ch) the judge stated that

> "It is well-established that the exception is not confined to crime or fraudulent misrepresentation but extends to fraud 'in a relatively wide sense': see *Barclays Bank plc v Eustice*."

In *Barrowfen*, alleged breaches of the duties of a director under the Companies Act 2006 came within the iniquity exception,

> "By analogy with BBGP I consider that the iniquity exception is engaged where breaches of sections 172 to 175 and 177 of the Companies Act 2006 are alleged against a director and the allegations involve fraud, dishonesty, bad faith or sharp practice or where the director consciously or deliberately prefers his or her own interests over the interests of the company and does so 'under a cloak of secrecy'".

It is irrelevant whether you are aware that you are being used for that purpose [*Banque Keyser Ullman v Skandia* [1986] 1 Lloyds Rep 336].

The crime/fraud exception is, essentially, a negation of LPP rather than an exception to it. LPP simply cannot attach as it is an abuse of the usual professional relationship between lawyer and client.

"The deception of the solicitors, and therefore the abuse of the normal solicitor/client relationship, will often be the hallmark of iniquity which negates the privilege." Popplewell, J JSC *BTA Bank v Ablyazov* [2014] EWHC 2788 (Comm) para 93.'

Further, information obtained on disclosure of documents in litigation which gives rise to a relevant suspicion about the opposing party, but which is subject to the implied undertaking that the documents may not be used for any purpose other than the conduct of the litigation, is not subject to any duty of disclosure.[1]

But as privileged material is excluded from the duty of disclosure it is important to understand what is, and what is not, covered by legal professional privilege.

1   *Bowman v Fels* [2005] 4 All ER 609, [2005] EWCA Civ 226 at [89].

Other offences

28.33

Other secondary offences relevant to solicitors involve tipping-off or otherwise prejudicing the course of an investigation.

Tipping-off

28.34

It is an offence if a person discloses (other than in strictly limited circumstances) that a disclosure has been made under section 337 or 338 if it is likely to prejudice any investigation that might be conducted following the disclosure, and if the information came to the person in the course of business in the regulated sector.[1]

It is an offence if a person discloses that an investigation into allegations that an offence has been committed under Part 7 of POCA 2002 is being contemplated or carried out, if the disclosure is likely to prejudice that investigation and the information came to the person in the course of business in the regulated sector.[2]

It is *not* an offence if a professional legal adviser makes the disclosure to a client and it is made for the purposes of dissuading the client from committing an offence.[3] It is a defence if the person making the disclosure does not know or suspect that disclosure is likely to prejudice any investigation.[4]

1   Section 333A(1) and (2) of POCA 2002. The circumstances in which disclosure may be made are set out in sections 333B, 333C and 333D of POCA 2002 and relate, in summary, to disclosures within the same organisation; between financial organisations and legal professionals in relation to a client or transaction common to both parties, if the purpose is only to prevent an offence being committed; and to disclosures to the authorities with a view to the detection, investigation or prosecution of offences.
2   Section 333A(3) of POCA 2002.
3   Section 333D(2).
4   Section 333D(3) and (4).

Prejudicing an investigation

28.35

It is an offence if a person outside the regulated sector who knows or suspects that a relevant investigation[1] is being conducted or is about to be conducted makes a disclosure that is likely to prejudice an investigation, or if that person falsifies, conceals, destroys or otherwise disposes of documents that are relevant to any investigation, or causes any of the above to take place. An investigation for these purposes is a confiscation investigation, a civil recovery investigation or a money laundering investigation.[2]

It is a defence if a disclosure is made by a legal adviser to a client, or a client's representative, in connection with the giving of legal advice or to any person in connection with legal proceedings or contemplated legal proceedings. However, this defence will not apply if the disclosure is made with the intention of furthering a criminal purpose.

1 Section 342(1) of POCA 2002. The various kinds of investigations are defined in section 341.
2 Section 342(2)(a) and (b).

Law Society guidance on tipping-off and prejudicing an investigation

28.36

The LSAG guidance contains helpful guidance at paragraphs 16.8–16.12:

> **'16.8 Tipping off Offences**
>
> Since 2007, s333A POCA has contained two offences for tipping off. There are also tipping off offences for terrorist property in the Terrorism Act, discussed in Section 17.
>
> *16.8.1 Tipping off – in the regulated sector*
>
> There are two tipping off offences in s333A of POCA. They apply only to businesses in the regulated sector.
>
> *16.8.1.2 Section 333A(1) – disclosing a suspicious activity report (SAR)*
>
> It is an offence to disclose to a third person that an internal or external SAR has been made by any person to the police, HM Revenue and Customs, the NCA or a nominated officer, if that disclosure might prejudice any investigation that might be carried out as a result of the SAR. This offence can only be committed:
>
> - after a SAR is made or a disclosure is made to the NCA;
> - if you know or suspect that by disclosing this information, you are likely to prejudice any investigation related to that SAR; and

- the information upon which the disclosure is based came to you in the course of business in the regulated sector.

16.8.1.3 Section 333A(3) – disclosing an investigation

It is an offence to disclose the fact that an investigation into a money laundering offence is being contemplated or carried out if that disclosure is likely to prejudice that investigation. The offence can only be committed if the information on which the disclosure is based came to the person in the course of business in the regulated sector, and it is known a law enforcement investigation is being contemplated or is underway.

The key point is that you can commit this offence, even when you are unaware that a SAR was submitted.

16.9 Prejudicing an investigation

S342(1) contains an offence to prejudice a confiscation, civil recovery or money laundering investigation, if the person making the disclosure knows or suspects that an investigation is being, or is about to be, conducted. S342(1) applies to those outside the regulated sector as well as those within the regulated sector.

You only commit this offence if you knew or suspected that the disclosure would, or would be likely to, prejudice any investigation.

16.10 Defences

16.10.1 Tipping off

The following disclosures are permitted:

- s333B – disclosures within an undertaking or group, including disclosures to a professional legal adviser or relevant professional adviser;
- s333C – disclosures between institutions, including disclosures from a professional legal adviser to another professional legal adviser;
- s333D – disclosures to your supervisory authority; and
- s333D(2) – disclosures made by professional legal advisers to their clients for the purpose of dissuading them from engaging in criminal conduct.

A person does not commit the main tipping off offence if he or she does not know or suspect that a disclosure is likely to prejudice an investigation.

16.10.2 Section 333B – disclosures within an undertaking or group etc.

It is not an offence if an employee, officer or partner of a practice discloses that a SAR has been made if it is to an employee, officer or partner of the same undertaking. A legal professional will not commit a tipping off offence if:

CHAPTER 28
MONEY LAUNDERING

- the disclosure is to a professional legal adviser or a relevant professional adviser;

- both the person making the disclosure and the person to whom it is made carry on business in an EEA [European Economic Area] state or in a country or territory imposing equivalent money laundering requirements; and

- those persons perform their professional activities within different undertakings that share common ownership, management or control.

16.10.3 Section 333C – disclosures between institutions etc.

A legal professional will not commit a tipping off offence if all the following criteria are met:

- The disclosure is made to another legal professional in an EEA state, or one with an equivalent AML regime;

- The disclosure relates to a client or former client of both parties, or a transaction involving them both, or the provision of a service involving them both;

- The disclosure is made for the purpose of preventing a money laundering offence; and

- Both parties have equivalent professional duties of confidentiality and protection of personal data.

16.10.4 Section 333D(2) – limited exception for professional legal advisers

A legal professional will not commit a tipping off offence if the disclosure is to a client and it is made for the purpose of dissuading the client from engaging in conduct amounting to an offence. This exception and the tipping off offence in s333A apply to those carrying on activities in the regulated sector.

16.11 Section 342(4) – professional legal adviser exemption

It is a defence to a s342(1) offence that a disclosure is made by a legal adviser to a client, or a client's representative, in connection with the giving of legal advice or to any person in connection with legal proceedings or contemplated legal proceedings. Such a disclosure will not be exempt if it is made with the intention of furthering a criminal purpose (s342(5)).

16.12 Making enquiries of a client

You should make preliminary enquiries of your client, or a third party, to obtain further information to help you to decide whether you have a suspicion. You may also need to raise questions during a retainer to clarify such issues.

There is nothing in POCA which prevents you making normal enquiries about your client's instructions, and the proposed retainer, in order to remove any concerns and enable the practice to decide whether to take on or continue the retainer. These enquiries will only be tipping off if:

- you disclose that you have already made a SAR or that a money laundering investigation is being carried out or contemplated; and

- those enquiries are likely to prejudice any subsequent investigation.

It is not tipping-off to include a paragraph about your obligations under the money laundering legislation in your practice's standard client care letter.'

Data protection

29.1

This chapter provides a brief introduction to the important and complex subject of data protection, specific guidance on aspects of the Data Protection Act (DPA) 2018 as it relates to solicitors, and some commentary on the interaction between confidentiality, privilege and data protection. It does not provide an all-encompassing guide to the subject, which is beyond the scope of this book. The focus in this chapter is on the regulation of solicitors and key obligations arising under the General Data Protection (UK GDPR)[1] as modified to apply in the UK by DPA 2018. The UK GDPR came into force on 25 May 2018.

Solicitors should be aware of the modifications to the express wording of the UK GDPR contained within DPA 2018 and should be careful to consider both the UK GDPR and DPA 2018 as a collective whole, since modifications made by DPA 2018 are of particular importance in the provision of legal services.

The UK GDPR and DPA 2018 contain a number of criminal offences relating to the misuse of personal data and give the Information Commissioner's Office (ICO) the power to impose potentially significant penalties for data breaches.

1   Regulation (EU) 2016/679 of the European Parliament and of the Council of 27 April 2016 on the protection of natural persons with regard to the processing of personal data and on the free movement of such data, and repealing Directive 95/46/EC (General Data Protection Regulation).

Protected data

29.2

The essential purpose of the UK GDPR and DPA 2018 is to give individuals greater control of, and access to, the information organisations hold about them. Solicitors and other legal services providers hold significant amounts of personal data for various reasons. 'Personal data' as protected by the UK GDPR and DPA 2018 is defined in article 4 of the UK GDPR as:

> 'any information relating to an identified or identifiable natural person ("data subject"); an identifiable natural person is one who can be identified, directly or indirectly, in particular by reference to an identifier such as a name, an identification number, location data, an online identifier or to one or more factors specific to the physical, physiological, genetic, mental, economic, cultural or social identity of that natural person'.

Solicitors will hold such information about a variety of individuals for various purposes – as employer, service provider, service user and regulated entity. The scope of the UK GDPR extends to all such information processed electronically in whole or in part and any such data processed other than by automated means which form or are intended to form part of a filing system.[1]

1   Article 2 of the UK GDPR.

Processing

29.3

Processing is defined as:

> 'any operation or set of operations which is performed on personal data or on sets of personal data, whether or not by automated means, such as collection, recording, organisation, structuring, storage, adaptation or alteration, retrieval, consultation, use, disclosure by transmission, dissemination or otherwise making available, alignment or combination, restriction, erasure or destruction'.[1]

The definition of processing is intentionally wide. Simply the act of storing personal data amounts to processing and must be permissible within the ambit of the UK GDPR. Processing of personal data in accordance with the UK GDPR must be justifiable on one or more of the grounds set out in article 6 of the UK GDPR. These are:

(a)   the data subject has given consent to the processing of his or her personal data for one or more specific purposes;[2]

(b)   processing is necessary for the performance of a contract to which the data subject is party or in order to take steps at the request of the data subject prior to entering into a contract;

(c)   processing is necessary for compliance with a legal obligation to which the controller is subject;

(d)   processing is necessary in order to protect the vital interests of the data subject or of another natural person;

(e)   processing is necessary for the performance of a task carried out in the public interest or in the exercise of official authority vested in the controller; and

(f)   processing is necessary for the purposes of the legitimate interests pursued by the controller or by a third party, except where such interests are overridden by the interests or fundamental rights and freedoms of the data subject which require protection of personal data, in particular where the data subject is a child.

1   Article 4 of the UK GDPR.
2   Article 6(1) of the UK GDPR. Note that consent must be freely given and affirmative (see article 4(11) of the UK GDPR). Consent must also be auditable and can be withdrawn at any time (see article 7 of the UK GDPR).

Special category data

29.4

Article 9 of the UK GDPR contains a prohibition on processing special category data, save in tightly defined specified circumstances. Special category data – broadly similar to the concept of 'sensitive personal data' under DPA 1998 – is defined as:

'personal data revealing racial or ethnic origin, political opinions, religious or philosophical beliefs, or trade union membership, and the processing of genetic data, biometric data for the purpose of uniquely identifying a natural person, data concerning health or data concerning a natural person's sex life or sexual orientation.'[1]

Note that biometric data is included but data relating to criminal convictions is not.

Solicitors are likely to hold special category data about (at least) staff and clients. Firms should be able to demonstrate that processing of such data complies with one or more of the article 6 requirements discussed above *and* falls within the conditions of article 9(2) of the UK GDPR, as modified by Schedule 6 to DPA 2018. These conditions are that:

(a)   the data subject has given explicit consent to the processing of that personal data for one or more specified purposes;

(b)   processing is necessary for the purposes of carrying out the obligations and exercising specific rights of the controller or of the data subject in the field of employment and social security and social protection law in so far as it is authorised by domestic law (see section 10 of DPA 2018) or a collective agreement pursuant to member state law providing for appropriate safeguards for the fundamental rights and the interests of the data subject;

(c)   processing is necessary to protect the vital interests of the data subject or of another natural person where the data subject is physically or legally incapable of giving consent;

(d)   processing is carried out in the course of its legitimate activities with appropriate safeguards by a foundation, association or any other not-for-profit body with a political, philosophical, religious or trade union aim and on condition that the processing relates solely to the members or to former members of the body or to persons who have regular contact with it in connection with its purposes and that the personal data is not disclosed outside that body without the consent of the data subjects;

(e)   processing relates to personal data which is manifestly made public by the data subject;

(f)   processing is necessary for the establishment, exercise or defence of legal claims or whenever courts are acting in their judicial capacity;

(g)   processing is necessary for reasons of substantial public interest and is authorised by domestic law (see section 10 of DPA 2018);

(h)   processing is necessary for the purposes of preventive or occupational medicine, for the assessment of the working capacity of the employee, medical diagnosis, the provision of health or social care or treatment or the management of health or social care systems and services on the basis of domestic law (see section 10 of DPA 2018) or pursuant to contract with a health professional and subject to the conditions and safeguards referred to in article 9.3 of the UK GDPR;

(i)   processing is necessary for reasons of public interest in the area of public health, such as protecting against serious cross-border threats to health or ensuring high standards of quality and safety of health care and of medicinal products or medical devices, on the basis of domestic law (see section 10 of

DPA 2018) which provides for suitable and specific measures to safeguard the rights and freedoms of the data subject, in particular professional secrecy; and

(j)   processing is necessary for archiving purposes in the public interest, scientific or historical research purposes or statistical purposes in accordance with article 89(1) of the UK GDPR (as supplemented by section 19 of DPA 2018) and is authorised by domestic law (see section 10 of DPA 2018).

In practice, the conditions most likely to be relevant to solicitors are: (a) explicit consent; (b) legal obligations relating to employment and social security; (e) public data; (f) pursuit of legal claims; and (g) substantial public interest.[2]

1   Article 9(1) of the UK GDPR.
2   Note that Part 2 of Schedule 1 to DPA 2018 contains additional requirements including that firms relying on this condition have appropriate policy documents in place.

Rights of the data subject

29.5

The UK GDPR extended the rights of data subjects and now provides for the following rights:

(1)   The right to be informed how and why data is processed and for how long it will be kept.[1]

(2)   The right of access – subject access requests must now be complied with within a month and at no cost to the data subject.[2]

(3)   The right to rectification.[3]

(4)   The right to erasure (the right to be forgotten): note that this is a qualified right and its availability will depend on the basis of processing.[4]

(5)   The right to restrict processing – this is also a qualified right and only available in certain circumstances.[5]

(6)   The right to data portability – this right only arises where processing is on the basis of consent or in performance of a contract and conducted electronically. It is, essentially, the right to receive a copy of the data in a usable electronic format.[6]

(7)   The right to object to processing – note that this is an absolute right as it relates to direct marketing and is otherwise qualified and capable of challenge. Data subjects should be given notice of their right to object to processing.[7]

(8)   Rights in relation to automated decision-making and profiling.[8]

1   Articles 13 and 14 of the UK GDPR.
2   See articles 12 and 15 and recitals 63 and 64 of the UK GDPR.
3   See articles 5, 12, 16 and 19 of the UK GDPR.
4   See article 17 of the UK GDPR.
5   See articles 18 and 19 of the UK GDPR.
6   See articles 13 and 20 of the UK GDPR.
7   See article 21 of the UK GDPR.
8   See article 22 of the UK GDPR.

Application to solicitors

29.6

As they relate to legal practices, the extent of the data subject's rights will depend on the nature of the data held and the purposes of the processing, since DPA 2018 contains a number of derogations from these rights. For example, data subjects may have restricted rights in relation to data collected for compliance with anti-money laundering (AML) legislation as it is likely to fall within a number of exemptions set out in Schedule 2 to DPA 2018, principally paragraphs 2(1) and 5(1).

More generally paragraph 19 of Schedule 2 to DPA 2018 contains potentially wide-ranging derogations in respect of information which is subject to legal professional privilege or in respect of which an obligation of confidence is owed to a client.

Further specific exemptions particularly relevant to solicitors are:

- paragraph 2: crime and taxation;
- paragraph 5: processing required by law or in connection with legal proceedings;
- paragraph 10: legal services regulation;
- paragraph 19: legal professional privilege;
- paragraph 20: self-incrimination;
- paragraph 21: corporate finance;
- paragraph 22: management forecasts;
- paragraph 23: negotiations; and
- paragraph 24: confidential references.

29.7

Few of the derogations are absolute and solicitors will need to consider the extent to which a data subject's rights have been curtailed by a relevant derogation. Since the UK GDPR must be construed in line with EU law, any derogations must be narrowly construed as a matter of principle.

The rationale underpinning the numerous derogations and modifications in DPA 2018 is to ensure that rights of access to information are not used in order to circumvent proper regulation and business management or to derail proper legal processes and/or cause harm.

Solicitors need to be aware of the derogations, their applications and limitations in order to ensure that they do not, for example, inadvertently breach client confidentiality by complying with a subject access request which should have been rejected.

29.8

For the most part, firms are likely to be data controllers for the purposes of the UK GDPR and DPA 2018. Firms need to have appropriate policies in place to ensure compliance. It may assist firms to address compliance by reference to categories of data held, to ensure consistency of approach and to mitigate risk. The considerations

CHAPTER 29
DATA PROTECTION

that apply to personal data held on personnel files, for example, are likely different from those that apply to data held on client files and different again from those that apply to marketing databases.

Firms and individual solicitors will also need to be aware of the personal data entrusted to employees (for example, client contact data on personal mobile devices) and ensure that appropriate training is given and policies cover such issues.

Data protection and confidentiality

29.9

Confidentiality and data protection are not synonymous. Confidentiality is a much broader concept. While it may be possible for potential conflicts to arise between professional obligations of confidence and the transparency requirements of the UK GDPR, solicitors can take comfort in the derogations contained in paragraph 19 of Schedule 2 to DPA 2018, which, among other things, restrict data subjects' rights of access to information in respect of which solicitors owe a duty of confidentiality to their clients. This exemption is likely to attach to most information on client files, save for information already in the public domain or in respect of which confidentiality has been waived or lost.

This does not mean, of course, that solicitors are not obliged to comply with notice requirements and subject access requests which relate to information which is not confidential. It will be interesting to see, in due course, how the derogation in paragraph 19 is applied in practice. Construed literally, the derogation appears to provide that there is simply no right for any data subject – including a client – to request any confidential information held on a confidential client file, even his or her own.

This may seem a strange construction; however, clients are plainly entitled to the information on their files through other means and a subject access request would be a singularly inefficient way to obtain information available in any event.

In the absence of any binding guidance on the construction of this derogation, solicitors may need to consider carefully how to approach subject access requests from those against whom a claim of confidentiality could not be maintained. This may be of particular relevance where, for example, the client is a company and a subject access request is made by a director.

29.10

It is conceivable that solicitors could fall into error in a number of ways when considering competing confidentiality and data protection obligations. For example:

(a)   refusing a legitimate subject access request solely on the grounds of confidentiality without considering the proper extent of the statutory derogations from the UK GDPR or failing in some other way to uphold the rights of data subjects due to an unjustifiable over-reliance on confidentiality – this could lead to complaints being made to the ICO by a data subject;

(b)   permitting data subjects too much access to and/or control over personal data held by the firm as a result of failing to take proper account of derogations from the UK GDPR – this could lead to a complaint of breach of confidence if disclosure of information is not required or permitted by law;

(c)   where data is held pursuant to an express or implied undertaking or within a confidentiality ring where the obligation of confidence is not owed to the client but to a third party. Solicitors may need to be particularly astute to record the proper basis for processing personal data to avoid creating conflicts between any contractual or quasi-contractual duties of confidentiality imposed and compliance with the UK GDPR; and

(d)   where clients – or other solicitors – provide material which contains unnecessary or excessive personal data, solicitors may need to consider whether they can properly accept it.

The starting point for solicitors is to understand the nature and extent of data protection obligations and to tie processing of personal data back to appropriate grounds. Embedding a culture of compliance and awareness through training should help to guard against problems arising.

Data protection and privilege

29.11

Solicitors can rely on the derogations in paragraph 19(a) of Schedule 2 to DPA 2018, in respect of subject access requests which impinge on legal professional privilege. Note that material attracting other forms of privilege such as litigation privilege appear to fall outside of the scope of this derogation.

In practice, the derogation under paragraph 19(b) relating to confidential information discussed above is likely to be of more use to solicitors, as it automatically includes material which may be subject to legal professional privilege.

Exporting data

29.12

Solicitors should be aware of how and where data is stored by suppliers and service providers. The UK GDPR imposes restrictions on the transfer of personal data internationally. Following Brexit, reliance on EU adequacy decisions for the purposes of international data transfers was frozen as at 31 December 2020. The UK now has power to issue its own adequacy decisions and to keep the position under review.

The EU issued an adequacy decision in relation to UK data protection rules on 21 June 2021 which is expected to remain in place until 2025. This means that data can be transferred from the UK into the European Economic Area (EEA) without additional safeguards in the majority of cases. Transfers outside the EEA must comply with rules on restricted transfers.

The ICO has issued guidance confirming that putting personal data on a website or on a UK server which may then be accessed in a non-EEA country may be treated as a restricted transfer.

Solicitors wishing to transfer data to non-EEA countries will need to assess the basis of the transfer and consider the following questions:

(1)   Has there been an adequacy decision?

(2)   Is the restricted transfer covered by appropriate safeguards?

(3)   Is there an exception?

The ICO has issued guidance on how to approach each of these questions, including details of adequacy decisions made and detailed information on appropriate safeguards.

Data protection officers

29.13

Most law firms are unlikely to need to appoint a data protection officer (DPO). The UK GDPR requires a DPO to be appointed by (a) public bodies; (b) organisations whose core functions include large-scale regular and systematic monitoring of individuals; and (c) organisations whose core functions include large-scale processing of special category data and data relating to criminal convictions. Firms conducting criminal work and any work which requires access to medical records, biometric data and other special category data will need to assess whether they meet this requirement. The ICO publishes some guidance on what factors will need to be considered but the question is, to a certain extent, a matter of judgement.

If a decision is taken to appoint a DPO, the DPO must be independent, adequately resourced, an expert in data protection and report to the highest level of management. The role will involve acting as the main contact for data subjects and the ICO, and advising on and monitoring compliance.

Reporting data breaches

29.14

The ICO defines a personal data breach as:

> 'a breach of security leading to the accidental or unlawful destruction, loss, alteration, unauthorised disclosure of, or access to, personal data. This includes breaches that are the result of both accidental and deliberate causes. It also means that a breach is more than just about losing personal data.'

Some data breaches trigger an obligation to report to the ICO – within 72 hours where feasible – and to notify data subjects. In deciding whether a breach is reportable, solicitors will need to consider whether and to what extent there is a risk to the rights and freedoms of the data subject arising from the breach. The ICO has detailed checklists on preparing for and responding to data breaches and highlights, in particular recital 85 of the UK GDPR as factors which must be borne in mind when assessing risk:

> 'A personal data breach may, if not addressed in an appropriate and timely manner, result in physical, material or non-material damage to natural

persons such as loss of control over their personal data or limitation of their rights, discrimination, identity theft or fraud, financial loss, unauthorised reversal of pseudonymisation, damage to reputation, loss of confidentiality of personal data protected by professional secrecy or any other significant economic or social disadvantage to the natural person concerned.'

A record should be kept of all data breaches – whether reportable or not – as well as the reasons for deciding whether or not a breach is reportable. Solicitors will need to consider whether the data breach is also a breach of confidentiality or is otherwise reportable to the Solicitors Regulation Authority (SRA) as a serious breach of regulatory arrangements. In practice it is likely that any breach which is reportable to the ICO will also be reportable to the SRA.

A report to the ICO should contain:

- a description of the nature of the personal data breach including, where possible:
  - the categories and approximate number of individuals concerned; and
  - the categories and approximate number of personal data records concerned;
- the name and contact details of the DPO (if your organisation has one) or other contact point where more information can be obtained;
- a description of the likely consequences of the personal data breach; and
- a description of the measures taken, or proposed to be taken, to deal with the personal data breach and, where appropriate, of the measures taken to mitigate any possible adverse effects.

Article 33 of the UK GDPR provides for the eventuality that not all required information may be available within the 72-hour reporting timeframe and allows for information to be provided in stages, provided it is supplied without delay.

CHAPTER 29
DATA PROTECTION

PART 8
Appendices

SRA Principles

[Last updated: 25 November 2019]

SRA Principles

Introduction

The SRA Principles comprise the fundamental tenets of ethical behaviour that we expect all those that we regulate to uphold. This includes all individuals we authorise to provide legal services (solicitors, RELs and RFLs), as well as authorised firms and their managers and employees. For licensed bodies, these apply to those individuals, and the part of the body (where applicable), involved in delivering the services we regulate in accordance with the terms of your licence.

Should the Principles come into conflict, those which safeguard the wider public interest (such as the rule of law, and public confidence in a trustworthy solicitors' profession and a safe and effective market for regulated legal services) take precedence over an individual client's interests. You should, where relevant, inform your client of the circumstances in which your duty to the Court and other professional obligations will outweigh your duty to them.

The Principles and Codes are underpinned by our Enforcement Strategy, which explains in more detail our approach to taking regulatory action in the public interest.

This introduction does not form part of the SRA Principles.

Principles

The principles are as follows:

You act:

1. in a way that upholds the constitutional principle of the rule of law, and the proper administration of justice.

2. in a way that upholds public trust and confidence in the *solicitors'* profession and in legal services provided by *authorised persons*.

3. with independence.

4. with honesty.

5. with integrity.

6. in a way that encourages equality, diversity and inclusion.

7. in the best interests of each *client*.

Supplemental notes

Made by the SRA Board on 30 May 2018.

Made under section 31 of the Solicitors Act 1974, section 9 of the Administration of Justice Act 1985 and section 83 of the Legal Services Act 2007.

SRA Code of Conduct for Solicitors, RELs and RFLs

[Last updated: 25 November 2019]

SRA Code of Conduct for Solicitors, RELs and RFLs

Introduction

The Code of Conduct describes the standards of professionalism that we, the SRA, and the public expect of individuals (solicitors, registered European lawyers and registered foreign lawyers) authorised by us to provide legal services.

They apply to conduct and behaviour relating to your practice, and comprise a framework for ethical and competent practice which applies irrespective of your role or the environment or organisation in which you work (subject to the Overseas Rules which apply to your practice overseas); although paragraphs 8.1 to 8.11 apply only when you are providing your services to the public or a section of the public.

You must exercise your judgement in applying these standards to the situations you are in and deciding on a course of action, bearing in mind your role and responsibilities, areas of practice, and the nature of your clients (which in an in house context will generally include your employer and may include other persons or groups within or outside your employer organisation).

You are personally accountable for compliance with this Code – and our other regulatory requirements that apply to you – and must always be prepared to justify your decisions and actions.

A serious failure to meet our standards or a serious breach of our regulatory requirements may result in our taking regulatory action against you. A failure or breach may be serious either in isolation or because it comprises a persistent or concerning pattern of behaviour. In addition to the regulatory requirements set by us in our Codes, Principles and our rules and regulations, we directly monitor and enforce the requirements relating to referral fees set out in section 56 of the Legal Aid, Sentencing and Punishment of Offenders Act 2012, and provisions relating to anti money laundering and counter terrorist financing, as set out in regulations made by the Treasury as in force from time to time.

All these requirements are underpinned by our Enforcement Strategy. That strategy explains in more detail our views about the issues we consider to be serious, and our approach to taking regulatory action in the public interest.

This introduction does not form part of the SRA Code of Conduct for Solicitors, RELs and RFLs.

Maintaining trust and acting fairly

1.1 You do not unfairly discriminate by allowing your personal views to affect your professional relationships and the way in which you provide your services.

1.2 You do not abuse your position by taking unfair advantage of *clients* or others.

1.3 You perform all *undertakings* given by you, and do so within an agreed timescale or if no timescale has been agreed then within a reasonable amount of time.

1.4 You do not mislead or attempt to mislead your *clients*, the *court* or others, either by your own acts or omissions or allowing or being complicit in the acts or omissions of others (including your *client*).

Dispute resolution and proceedings before courts, tribunals and inquiries

2.1 You do not misuse or tamper with evidence or attempt to do so.

2.2 You do not seek to influence the substance of evidence, including generating false evidence or persuading witnesses to change their evidence.

2.3 You do not provide or offer to provide any benefit to witnesses dependent upon the nature of their evidence or the outcome of the case.

2.4 You only make assertions or put forward statements, representations or submissions to the *court* or others which are properly arguable.

2.5 You do not place yourself in contempt of *court*, and you comply with *court* orders which place obligations on you.

2.6 You do not waste the *court's* time.

2.7 You draw the *court's* attention to relevant cases and statutory provisions, or procedural irregularities of which you are aware, and which are likely to have a material effect on the outcome of the proceedings.

Service and competence

3.1 You only act for *clients* on instructions from the *client*, or from someone properly authorised to provide instructions on their behalf. If you have reason to suspect that the instructions do not represent your *client's* wishes, you do not act unless you have satisfied yourself that they do. However, in circumstances where you have legal authority to act notwithstanding that it is not possible to obtain or ascertain the instructions of your *client*, then you are subject to the overriding obligation to protect your *client's* best interests.

3.2 You ensure that the service you provide to *clients* is competent and delivered in a timely manner.

3.3 You maintain your competence to carry out your role and keep your professional knowledge and skills up to date.

3.4 You consider and take account of your *client's* attributes, needs and circumstances.

3.5 Where you supervise or manage others providing legal services:

(a) you remain accountable for the work carried out through them; and

(b) you effectively supervise work being done for *clients*.

3.6   You ensure that the individuals you manage are competent to carry out their role, and keep their professional knowledge and skills, as well as understanding of their legal, ethical and regulatory obligations, up to date.

Client money and assets

4.1   You properly account to *clients* for any *financial benefit* you receive as a result of their instructions, except where they have agreed otherwise.

4.2   You safeguard money and *assets* entrusted to you by *clients* and others.

4.3   You do not personally hold *client money* save as permitted under regulation 10.2(b)(vii) of the Authorisation of Individuals Regulations, unless you work in an *authorised body*, or in an organisation of a kind *prescribed* under this rule on any terms that may be *prescribed* accordingly.

Business requirements

Referrals, introductions and separate businesses

5.1   In respect of any referral of a *client* by you to another *person*, or of any third party who introduces business to you or with whom you share your *fees*, you ensure that:

(a)   *clients* are informed of any financial or other interest which you or your business or employer has in referring the *client* to another *person* or which an *introducer* has in referring the *client* to you;

(b)   *clients* are informed of any fee sharing arrangement that is relevant to their matter;

(c)   the fee sharing agreement is in writing;

(d)   you do not receive payments relating to a referral or make payments to an *introducer* in respect of *clients* who are the subject of criminal proceedings; and

(e)   any *client* referred by an *introducer* has not been acquired in a way which would breach the *SRA's regulatory arrangements* if the *person* acquiring the *client* were regulated by the *SRA*.

5.2   Where it appears to the *SRA* that you have made or received a *referral fee*, the payment will be treated as a *referral fee* unless you show that the payment was not made as such.

5.3   You only:

(a)   refer, recommend or introduce a *client* to a *separate business*; or

(b)   divide, or allow to be divided, a *client's* matter between you and a *separate business*;

where the *client* has given informed consent to your doing so.

Other business requirements

5.4   You must not be a *manager, employee, member* or *interest holder* of a business that:

(a)   has a name which includes the word "solicitors"; or

(b)   describes its work in a way that suggests it is a *solicitors'* firm;

unless it is an *authorised body*.

5.5   If you are a *solicitor* who holds a practising certificate, an *REL* or *RFL*, you must complete and deliver to the *SRA* an annual return in the *prescribed* form.

5.6   If you are a *solicitor* or an *REL* carrying on *reserved legal activities* in a *non-commercial body*, you must ensure that:

   (a)   the body takes out and maintains indemnity insurance; and

   (b)   this insurance provides adequate and appropriate cover in respect of the services that you provide or have provided, whether or not they comprise *reserved legal activities*, taking into account any alternative arrangements the body or its *clients* may make.

Conflict, confidentiality and disclosure

Conflict of interests

6.1   You do not act if there is an *own interest conflict* or a significant risk of such a conflict.

6.2   You do not act in relation to a matter or particular aspect of it if you have a *conflict of interest* or a significant risk of such a conflict in relation to that matter or aspect of it, unless:

   (a)   the *clients* have a *substantially common interest* in relation to the matter or the aspect of it, as appropriate; or

   (b)   the *clients* are *competing for the same objective*,

   and the conditions below are met, namely that:

   (i)   all the *clients* have given informed consent, given or evidenced in writing, to you acting;

   (ii)   where appropriate, you put in place effective safeguards to protect your *clients'* confidential information; and

   (iii)   you are satisfied it is reasonable for you to act for all the *clients*.

Confidentiality and disclosure

6.3   You keep the affairs of current and former *clients* confidential unless disclosure is required or permitted by law or the *client* consents.

6.4   Where you are acting for a *client* on a matter, you make the *client* aware of all information material to the matter of which you have knowledge, except when:

   (a)   the disclosure of the information is prohibited by legal restrictions imposed in the interests of national security or the prevention of crime;

   (b)   your *client* gives informed consent, given or evidenced in writing, to the information not being disclosed to them;

   (c)   you have reason to believe that serious physical or mental injury will be caused to your *client* or another if the information is disclosed; or

   (d)   the information is contained in a privileged document that you have knowledge of only because it has been mistakenly disclosed.

6.5   You do not act for a *client* in a matter where that *client* has an interest adverse to the interest of another current or former *client* of you or your business or employer, for whom you or your business or employer holds confidential information which is material to that matter, unless:

(a)   effective measures have been taken which result in there being no real risk of disclosure of the confidential information; or

(b)   the current or former *client* whose information you or your business or employer holds has given informed consent, given or evidenced in writing, to you acting, including to any measures taken to protect their information.

Cooperation and accountability

7.1   You keep up to date with and follow the law and regulation governing the way you work.

7.2   You are able to justify your decisions and actions in order to demonstrate compliance with your obligations under the *SRA's regulatory arrangements*.

7.3   You cooperate with the *SRA*, other regulators, ombudsmen, and those bodies with a role overseeing and supervising the delivery of, or investigating concerns in relation to, legal services.

7.4   You respond promptly to the *SRA* and:

(a)   provide full and accurate explanations, information and documents in response to any request or requirement; and

(b)   ensure that relevant information which is held by you, or by third parties carrying out functions on your behalf which are critical to the delivery of your legal services, is available for inspection by the *SRA*.

7.5   You do not attempt to prevent anyone from providing information to the *SRA* or any other body exercising regulatory, supervisory, investigatory or prosecutory functions in the public interest.

7.6   You notify the *SRA* promptly if:

(a)   you are subject to any criminal charge, conviction or caution, subject to the Rehabilitation of Offenders Act 1974;

(b)   a *relevant insolvency event* occurs in relation to you; or

(c)   if you become aware:

(i)   of any material changes to information previously provided to the *SRA*, by you or on your behalf, about you or your practice, including any change to information recorded in the *register*; and

(ii)   that information provided to the *SRA*, by you or on your behalf, about you or your practice is or may be false, misleading, incomplete or inaccurate.

7.7   You report promptly to the *SRA* or another *approved regulator*, as appropriate, any facts or matters that you reasonably believe are capable of amounting to a serious breach of their *regulatory arrangements* by any *person* regulated by them (including you).

7.8   Notwithstanding paragraph 7.7, you inform the *SRA* promptly of any facts or matters that you reasonably believe should be brought to its attention in order that it may investigate whether a serious breach of its *regulatory arrangements* has occurred or otherwise exercise its regulatory powers.

7.9   You do not subject any *person* to detrimental treatment for making or proposing to make a report or providing or proposing to provide information based on a reasonably held belief under paragraph 7.7 or 7.8 above, or paragraph 3.9, 3.10, 9.1(d) or (e) or 9.2(b) or (c) of the SRA Code of Conduct for Firms, irrespective of whether the *SRA* or another *approved regulator* subsequently investigates or takes any action in relation to the facts or matters in question.

7.10   You act promptly to take any remedial action requested by the *SRA*. If requested to do so by the *SRA* you investigate whether there have been any serious breaches that should be reported to the *SRA*.

7.11   You are honest and open with *clients* if things go wrong, and if a *client* suffers loss or harm as a result you put matters right (if possible) and explain fully and promptly what has happened and the likely impact. If requested to do so by the *SRA* you investigate whether anyone may have a claim against you, provide the *SRA* with a report on the outcome of your investigation, and notify relevant persons that they may have such a claim, accordingly.

7.12   Any obligation under this section or otherwise to notify, or provide information to, the *SRA* will be satisfied if you provide information to your firm's *COLP* or *COFA*, as and where appropriate, on the understanding that they will do so.

When you are providing services to the public or a section of the public

Client identification

8.1   You identify who you are acting for in relation to any matter.

Complaints handling

8.2   You ensure that, as appropriate in the circumstances, you either establish and maintain, or participate in, a procedure for handling complaints in relation to the legal services you provide.

8.3   You ensure that *clients* are informed in writing at the time of engagement about:

   (a)   their right to complain to you about your services and your charges;

   (b)   how a complaint can be made and to whom; and

   (c)   any right they have to make a complaint to the *Legal Ombudsman* and when they can make any such complaint.

8.4   You ensure that when *clients* have made a complaint to you, if this has not been resolved to the *client's* satisfaction within 8 weeks following the making of a complaint they are informed, in writing:

   (a)   of any right they have to complain to the *Legal Ombudsman*, the time frame for doing so and full details of how to contact the *Legal Ombudsman*; and

   (b)   if a complaint has been brought and your complaints procedure has been exhausted:

      (i)   that you cannot settle the complaint;

      (ii)   of the name and website address of an alternative dispute resolution (ADR) approved body which would be competent to deal with the complaint; and

      (iii)   whether you agree to use the scheme operated by that body.

8.5   You ensure that complaints are dealt with promptly, fairly, and free of charge.

Client information and publicity

8.6   You give *clients* information in a way they can understand. You ensure they are in a position to make informed decisions about the services they need, how their matter will be handled and the options available to them.

8.7 You ensure that *clients* receive the best possible information about how their matter will be priced and, both at the time of engagement and when appropriate as their matter progresses, about the likely overall cost of the matter and any *costs* incurred.

8.8 You ensure that any *publicity* in relation to your practice is accurate and not misleading, including that relating to your charges and the circumstances in which *interest* is payable by or to *clients*.

8.9 You do not make unsolicited approaches to members of the public, with the exception of current or former *clients*, in order to advertise legal services provided by you, or your business or employer.

8.10 You ensure that *clients* understand whether and how the services you provide are regulated. This includes:

(a) explaining which activities will be carried out by you, as an *authorised person*;

(b) explaining which services provided by you, your business or employer, and any *separate business* are regulated by an *approved regulator*; and

(c) ensuring that you do not represent any business or employer which is not authorised by the *SRA*, including any *separate business*, as being regulated by the SRA.

8.11 You ensure that *clients* understand the regulatory protections available to them.

Supplemental notes

Made by the SRA Board on 30 May 2018.

Made under sections 31 and 32 of the Solicitors Act 1974, section 89 of, and paragraphs 2 and 3 of Schedule 14 to, the Courts and Legal Services Act 1990 and section 57(2) and (8) of the Legal Aid, Sentencing and Punishment of Offenders Act 2012.

APPENDIX 2

SRA Code of Conduct for Firms

[Law Society copyright. For the latest updates to the material, please see www.sra.org.uk.]

[Last updated: November 2019]

SRA Code of Conduct for Firms

Introduction

This Code of Conduct describes the standards and business controls that we, the SRA, and the public expect of firms (including sole practices) authorised by us to provide legal services. These aim to create and maintain the right culture and environment for the delivery of competent and ethical legal services to clients. These apply in the context of your practice: the way you run your business and all your professional activities (subject, if you are a licensed body, to any terms of your licence).

Paragraphs 8.1 and 9.1 to 9.2 set out the requirements of managers and compliance officers in those firms, respectively.

A serious failure to meet our standards or a serious breach of our regulatory requirements may lead to our taking regulatory action against the firm itself as an entity, or its managers or compliance officers, who each have responsibilities for ensuring that the standards and requirements are met. We may also take action against employees working within the firm for any breaches for which they are responsible. A failure or breach may be serious either in isolation or because it comprises a persistent or concerning pattern of behaviour.

In addition to the regulatory requirements set by us in our Codes, Principles and our rules and regulations, we directly monitor and enforce the requirements relating to referral fees set out in section 56 of the Legal Aid, Sentencing and Punishment of Offenders Act 2012, and provisions relating to anti money laundering and counter terrorist financing, as set out in regulations made by the Treasury as in force from time to time.

All of these requirements are underpinned by our Enforcement Strategy, which explains in more detail our views about the issues we consider to be serious, and our approach to taking regulatory action in the public interest.

This introduction does not form part of the SRA Code of Conduct for Firms.

Maintaining trust and acting fairly

1.1   You do not unfairly discriminate by allowing your personal views to affect your professional relationships and the way in which you provide your services.

1.2   You do not abuse your position by taking unfair advantage of *clients* or others.

1.3   You perform all *undertakings* given by you and do so within an agreed timescale or if no timescale has been agreed then within a reasonable amount of time.

1.4   You do not mislead or attempt to mislead your *clients*, the *court* or others, either by your own acts or omissions or allowing or being complicit in the acts or omissions of others (including your *client*).

1.5   You monitor, report and publish workforce diversity data, as *prescribed*.

Compliance and business systems

2.1   You have effective governance structures, arrangements, systems and controls in place that ensure:

   (a)   you comply with all the *SRA's regulatory arrangements*, as well as with other regulatory and legislative requirements, which apply to you;

   (b)   your *managers* and employees comply with the *SRA's regulatory arrangements* which apply to them;

   (c)   your *managers* and *interest holders* and those you employ or contract with do not cause or substantially contribute to a breach of the *SRA's regulatory arrangements* by you or your *managers* or employees;

   (d)   your *compliance officers* are able to discharge their duties under paragraphs 9.1 and 9.2 below.

2.2   You keep and maintain records to demonstrate compliance with your obligations under the *SRA's regulatory arrangements*.

2.3   You remain accountable for compliance with the *SRA's regulatory arrangements* where your work is carried out through others, including your *managers* and those you employ or contract with.

2.4   You actively monitor your financial stability and business viability. Once you are aware that you will cease to operate, you effect the orderly wind-down of your activities.

2.5   You identify, monitor and manage all material risks to your business, including those which may arise from your *connected practices*.

Cooperation and accountability

3.1   You keep up to date with and follow the law and regulation governing the way you work.

3.2   You cooperate with the *SRA*, other regulators, ombudsmen and those bodies with a role overseeing and supervising the delivery of, or investigating concerns in relation to, legal services.

3.3   You respond promptly to the *SRA* and:

   (a)   provide full and accurate explanations, information and documentation in response to any requests or requirements;

   (b)   ensure that relevant information which is held by you, or by third parties carrying out functions on your behalf which are critical to the delivery of your legal services, is available for inspection by the *SRA*.

3.4   You act promptly to take any remedial action requested by the *SRA*.

3.5   You are honest and open with *clients* if things go wrong, and if a *client* suffers loss or harm as a result you put matters right (if possible) and explain fully and promptly what has happened and the likely impact. If requested to do so by the *SRA* you investigate whether anyone may have a claim against you, provide the *SRA* with a report on the outcome of your investigation, and notify relevant persons that they may have such a claim, accordingly.

3.6   You notify the *SRA* promptly:

(a)   of any indicators of serious financial difficulty relating to you;

(b)   if a *relevant insolvency event* occurs in relation to you;

(c)   if you intend to, or become aware that you will, cease operating as a legal business;

(d)   of any change to information recorded in the *register*.

3.7   You provide to the *SRA* an information report on an annual basis or such other period as specified by the *SRA* in the *prescribed* form and by the *prescribed* date.

3.8   You notify the *SRA* promptly if you become aware:

(a)   of any material changes to information previously provided to the *SRA*, by you or on your behalf, about you or your *managers, owners* or *compliance officers*; and

(b)   that information provided to the *SRA*, by you or on your behalf, about you or your *managers, owners* or *compliance officers* is or may be false, misleading, incomplete or inaccurate.

3.9   You report promptly to the *SRA* or another *approved regulator*, as appropriate, any facts or matters that you reasonably believe are capable of amounting to a serious breach of their *regulatory arrangements* by any *person* regulated by them (including you) of which you are aware. If requested to do so by the *SRA* you investigate whether there have been any serious breaches that should be reported to the *SRA*.

3.10   Notwithstanding paragraph 3.9, you inform the *SRA* promptly of any facts or matters that you reasonably believe should be brought to its attention in order that it may investigate whether a serious breach of its *regulatory arrangements* has occurred or otherwise exercise its regulatory powers.

3.11   You do not attempt to prevent anyone from providing information to the *SRA* or any other body exercising regulatory, supervisory, investigatory or prosecutory functions in the public interest.

3.12   You do not subject any *person* to detrimental treatment for making or proposing to make a report or providing, or proposing to provide, information based on a reasonably held belief under paragraph 3.9 or 3.10 above or 9.1(d) or (e) or 9.2(b) or (c) below, or under paragraph 7.7 or 7.8 of the SRA Code of Conduct for Solicitors, RELs and RFLs, irrespective of whether the *SRA* or another *approved regulator* subsequently investigates or takes any action in relation to the facts or matters in question.

Service and competence

4.1   You only act for *clients* on instructions from the *client*, or from someone properly authorised to provide instructions on their behalf. If you have reason to suspect that the instructions do not represent your *client's* wishes, you do not act unless you have satisfied yourself that they do. However, in circumstances where you have legal authority to act notwithstanding that it is not possible to obtain or ascertain the instructions of your *client*, then you are subject to the overriding obligation to protect your *client's* best interests.

4.2   You ensure that the service you provide to *clients* is competent and delivered in a timely manner, and takes account of your *client's* attributes, needs and circumstances.

4.3 You ensure that your *managers* and employees are competent to carry out their role, and keep their professional knowledge and skills, as well as understanding of their legal, ethical and regulatory obligations, up to date.

4.4 You have an effective system for supervising *clients'* matters.

Client money and assets

5.1 You properly account to *clients* for any *financial benefit* you receive as a result of their instructions, except where they have agreed otherwise.

5.2 You safeguard money and *assets* entrusted to you by *clients* and others.

Conflict of interests

6.1 You do not act if there is an *own interest conflict* or a significant risk of such a conflict.

6.2 You do not act in relation to a matter or a particular aspect of it if you have a *conflict of interest* or a significant risk of such a conflict in relation to that matter or aspect of it, unless:

(a) the *clients* have a *substantially common interest* in relation to the matter or the aspect of it, as appropriate; or

(b) the *clients* are *competing for the same objective*,

and the conditions below are met, namely that:

(i) all the *clients* have given informed consent, given or evidenced in writing, to you acting;

(ii) where appropriate, you put in place effective safeguards to protect your *clients'* confidential information; and

(iii) you are satisfied it is reasonable for you to act for all the *clients*.

Confidentiality and disclosure

6.3 You keep the affairs of current and former *clients* confidential unless disclosure is required or permitted by law or the *client* consents.

6.4 Any individual who is acting for a *client* on a matter makes the *client* aware of all information material to the matter of which the individual has knowledge except when:

(a) the disclosure of the information is prohibited by legal restrictions imposed in the interests of national security or the prevention of crime;

(b) the *client* gives informed consent, given or evidenced in writing, to the information not being disclosed to them;

(c) the individual has reason to believe that serious physical or mental injury will be caused to the *client* or another if the information is disclosed; or

(d) the information is contained in a privileged document that the individual has knowledge of only because it has been mistakenly disclosed.

6.5 You do not act for a *client* in a matter where that *client* has an interest adverse to the interest of another current or former *client* for whom you hold confidential information which is material to that matter, unless:

(a) effective measures have been taken which result in there being no real risk of disclosure of the confidential information; or

(b) the current or former *client* whose information you hold has given informed consent, given or evidenced in writing, to you acting, including to any measures taken to protect their information.

Applicable standards in the SRA Code of Conduct for Solicitors, RELs and RFLs

7.1 The following paragraphs in the SRA Code of Conduct for Solicitors, RELs and RFLs apply to you in their entirety as though references to "you" were references to you as a firm:

(a) dispute resolution and proceedings before courts, tribunals and inquiries (2.1 to 2.7);

(b) referrals, introductions and *separate businesses* (5.1 to 5.3); and

(c) standards which apply when providing services to the public or a section of the public, namely client identification (8.1), complaints handling (8.2 to 8.5), and client information and publicity (8.6 to 8.11).

Managers in SRA authorised firms

8.1 If you are a *manager*, you are responsible for compliance by your firm with this Code. This responsibility is joint and several if you share management responsibility with other *managers* of the firm.

Compliance officers

9.1 If you are a *COLP* you must take all reasonable steps to:

(a) ensure compliance with the terms and conditions of your firm's authorisation;

(b) ensure compliance by your firm and its *managers*, employees or *interest holders* with the *SRA's regulatory arrangements* which apply to them;

(c) ensure that your firm's *managers* and *interest holders* and those they employ or contract with do not cause or substantially contribute to a breach of the *SRA's regulatory arrangements*;

(d) ensure that a prompt report is made to the *SRA* of any facts or matters that you reasonably believe are capable of amounting to a serious breach of the terms and conditions of your firm's authorisation, or the *SRA's regulatory arrangements* which apply to your firm, *managers* or employees;

(e) notwithstanding sub-paragraph (d), you ensure that the *SRA* is informed promptly of any facts or matters that you reasonably believe should be brought to its attention in order that it may investigate whether a serious breach of its *regulatory arrangements* has occurred or otherwise exercise its regulatory powers,

save in relation to the matters which are the responsibility of the *COFA* as set out in paragraph 9.2 below.

9.2 If you are a *COFA* you must take all reasonable steps to:

(a) ensure that your firm and its *managers* and employees comply with any obligations imposed upon them under the SRA Accounts Rules;

    (b)   ensure that a prompt report is made to the *SRA* of any facts or matters that you reasonably believe are capable of amounting to a serious breach of the SRA Accounts Rules which apply to them;

    (c)   notwithstanding sub-paragraph (b), you ensure that the *SRA* is informed promptly of any facts or matters that you reasonably believe should be brought to its attention in order that it may investigate whether a serious breach of its *regulatory arrangements* has occurred or otherwise exercise its regulatory powers.

Supplemental notes

Made by the SRA Board on 30 May 2018.

Made under section 31 of the Solicitors Act 1974, section 9 of the Administration of Justice Act 1985, section 83 of the Legal Services Act 2007, and section 57(2) and (8) of the Legal Aid, Sentencing and Punishment of Offenders Act 2012.

SRA Accounts Rules

[Law Society copyright. For the latest updates to the material, please see www.sra.org.uk.]

[Last updated: 25 November 2019]

SRA Accounts Rules

Introduction

These rules set out our requirements for when firms (including sole practices) authorised by us receive or deal with money belonging to clients, including trust money or money held on behalf of third parties. The rules apply to all firms we regulate, including all those who manage or work within such firms.

Firms will need to have systems and controls in place to ensure compliance with these rules and the nature of those systems must be appropriate to the nature and volumes of client transactions dealt with and the amount of client money held or received.

This introduction does not form part of the SRA Accounts Rules.

Part 1: General

Rule 1: Application section

1.1 These rules apply to *authorised bodies*, their *managers* and employees and references to "you" in these rules should be read accordingly.

1.2 The *authorised body's managers* are jointly and severally responsible for compliance by the *authorised body*, its *managers* and employees with these rules.

1.3 In relation to a *licensed body*, the rules apply only in respect of activities regulated by the *SRA* in accordance with the terms of its licence.

Part 2: Client money and client accounts

Rule 2: Client money

2.1 "*Client money*" is money held or received by you:

    (a) relating to *regulated services* delivered by you to a *client*;

    (b) on behalf of a third party in relation to *regulated services* delivered by you (such as money held as agent, stakeholder or held to the sender's order);

(c) as a trustee or as the holder of a specified office or appointment, such as donee of a power of attorney, Court of Protection deputy or trustee of an occupational pension scheme;

(d) in respect of your *fees* and any unpaid *disbursements* if held or received prior to delivery of a bill for the same.

2.2 In circumstances where the only *client money* you hold or receive falls within rule 2.1(d) above, and:

(a) any money held for *disbursements* relates to costs or expenses incurred by you on behalf of your *client* and for which you are liable; and

(b) you do not for any other reason maintain a *client account*;

you are not required to hold this money in a *client account* if you have informed your *client* in advance of where and how the money will be held. Rules 2.3, 2.4, 4.1, 7, 8.1(b) and (c) and 12 do not apply to *client money* held outside of a *client account* in accordance with this rule.

2.3 You ensure that *client money* is paid promptly into a *client account* unless:

(a) in relation to money falling within 2.1(c), to do so would conflict with your obligations under rules or regulations relating to your specified office or appointment;

(b) the *client money* represents payments received from the Legal Aid Agency for your *costs*; or

(c) you agree in the individual circumstances an alternative arrangement in writing with the *client*, or the third party, for whom the money is held.

2.4 You ensure that *client money* is available on demand unless you agree an alternative arrangement in writing with the *client*, or the third party for whom the money is held.

2.5 You ensure that *client money* is returned promptly to the *client*, or the third party for whom the money is held, as soon as there is no longer any proper reason to hold those funds.

Rule 3: Client account

3.1 You only maintain a *client account* at a branch (or the head office) of a *bank* or a *building society* in England and Wales.

3.2 You ensure that the name of any *client account* includes:

(a) the name of the *authorised body*; and

(b) the word "client" to distinguish it from any other type of account held or operated by the *authorised body*.

3.3 You must not use a *client account* to provide banking facilities to *clients* or third parties. Payments into, and transfers or withdrawals from a *client account* must be in respect of the delivery by you of *regulated services*.

Rule 4: Client money must be kept separate

4.1 You keep *client money* separate from money belonging to the *authorised body*.

4.2 You ensure that you allocate promptly any funds from *mixed payments* you receive to the correct *client account* or business account.

4.3 Where you are holding *client money* and some or all of that money will be used to pay your *costs*:

(a)   you must give a bill of *costs*, or other written notification of the *costs* incurred, to the *client* or the paying party;

(b)   this must be done before you transfer any *client money* from a *client account* to make the payment; and

(c)   any such payment must be for the specific sum identified in the bill of *costs*, or other written notification of the *costs* incurred, and covered by the amount held for the particular *client* or third party.

Rule 5: Withdrawals from client account

5.1   You only withdraw *client money* from a *client account*:

(a)   for the purpose for which it is being held;

(b)   following receipt of instructions from the *client*, or the third party for whom the money is held; or

(c)   on the *SRA's* prior written authorisation or in *prescribed* circumstances.

5.2   You appropriately authorise and supervise all withdrawals made from a *client account*.

5.3   You only withdraw *client money* from a *client account* if sufficient funds are held on behalf of that specific *client* or third party to make the payment.

Rule 6: Duty to correct breaches upon discovery

6.1   You correct any breaches of these rules promptly upon discovery. Any money improperly withheld or withdrawn from a *client account* must be immediately paid into the account or replaced as appropriate.

Rule 7: Payment of interest

7.1   You account to *clients* or third parties for a fair sum of *interest* on any *client money* held by you on their behalf.

7.2   You may by a written agreement come to a different arrangement with the *client* or the third party for whom the money is held as to the payment of *interest*, but you must provide sufficient information to enable them to give informed consent.

Rule 8: Client accounting systems and controls

8.1   You keep and maintain accurate, contemporaneous, and chronological records to:

(a)   record in client ledgers identified by the *client's* name and an appropriate description of the matter to which they relate:

(i)   all receipts and payments which are *client money* on the client side of the client ledger account;

(ii)   all receipts and payments which are not *client money* and bills of *costs* including transactions through the *authorised body's* accounts on the business side of the client ledger account;

(b)   maintain a list of all the balances shown by the client ledger accounts of the liabilities to *clients* (and third parties), with a running total of the balances; and

(c)   provide a cash book showing a running total of all transactions through *client accounts* held or operated by you.

8.2   You obtain, at least every five weeks, statements from *banks*, *building societies* and other financial institutions for all *client accounts* and business accounts held or operated by you.

8.3   You complete at least every five weeks, for all *client accounts* held or operated by you, a reconciliation of the *bank* or *building society* statement balance with the cash book balance and the client ledger total, a record of which must be signed off by the *COFA* or a *manager* of the firm. You should promptly investigate and resolve any differences shown by the reconciliation.

8.4   You keep readily accessible a central record of all bills or other written notifications of *costs* given by you.

Part 3: Dealing with other money belonging to clients or third parties

Rule 9: Operation of joint accounts

9.1   If, when acting in a *client's* matter, you hold or receive money jointly with the *client* or a third party, Part 2 of these rules does not apply save for:

(a)   rule 8.2 – statements from *banks*, *building societies* and other financial institutions;

(b)   rule 8.4 – bills and notifications of *costs*.

Rule 10: Operation of a client's own account

10.1   If, in the course of practice, you operate a *client's* own account as signatory, Part 2 of these rules does not apply save for:

(a)   rule 8.2 – statements from *banks*, *building societies* and other financial institutions;

(b)   rule 8.3 – reconciliations;

(c)   rule 8.4 – bills and notifications of *costs*.

Rule 11: Third party managed accounts

11.1   You may enter into arrangements with a *client* to use a *third party managed account* for the purpose of receiving payments from or on behalf of, or making payments to or on behalf of, the *client* in respect of *regulated services* delivered by you to the *client*, only if:

(a)   use of the account does not result in you receiving or holding the *client's* money; and

(b)   you take reasonable steps to ensure, before accepting instructions, that the *client* is informed of and understands:

(i)   the terms of the contractual arrangements relating to the use of the *third party managed account*, and in particular how any *fees* for use of the *third party managed account* will be paid and who will bear them; and

(ii)   the *client's* right to terminate the agreement and dispute payment requests made by you.

11.2   You obtain regular statements from the provider of the *third party managed account* and ensure that these accurately reflect all transactions on the account.

Part 4: Accountants' reports and storage and retention of accounting records

Rule 12: Obtaining and delivery of accountants' reports

12.1 If you have, at any time during an *accounting period*, held or received *client money*, or operated a joint account or a *client's* own account as signatory, you must:

(a) obtain an accountant's report for that *accounting period* within six months of the end of the period; and

(b) deliver it to the *SRA* within six months of the end of the *accounting period* if the accountant's report is qualified to show a failure to comply with these rules, such that money belonging to *clients* or third parties is, or has been, or is likely to be placed, at risk.

12.2 You are not required to obtain an accountant's report if:

(a) all of the *client money* held or received during an *accounting period* is money received from the Legal Aid Agency; or

(b) in the *accounting period*, the statement or passbook balance of *client money* you have held or received does not exceed:

(i) an average of £10,000; and

(ii) a maximum of £250,000,

or the equivalent in foreign currency.

12.3 In rule 12.2 above a "statement or passbook balance" is the total balance of:

(a) all *client accounts* held or operated by you; and

(b) any joint accounts and *clients'* own accounts operated by you,

as shown by the statements obtained under rule 8.2.

12.4 The *SRA* may require you to obtain or deliver an accountant's report to the SRA on reasonable notice if you cease to operate as an *authorised body* and to hold or operate a *client account*, or the *SRA* considers that it is otherwise in the public interest to do so.

12.5 You ensure that any report obtained under this rule is prepared and signed by an accountant who is a member of one of the *chartered accountancy bodies* and who is, or works for, a registered auditor.

12.6 The *SRA* may disqualify an accountant from preparing a report for the purposes of this rule if:

(a) the accountant has been found guilty by their professional body of professional misconduct or equivalent; or

(b) the *SRA* is satisfied that the accountant has failed to exercise due care and skill in the preparation of a report under these rules.

12.7 The *SRA* may specify from time to time matters that you must ensure are incorporated into the terms on which an accountant is engaged.

12.8 You must provide to an accountant preparing a report under these rules:

(a) details of all accounts held or operated by you in connection with your practice at any *bank*, *building society* or other financial institution at any time during the *accounting period* to which the report relates; and

(b) all other information and documentation that the accountant requires to enable completion of their report.

12.9 The accountant must complete and sign their report in the *prescribed* form.

Rule 13: Storage and retention of accounting records

13.1   You must store all *accounting records* securely and retain these for at least six years.

Supplemental notes

Made by the SRA Board on 30 May 2018.

Made under sections 32, 33A, 34, 37 of the Solicitors Act 1974, section 9 of the Administration of Justice Act 1985, and section 83(5)(h) of, and paragraph 20 of Schedule 11 to, the Legal Services Act 2007.

SRA Transparency Rules

[Last updated: 25 November 2019]

SRA Transparency Rules

Introduction

These rules set out the information authorised firms, and individuals providing services to the public from outside authorised firms, should make available to clients and potential clients.

The rules aim to ensure people have accurate and relevant information about a solicitor or firm when they are considering purchasing legal services and will help members of the public and small businesses make informed choices, improving competition in the legal market.

This introduction does not form part of the SRA Transparency Rules.

Rule 1: Costs information

1.1 An *authorised body*, or an individual practising in the circumstances set out in regulation 10.2(b)(i) to (vii) of the SRA Authorisation of Individuals Regulations, who publishes as part of its usual business the availability of any of the services set out at rule 1.3 to individuals or at rule 1.4 to businesses, must, in relation to those services, publish on its website cost information in accordance with rule 1.5 and 1.6.

1.2 Rule 1.1 does not apply to publicly funded work.

1.3 The services in relation to individuals are:

    (a) the conveyance of residential real property or real estate which comprise:

        (i) freehold or leasehold sales or purchases; or

        (ii) mortgages or re-mortgages;

    (b) the collection and distribution of *assets* belonging to a person following their death, where these are within the *UK* and the matters are not contested;

    (c) the preparation and submission of immigration applications, excluding asylum applications;

    (d) the provision of advice and representation at the First-tier Tribunal (Immigration and Asylum Chamber) in relation to appeals against Home Office visa or immigration decisions, excluding asylum appeals;

(e)   the provision of advice and representation at the Magistrates Court in relation to summary only road traffic offences dealt with at a single hearing;

(f)   the provision of advice and representation to employees in relation to the bringing of claims before the Employment Tribunal against an employer for unfair dismissal or wrongful dismissal.

1.4   The services in relation to businesses are:

(a)   the provision of advice and representation to employers in relation to defending claims before the Employment Tribunal brought by an employee for unfair dismissal or wrongful dismissal;

(b)   debt recovery up to the value of £100,000;

(c)   the provision of advice and assistance and representation in relation to licensing applications for business premises.

1.5   Costs information must include:

(a)   the total cost of the service or, where not practicable, the average cost or range of costs;

(b)   the basis for your charges, including any hourly rates or fixed fees;

(c)   the experience and qualifications of anyone carrying out the work, and of their supervisors;

(d)   a description of, and the cost of, any likely *disbursements*, and where the actual cost of a *disbursement* is not known, the average cost or range of costs;

(e)   whether any fees or *disbursements* attract VAT and if so the amount of VAT they attract;

(f)   details of what services are included in the price displayed, including the key stages of the matter and likely timescales for each stage, and details of any services that might reasonably be expected to be included in the price displayed but are not; and

(g)   if you use conditional fee or damages based agreements, the circumstances in which *clients* may have to make any payments themselves for your services (including from any damages).

1.6   Cost information published under this rule must be clear and accessible and in a prominent place on your website.

Rule 2: Complaints information

2.1   An *authorised body*, or an individual practising in the circumstances set out in regulation 10.2(b)(i) to (vii) of the SRA Authorisation of Individuals Regulations, must publish on its website details of its complaints handling procedure including, details about how and when a complaint can be made to the *Legal Ombudsman* and to the *SRA*.

Rule 3: Publication

3.1   An *authorised body*, or an individual practising in the circumstances set out in regulation 10.2(b)(i) to (vii) of the SRA Authorisation of Individuals Regulations, that does not have a website, must make the information set out in rules 1 to 2 available on request.

Rule 4: Regulatory information

4.1   An *authorised body* must display in a prominent place on its website (or, in the case of a *licensed body*, the website relating to its legal services, if separate) its *SRA* number and the *SRA's* digital badge.

4.2   An *authorised body's* letterhead and e-mails must show its *SRA* authorisation number and the words "authorised and regulated by the Solicitors Regulation Authority".

4.3   A *solicitor*, an *REL* or *RFL* who is providing legal services to the public or a section of the public other than through a firm that is regulated by the *SRA*:

    (a)   where they are not required to meet the *MTC*, must before engagement inform all *clients* of this fact and specify that alternative insurance arrangements are in place if this is the case (together with information about the cover this provides, if requested); and

    (b)   where applicable, must inform all *clients* that they will not be eligible to apply for a grant from the SRA Compensation Fund.

4.4   Rule 4.3 does not apply to a *solicitor*, an *REL* or *RFL* that is working in an *authorised non-SRA firm* or a *non-commercial body*.

Supplemental notes

Made by the SRA Board on 30 May 2018.

Made under section 31 of the Solicitors Act 1974, section 9 of the Administration of Justice Act 1985 and section 83 of, and Schedule 11 to, the Legal Services Act 2007.

APPENDIX 5

The prescribed organisations and terms under which solicitors, RELs and RFLs are allowed to hold client money in their own name

[Last updated: 25 November 2019]

The prescribed organisations and terms under which solicitors, RELs and RFLs are allowed to hold client money in their own name

Status

This mandatory statement prescribes the types of organisations where solicitors, RELs and RFLs who work in them can hold client money in their own name, pursuant to paragraph 4.3 of the SRA Code of Conduct for Solicitors, RELs and RFLs.

It also prescribes the terms that the SRA has determined should apply to the holding of client money in their own name by any such solicitors, RELs and RFLs.

Introduction

Paragraph 4.3 of the SRA Code for Solicitors, RELs and RFLs permits solicitors, RELs and RFLs to hold client money in their own name in certain limited circumstances, including if they work in an organisation of the kind prescribed by the SRA under the rule.

This statement sets out:

* the type of organisations prescribed by the SRA;
* and the relevant terms.

This statement may be revised or updated from time to time.

Prescribed organisations

For the purposes of paragraph 4.3 of the SRA Code for Solicitors, RELs and RFLs, you are permitted to hold client money in your own name if you are a solicitor. REL or RFL working in a non-commercial body. A non-commercial body is defined in the SRA Glossary as body that falls within section 23(2) of the Legal Services act 2007 (a "Prescribed Organisation").

Prescribed terms that apply

If you work in a Prescribed Organisation and you wish to be able to hold client money, you must comply, and make sure that the Prescribed Organisation complies with, the following terms. Please note that all defined terms referred to below are set out in the SRA Glossary.

Prescribed terms

1: Client money

1.1 *"Client money"* is money held or received by you:

(a) relating to *regulated services* delivered by you to a *client*;

(b) on behalf of a third party in relation to *regulated services* delivered by you (such as money held as agent, stakeholder or held to the sender's order);

(c) as a trustee or as the holder of a specified office or appointment, such as donee of a power of attorney, Court of Protection deputy or trustee of an occupational pension scheme;

(d) in respect of your *fees* and any unpaid *disbursements* if held or received prior to delivery of a bill for the same.

1.2 You ensure that *client money* is paid promptly into a *client account* unless:

(a) in relation to money falling within 1(c), to do so would conflict with your obligations under rules or regulations relating to your specified office or appointment;

(b) the *client money* represents payments received from the Legal Aid Agency for your *costs*; or

(c) you agree in the individual circumstances an alternative arrangement in writing with the *client*, or the third party, for whom the money is held.

1.3 You ensure that *client money* is available on demand unless you agree an alternative arrangement in writing with the *client* or the third party for whom the money is held.

1.4 You ensure that *client money* is returned promptly to the *client*, or the third party for whom the money is held, as soon as there is no longer any proper reason to hold those funds.

2: Client account

2.1 You only maintain a *client account* at a branch (or the head office) of a *bank* or a *building society* in England and Wales.

2.2 You ensure that the name of any *client account* includes:

(a) your name; and

(b) the word "client" to distinguish it from any other type of account held or operated by the Prescribed Organisation.

2.3 You must not use a *client account* to provide banking facilities to *clients* or third parties. Payments into, and transfers or withdrawals from a *client account* must be in respect of the delivery by you of *regulated services*.

3: Client money must be kept separate

3.1 You keep *client money* separate from money belonging to you or the Prescribed Organisation.

3.2 You ensure that you allocate promptly any funds from *mixed payments* you receive to the correct client account or any other accounts operated by the Prescribed Organisation.

3.3 Where you are holding *client* money and some or all of that money will be used to pay your *costs*:

(a) you must give a bill of *costs*, or other written notification of the *costs* incurred, to the client or the paying party;

(b) this must be done before you transfer any *client money* from a *client account* to make the payment; and

(c) any such payment must be for the specific sum identified in the bill of *costs*, or other written notification of the *costs* incurred, and covered by the amount held for the particular *client* or third party.

4: Withdrawals from client account

4.1 You only withdraw *client money* from a *client account*:

(a) for the purpose for which it is being held;

(b) following receipt of instructions from the *client*, or the third party for whom the money is held; or

(c) on the *SRA*'s prior written authorisation or in *prescribed* circumstances.

4.2 You appropriately authorise and supervise all withdrawals made from a *client account*.

4.3 You only withdraw *client money* from a *client account* if sufficient funds are held on behalf of that specific client or third party to make the payment.

5: Duty to correct breaches after discovery

5.1 You correct any breaches of these rules promptly upon discovery. Any money improperly withheld or withdrawn from a *client account* must be immediately paid into the account or replaced as appropriate.

6: Payment of interest

6.1 You account to *clients* or third parties for a fair sum of *interest* on any *client money* held by you on their behalf.

6.2 You may by a written agreement come to a different arrangement with the *client* or the third party for whom the money is held as to the payment of *interest*, but you must provide sufficient information to enable them to give informed consent.

7: Client accounting systems and controls

7.1 You keep and maintain accurate, contemporaneous, and chronological records to:

(a) record in client ledgers identified by the *client's* name and an appropriate description of the matter to which they relate:

(i) all receipts and payments in your name which are *client money* on the client side of the client ledger account;

(ii) all receipts and payments in your name which are not *client money* on the business side of the client ledger account;

(b)   maintain a list of all the balances shown by the client ledger accounts of the liabilities to *clients* (and third parties), with a running total of the balances; and

(c)   provide a cash book showing a running total of all transactions through *client accounts* held or operated by you.

7.2   You obtain, at least every five weeks, statements from *banks*, building societies and other financial institutions for all *client accounts* and business accounts held or operated by you.

7.3   You complete at least every five weeks, for all *client accounts* held or operated by you, a reconciliation of the *bank* or *building society* statement balance with the cash book balance and the client ledger total, a record of which must be signed by someone authorised to do so by the Prescribed Organisation. You should promptly investigate and resolve any differences shown by the reconciliation.

7.4   You keep readily accessible a central record of all bills or other written notifications of *costs* given by you.

8: Obtaining and delivery of accountants' reports

8.1   The *SRA* may require you to obtain or deliver an accountant's report to the *SRA* on reasonable notice if the SRA considers that it is in the public interest to do so. You must ensure that any such report is prepared and signed by an accountant who is a member of one of the *chartered accountancy bodies* and who is, or works for, a registered auditor.

8.2   The *SRA* may disqualify an accountant from preparing a report for the purposes of this rule if:

(a)   the accountant has been found guilty by their professional body of professional misconduct or equivalent; or

(b)   the *SRA* is satisfied that the accountant has failed to exercise due care and skill in the preparation of a report under these rules.

8.3   The *SRA* may specify from time to time matters that you must ensure are incorporated into the terms on which an accountant is engaged.

8.4   You must provide to an accountant preparing a report under these rules:

(a)   details of all client accounts held or operated by you in your own name at any *bank*, *building society* or other financial institution at any time during the *accounting period* to which the report relates; and

(b)   all other information and documentation that the accountant requires to enable completion of their report

8.5   You must store all accounting records in relation to client accounts held or operated in your name securely and retain these for at least six years.

The prescribed circumstances in which you can withdraw client money from client account to pay to a charity of your choice

[Last updated: 25 November 2019]

The prescribed circumstances in which you can withdraw client money from client account to pay to a charity of your choice

Rule 5.1 (c) of the SRA Accounts Rules

Status

Rule 5.1 (c) of the SRA Accounts Rules (Accounts Rules) provide that client money can only be withdrawn from a client account on the SRA's prior written authorisation or in prescribed circumstances.

This mandatory statement prescribes the circumstances in which such withdrawals can be made without our prior written authorisation. These circumstances are limited to withdrawals of residual client account balances of £500 or less on any one client matter provided the balance is paid to a charity of your choice and if you have met the conditions set out.

This statement must be complied with by all SRA authorised firms and their staff.

This statement may be revised or updated from time to time.

For amounts over £500 you will need our authority before removing this money from the client account. Please use our application form [www.sra.org.uk/solicitors/resources/withdrawal-of-residual-client-balances].

Introduction

The SRA Accounts Rules (Accounts Rules) require you to return client money promptly to the client, or third party for whom the money is held, (including refunds received after the client has been accounted to) as soon as there is no longer a proper reason to hold those funds (Rule 2.5).

A residual client account balance is money that you have not returned to your client at the end of a retainer and it is now difficult for you to do so as you cannot identify or trace the client.

Firms should, therefore, very rarely be holding residual client account balances.

However, you may withdraw residual client balances of £500 or less on any one client matter in the prescribed circumstances set out below.

Prescribed circumstances under Rule 5.1 (c)

You may withdraw residual client balances of £500 or less on any one client matter from a client account provided:

1.   the balance is paid to a charity of your choice

2.   you have taken reasonable steps to return the money to the rightful owner. The reasonableness of such steps will depend on:

     i.   the age of the residual balance;

     ii.   the amount of the residual balance;

     iii.   if you have access to the client's most up to date contact details;

     iv.   if not, the costs associated with tracing your client.

     We expect you to make more intensive efforts to locate the rightful owner for larger or more recent residual balances or for balances where more details are held about the client.

3.   you record the steps taken to return the money to the rightful owner and retain those records, together with all relevant documentation for at least six years;

4.   you keep appropriate accounting records, including:

     i.   a central register which records the name of the rightful owner on whose behalf the money was held, the amount, name of the recipient charity (and their charity number) and the date of the payment; and

     ii.   all receipts from the charity and confirmation of any indemnity provided against any legitimate claim subsequently made for the sum they have received.

5.   you do not deduct from the residual balance any costs incurred in attempting to trace or communicate with the rightful owner.

The records referred to in points 3 and 4 above may be requested by your reporting accountant who will look at whether you have followed these prescribed circumstances.

For amounts over £500 you will need our authority before removing this money from the client account. Please use our application form.

Additional guidance

You may choose to pay the money to a charity that does not offer you an indemnity but if it does not, you will be liable to pay the money to the client if they contact you later to claim it.

Some ways in which you may be able to trace your client include:

- making use of social media

- making a search of Companies House and/or the Probate Registry

- making use of the Department of Work and Pensions' letter forwarding service

- undertaking any free searches on the internet.

SRA warning notices

[Law Society copyright. Warning notices do not form part of the SRA Handbook, but we may have regard to them when exercising our regulatory functions.]

8.1 Bogus law firms and identity theft

[Updated 25 November 2019 (Date first published: 26 March 2012)]

Status

This document is to help you understand your obligations and how to comply with them. We may have regard to it when exercising our regulatory functions.

Who is this warning notice relevant to?

Consumers of legal services and those we regulate.

Our concerns

1.   There are serious and continuing risks to the public arising from the activities of criminals and criminal gangs who set up bogus law firms or bogus branch offices of genuine law firms. This is with the intention, usually, of stealing money, personal information or data. This warning notice provides information about the threat as well as advice about how to protect yourself and others from it.

2. We are using our resources to mitigate the risk in various ways including rigorous authorisation processes, use of intelligence, urgent investigation, removal of records from the Digital Register and publication of warnings.

3. It is important to bear in mind that we do not regulate the people who are perpetrating these frauds and our powers over them are relatively limited.

4. It is important to share some of the indicators of these frauds to maximise the chances of prevention.

5. If you become suspicious about a law firm for any reason, please contact us as a matter of extreme urgency since some frauds are carried out very quickly.

6. Bear in mind that you may come across these frauds in different contexts. You should keep an eye on any indication that a firm is being targeted or its name being used improperly. If you discover this, you should contact us immediately.

7. Some examples of factors that may give rise to suspicion are[1]

   - errors in letterheading – for example misspelling the name of the town in which a firm or office is supposedly based

   - no landline telephone number – note that numbers beginning with 07 are mobile telephone numbers

   - inconsistent telephone or fax numbers with those usually used by the firm

   - telephone calls being diverted to a call-back service

   - a firm apparently based in serviced offices

   - email addresses using generic email accounts – eg gmail – most law firms have addresses incorporating the name of their firm. If in doubt, check the genuine law firm's website to identify its contact email address. You may well notice a difference

   - sudden appearance in your locality of a firm with no obvious connection to the area, probably not interacting with other local firms at all

   - a firm appearing to open a branch office a considerable distance from its head office for no obvious reason

   - a firm based in one part of the country supposedly having a bank account in another part of the country – this is a strong indicator and has been seen several times

   - a client account apparently overseas – this is a breach of rule and is a major red flag

   - a firm's website which does not display the SRA's clickable Logo – all firms regulated by the SRA must display the SRA's clickable Logo on their website (see rule 1 of the Transparency Rules)

   - a strange or suspicious bank account name – such as the account not being in the name of the law firm you are supposedly dealing with either at all or by some variation.

8. This list is not exhaustive. Nor does the presence of one of the factors on it mean that you are dealing with a bogus law firm or solicitor. However, where you see the factors above you should act cautiously and take steps to safeguard your position.

9. If you become concerned, because of the possibility of the theft of the identity of a genuine solicitor, it is worth trying to speak to the solicitor concerned. For example, if the solicitor is supposedly at one particular office but is also based at a head office of the firm, you could speak to the head office preferably after verifying its genuine nature, perhaps by contact with the senior partner.

10. You should check whether the firm's website displays our clickable logo. Not all firms are regulated by us, but most are. All firms which the SRA does regulate must display

our clickable logo. However, presence of a clickable logo should not be taken as proof that a website is genuine. A fraudster may have copied a genuine image and displayed the copy on their website. More information on how you should use the clickable logo is available.

11. You should check our digital [register] since there are sometimes bogus law firms which have not sought registration with us and will not appear there; but bear in mind that the nature of identity theft is that fraudsters may have obtained some form of registration by fraudulent misstatement to us and therefore an entry on the digital register should not be taken as verification that the firm is genuine.

12. If you are sending money to a firm, we suggest you send a small amount first and then speak to someone you have been dealing with at the firm to ensure they have received it, before you send the rest of the money.

Our expectations

13. We encourage everyone to be vigilant for warning signs that a solicitor or firm's identity may have been stolen.

14. It is important that you report your suspicions to us immediately.

15. If you are an owner or manager of a law firm and you suspect your firm is being targeted or its name is being used improperly, as well as contacting the us, you should also contact your insurers and consider legal action (such as applying for an injunction) either to stop misleading statements or to freeze assets if money has gone missing. If there is any evidence of a crime having been committed, you should also inform the police.

16. There are risks to you and your firm, as found in *Lloyds TSB Bank PLC v Markandan and Uddin* [2012] EWCA Civ 65 where the firm that was said to be the victim of the fraud was still held liable for breach of trust in paying away mortgage monies.

17. If you are an owner or manager of a firm, there are some practical things you can do:

- Search your firm's name on the internet from time to time, since that might bring up details of a false office or false contact details for your firm – it may be worth considering doing the same with the names of some of your partners or staff

- Check your firm and individual details on the SRA Digital Register – in case someone has misused your name to set up a false office

- Be alert to suspicious incidents such as transactions that others seem to think your firm is dealing with when you are not

- Look out for alerts and warnings on our website about bogus firms

- Never send details of a change of bank account to your clients by email.

18. Do not assume that we or the police can take direct steps to protect your firm. We each will do what we can although we will be focused on fraud prevention and you must not exclude the possibility of urgently seeking an injunction particularly if you are in possession of the most direct evidence and indeed if action is required very urgently. In such circumstances, we will seek to assist as much as we properly can in light of the evidence and any order of the court.

Further help

If you require further assistance, please contact the *Professional Ethics helpline*.

NOTES

1. These do not necessarily individually establish a serious problem but are factors to be considered.

8.2 Compliance with the money laundering regulations – firm risk assessment

[Updated 25 November 2019 (Date first published: 7 May 2019)]

Status

This document is to help you understand your obligations and how to comply with them. We may have regard to it when exercising our regulatory functions.

Who is this warning notice relevant to?

This warning notice is relevant to firms and individuals we regulate who are subject to The Money Laundering, Terrorist Financing and Transfer of Funds (Information on the Payer) Regulations 2017 ("the money laundering regulations").

Statutory requirements

Regulation 18 of the money laundering regulations requires firms to take steps to identify the risks of money laundering and terrorist financing that are relevant to it.

Your firm-wide risk assessment must be in writing, kept up-to-date and provided to us upon request. It also must accurately set out what risks your firm is exposed to and you must also record the steps you have taken to prepare the risk assessment.

As part of the risk assessment, you must consider your risk arising from:

- your clients (e.g. whether any of them are Politically Exposed Persons or family members or known close associates of Politically Exposed Persons)

- the countries or geographic areas you operate in (e.g. any country that may bring a risk of corruption or may be considered a high-risk third country)

- your products or services (e.g. whether you are involved in conveyancing)

- transactions (e.g. are any of the transactions of a larger size)

- your delivery channels. (e.g. online or without any face to face contact)

You must also consider relevant materials that we publish, including, but not limited to this warning notice and our sectoral risk assessment.

Your firm's risk assessment should form the backbone of your policies, controls and procedures (required under the money laundering regulations 18, 19, 20 and 21) to prevent money laundering. It should be a useful document to your firm and staff, as it sets out your appetite for higher risk activities and should feed into your assessments of individual clients and matters.

Our concerns

We have a responsibility as an anti-money laundering supervisor to make sure those we supervise meet the requirements in the legislation and have appropriate policies, controls and procedures in place to prevent money laundering. Firm-wide risk assessments are a key component of this.

We undertake proactive monitoring to prevent and detect money laundering, including thematic reviews, desk-based monitoring and visits to firms. We have undertaken several recent thematic reviews, one in 2017 when the updated regulations came into force, and one in 2018 into firms acting as trust and company services providers (a high-risk area for money laundering).

More recently, we have called in and reviewed 400 risk assessments to understand what best practice looks like.

We are seeing too many firms that do not have a risk assessment in place, and those firms could be failing to prevent money laundering. An anti-money laundering firm-wide risk assessment is an important and obligatory part of the regulations. Failure to have one is both against the law and places your firm at greater risk of being used to launder money.

We also have a broad concern that firms have not taken into account our sectoral risk assessment as they are required to by Regulation 18(2)(a).

Our expectations

Preventing money laundering is a high priority for us. Money laundering allows criminals to change dirty money into clean assets and funds that have no obvious link to criminal activity. This supports serious crimes such as people and drug trafficking, which cause enormous harm to people, especially the vulnerable, as well as undermining the stability of our financial markets and the integrity of the legal services sector. Solicitors and law firms are in a position of privilege and act as gatekeepers to assets and markets that are tempting to criminals, so we expect the profession to take proactive action to avoid enabling financial crime.

It is clear from our work that many firms have still not put a compliant firm-based anti-money laundering risk assessment in place.

Of the 400 risk assessments we assessed, we have taken follow up action on around 20% which did not meet the required standards. We have also seen broad use of templates, some with prepopulated specimen text. In some cases near-identical risk assessments were submitted by different firms, something that is particularly concerning.

Of those risk assessments that are in place, we are seeing that many do not take into account the minimum risks that the regulations require firms to consider. In particular we are seeing a high number of risk assessments that do not consider:

- factors relating to doing business with clients from high-risk jurisdictions
- transactions or
- the delivery method of their services.

Some risk assessments we have seen are incomplete and miss off some of the areas required in the money laundering regulations. An example of this is that many firms do not understand their responsibilities when dealing with Politically Exposed Persons (PEPs) and their close associates and family members. Stating that your firm does not provide services to PEPs, as many firms have done, does not address the need to be able to identify PEPs and to put in place appropriate controls.

Failure to have a money laundering risk assessment in place for your firm is a significant breach of the money laundering regulations. We will take robust enforcement action where firms do not have one in place, where it is not sufficient to meet their responsibilities or where breaches are not rectified immediately.

8.3 Holiday sickness claims

[Updated 25 November 2019 (Date first published: 6 September 2017)]

Status

This guidance is to help you understand your obligations and how to comply with them. We may have regard to it when exercising our regulatory functions.

Who is this warning notice relevant to?

This warning notice is relevant to all those we regulate who act in personal injury cases, particularly holiday sickness claims.

The SRA Standards and Regulations

The principles and codes of conduct are underpinned by our Enforcement Strategy, which explains in more detail our approach to taking regulatory action in the public interest. The following principles are most relevant to this warning notice, however other principles and codes may apply.

- Principle 1: You act in a way that upholds the constitutional principle of the rule of law, and the proper administration of justice.

  You have obligations not only to clients but also to the court and to third parties with whom you have dealings on your clients' behalf.

- Principle 2: You act in a way that upholds public trust and confidence in the solicitors' profession and in legal services provided by authorised persons.

  You must behave in a way that maintains the trust the public places in you and in the provision of legal services. Members of the public should be able to place their trust in you. Any behaviour either within or outside your professional practice which undermines this trust damages not only you, but also the ability of the legal profession as a whole to serve society.

- Principle 4: You act with honesty

  Acting honestly in all your dealings with everyone is fundamental.

- Principle 5: You act with integrity.

  Personal integrity is central to your role as the client's trusted adviser and should characterise all your professional dealings with clients, the court, other lawyers and the public.

- Principle 7: You must act in the best interests of each client.

  You should always act in good faith and do your best for each of your clients

Our concerns

Following an increase in compensation claims since 2013, we have seen some behaviours that give us cause for concern such as:

- taking on matters whilst lacking competence and skill in the area of law
- failing to make sure they do not accept cases from introducers who are cold calling or failing to verify the source of the referral
- entering into improper referral arrangements and allowing their independence to be compromised by, for example favouring the interests of the referrer
- failing to properly identify clients and confirm client instructions including the verification of relevant documentation to support a claim
- bringing a claim without first investigating whether it is valid
- making unreasonable requests for disclosure from the defendant or their lawyers
- failing to objectively assess and investigate adverse evidence
- failing to properly advise clients about what is expected of them when making a claim
- submitting false or dubious claims in the hope of a settlement without further investigation by the defendant
- seeking unreasonable costs – either from the client or the defendant.

Those who conduct cases demonstrating one or more of these features may face regulatory action for breach of our Principles, Standards and Regulations. Our investigations involving holiday claims, have included improper links with claims management companies and payment for referrals of holiday sickness claims. We have also seen firms pursuing claims without the proper instructions from claimants.

Our expectations

Clear instructions

You must not pursue claims or continue with claims where you do not have the claimant's clear and express authority to do so (paragraph 3.1 of the code of conduct for solicitors, RELs and RFLs and paragraph 4.1 code of conduct for firms).

Merits of a claim

You must engage properly with all the merits of your clients' cases. Where there is evidence suggesting a claim is false or dubious in some way you must not act for them. We are clear that you must not bring cases, or continue with them where there is a serious concern about the honesty or reliability of the evidence (paragraphs 2.2, 2.4 and 2.6 of the codes of conduct for solicitors, RELs and RFLs and 7.1(a) of the code of conduct for firms). See further below on dishonest claims.

The extent to which you should verify a client's case is risk specific. Examples of risk factors in holiday sickness claims include:

- The claim is made some time after the alleged incident

- There was no report of the claim to the hotel

- There was no extensive sickness amongst others in the same accommodation – see *Wood v TUI Travel* [2017] EWCA Civ 11

- The claim comes from or involves people that have actively sought out/farmed for claims in a resort

- The client's contemporaneous report of the holiday was positive

- The client drank or ate excessively before or after becoming ill

The difficulties found in establishing holiday sickness claims is explained in the case of *Wood v TUI Travel* [2017] EWCA Civ 11 in which the Court of Appeal commented:

> "...it will always be difficult (indeed, very difficult) to prove that an illness is a consequence of food or drink which was not of a satisfactory quality, unless there is cogent evidence that others have been similarly affected and alternative explanations would have to be excluded..."

We expect you to engage with this and properly assess all the evidence before submitting claims.

Evidence

We have seen failures to make sure all documentary evidence is analysed. We have also seen highly improper advice to clients to delete evidence such as social media updates or pictures of the holiday.

In all litigation, we expect you to immediately inform clients of their duty to preserve evidence and allow you to review it fully and impartially. This is a critical duty to the administration of justice in ensuring unmeritorious claims are not made. You must therefore be rigorous in storing, retrieving, analysing and acting on evidence, including seeking and making appropriate disclosure. Claims should not be filed until your client has been properly advised on all relevant evidence, including the merits of their case and after your client has given clear instructions and authority, on a fully-informed basis to pursue their claim or not.

APPENDIX 8

If you take a narrow approach you may be treated as 'turning a blind eye' which can amount to dishonesty. In *Barlow Clowes v Eurotrust* [2005] UKPC 37 it was noted that a dishonest state of mind "may consist in suspicion combined with a conscious decision not to make inquiries which might result in knowledge". Dishonest claims are the most serious of all for you and your client. As well as disciplinary proceedings they can lead to costs against your client and even criminal proceedings.

If there are issues about a case that concern you, you must not turn a blind eye. You must properly engage with the issues and assess objectively if the case can properly be pursued.

An example of this might be allegations that claims are being generated or co-ordinated by organised criminals, as we have seen in 'cash for crash' cases. You cannot simply ignore such allegations, and nor can you simply assert that they consider them unproved or unfounded. We expect you to engage properly with them and bear in mind their duty to the administration of justice.

Cold calling

We have seen evidence of introducers and claims farmers approaching holiday makers to generate sickness claims. You have duties not to make unsolicited approaches to members of the public with the exception of current or former clients in order to advertise legal services (paragraph 8.9 of the code of Conduct for solicitors, RELs and RFLs and paragraph 7.1(c) of the code of conduct for firms). You remain accountable for compliance with our regulatory arrangements where your work is carried out through others, including managers, those you employ or contract with (paragraph 2.3 of the code of conduct for firms).

You should not have an arrangement with another party to cold call on your behalf since any client referred to you must not be referred in a way that breaches our regulatory arrangements (paragraph 5.1 (e) of the code of conduct for solicitors, RELs and RFLs and as applied by paragraph 7.1(b) in the code of conduct for firms.

Referral arrangements

You should take steps to make sure that you verify the source of any referral.

You should terminate any arrangement with an introducer or fee-sharer which causes or may cause you to breach the Principles or the Standards and Regulations, and/or that puts you in breach of the law.

Please see our previously published guidance on the Legal Aid, Sentencing and Punishment of Offenders Act 2012 (LASPO).

Where you have a referral arrangement that is not in breach of LASPO, you must still comply with paragraphs 5.1-5.3 of the code for conduct for solicitors, RELs and RFLs and/or paragraphs 7.1(b) of the code of conduct for firms. We have seen referrals made to a third party, such as a medical expert, when it is not in the client's best interests or where it is unlikely the claim can be properly progressed because the referral is made after a significant time has passed.

Further help

If you require further assistance, please contact the *Professional Ethics helpline*.

8.4 Improper use of client account as a banking facility

[Updated 25 November 2019 (Date first published: 18 December 2014/Updated 6 August 2018)]

Status

This warning notice highlights some key issues with regards to a law firm's client account being improperly used as a banking facility.

This document is to help you understand your obligations and how to comply with them. We may have regard to it when exercising our regulatory functions.

Who is this warning notice relevant to?

This warning notice is relevant to all law firms, their managers and employees who have any involvement in holding or using money received for clients or others.

For a number of years, we have warned that solicitors must not provide banking facilities to clients or others. This warning notice is a reminder of some of the key issues and risks of which you should be aware. We have also set out some case studies to help you comply with your obligations.

Our Standards and Regulations

Rule 3.3 of the SRA Accounts Rules provides that:

> "You must not use a client account to provide banking facilities to clients or third parties. Payments into, and transfers or withdrawals from a client account must be in respect of the delivery by you of regulated services".

"Regulated services" means: the legal and other professional services that you provide that are regulated by the SRA and includes, where appropriate, acting as a trustee or as the holder of a specified office or appointment.

Rule 3.3 reflects decisions of the Solicitors Disciplinary Tribunal that it is not a proper part of a solicitor's everyday business or practice to operate a banking facility for third parties, whether they are clients of the firm or not.

Concerns about the improper use of client account have been clearly and more broadly stated in case law. You should make sure that you are fully aware of the relevant case law including the cases of *Fuglers* (*Fuglers LLP v SRA* [2014] EWHC 179 (Admin)), *Patel* (*Premji Naram Patel v Solicitors' Regulation Authority* [2012] EWHC 3373 (Admin)), and *Zambia* (*Attorney General of Zambia v Meer Care & Desai* [2008] EWCA Civ 1007).

The Principles

A breach of rule 3.3 is a serious matter in itself.

If you allow your firm's client account to be used improperly this may also result in a breach of the SRA Principles by failing to act:

- in a way that upholds the constitutional principle of the rule of law, and the proper administration of justice: Principle 1

- in a way that upholds public trust and confidence in the solicitors' profession and in legal services provided by authorised persons: Principle 2

- with independence: Principle 3

- with integrity: Principle 5

Our concerns

Law firms, their managers and employees should not allow the firm's client account to be used to provide banking facilities to clients or third parties. You must also actively consider whether there are any risk factors suggesting that the transaction on which you are acting, even if it appears to be the normal work of a solicitor, is not genuine or is suspicious.

Some of the key issues you should be aware of include the following.

Providing banking facilities through a client account is objectionable in itself

The prohibition in rule 3.3 is simple and clear: "You must not use a client account to provide banking facilities to clients or third parties." The second sentence in the rule recognises that holding and moving money for clients may not be a breach where doing so is related to proper instructions regarding a transaction on which you are acting or in connection with the delivery of regulated services. These include legal and other professional services that you provide that are regulated by us.

The courts have confirmed that operating a banking facility for clients divorced from any legal or other professional work is in itself objectionable. You are not regulated as a bank to provide such facilities. If you do provide banking facilities for clients, you are trading on the trust and reputation from your status as a solicitor in doing so.

You must therefore only receive funds into your client account where there is a proper connection between receipt of the funds and the delivery by you of regulated services. It is not sufficient that there is simply an underlying transaction if you are not providing any regulated services, or if the handling of money has no proper connection to that service.

It should also be noted that any exemption or exclusion under the Financial Services and Markets Act 2000 is likely to be lost if a deposit is taken in circumstances which do not form part of your regulated services.

There must be a proper connection between the delivery by you of regulated services and the payments you are asked to make or receive

The rule is not intended to prevent usual practice in traditional work undertaken by solicitors such as conveyancing, company acquisitions, the administration of estates or dealing with formal trusts. So, it does not affect your ability to make usual and proper payments from client account when they are related to the transaction (such as the payment of estate agents' fees in a conveyancing transaction).

Whether there is such a proper connection will depend on the facts of each case. The fact that you have a retainer with a client is insufficient to allow you to process funds freely through client account. You need to think carefully about whether there is any justification for money to pass through your client account when it could be simply paid directly between the clients.

Historically, some solicitors have held funds for clients to enable them to pay the client's routine outgoings. This has been mainly for the clients' convenience such as where they are long term private clients or based abroad. In view of technological change, such as the ease of internet and telephone banking, we consider that allowing client account to be used in this way is no longer justifiable and a breach of rule 3.3. Clients can now operate their bank accounts from their own homes or indeed from anywhere in the world. Allowing clients simply to hold money in a client account gives rise to significant risks and may evade sophisticated controls and risk analyses that banks apply to money held for their customers.

Factors you should bear in mind when considering such issues include:

- Throughout the retainer, you should question why you are being asked to receive funds and for what purpose. The further the details of the transaction are from the norm or from the usual legal or professional services a solicitor provides, the higher the risk that you may breach rule 3.3.

- You should always ask why you are being asked to make a payment or why the client cannot make or receive the payment directly themselves. The client's convenience is not a legitimate reason, nor is not having access to a bank account in the UK. Risk factors could involve the payment of substantial sums to others, including family members, or to corporate entities, particularly overseas, if there is no reason why the client could not receive the money into their own account and transfer it from there.

- You have a separate obligation to return client money to the client or third party promptly, as soon as there is no longer any proper reason for you to hold those funds (rule 2.5 of the Accounts Rules). If you retain funds in client account after completion of a transaction, there is risk (depending on how long you hold the money) of breaching both rule 2.5 and 3.3.

Risk of insolvency

You should be aware that a client may ask you to hold or deal with money in client account to avoid their obligations under insolvency legislation. Banks commonly withdraw facilities when told that there has been a winding up petition.

You should be aware that a client may ask you to hold or deal with money in client account to avoid their obligations under insolvency legislation. Banks commonly withdraw facilities when told that there has been a winding up petition.

If a law firm allows its client account to be used as a banking facility in an insolvency situation to receive and process money, the client will improperly obtain a banking service which would otherwise be unavailable to it. There are also risks that in making payments to order. You may improperly favour one creditor over another.

Finally, section 127 of the Insolvency Act 1986 may apply to require creditors to reimburse payments from the client account in a subsequent liquidation. A solicitor who knowingly makes or facilitates such payments may be subject to a personal liability, in addition to the liability of the payee to reimburse the amount transferred.

Rule 3.3 and the risk of money laundering

Allowing a client account to be used as a banking facility carries with it the additional risk that you may assist money laundering. We directly monitor and enforce provisions relating to anti-money laundering and counter terrorist financing, as set out in regulations made by the Treasury as in force from time to time, including the Money Laundering, Terrorist Financing and Transfer of Funds (information on the payer) Regulations 2017 (MLRs).

You should be familiar with our warning notices on:

- Money laundering and terrorist financing

- Money laundering and terrorist financing – suspicious activity reports

- Compliance with the money laundering regulations – firm risk assessment

- Investment schemes (including conveyancing).

You must remain alert to any unusual or suspicious factors such as concern about the source of funds or what you are asked to do with them. Your obligation to comply with rule 3.3 offers an important 'first line of defence' against clients or others who seek to use your client account to launder money. It also helps you to secure professional independence from your client in compliance with Principle 3.

We have also seen firms making multiple transfers of money between the ledgers of different clients or companies without evidence of the purpose or legal basis for the transfers (such as Board resolutions or contracts). Transfers in such circumstances will be a breach of rule 3.3, particularly if they are simply carried out on request. It is an important principle of anti-money laundering regulation that transactions are properly recorded and can be reconstructed (see, for example, regulation 40(2)(b) of the Money Laundering, Terrorist Financing and Transfer of Funds (information on the payer) Regulations 2017). Such conduct would be of significant concern to us as it makes the tracking of money difficult and may be aggravated by the number and the value of such transfers.

Although, allowing client account to be used as a banking facility can facilitate money laundering, rule 3.3 exists independently of the anti-money laundering legislation and a breach of rule 3.3 does not require there to be evidence of laundering. If there is such evidence, we would expect a prosecution under the Proceeds of Crime Act 2002 (see for example

R v Khan (Shadab) [2010] EWCA Crim 2841 (four years' imprisonment)). It is no defence to, or mitigation, of a breach of rule 3.3 that there was no evidence of actual laundering. Indeed, such arguments indicate a lack of insight into the reasons for rule 3.3 and the risks it addresses.

For example:

- Rule 3.3 and the MLRs are to a large extent preventative provisions, intended to make it more difficult for people to use regulated businesses for improper purposes but also to deter law firms from helping such people.

- Any impropriety may be distant from the movement of money through a client account. In a classic laundering process, the movement through a client account may be the third or fourth stage of laundering the proceeds of a distant crime. But every stage contributes to the effectiveness of the laundering process.

- There are many potential forms of impropriety as well as money laundering. The Fuglers' case is one example in an insolvency context but there are many others such as hiding assets improperly in commercial or matrimonial disputes. You should also be aware of the risks in allowing your client account to be used to add credibility to questionable investment schemes.

- Movement of money through client account is attractive to those with an improper purpose:

  - Attempts by law enforcement or opposing litigants to obtain information may be blocked by a claim to privilege, even though the claim to privilege may be unsustainable on proper analysis with access to the documents.

  - It largely circumvents the sophisticated risk systems used by banks.

  - Solicitors, particularly in smaller firms, with a close relationship to an important client may be vulnerable to pressure to avoid making suspicious activity reports.

Enforcement action

You should be prepared to justify to us any decision that you make that it was appropriate for you to hold or move client money. Failure to have proper regard to this warning notice is likely to lead to disciplinary action.

Further help

If you require further assistance, please contact the *Professional Ethics helpline*.

8.5 Investment schemes including conveyancing

[Updated 17 August 2020 (Date first published: 23 June 2017)]

Status

This warning is to help you understand your obligations and how to comply with them. We may have regard to it when exercising our regulatory functions.

Who is this warning notice relevant to?

This warning notice is relevant to solicitors and all law firms, their managers and employees.

This warning is also relevant to members of the public who are considering paying money into what is promoted as an "investment" scheme where a law firm or solicitor is involved.

We have warned for a number of years about the risks posed by dubious or questionable investment schemes. This warning notice has been updated to reflect some of the recent key issues highlighted in our Risk Outlook and Thematic Report, including the risk that fraudsters are continually changing the look and feel of "investment" schemes to avoid features that have been warned about previously. Practitioners in many fields of law may therefore find that they are at risk of facilitating high risk or dubious investment schemes.

The SRA Standards and Regulations

If you are, or are considering, becoming involved in making, arranging or advising on any investments or other financial products that are regulated by the Financial Conduct Authority (FCA), you will need to make sure that you are entitled to carry on those activities.

If your involvement in these schemes is not directly linked to the legal services that law firms provide, you will need separate authorisation from the FCA.

If your involvement arises out of the delivery of legal services, then you will need make sure that the work can be carried out under the scope of our regulation (see SRA Financial Services (Scope) Rules).

In all cases, even if the investment or product is not an FCA-regulated product, you must comply with the requirements set out in the SRA Standards and Regulations.

In particular, you must act:

● in a way that upholds public trust and confidence in the solicitors' profession and in legal services provided by authorised persons (Principle 2)

● with independence (Principle 3)

● with integrity (Principle 5)

● in the best interests of each client (Principle 7)

Paragraph 1.2 of the SRA Codes of Conduct for solicitors, RELs and RFLs and for firms also requires you to make sure that you do not abuse your position by taking unfair advantage of clients or others, including prospective or actual buyers/investors.

You should also be mindful of your obligations to safeguard money and assets entrusted to you by clients or others (paragraph 4.2 and 5.2 of the SRA Codes respectively) and, as set out in the SRA Accounts Rules, specifically to make sure that client money is kept safe, and that your client account is not used as a banking facility (rule 3.3).

Our expectations

We expect you to act with integrity and protect consumers by robustly analysing the risks of any investment scheme you are involved in. The obligation rests on you as a firm to carry out all necessary checks and you should not rely on the word of the seller or other promoters of a scheme.

If you suspect that a transaction is potentially fraudulent, dubious or so high-risk that it is unfair to buyers or investors, you should provide full and frank advice to your clients and refuse or cease to act. We are particularly concerned about the dangers of schemes where your involvement or that of your law firm is used to give an impression of credibility or security for example, by being inappropriately named in promotional material or other literature relating to a scheme.

Our concerns

We continue to receive reports about law firms that are involved in dubious or questionable investment schemes. This is a key risk for consumers resulting in significant financial losses, which in some cases can be more than £1 million per scheme. We are seeing:

- Solicitors and law firms being used to give credibility to a scheme rather than because legal work is required. These sorts of schemes have been highlighted in previous warnings issued by us

- Funds transferring through a law firm's client account, without the transactions being connected to any underlying legal work, in breach of rule 3.3 of the SRA Accounts Rules (at risk of laundering money or otherwise improper payments being made)

- Dubious or risky schemes being presented as routine conveyancing or investment in "land" when the reality is very different

- No real legal work being carried out and legal fees are being generated when they are not necessary.

These concerns have been borne out by our thematic review. Further concerns identified include:

1. Investment schemes have evolved from high-yield financial arrangements or prime bank instrument fraud, into what appear to be more recognisable legal transactions such as the purchase of land when the reality is very different.

2. Sellers are changing the structure of schemes periodically to avoid detection.

3. Schemes are being labelled as, for example, mini-bonds, but are in fact speculative investments promising a high return and the buyers' money is not being used in the way the seller it says it will. Since 1 January 2020, the Financial Conduct Authority has temporarily banned promotions of 'speculative mini-bonds' to retail consumers, unless the investor is considered to be 'sophisticated' or have a high net worth.

We have set out at the end of this guidance a list of some of the red flag indicators all firms should be aware of.

Each of these issues are explored in more detail below.

Conveyancing or purported investment in land

Buyer-led financing of a development

Schemes are being promoted as involved in the routine buying of a property when in reality the buyer's money is being used to finance a high-risk development or refurbishment. This is of particular concern in unusual developments such as the buying of individual hotel rooms, rooms in care homes, or self-storage units. Our concerns also apply to any off plan "buyer-led" purchases. Off-plan means buying a property while it is still in the planning or construction stages, which involves the use of the buyer's money to fund a project or property development.

We are seeing cases of solicitors simply processing transactions for buyers while adopting the language of conveyancing. The effect is to mask what is really happening. For example, buyers provide money for a "deposit" which is released early to the seller upon some (often spurious) condition. The buyer's money is used to buy the property or finance its building or refurbishment.

The usual deposit in a conveyancing transaction is 10 percent. It is paid to make sure that the buyer will complete the contract. In some of the dubious schemes we have seen, the "deposit" has been 30 percent or even as high as 80 percent. These are not market standard deposits but involve pre-payment of the price and effectively providing finance to the developer. Our view is that such high deposits are particularly high risk because the buyer has very little protection if the development fails. Referring to them as deposits is part of the psychology of presenting a risky "investment" as routine conveyancing and which may lead buyers to believe that they are not parting with all of their money in one go. It tempts the buyer to invest further, even though the development may not have progressed. Psychologically, buyers might be reluctant to walk away from an investment if they have already paid a large proportion of the purchase price before exchange of contracts.

Buyers are not being advised, or properly advised, that these types of transaction often present a much higher risk than simply buying an existing house or apartment.

Such schemes have failed for a variety of reasons. These include for example:

- insufficient capital had been raised from deposits

- developers have gone into administration

- the development has simply not progressed

- money invested has been used by the developers for purposes not connected with the scheme

Where funding is provided for a substantial property development scheme by an institutional lender, that lender would typically have a high level of protection in place over the draw-down of funds. Where buyers' deposits are being used as an alternative source of finance to fund developments, their attention should be drawn to any differences between the level of protection in place over their funds and that which would typically be put in place by an institutional lender.

Where you are acting for the buyers in these types of transactions, you must advise your clients fully about the transaction and how it significantly differs from the simple conveyance of an existing property (if appropriate, advising against entering into the transaction). In addition to the issues outlined above we expect you to explain that:

1. Buying a property not yet built or completed ie buyer-led or subject to significant refurbishment, involves a substantial risk that the developer or seller could fail, and money will be lost.

2. Promises of substantial returns can be misleading. Standard warnings in publicity about the risk of capital loss are therefore not enough to make sure that you have properly advised your client upon the risks of the transaction.

Taking a lease of a room, a storage unit etc

Schemes are being promoted by which buyers take a lease of a supposed asset such as a hotel room, care home room, parking space or self- storage unit. This list is not exhaustive as fraudsters will continue to search for similar "assets".

These "fractional property" investments are where the buyer buys a portion or fraction of an investment property and receives a fraction of the rental income and a fraction of the capital growth. These schemes can involve a higher risk than the simple purchase of a property that has already been built. Such investments have been treated as standard conveyances. They were typically marketed as being 'a low-cost, high-yield investment product that's hands off and hassle free'.

However, in reality, buyers pay a substantial amount for the asset and also pay conveyancing costs, sometimes of several thousand pounds. There is no obvious reason for someone wanting to invest in a hotel to take out a lease and pay for the conveyancing of one room. It is difficult to see why such schemes require the involvement of a solicitor as this is not a 'conveyancing' transaction in the usual sense with a view to title being registered against a piece of land or property. All that seems to be done here is that the law firm is receiving money into their client account and sending it on to the seller. This would be regarded as a breach of rule 3.3 of the SRA Accounts Rules.

Buyers may be inappropriately reassured that taking out a "lease" means that they have a legal interest in the land or property when the reality is that their investment is dependent upon sharing the profits which would arise from the business being well managed.

We also see no particular reason why such investments should provide high returns and you must properly advise your clients of this and of the associated risk of their money being lost.

The Serious Fraud Office have previously investigated losses of up to £120m arising from the promotion of self-storage schemes.

Collective investment schemes – criminal liability

Many of these schemes are likely to be "collective investment schemes" under section 235 of the Financial Services and Markets Act 2000. Collective investment schemes are defined in the FCA Handbook Glossary (see link). If those involved in the schemes are not authorised by FCA, they will be committing a criminal offence and are likely to be imprisoned. You should exercise caution when being invited to be involved in any scheme that appears to involve a collective investment element.

Our view is that buyer-led schemes are likely to be regarded as collective investment schemes because the buyers are required to pool their money together, for example to finance the construction of a building. Some of these schemes might also amount to a 'Ponzi' scheme. This is a scheme which generates returns for early investors by acquiring new investors whose funds are then used to pay the initial investors a return on their deposits before the development completes.

If you are advising on such schemes, you will only be able to do so if you can satisfy the conditions set out in rule 2.1 of the SRA Financial Services (Scope) Rules.

If you are, however, involved in establishing, operating or winding up a collective investment scheme then you will need to be authorised by the FCA as these activities cannot be carried out under the scope of our regulation.

Unfair terms

The documentation in dubious schemes is often, but not always, obscure. It is frequently unfair to the consumer, and any solicitor involved in drafting or advising on terms which are unclear or favour one party over another should carefully consider their approach. The FCA has published examples of unfair terms on their website. The unfairness of the terms is often clear additional evidence that unfair advantage is being taken of the investor or buyer. In many cases, schemes will be targeted at foreign buyers who may have less time or be less able to question the terms of schemes that are being sold to them.

Evasion of rule 3.3 of the SRA Accounts Rules

As well as trying to give credibility to their scheme, fraudsters will provide false assurances that the "investment" will be kept secure in a law firm's client account. This facilitates the fraud and enables the money to be laundered.

Rule 3.3 prohibits law firms from using a client account to provide banking facilities to clients or third parties and makes it clear that payments into, and transfers from a client account must be in respect of the delivery by them of regulated services. Because of the artificial nature of the transaction or other fraudulent element, a firm's client account may be used solely to pass buyers' money through client account, which is prohibited.

You should carefully consider whether you are actually providing regulated services – regardless of how someone else may describe or brand your involvement in the scheme.

We have warned about the improper use of a client account as a banking facility and that warning notice should be read alongside this notice.

Insurance bonds

We have seen investment schemes promoted as being secured by insurance bonds which have proved worthless.

Where you are aware that the transaction is said to be secured by an insurance bond, you should satisfy yourself about its validity or enforceability and advise the client properly and fully. You should also make sure that you do not become involved in insurance distribution activities unless you comply with the SRA Financial Services (Scope) and SRA Financial Services (Conduct of Business) Rules. Risk factors include:

1.   The issuer of the bond is not regulated.

2.   The bond is only valid for a limited time period.

3.   The issuer is based in a jurisdiction where it is likely to be very difficult to enforce the bond.

4.   Where there is any doubt about the propriety or financial soundness of the issuer.

5.   The bond is written in terms unfamiliar to a lawyer in England and Wales.

6.   Reputable insurers do not offer bonds for the particular type of investment.

Your relationship with the seller and the buyers

Acting with independence

In the majority of dubious schemes, the law firm acts for the seller of the scheme, although they can used to act for buyers as well.

In some instances that we have seen, law firms already have a relationship with the seller, for example, as a client, through an existing business or referral relationship or in some cases through a personal friendship.

Just because you have an existing relationship with a client should not give you false reassurance about new instructions relating to an investment scheme. Placing reliance on the basis of a former relationship could have a detrimental effect on your independence and could lead you, for example, to fail to scrutinise the transaction and/or the parties involved. We are concerned that you might be at risk of turning a blind eye to concerning aspects of a scheme because of these existing relationships or due to concerns about losing a regular stream of guaranteed income.

The fact that similar schemes by similar people or businesses have previously succeeded does not mean that future schemes are necessarily genuine, or lower risk.

Who are you acting for?

We have seen some schemes where firms give the impression that they are providing some advice to the buyer. For example, we have seen examples where some buyers are not always clear that the panel firm they are referred to in promotional materials are acting for the seller rather than them.

Acting for both buyer and the seller in these cases is likely to constitute a conflict of interest and comprise serious misconduct (see paragraph 6.2 of the SRA Code of Conduct for solicitors, RELs and RFLs).

We have seen solicitors – supposedly acting for buyers – who appear more focused on ensuring the scheme continues so that they get paid rather than advising the buyer client properly.

If you are not acting for the buyers, you must make that absolutely clear to them.

However, the fact that you may act only for the seller does not mean that you owe no duties to buyers. You should strongly advise them to take their own independent advice from professionals they choose themselves. Attempts to prevent buyers from obtaining objective and independent advice is a very serious matter. Examples of this might include:

1.   Clear or subtle attempts to dissuade buyers from instructing their own solicitors – such as indications that they do not need legal advice or that the seller and their solicitors will "deal with everything".

2.   A requirement, or pressure, to instruct a particular firm (which may have past links with the developer or be motivated not to advise about the risks of the transaction to maintain a flow of work).

3.   A refusal by the seller to allow the buyer to seek their own advice on changes to terms and conditions – for example, where the terms are in any way unusual such as requiring a high "deposit" or its release to finance the development.

Limited retainers

You must act in your client's best interests and with integrity. We expect you, amongst other things, to point out clear and obvious risks that may not be obvious to your client. Clients should have sufficient information to make an informed decision about how their matter is handled and to give further instructions. Firms have argued that they were not required to advise clients on all aspects of a transaction because they had a "limited retainer". We have not seen a case where the retainer was limited at the client's (genuine) request. Limited retainers, particularly when dealing with consumers and small businesses, might be a warning of inherent issues with the scheme itself as it may be used to avoid involvement in, or advising clients about, more problematic areas. This approach is clearly not in the client's best interests.

Conclusion

You must not facilitate or arrange dubious or fraudulent investments. For all investments or products that are regulated by the FCA, you must make sure that you are permitted to do so. In all cases you must not take unfair advantage of clients or others (Paragraph 1.2 of the Code of Conduct for solicitors, RELs or RFLs). You must act with integrity (Principle 5). In addition, you must rigorously assess the transaction and refuse or cease to act if there is any doubt about the propriety of the transaction or whether buyers are being misled in any way. If you fail to make proper enquiries you could find yourself in breach of some or all of our Principles and standards. You could also be found to have acted dishonestly.

Red flags

Be alert to these sorts of issues:

- high deposits paid in instalments before exchange
- comparatively high returns
- complex and unfair agreement terms
- transactions require limited administrative work or only processing funds
- guaranteed buy-back of a product or property for profit
- having an interest in the scheme eg: panel firms and referrals
- sellers ask firms to promote the scheme or appear in marketing material
- exclusive offers on investment products that require secrecy
- buyers are mainly from another jurisdiction to the location of the scheme
- third party buyers do not have representation
- sellers ask firms to provide security for buyers' deposits
- high commissions due to sellers from deposits

Practical tips

1.   Be familiar with all of our warnings and the red flags that might guide you to consider your involvement in acting for the seller.

2.   Make sure that your firm is not represented or referred to in promotional material in a way that suggests that you endorse the scheme or that you are facilitating the receipt of money without providing any other legal services.

3. Look at how buyers have been contacted to make sure that they have not for example, been cold called or been targeted because of their vulnerability or because of their access to funds.

4. Analyse the scheme carefully and critically, with our warnings in mind. Firms may wish to consider using some of the same type of safeguards used for anti-money laundering checks to identify and assess the source of funds/wealth for parties involved in an investment scheme.

5. Refuse to act or cease to act if you have concerns.

6. Have an agreed firm wide approach to new investment business to manage risks to the firm and to buyers from dubious investment schemes.

7. Look critically at documents to assess what they mean and whether they are fair.

8. Avoid rationalising suspicious factors – such as by thinking "the warnings do not mention the type of transaction I have been asked to deal with, so it must be safe" or limiting retainers.

9. Do not allow your client account – or any account you control – to be used to receive investment money that could simply be sent by a buyer directly to the seller.

10. Satisfy yourself that the legal work is genuine and that your client account is not being used as a banking facility. Do not attempt to evade rule 3.3 of the SRA Accounts Rules by trying to manufacture a process of legal work or advice.

11. Carry out effective and thorough conflict checks including assessing any own conflicts especially when relying on previous relationships or because of receiving referrals as a 'panel law firm'.

12. Where an investment is high risk, not usual or not standard, advise your buyer client explicitly that that is the case even if it results in a matter not proceeding.

Enforcement action

Failure to comply with this warning notice is likely to lead to disciplinary action.

Further assistance

If you require further assistance with understanding your obligations in relation to supposed investment schemes please contact the *Professional Ethics Guidance team.*

8.6 Money laundering and terrorist financing

[Updated 25 November 2019 (Date first published: 8 December 2014)]

Status

This document is to help you understand your obligations and how to comply with them. We may have regard to it when exercising our regulatory functions.

Who is this warning notice relevant to?

This warning notice is relevant to all regulated persons who have a legal obligation to make sure that they:

● report any suspicious transactions

● do not facilitate money laundering or terrorist financing

This notice highlights warning signs which you should be aware of, and which may require you to take action in order to avoid committing a criminal offence or breaching your professional obligations under the SRA Standards and Regulations.

The Money Laundering, Terrorist Financing and Transfer of Funds (Information on the Payer) Regulations 2017 (MLR 2017) came into force on 26 June 2017 replacing the Money Laundering Regulations 2007. A new version of these regulations is due to come into effect in late 2019/early 2020. As a result law firms may need to make changes to their procedures and systems in order to remain compliant with their obligations. Read our guidance on the key changes introduced in the 2017 regulations to see the current requirements.

The SRA Standards and Regulations

Paragraph 7.1 of the Code of Conduct for Solicitors, RELs and RFLs requires you to keep up to date with and follow the law and regulation governing the way you work. This obligation includes making sure you comply with your legal obligations under the Proceeds of Crime Act 2002, the Terrorism Act 2000 and the MLR 2017.

You must make sure you do not facilitate money laundering, even when money does not pass through your firm's accounts. Your firm should have appropriate policies and procedures in place to protect it from being used for money laundering or terrorist financing as per requirements 2.1(a) and 2.5 of the Code of Conduct for Firms.

Our concerns

We supervise those we regulate for compliance with money laundering legislation. Firms must comply with the MLR 2017 and any future legislation that comes into force. We are concerned that some firms may not be complying by failing to have adequate systems and controls in place to prevent, detect and report money laundering.

The Financial Action Task Force (FATF), an independent inter-governmental body, issued a report in 2013 highlighting the vulnerabilities of legal professionals to money laundering and terrorist financing, in which it identified 42 'Red Flag Indicators'.

Being aware of these indicators or warning signs of money laundering and terrorist financing should assist you in applying a risk based approach to meeting your obligations under the MLR 2017 and other money laundering legislation. If red flag indicators are present in your dealings with a client, you should ask further questions and consider making a suspicious activity report to your firm's Money Laundering Reporting Officer (MLRO) or the National Crime Agency, as appropriate.

The warning signs highlighted by FATF include:

If the client:

- Is secretive or evasive about who they are, the reason for the transaction, or the source of funds.

- Uses an intermediary, or does not appear to be directing the transaction, or appears to be disguising the real client.

- Avoids personal contact without good reason.

- Refuses to provide information or documentation or the documentation provided is suspicious.

- Has criminal associations.

- Has an unusual level of knowledge about money laundering processes.

- Does not appear to have a business association with the other parties but appears to be connected to them.

If the source of funds is unusual, such as:

- Large cash payments.

- Unexplained payments from a third party.

- Large private funding that does not fit the business or personal profile of the payer.

- Loans from non-institutional lenders.

- Use of corporate assets to fund private expenditure of individuals.

- Use of multiple accounts or foreign accounts.

If the transaction has unusual features, such as:

- Size, nature, frequency or manner of execution.

- Early repayment of mortgages/loans.

- Short repayment periods for borrowing.

- An excessively high value is placed on assets/securities.

- It is potentially loss making.

- Involving unnecessarily complicated structures or steps in transaction.

- Repetitive instructions involving common features/parties or back to back transactions with assets rapidly changing value.

- The transaction is unusual for the client, type of business or age of the business.

- Unexplained urgency, requests for short cuts or changes to the transaction particularly at last minute.

- Use of a Power of Attorney in unusual circumstances.

- No obvious commercial purpose to the transaction.

- Instructions to retain documents or to hold money in your client account.

- Abandoning transaction and/or requests to make payments to third parties or back to source.

- Monies passing directly between the parties.

- Litigation which is settled too easily or quickly and with little involvement by you.

If the instructions are unusual for your business such as:

- Outside your or your firm's area of expertise or normal business, or if client is not local to you and there is no explanation as to why a firm in your locality has been chosen.

- Willingness of client to pay high fees.

- Unexplained changes to legal advisers.

- Your client appears unconcerned or lacks knowledge about the transaction.

If there are geographical concerns such as:

- Unexplained connections with and movement of monies between other jurisdictions.

- Connections with jurisdictions which are subject to sanctions or are suspect because drug production, terrorism or corruption is prevalent, or there is a lack of money laundering regulation.

FATF has also published detailed guidance on how legal professionals may apply a risk-based approach to their efforts to prevent money laundering and terrorist financing. The guidance focuses on risk identification, assessment, management and mitigation and may aid you in assessing and improving the relevant procedures and practices in your work.

Our expectations

We expect all firms and individuals regulated by us to comply with money laundering legislation including taking appropriate steps to conduct customer due diligence when required to do so by the MLR 2017. We expect firms and individuals to be aware of, and act properly upon, warning signs that a transaction may be suspicious.

Failure to comply with this warning notice may lead to disciplinary action, criminal prosecution, or both.

Further help

Read full guidance on the MLR 2017.

Read resources and information about AML compliance.

If you require further assistance, please contact the *Professional Ethics helpline*.

8.7 Money laundering and terrorist financing suspicious activity reports

[Updated 25 November 2019 (Date first published: 8 December 2014)]

Status

This document is to help you understand your obligations and how to comply with them. We may have regard to it when exercising our regulatory functions.

Who is this warning notice relevant to?

This warning notice is relevant to all regulated persons, especially Compliance Officers for Legal Practice (COLPs), Compliance Officers for Finance and Administration (COFAs) and firms' Money Laundering Reporting Officers and Money Laundering Compliance Officers.

The SRA Standards and Regulations

You have a duty to ensure you comply with money laundering legislation. Failure to do so may result in you breaching one or more of the Principles, including:

- Principle 1 – acting in a way that upholds the constitutional principle of the rule of law, and the proper administration of justice.

- Principle 2 – acting in a way that upholds public trust and confidence in the solicitors' profession and in legal services provided by authorised persons.

- Principle 7 – acting in the best interests of each client.

Paragraphs 3.3 and 3.6 of the Code of Conduct for Solicitors, RELs and RFLs, and paragraph 4.3 of the Code of Conduct for Firms require firms and individuals to make sure they are competent and keep their professional knowledge and skills up to date.

In order to comply with paragraph 2.1(a) and 2.5 of the Code of Conduct for Firms, we also expect firms to have systems and procedures in place which are adequate to prevent, detect and report money laundering; and that firms monitor the efficacy of such systems to make sure that any risks to compliance are identified and addressed. This includes ensuring that relevant staff are appropriately trained and regularly updated in respect of the relevant legislation and their professional obligations, including the National Crime Agency's (NCA) requirements.

Our concerns

We supervise individuals and firms we regulate for compliance with money laundering legislation. We have identified a significant risk of firms failing to have adequate systems and controls to prevent, detect and report money laundering.

Recently, the NCA produced an analysis of suspicious activity reports (SARs) it receives for consent to proceed with transactions (known as "consent SARs" or "defence against Anti-Money Laundering SARs (DAML)"). Under the Proceeds of Crime Act (POCA) 2002, you are required to submit a SAR to the NCA if you know or suspect, or have reason to know or suspect, that an individual is engaged in money laundering and the information has come to you in the course of your business. There are similar obligations to submit SARs in relation to terrorist financing offences under the Terrorism Act (TACT) 2000.

The analysis conducted by the NCA concluded that a disproportionately high percentage of reports received from the legal sector were of poor quality because firms were providing inadequate information. The NCA announced that, from 1 October 2014, consent SARs that do not contain reasons for suspicion, or a statement regarding criminal property, will be closed by the NCA upon receipt. The NCA has published detailed guidance on this new process.

Failure to make a disclosure to the NCA in appropriate circumstances can be a criminal offence and proceeding with a transaction in the absence of consent may result in the commission of a principal money laundering offence.

Our expectations

You should have regard to the Standards and Regulations, in particular paragraph 7.1 of the Code of Conduct for Solicitors, RELs and RFLs, and paragraph 3.1 of the Code of Conduct for Firms, to make sure you comply with the Money Laundering Regulations 2017, and with legislation such as your legal obligations under POCA 2002 and TACT 2000.

We expect all firms and individuals regulated by us to comply with the NCA guidance in relation to submitting consent SARs.

The NCA has stated that one of the causes behind delays in the turnaround of consent requests is the non-inclusion of one or more of the elements required (where known in your course of business) of a submission, namely:

1. The information or other matter that gives grounds for knowledge, suspicion or belief

2. A description of the property that is known, suspected or believed to be criminal property, terrorist property or derived from terrorist property

3. A description of the prohibited act for which consent is sought

4. If known, the identity of the person or persons known or suspected to be involved in money laundering or who committed or attempted to commit an offence under any of sections 15 to 18 of TACT 2000

5. If known, the whereabouts of the property that is known or suspected to be criminal property, terrorist property or derived from terrorist property

If under (4) and (5) the identity of the person or persons or the whereabouts of the property is not known, then any information believed or reasonably believed that may assist in identifying (4) or (5) or both should be provided in the SAR.

Failure to comply with this warning notice may lead to disciplinary action, criminal prosecution or both.

Further help

From us

For guidance on warning signs that a transaction may be suspicious see our Warning notice: Money laundering and terrorist financing.

From others

NCA guidance on completing SARs; making consent requests; and the closure of inadequate consent SARs:

- The SARS regime
- Submitting a suspicious activity report (SAR) within the regulated sector

Further information and assistance on your reporting obligations can be found at Chapter 8 of the Law Society practice note and in the Law Society advice article Help! I'm a new MLRO: making a report.

If you require further assistance, please contact the *Professional Ethics helpline*.

8.8 Offensive communications

[Updated 25 November 2019 (Date first published: 24 August 2017)]

Status

This document is to help you understand your obligations and how to comply with them. We may have regard to it when exercising our regulatory functions.

Who is this warning notice relevant to?

This guidance is relevant to you if:

- you are a solicitor, a registered European lawyer (REL) or a registered foreign lawyer (RFL) and your communications fall short of the standards expected of the profession, whether in the course of private practice, or practising in a non-LSA business (ie a business which is not regulated by any of the approved regulators or outside practice
- you work in an SRA-regulated practice as a manager, consultant, employee or trainee, whether as a lawyer or an unqualified person, in relation to communications made by you during the course of business or outside work
- you are an SRA-regulated firm, or the COLP in an SRA-regulated law firm.

The Standards and Regulations

You must comply with the Principles and in particular:

- Principle 2 – act in a way that upholds public trust and confidence in the solicitors' profession and in legal services provided by authorised persons
- Principle 3 – act with independence
- Principle 5 – act with integrity
- Principle 6 – act in a way that encourages equality, diversity and inclusion

You must also have regard to the relevant paragraphs in the Code of Conduct for Solicitors, RELs and RFLs and the Code of Conduct for Firms, but in particular those paragraphs referred to below.

Our concerns

We have experienced a significant increase in the number of complaints concerning inappropriate communications, specifically in relation to (but not limited to) emails and the use of social media, both inside and outside of practice.

Examples of the type of behaviour we have investigated, (and which we subsequently referred to the SDT), include:

- making offensive or pejorative comments relating to another person's race, sexual orientation or religion

- referring to women in derogatory terms and making sexually explicit comments
- making comments which harass or victimise the recipient
- using language intended to shock or threaten
- making offensive or abusive comments to another firm about that firm or its client, or to individuals who are unrepresented

The warning below focuses on social media, but also includes emails and texts. It is also relevant to communication by telephone or letter.

Our expectations

That individuals below regulated by us comply with the Principles and the Codes, as appropriate.

- A solicitor, REL or RFL, or
- You work in an SRA-regulated law firm in any capacity

We expect you to behave in a way that demonstrates integrity and maintains the trust the public places in you and in the provision of legal services.

In the context of letters, emails, texts or social media, this means ensuring that the communications you send to others or post online do not contain statements which are derogatory, harassing, hurtful, puerile, plainly inappropriate or perceived to be threatening, causing the recipient alarm and distress.

In addition to Principle 6 above, if you are a solicitor, a REL or an RFL, paragraph 1.1 of the Code for Solicitors, RELs and RFLs requires that you do not unfairly discriminate by allowing your personal views to affect your professional relationships and the way in which you provide your services.

We treat any communications which are offensive seriously, whether on the grounds of any of the 'protected characteristics' under the Equality Act 2010 or otherwise. The protected characteristics are age, race, disability, religion or belief, pregnancy or maternity, sex or sexual orientation, gender reassignment and marriage or civil partnership. Depending on the circumstances, you may be at risk under all of the Principles referred to above.

You should also note that where a court or tribunal makes a finding that you have committed an unlawful act of discrimination in a communication sent or posted by you, we will treat that as prima facie evidence of misconduct which may give rise to disciplinary proceedings.

Bear in mind that sending an offensive, threatening or harassing communication may also amount to a criminal offence (eg under section 1 of the Malicious Communications Act 1988, section 127 of the Communications Act 2003 or the Protection from Harassment Act 1997). Depending on the circumstances, committing any of these offences or failing to comply with the Equality Act 2010, could leave you at risk under Principles 2, 5 and 6.

Communications in the course of business

Inter-office emails

The Principles referred to above apply not only when communicating with third parties outside the firm, but also to emails addressed to colleagues within your firm. We expect you to act at all times with integrity and the fact that you intended such communications to be private will not excuse your conduct. Once sent, you have no control over what happens to your email and by using your firm's email system, you run the risk that others may be able to access those emails.

Likewise, you cannot justify your conduct on the grounds that you did not intend to cause offence, or that the recipient(s) of your email was not offended. One of our key concerns as a regulator is to uphold the public's confidence in the integrity and high standards of the

APPENDIX 8

profession. You may therefore be at risk of disciplinary action if you send an email which has the potential of causing offence to third parties and/or undermining public trust in the profession.

Entering into an exchange with others which you perceive or intend to be humorous can pose a particular risk, especially when your humour is at the expense of others; what may seem to be light-hearted banter to you may be offensive to a third party. You should ensure that you do not inadvertently cross the line and become offensive in any of the ways referred to above.

Communications with clients

Most firms these days communicate with their clients by email or text rather than by letter. However, there are inherent risks in this. Such forms of communication by their nature are more 'instant' and tend to be less formal than letters.

This can lead to the blurring of the line between client and friend and the informality, together with the expectation of a quick reply, makes it easy to overlook the need to consider carefully what you are saying.

Being on friendly terms with your client or using informal language is not of course a problem in itself, but you must be careful to ensure that your communications remain professional at all times, both in the tone and content. This is particularly so where it is foreseeable that the communication is likely to be disclosed to a wider audience at some point.

If a client makes derogatory, discriminatory or inappropriate references to others in their communications to you, you should not participate or endorse those comments, nor pass the offensive comments on if it is not necessary to do so. Where your client's comments are potentially in breach of the law, you should draw this to your client's attention.

Communications with other opposing lawyers and litigants in person

It is not uncommon for emails with the other side in relation to a client's matter to be robust, particularly in litigation. However, you should ensure such communications do not cross the line by using inflammatory language or being gratuitously offensive, either to the other side or about their client.

Your role is to act in the client's best interests; antagonising the other side is unlikely to achieve this. We expect you to remain objective and not allow the matter to become personal, regardless of the provocation or your client's instructions. You are not your client's 'hired gun' and you may be at risk under Principle 3 if you allow your independence to be compromised by being drawn into using offensive language or making offensive comments in order to meet your client's expectations.

It is equally important to remain professional when dealing with an individual who is representing themselves or has appointed a McKenzie Friend. In a recent decision, the SDT fined a solicitor for his heated and abusive exchange of emails with a litigant in person, calling this 'completely unacceptable'. The SDT said it was the solicitor's responsibility to maintain his professionalism regardless of what that person may have done.

Managers and supervisors

As a manager of an SRA-regulated firm, you are responsible for ensuring that all those in your firm comply with the Standards and Regulations (paragraph 2.3 of the Code for Firms). You will therefore be at risk under the Principles referred to above if you become aware of such emails, but do not take appropriate steps to stop the behaviour and deal with the sender(s) (for example, in accordance with your disciplinary policy).

This also applies if you are not a manager, but you are responsible for supervising a colleague's work and do not take steps to stop the behaviour.

Bear in mind also that as a manager of an SRA-regulated practice, if you are of the view that the sender's comments are capable of amounting to serious misconduct or which you believe should be brought to our attention for investigation, you have an obligation to report the individual(s) to us in accordance with paragraphs 3.9 and 3.10 of the Code for Firms For more information see our guidance on our reporting and notification requirements.

Solicitors, RELs and RFLs, wherever they are practising, have a similar obligation to report (paragraph 7.7, Code for Solicitors, RELs and RFLs). However, if you are not in an SRA-regulated practice, your duty to report will only arise if the person whose conduct gives rise to your concern is regulated by us or by one of the other approved regulators.

Conduct outside the course of business

Solicitors, RELs and RFLs

The above Principles continue to apply to you (as the context admits) outside your practice, whether in some other business capacity or in your personal life. It is in this sphere – namely outside of work – that we are currently receiving the majority of complaints.

The risk referred to above – namely that social media by its nature tends to encourage instant communication without the necessary forethought – tends to be greater when you are outside a work context. You must at all times be aware of the content you are posting and the need for professionalism.

This is especially true if you are participating in online discussion (whether this be on Facebook, Twitter, other social media, forums, blogs, etc) and you have identified yourself as, or are known to be, a solicitor. You should bear in mind the possibility that users will re-share the content you have posted on their own social network, potentially leading to rapid sharing with a huge number of users. Similarly, you cannot rely on your own privacy settings to prevent the posting from being passed on by others.

Even if you do not identify yourself as a solicitor, anonymity is not guaranteed; material which you post under a pseudonym may still be traced back to you or you may be identified as a solicitor if you include a photograph of yourself.

You should also consider carefully before retweeting an offensive comment. Unless you refute the content, you will be at risk of being seen as implicitly endorsing it. If it comes to your attention that a third party has accessed your computer and posted an inappropriate comment in your name on a social media network, you should take immediate steps to go online to refute the comment. It is advisable in any event to regularly audit your online presence to remove any material which makes you uncomfortable.

Trainees and other managers or employees

If you are the COLP or a manager of an SRA-regulated firm, you must take all reasonable steps to ensure that the firm complies with our regulatory arrangements. This includes ensuring that the firm has effective systems and controls in place:

- to meet the requirements of the Standards and Regulations (paragraph 2.1, Code for Firms), and

- to identify, monitor and manage all material risks to the business (paragraph 2.5)

If a member of your firm sends or posts an inappropriate or offensive communication, it not only puts you at risk under the Principles above, it also has the potential of causing significant damage to your firm, both in terms of reputation and financially; for example, if clients react by withdrawing their business or are deterred from instructing your firm. In some circumstances, you could also be liable for your employee's actions (eg if the communication amounts to victimising or harassing a third party).

To comply with the Code, you should assess the potential risks to your firm in light of the above, taking into account the nature and size of your firm to determine whether you need to put in place a social media policy or some other system or controls. It is likely to be easier

APPENDIX 8

to take disciplinary action against a staff member if you have a social media policy in place dealing with its improper use.

To be effective, you should ensure that members of your firm are conversant with any policy or system you put in place.

Remember: if a complaint is made against an individual in your firm, you may be asked to demonstrate how you ensured compliance with paragraphs 2.1 and 2.5 of the Code for Firms.

Enforcement action

If an issue arises, failure to have proper regard to this warning notice is likely to lead to disciplinary action.

For further information on our approach to taking regulatory action, see our Enforcement Strategy and in particular, our topic guide Use of social media and offensive communications. This sets out examples of common mitigating and aggravating features which we are likely to take into account in determining the seriousness of the breach.

Further guidance

For guidance on any of the above conduct matters, contact the *Professional Ethics helpline*.

For advice on creating a social media policy for your firm, see the Law Society's practice note.

The Crown Prosecution Service has issued guidance on hate crime, which can include offensive communications.

8.9 Payment Protection Insurance claims

[Updated 25 November 2019 (Date first published: 29 August 2017)]

Status

This warning notice is to help you understand your obligations and how to comply with them. We may have regard to it when exercising our regulatory functions.

Who is this warning notice relevant to?

This warning notice is relevant to all those we regulate acting in claims for mis-sold payment protection insurance (PPI).

The SRA Standards and Regulations

The principles require you to act:

- **Principle 1: in a way that upholds the constitutional principle of the rule of law, and the proper administration of justice.**

  You have obligations not only to clients but also to the court and to third parties with whom you have dealings on your clients' behalf.

- **Principle 2: in a way that upholds public trust and confidence in the solicitors' profession and in legal services provided by authorised persons**

  You must behave in a way that maintains the trust the public places in you and in the provision of legal services. Members of the public should be able to place their trust in you. Any behaviour either within or outside your professional practice which undermines this trust damages not only you, but also the reputation of the legal profession and its ability to serve society.

- **Principle 5: with integrity.**

  Personal integrity is central to your role as the client's trusted adviser and should characterise all your professional dealings with clients, the court, other lawyers and the public.

- **Principle 7: in the best interests of each client.**

  You should always act in good faith and do your best for each of your clients.

You should have regard to the requirements set out in the SRA Code of Conduct For Solicitors, RELs and RFLs, in particular those highlighted below.

Paragraph 1.2 and you do not abuse your position by taking unfair advantage of clients or others.

Paragraph 5.1(a) and that clients are informed of any financial or other interest which you or your business or employer has in referring the client to another person for which an introducer has in referring the client to you.

Paragraph 8.6 and that clients are given information in a way they can understand. You make sure they are in a position to make informed decisions about the services they need, how their matter will be handled and the options available to them.

You should also have regard to the requirements set out in the SRA Code of Conduct for Firms.

Our concerns

Following our previously issued guidance and engagement with Government departments, lenders and others involved in the handling of PPI, we are concerned that law firms are failing in their duties to act in accordance with the Standards and Regulations by:

- acting in matters without first investigating whether there is a valid claim

- making claims without knowledge of the policyholder/consumer

- failing to properly identify clients and confirm client instructions

- submitting false claims in the hope of a settlement without further investigation by the defendant

- charging unreasonable costs for a limited amount of work contrary to their fiduciary and regulatory duties.

Law firms who conduct cases which demonstrate one or more of these features may face regulatory action. This may also give us reason to suspect dishonesty by their principals or staff.

Client interests and charges

You should always have regard to the SRA's Principles and requirements set out in the Codes of Conduct. You should make sure that you act in your client's best interest and with integrity, treat your clients fairly and uphold the rule of law.

Your retainer is with your client and you are responsible to your client both under the law and our regulatory requirements. To make sure that you act in your clients' interests and deliver the required quality of service you should have clear instructions from your client and an agreed course of action. Your client should have all the necessary information to make informed decisions on how their matter should be dealt with (see paragraph 8.6 of the code of conduct for solicitors, RELs and RFLs). Unless you have regular contact with your client, you'll be at risk of failing to achieve the required standards.

Unless instructions are confirmed with the client at each stage of the retainer, throughout the life cycle of a case including whether to accept and offer to settle a claim, you'll be at risk of committing serious misconduct.

When agreeing your fees with a client you should make sure they are fair and reasonable (Solicitors (non-contentious business) remuneration order 2009 article 3) having regard to all the circumstances of the case.

The Financial Guidance and Claims Act 2018 ("the Act") received royal assent on 10 May 2018. The act prohibits fees of more than 20 percent, excluding VAT, being charged for PPI claims and prevents you from charging a client where no award has been recovered.

The cap is effective from 10 July 2018 and continues until permanent rules are made by us.

We expect you to have informed your clients about the fee cap and its effect.

Although legislation sets a fee cap of 20 percent, this does not allow for all clients to be charged at this rate. Our view is that, any fees charged that are greater than 15 percent of a client's damages are unreasonable, unless the work involved and the risk to the firm clearly demands a greater percentage of the damages.

Legal proceedings should not be issued to try to avoid or limit the impact of the fee cap. Proceedings should only be issued when it is in the client's interests. Attempts to avoid or limit the impact of the fee cap by issuing proceedings are likely to breach the principles and the standards in the Code of Conduct. It is unlikely that you would be acting in your clients' interests or treating them fairly if you have agreed to be paid a percentage of the client's damages that exceed fees that would have been payable had your usual hourly rate been charged.

In all circumstances, any fees you charge should be reasonable and proportionate to the work undertaken. This is particularly the case where the work carried out is limited, for example, to submitting a notice of claim and agreeing settlement. It is important that you do not exaggerate the time or effort involved in submitting a claim.

Claims Management Companies looking to engage with you and form an alternative business structure (ABS) firms will not avoid regulation as fees they charge will also be subject to the interim fee cap and then any permanent rules that we make. All SRA licensed ABSs must comply with the Standards and Regulations and will be subject to regulatory action if issues of professional misconduct are identified.

Cold calling

You must make sure that clients do not come to you through cold calling by your firm or a third party. Some third parties obtain client details illegally and you may be at risk of infringing applicable data protection legislation by the unauthorised use or handling of data. You should make sure the introducer is aware of your duties and you check regularly that their methods of marketing and contact do not put you in breach of the code (see paragraph 5.1(e) of the Code of Conduct for Solicitor RELs and RFLs). You could, for example ask clients how they were first contacted. If you fail to make the position clear you are at risk of non-compliance.

Referral arrangements

All referral arrangements must comply with the required standards set out in paragraphs 5.1 to 5.3 in the Code of Conduct for Solicitors, RELs and RFLs. You must be satisfied and be able to evidence that the agreement or the relationship with the referrer does not affect your ability to take proper and ongoing instructions from your client, or the way you deal with your client's information or manage you client's matter.

You have duty to:

- make sure that contracts or other arrangements between your client and a referrer are fair; and

- cease dealing with a referrer whose contractual terms or other conduct are contrary to your clients' interests or to the rule of law.

If you rely on an introducer, you should:

- only use the services of claims management companies authorised and regulated by the Financial Conduct Authority

- review your referral arrangements regularly, making sure this one referrer is not your sole source of work, and

- make sure the arrangement or behaviour of the introducer does not put you in breach of your duties.

Fraudulent claims and taking unfair advantage

You should not take unfair advantage of third parties or demand anything for yourself or on behalf of your client, such as compensation for mis-selling that is not legally recoverable.

When taking instructions from a client, as you progress a claim against a third party, you should make sure you have correct details of the client's identity and claim. No claim should have been made on behalf of a client unless you can evidence there is a sound basis for the claim, and you have valid instructions.

If you have issued a claim knowing it is not a valid one or have not investigated the validity of the claim, you will leave yourself open to disciplinary action for breach of the principles and standards expected of you.

You may also leave yourself and your clients open to criminal action for fraudulent claims.

Our expectations

We expect all those regulated by us comply with the principles and the standards expected of you.

Previously issued guidance relating to PPI claims is still relevant and should be read alongside this notice.

Questions and Answers relating to the interim fee cap

On 10 May 2018, the Financial Guidance and Claims Act 2018 ("the Act") received Royal Assent. The Act:

- prohibits fees of more than 20%, excluding VAT, being charged for PPI claims, and

- restricts SRA authorised firms and regulated individuals from charging a client where no award has been recovered.

The interim fee cap is effective from 10 July 2018 (two months from the date of Royal Assent).

These questions and answers form have been produced to help firms in understanding the effect of the interim fee cap and detail how we intend to monitor and enforce it.

Q1. Where is the interim fee cap set out in the Act?

Section 29 of the Act states:

"PPI claims and charges for claims management services: general

1. This section and sections 30 to 32 make provision for a fee cap to apply in certain circumstances to charges for regulated services provided in connection with a PPI claim.

2. The following provisions explain terms used in those sections.

3. The fee cap applicable to the amount charged for regulated services provided in connection with a PPI claim is 20% of the amount recovered for the claimant in satisfaction of the claim.

Accordingly, where nothing is recovered (whether or not a claim has been made or concluded) the fee cap is zero."

Q2. When does the fee cap come into effect and who does it apply to?

The fee cap comes into effect on 10 July 2018 and applies to all SRA authorised firms and regulated individuals.

It also applies to Claims Management Companies (CMCs) and persons regulated by the General Council of the Bar or the Chartered Institute of Legal Executives.

Q3. Does the fee cap apply to retainers/fee agreements entered into before 10 July?

No. The fee cap applies only to fee agreements that are entered into with a client from 10 July 2018.

Agreements which include terms relating to fees that exceed the cap will be unenforceable and the client will be able to recover the excess amount paid from you.

Q4. If the PPI claim is referred from a claims management company or another third party, can all parties charge a fee that does not exceed 20%?

No. Firms should make sure that, where the introducer has provided claims management services to the client or the client is referred to a third party to provide services relating to the PPI claim, that the collective fees to do not exceed the 20% fee cap

Q5. Are there specific rules relating to the interim fee cap?

No. The fee cap is set out in primary legislation.

A firm that charges more than 20% of a client's redress will be in breach of the SRA Standards and Regulations.

Q6. Does the fee cap of 20% include VAT?

No. The 20% cap is exclusive of VAT

Q7. Does the fee cap apply if hourly charging rates are applied?

Yes. If a client is charged fees at an hourly rate, firms will still be required to comply with the interim fee cap.

The total of fees that are charged on your hourly rate must therefore, not amount to more than 20% excluding VAT of the total amount of redress awarded.

Q8. Does this cap mean charging 20% in all cases is acceptable?

No. All firms have a regulatory duty to act in their client's best interests, which means all charges must be justifiable and equate to the level of work undertaken. If we find evidence a firms' charges are unjustified, even if they are below the cap, we may still take potential action.

Since many PPI claims can be handled in a straightforward manner by members of the public themselves, without attracting a fee, we would also expect solicitors to always advise their clients accordingly in all such cases.

Q9. Does the interim fee cap apply to claims if legal proceedings have been issued?

"Regulated claims management services" do not include any reserved legal activities mentioned in section 12(1) (a) or (b) of the Legal Services Act 2007 (exercise of a right of audience or the conduct of litigation).

This means that the interim fee cap does not apply to charges for work carried out in taking formal steps in proceedings which have been issued.

The 'Conduct of litigation' however, does not include any steps taken prior to the commencement of litigation; i.e. before proceedings are issued or to work carried out after the issue of proceedings which are not formal steps. Therefore, the fee cap will apply to charges for work done prior to the commencement of proceedings and to work done after other than charges for steps taken in the actual proceedings such as filing court documents.

Attempts to avoid the fee cap by issuing proceedings are likely to breach the SRA Standards and Regulations. Firms should also have regard to *Andrew & Ors v Barclays Bank plc* [2012] EWHC B13 (Mercantile). Proceedings should only be issued if it is in the client's best interests.

Q10. How will the interim fee cap be enforced?

Decisions about what action we take are decided on a case by case basis and will depend on for example, intent, harm caused, patterns of behaviour and vulnerability of the client.

Firms have an obligation to make sure that all fees are fair and reasonable and to uphold the rule of law.

Q11. When does the interim fee cap come to an end?

Section 33 of the Act requires us to make rules which will prohibit SRA authorised firms and regulated individuals from charging fees above a specified amount in relation to all relevant claims management agreements, and services provided in connection with all relevant claims management activities, which concern claims in relation to financial products or services.

The interim fee cap will continue until those rules are made and come into force.

Further help

Previously issued guidance on acting in PPI matters.

If you require further assistance, please contact the *Professional Ethics helpline*.

8.10 Referral fees, LASPO and SRA Principles

[Updated 25 November 2019 (Date first published: 11 October 2013)]

Status

This document is to help you understand your obligations and how to comply with them. We may have regard to it when exercising our regulatory functions.

Who is this warning notice relevant to?

This warning notice is relevant to you if you enter into or already have referral arrangements for personal injury work. Our codes of conduct are clear that, in addition to the regulatory requirements set by us in the Standards and Regulations, we directly monitor and enforce the requirements relating to referral fees set out in section 56 of the Legal Aid, Sentencing and Punishment of Offenders Act 2012 (LASPO).

The SRA Standards and Regulations

The principles and codes of conduct are underpinned by our Enforcement Strategy, which explains in more detail our approach to taking regulatory action in the public interest. The following principles are most relevant to this warning notice, however other principles and parts of the Standards and Regulations may apply.

- Principle 1: You act in a way that upholds the constitutional principle of the rule of law, and the proper administration of justice.

  You have obligations not only to clients but also to the court and to third parties with whom you have dealings on your clients' behalf;

- Principle 2: You act in a way that upholds public trust and confidence in the solicitors' profession and in legal services provided by authorised persons.

  You must behave in a way that maintains the trust the public places in you and in the provision of legal services. Members of the public should be able to place their trust in you. Any behaviour either within or outside your professional practice which undermines this trust damages not only you, but also the reputation of the legal profession and its ability to serve society;

- Principle 4: You act with honesty.

  Acting honestly in all your dealings is fundamental.

- Principle 5: You act with integrity.

  Personal integrity is central to your role as the client's trusted adviser and should characterise all your professional dealings with clients, the court, other lawyers.

- Principle 7: You act in the best interests of each client.

  You should always act in good faith and do your best for each of your clients.

In addition to complying with the Principles and LASPO, paragraphs 5.1 – 5.3 of the code of conduct for solicitors, RELs and RFLs and paragraph 7.1(b) of the code of conduct for firms set out obligations in relation to referrals to and by you.

You must make sure you do not have an own client conflict because of your relationship with an introducer (paragraph 6.1 of the code of conduct for solicitors, RELs and RFLs and paragraph 6.1 of the code of conduct for firms).

You must make sure you are authorised by and have clear instructions from your client in every case and that you are not influenced by an introducer (paragraphs 1.2 and 3.1 of the code of conduct for solicitors, RELs and RFLs and paragraphs 1.2 and 4.1 of the code of conduct for firms).

Our concerns

We know that the ban on referral fees has raised difficult issues in relation to its application and interpretation. We are also aware that, because of the wording of LASPO, it is possible to have arrangements that involve the introduction or referral of personal injury work without being in breach of LASPO. We are concerned, however, that by setting up arrangements in a way that does not breach LASPO, some of those we regulate are failing to consider their wider duties to clients and others, and in doing so may breach the Standards and Regulations. Examples include:

- agreeing with an introducer to deduct money from clients' damages;
- inappropriate outsourcing of work to introducers;

- referrals to other service providers which are not in the best interests of clients;

- failure to properly advise clients about the costs and how their claim should be funded; and

- lack of transparency about the arrangement.

Our expectations

We expect you to comply with LASPO and your obligations in the Standards and Regulations at all times. We will take enforcement action against you if you ignore the ban on the payment of referral fees or fail to address the issues and risks associated with referral arrangements, particularly where arrangements are detrimental to the interests of clients.

Where arrangements are permitted by law you must comply with paragraphs 5.1 to 5.3 of the code of conduct for solicitors, RELs and RFLs and paragraph 7.1 (b) of the code of conduct for firms.

You are required to inform your clients about any fee-sharing agreements you have and to have those agreements in writing. Clients must be informed where you have a financial or other interest either in referrals made to you or by you to others.

You must be satisfied and be able to evidence the fact that an arrangement with a referrer does not adversely affect your independence and your ability to advise your client.

You have a duty to ensure that contracts or other arrangements between your client and a referrer are fair. You must stop dealing with a referrer whose contractual terms or whose behaviours are contrary to your clients' interests or to the rule of law (paragraph 5 (e) of the code of conduct for solicitors, RELs and RFLs and paragraph 7.1(b) of the code of conduct for firms).

For this reason, you should review your referral arrangements regularly.

You should be aware that the onus is on you to show that a payment is not a referral fee if it appears to us that it is (paragraph 5.2 of the code of conduct for solicitors, RELs and RFLs and paragraph 7.1 of the code of conduct for firms).

You must also make sure clients give informed consent if you refer, recommend or introduce them to a separate business or divide a client's matter between you and a separate business (paragraph 5.3 of the code of conduct for solicitors, RELs and RFLs and paragraph 7.1(b) of the code of conduct for firms).

Deductions from clients' damages

Some claims management companies ("CMCs") are seeking to charge clients a proportion of their damages in return for being referred to a suitable law firm and/or for other claims management services. If you are asked by a CMC to deduct payments from your client's damages or forward the client's damages to the CMC you are unlikely to be able to comply with your obligations in the Standards and Regulations.

This is because any arrangement must be in the interests of your client. You must always consider if your ability to advise the client will be impaired by your relationship with the introducer. The Solicitors Disciplinary Tribunal has on a number of occasions criticised solicitors for failing to give independent advice to their clients where their own commercial interests in a referral arrangement conflict with the interests of the client. You must act with independence at all times.

In all cases, money can only be deducted from a client's damages with the client's informed consent, although even with consent deducting money in this way .is unlikely to ever to be in the client's interest.

This type of arrangement may place the introducer in breach of LASPO and you should not enter into any arrangement that could result in a third party acting in breach of the legislation or our regulatory arrangements (paragraph 5.1 (e) of the code of conduct for solicitors, RELs and RFLs and paragraph 7.1(b) of the code of conduct for firms).

Outsourcing/paying for services

We know that some arrangements involve the introducer carrying out a certain amount of work on the client's matter and a firm paying the introducer for carrying out this work.

Provided the payment is for a genuine service and is reasonable in all the circumstances, such a payment may not breach LASPO. However, payments for the receipt of or making of referrals cannot not be dressed up as a payment for services. Remember, the onus is on you to demonstrate a fee is not a referral fee (paragraph 5.2 of the code for Individuals and paragraph 7.1(b) of the code for firms).

Before entering into an arrangement, you need to consider carefully whether it is appropriate and reasonable for the introducer to be carry out work at all. We know that sometimes outsourcing might include advising the client on the appropriate means of funding the matter, explaining and signing the client up to a conditional fee agreement or damages-based agreement. Remember that you have a duty to make sure your clients receive enough information to make informed decisions about their matter and the way it will be handled. In our view, outsourcing work of this nature, or relying on a third party to provide the necessary information to the client, breaches the Standards and Regulations.

Inappropriate referrals

Some we regulate and introducers are arranging for clients to purchase insurance, medical reports or other products or services at inflated prices so that the firm or introducer receives a higher commission. In some cases, the firm may have an interest in the business providing the product or service. The receipt of these commissions, either by you or another person, may put you in breach of section 56(2) of LASPO. Where you refer your client to another service provider, the referral must be in the client's best interests and must not compromise your independence. Remember, you are also required to account to the client for any financial benefit you receive as a result of their instructions (Paragraph 4.1 of the code of conduct for solicitors, RELs and RFLs and paragraph 5.1 of the code of conduct for firms). Even if the client has been sold these products or service before instructing you, you must make sure you are not facilitating arrangements that are detrimental to clients' interests.

You should also consider whether any requirement by an introducer to use a particular provider compromises your independence and your ability to comply with your obligations.

Funding and fee agreements

There have been suggestions that some firms are not discussing with clients the options for funding their claim and in particular that they are not exploring whether the client has insurance that would cover their legal costs, so that the firm can charge an uplift on their fees. Remember, you must not take advantage of your clients and you have a duty to make clients aware of, and understand, the options for funding their claim and the terms of any fee agreement they enter into with you. (See, for example, paragraphs 1.2, 8.6 and 8.7 of the code of conduct for solicitors, RELs and RFLs and paragraphs 1.2 and 7.1(c) of the Code for Firms).

Transparency

Clients need to be in a position to make informed decisions about any referral to a firm or third party and about how their matter will be dealt with. Some introducers and firms have set up complex arrangements in order to make sure they do not breach LASPO, for example by making the client, rather than the third-party introducer, provide information to the firm about a potential claim. If you are involved in such an arrangement, you must make sure your client is not misled about who they are dealing with and who is providing particular services.

Further help

If you require further assistance, please contact the *Professional Ethics helpline.*

8.11 Risk factors in personal injury claims

[Updated 25 November 2019 (Date first published: 21 March 2016)]

Status

This document is to help you understand your obligations and how to comply with them. We may have regard to it when exercising our regulatory functions.

Who is this warning notice relevant to?

This warning notice is relevant to all those we regulate who receive and make personal injury referrals from or to third parties, work closely with them or act on their instructions.

The SRA Standards and Regulations

The principles and codes of conduct are underpinned by our Enforcement Strategy, which explains in more detail our approach to taking regulatory action in the public interest. The following principles are most relevant to this warning notice, however other principles and parts of the Standards and Regulations may apply:

- Principle 1: You act in a way that upholds the constitutional principle of the rule of law, and the proper administration of justice

  You have obligations not only to clients but also to the court and to third parties with whom might you have dealings on your client's behalf.

- Principle 2: You act in a way that upholds public trust and confidence in the solicitors' profession and in legal services provided by authorised persons.

  You must behave in a way that maintains the trust the public places in you and in the provision of legal services. Members of the public should be able to place their trust in you. Any behaviour either within or outside your professional practice which undermines this trust damages not only you, but also the reputation of the legal profession and its ability to serve society.

- Principle 3: You act with independence.

  Your duties to the court and proper administration of justice means you have to act independently in all you do.

- Principle 4: You act with honesty.

  Acting honestly in all your dealings is fundamental.

- Principle 5: You act with integrity.

  Integrity is central to your role as the client's trusted adviser and should characterise all your professional dealings with clients, the court, other lawyers and the public.

- Principle 7: You act in the best interests of each client.

  You should always act in good faith and do your best for each of your clients.

In addition to the principles above, you have duties to comply with relevant parts of the code of conduct for solicitors, RELs and RFLs and the code of conduct for firms.

Our concerns

We are concerned that some of those we regulate are failing in their duties to act in accordance with the Standards and Regulations by:

- allowing third parties to cold call potential clients

- entering into referral agreements that are in breach of the Legal Aid Sentencing and Punishment of Offenders Act 2012 (LASPO)

- taking and acting on instructions from third parties without making sure that the instructions originate from the client

- settling claims without a medical report

- paying damages or sending cheques to third parties without accounting properly to the client

- bringing personal injury claims without their clients' authority

- in some extreme cases, bringing claims without the knowledge of the named client claimant

- not training and supervising their staff adequately

Those we regulate who conduct cases demonstrating one or more of these features may face regulatory action.

Our expectations

We expect you to comply with LASPO AND your obligations in the Standards and Regulations at all times. If you work in litigation you are involved in the administration of justice and must be alert to any risk of receiving or pursuing fraudulent or questionable cases. Where you identify such a risk, you must act immediately to remove that risk.

Cold calling and publicity

You must make sure that clients do not come to you as a consequence of cold calling by you or a third party. Some third parties obtain client details illegally by the unauthorised handling of personal data.

The Standards and Regulations provide that you must not make unsolicited approaches to members of the public, save for approaches to current client or former clients (paragraph 8.9 of the code of conduct for solicitors, RELs and RFLs and paragraph 7.1 (c) of the code of conduct for firms).

You must make sure any introducer is aware of your obligations and you check regularly that their methods of marketing (see paragraph 5.1(e) of the code of conduct for solicitors, RELs and RFLs and paragraph 7.1(b) of the code of conduct for firms).

Any publicity in relation to your work, through you or a third party, must not be inaccurate or misleading (paragraph 8.8 of the code of conduct for solicitors, RELs and RFLs and paragraph 7.1(c) of the code of conduct for firms).

Referral arrangements

In personal injury matters, you must not enter into any arrangements contrary to LASPO.

Where arrangements are permitted by law you must comply with paragraphs 5.1 to 5.3 of the code of conduct for solicitors, RELs and RFLs and paragraph 7.1 (b) of the code of conduct for firms. You are required to inform your clients about any fee-sharing agreements you have and to have those agreements in writing. Clients must be informed where you have a financial or other interest either in referrals made to you or by you to others.

You must be satisfied and be able to evidence the fact that an arrangement with a referrer does not adversely affect your independence and your ability to advise your client.

You have a duty to ensure that contracts or other arrangements between your client and a referrer are fair. You must stop dealing with a referrer whose contractual terms or t whose behaviours are contrary to your clients' interests or to the rule of law (paragraph 5 (e) of the code of conduct for solicitors, RELs and RFLs and paragraph 7.1(b) of the code of conduct for firms). For this reason, you should review your referral arrangements regularly.

You should be aware that the onus is on you to show that a payment is not a referral fee if it appears to us that it is (paragraph 5.2 of the code of conduct for solicitors, RELs and RFLs and paragraph 7.1 of the code of conduct for firms).

You must also make sure clients give informed consent if you refer, recommend or introduce them to a separate business or divide a client's matter between you and a separate business (paragraph 5.3 of the code of conduct for solicitors, RELs and RFLs and paragraph 7.1(b) of the code of conduct for firms).

Third-party instructions

The nature of personal injury litigation and the role of introducers in this sector means the risks to clients, defendants and the administration of justice are high and you must exercise extra caution to ensure that you are acting on valid instructions. This means taking instructions from – or checking them – direct with your client (paragraph 3.1 of the code of conduct for solicitors, RELs and RFLs and paragraph 4.1 of the code of conduct for firms). This is an ongoing duty throughout the life of a case and will apply in particular to significant decisions such as whether to settle a claim and for how much.

The commercial interest of a referrer means that you cannot safely rely, without further scrutiny, on common practices such as instructions being given on behalf of another person by, for example, a trusted family member or one member of a couple or partnership.

Clients' interests

The Principles are clear that you must act in your clients' best interests and you must act with integrity. Your retainer is with your client and you are responsible to your client both in law and as a matter of conduct. To make sure you act in your clients' best interests and deliver a proper standard of service you must have clear instructions from your client and an agreed course of action. Your client should have all the necessary information to make informed decisions on how their matter should be dealt with (paragraph 8.6 of the code of conduct for solicitors, RELs and RFLs and paragraph 7.1(c) of the code of conduct for firms). Unless you have regular contact with your client, you will be at risk of failing to comply with your obligations.

Before issuing proceedings, you must have proper authority to do so. You must be fully satisfied that the terms of the claim properly reflect client instructions. Instructions should be confirmed at each stage of the retainer and authority to make, accept or reject an offer must be separately obtained. Acting without client instructions may leave you open to wasted costs orders (see paragraph 2.6 of the code of conduct for solicitors, RELs and RFLs and paragraph 7.1(a) of the code of conduct for firms) and negligence proceedings as well as disciplinary action. Unless instructions are confirmed with the client at each stage of the retainer, throughout proceedings, you will be at risk of committing misconduct (see paragraph 3.1 of the code of conduct for solicitors, RELs and RFLs and paragraph 4.1 of the code of conduct for firms).

Where your client clearly wishes – and confirms to you directly – that you act on instructions given by a third party, you must satisfy yourself it is in your client's interests to take instructions in this way. You should explain to your client that taking third party instructions means sharing of their confidential information and explain the implications and risks involved of doing this, for example. inaccurate information being acted on or the misuse of information by the third party.

Only if you are satisfied that the arrangement is in the best interests of the client and that there is no conflict between the interests of the client and the person giving instructions may you act in this way. You must be satisfied your client has given free and informed consent to you doing so.

APPENDIX 8

You should be mindful of any arrangements which may incentivise any referrer to take a particular course of action in the case, for example an early settlement, without regard to the best outcome for the client.

In personal injury matters the best information on the facts and consequences of the injury are highly likely to rest with the client. Blanket forms of authority based on bulk or standard terms present a greater risk to the interests of clients and the administration of justice, and are highly unlikely to comply with your obligations.

Identification

Because of the risks involved in bringing false claims, you must properly identify your client by obtaining and verifying proof of identity and address (see paragraph 8.1 of the code of conduct for solicitors, RELs and RFLs and paragraph 7.1(c) of the code of conduct for firms). Unusual or suspicious factors must be investigated fully. If any third party, including any agent, provides copy documentation such as a photocopy of a passport, you must ensure that the client confirms its authenticity directly to you.

Costs

Your client should be fully aware of the costs you are charging, the costs information you deliver should be transparent and clear. You have a duty to give clients' the best possible information both at the time of engagement and when appropriate as their matter progresses, about the likely overall cost of their matter (see paragraph 8.7 of the code of conduct for solicitors, RELs and RFLs and paragraph 7.1(c) the code of conduct for firms).

When giving costs information you should consider the best way to deliver the information to that client. The information may be in writing or discussed with the client first and followed up in writing. You should take extra care when instructed by vulnerable clients.

Accounting

Damages must be paid to the client unless you have a valid reason and valid instructions direct from your client to make payments to a third party. Before making such payments you should familiarise yourself with our warning notice on the improper use of a client account. You should not make payments where there is any concern that the client may be avoiding liabilities eg bank overdraft, benefits claw back. Cheques made payable to the client must be given or sent to the client at their address. Failure to properly account to a client may lead to regulatory action for failure to account for client money.

- 3.3 You ensure that the service you provide to clients is competent and delivered in a timely manner.

- 3.4 You maintain your competence to carry out your role and keep your professional knowledge and skills up to date.

- 8.6 You give clients information in a way they can understand. You ensure they are in a position to make informed decisions about the services they need, how their matter will be handled and the options available to them.

Should you delay in returning money to your client, you may find your client has moved on and you cannot now easily locate them. You may be able to pay such amounts to a charity (rule 5.1(c) of the Accounts Rules) but you may be required to ask us for permission to do so and in all cases, you will be required to make proportionate efforts to trace the client. Any such costs incurred by you are not recoverable and must be borne by you. Efficient systems to make sure you promptly pay damages to your client will reduce the need to incur such costs and time.

Misleading the court and other parties

You must not mislead or attempt to mislead your clients, the court or others, either by your own acts or omissions or allowing or being complicit in the acts or omissions of others (including your client) (paragraphs 1.4 of the codes of conduct).

As an individual (paragraphs 2.1–2.3 of the code of conduct for solicitors, RELs and RFLs), you have fundamental obligations not to:

- misuse or tamper with evidence or attempt to do so

- seek to influence the substance of evidence, including generating false evidence or persuading witnesses to change their evidence

- provide or offer to provide any benefit to witnesses dependent upon the nature of their evidence or the outcome of the case.

As a firm you are accountable for compliance with the SRA's regulatory arrangements where your work is carried out through others, including your managers and those you employ or contract with (paragraph 2.3 of the code of conduct for firms). You cannot turn a blind eye to misconduct on the part of others in your firm. You have an obligation to have an effective system for supervising client matters (paragraph 4.4 of the code of conduct for firms).

You should take care not to leave yourself open to accusations of misleading others such as where you are taking instructions from a third party.

You should be aware, for example, that claims subject to the pre-action protocol that are submitted through the claims portal require the legal representative to confirm their clients' instructions to make a claim. Completing the submission when you do not have instructions from the claimant will therefore leave you at risk of legal and disciplinary action.

There are some exceptional circumstances where a solicitor acts on third party instructions, for example, when acting for a minor or on behalf of a client who does not have capacity), or on the implied authority of the client to issue proceedings. This may be where the client has given clear instructions to act, but for some justifiable reason may be out of contact just before issuing proceedings and you are unable to confirm instructions. This causes particular difficulty where the limitation period is about to expire. In these circumstances make sure you can justify your position by evidencing your actions and be aware of the risks inherent in going ahead.

Before accepting a settlement on behalf of your client, make sure you have all necessary information for an informed decision to be made by the client. Be aware that if you settle a matter without first obtaining medical evidence you run the risk of failing in your duty to your client. Without medical evidence you cannot be sure of your client's prognosis and the full extent of their injuries. You leave yourself open to complaints about inadequate compensation and disciplinary action for failing in your duties.

When you receive a medical report, you should take care to fully understand the client's prognosis and be able to assess the information contained within the report. If you are in any doubt as to the honesty or competence of an expert witness, such as a doctor preparing a medical report, you must cease using the expert, review all cases involving that expert, and check the underlying facts direct with your clients.

Staff training and office systems

You have an obligation to make sure that you have effective governance structures, arrangements, systems and controls in place that ensure you comply with our regulatory arrangements , as well as with other regulatory and legislative requirements, which apply to you (paragraph 2.1(a) of the code of conduct for firms).

Before taking on a personal injury matter you should be sure that:

- you have well trained staff who are in a position to offer a proper standard of service to clients.

- systems in place to ensure that matters are triaged effectively by those who have experience in and an understanding of the litigation process.

- systems that allow for the diarising of limitation periods and court timetables.

- staff training that is reviewed regularly to ensure that skills and knowledge are updated.

- full and proper supervision of staff where work is overseen and support and further expertise is available to fee earners and case workers.

(See paragraph 4.3 and 4.4 of the code of conduct for firms)

Taking on files from another firm

Before taking on cases from other firms you should carry out due diligence on the files you will be acquiring. Some files may be in a poor state, with imminent time limits, you should ensure you have the necessary time and resources to deal with the matters on an urgent basis.

You should not take on cases where you do not have the necessary skills and experience.

Enforcement action

Failure to have proper regard to this warning notice is likely to lead to disciplinary action.

Further help

If you require further assistance, please contact the *Professional Ethics helpline*.

8.12 Tax avoidance your duties

[Updated 25 November 2019 (Date first published: 21 September 2017)]

Status

This document is to help you understand your obligations and how to comply with them. We may have regard to it when exercising our regulatory functions.

Who is this warning notice relevant to?

All those we regulate involved either directly or indirectly advising clients about tax, handling client matters or transactions involving them in the design, implementation, organisation or management of tax affairs, schemes or arrangements.

The SRA Standards and Regulations

Principle 1: You act in a way that upholds the constitutional principle of the rule of law, and the proper administration of justice.

You have obligations not only to clients but also to the court and to third parties with whom you have dealings on your clients' behalf.

Principle 2: You act in a way that upholds public trust and confidence in the solicitors' profession and in legal services provided by authorised persons.

Members of the public should be able to place their trust in you. Any behaviour either within or outside your professional practice which undermines this trust damages not only you, but also the ability of the legal profession as a whole to serve society.

Principle 5: You act with integrity.

Integrity is central to your role as the client's trusted adviser and should characterise all your professional dealings with clients, the court, other lawyers and the public.

Principle 7: You act in the best interests of each client.

You should always act in good faith and do your best for each of your clients.

In addition to the above principles, relevant paragraphs in the code of conduct for solicitors, RELs and RFLs and code of conduct for firms will apply to your dealings with clients. In particular:

- Paragraphs 1.4 of the codes provide that you must not mislead or attempt to mislead others, either by your own acts or omissions or allowing or being complicit in the acts or omissions of others (including your client).

- Paragraph 3.2 of the code of conduct for solicitors, RELs and RFLs says you must ensure the service you provide to clients is competent and delivered in a timely manner.

- Paragraph 3.4 of the code for conduct of solicitors, RELs and RFLs and 4.2 of the code of conduct for firms says you must consider and take account of your client's attributes, needs and circumstances.

- Paragraph 8.6 of the code for solicitors, RELs and RFLs provides that you must give clients information in a way they can understand and you ensure they are in a position to make informed decisions about the services they need, how their matter will be handled and the options available to them.

- Paragraph 4.3 of the code for firms says you must make sure your managers and employees are competent to carry out their roles, and keep their professional knowledge and skills, as well as understanding of their legal, ethical and regulatory obligations, up to date. Similarly, paragraph 3.3 of the code for solicitors, RELs and RFLs provides that you must maintain your own competence to carry out your role and keep your professional knowledge and skills up to date.

- Paragraph 1.2 of both codes requires that you do not abuse your position by taking unfair advantage of clients or others.

Our concerns

We have concerns about anyone we regulate facilitating tax avoidance schemes that are aggressive in ways that go beyond the intentions of Parliament.

In *SRA v Chan, Ali & Abode Solicitors Ltd* [2015] EWHC 2659 (Admin) the High Court decided that the following allegation was proved in relation to a scheme to save Stamp Duty Land Tax (SDLT):

> "They involved themselves in transactions and/or facilitated, permitted or acquiesced in the promotion and/or implementation of schemes to avoid the payment of Stamp Duty Land Tax ... in circumstances where the schemes were of a dubious nature and the respondents knew, or ought to have known concerns had been raised by both HMRC and counsel in relation to the nature of the transactions..."

The High Court also commented more widely in the case:

> "In my view, the evidence and the primary findings of fact of the tribunal – all eminently justified – compel a conclusion there was here a want of integrity and a failure to act with independence. They also compel a conclusion the respondents so acted as to diminish the trust the public would place in the respondents and the provision of legal services."

The tax system is a necessary part of our economic system, raising funds for public services and making for a healthy economy that serves society. You play an important role in helping taxpayers comply with their legal obligations.

You must also act with integrity in your own dealings with HMRC. In the case of *SRA v Scott* it was noted by the High Court that the solicitor: "...admitted there had been financial mismanagement of his firm in breach of Principle 8 of the SRA Principles 2011 (now paragraphs 2.1–2.5 of the Code for Firms), as evidenced by the firm's debt to HMRC of £232,317, which had led to the failure of the firm."

We have also seen a solicitor struck off the roll when allegations were found proven against him including that, "he declared to ...HMRC... that he (together with his wife) had bought a property for a price lower than that which he paid ...resulting in him paying too little in stamp duty land tax..., and being subjected to a penalty by HMRC."

Our expectations

Acting with integrity

You are in a position of trust and not only owe duties to your client but also wider duties under the Principles. You have a duty to act in clients' interests by giving sound and competent advice while ensuring your advice does not go beyond the lawful arrangement of the clients' affairs.

We expect you to act with integrity at all times and for your dealings, and those on your clients' behalf, with HMRC are conducted on an open and honest basis and that you do not seek to rely on their lack of knowledge of your client's tax position.

When advising a client on avoidance of tax schemes you should make clear that any avoidance arrangements the client enters into might deliver tax outcomes that were never envisaged or intended by Parliament and may be challenged. You should be clear as to the legal implications, the costs and penalties of non-compliance should the arrangement fail.

You should also consider your own position in facilitating such an arrangement. Should the arrangement be found to be abusive, your conduct may be called into question. To be involved in such arrangements is likely to reflect badly on you and to damage public confidence in those delivering legal services. You will leave yourself open to the risk of disciplinary proceedings as well as committing a criminal offence. Where you believe, as a consequence of your client's instructions, you are at risk then you should advise your client you cannot comply with their instructions and unless they change instructions you should terminate your retainer.

HMRC and the wider context

It is important that you are familiar with the underlying approach of HMRC which is changing rapidly. To make sure you are complying with your obligations above we expect you to familiar with the wider context of your work when dealing with tax affairs, schemes or arrangements.

HMRC will take action against what it refers to as "abusive tax avoidance schemes". This is explained by HMRC: "The General Anti Abuse Rule (GAAR) 2013 legislation comes into operation when the course of action taken by the taxpayer aims to achieve a favourable tax result that Parliament did not anticipate when it introduced the tax rules in question and, critically, where that course of action cannot reasonably be regarded as reasonable."

HMRC has also indicated it might challenge arrangements not caught by GAAR: "There may be tax avoidance arrangements that are challenged by HMRC using other parts of the tax code, but if they are not abusive, they are not within the scope of the GAAR."

The promotion or implementation of abusive arrangements (applying the definition set out in the GAAR, PCRT or otherwise) will lead both client and adviser into difficulties with HMRC and may leave you open to disciplinary action. The most common schemes we have seen in recent years have related to avoiding SDLT. We will continue to scrutinise any of these schemes carefully.

Legislation and the wider context

You might have clients who are using avoidance schemes. As a consequence of the Finance Act 2016, the Serial Tax Avoidance Regime came into force on 15 September 2016 and affected users of avoidance schemes from 6 April 2017. Under the regime sanctions and penalties are imposed on those using tax avoidance schemes. Anybody using an avoidance scheme is advised to provide information of the scheme to HMRC.

The Government has legislated for other anti-avoidance reform including "follower notices" and "accelerated payments" and intends to bring in a new penalty that can be applied to professionals who enable tax avoidance which HMRC later defeats. A penalty regime is already in force for those who enable offshore tax evasion or non-compliance, under s162 and Schedule 20 of the Finance Act 2016.

You must be fully familiar with all changes to ensure you comply with the Principles at all times, particularly the requirement to act with integrity.

Professional conduct in relation to taxation (PCRT)

Accountancy bodies have worked with HMRC to produce a statement of Professional Conduct in Relation to Taxation (PCRT). This is published on the websites of the accountancy bodies (and is liable to change). We welcome this statement and say that: "These standards reflect our own principles, particularly that solicitors must be honest and act with integrity, and uphold the rule of law."

We therefore expect you to be familiar with the PCRT and adhere to its standards.

Where you consider that a scheme is likely to be found to be abusive, you can advise a client to this effect. Where a scheme can reasonably be argued not to be abusive, you can advise a client to this effect, facilitate the scheme where so instructed by a client properly advised as to the risks, and litigate on behalf of a client as to the legality of the scheme where you can do so in a manner consistent with your duty to the Court.

It is for the relevant courts and tribunals to adjudicate on the legality of tax avoidance schemes. However, where schemes are found to be abusive, or where there is no finding but schemes contain indicators of abuse (such as, but not limited to, misleading conduct or the indicators set out in the GAAR or PCRT), and solicitors have facilitated such schemes, whether by providing supportive advice which advocates the use of such schemes, or does not sufficiently highlight the associated risks or otherwise, we will see this, on the face of things, as evidence of breach of the SRA Principles and are likely to investigate. If a solicitor gives advice to the effect that a scheme is likely to be found to be abusive and takes no steps to give effect to such a scheme, it is unlikely that enforcement action would be taken.

Further help

If you require further assistance, please contact the *Professional Ethics helpline*.

8.13 Use of non-disclosure agreements (NDAs)

[Updated 12 November 2020 (Date first published: 12 March 2018)]

Scope of the warning notice

This warning notice covers the use of non-disclosure agreements (NDAs) and we use this term to include any form of agreement or contract, or a clause within a wider agreement or contract, under which it is agreed that certain information will be kept confidential.

The guidance is relevant to all NDAs regardless of the context in which the NDA arises – we have seen examples of concerning clauses in employment matters, as well as disputes involving negligence claims and commercial transactions.

It applies whether you are acting on behalf of a client, for your own firm in your capacity as an employer or for yourself. It includes the terms or proposed terms of the NDA and your conduct in handling the matter.

Our concerns

We recognise that NDAs are often legitimately used to protect commercial interests, reputation and confidentiality. NDAs can operate to the mutual benefit of both parties to the agreement.

This warning notice and the SRA's Standards and Regulations, do not prohibit the use of NDAs. However, we are concerned to ensure that NDAs are not used to prevent reporting to us, other regulators and law enforcement agencies or making disclosures which are protected by law. We are also concerned to ensure that those we regulate do not take unfair advantage of the other party when dealing with NDAs.

This warning notice provides a reminder of some of the key issues and risks that you should be aware of when dealing with NDAs and highlights your professional obligations. When we use the term 'dealing with' NDAs in this notice, we are referring to negotiating, drafting, advising on, enforcing or being a party to an NDA.

Status

Whilst this guidance does not form part of the SRA Standards and Regulations, we may have regard to it when exercising our regulatory functions.

Who is this guidance relevant to?

This guidance is relevant to everyone we regulate, for example:

- managers and employees of law firms

- those responsible for managing human resources and complaints in law firms

- practitioners dealing with NDAs, including in house lawyers acting for their internal client.

The SRA Principles

Failure to report a serious breach of our regulatory requirements or other wrongdoing or criminal conduct, by you or your firm, or improperly using NDAs, may put you in breach of one or more of the SRA Principles set out below. These require you to act:

Principle 1: in a way that upholds the constitutional principle of the rule of law, and the proper administration of justice

Principle 2: in a way that upholds public trust and confidence in the solicitors' profession and in legal services provided by authorised persons

Principle 3: with independence

Principle 5: act with integrity.

The Principles are applicable in your practice and when you are acting in a personal capacity, although certain Principles will be less relevant in this context. For example, Principle 3, acting with independence, is unlikely to apply when you are acting on your own behalf.

The SRA Standards and Regulations

Where you are acting for a client in a matter which involves an NDA, you should have regard specifically to the paragraphs in the SRA Code of Conduct for Solicitors, RELs and RFLs and the Code of Conduct for Firms set out below:

- You do not abuse your position by taking unfair advantage of clients or others: paragraph 2 of the Code of Conduct for Solicitors, RELs and RFLs and paragraph 1.2 of the Code of Conduct for Firms

- You cooperate with the SRA, other regulators, ombudsmen, and those bodies with a role overseeing and supervising the delivery of, or investigating concerns in relation to, legal services: paragraph 3 of the Code of Conduct for Solicitors, RELs and RFLs and paragraph 3.2 of the Code of Conduct for Firms

- You do not attempt to prevent anyone from providing information to the SRA or any other body exercising regulatory, supervisory, investigatory or prosecutory functions in the public interest: paragraph 7.5 of the Code of Conduct for Solicitors, RELs and RFLs and paragraph 3.10 of the Code of Conduct for Firms

- You report promptly to the SRA, or another approved regulator, as appropriate, any facts or matters that you reasonably believe are capable of amounting to a serious breach of their regulatory arrangements by any person regulated by them (including you) of which you are aware: paragraph 7.7 of the Code of Conduct for Solicitors, RELs and RFLs and paragraph 3.9 of the Code of Conduct for Firms:

Please see our guidance on Reporting and notification obligations for further information on when you should make a report to us.

Our expectations

We expect you to act in accordance with your professional obligations as set out above when dealing with NDAs.

Any attempt to prevent a person from complaining or providing information to us will be a failure to meet our Principles and Standards, as described above. A practitioner who uses an NDA improperly or behaves in a way that is in breach of these requirements is at risk of disciplinary action.

Your duty to act in the best interest of your client does not override your professional obligations to uphold the proper administration of justice, act in a way that maintains public trust and confidence, and to act with independence and integrity. If your client's instructions are to act in a way that is inconsistent with our requirements, you will need to consider whether you can continue to act for them.

We consider that NDAs would be improperly used if you sought to:

- use an NDA as a means of preventing, or seeking to impede or deter, a person from:

  - co-operating with a criminal investigation or prosecution

  - reporting an offence to a law enforcement agency

  - reporting misconduct, or a serious breach of our regulatory requirements to us, or making an equivalent report to any other body responsible for supervising or regulating the matters in question

  - making a protected disclosure under the Public Interest Disclosure Act 1998.

- use an NDA to influence the substance of such a report, disclosure or co-operation

- use an NDA to prevent any disclosure required by law

- use an NDA to prevent proper disclosure about the agreement or circumstances surrounding the agreement to professional advisers, such as legal or tax advisors and/or medical professionals and counsellors, who are bound by a duty of confidentiality

- include or propose clauses known to be unenforceable

- use warranties, indemnities and clawback clauses in a way which is designed to, or has the effect of, improperly preventing or inhibiting permitted reporting or disclosures being made for example, asking a person to warrant that they are not aware of any reason why they would make a permitted disclosure, in circumstances where a breach of warranty would activate a clawback clause.

NDAs or other terms in an agreement which contains an NDA, must not stipulate or give the impression to the person expected to agree the NDA, that reporting or disclosure as set out above is prohibited.

In dealing with NDAs, we expect you:

- to use standard plain English and to make sure that the terms are clear and relevant to the issues and claims likely to arise

- to be clear in the NDA what disclosures can and cannot be made and to whom

- to provide clear advice to your client about the terms of the NDA to help ensure that there is no confusion about what is or is not permitted. Confirming such advice in writing may help the individual bringing the claim if issues arise at a later date and may also help you if a concern is later raised about your role in advising on the NDA

- if the agreement is or forms part of a settlement agreement under the Employment Rights Act 1996, to ensure that you are aware of the requirements governing those agreements, including for the employee to be in receipt of independent advice.

Duty not to take unfair advantage

Taking unfair advantage of an opposing party, whether unrepresented or represented by a lawyer, professional adviser, litigation friend, intermediary or other third party, would result in a breach of your professional obligations. This would include:

- taking advantage of an opposing party's lack of legal knowledge or where they have limited access to legal representation or advice, for example proposing or including a clause which you know to be unenforceable, or threatening to litigate upon such a clause

- applying undue pressure or using inappropriate aggressive or oppressive tactics in your dealings with the opposing party or their representative, for example, imposing oppressive and artificial time limits on a vulnerable opposing party to agree the terms of the NDA

- seeking to rely on your position as solicitor as a means of exerting power over the opposing party, for example, by discouraging them from taking legal advice

- preventing someone who has entered into an NDA from keeping or receiving a copy.

Where the opposing party is vulnerable or unrepresented, your obligations to make sure there is no abuse of position, or unfair advantage taken, will be heightened.

Enforcement action

Failure to comply with this warning notice may lead to disciplinary action.

Other sources of help

SRA Risk paper Walking The Line: The balancing of duties in litigation.

SRA Reporting and notification obligations.

SRA resources on the use of non-disclosure agreements.

Law Society practice note The Use of non disclosure agreements.

Further help

For guidance on conduct issues, contact the *Professional Ethics helpline*.

SRA guidance on new regulatory arrangements

Guidance on the SRA Standards and Regulations and SRA Handbook

[See www.sra.org.uk/solicitors/guidance for recently published or updated guidance relevant to the SRA Standards and Regulations. At the time of printing, this includes the list below.]

[Last updated: 16 August 2021]

- Access to and disclosure of an incapacitated person's will (13 March 2017; updated 25 November 2019)

- Accountant's report and the exemption to obtain one (1 August 2017; updated 25 November 2019)

- Acting with honesty (8 August 2016; updated 25 November 2019)

- Acting with integrity (23 July 2019; updated 25 November 2019)

- Adequate and appropriate indemnity insurance (12 September 2019; updated 25 November 2019)

- Admission as a solicitor (8 August 2016; updated 25 November 2019)

- Agreeing regulatory and disciplinary outcomes (8 August 2016; updated 25 November 2019)

- Approval of employment under s.41 and s.43 of the Solicitors Act 1974 (25 November 2019)

- Approval of role holders (8 August 2016; updated 12 March 2021)

- Bringing criminal proceedings (8 August 2016; updated 25 November 2019)

- Can my business be authorised? (4 July 2019; updated 12 March 2021)

- Client care letters (19 July 2019; updated 25 November 2019)

- Closing down your practice (10 May 2013; updated 25 November 2019)

- Confidentiality of client information (25 November 2019)

- Conflicts of interest (29 October 2019; updated 2 March 2020)

- Dealing with claims for mis-sold payment protection insurance (PPI) (4 January 2012; updated 25 November 2019)

- Decision-making, reviews and attendance procedures (25 November 2019)

- Do I need to operate a client account? (4 July 2019; updated 25 November 2019)

- Does my business need to be authorised? (4 July 2019; updated 25 November 2019)

- Does my employer need to be authorised by an approved regulator? (12 September 2017; updated 25 November 2019)

- Does your interest in a licensed body require approval? (7 March 2014; updated 8 March 2021)

- Drafting and preparation of wills (6 May 2014; updated 25 November 2019)

- European Lawyers practising in the UK (22 April 2016; updated 25 March 2021)

- Firm authorisation (4 July 2019; updated 25 November 2019)

- Firm closures due to financial difficulties (5 August 2020)

- Firm risk assessments (29 October 2019; updated 25 November 2019)

- Governments Technical Notice on the impact of a no deal EU exit scenario on EU lawyers practising in the UK (12 October 2018; updated 6 May 2020)

- Granting authority to withdraw residual client balances (8 August 2016; updated 8 October 2020)

- Guidance note on the impact on exempt European lawyers of the Government's Statutory Instrument on the basis of a 'no deal' EU exit scenario (10 December 2018; updated 25 November 2019)

- Helping you keep accurate client accounting records (4 July 2019; updated 25 November 2019)

- How we approach decisions to intervene (8 August 2016; 25 November 2019)

- How we deal with money when we intervene (Statutory Trusts) (8 August 2016; updated 5 July 2021)

- How we gather evidence in our regulatory and disciplinary investigations (25 November 2019)

- How we make decisions and the criteria we apply (5 November 2019)

- How we make our decision to authorise a firm (8 August 2016; updated 25 November 2019)

- How we recover our costs (8 August 2016; 25 November 2019)

- How we regulate non-authorised persons (8 August 2016; updated 25 November 2019)

- Identifying your client (issued 25 November 2019)

- If we are investigating you (issued 25 November 2019)

- Joint accounts and record keeping (4 July 2019; updated 25 November 2019)

- Law firms carrying on insurance distribution activities (27 September 2018; updated 25 November 2019)

- Legal Disciplinary Practices (25 November 2019)

- Making decisions to investigate concerns (8 August 2016; updated 25 November 2019)

- Making payments from the SRA Compensation Fund (Archived) (8 August 2016; updated 25 November 2019)

- Meeting our standards for good qualifying work experience (10 December 2020)

- Multi-disciplinary practices: Regulation of non-reserved legal activity (issued 14 September 2019; updated 5 March 2021)

- Not for profit sector: summary (23 July 2019; updated 25 November 2019)

- Offering inducements to potential clients or clients (25 June 2013; updated 25 November 2019)

- On-site investigations (inspections) (8 August 2016; updated 25 November 2019)

- Parallel investigations (8 August 2016; updated 25 November 2019)

- Planning for and completing an accountant's report (1 August 2017; updated 14 September 2020)

- Preparing to become a sole practitioner or an SRA-regulated freelance solicitor (4 July 2019; updated 25 November 2019)

- Public trust and confidence (25 November 2019)

- Publishing complaints procedure (5 November 2018; updated 25 November 2019)

- Publishing regulatory and disciplinary decisions (1 September 2016; updated 25 November 2019)

- Putting matters right when things go wrong, and own interest conflicts (25 November 2019)

- Q&As on the ban of personal injury referral fees (1 April 2013; updated 3 December 2019)

- Recovering costs and payments from third parties (8 August 2016; updated 25 November 2019)

- Referral fees, LASPO and SRA Principles (11 October 2013; updated 25 November 2019)

- Registered Foreign Lawyers (23 July 2019; updated 24 March 2021)

- Reporting and notification obligations (25 November 2019)

- Reporting duties under the SRA Overseas Rules (25 November 2019)

- Responsibilities of COLPs and COFAs (25 November 2019)

- Risk factors in immigration work (7 December 2016; updated 25 November 2019)

- Sole practitioners and small firms regulatory starter pack (8 January 2016; updated 25 November 2019)

- Solicitors and Compliance Officers for Legal Practice (COLPs) confirming qualifying work experience (10 December 2020)

- SRA consumer credit (22 December 2015; updated 11 November 2020)

- SRA investigations: Health issues and medical evidence (7 August 2020)

- Statement of our position regarding firms operating a client's own account (30 September 2019; updated 25 November 2019)

- Taking money for your firm's costs (14 September 2020)

- The Insurance Act 2015 (6 July 2016; updated 25 November 2019)

- The Money Laundering, Terrorist Financing and Transfer of Funds (2 March 2018; updated 25 November 2019)

- The Prohibition of referral fees in LASPO 56 60 (25 March 2013; updated 25 November 2019)

- The SRA's approach to equality, diversity and inclusion (17 July 2019; updated 25 November 2019)

- The SRA's approach to financial penalties (13 August 2013; updated 25 November 2019)

- Third party managed accounts (6 December 2017; updated 25 November 2019)

- Transparency in price and service (2 October 2018; updated 3 August 2021)

- UK's Exit from EU – Possible non-negotiated outcome at end of transition period (12 March 2020; updated 31 December 2020)

- UK's Exit from EU – the end of the implementation period and beyond (21 December 2020; updated 14 January 2021)

- Unregulated organisations – Conflict and confidentiality (23 July 2019; updated 25 November 2019)

- Unregulated organisations for employers of SRA-regulated lawyers (23 July 2019; updated 25 November 2019)

- Unregulated organisations – giving information to clients (23 July 2019; updated 25 November 2019)

- Unsolicited approaches (advertising) to members of the public (16 December 2019)

- Vocational training for trainee solicitors (25 November 2019)

- When do I need a practising certificate? (4 July 2019; updated 25 November 2019)

Topic guides

[See www.sra.org.uk/sra/corporate-strategy/sra-enforcement-strategy/enforcement-practice/]

- Anti-money laundering (3 April 2020)

- Competence and standard of service (25 November 2019)

- Criminal offences outside of practice (25 November 2019)

- Driving with excess alcohol convictions (25 November 2019)

- Enforcement in practice (3 April 2020)

- SRA Transparency Rules (February 2019; updated 25 November 2019)

- Use of social media and offensive communications (7 February 2019; updated 25 November 2019)

SRA guidance on publishing regulatory and disciplinary decisions

[Updated 25 November 2019 (Date first published: 1 September 2016. For the latest updates to the material, please see www.sra.org.uk.]

Publishing regulatory and disciplinary decisions

Status

This guidance explains the approach we take when deciding whether to publish regulatory and disciplinary decisions.

Who is this guidance for?

All SRA-regulated firms, their managers, role holders and employees.

All solicitors, registered European lawyers (RELs) or registered foreign lawyers (RFLs).

Purpose of this guidance

This offers guidance on the approach we take when deciding whether to publish regulatory and disciplinary decisions on our website.

This guidance should be read in the context of our decision making and other guidance. This will be updated from time to time.

Why do we publish regulatory and disciplinary decisions?

We act in the public interest and this includes providing appropriate protection for consumers and supporting the administration of justice and the rule of law. There is a public interest in being transparent about the decisions we make and why we have made them, in order to:

- raise awareness amongst those we regulate about the action we have taken, to improve understanding of our expectations, and deter them from action which would fall below our standards or breach our requirements
- make sure consumers and others, including prospective employers are able to access appropriate information to:
    - inform them about the closure of a firm as a result of an intervention
    - enable them to make informed choices about whom to instruct or to employ
    - decide whether behaviour of concern should be reported to us for action
- make sure we are properly accountable to the public for the decisions we make and show that we are acting proportionately and consistently; and
- maintain public confidence by demonstrating appropriate action is taken when things go wrong.

What do we publish?

Our Roll, Registers and Publication Regulations set out the types of regulatory and disciplinary decisions that we publish on our website.

Many of these decisions are made under our Regulatory and Disciplinary Procedure Rules. These rules provide that we will publish such decisions, unless we consider the particular circumstances outweigh the public interest in publication.

The types of regulatory and disciplinary decisions we publish include:

- authorisation

- any current suspension, for example, of a solicitor's practising certificate or a body's authorisation

- any other decision subject to publication under rule 9.2, such as when we issue proceedings against a solicitor before the Solicitors Disciplinary Tribunal (SDT)

- any other order made by the SDT; and

- the exercise of our powers of intervention.

We may also publish other further information if we consider that it helps us meet the regulatory objectives, for example, we publish:

- approval of employment of people who are subject to section 43 of the Solicitors Act 1974 or struck off or suspended solicitors, under s41 of the Solicitors Act 1974; or

- refusal to issue a practising certificate.

We may also publish other information about our work and key decisions where we consider it is in the public interest, such as the status of our ongoing investigations.

When might publication not be in the public interest?

Generally, we expect that the regulatory and disciplinary decisions covered in our rules will be published on our website as it is in the public interest for us to do so.

Each decision to publish will be taken on its own merits and we will take into account all of the relevant circumstances. These include any representations made by the person who is subject of the decision and, where appropriate, other relevant third parties.

So we may decide not to publish a decision if we are satisfied that:

- we would be unable to do so without:

    – disclosing someone's confidential or legally privileged information, such as a confidential or sensitive medical condition

    – prejudicing other investigations or legal proceedings

- in all the circumstances the impact of publication on the regulated person would be disproportionate. In particular, we need to consider Article 8 of the European Convention on Human Rights and balance the right to a private life with the legitimate aim of publication, as set out above.

These factors are not exhaustive, and we will take into account all other factors that we consider to be relevant.

Example I

We decide to fine a solicitor for a caution they receive in relation to a criminal offence committed outside of practice. The solicitor provides medical evidence to us which confirms that the stress of the publication of the fine will cause them to become a suicide risk. Taking these factors into account, we decide that publication is not in the public interest.

Nature of the publication

We will publish the decision on our website. We will usually include a short statement of the decision with brief factual details, such as where the person is currently working or was previously working, and the reasons for the decision.

We will take reasonable steps to avoid the publication of information relating to other identifiable persons. Where it is necessary to refer to clients or colleagues their details will be appropriately anonymised.

Where we have reached any such relevant decisions by agreement, these will normally be published in full. The aim is to give the public enough information so they can understand the nature of and reason for the agreement we have reached and the reason for the outcome.

For more detail on our approach to such agreements, see our guidance on Regulatory Settlement Agreements

Timing and length of publication

We will normally publish decisions promptly. In exceptional cases, we may publish the fact of a referral to the SDT prior to certification by them, if we consider it is in the public interest for us to do so.

Certain decisions we publish are subject to review, such as fines and conditions. Generally, we will not publish such decisions during any period for their review and until any review has been determined or withdrawn.

When we intervene into a firm, it is important to let the clients know the firm has closed as soon as possible, so we aim to publish such decisions immediately following the intervention.

With the exception of intervention decisions, we will generally give the regulated person or firm the opportunity to comment in advance about whether the decision should be published. We will take their views in to account when deciding whether to publish and will tell them our decision.

We may determine that it is not appropriate to publish the decision at the time it was made, for example, if this will risk prejudicing any ongoing proceedings. But we may then do so at a later date once those proceedings have concluded, or the risk is no longer material.

Generally, we will automatically remove decisions from our website three years after the date of publication – unless we consider that exceptionally it is not in the public interest for us to do so.

However, some publications such as section 43 orders or decisions by the SDT to strike off or suspend a solicitor for more than three years, will remain on our website until the suspension has ended, or a successful application is made for the section 43 order, suspension or strike off to be lifted. This allows the public or other interested parties to find out important information about individuals we regulate.

Example 2

We issue proceedings against a solicitor at the SDT for allegations around significant misuse of client money and failure to comply with our Accounts Rules.

After considering their representations, we decide that it is appropriate to publish details of the referral. We therefore publish a brief summary of the allegations on our website, making it clear that they have not yet been proven.

At the SDT hearing the solicitor is struck from the roll. We then update the referral decision, confirming the sanction imposed and including a link to the SDT's website should anyone require access to the full judgment (normally available six–eight weeks after the decision).

APPENDIX 10

We update the solicitor's details on our website to make it clear that they are now prohibited from practice. We will keep this in place until the solicitor has successfully applied to be restored to the roll.

Review of publication

Decisions may be amended or removed from our website where we consider that publication is no longer necessary in the public interest, or to correct or update the information. We may decide to do this ourselves. For example, we will update the summary of allegations to be made at the SDT if they have agreed to make an amendment to those allegations, and as a result the published summary is inaccurate.

If we are asked to remove a publication within the three-year period because of new information or a change in circumstances, we will consider if this is appropriate. In doing so, we will have regard to all the circumstances and consider the request in line with the factors relating to the decision to publish set out above.

Further help

If you require further assistance, please contact the *Professional Ethics Guidance helpline*.

CCBE Code of Conduct

[The Code is reproduced with the kind permission of the CCBE. For the latest updates to the material, please see www.ccbe.eu/.]

Code of Conduct for European Lawyers

This Code of Conduct for European Lawyers was originally adopted at the CCBE Plenary Session held on 28 October 1988, and subsequently amended during the CCBE Plenary Sessions on 28 November 1998, 6 December 2002 and 19 May 2006. The Code also takes into account amendments to the CCBE statutes formally approved at an Extraordinary Plenary Session on 20 August 2007.

Contents

EXPLANATORY MEMORANDUM

1. Preamble

1.1. The Function of the Lawyer in Society

In a society founded on respect for the rule of law the lawyer fulfils a special role. The lawyer's duties do not begin and end with the faithful performance of what he or she is instructed to do so far as the law permits. A lawyer must serve the interests of justice as well as those whose rights and liberties he or she is trusted to assert and defend and it is the lawyer's duty not only to plead the client's cause but to be the client's adviser. Respect for the lawyer's professional function is an essential condition for the rule of law and democracy in society.

A lawyer's function therefore lays on him or her a variety of legal and moral obligations (sometimes appearing to be in conflict with each other) towards:

—   the client;

—   the courts and other authorities before whom the lawyer pleads the client's cause or acts on the client's behalf;

—   the legal profession in general and each fellow member of it in particular;

—   the public for whom the existence of a free and independent profession, bound together by respect for rules made by the profession itself, is an essential means of safeguarding human rights in face of the power of the state and other interests in society.

1.2. The Nature of Rules of Professional Conduct

1.2.1. Rules of professional conduct are designed through their willing acceptance by those to whom they apply to ensure the proper performance by the lawyer of a function which is recognised as essential in all civilised societies. The failure of the lawyer to observe these rules may result in disciplinary sanctions.

1.2.2. The particular rules of each Bar or Law Society arise from its own traditions. They are adapted to the organisation and sphere of activity of the profession in the Member State concerned and to its judicial and administrative procedures and to its national legislation. It is neither possible nor desirable that they should be taken out of their context nor that an attempt should be made to give general application to rules which are inherently incapable of such application.

The particular rules of each Bar and Law Society nevertheless are based on the same values and in most cases demonstrate a common foundation.

1.3. The Purpose of the Code

1.3.1. The continued integration of the European Union and European Economic Area and the increasing frequency of the cross-border activities of lawyers within the European Economic Area have made necessary in the public interest the statement of common rules which apply to all lawyers from the European Economic Area whatever Bar or Law Society they belong to in relation to their cross-border practice. A particular purpose of the statement of those rules is to mitigate the difficulties which result from the application of "double deontology", notably as set out in Articles 4 and 7.2 of Directive 77/249/EEC and Articles 6 and 7 of Directive 98/5/EC.

1.3.2. The organisations representing the legal profession through the CCBE propose that the rules codified in the following articles:

- be recognised at the present time as the expression of a consensus of all the Bars and Law Societies of the European Union and European Economic Area;

- be adopted as enforceable rules as soon as possible in accordance with national or EEA procedures in relation to the cross-border activities of the lawyer in the European Union and European Economic Area;

- be taken into account in all revisions of national rules of deontology or professional practice with a view to their progressive harmonisation.

They further express the wish that the national rules of deontology or professional practice be interpreted and applied whenever possible in a way consistent with the rules in this Code.

After the rules in this Code have been adopted as enforceable rules in relation to a lawyer's cross-border activities the lawyer will remain bound to observe the rules of the Bar or Law Society to which he or she belongs to the extent that they are consistent with the rules in this Code.

1.4. Field of Application *Ratione Personae*

This Code shall apply to lawyers as they are defined by Directive 77/249/EEC and by Directive 98/5/EC and to lawyers of the Associate and Observer Members of the CCBE.

1.5. Field of Application *Ratione Materiae*

Without prejudice to the pursuit of a progressive harmonisation of rules of deontology or professional practice which apply only internally within a Member State, the following rules shall apply to the cross-border activities of the lawyer within the European Union and the European Economic Area. Cross-border activities shall mean:

(a)   all professional contacts with lawyers of Member States other than the lawyer's own;

(b)   the professional activities of the lawyer in a Member State other than his or her own, whether or not the lawyer is physically present in that Member State.

1.6. Definitions

In this Code:

"Member State" means a member state of the European Union or any other state whose legal profession is included in Article 1.4.

"Home Member State" means the Member State where the lawyer acquired the right to bear his or her professional title.

"Host Member State" means any other Member State where the lawyer carries on cross-border activities.

"Competent Authority" means the professional organisation(s) or authority(ies) of the Member State concerned responsible for the laying down of rules of professional conduct and the administration of discipline of lawyers.

"Directive 77/249/EEC" means Council Directive 77/249/EEC of 22 March 1977 to facilitate the effective exercise by lawyers of freedom to provide services.

"Directive 98/5/EC" means Directive 98/5/EC of the European Parliament and of the Council of 16 February 1998 to facilitate practice of the profession of lawyer on a permanent basis in a Member State other than that in which the qualification was obtained.

2. *General Principles*

2.1. Independence

2.1.1. The many duties to which a lawyer is subject require the lawyer's absolute independence, free from all other influence, especially such as may arise from his or her personal interests or external pressure. Such independence is as necessary to trust in the process of justice as the impartiality of the judge. A lawyer must therefore avoid any impairment of his or her independence and be careful not to compromise his or her professional standards in order to please the client, the court or third parties.

2.1.2. This independence is necessary in non-contentious matters as well as in litigation. Advice given by a lawyer to the client has no value if the lawyer gives it only to ingratiate him- or herself, to serve his or her personal interests or in response to outside pressure.

2.2. Trust and Personal Integrity

Relationships of trust can only exist if a lawyer's personal honour, honesty and integrity are beyond doubt. For the lawyer these traditional virtues are professional obligations.

2.3. Confidentiality

2.3.1. It is of the essence of a lawyer's function that the lawyer should be told by his or her client things which the client would not tell to others, and that the lawyer should be the recipient of other information on a basis of confidence. Without the certainty of confidentiality there cannot be trust. Confidentiality is therefore a primary and fundamental right and duty of the lawyer.

The lawyer's obligation of confidentiality serves the interest of the administration of justice as well as the interest of the client. It is therefore entitled to special protection by the State.

2.3.2. A lawyer shall respect the confidentiality of all information that becomes known to the lawyer in the course of his or her professional activity.

2.3.3. The obligation of confidentiality is not limited in time.

2.3.4. A lawyer shall require his or her associates and staff and anyone engaged by him or her in the course of providing professional services to observe the same obligation of confidentiality.

2.4. Respect for the Rules of Other Bars and Law Societies

When practising cross-border, a lawyer from another Member State may be bound to comply with the professional rules of the Host Member State. Lawyers have a duty to inform themselves as to the rules which will affect them in the performance of any particular activity.

Member organisations of the CCBE are obliged to deposit their codes of conduct at the Secretariat of the CCBE so that any lawyer can get hold of the copy of the current code from the Secretariat.

2.5. Incompatible Occupations

2.5.1. In order to perform his or her functions with due independence and in a manner which is consistent with his or her duty to participate in the administration of justice a lawyer may be prohibited from undertaking certain occupations.

2.5.2. A lawyer who acts in the representation or the defence of a client in legal proceedings or before any public authorities in a Host Member State shall there observe the rules regarding incompatible occupations as they are applied to lawyers of the Host Member State.

2.5.3. A lawyer established in a Host Member State in which he or she wishes to participate directly in commercial or other activities not connected with the practice of the law shall respect the rules regarding forbidden or incompatible occupations as they are applied to lawyers of that Member State.

2.6. Personal Publicity

2.6.1. A lawyer is entitled to inform the public about his or her services provided that the information is accurate and not misleading, and respectful of the obligation of confidentiality and other core values of the profession.

2.6.2. Personal publicity by a lawyer in any form of media such as by press, radio, television, by electronic commercial communications or otherwise is permitted to the extent it complies with the requirements of 2.6.1.

2.7. The Client's Interest

Subject to due observance of all rules of law and professional conduct, a lawyer must always act in the best interests of the client and must put those interests before the lawyer's own interests or those of fellow members of the legal profession.

2.8. Limitation of Lawyer's Liability towards the Client

To the extent permitted by the law of the Home Member State and the Host Member State, the lawyer may limit his or her liabilities towards the client in accordance with the professional rules to which the lawyer is subject.

3. Relations with Clients

3.1. Acceptance and Termination of Instructions

3.1.1. A lawyer shall not handle a case for a party except on that party's instructions. The lawyer may, however, act in a case in which he or she has been instructed by another lawyer acting for the party or where the case has been assigned to him or her by a competent body.

The lawyer should make reasonable efforts to ascertain the identity, competence and authority of the person or body who instructs him or her when the specific circumstances show that the identity, competence and authority are uncertain.

3.1.2. A lawyer shall advise and represent the client promptly, conscientiously and diligently. The lawyer shall undertake personal responsibility for the discharge of the client's instructions and shall keep the client informed as to the progress of the matter with which the lawyer has been entrusted.

A lawyer shall not handle a matter which the lawyer knows or ought to know he or she is not competent to handle, without co-operating with a lawyer who is competent to handle it.

3.1.3. A lawyer shall not accept instructions unless he or she can discharge those instructions promptly having regard to the pressure of other work.

3.1.4. A lawyer shall not be entitled to exercise his or her right to withdraw from a case in such a way or in such circumstances that the client may be unable to find other legal assistance in time to prevent prejudice being suffered by the client.

3.2. Conflict of Interest

3.2.1. A lawyer may not advise, represent or act on behalf of two or more clients in the same matter if there is a conflict, or a significant risk of a conflict, between the interests of those clients.

3.2.2. A lawyer must cease to act for both or all of the clients concerned when a conflict of interests arises between those clients and also whenever there is a risk of a breach of confidence or where the lawyer's independence may be impaired.

3.2.3. A lawyer must also refrain from acting for a new client if there is a risk of breach of a confidence entrusted to the lawyer by a former client or if the knowledge which the lawyer possesses of the affairs of the former client would give an undue advantage to the new client.

3.2.4. Where lawyers are practising in association, paragraphs 3.2.1 to 3.2.3 above shall apply to the association and all its members.

3.3. Pactum de Quota Litis

3.3.1. A lawyer shall not be entitled to make a *pactum de quota litis*.

3.3.2. By *"pactum de quota litis"* is meant an agreement between a lawyer and the client entered into prior to final conclusion of a matter to which the client is a party, by virtue of which the client undertakes to pay the lawyer a share of the result regardless of whether this is represented by a sum of money or by any other benefit achieved by the client upon the conclusion of the matter.

3.3.3. *"Pactum de quota litis"* does not include an agreement that fees be charged in proportion to the value of a matter handled by the lawyer if this is in accordance with an officially approved fee scale or under the control of the Competent Authority having jurisdiction over the lawyer.

3.4. Regulation of Fees

A fee charged by a lawyer shall be fully disclosed to the client, shall be fair and reasonable, and shall comply with the law and professional rules to which the lawyer is subject.

3.5. Payment on Account

If a lawyer requires a payment on account of his or her fees and/or disbursements such payment should not exceed a reasonable estimate of the fees and probable disbursements involved.

Failing such payment, a lawyer may withdraw from the case or refuse to handle it, but subject always to paragraph 3.1.4 above.

3.6. Fee Sharing with Non-Lawyers

3.6.1. A lawyer may not share his or her fees with a person who is not a lawyer except where an association between the lawyer and the other person is permitted by the laws and the professional rules to which the lawyer is subject.

3.6.2. The provisions of 3.6.1 above shall not preclude a lawyer from paying a fee, commission or other compensation to a deceased lawyer's heirs or to a retired lawyer in respect of taking over the deceased or retired lawyer's practice.

3.7. Cost of Litigation and Availability of Legal Aid

3.7.1. The lawyer should at all times strive to achieve the most cost effective resolution of the client's dispute and should advise the client at appropriate stages as to the desirability of attempting a settlement and/or a reference to alternative dispute resolution.

3.7.2. A lawyer shall inform the client of the availability of legal aid where applicable.

3.8. Client Funds

3.8.1. Lawyers who come into possession of funds on behalf of their clients or third parties (hereinafter called "client funds") have to deposit such money into an account of a bank or similar institution subject to supervision by a public authority (hereinafter called a "client account"). A client account shall be separate from any other account of the lawyer. All client funds received by a lawyer should be deposited into such an account unless the owner of such funds agrees that the funds should be dealt with otherwise.

3.8.2. The lawyer shall maintain full and accurate records showing all the lawyer's dealings with client funds and distinguishing client funds from other funds held by the lawyer. Records may have to be kept for a certain period of time according to national rules.

3.8.3. A client account cannot be in debit except in exceptional circumstances as expressly permitted in national rules or due to bank charges, which cannot be influenced by the lawyer. Such an account cannot be given as a guarantee or be used as a security for any reason. There shall not be any set-off or merger between a client account and any other bank account, nor shall the client funds in a client account be available to defray money owed by the lawyer to the bank.

3.8.4. Client funds shall be transferred to the owners of such funds in the shortest period of time or under such conditions as are authorised by them.

3.8.5. The lawyer cannot transfer funds from a client account into the lawyer's own account for payment of fees without informing the client in writing.

3.8.6. The Competent Authorities in Member States shall have the power to verify and examine any document regarding client funds, whilst respecting the confidentiality or legal professional privilege to which it may be subject.

3.9. Professional Indemnity Insurance

3.9.1. Lawyers shall be insured against civil legal liability arising out of their legal practice to an extent which is reasonable having regard to the nature and extent of the risks incurred by their professional activities.

3.9.2. Should this prove impossible, the lawyer must inform the client of this situation and its consequences.

4. Relations with the Courts

4.1. Rules of Conduct in Court

A lawyer who appears, or takes part in a case, before a court or tribunal must comply with the rules of conduct applied before that court or tribunal.

4.2. Fair Conduct of Proceedings

A lawyer must always have due regard for the fair conduct of proceedings.

4.3. Demeanour in Court

A lawyer shall while maintaining due respect and courtesy towards the court defend the interests of the client honourably and fearlessly without regard to the lawyer's own interests or to any consequences to him- or herself or to any other person.

4.4. False or Misleading Information

A lawyer shall never knowingly give false or misleading information to the court.

4.5. Extension to Arbitrators etc.

The rules governing a lawyer's relations with the courts apply also to the lawyer's relations with arbitrators and any other persons exercising judicial or quasi-judicial functions, even on an occasional basis.

5. Relations between Lawyers

5.1. Corporate Spirit of the Profession

5.1.1. The corporate spirit of the profession requires a relationship of trust and co-operation between lawyers for the benefit of their clients and in order to avoid unnecessary litigation and other behaviour harmful to the reputation of the profession. It can, however, never justify setting the interests of the profession against those of the client.

5.1.2. A lawyer should recognise all other lawyers of Member States as professional colleagues and act fairly and courteously towards them.

5.2. Co-operation among Lawyers of Different Member States

5.2.1. It is the duty of a lawyer who is approached by a colleague from another Member State not to accept instructions in a matter which the lawyer is not competent to undertake. The lawyer should in such case be prepared to help that colleague to obtain the information necessary to enable him or her to instruct a lawyer who is capable of providing the service asked for.

5.2.2. Where a lawyer of a Member State co-operates with a lawyer from another Member State, both have a general duty to take into account the differences which may exist between their respective legal systems and the professional organisations, competences and obligations of lawyers in the Member States concerned.

5.3. Correspondence between Lawyers

5.3.1. If a lawyer intends to send communications to a lawyer in another Member State, which the sender wishes to remain confidential or without prejudice he or she should clearly express this intention prior to communicating the first of the documents.

5.3.2. If the prospective recipient of the communications is unable to ensure their status as confidential or without prejudice he or she should inform the sender accordingly without delay.

5.4. Referral Fees

5.4.1. A lawyer may not demand or accept from another lawyer or any other person a fee, commission or any other compensation for referring or recommending the lawyer to a client.

5.4.2. A lawyer may not pay anyone a fee, commission or any other compensation as a consideration for referring a client to him- or herself.

5.5. Communication with Opposing Parties

A lawyer shall not communicate about a particular case or matter directly with any person whom he or she knows to be represented or advised in the case or matter by another lawyer, without the consent of that other lawyer (and shall keep the other lawyer informed of any such communications).

5.6.

(Deleted by decision of the Plenary Session in Dublin on 6 December 2002)

5.7. Responsibility for Fees

In professional relations between members of Bars of different Member States, where a lawyer does not confine him- or herself to recommending another lawyer or introducing that other lawyer to the client but instead him- or herself entrusts a correspondent with a particular matter or seeks the correspondent's advice, the instructing lawyer is personally bound, even if the client is insolvent, to pay the fees, costs and outlays which are due to the foreign correspondent. The lawyers concerned may, however, at the outset of the relationship between them make special arrangements on this matter. Further, the instructing lawyer may at any time limit his or her personal responsibility to the amount of the fees, costs and outlays incurred before intimation to the foreign lawyer of the instructing lawyer's disclaimer of responsibility for the future.

5.8. Continuing Professional Development

Lawyers should maintain and develop their professional knowledge and skills taking proper account of the European dimension of their profession.

5.9. Disputes amongst Lawyers in Different Member States

5.9.1. If a lawyer considers that a colleague in another Member State has acted in breach of a rule of professional conduct the lawyer shall draw the matter to the attention of that colleague.

5.9.2. If any personal dispute of a professional nature arises amongst lawyers in different Member States they should if possible first try to settle it in a friendly way.

5.9.3. A lawyer shall not commence any form of proceedings against a colleague in another Member State on matters referred to in 5.9.1 or 5.9.2 above without first informing the Bars or Law Societies to which they both belong for the purpose of allowing both Bars or Law Societies concerned an opportunity to assist in reaching a settlement.

Explanatory Memorandum

This Explanatory Memorandum was prepared at the request of the CCBE Standing Committee by the CCBE's deontology working party, who were responsible for drafting the first version of the Code of Conduct itself. It seeks to explain the origin of the provisions of the Code, to illustrate the problems which they are designed to resolve, particularly in relation to cross-border activities, and to provide assistance to the Competent Authorities in the Member States in the application of the Code. It is not intended to have any binding force in the interpretation of the Code. The Explanatory Memorandum was adopted on 28 October 1988 and updated on the occasion of the CCBE Plenary Session on 19 May 2006. The Explanatory Memorandum also takes into account amendments to the CCBE Statutes formally approved at an Extraordinary Plenary Session on 20 August 2007. The list of professions in the commentary on article 1.4 is subject to modification.

The original versions of the Code are in the French and English languages. Translations into other Community languages are prepared under the authority of the national delegations.

Commentary on Article 1.1 – The Function of the Lawyer in Society

The Declaration of Perugia, adopted by the CCBE in 1977, laid down the fundamental principles of professional conduct applicable to lawyers throughout the EC. The provisions of Article 1.1 reaffirm the statement in the Declaration of Perugia of the function of the lawyer in society which forms the basis for the rules governing the performance of that function.

Commentary on Article 1.2 – The Nature of Rules of Professional Conduct

These provisions substantially restate the explanation in the Declaration of Perugia of the nature of rules of professional conduct and how particular rules depend on particular local circumstances but are nevertheless based on common values.

Commentary on Article 1.3 – The Purpose of the Code

These provisions introduce the development of the principles in the Declaration of Perugia into a specific Code of Conduct for lawyers throughout the EU the EEA and Swiss Confederation, and lawyers of the Associate and Observer Members of the CCBE, with particular reference to their cross-border activities (defined in Article 1.5). The provisions of Article 1.3.2 lay down the specific intentions of the CCBE with regard to the substantive provisions in the Code.

Commentary on Article 1.4 – Field of Application Ratione Personae

The rules are stated to apply to all lawyers as defined in the Lawyers Services Directive of 1977 and the Lawyers Establishment Directive of 1998, and lawyers of the Associate and Observer Members of the CCBE. This includes lawyers of the states which subsequently acceded to the Directives, whose names have been added by amendment to the Directives. The Code accordingly applies to all the lawyers represented on the CCBE, whether as full Members, Associate Members or as Observer Members, namely:

Albania	Avokat
Andorra	Advocat
Armenia	Pastaban
Austria	Rechtsanwalt
Belgium	Avocat / Advocaat / Rechtsanwalt
Bosnia and Herzegovina	Advokat / Odvjetnik
Bulgaria	Advokat
Croatia	Odvjetnik
Cyprus	Dikegóros

Czech Republic	Advokát
Denmark	Advokat
Estonia	Vandeadvokaat
Finland	Asianajaja / Advokat
FYROM	Advokat
France	Avocat
Georgia	Advokati / Advokatebi
Germany	Rechtsanwalt
Greece	Dikegóros
Hungary	Ügyvéd
Iceland	Lögmaður
Ireland	Barrister / Solicitor
Italy	Avvocato
Latvia	Zverinats advokats
Liechtenstein	Rechtsanwalt
Lithuania	Advokatas
Luxembourg	Avocat / Rechtsanwalt
Malta	Avukat / Prokuratur Legali
Montenegro	Advokat
Moldova	Avocat
Netherlands	Advocaat
Norway	Advokat
Poland	Adwokat / Radca prawny
Portugal	Advogado
Romania	Avocat
Serbia	Advokat
Slovak Republic	Advokát / Advokátka
Slovenia	Odvetnik / Odvetnica
Spain	Abogado / Advocat / Abokatu / Avogado
Sweden	Advokat
Switzerland	Rechtsanwalt / Anwalt / Fürsprech / Fürsprecher / Advocat / avocat / avvocato /advocat
Turkey	Avukat
Ukraine	Advokat
United Kingdom	Advocate / Barrister / Solicitor

It is also hoped that the Code will be acceptable to the legal professions of other non-member states in Europe and elsewhere so that it could also be applied by appropriate conventions between them and the Member States.

Commentary on Article 1.5 – Field of Application Ratione Materiae

The rules are here given direct application only to "cross-border activities", as defined, of lawyers within the EU, the EEA and Swiss Confederation and lawyers of the Associate and

Observer Members of the CCBE – see above on Article 1.4, and the definition of "Member State" in Article 1.6. (See also above as to possible extensions in the future to lawyers of other states.) The definition of cross-border activities would, for example, include contacts in state A even on a matter of law internal to state A between a lawyer of state A and a lawyer of state B; it would exclude contacts between lawyers of state A in state A of a matter arising in state B, provided that none of their professional activities takes place in state B; it would include any activities of lawyers of state A in state B, even if only in the form of communications sent from state A to state B.

Commentary on Article 1.6 – Definitions

This provision defines a number of terms used in the Code, "Member State", "Home Member State", "Host Member State", "Competent Authority", "Directive 77/249/EEC" and "Directive 98/5/EC".

The reference to "where the lawyer carries on cross-border activities" should be interpreted in light of the definition of "cross-border activities" in Article 1.5.

Commentary on Article 2.1 – Independence

This provision substantially reaffirms the general statement of principle in the Declaration of Perugia.

Commentary on Article 2.2 – Trust and Personal Integrity

This provision also restates a general principle contained in the Declaration of Perugia.

Commentary on Article 2.3 – Confidentiality

This provision first restates, in Article 2.3.1, general principles laid down in the Declaration of Perugia and recognised by the ECJ in the *AM&S* case (157/79). It then, in Articles 2.3.2 to 4, develops them into a specific rule relating to the protection of confidentiality. Article 2.3.2 contains the basic rule requiring respect for confidentiality. Article 2.3.3 confirms that the obligation remains binding on the lawyer even if he or she ceases to act for the client in question. Article 2.3.4 confirms that the lawyer must not only respect the obligation of confidentiality him- or herself but must require all members and employees of his or her firm to do likewise.

Commentary on Article 2.4 – Respect for the Rules of Other Bars and Law Societies

Article 4 of the Lawyers Services Directive contains the provisions with regard to the rules to be observed by a lawyer from one Member State providing services on an occasional or temporary basis in another Member State by virtue of Article 49 of the consolidated EC treaty, as follows:

(a)   activities relating to the representation of a client in legal proceedings or before public authorities shall be pursued in each Host Member State under the conditions laid down for lawyers established in that state, with the exception of any conditions requiring residence, or registration with a professional organisation, in that state;

(b)   a lawyer pursuing these activities shall observe the rules of professional conduct of the Host Member State, without prejudice to the lawyer's obligations in the Member State from which he or she comes;

(c)   when these activities are pursued in the UK, "rules of professional conduct of the Host Member State" means the rules of professional conduct applicable to solicitors, where such activities are not reserved for barristers and advocates. Otherwise the rules of professional conduct applicable to the latter shall apply. However, barristers from Ireland shall always be subject to the rules of professional conduct applicable in the UK to barristers and advocates. When these activities are pursued in Ireland "rules of professional conduct of the Host Member State" means, in so far as they govern the oral presentation of a case in court, the rules of professional conduct applicable to barristers. In all other cases the rules of professional conduct applicable to solicitors shall apply. However, barristers and advocates from the UK shall always be subject to the rules of professional conduct applicable in Ireland to barristers; and

(d)   a lawyer pursuing activities other than those referred to in (a) above shall remain subject to the conditions and rules of professional conduct of the Member State from which he or she comes without prejudice to respect for the rules, whatever their source, which govern the profession in the Host Member State, especially those concerning the incompatibility of the exercise of the activities of a lawyer with the exercise of other activities in that state, professional secrecy, relations with other lawyers, the prohibition on the same lawyer acting for parties with mutually conflicting interests, and publicity. The latter rules are applicable only if they are capable of being observed by a lawyer who is not established in the Host Member State and to the extent to which their observance is objectively justified to ensure, in that state, the proper exercise of a lawyer's activities, the standing of the profession and respect for the rules concerning incompatibility.

The Lawyers Establishment Directive contains the provisions with regard to the rules to be observed by a lawyer from one Member State practising on a permanent basis in another Member State by virtue of Article 43 of the consolidated EC treaty, as follows:

(a)   irrespective of the rules of professional conduct to which he or she is subject in his or her Home Member State, a lawyer practising under his home-country professional title shall be subject to the same rules of professional conduct as lawyers practising under the relevant professional title of the Host Member State in respect of all the activities the lawyer pursues in its territory (Article 6.1);

(b)   the Host Member State may require a lawyer practising under his or her home-country professional title either to take out professional indemnity insurance or to become a member of a professional guarantee fund in accordance with the rules which that state lays down for professional activities pursued in its territory.

Nevertheless, a lawyer practising under his or her home-country professional title shall be exempted from that requirement if the lawyer can prove that he or she is covered by insurance taken out or a guarantee provided in accordance with the rules of the Home Member State, insofar as such insurance or guarantee is equivalent in terms of the conditions and extent of cover. Where the equivalence is only partial, the Competent Authority in the Host Member State may require that additional insurance or an additional guarantee be contracted to cover the elements which are not already covered by the insurance or guarantee contracted in accordance with the rules of the Home Member State (Article 6.3); and

(c)   a lawyer registered in a Host Member State under his or her home-country professional title may practise as a salaried lawyer in the employ of another lawyer, an association or firm of lawyers, or a public or private enterprise to the extent that the Host Member State so permits for lawyers registered under the professional title used in that state (Article 8).

In cases not covered by either of these Directives, or over and above the requirements of these Directives, the obligations of a lawyer under Community law to observe the rules of other Bars and Law Societies are a matter of interpretation of any relevant provision, such as the Directive on Electronic Commerce (2000/31/EC). A major purpose of the Code is to minimise, and if possible eliminate altogether, the problems which may arise from "double deontology", that is the application of more than one set of potentially conflicting national rules to a particular situation (see Article 1.3.1).

Commentary on Article 2.5 – Incompatible Occupations

There are differences both between and within Member States on the extent to which lawyers are permitted to engage in other occupations, for example in commercial activities.

APPENDIX 11

The general purpose of rules excluding a lawyer from other occupations is to protect the lawyer from influences which might impair the lawyer's independence or his or her role in the administration of justice. The variations in these rules reflect different local conditions, different perceptions of the proper function of lawyers and different techniques of rule-making. For instance in some cases there is a complete prohibition of engagement in certain named occupations, whereas in other cases engagement in other occupations is generally permitted, subject to observance of specific safeguards for the lawyer's independence.

Articles 2.5.2 and 3 make provision for different circumstances in which a lawyer of one Member State is engaging in cross-border activities (as defined in Article 1.5) in a Host Member State when he or she is not a member of the Host State legal profession.

Article 2.5.2 imposes full observation of Host State rules regarding incompatible occupations on the lawyer acting in national legal proceedings or before national public authorities in the Host State. This applies whether the lawyer is established in the Host State or not.

Article 2.5.3, on the other hand, imposes "respect" for the rules of the Host State regarding forbidden or incompatible occupations in other cases, but only where the lawyer who is established in the Host Member State wishes to participate directly in commercial or other activities not connected with the practice of the law.

Commentary on Article 2.6 – Personal Publicity

The term "personal publicity" covers publicity by firms of lawyers, as well as individual lawyers, as opposed to corporate publicity organised by Bars and Law Societies for their members as a whole. The rules governing personal publicity by lawyers vary considerably in the Member States. Article 2.6 makes it clear that there is no overriding objection to personal publicity in cross-border practice. However, lawyers are nevertheless subject to prohibitions or restrictions laid down by their home professional rules, and a lawyer will still be subject to prohibitions or restrictions laid down by Host State rules when these are binding on the lawyer by virtue of the Lawyers Services Directive or the Lawyers Establishment Directive.

Commentary on Article 2.7 – The Client's Interest

This provision emphasises the general principle that the lawyer must always place the client's interests before the lawyer's own interests or those of fellow members of the legal profession.

Commentary on Article 2.8 – Limitation of Lawyer's Liability towards the Client

This provision makes clear that there is no overriding objection to limiting a lawyer's liability towards his or her client in cross-border practice, whether by contract or by use of a limited company, limited partnership or limited liability partnership. However it points out that this can only be contemplated where the relevant law and the relevant rules of conduct permit – and in a number of jurisdictions the law or the professional rules prohibit or restrict such limitation of liability.

Commentary on Article 3.1 – Acceptance and Termination of Instructions

The provisions of Article 3.1.1 are designed to ensure that a relationship is maintained between lawyer and client and that the lawyer in fact receives instructions from the client, even though these may be transmitted through a duly authorised intermediary. It is the responsibility of the lawyer to satisfy him- or herself as to the authority of the intermediary and the wishes of the client.

Article 3.1.2 deals with the manner in which the lawyer should carry out his or her duties. The provision that the lawyer shall undertake personal responsibility for the discharge of the instructions given to him or her means that the lawyer cannot avoid responsibility by delegation to others. It does not prevent the lawyer from seeking to limit his or her legal liability to the extent that this is permitted by the relevant law or professional rules – see Article 2.8.

Article 3.1.3 states a principle which is of particular relevance in cross-border activities, for example when a lawyer is asked to handle a matter on behalf of a lawyer or client from another state who may be unfamiliar with the relevant law and practice, or when a lawyer is asked to handle a matter relating to the law of another state with which he or she is unfamiliar.

A lawyer generally has the right to refuse to accept instructions in the first place, but Article 3.1.4 states that, having once accepted them, the lawyer has an obligation not to withdraw without ensuring that the client's interests are safeguarded.

Commentary on Article 3.2 – Conflict of Interest

The provisions of Article 3.2.1 do not prevent a lawyer acting for two or more clients in the same matter provided that their interests are not in fact in conflict and that there is no significant risk of such a conflict arising. Where a lawyer is already acting for two or more clients in this way and subsequently there arises a conflict of interests between those clients or a risk of a breach of confidence or other circumstances where the lawyer's independence may be impaired, then the lawyer must cease to act for both or all of them.

There may, however, be circumstances in which differences arise between two or more clients for whom the same lawyer is acting where it may be appropriate for the lawyer to attempt to act as a mediator. It is for the lawyer in such cases to use his or her own judgement on whether or not there is such a conflict of interest between them as to require the lawyer to cease to act. If not, the lawyer may consider whether it would be appropriate to explain the position to the clients, obtain their agreement and attempt to act as mediator to resolve the difference between them, and only if this attempt to mediate should fail, to cease to act for them.

Article 3.2.4 applies the foregoing provisions of Article 3 to lawyers practising in association. For example a firm of lawyers should cease to act when there is a conflict of interest between two clients of the firm, even if different lawyers in the firm are acting for each client. On the other hand, exceptionally, in the "chambers" form of association used by English barristers, where each lawyer acts for clients individually, it is possible for different lawyers in the association to act for clients with opposing interests.

Commentary on Article 3.3 – Pactum de Quota Litis

These provisions reflect the common position in all Member States that an unregulated agreement for contingency fees (*pactum de quota litis*) is contrary to the proper administration of justice because it encourages speculative litigation and is liable to be abused. The provisions are not, however, intended to prevent the maintenance or introduction of arrangements under which lawyers are paid according to results or only if the action or matter is successful, provided that these arrangements are under sufficient regulation and control for the protection of the client and the proper administration of justice.

Commentary on Article 3.4 – Regulation of Fees

Article 3.4 lays down three requirements: a general standard of disclosure of a lawyer's fees to the client, a requirement that they should be fair and reasonable in amount, and a requirement to comply with the applicable law and professional rules.

In many Member States machinery exists for regulating lawyers' fees under national law or rules of conduct, whether by reference to a power of adjudication by the Bar authorities or otherwise. In situations governed by the Lawyers Establishment Directive, where the lawyer is subject to Host State rules as well as the rules of the Home State, the basis of charging may have to comply with both sets of rules.

Commentary on Article 3.5 – Payment on Account

Article 3.5 assumes that a lawyer may require a payment on account of the lawyer's fees and/ or disbursements, but sets a limit by reference to a reasonable estimate of them. See also on Article 3.1.4 regarding the right to withdraw.

Commentary on Article 3.6 – Fee Sharing with Non-Lawyers

In some Member States lawyers are permitted to practise in association with members of certain other approved professions, whether legal professions or not. The provisions of Article 3.6.1 are not designed to prevent fee sharing within such an approved form of association. Nor are the provisions designed to prevent fee sharing by the lawyers to whom the Code applies (see on Article 1.4 above) with other "lawyers", for example lawyers from non-Member States or members of other legal professions in the Member States such as notaries.

Commentary on Article 3.7 – Cost of Litigation and Availability of Legal Aid

Article 3.7.1 stresses the importance of attempting to resolve disputes in a way which is cost-effective for the client, including advising on whether to attempt to negotiate a settlement, and whether to propose referring the dispute to some form of alternative dispute resolution.

Article 3.7.2 requires a lawyer to inform the client of the availability of legal aid where applicable. There are widely differing provisions in the Member States on the availability of legal aid. In cross-border activities a lawyer should have in mind the possibility that the legal aid provisions of a national law with which the lawyer is unfamiliar may be applicable.

Commentary on Article 3.8 – Client Funds

The provisions of Article 3.8 reflect the recommendation adopted by the CCBE in Brussels in November 1985 on the need for minimum regulations to be made and enforced governing the proper control and disposal of clients' funds held by lawyers within the Community. Article 3.8 lays down minimum standards to be observed, while not interfering with the details of national systems which provide fuller or more stringent protection for clients' funds.

The lawyer who holds clients' funds, even in the course of a cross-border activity, has to observe the rules of his or her home Bar. The lawyer needs to be aware of questions which arise where the rules of more than one Member State may be applicable, especially where the lawyer is established in a Host State under the Lawyers Establishment Directive.

Commentary on Article 3.9 – Professional Indemnity Insurance

Article 3.9.1 reflects a recommendation, also adopted by the CCBE in Brussels in November 1985, on the need for all lawyers in the Community to be insured against the risks arising from professional negligence claims against them.

Article 3.9.2 deals with the situation where insurance cannot be obtained on the basis set out in Article 3.9.1.

Commentary on Article 4.1 – Rules of Conduct in Court

This provision applies the principle that a lawyer is bound to comply with the rules of the court or tribunal before which the lawyer practises or appears.

Commentary on Article 4.2 – Fair Conduct of Proceedings

This provision applies the general principle that in adversarial proceedings a lawyer must not attempt to take unfair advantage of his or her opponent. The lawyer must not, for example, make contact with the judge without first informing the lawyer acting for the opposing party or submit exhibits, notes or documents to the judge without communicating them in good time to the lawyer on the other side unless such steps are permitted under the relevant rules of procedure. To the extent not prohibited by law a lawyer must not divulge or submit to the court any proposals for settlement of the case made by the other party or its lawyer without the express consent of the other party's lawyer. See also on Article 4.5 below.

Commentary on Article 4.3 – Demeanour in Court

This provision reflects the necessary balance between respect for the court and for the law on the one hand and the pursuit of the client's best interest on the other.

Commentary on Article 4.4 – False or Misleading Information

This provision applies the principle that the lawyer must never knowingly mislead the court. This is necessary if there is to be trust between the courts and the legal profession.

Commentary on Article 4.5 – Extension to Arbitrators etc.

This provision extends the preceding provisions relating to courts to other bodies exercising judicial or quasi-judicial functions.

Commentary on Article 5.1 – Corporate Spirit of the Profession

These provisions, which are based on statements in the Declaration of Perugia, emphasise that it is in the public interest for the legal profession to maintain a relationship of trust and cooperation between its members. However, this cannot be used to justify setting the interests of the profession against those of justice or of clients (see also on Article 2.7).

Commentary on Article 5.2 – Co-operation among Lawyers of Different Member States

This provision also develops a principle stated in the Declaration of Perugia with a view to avoiding misunderstandings in dealings between lawyers of different Member States.

Commentary on Article 5.3 – Correspondence between Lawyers

In certain Member States communications between lawyers (written or by word of mouth) are normally regarded as to be kept confidential as between the lawyers. This means that the content of these communications cannot be disclosed to others, cannot normally be passed to the lawyers' clients, and at any event cannot be produced in court. In other Member States, such consequences will not follow unless the correspondence is marked as "confidential".

In yet other Member States, the lawyer has to keep the client fully informed of all relevant communications from a professional colleague acting for another party, and marking a letter as "confidential" only means that it is a legal matter intended for the recipient lawyer and his or her client, and not to be misused by third parties.

In some states, if a lawyer wishes to indicate that a letter is sent in an attempt to settle a dispute, and is not to be produced in a court, the lawyer should mark the letter as "without prejudice".

These important national differences give rise to many misunderstandings. That is why lawyers must be very careful in conducting cross-border correspondence.

Whenever a lawyer wants to send a letter to a professional colleague in another Member State on the basis that it is to be kept confidential as between the lawyers, or that it is "without prejudice", the lawyer should ask in advance whether the letter can be accepted on that basis. A lawyer wishing that a communication should be accepted on such a basis must express that clearly in the communication or in a covering letter.

A lawyer who is the intended recipient of such a communication, but who is not in a position to respect, or to ensure respect for, the basis on which it is to be sent, must inform the sender immediately so that the communication is not sent. If the communication has already been received, the recipient must return it to the sender without revealing its contents or referring to it in any way; if the recipient's national law or rules prevent the recipient from complying with this requirement, he or she must inform the sender immediately.

Commentary on Article 5.4 – Referral Fees

This provision reflects the principle that a lawyer should not pay or receive payment purely for the reference of a client, which would risk impairing the client's free choice of lawyer or the client's interest in being referred to the best available service. It does not prevent fee-sharing arrangements between lawyers on a proper basis (see also on Article 3.6 above).

In some Member States lawyers are permitted to accept and retain commissions in certain cases provided: a) the client's best interests are served, b) there is full disclosure to the client and c) the client has consented to the retention of the commission. In such cases the retention of the commission by the lawyer represents part of the lawyer's remuneration for the service provided to the client and is not within the scope of the prohibition on referral fees which is designed to prevent lawyers making a secret profit.

Commentary on Article 5.5 – Communication with Opposing Parties

This provision reflects a generally accepted principle, and is designed both to promote the smooth conduct of business between lawyers and to prevent any attempt to take advantage of the client of another lawyer.

Commentary on Article 5.6 – Change of Lawyer

Article 5.6 dealt with change of lawyer. It was deleted from the Code on 6 December 2002.

Commentary on Article 5.7 – Responsibility for Fees

These provisions substantially reaffirm provisions contained in the Declaration of Perugia. Since misunderstandings about responsibility for unpaid fees are a common cause of difference between lawyers of different Member States, it is important that a lawyer who wishes to exclude or limit his or her personal obligation to be responsible for the fees of a foreign colleague should reach a clear agreement on this at the outset of the transaction.

Commentary on Article 5.8 – Continuing Professional Development

Keeping abreast of developments in the law is a professional obligation. In particular it is essential that lawyers are aware of the growing impact of European law on their field of practice.

Commentary on Article 5.9 – Disputes amongst Lawyers in Different Member States

A lawyer has the right to pursue any legal or other remedy to which he or she is entitled against a colleague in another Member State. Nevertheless it is desirable that, where a breach of a rule of professional conduct or a dispute of a professional nature is involved, the possibilities of friendly settlement should be exhausted, if necessary with the assistance of the Bars or Law Societies concerned, before such remedies are exercised.

Council for Licensed Conveyancers Code of Conduct

[The Code is reproduced with the kind permission of the CLC. For the latest updates to the material, please see www.clc-uk.org.]

Council for Licensed Conveyancers Code of Conduct

[6 October 2011]

Introduction

This *Code of Conduct* was made in accordance with s.20 of the *Administration of Justice Act 1985*; s.53 of the *Courts and Legal Services Act 1999*; and s.83 of the *Legal Services Act 2007*.

All individuals and bodies regulated by the *CLC* must comply with this Code and its associated *regulatory arrangements*. In this Code "you" refers to individuals and bodies (and the employees and managers within them) regulated by the *CLC*. You must not permit anyone else to act or fail to act in such a way as to amount to a breach of this Code. Your main driver should be the delivery of positive *client outcomes*. The Code comprises *principles* and *specific requirements*, which taken together deliver positive *Outcomes* for your *Clients* and, particularly in relation to *Overriding Principle* 6, for others you deal with.

To effectively secure the protection of, and the provision of choice for, the consumer of legal services, you must at all times comply with the following *Overriding Principles*:

1. Act with independence and integrity;

2. Maintain high standards of work;

3. Act in the best interests of your *Clients*;

4. Comply with your duty to the court;

5. Deal with regulators and ombudsmen in an open and co-operative way;

6. Promote equality of access and service.

These are underpinned by *principles* of behaviour which must be demonstrated and *specific requirements* which must be complied with in order that the *Overriding Principles* are supported.

Disciplinary proceedings may be taken against you if the *CLC* believes there has been a breach of this Code, meaning that *clients* do not receive the standard of legal services they should reasonably expect to receive. The *CLC's* response will be informed by the *CLC's* Regulatory and *Enforcement* Policies.

In exceptional circumstances the *CLC* may waive a provision, or provisions, of the *regulatory arrangements* for an individual, body or circumstance for a particular purpose, or purposes, and with the *conditions* specified in the waiver.

Overriding Principle 1. Act with independence and integrity

Outcomes – you must deliver the following *Outcomes*:

1.1　*Clients* receive good quality independent information, representation and advice;

1.2　*Clients* receive an honest and lawful service;

1.3　*Client money* is kept separately and safely.

Principles – delivery of these *Outcomes* requires you to act in a principled way:

(a)　You do not allow your independence to be compromised.

(b)　You act honestly, professionally and decently.

(c)　You do not conduct yourself in a manner which may result in a breach of the law nor in any other manner which may bring the legal profession into disrepute.

(d)　You *carry on Reserved Legal Activity* only through a person entitled to *carry on* that activity.

(e)　You do not give false or misleading information relating to the provision of *Regulated Services*.

(f)　You do not allow fee arrangements to prejudice your independence or professional judgement.

(g)　You do not conduct business under a misleading name.

(h)　You keep *Client money* safe.

(i)　You do not publicise your business through unsolicited communications in person or by telephone.

(j)　Your advertising is clear, accurate and fair.

(k)　You keep *Client money* entirely separate from your money or the money of the entity.

(l)　You do not take unfair advantage of any person, whether or not a *Client* of the business.

Specific Requirements – you must also comply with the following *specific requirements*:

(m)　You comply with *anti-money laundering and prevention of financing terrorism legislation*.

(n)　When acting as a *CLC* licensee, you accept instructions only to act in a matter which is regulated by the *CLC*.

(o)　All business *communications*, websites and office premises display information confirming the entity is regulated by the *CLC* and the names of the *Managers* (identifying those who are *Authorised Persons*).

Overriding Principle 2. Maintain high standards of work

Outcomes – you must deliver the following *Outcomes*:

2.1　*Clients* are provided with a high standard of legal services;

2.2　*Client* matters are dealt with using care, skill and diligence;

2.3　Appropriate *arrangements*, resources, procedures, skills and commitment are in place to ensure *Clients* always receive a high standard of service.

Principles – delivery of these *Outcomes* requires you to act in a principled way:

(a)　You provide the level of service appropriate for, and agreed with, the *Client*.

(b)　You keep your skills and legal knowledge up-to-date.

(c)　You ensure all individuals within the entity are competent to do their work.

(d)   You supervise and regularly check the quality of work in *Client* matters.

(e)   You comply fully with any undertaking given by you.

(f)   You *systematically* identify and mitigate risks to the business and to *Clients*.

(g)   You promote ethical practice and compliance with regulatory requirements.

(h)   You enable staff to raise concerns which are acted on appropriately.

(i)   You maintain proper governance, management, supervision, financial, and risk management *arrangements* and *controls*.

(j)   You administer oaths, affirmations and declarations properly.

(k)   You deliver services in accordance with timetables reasonably agreed with the *Client*.

Specific Requirements – you must also comply with the following *specific requirements*:

(l)   *Control* of an entity is from a permanent fixed address in England or Wales.

(m)   A *Manager* who is an *Authorised Person* is responsible for ensuring that all of the entity's *employees* are properly supervised.

(n)   You make provision for alternative supervision *arrangements* in case of illness, accident or other unforeseen event.

(o)   You maintain proper records to evidence your *arrangements* and *controls* and how they are applied.

Overriding Principle 3. Act in the best interests of your Clients

Outcomes – you must deliver the following *Outcomes*:

3.1   Each *Client's* best interests are served;

3.2   *Clients* receive advice appropriate to their circumstances;

3.3   *Clients* have the information they need to make informed decisions;

3.4   *Clients* are aware of any referral arrangements and that they are consistent with your responsibilities both to them and to the *CLC*;

3.5   *Clients* are aware of any limitation or any condition resulting from your relationship with another party;

3.6   *Clients'* affairs are treated confidentially (except as required or permitted by law or with the *Client's* consent).

Principles – delivery of these *Outcomes* requires you to act in a principled way:

(a)   You only accept instructions and act in relation to matters which are within your professional competence.

(b)   You keep the interests of the *Client* paramount (except as required by the law or the *CLC's regulatory arrangements*).

(c)   You do not act for a *Client* where you judge it is not in their best interests for you to do so.

(d)   You do not accept instructions from a person nor continue to act for a *Client* whose interests conflict directly with your own, the entity's, or another *Client*.

(e)   You disclose *client* information only as the *Client* has instructed (or as required by the *CLC's regulatory arrangements* or by law), keeping effective records of any disclosures you make.

(f)   You only recommend a particular person, business or product when it is in the best interests of the *Client*.

(g) You cease acting in a matter if the *Client* so instructs or, in the absence of such instructions where it is reasonable to do so.

(h) You provide the *Client* with information which is accurate, useful and appropriate to the particular *Client*.

(i) You only provide *Regulated Services* whilst you have *CLC*-approved *professional indemnity insurance* in force.

(j) You provide the *Client* with all relevant information relating to any fee arrangements or fee changes.

(k) You advise *Clients* of the name and status of the person dealing with their matter and the name of the person responsible for overall supervision.

(l) You consult *Clients* on key decisions in a timely way.

(m) You *promptly* advise *Clients* of any significant changes to projected *costs*, timelines and strategies.

Specific Requirements – you must also comply with the following *specific requirements*:

(n) Where the entity represents parties with different interests in any transaction each party is at all times represented by different *Authorised Persons* conducting themselves in the matter as though they were members of different entities.

(o) You ensure there are adequate indemnity arrangements in respect of *claims* made against you for work carried out by you before you have ceased to practice by *purchasing professional indemnity insurance* for a minimum of 6 years from the expiry of the period of *professional indemnity insurance* stated in your evidence of insurance or policy document.

(p) If you seek to exclude or limit liability, you do so only to the extent that such exclusion or limitation is above the minimum level of cover provided by *CLC*-approved *professional indemnity insurance*; you must obtain the written informed consent of the *Client* for such exclusion or limitation to be effective.

(q) When offering and providing services which are not regulated by the *CLC*, you advise your *Client* of this and inform them in writing that the activity is not covered by *CLC*-approved *professional indemnity insurance* or the *CLC*-administered *Compensation Fund*.

(r) Before or when accepting instructions, you inform *Clients* in writing of the terms on which the instructions are accepted, a complete, accurate estimate of fees and *disbursements* to be charged and if and when they are likely to change.

(s) You *promptly* inform the *Client* in writing of the existence and amount of any sum payable (whether directly or indirectly) as a result of receipt of that *Client's* instructions.

(t) With the exception of *disbursements*, you do not delay completion because fees are outstanding to you.

(u) You discuss and agree with the *Client* how *costs* will be paid, whether directly by the *Client*, by public funding, through an insurance policy or otherwise.

Overriding Principle 4. Comply with your duty to the court

Note: this Principle will only be applicable if the *CLC's* application to regulate *advocacy* and *litigation* services is successful

Outcomes – you must deliver the following *Outcomes*:

4.1 You act in the interests of justice;

4.2 You act in good faith towards *Clients*.

Principles – delivery of these *Outcomes* requires you to act in a principled way:

(a)   You promote and protect the *client's* best interests.

(b)   You do not compromise your professional standards or independence.

(c)   You assist the court in the administration of justice.

(d)   You do not knowingly or recklessly mislead or deceive the court, or allow the court to be misled.

(e)   You ensure that the Court is informed of all relevant decisions and legislative provisions (whether this has a favourable or unfavourable effect on the case you are advancing).

(f)   You comply with any Court Order (unless an application for a stay is pending or the Order has been revoked by the Court).

(g)   You advise your *Client* to comply with Court Orders and of the consequences of failing to do so.

(h)   You properly protect sensitive evidence.

(i)   You safeguard the well being of children and other vulnerable persons.

Specific Requirement – you must also comply with the following specific requirement:

(j)   You ensure that the court is made aware of any relevant legal or factual matters which are likely to have a material effect on the outcome of the proceedings.

Overriding Principle 5. Deal with regulators and ombudsmen in an open and co-operative way

Outcome – you must deliver the following *Outcome*:

5.1   You act in accordance with your regulatory responsibilities.

Principles – delivery of these *Outcomes* requires you to act in a principled way:

(a)   You are open and honest in your dealings with us.

(b)   You comply with the *CLC Code of Conduct* and the *CLC's* other *regulatory arrangements*.

(c)   You comply *promptly* and fully with a *CLC* direction or request.

(d)   You comply with any *authorisation*, *permission* or *condition* endorsed on your *licence*, *Recognised Body Certificate* or *Licensed Body Licence*.

(e)   You co-operate with any *CLC* investigation.

(f)   You co-operate with any *Legal Ombudsman* investigation.

(g)   You comply *promptly* and fully with any *Legal Ombudsman* Order.

(h)   You co-operate with other regulators and ombudsmen.

Specific Requirements – you must also comply with the following *specific requirements*:

(i)   You make the *Compensation Fund* contribution determined by the *CLC*.

(j)   You *systematically* identify, monitor and manage risks to the delivery of this Code's *outcomes*.

(k)   You *promptly* notify insurers in writing of any facts or matters which may give rise to a *claim* under *CLC*-approved *professional indemnity insurance*.

(l)   You *promptly* notify the *CLC* in writing of any facts or matters which may give rise to a *claim* under its *Compensation Fund*.

(m) As a *CLC* licensee operating in an entity regulated by another regulator you must comply with that regulator's regulations at all times in a way which is reasonably consistent with this Code.

(n) You obtain permission from the *CLC* before offering *Reserved legal activities*:

– as a new business;

– in an entity regulated by another *Approved Regulator*; or

– through an entity with a *Manager* who is not a *CLC Lawyer*.

(o) You notify the *CLC* of any material breach of this Code, whether by you, the entity or any other person.

(p) You notify the *CLC* of a change as set out in the *CLC's* Notification Code.

Overriding Principle 6. Promote equality of access and service.

Outcomes – you must deliver the following *Outcomes*:

6.1 The service is accessible and responsive to the needs of individual *Clients*, including those who are vulnerable;[1]

6.2 No-one – *Client, employee*, colleague, job applicant, trainee or other party – you deal with feels discriminated[2] against (whether directly or indirectly), victimised or harassed;

6.3 You accept responsibility where the service you provide is not of the expected standard and provide appropriate redress for the *Client* where necessary;

6.4 Handling of *complaints* takes proper account of *Clients'* individual needs, including those who are vulnerable;

6.5 *Complaints* are dealt with impartially and comprehensively.

Principles – delivery of these *Outcomes* requires you to act in a principled way:

(a) You comply with *Equalities legislation*.

(b) You make reasonable adjustments to prevent persons with disabilities from being placed at a substantial disadvantage.

(c) You provide equal opportunities for all partners, *employees* or applicants in employment and training.

(d) You make all reasonable efforts to ensure your service is accessible and responsive to *Clients*, including those with vulnerabilities.

(e) The *complaints* procedure is clear, well-publicised and free.

(f) You treat *complaints* seriously and provide appropriate redress options.

(g) You deal with *complaints* fairly and within 28 days.

(h) You identify and address systemic *Client Complaints* issues.

Specific Requirements – you must also comply with the following *specific requirements*:

(i) Any allegation of (direct or indirect) discrimination, victimisation and harassment is investigated thoroughly, resulting, where appropriate, in disciplinary action.

(j) From the outset you advise *Clients* in writing of their right to make a complaint, how to make it, to whom, and the timeframes involved.

(k) You advise *Clients* in writing of their right to have their *complaint* escalated to the *Legal Ombudsman* and provide them with contact details and timeframes of that body.

(l) You keep a record of *complaints* received and any action taken as a result.

Notes

1   A *Client* may be vulnerable because of a range of characteristics, including (but not limited to): basic skills: literacy and numeracy; complexity and confusion: difficulty of accessing and understanding large amounts of information; disability or other impairment; mental health issues; distress or sudden change in circumstances e.g. bereavement, divorce, illness or loss of employment; low income; age; caring responsibilities; limited knowledge of, or limited skills in, use of English; balance of power: lack of competition and or choice; or inexperience or lack of knowledge of a particular subject. Vulnerability can only be assessed on a case-by-case basis.

2   On the grounds of age, disability, gender reassignment, marital and civil partnership status, pregnancy and maternity, race, religion or faith, sex or sexual orientation.

Regulators' Code

Regulators' Code

This Code was laid before Parliament in accordance with section 23 of the Legislative and Regulatory Reform Act 2006 ("the Act"). Regulators whose functions are specified by order under section 24(2) of the Act must have regard to the Code when developing policies and operational procedures that guide their regulatory activities. Regulators must equally have regard to the Code when setting standards or giving guidance which will guide the regulatory activities of other regulators. If a regulator concludes, on the basis of material evidence, that a specific provision of the Code is either not applicable or is outweighed by another relevant consideration, the regulator is not bound to follow that provision, but should record that decision and the reasons for it.

1. Regulators should carry out their activities in a way that supports those they regulate to comply and grow

1.1 Regulators should avoid imposing unnecessary regulatory burdens through their regulatory activities[1] and should assess whether similar social, environmental and economic outcomes could be achieved by less burdensome means. Regulators should choose proportionate approaches to those they regulate, based on relevant factors including, for example, business size and capacity.

1.2 When designing and reviewing policies, operational procedures and practices, regulators should consider how they might support or enable economic growth for compliant businesses and other regulated entities[2], for example, by considering how they can best:

- understand and minimise negative economic impacts of their regulatory activities;

- minimising the costs of compliance for those they regulate;

- improve confidence in compliance for those they regulate, by providing greater certainty; and

- encourage and promote compliance.

1.3 Regulators should ensure that their officers have the necessary knowledge and skills to support those they regulate, including having an understanding of those they regulate that enables them to choose proportionate and effective approaches.

1.4 Regulators should ensure that their officers understand the statutory principles of good regulation[3] and of this Code, and how the regulator delivers its activities in accordance with them.

2. Regulators should provide simple and straightforward ways to engage with those they regulate and hear their views

2.1 Regulators should have mechanisms in place to engage those they regulate, citizens and others to offer views and contribute to the development of their policies and service standards. Before changing policies, practices or service standards, regulators should consider the impact on business and engage with business representatives.

2.2 In responding to non-compliance that they identify, regulators should clearly explain what the non-compliant item or activity is, the advice being given, actions required or decisions taken, and the reasons for these. Regulators should provide an opportunity for dialogue in relation to the advice, requirements or decisions, with a view to ensuring that they are acting in a way that is proportionate and consistent.

This paragraph does not apply where the regulator can demonstrate that immediate enforcement action is required to prevent or respond to a serious breach or where providing such an opportunity would be likely to defeat the purpose of the proposed enforcement action.

2.3 Regulators should provide an impartial and clearly explained route to appeal against a regulatory decision or a failure to act in accordance with this Code. Individual officers of the regulator who took the decision or action against which the appeal is being made should not be involved in considering the appeal. This route to appeal should be publicised to those who are regulated.

2.4 Regulators should provide a timely explanation in writing of any right to representation or right to appeal. This explanation should be in plain language and include practical information on the process involved.

2.5 Regulators should make available to those they regulate, clearly explained complaints procedures, allowing them to easily make a complaint about the conduct of the regulator.

2.6 Regulators should have a range of mechanisms to enable and regularly invite, receive and take on board customer feedback, including, for example, through customer satisfaction surveys of those they regulate[4].

3. Regulators should base their regulatory activities on risk

3.1 Regulators should take an evidence based approach to determining the priority risks in their area of responsibility, and should allocate resources where they would be most effective in addressing those priority risks.

3.2 Regulators should consider risk at every stage of their decision-making processes, including choosing the most appropriate type of intervention or way of working with those regulated; targeting checks on compliance; and when taking enforcement action.

3.3 Regulators designing a risk assessment framework[5], for their own use or for use by others, should have mechanisms in place to consult on the design with those affected, and to review it regularly.

3.4 Regulators, in making their assessment of risk, should recognise the compliance record of those they regulate, including using earned recognition approaches and should consider all available and relevant data on compliance, including evidence of relevant external verification.

3.5 Regulators should review the effectiveness of their chosen regulatory activities in delivering the desired outcomes and make any necessary adjustments accordingly.

4. Regulators should share information about compliance and risk

4.1 Regulators should collectively follow the principle of "collect once, use many times" when requesting information from those they regulate.

4.2 When the law allows, regulators should agree secure mechanisms to share information with each other about businesses and other bodies they regulate, to help target resources and activities and minimise duplication.

5. Regulators should ensure clear information, guidance and advice is available to help those they regulate meet their responsibilities to comply

5.1 Regulators should provide advice and guidance that is focused on assisting those they regulate to understand and meet their responsibilities. When providing advice and guidance, legal requirements should be distinguished from suggested good practice and the impact of the advice or guidance should be considered so that it does not impose unnecessary burdens in itself.

5.2 Regulators should publish guidance, and information in a clear, accessible, concise format, using media appropriate to the target audience and written in plain language for the audience.

5.3 Regulators should have mechanisms in place to consult those they regulate in relation to the guidance they produce to ensure that it meets their needs.

5.4 Regulators should seek to create an environment in which those they regulate have confidence in the advice they receive and feel able to seek advice without fear of triggering enforcement action.

5.5 In responding to requests for advice, a regulator's primary concerns should be to provide the advice necessary to support compliance, and to ensure that the advice can be relied on.

5.6 Regulators should have mechanisms to work collaboratively to assist those regulated by more than one regulator. Regulators should consider advice provided by other regulators and, where there is disagreement about the advice provided, this should be discussed with the other regulator to reach agreement.

6. Regulators should ensure that their approach to their regulatory activities is transparent

6.1 Regulators should publish a set of clear service standards, setting out what those they regulate should expect from them.

6.2 Regulators' published service standards should include clear information on:

a) how they communicate with those they regulate and how they can be contacted;

b) their approach to providing information, guidance and advice;

c) their approach to checks on compliance[6], including details of the risk assessment framework used to target those checks as well as protocols for their conduct, clearly setting out what those they regulate should expect;

d) their enforcement policy, explaining how they respond to non-compliance;

e) their fees and charges, if any. This information should clearly explain the basis on which these are calculated, and should include an explanation of whether compliance will affect fees and charges; and

f) how to comment or complain about the service provided and routes to appeal.

6.3 Information published to meet the provisions of this Code should be easily accessible, including being available at a single point[7] on the regulator's website that is clearly signposted, and it should be kept up to date.

6.4 Regulators should have mechanisms in place to ensure that their officers act in accordance with their published service standards, including their enforcement policy.

6.5 Regulators should publish, on a regular basis, details of their performance against their service standards, including feedback received from those they regulate, such as customer satisfaction surveys, and data relating to complaints about them and appeals against their decisions.

1 The term 'regulatory activities' refers to the whole range of regulatory options and interventions available to regulators.

627

2   The terms 'business or businesses' is used throughout this document to refer to businesses and other regulated entities.

3   The statutory principles of good regulation can be viewed in Part 2 (21) on page 12: http://www.legislation.gov.uk/ukpga/2006/51/pdfs/ukpga_20060051_en.pdf.

4   The Government will discuss with national regulators a common approach to surveys to support benchmarking of their performance.

5   The term 'risk assessment framework' encompasses any model, scheme, methodology or risk rating approach that is used to inform risk-based targeting of regulatory activities in relation to individual businesses or other regulated entities.

6   Including inspections, audit, monitoring and sampling visits, and test purchases.

7   This requirement may be satisfied by providing a single web page that includes links to information published elsewhere.

Legal Ombudsman Scheme Rules

[The Legal Ombudsman Scheme Rules are reproduced with the kind permission of the Legal Ombudsman. For the latest updates to the material, please see www.legalombudsman. org.uk.]

[Last updated 1 April 2019]

Legal Ombudsman Scheme Rules

1 Introduction and definitions

Contents

1.1   ●   These scheme rules are about *complaints* made from 6 October 2010 to *authorised persons* including legal practitioners and others, authorised in England and Wales.

      ●   They explain which *complaints* are covered by the *Legal Ombudsman* and how it will deal with them.

      ●   This version includes amendments that apply to complaints referred to the Legal Ombudsman from 1 April 2019.

1.2   Parliament, in the *Act*:

      ●   created the Legal Services Board (to oversee *Approved Regulators*) and the Office for Legal Complaints (to establish the *Legal Ombudsman*);

      ●   gave the Lord Chancellor power to make orders, including orders modifying who would be able to bring a *complaint* to the *Legal Ombudsman*;

      ●   gave the Legal Services Board power to set requirements for the rules of *Approved Regulators* about how *authorised persons* handle *complaints*[1] and cooperate with an *ombudsman*;[2] and

      ●   gave the Office for Legal Complaints power to make rules affecting which *complaints* can be handled by the *Legal Ombudsman* and how those *complaints* will be handled.

1.3   These scheme rules include:

      ●   a summary of relevant provisions in the *Act*, as modified by orders made by the Lord Chancellor (though it is the *Act* and the orders themselves that count);

      ●   a summary of requirements on complaint-handling made by the Legal Services Board under the powers given to it by the *Act*; and

      ●   rules made by the Office for Legal Complaints under the powers given to it by the *Act*.

The endnotes identify the section of the *Act* that is being summarised, or under which an order, requirement or rule has been made; and which are the rules made by the Office of Legal Complaints for the Legal Ombudsman.

1.4   This book also includes some general guidance. There are six chapters –

    1:     Introduction and definitions:

–   contents of this book;

–   meaning of words that are underlined [italicised].

    2:     Who can complain about what:

–   who can complain;

–   what they can complain about.

    3:     What *authorised persons* must do:

–   dealing with *complaints* themselves;

–   cooperating with the *Legal Ombudsman*.

    4:     When *complaints* can be referred to the *Legal Ombudsman*:

–   after complaining to the *authorised person*;

–   time limit from act/omission;

–   *ombudsman* extending time limits.

    5:     How the *Legal Ombudsman* deals with *complaints*:

–   first contact;

–   grounds for dismissal;

–   referring a *complaint* to court;

–   referring to another *complaints* scheme;

–   related *complaints*;

–   resolution and investigation;

–   evidence;

–   procedural time limits;

–   hearings;

–   determinations and awards by an *ombudsman*;

–   acceptance/rejection of determinations;

–   publication;

–   enforcement.

    6:     Case fees payable by *authorised persons*.

Meaning of words that are underlined [italicised]

1.5   The *Act* means the Legal Services Act 2007.

1.6   *Complaint* means an oral or written expression of dissatisfaction which:

(a)   alleges that the complainant has suffered (or may suffer) financial loss, distress, inconvenience or other detriment; and

(b)   is covered by chapter two (who can complain about what).[3]

1.7   *Authorised person* means:

(a)   someone authorised, in England and Wales, to carry out a *reserved legal activity*[4] at the time of the relevant act/omission or covered under section 129 of the *Act*,[5] including:

- alternative business structures (licensed under part 5 of the *Act*);

- barristers;

- costs lawyers;

- chartered legal executives;

- licensed conveyancers;

- notaries;

- patent attorneys;

- probate practitioners;

- registered European lawyers;

- solicitors; or

- trade mark attorneys;

(b)　(under section 131 of the *Act*):

- a business that is responsible for an act/omission of an employee; and

- a partnership that is responsible for an act/omission of a partner.[6]

1.8　*Approved Regulator* means:

(a)　a regulator approved under schedule 4 of the *Act*, including:

- the Association of Chartered Certified Accountants (for reserved probate activities);

- the Association of Costs Lawyers, through the Costs Lawyer Standards Board;

- the Bar Council, through the Bar Standards Board (for barristers);

- the Chartered Institute of Patent Attorneys, through the Intellectual Property Regulation Board;

- the Council for Licensed Conveyancers;

- the Institute of Chartered Accountants in England and Wales (for reserved probate activities)

- the Institute of Chartered Accountants in Scotland (for reserved probate activities);

- CILEX Regulation, through the Chartered Institute of Legal Executives;

- the Chartered Institute of Trade Mark Attorneys, through the Intellectual Property Regulation Board;

- the Law Society, through the Solicitors Regulation Authority;

- the Master of the Faculties (for notaries); and

- the Legal Services Board (but only for any alternative business structures it licenses directly);

1.9　*Determination*[7] means a final decision that is made by an ombudsman on a complaint.

1.10　*Legal Ombudsman* means the ombudsman scheme established by the Office for Legal Complaints.

1.11　*Ombudsman* means:

(a)　any ombudsman from the *Legal Ombudsman*;[8] and

(b)　any *Legal Ombudsman* staff member to whom an *ombudsman* has delegated the relevant functions (but an *ombudsman* cannot delegate the functions of determining a *complaint* or of dismissing or discontinuing it for any of the reasons under paragraph 5.7).[9]

1.12 *Party* includes:

    (a)   a complainant (covered by chapter two);

    (b)   an *authorised person* (covered by chapter two) against whom the *complaint* is made;

    (c)   an *authorised person* (covered by chapter five) whom an *ombudsman* treats as a joint respondent to a *complaint*.[10]

1.13 *Public body* means any government department, local authority or any other body constituted for the purposes of the public services, local government or the administration of justice.[11]

1.14 *Reserved legal activity* (as defined in schedule 2 of the *Act*) means:

    (a)   exercising a right of audience;

    (b)   conducting litigation;

    (c)   reserved instrument activities;

    (d)   probate activities;

    (e)   notarial activities;

    (f)   administration of oaths.

2 Who can complain about what

Who can complain

2.1 A complainant must be one of the following:[12]

    (a)   an individual;

    (b)   a business or enterprise that was a micro-enterprise (European Union definition) when it referred the complaint to the *authorised person*;[13]

    (c)   a charity that had an annual income net of tax of less than £1 million when it referred the complaint to the *authorised person*;

    (d)   a club/association/organisation, the affairs of which are managed by its members/a committee/a committee of its members, that had an annual income net of tax of less than £1 million when it referred the complaint to the *authorised person*;

    (e)   a trustee of a trust that had an asset value of less than £1 million when it referred the complaint to the *authorised person*; or;

    (f)   a personal representative or beneficiary of the estate of a person who, before he/she died, had not referred the complaint to the *Legal Ombudsman*.

For (e) and (f) the condition is that the services to which the complaint relates were provided by the respondent to a person –

    (a)   who has subsequently died; and

    (b)   who had not by his or her death referred the complaint to the ombudsman scheme.

2.2 If a complainant who has referred a *complaint* to the *Legal Ombudsman* dies or is otherwise unable to act, the *complaint* can be continued by:[14]

    (a)   anyone authorised by law (for example:

        •   the executor of a complainant who has died; or

        •   someone with a lasting power of attorney from a complainant who is incapable); or

(b)   the residuary beneficiaries of the estate of a complainant who has died.[15]

2.3   A complainant must not have been, at the time of the act/omission to which the *complaint* relates:

(a)   a *public body* (or acting for a *public body*) in relation to the services complained about; or

(b)   an *authorised person* who procured the services complained about on behalf of someone else.[16] [17]

2.4   For example, where the *complaint* is about a barrister who was instructed by a solicitor on behalf of a consumer, the consumer can complain to the *ombudsman* but the solicitor cannot.

2.5   A complainant can authorise someone else in writing (including an *authorised person*) to act for the complainant in pursuing a *complaint*, but the *Legal Ombudsman* remains free to contact the complainant direct where it considers that appropriate.[18]

What they can complain about

2.6   The *complaint* must relate to an act/omission by someone who was an *authorised person* at that time[19] but:

(a)   an act/omission by an employee is usually treated also as an act/omission by their employer, whether or not the employer knew or approved;[20] and

(b)   an act/omission by a partner is usually treated also as an act/omission by the partnership, unless the complainant knew (at the time of the act/omission) that the partner had no authority to act for the partnership.[21]

2.7   The act/omission does not have to:

(a)   relate to a *reserved legal activity*;[22] nor

(b)   be after the *Act* came into force[23] (but see the time limits in chapter four).

2.8   The *complaint* must relate to services which the *authorised person*:

(a)   provided to the complainant; or

(b)   provided to another *authorised person* who procured them on behalf of the complainant; or

(c)   provided to (or as) a personal representative/trustee where the complainant is a beneficiary of the estate/trust;[24] or

(d)   offered, or refused to provide, to the complainant.[25]

2.9   A *complaint* is not affected by any change in the membership of a partnership or other unincorporated body.[26]

2.10   Where *authorised person* A ceases to exist and B succeeds to the whole (or substantially the whole) of A's business:

(a)   acts/omissions by A become acts/omissions of B;[27] and

(b)   *complaints* already outstanding against A become *complaints* against B[28]

unless an *Ombudsman* decides that this is, in his/her opinion, not fair and reasonable in all the circumstances of the case.

3 What authorised persons must do

Dealing with complaints themselves

3.1   *Authorised persons* including legal practitioners and others must comply with their *Approved Regulator's* rules on handling *complaints*, including any requirements specified by the Legal Services Board[29]

3.2 The Legal Services Board has required that:

(a) *authorised persons* tell all clients in writing at the time of engagement, or existing clients at the next appropriate opportunity that they can complain, how and to whom this can be done;

(b) this must include that they can complain to the *Legal Ombudsman* at the end of the *authorised person's* complaints process, the timeframe for doing so and full details of how to contact the *Legal Ombudsman*; and

(c) *authorised persons* tell all clients in writing at the end of the *authorised person's* complaints process that they can complain to the *Legal Ombudsman*, the timeframe for doing so and full details of how to contact the *Legal Ombudsman*.

3.3 The Legal Services Board expects that regulation of complaint-handling procedures by *Approved Regulators* will:

(a) give consumers confidence that:

- effective safeguards will be provided; and

- complaints will be dealt with comprehensively and swiftly, with appropriate redress where necessary;

(b) provide processes that are:

- convenient and easy to use (in particular for those that are vulnerable or have disabilities);

- transparent, clear, well-publicised, free and allow *complaints* to be made by any reasonable means;

- prompt and fair, with decisions based on sufficient investigation of the circumstances, and (where appropriate) offer a suitable remedy.

Cooperating with the Legal Ombudsman

3.4 *Authorised persons* must comply with their *Approved Regulator's* rules on cooperating with an *ombudsman*, including any requirements specified by the Legal Services Board.[30]

4 *When complaints can be referred to the Legal Ombudsman*

After complaining to the authorised person

4.1 Ordinarily, a complainant cannot use the *Legal Ombudsman* unless the complainant has first used the *authorised person's* complaints procedure (referred to in chapter three).[31]

Time limit from authorised person's final response

4.2 But a complainant can use the *Legal Ombudsman* if:[32]

(a) the *complaint* has not been resolved to the complainant's satisfaction within eight weeks of being made to the *authorised person*; or

(b) an *ombudsman* considers that there are exceptional reasons to consider the *complaint* sooner, or without it having been made first to the *authorised person*; or

(c) where an *ombudsman* considers that in-house resolution is not possible due to irretrievable breakdown in the relationship between an *authorised person* and the person making the *complaint*.

4.3   For example, an *ombudsman* may decide that the *Legal Ombudsman* should consider the *complaint* where the authorised person has refused to consider it, or where delay would harm the complainant.

4.4   (a)   This time limit applies only if the *authorised person's* written response to a *complaint* included prominently:

- an explanation that the *Legal Ombudsman* was available if the complainant remained dissatisfied;

- full contact details for the *Legal Ombudsman*; and

- a warning that the *complaint* must be referred to the *Legal Ombudsman* within six months of the date of the written response;

(b)   If (but only if) the conditions in (a) are satisfied, a complainant must ordinarily refer the *complaint* to the *Legal Ombudsman* within six months of the date of that written response.

Time limit from act/omission

4.5   Ordinarily:

(a)   the act or omission, or when the complainant should reasonably have known there was cause for complaint, must have been after 5 October 2010; and

(b)   the complainant must refer the *complaint* to the *Legal Ombudsman* no later than:

- six years from the act/omission; or

- three years from when the complainant should reasonably have known there was cause for complaint.[33]

4.6   In relation to 4.5(b):

(a)   where a complaint is referred by a personal representative or beneficiary of the estate of a person who, before he/she died, had not referred the complaint to the *Legal Ombudsman*, the period runs from when the deceased should reasonably have known there was cause for complaint; and

(b)   when the complainant (or the deceased) should reasonably have known there was a cause for complaint will be assessed on the basis of the complainant's (or the deceased's) own knowledge, disregarding what the complainant (or the deceased) might have been told if he/she had sought advice.

Ombudsman extending time limits

4.7   If an *ombudsman* considers that there are exceptional circumstances, he/she may extend any of these time limits to the extent that he/she considers fair.[34]

4.8   For example, an *Ombudsman*:

(a)   might extend a time limit if the complainant was prevented from meeting the time limit as a result of serious illness; and

(b)   is likely to extend a time limit where the time limit had not expired when the complainant raised the *complaint* with the *authorised person*.

5 How the Legal Ombudsman will deal with complaints[35]

5.1   The *Legal Ombudsman* may require a complainant to complete its complaint form.[36]

5.2   In the case of a partnership (or former partnership), it is sufficient for the *Legal Ombudsman* to communicate with any partner (or former partner).[37]

First contact

5.3   Unless:

(a)   the *authorised person* has already had eight weeks to consider the *complaint*; or

(b)   the *authorised person* has already issued a written response to the *complaint*; or

(c)   an *ombudsman* considers that there are exceptional reasons;

the *Legal Ombudsman* will:

(a)   refer the *complaint* to the *authorised person*;

(b)   notify the complainant; and

(c)   explain why to both of them.[38]

5.4   If the *authorised person* claims that all or part of the *complaint*:

(a)   is not covered by the Legal Ombudsman under chapter two; or

(b)   is out-of-time under chapter four; or

(c)   should be dismissed under paragraph 5.7;

an *ombudsman* will give all *parties* an opportunity to make representations before deciding.[39]

5.5   Otherwise, if an *ombudsman* considers that all or part of the *complaint*:

(a)   may not be covered by the *Legal Ombudsman* under chapter two; or

(b)   may be out-of-time under chapter four; or

(c)   should be dismissed under paragraph 5.7;

the *ombudsman* will give the complainant an opportunity to make representations before deciding.[40]

5.6   The *ombudsman* will then give the complainant and the *authorised person* his/her decision and the reasons for it.[41]

Grounds for dismissing or discontinuing a complaint[42]

5.7   An *ombudsman* may (but does not have to) dismiss or discontinue all or part of a *complaint* if, in his/her opinion:

(a)   it does not have any reasonable prospect of success, or is frivolous or vexatious; or

(b)   the complainant has not suffered (and is unlikely to suffer) financial loss, distress, inconvenience or other detriment; or

(c)   the *authorised person* has already offered fair and reasonable redress in relation to the circumstances alleged by the complainant and the offer is still open for acceptance; or

(d)   the complainant has previously complained about the same issue to the *Legal Ombudsman* or a predecessor complaints scheme (unless the *ombudsman* considers that material new evidence, likely to affect the outcome, only became available to the complainant afterwards); or

(e)   a comparable independent complaints (or costs-assessment) scheme or a court has already dealt with the same issue; or

(f)   a comparable independent complaints (or costs-assessment) scheme or a court is dealing with the same issue, unless those proceedings are first stayed (by the agreement of all parties or by a court order) so that the *Legal Ombudsman* can deal with the issue; or

(g)   it would be more suitable for the issue to be dealt with by a court, by arbitration or by another complaints (or costs–assessment) scheme;[43] or

(h)   the issue concerns an *authorised person's* decision when exercising a discretion under a will or trust; or

(i)   the issue concerns an *authorised person's* failure to consult a beneficiary before exercising a discretion under a will or trust, where there is no legal obligation to consult;

(j)   the issue involves someone else who has not complained and the *ombudsman* considers that it would not be appropriate to deal with the issue without their consent; or

(k)   it is not practicable to investigate the issue fairly because of the time which has elapsed since the act/omission; or

(l)   the issue concerns an act/omission outside England and Wales and the circumstances do not have a sufficient connection with England and Wales;[44]

(m)   the *complaint* is about an *authorised person's* refusal to provide a service and the complainant has not produced evidence that the refusal was for other than legitimate or reasonable reasons; or

(n)   there are other compelling reasons why it is inappropriate for the issue to be dealt with by the *Legal Ombudsman*.

Referring a complaint to court

5.8   Exceptionally (at the instance of an *ombudsman*) where the *ombudsman* considers that:

(a)   resolution of a particular legal question is necessary in order to resolve a dispute; but

(b)   it is not more suitable for the whole dispute to be dealt with by a court;

the *ombudsman* may (but does not have to) refer that legal question to court.[45]

5.9   Exceptionally, (at the instance of an *authorised person*) where:

(a)   the *authorised person* requests, and also undertakes to pay the complainant's legal costs and disbursements on terms the *ombudsman* considers appropriate; and

(b)   an *ombudsman* considers that the whole dispute would be more suitably dealt with by a court as a test case between the complainant and the *authorised person*;

the *ombudsman* may (but does not have to) dismiss the *complaint*, so that a court may consider it as a test case.[46]

5.10   By way of example only, in relation to a test case (at the instance of an *authorised person*) the *ombudsman* might require an undertaking in favour of the complainant that, if the complainant or the *authorised person* starts court proceedings against the other in respect of the *complaint* in any court in England and Wales within six months of the *complaint* being dismissed, the *authorised person* will:

(a)   pay the complainant's reasonable costs and disbursements (to be assessed if not agreed on an indemnity basis);

(b)   pay these in connection with the proceedings at first instance and also any subsequent appeal made by the *authorised person*; and

(c)   make interim payments on account if and to the extent that it appears reasonable to do so.

5.11   Factors the *ombudsman* may take into account in considering whether to refer a legal question to court, or to dismiss a *complaint* so that it may be the subject of a test case in court, include (but are not limited to):

(a)　any representations made by the *authorised person* or the complainant;

(b)　the stage already reached in consideration of the dispute.

(c)　how far the legal question is central to the outcome of the dispute;

(d)　how important or novel the legal question is in the context of the dispute;

(e)　the remedies that a court could impose;

(f)　the amount at stake; and

(g)　the significance for the *authorised person* (or similar *authorised persons*) or their clients.[47]

Referring to another complaints scheme

5.12　An *ombudsman* may refer a *complaint* to another complaints scheme if:

(a)　he/she considers it appropriate; and

(b)　the complainant agrees.[48]

5.13　If an *ombudsman* refers a *complaint* to another complaints scheme, the *ombudsman* will give the complainant and the *authorised person* reasons for the referral.[49]

Arrangements for assistance

5.14　The *Legal Ombudsman* may make such arrangements as it considers appropriate (which may include paying fees) for *Approved Regulators* or others to provide assistance to an *ombudsman* in the investigation or consideration of a *complaint*.[50]

Related complaints

5.15　The *Legal Ombudsman* may:

(a)　tell a complainant that a related *complaint* could have been brought against some other *authorised person*;[51] or

(b)　treat someone else who was an *authorised person* at the time of the act/omission as a joint respondent to the *complaint*.[52]

5.16　Where two or more *complaints* against different *authorised persons* relate to connected circumstances:

(a)　the *Legal Ombudsman* may investigate them together, but an *ombudsman* will make separate determinations;[53] and

(b)　the determinations may require the *authorised persons* to contribute towards the overall redress in the proportions the *ombudsman* considers appropriate.[54]

Resolution

5.17　The *Legal Ombudsman* will try to resolve *complaints* at the earliest possible stage, by whatever agreed outcome is considered appropriate.[55]

5.18　If a *complaint* is settled, abandoned or withdrawn, an *ombudsman* will tell both the complainant and the *authorised person*.[56]

Investigation

5.19　If the *Legal Ombudsman* considers that an investigation is necessary, it will:

(a)　ensure both *parties* have been given an opportunity of making representations;

(b)　send the *parties* a case decision[57] (which the *Act* calls an 'assessment'), with a time limit for response; and

(c)   if any *party* indicates disagreement within that time limit, arrange for an *ombudsman* to issue a final decision (which the *Act* calls a 'determination').[58]

5.20   If neither *party* indicates disagreement within that time limit, the *Legal Ombudsman* may treat the *complaint* as resolved by the case decision.[59]

Evidence

5.21   An apology will not of itself be treated as an admission of liability.[60]

5.22   An *ombudsman* cannot require anyone to produce any information or document which that person could not be compelled to produce in High Court civil proceedings, and the following provisions are subject to this.[61]

5.23   An *ombudsman* may give directions on:

(a)   the issues on which evidence is required; and

(b)   the way in which evidence should be given.[62]

5.24   An *ombudsman* may:

(a)   take into account evidence from *Approved Regulators* or the Legal Services Board;

(b)   take into account evidence from other third parties;

(c)   treat any finding of fact in disciplinary proceedings against the *authorised person* as conclusive;

(d)   include/exclude evidence that would be inadmissible/admissible in court;

(e)   accept information in confidence where he/she considers that is both necessary and fair;[63]

(f)   make a determination on the basis of what has been supplied;

(g)   draw inferences from any *party's* failure to provide information requested; and

(h)   dismiss a *complaint* if the complainant fails to provide information requested.[64]

5.25   An *ombudsman* may require a *party* to attend to give evidence and produce documents at a time and place specified by the *ombudsman*.[65]

5.26   An *ombudsman* may require a *party* to produce any information or document that the *ombudsman* considers necessary for the determination of a *complaint*.[66]

5.27   An *ombudsman* may:

(a)   specify the time within which this must be done;

(b)   specify the manner or form in which the information is to be provided; and

(c)   require the person producing the document to explain it.[67]

5.28   If the document is not produced, an *ombudsman* may require the relevant *party* to say, to the best of his/her knowledge and belief, where the document is.[68]

5.29   If an *authorised person* fails to comply with a requirement to produce information or a document, the *ombudsman*:

(a)   will tell the relevant *Approved Regulator*;

(b)   may require that *Approved Regulator* to tell the *ombudsman* what action it will take; and

(c)   may report any failure by that *Approved Regulator* to the Legal Services Board.[69]

5.30   Subject to this, if any *party* fails to comply with a requirement to produce information or a document, the *ombudsman* may enforce the requirement through the High Court.[70]

APPENDIX 14

Procedural time limits

5.31　An *ombudsman* may fix (and may extend) a time limit for any stage of the investigation, consideration and determination of a *complaint*.[71]

5.32　If any *party* fails to comply with such a time limit, the *ombudsman* may:

(a)　proceed with the investigation, consideration and determination;

(b)　draw inferences from the failure;

(c)　where the failure is by the complainant, dismiss the *complaint*; or

(d)　where the failure is by the *authorised person*, include compensation for any inconvenience caused to the complainant in any award.[72]

Hearings

5.33　An *ombudsman* will only hold a hearing where he/she considers that the *complaint* cannot be fairly determined without one. In deciding whether (and how) to hold a hearing, the *ombudsman* will take account of article 6 in the European Convention on Human Rights.[73]

5.34　A *party* who wishes to request a hearing must do so in writing, setting out:

(a)　the issues he/she wishes to raise; and

(b)　(if appropriate) any reasons why the hearing should be in private;

so the *ombudsman* may consider whether:

(a)　the issues are material;

(b)　a hearing should take place; and

(c)　any hearing should be in public or private.[74]

5.35　A hearing may be held by any means the *ombudsman* considers appropriate in the circumstances, including (for example) by phone.[75]

Determinations and awards by an ombudsman

5.36　An *ombudsman* will determine a *complaint* by reference to what is, in his/her opinion, fair and reasonable in all the circumstances of the case.[76]

5.37　In determining what is fair and reasonable, the *ombudsman* will take into account (but is not bound by):

(a)　what decision a court might make;

(b)　the relevant *Approved Regulator's* rules of conduct at the time of the act/omission; and

(c)　what the *ombudsman* considers to have been good practice at the time of the act/omission.[77]

5.38　The *ombudsman's* determination may contain one or more of the following directions to the *authorised person* in favour of the complainant:[78]

(a)　to apologise;

(b)　to pay compensation of a specified amount for loss suffered;

(c)　to pay interest on that compensation from a specified time;[79]

(d)　to pay compensation of a specified amount for inconvenience/distress caused;

(e)　to ensure (and pay for) putting right any specified error, omission or other deficiency;

(f)　to take (and pay for) any specified action in the interests of the complainant;

(g)   to pay a specified amount for costs the complainant incurred in pursuing the *complaint*;[80] [81]

(h)   to limit fees to a specified amount.

5.39   As a complainant does not usually need assistance to pursue a *complaint* with the *Legal Ombudsman*, awards of costs are likely to be rare.

5.40   If the determination contains a direction to limit fees to a specified amount, it may also require the *authorised person* to ensure that:[82]

(a)   all or part of any amount paid is refunded;

(b)   interest is paid on that refund from a specified time;[83]

(c)   all or part of the fees are remitted;

(d)   the right to recover the fees is waived, wholly or to a specified extent; or

(e)   any combination of these.

5.41   An *ombudsman* will set (and may extend) a time limit for the *authorised person* to comply with a determination (and may set different time limits for the *authorised person* to comply with different parts of a determination).[84]

5.42   Any interest payable under the determination will be at the rate:

(a)   specified in the determination; or

(b)   (if not specified) at the rate payable on High Court judgment debts.[85]

5.43   There is a limit of £50,000 on the total value that can be awarded by the determination of a *complaint* in respect of:[86]

(a)   compensation for loss suffered;

(b)   compensation for inconvenience/distress caused;

(c)   the reasonable cost of putting right any error, omission or other deficiency; and

(d)   the reasonable cost of any specified action in the interests of the complainant.

5.44   If (before or after the determination is issued) it appears that the total value will exceed £50,000, an *ombudsman* may direct which part or parts of the award are to take preference.[87]

5.45   That limit does not apply to:

(a)   an apology;

(b)   interest on specified compensation for loss suffered;[88]

(c)   a specified amount for costs the complainant incurred in pursuing the *complaint*;

(d)   limiting fees to a specified amount; or

(e)   interest on fees to be refunded.

Acceptance/rejection of determinations

5.46   The determination will:[89]

(a)   be in writing, signed by the *ombudsman*;

(b)   give reasons for the determination; and

(c)   require the complainant to notify the *ombudsman*, before a specified time, whether the complainant accepts or rejects the determination.

5.47   The *ombudsman* may require any acceptance or rejection to be in writing, but will have regard to any reason why the complainant may be unable to use writing.[90]

5.48   The *ombudsman* will send copies of the determination to the *parties* and the relevant *Approved Regulator*.[91]

5.49   If the complainant tells the *ombudsman* that he/she accepts the determination, it is binding on the *parties* and final.[92]

5.50   Once a determination becomes binding and final, neither *party* may start or continue legal proceedings in respect of the subject matter of the *complaint*.

5.51   If the complainant does not tell the *ombudsman* (before the specified time) that he/she accepts the determination, it is treated as rejected unless:

(a)   the complainant tells the *ombudsman* (after the specified time) that he/she accepts the determination; and

(b)   the complainant has not previously told the *ombudsman* that he/she rejects the determination; and

(c)   the *ombudsman* is satisfied that there are sufficient reasons why the complainant did not respond in time.[93]

5.52   If the complainant did not respond before the specified time, the *ombudsman* will notify the *parties* and the relevant *Approved Regulator* of the outcome, describing the provisions concerning late acceptance that are set out above.[94]

5.53   If the complainant accepts or rejects the determination, the *ombudsman* will notify the *parties* and the relevant *Approved Regulator* of the outcome.[95]

5.54   If a determination is rejected (or treated as rejected) by the complainant, it has no effect on the legal rights of any *party*.

Publication

5.55   The *Legal Ombudsman* may publish a report of its investigation, consideration and determination of a *complaint*. The report will not name (or otherwise identify) the complainant, unless the complainant agrees.[96]

Enforcement

5.56   A binding and final determination can be enforced through the High Court or a county court by the complainant.[97]

5.57   A binding and final determination can also be enforced through the High Court or a county court by an *ombudsman*, if:

(a)   the complainant agrees; and

(b)   the *ombudsman* considers it appropriate in all the circumstances.[98]

5.58   A court which makes an enforcement order must tell the *Legal Ombudsman*, and then an *ombudsman*:

(a)   will tell the relevant *Approved Regulator*;

(b)   may require that *Approved Regulator* to tell the *ombudsman* what action it will take; and

(c)   may report any failure by that *Approved Regulator* to the Legal Services Board.[99]

Misconduct

5.59   If (at any stage after the *Legal Ombudsman* receives a *complaint*) an *ombudsman* considers that the *complaint* discloses any alleged misconduct about which the relevant *Approved Regulator* should consider action against the *authorised person*, the *ombudsman*:

(a)   will tell the relevant *Approved Regulator*;

(b)   will tell the complainant that the *Approved Regulator* has been told;

(c)   may require that *Approved Regulator* to tell the *ombudsman* what action it will take; and

(d)   may report any failure by that *Approved Regulator* to the Legal Services Board.[100]

5.60   If an *ombudsman* considers that an authorised person has failed to cooperate with the *Legal Ombudsman*, the *ombudsman*:

(a)   will tell the relevant *Approved Regulator*;

(b)   may require that *Approved Regulator* to tell the *ombudsman* what action it will take; and

(c)   may report any failure by that *Approved Regulator* to the Legal Services Board.[101]

5.61   An *ombudsman*, the *Legal Ombudsman* and members of its staff will disclose to an *Approved Regulator* any information that it requests in order to investigate alleged misconduct or to fulfil its regulatory functions, so far as an *ombudsman* considers that the information:

(a)   is reasonably required by the *Approved Regulator*; and

(b)   has regard to any right of privacy of any complainant or third party involved (including rights of confidentiality or rights under the Data Protection Act 1998 or the Human Rights Act 1998).[102]

6 Case fees payable by authorised persons

6.1   A *complaint* is potentially chargeable unless:

(a)   it is out of jurisdiction; or

(b)   it is dismissed or discontinued under paragraph 5.7.[103]

6.2   A case fee is payable by the business/partnership[104] or individual *authorised person* for every potentially chargeable *complaint* when it is closed unless:

(a)   the *complaint* was:

- abandoned or withdrawn; or

- settled, resolved or determined in favour of the authorised person; and

(b)   the *ombudsman* is satisfied that the *authorised person* took all reasonable steps, under his/her complaints procedures, to try to resolve the *complaint*.[105]

6.3   The case fee is £400 for all chargeable *complaints*.[106]

6.4   The remaining costs of running the *Legal Ombudsman* are covered by a levy on *Approved Regulators* by the Legal Services Board.[107]

6.5   There is no charge to complainants.

1.   Section 112.
2.   Section 145.
3.   To distinguish complaints about service from those which relate solely to professional misconduct.
4.   Sections 12 and 129.
5.   This section covers the equivalent practitioners before the commencement of the Act.
6.   [OLC rule] Sections 133(8) and 147(7).
7.   Section 137.
8.   Section 122(5).
9.   Section 134.
10.   [OLC rule]. Where it is apparent that another legal practitioner was also involved. Section 133(3)(c).
11.   Section 128(7).
12.   Individuals are covered under section 128(3). The others are covered under the Legal Services Act 2007 (Legal Complaints)(Parties) Order 2010 made by the Lord Chancellor.
13.   Defined in European Commission Recommendation 2003/361/EC – broadly a business or enterprise with fewer than 10 employees and turnover or assets not exceeding €2 million.
14.   [OLC rule] Section 132(4).

15. To save their having to take out a grant of representation if one is not otherwise required.
16. Section 128(5).
17. The Lord Chancellor can exclude others under section 130.
18. [OLC rule] Section 133(1).
19. Section 128(1).
20. Section 131(1).
21. Section 131(2) and (3).
22. Section 128(1).
23. Section 125(2).
24. Section 128(4).
25. The Lord Chancellor can include others under section 128. Note, Legal Services Act 2007 (Legal Complaints) (Parties) Order 2012.
26. Section 132(1).
27. [OLC rule] Section 132(2).
28. [OLC rule] Section 132(3).
29. Section 112(2)
30. Section 145.
31. Section 126(1).
32. [OLC rule] Section 126(3).
33. [OLC rule].
34. [OLC rule] Section 133(2)(b).
35. Section 133(1).
36. [OLC rule] This gives the Ombudsman service the right to require a complaint form, but does not oblige it to do so.
37. [OLC rule] To make it clear that the Ombudsman service does not have to communicate with each partner individually.
38. [OLC rule] Section 135.
39. [OLC rule] Section 135.
40. [OLC rule] Section 135.
41. Section 135.
42. [OLC rule] Section 133(3)(a).
43. Where a complaint is about professional negligence or judgement, the OLC will consider (on a case-by-case basis) whether the issue is one that the OLC can deal with or whether the issue would be better dealt with in court.
44. [OLC rule] For example, a French client wishes to complain about advice on French law given in France by a French lawyer who is also qualified in England and Wales.
45. [OLC rule].
46. Paragraph 5.9 only applies if the legal practitioner so requests. The idea is that, in suitable cases, the legal practitioner can go to court, provided the complainant's legal costs are met. In other circumstances, an Ombudsman cannot force a legal practitioner to pay the complainant's costs of going to court.
47. [OLC rule].
48. [OLC rule] Section 133(3)(b).
49. [OLC rule] Section 135.
50. Schedule 15, paragraph 18.
51. Where it is apparent that the complaint was made against the wrong legal practitioner.
52. [OLC rule] Where it is apparent that another legal practitioner was also involved. Section 133(3)(c).
53. There need to be separate determinations because of the £50,000 limit.
54. [OLC rule].
55. [OLC rule].
56. Section 135.
57. Previously referred to as a recommendation report or a preliminary decision.
58. [OLC rule].
59. [OLC rule].
60. [OLC rule] To ensure legal practitioners are not discouraged from saying 'sorry'.
61. Sections 133(5) and 147(6).
62. [OLC rule].
63. Including, but not limited to, information which is "restricted information" under section 151.
64. [OLC rule].
65. [OLC rule] Section 133(3)(e).
66. Section 147(1) and (3).
67. Section 147(2) and (4).
68. Section 147(5).
69. Section 148.
70. Section 149.
71. [OLC rule].
72. [OLC rule].
73. [OLC rule].
74. [OLC rule].
75. [OLC rule]. The OLC has not exercised the power in section 133(3)(g) enabling it to make a rule about the OLC awarding expenses in connection with attending a hearing.
76. Section 137(1).
77. [OLC rule] Section 133(3)(f).
78. Section 137(2).

79. Section 137(4)(b).
80. [(g) is OLC rule] Section 133(3)(h).
81. The OLC has not exercised the power under section 133(3)(i) to make a rule requiring any party who has behaved unreasonably to pay costs to the Ombudsman service.
82. Section 137(2)(b)(ii).
83. Section 137(4)(b).
84. [OLC rule].
85. [OLC rule] Section 137(4).
86. Section 138(1) and (2). The Lord Chancellor can increase the limit under section 139. Note, Legal Services Act 2007 (Alteration of Limit) Order 2012.
87. [OLC rule].
88. Section 138(3).
89. Section 140(1) and (2).
90. [OLC rule].
91. Section 140(3).
92. Section 140(4).
93. [(c) is OLC rule] Section 140(5) and (6).
94. Section 140(7) and (8).
95. Section 140(7).
96. Section 150.
97. Section 141.
98. [OLC rule] Section 141(5).
99. Section 142.
100. Section 143.
101. Section 146.
102. [OLC rule] Section 144(1).
103. [OLC rule].
104. Note Section 131.
105. [OLC rule].
106. [OLC rule].
107. Sections 173 and 174.

The Solicitors (Disciplinary Proceedings) Rules 2019

[With consolidated amendments to 25 May 2020.]

Solicitors (Disciplinary Proceedings) Rules 2019

SI 2019/1185

Made 6th August 2019

Coming into force 25th November 2019

The Solicitors Disciplinary Tribunal, in exercise of the powers conferred by section 46 of the Solicitors Act 1974, makes the following Rules:

The Legal Services Board has approved the Rules in accordance with section 178 of the Legal Services Act 2007.

PART 1
INTRODUCTORY

1 Citation and commencement

These Rules may be cited as the Solicitors (Disciplinary Proceedings) Rules 2019 and come into force on 25th November 2019.

2 Scope

These Rules apply to—

    (a)   any application made to the Tribunal under any enactment, including the following provisions of the 1974 Act—

        (i)   section 43(1) (applications relating to the control of solicitors' employees and consultants);

        (ii)   section 43(3) (applications for review of orders made in respect of applications under section 43(1));

        (iii)   section 43(4) (applications for costs in relation to applications under section 43);

        (iv)   section 47(1)(a) to (f) (applications in relation to solicitors and former solicitors);

    (b)   any complaint made to the Tribunal under any enactment, including the following—

        (i)   section 43 of the Administration of Justice Act 1985 (legal aid complaints relating to solicitors);

        (ii)   section 31(2) of the 1974 Act (complaints in respect of failure to comply with rules as to professional practice, conduct and discipline);

        (iii)   section 32(3) of the 1974 Act (complaint in respect of failure to comply with accounts rules and trust accounts rules);

(iv)   section 34(6) of the 1974 Act (complaint in respect of failure by solicitor to comply with rules relating to accountants' reports);

(v)   section 34A(2) of the 1974 Act (complaint in respect of failure by employee of solicitor to comply with rules relating to professional practice, conduct and discipline);

(vi)   section 34A(3) of the 1974 Act (complaint in respect of failure by employee of solicitor to comply with rules relating to accountants' reports);

(vii)   section 37(4) of the 1974 Act (complaint in respect of failure by solicitor to comply with indemnity rules);

(viii)   section 44(2) of the 1974 Act (complaint in respect of contravention of order under section 43(2) in respect of solicitors' employees and consultants).

3 Interpretation

(1)   In these Rules—

"the 1974 Act" means the Solicitors Act 1974;

"the 2007 Act" means the Legal Services Act 2007;

"applicant" means a person making an application;

"application" means an application or complaint to which these Rules apply and which is made in accordance with these Rules;

"prescribed form" means the appropriate form published by the Tribunal on its website;

"authorised body" means—

(a)   a body which holds a licence in force under Part 5 of the 2007 Act granted by the Solicitors Regulation Authority;

(b)   a recognised body under section 9 of the Administration of Justice Act 1985;

(c)   a sole solicitor's practice recognised under section 9 of the Administration of Justice Act 1985;

"business day" means any day except a Saturday or Sunday, Christmas Day, Good Friday or a bank holiday in England and Wales under section 1 of the Banking and Financial Dealings Act 1971;

"case to answer" means an arguable case;

"clerk" means any clerk appointed under rules 8(1) and (2);

"the Clerk to the Tribunal" means the Clerk to the Tribunal who is in office at the date these Rules come into force, or the Clerk to the Tribunal subsequently appointed under rule 8(1);

"a lay application" means an application other than one—

(a)   made by the Society; or

(b)   to which Chapter 2 of Part 3 of these Rules applies;

"panel" means a panel appointed under rule 9(1) for the hearing of an application or any matter connected with an application;

"party" means an applicant or respondent;

"practice direction" means a direction made under rule 6(3);

"practice notice" means a notice made under rule 6(3);

"the President" means the President of the Tribunal, elected under rule 7(2);

"respondent" means any party to an application other than the applicant;

"the Society" means the Law Society and includes any duly constituted committee of the Law Society or any body or person exercising delegated powers of the Law Society, including the Solicitors Regulation Authority;

"solicitor members" and "lay members" have the same meaning as in section 46 of the 1974 Act;

"Statement" means a written statement (including a witness statement) signed by the individual making the statement and containing a declaration of truth in the following form—

"I believe that the facts and matters stated in this statement are true";

"the Tribunal" means the Solicitors Disciplinary Tribunal and where a panel has been appointed for the hearing of an application or any matter connected with it, includes a panel;

"Vice President" means a Vice President of the Tribunal, elected under rule 7(3).

(2) References in these Rules to solicitors include, where appropriate, former solicitors.

(3) References in these Rules to registered foreign lawyers are references to lawyers whose names are entered in the register of foreign lawyers maintained under section 89 of the Courts and Legal Services Act 1990 and include, where appropriate, those who have ceased to be registered in that register or whose registration has been suspended.

(4) Subject to paragraph (5), references in these Rules to registered European lawyers are references to—

(a) those lawyers—

(i) whose names were entered in the register of registered European lawyers maintained by the Society under regulation 15 of the European Communities (Lawyer's Practice) Regulations 2000, as it had effect immediately before IP completion day, at a time before IP completion day, but

(ii) in relation to whom regulation 6 of the Services of Lawyers and Lawyer's Practice (Revocation etc.) (EU Exit) Regulations 2020 does not apply;

(b) those lawyers whose names are entered in the register of registered European lawyers maintained by the Society under regulation 15 of the European Communities (Lawyer's Practice) Regulations 2000, as that regulation has effect by virtue of regulation 6 of the Services of Lawyers and Lawyer's Practice (Revocation etc.) (EU Exit) Regulations 2020 and includes, where appropriate, those who have ceased to be registered in that register or whose registration has been suspended.

(5) During the period when these Rules are in force before IP completion day, references in these Rules to registered European lawyers are references to lawyers whose names are entered in the register of European lawyers maintained by the Society under regulation 15 of the European Communities (Lawyer's Practice) Regulations 2000 and include, where appropriate, those who have ceased to be registered in that register or whose registration has been suspended.

4 The overriding objective

(1) The overriding objective of these Rules is to enable the Tribunal to deal with cases justly and at proportionate cost.

(2) The Tribunal must seek to give effect to the overriding objective when it—

(a) exercises any power under these Rules; or

(b) interprets any rule or practice direction.

APPENDIX 15

(3)   Dealing with a case justly and at proportionate cost includes, so far as is practicable—

(a)   ensuring that the parties are on an equal footing;

(b)   ensuring that the case is dealt with efficiently and expeditiously;

(c)   saving expense;

(d)   dealing with the case in ways which are proportionate to the nature, importance and complexity of the issues.

(4)   The parties are required to help the Tribunal to further the overriding objective set out above.

5 Standard of proof

The standard of proof that must be applied to proceedings considered under these Rules is the civil standard of proof.

6 Regulation of procedure and practice directions

(1)   Subject to the provisions of the 1974 Act, these Rules and any other enactment, the Tribunal may regulate its own procedure.

(2)   The Tribunal may dispense with any requirements of these Rules in respect of notices, Statements, witnesses, service or time in any case where it appears to the Tribunal to be just so to do.

(3)   The Tribunal (or a panel of Tribunal members consisting of no fewer than five members of whom no fewer than two must be lay members) may give such notices or make such directions concerning the practices or procedures of the Tribunal as are consistent with these Rules and as the panel considers appropriate.

(4)   Practice notices and practice directions may be promulgated under the authority of the President.

PART 2
CONSTITUTION

7 President and Vice Presidents

(1)   The President holding office at the date these Rules come into force may not hold the office of President for a total period exceeding six years and will only be eligible for re-election as President if he or she has not previously been re-elected as President.

(2)   The Tribunal, by a simple majority, must elect a solicitor member to be its President to hold office for a term not exceeding three years and the member so elected may be re-elected for a further term not exceeding three years.

(3)   The Tribunal, by a simple majority, must elect one solicitor member and one lay member to be its Vice Presidents for a term not exceeding three years and the members so elected may be re- elected for a further term not exceeding three years. The Vice Presidents may exercise any functions as are exercisable under these Rules by the President, as the President may direct.

(4)   The Tribunal must meet at least once in each calendar year and must publish an annual report, a copy of which must be sent to the Master of the Rolls, the Society and the Legal Services Board.

8 The Clerk to the Tribunal and other clerks and staff

(1)   The Tribunal must appoint a Clerk to the Tribunal.

(2)   The Tribunal may appoint other clerks to assist the Clerk to the Tribunal.

(3)   The Clerk to the Tribunal is responsible to the Tribunal for the administration of the Tribunal in an efficient manner, including the general supervision of the other clerks and other administrative staff; maintaining records and collecting statistics required by the Tribunal.

(4)   The Clerk to the Tribunal or any other clerk appointed by the Tribunal under this Rule must be a solicitor or barrister of not less than ten years' standing.

(5)   The office of the Clerk to the Tribunal must be vacated if—

  (a)   in the Tribunal's opinion, with which the Master of the Rolls agrees, the Clerk to the Tribunal is physically or mentally incapable of performing his or her duties; or

  (b)   the Clerk to the Tribunal—

    (i)   resigns; or

    (ii)   retires; or

    (iii)   is removed from office by a resolution of the Tribunal approved by the Master of the Rolls.

(6)   The Tribunal may prescribe the duties for which the clerks are to be responsible and those duties must include arrangements for—

  (a)   the submission of applications for certification as to whether or not there is a case to answer (see rule 13);

  (b)   making pre-listing arrangements;

  (c)   variation of directions;

  (d)   determining applications for adjournment of procedural or substantive hearings in accordance with rule 23(2);

  (e)   considering parties' non-compliance with directions and orders (see rule 20(3));

  (f)   securing a record of hearings (by electronic recording or other means) (see rule 39);

  (g)   advising the Tribunal on matters of law or procedure;

  (h)   preparing draft judgments for the consideration of the panel which heard an application (see rule 40);

  (i)   determining applications in respect of substituted service (see rule 46);

  (j)   drawing orders and findings and sending them to the Society.

9 Composition of panels

(1)   The Tribunal must appoint a panel of three members of the Tribunal for the hearing of any application. Two of the panel members must be solicitor members and one must be a lay member.

(2)   The President may appoint a member to be the chair of a panel.

(3)   If the President does not appoint a chair of a panel, a solicitor member must act as the chair.

10 Functions exercisable by a single solicitor member

A single solicitor member may exercise the functions set out in—

  (a)   rule 8(6) (c) (d) and (i) (duties for which clerks are responsible);

  (b)   rule 27(3) (directions relating to lodging of bundles);

  (c)   rule 22 (4) (f) and (g) (determining procedural applications)

APPENDIX 15

PART 3
APPLICATIONS

Chapter 1
Applications by the Law Society and lay applications

11 Application of Rules in Chapter 1

(1) Rules 12, 13 and 14 apply to applications made by the Society and to lay applications.

(2) Rule 15 applies to applications made by the Society.

(3) Rule 16 applies to lay applications.

12 Method and form of application

(1) An application to which this Rule applies must be sent to the Tribunal offices and must be made using the prescribed form.

(2) The application must be supported by a Statement setting out the allegations, the facts and matters supporting the application and each allegation contained within it and exhibiting any documents relied upon by the applicant.

(3) In the case of an application made by the Society, the application must be accompanied by—

(a) sufficient copies of the application and supporting documents to enable the Tribunal to retain one complete set and to serve one complete set on each respondent;

(b) a time estimate for the substantive hearing;

(c) a schedule of the Society's costs incurred up to and including the date on which the application is made.

(4) In the case of a lay application, the application must be accompanied by three copies of the application and supporting documents and one further copy for any second and each further respondent.

13 Certification of case to answer

(1) An application made in accordance with rule 12 must initially be considered by a solicitor member ("the initial solicitor member") for consideration of the question of whether there is a case to answer in respect of the allegations made in the application.

(2) If the initial solicitor member considers that there is a case to answer in respect of all the allegations made and is not of the opinion that the question is one of doubt or difficulty then the initial solicitor member must certify that there is a case to answer.

(3) If the initial solicitor member is minded not to certify that there is a case to answer in respect of all or some of the allegations made or is of the opinion that the question is one of doubt or difficulty, the question must be considered by a panel of three members of the Tribunal, two of whom must be solicitor members and one of whom must be a lay member. The initial solicitor member may be a member of the panel. If the panel considers that there is a case to answer in respect of any of the allegations made then it must certify that there is a case to answer in respect of those allegations.

(4) If the panel decides that there is no case to answer in respect of any of the allegations made, it may refuse or dismiss the application, or part of it, without requiring the respondent to answer the allegations and without hearing the applicant. The applicant must be provided with written reasons explaining the decision.

(5) If a panel or solicitor member certifies that a case to answer is established in respect of all or any of the allegations made, a clerk must serve a copy of each of the documents referred to in rule 12(3) or (4), as the case may be, on each respondent.

14 Supplementary Statements

(1)   An applicant who has made an application to which this Rule applies may, subject to paragraph (5), send supplementary statements to the Tribunal containing additional facts or matters on which the applicant seeks to rely or further allegations in support of the application.

(2)   A supplementary statement must be supported by a Statement setting out any new allegations, facts and matters supporting the application and each allegation contained within it and exhibiting any new documents relied upon by the applicant.

(3)   In the case of an application made by the Society, when a supplementary statement is sent to the Tribunal, the Society must provide—

(a)   sufficient copies of the supplementary statement and supporting documents to enable the Tribunal to retain one complete set and to serve a complete set on each respondent;

(b)   a revised time estimate for the substantive hearing;

(c)   a revised schedule of the Society's costs incurred up to and including the date on which the supplementary statement is sent;

(d)   any proposed directions for the future progression of the case, including any proposals to vary any existing directions.

(4)   In the case of a lay application, when a supplementary statement is sent to the Tribunal, the applicant must provide sufficient copies of the supplementary statement and supporting documents to enable the Tribunal to retain one complete set and to serve a complete set on each respondent.

(5)   The applicant will not be permitted to send a supplementary statement without leave of the Tribunal—

(a)   more than 12 months from the date of the application under rule 12;

(b)   less than 30 days before the date fixed for the substantive hearing of the application.

(6)   Rule 13 applies in respect of any supplementary statement containing additional facts or matters on which the applicant seeks to rely or further allegations in support of the application as it applies to an application made in accordance with rule 12.

15 Applications in respect of solicitors' employees

In a case where an application is made for an order under section 43(2) of the 1974 Act, the solicitor, recognised body, registered European lawyer or registered foreign lawyer by or for whose benefit the respondent is employed or remunerated—

(a)   may also be named or joined as a respondent to the application; and

(b)   must be joined as a respondent to the application if the Tribunal so directs.

16 Adjournment of application pending Law Society investigation

(1)   The Tribunal may adjourn the consideration of the question of whether to certify any application to which this Rule applies for an initial period of up to three months to enable the Society to carry out its own investigations and consider whether to—

(a)   initiate its own application; or

(b)   by agreement with the applicant, take over conduct of the application.

(2)   After the expiration of the initial adjournment period, the application may be referred to a panel on the first available date for further review and consideration, subject to the provisions of paragraph (3).

(3)   If at the expiration of the period specified by the Tribunal under paragraph (1) the Society has not made a decision as to whether to initiate or take over the conduct of an

application, the Tribunal may adjourn the matter for a further period of up to three months, after which the application must be referred to a panel on the first available date for further review and consideration.

Chapter 2
Applications by solicitors, etc.

17 Applications for restoration and termination of indefinite suspension

(1)   This Rule applies to applications made to the Tribunal under section 47 of the 1974 Act by—

    (a)   a former solicitor seeking restoration to the Roll of Solicitors kept by the Society under section 6 the 1974 Act;

    (b)   a person seeking restoration to the register of European lawyers or the register of foreign lawyers if his name has been withdrawn or removed from either register by the Tribunal;

    (c)   a solicitor, registered European lawyer or registered foreign lawyer seeking the termination of an indefinite period of suspension from practice imposed by the Tribunal.

(2)   An application to which this Rule applies must be sent to the Tribunal and must be made using the prescribed form.

(3)   The application must be supported by a Statement setting out the facts and matters supporting the application and exhibiting any documents relied upon by the applicant.

(4)   The Society must be a respondent to any application to which this Rule applies.

(5)   The applicant must serve on the Society-

    (a)   a copy of the application; and

    (b)   a Statement in support of the application.

(6)   Every application to which this Rule applies must be advertised by the applicant in the Law Society's Gazette and in a newspaper circulating in the area of the applicant's former practice (if available) and must also be advertised by the Tribunal on its website.

(7)   Any person may, no later than 21 days before the hearing date of an application to which this Rule applies, serve on the Tribunal and the parties to the application notice of that person's intention to oppose the allowing of the application and the Tribunal may allow the person to appear before it at the hearing of the application, call evidence and make representations upon which the Tribunal may allow the person to be cross-examined.

18 Application to vary or remove conditions on practice

(1)   This Rule applies to applications made to the Tribunal to vary or remove conditions on practice imposed by the Tribunal.

(2)   An application to which this Rule applies must be sent to the Tribunal and must be made using the prescribed form.

(3)   The application must be supported by a Statement setting out the facts and matters supporting the application and exhibiting any documents relied upon by the applicant.

(4)   The Society must be a respondent to any application to which this Rule applies.

19 Application for review of order relating to solicitors' employees and consultants

(1)   An application for a review of an order made under section 43(3)(a) of the 1974 Act must be sent to the Tribunal and must be made using the prescribed form.

(2)   The application must be supported by a Statement setting out the facts and matters supporting the application and exhibiting any documents relied upon by the applicant.

(3)   An application under section 43(3)(a) of the 1974 Act must be served on the Society and the Society must, within 28 days of the service of the application, send a Statement to the Tribunal setting out the facts and matters on which it relied in making the order under section 43(2) of the 1974 Act.

PART 4
CASE MANAGEMENT

20 Standard Directions

(1)   Following certification of a case to answer under rule 13, standard directions must be issued by a clerk and sent to the parties.

(2)   The standard directions may specify—

(a)   the date fixed for the substantive hearing of the matter;

(b)   the date by which a respondent must send to the Tribunal and serve on every other party an Answer to the allegations contained in the Statement served under rules 12 and 14 and a reply to the application and Statement served under rules 17, 18 and 19;

(c)   the date by which the respondent must send to the Tribunal and serve on every other party all documents on which the respondent intends to rely at the substantive hearing;

(d)   the date by which the parties must send to the Tribunal and serve on every other party a list of witnesses upon whose evidence they intend to rely at the substantive hearing;

(e)   the date by which the parties must notify the Tribunal of any intention to rely on expert evidence;

(f)   the date on which any case management hearing will take place;

(g)   the date by which the parties must send a statement of readiness to the Tribunal;

(h)   the date by which hearing bundles (and the number of copies) must be sent to the Tribunal;

(i)   any other standard direction which the Tribunal considers appropriate to ensure the management of matters in accordance with the overriding objective of these Rules mentioned in rule 4.

(3)   If a party fails to comply with the standard directions, any other direction or any of these Rules, the matter may be listed for a non-compliance hearing before a clerk, who may make appropriate directions, which may include listing the matter before the Tribunal which may direct that—

(a)   evidence which has not been sent or served as directed may not be relied upon without permission of the Tribunal;

(b)   an adverse costs order be made in default of compliance, which may be ordered to be paid immediately to any other party;

(c)   adverse inferences that the panel hearing the matter considers appropriate may be drawn at the substantive hearing from the failure to comply.

(4)   In this rule—

(a)   an "Answer" is a document which sets out—

(i)   which allegations in the Statement are admitted and which are denied; and

(ii)   the reasons for denial;

(b)   a "statement of readiness" is a document—

(i)   confirming that the parties are ready for the substantive hearing;

    (ii)   setting out what, if any, further directions are required by the parties; and

    (iii)   setting out whether the time estimate for the final hearing is the same as was anticipated when standard directions were issued or at any subsequent case management hearing, or otherwise providing a revised time estimate.

21 Case management hearings

(1)   A case management hearing must be arranged by the Tribunal or a clerk in cases where—

    (a)   a clerk considers that the holding of a case management hearing is justified by reason of the time estimate or revised time estimate provided by the Society under rule 12(3)(b) or 14(3)(b); or

    (b)   the clerk who reviews the application on receipt identifies issues which in the opinion of the clerk justify the holding of a case management hearing.

(2)   A case management hearing may be arranged by the Tribunal or a clerk at any other time before the hearing of an application.

(3)   A case management hearing may be heard by the Tribunal or a clerk and may take place by telephone, in person, or by such electronic means as may be approved by the Tribunal.

(4)   If the Tribunal notifies the parties in advance of a case management hearing that a further hearing is to be fixed or is likely to be fixed at the case management hearing, the parties must attend the case management hearing equipped with their dates to avoid and the dates to avoid of any witnesses.

(5)   If on receipt of a list of witnesses (see rule 20(2)(d)) or a statement of readiness (see rule 20(2)(g)) a clerk considers that a further case management hearing is required, a further case management hearing date may be fixed so that any further directions can be made.

22 Procedural applications

(1)   Any procedural application must be—

    (a)   made using the prescribed form; and

    (b)   sent to the Tribunal and served on every other party, together with any relevant supporting documentation.

(2)   The Tribunal, single solicitor member or clerk must issue written reasons for its decisions on procedural applications.

(3)   Any party aggrieved by a decision of a clerk under rule 8(6) may request that the application be re-determined by a panel or single solicitor member by notifying the Tribunal of this request within 14 days of receipt of the written reasons for the decision.

(4)   In this rule, a "procedural application" means an application for—

    (a)   a variation of directions;

    (b)   an adjournment of the hearing of an application (see rule 23);

    (c)   an amendment or withdrawal of an allegation (see rule 24);

    (d)   disclosure and discovery (see rule 26);

    (e)   leave to call or adduce expert evidence (see rule 30);

    (f)   a direction that special measures may be provided or used to assist vulnerable witnesses or respondents;

    (g)   a direction that a witness or respondent may give their evidence or otherwise participate in the proceedings by videolink or other electronic means;

    (h)   any other procedural application, including an application for a stay of proceedings for abuse of process, and general applications to exclude or adduce evidence.

23 Adjournments

(1)   An application for an adjournment of the hearing of an application must be supported by documentary evidence of the need for the adjournment.

(2)   An application for an adjournment made more than 21 days before the hearing date will be considered by a clerk or a single solicitor member on the papers.

(3)   An application for an adjournment made 21 days or less before the hearing date will be considered by the panel listed to sit on the substantive hearing on the papers unless it is in the interests of justice for the matter to be dealt with at an oral hearing.

24 Amendment or withdrawal of allegations

No allegation made in an application may be amended or withdrawn without leave of the Tribunal.

25 Agreed Outcome Proposals

(1)   The parties may up to 28 days before the substantive hearing of an application (unless the Tribunal directs otherwise) submit to the Tribunal an Agreed Outcome Proposal for approval by the Tribunal.

(2)   An Agreed Outcome Proposal must—

   (a)   contain a statement of the facts that are agreed between the relevant parties;

   (b)   set out the agreed proposed penalty and an explanation as to why the penalty would be in accordance with any guidance published by the Tribunal on sanctions imposed by the Tribunal;

   (c)   be signed by the relevant parties; and

   (d)   comply with any relevant practice direction made by the Tribunal in respect of Agreed Outcome Proposals.

(3)   If the Tribunal approves the Agreed Outcome Proposal in the terms proposed it must make an Order in those terms. The case must be called into an open hearing and the Tribunal must announce its decision.

(4)   If the Tribunal wishes to hear from the parties before making its decision the Tribunal may direct that there be a case management hearing which the parties to the proposed Agreed Outcome Proposal must attend for the purpose of making submissions before a final decision is reached. The case management hearing must be heard in private.

(5)   Where the Tribunal is not satisfied that it is appropriate to make an Order in accordance with paragraph (3) it must provide reasons to the parties who may then submit a revised proposal. If the Tribunal is satisfied with the revised proposal, it must make an Order in accordance with it.

(6)   Some or all of the same members of the panel appointed in respect of the application may consider the initial Agreed Outcome Proposal, any submissions made at a case management hearing and any revised proposal but may not subsequently participate in the panel for the substantive hearing (if there is one).

(7)   If on considering a submission under this rule the Tribunal decides not to make an Order in accordance with paragraph (3) it must make directions for the substantive disposal of the matter by a panel consisting of members who were not on the panel which considered the submission.

(8)   If on considering a submission under this rule the Tribunal decides not to make an Order and the Tribunal does not publish that decision or announce it in an open hearing, no information will be published or announced about the submission save that the Agreed Outcome Proposal was not approved.

26 Disclosure and discovery

(1)   If an application is made for the disclosure or discovery of material, the Tribunal may make an order that material be disclosed where it considers that the production of the material is necessary for the proper consideration of an issue in the case, unless the Tribunal considers that there are compelling reasons in the public interest not to order the disclosure.

(2)   Any order made by the Tribunal only applies to material that is in the possession or under the control of a party.

(3)   An order made under paragraph (1) does not oblige the parties to produce any material which they would be entitled to refuse to produce in proceedings in any court in England and Wales.

(4)   A party to proceedings before the Tribunal is required to disclose only—

    (a)   the documents on which the party relies;

    (b)   any documents which—

        (i)   adversely affect that party's own case;

        (ii)   adversely affect another party's case; or

        (iii)   support another party's case; and

    (c)   any documents which the party is required to disclose by a relevant practice direction.

PART 5
EVIDENCE

27 Evidence generally and service and sending of Evidence and bundles

(1)   Without prejudice to the general powers in Parts 2 and 3 of these Rules the Tribunal may give directions in relation to an application relating to any of the following—

    (a)   the exchange between parties of lists of documents which are relevant to the application, or relevant to particular issues, and the inspection of such documents;

    (b)   the provision by parties of statements of agreed matters;

    (c)   issues on which the Tribunal requires evidence or submissions;

    (d)   the nature and manner of the evidence or submissions that the Tribunal requires;

    (e)   the time at which any evidence or submissions are to be sent;

    (f)   the time to be allowed during the hearing for the presentation of any evidence or submission.

(2)   The Tribunal may—

    (a)   admit any evidence whether or not it would be admissible in a civil trial in England and Wales;

    (b)   exclude evidence that would otherwise be admissible where—

        (i)   the evidence was not provided within the time allowed by a direction given under these Rules or a practice direction; or

        (ii)   the evidence was otherwise provided in a manner that did not comply with a direction given under these Rules or a practice direction; or

        (iii)   it would otherwise be unfair, disproportionate or contrary to the interests of justice to admit the evidence.

(3)   Unless otherwise directed by the Tribunal, in cases where the Society is the applicant, it must send five copies of a paginated hearing bundle to the Tribunal no later than 14 days before the date listed for the substantive hearing.

28 Written Evidence

(1)   If no party requires the attendance of a witness, the Tribunal may accept the Statement of that witness as evidence in respect of the whole case or of any particular fact or facts.

(2)   Every Statement upon which any party proposes to rely must be sent to the Tribunal by that party and served on every other party on a date determined by the Tribunal which must be no less than 28 days before the date fixed for the hearing of the application. The Statement must be accompanied by a notice, using the prescribed form.

(3)   Any party on whom a notice has been served under paragraph (2) and who requires the attendance of the witness in question at the hearing must, no later than seven days after service of the notice require, in writing, the party by whom the notice was served to produce the witness at the hearing.

(4)   Any application for a witness summons must be made to the High Court.

(5)   If a Statement has not been served in accordance with paragraph 28(2) in relation to a witness, a party must apply to the Tribunal for permission—

(a)   to produce that Statement; and

(b)   for the witness to give evidence at the hearing.

(6)   Any party to an application may, by written notice, not later than 21 days before the date fixed for the hearing, request any other party to agree that any document may be admitted as evidence.

(7)   If a party desires to challenge the authenticity of a document which is the subject of paragraph (6), that party must, within seven days of receipt of the notice served under that paragraph, give notice that he or she does not agree to the admission of the document and that he or she requires that its authenticity be proved at the hearing.

(8)   If the recipient of a notice given under paragraph (6) does not give a notice in response within the period mentioned in paragraph (7), that recipient is deemed to have admitted the document unless otherwise ordered by the Tribunal.

29 Civil Evidence Act notices

(1)   Subject to the following provision of this Rule, the provisions of the Civil Evidence Act 1995 apply in relation to proceedings before the Tribunal in the same manner as they apply in relation to civil proceedings.

(2)   Any notice given under the provisions of the Civil Evidence Act 1995 as so applied must be given no later than the latest date for the service of witness statements under rule 28.

30 Expert evidence

(1)   No party may call an expert or adduce in evidence an expert's report at the substantive hearing of an application without leave of the Tribunal.

(2)   An application under this rule must be determined by a panel.

(3)   The Tribunal may permit expert evidence to be adduced where it considers that such evidence is necessary for the proper consideration of an issue or issues in the case.

(4)   If two or more parties wish to submit expert evidence on a particular issue, the Tribunal may direct that the evidence on that issue is to be given by a single joint expert.

(5)   The Tribunal may, at any stage, direct that a discussion take place between experts for the purpose of requiring the experts to identify and agree the expert issues in the proceedings and provide a joint schedule setting out the matters that are agreed and not agreed. The Tribunal may specify the issues which the experts must discuss.

(6)   Any expert evidence must be in the form of a Statement and must set out—

(a)   the expert's professional qualifications;

(b)   the substance of all material instructions (including a general description of the documents provided), whether written or oral, on the basis of which the Statement was written;

(c)   a declaration that the expert understands and has complied with the expert's duty to assist the Tribunal on matters within the expert's expertise and understands that this duty overrides any obligation to any party from whom the expert has received instructions or by whom they are paid.

31 Interpreters and Translators

(1)   If any witness, applicant or respondent requires the assistance of an interpreter to participate in a hearing the Tribunal must be notified of this fact by the party requiring the interpreter when sending the list of witnesses.

(2)   Where a witness statement has been translated from a language other than English it must be accompanied by a Statement confirming—

(a)   the language in which the original witness statement was made; and

(b)   that the translator has translated the witness statement into English to the best of the translator's skill and understanding.

32 Previous findings of record

(1)   A conviction for a criminal offence in the United Kingdom may be proved by the production of a certified copy of the certificate of conviction relating to the offence and proof of a conviction will constitute evidence that the person in question was guilty of the offence. The findings of fact upon which that conviction was based will be admissible as conclusive proof of those facts save in exceptional circumstances.

(2)   The judgment of any civil court, or any tribunal exercising a professional or disciplinary jurisdiction, in or outside England and Wales (other than the Tribunal) may be proved by producing a certified copy of the judgment and the findings of fact upon which that judgment was based are admissible as proof but not conclusive proof of those facts.

(3)   Where the Tribunal has made a finding based solely upon the certificate of conviction for a criminal offence which is subsequently quashed the Tribunal may, on the application of the Law Society or the respondent to the application in respect of which the finding arose, revoke its finding and make such order as to costs as appears to be just in the circumstances.

33 Adverse inferences

Where a respondent fails to—

(a)   send or serve an Answer in accordance with a direction under rule 20(2)(b); or

(b)   give evidence at a substantive hearing or submit themselves to cross-examination;

and regardless of the service by the respondent of a witness statement in the proceedings, the Tribunal is entitled to take into account the position that the respondent has chosen to adopt and to draw such adverse inferences from the respondent's failure as the Tribunal considers appropriate.

PART 6
HEARINGS AND COSTS

34 Publication of cause lists

(1)   A cause list will be published on the Tribunal's website before the case is due to be heard.

(2)   Any party or other person who claims to be affected by an application may apply to the Tribunal for the cause list to be anonymised on the grounds of—

(a)   exceptional hardship; or

(b)   exceptional prejudice

to a party, a witness or any person affected by the application.

(3) Any person making an application under paragraph (2) must serve a copy of that application together with a Statement in support on all parties to the proceedings, and—

(a) the application must be served no later than 28 days before the hearing in relation to which the application is made; and

(b) must be made using the prescribed form.

(4) The Tribunal may in its discretion consider the application on the papers or list it for an oral hearing.

(5) If the Tribunal is satisfied that either of the grounds in paragraph (2) are met, the Tribunal must direct that the cause list be anonymised in such a way that appears to it to be just and proper.

35 Public or private hearings

(1) Subject to paragraphs (2), (4), (5) and (6), every hearing of the Tribunal must take place in public.

(2) Any person who claims to be affected by an application may apply to the Tribunal for the hearing of the application to be conducted in private on the grounds of—

(a) exceptional hardship; or

(b) exceptional prejudice

to a party, a witness or any person affected by the hearing.

(3) Any person who makes an application under paragraph (2) must serve a copy of that application and a Statement in support on all parties to the proceedings. If there is no objection to the application from any of the parties, the Tribunal will consider the application on the papers unless it considers that it is in the interests of justice for the application to be considered at an oral hearing.

(4) If the Tribunal decides that the application made under paragraph (2) is to be considered at an oral hearing, that hearing will take place in private unless the Tribunal directs otherwise.

(5) The Tribunal may, before or during a hearing, direct without an application from any party that the hearing or part of it be held in private if—

(a) the Tribunal is satisfied that it would have granted an application under paragraph (2) had one been made; or

(b) the Tribunal considers that a hearing in public would prejudice the interests of justice.

(6) The Tribunal may give a direction excluding from any hearing or part of it any person—

(a) whose conduct the Tribunal considers is disrupting or likely to disrupt the hearing;

(b) whose presence the Tribunal considers is likely to prevent another person from giving evidence or making submissions freely;

(c) whose attendance at the hearing would otherwise prejudice the overriding objective of these Rules.

(7) Other than a party to the proceedings, a factual witness is excluded from the hearing until their evidence has been given, unless the parties agree or the Tribunal directs otherwise.

(8) Save in exceptional circumstances, where the Tribunal disposes of proceedings following a hearing held in private, it must announce its decision in a public session.

(9) The Tribunal may make a direction prohibiting the disclosure or publication of any matter likely to lead to the identification of any person whom the Tribunal considers should not be identified.

(10) The Tribunal may give a direction prohibiting the disclosure of a document or information to a person if it is satisfied that—

(a)   the disclosure would be likely to cause any person serious harm; and

(b)   it is in the interests of justice to make such a direction.

36 Proceeding in absence

If a party fails to attend and is not represented at the hearing and the Tribunal is satisfied that notice of the hearing was served on the party in accordance with these Rules, the Tribunal may hear and determine any application and make findings, hand down sanctions, order the payment of costs and make orders as it considers appropriate notwithstanding that the party failed to attend and is not represented at the hearing.

37 Application for re-hearing

(1)   At any time before the Tribunal's Order is sent to the Society under rule 42(1) or within 14 days after it is sent, a party may apply to the Tribunal for a re-hearing of an application if—

(a)   the party neither attended in person nor was represented at the hearing of the application; and

(b)   the Tribunal determined the application in the party's absence.

(2)   An application for a re-hearing under this rule must be made using the prescribed form accompanied by a Statement setting out the facts upon which the applicant wishes to rely together with any supporting documentation.

(3)   If satisfied that it is just to do so, the Tribunal may grant the application upon such terms, including as to costs, as it thinks fit. The re-hearing must be held before a panel comprised of different members from those who determined the original application.

38 Evidence and submissions during the hearing

(1)   The Tribunal may consent to a witness giving, or require any witness to give, evidence on oath or affirmation and may administer an oath or affirmation for that purpose.

(2)   The Tribunal may, at any hearing, dispense with the strict rules of evidence.

(3)   Without restriction on the general powers in Parts 2 and 3 of these Rules, the Tribunal may, pursuant to the overriding objective set out in rule 4(1), give directions in relation to—

(a)   the provision by the parties of statements of agreed matters;

(b)   issues on which it requires evidence to be given or submissions to be made and the nature and manner of the evidence or submissions it requires;

(c)   the time at which any evidence or submissions are to be given or made;

(d)   the time allowed during the hearing for the presentation of any evidence or submission;

(e)   the time allowed for cross-examination of a witness.

39 Recording of the hearing

(1)   All hearings of the Tribunal will be electronically audio-recorded.

(2)   Where hearings of the Tribunal are held in public, a copy of the recording must be disclosed to any person on request, subject to any direction by the Tribunal in relation to the release of the recording.

(3)   Where a hearing is held in private, a copy of the electronic recording may only be disclosed to the parties and only on the provision of an undertaking that the recording or any transcript of the hearing or any part of it will not be made public.

40 Decisions

(1)   The Tribunal may announce its decision at the conclusion of the hearing or may reserve its decision for announcement at a later date. In either case the announcement must be made in public unless rule 35(8) applies.

(2)   As soon as reasonably practicable after making a decision which finally disposes of all issues in the proceedings, the Tribunal must provide to each party a judgment containing written reasons for its decision, signed by a member of the Tribunal.

(3)   As soon as reasonably practicable following a case management hearing, the Tribunal will provide to each party a memorandum containing written reasons for its decisions, signed by a member of the Tribunal.

(4)   Decisions on applications made during the course of a substantive hearing must be announced in a public session and the written reasons must be contained in the judgment issued at the conclusion of the proceedings.

(5)   The Tribunal or a clerk may, at any time, correct a clerical error or omission in a judgment or memorandum.

41 Sanction

(1)   At the conclusion of the hearing, the Tribunal must make a finding as to whether any or all of the allegations in the application have been substantiated.

(2)   If the Tribunal makes a finding that any or all of the allegations in the application have been substantiated, the Tribunal must ask—

(a)   the clerk whether any allegations were found to have been substantiated against the respondent in any previous disciplinary proceedings before the Tribunal; and

(b)   the Society (in those cases where the Society is the applicant) whether it has imposed any sanction against the respondent in respect of conduct which has not been the subject of any previous disciplinary proceedings before the Tribunal.

(3)   The respondent will be entitled to make submissions by way of mitigation, including character references, in respect of the sanction, if any, to be imposed by the Tribunal.

(4)   The Tribunal must have regard to its guidance on sanctions in force at the time when determining the appropriate sanction.

42 The Order

(1)   The making of the Order that contains the Tribunal's decision must be announced by the Tribunal pursuant to Rule 40(1) and a copy of the Order signed by a member of the Tribunal must be sent by the Tribunal to the Society as soon as reasonably practicable following the hearing.

(2)   An Order takes effect once it has been announced by the Tribunal in public session or in private where rule 35(8) applies.

43 Costs

(1)   At any stage of the proceedings, the Tribunal may make such order as to costs as it thinks fit, which may include an order for wasted costs.

(2)   The amount of costs to be paid may either be decided and fixed by the Tribunal following summary assessment or directed by the Tribunal to be subject to detailed assessment by a taxing Master of the Senior Courts.

(3)   Without prejudice to the generality of paragraph (1), the Tribunal may make an order as to costs in circumstances where—

(a)   any application, allegation or appeal is withdrawn or amended;

(b)   some or all of the allegations are not proved against a respondent;

(c)   an appeal or interim application is unsuccessful.

(4)   The Tribunal must first decide whether to make an order for costs and must identify the paying party in any order made. When deciding whether to make an order for costs, against

which party, and for what amount, the Tribunal will consider all relevant matters including the following—

(a)   the conduct of the parties and whether any or all of the allegations were pursued or defended reasonably;

(b)   whether the Tribunal's directions and time limits imposed were complied with;

(c)   whether the amount of time spent on the matter was proportionate and reasonable;

(d)   whether any hourly rate and the amount of disbursements claimed is proportionate and reasonable;

(e)   the paying party's means.

(5)   If the respondent makes representations about the respondent's means, the representations must be supported by a Statement which includes details of the respondent's assets, income and expenditure (including but not limited to property, savings, income and outgoings) which must be supported by documentary evidence.

PART 7
MISCELLANEOUS

44 Sending and service of documents

(1)   Any document to be sent to the Tribunal or any other person or served on a party or any other person under these Rules, a practice direction or a direction given under these Rules must be—

(a)   sent by pre-paid first class post or by document exchange, or delivered by hand, to the Tribunal's or other person's office or as the case may be the address specified for the proceedings by the party (or if no such address has been specified to the last known place of business or place of residence of the person to be served); or

(b)   sent by email to the email address specified by the Tribunal or other person or specified for the proceedings by a party (or if no such address has been specified to the last known place of business or place of residence of the person to be served); or

(c)   sent or delivered by such other method as the Tribunal may direct.

(2)   Subject to paragraph (3), if a party specifies an email address for the electronic delivery of documents the Tribunal and other parties will be entitled to serve (and service will be deemed to be effective) documents by electronic means to that email address, unless the party states in writing that service should not be effected by those means.

(3)   If a party informs the Tribunal and every other party in writing that a particular form of communication, other than pre-paid post or delivery by hand, should not be used to send documents to that party, that form of communication must not be used.

(4)   Any recipient of a document sent by electronic means may request that the sender send a hard copy of the document to the recipient. The recipient must make such a request as soon as reasonably practicable after receiving the document electronically.

(5)   The Tribunal will proceed on the basis that the address, including an email address, provided by a party or its representative is and remains the address to which documents should be sent or delivered until receiving written notification to the contrary by that party or representative.

(6)   If a document submitted to the Tribunal is not written in English, it must be accompanied by an English translation and a Statement from the translator confirming that the translator carried out the translation and setting out the translator's qualifications.

45 Deemed Service

A document sent or served within the United Kingdom in accordance with these Rules or any relevant practice direction is deemed to be served on the day shown in the following table—

	Method of service	Deemed date of service
1.	First class post (or other service which provides for delivery on the next business day)	The second day after it was posted, left with, delivered to or collected by the relevant service provider provided that day is a business day; or if not, the next business day after that day.
2.	Document exchange	The second day after it was left with, delivered to or collected by the relevant service provider provided that day is a business day; or if not, the next business day after that day.
3.	Delivering the document by hand to or leaving it at an address	If it is delivered to or left at the address on a business day before 4.30p.m., on that day; or in any other case, on the next business day after that day.
4.	E-mail or other electronic method	If the e-mail or other electronic transmission is sent on a business day before 4.30p.m., on that day; or in any other case, on the next business day after the day on which it was sent.
5.	Fax	If the transmission of the fax is completed on a business day before 4.30p.m., on that day; or in any other case, on the next business day after the day on which it was transmitted.
6.	Personal service	If the document is served personally before 4.30p.m. on a business day, on that day; or in any other case, on the next business day after that day.

46 Substituted service by the applicant

(1)   If the applicant believes that there is no reasonable prospect of being able to effect service on a respondent using the methods set out in rule 44 it may apply to the Tribunal for a direction for substituted service. This application must be made in writing and set out—

(a)   the steps that have been taken to establish the address, place of business or email address of the respondent; and

(b)   the proposed alternative method of service.

(2)   The application may be determined by the Tribunal, a panel, a single solicitor member or a clerk, who may make a direction for substituted service if it is in the interests of justice to do so.

47 Calculating time

(1)   Subject to rule 45 an act required by these Rules, a practice direction or a direction given under these Rules to be done on or by a particular day must be done by 4:30 p.m. on that day unless otherwise directed.

(2)   If the time specified by these Rules, a practice direction or a direction given under these Rules for doing any act ends on a day other than a business day, the act is done in time if it is done on the next business day.

48 Representatives

(1)   Any party may appoint a legal representative to represent that party in the proceedings.

(2)   If a party appoints a legal representative, that party must send to the Tribunal and every other party written notice of the representative's name and address, together with a copy of the notice.

(3)   Anything permitted or required to be done by a party under these Rules may be done by the legal representative of that party, except signing a witness statement.

(4)   A party who receives due notice of the appointment of a legal representative—

(a)   must send to the legal representative any document which, at any time after the appointment, is required to be sent to the represented party, and need not send that document to the represented party; and

(b)   may proceed on the basis that the representative is and remains authorised as such until they receive written notification to the contrary from the representative or the represented party.

(5)   At a hearing a party may be accompanied by another person whose name and address has not been notified under paragraph (2) but who, with the permission of the Tribunal, may assist the party in presenting the party's case at the hearing.

(6)   Paragraphs (2) to (4) do not apply to a person who accompanies a party under paragraph (5).

(7)   In this rule "legal representative" means—

(a)   a solicitor;

(b)   a barrister;

(c)   a person who, for the purposes of the 2007 Act, is an authorised person in relation to an activity which constitutes the exercise of a right of audience or the conduct of litigation within the meanings given by Schedule 2 to that Act.

49 Amendments to the 2011 Appeals Rules

The Solicitors Disciplinary Tribunal (Appeals and Amendment) Rules 2011 are amended as follows—

(a)   In rule 2 (interpretation)—

(i)   for the definition of "the 2007 rules" substitute the following definition— ""the 2019 rules" means the Solicitors (Disciplinary Proceedings) Rules 2019";

(ii)   In the definition of "clerk", for "the 2007 rules" substitute "the 2019 rules";

(b)   In rule 5(1) for the words "listed in rule 3(11) of the 2007 Rules" substitute "listed in rule 8(6) of the Solicitors (Disciplinary Proceedings) Rules 2019";

(c)   In rule 5(2) for the words "rule 3(11) of the 2007 Rules" substitute "rule 8(6) of the Solicitors (Disciplinary Proceedings) Rules 2019";

(d)   In rule 27(1) for "5pm" substitute "4.30p.m.".

50 Revocation

The Solicitors (Disciplinary Proceedings) Rules 2007 are revoked.

51 Transitional provisions

These Rules do not apply to proceedings in respect of which an Application is made before the date on which these Rules come into force and those proceedings will be subject to the Solicitors (Disciplinary Proceedings) Rules 2007 as if they had not been revoked.

Signed by authority of the Solicitors Disciplinary Tribunal

Gate House, 1 Farringdon Street, London EC4M 7LG

6th August 2019

Edward Nally

President

Solicitors Disciplinary Tribunal

The Solicitors Disciplinary Tribunal (Appeals and Amendment) Rules 2011

[With consolidated amendments to 25 November 2019. For details see www. solicitorstribunal.org.uk/constitution-and-procedures/appeals]

Solicitors Disciplinary Tribunal (Appeals and Amendment) Rules 2011

SI 2011/2346

Made 22nd September 2011

Coming into force 1st October 2011

The Solicitors Disciplinary Tribunal in exercise of the powers conferred upon it by section 46 of the Solicitors Act 1974 as applied by paragraph 14C(2) of Schedule 2 to the Administration of Justice Act 1985 and section 44E(2) of the Solicitors Act 1974 and following the approval of the Legal Services Board makes the following Rules:

PART 1
INTRODUCTORY

1 Citation, commencement and application

(1) These Rules may be cited as the Solicitors Disciplinary Tribunal (Appeals and Amendment) Rules 2011 and shall come into force on 1st October 2011.

(2) These Rules (except rule 30) apply in relation to—

(a) appeals to the Tribunal under paragraph 14C of Schedule 2 to the Administration of Justice Act 1985;

(b) appeals to the Tribunal under section 44E of the 1974 Act (appeals against disciplinary action under section 44D); and

(c) appeals to the Tribunal in respect of decisions made by the Society which are appealable under Part 5 of the 2007 Act or the Society's licensing rules and which, by virtue of article 4(1) of the Legal Services Act 2007 (Appeals from Licensing Authority Decisions) (No.2) Order 2011 are appeals which may be heard and determined by the Tribunal.

2 Interpretation

In these Rules—

"the 1974 Act" means the Solicitors Act 1974;

"the 2007 Act" means the Legal Services Act 2007;

"the 2019 rules" means the Solicitors (Disciplinary Proceedings) Rules 2019;

"appeal" means a Schedule 2 appeal, a section 44E appeal or a licensing appeal;

"appellant" means—

    (a)   a person who makes an appeal to the Tribunal; or

    (b)   a person added or substituted as an appellant under rule 13(1);

"the Board" means the Legal Services Board;

"clerk" has the same meaning as in the 2019 rules;

a "licensing appeal" means an appeal of the type mentioned in rule 1(2)(c);

"Panel" means a panel appointed under rule 3 for the hearing of an appeal or any matter connected with an appeal;

"party" means the appellant or the respondent;

"practice direction" means a practice direction made under rule 10;

"the President" means the President of the Tribunal, appointed under rule 3 of the 2007 rules;

"respondent" means—

    (a)   the person who made the decision in respect of which an appeal is made; or

    (b)   a person added or substituted as a respondent under rule 13(1);

a "Schedule 2 appeal" means an appeal of the type mentioned in rule 1(2)(a);

a "section 44E appeal" means an appeal of the type mentioned in rule 1(2)(b);

"the Society" means the Law Society and includes any duly constituted committee of the Law Society or any body or person exercising delegated powers of the Law Society;

"the Society's licensing rules" means licensing rules made by the Society under section 83 of the 2007 Act (licensing rules);

"solicitor members" and "lay members" have the same meanings as in section 46 of the 1974 Act;

a "Stay" means a prohibition on the respondent implementing the decision in respect of which an appeal is made;

"the Tribunal" means the Solicitors Disciplinary Tribunal and where a Panel has been appointed for the hearing of an appeal or any matter connected with it, includes a Panel.

PART 2
CONSTITUTION OF APPEAL PANELS

3 Composition of panel

(1)   A Panel of at least three members of the Tribunal shall be appointed by the Tribunal for the hearing of any appeal.

(2)   Unless the President otherwise directs, the majority of the Panel members shall be solicitor members.

4 Appointment of chairman

The chairman of each Panel shall be appointed by the Tribunal and (unless the President determines otherwise) shall be a solicitor member.

5 Delegation

(1)   The duties to be performed by the clerks shall, in addition to the duties listed in rule 8(6) of the Solicitors (Disciplinary Proceedings) Rules 2019, include—

(a)   appointing panels under rule 3(1);

(b)   appointing a chairman of a Panel under rule 4; and

(c)   giving directions under rules 9, 13 and 19(1).

(2) Paragraph (1) is without prejudice to rule 8(6) of the Solicitors (Disciplinary Proceedings) Rules 2019.

(3)   No later than the date on which expires the period of 14 days beginning with the date on which the Tribunal sends notice to a party of a decision made by a clerk in exercise of functions of a judicial nature under paragraph (1), that party may send an application in writing to the Tribunal for that decision to be considered afresh by a Panel or a single solicitor member.

(4)   The following powers of the Tribunal may be exercised by a single solicitor member—

(a)   giving directions under rules 9, 13,14(2), (4) and (5), 15 and 19(1);

(b)   taking action under rule 11(2)(a) and (b);

(c)   making a decision under rule 14(1);

(d)   giving consent under rule 16(2).

PART 3
APPEAL PROCEDURE

6 Notice of appeal

(1)   An appellant must start proceedings for an appeal by sending or delivering a notice of appeal to the Tribunal.

(2)   In the case of a Schedule 2 appeal, the notice of appeal must be sent or delivered so that it is received by the Tribunal no later than the date on which expires the period of 28 days beginning with the date on which the appellant was notified in writing of the decision in question under paragraph 14B(4) of Schedule 2 to the Administration of Justice Act 1985.

(3)   In the case of a section 44E appeal, the notice of appeal must be sent or delivered so that it is received by the Tribunal no later than the date on which expires the period of 28 days beginning with the date on which the appellant was notified in writing of the decision in question under section 44D(4) of the 1974 Act.

(4)   The notice of appeal must set out—

(a)   the name and address of the appellant;

(b)   the name and address of the appellant's representative (if any);

(c)   an address where documents for the appellant may be sent or delivered;

(d)   the basis on which the appellant has standing to start proceedings before the Tribunal;

(e)   the name and address of the respondent;

(f)   details of the decision or act to which the proceedings relate;

(g)   the result the appellant is seeking;

(h)   the grounds on which the appellant relies;

(ha)   any application for an order for a Stay, if the appellant is allowed to make such an application under the Society's licensing rules;

(i)   whether the appellant would be content for the case to be dealt with without a hearing if the Tribunal considers it appropriate; and

(j)   any further information or documents required by a practice direction.

(4A) In the case of a licensing appeal made under the Society's licensing rules, if no time limit for the making of an appeal is prescribed under those rules, the notice of appeal must be sent or delivered so that it is received by the Tribunal no later than the date on which expires the period of 28 days beginning with the date on which the appellant was notified in writing of the decision which is the subject of the appeal.

(5) The appellant must send or deliver with the notice of appeal a copy of any written record of the decision in respect of which the appeal is made, and any statement of reasons for that decision that the appellant has or can reasonably obtain.

(6) The appellant must send or deliver three additional copies of the notice of appeal and any accompanying documents to the Tribunal at the same time as the appellant sends or delivers the notice of appeal to the Tribunal.

(7) The appellant must send or deliver a copy of the notice of appeal and any accompanying documents to the respondent at the same time as the appellant sends or delivers the notice of appeal to the Tribunal.

7 Response to notice of appeal

(1) The respondent must send or deliver to the Tribunal a response to the notice of appeal so that it is received no later than the date on which expires the period of 28 days beginning with the date on which the respondent received the notice of appeal.

(2) The response must set out at least—

(a) the name and address of the respondent;

(b) the name and address of the respondent's representative (if any);

(c) an address where documents for the respondent may be sent or delivered;

(d) any further information or documents required by a practice direction or a direction given under these Rules; and

(e) whether the respondent would be content for the case to be dealt with without a hearing if the Tribunal considers it appropriate.

(3) The response must include a statement as to whether the respondent opposes the appellant's case and, if so, any grounds for such opposition which are not contained in another document sent or delivered with the response.

(4) The respondent must send or deliver with the response—

(a) a copy of any written record of the decision, in respect of which the appeal is made, and any statement of reasons for that decision, that the appellant did not send or deliver with the notice of appeal and the respondent has or can reasonably obtain; and

(b) any documents relied upon by the respondent in making the decision in respect of which the appeal is made and which the respondent considers are relevant to the appeal.

(5) If the respondent sends or delivers the response to the Tribunal later than the time required by paragraph (1) or by any extension of time under rule 9(2)(a), the response must include a request for an extension of time and the reason why the response was not sent or delivered in time.

(6) The respondent must send or deliver three additional copies of the response and any accompanying documents to the Tribunal at the same time as the respondent sends or delivers the response to the Tribunal.

(7) The respondent must send or deliver a copy of the response and any accompanying documents to the appellant at the same time as it sends or delivers the response to the Tribunal.

8 Appellant's reply

(1)   The appellant may send or deliver to the Tribunal—

   (a)   a reply to the respondent's response; and

   (b)   any additional documents relied upon by the appellant in the reply.

(2)   Any reply and additional documents must be sent or delivered to the Tribunal so that they are received no later than the date on which expires the period of 14 days beginning with the date on which the appellant received the notice from the respondent.

(3)   If the appellant sends or delivers a reply to the Tribunal later than the time required by paragraph (2) or by any extension of time under rule 9(2)(a) the reply must include a request for an extension of time and the reason why the reply was not sent or delivered in time.

(4)   The appellant may send or deliver with the reply a list of documents on which the appellant relies in support of the appeal, and which the appellant did not send or deliver with the notice of appeal.

(5)   The appellant must send or deliver three additional copies of the reply and any accompanying documents to the Tribunal at the same time as the appellant sends or delivers the reply to the Tribunal.

(6)   The appellant must send or deliver a copy of any reply and any accompanying documents to the respondent at the same time as the appellant sends or delivers the reply to the Tribunal.

(7)   If the appellant has sent or delivered a list of documents under paragraph (4), the appellant must within 7 days of receiving a request from the respondent or the Tribunal—

   (a)   send or deliver to the respondent or Tribunal a copy of any document specified in the list (and in the case of the Tribunal, any additional copies of the document requested by the Tribunal, up to a maximum of four in number); or

   (b)   make such document available to the respondent or Tribunal to read or copy.

9 Directions and case management

(1)   The Tribunal may give a direction in relation to the conduct or disposal of appeal proceedings at any time, including a direction amending, suspending or setting aside an earlier direction.

(2)   In particular, and without restricting the general powers in paragraph (1) and rule 18, the Tribunal may—

   (a)   extend or shorten the time for complying with any rule, practice direction or direction, unless such extension or shortening would conflict with a provision of another enactment (or of any rule made under another enactment) containing a time limit;

   (b)   consolidate or hear together two or more sets of proceedings or parts of proceedings raising common issues, or treat a case as a lead case (whether under rule 15 or otherwise);

   (ba)   hear any application for an Order for a Stay;

   (c)   permit or require a party to amend a document;

   (d)   permit or require a party or another person to provide documents, information or submissions which are relevant to the proceedings to the Tribunal or a party;

   (e)   deal with an issue in the proceedings as a preliminary issue;

   (f)   hold a hearing to consider any matter, including a case management issue;

   (g)   decide the form of any hearing;

   (h)   adjourn or postpone a hearing;

   (i)   require a party to produce a bundle for a hearing;

APPENDIX 16

(j)   require a party to provide a skeleton argument;

(k)   decide the place and time of any hearing;

(l)   make requirements about documentation and inspection:

(m)   stay proceedings;

(n)   suspend the effect of its own decision pending the determination by the High Court of an application for permission to appeal against, and any appeal of, that decision.

(3) A clerk may appoint a time and place for the review of the progress of the matter and shall notify the parties of the date, time and place of any such review.

(4) A clerk may refer to the Tribunal any matter for a decision or directions and the Tribunal may itself or on the application of any party make a decision on such terms as to the Tribunal shall appear just—

(a)   to adjourn any hearing listed for directions or for a substantive hearing;

(b)   to agree to the amendment of any document or the correction of any matter;

(c)   to make any directions which shall appear necessary or appropriate to secure the timely hearing of the appeal.

(5) Any hearing under this rule shall be held in public unless rules 23(2) or (3) apply.

10 Practice directions

(1) The Tribunal (or a panel of Tribunal members consisting of not less than 5 members of whom no fewer than 2 shall be lay members) may give such notices or make such directions concerning the practices or procedures of the Tribunal as are consistent with these Rules and as shall seem appropriate.

(2) The Tribunal shall promulgate notices or directions given or made under paragraph (1) under the authority of the President.

11 Failure to comply with rules, practice directions or tribunal directions

(1) An irregularity resulting from a failure to comply with any provision of these Rules, a practice direction or a direction given under these Rules does not of itself render void the appeal or any step taken in the appeal.

(2) If a party has failed to comply with a requirement in these Rules, a practice direction or a direction given under these Rules, the Tribunal may take such action as the Tribunal considers just, which may include—

(a)   waiving the requirement;

(b)   requiring the failure to be remedied;

(c)   exercising its power under rule 12;

(d)   otherwise barring or restricting a party's participation in the appeal.

(3) The Tribunal may not bar or restrict a party's participation in the appeal under paragraph (2)(d) without first giving the party an opportunity to make representations in relation to the proposed action.

12 Striking out a party's case

(1) The Tribunal must strike out the whole or a part of an appeal if the Tribunal does not have jurisdiction in relation to the appeal or that part of it.

(2) The Tribunal may strike out the whole or a part of an appeal if—

(a)   the appellant has failed to comply with a direction given under these Rules which stated that failure by the appellant to comply with the direction could lead to the striking out of the appeal or part of it;

(b)   the appellant has failed to co-operate with the Tribunal to such an extent that the Tribunal cannot deal with the appeal fairly and justly; or

(c)   the Tribunal considers there is no reasonable prospect of the appellant's case, or part of it, succeeding.

(3)   The Tribunal may not strike out the whole or a part of the appeal under paragraph (1) or (2)(b) or (c) without first giving the appellant an opportunity to make representations in relation to the proposed striking out.

(4)   If the appeal, or part of it, has been struck out under paragraph (2)(a), the appellant may apply for the appeal, or part of it, to be reinstated.

(5)   An application under paragraph (4) must be made in writing and received by the Tribunal no later than the date on which expires the period of 28 days beginning with the date on which the Tribunal sent notification of the striking out to the appellant.

(6)   This rule applies to a respondent as it applies to an appellant except that—

(a)   a reference to the striking out of the whole or a part of the appeal is to be read as a reference to the striking out of the whole or a part of the response to the appeal; and

(b)   a reference to an application for the reinstatement of an appeal which has been struck out is to be read as a reference to an application for the reinstatement of a response to an appeal which has been struck out.

13 Addition, substitution and removal of parties

(1)   The Tribunal may give a direction adding, substituting or removing a party as an appellant or a respondent.

(2)   If the Tribunal gives a direction under paragraph (1) it may give such consequential directions as it considers appropriate.

(3)   A person who is not a party may apply to the Tribunal to be added or substituted as a party.

(4)   If a person who is entitled to be a party to an appeal by virtue of another enactment applies to be added as a party, and any conditions applicable to that entitlement have been satisfied, the Tribunal must give a direction adding that person as a respondent or, if appropriate, as an appellant.

14 Prevention of disclosure or publication of documents and information

(1)   The Tribunal may make a decision prohibiting the disclosure or publication of—

(a)   specified documents or information relating to any appeal proceedings; or

(b)   any matter likely to lead members of the public to identify any person whom the Tribunal considers should not be identified.

(2)   The Tribunal may give a direction prohibiting the disclosure of a document or information to a person if—

(a)   the Tribunal is satisfied that such disclosure would be likely to cause that person or some other person serious harm; and

(b)   the Tribunal is satisfied, having regard to the interests of justice, that it is proportionate to give such a direction.

(3)   If a party ("the first party") considers that the Tribunal should give a direction under paragraph (2) prohibiting the disclosure of a document or information to another party ("the second party"), the first party must—

(a)   exclude the relevant document or information from any documents that will be sent or delivered to the second party; and

    (b)   send or deliver to the Tribunal the excluded document or information, and the reason for its exclusion, so that the Tribunal may decide whether the document or information should be disclosed to the second party or should be the subject of a direction under paragraph (2).

(4)   If the Tribunal gives a direction under paragraph (2) which prevents disclosure to a party who has appointed a representative, the Tribunal may give a direction that the documents or information be disclosed to that representative if the Tribunal is satisfied that—

    (a)   disclosure to the representative would be in the interests of the party; and

    (b)   the representative will act in accordance with paragraph (5).

(5)   Documents or information disclosed to a representative in accordance with a direction under paragraph (4) must not be disclosed either directly or indirectly to any other person without the Tribunal's consent.

(6)   The Tribunal may, on its own initiative or on the application of a party, give a direction that certain documents or information must or may be disclosed to the Tribunal on the basis that the Tribunal will not disclose such documents or information to other persons, or specified other persons.

(7)   A party making an application for a direction under paragraph (6) may withhold the relevant documents or information from other parties until the Tribunal has granted or refused the application.

(8)   Unless the Tribunal considers that there is good reason not to do so, the Tribunal must send notice that a party has made an application for a direction under paragraph (6) to each other party.

(9)   The Tribunal must conduct proceedings and record its decision and reasons appropriately so as not to undermine the effect of a decision made under paragraph (1) or a direction given under paragraph (2) or (6).

15 Lead cases

(1)   This rule applies if—

    (a)   two or more appeals have been started before the Tribunal;

    (b)   in each such appeal the Tribunal has not made a decision finally disposing of all issues in the proceedings; and

    (c)   the appeals give rise to common or related issues of fact or law.

(2)   The Tribunal may give a direction—

    (a)   specifying one or more appeals falling under paragraph (1) as a lead case or lead cases; and

    (b)   staying the other appeals falling under paragraph (1) ("the related cases").

(3)   When the Tribunal makes a decision in respect of the common or related issues—

    (a)   the Tribunal must send or deliver a copy of that decision to each party in each of the related appeals; and

    (b)   subject to paragraph (4), that decision shall be binding on each of those parties.

(4)   No later than the date on which expires the period of 28 days beginning with the date on which the Tribunal sent or delivered a copy of the decision to a party under paragraph (3)(a), that party may apply in writing for a direction that the decision does not apply to, and is not binding on the parties to, a particular related appeal.

(5)   The Tribunal must give directions in respect of appeals which are stayed under paragraph (2)(b), providing for the disposal of or further directions in those appeals.

(6)   If the lead case or cases lapse or are withdrawn before the Tribunal makes a decision in respect of the common or related issues, the Tribunal must give directions as to—

(a)   whether another appeal or other appeals are to be specified as a lead case or lead cases; and

(b)   whether any direction affecting the related appeals should be set aside or amended.

16 Withdrawal

(1)   Subject to paragraph (2), an appellant may give notice of the withdrawal of its appeal, or any part of it, and the respondent may do likewise in respect of its case against the appeal—

(a)   at any time before a hearing to consider the disposal of the appeal (or, if the Tribunal disposes of the appeal without a hearing, before that disposal), by sending or delivering to the Tribunal a written notice of withdrawal; or

(b)   orally at a hearing.

(2)   Notice of withdrawal will not take effect unless the Tribunal consents to the withdrawal, which may be given subject to such order relating to costs as the Tribunal shall think fit.

(3)   A party which has withdrawn its appeal or case against the appeal may apply to the Tribunal for the appeal or case to be reinstated.

(4)   An application under paragraph (3) must be made in writing and be received by the Tribunal no later than the date on which expires the period of 28 days beginning with—

(a)   the date on which the Tribunal received the notice under paragraph (1)(a); or

(b)   the date of the hearing at which the appeal or case was withdrawn orally under paragraph (1)(b).

(5)   The Tribunal must notify each party in writing of a withdrawal under this rule.

17 Consent orders

(1)   The Tribunal may, at the request of the parties and only if it considers it appropriate, make a consent order disposing of the appeal proceedings and making such other appropriate provision as the parties have agreed.

(2)   Despite any other provision of these Rules, the Tribunal need not hold a hearing before making an order under paragraph (1), or provide reasons for the order.

18 General powers of Tribunal

(1)   Subject to the provisions of these Rules, the Tribunal may regulate its own procedure.

(2)   The Tribunal may dispense with any requirements of these Rules in respect of notices, statements or other documents, witnesses, service or time in any case where it appears to the Tribunal to be just so to do.

19 Disclosure, evidence and submissions

(1)   Without restriction on the general powers in rule 9 and 18, the Tribunal may give directions in relation to an appeal as to—

(a)   the exchange between parties of lists of documents which are relevant to the appeal, or relevant to particular issues, and the inspection of such documents;

(b)   the provision by parties of statements of agreed matters;

(c)   issues on which it requires evidence or submissions;

(d)   the nature of the evidence or submissions it requires;

(e)   whether the parties are permitted or required to provide expert evidence, and if so whether the parties must jointly appoint a single expert to provide such evidence;

(f)   any limit on the number of witnesses whose evidence a party may put forward, whether in relation to a particular issue or generally;

    (g)   the manner in which any evidence or submissions are to be provided, which may include a direction for them to be given—

        (i)   orally at a hearing; or

        (ii)   by written submissions or witness statement; and

    (h)   the time at which any evidence or submissions are to be sent or delivered.

(2)   The Tribunal may—

    (a)   admit evidence whether or not—

        (i)   the evidence would be admissible in a civil trial in the United Kingdom; or

        (ii)   the evidence was available to a previous decision maker; or

    (b)   exclude evidence that would otherwise be admissible where—

        (i)   the evidence was not provided within the time allowed by a direction given under these Rules or a practice direction;

        (ii)   the evidence was otherwise provided in a manner that did not comply with a direction given under these Rules or a practice direction; or

        (iii)   it would otherwise be unfair, disproportionate or unnecessary in the interests of justice to admit the evidence.

(3)   The Tribunal may consent to a witness giving, or require any witness to give, evidence on oath, and may administer an oath for that purpose.

20 Written evidence

(1)   The Tribunal may in its discretion, in respect of a whole case or of any particular fact or facts, proceed and act upon evidence given by Statement.

(2)   Every Statement upon which any party proposes to rely shall be sent or delivered to the clerk and to all other parties no later than 21 days before the date fixed for the hearing of the appeal together with a notice in the form of Form 1 in the Schedule.

(3)   Any party on whom a notice has been served under paragraph (2) and who requires the attendance, at the hearing, of the witness in question shall, no later than 9 days before the date of the hearing require, in writing, the other party to produce the witness at the hearing.

(4)   If no party requires the attendance of a witness in accordance with the provisions of this rule, the Tribunal may accept the Statement in question in evidence.

(5)   If any party intends to call as a witness any person who has not produced a Statement, he must, no later than 10 days before the date fixed for the hearing, notify the clerk and any other party to the proceedings of his intention and forthwith send or deliver a copy of a written proof of evidence to the other party and lodge five copies of the proof with the clerk.

(6)   In this rule, "Statement" means a written statement (including a witness statement) containing a statement that the party putting forward or making the Statement believes the facts stated in the Statement are true.

21 Decision with or without a hearing

(1)   The Tribunal must hold a hearing before making a decision which disposes of proceedings unless—

    (a)   each party has consented to the matter being determined without a hearing; and

    (b)   the Tribunal is satisfied that it can properly determine the issues without a hearing.

(2)   Despite anything to the contrary in these Rules, if the Tribunal holds a hearing to consider a preliminary issue, and following the disposal of that preliminary issue no further issue remains to be determined, the Tribunal may dispose of the proceedings without holding any further hearing.

22 Listing of appeal hearing

(1)   Unless the Tribunal has made directions in respect of the hearing of an appeal, a clerk shall appoint a date for the hearing by the Tribunal and shall give notice of the date to the parties.

(2)   The hearing shall not, unless all the parties have agreed or the Tribunal has so ordered, take place sooner than the date on which expires the period of 28 days beginning with the date of service of the notice appointing the date of the hearing.

23 Public or private hearings

(1)   Subject to paragraphs (2) and (3) every appeal hearing shall take place in public.

(2)   Any party and any person who claims to be affected by an appeal may seek a decision from the Tribunal that the hearing or part of it be conducted in private on the grounds of—

(a)   exceptional hardship; or

(b)   exceptional prejudice,

to a party, a witness or any person affected by the appeal.

(3)   If it is satisfied that those grounds are met, the Tribunal shall conduct the hearing or part of it in private and make such decision as shall appear to it to be just and proper.

(4)   The Tribunal may, before or during a hearing, direct that the hearing or part of it be held in private if—

(a)   the Tribunal is satisfied that it would have granted an application under paragraph (2) had one been made; or

(b)   in the Tribunal's view a hearing in public would prejudice the interests of justice.

(5)   The Tribunal may give a direction excluding from any hearing, or part of it—

(a)   any person whose conduct the Tribunal considers is disrupting or is likely to disrupt the hearing;

(b)   any person whose presence the Tribunal considers is likely to prevent another person from giving evidence or making submissions freely;

(c)   any person who the Tribunal considers should be excluded in order to give effect to the requirement at rule 14(9); or

(d)   any person where the purpose of the hearing would be defeated by the attendance of that person.

(6)   The Tribunal may give a direction excluding a witness from a hearing until that witness gives evidence.

24 Decisions

(1)   The Tribunal may announce a decision orally at a hearing of or relating to an appeal or may reserve its decision for announcement at a later date. In either case the announcement shall be made in public.

(2)   Subject to rule 14(9), the Tribunal must provide to each party as soon as reasonably practicable after making a decision which finally disposes of all issues in the proceedings—

(a)   an order stating the Tribunal's decision;

(b)   written reasons for the decision; and

(c)   notification of any right of appeal against the decision and the time within which, and manner in which, such right of appeal may be exercised.

(3)   The Tribunal may provide written reasons for any decision to which paragraph (2) does not apply.

(4)   An order under paragraph (2)(a) shall be signed by a member of the Tribunal upon the announcement of the decision and shall, subject to paragraph (5), be filed forthwith with the Society.

(5)   The Tribunal may suspend the filing of an order under paragraph (2)(a) if it appears to the Tribunal that there is good reason to do so, in which event the decision shall not take effect until the order is filed with the Society.

(6)   Subject to rule 14(9), the Tribunal may publicise a decision in such manner as it thinks fit.

25 Re-hearing where a party neither appears nor is represented

(1)   At any time before the date on which expires the period of 14 days beginning with the date on which an order was provided to the party under rule 24(2), a party may apply to the Tribunal for a re-hearing of an appeal if—

(a)   he neither attended in person nor was represented at the hearing of the appeal in question; and

(b)   the Tribunal determined the appeal in his absence.

(2)   An application for a re-hearing under this rule shall be made in the form of Form 2 in the Schedule and shall be supported by a statement setting out the facts upon which the applicant wishes to rely.

(3)   If satisfied that it is just so to do, the Tribunal may grant the application upon such terms, including as to costs, as it thinks fit. The re-hearing shall be held before a Panel comprised of different members from those who heard the original appeal.

PART 4
MISCELLANEOUS

26 Sending and delivery of documents

(1)   Any document to be sent or delivered to the Tribunal or to a party under these Rules, a practice direction or a direction given under these Rules must be—

(a)   sent by pre-paid first class post or by document exchange, or delivered by hand, to the address specified for the proceedings;

(b)   sent by fax (in the case of documents to be sent or delivered to the Tribunal, to the number specified for the proceedings); or

(c)   sent or delivered by such other method as the Tribunal may permit or direct.

(2)   Subject to paragraph (3), if a party provides a fax number, email address or other details for the electronic transmission of documents to them, that party must accept delivery of documents by that method.

(3)   If a party informs the Tribunal and all other parties that a particular form of communication, other than pre-paid post or delivery by hand, should not be used to send or deliver documents to that party, that form of communication must not be so used.

(4)   If the Tribunal or a party sends a document to a party or the Tribunal by email or any other electronic means of communication, the recipient may request that the sender send or deliver a hard copy of the document to the recipient. The recipient must make such a request as soon as reasonably practicable after receiving the document electronically.

(5)   The Tribunal and each party may assume that the address provided by a party or its representative is and remains the address to which documents should be sent or delivered until receiving written notification to the contrary.

(6)   If a document submitted to the Tribunal is not written in English, it must be accompanied by an English translation.

27 Calculating time

(1)   An act required by these Rules, a practice direction or a direction given under these Rules to be done on or by a particular day must be done by 4.30pm on that day.

(2)   If the time specified by these Rules, a practice direction or a direction given under these Rules for doing any act ends on a day other than a working day, the act is done in time if it is done on the next working day.

(3)   In this rule "working day" means any day except a Saturday or Sunday, Christmas Day, Good Friday or a bank holiday under section 1 of the Banking and Financial Dealings Act 1971.

28 Representatives

(1)   A party may appoint a representative (whether a legal representative or not) to represent that party in the proceedings.

(2)   If a party appoints a representative, that party (or the representative if the representative is a legal representative) must send or deliver to the Tribunal written notice of the representative's name and address, together with a copy of the notice.

(3)   A party who sends or delivers a notice under paragraph (2) must, at the same time, send or deliver a copy of the notice to the other party.

(4)   Anything permitted or required to be done by a party under these Rules, a practice direction or a direction given under these Rules may be done by the representative of that party, except signing a witness statement.

(5)   A person who receives due notice of the appointment of a representative—

(a)   must send or deliver to the representative any document which, at any time after the appointment, is required to be sent or delivered to the represented party, and need not send or deliver that document to the represented party; and

(b)   may assume that the representative is and remains authorised as such until they receive written notification that this is not so from the representative or the represented party.

(6)   At a hearing a party may be accompanied by another person whose name and address has not been notified under paragraph (2) but who, with the permission of the Tribunal, may act as a representative or otherwise assist in presenting the party's case at the hearing.

(7)   Paragraphs (2) to (5) do not apply to a person who accompanies a party under paragraph (6).

(8)   In this rule "legal representative" means a person who, for the purposes of the 2007 Act, is an authorised person in relation to an activity which constitutes the exercise of a right of audience or the conduct of litigation within the meaning of that Act, an advocate or solicitor in Scotland or a barrister or solicitor in Northern Ireland.

29 Costs

(1)   The Tribunal may, at any stage of an appeal, make such order as to costs as the Tribunal shall think fit, including an order—

(a)   disallowing costs incurred unnecessarily; or

(b)   that costs be paid by any party judged to be responsible for wasted or unnecessary costs, whether arising through failure to comply with time limits or otherwise.

(2)   The Tribunal may order that any party bear the whole or a part or a proportion of the costs.

(3)   The amount of costs to be paid may either be fixed by the Tribunal or be subject to detailed assessment by a Costs Judge.

(4)   The Tribunal may also make an order as to costs under this rule where any appeal is withdrawn or amended.

30 Amendment of 2007 rules

(1) The 2007 rules are amended as follows.

(2) In Form 6 in the Schedule, for "21 days" substitute "9 days".

Signed by authority of the Solicitors Disciplinary Tribunal

Jeremy Barnecutt

President

Solicitors Disciplinary Tribunal

22nd September 2011

SCHEDULE
FORMS

Rules 20(2) and 25(2)

FORM 1

FORM of NOTICE to accompany Statement of Evidence

Number . . . .

IN THE MATTER OF the Solicitors Disciplinary Tribunal (Appeals and Amendment) Rules 2011

AND IN THE MATTER OF

. . . .

TAKE NOTICE that the [appellant][respondent] proposes to rely upon the statement(s) listed below, copies of which are served herewith.

If you wish any person who has made one of these statements to be required to attend the hearing as a witness you must, not less than 9 days before the date set down for the hearing of the appeal, notify me and the Clerk to the Tribunal to that effect. In the event of your failure to do so the Tribunal may accept the statement in question in evidence.

LIST

Date of Statement   Name of Person who made the Statement

1.

2.

3.

Date: . . . .

Signed: . . . .

Address: . . . .

FORM 2

FORM of APPLICATION for a Rehearing

Number . . . .

IN THE MATTER OF the Solicitors Disciplinary Tribunal (Appeals and Amendment) Rules 2011

AND IN THE MATTER OF

. . . .

Number of Tribunal case in respect of which a rehearing is requested
. . . .

I APPLY under Rule 25(1) of the Solicitors Disciplinary Tribunal (Appeals and Amendment) Rules 2011 that the above-mentioned case be reheard by the Tribunal. The facts upon which I rely in support of this application are set out below:

(set out here full details of the facts on which the applicant for a rehearing relies and include the reasons why the person applying for the rehearing did not appear or was not represented before the Tribunal at the earlier hearing and set out all matters which he wishes to place before the Tribunal in mitigation or otherwise).

Dated: . . . .

Signature: . . . .

Address: . . . .

Solicitors Disciplinary Tribunal Guidance note on sanctions

[Reproduced with the kind permission of the Solicitors Disciplinary Tribunal. Issued by the SDT December 2020]

Guidance note on sanctions

[Eighth edition, December 2020]

Introduction

This Guidance Note consists of a distillation of current Solicitors Disciplinary Tribunal ("the Tribunal") sanctioning principles brought together in one document. Every case is fact-specific, and this Guidance Note consists of guidelines only; it is not intended in any way to fetter the discretion of the Tribunal when deciding sanction. The exercise of its powers and the imposition of sanctions are matters solely for determination by the Tribunal. The purpose of this Guidance Note is to assist the parties, the public and the legal profession in understanding the Tribunal's decision-making process.

The Tribunal is the statutory tribunal responsible for adjudicating upon applications and complaints made under the provisions of the Solicitors Act 1974 (as amended) ("the Act").

It is the function of the Tribunal to protect the public from harm, and to maintain public confidence in the reputation of the legal profession (and those that provide legal services) for honesty, probity, trustworthiness, independence and integrity. The public must be able to expect to receive a high standard of service from a competent and capable solicitor.

The Tribunal deals with an infinite variety of cases. Prescriptive, detailed guidelines for sanctions in individual cases are neither practicable nor appropriate. The Tribunal adopts broad guidance. Its focus is to establish the seriousness of the misconduct and, from that, to determine a fair and proportionate sanction.

The contents of the Guidance Note are reviewed at least annually.

Section A: Principles and procedure

Sanctions and orders available to the Tribunal

Solicitors

1. The Tribunal's jurisdiction and powers on an application are set out in Section 47 of the Act and include:

   - the imposition of a reprimand.

   - the imposition of an unlimited financial penalty payable to HM Treasury.

- the imposition of restrictions upon the way in which a solicitor can practise (not explicitly listed in Section 47, but implied by the words "the Tribunal shall have power to make such order as it may think fit" in the preamble to that Section, and see *Camacho v The Law Society* [2004] EWHC 1675 (Admin)).

- suspension from practice indefinitely or for a specified period or a suspended suspension.

- striking off the Roll.

2. The Tribunal is not restricted as to the number or combination of sanctions which it may impose.

3. Other orders which the Tribunal can make in respect of solicitors or former solicitors include:

- no order.

- termination of a period of suspension (see separate "Guidance Note On Other Powers of the Tribunal").

- restoration to the Roll following strike off (see separate "Guidance Note On Other Powers of the Tribunal").

- costs.

Solicitors' non-lawyer employees and managers

4. By Section 43(1) and (1A) of the Act the Tribunal has jurisdiction to deal with misconduct by those who are not admitted but are employed or remunerated by solicitors and others. The powers which the Tribunal may exercise in respect of such individuals are:

- no order.

- to make an order prohibiting, save with the prior consent of the regulator, any solicitor and others from employing or remunerating the person to whom the order relates, or from being a manager or having an interest in a recognised body.

- to review or revoke a Section 43 Order (see separate Guidance Note on Other Powers of the Tribunal).

5. Under Section 34A (2) and (3) of the Act there is provision for complaint to be made to the Tribunal in respect of an employee of a solicitor. The Tribunal's powers have been extended by Section 47(2E) of the Act. The Tribunal's powers in respect of complaints by the Solicitors Regulation Authority (SRA) concerning managers and employees of recognised bodies have been extended by an amendment by the Legal Services Act 2007 to Schedule 2 to the Administration of Justice Act 1985. When considering these matters the Tribunal has the power to make one or more of the following:

- an order directing payment of an unlimited financial penalty payable to HM Treasury.

- an order requiring the SRA to consider taking such steps as the Tribunal may specify in relation to the individual.

- if the individual is not a solicitor, a Section 43(2) Order.

- an order requiring the SRA to refer to an appropriate regulator any matter relating to the conduct of that employee.

6. The Tribunal has the power to make one or more of the following in respect of complaints made to the Tribunal concerning a recognised body:

- an order revoking the recognition of the recognised body.

- an order requiring the payment of a penalty by the recognised body.

Purpose of sanctions

7. The case of *Bolton v The Law Society* [1994] 1 WLR 512 sets out the fundamental principle and purposes of the imposition of sanctions by the Tribunal:

    "Any solicitor who is shown to have discharged his professional duties with anything less than complete integrity, probity and trustworthiness must expect severe sanctions to be imposed upon him by the Solicitors Disciplinary Tribunal."

    "... a penalty may be visited on a solicitor ... in order to punish him for what he has done and to deter any other solicitor tempted to behave in the same way ..."

    "... to be sure that the offender does not have the opportunity to repeat the offence; and"

    "... the most fundamental of all: to maintain the reputation of the solicitors' profession as one in which every member, of whatever standing, may be trusted to the ends of the earth ... a member of the public ... is ordinarily entitled to expect that the solicitor will be a person whose trustworthiness is not, and never has been, seriously in question. Otherwise, the whole profession, and the public as a whole, is injured. A profession's most valuable asset is its collective reputation and the confidence which that inspires." (per Bingham, then Master of the Rolls)

Tribunal's approach to sanction

8. Guidance on the Tribunal's approach to sanction is set out in *Fuglers and Others v Solicitors Regulation Authority* [2014] EWHC 179 (per Popplewell J) as follows:

    "28. There are three stages to the approach... The first stage is to assess the seriousness of the misconduct. The second stage is to keep in mind the purpose for which sanctions are imposed by such a tribunal. The third stage is to choose the sanction which most appropriately fulfils that purpose for the seriousness of the conduct in question."

Human rights, equality and diversity

9. The Tribunal is a "public authority" for the purposes of the Human Rights Act 1998, and it seeks to uphold and promote the principles of the European Convention on Human Rights in accordance with the Act. In deciding what sanction, if any, to impose the Tribunal should have regard to the principle of proportionality, weighing the interests of the public with those of the practitioner. The interference with the solicitor's right to practise must be no more than necessary to achieve the Tribunal's purpose in imposing sanctions. Reasons should be given for the sanction imposed, and the decision should usually be pronounced publicly.

10. The Tribunal is committed to equality of opportunity and aims to treat everyone who appears before it fairly and with respect, regardless of their background. Its processes and procedures are designed to be fair, objective, inclusive, transparent and free from unlawful discrimination. Tribunal Members and everyone acting for the Tribunal are expected to adhere to the spirit and letter of the Equality Act 2010 and other equality legislation.

Common procedural issues affecting sanction

Admission, but dispute as to facts

11. A respondent may admit the alleged misconduct, but dispute particular details. The Tribunal will hear from the parties to determine whether in its view the disputed

evidence would materially affect its sanction. If not, the Tribunal will proceed to determine sanction on the respondent's version of events. Where the dispute is such that it would materially affect sanction the Tribunal shall decide, having heard all the evidence, the factual basis upon which sanction will be based.

12. The Tribunal adopts the principle established in *R v Newton* [1983] Crim LR 198, and will only impose sanction upon a respondent where the particular misconduct is either admitted by, or proved against the respondent.

13. If at a hearing to establish the facts on which sanction is to be based (a "Newton hearing"), the respondent fails to adduce evidence in support of facts exclusively within his knowledge, this will entitle the Tribunal to draw such inference from that failure as it might see fit – *R v Underwood* [2005] 1 Cr.App.R. 13.

14. Once the factual basis has been established, the respondent will have the opportunity to make representations as to the level of sanction to be imposed before the Tribunal makes its final decision.

Multiple/Alternative allegations

15. Multiple allegations involving essentially the same wrongdoing committed concurrently and drafted in the alternative, or numerous similar examples of wrongdoing committed over a period of time, sometimes come before the Tribunal. When some or all of such allegations are found proved, it may be disproportionate and unjust to impose a sanction for each matter. In such a situation the Tribunal may in respect of matters found proved:

- impose a sanction, determined by the totality of the misconduct, which is specified as being in respect of all those matters; or

- impose a sanction on the more serious allegation/s, and make no separate order (or sanction) in respect of other more minor matters.

Sanction for each separate and distinct allegation

16. Where distinct and separate allegations are either admitted or proved, the Tribunal may:

- impose a particular sanction (determined by the totality of the misconduct) specified as being in respect of all matters; or

- determine the individual seriousness of each separate and distinct proven allegation, and the appropriate sanction in respect of each. Sanctions imposed will be proportionate to the totality of the misconduct.

Section B: Determining sanction

The starting point in determining sanction is to establish the seriousness of the allegation proved. The Tribunal will determine which of the sanction thresholds have been crossed, working from the lowest sanction upwards.

In determining seriousness the Tribunal must consider the respondent's culpability for their conduct and the harm caused or the harm that was intended or might reasonably be foreseen to have been caused by their actions.

When the Tribunal has identified the starting point it can add to or reduce this to reflect any aggravating or mitigating features which impact on the culpability of the respondent and harm caused to reach a provisional sanction.

On reaching a provisional sanction the Tribunal should take appropriate account of personal mitigation of the respondent before coming to a final decision.

The following list of factors is not exhaustive. Each case must be determined on its own facts and merits. Where a factor is considered to reach a decision on seriousness, it should not be considered again in deciding aggravating factors.

Assessing seriousness

17.   The Tribunal will assess the seriousness of the misconduct in order to determine which sanction to impose. Seriousness is determined by a combination of factors, including:

- the respondent's level of culpability for their misconduct.

- the harm caused by the respondent's misconduct.

- the existence of any aggravating factors.

- the existence of any mitigating factors.

Culpability

18.   The level of culpability ("responsibility for fault or wrong") will be influenced by such factors as (but not limited to):

- the respondent's motivation for the misconduct.

- whether the misconduct arose from actions which were planned or spontaneous.

- the extent to which the respondent acted in breach of a position of trust.

- the extent to which the respondent had direct control of or responsibility for the circumstances giving rise to the misconduct.

- the respondent's level of experience.

- whether the respondent deliberately misled the regulator (*Solicitors Regulation Authority v Spence* [2012] EWHC 2977 (Admin)).

Harm

19.   The Tribunal will determine the harm caused by the misconduct and in doing will assess:

- the impact of the respondent's misconduct upon those directly or indirectly affected by the misconduct, the public, and the reputation of the legal profession. The greater the extent of the respondent's departure from the "complete integrity, probity and trustworthiness" expected of a solicitor, the greater the harm to the legal profession's reputation.

- the extent of the harm that was intended or might reasonably have been foreseen to be caused by the respondent's misconduct.

Aggravating Factors

20.   Factors that aggravate the seriousness of the misconduct include (but are not limited to):

- dishonesty, where alleged and proved.

- misconduct involving the commission of a criminal offence, not limited to dishonesty.

- misconduct which was deliberate and calculated or repeated.

- misconduct continuing over a period of time.

- taking advantage of a vulnerable person.

APPENDIX 17

- misconduct motivated by, or demonstrating hostility, based on any protected or personal characteristics of a person.

- concealment of wrongdoing.

- placing the blame for the misconduct on others when the Tribunal has found that the respondent was responsible for that misconduct

- misconduct where the respondent knew or ought reasonably to have known that the conduct complained of was in material breach of obligations to protect the public and the reputation of the legal profession.

- previous disciplinary matter(s) before the Tribunal where allegations were found proved.

Mitigating Factors

21. Factors that mitigate the seriousness of the misconduct itself include (but are not limited to):

- misconduct resulting from deception or otherwise by a third party (including the client).

- the timing of and extent to which any loss arising from the misconduct is made good by the respondent.

- whether the respondent voluntarily notified the regulator of the facts and circumstances giving rise to misconduct.

- whether the misconduct was either a single episode, or one of very brief duration in a previously unblemished career.

- genuine insight, assessed by the Tribunal on the basis of facts found proved and the respondent's evidence.

- open and frank admissions at an early stage and/or degree of cooperation with the investigating body.

NOTE: Matters of purely personal mitigation are of no relevance in determining the seriousness of the misconduct. However, they will be considered by the Tribunal when determining the fair and proportionate sanction (see Section D, paragraphs 53 and 54).

Particular sanctions

22. Having determined the seriousness of the misconduct, the Tribunal will assess whether to make an order, and if so, which sanction to impose. The Tribunal, in making this assessment, will start from the least serious option.

No Order

23. The Tribunal may conclude that, having regard to all the circumstances, and where the Tribunal has concluded that the level of seriousness of the misconduct or culpability of the respondent is low, that it would be unfair or disproportionate to impose a sanction. In such circumstances, the Tribunal may decide not to impose a sanction, save for an order for costs.

Reprimand

24. A Reprimand will be imposed where the Tribunal has determined that the seriousness of the respondent's misconduct justifies a sanction at the lowest level and that the

protection of the public and the reputation of the legal profession does not require a greater sanction.

25. Relevant factors may include:

- the respondent's culpability is low.

- there is no identifiable harm caused to any individual.

- the risk of any such harm is negligible.

- the likelihood of future misconduct of a similar nature or any misconduct is very low.

- evidence of genuine insight, assessed by the Tribunal on the basis of facts found proved and the respondent's evidence.

- minor breaches of regulation not dealt with under the SRA's own disciplinary jurisdiction.

Fine

26. A Fine will be imposed where the Tribunal has determined that the seriousness of the misconduct is such that a Reprimand will not be a sufficient sanction, but neither the protection of the public nor the protection of the reputation of the legal profession justifies Suspension or Strike Off.

Level of Fine

27. The Tribunal will consider the following guidance in determining the appropriate level of Fine or combination of Fines to be imposed upon an individual and/or an entity:

- there is no limit to the level of Fine the Tribunal may impose. In deciding the level of Fine, the Tribunal will consider all the circumstances of the case, including aggravating and mitigating factors. The Tribunal will fix the Fine at a level which reflects the seriousness of and is proportionate to the misconduct.

- the respondent shall be expected to adduce evidence that their ability to pay a Fine is limited by their means (please refer to Practice Direction No. 6, clause 13 for cases issued prior to 24 November 2019 or Rule 43(5) of the Solicitors (Disciplinary Proceedings) Rules 2019 for cases issued on or after 25 November 2019; the terms of Standard Directions and/or specific Directions ordered by the Tribunal in the case).

- the factors to be considered include those outlined by Popplewell J at paragraph 35 of *Fuglers* (above), which may result in movement of the level of fine up or down the Indicative Fine Bands below. The Indicative Fine Bands provide broad starting points only. Factors to be considered include: (1) whether the seriousness of the misconduct, and giving effect to the purpose of the sanction, puts the case at or near the top, middle or bottom of the category (2) the level of fines imposed by other disciplinary tribunals or the High Court in analogous cases (3) the size or standing of the solicitor or firm in question (4) the means available to an individual or a firm. In considering means it is relevant to take into account the total financial detriment which is suffered, including any costs order, and any adverse financial impact of the decision itself.

28. In the absence of **evidence** of limited means, the Tribunal is entitled to assume that the respondent's means are such that they can pay the Fine which the Tribunal decides is appropriate.

29. Fines are payable to HM Treasury, which is responsible for enforcing payment, including the agreement of instalment terms.

Indicative Fine Bands (for individuals)

Fine Band	Overall Assessment of Seriousness of Conduct	Fine Range
Level 1	Lowest level for conduct assessed as sufficiently serious to justify a fine (rather than a reprimand)	£0–£2,000
Level 2	Conduct assessed as moderately serious	£2,001–£7,500
Level 3	Conduct assessed as more serious	£7,501–£15,000
Level 4	Conduct assessed as very serious	£15,001–£50,000
Level 5	Conduct assessed significantly serious but not so serious as to result in an order for suspension or strike off	£50,001 – unlimited

30. In determining the appropriate Fine for a firm the Tribunal will take into account the factors set out at paragraph 28 above. Any Fine imposed must be proportionate to the wrongdoing and be sufficient to meet the primary objectives of sanctions, including being a meaningful deterrent. The Tribunal will also take into consideration:

   - the seriousness of the misconduct

   - the size and financial resources of the firm and the effect of a Fine on its business. This assessment of resources should include considering the amount of revenue generated by the firm; the level of profitability per partner or registered individual and market share.

   - the loss to clients

   - the income generated by the misconduct

Restriction Order

31. A Restriction Order may be combined with any other sanction made by the Tribunal.

32. The Tribunal, in exercising its wide power to "make such order as it may think fit", may if it deems it necessary to protect the public, impose restrictions in the form of conditions upon the way in which a solicitor continues to practise. If the conditions are for an indefinite period it must be part of the order that the solicitor subject to the condition(s) has liberty to apply to the Tribunal to vary or discharge the conditions. Any breach of conditions imposed by the Tribunal would be a disciplinary offence which would generally merit a separate penalty. See in particular *Ebhogiaye v Solicitors Regulation Authority* [2013] EWHC 2445 (Admin).

33. Restricted practice will only be ordered if it is necessary to ensure the protection of the public and the reputation of the legal profession from future harm by the respondent.

34. A Restriction Order may be for either a finite or an indefinite period.

35. If the Tribunal makes an order for an indefinite period, it will specify as part of the order that the respondent may apply to the Tribunal to vary or rescind the restrictions either at any time or after the lapse of a defined period.

36. Examples of restrictions that may be imposed are as follows: The respondent may not:

   - practise as a sole practitioner or sole manager or sole owner of an authorised or recognised body.

   - be a partner or member of a Limited Liability Partnership (LLP), Legal Disciplinary Practice (LDP) or Alternative Business Structure (ABS) or other authorised or recognised body.

- be a Compliance Officer for Legal Practice or a Compliance Officer for Finance and Administration.

- hold client money.

- be a signatory on any client account.

- work as a solicitor other than in employment approved by the SRA.

37. In imposing any restriction the Tribunal must consider that restriction necessary and appropriate. The restrictions imposed should relate to the particular misconduct of the respondent.

Suspension

38. Suspension from the Roll will be the appropriate penalty where the Tribunal has determined that:

- the seriousness of the misconduct is such that neither a Restriction Order, Reprimand nor a Fine is a sufficient sanction or in all the circumstances appropriate.

- there is a need to protect both the public and the reputation of the legal profession from future harm from the respondent by removing their ability to practise, but

- neither the protection of the public nor the protection of the reputation of the legal profession justifies striking off the Roll.

- public confidence in the legal profession demands no lesser sanction.

- professional performance, including a lack of sufficient insight by the respondent (judged by the Tribunal on the basis of facts found proved and the respondent's evidence), is such as to call into question the continued ability to practise appropriately.

39. Suspension from the Roll, and thereby from practice, reflects serious misconduct.

40. Suspension can be for a fixed term or for an indefinite period. A term of suspension can itself be temporarily suspended.

Suspended Term of Suspension

41. Where the Tribunal concludes that the seriousness of the misconduct justifies suspension from the Roll, but it is satisfied that:

- by imposing a Restriction Order, the risk of harm to the public and the public's confidence in the reputation of the legal profession is proportionately constrained; and

- the combination of such an Order with a period of pending Suspension provides adequate protection and addresses the risk of harm to the public and the need to maintain the reputation of the profession

the Tribunal must suspend that period of suspension for so long as the Restriction Order remains in force (*SRA v Dar* [2019] EWHC 2831 (Admin)).

42. If the Restriction Order referred to above is breached, activation by the Tribunal of the term of suspension may follow.

43. In accordance with the guidance set out in *Solicitors Regulation Authority v James et al* [2018] EWHC 3058 (Admin) if the Tribunal imposes a suspended suspension the Tribunal should make clear that the suspension will be activated if further misconduct is committed.

44. If the period under restriction is successfully completed and the Restriction Order lifted, the pending suspension will cease to have effect.

APPENDIX 17

Fixed Term of Suspension

45.   Having concluded that the respondent should be immediately removed from practice, but that the protection of the public and the protection of the reputation of the legal profession do not require that they be struck off the Roll, the Tribunal will fix a term of suspension of such length both to punish and deter whilst being proportionate to the seriousness of the misconduct.

46.   The Tribunal can also impose a staged order with a fixed term of suspension followed by a period of restricted practice under a Restriction Order.

Indefinite Suspension

47.   Indefinite Suspension marks the highest level of misconduct that can appropriately be dealt with short of striking off the Roll. In deciding that an indefinite period of suspension is the fair and proportionate sanction, the Tribunal will have formed the view that:

- the seriousness of the misconduct is so high that striking off is the most appropriate sanction; but

- the presence of truly compelling and exceptional personal mitigation makes that course of action unjust; and/or

- there is a realistic prospect that the respondent will recover from, for example, illness, addiction, relevant medical condition etc. or respond to retraining so that they no longer represent a material risk of harm to the public or to the reputation of the profession.

Striking Off the Roll

48.   Where the Tribunal has determined that:

- the seriousness of the misconduct is at the highest level, such that a lesser sanction is inappropriate; and

- the protection of the public and/or the protection of the reputation of the legal profession requires it

the Tribunal will strike a solicitor's name off the Roll.

Sanction In Respect of a Registered European Lawyer (REL) or Registered Foreign Lawyer (RFL)

49.   RELs and RFLs are individuals registered with the SRA under applicable legislation. They are subject to the same rules of professional conduct and regulatory and disciplinary regime as apply to solicitors. The powers of the Tribunal in relation to sanction apply to RELs and RFLs. It should be noted that the Tribunal's powers to sanction a REL include additionally the withdrawal or suspension of their registration (see Section 26(2), The European Communities (Lawyer's Practice) Regulations 2000 as amended by The Services of Lawyers and Lawyer's Practice (Revocation etc.) (EU Exit) Regulations 2020).

50.   The sanction of withdrawal of registration in respect of a REL "possesses a gravity that lies between the sanctions of suspension and/or strike-off in the case of an English solicitor" (per Laws LJ in *Giambrone v Solicitors Regulation Authority* [2014] EWHC 1421 (Admin) at paragraph 55, and see also paragraph 60 per Foskett J).

Section C: Dishonesty

51.   The most serious misconduct involves dishonesty, whether or not leading to criminal proceedings and criminal penalties. A finding that an allegation of dishonesty has

been proved will almost invariably lead to striking off, save in exceptional circumstances (see *Solicitors Regulation Authority v Sharma* [2010] EWHC 2022 (Admin)).

Exceptional Circumstances

52. In considering what amounts to exceptional circumstances: relevant factors will include the nature, scope and extent of the dishonesty itself; whether it was momentary, or over a lengthy period of time; whether it was a benefit to the solicitor, and whether it had an adverse effect on others." (*Sharma* above). The exceptional circumstances must relate in some way to the dishonesty (*James* above)

53. The principal focus in determining whether exceptional circumstances exist is on the nature and extent of the dishonesty and the degree of culpability (*Sharma* and *R (Solicitors Regulation Authority) v Imran* [2015] EWHC 2572 (Admin)).

54. As a matter of principle nothing is excluded as being relevant to the evaluation, which could therefore include personal mitigation. In each case the Tribunal must when evaluating whether there are exceptional circumstances justifying a lesser sanction, focus on the critical questions of the nature and extent of the dishonesty and degree of culpability and engage in a balancing exercise as part of that evaluation between those critical questions on the one hand and matters such as personal mitigation, health issues and working conditions on the other. (*James* above).

55. Where dishonesty has been found mental health issues, specifically stress and depression suffered by the solicitor as a consequence of work conditions or other matters are unlikely without more to amount to exceptional circumstances:

> "The SDT having concluded that, notwithstanding mental health issues, each of the respondents was dishonest, I consider that it was contrary to principle for it then to conclude that those mental health issues could amount to exceptional circumstances".

> "….in my judgment, pressure of work or extreme working conditions whilst obviously relevant, by way of mitigation, to the assessment which the SDT has to make in determining the appropriate sanction, cannot either alone or in conjunction with stress or depression, amount to exceptional circumstances. Pressure of work or of working conditions cannot ever justify dishonesty by a solicitor…." per Flaux LJ in *James* (above)

Absence of Dishonesty

56. Striking off can be appropriate in the absence of dishonesty where, amongst other things:

- the seriousness of the misconduct is itself very high; and

- the departure by the respondent from the required standards of integrity, probity and trustworthiness is very serious.

57. In such cases, the Tribunal will have regard to the overall facts of the misconduct, and in particular the effect that allowing the respondent's name to remain on the Roll will have upon the public's confidence in the reputation of the legal profession – see in particular *Solicitors Regulation Authority v Emeana, Ijewere and Ajanaku* [2013] EWHC 2130 (Admin).

Misappropriation of client money falling short of Dishonesty

58. The Tribunal regards the breach of the absolute obligation to safeguard client money, which is quite distinct from the solicitor's duty to act honestly, as extremely serious.

59. The dishonest misappropriation of client money will invariably lead to strike off.

60.   Strike off can be appropriate in the absence of dishonesty. Where a respondent's failure properly to monitor client money leads to its misappropriation or misuse by others, such a serious breach of the obligation could warrant striking off.

> "....the tribunal had been at pains to make the point, which was a good one, that the solicitors' accounts rules existed to afford the public maximum protection against the improper and unauthorised use of their money and that, because of the importance attached to affording that protection and assuring the public that such protection was afforded, an onerous obligation was placed on solicitors to ensure that those rules were observed" per Bingham LCJ in *Weston v Law Society* [1998] Times, 15th July.

Section D: Personal mitigation

61.   Before finalising sanction, consideration will be given to any particular personal mitigation advanced by or on behalf of the respondent. The Tribunal will have regard to the following principles:

> "Because orders made by the tribunal are not primarily punitive, it follows that considerations which would ordinarily weigh in mitigation of punishment have less effect on the exercise of this jurisdiction than on the ordinary run of sentences imposed in criminal cases. It often happens that a solicitor appearing before the tribunal can adduce a wealth of glowing tributes from his professional brethren. He can often show that for him and his family the consequences of striking off or suspension would be little short of tragic. Often he will say, convincingly, that he has learned his lesson and will not offend again.
>
> .... All these matters are relevant and should be considered. But none of them touches the essential issue, which is the need to maintain among members of the public a well-founded confidence that any solicitor whom they instruct will be a person of unquestionable integrity, probity and trustworthiness. Thus it can never be an objection to an order of suspension in an appropriate case that the solicitor may be unable to re-establish his practice when the period of suspension is past. If that proves, or appears, likely to be so the consequence for the individual and his family may be deeply unfortunate and unintended. But it does not make suspension the wrong order if it is otherwise right. The reputation of the profession is more important than the fortunes of any individual member. Membership of a profession brings many benefits, but that is a part of the price." (*Bolton* above).

62.   Particular matters of personal mitigation that **may** be relevant and **may** serve to reduce the nature of the sanction, and/or its severity include that:

- the misconduct arose at a time when the respondent was affected by physical or mental ill-health that affected his ability to conduct himself to the standards of the reasonable solicitor. Such mitigation must be supported by medical evidence from a suitably qualified practitioner.

- the respondent was an inexperienced practitioner and was inadequately supervised by his employer.

- the respondent made prompt admissions and demonstrated full cooperation with the regulator.

Section E: Costs

63.   The Tribunal has the power to make such order as to costs as it thinks fit, including the payment by any party of costs or a contribution towards costs of such amount (if

any) as the Tribunal may consider reasonable (Section 47 of the Act). Such costs are those arising from or ancillary to proceedings before the Tribunal.

64. The Tribunal may make an order for the payment of a fixed amount of costs. This will be the usual order of the Tribunal where the parties are in agreement as to the liability for, and the amount of, those costs. Otherwise, the Tribunal will determine liability for costs, and either summarily assess those costs itself or refer the case for detailed assessment by a Costs Judge.

Costs against Respondent: allegations admitted/proved

General considerations

65. The Tribunal, in considering the respondent's liability for the costs of the applicant, will have regard to the following principles, drawn from *R v Northallerton Magistrates Court, ex parte Dove* (1999) 163 JP 894:

- it is not the purpose of an order for costs to serve as an additional punishment for the respondent, but to compensate the applicant for the costs incurred by it in bringing the proceedings and

- any order imposed must never exceed the costs actually and reasonably incurred by the applicant.

66. Before making any order as to costs, the Tribunal will give the respondent the opportunity to adduce financial information and make submissions. A respondent is not entitled as of right to an adjournment to produce evidence of means and the granting of an adjournment, which is at the Tribunal's discretion, may increase the overall costs awarded against the respondent. Respondents should therefore strictly comply with Practice Direction No. 6 for cases issued prior to 24 November 2019 or Rule 43(5) of the Solicitors (Disciplinary Proceedings) Rules 2019 for cases issued on or after 25 November 2019 and case-specific directions regarding the provision of evidence of means:

> "If a solicitor wishes to contend that he is impecunious and cannot meet an order for costs, or that its size should be confined, it will be up to him to put before the Tribunal sufficient information to persuade the Tribunal that he lacks the means to meet an order for costs in the sum at which they would otherwise arrive. ... where a solicitor admits the disciplinary charges brought against him, and who therefore anticipates the imposition of a sanction upon him, it should be incumbent upon him before the hearing to give advance notice to the SRA and to the Tribunal that he will contend either that no order for costs should be made against him, or that it should be limited in amount by reason of his own lack of means. He should also supply to the SRA and to the Tribunal, in advance of the hearing, the evidence upon which he relies to support that contention" (*Solicitors Regulation Authority v Davis and McGlinchey* [2011] EWHC 232 (Admin) per Mitting J and *Agyeman v Solicitors Regulation Authority* [2012] EWHC 3472 (Admin)).

67. A respondent will be expected to adduce evidence that their ability to pay costs is limited by their means (please refer to Practice Direction No. 6, clause 13, for cases issued prior to 24 November 2019 or Rule 43(5) of the Solicitors (Disciplinary Proceedings) Rules 2019 for cases issued on or after 25 November 2019; the terms of Standard Directions and/or specific Directions ordered by the Tribunal in the case).

68. Where the Tribunal decides that the respondent is, notwithstanding their limited means, properly liable for the applicant's costs (either in full or in part) and is satisfied that there is a reasonable prospect that, at some time in the future, their ability to pay those costs will improve, it may order the respondent to meet those costs but direct that such order is not to be enforced without leave of the Tribunal. Such orders will

APPENDIX 17

not be granted as a matter of course. A respondent must always provide evidence of means in support of an application for an order that any costs awarded by the Tribunal to the SRA should not be enforced without leave of the Tribunal. It should be noted that costs may be increased by an application by the SRA to enforce the same.

Costs against Respondent: some allegations not proved

69. Where the respondent is partially successful in defending the allegations pursued by the applicant, in considering the respondent's liability for costs the Tribunal will have regard to the following factors:

- the reasonableness of the applicant in pursuing an allegation on which it was unsuccessful.

- the manner in which the applicant pursued the allegation on which it was unsuccessful and its case generally.

- the reasonableness of the allegation, that is, was it reasonable for the applicant to pursue the allegation in all the circumstances.

- the extra costs in terms of preparation for trial, witness statements and documents and so on, taken up by pursuing the allegation upon which the applicant was unsuccessful.

- the extra Tribunal time taken in considering the unsuccessful allegation.

- the extent to which the allegation was inter-related in terms of evidence and argument with those allegations in respect of which the applicant was successful.

- the extra costs borne by the respondent in defending an allegation which was not found to be proved.

70. The Tribunal may award costs against a respondent even if it makes *no* finding of misconduct. In considering what costs to order, if any, the Tribunal will consider all relevant matters including the conduct of the parties.

71. The Tribunal must also take into account the decision of *Broomhead v Solicitors Regulation Authority* [2014] EWHC 2772 (Admin), in which Mr Justice Nicol stated as follows:

> "42. However, while the propriety of bringing charges is a good reason why the SRA should not have to pay the solicitor's costs, it does not follow that the solicitor who has successfully defended himself against those charges should have to pay the SRA's costs. Of course there may be something about the way the solicitor has conducted the proceedings or behaved in other ways which would justify a different conclusion. Even if the charges were properly brought it seems to me that in the normal case the SRA should have to shoulder its own costs where it has not been able to persuade the Tribunal that its case is made out. I do not see that this would constitute an unreasonable disincentive to take appropriate regulatory action."

Costs against Applicant

72. The starting point adopted by the Tribunal in considering whether costs should be awarded against the regulator (where that is the applicant in a particular case) is the principles set out in *CMA v Flynn Pharma* [2020] EWCA Civ 617. This case draws together previous decisions and sets out the principles at [79] as follows:

> "The applicable legal principles to be derived from these cases are, in my judgment, as follows:
>
> i)   Where a power to make an order about costs does not include an express general rule or default position, an important factor

in the exercise of discretion is the fact that one of the parties is a regulator exercising functions in the public interest.

ii)   That leads to the conclusion that in such cases the starting point or default position is that no order for costs should be made against a regulator who has brought or defended proceedings in the CAT acting purely in its regulatory capacity.

iii) The default position may be departed from for good reason.

iv)   The mere fact that the regulator has been unsuccessful is not, without more, a good reason. I do not consider that it is necessary to find "exceptional circumstances" as opposed to a good reason.

v)   A good reason will include unreasonable conduct on the part of the regulator, or substantial financial hardship likely to be suffered by the successful party if a costs order is not made.

vi)   There may be additional factors, specific to a particular case, which might also permit a departure from the starting point."

73.   There is no requirement for the proceedings to have been "a shambles from start to finish" (per Laws LJ, *Baxendale-Walker v The Law Society* [2007] EWCA Civ 233) or for "exceptional circumstances" – the question is whether there is good reason to depart from the starting point (no order for costs) and that can include unreasonable conduct on the part of the regulator.

74.   In relation to a possible "chilling effect" of an order against the regulator, [100] of *Flynn* states "in so far as it has potential to exist, I consider that it is already accommodated within the principles developed by the cases in this court."

75.   Where a respondent seeks to pursue an application for costs against the regulator, the Tribunal will have regard to the principles set out in *Flynn* above.

76.   The Tribunal will receive submissions from the parties at the substantive hearing, and will adjourn the hearing insofar as it relates to costs only for that purpose if necessary (but see paragraph 66 above).

APPENDIX 17

Extracts from the Solicitors Act 1974

[With consolidated amendments to 1 December 2020.]

Solicitors Act 1974

1974 CHAPTER 47

An Act to consolidate the Solicitors Acts 1957 to 1974 and certain other enactments relating to solicitors

[31st July 1974]

BE IT ENACTED by the Queen's most Excellent Majesty, by and with the advice and consent of the Lords Spiritual and Temporal, and Commons, in this present Parliament assembled, and by the authority of the same, as follows:—

PART I
RIGHT TO PRACTISE AS SOLICITOR

Qualifications and training

1 Qualifications for practising as solicitor

No person shall be qualified to act as a solicitor unless—

(a)   he has been admitted as a solicitor, and

(b)   his name is on the roll, and

(c)   he has in force a certificate issued by the Society in accordance with the provisions of this Part authorising him to practise as a solicitor (in this Act referred to as a "practising certificate").

1A Practising certificates: employed solicitors

A person who has been admitted as a solicitor and whose name is on the roll shall, if he would not otherwise be taken to be acting as a solicitor, be taken for the purposes of this Act to be so acting if he is employed in connection with the provision of any legal services—

(a)   by any person who is qualified to act as a solicitor;

(b)   by any partnership at least one member of which is so qualified;

(c)   by a body recognised under section 9 of the Administration of Justice Act 1985 (incorporated practices); or

(d)   by any other person who, for the purposes of the Legal Services Act 2007, is an authorised person in relation to an activity which is a reserved legal activity (within the meaning of that Act).

13 Appeals etc in connection with the issue of practising certificates

(1)   A person who makes an application under section 9 may appeal to the High Court against—

    (a)   a decision to refuse the application for a practising certificate,

    (b)   [...] or

    (c)   a decision to impose a condition on a practising certificate issued in consequence of the application.

(2)   A person who holds a practising certificate subject to a condition within section 10(4)(b) may appeal to the High Court against any decision by the Society to refuse to approve the taking of any step for the purposes of that condition.

(3)   The Society may make rules which provide, as respects any application under section 9 that is neither granted nor refused by the Society within such period as may be specified in the rules, for enabling an appeal to be brought under this section in relation to the application as if it had been refused by the Society.

(4)   On an appeal under subsection (1), the High Court may—

    (a)   affirm the decision of the Society,

    (b)   [*repealed*]

    (c)   direct the Society to issue a certificate to the applicant free from conditions or subject to such conditions as the High Court may think fit,

    (d)   direct the Society not to issue a certificate,

    (e)   if a certificate has been issued, by order suspend it,

    (f)   [...] or

    (g)   make such other order as the High Court thinks fit.

(5)   On an appeal under subsection (2), the High Court may—

    (a)   affirm the decision of the Society,

    (b)   direct the Society to approve the taking of one or more steps for the purposes of a condition within section 10(4)(b), or

    (c)   make such other order as the High Court thinks fit.

(6)   In relation to an appeal under this section the High Court may make such order as it thinks fit as to payment of costs.

(7)   The decision of the High Court on an appeal under subsection (1) or (2) shall be final.

13A Imposition of conditions while practising certificates are in force

(1)   Subject to the provisions of this section, the Society may in the case of any solicitor direct that his practising certificate for the time being in force (his "current certificate") shall have effect subject to such conditions as the Society may think fit.

(2)   The power conferred by subsection (1) is exercisable in relation to a solicitor at any time during the period for which the solicitor's current certificate is in force if—

    (a)   [*repealed*]

    (b)   it appears to the Society that the case is of a prescribed description.

(3)   "Prescribed" means prescribed by regulations under section 28.

(6)   A solicitor in whose case a direction is given under this section may appeal to the High Court against the decision of the Society.

(7)   On an appeal under subsection (6), the High Court may—

(a)   affirm the decision of the Society; or

(b)   direct that the appellant's current certificate shall have effect subject to such conditions as the High Court thinks fit; or

(c)   by order revoke the direction; or

(d)   make such other order as it thinks fit.

(7A) The decision of the High Court on an appeal under subsection (6) shall be final.

(8)   Subsections (4) and (5) of section 10 apply for the purposes of subsection (1) of this section as they apply for the purposes of that section.

(9)   A solicitor who holds a practising certificate subject to a condition imposed under subsection (1) which prohibits that solicitor from taking any steps specified in the condition, except with the approval of the Society, may appeal to the High Court against any decision by the Society to refuse to approve the taking of any step for the purposes of that condition.

(10) On an appeal under subsection (9), the High Court may—

(a)   affirm the decision of the Society,

(b)   direct the Society to approve the taking of one or more steps for the purposes of the condition, or

(c)   make such other order as the High Court thinks fit.

(11) The decision of the High Court on an appeal under subsection (9) shall be final.

(12) In relation to an appeal under this section the High Court may make such order as it thinks fit as to payment of costs.

13B Suspension of practising certificates where solicitors convicted of fraud or serious crime

(1)   Where—

(a)   a solicitor has been convicted of—

(i)   an offence involving dishonesty or deception; or

(ii)   an indictable offence; and

(b)   the Society has made an application to the Tribunal under section 47 with respect to him,

the Society may direct that any practising certificate of his which is for the time being in force be suspended.

(2)   Any such suspension shall be for such period, not exceeding six months, as the Society shall specify in the direction.

(3)   If, before the specified period expires—

(a)   the Tribunal determines the Society's application;

(b)   the conviction is quashed or set aside; or

(c)   the Society withdraws its application to the Tribunal,

the suspension shall cease to have effect.

(4)   Where the specified period comes to an end without any of the events mentioned in subsection (3) having occurred, the Society may direct that the suspension be continued for such period, not exceeding six months, as it shall specify in the direction.

(5)   A suspension under this section may only be extended once under subsection (4).

(6)   Nothing in this section is to be taken as in any way affecting the Tribunal's power to suspend a solicitor from practice.

(7)   A solicitor in whose case a direction is given under subsection (1) or (4) may appeal to the High Court against the direction within one month of being notified of it.

(8)   In an appeal under subsection (7), the High Court may—

(a)   affirm the suspension;

(b)   direct that the appellant's certificate shall not be suspended, but shall have effect subject to such conditions as the High Court thinks fit;

(c)   by order revoke the direction; or

(d)   make such other order as it thinks fit.

(9)   In relation to an appeal under subsection (7) the High Court may make such order as it thinks fit as to payment of costs.

(10) The decision of the High Court on an appeal under subsection (7) shall be final.

15 Suspension of practising certificates

(1)   The making by the Tribunal or by the court of an order suspending a solicitor from practice shall operate, and an adjudication in bankruptcy of a solicitor or the making of a debt relief order (under Part 7A of the Insolvency Act 1986) in respect of a solicitor shall operate immediately, to suspend any practising certificate of that solicitor for the time being in force.

(1A) Where the power conferred by paragraph 6(1), 6A(1) or 9(1) of Schedule 1 has been exercised in relation to a solicitor by virtue of paragraph 1(1)(a)(i), (aa), (c) (so far as it applies to rules made by virtue of section 31 or 32) or (e) of that Schedule, the exercise of that power shall operate immediately to suspend any practising certificate of that solicitor for the time being in force.

(1B) Subsection (1A) does not apply if, at the time when the power referred to there is exercised, the Society directs that subsection (1A) is not to apply in relation to the solicitor concerned.

(1C) If, at the time when the power referred to in subsection (1A) is exercised, the Society gives a direction to that effect, the solicitor concerned may continue to act in relation to any matter specified in the direction as if his practising certificate had not been suspended by virtue of subsection (1A), but subject to such conditions (if any) as the Society sees fit to impose.

(2)   For the purposes of this Act, a practising certificate shall be deemed not to be in force at any time while it is suspended.

16 Duration of suspension of practising certificates

(1)   Where a practising certificate is suspended, it expires on such date as may be prescribed by regulations under section 28.

(2)   The suspension of a practising certificate by virtue of section 15(1) by reason of an adjudication in bankruptcy shall terminate if the adjudication is annulled and an office copy of the order annulling the adjudication is served on the Society.

(2A) The suspension of a practising certificate by virtue of section 15(1) by reason of the making of a debt relief order shall terminate—

(a)   if the debt relief order is revoked on the ground mentioned in section 251L(2)(c) or (d) of the Insolvency Act 1986 and a copy of the notice provided to the debtor under Rule 9.18 of the Insolvency (England and Wales) Rules 2016 is served on the Society or the debt relief order is revoked by the court under section 251M(6)(e) of that Act and a copy of the court order is served on the Society;

(b)   if the debt relief order is revoked and a period of one year has elapsed beginning with the effective date of that order.

(3)   Where a solicitor's practising certificate is suspended—

(a)   by an order under section 13(4); or

(b)   by virtue of section 15(1) by reason of his adjudication in bankruptcy or the making of a debt relief order (under Part 7A of the Insolvency Act 1986) in respect of him; or

(c)   by virtue of section 15(1) by reason of his suspension from practice and the period of his suspension from practice expires before the date on which his certificate will expire,

(d)   by virtue of section 15(1A)

the solicitor may at any time before the certificate expires (and, in the case of adjudication in bankruptcy, while the adjudication remains unannulled) apply to the Society to terminate the suspension.

(4)   On an application under subsection (3), the Society may in its discretion—

(a)   by order terminate the suspension either unconditionally or subject to such conditions as the Society may think fit; or

(b)   refuse the application.

(5)   If on an application by a solicitor under subsection (3) the Society refuses the application or terminates the suspension subject to conditions, the solicitor may appeal against the decision of the Society to the High Court, which may—

(a)   affirm the decision; or

(b)   terminate the suspension either unconditionally or subject to such conditions as it may think fit.

(6)   In relation to an appeal under subsection (5) the High Court may make such order as it thinks fit as to payment of costs.

(7)   The decision of the High Court on an appeal under subsection (5) shall be final.

17 Publicity in relation to suspension of practising certificates

(1)   Where a solicitor's practising certificate is suspended by an order under section 13(4), or by virtue of section 15(1) by reason of his adjudication in bankruptcy, the Society shall forthwith cause notice of that suspension to be published and a note of it to be entered against the name of the solicitor on the roll.

(2)   Where any such suspension of a practising certificate as is mentioned in subsection (1) is terminated under section 16(2), (4) or (5), the Society shall forthwith cause a note of that termination to be entered against the name of the solicitor on the roll and, if so requested in writing by the solicitor, a notice of it to be published.

Supplementary

28 Regulations

(1)   The Society may make regulations about the following matters, namely—

(a)   admission as a solicitor;

(b)   the keeping of the roll;

(c)   practising certificates;

(d)   the keeping of the register under section 10A.

(2)   [*repealed*]

(3)   [*repealed*]

(3A) Regulations about the keeping of the roll may (among other things)—

    (za)   make provision about the form in which the roll is to be kept and the manner in which entries are to be made, altered and removed;

    (a)   provide for the Society, at such intervals as may be specified in the regulations, to enquire of solicitors of any class so specified whether they wish to have their names retained on the roll;

    (b)   require solicitors of any such class, at such intervals as aforesaid, to pay to the Society a fee in respect of the retention of their names on the roll of such amount as may be prescribed by the regulations;

    (c)   authorise the Society to remove from the roll the name of any solicitor who—

        (i)   fails to reply to any enquiry made in pursuance of paragraph (a) or to pay any fee payable by virtue of paragraph (b), or

        (ii)   replies to any such enquiry by indicating that he does not wish to have his name retained on the roll;

    (d)   authorise the Society to remove from the roll the name of any solicitor who has died;

    (e)   require the information on the roll to be made available to the public;

    (f)   specify the manner in which information is to be made so available and require it to be made so available during office hours and without charge.

(3B) Regulations about practising certificates may (among other things)—

    (a)   prescribe the form and manner in which applications for, or relating to, practising certificates are to be made;

    (b)   prescribe information which must be included in or accompany such applications;

    (c)   make provision about time limits for dealing with such applications, and confer on a person power to extend or bring forward such a time limit in prescribed circumstances;

    (d)   prescribe the requirements which applicants for practising certificates must satisfy before they may be issued with a practising certificate;

    (e)   prescribe descriptions of applicants, and conditions in relation to them, for the purposes of section 10(2) (circumstances in which practising certificates must be issued subject to prescribed conditions);

    (f)   [*repealed*];

    (g)   prescribe circumstances for the purposes of section 10(3) (circumstances in which application may be refused etc in the public interest);

    (h)   make provision about when conditions imposed on practising certificates take effect (including provision conferring power on the Society to direct that a condition is not to have effect until the conclusion of any appeal in relation to it);

    (i)   make provision for the commencement, duration, replacement, withdrawal and expiry of practising certificates;

    (j)   prescribe circumstances for the purposes of section 13A(2) (circumstances in which conditions can be imposed during period of practising certificate);

    (k)   require solicitors who hold practising certificates to notify the Society of such matters as may be prescribed, at such times, or in such circumstances as may be prescribed.

(3C) Regulations about the keeping of the register under section 10A may (among other things)—

    (a)   make provision about the form in which the register is to be kept and the manner in which entries are to be made, altered and removed;

(b)   require information of a specified kind to be included in entries in the register;

(c)   require information (or information of a specified description) on the register to be made available to the public;

(d)   specify the manner in which it is to be made so available and require it to be made so available during office hours and without charge.

(3D) Regulations under this section may make provision for appeals to the High Court against decisions made by the Society under the regulations.

(3E) In relation to an appeal under regulations made by virtue of subsection (3D), the High Court may make such order as it thinks fit as to payment of costs.

(3F) The decision of the High Court on such an appeal shall be final.

(3G) Regulations under this section may—

(a)   provide for a person to exercise a discretion in dealing with any matter;

(b)   include incidental, supplementary and consequential provision;

(c)   make transitory or transitional provision and savings;

(d)   make provision generally or only in relation to specified cases or subject to specified exceptions;

(e)   make different provision for different cases.

(4)   [*repealed*]

(5)   [*repealed*]

PART II
PROFESSIONAL PRACTICE, CONDUCT AND DISCIPLINE OF SOLICITORS AND CLERKS

Practice rules

31 Rules as to professional practice, conduct and discipline

(1)   Without prejudice to any other provision of this Part the Society may make rules for regulating in respect of any matter the professional practice, conduct, fitness to practise and discipline of solicitors and for empowering the Society to take such action as may be appropriate to enable the Society to ascertain whether or not the provisions of rules made, or of any code or guidance issued, by the Society are being, or have been, complied with.

(1A) The powers conferred on the Society by subsection (1) include power to make, in relation to solicitors, provision of a kind which the Society would be prohibited from making but for section 157(5)(c) of the Legal Services Act 2007 (exception from prohibition on approved regulators making provision for redress).

(1B) Rules under this section must provide that a solicitor may not practise as a sole solicitor unless there is in force in relation to that solicitor's practice a recognition under section 9 of the Administration of Justice Act 1985.

(1C) Rules under this section may provide that, for the purposes of the rules, this Act and the Administration of Justice Act 1985, a solicitor is not to be regarded as practising as a sole solicitor in such circumstances as may be prescribed by the rules.

(2)   If any solicitor fails to comply with rules made under this section, any person may make a complaint in respect of that failure to the Tribunal.

(3)   [*repealed*]

(4)   [*repealed*]

Accounts etc

32 Accounts rules and trust accounts rules

(1)   The Society shall make rules—

   (a)   as to the opening and keeping by solicitors of accounts at banks or with building societies for money within subsection (1A);

   (aa)   as to the operation by solicitors of accounts kept by their clients or other persons at banks or with building societies or other financial institutions;

   (b)   as to the keeping by solicitors of accounts containing information as to money received, held or paid by them for or on account of their clients or other persons (including money received, held or paid under a trust); and

   (c)   empowering the Society to take such action as may be necessary to enable it to ascertain whether or not the rules are being, or have been, complied with.

(1A) The money referred to in subsection (1) is money (including money held on trust) which is received, held or dealt with for clients or other persons.

(2)   [*repealed*]

(3)   If any solicitor fails to comply with rules made under this section, any person may make a complaint in respect of that failure to the Tribunal.

(4)   The Society shall be at liberty to disclose a report on or information about a solicitor's accounts obtained in the exercise of powers conferred by rules made under subsection (1) for use in investigating the possible commission of an offence by the solicitor or any of his employees and for use in connection with any prosecution of the solicitor or any of his employees consequent on the investigation.

(5)   Rules under this section may specify circumstances in which solicitors or any class of solicitors are exempt from the rules or a part of the rules.

(6)   [*repealed*]

33 Interest on clients' money

(1)   Rules under section 32 may require a solicitor to pay interest, or sums in lieu of and equivalent to interest, to a client, any other person or any trust, for whom the solicitor holds money.

(2)   The cases in which a solicitor may be required by the rules to act as mentioned in subsection (1) may be defined, among other things, by reference to the amount of any sum received or the period for which it is or is likely to be retained or both.

(3)   Except as provided by the rules, a solicitor is not liable to account to any client, other person or trust for interest received by the solicitor on money held at a bank or building society in an account which is for money received or held for, or on account of—

   (a)   the solicitor's clients, other persons or trusts, generally, or

   (b)   that client, person or trust, separately.

(4)   Rules under section 32 may—

   (a)   prescribe the circumstances in which a solicitor may make arrangements to limit or exclude an obligation imposed on the solicitor by rules made by virtue of this section, and

   (b)   prescribe the requirements to be met by and in relation to those arrangements.

33A Inspection of practice bank accounts etc

(1)   The Society may make rules empowering the Society to require a solicitor to produce documents relating to any account kept by him at a bank or with a building society—

   (a)   in connection with his practice; or

(b)   in connection with any trust of which he is or formerly was a trustee,

for inspection by a person appointed by the Society pursuant to the rules.

(2)   The Society shall be at liberty to disclose information obtained in exercise of the powers conferred by rules made under subsection (1) for use in investigating the possible commission of an offence by the solicitor and for use in connection with any prosecution of the solicitor consequent on the investigation.

34 Accountants' reports

(1)   The Society may make rules requiring solicitors to provide the Society with reports signed by an accountant (in this section referred to as an "accountant's report") at such times or in such circumstances as may be prescribed by the rules.

(2)   The rules may specify requirements to be met by, or in relation to, an accountant's report (including requirements relating to the accountant who signs the report).

(6)   If any solicitor fails to comply with the provisions of any rules made under this section, a complaint in respect of that failure may be made to the Tribunal by or on behalf of the Society.

(7)   [*repealed*]

(8)   [*repealed*]

(9)   Where an accountant, during the course of preparing an accountant's report—

(a)   discovers evidence of fraud or theft in relation to money held by a solicitor for a client or any other person (including money held on trust) or money held in an account of a client of a solicitor, or an account of another person, which is operated by the solicitor, or

(b)   obtains information which the accountant has reasonable cause to believe is likely to be of material significance in determining whether a solicitor is a fit and proper person to hold money for clients or other persons (including money held on trust) or to operate an account of a client of the solicitor or an account of another person,

the accountant must immediately give a report of the matter to the Society.

(10) No duty to which an accountant is subject is to be regarded as contravened merely because of any information or opinion contained in a report under subsection (9).

Sole solicitors

34A Employees of solicitors

(1)   Rules made by the Society may provide for any rules made under section 31, 32, 33A or 34 to have effect in relation to employees of solicitors with such additions, omissions or other modifications as appear to the Society to be necessary or expedient.

(2)   If any employee of a solicitor fails to comply with rules made under section 31 or 32, as they have effect in relation to the employee by virtue of subsection (1), any person may make a complaint in respect of that failure to the Tribunal.

(3)   If any employee of a solicitor fails to comply with rules made under section 34, as they have effect in relation to the employee by virtue of subsection (1), a complaint in respect of that failure may be made to the Tribunal by or on behalf of the Society.

34B Employees of solicitors: accounts rules etc

(1)   Where rules made under section 32(1) have effect in relation to employees of solicitors by virtue of section 34A(1), section 85 applies in relation to an employee to whom the rules have effect who keeps an account with a bank or building society in pursuance of such rules as it applies in relation to a solicitor who keeps such an account in pursuance of rules under section 32.

(2)   Subsection (3) applies where rules made under section 32—

   (a)   contain any such provision as is referred to in section 33(1), and

   (b)   have effect in relation to employees of solicitors by virtue of section 34A(1).

(3)   Except as provided by the rules, an employee to whom the rules are applied is not liable to account to any client, other person or trust for interest received by the employee on money held at a bank or building society in an account which is for money received or held for, or on account of—

   (a)   clients of the solicitor, other persons or trusts, generally, or

   (b)   that client, person or trust, separately.

(4)   Subsection (5) applies where rules made under section 33A(1) have effect in relation to employees of solicitors by virtue of section 34A(1).

(5)   The Society may disclose a report on or information about the accounts of any employee of a solicitor obtained in pursuance of such rules for use—

   (a)   in investigating the possible commission of an offence by the solicitor or any employees of the solicitor, and

   (b)   in connection with any prosecution of the solicitor or any employees of the solic-itor consequent on the investigation.

(6)   Where rules made under section 34 have effect in relation to employees of solicitors by virtue of section 34A(1), section 34(9) and (10) apply in relation to such an employee as they apply in relation to a solicitor.

Intervention in solicitor's practice, Compensation Fund and professional indemnity

35 Intervention in solicitor's practice

The powers conferred by Part II of Schedule 1 shall be exercisable in the circumstances specified in Part I of that Schedule.

Restrictions on employment of certain persons

41 Employment by solicitor of person struck off or suspended

(1)   No solicitor shall, except in accordance with a written permission granted under this section, employ or remunerate in connection with his practice as a solicitor any person who to his knowledge is disqualified from practising as a solicitor by reason of the fact that—

   (a)   his name has been struck off the roll, or

   (b)   he is suspended from practising as a solicitor, or

   (c)   his practising certificate is suspended while he is an undischarged bankrupt.

(1A) No solicitor shall, except in accordance with a written permission granted under this section, employ or remunerate in connection with his practice as a solicitor any person if, to his knowledge, there is a direction in force under section 47(2)(g) in relation to that person.

(1B) Where—

   (a)   a solicitor ("the employed solicitor") is employed by another solicitor in accord-ance with a written permission granted under this section, and

   (b)   the employed solicitor is disqualified from practising as a solicitor by reason of a fact mentioned in subsection (1)(b) or (c),

section 20(1) does not apply in relation to anything done by the employed solicitor in the course of that employment.

(2) The Society may grant a permission under this section for such period and subject to such conditions as the Society thinks fit.

(3) A solicitor aggrieved by the refusal of the Society to grant a permission under subsection (2), or by any conditions attached by the Society to the grant of any such permission, may appeal to the High Court which may—

(a) confirm the refusal or the conditions, as the case may be; or

(b) grant a permission under this section for such period and subject to such conditions as it thinks fit.

(4) If any solicitor acts in contravention of this section or of any conditions subject to which a permission has been granted under it, the Tribunal or, as the case may be, the High Court may—

(a) order that his name be struck off the roll,

(b) order that he be suspended from practice for such period as the Tribunal or court thinks fit, or

(c) make such other order in the matter as it thinks fit.

(4A) In relation to an appeal under subsection (3) the High Court may make such order as it thinks fit as to payment of costs.

(4B) The decision of the High Court on an appeal under subsection (3) shall be final.

(5) [*repealed*]

42 Failure to disclose fact of having been struck off or suspended

(1) Any person who, while he is disqualified from practising as a solicitor by reason of the fact that—

(a) his name has been struck off the roll, or

(b) he is suspended from practising as a solicitor, or

(c) his practising certificate is suspended while he is an undischarged bankrupt,

seeks or accepts employment by a solicitor in connection with that solicitor's practice without previously informing him that he is so disqualified shall be guilty of an offence and liable on summary conviction to a fine not exceeding level 3 on the standard scale.

(1A) Any person—

(a) with respect to whom a direction is in force under section 47(2)(g); and

(b) who seeks or accepts employment by a solicitor in connection with that solicitor's practice without previously informing him of the direction,

shall be guilty of an offence and liable on summary conviction to a fine not exceeding level three on the standard scale.

(2) Notwithstanding anything in the Magistrates' Courts Act 1980, proceedings under this section may be commenced at any time before the expiration of six months from the first discovery of the offence by the prosecutor, but no such proceedings shall be commenced except by, or with the consent of, the Attorney General.

43 Control of solicitors' employees and consultants

(1) Where a person who is or was involved in a legal practice but is not a solicitor—

(a) has been convicted of a criminal offence which is such that in the opinion of the Society it would be undesirable for the person to be involved in a legal practice in one or more of the ways mentioned in subsection (1A), or

(b) has, in the opinion of the Society, occasioned or been a party to, with or without the connivance of a solicitor, an act or default in relation to a legal practice which involved conduct on his part of such a nature that in the opinion of the Society it would be undesirable for him to be involved in a legal practice in one or more of the ways mentioned in subsection (1A),

the Society may either make, or make an application to the Tribunal for it to make, an order under subsection (2) with respect to that person.

(1A) A person is involved in a legal practice for the purposes of this section if the person—

(a)   is employed or remunerated by a solicitor in connection with the solicitor's practice;

(b)   is undertaking work in the name of, or under the direction or supervision of, a solicitor;

(c)   is employed or remunerated by a recognised body;

(d)   is employed or remunerated by a manager or employee of a recognised body in connection with that body's business;

(e)   is a manager of a recognised body;

(f)   has or intends to acquire an interest in such a body.

(2)   An order made by the Society or the Tribunal under this subsection is an order which states one or more of the following—

(a)   that as from the specified date—

    (i)   no solicitor shall employ or remunerate, in connection with his practice as a solicitor, the person with respect to whom the order is made,

    (ii)   no employee of a solicitor shall employ or remunerate, in connection with the solicitor's practice, the person with respect to whom the order is made,

    (iii)   no recognised body shall employ or remunerate that person, and

    (iv)   no manager or employee of a recognised body shall employ or remunerate that person in connection with the business of that body,

    except in accordance with a Society permission;

(b)   that as from the specified date no recognised body or manager or employee of such a body shall, except in accordance with a Society permission, permit the person with respect to whom the order is made to be a manager of the body;

(c)   that as from the specified date no recognised body or manager or employee of such a body shall, except in accordance with a Society permission, permit the person with respect to whom the order is made to have an interest in the body.

(2A) The Society may make regulations prescribing charges to be paid to the Society by persons who are the subject of an investigation by the Society as to whether there are grounds for the Society—

(a)   to make an order under subsection (2), or

(b)   to make an application to the Tribunal for it to make such an order.

(2B) Regulations under subsection (2A) may—

(a)   make different provision for different cases or purposes;

(b)   provide for the whole or part of a charge payable under the regulations to be repaid in such circumstances as may be prescribed by the regulations.

(2C) Any charge which a person is required to pay under regulations under subsection (2A) is recoverable by the Society as a debt due to the Society from the person.

(3)   Where an order has been made under subsection (2) with respect to a person by the Society or the Tribunal—

(a)   that person or the Society may make an application to the Tribunal for it to be reviewed, and

(b)   whichever of the Society and the Tribunal made it may at any time revoke it.

(3A) On the review of an order under subsection (3) the Tribunal may order—

(a)   the quashing of the order;

(b)   the variation of the order; or

(c)   the confirmation of the order;

and where in the opinion of the Tribunal no prima facie case for quashing or varying the order is shown, the Tribunal may order its confirmation without hearing the applicant.

(4)   The Tribunal, on the hearing of any application under this section, may make an order as to the payment of costs by any party to the application.

(5)   Orders made under subsection (2) by the Society, or made, varied or confirmed under this section by the Tribunal and filed with the Society, may be inspected during office hours without payment.

(5A) In this section—

"manager", in relation to a recognised body, has the same meaning as it has in relation to a body in the Legal Services Act 2007 (see section 207 of that Act);

"recognised body" means a body recognised under section 9 of the Administration of Justice Act 1985;

"specified date" means such date as may be specified in the order;

"Society permission" means permission in writing granted by the Society for such period and subject to such conditions as the Society may think fit to specify in the permission.

(5B) A person has an interest in a recognised body for the purposes of this section if the person has an interest in that body within the meaning of Part 5 of the Legal Services Act 2007 (see sections 72 and 109 of that Act).

(6)   [*repealed*]

(7)   For the purposes of this section an order discharging a person absolutely or conditionally in respect of an offence shall, notwithstanding anything in section 82 of the Sentencing Code, be deemed to be a conviction of the offence for which the order was made.

44 Offences in connection with orders under section 43(2)

(1)   It is an offence for a person in respect of whom there is in force an order under section 43(2) which contains provision within section 43(2)(a)—

(a)   to seek or accept any employment or remuneration from a solicitor, or an employee of a solicitor, in connection with the practice carried on by that solicitor without previously informing the solicitor or employee of the order;

(b)   to seek or accept any employment or remuneration from a recognised body, or a manager or employee of a recognised body, in connection with that body's business, without previously informing the body, or manager or employee, of the order.

(1A) It is an offence for a person in respect of whom there is in force an order under section 43(2) which contains provision within section 43(2)(b) to seek or accept a position as a manager of a recognised body, without previously informing that body of the order.

(1B) It is an offence for a person in respect of whom there is in force an order under section 43(2) which contains provision within section 43(2)(c) to seek or accept an interest in a recognised body from any person, without previously informing that person and (if different) the recognised body of the order.

APPENDIX 18

(1C) A person guilty of an offence under subsection (1), (1A) or (1B) is liable on summary conviction to a fine not exceeding level 3 on the standard scale.

(2)   Where an order under section 43(2) is in force in respect of a person, then, if any solicitor knowingly acts in contravention of that order or of any conditions subject to which permission for the taking of any action has been granted under it, a complaint in respect of that contravention may be made to the Tribunal by or on behalf of the Society.

(3)   Any document purporting to be an order under section 43(2) and to be duly signed in accordance with section 48(1) shall be received in evidence in any proceedings under this section and be deemed to be such an order without further proof unless the contrary is shown.

(4)   Notwithstanding anything in the Magistrates' Courts Act 1980, proceedings under subsection (1) may be commenced at any time before the expiration of six months from the first discovery of the offence by the prosecutor, but no such proceedings shall be commenced, except with the consent of the Director of Public Prosecutions, by any person other than the Society or a person acting on behalf of the Society.

(5)   In this section—

> "manager" has the same meaning as in section 43;

> "recognised body" means a body recognised under section 9 of the Administration of Justice Act 1985;

and for the purposes of subsection (1B) a person seeks or accepts an interest in a recognised body if the person seeks or accepts an interest which if it were obtained by the person would result in the person having an interest in that body within the meaning of Part 5 of the Legal Services Act 2007 (see sections 72 and 109 of that Act).

44A

[*repealed*]

Examination of files

44B Provision of information and documents by solicitors etc

(1)   The Society may by notice require a person to whom this section applies—

(a)   to provide information, or information of a description, specified in the notice, or

(b)   produce documents, or documents of a description, specified in the notice.

(2)   This section applies to—

(a)   a solicitor;

(b)   an employee of a solicitor;

(c)   a recognised body;

(d)   an employee or manager of, or a person with an interest in, a recognised body.

(3)   The Society may give a notice under this section only if it is satisfied that it is necessary to do so for the purpose of investigating—

(a)   whether there has been professional misconduct by a solicitor;

(b)   whether a solicitor, or an employee of a solicitor, has failed to comply with any requirements imposed by or by virtue of this Act or any rules made by the Society;

(c)   whether a recognised body, or any of its managers or employees has failed to comply with any requirement imposed by or by virtue of the Administration of Justice Act 1985 or any rules made by the Society and applicable to the body, manager or employee by virtue of section 9 of that Act;

(d)   whether there are grounds for making, or making an application to the Tribunal for it to make, an order under section 43(2) with respect to a person who is or was involved in a legal practice (within the meaning of section 43(1A)).

(4)   A notice under this section—

(a)   may specify the time and place at which, and manner and form in which, the information is to be provided or document is to be produced;

(b)   must specify the period within which the information is to be provided or the document produced;

(c)   may require the information to be provided or document to be produced to the Society or to a person specified in the notice.

(5)   The Society may pay to any person such reasonable costs as may be incurred by that person in connection with the provision of any information, or production of any document, by that person pursuant to a notice under this section.

(6)   Paragraphs 9(3) and (4) and 13, 15 and 16 of Schedule 1 apply in relation to the powers to obtain information conferred by this section, but for this purpose—

(a)   paragraph 9 of that Schedule has effect as if—

    (i)   in sub-paragraph (3) for "such documents" there were substituted "information to which a notice given to him under section 44B applies",

    (ii)   in that sub-paragraph for "sub-paragraph (1)" there were substituted "the notice", and

    (iii)   in sub-paragraph (4) for "produce" (in the first place) to the end there were substituted "provide information pursuant to a notice under section 44B to provide the information to any person appointed by the Society at such time and place as may be specified in the order.", and

(b)   the reference to the solicitor or his personal representative in paragraph 13 of that Schedule is to be construed as a reference to the person to whom the notice was given under this section.

(7)   Paragraphs 9 (other than sub-paragraphs (1) and (3)), 12, 13, 15 and 16 of Schedule 1 apply in relation to the powers to obtain documents conferred by this section as they apply in relation to the powers conferred by paragraph 9(1) of that Schedule, except that for this purpose—

(a)   any reference in paragraph 9 of that Schedule to a person appointed, or to a requirement, under sub-paragraph (1) of that paragraph is to be construed as a reference to a person appointed, or to a requirement to produce documents, under this section,

(b)   any reference in that paragraph to any such documents as are mentioned in paragraph 9(1) of that Schedule is to be construed as a reference to any documents to which a notice under this section applies,

(c)   the references to the solicitor or his firm in paragraph 9(5) and (6) of that Schedule, and the reference to the solicitor or personal representative in paragraph 9(7) of that Schedule, are to be construed as references to the person to whom the notice was given under this section, and

(d)   the reference in paragraph 9(12) of that Schedule to the Society is to be construed as including a reference to a person specified under subsection (4)(c).

(8)   Where powers conferred by Part 2 of Schedule 1 to the 1974 Act are exercisable in relation to a person within paragraph (a), (b), (c) or (d) of subsection (2), they continue to be so exercisable after the person has ceased to be a person within the paragraph in question.

(9)   In this section—

    "manager" has the same meaning as in the Legal Services Act 2007 (see section 207 of that Act);

"recognised body" means a body recognised under section 9 of the Administration of Justice Act 1985;

and the reference to a person who has an interest in a recognised body is to be construed in accordance with sections 72 and 109 of the Legal Services Act 2007.

44BA Power to require explanation of document or information

(1)   The Society may, by notice, require a person to whom a notice is given under section 44B (or a representative of the person) to attend at a time and place specified in the notice to provide an explanation of any information provided or document produced pursuant to the notice.

(2)   The Society may pay to any person such reasonable costs as may be incurred by that person in connection with that person's compliance with a requirement imposed under subsection (1).

(3)   Paragraphs 9(3) and (4) and 13, 15 and 16 of Schedule 1 apply in relation to a notice under this section, except that for this purpose—

   (a)   paragraph 9 of that Schedule has effect as if—

      (i)   in sub-paragraph (3) for "having" to "sub-paragraph (1)" there were substituted "refuses, neglects or otherwise fails to comply with a requirement under section 44BA(1)", and

      (ii)   in sub-paragraph (4) for "produce" (in the first place) to the end there were substituted "provide an explanation of any information provided or document produced pursuant to a notice under section 44B (or a representative of such a person) to attend at a time and place specified in the order to provide an explanation of any information so provided or document so produced.", and

   (b)   the reference to the solicitor or his personal representative in paragraph 13 of that Schedule is to be construed as a reference to the person to whom the notice was given under this section.

44BB Provision of information and documents by other persons

(1)   The High Court, on the application of the Society, may order a person to whom section 44B does not apply—

   (a)   to provide information, or information of a description, specified in the notice, or

   (b)   to produce documents, or documents of a description, specified in the notice.

(2)   The High Court may make an order under this section only if it is satisfied—

   (a)   that it is likely that the information or document is in the possession or custody of, or under the control of, the person, and

   (b)   that there is reasonable cause to believe that the information or document is likely to be of material significance to an investigation into any of the matters mentioned in section 44B(3)(a) to (d).

(3)   An order under this section may direct the Society to pay to a person specified in the order such reasonable costs as may be incurred by that person in connection with the provision of any information, or production of any document, by that person pursuant to the order.

(4)   Section 44B(4) applies in relation to an order under this section as it applies in relation to a notice under section 44B.

(5)   Paragraphs 9(5A) and (7) to (12), 12, 13, 15 and 16 of Schedule 1 apply in relation to an order under this section as they apply in relation to an order under paragraph 9(4) of that Schedule, except that for this purpose—

(a) the reference to the solicitor or personal representative in paragraph 9(7) of that Schedule is to be construed as a reference to the person in respect of whom the order under this section is made,

(b) the reference in paragraph 9(12) of that Schedule to the Society is to be read as including a reference to a person specified under section 44B(4)(c) (as applied by subsection (4) of this section), and

(c) the reference to the solicitor or his personal representative in paragraph 13 of that Schedule is to be construed as a reference to the person to whom the notice was given under this section.

44BC Information offences

(1) It is an offence for a person who knows or suspects an investigation into any of the matters mentioned in section 44B(3)(a) to (d) is being or is likely to be conducted—

(a) to falsify, conceal, destroy or otherwise dispose of a document which the person knows or suspects is or would be relevant to the investigation, or

(b) to cause or permit the falsification, concealment, destruction or disposal of such a document.

(2) In proceedings for an offence under subsection (1) it is a defence for the accused to show that the accused had no intention of concealing facts disclosed by the documents from the person conducting the investigation.

(3) It is an offence for a person, in purported compliance with a requirement imposed on the person under section 44B, 44BA or 44BB—

(a) to provide information which the person knows to be false or misleading in a material particular, or

(b) recklessly to provide information which is false or misleading in a material particular.

(4) A person who is guilty of an offence under subsection (1) or (3) is liable—

(a) on summary conviction, to imprisonment for a term not exceeding 12 months or a fine not exceeding the statutory maximum, or both;

(b) on conviction on indictment, to imprisonment for a term not exceeding 2 years or a fine, or both.

(5) In relation to an offence under subsection (1) or (3) committed before the commencement of paragraph 24(2(of Schedule 22 to the Sentencing Act 2020 the reference in subsection (4)(a) to 12 months is to be read as a reference to 6 months.

Costs of investigations

44C Power to charge for costs of investigations

(1) The Society may make regulations prescribing charges to be paid to the Society by solicitors who are the subject of a discipline investigation.

(2) A "discipline investigation" is an investigation carried out by the Society into—

(a) possible professional misconduct by a solicitor, or

(b) a failure or apprehended failure by a solicitor to comply with any requirement imposed by or by virtue of this Act or any rules made by the Society.

(3) Regulations under this section may—

(a) make different provision for different cases or purposes;

(b) provide for the whole or part of a charge payable under the regulations to be repaid in such circumstances as may be prescribed by the regulations.

(4)   Any charge which a solicitor is required to pay under regulations under this section is recoverable by the Society as a debt due to the Society from the solicitor.

(5)   This section (other than subsection (2)(a)) applies in relation to an employee of a solicitor as it applies in relation to a solicitor.

Disciplinary powers of the Society

44D Disciplinary powers of the Society

(1)   This section applies where the Society is satisfied—

(a)   that a solicitor or an employee of a solicitor has failed to comply with a requirement imposed by or by virtue of this Act or any rules made by the Society, or

(b)   that there has been professional misconduct by a solicitor.

(2)   The Society may do one or both of the following—

(a)   give the person a written rebuke;

(b)   direct the person to pay a penalty not exceeding £2,000.

(3)   The Society may publish details of any action it has taken under subsection (2)(a) or (b), if it considers it to be in the public interest to do so.

(4)   Where the Society takes action against a person under subsection (2)(b), or decides to publish under subsection (3) details of any action taken under subsection (2)(a) or (b), it must notify the person in writing that it has done so.

(5)   A penalty imposed under subsection (2)(b) does not become payable until—

(a)   the end of the period during which an appeal against the decision to impose the penalty, or the amount of the penalty, may be made under section 44E, or

(b)   if such an appeal is made, such time as it is determined or withdrawn.

(6)   The Society may not publish under subsection (3) details of any action under subsection (2)(a) or (b)—

(a)   during the period within which an appeal against—

(i)   the decision to take the action,

(ii)   in the case of action under subsection (2)(b), the amount of the penalty, or

(iii)   the decision to publish the details,

may be made under section 44E, or

(b)   if such an appeal has been made, until such time as it is determined or withdrawn.

(7)   The Society must make rules—

(a)   prescribing the circumstances in which the Society may decide to take action under subsection (2)(a) or (b);

(b)   about the practice and procedure to be followed by the Society in relation to such action;

(c)   governing the publication under subsection (3) of details of action taken under subsection (2)(a) or (b);

and the Society may make such other rules in connection with the exercise of its powers under this section as it considers appropriate.

(8)   Before making rules under subsection (7), the Society must consult the Tribunal.

(9)   A penalty payable under this section may be recovered as a debt due to the Society, and is to be forfeited to Her Majesty.

(10) The Lord Chancellor may, by order, amend paragraph (b) of subsection (2) so as to substitute for the amount for the time being specified in that paragraph such other amount as may be specified in the order.

(11) Before making an order under subsection (10), the Lord Chancellor must consult the Society.

(12) An order under subsection (10) is to be made by statutory instrument subject to annulment in pursuance of a resolution of either House of Parliament.

(13) This section is without prejudice to any power conferred on the Society or any other person to make an application or complaint to the Tribunal.

44E Appeals against disciplinary action under section 44D

(1)   A person may appeal against—

(a)   a decision by the Society to rebuke that person under section 44D(2)(a) if a decision is also made to publish details of the rebuke;

(b)   a decision by the Society to impose a penalty on that person under section 44D(2) (b) or the amount of that penalty;

(c)   a decision by the Society to publish under section 44D(3) details of any action taken against that person under section 44D(2)(a) or (b).

(2)   Subsections (9)(b), (10)(a) and (b), (11) and (12) of section 46 (Tribunal rules about procedure for hearings etc) apply in relation to appeals under this section as they apply in relation to applications or complaints, except that subsection (11) of that section is to be read as if for "the applicant" to "application)" there were substituted "any party to the appeal".

(3)   Rules under section 46(9)(b) may, in particular, make provision about the period during which an appeal under this section may be made.

(4)   On an appeal under this section, the Tribunal has power to make such order as it thinks fit, and such an order may in particular—

(a)   affirm the decision of the Society;

(b)   revoke the decision of the Society;

(c)   in the case of a penalty imposed under section 44D(2)(b), vary the amount of the penalty;

(d)   in the case of a solicitor, contain provision for any of the matters mentioned in paragraphs (a) to (d) of section 47(2);

(e)   in the case of an employee of a solicitor, contain provision for any of the matters mentioned in section 47(2E);

(f)   make such provision as the Tribunal thinks fit as to payment of costs.

(5)   Where by virtue of subsection (4)(e) an order contains provision for any of the matters mentioned in section 47(2E)(c), section 47(2F) and (2G) apply as if the order had been made under section 47(2E)(c).

(6)   An appeal from the Tribunal shall lie to the High Court, at the instance of the Society or the person in respect of whom the order of the Tribunal was made.

(7)   The High Court shall have power to make such order on an appeal under this section as it may think fit.

(8)   Any decision of the High Court on an appeal under this section shall be final.

(9)   This section is without prejudice to any power conferred on the Tribunal in connection with an application or complaint made to it.

45

[*repealed*]

Disciplinary proceedings before Solicitors Disciplinary Tribunal

46 Solicitors Disciplinary Tribunal

(1) Applications and complaints made by virtue of any provision of this Act shall be made, except so far as other provision is made by this Act or by any regulations under it, to the tribunal known as the "Solicitors Disciplinary Tribunal".

(2) The Master of the Rolls shall appoint the members of the Tribunal.

(3) The Tribunal shall consist—

(a) of practising solicitors of not less than ten years' standing (in this section referred to as "solicitor members"); and

(b) of persons who are neither solicitors nor barristers (in this section referred to as "lay members").

(4) A member of the Tribunal shall hold and vacate his office in accordance with the terms of his appointment and shall, on ceasing to hold office, be eligible for re-appointment.

(5) The Tribunal may pay its members such remuneration, fees or allowances as it may determine with the approval of the Legal Services Board.

(5A) The Tribunal may do anything calculated to facilitate, or incidental or conducive to, the carrying out of any of its functions.

(6) [*repealed*]

(7) [*repealed*]

(8) [*repealed*]

(9) The Tribunal may make rules—

(a) empowering the Tribunal to elect a solicitor member to be its president; and

(b) about the procedure and practice to be followed in relation to the making, hearing and determination of applications and complaints (including provision about the composition of the Tribunal).

(10) Without prejudice to the generality of subsection (9)(b), rules made by virtue of that paragraph may in particular—

(a) empower the president of the Tribunal to appoint a chairman for the hearing and determination of any application or complaint;

(b) provide that, if the president does not appoint a chairman, a solicitor member shall act as chairman; and

(c) provide, in relation to any application or complaint relating to a solicitor, that, where in the opinion of the Tribunal no prima facie case in favour of the applicant or complainant is shown in the application or complaint, the Tribunal may make an order refusing the application or dismissing the complaint without requiring the solicitor to whom it relates to answer the allegations and without hearing the applicant or complainant.

(11) For the purposes of any application or complaint made to the Tribunal under this Act, the Tribunal may administer oaths, and the applicant or complainant and any person with respect to whom the application or complaint is made (or, in the case of an application under section 47(1)(b), any of the parties to the application) may issue writs of subpoena ad testificandum and duces tecum, but no person shall be compelled under any such writ to produce any document which he could not be compelled to produce on the trial of an action.

(12) The power to make rules conferred by subsection (9) shall be exercisable by statutory instrument, and the Statutory Instruments Act 1946 shall apply to a statutory instrument containing such rules in like manner as if the rules had been made by a Minister of the Crown.

46A Funding of the Tribunal

(1)   The Tribunal must submit to the Society in respect of each year a budget for the year approved by the Legal Services Board.

(2)   A budget for a year is a statement of the amount of money which the Tribunal estimates is required to enable it to meet all of its expenditure in that year (having regard to any amounts received but not spent in previous years).

(3)   Before approving a statement for the purposes of subsection (1) the Legal Services Board must consult the Society.

(4)   The budget for a year must be submitted to the Society under subsection (1) no later than the date in the preceding year specified by the Society for the purposes of this subsection.

(5)   Before specifying a date for this purpose the Society must consult the Tribunal.

(6)   The amount specified in a budget submitted under subsection (1) must be paid by the Society to the Tribunal—

    (a)   in such instalments and at such times as may be agreed between the Society and the Tribunal, or

    (b)   in the absence of such agreement, before the beginning of the year to which the budget relates.

(7)   The Society may pay the Tribunal such other amounts as the Society considers appropriate.

(8)   In this section "year" means a calendar year.

47 Jurisdiction and powers of Tribunal

(1)   Any application—

    (a)   to strike the name of a solicitor off the roll;

    (b)   to require a solicitor to answer allegations contained in an affidavit;

    (c)   to require a former solicitor whose name has been removed from or struck off the roll to answer allegations contained in an affidavit relating to a time when he was a solicitor;

    (d)   by a solicitor who has been suspended from practice for an unspecified period, by order of the Tribunal, for the termination of that suspension;

    (e)   by a former solicitor whose name has been struck off the roll to have his name restored to the roll;

    (f)   by a former solicitor in respect of whom a direction has been given under subsection (2)(g) to have his name restored to the roll,

shall be made to the Tribunal; but nothing in this subsection shall affect any jurisdiction over solicitors exercisable by the Master of the Rolls, or by any judge of the High Court, by virtue of section 50.

(2)   Subject to subsections (2E) and (3) and to section 54, on the hearing of any application or complaint made to the Tribunal under this Act, other than an application under section 43, the Tribunal shall have power to make such order as it may think fit, and any such order may in particular include provision for any of the following matters—

    (a)   the striking off the roll of the name of the solicitor to whom the application or complaint relates;

(b)   the suspension of that solicitor from practice indefinitely or for a specified period;

(c)   the payment by that solicitor or former solicitor of a penalty, which shall be forfeit to Her Majesty;

(d)   in the circumstances referred to in subsection (2A), the exclusion of that solicitor from criminal legal aid work (either permanently or for a specified period);

(e)   the termination of that solicitor's unspecified period of suspension from practice;

(f)   the restoration to the roll of the name of a former solicitor whose name has been struck off the roll and to whom the application relates;

(g)   in the case of a former solicitor whose name has been removed from the roll, a direction prohibiting the restoration of his name to the roll except by order of the Tribunal;

(h)   in the case of an application under subsection (1)(f), the restoration of the applicant's name to the roll;

(i)   the payment by any party of costs or a contribution towards costs of such amount as the Tribunal may consider reasonable.

(2A) An order of the Tribunal may make provision for the exclusion of a solicitor from criminal legal aid work as mentioned in subsection (2)(d) where the Tribunal determines that there is good reason for doing so arising out of—

(a)   his conduct, including conduct in the capacity of agent for another solicitor, in connection with the provision for any person of services provided under arrangements made for the purposes of Part 1 of the Legal Aid, Sentencing and Punishment of Offenders Act 2012; or

(b)   his professional conduct generally.

(2B) Where the Tribunal makes any such order as is referred to in subsection (2A) in the case of a solicitor who is a member of a firm of solicitors, the Tribunal may, if it thinks fit, order that any other person who is for the time being a member of the firm shall be excluded (either permanently or for a specified period) from criminal legal aid work.

(2C) The Tribunal shall not make an order under subsection (2B) unless an opportunity is given to him to show cause why the order should not be made.

(2D) Any person excluded from criminal legal aid work by an order under this section may make an application to the Tribunal for an order terminating his exclusion.

(2E) On the hearing of any complaint made to the Tribunal by virtue of section 34A(2) or (3), the Tribunal shall have power to make one or more of the following—

(a)   an order directing the payment by the employee to whom the complaint relates of a penalty to be forfeited to Her Majesty;

(b)   an order requiring the Society to consider taking such steps as the Tribunal may specify in relation to that employee;

(c)   if that employee is not a solicitor, an order which states one or more of the matters mentioned in paragraphs (a) to (c) of section 43(2);

(d)   an order requiring the Society to refer to an appropriate regulator any matter relating to the conduct of that employee.

(2F) Subsections (1) to (1C), (3) and (4) of section 44 apply in relation to an order under subsection (2E)(c) as they apply in relation to an order under section 43(2).

(2G) Section 44(2), paragraph 16(1)(d) and (1A)(d) of Schedule 2 to the Administration of Justice Act 1985 and paragraph 15(3A) of Schedule 14 to the Courts and Legal Services Act 1990 apply in relation to an order under subsection (2E)(c) as they apply in relation to an order under section 43(2).

(2H) For the purposes of subsection (2E)(d) an "appropriate regulator" in relation to an employee means—

(a)   if the employee is an authorised person in relation to a reserved legal activity (within the meaning of the Legal Services Act 2007), any relevant approved regulator (within the meaning of that Act) in relation to that employee, and

(b)   if the employee carries on activities which are not reserved legal activities (within the meaning of that Act), any body which regulates the carrying on of such activities by the employee.

(3)   On proof of the commission of an offence with respect to which express provision is made by any section of this Act, the Tribunal shall, without prejudice to its power of making an order as to costs, impose the punishment, or one of the punishments, specified in that section.

(3A) Where, on the hearing of any application or complaint under this Act, the Tribunal is satisfied that more than one allegation is proved against the person to whom the application or complaint relates it may impose a separate penalty (by virtue of subsection (2)(c)) with respect to each such allegation.

(3B) For the avoidance of doubt, nothing in this section permits the Tribunal to make an order requiring redress to be made in respect of any act or omission of any person.

(3C) In this section "criminal legal aid work" means the provision under arrangements made for the purposes of Part 1 of the Legal Aid, Sentencing and Punishment of Offenders Act 2012 of—

(a)   advice or assistance described in section 13 or 15 of that Act, or

(b)   representation for the purposes of criminal proceedings.

(4)   [*repealed*]

(5)   [*repealed*]

(6)   [*repealed*]

47A

[*repealed*]

48 Orders of Tribunal

(1)   An order of the Tribunal shall be filed with the Society, and a statement of the Tribunal's findings, signed by the chairman or by some other member of the Tribunal authorised by him in that behalf, shall either be prefaced to the order or added to the file containing the order as soon as may be after the order has been made.

(2)   Where an order which has been filed includes provision for any of the matters referred to in paragraphs (a) to (i) of section 47(2), the Society—

(a)   shall cause a note of the effect of the order to be entered on the roll against the name of the solicitor or former solicitor with respect to whom the application or complaint was made; and

(b)   except where it only makes provision for matters referred to in paragraph (e), (ea), (f), (h) or (i) of section 47(2), shall forthwith upon filing the order cause a notice stating its effect to be published.

(3)   Any file kept by the Society under this section may be inspected during office hours without payment.

(4)   An order which has been filed shall be treated, for the purpose of enforcement, as if it had been made by the High Court.

(5)   In the case of orders of the Tribunal under section 44E, the reference in subsection (2)(a) to the application or complaint is to be read as a reference to the Tribunal's order.

49 Appeals from Tribunal

(1)   An appeal from the Tribunal shall lie to the High Court.

(2)   Subject to subsection (3) and to section 43(5) of the Administration of Justice Act 1985, an appeal shall lie at the instance of the applicant or complainant or of the person with respect to whom the application or complaint was made.

(3)   An appeal against an order under section 43(3A) shall lie only at the instance of the person with respect to whom the order was made.

(4)   The High Court shall have power to make such order on an appeal under this section as it may think fit.

(5)   Subject to any rules of court, on an appeal against an order made by virtue of rules under section 46(10)(c) without hearing the applicant or complainant, the court—

(a)   shall not be obliged to hear the appellant, and

(b)   may remit the matter to the Tribunal instead of dismissing the appeal.

(6)   Any decision of the High Court—

(a)   on an application under section 43(3) or 47(1)(d), (e), (ea) or (f), or

(b)   against an order under section 43(3A),

shall be final.

(7)   [*repealed*]

49A Appeals to the Tribunal instead of the High Court

(1)   The Society may, with the approval of the Tribunal, make rules which provide that in such circumstances as may be prescribed by the rules an appeal under any of the provisions listed in subsection (2) lies to the Tribunal and not to the High Court.

(2)   Those provisions are—

(a)   section 8(4);

(b)   section 13A(6);

(c)   section 16(5);

(d)   section 28(3D);

(e)   section 41(3);

(f)   paragraph 14 of Schedule 14 to the Courts and Legal Services Act 1990 (foreign lawyers: appeals against conditions or refusals).

(3)   Any decision of the Tribunal on an appeal by virtue of rules made under this section shall be final.

Disciplinary proceedings before Senior Courts

50 Jurisdiction of Senior Courts over solicitors

(1)   Any person duly admitted as a solicitor shall be an officer of the Senior Courts.

(2)   Subject to the provisions of this Act, the High Court, the Crown Court and the Court of Appeal respectively, or any division or judge of those courts, may exercise the same jurisdiction in respect of solicitors as any one of the superior courts of law or equity from which the Senior Courts were constituted might have exercised immediately before the passing of the Supreme Court of Judicature Act 1873 in respect of any solicitor, attorney or proctor admitted to practise there.

(3)   An appeal shall lie to the Court of Appeal from any order made against a solicitor by the High Court or the Crown Court in the exercise of its jurisdiction in respect of solicitors under subsection (2).

51 Procedure upon certain applications to High Court

(1)   Where an application to strike the name of a solicitor off the roll or to require a solicitor to answer allegations contained in an affidavit is made to the High Court, then, subject to section 54, the following provisions of this section shall have effect in relation to that application.

(2)   The court shall not entertain the application except on production of an affidavit proving that the applicant has served on the Society fourteen clear days' notice of his intention to make the application, together with copies of all affidavits intended to be used in support of the application.

(3)   The Society may appear by counsel on the hearing of the application and any other proceedings arising out of or in reference to the application, and may apply to the court—

(a)   to make absolute any order nisi which the court may have made on the application;

(b)   to make an order that the name of the solicitor be struck off the roll; or

(c)   to make such other order as the court may think fit.

(4)   The court may order the costs of the Society of or relating to any of the matters mentioned in subsections (2) and (3) to be paid by the solicitor against whom, or by the person by whom, the application was made, or was intended to be made, or partly by one and partly by the other of them.

Disciplinary proceedings—general

54 Restrictions on powers to strike names off roll

(1)   No solicitor shall be liable to have his name struck off the roll on account of any failure to comply with the requirements with respect to persons seeking admission as solicitors of any training regulations or on account of any defect in his admission and enrolment, unless—

(a)   the application to strike his name off the roll is made within twelve months of the date of his enrolment; or

(b)   fraud is proved to have been committed in connection with the failure or defect.

(2)   No solicitor shall be liable to have his name struck off the roll by reason only—

(a)   that a solicitor who undertook a training responsibility for him under training regulations neglected or omitted to take out a practising certificate; or

(b)   that the name of a solicitor who undertook such a responsibility for a period has been removed from or struck off the roll after the end of that period.

55 Applications to require solicitor to answer allegations

For the avoidance of doubt it is hereby declared that an application by any person to require a solicitor to answer allegations contained in an affidavit, whether that application is made to the Tribunal or to the High Court, may be treated as an application to strike the name of that solicitor off the roll on the grounds of the matters alleged.

SCHEDULE 1
Intervention in Solicitor's Practice

Section 35

PART I
CIRCUMSTANCES IN WHICH SOCIETY MAY INTERVENE

1   (1)   Subject to sub-paragraph (2), the powers conferred by Part II of this Schedule shall be exercisable where—

(a)   the Society has reason to suspect dishonesty on the part of—

    (i)   a solicitor, or

    (ii)   an employee of a solicitor, or

    (iii)   the personal representatives of a deceased solicitor,

    in connection with that solicitor's practice or former practice or in connection with any trust of which that solicitor is or formerly was a trustee or that employee is or was a trustee in his capacity as such an employee;

(aa)   the Society has reason to suspect dishonesty on the part of a solicitor ("S") in connection with—

    (i)   the business of any person of whom S is or was an employee, or of any body of which S is or was a manager, or

    (ii)   any business which is or was carried on by S as a sole trader;

(b)   the Society considers that there has been undue delay on the part of the personal representatives of a deceased solicitor who immediately before his death was practising as a sole solicitor in connection with that solicitor's practice or in connection with any trust;

(c)   the Society is satisfied that a solicitor has failed to comply with rules made by virtue of section 31, 32 or 37(2)(c);

(d)   a solicitor has been made bankrupt or has made a composition or arrangement with his creditors;

(e)   a solicitor has been committed to prison in any civil or criminal proceedings;

(ee)   the Society is satisfied that a sole solicitor is incapacitated by illness, injury or accident to such an extent as to be unable to attend to his practice;

(f)   a solicitor lacks capacity (within the meaning of the Mental Capacity Act 2005) to act as a solicitor and powers under sections 15 to 20 or section 48 of that Act are exercisable in relation to him; or

(g)   the name of a solicitor has been removed from or struck off the roll or a solicitor has been suspended from practice;

(h)   the Society is satisfied that a solicitor has abandoned his practice;

(i)   [*repealed*]

(j)   any power conferred by this Schedule has been exercised in relation to a sole solicitor by virtue of sub-paragraph (1)(a) and he has acted as a sole solicitor within the period of eighteen months beginning with the date on which it was so exercised;

(k)   the Society is satisfied that a person has acted as a solicitor at a time when he did not have a practising certificate which was in force;

(l)   the Society is satisfied that a solicitor has failed to comply with any condition, subject to which his practising certificate was granted or otherwise has effect, to the effect that he may act as a solicitor only—

    (i)   in employment which is approved by the Society in connection with the imposition of that condition;

    (ii)   as a member of a partnership which is so approved;

    (iii)   as a manager of a body recognised by the Society under section 9 of the Administration of Justice Act 1985 and so approved; or

    (iv)   in any specified combination of those ways;

(m)   the Society is satisfied that it is necessary to exercise the powers conferred by Part 2 of this Schedule (or any of them) in relation to a solicitor to protect—

(i)   the interests of clients (or former or potential clients) of the solicitor or his firm, or

(ii)   the interests of the beneficiaries of any trust of which the solicitor is or was a trustee.

(1A) In sub-paragraph (1) "manager" has the same meaning as in the Legal Services Act 2007 (see section 207 of that Act).

(2)   *[repealed]*

2   On the death of a sole solicitor paragraphs 6 to 8 shall apply to the client accounts of his practice.

3   The powers conferred by Part II of this Schedule shall also be exercisable, subject to paragraphs 5(4) and 10(9), where—

(a)   the Society is satisfied that there has been undue delay—

(i)   on the part of a solicitor in connection with any matter in which the solicitor or his firm is or was acting on behalf of a client or with any trust, or

(ii)   on the part of an employee of a solicitor in connection with any trust of which the employee is or was a trustee in his capacity as such an employee; and

(b)   the Society by notice in writing invites the solicitor to give an explanation within a period of not less than 8 days specified in the notice; and

(c)   the solicitor fails within that period to give an explanation which the Society regards as satisfactory; and

(d)   the Society gives notice of the failure to the solicitor and (at the same or any later time) notice that the powers conferred by Part II of this Schedule are accordingly exercisable.

4   (1)   Where the powers conferred by Part II of this Schedule are exercisable in relation to a solicitor, they shall continue to be exercisable after his death or after his name has been removed from or struck off the roll.

(2)   The references to the solicitor or his firm in paragraphs 5(1), 6(2) and (3), 6A, 8, 9(1), (5) and (6) and 10(2) and (7) include, in any case where the solicitor has died, references to his personal representatives.

PART II
POWERS EXERCISABLE ON INTERVENTION

Money

5   (1)   The High Court, on the application of the Society, may order that no payment shall be made without the leave of the court by any person (whether or not named in the order) of any money held by him (in whatever manner and whether it was received before or after the making of the order) on behalf of the solicitor or his firm.

(2)   No order under this paragraph shall take effect in relation to any person to whom it applies unless the Society has served a copy of the order on him (whether or not he is named in it) and, in the case of a bank or other financial institution, has indicated at which of its branches the Society believes that the money to which the order relates is held.

(3)   A person shall not be treated as having disobeyed an order under this paragraph by making a payment of money if he satisfies the court that he exercised due diligence to ascertain whether it was money to which the order related but nevertheless failed to ascertain that the order related to it.

(4)   This paragraph does not apply where the powers conferred by this Part of this Schedule are exercisable by virtue of paragraph 3.

6   (1)   Without prejudice to paragraph 5, if the Society passes a resolution to the effect that any sums of money to which this paragraph applies, and the right to recover or receive them, shall vest in the Society, all such sums shall vest accordingly (whether they were received by the person holding them before or after the Society's resolution) and shall be held by the Society on trust to exercise in relation to them the powers conferred by this Part of this Schedule and subject thereto and to rules under paragraph 6B upon trust for the persons beneficially entitled to them.

(2)   This paragraph applies—

  (a)   where the powers conferred by this paragraph are exercisable by virtue of paragraph 1, to all sums of money held by or on behalf of the solicitor or his firm in connection with:

  (i)   his practice or former practice,

  (ii)   any trust of which he is or formerly was a trustee, or

  (iii)   any trust of which a person who is or was an employee of the solicitor is or was a trustee in the person's capacity as such an employee;

  (b)   where they are exercisable by virtue of paragraph 2, to all sums of money in any client account; and

  (c)   where they are exercisable by virtue of paragraph 3, to all sums of money held by or on behalf of the solicitor or his firm in connection with the trust or other matter in connection with which the Society is satisfied there has been undue delay as mentioned in sub-paragraph (a) of that paragraph.

(3)   The Society shall serve on the solicitor or his firm and on any other person having possession of sums of money to which this paragraph applies a certified copy of the Council's resolution and a notice prohibiting the payment out of any such sums of money.

(4)   Within 8 days of the service of a notice under sub-paragraph (3), the person on whom it was served, on giving not less than 48 hours' notice in writing to the Society and (if the notice gives the name of the solicitor instructed by the Society) to that solicitor, may apply to the High Court for an order directing the Society to withdraw the notice.

(5)   If the court makes such an order, it shall have power also to make such other order with respect to the matter as it may think fit.

(6)   If any person on whom a notice has been served under sub-paragraph (3) pays out sums of money at a time when such payment is prohibited by the notice, he shall be guilty of an offence and liable on summary conviction to a fine not exceeding level 3 on the standard scale.

6A   (1)   Without prejudice to paragraph 5, if the Society passes a resolution to the effect that any rights to which this paragraph applies shall vest in the Society, those rights shall vest accordingly.

(2)   This paragraph applies to any right to recover or receive debts due to the solicitor or his firm in connection with his practice or former practice.

(3)   Any sums recovered by the Society by virtue of the exercise of rights vested under sub-paragraph (1) shall vest in the Society and shall be held by it on trust to exercise in relation to them the powers conferred by this Part of this Schedule and, subject to those powers and to rules under paragraph 6B, upon trust for the persons beneficially entitled to them.

(4)   The Society shall serve on the solicitor or his firm, and any person who owes a debt to which the order applies, a certified copy of the Society's resolution.

6B (1)   The Society may make rules governing its treatment of sums vested in it under paragraph 6 or 6A(3).

(2)   The rules may in particular make provision in respect of cases where the Society, having taken such steps to do so as are reasonable in all the circumstances of the case, is unable to trace the person or persons beneficially entitled to any sum vested in the Society under paragraph 6 or 6A(3) (including provision which requires amounts to be paid into or out of compensation funds (within the meaning of section 36A)).

7   (1)   If the Society takes possession of any sum of money to which paragraph 6 or 6A(3) applies, the Society shall pay it into a special account in the name of the Society or of a person nominated on behalf of the Society, or into a client account of a solicitor nominated on behalf of the Society, and any such person or solicitor shall hold that sum on trust to permit the Society to exercise in relation to it the powers conferred by this Part of this Schedule and subject thereto and to rules under paragraph 6B on trust for the persons beneficially entitled to it.

(2)   A bank or other financial institution at which a special account is kept shall be under no obligation to ascertain whether it is being dealt with properly.

8   Without prejudice to paragraphs 5 to 7, if the High Court is satisfied, on an application by the Society, that there is reason to suspect that any person

(a)   holds money on behalf of the solicitor or his firm, or

(b)   has information which is relevant to identifying any money held by or on behalf of the solicitor or his firm,

the court may require that person to give the Society information as to any such money and the accounts in which it is held.

Documents

9   (1)   The Society may give notice to the solicitor or his firm requiring the production or delivery to any person appointed by the Society at a time and place to be fixed by the Society—

(a)   where the powers conferred by this Part of this Schedule are exercisable by virtue of paragraph 1, of all documents in the possession or under the control of the solicitor or his firm in connection with his practice or former practice or with any trust of which the solicitor is or was a trustee; and

(b)   where they are exercisable by virtue of paragraph 3, of all documents in the possession or under the control of the solicitor or his firm in connection with the trust or other matters of which the Society is satisfied (whether or not they relate also to other matters).

(2)   The person appointed by the Society may take possession of any such documents on behalf of the Society.

(3)   Except in a case where an application has been made to the High Court under sub-paragraph (4), if any person having possession or control of any such documents refuses, neglects or otherwise fails to comply with a requirement under sub-paragraph (1), he shall be guilty of an offence and liable on summary conviction to a fine not exceeding level 3 on the standard scale.

(4)   The High Court, on the application of the Society, may order a person required to produce or deliver documents under sub-paragraph (1) to produce or deliver them to any person appointed by the Society at such time and place as may be specified in the order, and authorise him to take possession of them on behalf of the Society.

(5)   If on an application by the Society the High Court is satisfied that there is reason to suspect that documents in relation to which the powers conferred by sub-paragraph (1) are exercisable have come into the possession or under the control of some person other than the

solicitor or his firm, the court may order that person to produce or deliver the documents to any person appointed by the Society at such time and place as may be specified in the order and authorise him to take possession of them on behalf of the Society.

(5A) In the case of a document which consists of information which is stored in electronic form, a requirement imposed by a notice under sub-paragraph (1) or an order under sub-paragraph (4) or (5), is a requirement to produce or deliver the information in a form in which it is legible or from which it can readily be produced in a legible form.

(6) On making an order under this paragraph, or at any later time, the court, on the application of the Society, may authorise a person appointed by the Society to enter any premises (using such force as is reasonably necessary) to search for and take possession of

(a)   any documents to which the order relates;

(b)   any property—

(i)   in the possession of or under the control of the solicitor or his firm, or

(ii)   in the case of an order under sub-paragraph (5), which was in the possession or under the control of such a person and has come into the possession or under the control of the person in respect of whom the order is made,

which the Society reasonably requires for the purpose of accessing information contained in such documents, and to use property obtained under paragraph (b) for that purpose.

(7) The Society, on taking possession of any documents or other property under this paragraph, shall serve upon the solicitor or personal representatives and upon any other person from whom they were received on the Society's behalf or from whose premises they were taken a notice that possession has been taken on the date specified in the notice.

(8) Subject to sub-paragraph (9) a person upon whom a notice under sub-paragraph (7) is served, on giving not less than 48 hours' notice to the Society and (if the notice gives the name of the solicitor instructed by the Society) to that solicitor, may apply to the High Court for an order directing the Society to deliver the documents or other property to such person as the applicant may require.

(9) A notice under sub-paragraph (8) shall be given within 8 days of the service of the Society's notice under sub-paragraph (7).

(10) Without prejudice to the foregoing provisions of this Schedule, the Society may apply to the High Court for an order as to the disposal or destruction of any documents or other property in its possession by virtue of this paragraph or paragraph 10.

(11) On an application under sub-paragraph (8) or (10), the Court may make such order as it thinks fit.

(12) Except so far as its right to do so may be restricted by an order on an application under sub-paragraph (8) or (10), the Society may take copies of or extracts from any documents in its possession by virtue of this paragraph or paragraph 10 and require any person to whom it is proposed that such documents shall be delivered, as a condition precedent to delivery, to give a reasonable undertaking to supply copies or extracts to the Society.

Mail and other forms of communication

10   (1)   The High Court, on the application of the Society, may from time to time make a communications redirection order.

(2)   A communications redirection order is an order that specified communications to the solicitor or his firm are to be directed, in accordance with the order, to the Society or any person appointed by the Society.

(3)   For the purposes of this paragraph—

(a)   "specified communications" means communications of such description as are specified in the order;

(b)   the descriptions of communications which may be so specified include—

    (i)   communications in the form of a postal packet;

    (ii)   electronic communications;

    (iii)   communications by telephone.

(4)   A communications redirection order has effect for such time not exceeding 18 months as is specified in the order.

(5)   Where a communications redirection order has effect, the Society or the person appointed by the Society may take possession or receipt of the communications redirected in accordance with the order.

(6)   Where a communications redirection order is made, the Society must pay to—

(a)   in the case of an order relating to postal packets, the postal operator concerned, and

(b)   in any other case, the person specified in the order,

the like charges (if any) as would have been payable for the redirection of the communications to which the order relates if the addressee had permanently ceased to occupy or use the premises or other destination of the communications and had applied to the postal operator or the specified person (as the case may be) to redirect the communications to him as mentioned in the order.

(7)   The High Court may, on the application of the Society, authorise the Society, or a person appointed by it, to take such steps as may be specified in the order in relation to any website purporting to be or have been maintained by or on behalf of the solicitor or his firm if the High Court is satisfied that the taking of those steps is necessary to protect the public interest or the interests of clients (or potential or former clients) of the solicitor or his firm.

(8)   In this paragraph "postal operator" and "postal packet" have the meaning given by section 27 of the Postal Services Act 2011.

(9)   This paragraph does not apply where the powers conferred by this Part of this Schedule are exercisable by virtue of paragraph 3.

Trusts

11   (1)   If the solicitor or his personal representative is a trustee of a trust, the Society may apply to the High Court for an order for the appointment of a new trustee in substitution for him.

(2)   The Trustee Act 1925 shall have effect in relation to an appointment of a new trustee under this paragraph as it has effect in relation to an appointment under section 41 of that Act.

General

12   The powers in relation to sums of money, documents and other property conferred by this Part of this Schedule shall be exercisable notwithstanding any lien on them or right to their possession.

13   Subject to any order for the payment of costs that may be made on an application to the court under this Schedule, any costs incurred by the Society for the purposes of this Schedule, including, without prejudice to the generality of this paragraph, the costs of any person exercising powers under this Part of this Schedule on behalf of the Society, shall be paid by the Solicitor or his personal representatives and shall be recoverable from him or them as a debt owing to the Society.

13A (1)   The High Court, on the application of the Society, may order a former partner of the solicitor to pay a specified proportion of the costs mentioned in paragraph 13.

(2)   The High Court may make an order under this paragraph only if it is satisfied that the conduct (or any part of the conduct) by reason of which the powers conferred by this Part were exercisable in relation to the solicitor was conduct carried on with the consent or connivance of, or was attributable to any neglect on the part of, the former partner.

(3)   In this paragraph "specified" means specified in the order made by the High Court.

14   Where an offence under this Schedule committed by a body corporate is proved to have been committed with the consent or connivance of, or to be attributable to any neglect on the part of, any director, manager, secretary or other similar officer of the body corporate or any person who was purporting to act in any such capacity, he, as well as the body corporate, shall be guilty of that offence and shall be liable to be proceeded against and punished accordingly.

15   Any application to the High Court under this Schedule may be disposed of in chambers.

16   The Society may do all things which are reasonably necessary for the purpose of facilitating the exercise of its powers under this Schedule.

Extracts from the Administration of Justice Act 1985

[With consolidated amendments to 31 December 2020.]

Administration of Justice Act 1985

1985 CHAPTER 61

An Act to make further provision with respect to the administration of justice and matters connected therewith; to amend the Solicitors Act 1974; to regulate the provision of solicitors' services in the case of incorporated practices; to regulate the provision of conveyancing services by persons practising as licensed conveyancers; to make further provision with respect to complaints relating to the provision of legal aid services; to amend the law relating to time limits for actions for libel and slander; and to make further provision with respect to arbitrations and proceedings in connection with European patents

[30th October 1985]

BE IT ENACTED by the Queen's most Excellent Majesty, by and with the advice and consent of the Lords Spiritual and Temporal, and Commons, in this present Parliament assembled, and by the authority of the same, as follows:–

Legal services bodies and sole solicitors' practices

9 Recognition of legal services bodies and of sole solicitors' practices

(1)   The Society may make rules—

    (a)   making provision as to the management and control of legal services bodies;

    (b)   prescribing the circumstances in which—

        (i)   legal services bodies may be recognised by the Society as being suitable bodies to undertake the provision of any solicitor services or other relevant legal services; and

        (ii)   sole solicitors' practices may be recognised by the Society as being suitable to undertake the provision of any such services;

    (c)   prescribing the requirements which (subject to any exceptions provided by the rules) must at all times be satisfied by bodies and sole solicitors' practices so recognised if they are to remain so recognised; and

    (d)   regulating the conduct of the affairs of such bodies and sole solicitors' practices.

(1A) Where the Society makes rules under subsection (1), it must by rules under subsection (1)(c) prescribe the requirement that (subject to any exceptions provided by the rules) recognised bodies and recognised sole solicitors' practices must not provide services other than—

    (a)   solicitor services, or

    (b)   solicitor services and other relevant legal services.

(1B) "Relevant legal services" means—

(a)   solicitor services, and

(b)   where authorised persons other than solicitors or registered European lawyers are managers or employees of, or have an interest in, a recognised body, or are employees in a recognised sole solicitor's practice, services of the kind provided by individuals practising as such authorised persons (whether or not those services involve the carrying on of reserved legal activities within the meaning of the Legal Services Act 2007).

(1C) The Society may by rules under this section provide that services specified, or of a description specified, in the rules are not to be treated as solicitor services or other relevant legal services.

(2)   Rules made by the Society may also make provision—

(a)   for the manner and form in which applications for recognition under this section, or for the renewal of such recognition, are to be made, and requiring such applications to be accompanied by a fee of such amount as the Society may from time to time determine;

(aa)   for the manner and form in which other applications under the rules are to be made, and requiring such applications to be accompanied by a fee of such amount as the Society may from time to time determine;

(ab)   requiring recognised bodies, recognised sole solicitors' practices or descriptions of such bodies or practices, to pay periodical fees of such amount as the Society may from time to time determine;

(b)   for regulating the names that may be used by recognised bodies or recognised sole solicitors' practices;

(c)   about the time when any recognition, or renewal of recognition, takes effect and the period for which it is (subject to the provisions made by or under this Part) to remain in force;

(d)   for the suspension or revocation of any such recognition, on such grounds and in such circumstances as may be prescribed by the rules;

(e)   about the effect on the recognition of a partnership or other unincorporated body ("the existing body") of any change in the membership of the existing body, including provision for the existing body's recognition to be transferred where the existing body ceases to exist and another body, or a sole solicitor's practice, succeeds to the whole or substantially the whole of its business;

(eza)   about the effect on the recognition of a sole solicitor's practice where the sole solicitor ceases to practise as a sole principal and—

(i)   another sole solicitor succeeds that sole solicitor as sole principal in the practice; or

(ii)   a body or another sole solicitor succeeds to the whole or substantially the whole of the practice's business;

(ea)   for the keeping by the Society of a register containing the names and places of business of all bodies and sole solicitors' practices which are for the time being recognised under this section, and such other information relating to them as may be specified in the rules;

(eb)   for information (or information of a specified description) on such a register to be made available to the public, including provision about the manner in which, and times at which, information is to be made so available;

(f)   for rules made under any provision of the 1974 Act to have effect in relation to recognised bodies or recognised sole solicitors' practices with such additions, omissions or other modifications as appear to the Society to be necessary or expedient;

(fa)   about the education and training requirements to be met by managers and employees of recognised bodies or employees in recognised sole solicitors' practices;

(fb)   for rules made under any provision of the 1974 Act to have effect in relation to managers and employees of recognised bodies or employees in recognised sole solicitors' practices with such additions, omissions or other modifications as appear to the Society to be necessary or expedient;

(fc)   requiring recognised bodies to appoint a person or persons to monitor compliance, by the recognised body, its managers and its employees, with requirements imposed on them by or by virtue of this Act or any rules applicable to them by virtue of this section;

(fd)   requiring the sole solicitor in a recognised sole solicitor's practice to appoint a person or persons to monitor compliance, by the sole solicitor and the employees in the practice, with requirements imposed on them by or by virtue of this Act, the 1974 Act or any rules applicable to them by virtue of this section or the 1974 Act;

(g)   [*repealed*]

(h)   for the manner of service on recognised bodies, or on sole solicitors in relation to recognised sole solicitors' practices, of documents authorised or required to be served under or by virtue of this Part.

(2ZA) Rules under subsection (2)(fd) may provide that the person appointed under that paragraph may be the sole solicitor.

(2A) If rules under this section provide for the recognition of legal services bodies which have one or more managers who are not legally qualified, the rules must make provision—

(a)   for the recognition of such bodies to be suspended or revoked, on such grounds and in such circumstances as may be prescribed by the rules;

(b)   as to the criteria and procedure for the Society's approving, as suitable to be a manager of a recognised body, an individual who is not legally qualified (and for the Society's withdrawing such approval).

(2B) Rules under this section may make provision for appeals to the High Court against decisions made by the Society under the rules—

(a)   to suspend or revoke the recognition of any body or sole solicitor's practice;

(b)   not to approve, as suitable to be the manager of a recognised body, an individual who is not legally qualified (or to withdraw such approval).

(2C) The rules may provide for appeals against decisions within subsection (2B)(b) to be brought by the individual to whom the decision relates (as well as the body).

(2D) In relation to an appeal under rules made by virtue of subsection (2B), the High Court may make such order as it thinks fit as to payment of costs.

(2E) The decision of the High Court on such an appeal shall be final.

(2F) Where the Society decides to recognise a body or a sole solicitor's practice under this section it must grant that recognition subject to one or more conditions if—

(a)   the case is of a kind prescribed for the purposes of this section by rules made by the Society, and

(b)   the Society considers that it is in the public interest to do so.

(2G) While a body or a sole solicitor's practice is recognised under this section, the Society—

(a)   must direct that the recognition is to have effect subject to one or more conditions if—

(i)   the case is of a prescribed kind, and

(ii)   the Society considers that it is in the public interest to do so;

(b)   may, in such circumstances as may be prescribed, direct that the recognition is to have effect subject to such conditions as the Society may think fit.

"Prescribed" means prescribed by rules made by the Society.

(2H) The conditions which may be imposed under subsection (2F) or (2G) include—

(a)   conditions requiring the body or the sole solicitor to take specified steps that will, in the opinion of the Society, be conducive to the carrying on of an efficient business;

(b)   conditions which prohibit the body or the sole solicitor from taking any specified steps except with the approval of the Society;

(c)   if rules under this section provide for the recognition of legal services bodies which have one or more managers who are not legally qualified, a condition that all the managers of the body must be legally qualified.

"Specified" means specified in the condition.

(2I) Rules made by the Society may make provision about when conditions imposed under this section take effect (including provision conferring power on the Society to direct that a condition is not to have effect until the conclusion of any appeal in relation to it).

(2J) Section 86A of the 1974 Act applies to rules under this section as it applies to rules under that Act.

(2K) Rules under this section may contain such incidental, supplemental, transitional or transitory provisions or savings as the Society considers necessary or expedient.

(3) Despite section 24(2) of the 1974 Act, section 20 of that Act (prohibition on unqualified person acting as solicitor) does not apply to a recognised body; and nothing in section 24(1) of that Act applies in relation to such a body.

(4) *[repealed]*

(5) A certificate signed by an officer of the Society and stating that any body or sole solicitor's practice is or is not, or was or was not at any time, recognised under this section shall, unless the contrary is proved, be evidence of the facts stated in the certificate; and a certificate purporting to be so signed shall be taken to have been so signed unless the contrary is proved.

(6) Schedule 2 (which makes provision with respect to the application of provisions of the 1974 Act to recognised bodies, with respect to other matters relating to such bodies, and with respect to matters relating to recognised sole solicitors' practices) shall have effect.

(7) Subject to the provisions of that Schedule, the Lord Chancellor may by order made by statutory instrument subject to annulment in pursuance of a resolution of either House of Parliament provide for any enactment or instrument passed or made before or in the same session as the Legal Services Act 2007 was passed and having effect in relation to solicitors to have effect in relation to recognised bodies with such additions, omissions or other modifications as appear to the Lord Chancellor to be necessary or expedient.

(8) In this section—

"the 1974 Act" means the Solicitors Act 1974;

"authorised person" means an authorised person in relation to an activity which is a reserved legal activity (within the meaning of the Legal Services Act 2007);

references to employment in a recognised sole solicitor's practice are references to employment by a sole solicitor for the purposes of a practice recognised under this section;

"the Society" has the meaning given by section 87(1) of the 1974 Act;

"legally qualified" and "legal services body" have the meaning given by section 9A;

"manager", in relation to a body, has the same meaning as in the Legal Services Act 2007 (see section 207 of that Act);

"recognised body" means a body for the time being recognised under this section;

"recognised sole solicitor's practice" means a sole solicitor's practice for the time being recognised under this section;

"registered European lawyer" means a person who is registered with the Law Society under regulation 17 of the European Communities (Lawyer's Practice) Regulations 2000, as that regulation has effect by virtue of regulation 6 of the Services of Lawyers and Lawyer's Practice (Revocation etc) (EU Exit) Regulations 2020;

"sole solicitor" has the meaning given by section 87(1) of the 1974 Act;

"solicitor services" means professional services such as are provided by individuals practising as solicitors or lawyers of other jurisdictions;

and a person has an interest in a body if the person has an interest in the body within the meaning of Part 5 of the Legal Services Act 2007 (see sections 72 and 109 of that Act).

(9)   [*repealed*]

9A Legal services bodies

(1)   For the purposes of section 9, a "legal services body" means a body (corporate or unincorporate) in respect of which—

(a)   the management and control condition, and

(b)   the relevant lawyer condition,

are satisfied.

(2)   The management and control condition is satisfied if—

(a)   at least 75% of the body's managers are legally qualified,

(b)   the proportion of shares in the body held by persons who are legally qualified is at least 75%,

(c)   the proportion of voting rights in the body which persons who are legally qualified are entitled to exercise, or control the exercise of, is at least 75%,

(d)   all the persons with an interest in the body who are not legally qualified are managers of the body, and

(e)   all the managers of the body who are not legally qualified are individuals approved by the Society as suitable to be managers of a recognised body.

(3)   The Society may by rules under section 9 provide that, in relation to specified kinds of bodies, subsection (2) applies as if the references to 75% were to such greater percentage as may be specified (and different percentages may be specified for different kinds of bodies).

(4)   The relevant lawyer condition is satisfied in relation to a body if at least one manager of the body is—

(a)   a solicitor,

(b)   a registered European lawyer, or

(c)   a qualifying body.

(5)   For that purpose a qualifying body is a body in respect of which—

(a)   the management and control condition is satisfied,

(b)   the relevant lawyer condition is satisfied by virtue of subsection (4)(a) or (b), and

(c)   the services condition is satisfied.

(6)   For the purposes of this section the following are legally qualified—

(a)   an authorised person who is an individual;

(b)   a registered foreign lawyer (within the meaning of section 89 of the Courts and Legal Services Act 1990 (c 41));

(c)   an advocate or solicitor in Scotland;

(ca)   a member of the Bar of Northern Ireland or a solicitor of the Court of Judicature of Northern Ireland;

(d)   an authorised person which is a body in respect of which—

(i)   the services condition is satisfied, and

(ii)   the management and control condition would be satisfied if the references in subsection (2) to persons who are legally qualified were to persons who are legally qualified by virtue of paragraphs (a) to (ca);

(e)   a body which provides professional services such as are provided by individuals who are authorised persons or lawyers of other jurisdictions, and in respect of which the management and control condition would be satisfied if the references in subsection (2) to persons who are legally qualified were to persons who are legally qualified by virtue of paragraphs (a) to (ca);

(f)   a legal partnership which—

(i)   was in existence immediately before the commencement of this paragraph,

(ii)   since that time has continued to be a partnership of the kind mentioned in rule 12.01(1)(b), 12.02(1)(b) or 12.04(1)(c)(i) of the pre-commencement conduct rules (framework of practice), and

(iii)   has not, since that time, had a body corporate (other than a body within paragraph (g)) as a member;

(g)   a body corporate which—

(i)   was recognised under section 9 immediately before the commencement of this paragraph, and

(ii)   has since that time continued to satisfy the requirements of rule 14.03(1) and 14.04(1) to (3) or the requirements of rule 14.05(1) to (3) of the pre-commencement conduct rules (restrictions on directors, owners etc of incorporated practices);

(h)   a body which—

(i)   is an authorised person and satisfies the services condition, or

(ii)   provides professional services such as are provided by individuals who are authorised persons or lawyers of other jurisdictions,

and which satisfies the requirements of rules under subsection (6C).

(6A) For the purposes of subsection (6)(f), a partnership is to be treated as the same partnership despite a change in membership, if any person who was a member before the change remains a member.

(6B) For the purposes of subsection (6)(f) and (g), the references in the pre-commencement conduct rules to a recognised body are to be construed as references to a body which was recognised under section 9 immediately before the commencement of subsection (6)(f) and (g).

(6C) The Society must make rules for the purposes of paragraph (h) of subsection (6) prescribing the requirements relating to management and control which must be satisfied by or in relation to a body for it to fall within that paragraph.

(7) For the purposes of this section, the services condition is satisfied in relation to a body if the body provides only services which may be provided by a recognised body (having regard to rules under section 9(1A) and (1C)).

(8) For the purposes of this section—

"authorised person" has the same meaning as in section 9;

"legal partnership" means a partnership in which a solicitor, a registered European lawyer or a recognised body is permitted to practise by virtue of rules made under section 31 of the Solicitors Act 1974 (c 47), as those rules had effect immediately before the commencement of subsection (6)(f);

"manager", in relation to a body, has the meaning given by section 9;

"pre-commencement conduct rules" means rules under Part 2 of the Solicitors Act 1974 or section 9 of this Act, known as the Solicitors' Code of Conduct 2007, as those rules had effect immediately before the commencement of subsection (6)(f) and (g);

"recognised body" has the same meaning as in section 9 (subject to subsection (6B) above);

"registered European lawyer" has the same meaning as in section 9;

"shares" has the same meaning as for the purposes of Part 5 of the Legal Services Act 2007 (see sections 72 and 109 of that Act);

"the Society" has the meaning given by section 87(1) of the Solicitors Act 1974;

"specified" means specified in rules made by the Society;

and a person has an interest in a body if the person has an interest in the body for the purposes of section 9.

10 Penalty for pretending to be a body recognised under s 9

(1) A body shall not describe itself or hold itself out as a body for the time being recognised under section 9 unless it is so recognised.

(2) Any body which contravenes subsection (1) shall be guilty of an offence and liable on summary conviction to a fine not exceeding the fourth level on the standard scale.

(3) Where an offence under this section committed by a body corporate is proved to have been committed with the consent or connivance of or to be attributable to any neglect on the part of an officer of the body corporate, that officer (as well as the body corporate) is guilty of the offence and is liable to be proceeded against and punished accordingly.

(4) Where the affairs of a body corporate are managed by its members, subsection (3) applies in relation to the acts and defaults of a member in connection with the member's functions of management as it applies to an officer of the body corporate.

(5) Proceedings for an offence under this section alleged to have been committed by an unincorporated body are to be brought in the name of that body (and not in that of any of its members) and, for the purposes of any such proceedings, any rules of court relating to the service of documents have effect as if that body were a corporation.

(6) A fine imposed on an unincorporated body on its conviction of an offence under this section is to be paid out of the funds of that body.

(7) If an unincorporated body is charged with an offence under this section, section 33 of the Criminal Justice Act 1925 (c 86) and Schedule 3 to the Magistrates' Courts Act 1980 (c 43) (procedure on charge of an offence against a corporation) have effect in like manner as in the case of a corporation so charged.

(8) Where an offence under this section committed by an unincorporated body (other than a partnership) is proved to have been committed with the consent or connivance of, or to be

attributable to any neglect on the part of, any officer of the body or any member of its governing body, that officer or member as well as the unincorporated body is guilty of the offence and liable to be proceeded against and punished accordingly.

(9)   Where an offence under this section committed by a partnership is proved to have been committed with the consent or connivance of, or to be attributable to any neglect on the part of, a partner, that partner as well as the partnership is guilty of the offence and liable to be proceeded against and punished accordingly.

(10) In this section "officer", in relation to a body corporate, means—

(a)   any director, secretary or other similar officer of the body corporate, or

(b)   any person who was purporting to act in any such capacity.

10A Penalty for sole solicitor pretending that practice is recognised

(1)   A sole solicitor shall not describe or hold out the sole solicitor's practice as a practice for the time being recognised under section 9 unless it is so recognised.

(2)   Any person who contravenes subsection (1) is guilty of an offence and liable on summary conviction to a fine not exceeding level 4 on the standard scale.

(3)   In this section "sole solicitor" has the same meaning as in section 9.

SCHEDULE 2
Legal services practices: Supplementary Provisions

Section 9

Interpretation

1   (1)   Subject to sub-paragraph (2), references in this Schedule to a recognised body or a recognised sole solicitor's practice are references to a body or sole solicitor's practice for the time being recognised under section 9 of this Act.

(2)   References in this Schedule to a recognised body or a recognised sole solicitor's practice in relation to—

(a)   a complaint (other than such a complaint as is mentioned in paragraph 16(1)(a));

(b)   [*repealed*]

include references to a body or sole solicitor's practice that was recognised under section 9 of this Act at the time when the conduct to which the complaint relates took place.

(2A) References in this Schedule to a manager or employee of a recognised body, or to an employee in a recognised sole solicitor's practice, in relation to a complaint (other than such a complaint as is mentioned in paragraph 16(1A)(a)), include references to a person who was such a manager or employee at the time when the conduct to which the complaint relates took place.

(2B) In this Schedule references to employment in a recognised sole solicitor's practice have the same meaning as in section 9.

(3)   [*repealed*]

(4)   In section 87(1) of the 1974 Act the definitions of "client", "contentious business" and "non-contentious business" shall apply for the purposes of this Schedule; and for the purposes of—

(a)   any provision of this Schedule in so far as it has effect in relation to a recognised body; and

(b)   any provision of the 1974 Act in so far as it has effect in relation to a recognised body by virtue of this Schedule, they shall apply as if for any reference to a solicitor there were substituted a reference to a recognised body.

(5) Subject to sub-paragraphs (4) and (6), any expression used in this Schedule which is also used in the 1974 Act has the same meaning as in that Act.

(6)   In this Schedule—

"manager", in relation to a body, has the same meaning as in the Legal Services Act 2007 (see section 207 of that Act);

"registered European lawyer" has the same meaning as in section 9A;

"the 1974 Act" means the Solicitors Act 1974.

Appeal against refusal of Society to grant recognition etc

2   (1)   A body may appeal to the High Court against—

(a)   a decision to refuse an application by the body for recognition under section 9;

(b)   a decision to impose a condition under subsection (2F) of that section on the body's recognition under that section;

(c)   a decision to impose a condition under subsection (2G) of that section on the body's recognition under that section.

(1A) A sole solicitor may appeal to the High Court against—

(a)   a decision to refuse an application for recognition of the solicitor's practice under section 9;

(b)   a decision to impose a condition under subsection (2F) of that section on the recognition of the solicitor's practice under that section; and

(c)   a decision to impose a condition under subsection (2G) of that section on the recognition of the solicitor's practice under that section.

(2)   A recognised body whose recognition is subject to a condition within section 9(2H)(b) may appeal to the High Court against any decision by the Society to refuse to approve the taking of any step for the purposes of that condition.

(2A) Where the recognition of a recognised sole solicitor's practice is subject to a condition within section 9(2H)(b), the sole solicitor may appeal to the High Court against any decision by the Society to refuse to approve the taking of any step for the purposes of that condition.

(3)   Rules made by the Society may make provision, as respects any application for recognition that is neither granted nor refused by the Society within such period as may be specified in the rules, for enabling an appeal to be brought under this paragraph in relation to the application as if it had been refused by the Society.

(4)   On an appeal under sub-paragraph (1)(a) or (b) or (1A)(a) or (b), the High Court may—

(a)   affirm the decision of the Society,

(b)   direct the Society to grant the body or sole solicitor's practice recognition under section 9 free from conditions or subject to such conditions as the High Court may think fit,

(c)   direct the Society not to recognise the body or sole solicitor's practice,

(d)   if the Society has recognised the body or sole solicitor's practice, by order suspend the recognition, or

(e)   make such other order as the High Court thinks fit.

(5)   On an appeal under sub-paragraph (1)(c) or (1A)(c), the High Court may—

(a)   affirm the decision of the Society,

(b)   direct that the recognition under section 9 is to have effect subject to such conditions as the High Court may think fit,

(c)   by order revoke the direction given by the Society under section 9(2G), or

(d)   make such other order as the High Court thinks fit.

(6)   On an appeal under sub-paragraph (2) or (2A), the High Court may—

(a)   affirm the decision of the Society,

(b)   direct the Society to approve the taking of one or more steps for the purposes of a condition within section 9(2H)(b), or

(c)   make such other order as the High Court thinks fit.

(7)   In relation to an appeal under this paragraph, the High Court may make such order as it thinks fit as to payment of costs.

(8)   The decision of the High Court on an appeal under this paragraph is final.

Accounts rules

3   (1)   This paragraph applies where rules made under section 32(1) of the 1974 Act are applied—

(a)   to recognised bodies in accordance with section 9(2)(f) of this Act, or

(b)   to managers or employees of such bodies in accordance with section 9(2)(fb) of this Act.

(2)   The Society may disclose a report on or information about the accounts of a recognised body, or a manager or employee of a recognised body, obtained in pursuance of such rules for use—

(a)   in investigating the possible commission of an offence by the body or any of its managers or employees, and

(b)   in connection with any prosecution of the body or any of its managers or employees consequent on the investigation.

Interest on clients' money

4   (1)   Where rules made under section 32 of the 1974 Act and containing any such provision as is referred to in section 33(1) of that Act are applied to recognised bodies in accordance with section 9(2)(f) of this Act, then, except as provided by the rules, a recognised body is not liable to account to any client, other person or trust for interest received by the recognised body on money held at a bank or building society in an account which is for money received or held for, or on account of—

(a)   clients of the recognised body, other persons or trusts, generally, or

(b)   that client, person or trust separately.

(2)   *[repealed]*

4ZA   Where rules made under section 32 of the 1974 Act and containing any such provision as is referred to in section 33(1) of that Act are applied to managers or employees of recognised bodies in accordance with section 9(2)(fb), then, except as provided by the rules, a manager or employee to whom the rules are applied is not liable to account to any client, other person or trust for interest received by the manager or employee on money held at a bank or building society in an account which is for money received or held for, or on account of—

(a)   clients of the recognised body, other persons or trusts, generally, or

(b)   that client, person or trust, separately.

Inspection of bank accounts

4A (1)   This paragraph applies where rules made under section 33A(1) of the 1974 Act are applied—

(a)   to recognised bodies in accordance with section 9(2)(f) of this Act, or

(b)   to managers or employees of such bodies in accordance with section 9(2)(fb) of this Act.

(2)   The Society may disclose information about the accounts of a recognised body, or a manager or employee of a recognised body, obtained in pursuance of such rules for use—

(a)   in investigating the possible commission of an offence by the body or any of its managers or employees, and

(b)   in connection with any prosecution of the body or any of its managers or employees consequent on the investigation.

Accountants' reports

5   Where rules made under section 34 of the 1974 Act are applied to recognised bodies in accordance with section 9(2)(f), section 34(9) and (10) of that Act apply in relation to a recognised body as they apply in relation to a solicitor.

5A   Where rules made under section 34 of the 1974 Act are applied to managers or employees of recognised bodies in accordance with section 9(2)(fb), section 34(9) and (10) of that Act apply in relation to a manager or employee to which the rules are applied as they apply in relation to a solicitor.

Compensation Fund

6   (1)   Section 36 of the 1974 Act applies in relation to recognised bodies as if for paragraphs (a) and (b) of subsection (1) there were substituted—

"(a)   an act or omission of a recognised body or former recognised body;

(b)   an act or omission of a manager or employee, or former manager or employee, of a recognised body or former recognised body;".

(2)   Section 36A(2) and (3) of the 1974 Act applies in relation to recognised bodies as it applies in relation to solicitors.

Solicitor who is justice of the peace not to act in certain proceedings

7   In section 38 of the 1974 Act references to any partner of a solicitor shall be construed, in relation to a solicitor who is a manager of a recognised body, as references to any other solicitor who is a manager of that body.

8   [*repealed*]

Restriction on employment of person struck off roll or suspended

9   (1)   Section 41 of the 1974 Act (except subsection (4)) shall apply to a recognised body (and any manager or employee of it) and its business as such as it applies to a solicitor and his practice as such.

(2)   No recognised body (or manager or employee of such a body) may, except in accordance with a written permission granted by the Society under this paragraph, permit a person to whom sub-paragraph (3) applies to—

(a)   be a manager of the body, or

(b)   have an interest in the body;

and for this purpose a person has an interest in the body if he has an interest in the body within the meaning of Part 5 of the Legal Services Act 2007 (see sections 72 and 109 of that Act).

(3) This sub-paragraph applies to a person who to the knowledge of the recognised body (or, as the case may be, the manager or employee) is a person—

(a) who is disqualified from practising as a solicitor by reason of one of the facts mentioned in section 41(1)(a), (b) or (c) of the 1974 Act (name struck off the roll, suspension etc), or

(b) in respect of whom there is a direction in force under section 47(2)(g) of that Act (prohibition on restoration to roll).

(4) Permission granted for the purposes of sub-paragraph (2) may be granted for such period and subject to such conditions as the Society thinks fit.

(5) A person aggrieved by the refusal of the Society to grant permission under sub-paragraph (4), or by any conditions attached by the Society to the grant of any such permission may appeal to the High Court which may—

(a) confirm the refusal or the conditions, as the case may be, or

(b) grant a permission under this paragraph for such period and subject to such conditions as it thinks fit.

(6) In relation to an appeal under sub-paragraph (5) the High Court may make such order as it thinks fit as to payment of costs.

(7) The decision of the High Court on an appeal under sub-paragraph (5) is final.

Failure to disclose fact of having been struck off or suspended

10 (1) Section 42(1) and (1A) of the 1974 Act shall apply in relation to employment by a recognised body (or any manager or employee of such a body) in connection with its business as it applies in relation to employment by a solicitor in connection with his practice.

(2) It is an offence for a person ("P") to whom sub-paragraph (3) applies—

(a) to seek or accept from any person an interest in a recognised body, without previously informing that person (and, if different, the recognised body) that P is a person to whom that sub-paragraph applies, or

(b) to seek or accept a position as a manager of a recognised body, without previously informing that body that P is such a person.

(3) This sub-paragraph applies to a person—

(a) who is disqualified from practising as a solicitor by reason of one of the facts mentioned in section 41(1)(a), (b) or (c) of the 1974 Act (name struck off the roll, suspension etc), or

(b) in respect of whom there is a direction in force under section 47(2)(g) of that Act (prohibition on restoration to roll).

(4) A person guilty of an offence under sub-paragraph (2) is liable on summary conviction to a fine not exceeding level 3 on the standard scale.

(5) Subsection (2) of section 42 of the 1974 Act applies in relation to an offence under sub-paragraph (2) as it applies in relation to an offence under that section.

(6) For the purposes of sub-paragraph (2)(a) a person seeks or accepts an interest in a recognised body if the person seeks or accepts an interest which if it were obtained by the person would result in the person having an interest in that body within the meaning of Part 5 of the Legal Services Act 2007 (see sections 72 and 109 of that Act).

11   [*repealed*]

12   [*repealed*]

13   [*repealed*]

Information about suitability for recognition

14   (1)   The Society may give a notice under this paragraph if it is satisfied that it is necessary to do so for the purpose of investigating whether—

(a)   a recognised body continues to be suitable to be recognised under section 9, or

(b)   a manager of a recognised body who is not legally qualified (within the meaning of section 9A) continues to be suitable to be a manager of a recognised body.

(2)   A notice under this paragraph is a notice which requires a person within sub-paragraph (3)—

(a)   to provide information, or information of a description, specified in the notice, or

(b)   to produce documents, or documents of a description, specified in the notice.

(3)   The persons are—

(a)   the recognised body;

(b)   an employee or manager of the recognised body;

(c)   a person who has an interest in the recognised body (within the meaning of the Legal Services Act 2007 (see sections 72 and 109 of that Act)).

(4)   For the purposes of this paragraph, section 44B(4) to (7) of the 1974 Act applies—

(a)   in relation to a notice under this paragraph as if it were a notice under section 44B of that Act, and

(b)   in relation to a person given a notice under this paragraph as if that person were a person given a notice under that section,

and references in subsections (6) and (7) of that section to powers conferred by that section are to be read as references to powers conferred by this paragraph.

(5)   Where powers conferred by Part 2 of Schedule 1 to the 1974 Act are exercisable in relation to a person within paragraph (a), (b) or (c) of sub-paragraph (3), they continue to be so exercisable after the person has ceased to be a person within the paragraph in question.

(6)   Section 44BA of the 1974 Act (power to require explanation of document or information) applies in relation to a notice under this paragraph and the person to whom such a notice is given as it applies in relation to a notice under section 44B of the 1974 Act and the person to whom such a notice is given.

(7)   Subsection (1) of section 44BC of that Act (falsification of documents etc) applies in relation to an investigation of the kind mentioned in sub-paragraph (1) as it applies in relation to the investigations mentioned in that subsection, and subsections (2), (4) and (5) of that section apply accordingly.

(8)   Subsection (3) of that section (provision of false information etc) applies in relation to a requirement imposed under this paragraph as it applies in relation to a requirement imposed by section 44B of that Act, and subsections (4) and (5) of that section apply accordingly.

14ZA   (1)   The Society may give a notice under this paragraph if it is satisfied that it is necessary to do so for the purpose of investigating whether a recognised sole solicitor's practice continues to be suitable to be recognised under section 9.

(2)   A notice under this paragraph is a notice which requires a person within sub-paragraph (3)—

(a)   to provide information, or information of a description, specified in the notice, or

(b)   to produce documents, or documents of a description, specified in the notice.

(3)   The persons are—

(a)   the sole solicitor; and

(b)   an employee in the recognised sole solicitor's practice.

(4)   For the purposes of this paragraph, section 44B(4) to (7) of the 1974 Act applies—

(a)   in relation to a notice under this paragraph as if it were a notice under section 44B of that Act, and

(b)   in relation to a person given a notice under this paragraph as if that person were a person given a notice under that section,

and references in subsections (6) and (7) of that section to powers conferred by that section are to be read as references to powers conferred by this paragraph.

(5)   Where powers conferred by Part 2 of Schedule 1 to the 1974 Act are exercisable in relation to a person within paragraph (a) or (b) of sub-paragraph (3), they continue to be so exercisable after the person has ceased to be a person within the paragraph in question.

(6)   Section 44BA of the 1974 Act (power to require explanation of document or information) applies in relation to a notice under this paragraph and the person to whom such a notice is given as it applies in relation to a notice under section 44B of the 1974 Act and the person to whom such a notice is given.

(7)   Subsection (1) of section 44BC of that Act (falsification of documents etc) applies in relation to an investigation of the kind mentioned in sub-paragraph (1) as it applies in relation to the investigations mentioned in that subsection, and subsections (2), (4) and (5) of that section apply accordingly.

(8)   Subsection (3) of that section (provision of false information etc) applies in relation to a requirement imposed under this paragraph as it applies in relation to a requirement imposed by section 44B of that Act, and subsections (4) and (5) of that section apply accordingly.

Power to charge for costs of investigation

14A (1)   The Society may make regulations prescribing charges to be paid to the Society by recognised bodies who are the subject of a discipline investigation or by the sole solicitor in a recognised sole solicitor's practice which is subject to a discipline investigation.

(2)   A discipline investigation is an investigation carried out by the Society into a failure or apprehended failure by a recognised body, or by a sole solicitor, or any employee, in a recognised sole solicitor's practice, to comply with any requirement imposed by or by virtue of this Act or any rules applicable to them by virtue of section 9.

(3)   Regulations under this paragraph may—

(a)   make different provision for different cases or purposes;

(b)   provide for the whole or part of a charge payable under the regulations to be repaid in such circumstances as may be prescribed by the regulations.

(4)   Any charge which a recognised body or a sole solicitor is required to pay under regulations under this paragraph is recoverable by the Society as a debt due to the Society from the recognised body or from that sole solicitor.

(5)   This paragraph applies in relation to a manager or employee of a recognised body as it applies in relation to a recognised body.

Disciplinary powers of the Society

14B (1)   This paragraph applies where the Society is satisfied that—

(a)   a recognised body, or a manager or employee of a recognised body, or

(b)   a sole solicitor, or any employee, in a recognised sole solicitor's practice, has failed to comply with a requirement imposed by or by virtue of this Act or any rules applicable to that person by virtue of section 9 of this Act.

(2)   The Society may do one or both of the following—

(a)   give the person a written rebuke;

(b)   direct the person to pay a penalty not exceeding £2,000.

(3)   The Society may publish details of any action it has taken under sub-paragraph (2)(a) or (b), if it considers it to be in the public interest to do so.

(4)   Where the Society takes action against a person under sub-paragraph (2)(b), or decides to publish under sub-paragraph (3) details of such action under sub-paragraph (2)(a) or (b), it must notify the person in writing that it has done so.

(5)   A penalty imposed under sub-paragraph (2)(b) does not become payable until—

(a)   the end of the period during which an appeal against the decision to impose the penalty, or the amount of the penalty, may be made under paragraph 14C, or

(b)   if such an appeal is made, such time as it is determined or withdrawn.

(6)   The Society may not publish under sub-paragraph (3) details of any action under sub-paragraph (2)(a) or (b)—

(a)   during the period within which an appeal against—

(i)   the decision to take the action,

(ii)   in the case of action under sub-paragraph (2)(b), the amount of the penalty, or

(iii)   the decision to publish the details,

may be made under paragraph 14C, or

(b)   if such an appeal has been made, until such time as it is determined or withdrawn.

(7)   The Society must make rules—

(a)   prescribing the circumstances in which the Society may decide to take action under sub-paragraph (2)(a) or (b);

(b)   about the practice and procedure to be followed by the Society in relation to such action;

(c)   governing the publication under sub-paragraph (3) of details of action taken under sub-paragraph (2)(a) or (b);

and the Society may make such other rules in connection with the exercise of its powers under this paragraph as it considers appropriate.

(8)   Before making rules under sub-paragraph (7), the Society must consult the Tribunal.

(9)   A penalty under this paragraph may be recovered as a debt due to the Society, and is to be forfeited to Her Majesty.

(10)   The Lord Chancellor may, by order, amend paragraph (b) of sub-paragraph (2) so as to substitute for the amount for the time being specified in that paragraph such other amount as may be specified in the order.

(11)   Before making an order under sub-paragraph (10), the Lord Chancellor must consult the Society.

(12)   An order under sub-paragraph (10) is to be made by statutory instrument subject to annulment in pursuance of a resolution of either House of Parliament.

(13)   This paragraph is without prejudice to any power conferred on the Society, or any other person, to make an application or complaint to the Tribunal.

14C (1) A person may appeal against—

(a) a decision by the Society to rebuke that person under paragraph 14B(2)(a) if a decision is also made to publish details of the rebuke;

(b) a decision by the Society to impose a penalty on that person under paragraph 14B(2)(b) or the amount of that penalty;

(c) a decision by the Society to publish under paragraph 14B(3) details of any action taken against that person under paragraph 14B(2)(a) or (b).

(2) Subsections (9)(b), (10)(a) and (b), (11) and (12) of section 46 of the 1974 Act (Tribunal rules about procedure for hearings etc) apply in relation to appeals under this paragraph as they apply in relation to applications or complaints, except that subsection (11) of that section is to be read as if for "the applicant" to "application)" there were substituted "any party to the appeal".

(3) Rules under section 46(9)(b) of the 1974 Act may, in particular, make provision about the period during which an appeal under this paragraph may be made.

(4) On an appeal under this paragraph, the Tribunal has power to make an order which—

(a) affirms the decision of the Society;

(b) revokes the decision of the Society;

(c) in the case of a penalty imposed under paragraph 14B(2)(b), varies the amount of the penalty;

(d) in the case of a recognised body, contains provision for any of the matters mentioned in paragraph 18(2);

(e) in the case of a manager or employee of a recognised body, or in the case of a sole solicitor, or an employee, in a recognised sole solicitor's practice, contains provision for any of the matters mentioned in paragraph 18A(2);

(f) makes such provision as the Tribunal thinks fit as to payment of costs.

(5) Where, by virtue of sub-paragraph (4)(e), an order contains provision for any of the matters mentioned in sub-paragraph (2)(c) of paragraph 18A, sub-paragraphs (5) and (6) of that paragraph apply as if the order had been made under sub-paragraph (2)(c) of that paragraph.

(6) An appeal from the Tribunal shall lie to the High Court, at the instance of the Society or the person in respect of whom the order of the Tribunal was made.

(7) The High Court shall have power to make such order on an appeal under this paragraph as it may think fit.

(8) Any decision of the High Court on an appeal under this section shall be final.

(9) This paragraph is without prejudice to any power conferred on the Tribunal in connection with an application or complaint made to it.

15 [*repealed*]

Complaints to Tribunal with respect to recognised bodies and recognised sole solicitors' practices

16 (1) The Tribunal shall have jurisdiction to hear and determine any of the following complaints made to it under this paragraph with respect to a recognised body, namely—

(a) a complaint that the body has (while a recognised body) been convicted by any court of a criminal offence which renders it unsuitable to be recognised under section 9 of this Act;

(b) a complaint that the body has failed to comply with any requirement imposed by or by virtue of this Act or with any rules applicable to it by virtue of section 9 of this Act;

(c) a complaint that the body has acted in contravention of section 41 of the 1974 Act or paragraph 9(2) of this Schedule or of any conditions subject to which a permission has been granted under section 41 of that Act or that paragraph of this Schedule; or

(d) a complaint that the body has knowingly acted in contravention of any such order as is mentioned in section 44(2) of the 1974 Act or of any conditions subject to which a permission has been granted under such an order.

(1A) The Tribunal shall have jurisdiction to hear and determine any of the following complaints made to it under this paragraph with respect to a manager or employee of a recognised body ("the relevant person")—

(a) a complaint that the relevant person has been convicted by any court of a criminal offence which renders that person unsuitable to be a manager or employee (or both) of a recognised body;

(b) a complaint that the relevant person has failed to comply with any requirement imposed by or by virtue of this Act or any rules applicable to the relevant person by virtue of section 9 of this Act;

(c) a complaint that the relevant person has acted in contravention of section 41 of the 1974 Act or paragraph 9(2) of this Schedule or of any conditions subject to which a permission has been granted under that section or for the purposes of paragraph 9(2) of this Schedule;

(d) a complaint that the relevant person has knowingly acted in contravention of an order under section 43(2) of the 1974 Act or of any conditions subject to which a permission has been granted under such an order.

(1B) The Tribunal has jurisdiction to hear and determine any of the following complaints made to it under this paragraph with respect to the sole solicitor, or an employee, in a recognised sole solicitor's practice ("the relevant person")—

(a) a complaint that the relevant person has been convicted by any court of a criminal offence which renders that person unsuitable to be the sole solicitor, or an employee, in a recognised sole solicitor's practice (or both);

(b) a complaint that the relevant person has failed to comply with any requirement imposed by or by virtue of this Act or any rules applicable to the relevant person by virtue of section 9 of this Act.

(2) A complaint may be made to the Tribunal under this paragraph by any person.

Procedure on applications and complaints

17 In subsections (9) to (11) of section 46 of the 1974 Act—

(a) any reference to an application or complaint shall be construed as including a reference to any such application as is mentioned in paragraph 21(1) or any such complaint as is mentioned in paragraph 16(1), (1A) or (1B);

(b) any reference to an application or complaint made under that Act shall be construed as including a reference to any such application or complaint as aforesaid made under this Schedule; and

(c) in the case of subsection (10)(c), any reference to a solicitor shall be construed as including a reference to a recognised body or, in the case of such a complaint as is mentioned in paragraph 16 (1A) or (1B), to a manager or employee of such a body or (as the case may be) to an employee in a recognised sole solicitor's practice.

Powers of Tribunal with respect to recognised bodies

18 (1)   Where on the hearing of any complaint made to it under this Schedule (other than paragraph 16(1A)) the Tribunal is satisfied that a recognised body—

    (a)   has been convicted as mentioned in paragraph (a) of paragraph 16(1); or

    (b)   has failed to comply with any requirement imposed by or by virtue of this Act or with any such rules as are mentioned in paragraph (b) of paragraph 16(1); or

    (c)   has acted as mentioned in paragraph (c) or (d) of that provision;

    (d)   [*repealed*]

the Tribunal may, if it thinks fit, make one or more of the orders referred to in sub-paragraph (2).

(2)   Those orders are—

    (a)   an order revoking the recognition under section 9 of this Act of the body to which the complaint relates;

    (b)   an order directing the payment by that body of a penalty, to be forfeited to Her Majesty;

    (c)   an order requiring that body to pay the costs incurred in bringing against it the proceedings before the Tribunal or a contribution towards those costs, being a contribution of such amount as the Tribunal considers reasonable.

(2A) Where, on the hearing of any application or complaint made to it under this Schedule, the Tribunal is satisfied that more than one allegation is proved against the recognised body to whom the application or complaint relates, it may impose a separate penalty (by virtue of sub-paragraph (2)(b)) with respect to each such allegation.

(3)   [*repealed*]

(4)   [*repealed*]

18A (1)   Where, on the hearing of any complaint made to it under paragraph 16(1A) or (1B) of this Schedule, the Tribunal is satisfied that a manager or employee of a recognised body, or the sole solicitor, or an employee, in a recognised sole solicitor's practice—

    (a)   has been convicted as mentioned in paragraph (a) of paragraph 16(1A) or (as the case may be) paragraph (a) of paragraph 16(1B),

    (b)   has failed to comply with any requirement imposed by or by virtue of this Act or any rules applicable to the relevant person by virtue of section 9 of this Act, or

    (c)   (in the case of a manager or employee of a recognised body) has acted as mentioned in paragraph (c) or (d) of paragraph 16(1A),

the Tribunal may, if it thinks fit, make one or more of the orders referred to in sub-paragraph (2).

(2)   Those orders are—

    (za)   in the case of a complaint relating to a sole solicitor, or an employee, in a recognised sole solicitor's practice, an order revoking the recognition under section 9 of this Act of the sole solicitor's practice;

    (a)   an order directing the payment by the relevant person of a penalty to be forfeited to Her Majesty;

    (b)   an order requiring the Society to consider taking such steps as the Tribunal may specify in relation to the relevant person;

    (c)   if the person is not a solicitor, an order which states one or more of the matters mentioned in sub-paragraph (3);

(d)   an order requiring the Society to refer to an appropriate regulator any matter relating to the conduct of the relevant person.

(3)   The matters referred to in sub-paragraph (2)(c) are—

(a)   that as from the specified date—

(i)   no solicitor or employee of a solicitor shall employ or remunerate, in connection with the practice carried on by that solicitor, the person with respect to whom the order is made, and

(ii)   no recognised body, or manager or employee of such a body, shall employ or remunerate that person, in connection with the business of the recognised body,

except in accordance with a Society permission;

(b)   that as from the specified date no recognised body or manager or employee of such a body shall, except in accordance with a Society permission, permit the person with respect to whom the order is made to be a manager of the body;

(c)   that as from the specified date no recognised body or manager or employee of such a body shall, except in accordance with a Society permission, permit the person with respect to whom the order is made to have an interest in the body.

(4)   For this purpose a person has an interest in a body if the person has an interest in the body within the meaning of Part 5 the Legal Services Act 2007 (see sections 72 and 109 of that Act).

(5)   Subsections (1) to (1C), (3) and (4) of section 44 of the 1974 Act (offences in connection with orders under section 43(2) of that Act) apply in relation to an order under sub-paragraph (2)(c) as they apply in relation to an order under section 43(2) of that Act, except that references in those subsections to provision within section 43(2)(a), (b) or (c) of that Act are to be read as references to provision within sub-paragraph (3)(a), (b) or (c).

(6)   Section 44(2) of the 1974 Act, paragraph 16(1)(d) and (1A)(d) of this Schedule and paragraph 15(3A) of Schedule 14 to the Courts and Legal Services Act 1990 apply in relation to an order under sub-paragraph (2)(c) as they apply in relation to an order under section 43(2) of the 1974 Act.

(7)   For the purposes of sub-paragraph (2)(d) an "appropriate regulator" in relation to the relevant person means—

(a)   if the person is an authorised person in relation to a reserved legal activity for the purposes of the Legal Services Act 2007, any relevant approved regulator (within the meaning of that Act) in relation to that person, and

(b)   if the person carries on activities which are not reserved legal activities, any body which regulates the carrying on of such activities by the person.

19   [*repealed*]

Powers of Tribunal in respect of legal aid complaints

20   (1)   Where the Tribunal makes any such order as is referred to in subsection (2A) of section 47 of the 1974 Act in the case of a solicitor who is a manager or employee of a recognised body, the Tribunal may, if it thinks fit, order that any solicitor who is for the time being a manager of that body shall be excluded (either permanently or for a specified period) from criminal legal aid work (as defined in that section).

(1A)   Where the Tribunal makes any such order as is referred to in section 47(2A) of the 1974 Act in the case of a solicitor who is an employee in a recognised sole solicitor's practice, the Tribunal may, if it thinks fit, order that any solicitor who is for the time being the sole solicitor in that practice shall be excluded (either permanently or for a specified period) from criminal legal aid work (as defined in that section).

(2) [*repealed*]

Revocation of recognition by reason of default by director

21 (1) Where—

(a)   any order is made by the Tribunal under section 47 of the 1974 Act in the case of a manager of a recognised body or of the sole solicitor in a recognised sole solicitor's practice; or

(b)   an order is made by the High Court or the Court of Appeal that the name of a manager of a recognised body, or of the sole solicitor in a recognised sole solicitor's practice, be struck off the roll or that such a manager or sole solicitor be suspended from practice as a solicitor; or

(c)   any such order as is mentioned in paragraph (a) or (b) is made in the case of a person employed by a recognised body and the act or omission constituting the ground on which the order was made was instigated or connived at by a manager of the recognised body or, if the act or omission was a continuing act or omission, a manager of the body had or reasonably ought to have had knowledge of its continuance, or

(d)   any such order as is mentioned in paragraph (a) or (b) is made in the case of a person employed in a recognised sole solicitor's practice and the act or omission constituting the ground on which the order was made was instigated or connived at by the sole solicitor, or, if the act or omission was a continuing act or omission, the sole solicitor had or reasonably ought to have had knowledge of its continuance,

the Tribunal may, on an application made with respect to the recognised body or the recognised sole solicitor's practice by or on behalf of the Society, by order revoke its recognition under section 9 of this Act.

(2)   The Tribunal shall not take a case into consideration during any period within which proceedings by way of appeal may be brought which may result in sub-paragraph (1) being rendered inapplicable in that case, or while any such proceedings are pending.

(3)   Any reference to a manager of a recognised body, or to a sole solicitor in a recognised sole solicitor's practice, in any of paragraphs (a) to (c) of sub-paragraph (1) includes a reference to a person who was a manager of the body, or the sole solicitor in the practice, at the time of the conduct leading to the making of the order referred to in that paragraph.

(4)   The reference in paragraph (c) of sub-paragraph (1) to a person employed by a recognised body, or in a sole solicitor's practice, includes a reference to a person who was so employed at the time of the conduct leading to the making of the order referred to in that paragraph.

Costs: general modification of provisions of Part III of 1974 Act

22 (1) In the provisions to which this paragraph applies—

(a)   any reference to a solicitor or to a client of a solicitor shall be construed as including a reference to a recognised body or to a client of such a body; and

(b)   any reference to a client's solicitor shall be construed as including a reference to any recognised body acting for a client.

(2)   This paragraph applies to the following provisions of the 1974 Act (which relate to the remuneration of solicitors in respect of contentious and non-contentious business), namely—

section 56 (except subsections (1)(e) and (5));

sections 57 to 59;

section 60 (except subsection (5));

sections 61 and 62;

sections 64 and 65;

section 67;

section 69(1); and

sections 70 to 74.

Orders as to remuneration for non-contentious business

23 (1)   In relation to an order under section 56 of the 1974 Act prescribing (by virtue of paragraph 22) general principles to be applied when determining the remuneration of recognised bodies in respect of non-contentious business, subsection (5) of that section shall have effect as if—

(a)   in paragraph (a), for "the solicitor" there were substituted "the recognised body"; and

(b)   in paragraph (d), the reference to the solicitor or any employee of the solicitor who is an authorised person were a reference to any manager or employee of the recognised body who is an authorised person.

(2)   In this paragraph "authorised person" means a person who is an authorised person in relation to an activity which is a reserved legal activity, within the meaning of the Legal Services Act 2007 (see section 18 of that Act).

Effect of contentious business agreements

24 (1)   This paragraph applies in relation to a contentious business agreement made between a recognised body and a client.

(2)   A provision in the agreement that the body shall not be liable for the negligence of any of its managers or employees shall be void if the client is a natural person who, in entering that agreement, is acting for purposes which are outside his trade, business or profession.

(3)   A provision in the agreement that the body shall be relieved from any responsibility to which it would otherwise be subject in the course of carrying on its business as a recognised body shall be void.

(4)   A provision in the agreement that any manager of the body shall be relieved from any responsibility to which the manager would otherwise be subject in the course of the carrying on by the body of its business as a recognised body shall be void.

Effect on contentious business agreement of supervening incapacity of recognised body to act for client

25 (1)   If, after some business has been done under a contentious business agreement made between a recognised body and a client but before the body has wholly performed it, the body ceases to be capable of wholly performing it by reason of one of the following events, namely—

(a)   the body ceases (for any reason) to be a recognised body;

(b)   a relevant insolvency event occurs in relation to the body; or

(c)   the client terminates the retainer or employment of the body in favour of another recognised body or a solicitor (as, notwithstanding the agreement, he shall be entitled to do),

any party to, or the representative of any party to, the agreement may apply to the court, and the court shall have the same jurisdiction as to enforcing the agreement so far as it has been performed, or setting it aside, as the court would have had if the recognised body were still capable of wholly performing it.

(2)   The court, notwithstanding that it is of the opinion that the agreement is in all respects fair and reasonable, may order the amount due in respect of business under the agreement to be ascertained by assessment, and in that case—

(a)   the costs officer, in ascertaining that amount, shall have regard so far as may be to the terms of the agreement; and

(b)   payment of the amount found by him to be due may be enforced in the same manner as if the agreement had been wholly performed.

(3)   If in such a case as is mentioned in sub-paragraph (1)(c) an order is made for the assessment of the amount due to the recognised body in respect of the business done under the agreement, the court shall direct the costs officer to have regard to the circumstances under which the termination of the body's retainer or employment has taken place, and the costs officer, unless he is of the opinion that there has been no default, negligence, improper delay or other conduct on the part of any manager or employee of the body affording the client reasonable ground for terminating its retainer or employment, shall not allow to the body the full amount of the remuneration agreed to be paid to it.

(4)   For the purposes of this paragraph a relevant insolvency event occurs in relation to a recognised body if—

(a)   a resolution for a voluntary winding-up of the body is passed without a declaration of solvency under section 89 of the Insolvency Act 1986;

(b)   the body enters administration within the meaning of paragraph 1(2)(b) of Schedule B1 to that Act;

(c)   an administrative receiver within the meaning of section 251 of that Act is appointed;

(d)   winding up becomes a creditors' voluntary winding up under section 96 of that Act (conversion to creditors' voluntary winding up);

(e)   an order for the winding up of the body is made.

Assessments with respect to contentious business

26   (1)   Subject to the provisions of any rules of court, on every assessment of costs in respect of any contentious business done by a recognised body, the costs officer may—

(a)   allow interest at such rate and from such time as he thinks just on money disbursed by the body for the client, and on money of the client in the possession of, and improperly retained by, the body or any manager or employee of the body; and

(b)   in determining the remuneration of the body, have regard to the skill, labour and responsibility on the part of any authorised person, being a manager or employee of the body, which the business involved.

(2)   In this paragraph "authorised person" means an authorised person, in relation to an activity which is a reserved legal activity, within the meaning of the Legal Services Act 2007.

Power of court to order delivery of bill of costs, etc.

27   Any jurisdiction—

(a)   of the High Court to make any such orders as are referred to in subsection (1) of section 68 of the 1974 Act in relation to a solicitor (whether or not business has been done by him in the High Court); or

(b)   of the county court or the family court to make any such orders as are referred to in subsection (2) of that section in relation to a solicitor,

shall be exercisable in like manner in relation to a recognised body.

Power of court to order recognised body to pay over clients' money

28   Any jurisdiction of the High Court to make, in the case of a solicitor who is acting or has acted as such for a client, an order requiring the payment or delivery up of, or otherwise relating to, money or securities which the solicitor has in his possession or control on behalf of the client shall be exercisable in like manner in the case of a recognised body which is acting or has acted as such for a client or any manager or employee of such a body.

Actions to recover costs

29 (1)   Subsection (2A) of section 69 of the 1974 Act shall have effect in relation to a bill of costs delivered by a recognised body as if for paragraphs (a) and (b) there were substituted—

"(a)   signed on behalf of the recognised body by any manager or employee of the body authorised by it to do so, or

(b)   enclosed in, or accompanied by, a letter which is so signed and refers to the bill."

(2)   Subsection (2E) of that section shall have effect in relation to such a bill as if for "the solicitor" there were substituted "the recognised body".

Power of Society to inspect files relating to certain proceedings

30   Section 83 of the 1974 Act shall apply in relation to proceedings which have been brought with respect to a recognised body for any of the following purposes, namely—

(a)   for the winding-up of the body;

(b)   for the appointment of an administrative receiver within the meaning of section 251 of the Insolvency Act 1986; or

(c)   for the appointment of an administrator under Schedule B1 to the Insolvency Act 1986,

as it applies in relation to proceedings in bankruptcy which have been taken against a solicitor.

Bank accounts

31   Where rules made under section 32(1) of the 1974 Act are applied to recognised bodies in accordance with section 9(2)(f) of this Act, section 85 of the 1974 Act shall apply in relation to a recognised body which keeps an account with a bank or building society in pursuance of any such rules as it applies in relation to a solicitor who keeps such an account in pursuance of rules under section 32.

31A Where rules made under section 32(1) of the 1974 Act are applied to managers or employees in accordance with section 9(2)(fb) of this Act, section 85 of the 1974 Act shall apply in relation to a manager or employee to whom the rules are applied who keeps an account with a bank or building society in pursuance of any such rules as it applies in relation to a solicitor who keeps such an account in pursuance of rules under section 32.

Intervention by Society

32 (1)   Subject to sub-paragraph (2), where—

(a)   the Society is satisfied that a recognised body or a manager of such a body has failed to comply with any rules applicable to the body or manager by virtue of section 9 of this Act; or

(b)   a person has been appointed receiver or manager of property of a recognised body; or

(c)   a relevant insolvency event occurs in relation to a recognised body; or

(d)   the Society has reason to suspect dishonesty on the part of any manager or employee of a recognised body in connection with—

      (i)   that body's business,

      (ii)   any trust of which that body is or was a trustee,

      (iii)   any trust of which the manager or employee is or was a trustee in his capacity as such a manager or employee, or

      (iv)   the business of another body in which the manager or employee is or was a manager or employee or the practice (or former practice) of the manager or employee; or

  (da)   the Society considers that there has been undue delay on the part of the personal representatives of a deceased solicitor who immediately before death was practising as the sole principal of a recognised body in connection with the recognised body's business or in connection with any trust; or

  (db)   the Society is satisfied that a solicitor practising as the sole principal of a recognised body is incapacitated by illness, injury or accident to such an extent as to be unable to attend to the solicitor's practice or to the recognised body's business; or

  (e)   the Society is satisfied that it is necessary to exercise the powers conferred by Part 2 of Schedule 1 to the 1974 Act (or any of them) in relation to a recognised body to protect—

      (i)   the interests of clients (or former or potential clients) of the recognised body,

      (ii)   the interests of the beneficiaries of any trust of which the recognised body is or was a trustee, or

      (iii)   the interests of the beneficiaries of any trust of which a person who is or was a manager or employee of the recognised body is or was a trustee in that person's capacity as such a manager or employee;

the powers conferred by Part II of Schedule 1 to the 1974 Act shall be exercisable in relation to the recognised body and its business in like manner as they are exercisable in relation to a solicitor and his practice.

(1A) For the purposes of this paragraph a relevant insolvency event occurs in relation to a recognised body if—

  (a)   a resolution for a voluntary winding-up of the body is passed without a declaration of solvency under section 89 of the Insolvency Act 1986;

  (b)   the body enters administration within the meaning of paragraph 1(2)(b) of Schedule B1 to that Act;

  (c)   an administrative receiver within the meaning of section 251 of that Act is appointed;

  (d)   a meeting of creditors is held in relation to the body under section 95 of that Act (creditors' meeting which has the effect of converting a members' voluntary winding up into a creditors' voluntary winding up);

  (e)   an order for the winding up of the body is made.

(2)   *[repealed]*

32A On the death of a solicitor practising as the sole principal of a recognised body, paragraphs 6 to 8 of Schedule 1 to the 1974 Act shall apply to the client accounts of the recognised body.

33   The powers conferred by Part II of Schedule 1 to the 1974 Act shall also be exercisable as mentioned in paragraph 32(1) of this Schedule where—

  (a)   the Society is satisfied that there has been undue delay—

      (i)   on the part of a recognised body in connection with any matter in which it is or was acting on behalf of a client or with any trust of which it is or was a trustee, or

    (ii)   on the part of a person who is or was a manager or employee of a recognised body in connection with any trust of which the manager or employee is or was a trustee in his capacity as such a manager or employee;

(b)   the Society by notice in writing invites the body to give an explanation within such period following the giving of the notice as may be specified in it, being a period of not less than eight days; and

(c)   the body fails within that period to give an explanation which the Society regards as satisfactory; and

(d)   the Society gives notice of the failure to the body and (at the same or any later time) notice that the powers conferred by Part II of Schedule 1 to the 1974 Act are accordingly exercisable in its case by virtue of this paragraph.

34 (1)   Where the recognition of a body under section 9 of this Act—

(a)   has been revoked in accordance with rules under that section or by an order of the Tribunal under this Schedule; or

(b)   has expired and no further recognition of that body has been granted under that section,

the powers conferred by Part II of Schedule 1 to the 1974 Act shall be exercisable in relation to the body and its former business as a recognised body as they are exercisable in relation to a solicitor and his practice.

(2)   Where the powers conferred by Part II of Schedule 1 to the 1974 Act are exercisable in relation to a recognised body in accordance with paragraph 32 or 33 of this Schedule they shall continue to be so exercisable after that body's recognition under section 9 of this Act has been revoked or has otherwise ceased to be in force.

35 In connection with the application of Part II of Schedule 1 to the 1974 Act for the purposes of this Schedule, in that Part of that Schedule—

(a)   any reference to the solicitor or to his practice shall be construed as including a reference to the body in relation to which the powers conferred by that Part of that Schedule are exercisable by virtue of paragraph 32, 32A, 33 or 34(1) of this Schedule or to its business (or former business) as a recognised body;

(b)   any reference to paragraph 1 of that Schedule shall be construed as including a reference to paragraph 32 or 34(1) of this Schedule;

(ba)   any reference to paragraph 2 of that Schedule shall be construed as including a reference to paragraph 32A of this Schedule;

(c)   any reference to paragraph 3 of that Schedule shall be construed as including a reference to paragraph 33 of this Schedule;

(d)   paragraph 6(2)(a) of that Schedule is to be construed as including a reference to sums of money held by or on behalf of the recognised body in connection with any trust of which a person who is or was a manager of the recognised body is or was a trustee in his capacity as such a manager;

(e)   paragraph 9 of that Schedule is to be construed—

    (i)   as if sub-paragraph (1) included a reference to documents in the possession or under the control of the recognised body in connection with any trust of which a person who is or was a manager or employee of the recognised body is or was a trustee in his capacity as such a manager or employee, and

    (ii)   as applying to such a manager or employee and documents and property in his possession or under his control in connection with such a trust as it applies to a solicitor and documents and property in the possession or under the control of the solicitor;

(f)   paragraph 11(1) of that Schedule is to be construed as including a power for the Society to apply to the High Court for an order for the appointment of a new trustee to a trust in substitution for a person who is a trustee, in his capacity as a manager or employee of the recognised body; and

(g)   paragraph 13A of that Schedule is to be read as if the references to a former partner were references—

(i)   in the case of a recognised body which is a partnership, to a former partner in the partnership, and

(ii)   in any other case to a manager or former manager of the recognised body.

Privilege from disclosure etc.

36   (1)   Where a recognised body acts as such for a client, any communication, document, material or information is privileged from disclosure in like manner as if the recognised body had at all material times been a solicitor acting for the client.

(2)   Any enactment or instrument making special provision in relation to a solicitor or other legal representative as to the disclosure of information, or as to the production, seizure or removal of documents, with respect to which a claim to professional privilege could be maintained shall, with any necessary modifications, have effect in relation to a recognised body as it has effect in relation to a solicitor.

(3)   In sections 748(4), 749 and 771(5) and (6) of the Income Tax Act 2007 and section 832(5) and (6) of the Corporation Tax Act 2010 any reference to a solicitor's client shall, in relation to a solicitor who is a manager or employee of a recognised body, be construed as a reference to a client of that body.

(4)   This paragraph does not apply to a recognised body which holds a licence under Part 5 of the Legal Services Act 2007 (alternative business structures).

Modification of enactments relating to conveyancing etc.

37   In the following provisions, namely—

(a)   sections 10(2), 48 and 182 of the Law of Property Act 1925;

(b)   [*repealed*]

(c)   section 12 of the Land Charges Act 1972;

(d)   section 13 of the Local Land Charges Act 1975;

any reference to a solicitor shall be construed as including a reference to a recognised body, and any reference to a person's solicitor shall be construed as including a reference to a recognised body acting for that person.

Extracts from the Courts and Legal Services Act 1990

[With consolidated amendments to 1 January 2010 and prospective amendments in section 89.]

Courts and Legal Services Act 1990

1990 CHAPTER 41

An Act to make provision with respect to the procedure in, and allocation of business between, the High Court and other courts; to make provision with respect to legal services; to establish a body to be known as the Lord Chancellor's Advisory Committee on Legal Education and Conduct and a body to be known as the Authorised Conveyancing Practitioners Board; to provide for the appointment of a Legal Services Ombudsman; to make provision for the establishment of a Conveyancing Ombudsman Scheme; to provide for the establishment of Conveyancing Appeal Tribunals; to amend the law relating to judicial and related pensions and judicial and other appointments; to make provision with respect to certain officers of the Supreme Court; to amend the Solicitors Act 1974; to amend the Arbitration Act 1950; to make provision with respect to certain loans in respect of residential property; to make provision with respect to the jurisdiction of the Parliamentary Commissioner for Administration in connection with the functions of court staff; to amend the Children Act 1989 and make further provision in connection with that Act; and for connected purposes

[1st November 1990]

BE IT ENACTED by the Queen's most Excellent Majesty, by and with the advice and consent of the Lords Spiritual and Temporal, and Commons, in this present Parliament assembled, and by the authority of the same, as follows:–

...

PART IV
SOLICITORS

89 Foreign lawyers: recognised bodies and partnerships with solicitors

(1)   The Law Society shall maintain a register of foreign lawyers for the purposes of this section.

(2)   A foreign lawyer who wishes to be registered under this section must apply to the Society in accordance with the requirements of Part I of Schedule 14.

(3)   The power to make rules under—

    (a)   the following provisions of the Solicitors Act 1974—

        (i)   section 31 (professional practice, conduct and discipline);

        (ii)   section 32 (accounts and trust accounts);

        (iii)   section 34 (accountants' reports);

(iv)   sections 36 and 36A (compensation grants); and

(v)   section 37 (professional indemnity); and

(b)   section 9 of the Administration of Justice Act 1985 (incorporated practices),

shall also be exercisable in relation to registered foreign lawyers.

(4)   Subject to the provisions of Schedule 14, any such power may be exercised so as to make different provision with respect to registered foreign lawyers to the provision made with respect to solicitors.

(5)   Subject to the provisions of Schedule 14, the Lord Chancellor may by order provide that any enactment or instrument—

(a)   passed or made before or in the same Session as the Legal Services Act 2007 was passed;

(b)   having effect in relation to solicitors; and

(c)   specified in the order,

shall have effect with respect to registered foreign lawyers as it has effect with respect to solicitors.

(6)   An order under subsection (5) may provide for an enactment or instrument to have effect with respect to registered foreign lawyers subject to such additions, omissions or other modifications as the Lord Chancellor sees fit to specify in the order.

(7)   Subject to the provisions of Schedule 14, the Lord Chancellor may by order provide that any enactment or instrument—

(a)   passed or made before or in the same Session as the Legal Services Act 2007 was passed;

(b)   having effect in relation to recognised bodies; and

(c)   specified in the order,

shall, in its application in relation to recognised bodies whose managers include one or more registered foreign lawyers, have effect with such additions, omissions or other modifications as the Lord Chancellor sees fit to specify in the order.

(8)   Schedule 14 shall have effect for the purposes of supplementing this section.

(8A) Rules and regulations made by the Law Society under, or by virtue of, this section or Schedule 14 which are not regulatory arrangements within the meaning of the Legal Services Act 2007 are to be treated as such arrangements for the purposes of that Act.

(9)   In this section and in Schedule 14—

"foreign lawyer" means a person who is not a solicitor or barrister but who is a member, and entitled to practise as such, of a legal profession regulated within a jurisdiction outside England and Wales;

"manager", in relation to a body, has the same meaning as in the Legal Services Act 2007 (see section 207 of that Act);

"multi-national partnership" means a partnership whose members consist of one or more registered foreign lawyers and one or more other lawyers as permitted by rules made under section 31 of the Solicitors Act 1974;

"recognised body" has the same meaning as in section 9 of the Administration of Justice Act 1985 (management and control by solicitors of incorporated practices); and

"registered foreign lawyer" means a foreign lawyer who is registered under this section.

SCHEDULE 14
Foreign Lawyers: Partnerships and Recognised Bodies

Section 89

PART I
REGISTRATION

General

1   In this Schedule—

"the Act of 1974" means the Solicitors Act 1974;

"the register" means the register maintained by the Society under section 89;

"registration" means registration in that register;

"the Society" means the Law Society; and

"the Tribunal" means the Solicitors Disciplinary Tribunal.

Application for registration

2   (1)   An application for registration or for renewal of registration—

(a)   shall be made to the Society in such form as the Society may prescribe; and

(b)   shall be accompanied by such fee as the Society may, with the concurrence of the Legal Services Board, prescribe.

(2)   Where such an application is duly made by a foreign lawyer, the Society may register the applicant if it is satisfied that the legal profession of which the applicant is a member is one which is so regulated as to make it appropriate for members of that profession to be managers of recognised bodies.

(3)   [*repealed*]

(4)   The Society may make regulations, with the concurrence of the Legal Services Board, with respect to—

(a)   the keeping of the register (including the form of the register and the manner in which entries are to be made, altered or removed); and

(b)   applications for registration or renewal of registration; and

(c)   the making available to the public of the information contained in the register (including the manner in which, and hours during which, the information is to be made so available and whether the information is to be made available free of charge).

(5)   [*repealed*]

2A   (1)   The Society may direct that a foreign lawyer's registration is to have effect subject to such conditions as the Society thinks fit to impose.

(2)   A direction under sub-paragraph (1) may be given in respect of a foreign lawyer

(a)   at the time he is first registered, or

(b)   at any time when the registration has effect.

Duration of registration

3   (1)   Every registration shall have effect from the beginning of the day on which it is entered in the register.

(2)   The Society may make regulations—

(a)   prescribing the date ("the renewal date") by which each registered foreign lawyer must apply for his registration to be renewed; and

(b)   requiring every entry in the register to specify the renewal date applicable to that registration.

(3) Any such regulations may—

  (a) provide different renewal dates for different categories of registered foreign lawyer or different circumstances;

  (b) provide for the Society to specify, in the case of individual registered foreign lawyers, different renewal dates to those prescribed by the regulations;

  (c) make such transitional, incidental and supplemental provision in connection with any provision for different renewal dates as the Society considers expedient.

(4) Where a foreign lawyer is registered, the Society may cancel his registration if—

  (a) the renewal date for his registration has passed but he has not applied for it to be renewed; or

  (b) he has applied to the Society for it to be cancelled.

Evidence as to registration

4 Any certificate purporting to be signed by an officer of the Society and stating that a particular foreign lawyer—

  (a) is, or is not, registered; or

  (b) was registered during a period specified in the certificate,

shall, unless the contrary is proved, be evidence of that fact and be taken to have been so signed.

PART II
REGISTERED FOREIGN LAWYERS: SUPPLEMENTARY PROVISIONS

Intervention in practices

5 (1) In this paragraph "the intervention powers" means the powers conferred by Part II of Schedule 1 to the Act of 1974 (intervention in solicitors' practices) as modified by this Schedule or under section 89.

(2) Subject to sub-paragraphs (3) and (4), the intervention powers shall be exercisable in relation to a person who is or has been a registered foreign lawyer and the practice of the multi-national partnership of which he is or was a member as they are exercisable in relation to a solicitor and his practice.

(3) The intervention powers are only exercisable where—

  (a) the Society has reason to suspect dishonesty on the part of the registered foreign lawyer, or on the part of an employee of the multi-national partnership, in connection with—

    (i) the practice of that partnership; or

    (ii) any trust of which the registered foreign lawyer is or was a trustee;

  (b) in the case of a registered foreign lawyer who has died, the Society has reason to suspect dishonesty on the part of his personal representative, in connection with—

    (i) the practice of the multi-national partnership; or

    (ii) any trust of which the registered foreign lawyer was a trustee;

  (ba) the Society has reason to suspect dishonesty on the part of the registered foreign lawyer ("L") in connection with—

    (i) the business of any person of whom L is or was an employee, or of any body of which L is or was a manager, or

    (ii) any business which is or was carried on by L as a sole trader;

(c)   the Society is satisfied that the registered foreign lawyer has failed to comply with rules made under section 32 or 37(2)(c) of the Act of 1974;

(d)   a bankruptcy order (as defined in paragraph 10(3)) has been made against him or he has made a composition or arrangement with his creditors;

(e)   he has been committed to prison in any civil or criminal proceedings;

(ea)   the Society is satisfied that he has abandoned his practice;

(f)   he lacks capacity (within the meaning of the Mental Capacity Act 2005) to act as a registered foreign lawyer and powers under sections 15 to 20 or section 48 are exercisable in relation to him;

(g)   his name has been struck off the register or his registration has been suspended or cancelled;

(h)   he has purported to act as a member of a multi-national partnership at a time when he was not registered;

(i)   the Society is satisfied that he has failed to comply with any condition, subject to which he is registered, to the effect that—

    (i)   he may only be a member of a partnership which is approved by the Society; or

    (ii)   he may only be a manager of a recognised body which is so approved; or

    (iii)   he may only be such a member or such a manager;

(j)   the Society is satisfied that it is necessary to exercise the intervention powers (or any of them) in relation to the registered foreign lawyer to protect—

    (i)   the interests of clients (or former or potential clients) of the registered foreign lawyer or the multi-national partnership, or

    (ii)   the interests of the beneficiaries of any trust of which the registered foreign lawyer is or was a trustee.

(4)   [*repealed*]

(5)   The intervention powers (other than those conferred by paragraphs 5 and 10 of Part II of Schedule 1 to the Act of 1974) shall also be exercisable where—

(a)   the Society is satisfied that there has been undue delay on the part of a registered foreign lawyer in connection with—

    (i)   any matter in which he, or the multi-national partnership of which he is or was a member, was instructed on behalf of a client; or

    (ii)   any trust;

(b)   the Society by notice invites the registered foreign lawyer to give an explanation within a period (of not less than 8 days) specified in the notice;

(c)   the registered foreign lawyer fails within that period to give an explanation which the Society regards as satisfactory; and

(d)   the Society gives notice of the failure to the registered foreign lawyer and notice that the intervention powers are accordingly exercisable.

(6)   Where the intervention powers are exercisable in relation to a registered foreign lawyer, they shall continue to be exercisable—

(a)   at any time when his registration is suspended;

(b)   after his name has been struck off the register or his registration has been cancelled; or

(c)   after his death.

APPENDIX 20

(7) Part II of Schedule 1 to the Act of 1974 shall have effect in relation to the intervention powers exercisable by virtue of this Schedule, subject to—

(a)   any express modifications made under section 89; and

(b)   any modifications necessary in the light of this paragraph.

(8)   For the purposes of this paragraph, Part II of Schedule 1 to the Act of 1974 shall be read with paragraph 4(2) of Part I of that Schedule.

(9)   The notices required to be given by this paragraph must be in writing but need not be given at the same time.

(10) In this paragraph "manager", in relation to a recognised body, has the same meaning as in the Legal Services Act 2007 (see section 207 of that Act).

The Compensation Fund

6   Section 36 of the 1974 Act applies in relation to registered foreign lawyers as if for paragraphs (a) and (b) of subsection (1) there were substituted—

"(a)   an act or omission of a registered foreign lawyer or former registered foreign lawyer;

(b)   an act or omission of an employee or former employee of a registered foreign lawyer or former registered foreign lawyer;".

Contributions to the Fund

7   Section 36A(2) and (3) of the 1974 Act applies in relation to registered foreign lawyers as it applies in relation to solicitors.

Accountants' reports

8   Section 34 of the Act of 1974 applies in relation to registered foreign lawyers as it applies in relation to solicitors.

9   [*repealed*]

Effect of bankruptcy

10   (1)   The registration of any foreign lawyer against whom a bankruptcy order is made shall be suspended on the making of that order.

(2)   The suspension of any registration by reason of a bankruptcy order shall terminate if the order is annulled and an office copy of the order annulling it is served on the Society.

(3)   In sub-paragraph (1), "bankruptcy order" includes any order which is not a bankruptcy order but which has the same, or a similar, effect under the law in force in any territory outside England and Wales.

Effect of disciplinary action

11   (1)   Where a registered foreign lawyer is struck off, or suspended from practice, his registration shall be suspended.

(2)   In sub-paragraph (1) "struck off" and "suspended from practice" mean—

(a)   any action taken within the jurisdiction by reference to which the registered foreign lawyer is qualified to be registered; or

(b)   where the registered foreign lawyer is qualified to be registered by reference to more than one jurisdiction, any action taken within any one of those jurisdictions, which is the equivalent, respectively, of a solicitor being struck off the roll or suspended from practice under the Act of 1974.

Re-instatement of disciplined foreign lawyer

12 (1)   Where a person's registration has been suspended by virtue of paragraph 11, it shall be revived—

(a)   if his right to practise in the jurisdiction in question is restored; and

(b)   a copy of the instrument restoring his right, certified to be a true copy by an officer of the appropriate court in the jurisdiction in question, or the professional body concerned, is served on the Society.

(2)   Where a person whose registration is suspended by virtue of paragraph 11 applies to the Society for the suspension to be terminated, the Society may terminate it subject to such conditions, if any, as it thinks fit to impose.

Effective date of revived registration

13   Where a foreign lawyer's registration is revived (whether as the result of the termination of its suspension, restoration by order of the Tribunal or for any other reason), that revival shall take effect on such date, and subject to such conditions, as the Society may direct.

Appeal against conditions or refusals

14 (1)   Any foreign lawyer may appeal to the High Court against—

(a)   the refusal of the Society to register him or to renew his registration;

(b)   the refusal of the Society to terminate the suspension of his registration on an application made by him under paragraph 12;

(c)   the failure of the Society to deal with any application by him for registration, renewal of registration or the termination (under paragraph 12(2)) of a suspension within a reasonable time;

(d)   any condition imposed by the Society under paragraph 2A, 12(2) or 13; or

(e)   a decision of the Society to remove his name from the register.

(2)   [*repealed*]

(3)   On an appeal under this paragraph, the High Court may make such order as it thinks fit.

(4)   In relation to an appeal under this paragraph the High Court may make such order as it thinks fit as to payment of costs.

(5)   The decision of the High Court on an appeal under this paragraph shall be final.

Jurisdiction and powers of Disciplinary Tribunal

15 (1)   Subject to paragraph 16, section 46 of the Act of 1974 (Solicitors Disciplinary Tribunal) shall apply, with the necessary modifications, in relation to applications and complaints made by virtue of any provision of this Schedule as it applies in relation to applications and complaints made by virtue of any provision of that Act.

(2)   Any application—

(a)   to strike the name of a foreign lawyer off the register;

(b)   to require a registered foreign lawyer to answer allegations in an affidavit;

(c)   to suspend the registration of a foreign lawyer for a specified or indefinite period;

 (d) by a foreign lawyer whose name has been struck off the register by order of the Tribunal to have his name restored to the register;

 (e) by a foreign lawyer whose registration has been suspended for an indefinite period by order of the Tribunal for the termination of that suspension,

shall be made to the Tribunal.

(3) Any person who alleges that a registered foreign lawyer has failed to comply with any rule made under section 31, 32, 34, or 37 of the Act of 1974 may make a complaint to the Tribunal.

(3A) Any person who alleges that a registered foreign lawyer has knowingly acted in contravention of any order under section 43(2) of the Act of 1974 or of any conditions subject to which a permission has been granted under such an order may make a complaint to the Tribunal.

(4) On the hearing of any application or complaint made to the Tribunal with respect to a foreign lawyer, the Tribunal shall have power to make such order as it may think fit, and any such order may in particular include provision for any of the following matters—

 (a) the striking off the register of the name of the foreign lawyer to whom the application or complaint relates;

 (b) the suspension of that foreign lawyer's registration indefinitely or for a specified period;

 (c) the payment by that foreign lawyer of a penalty, which shall be forfeit to Her Majesty;

 (d) the termination of that foreign lawyer's unspecified period of suspension from registration;

 (e) the restoration to the register of the name of a foreign lawyer which has been struck off the register;

 (f) the payment by any party of costs or a contribution towards costs of such amount as the Tribunal may consider reasonable.

(5) [*repealed*]

Foreign lawyers assisting the Tribunal

16 (1) For the purposes of section 46 of the Act of 1974 (Solicitors Disciplinary Tribunal), the Tribunal may make rules providing for it to be assisted, in dealing with any application or complaint of a kind mentioned in paragraph 15, by a member of the legal profession in the jurisdiction by reference to which the foreign lawyer is or was qualified to be registered.

(2) Rules under sub-paragraph (1) shall not be made without the concurrence of the Legal Services Board.

(3) Subsection (12) of section 46 of the Act of 1974 (rules to be made by statutory instrument etc) shall apply to rules made under this paragraph as it applies to rules made under subsection (9) of that section.

Appeals from Tribunal

17 (1) An Appeal from the Tribunal shall lie to the High Court.

(2) The High Court shall have power to make such order on an appeal under this paragraph as it may think fit.

(3) Any decision of the High Court on an appeal in the case of an order on an application under paragraph 15(2)(d) or (e), or the refusal of any such application, shall be final.

Extracts from the Legal Services Act 2007

[With consolidated amendments to 1 December 2020.]

Legal Services Act 2007

2007 CHAPTER 29

An Act to make provision for the establishment of the Legal Services Board and in respect of its functions; to make provision for, and in connection with, the regulation of persons who carry on certain legal activities; to make provision for the establishment of the Office for Legal Complaints and for a scheme to consider and determine legal complaints; to make provision about claims management services and about immigration advice and immigration services; to make provision in respect of legal representation provided free of charge; to make provision about the application of the Legal Profession and Legal Aid (Scotland) Act 2007; to make provision about the Scottish legal services ombudsman; and for connected purposes.

[30th October 2007]

Be it enacted by the Queen's most Excellent Majesty, by and with the advice and consent of the Lords Spiritual and Temporal, and Commons, in this present Parliament assembled, and by the authority of the same, as follows:—

PART 1
THE REGULATORY OBJECTIVES

1   The regulatory objectives

(1)   In this Act a reference to "the regulatory objectives" is a reference to the objectives of—

    (a)   protecting and promoting the public interest;

    (b)   supporting the constitutional principle of the rule of law;

    (c)   improving access to justice;

    (d)   protecting and promoting the interests of consumers;

    (e)   promoting competition in the provision of services within subsection (2);

    (f)   encouraging an independent, strong, diverse and effective legal profession;

    (g)   increasing public understanding of the citizen's legal rights and duties;

    (h)   promoting and maintaining adherence to the professional principles.

(2)   The services within this subsection are services such as are provided by authorised persons (including services which do not involve the carrying on of activities which are reserved legal activities).

(3)   The "professional principles" are—

    (a)   that authorised persons should act with independence and integrity,

(b)   that authorised persons should maintain proper standards of work,

(c)   that authorised persons should act in the best interests of their clients,

(d)   that persons who exercise before any court a right of audience, or conduct litigation in relation to proceedings in any court, by virtue of being authorised persons should comply with their duty to the court to act with independence in the interests of justice, and

(e)   that the affairs of clients should be kept confidential.

(4)   In this section "authorised persons" means authorised persons in relation to activities which are reserved legal activities.

PART 2
THE LEGAL SERVICES BOARD

Constitution

2   The Legal Services Board

(1)   There is to be a body corporate called the Legal Services Board ("the Board").

(2)   Schedule 1 is about the Board.

General functions

3   The Board's duty to promote the regulatory objectives etc

(1)   In discharging its functions the Board must comply with the requirements of this section.

(2)   The Board must, so far as is reasonably practicable, act in a way—

(a)   which is compatible with the regulatory objectives, and

(b)   which the Board considers most appropriate for the purpose of meeting those objectives.

(3)   The Board must have regard to—

(a)   the principles under which regulatory activities should be transparent, accountable, proportionate, consistent and targeted only at cases in which action is needed, and

(b)   any other principle appearing to it to represent the best regulatory practice.

4   Standards of regulation, education and training

The Board must assist in the maintenance and development of standards in relation to—

(a)   the regulation by approved regulators of persons authorised by them to carry on activities which are reserved legal activities, and

(b)   the education and training of persons so authorised.

5   Corporate governance

In managing its affairs, the Board must have regard to such generally accepted principles of good corporate governance as it is reasonable to regard as applicable to it.

6   Annual report

(1)   The Board must prepare a report ("the annual report") for each financial year.

(2)   The annual report must deal with—

(a)   the discharge of the Board's functions,

(b)   the extent to which, in the Board's opinion, the Board has met the regulatory objectives, and

(c)   such other matters as the Lord Chancellor may from time to time direct.

(3)   As soon as reasonably practicable after the end of each financial year, the Board must give the Lord Chancellor a copy of the annual report prepared for that year.

(4)   The Lord Chancellor must lay a copy of the annual report before Parliament.

(5)   In this section "financial year" means—

(a)   the period beginning with the day on which the Board is established and ending with the next following 31 March, and

(b)   each successive period of 12 months.

7 Supplementary powers

The Board may do anything calculated to facilitate, or incidental or conducive to, the carrying out of any of its functions.

8 The Consumer Panel

(1)   The Board must establish and maintain a panel of persons (to be known as "the Consumer Panel") to represent the interests of consumers.

(2)   The Consumer Panel is to consist of such consumers, or persons representing the interests of consumers, as the Board may appoint with the approval of the Lord Chancellor.

(3)   The Board must appoint one of the members of the Consumer Panel to be the chairman of the Panel.

(4)   The Board must secure that the membership of the Consumer Panel is such as to give a fair degree of representation to both—

(a)   those who are using (or are or may be contemplating using), in connection with businesses carried on by them, services provided by persons who are authorised persons in relation to activities which are reserved legal activities, and

(b)   those who are using (or are or may be contemplating using) such services otherwise than in connection with businesses carried on by them.

(5)   The Consumer Panel must not include any person who is—

(a)   a member of the Board or of its staff;

(b)   a member of the Office for Legal Complaints (see Part 6), an ombudsman appointed by it or a member of its staff appointed under paragraph 13 of Schedule 15;

(c)   a member of the governing body, or of the staff, of an approved regulator;

(d)   an authorised person in relation to an activity which is a reserved legal activity;

(e)   an authorised person (within the meaning given in section 31 of the Financial Services and Markets Act 2000 (authorised persons)) in relation to regulated claims management activity (within the meaning given by section 417(1) of that Act (definitions));

(f)   an advocate in Scotland;

(g)   a solicitor in Scotland;

(h)   a member of the Bar of Northern Ireland; or

(i)   a solicitor of the Court of Judicature of Northern Ireland.

(6)   The chairman and other members of the Consumer Panel are to be—

(a)   appointed for a fixed period, and on other terms and conditions, determined by the Board, and

(b)   paid by the Board in accordance with provision made by or under the terms of appointment.

APPENDIX 21

(7)   But a person may be removed from office in accordance with those terms and conditions only with the approval of the Lord Chancellor.

(8)   A person who ceases to be chairman or another member of the Consumer Panel may be re-appointed.

9   Committees and the procedure of the Consumer Panel

(1)   The Consumer Panel may make such arrangements as it thinks fit for committees established by the Panel to give advice to the Panel about matters relating to the carrying out of the Panel's functions.

(2)   The Consumer Panel may make such other arrangements for regulating its own procedure, and for regulating the procedure of the committees established by it, as it thinks fit.

(3)   Those arrangements may include arrangements as to quorums and as to the making of decisions by a majority.

(4)   The committees established by the Consumer Panel may include committees the membership of which includes persons who are not members of the Panel.

(5)   The membership of every committee established by the Consumer Panel must contain at least one person who is a member of the Panel.

(6)   Where a person who is not a member of the Consumer Panel is a member of a committee established by it, the Board may pay to that person such remuneration and expenses as the Board may determine.

10   Representations by the Consumer Panel

(1)   The Board must consider any representations made to it by the Consumer Panel.

(2)   If the Board disagrees with a view expressed, or proposal made, in the representations, it must give the Consumer Panel a notice to that effect stating its reasons for disagreeing.

(3)   The Consumer Panel may publish such information as it thinks fit about any representations made by it to the Board.

(4)   Where the Consumer Panel publishes information about any representations made by it, the Board must publish any notice it gives under subsection (2) in respect of those representations.

11   Advice and research functions of the Consumer Panel

(1)   The Consumer Panel may, at the request of the Board—

   (a)   carry out research for the Board;

   (b)   give advice to the Board.

(2)   The Board must consider any advice given and the results of any research carried out under this section.

(3)   The Consumer Panel may publish such information as it thinks fit about advice it gives, and about the results of research carried out by it, under this section.

PART 3
RESERVED LEGAL ACTIVITIES

Reserved legal activities

12   Meaning of "reserved legal activity" and "legal activity"

(1)   In this Act "reserved legal activity" means—

   (a)   the exercise of a right of audience;

   (b)   the conduct of litigation;

    (c)   reserved instrument activities;

    (d)   probate activities;

    (e)   notarial activities;

    (f)   the administration of oaths.

(2)   Schedule 2 makes provision about what constitutes each of those activities.

(3)   In this Act "legal activity" means—

    (a)   an activity which is a reserved legal activity within the meaning of this Act as originally enacted, and

    (b)   any other activity which consists of one or both of the following—

          (i)   the provision of legal advice or assistance in connection with the application of the law or with any form of resolution of legal disputes;

          (ii)   the provision of representation in connection with any matter concerning the application of the law or any form of resolution of legal disputes.

(4)   But "legal activity" does not include any activity of a judicial or quasi-judicial nature (including acting as a mediator).

(5)   For the purposes of subsection (3) "legal dispute" includes a dispute as to any matter of fact the resolution of which is relevant to determining the nature of any person's legal rights or liabilities.

(6)   Section 24 makes provision for adding legal activities to the reserved legal activities.

Carrying on the activities

13   Entitlement to carry on a reserved legal activity

(1)   The question whether a person is entitled to carry on an activity which is a reserved legal activity is to be determined solely in accordance with the provisions of this Act.

(2)   A person is entitled to carry on an activity ("the relevant activity") which is a reserved legal activity where—

    (a)   the person is an authorised person in relation to the relevant activity, or

    (b)   the person is an exempt person in relation to that activity.

(3)   Subsection (2) is subject to section 23 (transitional protection for non-commercial bodies).

(4)   Nothing in this section or section 23 affects section 84 of the Immigration and Asylum Act 1999 (c 33) (which prohibits the provision of immigration advice and immigration services except by certain persons).

Offences

14   Offence to carry on a reserved legal activity if not entitled

(1)   It is an offence for a person to carry on an activity ("the relevant activity") which is a reserved legal activity unless that person is entitled to carry on the relevant activity.

(2)   In proceedings for an offence under subsection (1), it is a defence for the accused to show that the accused did not know, and could not reasonably have been expected to know, that the offence was being committed.

(3)   A person who is guilty of an offence under subsection (1) is liable—

    (a)   on summary conviction, to imprisonment for a term not exceeding 12 months or a fine not exceeding the statutory maximum (or both), and

(b)   on conviction on indictment, to imprisonment for a term not exceeding 2 years or a fine (or both).

(4)   A person who is guilty of an offence under subsection (1) by reason of an act done in the purported exercise of a right of audience, or a right to conduct litigation, in relation to any proceedings or contemplated proceedings is also guilty of contempt of the court concerned and may be punished accordingly.

(5)   In relation to an offence under subsection (1) committed before the commencement of paragraph 24(2) of Schedule 22 to the Sentencing Act 2020, the reference in subsection (3)(a) to 12 months is to be read as a reference to 6 months.

15   Carrying on of a reserved legal activity: employers and employees etc

(1)   This section applies for the interpretation of references in this Act to a person carrying on an activity which is a reserved legal activity.

(2)   References to a person carrying on an activity which is a reserved legal activity include a person ("E") who—

(a)   is an employee of a person ("P"), and

(b)   carries on the activity in E's capacity as such an employee.

(3)   For the purposes of subsection (2), it is irrelevant whether P is entitled to carry on the activity.

(4)   P does not carry on an activity ("the relevant activity") which is a reserved legal activity by virtue of E carrying it on in E's capacity as an employee of P, unless the provision of relevant services to the public or a section of the public (with or without a view to profit) is part of P's business.

(5)   Relevant services are services which consist of or include the carrying on of the relevant activity by employees of P in their capacity as employees of P.

(6)   Where P is an independent trade union, persons provided with relevant services do not constitute the public or a section of the public where—

(a)   the persons are provided with the relevant services by virtue of their membership or former membership of P or of another person's membership or former membership of P, and

(b)   the services are excepted membership services.

(7)   Subject to subsection (8), "excepted membership services" means relevant services which relate to or have a connection with—

(a)   relevant activities of a member, or former member, of the independent trade union;

(b)   any other activities carried on for the purposes of or in connection with, or arising from, such relevant activities;

(c)   any event which has occurred (or is alleged to have occurred) in the course of or in connection with such relevant activities or activities within paragraph (b);

(d)   activities carried on by a person for the purposes of or in connection with, or arising from, the person's membership of the independent trade union;

and such other relevant services as the Lord Chancellor may by order specify.

(8)   The Lord Chancellor may by order make provision about the circumstances in which relevant services do or do not relate to, or have a connection with, the matters mentioned in paragraphs (a) to (d) of subsection (7).

(9)   Subject to that, the Lord Chancellor may by order make provision about—

(a)   what does or does not constitute a section of the public;

(b)   the circumstances in which the provision of relevant services to the public or a section of the public does or does not form part of P's business.

(10) The Lord Chancellor may make an order under subsection (7), (8) or (9) only on the recommendation of the Board.

(11) If P is a body, references to an employee of P include references to a manager of P.

(12) In subsection (7), "relevant activities", in relation to a person who is or was a member of an independent trade union, means any employment (including self-employment), trade, occupation or other activity to which the person's membership of the trade union relates or related.

16   Offence to carry on reserved legal activity through person not entitled

(1)   Where subsection (2) applies it is an offence for a person ("P") to carry on an activity ("the relevant activity") which is a reserved legal activity, despite P being entitled to carry on the relevant activity.

(2)   This subsection applies if—

(a)   P carries on the relevant activity by virtue of an employee of P ("E") carrying it on in E's capacity as such an employee, and

(b)   in carrying on the relevant activity, E commits an offence under section 14.

(3)   If P is a body, references in subsection (2) to an employee of P include references to a manager of P.

(4)   In proceedings for an offence under subsection (1), it is a defence for the accused to show that the accused took all reasonable precautions and exercised all due diligence to avoid committing the offence.

(5)   A person who is guilty of an offence under subsection (1) is liable—

(a)   on summary conviction, to imprisonment for a term not exceeding 12 months or a fine not exceeding the statutory maximum (or both), and

(b)   on conviction on indictment, to imprisonment for a term not exceeding 2 years or a fine (or both).

(6)   A person who is guilty of an offence under subsection (1) by reason of an act done in the purported exercise of a right of audience, or a right to conduct litigation, in relation to any proceedings or contemplated proceedings is also guilty of contempt of the court concerned and may be punished accordingly.

(7)   In relation to an offence under subsection (1) committed before the commencement of paragraph 24(2) of Schedule 22 to the Sentencing Act 2020, the reference in subsection (5)(a) to 12 months is to be read as a reference to 6 months.

17   Offence to pretend to be entitled

(1)   It is an offence for a person—

(a)   wilfully to pretend to be entitled to carry on any activity which is a reserved legal activity when that person is not so entitled, or

(b)   with the intention of implying falsely that that person is so entitled, to take or use any name, title or description.

(2)   A person who is guilty of an offence under subsection (1) is liable—

(a)   on summary conviction, to imprisonment for a term not exceeding 12 months or a fine not exceeding the statutory maximum (or both), and

(b)   on conviction on indictment, to imprisonment for a term not exceeding 2 years or a fine (or both).

(3) In relation to an offence under subsection (1) committed before the commencement of paragraph 24(2) of Schedule 22 to the Sentencing Act 2020, the reference in subsection (2)(a) to 12 months is to be read as a reference to 6 months.

18 Authorised persons

(1) For the purposes of this Act "authorised person", in relation to an activity ("the relevant activity") which is a reserved legal activity, means—

(a) a person who is authorised to carry on the relevant activity by a relevant approved regulator in relation to the relevant activity (other than by virtue of a licence under Part 5), or

(b) a licensable body which, by virtue of such a licence, is authorised to carry on the relevant activity by a licensing authority in relation to the reserved legal activity.

(2) A licensable body may not be authorised to carry on the relevant activity as mentioned in subsection (1)(a).

(3) But where a body ("A") which is authorised as mentioned in subsection (1)(a) becomes a licensable body, the body is deemed by virtue of this subsection to continue to be so authorised from that time until the earliest of the following events—

(a) the end of the period of 90 days beginning with the day on which that time falls;

(b) the time from which the relevant approved regulator determines this subsection is to cease to apply to A;

(c) the time when A ceases to be a licensable body.

(4) Subsection (2) is subject to Part 2 of Schedule 5 (by virtue of which licensable bodies may be deemed to be authorised as mentioned in subsection (1)(a) in relation to certain activities during a transitional period).

(5) A person other than a licensable body may not be authorised to carry on the relevant activity as mentioned in subsection (1)(b).

(6) But where a body ("L") which is authorised as mentioned in subsection (1)(b) ceases to be a licensable body, the body is deemed by virtue of this subsection to continue to be so authorised from that time until the earliest of the following events—

(a) the end of the period of 90 days beginning with the day on which that time falls;

(b) the time from which the relevant licensing authority determines this subsection is to cease to apply to L;

(c) the time when L becomes a licensable body.

19 Exempt persons

In this Act, "exempt person", in relation to an activity ("the relevant activity") which is a reserved legal activity, means a person who, for the purposes of carrying on the relevant activity, is an exempt person by virtue of—

(a) Schedule 3 (exempt persons), or

(b) paragraph 13 or 18 of Schedule 5 (additional categories of exempt persons during transitional period).

20 Approved regulators and relevant approved regulators

(1) In this Act, the following expressions have the meaning given by this section—

"approved regulator";

"relevant approved regulator".

(2) "Approved regulator" means—

    (a)   a body which is designated as an approved regulator by Part 1 of Schedule 4 or under Part 2 of that Schedule (or both) and whose regulatory arrangements are approved for the purposes of this Act, and

    (b)   if an order under section 62(1)(a) has effect, the Board.

(3) An approved regulator is a "relevant approved regulator" in relation to an activity which is a reserved legal activity if—

    (a)   the approved regulator is designated by Part 1, or under Part 2, of Schedule 4 in relation to that reserved legal activity, or

    (b)   where the approved regulator is the Board, it is designated in relation to that reserved legal activity by an order under section 62(1)(a).

(4) An approved regulator is a "relevant approved regulator" in relation to a person if the person is authorised by the approved regulator to carry on an activity which is a reserved legal activity.

(5) Schedule 4 makes provision with respect to approved regulators other than the Board.

In that Schedule—

    (a)   Part 1 designates certain bodies as approved regulators in relation to certain reserved legal activities,

    (b)   Part 2 makes provision for bodies to be designated by order as approved regulators in relation to one or more reserved legal activities, and

    (c)   Part 3 makes provision relating to the approval of changes to an approved regulator's regulatory arrangements.

(6) An approved regulator may authorise persons to carry on any activity which is a reserved legal activity in respect of which it is a relevant approved regulator.

…

PART 4
REGULATION OF APPROVED REGULATORS

Introductory

27 Regulatory and representative functions of approved regulators

(1) In this Act references to the "regulatory functions" of an approved regulator are to any functions the approved regulator has—

    (a)   under or in relation to its regulatory arrangements, or

    (b)   in connection with the making or alteration of those arrangements.

(2) In this Act references to the "representative functions" of an approved regulator are to any functions the approved regulator has in connection with the representation, or promotion, of the interests of persons regulated by it.

General duties of approved regulators

28 Approved regulator's duty to promote the regulatory objectives etc

(1) In discharging its regulatory functions (whether in connection with a reserved legal activity or otherwise) an approved regulator must comply with the requirements of this section.

(2) The approved regulator must, so far as is reasonably practicable, act in a way—

    (a)   which is compatible with the regulatory objectives, and

APPENDIX 21

(b)   which the approved regulator considers most appropriate for the purpose of meeting those objectives.

(3)   The approved regulator must have regard to—

(a)   the principles under which regulatory activities should be transparent, accountable, proportionate, consistent and targeted only at cases in which action is needed, and

(b)   any other principle appearing to it to represent the best regulatory practice.

...

Regulatory conflict

52   Regulatory conflict with approved regulators

(1)   The regulatory arrangements of an approved regulator must make such provision as is reasonably practicable to prevent regulatory conflicts.

(2)   For the purposes of this section and section 53, a regulatory conflict is a conflict between—

(a)   a requirement of the approved regulator's regulatory arrangements, and

(b)   a requirement of the regulatory arrangements of another approved regulator.

(3)   Subsection (4) applies where a body is authorised by an approved regulator ("the entity regulator") to carry on an activity which is a reserved legal activity.

(4)   If a conflict arises between—

(a)   a requirement of the regulatory arrangements of the entity regulator, in relation to the body authorised by the entity regulator or an employee or manager of the body ("an entity requirement"), and

(b)   a requirement of the regulatory arrangements of another approved regulator in relation to an employee or manager of the body who is authorised by it to carry on a reserved legal activity ("an individual requirement"),

the entity requirement prevails over the individual requirement.

...

PART 5
ALTERNATIVE BUSINESS STRUCTURES

Introductory

71   Carrying on of activities by licensed bodies

(1)   The provisions of this Part have effect for the purpose of regulating the carrying on of reserved legal activities and other activities by licensed bodies.

(2)   In this Act "licensed body" means a body which holds a licence in force under this Part.

72   "Licensable body"

(1)   A body ("B") is a licensable body if a non-authorised person—

(a)   is a manager of B, or

(b)   has an interest in B.

(2)   A body ("B") is also a licensable body if—

(a)   another body ("A") is a manager of B, or has an interest in B, and

(b)   non-authorised persons are entitled to exercise, or control the exercise of, at least 10% of the voting rights in A.

(3)   For the purposes of this Act, a person has an interest in a body if—

(a)   the person holds shares in the body, or

(b)   the person is entitled to exercise, or control the exercise of, voting rights in the body.

(4)   A body may be licensable by virtue of both subsection (1) and subsection (2).

(5)   For the purposes of this Act, a non-authorised person has an indirect interest in a licensable body if the body is licensable by virtue of subsection (2) and the non-authorised person is entitled to exercise, or control the exercise of, voting rights in A.

(6)   In this Act "shares" means—

(a)   in relation to a body with a share capital, allotted shares (within the meaning of the Companies Acts);

(b)   in relation to a body with capital but no share capital, rights to share in the capital of the body;

(c)   in relation to a body without capital, interests—

(i)   conferring any right to share in the profits, or liability to contribute to the losses, of the body, or

(ii)   giving rise to an obligation to contribute to the debts or expenses of the body in the event of a winding up;

and references to the holding of shares, or to a shareholding, are to be construed accordingly.

Licensing

84   Application for licence

(1)   A licensing authority other than the Board must determine any application for a licence which is made to it.

(2)   The Board (acting in its capacity as a licensing authority) may determine an application for a licence which is made to it only if the applicant is entitled to make the application by virtue of a decision of the Board (acting otherwise than in its capacity as a licensing authority) under Schedule 12.

(3)   A licensing authority may not grant an application for a licence unless it is satisfied that if the licence is granted the applicant will comply with its licensing rules.

(4)   If the licensing authority grants an application for a licence, it must issue the licence as soon as reasonably practicable.

(5)   The licence has effect from the date on which it is issued.

(6)   References in this section to an application for a licence are to an application for a licence which is—

(a)   made to a licensing authority by a licensable body, in accordance with the authority's licensing rules, and

(b)   accompanied by the required application fee (if any).

85   Terms of licence

(1)   A licence issued under section 84 must specify—

(a)   the activities which are reserved legal activities and which the licensed body is authorised to carry on by virtue of the licence, and

(b)   any conditions subject to which the licence is granted.

(2)   If an order under section 106 has been made in relation to the licensed body, the licence must also specify the terms of the order.

(3)   In the case of a licensing authority other than the Board, the licence may authorise the licensed body to carry on activities which are reserved legal activities only if the licensing authority is designated in relation to the reserved legal activities in question.

(4)   A licence must be granted subject to the condition that—

(a)   any obligation which may from time to time be imposed on the licensed body or a person within subsection (5) by or under the licensing authority's licensing rules is complied with, and

(b)   any other obligations imposed on the licensed body or a person within that subsection by or under this or any other enactment (whether passed before or after this Act) are complied with.

(5)   The persons mentioned in subsection (4) are the managers and employees of a licensed body, and non-authorised persons having an interest or an indirect interest, or holding a material interest, in the licensed body (in their capacity as such).

(6)   A licence may be granted subject to such other conditions as the licensing authority considers appropriate.

(7)   Those conditions may include conditions as to the non-reserved activities which the licensed body may or may not carry on.

(8)   In this Part references to the terms of the licence are to the matters listed in subsections (1) and (2).

86   Modification of licence

(1)   A licensing authority may modify the terms of a licence granted by it—

(a)   if the licensed body applies to the licensing authority, in accordance with its licensing rules, for it to do so;

(b)   in such other circumstances as may be specified in its licensing rules.

(2)   If a licensed body is a body to which section 106 applies, the licensing authority may modify the terms of its licence in accordance with sections 106 and 107.

(3)   A licensing authority modifies the terms of a licensed body's licence by giving the licensed body notice in writing of the modifications; and the modifications have effect from the time the licensing authority gives the licensed body the notice or such later time as may be specified in the notice.

(4)   The licensing authority's power under this section is subject to—

(a)   section 85(3) and (4), and

(b)   licensing rules made under paragraph 6 of Schedule 11.

…

Regulation of licensed bodies

…

93   Information

(1)   The relevant licensing authority in relation to a licensed body may by notice require a person within subsection (2)—

(a)   to provide information, or information of a description, specified in the notice, or

(b)   produce documents, or documents of a description, specified in the notice, for the purpose of enabling the licensing authority to ascertain whether the terms of the licensed body's licence are being, or have been, complied with.

(2)   The persons are—

(a)   the licensed body;

(b)   any manager or employee (or former manager or employee) of the licensed body;

(c)   any non-authorised person who has an interest or an indirect interest, or holds a material interest, in the licensed body.

(3)   A notice under subsection (1)—

(a)   may specify the manner and form in which any information is to be provided;

(b)   must specify the period within which the information is to be provided or the document produced;

(c)   may require the information to be provided, or the document to be produced, to the licensing authority or to a person specified in the notice.

(4)   The licensing authority may, by notice, require a person within subsection (2) (or a representative of such a person) to attend at a time and place specified in the notice to provide an explanation of any information provided or document produced under this section.

(5)   The licensing authority may pay to any person such reasonable costs as may be incurred by that person in connection with—

(a)   the provision of any information, or production of any document, by that person pursuant to a notice under subsection (1), or

(b)   that person's compliance with a requirement imposed under subsection (4).

(6)   The licensing authority, or a person specified under subsection (3)(c) in a notice, may take copies of or extracts from a document produced pursuant to a notice under subsection (1).

(7)   For the purposes of this section and section 94, references to a licensed body include a body which was, but is no longer, a licensed body.

94   Enforcement of notices under section 93

(1)   Where a person is unable to comply with a notice given to the person under section 93, the person must give the licensing authority a notice to that effect stating the reasons why the person cannot comply.

(2)   If a person refuses or otherwise fails to comply with a notice under section 93, the licensing authority may apply to the High Court for an order requiring the person to comply with the notice or with such directions for the like purpose as may be contained in the order.

95   Financial penalties

(1)   A licensing authority may, in accordance with its licensing rules, impose on a licensed body, or a manager or employee of a licensed body, a penalty of such amount as it considers appropriate.

(2)   The amount must not exceed the maximum amount prescribed under subsection (3).

(3)   The Board must make rules prescribing the maximum amount of a penalty which may be imposed under this section.

(4)   Rules may be made under subsection (3) only with the consent of the Lord Chancellor.

(5)   A penalty under this section is payable to the licensing authority.

(6)   For the purposes of this section—

(a)   references to a licensed body are to a body which was a licensed body at the time the act or omission in respect of which the penalty is imposed occurred, and

(b)   references to a manager or employee of a licensed body are to a person who was a manager or employee of a licensed body at that time,

(whether or not the body subsequently ceased to be a licensed body or the person subsequently ceased to be a manager or employee).

(7)   In sections 96 and 97 references to a "penalty" are to a penalty under this section.

96   Appeals against financial penalties

(1)   A person on whom a penalty is imposed under section 95 may, before the end of such period as may be prescribed by rules made by the Board, appeal to the relevant appellate body on one or more of the appeal grounds.

(2)   The appeal grounds are—

(a)   that the imposition of the penalty is unreasonable in all the circumstances of the case;

(b)   that the amount of the penalty is unreasonable;

(c)   that it is unreasonable of the licensing authority to require the penalty imposed or any portion of it to be paid by the time or times by which it was required to be paid.

(3)   On any such appeal, where the relevant appellate body considers it appropriate to do so in all the circumstances of the case and is satisfied of one or more of the appeal grounds, that body may—

(a)   quash the penalty,

(b)   substitute a penalty of such lesser amount as it considers appropriate, or

(c)   in the case of the appeal ground in subsection (2)(c), substitute for any time imposed by the licensing authority a different time or times.

(4)   Where the relevant appellate body substitutes a penalty of a lesser amount it may require the payment of interest on the substituted penalty at such rate, and from such time, as it considers just and equitable.

(5)   Where the relevant appellate body specifies as a time by which the penalty, or a portion of the penalty, is to be paid a time before the determination of the appeal under this section it may require the payment of interest on the penalty, or portion, from that time at such rate as it considers just and equitable.

(6)   A party to the appeal may appeal to the High Court on a point of law arising from the decision of the relevant appellate body, but only with the permission of the High Court.

(7)   The High Court may make such order as it thinks fit.

(8)   Except as provided by this section, the validity of a penalty is not to be questioned by any legal proceedings whatever.

97   Recovery of financial penalties

(1)   If the whole or any part of a penalty is not paid by the time by which, in accordance with licensing rules, it is required to be paid, the unpaid balance from time to time carries interest at the rate for the time being specified in section 17 of the Judgments Act 1838 (c. 110).

(2)   Where a penalty, or any portion of it, has not been paid by the time by which, in accordance with licensing rules, it is required to be paid and—

(a)   no appeal relating to the penalty has been made under section 96 during the period within which such an appeal can be made, or

(b)   an appeal has been made under that section and determined or withdrawn,

the licensing authority may recover from the person on whom the penalty was imposed, as a debt due to the licensing authority, any of the penalty and any interest which has not been paid.

(3)   A licensing authority must pay into the Consolidated Fund any sum received by it as a penalty (or as interest on a penalty).

98   Referral of employees etc to appropriate regulator

(1)   The relevant licensing authority may refer to an appropriate regulator any matter relating to the conduct of—

(a)   an employee or manager of a licensed body;

(b)   a person designated as a licensed body's Head of Legal Practice or Head of Finance and Administration.

(2)   The licensing authority may also refer any matter relating to the conduct of such a person to the Board.

(3)   Appropriate regulators are—

(a)   if the person is an authorised person in relation to a reserved legal activity, any relevant approved regulator in relation to that person, and

(b)   if the person carries on non-reserved activities, any person who exercises regulatory functions in relation to the carrying on of such activities by the person.

99   Disqualification

(1)   A licensing authority may in accordance with its licensing rules disqualify a person from one or more of the activities mentioned in subsection (2) if—

(a)   the disqualification condition is satisfied in relation to the person, and

(b)   the licensing authority is satisfied that it is undesirable for the person to engage in that activity or those activities.

(2)   The activities are—

(a)   acting as Head of Legal Practice of any licensed body,

(b)   acting as Head of Finance and Administration of any licensed body,

(c)   being a manager of any licensed body, or

(d)   being employed by any licensed body.

(3)   The disqualification condition is satisfied in relation to a person if, in relation to a licensed body licensed by the licensing authority, the person (intentionally or through neglect)—

(a)   breaches a relevant duty to which the person is subject, or

(b)   causes, or substantially contributes to, a significant breach of the terms of the licensed body's licence.

(4)   The relevant duties are—

(a)   the duties imposed on a Head of Legal Practice by section 91,

(b)   the duties imposed on a Head of Finance and Administration by section 92,

(c)   the duties imposed by section 176 on regulated persons (within the meaning of that section), and

(d)   the duty imposed on non-authorised persons by section 90.

…

APPENDIX 21

PART 6
LEGAL COMPLAINTS

Complaints procedures of authorised persons

112   Complaints procedures of authorised persons

(1)   The regulatory arrangements of an approved regulator must make provision requiring each relevant authorised person—

    (a)   to establish and maintain procedures for the resolution of relevant complaints, or

    (b)   to participate in, or make arrangements to be subject to, such procedures established and maintained by another person,

and provision for the enforcement of that requirement.

(2)   The provision made for the purposes of subsection (1) must satisfy such requirements as the Board may, from time to time, specify for the purposes of that subsection.

(3)   In this section—

    "relevant authorised person", in relation to an approved regulator, means a person in relation to whom the approved regulator is a relevant approved regulator;

    "relevant complaint", in relation to a relevant authorised person, means a complaint which—

        (a)   relates to an act or omission of that person, and

        (b)   may be made under the scheme provided for by this Part

(4)   The Board must publish any requirements specified by it for the purposes of subsection (2).

(5)   This section applies in relation to the licensing rules of the Board as it applies in relation to the regulatory arrangements of an approved regulator except that subsection (3) has effect as if for the definition of "relevant authorised person" there were substituted—

    "'relevant authorised person', in relation to the Board, means a person licensed by the Board under Part 5;".

Overview of the scheme

113   Overview of the scheme

(1)   This Part provides for a scheme under which complaints which—

    (a)   relate to an act or omission of a person ("the respondent") in carrying on an activity, and

    (b)   are within the jurisdiction of the scheme (see section 125),

may be resolved quickly and with minimum formality by an independent person.

(2)   Under the scheme—

    (a)   redress may be provided to the complainant, but

    (b)   no disciplinary action may be taken against the respondent.

(3)   Section 157 prevents provision relating to redress being included in the regulatory arrangements of an approved regulator, or licensing rules made by the Board in its capacity as a licensing authority.

(4)   But neither the scheme nor any provision made by this Part affects any power of an approved regulator, or the Board in its capacity as a licensing authority, to take disciplinary action.

(5) "Disciplinary action" means the imposition of sanctions, in respect of a breach of conduct rules or discipline rules, on a person who is an authorised person in relation to an activity which is a reserved legal activity.

Jurisdiction and operation of the ombudsman scheme

125 Jurisdiction of the ombudsman scheme

(1) A complaint which relates to an act or omission of a person ("the respondent") in carrying on an activity is within the jurisdiction of the ombudsman scheme if—

  (a)   the complaint is not excluded from the jurisdiction of the scheme by section 126, or by scheme rules made under section 127,

  (b)   the respondent is within section 128, and

  (c)   the complainant is within section 128 and wishes to have the complaint dealt with under the scheme.

(2)   In subsection (1) references to an act or omission include an act or omission which occurs before the coming into force of this section.

(3)   The right of a person to make a complaint under the ombudsman scheme, and the jurisdiction of an ombudsman to investigate, consider and determine a complaint, may not be limited or excluded by any contract term or by notice.

126 Complaints excluded because respondent's complaints procedures not used

(1)   A complaint is excluded from the jurisdiction of the ombudsman scheme if the complainant has not first used the respondent's complaints procedures in relation to the complaint.

(2)   The respondent's complaints procedures are the procedures established by the respondent, or which the respondent participates in or is subject to, in accordance with regulatory arrangements (or licensing rules of the Board) made in accordance with section 112.

(3)   Scheme rules may provide that subsection (1) does not apply in specified circumstances.

127 Complaints excluded by scheme rules

(1)   Scheme rules may make provision excluding complaints of a description specified in the rules from the jurisdiction of the ombudsman scheme.

(2)   But they may not make provision excluding a complaint from the jurisdiction of the ombudsman scheme on the ground that it relates to a matter which has been or could be dealt with under the disciplinary arrangements of the respondent's relevant authorising body.

128 Parties

(1)   The respondent is within this section if, at the relevant time, the respondent was an authorised person in relation to an activity which was a reserved legal activity (whether or not the act or omission relates to a reserved legal activity).

(2)   The complainant ("C") is within this section if C—

  (a)   meets the first and second conditions, and

  (b)   is not excluded by subsection (5).

(3)   The first condition is that C is—

  (a)   an individual, or

  (b)   a person (other than an individual) of a description prescribed by order made by the Lord Chancellor in accordance with a recommendation made under section 130.

(4)   The second condition is that—

    (a)   the services to which the complaint relates were provided by the respondent to C;

    (b)   the services to which the complaint relates were provided by the respondent to an authorised person who procured them on C's behalf;

    (c)   the services to which the complaint relates were provided by the respondent—

        (i)   in the respondent's capacity as a personal representative or trustee, or

        (ii)   to a person acting as a personal representative or trustee,

    and C is a beneficiary of the estate or trust in question; or

    (d)   C satisfies such other conditions, in relation to the services to which the complaint relates, as may be prescribed by order made by the Lord Chancellor in accordance with a recommendation made under section 130.

(5)   C is excluded if, at the relevant time—

    (a)   C was an authorised person in relation to an activity which was a reserved legal activity and the services to which the complaint relates were procured by C on behalf of another person,

    (b)   C was a public body or was acting on behalf of such a body in relation to the services to which the complaint relates, or

    (c)   C was a person prescribed, or of a description prescribed, as excluded by order made by the Lord Chancellor in accordance with a recommendation made under section 130.

(6)   In subsection (4)(b) "authorised person" means an authorised person in relation to any activity which is a reserved legal activity.

(7)   In this section—

"public body" means any government department, local authority or other body constituted for purposes of the public services, local government or the administration of justice;

"relevant time", in relation to a complaint, means the time when the act or omission to which the complaint relates took place.

129   Pre-commencement acts and omissions

(1)   For the purposes of section 128 a person is to be regarded as an authorised person in relation to an activity which is a reserved legal activity, at a time before section 125 comes into force, if the person was at that time—

    (a)   a person of the kind mentioned in paragraph 2(4) of Schedule 15,

    (b)   a body recognised under section 9 or 32 of the Administration of Justice Act 1985 (c. 61) (recognised bodies), or

    (c)   a legal partnership, a conveyancing partnership, a patent attorney body or a trade mark attorney body.

(2)   In this section—

"conveyancing partnership" has the meaning given by paragraph 11(5) of Schedule 5;

"legal partnership" has the meaning given by paragraph 7(4) of that Schedule;

"patent attorney body" has the meaning given by paragraph 14(7) of that Schedule;

"trade mark attorney body" has the meaning given by paragraph 16(7) of that Schedule.

130   Orders under section 128

(1)   An interested body may, at any time, recommend to the Lord Chancellor that the Lord Chancellor make an order under section 128(3)(b), (4)(d) or (5)(c).

(2)   An interested body must, if requested to do so by the Lord Chancellor, consider whether or not it is appropriate to make a recommendation under subsection (1).

(3)   An interested body must, before making a recommendation under subsection (1)—

(a)   publish a draft of the proposed recommendation,

(b)   invite representations regarding the proposed recommendation, and

(c)   consider any such representations which are made.

(4)   Where the Lord Chancellor receives a recommendation under subsection (1), the Lord Chancellor must consider whether to follow the recommendation.

(5)   If the Lord Chancellor decides not to follow the recommendation, the Lord Chancellor must publish a notice to that effect which includes the Lord Chancellor's reasons for the decision.

(6)   In this section "interested body" means—

(a)   the OLC,

(b)   the Board, or

(c)   the Consumer Panel.

131   Acts and omissions by employees etc

(1)   For the purposes of this Part and the ombudsman scheme, any act or omission by a person in the course of the person's employment is to be treated as also an act or omission by the person's employer, whether or not it was done with the employer's knowledge or approval.

(2)   For the purposes of this Part and the ombudsman scheme, any act or omission by a partner in a partnership in the course of carrying on, in the usual way, business of the kind carried on by the partnership is to be treated as also an act or omission by the partnership.

(3)   But subsection (2) does not apply if the partner had no authority to act for the partnership and the person purporting to rely on that subsection knew, at the time of the act or omission, that the partner had no such authority.

132   Continuity of complaints

(1)   The ability of a person to make a complaint about an act or omission of a partnership or other unincorporated body is not affected by any change in the membership of the partnership or body.

(2)   Scheme rules must make provision determining the circumstances in which, for the purposes of the ombudsman scheme, an act or omission of a person ("A") is, where A ceases to exist and another person ("B") succeeds to the whole or substantially the whole of the business of A, to be treated as an act or omission of B.

(3)   Rules under subsection (2) must, in relation to cases where an act or omission of A is treated as an act or omission of B, make provision about the treatment of complaints under the ombudsman scheme which are outstanding against A at the time A ceases to exist.

(4)   Scheme rules must make provision permitting such persons as may be specified in the rules to continue a complaint made by a person who has died or is otherwise unable to act; and for that purpose may modify references to the complainant in this Part and in scheme rules.

133   Operation of the ombudsman scheme

(1)   Scheme rules must set out the procedure for—

(a)   the making of complaints under the ombudsman scheme, and

(b)   the investigation, consideration and determination of complaints by an ombudsman.

(2) Scheme rules—

   (a)   must provide that a complaint is to be entertained under the ombudsman scheme only if the complainant has made the complaint under that scheme before the applicable time limit (determined in accordance with the scheme rules) has expired, and

   (b)   may provide that an ombudsman may extend that time limit in specified circumstances.

(3) Scheme rules made under subsection (1) may (among other things) make provision—

   (a)   for the whole or part of a complaint to be dismissed, in specified circumstances, without consideration of its merits;

   (b)   for the reference of a complaint, in specified circumstances and with the consent of the complainant, to another body with a view to it being determined by that body instead of by an ombudsman;

   (c)   for a person who, at the relevant time (within the meaning of section 128(7)) was an authorised person in relation to an activity to be treated in specified circumstances, for the purposes of the scheme and this Part, as if that person were a co-respondent in relation to a complaint;

   (d)   about the evidence which may be required or admitted and the extent to which it should be oral or written;

   (e)   for requiring parties to the complaint to attend to give evidence and produce documents, and for authorising the administration of oaths by ombudsmen;

   (f)   about the matters which are to be taken into account in determining whether an act or omission was fair and reasonable;

   (g)   for an ombudsman, in such circumstances as may be specified, to award expenses to persons in connection with attendance at a hearing before an ombudsman;

   (h)   for an ombudsman to award costs against the respondent in favour of the complainant;

   (i)   for an ombudsman to award costs against the complainant or the respondent in favour of the OLC for the purpose of providing a contribution to resources deployed in dealing with the complaint, if in the ombudsman's opinion that person acted so unreasonably in relation to the complaint that it is appropriate in all the circumstances of the case to make such an award;

   (j)   for the purpose of facilitating the settlement of a complaint with the agreement of the parties to it;

   (k)   for specified persons to be notified of complaints, determinations and directions under the ombudsman scheme.

(4) The circumstances specified under subsection (3)(a) may include the following—

   (a)   the ombudsman considers the complaint or part to be frivolous or vexatious or totally without merit;

   (b)   the ombudsman considers that the complaint or part would be better dealt with under another ombudsman scheme, by arbitration or by other legal proceedings;

   (c)   the ombudsman considers that there has been undue delay in the making of the complaint or part, or the provision of evidence to support it;

   (d)   the ombudsman is satisfied that the matter which is the subject of the complaint or part has previously been dealt with under another ombudsman scheme, by arbitration or by other legal proceedings;

   (e)   the ombudsman considers that there are other compelling reasons why it is inappropriate for the complaint or part to be dealt with under the ombudsman scheme.

(5)   No person may be required by scheme rules—

(a)   to provide any information or give any evidence which that person could not be compelled to provide or give in evidence in civil proceedings before the High Court, or

(b)   to produce any document which that person could not be compelled to produce in such proceedings.

(6)   Scheme rules may authorise an ombudsman making an award of costs in accordance with rules within subsection (3)(h) or (i) to order that the amount payable under the award bears interest, from a time specified in or determined in accordance with the order, at a rate specified in or determined in accordance with the rules.

(7)   An amount due under an award made in favour of a person by virtue of provision made under subsection (3)(g), (h) or (i) is recoverable as a debt due to that person.

(8)   In this section—

"party", in relation to a complaint, means—

(a)   the complainant,

(b)   the respondent, and

(c)   any other person who in accordance with scheme rules is to be regarded as a party to the complaint;

"specified" means specified in scheme rules.

134   Delegation of an ombudsman's functions

(1)   An ombudsman may delegate to a member of the OLC's staff appointed under paragraph 13 of Schedule 15—

(a)   any function of the ombudsman in relation to the making, investigation or consideration of a complaint;

(b)   any other function conferred on the ombudsman by or by virtue of this Part.

(2)   Nothing in subsection (1) applies to the following functions—

(a)   the function of determining a complaint;

(b)   the function of deciding that a complaint should be dismissed by virtue of rules under section 133(3)(a);

(c)   the Chief Ombudsman's power to consent to the appointment of an assistant ombudsman under section 122;

(d)   the duties imposed on the Chief Ombudsman by section 123 (Chief Ombudsman's report).

135   Notification requirements

(1)   This section applies where a complaint—

(a)   is excluded from the jurisdiction of the ombudsman scheme under section 126, or by virtue of scheme rules made under section 127;

(b)   is dismissed, or referred to another body, by virtue of scheme rules;

(c)   is settled, withdrawn or abandoned (or treated as withdrawn or abandoned by virtue of scheme rules).

(2)   The ombudsman must notify—

(a)   the complainant;

(b)   the respondent;

APPENDIX 21

(c)   any relevant authorising body, in relation to the respondent, notified of the complaint in accordance with rules within section 133(3)(k),

and, in a case within subsection (1)(a) or (b), must give reasons for the exclusion, dismissal or referral.

136   Charges payable by respondents

(1)   Scheme rules must require respondents, in relation to complaints under the ombudsman scheme, to pay to the OLC such charges as may be specified in the rules.

(2)   The rules must provide for charges payable in relation to a complaint to be waived (or wholly refunded) where—

(a)   the complaint is determined or otherwise resolved in favour of the respondent, and

(b)   the ombudsman is satisfied that the respondent took all reasonable steps to try to resolve the complaint under the respondent's complaints procedures.

(3)   The rules may make provision as to—

(a)   the circumstances in which a complaint is to be treated as determined or otherwise resolved in favour of the respondent (which may include circumstances where a complaint is settled, withdrawn or abandoned (or treated as withdrawn or abandoned by virtue of scheme rules));

(b)   matters to be taken into account by the ombudsman for the purposes of subsection (2)(b).

(4)   The respondent's complaints procedures are the procedures established by the respondent, or which the respondent participates in or is subject to, in accordance with regulatory arrangements (or licensing rules of the Board) made in accordance with section 112.

(5)   The rules may, among other things—

(a)   provide for the OLC to reduce or waive a charge in such other circumstances as may be specified;

(b)   set different charges for different stages of the proceedings on a complaint;

(c)   provide for charges to be wholly or partly refunded in such other circumstances as may be specified;

(d)   provide that if the whole or any part of a charge is not paid by the time by which it is required to be paid under the rules, the unpaid balance from time to time carries interest at the rate specified in, or determined in accordance with, the rules.

(6)   Any charge which is owed to the OLC by virtue of rules made under this section may be recovered as a debt due to the OLC.

Determinations under the scheme

137   Determination of complaints

(1)   A complaint is to be determined under the ombudsman scheme by reference to what is, in the opinion of the ombudsman making the determination, fair and reasonable in all the circumstances of the case.

(2)   The determination may contain one or more of the following—

(a)   a direction that the respondent make an apology to the complainant;

(b)   a direction that—

(i)   the fees to which the respondent is entitled in respect of the services to which the complaint relates ("the fees") are limited to such amount as may be specified in the direction, and

      (ii)   the respondent comply, or secure compliance, with such one or more of the permitted requirements as appear to the ombudsman to be necessary in order for effect to be given to the direction under sub-paragraph (i);

(c)   a direction that the respondent pay compensation to the complainant of such an amount as is specified in the direction in respect of any loss which has been suffered by, or any inconvenience or distress which has been caused to, the complainant as a result of any matter connected with the complaint;

(d)   a direction that the respondent secure the rectification, at the expense of the respondent, of any such error, omission or other deficiency arising in connection with the matter in question as the direction may specify;

(e)   a direction that the respondent take, at the expense of the respondent, such other action in the interests of the complainant as the direction may specify.

(3)   For the purposes of subsection (2)(b) "the permitted requirements" are—

(a)   that the whole or part of any amount already paid by or on behalf of the complainant in respect of the fees be refunded;

(b)   that the whole or part of the fees be remitted;

(c)   that the right to recover the fees be waived, whether wholly or to any specified extent.

(4)   Where—

(a)   a direction is made under subsection (2)(b) which requires that the whole or part of any amount already paid by or on behalf of the complainant in respect of the fees be refunded, or

(b)   a direction is made under subsection (2)(c),

the direction may also provide for the amount payable under the direction to carry interest from a time specified in or determined in accordance with the direction, at the rate specified in or determined in accordance with scheme rules.

(5)   The power of the ombudsman to make a direction under subsection (2) is not confined to cases where the complainant may have a cause of action against the respondent for negligence.

138   Limitation on value of directions under the ombudsman scheme

(1)   Where a determination is made under the ombudsman scheme in respect of a complaint, the total value of directions under section 137(2)(c) to (e) contained in the determination must not exceed £50,000.

(2)   For this purpose the total value of such directions is the aggregate of—

(a)   the amount of any compensation specified in a direction under subsection (2)(c) of section 137, and

(b)   the amount of any expenses reasonably incurred by the respondent when complying with a direction under subsection (2)(d) or (e) of that section.

(3)   For the purposes of determining that total value, any interest payable on an amount within subsection (2)(a) of this section, by virtue of section 137(4), is to be ignored.

139   Alteration of limit

(1)   The Lord Chancellor may by order amend section 138(1) in accordance with a recommendation made by an interested body under subsection (2).

(2)   An interested body may, at any time, recommend to the Lord Chancellor that section 138(1) should be amended so as to substitute the amount specified in the recommendation for the amount for the time being specified in that provision.

(3)   An interested body must, if requested to do so by the Lord Chancellor, consider whether or not it is appropriate to make a recommendation under subsection (2).

(4)   An interested body must, before making a recommendation under subsection (2)—

(a)   publish a draft of the proposed recommendation,

(b)   invite representations regarding the proposed recommendation, and

(c)   consider any such representations which are made.

(5)   Where the Lord Chancellor receives a recommendation under subsection (2), the Lord Chancellor must consider whether to follow the recommendation.

(6)   If the Lord Chancellor decides not to follow the recommendation, the Lord Chancellor must publish a notice to that effect which includes the Lord Chancellor's reasons for the decision.

(7)   In this section "interested body" means—

(a)   the OLC,

(b)   the Board, or

(c)   the Consumer Panel.

140   Acceptance or rejection of determination

(1)   When an ombudsman has determined a complaint the ombudsman must prepare a written statement of the determination.

(2)   The statement must—

(a)   give the ombudsman's reasons for the determination,

(b)   be signed by the ombudsman, and

(c)   require the complainant to notify the ombudsman, before a time specified in the statement ("the specified time"), whether the complainant accepts or rejects the determination.

(3)   The ombudsman must give a copy of the statement to—

(a)   the complainant,

(b)   the respondent, and

(c)   any relevant authorising body in relation to the respondent.

(4)   If the complainant notifies the ombudsman that the determination is accepted by the complainant, it is binding on the respondent and the complainant and is final.

(5)   If, by the specified time, the complainant has not notified the ombudsman of the complainant's acceptance or rejection of the determination, the complainant is to be treated as having rejected it.

(6)   But if—

(a)   the complainant notifies the ombudsman after the specified time that the determination is accepted by the complainant,

(b)   the complainant has not previously notified the ombudsman of the complainant's rejection of the determination, and

(c)   the ombudsman is satisfied that such conditions as may be prescribed by the scheme rules for the purposes of this subsection are satisfied,

the determination is treated as if it had never been rejected by virtue of subsection (5).

(7)   The ombudsman must give notice of the outcome to—

(a)   the complainant,

(b)   the respondent, and

(c)   any relevant authorising body in relation to the respondent.

(8)   Where a determination is rejected by virtue of subsection (5), that notice must contain a general description of the effect of subsection (6).

(9)   A copy of the determination on which appears a certificate signed by an ombudsman is evidence that the determination was made under the scheme.

(10) Such a certificate purporting to be signed by an ombudsman is to be taken to have been duly signed unless the contrary is shown.

(11) Neither the complainant nor the respondent, in relation to a complaint, may institute or continue legal proceedings in respect of a matter which was the subject of a complaint, after the time when a determination by an ombudsman of the complaint becomes binding and final in accordance with this section.

141   Enforcement by complainant of directions under section 137

(1)   This section applies where—

(a)   a determination is made in respect of a complaint under the ombudsman scheme,

(b)   one or more directions are made under section 137(2), and

(c)   the determination is final by virtue of section 140(4).

(2)   An amount payable in accordance with—

(a)   a direction under subsection (2)(b) of section 137 which requires that the whole or part of any amount already paid by or on behalf of the complainant in respect of the fees be refunded, or

(b)   a direction under subsection (2)(c) of that section,

including any interest payable by virtue of subsection (4) of that section, is recoverable, if a court so orders on the application of the complainant or an ombudsman, as if it were payable under an order of that court.

(3)   If the respondent fails to comply with any other direction under section 137(2), the complainant or an ombudsman may make an application to the court under this subsection.

(4)   If, on an application under subsection (3), the court decides that the respondent has failed to comply with the direction in question, it may order the respondent to take such steps as the court directs for securing that the direction is complied with.

(5)   An ombudsman may make an application under subsection (2) or (3) only in such circumstances as may be specified in scheme rules, and with the complainant's consent.

(6)   If the court makes an order under subsection (2) on the application of an ombudsman, the ombudsman may in such circumstances as may be specified in scheme rules and with the complainant's consent recover the amount mentioned in that subsection on behalf of the complainant.

(7)   In this section "court" means the High Court or the county court.

142   Reporting court orders made against authorised persons

(1)   Where a court makes an order under section 141, it must give the OLC notice to that effect.

(2)   Where the order is made against a person who is an authorised person in relation to any activity which is a reserved legal activity, the OLC must make arrangements to ensure that an ombudsman gives to each relevant authorising body, in relation to that person, a report which states that the order has been made.

APPENDIX 21

(3)   A report under subsection (2) may require the relevant authorising body to report to the ombudsman the action which has been or is to be taken by it in response to the report under subsection (2) and the reasons for that action being taken.

(4)   If an ombudsman, having regard to any report produced by the relevant authorising body in compliance with a requirement imposed under subsection (3), or any failure to comply with such a requirement, considers—

(a)   that there has been a serious failure by the relevant authorising body to discharge its regulatory functions, or

(b)   if such a requirement has been imposed on the body on more than one occasion, that the relevant authorising body has persistently failed adequately to discharge its regulatory functions,

the ombudsman may make a report to that effect to the Board.

Reporting misconduct

143   Reporting possible misconduct to approved regulators

(1)   This section applies where—

(a)   an ombudsman is dealing, or has dealt, with a complaint under the ombudsman scheme, and

(b)   the ombudsman is of the opinion that the conduct of the respondent or any other person in relation to any matter connected with the complaint is such that a relevant authorising body in relation to that person should consider whether to take action against that person.

(2)   The ombudsman must give the relevant authorising body a report which—

(a)   states that the ombudsman is of that opinion, and

(b)   gives details of that conduct.

(3)   The ombudsman must give the complainant a notice stating that a report under subsection (2) has been given to the relevant authorising body.

(4)   A report under subsection (2) may require the relevant authorising body to report to the ombudsman the action which has been or is to be taken by it in response to the report and the reasons for that action being taken.

(5)   The duty imposed by subsection (2) is not affected by the withdrawal or abandonment of the complaint.

(6)   If an ombudsman, having regard to any report produced by the relevant authorising body in compliance with a requirement imposed under subsection (4), or any failure to comply with such a requirement, considers—

(a)   that there has been a serious failure by the relevant authorising body to discharge its regulatory functions, or

(b)   if such a requirement has been imposed on the body on more than one occasion, that the relevant authorising body has persistently failed adequately to discharge its regulatory functions,

the ombudsman may make a report to that effect to the Board.

Co-operation with investigations

144   Duties to share information

(1)   Scheme rules must make provision requiring persons within subsection (3) to disclose to an approved regulator information of such description as may be specified in the rules, in such circumstances as may be so specified.

(2)   The regulatory arrangements of an approved regulator must make provision requiring the approved regulator to disclose to persons within subsection (3) information of such description as may be specified in the arrangements, in such circumstances as may be so specified.

(3)   The persons are—

(a)   the OLC;

(b)   an ombudsman;

(c)   a member of the OLC's staff appointed under paragraph 13 of Schedule 15.

(4)   Provision made under subsection (1) or (2) must satisfy such requirements as the Board may, from time to time, specify.

(5)   In specifying requirements under subsection (4) the Board must have regard to the need to ensure that, so far as reasonably practicable—

(a)   duplication of investigations is avoided;

(b)   the OLC assists approved regulators to carry out their regulatory functions, and approved regulators assist with the investigation, consideration and determination of complaints under the ombudsman scheme.

(6)   The Board must publish any requirements specified by it under subsection (4).

(7)   The OLC must—

(a)   before publishing under section 205(2) a draft of rules it proposes to make under subsection (1), consult each approved regulator to which the proposed rules apply, and

(b)   when seeking the Board's consent to such rules under section 155, identify any objections made by an approved regulator to the rules and not withdrawn.

(8)   An approved regulator must—

(a)   consult the OLC before making provisions in its regulatory arrangements of the kind mentioned in subsection (2), and

(b)   where an application is made for the Board's approval of such provisions, identify any objections made by the OLC to the provisions and not withdrawn.

(9)   [*repealed*]

145   Duties of authorised persons to co-operate with investigations

(1)   The regulatory arrangements of an approved regulator must make—

(a)   provision requiring each relevant authorised person to give ombudsmen all such assistance requested by them, in connection with the investigation, consideration or determination of complaints under the ombudsman scheme, as that person is reasonably able to give, and

(b)   provision for the enforcement of that requirement.

(2)   The provision made for the purposes of subsection (1) must satisfy such requirements as the Board may, from time to time, specify for the purposes of that subsection.

(3)   The Board must publish any requirements specified by it under subsection (2).

(4)   In this section "relevant authorised person"—

(a)   in relation to an approved regulator, has the same meaning as in section 112, and

(b)   [*repealed*].

146   Reporting failures to co-operate with an investigation to approved regulators

(1)   This section applies where an ombudsman is of the opinion that an authorised person has failed to give an ombudsman all such assistance requested by the ombudsman, in

connection with the investigation, consideration or determination of a complaint under the ombudsman scheme, as that person is reasonably able to give.

(2)   The ombudsman must give each relevant authorising body, in relation to that person, a report which—

    (a)   states that the ombudsman is of that opinion, and

    (b)   gives details of the failure.

(3)   A report under subsection (2) may require the relevant authorising body to report to the ombudsman the action which has been or is to be taken by it in response to the report under that subsection and the reasons for that action being taken.

(4)   The duty imposed by subsection (2) is not affected by the withdrawal or abandonment of the complaint.

(5)   If an ombudsman, having regard to any report produced by the relevant authorising body in compliance with a requirement imposed under subsection (3), or any failure to comply with such a requirement, considers—

    (a)   that there has been a serious failure by the relevant authorising body to discharge its regulatory functions, or

    (b)   if such a requirement has been imposed on the body on more than one occasion, that the relevant authorising body has persistently failed adequately to discharge its regulatory functions,

the ombudsman may make a report to that effect to the Board.

(6)   In this section "authorised person" means an authorised person in relation to any activity which is a reserved legal activity.

Information

147   Information and documents

(1)   An ombudsman may, by notice, require a party to a complaint under the ombudsman scheme—

    (a)   to produce documents, or documents of a description, specified in the notice, or

    (b)   to provide information, or information of a description, specified in the notice.

(2)   A notice under subsection (1) may require the information or documents to be provided or produced—

    (a)   before the end of such reasonable period as may be specified in the notice, and

    (b)   in the case of information, in such manner or form as may be so specified.

(3)   This section applies only to information and documents the provision or production of which the ombudsman considers necessary for the determination of the complaint.

(4)   An ombudsman may—

    (a)   take copies of or extracts from a document produced under this section, and

    (b)   require the person producing the document to provide an explanation of it.

(5)   If a person who is required under this section to produce a document fails to do so, an ombudsman may require that person to state, to the best of that person's knowledge and belief, where the document is.

(6)   No person may be required under this section—

    (a)   to provide any information which that person could not be compelled to provide or give in evidence in civil proceedings before the High Court, or

    (b)   to produce any document which that person could not be compelled to produce in such proceedings.

(7)   In this section "party", in relation to a complaint, means—

(a)   the complainant;

(b)   the respondent;

(c)   any other person who in accordance with the scheme rules is to be regarded as a party to the complaint.

148   Reporting failures to provide information or produce documents

(1)   This section applies where an ombudsman is of the opinion that an authorised person has failed to comply with a requirement imposed under section 147(1).

(2)   The ombudsman must give each relevant authorising body, in relation to that person, a report which—

(a)   states that the ombudsman is of that opinion, and

(b)   gives details of the failure.

(3)   A report under subsection (2) may require the relevant authorising body to report to the ombudsman the action which has been or is to be taken by it in response to the report under that subsection and the reasons for that action being taken.

(4)   The duty imposed by subsection (2) is not affected by the withdrawal or abandonment of the complaint in relation to which the requirement was imposed under section 147(1).

(5)   If an ombudsman, having regard to any report produced by the relevant authorising body in compliance with a requirement imposed under subsection (3), or any failure to comply with such a requirement, considers—

(a)   that there has been a serious failure by the relevant authorising body to discharge its regulatory functions, or

(b)   if such a requirement has been imposed on the body on more than one occasion, that the relevant authorising body has persistently failed adequately to discharge its regulatory functions,

the ombudsman may make a report to that effect to the Board.

(6)   In this section "authorised person" means an authorised person in relation to any activity which is a reserved legal activity.

149   Enforcement of requirements to provide information or produce documents

(1)   This section applies where an ombudsman is of the opinion that a person ("the defaulter") has failed to comply with a requirement imposed under section 147(1).

(2)   The ombudsman may certify the defaulter's failure to comply with the requirement to the court.

(3)   Where an ombudsman certifies a failure to the court under subsection (2), the court may enquire into the case.

(4)   If the court is satisfied that the defaulter has failed without reasonable excuse to comply with the requirement, it may deal with—

(a)   the defaulter, and

(b)   in the case of a body, any manager of the body,

as if that person were in contempt.

(5)   Subsection (6) applies in a case where the defaulter is an authorised person in relation to any activity which is a reserved legal activity.

(6)   The ombudsman ("the enforcing ombudsman") may not certify the defaulter's failure to the court until a report by that or another ombudsman has been made as required by section 148(2) and the enforcing ombudsman is satisfied—

(a)   that each relevant authorising body to whom such a report was made has been given a reasonable opportunity to take action in respect of the defaulter's failure, and

(b)   that the defaulter has continued to fail to provide the information or produce the documents to which the requirement under section 147 related.

(7)   In this section "court" means the High Court.

150   Reports of investigations

(1)   The OLC may, if it considers it appropriate to do so in any particular case, publish a report of the investigation, consideration and determination of a complaint made under the ombudsman scheme.

(2)   A report under subsection (1) must not (unless the complainant consents)—

(a)   mention the name of the complainant, or

(b)   include any particulars which, in the opinion of the OLC, are likely to identify the complainant.

151   Restricted information

(1)   Except as provided by section 152, restricted information must not be disclosed—

(a)   by a restricted person, or

(b)   by any person who receives the information directly or indirectly from a restricted person.

(2)   In this section and section 152—

"restricted information" means information (other than excluded information) which is obtained by a restricted person in the course of, or for the purposes of, an investigation into a complaint made under the ombudsman scheme (including information obtained for the purposes of deciding whether to begin such an investigation or in connection with the settlement of a complaint);

"restricted person" means—

(a)   the OLC,

(b)   an ombudsman, or

(c)   a person who exercises functions delegated under paragraph 22 of Schedule 15.

(3)   For the purposes of subsection (2) "excluded information" means—

(a)   information which is in the form of a summary or collection of information so framed as not to enable information relating to any particular person to be ascertained from it;

(b)   information which at the time of the disclosure is or has already been made available to the public from other sources;

(c)   information which was obtained more than 70 years before the date of the disclosure.

152   Disclosure of restricted information

(1)   A restricted person may disclose restricted information to another restricted person.

(2)   Restricted information may be disclosed for the purposes of the investigation in the course of which, or for the purposes of which, it was obtained.

(3)   Section 151 also does not preclude the disclosure of restricted information—

(a) in a report made under—

    (i) section 143(2) (report of possible misconduct to approved regulators),

    (ii) section 146(2) (report of failure to co-operate with investigation),

    (iii) section 148 (reporting failures to provide information or produce documents), or

    (iv) section 150 (reports of investigations),

(b) for the purposes of enabling or assisting the Board to exercise any of its functions,

(c) to an approved regulator for the purposes of enabling or assisting the approved regulator to exercise any of its regulatory functions,

(d) with the consent of the person to whom it relates and (if different) the person from whom the restricted person obtained it,

(e) for the purposes of an inquiry with a view to the taking of any criminal proceedings or for the purposes of any such proceedings,

(f) where the disclosure is required by or by virtue of any provision made by or under this Act or any other enactment or other rule of law,

(g) to such persons (other than approved regulators) who exercise regulatory functions as may be prescribed by order made by the Lord Chancellor, for such purposes as may be so prescribed.

(4) Subsections (2) and (3) are subject to subsection (5).

(5) The Lord Chancellor may by order prevent the disclosure of restricted information by virtue of subsection (2) or (3) in such circumstances, or for such purposes, as may be prescribed in the order.

153 Data protection

In section 31 of the Data Protection Act 1998 (c. 29) (regulatory activity), after subsection (4B) (inserted by section 170) insert—

"(4C) Personal data processed for the purposes of the function of considering a complaint under the scheme established under Part 6 of the Legal Services Act 2007 (legal complaints) are exempt from the subject information provisions in any case to the extent to which the application of those provisions to the data would be likely to prejudice the proper discharge of the function."

Defamation

154 Protection from defamation claims

For the purposes of the law of defamation—

(a) proceedings in relation to a complaint under the ombudsman scheme are to be treated as if they were proceedings before a court, and

(b) the publication of any matter by the OLC under this Part is absolutely privileged.

PART 8
MISCELLANEOUS PROVISIONS ABOUT LAWYERS ETC

Duties of regulated persons

176 Duties of regulated persons

(1) A person who is a regulated person in relation to an approved regulator has a duty to comply with the regulatory arrangements of the approved regulator as they apply to that person.

(2)   A person is a regulated person in relation to an approved regulator if the person—

(a)   is authorised by the approved regulator to carry on an activity which is a reserved legal activity, or

(b)   is not so authorised, but is a manager or employee of a person who is so authorised.

(3)   This section applies in relation to the Board in its capacity as a licensing authority and its licensing rules, as it applies in relation to an approved regulator and its regulatory arrangements.

SCHEDULE 2
The reserved legal activities

Section 12

Introduction

1   This Schedule makes provision about the reserved legal activities.

2   In this Schedule "the appointed day" means the day appointed for the coming into force of section 13 (entitlement to carry on reserved legal activities).

Rights of audience

3   (1)   A "right of audience" means the right to appear before and address a court, including the right to call and examine witnesses.

(2)   But a "right of audience" does not include a right to appear before or address a court, or to call or examine witnesses, in relation to any particular court or in relation to particular proceedings, if immediately before the appointed day no restriction was placed on the persons entitled to exercise that right.

Conduct of litigation

4   (1)   The "conduct of litigation" means—

(a)   the issuing of proceedings before any court in England and Wales,

(b)   the commencement, prosecution and defence of such proceedings, and

(c)   the performance of any ancillary functions in relation to such proceedings (such as entering appearances to actions).

(2)   But the "conduct of litigation" does not include any activity within paragraphs (a) to (c) of sub-paragraph (1), in relation to any particular court or in relation to any particular proceedings, if immediately before the appointed day no restriction was placed on the persons entitled to carry on that activity.

Reserved instrument activities

5   (1)   "Reserved instrument activities" means—

(a)   preparing any instrument of transfer or charge for the purposes of the Land Registration Act 2002 (c 9);

(b)   making an application or lodging a document for registration under that Act;

(c)   preparing any other instrument relating to real or personal estate for the purposes of the law of England and Wales or instrument relating to court proceedings in England and Wales.

(2)   But "reserved instrument activities" does not include the preparation of an instrument relating to any particular court proceedings if, immediately before the appointed day, no restriction was placed on the persons entitled to carry on that activity.

(3)   In this paragraph "instrument" includes a contract for the sale or other disposition of land (except a contract to grant a short lease), but does not include—

(a)   a will or other testamentary instrument,

(b)   an agreement not intended to be executed as a deed, other than a contract that is included by virtue of the preceding provisions of this sub-paragraph,

(c)   a letter or power of attorney, or

(d)   a transfer of stock containing no trust or limitation of the transfer.

(4)   In this paragraph a "short lease" means a lease such as is referred to in section 54(2) of the Law of Property Act 1925 (c 20) (short leases).

Probate activities

6   (1)   "Probate activities" means preparing any probate papers for the purposes of the law of England and Wales or in relation to any proceedings in England and Wales.

(2)   In this paragraph "probate papers" means papers on which to found or oppose—

(a)   a grant of probate, or

(b)   a grant of letters of administration.

Notarial activities

7   (1)   "Notarial activities" means activities which, immediately before the appointed day, were customarily carried on by virtue of enrolment as a notary in accordance with section 1 of the Public Notaries Act 1801 (c 79).

(2)   Sub-paragraph (1) does not include activities carried on—

(a)   by virtue of section 22 or 23 of the Solicitors Act 1974 (c 47) (reserved instrument activities and probate activities), or

(b)   by virtue of section 113 of the Courts and Legal Services Act 1990 (c 41) (administration of oaths).

Administration of oaths

8   The "administration of oaths" means the exercise of the powers conferred on a commissioner for oaths by—

(a)   the Commissioners for Oaths Act 1889 (c 10);

(b)   the Commissioners for Oaths Act 1891 (c 50);

(c)   section 24 of the Stamp Duties Management Act 1891 (c 38).

SCHEDULE 3
Exempt persons

Section 19

Rights of audience

1   (1)   This paragraph applies to determine whether a person is an exempt person for the purpose of exercising a right of audience before a court in relation to any proceedings (subject to paragraph 7).

(2)   The person is exempt if the person—

(a)   is not an authorised person in relation to that activity, but

(b)   has a right of audience granted by that court in relation to those proceedings.

(3)   The person is exempt if the person—

(a)   is not an authorised person in relation to that activity, but

(b)   has a right of audience before that court in relation to those proceedings granted by or under any enactment.

(4)   The person is exempt if the person is the Attorney General or the Solicitor General and—

(a)   the name of the person is on the roll kept by the Law Society under section 6 of the Solicitors Act 1974 (c 47), or

(b)   the person has been called to the Bar by an Inn of Court.

(5)   The person is exempt if the person is the Advocate General for Scotland and is admitted—

(a)   as a solicitor in Scotland under section 6 of the Solicitors (Scotland) Act 1980 (c 46), or

(b)   to practise as an advocate before the courts of Scotland.

(6)   The person is exempt if the person—

(a)   is a party to those proceedings, and

(b)   would have a right of audience, in the person's capacity as such a party, if this Act had not been passed.

(7)   The person is exempt if—

(a)   the person is an individual whose work includes assisting in the conduct of litigation,

(b)   the person is assisting in the conduct of litigation—

(i)   under instructions given (either generally or in relation to the proceedings) by an individual to whom sub-paragraph (8) applies, and

(ii)   under the supervision of that individual, and

(c)   the proceedings are not reserved family proceedings and are being heard in chambers—

(i)   in the High Court or county court, or

(ii)   in the family court by a judge who is not, or by two or more judges at least one of whom is not, within section 31C(1)(y) of the Matrimonial and Family Proceedings Act 1984 (lay justices).

(8)   This sub-paragraph applies to—

(a)   any authorised person in relation to an activity which constitutes the conduct of litigation;

(b)   any person who by virtue of section 193 is not required to be entitled to carry on such an activity.

(9)   The person is an exempt person in relation to the exercise of a right of audience in proceedings on an appeal from the Comptroller-General of Patents, Designs and Trade Marks to the Patents Court under the Patents Act 1977 (c 37), if the person is a solicitor of the Court of Judicature of Northern Ireland.

(10)   For the purposes of this paragraph—

"family proceedings" has the same meaning as in the Matrimonial and Family Proceedings Act 1984 (c 42) and also includes any proceedings in the family court and any other proceedings which are family proceedings for the purposes of the Children Act 1989 (c 41);

"reserved family proceedings" means such category of family proceedings as the Lord Chancellor may, after consulting the President of the Law Society and with the concurrence of the President of the Family Division, by order prescribe;

and any order made under section 27(9) of the Courts and Legal Services Act 1990 (c 41) before the day appointed for the coming into force of this paragraph is to have effect on and after that day as if it were an order made under this sub-paragraph.

Conduct of litigation

2   (1)   This paragraph applies to determine whether a person is an exempt person for the purpose of carrying on any activity which constitutes the conduct of litigation in relation to any proceedings (subject to paragraph 7).

(2)   The person is exempt if the person—

(a)   is not an authorised person in relation to that activity, but

(b)   has a right to conduct litigation granted by a court in relation to those proceedings.

(3)   The person is exempt if the person—

(a)   is not an authorised person in relation to that activity, but

(b)   has a right to conduct litigation in relation to those proceedings granted by or under any enactment.

(4)   The person is exempt if the person—

(a)   is a party to those proceedings, and

(b)   would have a right to conduct the litigation, in the person's capacity as such a party, if this Act had not been passed.

(5)   The person is an exempt person in relation to any activity which is carried on in or in connection with proceedings on an appeal from the Comptroller-General of Patents, Designs and Trade Marks to the Patents Court under the Patents Act 1977 (c 37), if the person is a solicitor of the Court of Judicature of Northern Ireland.

Reserved instrument activities

3   (1)   This paragraph applies to determine whether a person is an exempt person for the purpose of carrying on any activity which constitutes reserved instrument activities (subject to paragraph 7).

(2)   The person is exempt if the person prepares the instruments or applications in the course of the person's duty as a public officer.

(3)   The person ("E") is exempt if—

(a)   E is an individual,

(b)   E carries on the activity at the direction and under the supervision of another individual ("P"),

(c)   when E does so, P and E are connected, and

(d)   P is entitled to carry on the activity, otherwise than by virtue of sub-paragraph (10).

(4)   For the purposes of sub-paragraph (3), P and E are connected if—

(a)   P is E's employer,

(b)   P is a fellow employee of E,

(c)   P is a manager or employee of a body which is an authorised person in relation to the activity, and E is also a manager or employee of that body.

(5)   If the person is an accredited person, the person is exempt to the extent that the activity consists of the preparation of any instrument—

(a)   which creates, or which the person believes on reasonable grounds will create, a farm business tenancy (within the meaning of the Agricultural Tenancies Act 1995 (c 8)), or

(b)   which relates to an existing tenancy which is, or which the person believes on reasonable grounds to be, such a tenancy.

(6)   In sub-paragraph (5) "accredited person" means a person who is—

(a)   a Fellow of the Central Association of Agricultural Valuers, or

(b)   a Member or Fellow of the Royal Institution of Chartered Surveyors.

(7)   The person is exempt to the extent that the activity carried on by the person is also a reserved legal activity within sub-paragraph (8) and the person is—

(a)   authorised to carry on that activity (other than under Part 5) by a relevant approved regulator in relation to the activity,

(b)   authorised to carry on that activity by a licence under Part 5, or

(c)   an exempt person in relation to that activity by virtue of paragraph 1 or 2 of this Schedule.

(8)   The activities are—

(a)   the exercise of a right of audience;

(b)   the conduct of litigation.

(9)   The person is exempt if the person is employed merely to engross the instrument or application.

(10)   The person is exempt if the person is an individual who carries on the activity otherwise than for, or in expectation of, any fee, gain or reward.

(11)   The person is exempt if—

(a)   the person is a person qualified to practise as a solicitor in Scotland in accordance with section 4 of the Solicitors (Scotland) Act 1980 (c 46), and

(b)   the reserved instrument activities fall within paragraph 5(1)(c) of Schedule 2 (preparation of certain instruments relating to real or personal property or legal proceedings).

Probate activities

4   (1)   This paragraph applies to determine whether a person is an exempt person for the purpose of carrying on any activity which constitutes probate activities (subject to paragraph 7).

(2)   The person ("E") is an exempt person if—

(a)   E is an individual,

(b)   E provides the probate activities at the direction and under the supervision of another individual ("P"),

(c)   when E does so, P and E are connected, and

(d)   P is entitled to carry on the activity, otherwise than by virtue of sub-paragraph (4).

(3)   For the purposes of sub-paragraph (2), P and E are connected if—

(a)   P is E's employer,

(b)   P is a fellow employee of E,

(c)   P is a manager or employee of a body which is an authorised person in relation to the activity, and E is also a manager or employee of that body.

(4)   The person is exempt if the person is an individual who carries on the activity otherwise than for, or in expectation of, any fee, gain or reward.

Notarial activities

5   (1)   This paragraph applies to determine whether a person is an exempt person for the purpose of carrying on any activity which constitutes notarial activities (subject to paragraph 7).

(2)   The person is exempt if the person is not an authorised person in relation to that activity under this Act, but is authorised to carry on that activity by or by virtue of any other enactment.

(3)   The person is exempt if section 14 of the Public Notaries Act 1801 (c 79) applies to the person, and—

(a)   where that section applies by virtue of the person holding or exercising an office or appointment, the person carries on the activity for ecclesiastical purposes;

(b)   where that section applies by virtue of the person performing a public duty or service under government, the person carries on the activity in the course of performing that duty or service.

(4)   The person is exempt if the person is an individual who carries on the notarial activities otherwise than for or in expectation of a fee, gain or reward.

Administration of oaths

6   (1)   This paragraph applies to determine whether a person is an exempt person for the purpose of carrying on any activity which constitutes the administration of oaths (subject to paragraph 7).

(2)   The person is exempt if the person is not an authorised person in relation to that activity under this Act, but is authorised to carry on that activity by or by virtue of any other enactment.

(3)   The person is exempt if the person has a commission under section 1(1) of the Commissioners for Oaths Act 1889 (c 10).

European lawyers

7   A European lawyer (within the meaning of the European Communities (Services of Lawyers) Order 1978 (SI 1978/1910), as it has effect by virtue of regulation 5 of the Services of Lawyers and Lawyer's Practice (Revocation etc) (EU Exit) Regulations 2020) is an exempt person for the purposes of carrying on an activity which is a reserved legal activity and which the European lawyer is entitled to carry on by virtue of that order, as it has effect by virtue of that regulation.

Employers etc acting through exempt person

8   (1)   This paragraph applies where—

(a)   a person ("P") carries on an activity ("the relevant activity") which is a reserved legal activity,

(b)   P carries on the relevant activity by virtue of an employee of P ("E") carrying it on in E's capacity as such an employee, and

(c)   E is an exempt person in relation to the relevant activity.

(2)   P is an exempt person in relation to the relevant activity to the extent that P carries on that activity by virtue of E so carrying it on.

APPENDIX 21

(3)   This paragraph does not apply where E—

   (a)   carries on the relevant activity at the direction and under the supervision of an authorised person in relation to that activity, and

   (b)   is exempt in relation to that activity by virtue of paragraph 1(7), 3(3) or 4(2).

(4)   If P is a body, in this paragraph references to an employee of P include references to a manager of P.

Further exempt persons

9   (1)   The Lord Chancellor may, by order, amend this Schedule so as to provide—

   (a)   for persons to be exempt persons in relation to any activity which is a reserved legal activity (including any activity which is a reserved legal activity by virtue of an order under section 24 (extension of reserved legal activities)),

   (b)   for persons to cease to be such persons, or

   (c)   for the amendment of any provision made in respect of an exempt person.

(2)   The Lord Chancellor may make an order under sub-paragraph (1) only on the recommendation of the Board.

Sources of help

What do you do when a letter arrives from the Solicitors Regulation Authority or Legal Ombudsman (LeO) with some kind of complaint, or if you are subject to a forensic investigation by the SRA, or if you face disciplinary proceedings? Where do you turn for assistance?

The first point to make is that doing nothing is not an option. Both the LeO and the SRA apply strict time limits; adjudications will be adverse if you do not provide your explanations – your side of the story – for the benefit of the adjudicator or ombudsman. Do not assume that you will be given extensions of time – any request for more time will have to be fully justified and will be considered on the premise that complying with the requirements of the regulator will be a matter of priority. At the other extreme, failing to appear at the Solicitors Disciplinary Tribunal in your own defence may be a terminal mistake.

Specialist assistance

In any matter of complexity or apparent seriousness it is desirable to obtain specialist assistance, and there are relatively few with the requisite expertise.

The ethics helpline formerly operated by the Law Society is now under the jurisdiction of the SRA. It is not known to what extent information received as a result of advice being sought will be treated as information about the person enquiring, for the purposes of regulatory action.

The **Solicitors' Assistance Scheme** is independent of the Law Society and SRA. Established over thirty years ago, it comprises around 80 volunteers from all over England and Wales, most of whom are practising solicitors with a high degree of skill and experience. The scheme members offer a minimum of one hour of pro bono advice and assistance. Any further advice and assistance will be offered at the discretion of the scheme member, or will be by way of a formal retainer.. They can be contacted via email at **help@thesas.org.uk** and via the website **www.thesas.org.uk**.

Professional indemnity insurance no longer provides cover for the costs of defending disciplinary or regulatory proceedings.

LawCare promotes and supports good mental health and wellbeing in the legal community. It provides information and support to anyone in the legal community experiencing mental health and wellbeing problems. The contact number for solicitors, law students and legal executives in England and Wales is 0800 279 6888. Their website is **www.lawcare.org.uk**.

The Law Society's **Practice Advice Service** is a dedicated support-line for solicitors, trainees and employees of law firms. It is staffed by a team of experienced solicitors who deal with enquiries using their own knowledge and a variety of information sources, as well as the experience of other specialists within the Law Society. They are able to assist with enquiries on legal practice in many areas including anti-money laundering; solicitors' costs; multi-party actions; conveyancing; conditional fee agreements; probate; and rights of audience in the Crown Court. Advice by the Practice Advice Service does not constitute legal advice and cannot be relied upon as such. The contact number is 020 7320 5675 and e-mail **practiceadvice@lawsociety.org.uk**.

Financial assistance

Less relevant to the regulatory context, but a potential source of financial assistance for those in need, is **SBA – The Solicitors' Charity**, formerly known as the Solicitors Benevolent Association, which is the principal nationwide charity for solicitors in England and Wales. SBA is run by solicitors, for solicitors and their families, SBA has been working at the heart of the legal profession for over 150 years. It is dedicated to helping solicitors past and present, and their families, in times of need. The Association's email address is **caseworker@thesolicitorscharity .org**, or see its website **www.thesolicitorscharity.org**.

Index

805